Coins and Currency

ALSO BY MARY ELLEN SNODGRASS
AND FROM MCFARLAND

Encyclopedia of World Scriptures (2001)

Who's Who in the Middle Ages (2001)

Coins and Currency

An Historical Encyclopedia

by Mary Ellen Snodgrass

McFarland & Company, Inc., Publishers
Jefferson, North Carolina, and London

All photographs not otherwise credited
are by the author

LIBRARY OF CONGRESS CATALOGUING-IN-PUBLICATION DATA

Snodgrass, Mary Ellen.
Coins and currency : an historical encyclopedia /
by Mary Ellen Snodgrass.
p. cm.
Includes bibliographical references and index.

ISBN 0-7864-1450-2 (illustrated case binding : 60# alkaline paper) ∞

1. Coins — History — Encyclopedias.
2. Money — History — Encyclopedias. I. Title.
CJ59.S66 2003 737.4'03 — dc21 2003009256

British Library cataloguing data are available

Cover photograph: Paper money ©2002 Comstock. Front cover coin: reverse of the Kona dollar. Background coins: reverse of the Bermuda five-cent piece and a Tahitian coin

Manufactured in the United States of America

McFarland & Company, Inc., Publishers
Box 611, Jefferson, North Carolina 28640
www.mcfarlandpub.com

Acknowledgments

A reference work covering the world's money from its inception requires multiple sources of information. In addition to libraries, government treasury agents, coin collectors, and knowledgeable individuals, I am grateful to coin dealers around the globe who have advised and informed me. Many have offered detailed explanations and tutorials as well as photographs and artwork from their private collections. I list these individuals below.

Dr. Richard A. Bagg, Numismatist
Bowers and Merena Galleries
P.O. Box 1224
Wolfeboro, New Hampshire 03894
Tele: 800-458-4646
Fax: 603-569-5319
rick@Bowersandmerena.com
http://www.bowersandmerena.com/

Frank Bakos Ancient Coins and Artefacts
37 Gayner Road
Filton, Bristol
England B270SP
Tel: 0117 9699716
Email: f.bakos@virgin.net
http://freespace.virgin.net/frank.bakos/index.html

Alexander Basok, Numismatist
Rusty Pennies
1954 First Street #186
Highland Park, Illinois 60035
Tele: 847-444-1163
Fax: 847-444-1165
Email: basok@rustypennies.com
http://www.rustypennies.com

Javier Blake, President
Currency of Note, Inc.
8362 Pines Boulevard PMB 194
Pembroke Pines, Florida 33024-6600
Tele: 877-CCNOW-77
Fax: 954-436-9924
Email: order@currencyofnote.com
http://www.currencyofnote.com/

Beth Bradshaw
reference librarian
Patrick Beaver Library
Hickory, North Carolina

Guy Clark
Ancient Coins and Antiquities
P.O. Box 6151
Norfolk, Virginia 23508-6151
Tele: 757-622-3474
Email: guyclark@pilot.infi.net

Samuel E. Cox, Customer Service Manager
Worldwide Treasure Bureau
P.O. Box 5012
Visalia, California 93278
Tele: 800-437-0222
http://www.qksrv.net/click-978793-3962683

Steve Deeds
Superior Galleries
9478 West Olympic Boulevard
Beverly Hills, California 90212
Tele: 800-421-0754
310-203-9855
Fax: 310-203-0496
http://www.superiorgalleries.com/

Dan Drew
Drew's Rare and Unusual Coins
P.O. Box 48755
Athens, Georgia 30604
Email: drew905@mac.com
http://personalwebs.myriad.net/drew905/default.html

Dick Dunn, secretary-treasurer
Canadian Paper Money Society
P.O. Box 562
Pickering, Ontario
Canada L1V 2R7
Tele: 905-509-1146
Email: cpms@idirect.com
http://www.nunetcan.net/cpms.htm

Philippe Elsen, Numismatist
Numismatique
Avenue de Tervueren, 65
1040 Bruxelles, Belgique
Tele:32-2-734-63.56
Fax: 3-2-735-77-78
Email: numismatique@elsen.be
http://www.elsen.be/about_staff.html

Lyle Engleson, Photographer
Ira & Larry Goldberg Coins & Collectibles, Inc.
350 South Beverly Drive, Suite 350
Beverly Hills, California 90212
Tele: 310-551-COIN
800-978-COIN
Email: info@goldbergcoins.com
http://www.goldbergcoins.com

Tom Flowers, President
Mintmark.com
P.O. Box 48
Ortega Station 172
Jacksonville, Florida 32210
Tele: 877-443-9147
Email: currency@mintmark.com
http://www.mintmark.com

Medea Gabunia
Exhibitions, Georgia Gateway
Email: geobuy@yahoo.com
www.georgia-gateway.org/ENG/Marketplace/Exhibition/index.html.

Avis Gachet, Book Buyer
Wonderland Books
5008 Hickory Boulevard
Hickory, North Carolina 28601
Fax: 828-396-2710
Email: wonland@twave.net
http://www.abebooks.com/home/WONLAND/

Vic Gardner, Numismatist
Lion Coins
4 Lindsgate Drive
Timperley Altrincham
Cheshire, England WA15 6RB
Tele: 44-7970-207938
http://www.LionCoins.com

Ron Guth, President
CoinFacts.com, Inc.
P.O. Box 900
La Jolla, California 92038
Tele: 619-972-9449
Fax: 419-710-7699
Email: ron@coinfacts.com
http://www.coinfacts.com/

Jim Halperin, Owner
Cathy Hadd, Numismatist
Carl Watson, Art Editor
Mark Van Winkle, Chief Cataloger
Heritage Coins
Heritage Plaza
100 Highland Park Village, Second Floor
Dallas, Texas 75205-2788
Tele: 800-US-COINS
214 528-3500
Email: Mark@HeritageCoin.com
http://www.heritagecoin.com

Andrew Howitt, Historian
HistoryinCoins.com
30 Brewsters Close
Bingham, Nottinghamshire
England NG138BA
http://www.bottles.freeserve.co.uk/fsp.html

David Kaplan, Historian
Coins from Famous People in History

P.O. Box 1081
Syosset, New York 11791
Email: DKaplan888@aol.com
http://members.aol.com/dkaplan888/main.html

Desmond Kenny, book dealer
Galway, Ireland

Matt Kilbourne
U.S. Mint
Washington, D.C.

Lynne Lail, customer service
Bank of Granite
Hickory, North Carolina

Ron Landis, Chief Engraver
Gallery Mint Museum
P.O. Box 706
Eureka Springs, Arkansas 72632
Tele: 888-558-MINT
Email: gmm@arkansas.net
http://www.coin-gallery.com/gmm/

Dana Linett
P.O. Box 3341
La Jolla, California 92038
Tele: 858-459-4159
Fax: 858-459-4373
Email: History@EarlyAmerican.com
http://www.earlyamerican.com/

Thomas K. Mallon-McCorgray
The Coins and History of Asia
Email: tkmallon@grifterrec.com
http://www.grifterrec.com/coins/coins.html

Diana Norman, novelist and journalist
Datchworth, Stevenage
England

Louis Nunnery, coin collector
Newton, North Carolina

Ken Prophet
Canadian Numismatic Journal
Barrie, Ontario

Mia Romcevic
Athina S. A. Numismatics
21, Rue du Mont-Blanc
1201 Geneva, Switzerland
Tele: (+41) 22 738 71 55
Fax: (+41) 22 738 71 56
Email: coins@athina.ch
http://www.athina.ch/

Wanda Rozzelle, reference librarian
Catawba County Library
Newton, North Carolina

Chris Rudd
Celtic Coins
P.O. Box 222
Aylsham, Norfolk
England NR116TY
Tele: 01263-735007
Fax: 01263-731777
Email: chrisrudd@celticcoins.com
http://www.celticcoins.com

Russian Coin World
www.russiancoinworld.homestead.com/

Jon Saxton
Triton Technologies International, Ltd.
9701 Shore Road #6K
Brooklyn, New York 11209
Email: spam.free@verizon.net
http://www.triton.vg/

Mark Schumacher, reference librarian
Jackson Library, UNC-G
Greensboro, North Carolina

John Stafford-Langan
Irish Coinage
Email: john.stafford-langan@horizon.ie
http://www.bottles.freeserve.co.uk/fsp.html

Mike and Viv Vosper, Numismatists
Mike R. Vosper Coins
P.O. Box 32
Hockwold, Brandon, Suffolk
England IP26 4HX
Tele & Fax: 44-0-1842-828292
E-mail: mike.vosper@vosper4coins.co.uk

Special thanks go to Linda Campbell Franklin, who located material on the Middle Ages and Byzantine history for this work and for an earlier one, *Who's Who in the Middle Ages* (McFarland, 2001).

Contents

List of Entry Headings

Preface

Coins and Currency is an alphabetical encyclopedia to the use of money throughout world history. The entries cover people, places, and terms associated with points in world affairs when human action has intersected with money. The reader will find individual entries on periods of monetary history (e.g., the Middle Ages and Renaissance) as well as on special monetary coinage (e.g., elephant tokens, drum money, papal coins) and an overview of world coinage. Some entries tell the stories of particular coins, including the talent, shekel, *manilla,* Mercury dime, amulet coins, and Susan B. Anthony dollar. Coin artists such as Augustus Saint-Gaudens, Caradosso, Benvenuto Cellini, and Anthony de Francisci are covered, as are two families of engravers, the Wyons of England and the Roettiers of France. Throughout the text, tables of monetary slang, shipwrecks, assay and mint marks, counterfeiters, world coinage, and shifting values of Roman coins in the republic and empire provide a wealth of knowledge at a glance. Translations of terms and inscriptions in foreign languages provide a clearer understanding of the image or message that the coiner intended.

Entries in this book show how money has figured in scripture, such as talmudic discussions of usury and biblical passages that mention the widow's mite, Judas's 30 pieces of silver, Jesus's driving the money changers out of the temple, and the price that Abraham paid for Sarah's tomb; writings by famous historical figures, such as Benjamin Franklin and Thomas Jefferson, who wrote on the creation of a U.S. monetary system; and the works of authors like Amy Tan, Francis Bacon, Mark Twain, Al-Kwarizmi, Edgar Allan Poe, Mary Ann Evans, L. Frank Baum, and Fra Luca Pacioli, creator of the double-entry bookkeeping system. For readers seeking sociological details of monetary exchange, entries on such subjects as blood money, gold rushes, Wells Fargo, the gold standard, hoarding, Fibonacci's democratization of the number system, and cocoa bean and coconut moneys illuminate particular needs and longings for money and the things that it buys. For readers looking for heroics in the history of money, entries on salvor Mel Fisher, archeologist Peter Throckmorton, orator William Jennings Bryan, statesman Alexander Hamilton, numismatist Franz Seraph Streber, and financier William Paterson summarize the lives of people endowed with vision, zeal, and good ideas.

Each entry lists source material gleaned from print and electronic media. I am grateful for the starting places — Larry Allen's *Encyclopedia of Money,* Joe Cribb's *Money* and *The Coin Atlas*, Glyn Davies's *A History of Money from Ancient Times to the Present Day*, Ya'akov Meshorer's *Ancient Jewish Coinage*, Q. David Bowers's *Adventures with Rare Coins*, and Paul Einzig's *Primitive Money*—as well as the specialized reference works, notably Jay Robert Nash's *Encyclopedia of World Crime*, Nigel Pickford's *The Atlas of Ship Wrecks and Treasure*, John Cannon and Ralph Griffiths's *Oxford Illustrated History of the British Monarchy*, George F. Bass's *Ships and Shipwrecks of the Americas: A History Based on Underwater Archaeology*, Peter Kemp's *The Oxford Companion to Ships and the Sea*, Lloyd R. Laing's *Coins and Archaeology*, David Sinclair's *The Pound*, and an intriguing compendium of numismatic gossip, Robert R. Van Ryzin's *Twisted Tails: Sifted Fact, Fantasy and Fiction from U.S. Coin History*. Broadening my understanding of monetary history were exceptional pictorial sources, particularly Elvira Clain-Stefanelli and Vladimir Clain-Stefanelli's *The Beauty and Lore of Coins, Currency, and Medals*, Edward Thomas's *Numismata Orientalia*, Brenda Ralph Lewis's *Coins and Currency*, and electronic picture stories at web sites entitled "The British Royal Mint," "The Bureau of Engraving and Printing," and "The U.S. Mint." Each of these sources points the way to more thorough studies of coin art, history, and lore.

For the student, historian, teacher, researcher, general reader, and coin hound, the back matter of *Coins and Currency* includes a time line that places in chronological order some of the important events in monetary history, such as the placement of Christian symbols and Islamic verses on coins, Dr. Selma Burke's attempt to design a Rosa Parks coin, treasure legislation prohibiting rifling of historic underwater shipwrecks, the development of Fidel Castro's interest in coin salvage, Adolf Burger's assistance in locating Nazi counterfeit banknotes, and the emergence of the euro as a world currency. For quick reference to common coin terminology, a glossary supplies a definition of necessary terms (e.g., planchet, uniface, web press, plate money, bracteate) and a simplified explanation of such technological advances as archeomagnetic dating, siderography, and sonar profiling. The bibliography is an exhaustive list of my sources.

Introduction

Money is a fact of life. No era's history is free of exchange media. There were Celtic coins awaiting Julius Caesar's legionaries when they arrived in Britannia, bullet coins in circulation at the harbor market when Anna Leonowens reached Mongkut's Siam, and stone money already hacked free from quarries when Captain David O'Keefe first met the Yap of Oceania. The full panorama of rice money in southeast Asia, playing card scrip in Canada, archeologists gathering encrusted rounds of gold from the deep waters around the sunken *Atocha*, and hands at the Paris Mint winding a screw press reminds the student of history that human endeavors refuse to fit neatly into categories. From a study of coins and currency in history, the reader learns that the many sides to human personalities intertwine the exploiter and the exploited, the greedy and the great-hearted.

As human action (like spearing elk and conies for dinner) moved toward *interaction* (like trading baskets for barley and ollas for plow points) it became necessary to standardize units of exchange — amber beads, knife blades, saw grass mats — and to create abstract transportable forms of wealth such as feathered strips, shell fishhooks, lumps of bronze, and iron wheels. From marten and beaver skins, whale and dog teeth, and sea salt blocks to electrum and silver circlets, money advanced according to the demands of complex societies. Greek coinage, the height of beauty and efficiency in the ancient world, preserved not only the silver *drachmas* with which shoppers bought Samian wine and olive oil, but also extolled the images of Athena and Zeus along with Hercules, the dolphin, and the other cultural icons that identified the Greek value system.

Beyond their worth to economics and culture, early coins served their creators as tools of propaganda. Across Egypt, Rome, Persia, and Byzantium, portrait coins boasted of conquerors and governors like Alexander III the Great, Julius Caesar, Constantine the Great, and Justinian the lawgiver. Other nations learned the intricacies of classic Mediterranean coinage as camels bore coin pouches over the spice trade routes and lateen sails carried shippers and their stock of *tetradrachmas* to ports in Arabia, Ceylon, and Sumatra. Far to the northwest, Celtic smithies emulated on potin the gestures and style of classic coinage. Though struck with lesser artistry than that of Attica and Syracusa, Celtic coinage displayed no less fervor.

The intrusion of organized religion into coinage shifted emphasis from scepters and robes to holy fires and nimbate holy figures—Ahura Mazda, Siva, Lakshmi, Christ, the Virgin Mary, saints, and angels—and audaciously pictured earthly satraps receiving coronets and blessings from heavenly beings. Unlike Zoroastrianism, Christianity, Hinduism, and Buddhism, the advance of Islam produced a singular shift in coinage. Basing their decisions on Koranic principles, which reject artistic representation of the Prophet Mohammed or of Allah, rulers like Saladin and Jahangir of India abandoned past traditions of ego and self-adulation to embrace pictureless coins enwrapped in Arabic script. The artistic side of Islam found expression in the beauty of holy writ composed in flowing calligraphy and in the grandeur of the *tughra*, a signature compressed into a unitized figure as bemusing as a puzzle, as definitive as a knotted tassel. The spread of Muslims over the map altered coinage in the Middle East, across Afghanistan, and into the Indian subcontinent and, at the same time, west from Mecca over northern and central Africa and into Sicily and Iberia.

Following Christopher Columbus's world-changing voyage to the Caribbean, the lust for gold marked human endeavors in a new round of jealousy, perfidy, enslavement, and piracy. While peons in Central and South America struck ore into doubloons and *maravedís* so Spain could wallow in cascades of gold and silver, envious rival nations awaited the transport across the Atlantic of each season's coinage. To rearrange the allotment of treasure, the bold Queen Elizabeth I of England dispatched her privateers to steal the new issue and carry it to English coin smithies for counterstamping and adding to the treasury. Licensed stealing on the Spanish Main elevated men like Piet Heyn and George Anson to national heroism and earned Sir Francis Drake his knighthood. Simultaneously, audacious thieves like Blackbeard, William Kidd, Mary Read, Black Bart Roberts, Anne Bonny, and Henry Morgan flew the Jolly Roger in place of a national ensign. They took the same liberties with ownership, but omitted the counterstamp. Reveling in cash from any source, pirates spread their largesse in buccaneer capitals over the Caribbean isles and up the Atlantic coast, leaving behind a treasure in folklore.

While pirates frolicked in cash, for European colonists, specie of any type or provenance was a rarity. As welcome as the trade goods and services they bought, a motley array of tuppences, *sous*, *stuivers*, *écus*, and cobs served settlers along the St. Lawrence Seaway, down the Mississippi Valley, throughout New England, and south to the Carolinas. While individual wallets dwindled, the cash boxes of colonial entrepreneurs grew fat on the transatlantic circulation of pieces of eight, shillings, and *guilders*. Coins supplemented the more onerous Iroquois wampum, beaver fur baled by the *coureurs de bois*, Georgia leaf tobacco hacked and bundled by African slaves, and various other commodity moneys. In comparison to cash, crude and perishable trade and barter items sparked arguments and produced quandaries over transfer, evaluation, and storage. In subsequent decades, improvements in coin technology worked at the problems of badly worn pennies and small change shortages for everyday commerce as well as threats of counterfeit coinage and outright thievery through sweating and coin clipping and shaving.

Gradually, elegant moneys enhanced national prestige with symbolism and fine crafting and memorable inscriptions. The sophisticated *ducat, dinar, koban, florin*, and private specie generated by the papal Zecca replaced crude maul-hammered pieces from medieval forges. World travelers made the mental connection between the French and the *franc*, Germany and its *thaler*, Japan and its *oban*, and the English with their long-lived crowns, shillings, and pennies. The cascade of *louis d'ors, dirhams, pice, yen*, and *rupees* from around the world filled the pockets of international merchants and enabled buyers and sellers from a mix of nations and cultures to meet on equal footing and contract business with confidence.

The advance of banking from Egyptian grain depots to the Royal Exchange, Paris Bourse, and Federal Reserve Bank moved money into new realms. Paper notes, scrip, and siege and fiat money produced new cautions in the minds of people who were accustomed to weighing coins on a balance beam scale and computing their worth based on the value of precious metals. Unlike silver in the hand, promissory notes and bank-to-bank trading required more knowledge of economics and of the political alliances that bound country to country in peace and prosperity. World wars and border enmities kept the status quo in perpetual tilt, requiring embassies to iron out the details to keep commerce flowing.

Into the last decades of the twentieth century, money ranged free of die stamp and printing press to become functions of the stroke of a key, the swipe of a credit card. As the twenty-first century began, the incipient distribution of one currency for 12 European countries had created a new wrinkle in international cooperation. Backers of the euro share a mutual trust that reduction of the number of specie and note types will lessen errors in exchange that date back to the Mamluks and Ionians swapping coppers at dockside. Ironically, at the same time that moneyers have looked ahead to new alloys and security devices to ease difficulties in marketing and savings, designers have returned to the early Greek, Renaissance Italian, and art deco touchstones of beauty, physical appeal, and intrinsic symbolism.

In conclusion, the highs and lows of monetary history parallel the best and worst in human behaviors. Like Marley's ghost, the Mammon of past and present perpetually shadows the mores of the people who coin, print, and hoard money. The grand *antoniniani* of the Roman Empire, debased *sestertii,* and glittering Maltese *zecchini* share space on the page with low-quality *tympf,* pirate swag, Brinks and Wells Fargo robberies, and the Holocaust scrip cranked out on concentration camp printing presses. Art, drama, literature, and film record the myriad faces of monetary ethics, lauding the epiphanies of Daniel Defoe's Robinson Crusoe, Charles Dickens's Ebenezer Scrooge, and George Eliot's Silas Marner while holding up as warnings Jan Vermeer's procuress, Robert Louis Stevenson's Long John Silver, the Western scenario of Butch Cassidy robbing the Katy Flier, and William Shakespeare's stagy Shylock, the embodiment of crude, destructive stereotyping of the Jewish moneylender.

The story of currency in history spreads into the far corners of zeal and ambition — from the fevered hope of diggers of the money pit and panners of Yukon streams to the religious fervor of the Knights Hospitallers and Stuart kings stroking scrofulous patients with amulet coins; from the artisans who created Santa Cruz feather money and African kissi pennies to the dreamers who envisioned moneyless utopias and the criminals who dabbed in money laundering, scams, and forgery. Currency, of itself, has no value beyond the paper and metal in its makeup. It is the human overlay of hope that turns thin coins into an *obolus* on each sightless eye to pay the way for the deceased into the underworld; it is altruism and love of humankind that turns coins into a March of Dimes to defeat polio and birth defects. Offsetting the Anglo-Saxon bribery of Viking raiders, Irish swapping of slave women as cash, and bribes and hush money slipped from palm to palm, monetary history highlights the specie of old as treasure for the diver, metal detector, numismatist, and hobby coin collector. For the admirer and the curious, bright circlets on chains and watch fobs and trays and cases of fine coins set aglitter under the museum's bright lights bear testimony to the allure of money for all times.

THE ENCYCLOPEDIA

Admiral Gardner

The 813-ton English cargo vessel *Admiral Gardner* sank in the English Channel after setting sail from Dover on January 25, 1809. On its sixth voyage to colonial India, the ship, accompanied by sister ships *Britannia* and *Carnatic*, bore 54 tons of copper ten- and 20-cash pieces for Madras, India, which coiners had struck in 1808 at the Soho Works in Birmingham. Brassware manufacturer Matthew Boulton intended them for the East India Company as pay for workers in Bengal and Madras. Each coin bore the seal and motto of the British Empire, the legend "East India Company," and the date 1808.

Built on the Thames in 1796 by John Woolmore and named for Alan Gardner, Member of Parliament, the *Admiral Gardner* was one of a fleet of company ships that resembled Royal Naval vessels in size and equipment. Designed for shipping heavy loads, it carried a smaller crew and fewer arms than battleships required. Captain William John Eastfield was unable to maneuver the heavy craft in a freak gale off Dover and grounded his ship off South Foreland on the Goodwin Sands. By dawn, his cargo was lost to the sea. On February 11, 1809, London publisher Thomas Tegg captured the event in a pamphlet illustrated with a dramatic view of the listing ship bashed by waves.

Ironically, during the Industrial Revolution, it was Boulton, a respected philanthropist and industrialist honored as a fellow of the Royal Society, who solved some of England's minting difficulties in meeting the empire's demands for bronze coins. The issuance of privately minted coins like Boulton's enabled employers to pay laborers, who suffered the brunt of hard work rewarded by money deflated to half value. To ease the shortage in India, he had accepted a contract to supply coins and to ship minting machines to East India Company field operations in Calcutta and Madras. Allied with inventor James Watt in 1768, Boulton had become a partner in the growing steam engine operation, which successfully drained the shafts of tin mines in Cornwall and updated coinage from hand striking to a rapid, accurate mechanized process.

The day after the loss of the *Admiral Gardner*, Captain Eastfield wrote a report to William Ramsey of India House from Deal, Kent. Eastfield expressed regret and recounted details of the ship's departure on the flood tide at sunset. At 7:00 P.M., he summoned all hands to battle rain and northwesterly winds. Shortly before 11:00 P.M., he heard the pilot exclaiming that the ship had struck shore in five fathoms of water. The situation was so desperate that the pilot lost two fingers in cutting away the sheet. The gallant struggle sapped the crew, who realized by 6:30 A.M. that the ship was lost. At 3:35 P.M. the next afternoon, as the ship filled with water, rescuers from Deal saved all on board but one. The event appears to have ruined Eastfield's health. He died that same year.

The remains of the *Admiral Gardner* gained new interest in 1984, when an English fisherman realized that the obstacle snagging his net four miles off shore must be the ship's ruins. In June 1985, diving operations in 45–60 feet of water retrieved 1,250,000 coins from the hold of the wreck, which had dwindled to deck, frame, and ribs. Mounting squabbles with preservationists over protecting the site slowed recovery of treasure, which turned up copper ingots, iron bars, cannon balls, anchors, and barrels of uncirculated coins marked in Roman numerals as "X Cash" and "XX Cash." The reverse of each coin displayed the etymology of "cash," which derived from *kasu*, the Tamil word for "coin." The incised Latin motto of the East India Company read "*Auspicio Regis et Senatus Angliae*" ("By Authority of the King and the English Parliament"). Passed to a maritime official called the receiver of wreck were recovered items, including one complete barrel of 28,000 coins, which preservers treated at Portsmouth to prevent corrosion. To maintain the site as a historical treasure, the government curtailed salvage operations under the Protection of Wrecks Act of 1973. Supplying additional data were journals, ledgers, and pay books housed at the U.K. National Register of Archives.

See also **Matthew Boulton.**

SOURCES: "*Admiral Gardner,*" http://www.ships.clara.net/lost/lost_a/admgard/index.htm. • *Biography Resource Center*. Farmington Hills, Mich.: Gale Group, 2001. • Kemp, Peter, ed. *The Oxford Companion to Ships and the Sea*. Oxford: Oxford University Press, 1988. • *Merriam-Webster's Biographical Dictionary*. Springfield, Mass.: Merriam-Webster, 1995. • Rocco, Fiammetta. "Keeping the Flame." *Institutional Investor*, December 1988, 31–32. • *World of Invention*, 2nd ed. Farmington Hills, Mich.: Gale Group, 1999.

African money

From early times, the African economy depended on trade and barter before developing as legal tender such primitive currency as cowries, brass rings and rods, iron bars, gold ore, feathers, salt, slaves, ivory, and kola nuts. To the northeast in Egypt, the use of bronze money rings strung on metal loops and worn as armlets and necklaces supplied shoppers at Tanis with small change. To substantiate value, merchants weighed them on balance beam scales. In 1300 B.C., Egyptian moneyers created true coins.

A social guarantee of security, the traditional dowry appears in Egyptian writings from the 600s B.C. Portable goods made up bridewealth, the massed gift of farm animals, household goods, and money that prospective husbands offered to future in-laws. Bridewealth was the focus of *shep en sehemet* ("marriage contracts"), a formal accounting of agricultural benefits, property, goods, and money passed from groom to bride's father, male to male, and implied a political union of families. Most welcome among the gifts were primitive media of exchange — lengths of cloth, copper bracelets and torques, wood and amber beads, hoes and knife blades, goats and sheep, and cattle. Some pledges were so financially burdensome that they required years to fulfill. While the groom made payments on his debt, the obligation rewarded him with the patriarchal and social benefits of marriage and encouraged a stable relationship free from non-support, desertions, separations, and divorce.

The first genuine coins struck in Africa appeared in Libya around 500 B.C. In 470 B.C., native coiners created irregular pieces with a bold, bearded profile of Zeus wearing a ram's horn headdress. The Egyptian king Ptolemy XII abandoned impersonal and divine motifs for his own portrait coin rendered in the style of Philip II of Macedon and his son, Alexander III the Great. Greek design influenced Numidian portrait coins of great kings, notably the vicious Jugurtha, whom the Roman general Sulla captured and the consul Marius marched in the streets of Rome before executing in 104 B.C. In Mauretania, the coins of Juba II honored the king and his first wife, Cleopatra Selene, daughter of Mark Antony

This portrait coin from North Africa was minted in 322 B.C., a decade after the conquest of Egypt by Alexander III the Great of Macedon. (Guy Clark, Ancient Coins and Antiquities, Norfolk, Virginia)

and Cleopatra. By the beginning of the reign of Augustus Caesar, these kingdoms ceased to exist as Rome swallowed them up in an empire that ringed the Mediterranean.

To the south, an area never subjugated by Greece or Rome, sub–Saharan Africans traded in goats and cattle and established a goat standard in Uganda and Tanzania and along the equator. Before manufactured coins and paper money reached the continent, black Africa produced a wide range of folk currencies based on natural resources and artisanal crafting, especially in the Congo and along the Gold Coast. Shoppers used cowries, beads, brass or copper wires, and metal bars for small change and iron-bladed knives, axes, sickles, and sabers for larger purchases. Style of trade items varied by locale and tribe:

A profile coin from 25 B.C. of Juba II of Mauritania, husband of Cleopatra Selene, the daugher of Cleopatra and Mark Anthony, beats the Latin inscription "REX IUBA" [King Juba]. (Guy Clark, Ancient Coins and Antiquities, Norfolk, Virginia)

Nation and People	*Types of Money*
Abyssinia	
Abyssinians	brick salt
Algeria	cardboard coins
Angola	macuta copper bars, beer, shells, glass beads, fiber mats, red timber
Kissama	salt bars
Benin	cotton cloth, cowries, *manillas*
Fon	peg ingots
Cameroon	wives, goats, sheep, beads, cowries, soap, fishhooks, gunpowder, brass rings, black spotted peas, brass animal shapes, salt money
Bafia	iron triangles and clubs
Bakwiri	cattle, women
Banaka	rifles, gunpowder, tobacco, salt, rum, cotton, sheep
Bapuku	rifles, gunpowder, tobacco, salt, rum, cotton
Basa	tobacco
Batanga	sheep
Bulu	cloth
Dikwa	throwing axes
Fulani	bar ingots
Kapsiki	throwing knives
Kirdi	sickle blades, throwing axes and knives
Marghi	throwing knives
Matakam	double spiral pins, hoe blades
Podokwo	sickle blades
Central Africa	
Bwaka	hoe blades
Ekonda	leg cuffs
Fang	hoe blades, axes
Jonga	double gongs
Katanga	*handa* ingots, crosses
Kusu	U-shaped *konga* bars
Kwele	hoe blades, *mandjong* ("crossbow arrows")
Lokele	sword blades
Mbole	arch bullion, c-shaped anklets, hoe blades
Ngelima	arch bullion, hoe blades
Nkutshu	double gongs
Sara	throwing knives
Songo-Meno	*konga* ("u-bars")
Turumbu	spear blades, sword blades
Chad	
Koma	throwing knives
Masa	throwing knives
Sara	throwing knives
Congo (Zaire)	slaves, wire coils, shovels, arrows, raffia mats, cowries, beads, tobacco, salt, guns, iron bells, U-shaped copper bars, braided elephant tail hair, bracelets, human teeth

Babunda	rubber
Bagirmi	cotton cloth strips, iron throwing disks
Bakongo	iron bars
Bapindji	rubber
Bwaka	hoe blades
Ekonda	leg cuffs
Jonga	double gongs, flanged gongs
Kasai	shells
Katanga	*handa* ingots, crosses
Kuba	cowries, copper *bakuba* anklets
Kusu	u-shaped *konga* bars
Kwango	shells
Kwele	hoe blades, *mandjong* ("crossbow arrows")
Lele	raffia cloth
Lokele	sword blades
Lulua	*zappozap* axes
Mbole	arch bullion, c-shaped anklets, hoe blades
Ngelima	arch bullion, hoe blades
Nkutshu	double gongs, wrought iron *iwenga* blades
Nsapo	zappozap axes
Songo-Meno	u-shaped *konga* bars
Turumbu	*liganda* spear blades, sword blades
Wadai	cattle, cotton cloth
Wangata	iron leg coils and armbands
Dahomey	cowries
Ethiopia	iron blades, salt money, cartridges, flint, *barjookes* beads made from glass bottles, guns
Borana	cloth, metal bracelets, metal cubes, beads, tobacco, cowries, livestock
Somali	camels, tobacco, blue cotton cloth, millet
Gabon	ivory, sandalwood, ebony, iron knives
Fang	hoe blades
Kwele	hoe blades, *mandjong* crossbow arrows, ivory
Kota	iron axes, sickles
Gambia	
Mandingo	cloth, kola nuts, cattle
Senegambia	gold dust, ostrich feathers
Ghana	slaves, cowries, beads, iron needles, iron disks
Ashanti	gold dust, brass animal shapes
Guinea	slaves, silver and copper fetishes, rice, pepper
Bini	iron bangles
Kissi	kissi pennies
Toma	kissi pennies
Ivory Coast	gold dust, cowries
Agni	tobacco, salt, cloth, hoes, beads
Kenya	cattle, goats
Elgeyo	cows
Kikuyu	goats, sheep
Masai	cattle
Turkana	cows
Wakamba	cattle
Liberia	palm oil, palm kernels
Kissi	kissi pennies, glass lozenges
Kpele	salt, iron rods, slaves, cattle, kola nuts
Kru	knobbed cylinder rings
Toma	kissi pennies, glass lozenges
Libya	corn, silk string
Madagascar	pieces of silver coins, cattle, oxen
Mali	slab salt
Mozambique	rectangular gold *maticae*, calico, beads, lead and copper bracelets, copper and brass wire, cowries, millet, ammunition, gunpowder, brass disks, iron needles
Wabena	cattle, goats, poultry, ducks, dogs, hoes, cloth, rifles
Niger	
Tuareg	knobbed ring bracelets
Nigeria	slaves, palm oil, copper and brass rods, yams, palm kernels, black spotted peas, iron bars, wooden beads, cloth strips, feathers, fine copper wire, bottles of gin, tin straws
Chamba	rings with butterfly ends
Fulani	bar ingots
Idoma	iron blades
Igbo (Ibo)	coil bracelets, copper rings, cowries, manillas
Mfumte	iron blades
Munshi	brass beads with loops for hanging
Yoruba	cylindrical pointed collars, cowries
Portuguese	
East Africa	hoes, cattle
Sierra Leone	gunpowder, flints, silver bars, salt money
Bubi	shell disks
Kissi	kissi pennies

Sherbo	iron strips
Toma	kissi pennies
South Africa	
Basuto	beads, coral, rifles, ivory, spears points, cattle
Hottentot	brass rods, glass beads, tobacco, wire, pipes, copper plates
Kaffir	metal rings, cattle
Malepa	clay pots
Sudan	hoe blades, ring money, bundles of cotton thread, slaves, onions, cotton thread, copper cylinders, millet
Darfur	amorphous iron lumps, tin plates
Dinka	cattle
Fader	tin rings, cotton fabric
Guely	salt bars
Kouca	tobacco
Mombattu	semicircular rings, amorphous iron lumps
Nuer	cattle, sheep
Shilluk	cattle
Tanzania	livestock, poultry, blue and white cylindrical beads, cowries, brass wire, iron arrowheads
Ruanda-Urundi	cattle
Swahili	copper coins
Wahima	cotton cloth
Togo	hoes, onions, pepper, salt, oil, poultry, rubber balls, iron bells
Moba	cowries
Uganda	beer, cowries, cattle
Ankole	cattle
Baganda	cattle, goats
Chiga	iron hoes, ivory discs
Iteso	cattle
Kuku	arrows
Lango	cattle, grain, beer
Madi	arrows
Makaraka	spearheads
West Africa	
Chamba	rings with butterfly ends
Dikwa	throwing axes
Fon	peg ingots
Idoma	iron blades
Igbo (Ibo)	coil bracelets, cowries, *manillas*
Kapsiki	throwing knives
Kirdi	sickle blades, throwing axes and knives
Kissi	kissi pennies
Kru	knobbed cylinder rings
Marghi	throwing knives
Matakam	double spiral pins, hoe blades
Mfumte	iron blades
Podokwo	sickle blades
Sara	throwing knives
Toma	kissi pennies
Tuareg	knobbed ring bracelets
Yoruba	cylindrical pointed collars
Zambia	calico cloth, salt
Mambwe	livestock
Zanzibar	cotton *doti* cloth, wire, cloth, beads
Zimbabwe	metal H-shaped crosses

From A.D. 200, Aksum introduced the first indigenous African coinage. Traders carried its specie as far east as Yemen. Until the 600s A.D., coiners struck pieces from bronze, silver, and gold and patterned sizes and legends on Roman originals. Details from Aksumite money written in Ethiopic or *Lessana Ge'ez* ("language of the free") have enabled historians to study the periods and accomplishments of dynasties. The most effective ruler, Ezana, who came to power around A.D. 320, ruled from western Ethiopia into southern Arabia and exacted tribute from client chiefs and kings. After Ezana's conversion to Christianity, perhaps by his teacher, the Syrian missionary called Frumentius, Aksumite moneyers replaced symbols of animism, fetishism, and polytheism with the Christian cross. A pragmatic shift, the Aksumite alliance with the prevailing religion of the Roman Empire brought the nation into closer relationship with the Mediterranean world.

Coastal countries were the first to develop trade with the African heartland. In the

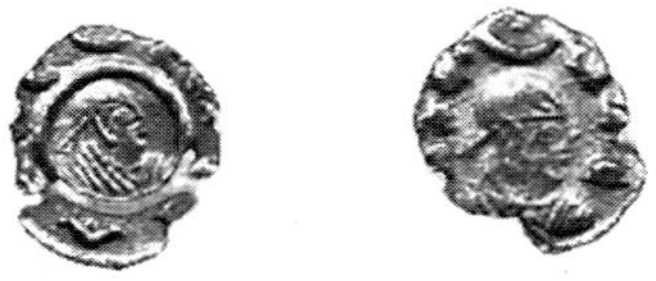

In A.D. 330, the African kingdom of Aksum, which introduced the first indigenous African coinage, produced this portrait piece, which traders carried as far east as Yemen. (Guy Clark, Ancient Coins and Antiquities, Norfolk, Virginia)

1000s, Arab merchants entered Kenya bearing Islamic coins to trade for ivory and slaves. For the first time, Africans contemplated the religious markings that praised Allah, the god of the Koran. In 1324, Mansa Musa, the grandnephew of Sundiata and emperor of Mali, made an obligatory *hajj* (pilgrimage) from his capital of Nian on the Upper Niger River to Mecca. For the first time, the outside world glimpsed his great wealth. Before Sultan Al-Malik an-Nasir at Cairo and at Mecca, he passed in procession in fine attire on horseback before stunned Arabs, who marveled at his retinue of 60,000 retainers and 12,000 slaves uniformed in brocaded silk. In the packs of 80 camels were loads of gold, which so flooded Cairo's market stalls that it depressed the gold market.

In 1352, travel writer ibn Battuta, author of *Tuhfat al-Nuzzar fi Ghara'ib al-Amsar wa'Ajaib al'Asfar* (*On Curiosities of Cities and Wonders of Travel*) (1354), visited Kilwa, a thriving port city in Tanzania that he described as beautiful, well-constructed, and elegant. A commercial center, it was the nexus of trade between central Africa and merchants from Arabia and India. The city was the first in Africa to have a mint, where sultans cast coins in six denominations. The harbor was still impressive in 1500, when Portuguese explorer Pedro Alvares Cabral visited.

Battuta journeyed by caravan for 63 days south across the Sahara Desert from Fez to Mali. He discovered that *bilad al-sudan* ("black Africa") was enjoying a financial boom from the gold mines at Bambuk and Bure. Because Christian governments in Europe stabilized their treasuries with west African gold, Mali prospered. Ibn Battuta discovered that the Malians could afford large armies and could conquer neighboring fields and pastures, thus enlarging the tax base. Amidst a wealth of gold, he observed that the Malians and Sudanese used as currency cowrie shells from the Maldives. As African trade with Muslim caravans imported Islam, the Arabs' ready money paid for the building of mosques and won African converts from paganism.

The Congo prospered from its copper deposits in the Katanga region, where money first appeared as amorphous hunks of ore. At the beginning of the 15th century, workers formed copper into X's and H's around ten inches high and weighing up to nine pounds. In sand molds, artisans shaped molten copper into perpendicular shapes called *baluba* crosses. As money, the crosses circulated in central Africa or were melted down for reshaping. The bundling of slender wires answered the need for small change.

In 1541, Portuguese traveler Duarte (or Odoardo) Lopez (or Lopes) wrote *Relazione del Reame di Congo delle Circonvicine Contrade* (*A Report on the Kingdom of the Congo and Surrounding Countries*), which explained the provenance of an unusual decorative currency from elephant country. Natives lured or drove the beasts into blinds too narrow to allow the animals to turn around. Daring pursuers followed and lopped off elephant tails, one of which would buy up to three slaves. From elephant hair, the hunters braided bracelets. A similar trade in giraffe tails threatened the animal's survival until the East African governments banned the tails as money.

Iron was a common material for hoe money, the generic name for implements, knives, and blades used as currency and also as emblems of status and power at tribal ceremonies. Iron was also the choice for nuptial gifts among the Turumbu of the Congo and Central Africa. They valued iron spear blades as a standard bride price, which established the economic class of the groom at the same time that it compensated parents for the loss of their daughter's labor. If the marriage foundered, the bride's parents could demand return of the blades, which became an insurance policy protecting women from penury when they fled abusive or adulterous mates or abandoned homes.

An unusual blend of jewelry and convenient storage of worth was the *manilla*, a bronze bangle bracelet, anklet, or torque shaped out of bar metal. In Mali, the display of thin-bladed gold *kwottenai* ("earrings") served a similar purpose as a reservoir of wealth and security for women and the daughters to whom they pass their jewelry. Beaten from gold ingots into crescents, these earrings bore human figures and images from nature that enhanced both the beauty and prestige of the wearer. Like signet rings or pearl necklaces in the West, *kwottenai* became the woman-to-woman heritage that linked generations. A variant on the concept of wearable currency was the twisted copper wire bracelet or neck-piece, often finished at the ends with fancy knots. Worth hinged on length rather than weight, thus making exchanges easy to negotiate without scales.

Original to the Kissi people was the kissi penny, also called ghisi, gitzi, and gizzie iron, a long coin comprised of iron rods from seven to twelve inches long and twisted into an anthropomorphic unit. Valued from the 1800s to around 1950 in Guinea, Liberia, and Sierra Leone, these unusual trade pieces carried a folk superstition that each humanoid shape held a soul. If the rods broke, the loss of the soul devalued the coin. Only a shaman could regenerate the spirit.

In the 1870s, British general Charles George Gordon attempted to familiarize the Sudanese with the convenience of modern coins. To end the feudal system, he tutored chiefs in the value of money over beads, calico, and other trade items and acted out simple exchanges, such as two dollars for an ivory tusk and two bells for a dollar. Gordon explained that individual wealth would elevate the Sudanese from vassals to citizens. Eventually, the experiment in offering both beads and coins to workers resulted in rejection of beads. Peasants developed thrift and vowed to save their coins until they had enough to buy expensive items.

In 1938, for the British Royal Institute of International Affairs, Lord William Malcolm Hailey devised a similar training system in *African Survey: A Study of Problems Arising in Africa South of the Sahara*. He intended to halt dependence on cattle for currency because pasturing too many animals depleted grass from the land and turned the region into a dust bowl. To save arable soil, Hailey proposed that moneyers present coins stamped with the likeness of a cow or goat to make the psychological connection between actual and symbolic worth. The effort did not expunge centuries of exploitation of conquered people. A French cartoonist satirized the condescending British by depicting a colonial overlord turning the capstan of a screw press, which squashes the body of a black African slave while generating gold coins. A pompous Church of England clergyman stands alongside the operation reading from a prayer book.

As colonialism died out, by the 1900s, more sophisticated coinage appeared in Angola, Ghana, Liberia, and Sierra Leone, where designers featured symbols relating to liberation and the end of the slave trade. A Liberian copper penny pictured a dramatic scenario — an African male welcoming home former citizens freed from bondage. Modernization removed the nature-based imagery of the past. A 25-*ghirsh* coin struck on cupronickel in Sudan in 1968 pictured a suitably bureaucratic scenario, a postman with upraised staff hurrying his camel along a desert mail route.

Throughout the 20th century, African colonies tended to trade in the coin of the European overlord or in local coinage that imitated the mottoes and motifs of the parent country. Smaller, less affluent countries contracted their coinage from outside their boundaries, primarily from London's Royal Mint while such large, prosperous nations as Ghana, Malawi, and Zambia established their own minting operations. Zambia struck a 12-sided coin picturing an ear of corn in support of the United Nations Food and Agriculture Organization.

Prosperity has not progressed unhampered. Late in the 1980s, Angola supported a failing economy by accepting imported beer as a substitute for the faltering *kwanza*. As trade on the *Roque Santeiro* ("black market") plunged commerce into a primitive state, workers accepted company scrip in lieu of legal tender and converted it into cases of Beck's, Heineken, or Stella Artois. In current times, African moneys include the revived Angolan *kwanza* as well as the *cedi*, *cent*, *centavo*, *centime, butat, dalasi, dinar, dirham, franc, lwei, khoum, kobo, kopek, kwacha, leone, lisente, loti, metical, millième, naira, nakfa, ngwee, ouguiya, pesewa, piastre, pound, pula, rand, rouble, rupee, shilling, tambala,* and *thebe.*

See also **cowrie; Egyptian money; fish-hook money; Islamic money; krugerrand; *manilla*; paper money; portrait coins; Rix dollars; salt money; *thaler*; tooth money; *Whydah*; world money.**

SOURCES: Allen, Larry. *Encyclopedia of Money.* New York: Checkmark Books, 2001. • "The Artistry of African Currency." http://www.nmafa.si.edu/exhibits/site/manillas.htm. • Bullis, Douglas. "The Longest Hajj: The Journeys of Ibn Battuta." *Aramco World,* July/August 2000, 2–39. • Clain-Stefanelli, Elvira, and Vladimir Clain-Stefanelli. *The Beauty and Lore of Coins, Currency, and Medals.* Croton-on-Hudson, N.Y.: Riverwood Publishers, 1974. • Cribb, Joe. *Money.* Toronto: Stoddart, 1990. • Davidson, Basil. *African Kingdoms.* New York: Time, Inc., 1966. • Davies, Glyn. *A History of Money from Ancient Times to the Present Day.* Cardiff: University of Wales Press, 1994. • Einzig, Paul. *Primitive Money.* Oxford: Pergamon Press, 1966. • *Encyclopedia of African History and Culture.* New York: Facts On File, Inc., 2001. • Ibn Battuta. *The Travels of Ibn Battuta.* Cambridge: Cambridge University Press, 1971. • James, Peter, and Nick Thorpe. *Ancient Inventions.* New York: Ballantine, 1994. • Lewis, Brenda Ralph. *Coins & Currency.* New York: Random House, 1993. • Opitz, Charles J. *Odd and Curious Money.* Ocala, Fla.: First Impressions, 1986. • Taylor, Paul. "Wholesale Corruption." *Washington Post,* September 28, 1993, p. A29. • Tibbles, Anthony. "TransAtlantic Slavery." *Antiques,* June 1999. • "Trading with Europeans." http://educate.si.edu/resources/lessons/siyc/currency/essay5.html.

Alexius I Comnenus

To stave off Islamic attack on Byzantium, the Emperor Alexius I Comnenus initiated a vigorous campaign to bolster the military, even at the cost of debased currency. Born around 1048, he came to power in 1081 before the organization of the First Crusade. As financial and internal affairs tottered toward ruin, he shored up the military to secure his throne against two threats, the Normans and Seljuk Turks. In a letter imploring aid from the Germans against Robert the Norman, Alexius wrote in desperation, describing his dispatch of money:

> For surely God will never allow the scourge of sinners to fall upon His own inheritance to such an extent. The gifts our Majesty agreed to send to your mighty Highness, to wit the 144,000 "nummi" ... [consisting] of coins stamped with the head of Romanus and of ancient quality. And when your Highness has accomplished the oath, the remaining 216,000 "nummi" as well as the stipend of the twenty dignities conferred, shall be sent to your Highness by your trusty servant Bagelardus ["Medieval Sourcebook: Anna Comnena," Book II].

Such was the cost that Alexius gladly paid to shore up his western frontier.

After appealing to Pope Urban II, Alexius supported the First Crusade, initiated by Peter the Hermit in 1096. To secure the state treasury, Alexius resorted to dire measures. He superintended a debasement of gold scyphate *nomismata,* cup-shaped coins that he ordered with his likeness, and demanded the razing of public statues to be scrapped for their bronze. Many of the details of his reign survive in the *Alexias* or *Alexiad* (1148), composed by his daughter, historian Anna Comnena. In Book V, she lists the methods of procuring funds, beginning with the collection of gold and silver articles for melting at the imperial mint. She extols the example of her mother, the Empress Irene, who "deposited the sum that remained to her of her parents' patrimony, hoping thereby to instigate others to do the same; for she was extremely anxious for the Emperor, seeing the straits into which his affairs had fallen" ("Medieval Sourcebook: Anna Comnena," Book V).

Anna continues with a catalog of the donations of friends of the imperial family. When mercenaries clamored for pay and bonuses, in the absence of good will from Rome, Alexius debated public and private schemes of fund-raising, then perused ancient laws concerning liquidation of Church property. Because canon law sanctioned sale of sacred properties for the ransoming of prisoners of war, he began turning church vessels into coin. In Anna's words, Leo, bishop of the church at Chalcedon, "tore off the silver and gold ornaments on the doors of the church in Chalcoprateia" (*ibid.*).

In Book VI, Anna notes the price her father paid for stripping the church and coining money to fund the military. When he returned from battle to his palace in Constantinople,

> The mutterings against him in the highways and byways did not escape his notice, and the hearing of them wounded his soul because the number of backbiters railing against him had increased greatly although he had not committed any serious offence [*ibid.*].

She justifies the liquidation of private and church wealth as a last-ditch effort to acquire moneys that he intended to pay back. She emphasizes that her father intended to readorn the churches at war's end. When Alexius died on August 16, 1118, of a heaviness of the chest that he had contracted in two years of combat, he left the Byzantine Empire and its state church diminished and war-worn, but secure.

***See also* Byzantine coins; scyphate coins.**

SOURCES: Clain-Stefanelli, Elvira, and Vladimir Clain-Stefanelli. *The Beauty and Lore of Coins, Currency, and Medals*. Croton-on-Hudson, N.Y.: Riverwood Publishers, 1974. • *Encyclopedia of World Biography*. Detroit: Gale Group, 1998. • Hastings, James, ed. *Encyclopedia of Religion and Ethics*. New York: Charles Scribner's Sons, 1951. • "Medieval Sourcebook: Anna Comnena: The Alexiad." http://www.fordham.edu/HALSALL/basis/annacomnena-alexiad00.html. • *New Catholic Encyclopedia*. San Francisco: Catholic University of America, 1967. • Snodgrass, Mary Ellen. *Who's Who in the Middle Ages*. Jefferson, N.C.: McFarland, 2001. • Starr, Chester G. *A History of the Ancient World*. New York: Oxford University Press, 1991.

Al-Khwarizmi

The father of algebra, decimals, and algorithms, astronomer and geographer Muhammad Ibn Musa Al-Khwarizmi (also lgorizm or Muhammad Bin Musa Al-Khwarizmi) created the basis of modern number theory, banking, and commerce. Born in A.D. 770 at Keva on the Oxus River in Uzbekistan, he came of age in Baghdad and apprenticed on the staff of Kalif Al-Mamun. By mastering the Hindu and Greek math of Brahmagupta and Pythagoras, he invented linear and quadratic equations, differential calculus, conics, and trigonometric tables for the sine and tangent functions. As an aid to star study, he compiled star tables that Adelard of Bath and Gerard of Cremona introduced to Europe three centuries later in Latin translations.

Al-Khwarizmi's two math texts supplied classrooms into the 1500s. As overseer of 70 geographers, he was the first to fit a globe with a world map and pioneered degree measurements for cartographers. He is best known for mapping the heavens and for publishing *Hisab al-Jabr w-al-Muqabalah* (*The Science of Restoration and Reduction*) (ca. A.D. 800), and handbooks to sundials, clocks, and astrolabes. Along with the writings of Italian theorist Leonardo Fibonacci, who introduced Arabic numerals in Europe, these sophisticated number studies democratized business math, enabling money changers, bankers, and loan officers to express the complexities of cost, overhead, and interest and of changing money among currencies.

***See also* Leonardo Fibonacci.**

SOURCES: Allen, Larry. *Encyclopedia of Money*. New York: Checkmark Books, 2001. • Crombie, A. C. *Medieval and Early Modern Science*. Cambridge, Mass.: Harvard University Press, 1967. • Snodgrass, Mary Ellen. *Who's Who in the Middle Ages*. Jefferson, N.C.: McFarland, 2001. • Wasilewska, Ewa, "On the Money," *The World & I*, November 1, 1998, 222. • Weatherford, Jack. *The History of Money: From Sandstone to Cyberspace*. Pittsburgh, Pa.: Three Rivers Press, 1998

American eagle

The American eagle is a long-lived symbol. Bearing the mintmark EB, it appeared on coppers that Ephraim Brasher struck at Thomas Machin's Mill in Newburgh, New York. Called excelsiors or Eboracs, they pictured the New York state seal and the American eagle grasping arrows and an olive branch in a star-decked pose that became the U.S. seal.

The eagle that graced U.S. coins after

1855 derives from a real bird that nested in the Philadelphia mint pressroom in the late 1840s. For six years, Peter, as the mint bird was called, welcomed staff attention as the facility's pet and familiarized himself with the neighboring houses and children on the street. During operating hours, he perused the vault and observed the coinage machinery at close range, once getting too close to the flywheel and incurring a fatal injury. The staff hired a taxidermist to repair the broken wing and to stuff and mount Peter for display in a glass case in the cabinet room. His noble plumage and defiant gaze, duplicated by a long line of mint artisans, remained fixtures of national specie.

Complaints from ornithologists suggested that the first coin sculptor stylized the bird. Instead of a true image of Peter, they claimed that the eagle's wings were appropriate, but the head looked like a hawk's and the body like a dove's. Despite nitpicking, citizens approved the eagle as a symbol of American strength and resolve, thus carrying on a tradition of aquiline qualities that the ancient Greeks and Romans had admired. In 1916, Adolph A. Weinman backed the Walking Liberty half-dollar with a bold eagle, its legs emulating that of the striding Lady Liberty and its wings outstretched as though readying for flight. From the presence of Peter's likeness on large denominations, workers receiving their pay in cash remarked, "The eagle has flown."

See also **Ephraim Brasher; Great Seal of the United States.**

SOURCES: "The Bureau of Engraving and Printing," http://www.bep.treas.gov/. • Clain-Stefanelli, Elvira, and Vladimir Clain-Stefanelli. *The Beauty and Lore of Coins, Currency, and Medals.* Croton-on-Hudson, N.Y.: Riverwood Publishers, 1974. • "The Great Seal of the United States." http://greatseal.com/. • "The Great Seal of the United States." Washington, D.C.: U.S. Department of State Dispatch, 1996. • Reed, Mort. *Cowles Complete Encyclopedia of U.S. Coins.* New York: Cowles Book Company, 1969. • Reinfeld, Fred. *Treasury of the World's Coins.* New York: Sterling Publishing, 1953.

amulet coins

Amulet coins, like talismans, convince the gullible that they carry protective and healing powers, for example, Byzantine coins called *monetae Sanctae Helenae* ("St. Helena's money") that parents revered for preventing epilepsy and the 16th-century coin bearing Christ's profile and a Hebrew inscription, which also purportedly warded off seizures. The Chinese made amulets from holy scrap metal. In the A.D. 900s, coiners melted down Buddhist statues to produce bronze *tong bao* charm coins believed to heal the sick and comfort parturient women. The coins bore mottoes extolling health and prosperity.

Hindu amulet coins obtained protective powers both from precious metals and from the engraving of sacred figures and godly symbols. In Nepal, a parturient woman could get relief during protracted labor by gazing on a *rupee* displaying Siva's images. Another Indian application of amulet coins was to soak them in water and dispense the liquid to women in labor as a soothing elixir. Buddhists of the Himalayas also put faith in the powers of Venetian *sequins* and coins picturing Queen Victoria.

In Northern India, amulet tokens from the coinage of Akbar the Great around 1591 presented Islam's *charyari* ("four friends"), the four caliphs who succeeded Mohammed:

- Abu Bakr, Mohammed's friend and adviser who accompanied him on the flight to Medina and the father of wife Ayesha
- 'Umar I (or Omar) ibn Al-Khattab, the savior of Mohammed's revelations from loss on the battlefield and the father of the prophet's wife Hafsa
- 'Uthman (or Othman) ibn Affan, who retrieved the copies of the prophet's revelations from Mohammed's wife Hafsa for publication as the Koran
- 'Ali, the disciple who was buried near the prophet at the *Masjid al-Nabi* ("Mosque of the Prophet") in Medina.

The four caliphs superintended religious matters during the spread of Arab power from Syria, Iraq, Persia, and Egypt to Central Asia, North Africa, and southern Europe and during the assembly and issuance of the Koran. Families made protective medallions for their children from these biographical coins to bring good fortune.

In the Punjab, likenesses of the god Rama, his wife Sita, and Hanuman, the monkey deity, adorned cup-shaped *rama-tankas* ("Rama coins") (also *rama-tenki*). Inscriptions of "*Ram nam*" ("the name of God") indicated a sacred significance of these pieces at Hindu temple ritual. According to local legend, at the court of Abdul Hassan Tana Shah, around A.D. 1650, Gopanna, a devotee of Lord Rama, channeled tax collections from the state treasury to the temple for repairs. The courts found him guilty of misuse of royal moneys and sentenced him to a term in the dungeon of Golconda, a fortress west of Hyderabad. Still devout, Gopanna was praying in his cell when Lord Rama appeared and made restitution for the missing money with gold coins stamped with holy images. Tana Shah immediately freed Gopanna and reinstated him to his former rank. The sacred *rama-tankas* remained at the temple as proof of Gopanna's piety. The anthems that Gopanna sang to Rama became classic Hindu liturgical music.

During the early Christian era, pilgrims to the Holy Land obtained *eulogiai*, uniface good-luck tokens that conferred on the bearer ample blessings and protection from demons and the evil eye. Shaped out of clay to resemble Roman coins, the tokens may also have borne curative powers, a wise precaution for travelers passing through metropolitan territories rife with cholera and plague. Whatever their allure, Christian patriarchs inveighed against such pagan practice. The golden-mouthed preacher John Chrysostom of Antioch, whom the Emperor Arcadius appointed archbishop of Constantinople in A.D. 398, chastised audiences for wearing bronze amulet coins of Alexander III the Great on their heads and feet.

The superstitious circumvented Christian hardliners like John by incising on their Alexandrine talismans the *chi-rho*, the monogram of "Christ," which looks like an X superimposed on a P, thus achieving protection from both new and old traditions. In later periods, gifts of quasi-religious amulet coins picturing Christ officiating at a wedding conferred blessing on newlyweds. Throughout the Middle Ages, particularly for those people going on one of nine crusades waged between 1096 and 1291, the wearing of a St. George coin or charm protected the bearer on journeys. The English and French touch coins of the late medieval period supposedly bore the magical power of a monarch who could cure scrofula, a tubercular condition of the neck glands.

At the Slovakian city of Kremnitz (or Kremnica), Hungary, minting flourished after a major gold strike in 1320. Within five years, the monarchs of Bohemia and Hungary adopted a union money system as a means of bypassing the commercial dominance of Vienna. They based their coinage on the gold florin and the silver groat or *groschen*. Slovakian engravers created coins picturing biblical scenes, with Old Testament and New Testament depicted on opposite sides. Soldiers preferred the coins of Count David of Mansfeld or of Kremnitz as protection from wounds or from begin unseated from their mounts in battle.

After the Reformation, European engravers produced medals and medallions containing biblical phrases, symbols, and good luck wishes. The Viennese preferred amulets focusing on the life of Christ, such as Christmas disks showing the infant Christ in a manger and Easter coins featuring the Pascal lamb. On the *ducat* and *thaler*, was St. George, queller of a dragon, who supposedly warded off wounds. A cross entwined with snakes, taken from the Greek caduceus staff of Hermes, guarded people during outbreaks of plagues. Other coins pictured St. Roch, who healed Italians in 1348 during the Black Death; St. Rosalia, whose bones saved Palermo from an epidemic; and St. Sebastian, who survived multiple arrows shot by the soldiers of the Emperor Diocletian.

Other examples of superstition relating to coins involved numerous suppositions about magic. Shavings from the *ducats* of Matthias I, the king of Hungary after 1457, warded off cramp for young children. German "Jesus pennies" prevented epilepsy. The German alchemist medal of the 1600s struck with mystic symbols served Leonhard Thurneisser, a Basel healer, as an advertisement of his skill at transmuting base metal into a healing substance. Late in the 17th century, the Chinese made coin swords by suspending money from iron staffs to wave away evil and disease. Although the bearer could spend the parts as cash, the sword was worth more whole than broken down into individual coins.

Beyond the Renaissance, amulet coins continued to comfort the superstitious. Pilgrims to Canterbury Cathedral in Kent, England, or to the church of St. Wenceslas at Prague, Czechoslovakia, revered relic coins bearing images of the Virgin Mary or of Christian martyrs. In France around 1700, subjects of Louis XIV bought allegorical tokens for their protective power rather than their artistry. According to missionaries to Oceania, the Maori of New Zealand transferred physical suffering to a coin, which could be tossed into a flame or the ocean.

See also **bracteate; Chinese money; Hunley; Macedonian coins; medieval coins; papal coins; Peter I; Russian money; spirit money; *thaler*; touch coin.**

SOURCES: Allen, Larry. *Encyclopedia of Money*. New York: Checkmark Books, 2001. • Clain-Stefanelli, Elvira, and Vladimir Clain-Stefanelli. *The Beauty and Lore of Coins, Currency, and Medals*. Croton-on-Hudson, N.Y.: Riverwood Publishers, 1974. • Hastings, James, ed. *Encyclopedia of Religion and Ethics*. New York: Charles Scribner's Sons, 1951. • *New Catholic Encyclopedia*. San Francisco: Catholic University of America, 1967. • Shanks, Hershel. "Solomon's Blessings." Biblical Archaeology Review, September/October 2001, pp. 46–47.

Anglo-Saxon coins

As characterized in medieval verse encomia in *Beowulf* (ca. A.D. 600), *Brunanburh* (A.D. 936), *The Saga of Burnt Njáll* (ca. 1220), and *The Saga of Gunnlaug Serpent-tongue* (ca. 1250), the Anglo-Saxons were renowned for generosity. Public ceremonies at the state hall in recognition of worthy warriors involved distribution of metal rings, arm bracelets, torques, and coils, which could be lopped into pieces for small change. The chieftain who distributed bounty was called the ring-giver, a virtue extolled in the prologue to *Beowulf* in which the noble ring-giving king Beo goes to his watery burial heaped with treasure. Ring money permeated the chronicles of the Angles, Danes, and Swedes. The presenter of rings was a term of honor for a dispenser of plunder that Beowulf, the oldest English epic hero, mentioned in his dying speech to Hrothgar.

The first genuine coins in circulation among Anglo-Saxons were the gold *solidi* the invading Romans brought in the mid–first century B.C. and the Merovingian Gallic *tremisses* (crowns), which reached England after A.D. 550. Following a 236-year hiatus of minting by the Celts, Anglo-Saxon England ended the long dry spell with coins struck by a churchman and medalist, Bishop Liudard. He arrived from France in A.D. 560 as royal escort to Bertha to wed Ethelbert, the ten-year-old king of Kent and the first rex Anglorum (king of the Angles). At the height of Anglo-Saxon invasions of Britain, Liudard resumed coin production around A.D. 561.

Around A.D. 600, copies of French *tremisses* appeared from mints in Kent and Londinium. Called *thrymas*, these shilling pieces were struck from gold ore. During Ethelbert's long reign, Bishop Mellitus of London, an emissary from the Anglo-Saxon throne to the papacy, began minting gold coins in London from A.D. 604 to 616. In 1939, the valuable Sutton Hoo burial site excavated at Woodbridge, Suffolk, in southeastern England turned up the remains of a king, perhaps Raedwald of East Anglia. He was buried about A.D. 625 with his ship and horse, silver dishes, and bronze and gold-hilted sword and shield. The cache of gold *tremisses* within his leather money belt were struck at 37 mints across France, providing historians with a glimpse of coinage that migrated north during trade with Britain.

By A.D. 630, Saxon mints were hammering out a sizeable number of coins, which stimulated commerce. As quantity increased, quality suffered. In A.D. 675, the base shifted from gold and gold alloy to silver. The primitive *sceat* (also *sceatta*), a small, lightweight hammered coin of low quality silver, few inscriptions, and little artistic appeal, emerged in the late A.D. 600s. Exceptions to these uninspired disks were the royal issue of Eadbert of Northumbria after A.D. 738 and of Beonna of East Anglia around A.D. 750, each of which bore a royal name.

On January 18, 1999, a team of 16 members of the Ashington and Bedlington Detector Club unearthed a hoard of 162 Saxon *sceatta* near Bamburgh, the ancient capital of the North and a strong fortress against invaders that the Celts called Dinguaroy. This valuable cache preserved for history the early everyday coinage of the Anglo-Saxons. Scattered by years of plowing, the coins emerged in twos and threes and one find of 33 in a 70 × 40–yard expanse.

In A.D. 752, when Pepin III (or Pepin the Short), father of Charlemagne, became sole Frankish monarch, he issued the first *denier*, a long-lived silver coin on which the English modeled their silver penny. Around A.D. 765, Heaberth of Kent issued the first of the English version of the *denier*. The penny supplanted the *sceat* in southern England and penetrated as far north as Northumbria, where a royal issue of base *stycas*, the regional version of *sceats*, displayed the king's name along with that of the moneyer. Once circulated from church mints at Canterbury and York as well as from state treasuries, the *sceat* gradually shifted from silver to bronze before disappearing from circulation by A.D. 800.

Greater demand on the treasury in A.D. 871 caused Alfred the Great to establish eight new mints and to increase coinage. With the money, he paid mercenaries to garrison Wessex towns against Danish insurgents. The terror continued until Alfred overcame Guthrum, the Danish monarch, at the battle of Edlington in A.D. 878, and freed England from Scandinavian invasions. To publicize his likeness and capital city, Alfred issued a penny struck with his crowned head and the name of London. He appears to have chosen a weight and design that would satisfy the Danes and enclosed in a peace treaty a coin conversion chart as though using the opportunity to boost international trade.

When Alfred's successor, Edward the Elder, came to power in A.D. 899, he and his sister Ethelflaed (also Aedelfleda) strengthened fortifications at Mercia, the vast buffer zone that separated Londoners from the Celts of Wales. To impress on Mercian subjects the importance of strong defenses, the royal siblings minted pennies picturing lookout towers. Flanking the architecture were two lines of lettering naming the moneyer, Eadmund.

Around A.D. 905, some six years after the death of Alfred the Great, Danish raiders attacking northern England appear to have seized jewelry, silver ingots, and 8,000 coins struck by Alfred's moneyers. On the run from pursuers, they buried their loot on the bank of the Ribble River at Preston, a market center in Lancashire. On May 15, 1840, workers repairing a wall discovered the cache, which historians call the Cuerdale hoard. The gray mud that coated the remains of the wood chest preserved for over nine centuries the high quality of Anglo-Saxon coin artistry, particularly 1,800 coins minted by Eadmund and 3,000 pennies bearing the unidentified royal cipher of "Cnut Rex Cunnetti" (Cnut, King of Cnut's people). The haphazard burial of the trove attests to hard times for the Anglo-Saxons after the loss of a strong king and protector.

By A.D. 924, when Alfred's grandson Athelstan (also Aethelstan or Ethelstane) came to power, he warded off Viking raiders, earning for himself the title of Rex Totius Britannia ("King of All Britain"). A warrior-king much stronger than his father, Edward the Elder, Athelstan earned a reputation in the united realm as the "ring-giver," the ancient compounded title indicating his importance to men who fought wars for a share of the plunder (Clain-Stefanelli, and Clain-Stefanelli 1974, 21). According to the Oxford Illustrated History of the British Monarchy, coins aided the Anglo-Saxons in their quest for control:

> It was a system that enabled the king to exploit the wealth of a much enlarged kingdom. It made possible the great crusade against the Vikings, and it enabled English kings to raise very substantial sums of money indeed with which to bribe the Vikings [Cannon and Griffiths 1988, p. 68].

Under concerted Anglo-Saxon might, the Danelaw, the northern, central, and eastern region of England colonized by Viking armies in the late A.D. 800s, ceased to bleed Athelstan's subjects of their resources. The king's crack troops also kept the Danes from exacting punishments on those who withheld blood money by slitting their noses, the origin of the term "pay through the nose." For his peaceful nation, Athelstan stimulated trade, built a hospital, restored abbeys, and issued a national currency, which he legitimized under the Statute of Greatley in A.D. 928. As a result, England became the first European nation since the Romans to enjoy a unified monetary system.

At Jorvik ("York"), according to the Fagrskinna Saga, Eric Bloodaxe, a battle-winning pagan hero, established a violent reign in the mid–A.D. 900s that resonated in Scandinavian verse. Exiled from Norway by his father, King Harold Fairhair, Eric settled at Northumbria, where he led the kingdom to independence from King Eadred. To symbolize his strong-armed approach to governance, Eric established a mint producing militant silver pennies depicting a naked sword between two lines of lettering extolling himself as "Eric Rex."

Safety from bruisers like Eric did not come cheap. Farther south, demands on mints from commerce and warfare forced Athelstan and Edgar, his successor, to beef up coining operations. Athelstan decreed 30 state mints plus branch operations at outlying boroughs not named in his master scheme. Under Edgar (or Eadgar) the Peaceful, a strong monarch and creative administrator crowned in A.D. 959, the English government upped the number of mints to 40.

Edgar's silver penny presented a handsome crowned monarch in profile and a broad inscription proclaiming him "*Eadgar Rex Anglorum*" ("Edgar King of the English"). He standardized stamps and regulated the size, weight, uniformity, and quality of coinage, a monetary system that remained the model of fiscal administration for two centuries. In comparison with the crude, off-struck coinage of Eric Bloodaxe and of Hywel ap Cadell (also Hywel Dda or Hywel the Good) of Wales, Edgar's pennies looked almost refined. From the royal mint at Cambridge, he controlled monetary circulation and focused on trade as a central issue of his serene, civic-minded reign, which lasted until 975. His economic savvy produced a six-year cycle by which the mint melted and recoined money to maintain its uniformity and to bolster the royal treasury. His uniform money system survived until the Royal Mint initiated decimal currency on February 15, 1971.

Edgar's peace proved illusory. The resumption of Viking raids during the reign of Ethelred II the Unready (also Aethelred the Unraedy) generated a new cry for cash. In A.D. 978, the king set in motion 75 royal mints — 2½ times the number Athelstan required. Together, they produced 40 million pennies to pay the danegeld (Dane tribute), a bribery system that decreased the Vikings' need to plunder or to raise ransom by kidnap. To assure quality that would satisfy the Danes, Ethelred passed a law threatening capital punishment to the counterfeiter, shaver, or clipper of coins.

From 24,000 tons of silver, Ethelred began amassing a war chest of coins in astonishing amounts:

year	*amount*
991	£22,000
993	£16,000
1001	£24,000
1005	£36,000
1012	£48,000

During the step-up in production, those citizens holding obsolete or worn pennies could turn them in for new coins at any mint location. Ethelred's vigorous mint output spurred envy in the Swedish King Olof Skottkonung, who, in 995, imported Anglo-Saxon coin masters to strike silver pennies at his Sigtuna mint.

King Ethelred relieved citizens of some of their savings by instituting the *heregeld* (soldier debt), a tax levied in 1012 to pay for additional mercenaries and ships to put up a militant front before the rapacious Vikings. Vast numbers of new coins, picturing Ethelred in profile encircled by the legend "Aethelred Rex Anglorum" (Ethelred King of the English), circulated widely in Scandinavia, a testimony to the reign of a stoutly English king and to the bleeding of the English by their enemies. The situation worsened the next year, when Ethelred ceded his throne temporarily to the Danish pirate king Sweyn Forkbeard and his son and heir Canute I. From Normandy, Ethelred raised a force and fought his way back to power, but survived only a few years.

The *geld* remained in effect until 1162, when the Danes' internal strife and encroaching German tribes lessened the danger of Viking raids on England. By the reign of Edward the Confessor, which ended in 1066, England satisfied the onerous tax off the productivity of 87 mints, extending from Castle Gotha in the southwestern tip of Cornwall north to York. To get the most out of his pennies, Edward increased mint profits by halving the cycle of meltdown and reminting.

See also **Appledore hoard; Athelstan; blood money; Canute I; cloth money; counterfeiting; Edward the Confessor; Egbert; Offa of Mercia; penny; ring money.**

SOURCES: Allen, Larry. *Encyclopedia of Money*. New York: Checkmark Books, 2001. • Cannon, John, and Ralph Griffiths. *Oxford Illustrated History of the British Monarchy*. Oxford: Oxford University Press, 1988. • Clain-Stefanelli, Elvira, and Vladimir Clain-Stefanelli. *The Beauty and Lore of Coins, Currency, and Medals*. Croton-on-Hudson, N.Y.: Riverwood Publishers, 1974. • Clark, John. *A History of Epic Poetry*. New York: Haskell House, 1973. • Cribb, Joe. *Money*. Toronto: Stoddart, 1990. • Cribb, Joe, Barrie Cook, and Ian Carradice. *The Coin Atlas*. London: Little, Brown and Co., 1999. • "The Cuerdale Hoard." http://www.treasure-hunting.co.uk. • Davies, Glyn. *A History of Money from Ancient Times to the Present Day*. Cardiff: University of Wales Press, 1994. • Einzig, Paul. *Primitive Money*. Oxford: Pergamon Press, 1966. • Hastings, James, ed. *Encyclopedia of Religion and Ethics*. New York: Charles Scribner's Sons, 1951. • Lewis, Brenda Ralph. *Coins & Currency*. New York: Random House, 1993. • "Medieval Sourcesbook: The Anglo-Saxon Dooms, 560–975." http://www.fordham.edu/halsall/source/560-975dooms.html. • *New Catholic Encyclopedia*. San Francisco: Catholic University of America, 1967. • Parker, Michael St. John. *Britain's Kings and Queens*. Andover, Hants: Pitkin, 1994. • Reinfeld, Fred. *Treasury of the World's Coins*. New York: Sterling Publishing, 1953. • Rice, David Talbot, ed. *The Dawn of European Civilization: The Dark Ages*. New York: McGraw-Hill, 1965. • Sinclair, David. *The Pound*. London: Century Books, 2000. • Snodgrass, Mary Ellen. *Who's Who in the Middle Ages*. Jefferson, N.C.: McFarland, 2001. • Tyler, Elizabeth. "Treasures and Convention in Old English Verse." *Notes and Queries*, March 1996.

Appledore hoard

In August and September 1997, treasure hunters Phil Collins and Bert Douch's discovery near Dungeness in Kent, England, of a cache of 500 silver pennies and 30 halves cut from pennies preserved for monetary history the most significant examples of late Anglo-Saxon coinage. With the help of the landowner and his wife, the two men scoured the area with metal detectors and watched their trove expand. The farmer plowed the field to further loosen the soil, enabling Collins and Douch to locate more of the subterranean stash.

The collection, known as the Appledore hoard, appeared to have been buried in a red terra cotta pot, which the plow obliterated over time. Under the Treasure Act of 1996, the stash passed to the British Museum for analysis and evaluation. The coins dated from the early 1000s and the reign of Canute I, England's first Scandinavian monarch, and were worth £750,000. For their historic value, the government declared them an official treasure trove.

Most of the coins were the Expanding

Cross faces issued from 1051 to 1052 during the reign of Edward the Confessor. They bore the names of southeastern mint locations, including Canterbury, Dover, Hastings, Romney, and Sandwich as well as northern sites in Chester, Lincoln, and York. At the time of their minting, one silver penny would have paid a manual worker's monthly wage. In proof of Gresham's law, which declares that people tend to hoard attractive, high-quality coins, some pieces appear to have been new when they were hoarded. Except for some damage from plowing, all were in excellent condition.

Historical surmise, based on the *Anglo-Saxon Chronicle*, connects the trove with the rebellion of Earl Godwin of Wessex and his sons, who fled the area. Godwin went to Bruges and his son Harold to Ireland. Upon their return in 1052, Godwin landed at Appledore near Dungeness and resumed his voyage west to join King Harold I before returning to Dungeness to summon supporters from Dover, Folkestone, Hastings, Hythe, Romney, and Sandwich. The hoard may have been cash hastily concealed to protect it from rebel seizure.

SOURCES: "The Man with the Midas Touch." (London) *Times*, March 14, 1998, 16. • "Saxon Coins Could Be Worth £750,000." *Weekly Telegraph*, August 20, 1997. • Sinclair, David. *The Pound*. London: Century Books, 2000.

assay marks

The assaying of ores to determine metal content is a complex chemical study involving dissolving a sample bead to observe the separation of elements. Written records of Jesuit assayers in Chocó, Colombia, in the 1500s speak of dense gray pebbles in alluvial gold that adulterated and weakened the metal. The writers named the gray adulterant *platina del Pinto* for the Pinto River, a branch of the San Juan River.

Assay marks carry authority and validity, as with the I and the J initials of the assayers Ignacio Zenón Gélves and Juan Martínez de Roxas and the F and M referring to Francisco Arance y Cobos and Mariano Rodríguez, all of whom produced the Spanish pistareen, and the bold EB set in an oval, of American colonial assayer and metalsmith Ephraim Brasher, who accepted commissions from George Washington. The Brasher monogram appeared on the breast of the American eagle on his famous gold doubloon. In the early 18th century, one of England's most prominent assayers, Sir Isaac Newton, performed meticulous examinations of precious metals over his thirty years as master of the mint and personally wrote reports on quality.

For antiques specialists and numismatists, assay marks like those of Brasher and Newton are like fingerprints identifying a particular item or coin with a specific time and place. From country to country, markings vary. They may incorporate any or all of these details — symbols for place of assay, date of assay in letters or letters and numbers, maker's mark, importation or exportation mark, and tax or duty mark.

The assayer's mark, like a mint mark, is often a clue to the provenance of recovered coins and treasure from early times. Numismatist Alfredo Díaz Gámez used his knowledge of the assayer's mark or stamp to trace a single silver coin from unidentified undersea wreckage from the Caribbean. Aided by Carisub, the marine archeology division of Cuba, divers recovered coins from the reign of Philip II of Spain. Gámez recognized the shape of the letter R on coins that indicated an assayer working between 1605 and 1613. Because of Gámez's careful study, he could identify the remains as the Spanish galleon *Nuestra Señora del Rosario*, which two pirates ships sank at a long reef off northwestern Cuba in 1590 with a trove of gold chains, jewelry, and silver coins.

***See also* Ephraim Brasher; Central America; hallmark; mintmark; Sir Isaac Newton; Templeton Reid; silver strikes; touchstone; trial of the pyx; U.S. Treasury.**

SOURCES: Allen, Thomas B. "Cuba's Golden Past." *National Geographic*, July 2001, 74–91. • "Atocha Dive Expeditions." *Skin Diver*, December 1999, 96. • Bowden, Tracy. "Gleaning Treasure from the Silver Bank." *National Geographic*, July 1996, 90–105. • Cockburn, Alexander. "Beat the

Devil: Imperial Addictions." *The Nation*, August 3, 1985, 70–71. • Cribb, Joe. *Money*. Toronto: Stoddart, 1990. • Pickford, Nigel. *The Atlas of Ship Wrecks & Treasure*. New York: Dorling Kindersley, 1994.

assignat

During the French Revolution, the recently formed republican treasury printed *assignats*, a daintily scrolled and illustrated paper currency in a numbered series bearing five percent interest and pledging nationalized church property as security. During an era of hoarding, which brought market inventories to a dangerous low in food, clothing and shoes, nails, and medicines, *assignats* funded the interim government and maintained commerce from 1790 until 1793. The ornately bordered paper bills displayed the denomination, the date based on the republic's new calendar, and a description, "Hypothéqué sur les Domaines Nationaux" (mortgaged on national domains). By 1795, the treasury had issued *assignats* valued at eleven billion *livres*.

When the value of *assignats* fell to 10 percent of their face value, treasury printers went on strike, demanding that they be paid in loaves of bread rather than the flimsy paper money they produced. On February 18, 1796, when around 40 billion *assignats* shrank in value, officials of the revolutionary government burned notes and printing plates and presses in a dramatic public spectacle at the Place Vendôme, an octagonal piazza surrounded by shops and stalls. Before disgruntled citizens, the five-man board of governors had to admit failure and suspend circulation of the despised *assignats*.

To provide the French with currency, in March, treasury officials created a new form of paper money, the *mandat territoraux* (land warrants), each worth 30 *assignats*. Almost as rapidly as that of the previous paper bills, the value of the mandat fell to 10 assignats. In truth, until the rise of Napoleon Bonaparte and the return of metal coins on February 4, 1797, the French had no viable currency.

***See also* franc.**

SOURCES: Allen, Larry. *Encyclopedia of Money*. New York: Checkmark Books, 2001. • Bernier, Olivier. *The World in 1800*. New York: John Wiley & Sons, 2001. • Clain-Stefanelli, Elvira, and Vladimir Clain-Stefanelli. *The Beauty and Lore of Coins, Currency, and Medals*. Croton-on-Hudson, N.Y.: Riverwood Publishers, 1974. • Cribb, Joe. *Money*. Toronto: Stoddart, 1990. • Cribb, Joe, Barrie Cook, and Ian Carradice. *The Coin Atlas*. London: Little, Brown and Co., 1999. • Davies, Glyn. *A History of Money from Ancient Times to the Present Day*. Cardiff: University of Wales Press, 1994. • Kunzig, Robert. "Euroland or Bust." *Discover*, October 1998. • Weatherford, Jack. *The History of Money: From Sandstone to Cyberspace*. Pittsburgh, Pa.: Three Rivers Press, 1998.

Athelstan

The first king of the British Isles to mint portrait coins, Athelstan (also Aethelstan or Ethelstane) assured a war-like reputation for the Anglo-Saxons. The illegitimate offspring of Edward the Elder and his mistress and the grandson of Alfred the Great, the first great Anglo-Saxon coiner, Athelstan came from noble ancestry. After he merged Wessex with Mercia during his crowning in 924 at Kingston-upon-Thames, he had ample reason to relish the title of the first *Rex Totius Britanniae* ("King of All Britain"). Exhibiting his pride were silver pennies showing him crowned with a corona, a Mediterranean motif begun by Philip II of Macedon, father of Alexander III the Great.

Assuring the longevity of his realm, Athelstan expelled the Vikings from Northumbria and pressed on in his conquests west of the Wye River. The height of the kingdom's military success came in A.D. 937, when he vanquished the combined Irish, Norsemen, Scots, and Welsh manpower under Constantine of Scotland. Athelstan's method of shoring up alliances was the betrothal of his five sisters to potential challengers.

A founder of mints and a hospital at York in A.D. 936, Athelstan worked vigorously toward codifying laws, rebuilding monasteries, and extending commerce through the circulation of silver pennies. He issued a chillingly uncompromising edict at the council at Grateley in A.D. 928 stating:

> That there be one money over all the king's dominion, and that no man mint except within port. And if the moneyer be guilty, let the hand be struck off that wrought the offence, and be set up on the money-smithy but if it be an accusation, and he is willing to clear himself, then let him go to the hot-iron, and clear the hand therewith with which he is charged that fraud to have wrought. And if at the ordeal he should be guilty, let the like be done as here before ordained ["Anglo-Saxon Dooms"].

At his death on October 27, A.D. 939, and burial at Malmesbury, the king left in operation a chain of mints, the first unified state monetary system since the Roman Empire:

locations	*number*	*type*
Canterbury	4	royal
	2	bishop's
	1	abbot's
Chichester	1	royal
Exeter	2	royal
Hampton	2	royal
Hastings	1	royal
Lewes	2	royal
London	8	royal
Shaftesbury	2	royal
Wareham	2	royal
Winchester	6	royal
total	33	30 royal, 3 ecclesiastical

Each of the remaining boroughs were allowed one minting operation. Athelstan obviously pinned his hopes for state survival in part on a unified English currency. His coins were homely, but standardized, probably because he set rigorous criteria of skill and strength for his coining staff.

SOURCES: Cannon, John, and Ralph Griffiths. *Oxford Illustrated History of the British Monarchy.* Oxford: Oxford University Press, 1988. • Clain-Stefanelli, Elvira, and Vladimir Clain-Stefanelli. *The Beauty and Lore of Coins, Currency, and Medals.* Croton-on-Hudson, N.Y.: Riverwood Publishers, 1974. • Davies, Glyn. *A History of Money from Ancient Times to the Present Day.* Cardiff: University of Wales Press, 1994. • Hastings, James, ed. *Encyclopedia of Religion and Ethics.* New York: Charles Scribner's Sons, 1951. • "Medieval Sourcesbook: The Anglo-Saxon Dooms, 560-975." http://www.fordham.edu/halsall/source/560-975dooms.html. • *New Catholic Encyclopedia.* San Francisco: Catholic University of America, 1967. • Parker, Michael St. John. *Britain's Kings and Queens.* Andover, Hants: Pitkin, 1994. • Rice, David Talbot, ed. *The Dawn of European Civilization: The Dark Ages.* New York: McGraw-Hill, 1965. • Sinclair, David. *The Pound.* London: Century Books, 2000. • Snodgrass, Mary Ellen. *Who's Who in the Middle Ages.* Jefferson, N.C.: McFarland, 2001.

Atocha

In 1622, a major cache of Spanish cobs went down with the guardian galleon *Nuestra Señora de Atocha* and sister ship *Santa Margarita,* two the 28 ships that comprised the Tierra Firme fleet. Borne by trade winds, eight succumbed to harsh weather and disappeared into the quicksands of the Gulf of Mexico on what is now the Outer Continental Shelf. The fleet, departing late for its annual convoy, was two days into the voyage from Portbello, Panama, to Cartagena, Colombia, Havana, Cuba, and Cadiz, Spain, with newly minted coins.

Philip IV of Spain built the 550-ton *Atocha* in Havana to be his marine fortress and appointed Vice-Admiral Pedro Pasquier de Espanza to command its 18 gunners and 20 bronze cannon. The *Atocha* and its sister ship, heavily guarded against privateers and foreign navies, rendezvoused with the 26 other vessels in the convoy in Havana and entered the Gulf Stream for the transatlantic journey. The doom of the two ships was a hurricane on September 6, 1622, on a reef 35 miles off Upper Matecumbe and Lower Matecumbe, two islands near Key West, Florida.

In addition to wealthy grandees and important Catholic prelates making the crossing to the mother country, the *Atocha* carried tobacco, indigo, cochineal, rosewood, copper ingots, and a royal treasure of two million pesos minted in Portobello, Panama. The money secured on board included a slave head tax, court fines, coins earned from papal indulgences, contraband gold, money chains forged of gold links, and 21,323 pieces of eight owed to Christopher Columbus's heirs. The companion ship bore 34 gold bars, 419 silver ingots, and 118,000 newly minted *reales,* crudely hammered silver coins called cobs.

The ship's end came swiftly beyond the Florida straits after the rudder broke, freeing the high-sterned vessel to slew around toward treacherous reefs of the lower Florida Keys. Crew and passengers aboard the *Santa Margarita* watched the final moments of the *Atocha* before their own vessel suffered the same fate. Of some 470 aboard the two galleons, only 72 managed to swim to shore. Surviving from the 123 crewmen, 82 soldiers, and 48 passengers aboard the *Atocha*, were a sailor, two apprentice seamen, a slave, and a ship's boy, all five who had tied themselves to the mizzenmast during the storm.

The Spanish were intent on recovering the newly minted coins, but a second hurricane hampered salvage operations by scattering the wreckage and burying the *Atocha* in sand. The loss was a lethal blow to the treasury. To save the nation from financial ruin, in 1624, Francisco Nuñez Melian returned to the spot where the mizzenmast protruded from the sea and dragged the bottom with grappling hooks in an effort to retrieve from the battered hulk bronze cannon, silver ingots, 600 pounds of gold, and 67,000 silver coins. Failing to locate the mother lode, he filed a report and map locating the wreckage. Captain Juan de Anuez worked until 1641 to recover more of the trove; however, 17th-century methods could not bring enough of the haul to the surface to rescue Spain from an economic depression.

U.S. treasure hunter Mel Fisher acquired Melian's memorandum in 1970 and labored 15 years to recover the *Atocha*. At length, he found the mother lode, a huge shelf of bars lying in place on the ocean floor atop the beams framing the hull. Aided by archeologist R. Duncan Mathewson, he began deep-water salvage on July 20, 1985, and retrieved for numismatists' perusal some of the cobs that were in circulation from Canada to the West Indies in the 17th and 18th centuries. Seriously deteriorated and further compromised in the restoration process, the silver coins nonetheless exemplified the Spanish treasury's monetary problems with stamped coins that lacked fine detailing and edging. The cache, valued at $400 million, became the world's largest undersea recovery. Its salvage prefaced an outcry from historians against plundering ancient shipwrecks and inaugurated a new academic discipline, underwater archeology.

See also **cobs; Mel Fisher; treasure ships; underwater archeology.**

SOURCES: "Atocha Dive Expeditions." *Skin Diver*, December 1999, 96. • Bass, George F., ed. *Ships and Shipwrecks of the Americas: A History Based on Underwater Archaeology*. London: Thames and Hudson, 1996. • Bowden, Tracy. "Gleaning Treasure from the Silver Bank." *National Geographic*, July 1996, 90–105. • Cockburn, Alexander. "Beat the Devil: Imperial Addictions." *The Nation*, August 3, 1985, 70–71. • *Contemporary Newsmakers 1985*. Detroit: Gale Research, 1986. • Pickford, Nigel. *The Atlas of Ship Wrecks & Treasure*. New York: Dorling Kindersley, 1994. • Sandz, Victoria. *Encyclopedia of Western Atlantic Shipwrecks and Sunken Treasure*. Jefferson, N.C.: McFarland, 2001. • "Treasure Hunter Who Went for the Gold." *U.S. News & World Report*, August 5, 1985, 13.

Bailly, Joseph Alexis

An able designer but elusive figure in the history of U.S. coins, sculptor Joseph Alexis Bailly styled the 1873 dollar and the 1874 25-cent piece. The son of furniture and cabinet maker Joseph Philador Bailly, Joseph Bailly was born in Paris, France, on January 21, 1825. After apprenticing with his father and studying at the French Institute under Baron Bozio, Bailly was drafted into the army after the overthrow of the constitutional monarchy initiated the Revolution of 1848. While on duty in the Garde Mobile, at age 25, he fled France after shooting an officer and lived briefly in New York and Buenos Aires.

In the French Quarter of New Orleans, Louisiana, Bailly set up as a sculptor, cameo carver, and engraver. He married Louisa David of Brie, France, and traveled to Buenos Aires, New York, and Philadelphia. In 1850, he set up shop in Philadelphia, site of the U.S. mint. For the next three decades, he carved in wood and stone, made bronze tomb effigies, sculpted cameos and marble portrait statuary, and created medallions and plaques. He was named to the Philadelphia Academy in 1856, taught at the Pennsylvania Academy of Fine Arts, and produced work on display in Philadelphia and Washington, D.C.

In the employ of James Pollock, director of minting, in 1873, Bailly appears to have created the bas-relief of Miss Liberty on the trade dollar. The pose displays her seated on a globe with William Barber's fierce eagle on the reverse. The next year, Pollock commissioned Bailly to design a 20-cent piece. For a model, he reprised his classically draped liberty image, picturing her seated and ringed with stars with somber expression, upswept hair, and a staff of state in her right hand.

Among Bailly's most memorable works are sculptures of American notables Benjamin Franklin, Ulysses S. Grant, George Meade, George Washington, and Reverend John Witherspoon. In his 28th year as a sculptor, Bailly completed a mounted statue of Venezuela's President Antonio Guzmán Blanco, the nation's absolute ruler from 1870 to 1889. The likeness was displayed at the 1876 Philadelphia Centennial Exhibition. Bailly died of heart attack in Philadelphia on June 15, 1883. Bailly's family portrait busts of William Emlen Cresson and his wife survive in the Pennsylvania Academy of Fine Arts.

SOURCES: *Biography Resource Center*. Farmington Hills, Mich.: The Gale Group. 2001. • Johnson, Allen, ed. *Dictionary of American Biography*. New York: Charles Scribner's Sons, 1928. • "Joseph Alexis Bailly," *Philadelphia Public Art*, http://www.philart.net/cgi-bin/control.cgi. • Marotta, Michael E., "Coin Gallery Online," http://www.coin-gallery.com/ cgmarotta.htm. • Taxay, Don. *The U.S. Mint and Coinage*. New York: Arco Publishing, 1966. • "United States Pattern Coins: The Bass Collection," http://www.harrybassfoundation.org/basscatalogs/BASSSALE1/b1-2-a.htm. • Wilson, James Grant, and John Fiske, eds. *Appleton's Cyclopedia of American Biography*. Detroit: Gale Research, Detroit, 1968.

Bank of England

English banking owes its beginnings to London goldsmiths, a unified guild that crowded out competition from Germany, Holland, and Italy. In 1633, the artisans established pre-modern services of storing and securing money and bullion as well as jewels and plate, making loans to individuals and governments, transferring funds among accounts, and exchanging foreign money. Deposit receipts began circulating as paper notes, the forerunners of true banknotes. Because the financial house issued checks, the English derived the term "exchequer" to indicate a national bank. By 1776, banknotes were more common than coins.

Established by Parliament at Mercers' Hall, London, the Bank of England, fondly called the "Old Lady of Threadneedle Street," emerged during the War of the Grand Alliance as an agency that allowed the crown to wage war on Louis XIV's holdings in Holland by financing armaments and mercenaries. In 1688, during the reign of William and Mary, Scottish financier and investor William Paterson of Dumfriesshire proposed shoring up weak national finances by loaning the government £1,200,000 with a return of eight percent per annum. Additional moneys came from the royal couple and 1,267 individual shareholders. Those contributing the maximum 10,000 pounds were the Earl of Portland, James de la Brettoniere, William Brownlowe, Thomas Howard, Thomas Mulsoe, Anthony Humberstone, Anthony Parsons, Sir John Houblon, Abraham Houblon, Theodore Janssen, and Sir William Scawen. The shareholders christened their new venture the Governor and Company of the Bank of England.

With the backing of merchants and goldsmiths, the 26 directors incorporated as the bank's board, which admitted wholesaler Michael Godfrey and members of the city livery companies, some of whom were members of Parliament. For leadership, the directorate elected Sir John Houblon as governor and Michael Godfrey as deputy governor. The strongly anti-papist, pro–Whig bank was operated by 17 tellers and two janizaries. By a royal charter inked on July 27, 1694, the financial institution monopolized joint-stock operations in England and Wales.

Resituated in Grocers' Hall, then, in 1733, in a sedate stone building on Threadneedle Street designed by George Sampson, the Bank of England continued to manage government moneys as the London commercial district grew up around it. At the core, the staff received deposits, issued banknotes in England and Wales, and maintained English authority in European money dealings. Rechartered in 1781 as the public exchequer, its integrity held firm, even during the economic fluctuations caused by the French Revolution of 1789 and the Napoleonic Wars, when the bank issued paper notes in place of gold and silver coins. To protect dwindling gold reserves, in 1791, the government began a period of restrictions on gold payouts. The suspension of gold specie withdrawals and issuance of tokens lasted from 1797 until 1821.

As England's money clearinghouse during the 1800s, the Bank of England was so crucial to the nation that it was guarded by the military. The directorate began printing paper money, which it monopolized under the Bank Charter Act of 1833, and superintended Britain's gold reserves and foreign exchange. After abandoning the gold standard in 1931, the bank transferred bullion reserves to the British treasury. Under the Bank Charter Act of 1844, the issuance of banknotes became a separate department. Over the Victorian era to the beginning of World War I, the bank maintained financial stability and prosperity unknown in other countries' commercial centers. Over the globe, including England's holdings in Australia, British Honduras, Canada, the Caribbean, Egypt, Gibraltar, Guiana, Hong Kong, the Indian subcontinent, Ireland, Malaysia, Malta, New Zealand, Nigeria, Rhodesia, Singapore, South Africa, and the Sudan, the pound sterling held steady for seven decades, furthering trade and industrialization.

At the beginning of World War I, the bank became England's only source of paper money. In 1946, the bank left private hands and became the public's bank and the adviser, agent, and debt manager to the royal treasury. For much of the world, the bank served as a model of centralized financial services. In retrospect, historian John Kenneth Galbraith, author of *Money: Whence It Came and Where It Went* (1975), saluted the Bank of England with a just comparison: "Of all institutions concerned with economics, none has for so long enjoyed such prestige. It is, in all respects, to money as Saint Peter's is to the Faith. And the reputation is deserved, for most of the art as well as much of the mystery associated with the management of money originated there" (Weatherford 1998, p. 159). After the world wars, financial systems in other countries—Germany, Japan, Switzerland, the U.S.—eclipsed the revered Bank of England and its pound.

See also **Matthew Boulton; Adolf Burger; counterfeiting; counterstamp; Alexander Hamilton; William Paterson; tokens; Wyon family.**

SOURCES: Allen, Larry. *Encyclopedia of Money*. New York: Checkmark Books, 2001. • "The Bank of England." http://www.bankofengland.co.uk/history.htm. • Braudel, Fernand. *The Wheels of Commerce*. New York: Harper and Row, 1982. • Cribb, Joe. *Money*. Toronto: Stoddart, 1990. • Cribb, Joe, Barrie Cook, and Ian Carradice. *The Coin Atlas*. London: Little, Brown and Co., 1999. • Davies, Glyn. *A History of Money from Ancient Times to the Present Day*. Cardiff: University of Wales Press, 1994. • Galbraith, John Kenneth. *Money: Whence It Came, Where It Went*. Boston: Houghton Mifflin, 1975. • Jacobs, Wayne L. "The Mystery of the Disappearing P. E. I. 'Dumps.'" *Canadian Numismatic Association Journal*, November 2001, 433–438. • Magnusson, Magnus. *Cambridge Biographical Dictionary*. Cambridge: University of Cambridge, 1990. • Sinclair, David. *The Pound*. London: Century Books, 2000. • Snodgrass, Mary Ellen. *Who's Who in the Middle Ages*. Jefferson, N.C.: McFarland, 2001. • Stephen, Sir Leslie, and Sir Sidney Lee, eds. *Dictionary of National Biography*. London: Oxford University Press, 1922. • Weatherford, Jack. *The History of Money: From Sandstone to Cyberspace*. Pittsburgh, Pa.: Three Rivers Press, 1998.

banking

A millennium before true coined money, around 3100 B.C., banking began in Uruk along the Euphrates and Tigris rivers in Mesopotamia. Over eight centuries later, the treasury of Cappadocia issued uniform silver ingots along with a guarantee of standard weight and purity. As a result of state backing, money earned the respect of traders and peasants. In an age of prosperity, merchants and financiers used palaces and temples as storage centers for grain, cattle, tools, and precious metals, all exchange items enhancing trade and barter. Clerks depositing valuable stores issued receipts that doubled as a form of currency to pay priests, merchants, and tax agents. Some 1,500 years after the emergence of Mesopotamian banking, the evolution of multiple-service banking via tallies and records written in cuneiform script and the issuance of uniform metal ingots preceded bank loans on notes of deposit. To assure honesty, the Code of Hammurabi, a body of Babylonian laws set down in cuneiform around 1750 B.C., regulated banking procedures.

By the seventh century B.C., the house of Egibi established a customer-friendly bank in Babylon that offered clients pawnbroking, checking, money changing, investments, real estate, slave markets, and shipping. During the Babylonian captivity of the Jews from 598 to 538 B.C., a scion of the original family, Yacob Egibi, founded modern banking by lending cash in exchange for repayment with interest. Controlling the crossroads of Cyprus, Elam, Egypt, Phoenicia, and Syria, the Egibi family flourished in business for two centuries and established branch banks to handle their complex monetary affairs. Company accountants left 2,000 tablets written in Akkadian from the time of Marduk-nasir-apli, discovered in terracotta jars in 1874. These invaluable texts contain the contracts and records of the house of Egibi's international trade, some of which was transacted in metal ingots. A second house, the bank of Murashshu and sons at Nippur, ventured into leasing, civil engineering, water rights, and monopolies in brewing and fisheries, all producing cash profits.

The Greeks, who were the next fiscal innovators, used temples as treasuries or storehouses for money and valuables and offered on-site money changing. The first Greek merchant banker identified by name was Pythius, who managed commercial funding in the eastern Mediterranean around 600 B.C. Outside Athens, Pasion of Archarnae, a former slave, rose to become the area's most influential and wealthiest banker and insurer of commodities as Athens evolved as the Mediterranean superstore for oil, wine, and grain. His high fees alleviated the risks of bottomry, the insuring of ships against wrecks and piracy, and also covered runs on the bank and the likelihood of dealing in foreign coins that might be shaved, clipped, or counterfeit.

To the south, the Egyptian banking system, headquartered at Alexandria, remained the financial mainstay even under Alexander III the Great, who seized Memphis in November 332 B.C. and circulated Greek coins as soldiers' pay. In Ptolomaic times after 323 B.C., the Egyptians developed private banking firms, which provided secure vaults for deposit of coinless wealth, usually in wheat and barley, and charted transfers by a credit and debit set-up that preceded Fra Luca Pacioli's ingenious double-entry bookkeeping system by over 1500 years. The banking officer, called the *oikonomus* (household manager), supervised the warehousing and safekeeping of perishables and provided governors with a constant watch over community assets at palace and temple storehouses.

At Rome, the chief banking services were the work of *argentarii* (money changers), who oiled the wheels of trade in a multinational city that tended to prefer coins in hand to deposits in the bank. In 100 B.C., the *equites* (knight class) owned and operated banks that stored foreign and domestic specie. To the *equites,* the post was lucrative, both in earnings and political influence. To acquire the title of banker, seekers established their eligibility by proving to the state censors a personal monetary worth above 400,000 *sesterces.* The system implied that those who had money were the most likely to respect and guard the funds of others.

Within a virtually impregnable city, financiers in republican Rome took advantage of their urban location near the center of power. For short-term loans, city bankers established high rates of usury that were a bargain compared to the charge in outlying territories. Exchange bills functioned like checks by transferring amounts between accounts without actually counting out coins from palm to palm. Thus, chests of money stayed secure in the vaults while authorized receipts of deposit circulated like currency.

By the beginning of the empire, Augustus had fine-tuned Roman banking well enough to reorganize the procedures introduced in Egyptian banks. Imperial financial institutions worked out schedules similar to modern exchange rates. Clerks shuffled a dizzying array of Mediterranean coinage, including the tiny *minimi* (smallest), a third-century A.D. slang term for small, artless knock-offs of genuine Roman coins. During the Byzantine era, when Roman power shifted to the east to Constantinople, the Emperor Justinian codified quasi-legal banking rules into law, which remained in effect into the Middle Ages.

As is true throughout history, the emergence of power struggles produced a desperate need for liquidity. A major stimulus to Medieval banking occurred in 1096 with the launching of the First Crusade, which lasted until 1099. To acquire cash for equipping and feeding forces and their mounts and for issuing salaries, banks enabled individuals and armies traveling across Europe to the Holy Lands to transfer sums of money by bills of exchange, the beginning of Europe's long-distance bank network. Serving as underwriters and shippers under new and more demanding circumstances than daily commerce were the Knights Templar. A parallel brotherhood, the Knights Hospitallers, pawned their wealth and petitioned for donations to ransom captive Christians held prisoner in the Levant.

Because limited coins in circulation could not keep pace with the spiraling financial demand, the first country-to-country coinless deal derived from an exchange contract signed in 1156 in Genoa with a bank in Constantinople. The massive flow of subsequent bills of exchange, foreign currencies, and bullion spawned banking centers:

city	*bank*
Barcelona	Lonja, built by Pedro the Ceremonious in 1393
Bergen, Norway	Hanseatic College of Merchants
Florence	Mercato Nuevo in the Piazza Mentana
Frankfurt	*Fischmarkt* (Fish Market)
Genoa	Casa di San Giorgio
Lille	Beauregard
Lyons	Place des Changes
Marseilles	Loge, established in 1653
Palermo	Loggia
Piacenza	College of Merchants
Stockholm	Riksbank
Valencia	Lonja
Verona	Mercato a Termine

A major player in late medieval banking was the papacy, which negotiated annual transfers across Europe.

Some medieval commercial consortia began outdoors, as with the Luccan money changers at the entrance to St. Martin's Church. Cadiz merchants functioned informally at open-air markets until they built a bank in 1596 on the Calle Nueva. In Seville, merchants formed an outdoor bank at the cathedral *gradas* (steps); Lisbon was known from 1294 for its banking street, the Rua Nova. At Liège, high finance began in the late 1500s at the Public Weighhouse and at the Quai de la Beach under the overhang of the episcopal palace. Also informal were the Leipzig arcade and public scale, the Dunkerque townhouse square, and the roofless Canton des Flamands of La Rochelle, which functioned until the opening of a building in 1761.

From the early 1200s, Venice, the cradle of capitalism, had exploited its location on major trade routes along the Mediterranean by developing commerce in Murano glass, beads, mosaics, jewelry, leather goods, imitation *objets d'art*, brocades, damask, and lace. In addition to banking services, the merchant aristocracy issued insurance and bills of exchange, commissioned gold *ducats* and *sequins*. Clerks kept accounts with double-entry bookkeeping, a system first described in Tuscan mathematician Fra Luca Pacioli's treatise *Summa de Arithmetica, Geometria, Proportioni, et Proportionalità* (*On Arithmetic, Geometry, Ratios, and Proportionality*) (1494).

On Italy's west coast, and in Florence, the "Athens of the West," evolved the banking dynasties of banking houses of Bardi, Medici, Peruzzi, and Rucellai. On the basis of free-flowing cash, Florence became an art and culture center and spawned a maritime empire. Financiers followed successful Venetian monetary practice in 1252 by stamping an original gold coin called the *florin*, which bore a modest flower symbolizing a city overburdened with ego. From international dealings, Mediterranean acumen at money-handling spread to northwestern Europe and turned Holland and England into world-class money markets.

In 1298 during the financing of a naval war with Venice, Genoa's commercial rival, the Genoan Casa di San Giorgio ("House of St. George") or Banca di San Giorgio devised a system of promissory notes to depositors. In exchange for bullion, bank tellers issued the first hand-written banknotes and promised to redeem paper bills with customs collected in its harbor, precious metals, or bank stock. In the 1300s, the Casa served as a local cash depository for merchants enriched by European and Levantine trade in spices, dye, medicine, cloth, metals, African wool, skins, coral, and gold. Formally organized in 1407 at a waterfront palazzo on the Piazza Caricamento as an association of eight state creditors, the institution functioned apart from the office of Doge Michele Steno as a private source of short-term loans, investments, and tax collection.

Genoa's Casa di San Giorgio was so profitable that the city coined a self-congratulatory motto, "*Genuensis ergo mercator*" ("[I am] Genoese, Therefore a Trader"). A late 15th-century Casa chancellor, Antonio Gallo, arranged dealings with Columbus and his kinsmen, Amico and Matteo de Columbo, and wrote Christopher Columbus's biography around 1495. Gallo aided Columbus as intermediary with city merchants, especially Lodisio d'Oria and Jacobo di Negro, who partially bankrolled Columbus's 1492 expedition to the New World.

The consummate banker of the Renaissance, Cosimo de' Medici, inherited an international banking cartel from his father, Giovanni di Bicci. Cosimo's staff met daily outdoors at trestle tables in Florence and spread double-entry ledgers on green cloths. They issued traveler's checks, exchanged coins from over 20 Italian state currencies, and lent money locally to vintners and grocers as well as to dukes, kings, and popes. Pius II, Cosimo's largest client, used Cosimo as an agent of church revenue, which his bank dispatched to the church treasury in local specie. Cosimo's bank spread to branch offices in Avignon, Bruges, Geneva, London, Milan, Pisa, Rome, and Venice. By turning the gold *florin* into Europe's prime currency, he also elevated finance to a cornerstone of world politics.

Perhaps out of Cosimo's guilt over the taint of usury, the great wealth of the Medicis produced acts of altruism and civic generosity. In the 1430s, Cosimo impressed Doge Francesco Foscari, Francesco Sforza, and Pope Nicholas V with his political and artistic patronage. Lavish expenditure on rare coins and artistic masterpieces, monastery and church rebuilding, copying of manuscripts and establishment of libraries, and nepotism entrenched the family in the good graces of people in Avignon, Bruges, Milan, London, Lyon, and Pisa. Cosimo's inattentive grandson, Lorenzo the Magnificent, perpetuated the cultural connection between bank profits and civic gift-giving until his managers squandered the family wealth and brought down the bank in 1494.

Influencing the money policies of continental Europe and Great Britain as early as 1585 was the Bank of Amsterdam, established on the Damplatz in 1631. It incorporated a money market, investment brokerage, and stock exchange and extended money marketing thrice weekly to a separate Corn Exchange. The impressive bourse, which featured a classic internal colonnade, grand clock tower, shops, and open courtyard, emulated the open-air basilicas of ancient Rome, the centers of money changing and varied commerce. By 1722, the Amsterdam bourse's 1,000 brokers received 4,500 clients daily in the public room during two hours of business. Activity declined on Saturdays, the Jewish sabbath. In 1778, bourse account manager Louis Greffulhe kept notes on the rise of large-scale speculation in colonial commodities and hedged his own bets with inside information from his London connections and from a Jewish house, J. and Abraham Garcia.

Based on successful operations in Genoa and Venice, the Amsterdam bank standardized Dutch currency and edged out Antwerp as a north European financial center. Fueled by the success of the Dutch East India Company and the West India Company, into the early 17th century, Amsterdam and its fluid currency financed colonial expansion in the Western Hemisphere and Asia. Much praised by Adam Smith in *Inquiry into the Nature and Causes of the Wealth of Nations* (1776), the first masterpiece of political economy, Dutch banking was the foundation of modern money. Its Amsterdam location became the warehouse of Europe's bullion.

Over time, for a city to thrive during the Renaissance it had to accommodate a wide range of financial dealings. London's bourse, from the Latin *bursa* ("moneybag"), evolved into the Royal Exchange in 1579. Paris had its Bourse, which began at the Place aux Changes before moving in 1724 to the Palais de Nevers. A warning to the over-eager was the failed Ayr Bank of Scotland, an idealistic land-based corporation that lent too liberally, issued too many banknotes, and collapsed in 1772, bankrupting its founders.

The acceptance of banks as adjuncts to successful cities colored the report of Lees Both, Russian ambassador to Gibraltar, who, in 1782, carped that the island had no exchange like the places in major trading cities where merchants did business. The reason that Gibraltar, Livorno, and other harbors developed no formal bank or *bureau de change* was their reliance on black marketeering and contraband. For obvious reasons, under-the-table business in these locales required no receipts and left no records.

Bankers tended to produce their own culture. Betting and lotteries nourished *coffy huisen* ("coffeehouses"), where financiers warmed themselves at stoves, read, played cards, shared news, and enjoyed tobacco, chocolate, tea, and coffee. In 1688, English insurer Lloyd's of London, began as Edward Lloyd's coffeehouse, where maritime financiers and shipowners conversed and discussed business; in New York City, two dozen entrepreneurs and money men meeting under a buttonwood tree in 1792 began frequenting the Tontine Coffee House and founded the New York Stock Exchange.

The U.S. banking system got off to a rocky start with serious disagreements between Alexander Hamilton, first secretary of the treasury, and his critics, notably Secretary of State Thomas Jefferson and colonial financier Robert Morris. After Hamilton initiated the Bank of the United States in 1791, a pattern of folk institutions multipled in the colonies, where no system or rule guided the backing of printed paper money. As numbers rose from three banks in 1790 to 788 in 1830, detractors ridiculed unscrupulous operations as "wildcat banks." The establishment of questionable financial institutions ended during the presidency of Andrew Jackson, who required payment in coin rather than frivolous paper bills.

In Hamburg, the rise of German banking in the 1770s stimulated thrift through individual savings accounts. Establishing rural credit cooperatives, Friedrich Wilhelm Raffeisen set up a system that blossomed rapidly before World War II. Paralleling the phenomenon were the industrial cooperatives begun in 1850 by Herman Schultze-Delitzsch.

For the French economy, Napoleon created the Bank of France in 1800 as a means of raising money and managing the national debt. The institution distributed the newly created *franc* and took over the issuance of banknotes, once the job of the *Caisse des Comptes Courants* and the *Caisse d'Escompte du Comerce*. By 1803, the French national bank monopolized the printing of banknotes, a trust it jeopardized in 1804 by issuing too much paper money. Gradually earning the citizens' trust, it opened provincial branches and, in 1848, earned for its notes the designation of legal tender.

In the estimation of German social and economic analyst Oswald Spengler, author of the monumental two-volume *The Decline of the West: Perspectives on World History* (1918–1922), banking receded in importance at the end of the 1800s. He summarized: "The last century [the 19th] was the winter of the West, the victory of materialism and scepticism, of socialism, parliamentarianism, and money. But in this century blood and instinct will regain their rights against the power of money and intellect" (Spengler). In his estimation, money had fallen behind international politics as a world power.

***See also assignat;* Bank of England; Leonardo Fibonacci; giro system; Alexander Hamilton; Knights Templar; John Law; *mark;* Hugh McCulloch; money laundering; moneylending; Robert Morris; paper money; Pasion of Archarnae; William Paterson; Sir William Petty; Roman coins — Monarchy and republic; U.S. Treasury.**

SOURCES: Allen, Larry. *Encyclopedia of Money*. New York: Checkmark Books, 2001. • "Ancient History Sourcebook: A Collection of Contracts from Mesopotamia, c. 2300–428 BCE." http://www.fordham.edu/HALSALL/ANCIENT/mesopotamia-contracts.html. • Barton, George Aaron. *Assyrian and Babylonian Literature*. New York: D. Appleton & Company, 1904. • Braudel, Fernand. *The Wheels of Commerce*. New York: Harper and Row, 1982. • Casson, Lionel. *The Ancient Mariners*. Princeton, N.J.: Princeton University Press, 1991. • Clain-Stefanelli, Elvira, and Vladimir Clain-Stefanelli. *The Beauty and Lore of Coins, Currency, and Medals*. Croton-on-Hudson, N.Y.: Riverwood Publishers, 1974. • Crombie, A. C. *Medieval and Early Modern Science*. Cambridge, Mass.: Harvard University Press, 1967. • Davies, Glyn. *A History of Money from Ancient Times to the Present Day*. Cardiff: University of Wales Press, 1994. • "Family Archives from Neo-Babylonian and Early Achaemenid Babylon." *Centre for the Study of Ancient Documents Newsletter*, June 3, 1998. • Galbraith, John Kenneth. *Money: Whence It Came, Where It Went*. Boston: Houghton Mifflin, 1975. • *Handbook to Life in Ancient Rome*. New York: Facts On File, Inc., 1994. • Jurdjevig, Mark. "Civic Humanism and the Rise of the Medici." *Renaissance Quarterly*, Winter 1999. • Lothar, Corinna. "Sun Shines brightly on Liguria La Superba." *Washington Times*, April 21, 2001. • "Modern History Sourcebook: Oswald Spengler: The Decline of The West, 1922." http://www.fordham.edu/halsall/mod/spengler-decline.html. • Napier, H. Albert, et al. *Creating a Winning E-Business*. Detroit: Thomson Learning, 2001. • Pickford, Nigel. *The Atlas of Ship Wrecks & Treasure*. New York: Dorling Kindersley, 1994. • Severy, Merle, ed. *The Renaissance*. Washington, D.C.: National Geographic Society, 1977. • Shaw, Christine. "Counsel and Consent in Fifteenth-Century Genoa." *English Historical Review*, September 1, 2001. • Snodgrass, Mary Ellen. *Who's Who in the Middle Ages*. Jefferson, N.C.: McFarland, 2001. • Wasilewska, Ewa. "On the Money." *The World & I*, November 1, 1998, 222. • Weatherford, Jack. *The History of Money: From Sandstone to Cyberspace*. Pittsburgh, Pa.: Three Rivers Press, 1998.

Barber, Charles Edward

Prolific engraver Charles Edward Barber established his place in U.S. coinage with a B stamped on the neck of the profile adorning the 1892 dime, quarter, and half-dollar. He became the sixth on-site sculptor at the Philadelphia Mint in 1879, replacing his father, Chief Engraver William Barber. Assisted by George T. Morgan, the younger Barber is renowned for designing the 1883 Hawaiian silver coin, the 1886 Liberty Head nickel, the 1892 Columbian half dollar, and the 1892 dime, quarter, and half dollar, plus commemorative medallions and some unsigned dies, including the four-dollar Flowing Hair Stella and Washlady likenesses. He is best known for replacing the familiar seated Liberty motif introduced by Joseph Alexis Bailly.

A native of London, Charles Barber, the son and grandson of master engravers, was born in 1840. His family emigrated to America when he was twelve and lived in Boston, where, in 1860, his father was a letter cutter. The family settled in Philadelphia, where his father, then a silvermaster and diesmith, worked at the U.S. Mint. Apprenticed to his father, Charles Barber went to work as a modest assistant. He married Martha E. Jones in 1875 and sired a daughter, Edith. During a period of prosperity, he had an astounding influence on U.S. currency.

Upon the death of the elder Barber, Charles, then 39 years old, succeeded as head engraver despite some consideration of Morgan for the job. At Barber's height, he created coins for Cuba and Venezuela, the 1893 Isabella quarter, the 1900 Lafayette dollar, and the Panama-Pacific $2.50 gold and the 50-cent silver pieces. With Morgan's assistance, he styled the 1903 Louisiana Purchase Exposition commemorative gold dollar, modeled on work by engraver John Reich and on a bust by rococo sculptor Jean-Antoine Houdon. Barber died on February 18, 1917.

Overall, Barber's work was satisfactory, but not artistic. In 1905, he was involved in a controversy with President Theodore Roosevelt, who disdained Barber's work. In his stead, the president preferred that Dublin-born sculptor Augustus Saint-Gaudens, the premiere American artist of his day, who designed all new American coins valued from a penny to 20 dollars. Barber accommodated the sculptor's dramatic bas-relief by replacing the mint's Hill reducing machine with a Janvier lathe, a three-dimensional pantograph that diminished depth considerably from the original plaster model. The reduction made practical a deeply incised design that would not have stood up to everyday coin wear in its original form.

See also **William Barber; George T. Morgan; Bela Lyon Pratt; U.S. coins.**

SOURCES: Ahwash, Kamal M. *Encyclopedia of United States Liberty Seated Dimes 1837–1891.* Wallingford, Pa.: Kamal Press, 1974. • Bowers, Q. David. *Adventures with Rare Coins.* Los Angeles: Bowers & Ruddy Galleries, Inc., 1979. • Breen, Walter. *Walter Breen's Complete Encyclopedia of U.S. and Colonial Coins.* New York: F.C.I. Press/Doubleday, 1988. • Reed, Mort. *Cowles Complete Encyclopedia of U.S. Coins.* New York: Cowles Book Company, 1969. • Reiter, Ed. "Numismatics: The Roman Touch." *New York Times,* January 16, 1983, p. H40. • Rochette, Ed. "Four Hundred Cents to the Stella Dollar!" *Antiques & Collecting Hobbies,* December 1986, p. 72. • Taxay, Don. *The U.S. Mint and Coinage.* New York: Arco Publishing, 1966. • Van Ryzin, Robert R. *Twisted Tails: Sifted Fact, Fantasy and Fiction from U.S. • Coin History.* Iola, Wisc.: Krause Publications, 1995.

Barber, William

Named the fifth on-site sculptor at the Philadelphia Mint in 1879, Chief Engraver William Barber entered U.S. coin manufacture at a significant time in its history. The son of master engraver John Barber, he was born in London on May 2, 1807, and apprenticed early in the family art. As an employee of De La Rue & Company, in his early twenties, he began producing die-stamped labels and cards and silver-plated tableware. He emigrated from London in September 1852, then worked at letter cutting and designing trade plates and political medals in Boston in 1860.

During the Civil War, William Barber designed gold and silver items for Gorham & Company with the aid of his son, Charles Edward Barber, who became his apprentice in engraving. Settled in Philadelphia in 1865, William worked in U.S. coinage and rose to the top post in January 1869 at the death of his predecessor, James Barton Longacre, who had flourished as the chief engraver for a quarter century.

Under Barber's decade of leadership, the mint continued to adapt Longacre's motifs and eventually added new dies for the 1874 20-cent piece, commercial and trade dollars, and silver coins. Assisting Barber were sculptors George T. Morgan and William H. Key. Most prized of Barber's originals is the 1872 Amazonian silver coin. By 1877, he was earning an annual salary of $3,000. He died on August 31, 1879, following a seaside vacation to Atlantic City, New Jersey.

See also **Charles Edward Barber; James Barton Longacre; George T. Morgan; Anthony C. Paquet.**

SOURCES: Ahwash, Kamal M. *Encyclopedia of United States Liberty Seated Dimes 1837–1891.* Wallingford, Pa.: Kamal Press, 1974. • Breen, Walter. *Walter Breen's Complete Encyclopedia of U.S. and Colonial Coins.* New York: F. C. I. Press/Doubleday, 1988. • Reiter, Ed. "Numismatics: The Roman Touch." *New York Times,* January 16, 1983, p. H40. • Rochette, Ed. "Four Hundred Cents to the Stella Dollar!" *Antiques & Collecting Hobbies,* December 1986, p. 72. • Taxay, Don. *The U.S. Mint and Coinage.* New York: Arco Publishing, 1966.

bas-relief

Sculptured or incised relief, called *basso-relievo*, projects quasi-three-dimensional shapes from the surrounding plane surface. Classification of shaping depends upon the degree of undercutting of outlines and the height and detachment of figures from the background to give the illusion of a full shape. Integral in the art of Assyria, Egypt, and the Middle East, relief work adorns tombs and monuments from early times. The use of contoured portraiture characterized imperial Roman art from A.D. 100 to 200 and subsequent religious adornment in the churches of northwestern Europe and Britain.

Because of the limitations of coin and medal art, bas-relief became the standard shaping of money after Philip of Macedon introduced Greek portrait coins early in the fourth century B.C. Following a similar system of self-aggrandizement to impress his Persian subjects, King Shapur II, a Sasanian monarch, had himself pictured at full gallop on a royal hunt. His mounted figure and carefully incised face, beard, and hair complement a drawn bow and the fleeing quarry, a tusked boar. The image corroborates an eyewitness account:

> He himself, mounted on his charger, and being taller than the rest, led his whole army, wearing instead of a crown a golden figure of a ram's head inlaid with jewels; being also splendid from the retinue of men of high rank and of different nations which followed him ["Shapur II"].

The noble bearing and demeanor are well suited to three-dimensional art, which expresses a dynamism and motion not found in painting and mosaic.

New World artisans brought bas-relief to a height of artistic expression, notably, a simplified view of the Sierra Madre dominated by a textured sunburst on the Guatemalan gold coinage of 1820. The 1828 eight-*escudo* piece featured a stylized sun surrounded by light and by raised dots and lettering on the legend, which read "Provincias del Rio de la Plata." Mexican moneyers incised the traditional eagle holding a snake on low relief coin designs of 1824 and 1846 as a tribute to Aztec myths surrounding the founding of Tenochtitlán, the nucleus of Mexico city. At Cuzco, Peru, in 1837, the mint produced a silver eight-*real* piece featuring a sunburst topped with four stars. On the back, a complex scene pictured a volcano, Spanish galleon, horn of plenty, stone building, and the legend "Firme por la Union" (for a strong union). A Brazilian coin from 1900 showed the grand, all-embracing gesture of Portuguese expeditioner Pedro Alvares Cabral with flowing cloak and staff. He stands alongside a beneficent star above a curved banner stating his name. The Portuguese legend honors the "*4th Centenario do Descobrimento do Brasil*" ("400th Anniversary of the Discovery of Brazil"). A nobly curved silhouette of Incan dynastic founder Manco Capac (also Manqo Qhapaq) with feathered crown and bold circular earring, graced a Peruvian coin struck in 1930, another South American collectors' item.

The first U.S. coins issued from 1792 to 1836 were products of master dies engraved from an original sketch of the main design in the exact size. The engraving staff later added stars, legends, rims, and dates, which varied to suit individual scenarios. To reduce wear and assure a clean image, workers made dies of pressure-hardened steel. Each cylindrical blank received a nitric acid wash and was ground into a cone shape at one end. The surface required filing and polishing with an oil stone before the engraver applied a thin film of transfer wax. After placing a copy of the sketch over the top layer, the engraver burnished lines into the wax with a spoon-ended mallet.

After peeling the paper free, coin artists incised designs with a graving tool, shaping depth lines to create a bas-relief. Like the lapidary or watchmaker, the engravers' choice of tools ranged from flat, round, and diamond tips to the onglette, shaped like a Gothic arch. The careful inciser halted periodically to stamp the three-dimensional shape in clay as a check on quality and depth. When the master die passed inspection, it was ready for tempering under extremes of heat and cold and positioning on a hub for stamping the working dies. In 1836, the U.S. Mint staff ceased the tedious hand-incising method and installed a portrait lathe, which copied original art onto master dies. In 1867, the equipping of machinery with the Hill reducing machine further improved and simplified die-making. The Janvier lathe, installed in 1907, applied pantographic reduction to intricate master designs.

Variances in the degree of relief aided treasuries in controlling wear to raised detailing. In the 19th century, the Roman Republic issued a complex emblem picturing the widespread wings of the state eagle and the encircling laurel wreath atop a fasces and furled state banner laid horizontally on the altar of peace, marked with a Jacobin cap and dagger. The minutely detailed bas-relief honors the revolution of 1799. Another beauty, the elephant coin struck after 1851 during the reign of Phra Maha Mongkut of Siam pictured a swirl of nine leaf shapes encircling a raised elephant at center within a deeply incised fluted edge. In contrast, subsequent Siamese elephant coins did not create enough thrust, particularly the two-dimensional effect of a three-headed crowned elephant adorning *ticals* of the early 20th century.

An artful blend of high and low relief highlights the grace and humanism of a gold fifty *lei* piece struck in 1922 by the Romanian queen Marie Wettin of Saxe-Coburg-Gotha, granddaughter of Queen Victoria and heroic Red Cross nurse during epidemics of typhus and cholera. Marie's appealingly youthful silhouette is draped in veil and robe, adorned with chains and pendants from her earrings, and encircled by the legend "*Maria Regina i Romanilor*" ("Queen Mary of Romania"). Angles and shadowing focus attention on a deeply incised facial outline and multipointed crown.

Religious emblems thrive on nuances of bas-relief. In 1899, Jules C. Chaplain, designer for the Paris mint, copied the Ethiopian "lion of Judah" incised in low projection by Austrian mint artist F. X. Pawlik for the *talari*. Tempering the animal's feral musculature and defiant stance are the crozier and banner, balanced by an elongated looped tail. A spare, dramatic Israeli coin sculpted by Myriam Caroly in 1958 pictured a seven-branch menorah on tripod. Inset in a rounded lozenge in starkly even relief, the bold figure, anchored by a single vertical, characterizes Jewish faith with art deco grace.

A series of three Thai coins struck in 1983 to honor the 700th anniversary of the Siamese alphabet featured a balance of low and high relief. On the front of the 10-*baht* coin, the bold incision of a seated Buddha dwarfs a temple and table. The curve of limbs, shoulders, and face characterize the deity's human qualities. On the reverse, the artist sculpted the country's alphabet in low relief.

In 1984, Denmark circulated simple, flat raised motifs in art deco style on its 25-*øre* coin, which had a hole in the center. Instead of words, the obverse pictured a crown above the ornate monogram M2R, referring to Queen Margarethe II. Balancing the royal emblem was a branch and leaves incised with a natural flow of veins and scalloped edges. The coin back names the country and denomination in simple, stark relief adorned only with parallel curved lines.

***See also* Victor D. Brenner; Benvenuto Cellini; *drachma;* Leone Leoni; Gaspare Molo; pantograph; papal coins; Benedetto Pistrucci; portrait coins; Augustus Saint-Gaudens; Jean Varin; Adolph A. Weinman; Charles Cushing Wright; Wyon family.**

SOURCES: "Celebrating the American Medal." *American Numismatic Society Newsletter*, Fall 1997. • Clain-Stefanelli, Elvira, and Vladimir Clain-Stefanelli. *The Beauty and Lore of Coins, Currency, and Medals.* Croton-on-Hudson, N.Y.: Riverwood Publishers, 1974. • Lewis, Brenda Ralph. *Coins & Currency.* New York: Random House, 1993. • Reed, Mort. *Cowles Complete Encyclopedia of U.S. Coins.* New York: Cowles Book Company, 1969. • "Shapur II." http://bcd.britannica.com/bcom/eb/... /0,5716,68882,00.html.

Bass, George

A founder of seabed archeology, George Fletcher Bass pursued the discipline for 40 years and established standards for exploring undersea artifacts. Off the shores of Turkey in 1959, he directed the first undersea excavation conducted under terrestrial regulations. From his scholarly beginnings, he advanced to professor of preclassical, classical, and nautical archeology at Texas A & M and, in 1973, founded and chaired the Institute of Nautical Archaeology, which has explored shipwrecks dating from the 1700s B.C. to the A.D. 1800s His expeditions have taken him to land digs in Greece, Italy, and Turkey and to submerged sites in the Mediterranean and Caribbean seas, Maine, and Virginia.

Born in Columbia, South Carolina, on December 9, 1932, to Virginia Wauchope and Robert D. Bass, an English professor, Bass learned scholarly habits and attitudes in childhood. Early on, he developed an interest in marine archeology from the experiences of his uncle Robert Wauchope, who studied archeology at Harvard University. Bass completed an undergraduate degree at Johns Hopkins University before pursuing a Ph.D. in classical archaeology.

In 1959, Bass was specializing in Bronze Age Aegean artifacts at the University of Pennsylvania about the time that amateur archeologist Dr. Peter Throckmorton of Maine discovered the late Bronze Age wreck of a royal seagoing trader that sank in a storm around 1317 B.C. off Cape Gelidonya at Ulu Burun, Turkey. He asked the university for advice on applying land excavation techniques to seabed artifacts. In reply, Bass volunteered to study diving at the YMCA and direct Throckmorton's team in salvaging the ancient ship.

Working 90 feet down with co-director Cemal Pulak, Bass and his wife Ann spent 11 summers at his Turkish *pied-à-terre* making 22,500 dives. He adapted more leisurely land study methods to two 20-minute dives per day. Among the artifacts the couple catalogued over a decade in Turkey were bronze tools, incense jars from Canaan, a wax-paged book, elephant tusks, and hippopotamus teeth. Bass discovered the oldest wax-coated writing tablet, a gold scarab that had belonged to Queen Nefertiti, Canaanite jewelry, and the oldest glass ingots, forerunners of coins. In addition, salvors located additional forms of precoinage — stacks of small metal disks called bun ingots, ovoid bronze ingots, and corroded tin ingots that had lost their shape from contact with saltwater. Some the users had broken into small pieces, perhaps converting whole ingots into small change to facilitate trade.

Bass's enthusiasm for the expedition was evident in his description of the wreck and its time period:

> There has been no more important a preclassical Mediterranean site excavated in recent decades than the Ulu Burun shipwreck in Turkey, with its 18,000 artifacts from nearly a dozen different cultures, twenty tons in all, precisely dated to within a few years of 1300 B.C. by the tree rings in a log, perhaps firewood, carried on board. This site is revolutionizing our picture of the Late Bronze Age — the time of the Trojan War, King Tut, and the Exodus [Bass, "25 Year History"].

He concluded that the examination of this one wreck justified the creation of an undersea archaeological institute and outlined ongoing excavation of undersea wreck sites. Now divers are, for the first time, excavating a wreck from the Golden Age of classical Greece off Tektas Burnu, Turkey; the world's oldest shipwreck in the Western Hemisphere in Lake Champlain; and a Roman-era fishing boat in Israel. From these studies, he anticipated contributing to the history of ships, technology, art, and money and commerce.

In addition to publishing articles in *The Oxford Encyclopedia of Archaeology in the Near East*, *Archaeology*, *American Journal of Archaeology*, *Journal of Glass Studies*, *Archaeological News*, *Studies in Mediterranean Archaeology*, *Anatolian Studies*, *Medieval Archaeology*, *Encyclopedia of Underwater and Maritime Archaeology*, and *National Geographic*, Bass issued a book on the project in Turkey, *Cape Gelidonya: A Bronze Age Shipwreck* (1965), and followed with *Archaeology Under Water* (1966), *The Smithsonian Twentieth-Century Treasury of Science* (1966), *Archaeology Beneath the Sea* (1975), *Yassi Ada* (1982), *The Bronze Age Shipwreck at Ulu Burun* (1995), and *Ship-*

wrecks in the Bodrum Museum of Underwater Archaeology (1996). He also edited *A History of Seafaring: Based on Underwater Archaeology* (1972), *Ships and Shipwrecks of the Americas: A History Based on Underwater Archaeology* (1988), and *A History of Seafaring in the Americas Based on Underwater Archaeology* (2001). His groundbreaking work earned him the John Olivers La Gorce gold medal and the 1988 Centennial Award from the National Geographic Society, the Archaeological Institute of America gold medal, the Lowell Thomas Award, and a visiting professorship at Cambridge University. He holds the Abell Chair and the Yamini Chair in Nautical Archaeology at Texas A & M and takes pride in training undersea archeologists from Albania, Belgium, Canada, China, Denmark, England, France, Greece, Jamaica, Japan, Peru, South Africa, Switzerland, and Turkey.

***See also* Peter Throckmorton; underwater archeology.**

SOURCES: Banks, Suzy. "George F. Bass." *Texas Monthly*, September 2000, p. 171. • Bass, George F. "Cape Gelidonya: A Bronze Age Shipwreck." *Transactions of the American Philosophical Society* 57, part 8, Philadelphia, 1967. • Bass, George F., ed. *Ships and Shipwrecks of the Americas: A History Based on Underwater Archaeology*. London: Thames and Hudson, 1996. • Bass, George F. "25 Year History of INA Research," http://ina.tamu.edu/25yearhis1.htm. • *Contemporary Authors Online*. Farmington Hills, Mich.: Gale Group, 2000. • Fielding, Andrew. "History from the Sea." *New Scientist*, January 14, 1988. • Gifford, John A. "Ships and Shipwrecks of the Americas," *American Antiquity*, April 1998, pp. 361–362. • Kaufman, R. "The Sea Remembers." *Library Journal*, January 1988, p. 85. • Sullivan, Mark. "Sunken Vessel Near Turkey Believed to Date to 1,500 B.C." *New York Times*, October 30, 1982. • Throckmorton, Peter. "Oldest Known Shipwreck Yields Bronze Age Cargo." *National Geographic*, May 1962, pp. 696–711.

Bechtler, Christoph

When the United States enjoyed its first gold rush in the 1820s in the years preceding the creation of a national mint, gold was plentiful in Georgia and Western North Carolina. As of 1830, North Carolina alone boasted 56 gold mines. Because the largest strikes were in rural Cabarrus County, transportation of ore to the Philadelphia Mint was cumbrous, expensive, and unsafe. To facilitate the standardizing of coining gold dust and nuggets, in 1831, Alt Christoph Bechtler, a German-American watchmaker, jeweler, gunsmith, and diemaker, who had arrived from Baden the previous year, added mintmaster to his list of talents.

Born in Pfortzheim in 1782, Bechtler migrated to New York with his son Augustine and nephew Christoph Bechtler, Jr. Although the elder Bechtler spoke no English, he opened a private assaying, metallurgy, and minting business in rural Rutherfordton, North Carolina, and created dies for stamping the nation's first one-dollar gold coins. To expand the Bechtler Mint, he placed advertisements in the North Carolina *Spectator and Western Advertiser* proposing striking coins from private stock of unrefined gold ore.

For nineteen years, Bechtler's factory coined gold eagle dollars as well as quarters, halves, and 2.5-dollar and five-dollar denominations more efficiently and cost effectively than the U.S. Mint. He standardized styles and values:

series	*date*	*size*	*markings*
1st	July–September 1831	20 carats	assayer; North Carolina Gold
2nd	fall 1831	20 carats	—
3rd	winter 1831–July 1834	20 carats	N Carolina
4th	August 1834–1840	20 carats	August 1, 1834
5th	1834–1840	21 carats	—
6th	August 1834–1840	22 carats	Georgia Gold
7th	1840–1842	—	Behtler (without a C)

As of 1840, his operation had minted coins worth $2.2 million. From the 1840s to 1852, Bechtler's son and partner, Augustine Bechtler, contributed to the business under the supervision of a nephew, Christopher Bechtler, Jr. At a steady pace, the operation turned out

$4,000 to $5,000 each week. The Bechtler coinage earned the respect of users for its consistent value, distinctive design, and wide circulation in an area underserved by the U.S. Treasury.

Although private minting was legal, Bechtler's factory came under the scrutiny of federal treasury investigators, who studied the problem of circulating coins from the Philadelphia mint in the South. As more prospecting increased the amount of gold in the hands of speculators, the congressional leaders from North Carolina proposed establishing a U.S. branch mint at Charlotte, the major city of Mecklenburg County and of the piedmont. On March 3, 1835, President Andrew Jackson sanctioned the coinage of gold in Charlotte, which increased in 1849 to the striking of gold dollars in a liberty head pattern created by engraver James Barton Longacre. Another branch opened in Dahlonega, Georgia, increasing the number of gold coins that the federal government could turn out. Nonetheless, even though Congress approved gold coinage in one- and 20-dollar denominations in 1836, the federal minting program met with strong objection from Robert Maskell Patterson, the former mathematics professor and mint director who introduced U.S. coinage by steam-powered press.

Because Bechtler charged only 2–2.5 percent for coining bullion and maintained an impeccable reputation, he remained the major supplier of Southern coins until his death around 1842. Quality and integrity declined under Augustine's minting. After his retirement, Christoph Bechtler, Jr.'s, inept handling of the operation curtailed the flow of Bechtler money in 1857. Another change in coinage resulted from the California gold rush of 1849, which began pouring gold dust and bullion into the economy from the West Coast. During the Civil War, when paper money devalued rapidly, Bechtler gold remained unimpeached for quality and value.

SOURCES: Akers, David W. *United States Gold Coins*. Englewood, Ohio: Paramount Publications, Englewood, Ohio, 1975. • Alexander, David T., Thomas K. DeLorey, and P. Bradley Reed. *Coin World Comprehensive Catalog & Encyclopedia of United States Coins*. New York: World Almanac–Pharos Books, 1990. • "The Bechtler Private Mint." http://www.raregold.com/r-bech.htm. • *Biography Resource Center*. Farmington Hills, Mich.: Gale, 2001. • Bowers, Q. David. *The History of United States Coinage as Illustrated by the Garrett Collection*. Wolfeboro, N.H.: Bowers & Merena Galleries, 1979. • Breen, Walter. *Walter Breen's Complete Encyclopedia of U.S. and Colonial Coins*. New York: F. C. I. Press/Doubleday, 1988. • Clain-Stefanelli, Elvira, and Vladimir Clain-Stefanelli. *The Beauty and Lore of Coins, Currency, and Medals*. Croton-on-Hudson, N.Y.: Riverwood Publishers, 1974. • Hammett, A. B. J. *The History of Gold*. Kerriville, Tex.: Braswell Printing, Co., 1966. • "Legacy of Gold." *Charlotte Observer*, March 15, 1999. • "The North Carolina Collection's Currency Holdings." *North Carolina Collection Gallery*, http://www.lib.unc.edu/ncc/gallery/currency.html. • Sherrill, Sarah B. "North Carolina Gold Coins." *Antiques*, October 1980, 638–639. • Taxay, Don. *The U.S. Mint and Coinage*. New York: Arco Publishing, 1966.

bezant

A saucer-shaped Byzantine coin, the *bezant* (or *besant*) takes its name from the coastal town that became Istanbul. The name for the coin connects with history that covers 2,600 years. Later forms of the word "bezant," Byzantine and Byzantium, derive from the original capital city, which Greek colonists founded at the end of the 8th century B.C. The Greeks named it for the hero Byzas of Megara, who captured the peninsula on the Bosporus from Thracian tribes about 657 B.C. and built it into a thriving port city. The main mints producing *bezants* were Antioch, Alexandria, Catania, Constantinople, Cyzicus, Nicomedia, Ravenna, Syracuse, and Thessalonica. Because of its purity, the coin served for some eight centuries, making it among the longest-lived of the world's currencies.

The coins of the year A.D. 1000 were flat, sometimes oval in shape, and stamped with portraits front and back. Based on the Roman *solidus* struck by Constantine I the Great, the first Christian emperor, into the 1200s, the *bezant* remained a trade coin at Constantinople, the *entrepôt* of the Middle East. Because Constantine found religion a political expedient, his moneyers designed *bezants* with predominantly Christian portraiture and symbolism, especially views of Christ, the Virgin Mary, and saints.

Bezants permeate the history of Christian-Islamic face-offs in the Middle East. In 1035, Robert of Normandy, who led a pilgrimage to the Holy Land, rescued his followers at the Jerusalem gates by paying their entrance fee of one gold *bezant* each. After Saladin took Jerusalem on October 2, 1187, Richard I the Lion-Hearted redeemed sacred relics stored at the church of the Holy Sepulchre for 50,000 *bezants*. Saladin, a fair-minded Kurdish warrior-king, maintained a workable relationship with Christians and disguised himself for an on-site survey of the hospital run by the Knights of St. John at Acre. After observing their charity and merciful treatment of all patients, Christian and Muslim, Saladin granted the brotherhood a yearly stipend of 1,000 gold *bezants*. In subsequent struggles over ownership of sanctified territory, crusaders and their suppliers brought Middle Eastern *bezants* home to Europe when they returned from the Holy Land.

As a means of expediting trade with Middle Eastern merchants, Christians involved in the first four crusades—1095, 1096–1099, 1147–1149, and 1189–1192—minted their own *bezants*. When money was scarce, Balian d'Ibelin of Beirut and Sidon, the commander of the Christian forces at Jerusalem and the Latin go-between who negotiated the surrender of Jerusalem to Saladin, received authority from the Patriarch Heraclius to strike coins. Balian stripped silver from the roof of the Church of the Holy Sepulchre. Along with bullion from the church treasury and money that King Henry II of England pledged to the Knights Hospitallers, Balian produced new coins that he used to buy weapons.

These war-time coins lacked the fine borders of earlier coinage and were too thin to allow for reeded edging. For legends, Christian coiners used as models the *deniers* and *dirhans* of Palestine and Syria and applied the Arabic calligraphy common to Islamic tradition, which forbade human iconography. Ironically, because coin designers declined to learn Arabic or have it translated, they failed to recognize the scrolled lettering as the Islamic creed, "There is no God but God, and there is no other" (Hastings 1951, III, p. 709). Thus, Europeans campaigning to retrieve the Holy Land from Saracen hands inadvertently helped to spread Islamic fervor over Europe and North Africa.

See also **Islamic coins; medieval coins; paper money.**

SOURCES: Clain-Stefanelli, Elvira, and Vladimir Clain-Stefanelli. *The Beauty and Lore of Coins, Currency, and Medals*. Croton-on-Hudson, N.Y.: Riverwood Publishers, 1974. • Cribb, Joe. *Money*. Toronto: Stoddart, 1990. • Cribb, Joe, Barrie Cook, and Ian Carradice. *The Coin Atlas*. London: Little, Brown and Co., 1999. • Hastings, James, ed. *Encyclopedia of Religion and Ethics*. New York: Charles Scribner's Sons, 1951. • "Islamic Coins," http://www.islamiccoinsgroup.50g.com/jims.htm. • Lewis, Brenda Ralph. *Coins & Currency*. New York: Random House, 1993. • Loud, G. A. "Coinage, Wealth and Plunder in the Age of Robert Guiscard." *English Historical Review*, September 1999. • Nashabe, Hisham, ed. *Studia Palaestina*. Beirut: Institute for Palestine Studies, Beirut, 1988. • Pollak, Henry. *Coinage & Conflict*. Clifton, N.J.: Coin & Currency Institute, 2001. • Reinfeld, Fred. *Treasury of the World's Coins*. New York: Sterling Publishing, 1953. • Schaff, Philip. *History of the Christian Church*. New York: Scribner's, 1888.

bible currency

As elements of monetary transactions and temple tithes, barter and coins figure in numerous scenarios in the Old and New Testaments. When Abram and his wife Sarai arrived in Palestine from Ur around 1950 b.c., trade in silver was transacted in quantities of rings and bangles weighed on a balance beam scale. According to Judean, Ephraimite, and priestly oral traditions condensed in Genesis, the first book of the Pentateuch, long after the couple changed their names to Abraham and Sarah, he purchased a burial plot for her at Hebron. Because he was a stranger in Canaan, he negotiated for the cave of Machpelah and surrounding fields with Ephron ben Zohar the Hittite, a non–Semitic seller. The cost was "four hundred silver shekels, according to the weights current among the merchants" (Genesis 23:16). The money changed hands at the city gate, the place where elders gathered to supervise the transfer of title.

The shekel, which remains the monetary unit of Israel, figured later in the book of Genesis during the harsh sibling rivalry of Jacob's twelve sons, which is set at Dothan around 1800 B.C. As described in Genesis 37:12–36, the envious Judah convinced the other plotters to sell 17-year-old Joseph, Jacob's favorite, to Ishmaelite traders from Gilead, who were bound for Egypt with spices, balm, and myrrh. Retrieving Joseph from a pit, brothers exchanged brother for silver at the rate of 20 silver shekels for one male slave. The money would have taken the form of ingots that required the buyer to measure them on a scale against bronze and stone weights. The total was appreciable — enough to buy ten quality rams.

The act of selling a brother for silver prefigures Joseph's rise to Egypt's premier banker and keeper of the pharaoh's circular granaries. When the tables turned and Jacob's wicked sons journeyed from Judea to Egypt in search of food to sustain the family during a famine, Joseph accused the brothers of spying and had his minions hide the brothers' money in their grain sacks. The amazement of the brothers contrasts the firm morals of their father Jacob, who sent them a second time for Egyptian grain along with the fruits of the land — balm, honey, spices, myrrh, almonds — and twice the purchase price in cash. In Genesis 43:12, Jacob instructed, "Take double money in your hand; and the money that was brought again in the mouth of your sacks, carry it again in your hand; peradventure it was an oversight."

Joseph again tricked the brothers by inviting them to a meal, Jew with Egyptian, by welcoming his youngest brother Benjamin, and by filling their sacks with grain along with the money they paid for it. Household servants also placed in Benjamin's sack a silver chalice, a sacred divining vessel in which Joseph swirled oil on water and interpreted the patterns, which would have revealed the coming of spies and thieves from Canaan. Feigning outrage, he roared, "Wherefore have ye rewarded evil for good?" (Genesis 44:4). He tormented the older brothers by letting them depart, but forced them to leave the youngest as a slave in recompense. At length, Joseph revealed his identity. In 1960, Pope John XXIII welcomed Jewish guests to the Vatican with a phrase from the story, "I am Joseph, your brother," a metaphoric statement of kinship and conciliation between Christians and Jews.

As described in I Kings 10 and II Chronicles 9, an exchange of gift goods marked the state visit of the Queen of Sheba (also Saba or Seba), most likely from southwestern Arabia or Ethiopia, to Solomon around 950 B.C. She arrived with a grand retinue of camels bearing state gifts. After she tested him with riddles and inquiries, she found him a suitable monarch for negotiations. To mark their colloquy, she presented him spices, precious stones, almug wood (sandalwood) for carving terrace pillars and musical instruments, and 120 gold talents, which weighed around 25 tons and were valued at $3,600,000. Solomon, who earned around $20 million annually, was rich enough to turn his own store of raw gold into 200 targets, 300 shields, and plating for an ivory throne adorned with lions. The state bargaining complete, the Queen of Sheba returned home satisfied. Her state visit to Solomon appears as a motif in William Shakespeare's *Henry VIII* and in the novels of Sir Walter Scott and Thomas Hardy.

After the age of Ezra in the fifth century B.C., the compilation of semi-sacred or quasi-sacred texts produced the Old Testament Apocrypha, which flesh out Jewish history over the next three centuries. Maccabees I & II summarize the epic heroism of the short-lived zealot priest Mattathias of Modein and his sons John Gaddi, Simon Thassi, Eleazar Avaran, Jonathan Apphus, and Judah Maccabee (or Judas Maccabaeus), the legendary Hasmonian leader of guerrilla warfare. The first half of the text, composed in Hebrew by an unnamed Palestinian Jew writing in Hebrew, derives from an era of combat around the mid- to late-second century B.C.

Antagonizing the Jews in Egypt and Judea at a dramatic moment during the post–Alexandrian era, the Seleucid king Antiochus IV faced off against the Hasmonians. At a high point in the action in chapter 15 of I Maccabees, the king instructed the high priest and ethnarch Simon to coin money with his own stamp in Jewish style, that is, according to the first of the Ten Commandments, which forbids the engraving of human likeness as an affront to God. Antiochus concluded, "As concerning Jerusalem and the sanctuary, let them be free" (I Maccabees 15:6). The resulting coinage constituted the first true Jewish coin. A primitive bronze piece, it featured an anchor on the face and the Jerusalem lily on the reverse.

Also biographical in style and imagery, New Testament coinage offers numerous glimpses of the lifestyle of Christ and his followers. Around A.D. 5, a Syrian coin minted at Antioch pictured the goddess Tyche or Good Luck opposite a ram leaping toward an oversized star. The ram symbolizes both Judea and Aries, the sign of the zodiac associated with regeneration and spring, the time of year when some historians believe that Christ was born. Astronomers surmise that the star on the coin is the mythic Star of Bethlehem mentioned in the book of the first gospel writer, the publican Matthew.

During the ministry of Christ, Matthew wrote a thorough biography of a preacher and wonder-worker he assumed to be Jewish royalty, the savior foretold by the prophet Isaiah. Matthew gleaned data from the gospel of Mark and composed in Aramaic a full life story, sermon anthology, and word-for-word citations from Christ's conversations and sermons. A parallel biography, composed by Luke, a beloved Gentile physician who wrote around A.D. 90, pictured the long trek to Bethlehem, where Joseph, anticipating the arrival of his firstborn, paid the Roman head tax. Joseph probably used the *denarius* that Augustus issued, ironically, the same silver coin that paid the soldiers who tyrannized and harassed Palestinian Jews.

Both Matthew and Mark described Jesus's concern for the multitudes, whom he intended to feed. In Mark's version (8:1–9), Jesus sent his disciples to buy food for 4,000 followers. The disciples quantified the amount as "two hundred pennyworth of bread," a reference to the Roman *denarius* that Tiberius commissioned in A.D. 14, which was one day's wages for a skilled laborer. Jesus cut through the math with a miracle, the transformation of five barley loaves and a few fish into a sufficient meal plus seven baskets of leftovers. The story influenced the writings of St. Augustine and Geoffrey Chaucer and Somerset Maugham's four-act comedy *Loaves and Fishes* (1924).

The account of Lazarus's resurrection, another episode in Jesus's biography, returns to the *denarius* as the standard monetary denomination of the era. The episode appears in the fourth gospel, written by John, "God's eagle," the beloved follower who was one of the "sons of thunder." A spiritual author who composed about the end of the first century a.d., contemporaneous with Luke, John may have been either a brother of James ben Zebedee, a disciple of John the Baptist, or Jesus's nephew, the son of Salome, Mary's sister. John's writing comes from the end of the first century A.D. and expresses deep affection for the solitary redeemer, whom John loved as a friend, companion, and adviser.

According to John 11–12:1–8, as Jesus journeyed beyond the Jordan river, he received a message that Lazarus, Mary and Martha's brother, was ill. Thomas was concerned that Jesus should not return to that part of Judea, but Jesus insisted on hurrying to Bethany. Outside the city, he learned that Lazarus had died and been entombed for four days in a cave sealed with a great stone. Jesus amazed all by summoning the dead man back to life.

The second episode took place six days before Pasach (Passover) when Jesus visited his three friends at home for dinner. Mary of Bethany expressed hospitality, gratitude, and love by anointing his feet with what Mark describes as an alabaster box containing precious spikenard and by wiping his feet with her hair. Judas Iscariot denounced the act as an extravagance worth 300 *denarii*, nearly a year's wages for a laborer, which Mary should have donated to the poor. In John 12:7–8, Jesus reminded Judas that Mary's act was appropriate homage to Jesus, whose earthly time was coming to an end. Matthew pictured her piety and generosity as a foreshadowing of Jesus's martyrdom and herbal preparation for burial, which was only days away.

Matthew depicts Jesus at his most important appearance in Jerusalem. The city itself was a commercial center, offering open-air shops in the lower city for sale of baked goods, pottery, fabric, metal and wood crafts, jewelry, oil and perfume, and food. The clink of coins from many nations marked the buying of souvenirs and the sale of food and drink at taverns. Beyond, the open-air theater built by Herod the Great offered top entertainment from Greece and Rome. On the Sabbath, the Jewish sector fell silent as commerce halted at sundown for worship in the city's 480 synagogues.

In the matter of commerce, Matthew emphasizes Jesus's savvy verbal parrying of the Pharisees, a set of legalistic middle-class sticklers for the letter of the law. The text mentions Jesus's anger at Gentile money changers plying a lucrative trade in Judaism's holiest site, the Temple of Jerusalem. The reason for the exchange of foreign coins for shekels was the Jewish law forbidding in the Jewish communities of Palestine any coins and other public manifestations that carried the image of Tiberius Claudius Nero, the second Roman Emperor. Such coins came into two types of transactions: the donation of money in lieu of animal sacrifice and the paying of annual temple dues of a silver half-shekel weighing a half ounce, the amount owed by male Jews over age twenty and paid each Pesach. Such a gift in Roman portrait coins violated the first of the Ten Commandments, which bans graven images of deities.

Set on a Christian holiday now called Palm Sunday, the event known as the "driving of the money changers from the temple" pictures Jesus venting anger at the swapping of coins and weighing of gold and silver for profit, a practice accompanying the sale of doves and pigeons as well as lambs and cattle to be sacrificed on the altar. In Matthew's words:

> And Jesus went into the temple of God, and cast out all them that sold and bought in the temple, and overthrew the tables of the money changers, and the seats of them that sold doves. And said unto them, "It is written, My house shall be called the house of prayer; but ye have made it a den of thieves" [Matthew 21:12–13].

According to Mark, this cleansing of the temple of corrupt trade transpired the next day after Jesus's triumphant entry into the city during Pesach.

Whatever the time, the place is the dominant factor in the event. It establishes Jesus's tie with the Jewish hierarchy, for Pharisees, according to the Talmud, also condemned commerce in the house of Yahweh as sacrilege. Nonetheless, the temple's Levite priests and their staff of cantors, doormen, and servants depended on a share of the money changing, which they levied on anyone wishing to set up an exchange. The money changers apparently charged over 12 percent interest and targeted, in particular, the poor and unwary for the swapping of Roman currency for shekels minted at Tyre. The temple hierarchy monitored these financial transactions and maintained a designated spot in the outer Court of the Gentiles as the only place that coin handlers could set up their booths.

A tribute penny issued under Tiberius appears in a second segment of the gospel of Matthew. As the Pharisees searched for some complaint to halt the interference of Jesus in established Jewish practice, they posed a trick question concerning the lawfulness of paying taxes to Rome. Calling them hypocrites, Jesus requested a coin — a silver *denarius*, the standard coin for paying taxes, picturing Tiberius and the blasphemous legend "*Pontifex Maxim(us)*" ("Chief Priest"). Jesus asked whose likeness appeared on it. When the Pharisees identified the Emperor Tiberius, Jesus replied, "Render therefore unto Caesar the things which are Caesar's; and unto God the things that are Gods" (Matthew 22:21). The logic of

Jesus's answer is both pragmatism and a wily avoidance of self-incrimination. Rather than refuse to pay taxes levied by the Roman governor, he separated a citizen's obligations to state and church.

Jesus's educative parable of the widow's mite from Mark 12:41–44 returns to the public show of donations at the Temple of Jerusalem. Written around A.D. 70, probably by John Mark, one of the first Christians living in Jerusalem, the gospel contained only sixteen chapters and may have been completed in Rome at the end of Peter's pulpit career. Used as source material by both Matthew and Luke, the book appears to draw on Peter's sermons.

The story, set during Paschal week, describes a heavy attendance by women making offerings in thanks for temple services. According to the Mishnah, a basic compilation of Jewish moral law, the temple sanctuary displayed thirteen chests in the shape of a *shofar* (ram's horn). Six of the thirteen received free-will donations. Jesus insisted on evaluating these gifts in terms of ability to pay. Thus, the unnamed widow, who donated her "mite" (actually two bronze *lepta*), paid all that she had, a grand gift in comparison with the self-important rich making a public show of dropping huge sums.

The two small bronze coins in question were small change minted in the time of Pontius Pilate, the Roman procurator of Judea in the decade after A.D. 26. Worth 1/12 of a cent, the *lepton* was the smallest denomination of the period and, in concession to Hebrew law, pictured a palm branch rather than the portrait of an emperor. Pilate's *lepton* bore the picture of a *simpulum* (wine ladle) used at Roman sacrifices; on the flip side were three grain heads. The gift of the two *lepta* recurs in a wide span of literature — the sermons of St. John Chrysostom and the writings of William Langland, St. Thomas More, John Dryden, Jonathan Swift, Byron, Jane Austen, Herman Melville, George Bernard Shaw, and James Joyce.

Luke, who was predisposed toward a humanitarian and egalitarian point of view toward women and the poor, wrote with a scholarly flair overlaid with warmth and understanding. He describes another parable that Jesus delivered to the scribes and Pharisees in terms they would appreciate. In characterizing the salvation of the lost, he asks,

> What woman having ten pieces of silver, if she lose one piece, doth not light a candle, and sweep the house, and seek diligently till she find it? And when she hath found it, she calleth her friends and her neighbors together, saying, Rejoice with me; for I have found the piece which I had lost [Luke 15:8–9].

The coin that Luke refers to may have been the same tribute *denarius* that Jesus had used to outwit the Pharisees questioning payment of taxes. The illustrative story demonstrates in Luke what the Italian epicist Dante Alighieri extolled as "il scriba della gentilezza di Cristo" (the scribe of the kindness of Christ) (Cahill 1999, p. xvi).

As the drama of the betrayal and arrest of Jesus played out, Judas Iscariot, the same disciple who had rebuked Mary of Bethany for wasting money on perfumed ointment, conspired with the chief priests and captains to hand over Jesus to the Sanhedrin, the Jewish high court headed by Caiaphas, the high priest. Judas's venality colors Matthew's account of a sordid exchange of bounty:

> Judas Iscariot went unto the chief priests, and said unto them, "What will ye give me, and I will deliver him unto you?" And they covenanted with him for thirty pieces of silver. And from that time he sought opportunity to betray him [Matthew 26:14–16].

For betraying Christ, Judas earned the notorious thirty pieces of silver, probably paid in Phoenician coins minted at Tyre depicting Melkarth, the Phoenician version of the Greek strongman Hercules. (Guy Clark, Ancient Coins and Antiquities, Norfolk, Virginia)

For his treachery, Judas earns the notorious 30 coins, probably paid in Phoenician *shekels* or *tetradrachms* minted at Tyre, which were valued at four *denarii* per shekel or approximately 120 days' wages. The coins bore the bust of Melkarth, the Phoenician version of the strongman Hercules.

In John's telling, at the Last Supper, Jesus shared the Pesach dish with Judas and sent him on his secret mission to Jewish authorities. The disciples assumed that, because Judas carried the group purse, he must be making some purchase on Jesus's behalf. The sell-out of Jesus became one of the most cited biblical episodes, which recurs in *The Voyage of St. Brendan* (ca. 1121) and in the works of Erasmus, Martin Luther, Cynewulf, Dante, William Langland, William Shakespeare, Ben Jonson, Geoffrey Chaucer, George Eliot, and Emily Brontë. In more recent times, the betrayal figured in Robert Penn Warren's *All the King's Men* (1946), Nikos Kazantzakis's *The Greek Passion* (1954) and *The Last Temptation of Christ* (1955), and in Norman Mailer's *The Executioner's Song* (1980).

The Judas penny, an amulet coin of spurious history, spread to all points of Christendom from the hands of pilgrims to the Holy Land. Fake copies bore the words "*Imago Caesaris*" ("Caesar's likeness"), which misidentified a bust of the sun god Apollo as the emperor whose coin Christ requested during his test by the Pharisees. Devout Christians singled out a Syracusan ten-*drachm* coin from 400 B.C. as the Judas penny and had it set into gold jewelry. Other pseudo-biblical coins include gold pieces from the magi's chests. These amulet pieces, revered as protectors of women during childbirth, were enshrined at Sens Cathedral, Notre Dame du Puy, Visitandines in Aix, St. Denis, Santa Croce and the Annunziata in Florence, Montserrat in Catalonia, and the Abbey of the Trinity and St. Sergius in Moscow.

See also **coins and currency in drama and film; Mammon; medieval coins; money-lending; shekel; talent; trade and barter.**

SOURCES: Abbott, Walter M., et al. *The Bible Reader*. New York: Bruce Publishing Co., 1969. • Alexander, David, and Pat Alexander, eds. *Eerdmans' Handbook to the World's Religions*. Grand Rapids, Mich.: William B. Eerdmans Publishing Co., 1982. • Anderson, Bernhard W. *Understanding the Old Testament*. Englewood Cliffs, N.J.: Prentice-Hall, Inc., 1966. • *The Apocrypha of the Old Testament*. New York: American Bible Society, n. d. • Cahill, Thomas, intro. *The Gospel According to Luke*. New York: Grove Press, 1999. • Clain-Stefanelli, Elvira, and Vladimir Clain-Stefanelli. *The Beauty and Lore of Coins, Currency, and Medals*. Croton-on-Hudson, N.Y.: Riverwood Publishers, 1974. • Davies, Glyn. *A History of Money from Ancient Times to the Present Day*. Cardiff: University of Wales Press, 1994. • Einzig, Paul. *Primitive Money*. Oxford: Pergamon Press, 1966. • Hastings, James, ed. *Encyclopedia of Religion and Ethics*. New York: Charles Scribner's Sons, 1951. • Jeffrey, David Lyle, gen. ed. *A Dictionary of Biblical Tradition in English Literature*. Grand Rapids, Mich.: William B. Eerdmans Publishing Co., 1992. • Kee, Howard Clark, Franklin W. Young, and Karlfried Froehlich. *Understanding the New Testament*. Englewood Cliffs, N.J.: Prentice-Hall, 1965. • Komroff, Manuel, ed. *The Apocrypha or Non-Canonical Books of the Bible*. New York: Tudor Publishing Co., 1937. • Lockyer, Herbert. *All the Women of the Bible*. Grand Rapids, Mich.: Zondervan Publishing, 1988. • Maxey, Al. "The Lord's Supper: A Historical Overview." http://www.zianet.com/maxey/Supper5.htm. • May, Herbert G., and Bruce M. Metzger, eds. *The Oxford Annotated Bible*. New York: Oxford University Press, 1962. • Meshorer, Ya'akov. *Coins of the Ancient World*. Jerusalem: Jerusalem Publishing House, 1974. • Metzger, Bruce M. *The Apocrypha of the Old Testament*. New York: Oxford University Press, 1965. • Molnar, Michael R. *The Star of Bethlehem: The Legacy of the Magi*. New Brunswick, N.J.: Rutgers University Press, 1999. • Pollak, Henry. *Coinage & Conflict*. Clifton, N.J.: Coin & Currency Institute, 2001. • Reinfeld, Fred. *Treasury of the World's Coins*. New York: Sterling Publishing, 1953. • Snodgrass, Mary Ellen. *Encyclopedia of World Scripture*. Jefferson, N.C.: McFarland, 2001. • Wigoder, Geoffrey. *The Encyclopedia of Judaism*. New York: Macmillan, 1989.

bimetallism

The use of coins of both gold and silver constitutes a bimetallic money system, such as that of Genoa, the medieval city that struck the *genovino d'oro*, the first gold coin of the era, in 1252. Croesus, the reformer of Lydian money after 570 B.C., halted the striking of coins from natural electrum and upgraded Lydian money to the world's first bimetallic system by inventing *staters* in silver and gold. In 1504, the Anjou kings of Naples produced bimetallic coinage, which had ceased in 1278. To dubious peasants, Neopolitan treasury officials eased introduction of the *salut d'oro* and *salut d'argento* with pious religious designs featuring the Virgin Mary.

In admiration of the Florentine *florin*, Plantagenet king Henry III, successor to King John, altered English coinage to bimetallism by initiating his own gold coin to augment silver pieces. The undoing of Henry's bimetallism was his reputation for ignoring tradition. His public relations campaign failed to stimulate confidence in the peasantry, which rejected gold in favor of silver, the metal they recognized and trusted. Following a European trend toward gold coinage, Edward III, who came to the throne two generations later, was the next to propose bimetallism for England with a gold series comprised of the leopard, helm, and *florin*, the latter named for the floral emblem on a Florentine coin. Again, the people rejected everything but silver.

See also **William Jennings Bryan; *daric*; *écu*; English money; *florin*; Alexander Hamilton; Thomas Jefferson; Lydian coins; paper money; U.S. coins; Wizard of Oz.**

SOURCES: Cannon, John, and Ralph Griffiths. *Oxford Illustrated History of the British Monarchy.* Oxford: Oxford University Press, 1988. • Clain-Stefanelli, Elvira, and Vladimir Clain-Stefanelli. *The Beauty and Lore of Coins, Currency, and Medals.* Croton-on-Hudson, N.Y.: Riverwood Publishers, 1974. • Cribb, Joe. *Money.* Toronto: Stoddart, 1990. • Davies, Glyn. *A History of Money from Ancient Times to the Present Day.* Cardiff: University of Wales Press, 1994.

Blackbeard

One of North America's most hunted criminals both before and after death, Blackbeard epitomized piracy. Long of limb and stout at brandishing weapons or swear words, he crossed his chest and shoulders with scarlet bandoliers holding three pairs of pistols. Using a natural growth of black hair, he cowed victims with his flowing beard, which he tied in grosgrain and plaited with hemp and saltpeter. He lit the ends like fuses, and twisted some plaits around his ears and stuck others out from his hat. By preying on the shipping lanes between Great Britain and North America, especially those to and from the Caribbean isles, he developed a two-year reign of terror into enduring legends of stolen booty, chests of treasure, and hidden wealth counted out in Spanish pieces of eight. His story ended in a hand-to-hand contest and the loss of his first ship, a three-master square-rigger, long a victim of the "Graveyard of the Atlantic," a sandy stretch two miles off Beaufort, North Carolina.

Born Edward Teach (also Tach, Thach, or Thatch) in 1680 in Bristol, England (or possibly Jamaica), Blackbeard appears to have been the son of gentry because of his ability to read and write. His brother joined the Jamaican military as an artillery officer. In early boyhood, Edward chose to go to sea.

Licensed as a privateer out of Jamaica, Blackbeard robbed ships from 1701 to 1713 during the War of the Spanish Succession, also called Queen Anne's War. At the end of hostilities, he continued his thievery as an outright pirate, targeting passengers and cargo of vessels departing Virginia and the Carolinas. He and his fleet of smaller pirate ships were especially adept at navigating perpetually shifting keyhole inlets to the Pamlico Sound area, the inland waters between North Carolina's shore and its chain of coastal islands called the Outer Banks, the roughest waters on the Eastern Seaboard.

Blackbeard's methods made the most of nature. When followed, he ducked into shallow areas that those unfamiliar with the shoals, sandbars, and backwaters could not afford to navigate without risking grounding or worse. In winter, he left "Teach's Hole" and ranged farther south to the Caribbean Sea. He captured the *Revenge* from Stede Bonnet, a British pirate and planter on Barbados, and forced Bonnet into service on the same vessel. When Bonnet accepted a royal amnesty, he searched the Carolinas for Blackbeard, who had stolen Bonnet's plunder.

In 1716, when Blackbeard served on the ship of Captain Benjamin Hornigold (or Thornigold), he made his initial mark on history. At New Providence, a Bahamian island between Andros and Eleuthera, the band sought Nassau, where the absence of royal law allowed the pirates relaxation at brothels, taverns, and grog shops. Following a brief vacation, the outlaws traveled northeast up the Atlantic seaboard to the Chesapeake Bay, the Atlantic coast's largest and busiest inlet, and began waylaying ships laden with cotton, flour, rum, silks, tools, wine, and gold bullion.

The next year off St. Vincent in the Windward Islands, with Hornigold's help, Blackbeard established his own captaincy aboard a stolen 26-gun slaver originally called the *Concorde de Nantes,* bound from Nantes, France, to Martinique. In gentlemanly fashion, Blackbeard gave the captain a small ship to carry his load of Senegalese slaves on to his destination. By outfitting the 103-foot *Concorde* with 40 cannon and staffing it with a crew of up to 150 mixed-race sailors, he created a floating arsenal he called the *Queen Anne's Revenge.* Although Captain Woodes Rogers, the Bahamian governor, offered amnesty to pirates who pled guilty and begged mercy of the British court, Blackbeard was just beginning a lucrative career in intimidation and murder on the Atlantic.

Blackbeard gained a reputation for merciless treatment of captives, whom he maimed with his cutlass. Given to gang rape, slicing out entrails, blinding, and hacking off ears and fingers, he was notorious for hideous cruelties that also victimized crew members who displeased him. In 1718, he departed winter quarters at Charles Town, South Carolina, and anchored his flagship and three sloops in the harbor, where his men elected officers and established percentages of the take due each pirate. To increase their income, Blackbeard harried and ransacked any vessel leaving or approaching the harbor. He made a deal with local people to trade kidnap victims, many of whom were prominent citizens, for medicines to rid his 400 men of fever. If the mainlanders refused, they would receive dismembered bodies and the burning hulls of the captured ships. When townspeople agreed to his demands, he kept his bargain, swapping for curatives his collection of prisoners, whom he had stripped of money, gold jewelry, and most of their clothing.

Blackbeard lost the *Queen Anne's Revenge* a week later on a sandbar off Topsail Island, North Carolina, 1.5 miles south of Fort Macon. According to one theory, he deliberately grounded the ship opposite Beaufort and marooned its sailors to rid himself of excess baggage. On the *Adventure,* equipped with ten guns, he sailed up the Pamlico River to the colonial capital of Bath, where he wed Mary Ormond. He successfully negotiated for a pardon from Governor Charles Eden, an emissary of George I under the Lords Proprietors. In exchange for a share of the swag, Blackbeard renewed his privateer's license, which he used as a shield against arrest. Unimpeded by law, he captured and plundered at will from ships and coastal rice and tobacco plantations and passed along a portion of money and goods to Eden through Tobias Knight, the governor's assistant and customs agent.

To end Blackbeard's marine banditry, Atlantic traders appealed to Governor Alexander Spotswood of Virginia, who posted a £100 bounty for the pirate or his crew, primarily to prevent their attacking Norfolk. Two shallow-draft ships — the *Jane* and the *Roger*— patrolled the coastal shores for Blackbeard. Commanded by Lieutenant Robert Maynard, a naval party of around 60, armed with swords and knives, trailed the pirate band of 20 to Ocracoke Island and awaited dawn at a spot now called Teach Hole Channel. Temporarily hampered when the attack boats ran aground, on November 22, 1718, Maynard's officers pushed off with oars toward the *Adventure.* Direct hits by pirate cannon wracked the naval vessels. Maynard and his survivors hid below deck, then assailed Blackbeard at close range with swords when he boarded one of the boats.

At Blackbeard's death, piracy in the West Indies received a sobering blow. His body sustained five shots and twenty slashes before a sailor lopped off his head, which Maynard swung from a bowsprit to establish a claim for the reward. Of the fifteen captured pirates, thirteen were hanged at Williamsburg, Virginia, and their bodies left to rot in chains as a warning to other would-be sea predators. To a public inquiry, Governor Eden, a collaborator in Blackbeard's return to plunder, brazened out his deal with the pirate chief, who had captured and robbed, in all, some 40 ships.

The gist of the pirate's career reached popularity with the public through Captain Charles Johnson's two-volume *A General History of the Robberies and Murders of the Most Notorious Pyrates* (1724, 1728), a sourcebook for Robert Louis Stevenson's *Treasure Island* (1883). Also surviving Blackbeard were hosts of collected pirate tales about his decapitated remains, the play *Blackbeard or The Captive Princess* (1798), and local legends about caches of gold coins and jewelry near Blackbeard Creek on Blackbeard Island, one of Georgia's Sea Isles, as well as on Beaufort Inlet and Old Topsail Inlet in North Carolina. Other likely locales for searches include Hammock House at Beaufort and Old Brick House at Elizabeth City, North Carolina, and farther south on Goose Creek up the Pamlico River at Bath. Casting doubt on the existence of buried treasure is historian Lindley Butler, author of *Pirates, Privateers and Rebel Raiders of the Carolian Coast* (2001).

On November 21, 1996, Mike Daniel and his undersea expeditioners from Boca Raton, Florida, recovered a sunken hull off Beaufort that may be the remains of the flagship *Queen Anne's Revenge*, which people believe went down in 1718 in 20 feet of water with chests of coins in the hold. Using submerged detection devices, archeologists located gold flakes, lead shot, broken glass wine bottles, ballast stones, brass dividers, pewter plates, musket parts, three anchors, 21 cannon, and a ship's bell from the *I.H.S. Maria*, dated 1709. Although experts on pirate and maritime history declared that Blackbeard and his officers had stashed most of the haul or distributed it among 400 crewmen, salvage operations and treasure hunting extended into 2002. Public curiosity gravitated to the ship's remains, now on display at the North Carolina Maritime Museum at Beaufort.

See also **piracy; sixpence.**

SOURCES: *Biography Resource Center*. Farmington Hills, Mich.: Gale, 2001. • Bond, Constance. "A Fury from Hell or Was He?" *Smithsonian*, February 2000, p. 62. • Bordsen, John. "Prowling with Pirates." *Charlotte Observer*, August 12, 2001, 1G, 8G. • Broad, William. "Archaeologists Revise Portrait of Buccaneers as Monsters." *New York Times*, March 11, 1997, C1, 9. • Butler, Lindley S. "Blackbeard's Revenge." *American History*, August 2000, p. 18. • "Clues Pointing Toward Ship as Blackbeard's Researchers '95 Percent Certain.'" *Washington Daily News*, October 30, 1997. • Cordingly, David. *Under the Black Flag*. San Diego, Calif.: Harvest Books, 1995. • *Encyclopedia of World Biography*. Detroit: Gale Group, 1998. • Kemp, Peter, ed. *The Oxford Companion to Ships and the Sea*. Oxford: Oxford University Press, 1988. • Lee, Robert E. *Blackbeard the Pirate*. Winston-Salem, N.C.: John F. Blair, 1974. • Nash, Jay Robert. *Encyclopedia of World Crime*. 6 vols. Wilmette, Ill.: CrimeBooks Inc., 1990. • Roberts, Nancy. *Blackbeard and Other Pirates of the Atlantic Coast*. New York: John F. Blair, Publisher, 1993. • Sandz, Victoria. *Encyclopedia of Western Atlantic Shipwrecks and Sunken Treasure*. Jefferson, N.C.: McFarland, 2001.

blood money

A step up from the code of vengeance calling for a compensatory "eye for an eye," historically, blood money substituted a sum of money or goods with which the murderer appeased the victim's family or clan. The value to civilization was a halt to the spiraling feuding, vendettas, and violence that payback traditionally set in motion. The Code of Hammurabi, a body of Babylonian laws set down in cuneiform script around 1750 B.C., stated in explicit amounts the penalties and fines in minas and shekels and/or goods owed for specific cases of wrongful death, e. g., murdering or accidentally killing a woman or slave, murdering a freeman, and causing the death of the unborn.

After the 700s B.C., independent Greek city-states refined their traditional justice system governing blood money. To avoid extended rounds of violence, presiding justices, who were heavily biased in favor of the rich and powerful, decided appropriate compensation. The Romans evolved a similar penal system built on the Greek model and developed a compulsory cash requital in place of retaliation and vengeance. The coins that changed hands even-handedly compensated the injured party for loss and damages.

The Anglo-Saxons collected from clan members a fair share of ring money comprising the *wergild* (also *weregild* or *wergeld*) (value in gold) owed to a victim's relatives or clan. Based on a system of reciprocity, the standard of contribution determined the amount of "man price" based on the nearness of kin and awarded the sum to the victim's family and/or clan on a similar proportional basis. Under the meticulous laws of King Ethelbert of Kent, after A.D. 560, payment of blood money also settled numerous varieties of adultery, assault, manslaughter, and theft. According to the wording of the original royal doom, "If a freeman lie with a freeman's wife, let him pay for it with his *wergeld*, and provide another wife with his own money, and bring her to the other" ["Anglo-Saxon Dooms"].

Under Alfred the Great after A.D. 871, the law allowed an injured husband to fight his wife's seducer without incurring *wergild* if the husband witnessed the adultery. Among the Franks, the *Lex Salica* ("Salic Law"), codified under Clovis around A.D. 496, specified which relatives received compensation. In the case of a father's murder, the sons shared half of the money, with the other relatives dividing the remaining half. In cases of a victim who had no relatives, that portion owed to them reverted to the *fisc* [state treasury]. When Charlemagne came to power in A.D. 771, his legislation to the Franks preserved the barbaric law codes of the past, including ordeals, trial by combat, punishment by mutilation, and the *wergild*.

Types of compensation varied worldwide. Usually, plaintiffs prized valuable or rare goods or commodities, such as cowries in the Congo and sacred *diwara* or *tambu* shells in New Britain, New Guinea, where payment in 20 to 50 strings or coils of shells requited unlawful death. Fijians chose whale teeth; Samoans offered mats. On the Solomon Islands, requital required the payment of shell money, with red carrying the highest value. On the Reef and Santa Cruz islands, blood guilt required payment in the red plumage of the *Trichoglossus massena* parrot or the honey-eating *Mzeomela cardinalis*. In 1871, a Reef Island killer used four coils worked in scarlet feathers to compensate for the murder of Bishop Patterson. On the Pacific coast of North America, the Haida settled blood claims with shell money much as the Karok used shells to soothe the outraged third party in a love triangle. Among the Umatilla and Kwakiutl, a system of blood money payment comparable to the Anglo-Saxon *wergild* contributed to the return of peace.

Among the Irish, Kenyans, Scots, Somali, Swedes, and Welsh, livestock served as blood money. The Welsh system stated in number of cows the worth of the murder victim: 1,000 for royalty; 126 for an ordinary tribe member. Because of the limited amount of money in circulation, Scots requited murder with 126 cattle, rather than to round up the 9,072 pennies that equaled the victim's worth. The medieval Swedes offered more leeway — in the case of a slaughtered slave, a master might accept either a cash fine of six marks in pennies or else two yoke of oxen or the equivalent in woolens. In Sudan, the Somali dealt strictly in camels, demanding 100 mares to repay the murder of a man and 50 for killing a woman. Damages for blinding, disabling, even bruising ranged in cost from 50 to 30 and down to three camels.

***See also* cloth and fiber money; leather money; ring and bullet money; shekels; Roman coins — Monarchy and republic; shell money.**

SOURCES: Allen, Larry. *Encyclopedia of Money*. New York: Checkmark Books, 2001. • Davies, Glyn. *A History of Money from Ancient Times to the Present Day*. Cardiff: University of Wales Press, 1994. • Einzig, Paul. *Primitive Money*. Oxford: Pergamon Press, 1966. • *Encyclopedia of the Ancient Greek World*. New York: Facts On File, Inc., 1995. • Henderson, Ernest F. *Select Historical Documents of the Middle Ages*. London: George Bell and Sons, 1896. • "Medieval Source Book: The Anglo-Saxon Dooms, 560–975." http://www.fordham.edu/halsall/source/560-975dooms.html. • Pritzker, Barry M. *A Native American Encyclopedia: History, Culture, and Peoples*. Oxford: Oxford University Press, 2000. • Sinclair, David. *The Pound*. London: Century Books, 2000.

Bonny, Anne

A noted pirate and expert fencer, Anne Bonny (also Bonney), alias "Bonn," gained an intriguing reputation for committing a male-dominated crime. Aboard the ship of John "Calico Jack" Rackham (or Rackam), a small-time privateer, Bonny and comrade Mary Read engaged in theft while dressed in the guise of male freebooters. Armed with cutlass and pistols, the two women established a place for female thieves on the high seas.

The bastard daughter of Irish attorney William Cormac and his maid Peg Brennan, Bonny was born on March 8, 1697, in Cork, Ireland. Brennan lost her job after Cormac's wife accused her of pilfering spoons. Cormac attempted to cover the shame of Anne's birth by rearing her as a relative apprenticed to his office. When disclosure humiliated him, he and Brennan took the child and emigrated to Charles Town, South Carolina. He flourished in trade and through ownership of a plantation.

Legend assigns to Anne Bonny stories of shooting a servant to death, burning a plantation, and walloping a would-be rapist. At age 16, she defied her father and married an itinerant sailor, James Bonny, from Bristol, England, whom she had met through Captain Raynor in Charles Town. After Cormac disowned her, she settled at New Providence, a Bahamian haven for pirates. Because the life of a marine criminal appealed to Bonny, her husband's work on the waterfront as a paid informer for Governor Woodes Rogers distressed her.

When Rogers offered an amnesty from King George I to pirates as a means of curtailing the plundering of English merchant vessels, Bonny met the colorful Rackham, who came to port to request a pardon. She took a chance on upgrading her lackluster life with adventure and profit as Rackham's mistress. He offered her husband money in lieu of a legal divorce. James Bonny reported his wife's desertion to Rogers, who threatened her with public whipping if she did not return to lawful wedlock.

Bonny joined Rackham in commandeering the *Queen Royal* in New Providence harbor, enlisting a willing crew and setting out to prey on prize merchant ships. They robbed their victims of personal cash, jewelry, strongboxes, and usable or saleable goods. In 1718, she accepted the general amnesty and returned to Cuba to give birth to their child. Her infant daughter died, leaving her alone and unfulfilled. In July 1719, she returned to Rackham and sea roving.

Bonny became the lover of Mary Read, a fellow cross-dressing pirate whose past mirrored her own. After the crew seized the English ship *William*, Rogers declared Rackham, Read, and Bonny outlaws. The crew kept the *William* and used it to victimize more merchant vessels and fishing trawlers. In Jamaica's Negril Bay, Captain Jonathon Barnet and his British law enforcers destroyed the rigging of the pirate ship and boarded it in October 1720. Bonny and Read set a better example of valor under fire than their rum-sogged male shipmates, who crept below deck out of sight.

Before Governor Nicholas Lawes at the Grand Court at St. Jaco de la Vega (now Spanish Town), Jamaica, in 1720, Bonny ran afoul of islanders who were sorely tired of pirates and rampant thievery. To avoid the gibbet and public display of her remains, the fate of Rackham and the captured crewmen hanged on Deadman's Cay on November 28, she and Read pled pregnancy. After Read died in prison on December 4, Bonny gave birth in jail and was released, ostensibly through the intervention of Governor Rogers. She may have settled on a South Carolina plantation. Her legend figured in Captain Charles Johnson's two-volume *A General History of the Robberies and Murders of the Most Notorious Pyrates*

(1724, 1728), a sourcebook for Robert Louis Stevenson's adventure novel *Treasure Island* (1883).

See also **Mary Read.**

SOURCES: Bordsen, John. "Prowling with Pirates." *Charlotte Observer*, August 12, 2001, 1G, 8G. • Cordingly, David. *Under the Black Flag*. San Diego, Calif.: Harvest Books, 1995. • *Gay & Lesbian Biography*. Detroit: St. James Press, 1997. • Nash, Jay Robert. *Encyclopedia of World Crime*. 6 vols. Wilmette, Ill.: CrimeBooks Inc., 1990. • Rediker, Marcus. *Between the Devil and the Deep Blue Sea*. Cambridge: Cambridge University Press, 1987. • Rediker, Marcus. "When Women Pirates Sailed the Seas." *Wilson Quarterly*, Autumn 1993, 102–111.

Boulton, Matthew

A pioneer of steam-powered coin stamping, jeweler and engineer Matthew Boulton became one of the heroes of the early Industrial Revolution. The financier of James Watt's steam projects, Boulton put his wealth to good use as co-founder of the Lunar Society of Birmingham and builder of Birmingham's theater in 1807. At his death on August 17, 1809, only seven months after his newly minted copper coins vanished into the sea with the foundering of the *Admiral Gardner* off Deal, Kent, Boulton was involved in the rebuilding of the Tower Mint and had earned the respect of manufacturers and Europe's mintmasters.

Born on September 3, 1728, in Birmingham, Boulton followed his father's trade in buckle- and button-making and the stamping of Sheffield flatware from sheet metal. Upon inheriting the family firm, in 1761, he ventured into additional plants in Soho and Smethwick, near Birmingham, for making ormolu, watch chains, filigree, gold inlays, and silver plate. After increasing his understanding of technology, he invented the steel inlay process. In 1766, he settled at Soho House in Handsworth, where he amassed fossils for study and welcomed to the Lunar Society scientists, engineers and thinkers the caliber of Erasmus Darwin, Samuel Galton, Joseph Priestley, Jonathan Stokes, James Watt, and Josiah Wedgwood.

In 1767, Boulton teamed with Watt, a Scottish inventor, to develop steam-powered factory machinery using the Newcomen engine. Boulton's expertise in coinage got him an appointment as treasury agent in Birmingham to collect worn-out specie. He was so appalled at the state of coinage that he devoted his career to improving it. After acquiring the patents vacated by John Roebuck, Boulton joined Watt in 1775 as a builder of steam engines for sale to northwestern European entrepreneurs. The engine enabled him to work toward a reverse of Gresham's law by producing ample high-grade coins to drive counterfeiters out of business.

Aided by French inventor and engraver Jean Pierre Droz (or Drost) and German portrait artist Konrad Heinrich Kuchler, at a private mint at Soho, Birmingham, Boulton refined his understanding of coinage at a time when London's Royal Mint struggled to keep pace with the burgeoning economy. With a steam-driven machine, he could automatically feed in planchets and stamp up to 150 small coins per minute. In 1787, under contract to director Robert Wissett of the United East India Company, Boulton minted coins for the colony of Bencoolen, Sumatra, and received an order for tokens from Monnerons, a French banking firm. By 1791, he had worked out difficulties with the coin ejection system and begun striking pennies for Sierra Leone.

The next year, Boulton summarized the resources of his mint, which employed eight large machines to strike either coins or medals. He described the technology in simple terms:

> Each machine is capable of being adjusted in a few minutes so as to strike any number of pieces of money from 50 to 120 per minute.... Each piece being struck in a steel collar, the whole number are perfectly round and of equal diameter. Each machine requires the attendance of one boy of only 12 years of age, and he has no labour to perform. He can stop his press in one instant, and set it going again the next [Grierson 1975, p. 119].

Boulton added that his machine was capable of striking various sizes of coins, from large English crowns to French *sous*. He exulted that his device operated with less friction, wear, and noise and fewer breakdowns than less automated devices. His intention was to distribute his coppers through the canals, a concern in which he held stock.

By 1794, Boulton had added thick, wide rims, incuse or inset legends, lettered or engrained edging to halt counterfeiting, and low relief, which made the dies longer lasting. In 1797, he earned a government commission as private contractor authorized to replace with his steam-powered press 50 tons of copper pence and twopence laboriously hand-struck on hand-cut blanks. For the task, he applied the engravings of master sculptors Alexandre Ponthon, Rambert Dumarest, and Konrad Heinrich Kuchler. Boulton fumed at evidence that his copper cartwheels had been counterfeited in Birmingham by Thomas Barber. After the man's arrest and the confiscation of his tools and dies, he came to trial in Warwick and was acquitted.

Boulton's steam-driven coiner outpaced the tedious minting by *balancier* or screw press, which had dominated coinage for two centuries. His largest coins, copper cartwheels, became army pay in Chatham, Deptford, Greenwich, Portsmouth, Skegness, Southampton, and Woolwich. The first English specie in three decades to bear a royal portrait, they ushered in modern English coinage. Over the next nine years, the initial contract extended to 4,200 tons of copper. The boost to the English monetary system disrupted counterfeiters and affirmed national faith in English coins by establishing a more consistent copper coinage for Great Britain and its colonial Indian mints at Bombay, Calcutta, and Madras.

At the rate of up to 920 strikes per minute, as compared to 30 per minute by the screw press, Boulton made token money for English, Scottish, and Irish towns and two- and five-*sou* tokens for the East India Company, contracted by John Motteux for the Monnerons, a French merchant family, and designed by Augustin Dupré. Boulton also minted coins for banks in England, France, Scotland, and Wales and aided the Bank of England in May 1804 by overstriking Spanish dollars with official designs and five shillings markings. The project kept Boulton occupied until 1815.

In 1816, Boulton complained to the Lords of the Privy Council about the ubiquity of counterfeit coinage. He charged that illegal moneys cost the public, even from pieces as small as the halfpence. The involvement of industrialists shocked him:

> It is now too common among many of the lower class of manufacturers and traders to purchase these counterfeit halfpence at little more than half their nominal value and pay with this money their workmen and labourers [Powell 1993].

He noted that the scarcity of genuine coppers and the ease with which fake coins were produced "have hitherto rendered all means of suppressing this illegal and injurious act fruitless" (*ibid.*).

Boulton earned contracts in the Western Hemisphere from Bermuda, Newfoundland, St. Helena, and the United States and negotiated for more in South America. He also supplied mechanical presses to Denmark, India, Mexico, and Spain. In 1809, mint authorities grudgingly dubbed him Matthew Boulton, Esquire, a slighting reward for his contribution to coinage. The machine he designed for the Royal Mint moved from the old Tower Mint to Tower Hill in 1810 and stayed in production until 1882. For the Russian mint at St. Petersburg, he aligned a process to roll, cut, and press each metal strip to eject coins at the other end. The company of Boulton and Watt passed to Boulton's son, Matthew Robinson Boulton. Matthew Boulton College, Birmingham's first technical school, commemorated the visionary inventor and entrepreneur when it opened in November 1893.

***See also Admiral Gardner;* incuse; penny; Benedetto Pistrucci; U.S. coins.**

SOURCES: *Biography Resource Center*. Farmington Hills, Mich.: Gale Group, 2001. • Crystal, David, ed. *The Cambridge Biographical Dictionary*. Cambridge: University of Cambridge, 1996. • Davies, Glyn. *A History of Money from Ancient Times to the Present Day*. Cardiff: University of Wales Press, 1994. • da Vinci, Leonardo. *The Codex*

Leicester, Notebook of a Genius. Sydney, Aust.: Powerhouse Publishing, 2000. • Grierson, Philip. *Numismatics.* London: Oxford University Press, 1975. • Jacobs, Wayne L. "The Mystery of the Disappearing P.E.I. 'Dumps.'" *Canadian Numismatic Association Journal,* November 2001, 433–438. • Kemp, Peter, ed. *The Oxford Companion to Ships and the Sea.* Oxford: Oxford University Press, 1988. • "Matthew Boulton and the Development of Modern Coinage." http://www.geocities.com/mboulton1797/. • Powell, John. "The Birmingham Coiners, 1770–1816." *History Today,* July 1993, pp. 49–55. • Reinfeld, Fred. *Treasury of the World's Coins.* New York: Sterling Publishing, 1953. • Ritchie-Calder, Lord. "The Lunar Society of Birmingham." *Scientific American,* June 1982, 136–145. • Rocco, Fiammetta. "Keeping the Flame." *Institutional Investor,* December 1988, 31–32. • Schofield, Robert E. *The Lunar Society of Birmingham: A Social History of Provincial Science and Industry in Eighteenth-Century England.* Oxford: Clarendon Press, 1963. • Taxay, Don. *The U.S. Mint and Coinage.* New York: Arco Publishing, 1966. • *World of Invention,* 2nd ed. Farmington Hills, Mich.: Gale Group, 1999.

bracteate

As medieval coin style moved away from past models of the Greeks and Romans to thinner, lighter pieces, the bracteate, a uniface coin, came into being. Invented in Poland, it remained popular until 1350. The name derived from the Latin *bractea* (thin metal piece), which explains its application to paper-thin copper, silver, or gold coins stamped with incuse dies. The concept of single-surface *denarii* or *pfennigs* originated in Hesse and Thuringia and extended to Bohemia, Hungary, Poland, and Sweden. Called a *hohlpfennig* (hollow penny) or "thin *pfennig*" in German, it came into style in Denmark around A.D. 975; in the Holy Roman Empire in 1120; in Götland and Kalmar, Sweden, after 1150; and in Norway a decade later during the reign of Harold Hardrade. The name "bracteate" did not apply until the 1700s.

Preceding bracteate coins was the protective amulet bracteate. A famous example, the Vadstena Bracteate, struck in Östergötland, Sweden, in the fifth century A.D., was a gold ornamental medallion. It bore rich motifs and a 24-character runic alphabet, called a futhark, arrayed in three groups of eight symbols along with the indecipherable phrase "tuwa tuwa," which may have been an onomatopoetic incantation. Copies of the amulet were unearthed at Motala and Grumpan, Sweden.

Polish artisans began hammering airy, flexible bracteates during the A.D. 900s. Because the coins quickly lost their sharp imagery as the act of stamping compromised the metal's integrity, designs were simple. One beauty, the Tuvasgården bracteate, displayed a stylized hare rather than the typical birds of prey or mythic beasts. Most pictured standard diadem-and-scepter motifs or the crozier and mitre of a bishop. Because of the coin's fragility, consumers easily snipped it into small change. However, the coins did not survive rough wear or repeated circulation. Historians studying hoards of European coins discovered that 30 years was the longest span that a bracteate circulated.

The bracteate was virtually useless to merchants but valuable to kings, potentates, and prelates. After 1167, Knut Eriksson commissioned a uniface bracteate from the Sigtuna mint showing the head and shoulders of the ruler, who holds a spear. The brutal King Mieszko III the Elder of Cracow ordered new coins after 1173. At his mint, those Jews who had supported his power grab became the royal diemasters. They struck pure silver bracteates, which they inscribed in Hebrew only on the front surface or left without legends in a form known as mute bracteates. By the end of the 12th century, the German gothic bracteate coinage of Brunswick-Luneburg, Falkenstein, Gandersheim, Reichenau, and Saxony demonstrated the extremes of departure from the heavy, serious *staters, denarii,* and *sestertii* of the past.

Bracteates varied widely in esthetics and form and pictured saints and civil and ecclesiastical rulers, riders in Hesse and Thuringia, lions in Brunswick and Czech lands, falcons in Falkenburg, linden boughs in Bohemia, as well as fish, battlements, landmarks, and millwheels. One of the most pictorial bracteates was the silver *denarius* of Frederick II of Hohenstaufen, minted as propaganda at Ulm after he was crowned emperor of Germany in 1212 and picturing him face-forward alongside his wife, Queen Constance of Sicily. After 1250, the Hapsburgs of Laufenburg issued an ungainly bracteate. A silver *denar*, it featured a raised rim and rough edges shaped into a square. Stamped in a *repoussé* style, the coin began as a square of metal pressed from the back with a deeply incised reverse die. Because of the die's unusual face, it resembled the wax seal applied to wine bottles, government documents, and excise tax receipts.

***See also* Irish money; medieval coins; penny.**

SOURCES: Clain-Stefanelli, Elvira, and Vladimir Clain-Stefanelli. *The Beauty and Lore of Coins, Currency, and Medals.* Croton-on-Hudson, N.Y.: Riverwood Publishers, 1974. • Cribb, Joe. *Money.* Toronto: Stoddart, 1990. • Cribb, Joe, Barrie Cook, and Ian Carradice. *The Coin Atlas.* London: Little, Brown and Co., 1999. • Davies, Glyn. *A History of Money from Ancient Times to the Present Day.* Cardiff: University of Wales Press, 1994. • Grierson, Philip. *Numismatics.* London: Oxford University Press, 1975. • Hastings, James, ed. *Encyclopedia of Religion and Ethics.* New York: Charles Scribner's Sons, 1951. • Lewis, Brenda Ralph. *Coins & Currency.* New York: Random House, 1993. • Reinfeld, Fred. *Treasury of the World's Coins.* New York: Sterling Publishing, 1953.

Bramante, Donato

One of the great achievers of the Italian Renaissance, Donato (also Donino or Donnino) Bramante accomplished artistic works and architectural triumphs in Milan and Rome as well as the invention of the first coin press. Born in Monte Asdruvaldo, Urbino, in 1444, he obeyed his father by studying art and by assisting Piero della Francesca (or di' Franceschi), perhaps the most popular artist of his day. From murals to architectural perspective, Bramante advanced in mastery of the complex relationship between fresco and design. In 1488, he helped to plan and build the cathedral at Pavia, followed two years later by the design of a tower for the Milan Cathedral.

Reaching out to the disciplines of poetry, music, and theatrical staging as well as city planning, coinage, and military fortification, Bramante allowed humanism full play in his many interests. Under Pope Julius II in 1503, he began remodeling and designing additions to the Vatican complex and planned St. Peter's Basilica. In old age, Bramante served Pope Leo X by designing a city water system and plotting flood control for Rome. In 1508, Bramante created a screw press for coinage, an idea that Benvenuto Cellini developed a generation later. The innovation did not reach its full potential until 1550, when silversmith Marx Schwab of Augsburg, Germany, made a heavy-duty device for the printing industry. One of his first customers was Henri II of France.

***See also* Benvenuto Cellini; screw press.**

SOURCES: Cribb, Joe. *Money.* Toronto: Stoddart, 1990. • Davies, Glyn. *A History of Money from Ancient Times to the Present Day.* Cardiff: University of Wales Press, 1994. • *Encyclopedia of Art.* New York: McGraw-Hill Book Co., 1968. • Laing, Lloyd R. *Coins and Archaeology.* New York: Schocken Books, 1969.

Brasher, Ephraim

Metalsmith and assayer Ephraim Brasher, a specialist in gold and silver and member of New York's silversmiths society, struck the first gold U.S. coin. He had a solid reputation for skill and honesty and received commissions to make silver skewers for his neighbor, George Washington. During a severe shortage of coins to facilitate colonial commerce, Brasher assayed precious metals, authenticated foreign specie, and provided private mintage in copper, silver, and gold. Because of his renown, his mint mark, a bold EB set in an oval, carried authority and validity.

In 1787, six years before the opening of the U.S. Mint in Philadelphia, Brasher petitioned the New York State treasury to allow him to join fellow metalsmith John Bailey in minting copper coins. Brasher also subcontracted with Matthais Ogden of the Elizabethtown mint to produce New Jersey coppers. Most valuable of Brasher's coinage are gold doubloons featuring a sunrise and the legend "*Excelsior, Nova Eboraca, Columbia*" ("Loftier, New York, Columbia.") "Columbia" was a Latinized version of Christopher Columbus's surname that served as the Latin equivalent of "United States."

Brasher modeled his new coins after the Spanish eight-*escudo* piece minted in Lima, Peru. At Thomas Machin's mill in Newburgh, New York, Brasher struck similar coins in copper called excelsiors or Eboracs. They pictured the New York state seal and the American eagle grasping arrows and an olive branch in a star-decked pose that became the U.S. seal. He remained active in U.S. coinage in 1792 by assaying precious metals for the federal treasury.

In 1942, American detective novelist Raymond Chandler featured in a novel, *The High Window,* the most famous of Brasher's doubloons, the only piece on which his mintmark appears on the eagle's breast. The third of Chandler's famous Philip Marlowe mystery series, the novel contains an ominous search plot set in Pasadena, California. The story was the basis for two films, *Time to Kill* (1942) and a low-budget remake, *The Brasher Doubloon* (1947), starring George Montgomery as Detective Marlowe. Coinciding with the filming of the second movie, Chandler reissued the novel in its movie edition, *The Brasher Doubloon: A Philip Marlowe Mystery* (1946). The novel was the third segment of the four-part *Raymond Chandler Omnibus* (1964), a selection of his four top novels.

The famed Brasher doubloon, one of the goldsmith's seven extant coins, remained in the numismatic collection of the Sterling Memorial Library at Yale University until 1965, when hooded robbers snatched it. The gang's *modus operandi* duplicated that of Chandler's in *The High Window.* Two years later, a private eye located the coin in the hands of a Chicago numismatist and coin dealer, but never identified the thieves. Because the doubloon presented the university with security problems, in January 1981, university president A. Bartlett Giametti announced its sale for $650,000. The proceeds assisted in the financing of a new archive, the Seeley G. Mudd Library, which houses United Nations and U.S. government documents. Other of the Brasher doubloons remain at the Smithsonian Institution, American Numismatic Society, and private collections.

SOURCES: Clain-Stefanelli, Elvira, and Vladimir Clain-Stefanelli. *The Beauty and Lore of Coins, Currency, and Medals.* Croton-on-Hudson, N.Y.: Riverwood Publishers, 1974. • Kleeberg, John, ed. *The Money of Pre-Federal America.* New York: American Numismatic Society, 1992. • Reiter, Ed. "A Quick Sale for Yale's Brasher Doubloon." *New York Times,* January 18, 1981, p. D32. • *St. James Guide to Crime & Mystery Writers,* 4th ed. Detroit: St. James Press, 1996. • "Yale Sells Storied Coin." *American Libraries,* February 1981, p. 65.

Brenner, Victor D.

In 1906, the U.S. Congress commissioned the original Lincoln penny, the nation's most common coin, which was the design of Lithuanian-American medalist and sculptor Victor David Brenner, a great admirer of the sixteenth U.S. president. Replacing the familiar Indian head cent, the new coin honored Lincoln on his 100th birthday. The penny achieved two radical departures from national coin art: it was the first to feature a president and the first to display the motto "In God We Trust." Congress authorized the motto on March 3, 1865, only six weeks before Lincoln died from a gunshot wound inflicted the previous night at Ford Theatre in Washington by actor John Wilkes Booth. Brenner also contributed to American coins by designing the Roosevelt dime.

Born on June 12, 1871, near the Baltic Sea in the village of Shavli, Russia, Brenner was the son of Sarah Margolis and metalworker George Brenner and grandson of a blacksmith. Ambitious and idealistic, Brenner was homeschooled in Talmud, language, and history. After observing his father chiseling headstones, engraving jewelry, carving soapstone, and cutting out silhouettes, at age 13, Brenner learned the more refined arts of seal-making, line-engraving, and sculpted portraiture. In

1889, he traveled to Riga to study ring and brooch engraving. A year later, he emigrated to the United States.

In classes at the Cooper Union night school, Brenner perfected his command of classic pose and French styling. After training at the Art Students' League and National Academy of Design, at age 23, he established a business in die-cut jewelry and silver. His earnings paid his family's fare to the United States. Officials of the American Numismatic Society learned of his art from a professor at the City College, who was impressed by a badge picturing German composer Ludwig van Beethoven. The discovery was the beginning of Brenner's fame as a medalist.

At age 27, Brenner entered an apprenticeship with master medalists and bas-relief specialists Charpentier and Roty in Paris. Brenner also sought experience under the tutelage of Dubois, Puech, and Verlet at the Académie Julien. In 1900, Brenner won a bronze medal at the Paris Exposition and an honorable mention at the Paris Salon. Back at his New York workshop, he set up a practice in medal and badge making and die cutting to pay for another study tour in Paris. For the Fine Arts Federation of New York, in 1904, he sculpted the classical figure of Athena bearing Nike, goddess of victory, in her outstretched hand and clutching symbols of painting, sculpture, and architecture. By 1906, he considered himself an artist.

The opportunity to design the Lincoln coin, which Congress proposed in 1886, had gone unmet while the U.S. Mint turned out five-cent coins. As Brenner sculpted the Panama Canal Service medal to honor builders of the project, he incised President Theodore Roosevelt's portrait on the reverse. The president surveyed Brenner's studio and admired his Lincoln plaque. It emphasized the lanky president's cheek and jaw as displayed on Matthew B. Brady's photograph of the president taken at Brady's studio on February 9, 1864. Roosevelt recommended that Secretary of the Treasury Franklin MacVeagh award Brenner the commission for the nation's first presidential penny.

Brenner had to fight for the acceptance of Lincoln's likeness. The First Coinage Act of 1792 required "an impression emblematic of Liberty." Although coin art had traditionally relied on allegorical representations, Brenner argued that Lincoln himself, who guided the nation during the Civil War, was a human embodiment of liberty. Mint staff admired the pose, the only portrait coin that faces right, and the wheat heads, one of three that Brenner sculpted for the reverse. Between the two stalks, he added "*E Pluribus Unum*" ("One [nation] out of many [states]"), the national Latin motto, which he arced around the upper rim.

The coin, originally produced at the Philadelphia mint, earned approval on July 14, 1909, the Lincoln Centennial Year. When the public received the first coins on August 2, the design raised a furor. Admirers of Lincoln felt that he deserved to be displayed on a coin of higher monetary value. Those who championed his respect for commoners riposted that the penny was the perfect choice because it figured in daily change making. A contingent of Southerners, still smarting over the outcome of the Civil War and Lincoln's decision to free the slaves, challenged the coin on the grounds that the Lincoln portrait resembled the proud monarchs on European currency. Those championing native Americans resented the removal of the Indian Head Penny from mint production.

More objectionable was the addition of Brenner's signature, which appeared on the master plaque. Because long-time mint employees resented the Russian immigrant's egotism in applying his name to the finished model, they reduced the monogram to his initials, then censored the VDB after the minting of the first 22 million coins, claiming that the letters stood out too prominently. President William Howard Taft took the side of those requesting that the medalist be anonymous, but the change could not halt full-time production of so popular a coin.

After 1909, pennies minted in Denver, San Francisco, and Philadelphia appeared with the initial B or with no acknowledgement of the medalist. That same year, Brenner wrote the president of the American Numismatic Association (ANA) an explanation: "The name of the artist on a coin is essential for the student of history as it enables him to trace environments and conditions of the time said coin was produced" (Van Ryzin 1995, p. 171). Good-naturedly Brenner added that the undercurrent of complaints had boosted the study of numismatic art. The ANA passed a resolution calling for historic accuracy to convey to future generations of the identity of the coiner.

The contretemps over Brenner's initials led to a run on the first 25 million coins available at banks and subtreasuries in Boston, Chicago, New York, Philadelphia, and St. Louis. As the price rose to as much as a dollar for each initialed penny, *Collier's* magazine featured a photo of Wall Street newsboys doing their own investing in pennies with a markup of 24 cents. In 1918, mint officials returned a discreet reinscription of the initials VDB to the penny's front view under Lincoln's shoulder.

Brenner completed several busts and, in 1911, the Mary Schenley Memorial Fountain, "Song to Nature," which stands outside the Frick Fine Arts building in Pittsburgh in recognition of her donation of land for the park. His success brought commissions from the American Numismatic Society, Art Institute of Chicago, and National Academy of Design, resulting in hundreds of bronze or silver plaques and medals, some single-sided and others double. In 1920, the American Numismatic Society displayed 69 of Brenner's original commemoratives and club and society plaques at an international exhibition, gaining for the artist a reputation for first-rate verisimilitude, especially the nude on the Sorolla medal, a University of Wisconsin plaque, and a draped likeness on the Fine Arts Federation plaque.

Following mutually satisfying associations with the Architectural League of New York, American Numismatic Society, and National Sculpture Society and exhibits at Boston's Museum of Fine Arts, the Paris Mint, Luxembourg Museum, New York's Metropolitan Museum, Munich Glyptothek, and Vienna Numismatic Society, he retired after suffering a debilitating illness and died in New York City on April 5, 1924. In October 1999, the Fleischer Museum in Scottsdale, Arizona, in conjunction with the National Sculpture Society, included Brenner's Lincoln portrait among the 110 displayed at an end-of-the-millennium exhibit entitled "Masterworks of American Sculpture: Selections from the Members of the National Sculpture Society, 1875–1999." In April 2001, President Bill Clinton signed the Abraham Lincoln Bicentennial Commission Act, establishing a 15-member panel to determine how to celebrate the bicentennial of Abraham Lincoln's birth in 2009. Clinton charged the commission with planning a Lincoln bicentennial penny as a tribute to honor America's favorite president.

***See also* Lincoln head penny; U.S. coins.**

SOURCES: "Americans for Common Cents." http://www.pennies.org/. • Clain-Stefanelli, Elvira, and Vladimir Clain-Stefanelli. *The Beauty and Lore of Coins, Currency, and Medals*. Croton-on-Hudson, N.Y.: Riverwood Publishers, 1974. • Greene, Bob. "Heads You Lose, Tails You Lose." *Esquire*, April 1981. • "Hey Wiseguy — A Head Puzzler." *Peoria Journal Star*, December 4, 2000. • "Lincoln Bicentennial Commission Asked to Consider Minting New Penny." *PR Newswire*, April 7, 2000. • *The Memorial Book for the Jewish Community of Yurburg, Lithuania*. Tel Aviv, Israel: Organization of Former Residents of Yurburg, 1991. • *Merriam-Webster's Biographical Dictionary*. Springfield, Mass.: Merriam-Webster, 1995. • Reed, Mort. *Cowles Complete Encyclopedia of U.S. Coins*. New York: Cowles Book Company, 1969. • Reiter, Ed. "Circulated Coins." *New York Times*, November 4, 1984. • Reiter, Ed. "New Coin May Place Washington on Horseback." *New York Times*, February 21, 1982. • Taxay, Don. *The U.S. Mint and Coinage*. New York: Arco Publishing, 1966. • Van Ryzin, Robert R. *Twisted Tails: Sifted Fact, Fantasy and Fiction from U.S. Coin History*. Iola, Wisc.: Krause Publications, 1995.

Brinks robberies

In its daily transportation of the nation's cash, the U.S. security firm of Brinks, Incorporated, has faced clever thieves since its founding in 1859. The firm was founded by Washington P. Brink of Vermont and headquartered in Chicago to transport in-town shipments of goods and baggage, including the possessions of Abraham Lincoln. In 1891, Brinks received its first payroll contract from Western Electric. Staffed at 160 locations by former police and soldiers, it developed into an international contract carrier and armored car service to haul money and valuables as well as federal currency; it also offered automatic teller machine services, door-to-door air courier delivery, and automated coin sorting and wrapping in the United States and 50 foreign countries. After two operatives died in a 1917 holdup, the company began designing its own vehicles.

A complicated theft of over $2.75 million in cash in Boston on January 17, 1950, derived from the plotting of Anthony Pino and Joseph F. McGinnis. With a gang of petty crooks — Henry J. Baker, John S. Banfield, Vincent J. Costa, James Ignatius Flaherty, Michael V. Geagan, Stanley H. Gusciora, Adolph Maffie, James O'Keefe, and Thomas F. Richardson — the planners moved in on Brink's headquarters, where lax security at a side door allowed secret entry to the bundling of millions in cash. After an 18-month study of operations and practice runs, the gang forged door keys and struck when the company amassed a large amount of cash. The lead group overpowered and tied and taped the head cashier and his staff, then began shoveling money into bags. Out of $2,775,395 stolen, $1,218,211.29 was in bills and coins weighing 1,200 pounds. In their haste, the thieves overlooked a security box containing one million dollars in cash.

At their hideout in Roxbury, McGinnis and Pino supervised the destruction of securities and any bills that might be marked. Each member received a share, totaling $100,000. The FBI was stymied in their search for clues until early April, when O'Keefe, sentenced to prison for another heist, alerted the police. He offered to expose the theft in exchange for his freedom. The gang received lengthy prison terms. To their chagrin, Joseph F. Dineen, a journalist for the Boston *Globe*, earned $150,000 for a contract with Paramount for his novel *Six Rivers to Cross* (1955), which he based on the robbery. The 1955 film version starred Tony Curtis, George Nader, Jay C. Flippen, and Sal Mineo.

The noon robbery of a Brink's armored truck in Montreal on March 30, 1976, produced the largest haul in the company's history — $2.8 million. In an alley alongside the Royal Bank of Canada, the thieves wielded an anti-aircraft machine gun to wrest the vehicle from Gilles Lachapelle. The gang drove their white van and the Brink's truck to Nun's Island. Two months later, Canadian authorities apprehended six gang members.

In 1981, Kuwasi Balagoon, Kathy Boudin, Samuel Brown, Judith A. Clark, and David J. Gilbert robbed a Brink's armored truck at a mall in Nanuet, New York. The police chase and shooting of two officers ended in capture and a 75-years-to-life sentence. Four others were convicted of conspiracy, robbery, and other crimes.

***See also* euro.**

SOURCES: "The Brinks Robbery." http://www.fbi.gov/fbinbrief/historic/famcases/brinks/brinks.htm. • Considine, Bob. *The Men Who Robbed Brinks*. New York: Random House, 1961. • Nash, Jay Robert. *Encyclopedia of World Crime*. 6 vols. Wilmette, Ill.: CrimeBooks Inc., 1990.

Briot, Nicholas

A talented French portraitist, engraver, diemaker, and machinist, Nicholas (or Nicolas) Briot, the mechanizer of die-stamped coins, introduced modern minting in France and England. He was born in Bassiguy, France, in 1579 and mastered German press mechanics with the *balancier* (screw press). He became chief engraver of the French mint at Lyon at age thirty. He is best known for supplying a royal portrait profile of Louis XIII Le Juste to coins and adding the distinctive triple *fleur-de-lis* to the reverse side.

In 1615, Briot published *Raisons, Moyens, et Propositions pour Faire Toutes Les Monnaies du Royaume, à l'Avenir, Uniformes, et Faire Cesser Toutes Fabrications, &* (*Reasons, Meth-*

ods, and Proposals for Making All Royal Coins Uniform and for Ceasing Hand Striking, Etc.). A year later, he began testing the simplified one-stroke coining method on the franc and demi-franc, which bore the saucy inscription "*Espreuve Faicto Par L'Exprès Commandement du Roy Louis XIII*" ("Proof Rendered by the Express Command of King Louis XIII"). Briot's mechanized process, an advanced mint technology that he developed with the aid of Jean Varin, threatened to replace the medieval hand-hammered minting that produced non-standardized likenesses and uneven coins at a slower rate. His proposal to turn coinage into a factory operation met with stiff opposition from chief moneyers, who rejected technology in favor of hand-made coins. Mint staff also protested because the change from hand-striking would have cost Parisian coiners their jobs.

Although Briot countered that hammering was obviously less precise, the old guard held firm against any newly invented method of striking coins. Persecuted by creditors and hounded by death threats, Briot left France. In 1625, he accepted a post offered by Charles I of England. Under the direction of Thomas Rawlins, England's chief royal engraver, Briot introduced screw presses and, once more, faced artisans' hostility to milled coins.

At London's Tower Mint, Briot was able to perfect his coin milling machine and to apply its rapid stamping on commemorative medals. By 1628, he had advanced to chief engraver. On December 16, the king extended "the privilege to be a free denizen, and also full power and authority to frame and engrave the first designs and effigies of the king's image in such size and forms as are to serve in all sorts of coins of gold and silver" (Stephen and Lee 1922, 1259). Still competing with traditional hand-striking methods, in 1631, Briot operated the milling machines that turned out silver coins in both London and Edinburgh. Simultaneously, he produced medals, dies, and molds, including the "Dominion of the Sea" medal and two coronation medals, each signed with his surname or N.B.

Briot signed his most famous coins, the British crown and half-crown, with a B, sometimes accompanied by an anchor or flower. Outstanding in his work was a handsome sixpence featuring the likeness of Charles I, which is preserved in the Tregwynt hoard discovered in Pembrokeshire, England, in 1996. When Charles I was crowned in Edinburgh, it was Briot's masterful medals and coins that he threw to the crowd that lined the way.

Briot remained in London until 1633, when he was named chief engraver, and served as mintmaster in Scotland from 1635 until 1639. During the English civil war, he supervised coin milling at Oxford and York. He died at Oxford in 1646. Upon the restoration of the monarchy in 1660, Briot's widow, Esther Briot, received back pay issued to the former staff of Charles I.

***See also* coinage; English coins; screw press; Thomas Simon.**

SOURCES: Allen, Larry. *Encyclopedia of Money*. New York: Checkmark Books, 2001. • "Aspects de la naissance d'une monnaie nouvelle à la Renaissance." http://www.i-numis.com/europe/articles/moderne/moderne2-fr.html. • "CGB.Fr Numismatiques." http://www.ordonnances.org/regnes/louis13/1622_1632.html. • "Coins of the Louis Kings." http://www.cgb.fr/monnaies/articles/mon naiesfrance/roislouisgb.html. • Davies, Glyn. *A History of Money from Ancient Times to the Present Day*. Cardiff: University of Wales Press, 1994. • *Encyclopedia of Art*. New York: McGraw-Hill Book Co., 1968. • "Louis XIII le Juste." http://www.cgb.fr/monnaies/vso/v12/fr/monnaies8287.html. • *Merriam-Webster's Biographical Dictionary*. Springfield, Mass.: Merriam-Webster, 1995. • "Monnaies Royales Françaises." http://www.epromat.com/poindessault/ve26/p2605.htm. • Sardin, Frédérique. "Les légendes en creux fautées sur les tranches des monnaies françaises en or et en argent du XIXe siècle." http://www. amisdufranc.org/articles/varietes/tranches_fautees.html. • Sargent, Thomas J., and Francois R. Velde. *The Evolution of Small Change*. Chicago: Federal Reserve Bank, 1997. • Stephen, Sir Leslie, and Sir Sidney Lee, eds. *Dictionary of National Biography*. London: Oxford University Press, 1922. • "The Story of the Sixpence." http://www.24carat.co.uk/sixpencesstory.html.

Bryan, William Jennings

The famed American orator and self-proclaimed Bible expert at the Scopes Monkey Trial, William Jennings Bryan exploited a folksy background and homey, bible-based values as a means of inflaming populist politics. Born March 19, 1860, on a farm in Salem, Illinois (which was the source of his nickname, the "boy orator from the Platte"), he attended an academy at Jacksonville, graduated from Illinois College at age 21, and read law at Chicago's Union College of Law. A pompous Democratic congressman, he refined his platform skills on a regular round of Chautauqua speaking engagements.

Bryan earned his reputation as a demagogue at age 36 for defending the common man during the debate over free coinage of silver, the result of the Coinage Act of 1873, which dropped bimetallism and replaced it with the gold standard. After the shift fueled the 1890 economic depression, protest emerged in the prairie states and among debtors and the unemployed, who renamed the congressional shift the "Crime of '73." Bryan's famous "Cross of Gold" speech, delivered at the Chicago Democratic National Convention held at the Chicago Colosseum on July 9, 1896, was a slur against backers of President Grover Cleveland and an attempt to stir the emotions of Midwestern voters. His text, which appeared on July 10 in the *Chicago Daily Tribune,* summarized the silver movement. In his last utterance at the lectern, he thundered, "You shall not press down upon the brow of labor this crown of thorns, you shall not crucify mankind upon a cross of gold" (*Gale Encyclopedia of U.S. Economic History,* 1999). His audience stamped and cheered for thirty minutes as he struck the pose of the crucified Christ with arms outstretched. In the streets, people chanted his name as he ascended a barouche.

The emotion of Bryan's peroration along with his traveling over 18,000 miles to address humble audiences earned him a presidential nomination and a new sobriquet, "the Great Commoner." Billing himself as a crusader for silver and enemy of the Eastern moneymen of Wall Street, like David against Goliath, he intended to polarize voters and carry the rural South and West. He made a moving case for the treasury's high-handedness in establishing a deflationary policy without public debate. However, his crusade for the silver-rich western states was politically detrimental because it favored a sparsely populated voting bloc.

Bryan's ploy failed because his campaign came too late; he lost to Ohio governor William McKinley. In 1900, the U.S. passed the Gold Standard Act, officially ending dependence on silver to back paper money. Still game for politics, Bryan ran for president a second time two years after serving as colonel of a Nebraska infantry regiment during the Spanish-American War. He established the *Commoner,* a populist newspaper, and, in 1908, lost a third presidential campaign against William Howard Taft. After a four-year term as secretary of state, Bryan resigned in 1915 to protest Woodrow Wilson's involvement of the United States in World War I.

On July 9, 1925, Bryan made a public splash by addressing the Dayton board of education the day before the Scopes trial in Dayton, Tennessee, where farmers still cherished the populist splendor of the "Cross of Gold" speech. The trial turned into an early media circus and another opportunity for Bryan to posture as a humble religious man dedicated to speaking for lowly farm folk. After the jury found John T. Scopes guilty of breaking a law against teaching evolution in public schools, Bryan addressed 8,000 fundamentalists at Jasper, Tennessee, then returned to Dayton, Ohio, and died in his sleep on July 26, 1925.

See also* gold standard; *Wizard of Oz.

SOURCES: Allen, Robert. *William Jennings Bryan.* Milford, Mich.: Mott Media, 1992. • *Gale Encyclopedia of U.S. Economic History.* Farmington Hills, Mich.: Gale Group, 1999. • Harpine, William D. "Bryan's "Cross of Gold": The Rhetoric and Polarization at the 1896 Democratic Convention." *Quarterly Journal of Speech,* August 1, 2001, pp. 291–304. • Reid, Ronald F. *Three Centuries of American Rhetorical Discourse.* Prospect Heights, Ill.: Waveland Press, 1988. • Taxay, Don. *The U.S. Mint and Coinage.* New York: Arco Publishing, 1966. • Vitullo-Martin, Julia. "Monkey Business: What Really Happened in Tennessee." *Commonweal,* October 8, 1999. • Weatherford, Jack. *The History of Money: From Sandstone to Cyberspace.* Pittsburgh, Pa.: Three Rivers Press, 1998.

Buell, Abel

Silversmith, typemaster, and ex-con Abel Buell (or Buel) contributed technology and style to U.S. coinage. A Connecticut native born in Killingworth on February 1, 1741, he learned engraving in boyhood from Ebenezer Chittenden, a master smith. At age 21, Buell opened a shop in his hometown and received a commission to draft a five-shilling state note. Because he enlarged the face value to five pounds, in March 1764, he was sentenced at a Norwich courtroom to imprisonment, branding, and loss of property. To overcome the stigma of crime, he worked at refining a lapidary polishing machine and mastered type founding.

By 1769, Buell was at work in Boston typesetting and designing ad copy and establishing a type foundry in New Haven. In 1770, he advanced to copperplate engraving. In flight from the state of Connecticut because of mishandling funds, he stayed on the run until 1778, when he reunited with his second wife, Aletta Devoe Buell, who had maintained his silversmithy, called "At the Sign of the Coffee Pot."

In 1781 Buell became the first American to manufacture type commercially. He invested in packet boat transport, marble quarrying, jewelry, and engineering. At age 43, he earned a commission from Bernard Romano for incising a wall map of U.S. territories as reflected by the peace of 1783. In 1785, Buell invented a coining machine and organized a penny manufactory for Connecticut and Vermont, which he operated with the aid of his son William, whom he taught to incise dies.

For all his faults, Buell contributed to U.S. monetary history. In 1787, he struck the post-colonial Fugio Cent, the first coin issued under the authorization of the United States. It bears the mottoes "We Are One" and "Mind Your Business." His Vermont penny carried the legend "*Stella Quarta Decima*" ("14th star"), a prediction of its entry into the Union. Late in his career, he made armor and returned to silversmithing in 1805 at Stockbridge, Massachusetts. Buell died on March 10, 1822.

SOURCES: *Columbia Encyclopedia*, Edition 6. Farmington, Mich.: Gale Group, 2000. • Johnson, Allen, ed. *Dictionary of American Biography*. New York: Charles Scribner's Sons, 1928. • *Merriam-Webster's Biographical Dictionary*. Springfield, Mass.: Merriam-Webster, 1995. • Newman, Ewell L., "Abel Buell: Errant Genius," *Imprint*, February 1976, pp. 7–8. • Pollak, Henry. *Coinage & Conflict*. Clifton, N.J.: Coin & Currency Institute, 2001.

Burger, Adolf

In Nazi Germany during World War II, Jewish inmate Adolf Burger played a key role in the plot of Heinrich Himmler, who conspired to counterfeit 8,965,080 banknotes in five-, ten-, 20-, and 50-pound denominations. Known as "Operation Bernhard," the military scheme was intended to destabilize the British treasury and bankrupt the Allies. The German ruse bore the name of its director, Major Bernhard Krüger of the S.S., the initials of the elite *Schutzstaffel* that served as Adolf Hitler's bodyguard. At the printshop of Sachsenhausen, a concentration camp north of Berlin, clever counterfeiters forced Jewish conscript bookbinders, engravers, and printers to produce phony bills, English and Russian postage stamps, driver's licenses, professional degrees, and propaganda pamphlets.

In 1944, the S.S. transferred to Sachsenhausen Czech printer Adolf Burger and eight other inmates from France, Holland, and Poland to assist Operation Bernhard. Burger worked for three weeks at copying Yugoslav currency, then joined the 142 workers making British money. Essential to believable counterfeit bills was the paper used by British moneyers. To substitute, the Germans imported flax rags from Turkey, which they first soiled with machine oil. The workshop offered photo equipment, brushes, needles, and pins as tools for the intricate reproduction, which required duplicating print plates and mastering serial enumeration of notes. For a test run, agents posing as emissaries of the *Deutsche Reichsbank* (German state bank) had Swiss bankers inspect the notes and report on their authenticity. The Swiss, after conferring with the Bank of England, declared them genuine.

Near war's end, the S.S. resituated their counterfeiting operating at Mauthausen, a concentration camp in northern Austria, where the staff turned their operation into a factory making U.S. 100-dollar bills. One specialist forger, Russian-Jewish inmate Solomon Smolianoff, earned the German Iron Cross for his contribution to the scheme. With the proceeds of illicit pounds, the German war machine outfitted its commandos and enlisted more spies. The Bank of England retaliated by recalling its paper notes and, in 1944, reissuing them in color on different paper.

When allied forces liberated Mathausen in 1945, the S.S. dismantled the camp and hid the evidence of their attempt at economic sabotage in the Austrian Alps at Lake Toplitz. Burger borrowed a camera from a German peasant, photographed the camp and its team of forgers, and published a bestseller of the Holocaust, *Des Teufels Werkstatt* (*The Devil's Workshop*) (1980), source of a TV documentary on prison-labor counterfeiting. In November 2001, he assisted historians in identifying boxes of counterfeit Bank of England cash that oceaneers in a miniature submarine retrieved from the lake at a depth of 348 feet. French paper restorers Bernard Lebeau and Florence Hereenschmidt salvaged the notes, which still bore fake watermarks. Salvors preserved the best of the notes for an exhibit at the Simon Wiesenthal Museum of Tolerance in Los Angeles. *60 Minutes II* featured the four-week hunt for Nazi forgeries on November 21, 2001.

SOURCES: Allen, Larry. *Encyclopedia of Money*. New York: Checkmark Books, 2001. • Gilbert, Martin. *Atlas of the Holocaust*. New York: William Morrow and Co., 1993. • "Lake Search Yields Counterfeit Bills, but No Nazi Gold." Bergen, N.J., *Record*, November 23, 2000. • Levy, Alan. "Adolf Burger: The Forger as a Work of Art." *Prague Post*, November 1, 2000. • "The Search for Answers." *CBS News*, November 21, 2001. • Wheal, Elizabeth-Anne, Stephen Pope, and James Taylor. *Encyclopedia of the Second World War*. New York: Castle Books, 1989.

Burke, Dr. Selma

A curious quirk of history has left unsigned Dr. Selma Hortense Burke's portrait on the Roosevelt dime. Born in Mooresville, North Carolina, on December 31, 1900, she was the granddaughter of Samuel S. Jackson, a slave of General Stonewall Jackson, and the last of the ten children of Mary Jackson and Neal Burke. Her introduction to art came from her artist grandmother and from her father, a minister, railroad brakeman, and chef on ocean liners. Among his gifts from his travels were African carvings purchased in Africa, the Caribbean, Europe, and South America. His two missionary brothers also collected religious tokens and carvings during their assignments in Africa. At their death in 1913, their belongings passed to Dr. Burke's family.

While making whitewash in girlhood, Burke took an interest in sculpture. She pursued her hobby by carving an angel on a black walnut limb and by shaping local river clay into a menagerie of animals. She wanted to be an artist, but took her mother's advice and aimed for a career in nursing while studying at the Nannie Burroughs School for Girls in Washington, D.C. Educator William Arial, the superintendent of schools, became her mentor and coached her in the arts. Under his patronage, she entered the Slater Normal and Industrial School in Winston-Salem, North Carolina, and, at age 24, earned an R.N. at the St. Agnes School of Nursing at St. Augustine College in Raleigh. She became the first black registered nurse in Mecklenburg County, North Carolina.

While working in Philadelphia, Burke studied surgical nursing at Women's Medical College. In 1925, she married Durant Woodward, who died within the year. In 1929, she began working for the heiress of the Otis Elevator Company in Cooperstown, New York. To perpetuate an interest in art, Burke retrieved a sculptor's sketches from the trash, attended performances at Carnegie Hall and the Metropolitan Opera, and modeled for photographers Alfred Stieglitz and Edward Steichen. In 1935, she settled in New York

City and posed for art classes at Sarah Lawrence College. Through marriage to poet Claude McKay and friendship with radical labor leader Max Eastman, she met the distinguished blacks of the Harlem Renaissance.

On a scholarship Burke earned after demonstrating technique to a student, she studied sculpture at Columbia University and won the Julius Rosenwald Award of $1,500 and, in 1936, a Boehler Foundation fellowship. She traveled Europe, learned ceramics in Vienna, and studied nude modeling in Paris under sculptor Aristide Maillol and painter Henri Matisse. Divorced from McKay, she completed an M.F.A. from Columbia in 1941 and organized works for a first exhibit at New York City's McMillen Galleries in New York.

After Burke joined the war effort by driving a truck at the Brooklyn Naval Yard, in 1943, she was hospitalized with a back injury. While recuperating, she learned that the District of Columbia Fine Arts Commission was sponsoring a national competition to produce a profile of President Franklin D. Roosevelt to be used for the 1945 March of Dimes campaign. Out of a field of twelve entrants, Burke won the commission. She discarded print images from newspapers and books because they didn't provide the angle she needed.

In a letter, Burke requested an appointment for a live sitting. She introduced herself as a student at Columbia University and an artist familiar with sculptor Jean-Antoine Houdon's bust of George Washington. When the president agreed to pose, she began making eight charcoal sketches during 45 minutes' work at the cabinet room on February 22, 1945, six weeks before the president's sudden death at Warm Springs, Georgia. Because she forgot to bring sketchbooks, she drew on butcher paper, which she hastily purchased at the A & P before her train ride south. To set her model at ease, she chatted with him about Father Divine, leader of New York City's Peace Mission.

To complete the drawing, Burke required one more White House visit on April 20, but the president died on April 12. Out of respect, she framed the original to hang in her studio. Cast in bronze and mounted at the Recorder of Deeds Building in Washington, the completed plaque, which was 3.5' by 2.5', depicted freedoms from want and war and the freedoms of speech and worship. The president's wife, Eleanor Roosevelt, thought the pose was too youthful, but Burke replied that she wanted to capture the strength of a Roman gladiator to convey the immense demands on a man who led the Allies through World War II.

The profile, called "The Four Freedoms," got its first public showing in July at the Modern Age Gallery. On September 24, 1945, the public viewed Burke's portrait plaque, which was unveiled by President Harry S Truman and Frederick S. Weaver, deputy recorder of deeds and the grandson of abolitionist orator Frederick Douglass. Truman declared the likeness a true image of the man.

The profile graced the Roosevelt dime, which was first minted in 1946, replacing the Adolph A. Weinman Mercury dime. The confusion about the sculptor's identity arose after John R. Sinnock, chief engraver at the U.S. Mint, placed his initials on the profile. A friend warned Burke that Sinnock intended to take credit for the profile. Burke concluded that, because political leadership had shifted from Democrat to Republican and because of her race and liberal politics, the concealment of her name and artistry was not surprising. When she pressed her case against Sinnock for plagiarism, FBI Director J. Edgar Hoover began investigating her. In March 1946, Sinnock claimed in an article in *Numismatic Scrapbook Magazine* that he sculpted the image of Roosevelt from two original life studies.

Burke began teaching students at her home studio and in workshops and public school and college classrooms, including Swarthmore College, Livingstone College, Harvard University, the A. W. Mellon Foundation, the Friends Charter School in Pennsylvania, St. George's School in New York, and Old Solebury School in Bucks County, Pennsylvania. After her marriage to architect Herman Kobbe in 1949, she lived and worked at a farm near an artists' enclave in New Hope, Pennsylvania, and promoted the Pennsylvania Council on the Arts. In 1971, she completed requirements for a Ph.D. from Livingstone College. On June 20, 1975, Governor Milton Schapp honored her contributions to the arts by proclaiming Selma Burke Day.

In widowhood, Burke founded Pittsburgh's Selma Burke Art Center and the Selma Burke School of Sculpture in New York, where staff offered a full curriculum in the arts, puppetry, and TV production. She remained active in school and foundation work until her retirement in 1982. The corpus of her works includes some 20 sculptures in bronze, clay, rock, and wood of such notables as educator Booker T. Washington, jazz great Duke Ellington, financier Charles Schwab, abolitionist John Brown, educator Mary McLeod Bethune, freedom fighter Dr. Martin Luther King, Jr., and President Calvin Coolidge. She earned honorary degrees from Wake Forest University, Moore College, Johnson C. Smith University, Spelman College, Winston-Salem State University, and the University of North Carolina.

At age 90, Burke received acclaim from Pennsylvania Governor Robert P. Casey. He noted her travels to study with great artists and her assistance to the next generation of sculptors. He added, "Your ten cents can be found in every community across the nation. But that dime is worth so much more than its monetary value" (Van Ryzin 1995, p. 161). That fall, James Roosevelt, son of the former president, wrote Burke his personal thanks for the coin: "Although Americans may not recognize the name or face of the person who sculpted it, the face of my father on the U.S. dime is a constant testimonial to a great man who envisioned a great country" (*ibid.*). Shortly before her death from cancer on August 29, 1995, at her home in New Hope, Pennsylvania, she was designing a half-dollar coin to honor Alabama hero Rosa Parks. Burke acquired a Yaddo Foundation fellowship, Julius Rosenwald Award, an honorarium from the Women's Caucus for Art, the Pearl S. Buck Foundation Woman's Award, Distinguished Daughter of Pennsylvania award, Essence Magazine Award, and Candace Award.

***See also* March of Dimes; U.S. coins.**

SOURCES: Chappell, Kevin. "Sculptor Who Created Roosevelt's Imprint on the Dime Tells Kids How Love of Art Has Shaped Her Life." Knight-Ridder/Tribune News Service, December 7, 1994. • *Contemporary Black Biography*. Detroit: Gale Research, 1997. • Davis, Mark. "Selma Burke, the 'Grande Dame' of African American Artists, Is Honored." Knight-Ridder/Tribune News Service, December 8, 1993. • Hine, Darlene Clark, et al., eds. *Black Women in America*. Bloomington: Indiana University Press, 1993. • "Obituary." *Jet*, September 18, 1995, p. 58. • Reed, Mort. *Cowles Complete Encyclopedia of U.S. Coins*. New York: Cowles Book Company, 1969. • Taxay, Don. *The U.S. Mint and Coinage*. New York: Arco Publishing, 1966. • Van Ryzin, Robert R. *Twisted Tails: Sifted Fact, Fantasy and Fiction from U.S. Coin History*. Iola, Wisc.: Krause Publications, 1995.

Byzantine coins

Imperial power passed east from the dying Roman Empire to Constantinople after the barbarian Alans, Burgundians, Suevians, and Vandals overran Rome in December A.D. 406. As a result, money matters proved more stable than they had been under the last emperors. In the old empire, minting had gradually declined except for the Roman and Italian operations. For financial reasons, the barbarian powerholders in the West had to evolve their own characteristic coinage, including the silver *miliaresion* and the short-lived *hexagram*. Byzantine coinage, bearing the imperial legend "*basileus Romaion*" (king of the Romans) did not fluctuate like earlier Roman money systems. Its beauty remained classic for centuries and influenced the Russian coinage of the princes of Kiev.

In A.D. 450, during the last year of the rule of Theodosius II, a marriage coin connected Christ with the success of holy wedlock. For the wedding of his pious sister Pulcheria to Marcian, the emperor commissioned a coin inscribed "*Feliciter Nubtiis*" ("Luck to the newlyweds"). The image shows the couple with Christ resting his hands on their shoulders. The scenario did not recur until after

Byzantine coins featured pious poses and crosses expressing the Roman Empire's embrace of Christianity. Gradually, medieval art impersonalized iconography and replaced human features with crosses (Guy Clark, Ancient Coins and Antiquities, Norfolk, Virginia)

This portrait coin from A.D. 527 pictures the Byzantine Emperor Justinian I, who protected all of Europe from the advance of Arabs and Turks and shielded Christianity from the threat of Islam. (Guy Clark, Ancient Coins and Antiquities, Norfolk, Virginia)

A.D. 685 under Justinian II, during the rise of militant Islamics and their anti–Christian coin mottoes.

Similar pious poses expressed the rise of Christianity by featuring Christ enthroned, holding a bible, crowning monarchs, or standing before a kneeling emperor. Additional religious depictions feature the nimbate Virgin Mary seated and holding the infant Christ, standing with an emperor, or holding a cross. The growth of the pantheon of saints added to standard coin art the saints Alexander, Constantine, George, Theodore, and Michael. Gradually, medieval art impersonalized pious iconography and replaced human features with crosses.

After A.D. 450, Marcian, a soldier-emperor and the last of the Theodosian dynasty, faced Attila the Hun, who demanded annual tribute in cash. Marcian sneered that he had iron, but not gold. After the Huns moved on to attack Rome, Marcian built up his treasury and reformed coinage as an adjunct to economic reform. He struck a gold *solidus* picturing himself girded for war opposite winged Victory uplifting a long cross. His reforms were so valuable to the citizens that they shouted at subsequent emperors, "Reign like Marcian!" His reign earned the title of the "Golden Age of the Eastern Empire."

The last emperor to rule east and west, Justinian I the Great, who came to power in A.D. 526, became Byzantium's prime civilizer and lawgiver. At the height of the empire's grandeur, he protected the realm from Vandal and Goth invasions and, with the help of the Empress Theodora, quelled the Nika riot in his own city. By modernizing trade and strengthening the infrastructure, he readied the city for great achievements, especially the codification of the *Corpus Juris Civilis* (Body of Civil Law).

A one-pound gold commemorative coin pictures Justinian in armor and helmet on a prancing steed. Ahead, a barefoot Victory lifts his war trophies. Encircling the scenario are words summarizing his achievements: "*Salus et Gloria Romanorum*" ("Safety and glory of the Romans"). In truth, the safety he offered his people protected all of Europe from the advance of Arabs and Turks and shielded Christianity from the threat of Islam.

Around A.D. 580, Tiberius II Constantinus displayed the cross of Calvary on the reverse of coins he paid to Chilperic, the Frankish king who supplied Byzantium with hired soldiers. The tradition of religious figures ended under Leo III (or Leo the Isaurian), the

In A.D. 685, the Byzantine Emperor Justinian II fought the rise of militant Islamics by circulating coins marked by pious Christian imagery. (Guy Clark, Ancient Coins and Antiquities, Norfolk, Virginia)

Syrian-born emperor who initiated iconoclasm, the opposition to icons and physical representations of divinity on art, architecture, or coinage. Upon his election to power in A.D. 717, he vigorously challenged Islam and Judaism. In A.D. 726, he ordered idols, mosaics, and holy pictures destroyed and, against strong criticism by the Roman papacy, maintained iconoclasm until his death on June 18, A.D. 741.

After A.D. 811, the gold *nomisma* (or *noumisma)*, a thin, stackable scyphate or cup-shaped coin with a ragged edge, replaced the *solidus* as the Byzantine equivalent. Citizens dubbed the *nomisma* the *michalatus* after its initiator, the Emperor Michael I Rhangabe, successor of Nicephorus I. The coin maintained purity for two centuries, when mint-masters produced it from electrum, a pale yellow alloy of gold and silver. The series backed the portrait of Michael with a Greek cross and religious inscription.

A century later, after designers abandoned Leo's spartan designs, coin art returned to the depiction of imperial and religious figures, beginning with images of Christ. In A.D. 972, John Zimisces pictured his imperial crowning on a silver coin as an act of the Virgin Mary while God reached his hand toward earth in a sign of blessing. The prayerful pose of the Virgin Mary was first ordered by Pope Leo VI. After Christianity reached Kiev in A.D. 988, circulation of Byzantine coins influenced design of Russian silver pieces.

One regal Byzantine pose, that of Romanus III Argyrus after 1028, placed the emperor with royal robe, crown, and orb alongside the haloed image of the Virgin Mary. After his coronation in 1185, Isaac II Angelus struck a scyphate coin showing the Archangel Michael bestowing the diadem. On the *nomismata* of Michael IV, Alexius I, and John II appeared Christ enthroned as *rex regnantium* ("king of kings"), a title that characterized the cohesive power of Christianity as a state church. The broad, thin-rimmed coin influenced the *grosso matapan* that Doge Giovanni Dandalo introduced in Venice after 1280.

From the time of Emperor Michael IV, a former money changer, after 1034, coin purity declined. The rate of debasement accelerated in 1204 at the end of the Fourth Crusade. An unusual falsehood was the lie that John III Ducas Vatatzes, the emperor of Nicea, claimed on his coins. Although he styled himself "*porphyrogenitus*" ("born to the purple"), he actually acquired rule by supplanting Constantine, son of Theodore I Lascaris, the rightful ruler, and by imprisoning and murdering two more sons, Alexius and Isaac. John strengthened the claim through marriage to Theodore's daughter Irene. As trust in coins weakened, during the mid–1200s, traveler William of Rubruck (also Willem van Ruysbroeck, Rubruquis, or Ruisbroek), a Franciscan missionary to Tatary, observed suspicion among his bearers concerning the quality of money. They rubbed dubious coins between their fingers and sniffed at them to determine the copper content.

During the tumble of Byzantine coinage from precious metals into base copper, one coin stood out for its excellence. In 1231, the Holy Roman Emperor Frederick II, then king of Sicily, commissioned the *augustalis*, a portrait coin that was the first to influence commerce since the demise of Roman imperial specie. Roman in style, pose, and lettering, it returned gold bullion to Western European mints in the form of Tunisian ores. The regal coin outshone in beauty and worth the declining silver *denier* and the ubiquitous Arab *dinar*. Minting of the *augustalis* coincided with the publication of the emperor's law text, *Liber Augustalis*, a bastion of medieval law creating the secular state in Sicily. The gold piece thrived for a half century, giving place to the Renaissance coinage of gold *ducats* in Venice and *florins* in Florence.

The final years of the Byzantine Empire reduced once-grand emperors to bribery and beggary to maintain a semblance of power. As Europe menaced from the west and Saracens from the east, monarchs hanging on by threads gave little thought to ennobling themselves on ornate portrait coins. Subsequent mintings produced crude, ill-struck pieces far inferior to the artful coins emerging from the Renaissance treasuries of Florence, Genoa, and Venice. In 1453, when the Ottoman Turks, led by Mohammed II, seized Constantinople, historian Leonard of Chios, Mytilene's archbishop, summarized the face-off between authorities and the working class in *Historia Captae a Turcis Constantinopolis* (*History of the Turkish Seizure of Constantinople*) (1544). To persuade soldiers and common laborers to work, Emperor Constantine XI Palaeologus collected sacred vessels for melting and shaping into acceptable coins for their pay.

See also **hoarding; Peter I; scyphate coins.**

SOURCES: Allen, Larry. *Encyclopedia of Money*. New York: Checkmark Books, 2001. • Bunson, Matthew. *A Dictionary of the Roman Empire*. New York: Oxford University Press, 1991. • Clain-Stefanelli, Elvira, and Vladimir Clain-Stefanelli. *The Beauty and Lore of Coins, Currency, and Medals*. Croton-on-Hudson, N.Y.: Riverwood Publishers, 1974. • Cribb, Joe. *Money*. Toronto: Stoddart, 1990. • Davies, Glyn. *A History of Money from Ancient Times to the Present Day*. Cardiff: University of Wales Press, 1994. • Evans, James Allan. "View from a Turkish Monastery: An Overview of the Byzantine World." *Athena Review*, Vol. 3, 2001, 16–25. • Hastings, James, ed. *Encyclopedia of Religion and Ethics*. New York: Charles Scribner's Sons, 1951. • Howatson, M. C., ed. *The Oxford Companion to Classical Literature*. Oxford: Oxford University Press, 1991. • Lyttelton, Margaret, and Werner Forman. *The Romans: Their Gods and Their Beliefs*. London: Orbis Publishing, 1984. • Meshorer, Ya'akov. *Coins of the Ancient World*. Jerusalem: Jerusalem Publishing House, 1974. • *New Catholic Encyclopedia*. San Francisco: Catholic University of America, 1967. • Pliny. *The Natural History*. New York: McGraw-Hill, 1962. • Pollak, Henry. *Coinage & Conflict*. Clifton, N.J.: Coin & Currency Institute, 2001. • Reinfeld, Fred. *Treasury of the World's Coins*. New York: Sterling Publishing, 1953. • Snodgrass, Mary Ellen. *Who's Who in the Middle Ages*. Jefferson, N.C.: McFarland, 2001. • Starr, Chester G. *A History of the Ancient World*. New York: Oxford University Press, 1991.

Canadian money

In colonial Canada, commodity exchange was legal tender in a land where coins were yet to be minted. In settled areas, until true Canadian coinage was possible, reliance on French coinage was the rule as well as instances of wampum and hide and skin currency, such as the moose- and bearskin money recognized in Quebec Province in 1673. In Nova Scotia, maple sugar and timber were as valid as blankets among the Eskimo, dried cod in Newfoundland, and salt, wheat, corn, peas, pork. In British Columbia, polar bear teeth substituted for coins. Token money served the Hudson Bay Company, which was organized in 1670 at the request of disgruntled *voyageurs* Médard Chouart des Groseilliers and Pierre Esprit Radisson. The fur-trading monopoly issued coins worth ⅛ of a beaver skin for use in the outback.

In 1670, silver 5-*sols* and 15-*sols* circulated in the French possessions in the territory of the French West India Company, including Acadia, French Canada, French Newfoundland, and French West Indies. Struck by the Paris mint and introduced on February 19, these "*Gloriam Regni Tui Dicent*" ("They will speak glory of your reign") coins, designed by Jean Varin in honor of Louis XIV, equaled the weight, worth, and quality of French coins, but were legal tender only in the Western Hemisphere. This stricture limited their use for the purchase of imported goods. A decade later, a change in laws widened the area in which the coins were accepted.

As trade goods flourished, colonial Canadians saw the influx of Spanish-American coins minted in Lima, Peru; Mexico City, Mexico; and Potosí, Bolivia, valued at one, two, four, and eight *reales* (or *piastres)*. Their use was evidence of inter-colonial commerce with French *coureurs de bois* (woodsmen) and Dutch and English merchants. By 1681, a decree regarding circulation of such foreign coins combatted problems with clipping and shaving by requiring that they be weighed. The solution suited pharmacists, merchants, and government officials, but failed to protect ordinary citizens, who had no balance-beam scale handy at every monetary exchange. To simplify matters, two years later, the council at Quebec moved to have the clerk of court stamp coins with their weight in the presence of the attorney general, clerk of court, and council members. For authentication, John Soullard engraved appropriate dies.

To expedite monetary exchange in small sums, merchants replaced coins with *Bon Pour* ("Good For") notes and tokens, for example, the "beaver money" that the Hudson Bay Company stamped on brass tokens in one-shilling amounts and "broomsticks," a thick, stubby wood circlet that looked like it had been lopped from a broom handle (Cribb 1990, 48). Provincial tokens — called half-pennies in English-speaking locales and *sous* in French Quebec — served as small change in tandem with American dollars and Spanish *pesos* or pieces of eight. The surge of uncoordinated minting produced indigenous coinage in New Brunswick, Newfoundland, Nova Scotia, Ontario, Prince Edward Island, and Quebec.

At the next stage of regional coinage, when shipments failed to arrive from the treasury in 1685, Jacques de Meulles issued playing card money as scrip to pay soldiers. Whereas the New England Puritans would have damned playing cards as sinful, the issuance of the cards suited the semi-literate Canadian *habitants* and provided light, portable, and adaptable exchange media for daily use. In 1702, war with England forced the French to halt the shipment of silver coins to redeem the cards. The outstanding debt to soldiers continued until 1714, when France began redeeming two-million *livres* in cards at half the face value. The offer extended until 1720, when the playing cards were declared worthless.

On Prince Edward Island, widespread hoarding of English coins forced businesses to operate by barter. Chief among exchange items were wheat and the pelts of beaver, moose, and wildcat. As the French lost their hold on the Atlantic seaboard, in 1713, British occupation forces in Nova Scotia requested that the home office discontinue the allotment of rum as pay and send instead coins or paper bills. In the estimation of officers, rum encouraged rowdiness and blasphemy rather than sober military service. The English colonies, with a population over 1,000,000 compared to 70,000 in New France, built a strong economy based on agriculture and growing trade with the West Indies and the mother country.

Because commerce made demands on the makeshift monetary situation, scrip carried the Canadians until the treasury could set up a standardized system. A local money system of army bills emerged in eastern Canada during the War of 1812, when the military office in Quebec City issued uniface notes worth four, 25, 100, and 400 dollars. Over the next two years, additional issue increased the number of small denominations. With the signing of a peace treaty on December 24, 1814, the need for army bills ceased.

Canada's treasury continued to rely on an irregular system of English and French coins and tokens until 1858, when national coinage first emulated the U.S. decimal-based system with the first penny and five-, ten-, and 20-cent coins. The Victorian penny was the design of Leonard Charles Wyon, a scion of an illustrious English family of coiners, who was assisted by George William De Saulles. Struck before formal confederation of the Canadian provinces, the penny earned scorn for the skimpy evaluation of 100 coins to the pound of bronze as contrasted to the British standard of 80 to the pound. The treasury did not correct the valuation until 1876.

In 1868, the Currency Act made the dollar the official monetary unit of the Dominion of Canada. Until the establishment of the Royal Canadian Mint in Ottawa in 1908, national coinage was the work of outside agencies, with much of the Yukon and British Columbia's gold ore being exported to the United States. After three years of construction, the new facility on Sussex Drive in Ottawa opened on January 2, 1908, with Arthur H. W. Cleave superintending the Canadian branch of the British Royal Mint and Dr. James Bonar as first deputy master of the mint. The treasury produced its first specie, a 50-cent piece. Its first gold coin, the sovereign, featured the design of Benedetto Pistrucci, Italian cameo engraver and medalist who became the London mint's chief engraver in 1817 and chief medalist in 1828. The incuse die stamped a raised image of St. George, England's popular patron saint, trampling a dragon.

The subsequent monetary system ranged coins in value from a penny, five-, ten-, 20-, 25-, and 50-cent pieces to one, five, and ten dollars, with the half-dollar carrying the brunt of everyday public use into the Edwardian era. In 1911, the oversized penny underwent a redesign by Sir E. B. MacKennal, an Australian sculptor, and W. H. J. Blakemore. The coin pictured George V, but omitted from the legend the *de rigueur* Latin phrase "*Dei Gratia*," ("By the Grace of God"). The public greeted the oversight by dubbing the pennies "godless coins." A year later, an upgraded die supplied the phrase. As of December 1, 1931, British overseers departed, leaving the Canadian mint completely under domestic management.

In 1935, the Canadian treasury issued silver dollars on a commemorative design featuring George V and a *voyageur*. It was the start of a series of such dollars picturing significant moments in the nation's bi-national beginnings as part French and part English. In 1937, the abdication of Edward VIII produced a quandary calling for the reclamation of pennies and 10-cent pieces. Only 25-cent pieces appeared with his portrait. English engravers quickly made likenesses of George VI's image, which had to be cut in England. Two years later, a special silver dollar noted visits by George VI and Queen Elizabeth with the likeness of the Canadian Parliament building and the legend "*Fide Suorum Regnat*" ("He Rules by the Faith of His People"). Throughout the late 1930s to 1943, Canadian mints relied on engravings by British sculptor George Edward Kruger-Gray, a Royal College of Art graduate, who also created a badge for the Royal Naval Patrol Service and coins for Australia, Bermuda, Cyprus, Great Britain, Jersey, Mauritius, New Guinea, New Zealand, South Africa, and Southern Rhodesia.

With the establishment of India's independence in 1947, the Canadian mintmaster removed the abbreviation "Ind Imp" (India's Emperor) from subsequent coins. The merger of Newfoundland with Canada in 1949 resulted in a silver dollar that Thomas Shingles, chief engraver of the Royal Canadian Mint, crafted showing H.M.S. *Matthew*, explorer John Cabot's ship that he sailed to Newfoundland in 1497. One of the first Canadian commemorative coins, it bore a propitious Latin phrase "*Floreat Terra Nova*" ("May the New Land Flourish").

Controversy dogged coin picturing Britain's queen. An off-shoulder portrait of Queen Elizabeth II in 1954 forced engravers to redesign the die with a more modest draping over the shoulder. Another unfortunate royal issue, a dollar bill, pictured such convoluted curls that the superstitious claimed to see the face of Satan in her hair. Because people rejected the bills, the treasury retired them from circulation.

Wartime shortages of nickel in 1954 resulted in the five-cent piece being struck on chrome-plated steel. A commemorative issued in 1958 recalling the centennial of British Colombia's entrance as a territory featured a beaver totem common to Pacific Coastal tribes. Natives avoided the coins because the shape was a death totem. A 1964 coin remarked the centennial of the Charlottetown Conference of 1864, when Canadians first negotiated their confederation.

In 1967, the Canadian centennial year, the treasury approved a series of coins depicting animals — bear, beaver, Canadian goose, duck, elk, horned owl, lynx, mackerel, wolf— found in the Western Hemisphere and struck the first 20-dollar gold piece, created in London at the Royal Mint, at the Heaton Mint in Birmingham, and at the Royal Canadian Mint in Ottawa. Outlying provinces — Prince Edward Island, New Brunswick, Newfoundland, and Nova Scotia — continue to produce their own coinage. One example, a 1950 five-cent piece, honored Swedish chemist A. F. Cronstedt, discoverer of nickel. In 1973, a quarter featuring an officer on horseback recognized the centennial of the Royal Canadian Mounted Police, who brought law and order to the nation's far west. In 1989, issuance of a dollar coin picturing *coureurs de bois* (woodsmen) paddling a canoe added the legend "Fleuve

In 1967, the Canadian centennial year, the treasury approved a series of notes and coins depicting animals found in the Western Hemisphere.

Mackenzie River," a repetition of "river" in French and English, the nation's two official languages.

The mint's centennial in 1998 was the occasion for a new half dollar featuring Elizabeth II. The next year, the mint distributed a silver dollar celebrating the 225th anniversary of the sighting of the Queen Charlotte islands by Spanish explorer Juan Perez. The surface depicted his frigate, the *Santiago*, and the date 1774.

Noting the arrival of a new millennium, on January 6, 2000, the Canadian mint sponsored a coin design contest judged by an independent panel of post-secondary art and design students, who selected 12 winners from 33,000 entries. Alfonso Gagliano, Minister of Public Works and Government Services and supervisor of the Royal Canadian Mint, joined mintmaster Danielle Wetherup in announcing the twelve winners of a design contest for new quarters. The sketches displayed the theme of national pride and heritage in abstract terms, beginning with pride, by freelance artist Donald F. Warkentin of Winnipeg. Unveiled at the rate of one per month, the designs were the creations of ordinary citizens, including youth, who set the tone for the next century. A later winner, Thunder Bay teenager Laura Paxton, portrayed six children holding the Canadian flag. One child is in a wheelchair, another on crutches.

A new half-dollar featured the red-tailed hawk, a migratory species that includes Harlan's (harlani) hawk and Krider's hawk, both common to the prairies. Designed by Quebec artist Pierre Leduc, the image is opposite the face portrait Queen Elizabeth II, engraved by Dora de Pédery-Hunt, who also sculpted a gold florin featuring the mayflower, emblem of Nova Scotia. The Royal Canadian Mint also issued a sterling silver hologram cameo 20-dollar piece celebrating Canadian achievement in transportation. The first three coins in the series, designed by Cape Breton artist J. Franklin Wright, featured the schooner *Blue Nose*, built in Lunenburg, Nova Scotia, in 1921 and winner of Halifax Herald International Fisherman's trophies annually from 1921 to 1938.

***See also* Brinks robbery; cloth and**

***Left:* This Canadian dime minted in 1999 pictures the Bluenose sailing vessel and commemorates the nation's shipbuilding industry. *Right:* A Canadian penny struck in 1999 features the maple leaf, a national symbol.**

fiber money; colonial coins; commemorative coins; counterfeiting; counterstamp; dollar; fur money; gold rush; leather and hide money; paper money; pistareen; Benedetti Pistrucci; *sou*; tokens; tooth money; Jean Varin; wampum; Wyon family.

SOURCES: Aaron, Robert. "'Invisible' 25-cent Coins Are Celebrations of Millennium." *Toronto Star*, July 1, 2000. • Aaron, Robert. "Let a Canadian Redesign Our Penny." *Toronto Star*, September 26, 2000. • Aaron, Robert. "Coins." *Toronto Star*, October 30, 2000. • Allen, Larry. *Encyclopedia of Money*. New York: Checkmark Books, 2001. • Babbitt, John S. "Coins and Currency on U.S. Stamps." *Stamps*, January 21, 1995. • "The Canadian Coin Reference Site." http://www. canadiancoin.com/. • Clain-Stefanelli, Elvira, and Vladimir Clain-Stefanelli. *The Beauty and Lore of Coins, Currency, and Medals*. Croton-on-Hudson, N.Y.: Riverwood Publishers, 1974. • Cribb, Joe. *Money*. Toronto: Stoddart, 1990. • Einzig, Paul. *Primitive Money*. Oxford: Pergamon Press, 1966. • Jacobs, Wayne L. "Canada's First Coinage." *Canadian Numismatic Association Journal*, July/August 1995. • Lewis, Brenda Ralph. *Coins & Currency*. New York: Random House, 1993. • Martindale, Nancy E. "The Cash Notes of 'The Oldest Colony.'" *Canadian Numismatic Association Journal*, November 2001, 424–427. • Martindale, Nancy E. "War of 1812 Spurred the Need for Army Bills." *Canadian Numismatic Association Journal*, October 2001, 373–377. • Opitz, Charles J. *Odd and Curious Money*. Ocala, Fla.: First Impressions, 1986. • Standish, David. *The Art of Money*. San Francisco: Chronicle Books, 2000. • Weatherford, Jack. *The History of Money: From Sandstone to Cyberspace*. Pittsburgh, Pa.: Three Rivers Press, 1998. • "Year 2000 25-cent Coins Unveiled by RCM." *Canadian Coin News*, January 25– February 7, 2000.

Canute I

Also known as Cnut, Knut, and Canute the Great, the Danish king Canute I was a vigorous, ruthless uniter of diverse peoples. Born to Sigrid of Sweden and Sweyn Forkbeard (also Swend Tweskideg) of Denmark around A.D. 995, Canute commanded the Viking realm and established peace in England after the predations of his pirate father. After decades of plunder and bloodshed, he established the Danelaw, the northern, central, and eastern region of England colonized by Viking armies in the late A.D. 800s, and extended a strong lineage from the Shieldings and Knytlings to his own sons, Harald Harefoot and Harthacanute.

A warrior from the age of fourteen, Canute superintended his father's English fleet at Gainsborough. In 1016, during a period of uncertainty, he assumed a shaky throne and had to fight off Ethelred the Unready, whom his father had unseated three years before. Canute triumphed and conquered East Anglia, Mercia, and Wessex. Upon establishing rule, he combined Danish, English, pagan, and Christian advisories and protected his subjects by controlling the borders of Cornwall, Scotland, and Wales. He coined a series of *sceattas*, *ores*, and *mancuses* at Norse-held mints in Dublin, where workers with little interest in art hammered out silver pennies picturing Canute in a nondescript profile pose mimicking a Roman emperor in corona.

With the proceeds of the *heregeld* (soldier debt), which Canute inherited, he maintained a strong treasury to assure war supplies, mercenaries, a fleet of battleships, and bribes of 20 million pennies to pay off advancing Viking raiders. He increased coinage with branch mints at Hederby, Lund, Orbaek, Ribe, and Viborg, Denmark. In 1018 alone, he amassed £72,000 in coin with an additional £10,500 acquired in London.

While attending a church council at Rome in 1027, Canute strengthened the payment of Peter's pence, an annual stipend or tithe to the church. He created a silver coinage that quickly linked England and Denmark as trading partners and extended free trade as far west as Ireland and north into Scotland. His three coins — the quatrefoil, pointed helmet, and short cross — survived into the thirteenth century. He died of a wasting liver disease at Shaftesbury on November 12, 1035, and was interred at Winchester. He left his empire, a strong currency, and efficient treasury to Edward the Confessor, a less able king and money manager who abolished the *heregeld* in 1051.

In March 1853, Tucker Coles discovered a hoard of 200 silver pennies from Ethelred and Canute's time and that of Canute's son Harald. Located as builders excavated a path at Wedmore, England, the cache appears to have been buried in an earthen crock before 1040. Historians surmise that the money may have been the savings of someone who died without divulging the crock's location. The British Museum took charge of the coins.

See also **Anglo-Saxon coins; penny; Peter's pence.**

SOURCES: Cannon, John, and Ralph Griffiths. *Oxford Illustrated History of the British Monarchy.* Oxford: Oxford University Press, 1988. • Cribb, Joe. *Money*. Toronto: Stoddart, 1990. • Cribb, Joe, Barrie Cook, and Ian Carradice. *The Coin Atlas.* London: Little, Brown and Co., 1999. • Davies, Glyn. *A History of Money from Ancient Times to the Present Day.* Cardiff: University of Wales Press, 1994. • *Encyclopedia of World Biography*. Detroit: Gale Research, 1998. • *New Catholic Encyclopedia.* San Francisco: Catholic University of America, 1967. • Reinfeld, Fred. *Treasury of the World's Coins.* New York: Sterling Publishing, 1953. • Sinclair, David. *The Pound.* London: Century Books, 2000. • Snodgrass, Mary Ellen. *Who's Who in the Middle Ages*. Jefferson, N.C.: McFarland, 2001.

La Capitana

In 1997, salvor Bob McClung won a race among several salvage firms to locate the Spanish treasure ship *La Capitana Jesus Maria de la Limpia Concepción*, a 130-foot flagship of the Spanish Armada of the Southern Seas. Built in Guayaquil, Ecuador, in 1644, it was the largest of Spain's fleet of money galleons. In the standard pattern of West Coast treasure ships, it was headed to Panama, where muleteers portaged its stores of newly hammered silver coins across the isthmus for the final leg of the journey across the Caribbean and Atlantic to Spain.

The *Capitana* ran aground, sheared its rudder, and sank off Chanduy, Ecuador, in 1654 after leaving Peru with 200 strongboxes of coins, 600 passengers, and evidence of a counterfeiting plot. A salvage operation conducted off the galleon *Nuestra Señora de las Maravillas* two years later ended in tragedy when it capsized off the Bahamas, becoming the world's second largest treasure relic. In 1687, William Phips, a sailor from New England, made a second recovery attempt of the immense *Capitana* treasure by hiring pearl divers to perform the undersea search. Although his mission failed, James II of England awarded him a knighthood and the governorship of Massachusetts.

In the 1960s, when critics dubbed the *Maravillas* a ghost wreck, diver and underwater archeologist Robert F. Marx pursued the shipwreck based on his reading of a book that Dr. Ribadeneyra, an eyewitness, published in Madrid in 1657. Marx located the hulk in 1972 and retrieved gold disks, silver, thousands of coins, emeralds, and a silver plate stamped with Dr. Ribadeneyra's blazon. The excavation ceased after the Bahamian government banned Marx's diving operation and impounded recovered loot.

Three decades later, McClung and his fellow salvors made repeated dives 35 feet into murky, shark-infested waters to retrieve timbers, amphorae, silver ingots, bronze cannon balls, emeralds, one gold *escudo,* and 4,000 silver pieces of eight, the products of the New World mint at Potosí, Bolivia. Mint dates between 1648 and 1652 confirmed the find as the *Capitana*. The project ended in a muddle for SubAmerica Discoveries, Incorporated, of Reston, Virginia, a company that underwrote the recovery of treasure worth $400 million, according to the assessment of naval archaeologist John de Bry, director of the Center for Historical Archaeology. The Ecuadorean government impounded the treasure and held it for over a year until agents could inventory goods and coins, confirm the appraisal, and make an amicable split with McClung, whose backers negotiated for half. After a difficult wait, McClung received his share, 2.5 percent of the undersea hoard.

SOURCES: Bowden, Tracy. "Gleaning Treasure from the Silver Bank." *National Geographic*, July 1996, 90–105. • Cockburn, Alexander. "Beat the Devil: Imperial Addictions." *Nation*, August 3, 1985, 70–71. • Jones, Bart. "Modern Day Pirates?" *Hannibal Post-Courier,* June 27, 1998. • Pickford, Nigel. *The Atlas of Ship Wrecks & Treasure*. New York: Dorling Kindersley, 1994. • Sandz, Victoria. *Encyclopedia of Western Atlantic Shipwrecks and Sunken Treasure*. Jefferson, N.C.: McFarland, 2001. • Schemo, Diana Jean. "Recovery of Spanish

Galleon off Ecuador's Coast Raises Controversy and Romance." *New York Times,* April 14, 1997. • "Treasure Hunter Who Went for the Gold." *U.S. News & World Report,* August 5, 1985, 13. • Velazquez, José. "Salvagers Recover Thousands of Coins from Galleon Sunk off Ecuador." *News Times,* April 4, 1997.

Caradosso

A master medalist, gem carver, and jewelry appraiser, Christoforo Ambrogio Foppa, known as Caradosso, established his reputation for High Renaissance coin art with the portrait coin of Ludovico "il Moro" Sforza, Duke of Milan. Born in Mondonico (or Pavia) around 1442, the sculptor learned gold working from his father, goldsmith Gian Maffeo Foppa. He followed his father into the duke's service in 1480 as court goldsmith and designer and became the duke's personal jeweler. Caradosso also served King Matthias I Corvinus of Hungary and traveled Italy on buying trips for members of the Milanese court. After a decline in the duke's finances in 1500, Caradosso served wealthy families in Lombardy and Mantua, particularly Isabella d'Este, a purveyor of art.

Caradosso's artistry influenced Florentine sculptor Benvenuto Cellini, notably, a commemorative medal featuring Bramante's design of St. Peter's Basilica, which Caradosso struck in 1506. Carodosso was a founding member of the Universitá degli Oretici, a guild of goldsmiths formed in 1509. Later in his career, he worked for two art-loving popes, Julius II and Leo X. For a magnificent papal miter, Caradosso earned 200,000 *ducats*. In addition, he sculpted surfaces of the sacristy of San Satir as well as clasps, badges, inkwells, croziers, reliquaries, pendants, commemorative coins, and portrait medals picturing the magnates of the High Italian Renaissance — Francesco Sforza, Donato Bramante, Pope Julius II, and Gian Giacomo Trivulzio.

SOURCES: Clain-Stefanelli, Elvira, and Vladimir Clain-Stefanelli. *The Beauty and Lore of Coins, Currency, and Medals.* Croton-on-Hudson, N.Y.: Riverwood Publishers, 1974. • Jansen, H. W., and Anthony F. Janson. *History of Art.* New York: Harry N. Abrams, Incorporated, 1997. • *New Catholic Encyclopedia.* San Francisco: Catholic University of America, 1967. • Turner, Jane Shoaf. *Grove Dictionary of Art.* New York: St. Martin's Press, 2000.

Carausius

After a long hiatus under Roman domination, a resurgence of British mintage occurred under Marcus Aurelius Mausaeus Carausius, a Roman naval pilot born in Menapia, Belgae, who headquartered in Bononia (Boulogne) and established an independent British state. Under co-emperors Diocletian and Maximian, he commanded the *Classis Britannica* (channel fleet), a North Sea flotilla of marauders along Spain and Gaul assigned to seize loot from Frankish and Saxon pirates. He engineered a method of enriching himself by letting the pirates fill their coffers with coins before intercepting them and confiscating their stolen goods.

Outlawed by Maximian as a buccaneer chief, Carausius retreated to Britain. Late in A.D. 286, he proclaimed himself the Augustus and commandeered trade. Grudgingly legitimized around A.D. 290, he coined copper, silvered bronze, silver, and gold at Londinium and at a second English site, probably Camulodunum (Colchester), Clausentum (Bitterne), or Corinium (Cirencester), as well as in Gaul at Rouen, where he had extended his power. Seeking credibility at home and in Rome during a low in imperial minting, Carausius melted down his plunder for coins, an age-old propaganda device that worked well in Britannia. Among the first pieces he commissioned was a radiate bronze piece suggesting the dawn of a new day.

On new gold and silver specie, Carausius highhandedly declared himself "Restorer of the Romans" and inscribed "*Pax Aug*" ("Imperial Peace") and lofty lines from the *Aeneid* (ca. 30 B.C.) of Virgil, epicist of the Emperor Augustus. Carausius authorized a trio of imperial profiles and the inscription "*Carausius et Fratres Sui*" ("Carausius and His Brothers"), implying a cozy triumvirate with Diocletian and Maximian. Carausius's portrait bust appeared on a double *denarius* with crown and laurel wreath and a satyr on the reverse; one *antoninianus* found in Hampshire bears the abbreviation "*Imp Carausius Tr Pf Aug*" ("Emperor Carausius Tribune Pontifex Augustus").

Carausius used coins for self-ennoblement, as demonstrated by the legend "*Expectate Veni*" ("Come, Awaited One"). He maintained his hold of the English Channel and the southeastern shore of England via a crack troop until his murder in 293 by Caius Allectus, his minister and second in command. Until Allectus died in battle in 296, he continued coin production, overstamping his name on the coins that Carausius had styled. Among his issue was a bronze *quinarius*.

SOURCES: Bédoyère, Guy de la, "Carausius, Rebel Emperor of Roman Britain," *The Numismatic Chronicle*, 1998, 79–88. • Cribb, Joe. *Money*. Toronto: Stoddart, 1990. • Cribb, Joe, Barrie Cook, and Ian Carradice. *The Coin Atlas*. London: Little, Brown and Co., 1999. • "Mausaeus Carausius." http://www.roman-empire.net/decline/carausius-index.html. • Noot, Arthur E. "Carausius Carved an Empire from within an Empire." *The Celator*, February 1996.

Catherine II

Russia's greatest female monarch, Catherine II, also called Catherine the Great, applied intelligence and a keen appreciation for economy to the advancement of the state. The daughter of Johanna Elisabeth of Holstein-Gottorp and Christian August, Prince of Anholt-Zerbst, Catherine was born April 21, 1729, in Stettin, Prussia. She received tutoring in French and German, history, religion, and music, and set her sights on the imperial crown at age fifteen during her first visit to Russia.

To marry Grand Duke Peter, Catherine had to renounce the Lutheran faith, convert to Russian Orthodoxy, and change her name to Yekaterina Alexeyevna, all in the pursuit of power. Likewise negotiable was her relationship with her husband, who became Emperor Peter III. He reputedly fathered Anne and Paul, but otherwise maintained a sham domestic relationship. When he insulted her publicly and began to plot a divorce, she made up her mind, "Either I die, or I begin to rule" (Pavlenko 1996).

Well educated and politically savvy from girlhood, in 1761, Catherine came to power at age 33 and ruled for about that many years. Crucial to her plan for the Russian Empire was a thorough modernization, which included a stronger bureaucracy and emulation of Western ideals. A wide knowledge of the writings of Plutarch, Tacitus, Machiavelli, Diderot, Montesquieu, and Voltaire made her an enlightened despot, but it was her attention to Russian customs and expectations that endeared her to the people. Unlike her husband, who belittled the nation, she solidifed a following. Bolstered by a faithful army and the support of Gregory Orlov, her paramour, she toppled her husband in 1762 and kept him under arrest until his death in a struggle with palace guards. In their last bitter confrontations, he warned, "She will squeeze you like a lemon and then she will throw you away" (Madariaga 2001).

Left to rule alone, Catherine, emulating the reign of Henri IV of France, wisely appeased the nobility, controlled the Russian military, secularized the church, and opposed serfdom. On the advice of Count Nikita Panin, she initiated reforms to rid Russia of feudal laws and the practice of torture. In addition to equalizing citizen rights in the style of the English Magna Carta of 1215, she placed a legislative commission in charge of updating statutes. Ultimately, her patience ran out and she dismissed the inept commissioners who failed to take seriously her intent to put the nation on a par with Western European states.

Catherine adopted from British economist Adam Smith and enlightened view on trade and customs. In 1766, she set up a new coinage and encouraged a free flow of European monies by welcoming outsiders to settle in Russia. To fund war with Turkey and subsequent engagements in Persia, Poland, and Sweden, she introduced inconvertible paper money in 1768 with the creation of the *rouble-assignat*. At the Sestoretsk arms factory, in

1770, she minted thick, broad-rimmed copper *rubles* intended to supplant flimsy paper bills. Barren of a royal portrait, the face featured a laurel circlet and "ruble money" in cyrillic; the reverse pictured the double-headed Russian eagle.

In 1776, Catherine founded a Siberian mint and staffed and equipped it from the royal coinworks at Ekaterinburg. The *kopeks* she produced boosted trade to further the League of Armed Neutrality, an anti–British alliance she founded in support of the American colonists during their revolt against England. On the obverse of the one-*kopek* piece, she placed an ornate monogram topped with a crown. The reverse pictured the ermine, a slender, unassuming animal whose pelts undergirded the Russian economy.

In alliance with Poland, Catherine won a war against the Turks. She cleared the way to the Black Sea for Russian traders, but failed to annex northern Turkey to her empire. When her Baltic fleet entered the Mediterranean in 1769, she exulted to the British ambassador, "We have aroused the sleeping cat, and the cat is going to attack the mice and you will see what you will see, and people will talk about us and nobody expected us to make such a rumpus" (Madariaga 2001).

On the domestic scene, Catherine encouraged the arts and private publication, promoted establishment of the Bolshoi Theatre, and drew up a plan for an ambitious universal education system as well as hospitals and almshouses. In her reign, she managed to open an Academy of Sciences and more schools about the country, but left much of her vision for the nation to subsequent rulers. Still undecided on the matter of a successor — either her son Paul or grandson Alexander — she died on November 6, 1796, of stroke and was buried in St. Petersburg.

SOURCES: Allen, Larry. *Encyclopedia of Money*. New York: Checkmark Books, 2001. • Clain-Stefanelli, Elvira, and Vladimir Clain-Stefanelli. *The Beauty and Lore of Coins, Currency, and Medals*. Croton-on-Hudson, N.Y.: Riverwood Publishers, 1974. • *Encyclopedia of World Biography*. Detroit: Gale Research, 1998. • *Historic World Leaders*. Detroit: Gale Research, 1994. • Madariaga, Isabel de, "Catherine the Great: A Personal View," *History Today*, November 1, 2001. • Pavlenko, Nikolai, "A Woman of Substance," *Russian Life*, November 1996. • Reinfeld, Fred. *Treasury of the World's Coins*. New York: Sterling Publishing, 1953.

Cellini, Benvenuto

A major Florentine artist, sculptor, and goldsmith, Benvenuto Cellini applied classical themes and treatments to numerous Renaissance sculptures and medals. A highly cultured student of the arts, he preserved much of his artistry in an incisive autobiography, *La Vita de Benvenuto Cellini Scritta da Lui Modesimo* (*The Life of Benvenuto Cellini Written by Himself*), which he began at age 58. While at Rome, he struck a gold coin and presented it to Pope Paul III along with the coins produced under previous prelates. On the strength of its beauty and quality, the pope appointed Cellini the master of the mint press at Rome.

The son of an architect and musical instrument maker, Cellini was born on November 3, 1500. In his early teens, he apprenticed in goldsmithing with Antonio di Sandro, called " Marcone," and quickly established a clientele among the elite. He had to interrupt his training around 1516 because of engaging in a public fray. After a period of collaboration with Francesco Castoro in Siena, he settled in Rome, but traveled widely in Italy to Bologna, Naples, Pisa, and Venice before returning home to Florence. Under commission of popes, he crafted jewelry, *objets d'art,* and portrait medals, notably a gold medallion with carved stone showing Leda and the swan, the mythic parents of Helen of Troy, which he executed for Gonfaloniere Gabbrello Cesarino. Cellini also designed artistic shillings, the popular portrait coins of the day, the *testoni*, which the English called testoons and the French *testons*.

For Pope Clement VII, Cellini had served as stamp master and created some of his most impressive small pieces, particularly a button for his cope, a chalice, dies, and coins. In 1530, he struck a commemorative peace medal picturing the bareheaded pope in profile surrounded by the legend "Clemens VII Pont. Max," meaning "Clement VII Pontifex Maximus," the Latin term for chief priest. Cellini also made devotional medals and coins for the papal mint and incised them with his personal cipher. Because of involvement in hostilities against imperial forces, he served a prison sentence in Rome's grim Castel Sant'Angelo. More scrapes with the law over a revenge killing sent Cellini into hiding until he could seek the protection of Pope Paul III. Although the pope had received a complaint that Cellini was wanted for murder, Paul declared his future coiner above the law. Cellini composed personal memoirs on the cutting of steel dies for stamping the coinage of the Vatican and elsewhere.

While Cellini sheltered in Florence in 1535, he worked for Alessandro de' Medici. Cellini stated in his autobiography:

> He gave me orders at once to strike dies for his coinage; and the first I made was a piece of forty soldi, with the Duke's head on one side and San Cosmo and San Damian on the others. This was in silver, and it gave so much satisfaction that the duke did not hesitate to say they were the best pieces of money in Christendom. The same said all Florence and every one who saw them [Hipkiss, 1937].

At age forty, Cellini fled to France and worked for his next protector, Francis I, as designer and decorator of Fontainebleau, an ornate château for which he cast a notable bronze nymph. He carved bas-reliefs, silver vases, and bronze busts of mythic deities of Jupiter, Mars, and Vulcan. Around 1538, he applied the screw press concept to coinage, an innovation originated in 1508 by architect Donato Bramante. In 1543, Cellini molded a salt cellar of Neptune and Ceres, a copy for an earlier model he had made for Cardinal Ippolito d'Este of Ferrara. Cellini's goldsmithing techniques passed to the French and from them to other European moneyers.

Resettled in Florence in 1545, Cellini made modest advances in marble statues. He showed more artistic control with a bronze portrait bust of banker Duke Cosimo de' Medici of Tuscany and a masterly pose featuring the Greek hero Perseus uplifting the gorgon Medusa's head for the Loggia dei Lanzi. The alliance with Cosimo did not last. A difficult friend and colleague, Cellini abandoned earlier relationships and developed a comradeship with Michelangelo.

Cellini gradually abandoned his pugnacious underside and, in 1558, sought entrance into the priesthood. At age 65, he began compiling *Trattato della Scultura* (*Treatise on Sculpture*) (1568) and, the same year, a text on metalwork, *Trattato dell' Oreficeria* (*Treatise on Goldsmithing*). A curious blend of artisan and scrapper, he died on February 13, 1571, in Florence. In 1937, the Museum of Fine Arts in Boston, Massachusetts, announced Dr. George L. Walton's gift to the collection of Cellini's 40 *solidus*, struck in Florence from 1530 to 1537.

***See also lira;* papal coins; portrait coins**

SOURCES: Allen, Larry. *Encyclopedia of Money*. New York: Checkmark Books, 2001. • Clain-Stefanelli, Elvira, and Vladimir Clain-Stefanelli. *The Beauty and Lore of Coins, Currency, and Medals*. Croton-on-Hudson, N.Y.: Riverwood Publishers, 1974. • Cole, Michael. "Cellini's Blood." *Art Bulletin*, June 1999, pp. 215–216. • *Encyclopedia of World Biography*. Detroit: Gale Research, 1998. • Hipkiss, Edwin J. "A Florentine Coin of the Sixteenth Century." *Bulletin of the Museum of Fine Arts*, February 1937. • *Historic World Leaders*. Detroit: Gale Research, 1994. • *International Dictionary of Art and Artists*. Detroit: St. James Press, 1990. • Reinfeld, Fred. *Treasury of the World's Coins*. New York: Sterling Publishing, 1953.

Celtic coins

The Celts of Gaul and Brittany possessed coins centuries before their introduction to Roman coinage. According to Hubert Howe Bancroft's *The Book of the Fair* (1893)—a summary of exhibits at the World's Columbian Exhibition—the author saw

> ring money which to Gaul and Briton served for ornament or cash, often forming his entire worldly wealth. Of these was unearthed in Staffordshire, England, nearly two centuries ago, a specimen containing twenty-six ounces of pure gold, some four feet long, and with all the ductility of the virgin metal [Bancroft 1893, chapter 7].

This Celtic portrait coin minted on the Danube in 200 B.C. depicts a warrior on horseback, a common military motif. (Guy Clark, Ancient Coins and Antiquities, Norfolk, Virginia)

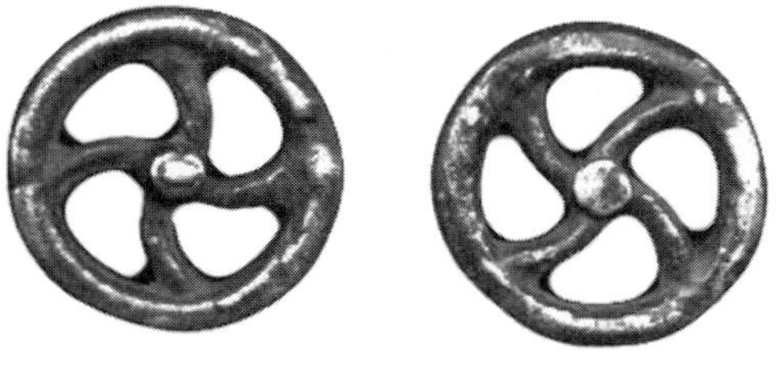

This Celtic coin from 100 B.C. takes the three-dimensional shape of a four-spoked wheel. (Guy Clark, Ancient Coins and Antiquities, Norfolk, Virginia)

Shaped as armbands, bracelets, and torques, these pre-monetary pieces were portable and easily weighed to determine intrinsic worth.

In addition to regular trade in sword blades, lead hatchets, and bronze wheels and axes, called *celts*, some tribes minted bronze, silver, and gold coins as well as tokens made of *potin*, a grayish alloy of copper, lead, zinc, and tin. The earliest, dated after 325 B.C., were struck in Belgica in imitation of the classic Greek designs of Philip II of Macedon's gold *stater* and silver *tetradrachm*. The last center of Celtic money development was Britannia, which maintained independent minting until its conquest by the Romans. Around 150 B.C., Gallo-Belgic coinage of the Ambiani reached Britannia. Extravagant in design, it featured a human profile outlined in quantities of hair, a proportion and style unique to Celtic stylists. Within a half century, British coiners around Kent were producing the first local coins, portrait pieces known as the Thurrock potins.

Celtic production methods employed both professional casting and hammering. Casting, the preferred method in southeast Britannia, began with shaping inter-connected molds to allow melted metal to flow evenly from one indentation to another. When the metal hardened, the caster separated the circles and removed the sprues, the tips that remained from the original branching. Marring quality was the successive use of the same mold, which gradually lost its definition and produced blurred images.

Hammering required individual attention to the shaping of each coin. To standardize value, moneyers placed exact amounts of powdered metal or nuggets in clay molds. After heating and flattening, the flan was ready for striking between concave obverse and reverse dies incised on iron or bronze. Counterfeiters emulated the coins by dipping flans in molten gold or silver or by hammering in place a thin sheet of precious metal to the core. For dies, they pressed coins into malleable metal to impress the pattern.

Common Celtic design motifs included abstract wavy lines, circles and wheels, tridents, grain heads, eagles, boars, bulls, and horses as well as the Roman deities and names of Celtic tribes, e.g., Iceni. The earliest example, struck by the Nervii, featured a horse and wheel. One gold coin minted in 100 B.C. pictured the profile of the sun god Apollo with elaborate hair cascading like ocean waves. Less artful than Continental Celtic coinage, the money produced north of the Thames was commissioned by Addedomaros, a chieftain of the Trinovantes, around 35 B.C., and by Tasciovanus of Verulamium, who added "Tasci Ricon," an abbreviation of his name and title.

To the north in Lincolnshire and Norfolk, the Trinovanti and Catuvellauni began striking unpatterned coins late in the first century B.C. Later pieces featured the horse and boar and abbreviated names of chiefs. To the west in Dorset, the Durotriges and Dobunni continued the focus on horses, which they copied from the Atrebates, a tribe of south-central Britain on the southern banks of the Thames. Historians deduce that Bodvoc or Corio, rulers of the Dobunni, were the first

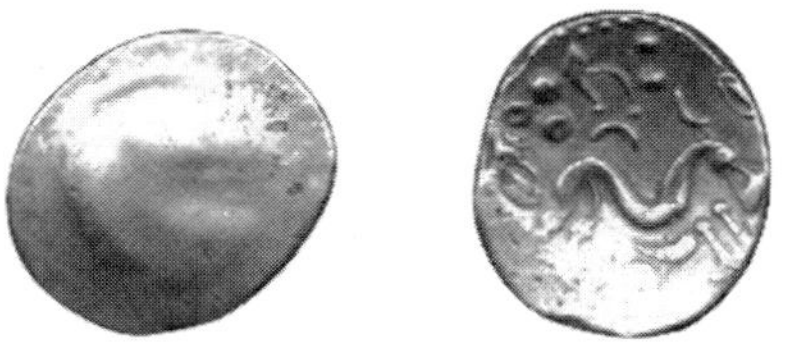

This piece from 60 B.C. displays the Gallo-Belgic style of coinage of the Ambiani, whose artistry influenced the minting styles of Britannia. (Guy Clark, Ancient Coins and Antiquities, Norfolk, Virginia)

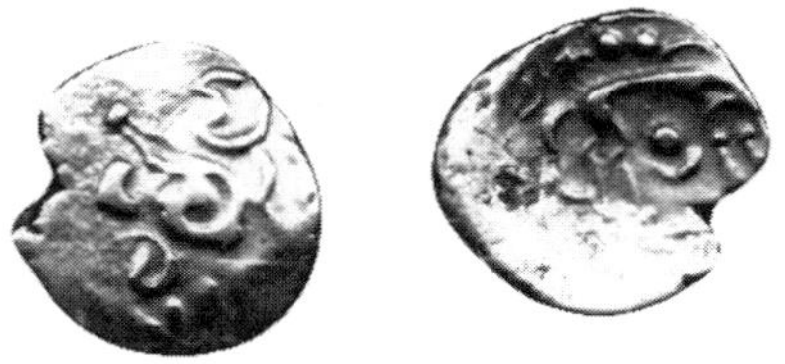

Less artful than Continental celtic coinage, this piece was minted by the Iceni, a tribe of ancient Britain, in 60 B.C., the year that their Queen Boudicca led a revolt against Roman troops. (Guy Clark, Ancient Coins and Antiquities, Norfolk, Virginia)

Celtic chieftains to want their names to appear on coins. Bodvoc added a silhouette on his silver pieces, most likely as a political statement.

According to expert Dr. Philip de Jersey, author of *Coinage in Iron Age Armorica* (1994), around 75 B.C., the Celtic *stater* also served the Armoricans on the Channel Islands. Resembling Coriosolite items made in Northern Gaul, these coins were a blend of a little silver and tin with 75 percent copper. Emulating Greek minting styles of Philip II of Macedon and Alexander the Great, Celtic engravers executed a head with plaits and a mounted horseman on the reverse. One notable portrait coin from 48 B.C. pictures a Gallic chieftain and, on the reverse, a Celtic war chariot with two rearing horses in the heroic style of Roman coinage.

The nature of Celtic coins intrigued the Romans on their first forays into northeastern Europe. On his mission to Britannia, Julius Caesar, Roman commander in chief and author of *Gallic Commentaries* (58 B.C.), gathered details on Celtic currency dating to the Iron Age. Among the coins he witnessed in use were primitive iron bar coins as well as the refined silver *staters* of the maritime tribe of Armorica, which dated to 75 B.C.

With the coming of a sophisticated Roman overlord, Celt's monetary systems were subsumed under the coinage of Rome, although they also used moneys acquired by trade with other Mediterranean nations. Central to Julius Caesar's conquest of Gaul was Vercingetorix, the Celtic chief whom Caesar's 12 legions crushed in 52 B.C., whose portrait appeared on a coin. After presentation in a martial parade through Rome, Vercingetorix survived in prison until his execution in 46 B.C. When the invaders departed Celtic territory, northern traders retained the Roman brass and copper *minissimi* (smallest coins), which were equivalent to their own low-value coins.

A generation later, the Cantii of southeastern England formed *potin* coins of bronze and tin with symbolic shapes, including a bull, the popular figure of worshippers of Mithras, the soldiers' god. In this same general period, Swiss celts living in the Alps stamped bronze coins with spoked wheels front and back. Farther west in France, a hammered bronze coin picturing a bear claw and horse motif circulated with either a silver or gold surface.

In the early first century A.D. north of the Thames River, coins of the Catuvellauni, the most powerful Belgic tribe, pictured a chieftain, Cunobelinus, whom William Shakespeare made the protagonist of the play *Cymbeline* (ca. 1608). Called "*Britannorum Rex*" ("King of the Britons") by Roman biographer Suetonius, Cunobelinus who united the Trinovanti and the Catuvellauni tribes around A.D. 10, ordered gold *staters* stamped at a mint in Camulodunum, the Celtic name for Colchester, Essex, where he emulated Roman portrait coins.

The face of Cunobelinus's coin featured a two-horse war chariot, the method the Celts used to overwhelm an enemy, strike, and dash out of the way of retaliation. Moving toward peaceful subjects, his later coinage placed a grain head near an abbreviation of his name; subsequent coins developed horse motifs. On a gold coin struck after A.D. 10, his moneyers pictured a prancing horse above the word "Cuno," an abbreviation of his name. His innovative reign boosted an agrarian people to economic successs.

Into the second century A.D., payment of Roman occupation forces brought imperial coins into the British Isles. Discoveries of hoards in Scotland established the pervasive use of the silver *denarius* and copper *as* and *sestertius* for military salaries. Celtic traders also dealt in the bronze coinage of Hadrian and Antoninus Pius, two of the "good emperors," who financed the structure of walls sealing off the island nation's northern frontier. In honor of the engineering feat, coins circulating primarily in Celtic England bore images of the walls with the allegorical image of Britannia sitting on rocks.

Local production of Roman coins under the usurpers Carausius and Allectus in the last decades of the third century A.D. ended the necessity for hauling payloads overland from Roman mints. At a Londinium coinsmithy and one unidentified location, coins carried letters indicating the usurpers' mintage in Britain. After Constantius I overthrew Allectus in A.D. 296, the mints remained in operation and reverted to producing the standard coin of the Roman Empire.

Coins figure in Celtic art in depictions of divinities. Sculptors chiseled images of the *genii cucullati* ("hooded spirits") on reliefs adorning the Romano-Celtic sanctuary at Wabelsdorf, Austria. In stone bas-relief, large and small spirits, each wearing a *cucullus* ("hood"), appear either alone or in company. They carry scrolls, eggs, or sacks of coins, which symbolize both fertility and wealth. Another Celtic deity, the Rosmerta, an associate of Mercury, the god of commerce, exuded confidence as the great provider. She represented prosperity and abundance, symbolized by the cornucopia, *patera* (serving dish), *caduceus* (ceremonial wand), and moneybags fat with coins.

The compilation of a Celtic coin index began in 1960, when metal detectors unearthed historic coins at a rapid rate, boosting such treasure troves as the Snettisham find in Norfolk, East Anglia, in 1948. To catalog these finds, Derek Allen and Sheppard Frere amassed photos and exhaustive data on 8,000 examples housed in British museums. In the 1980s, author Barry Cunliffe, professor of European archaeology and lecturer in Celtic studies at Oxford, superintended their catalog, which Dr. Philip de Jersey of the Institute of Archaeology at Oxford University, placed on electronic database in 1992. Completing a historic overview was the addition of photographs, which began four years later.

***See also* Carausius; potin; ring and bullet money.**

SOURCES: Allen, Larry. *Encyclopedia of Money.* New York: Checkmark Books, 2001. • Bancroft, Hubert Howe. *The Book of the Fair.* Chicago: The Bancroft Company, 1893. • Clain-Stefanelli, Elvira, and Vladimir Clain-Stefanelli. *The Beauty and Lore of Coins, Currency, and Medals.* Croton-on-Hudson, N.Y.: Riverwood Publishers, 1974. • Cribb, Joe. *Money.* Toronto: Stoddart, 1990. • Cribb, Joe, Barrie Cook, and Ian Carradice. *The Coin Atlas.* London: Little, Brown and Co., 1999. • Davies, Glyn. *A History of Money from Ancient Times to the Present Day.* Cardiff: University of Wales Press, 1994. • *Dictionary of Roman Religion.* New York: Facts On File, Inc., 1996. • de Jersey, Philip. *Coinage in Iron Age Armorica.* Oxford: Oxford University Press, 1994. • Einzig, Paul. *Primitive Money.* Oxford: Pergamon Press, 1966. • Head, Barclay V. *Historia Numorum.* Chicago: Argonaut, 1911. • Laing, Lloyd R. *Coins and Archaeology.* New York: Schocken Books, 1969. • Lewis, Brenda Ralph. *Coins & Currency.* New York: Random House, 1993.

Central America

One of the great treasure ships of all time, the U.S. mail steamer *Central America* sank off Cape Hatteras, North Carolina, after foundering in a hurricane on September 11, 1857. The loss was the worst maritime disaster of the 1800s. The 425 who drowned in 8,000 feet of water included U.S. Navy captain William Lewis Herndon, who had managed to lower all but one of the men aboard on ropes to a passing vessel, the *Marine.* With the *Central America* perished hopes of delivering 21 tons of gold dust, nuggets, bars, ingots, and coins from the goldfields of California to New York banks in time to stop the Panic of 1857. Historians link the sinking with the destabilization of the U.S. economy and the nation and the outbreak of the Civil War.

Launched in 1852, the three-masted sidewheeler *Central America* had completed 43 three-week trips from New York to Panama, snaking midway between Cuba and Florida before entering the Atlantic Ocean for the journey north. In all, the mail ship ferried about one-third of the bullion and gold coin issuing from California mines to the East. Passengers were the second most important cargo, with some 410,000 moving west from 1849 to 1860 over the Isthmus of Panama, the quickest and safest route. Fares ranged upward from $150 to $300 for steerage, second-, and first-class passengers. The wealthiest numbered some of the elite travelers to the American West.

The last journey, begun on September 3 at Aspinwall, Panama, transported three tons of bullion, ingots, and privately minted double eagle coins in the safekeeping of the purser for a total worth of $1,595,497.13. Unlisted on the ship's manifest were the money belts, cash boxes, carpetbags, trunks, and secret stashes belonging to individuals who trusted only themselves with their gold. Other items were beyond assessment, notably, a sheaf of sketches and paintings of birds and mammals in the American Southwest by John Woodhouse Audubon, son of naturalist John James Audubon. After departing Havana harbor on September 8, the ship pushed on about 9:25 A.M., straight into the path of a hurricane.

Facing certain destruction and drowning, some passengers abandoned personal treasure to join bucket brigades and bailed out the mailship's listing hull. One selfless father, Alvin Ellis, dipped water while his wife Lynthia and their children, Lillie, Charles, and little Alvin, were being rescued. After high seas extinguished boilers, the *Central America* wallowed at the will of waves and winds. At daylight, the *Ellen* picked up some who bobbed on floating timbers and hatchways. Out of 578 passengers and crew aboard, only 153 escaped.

In 1986, salvor Thomas G. Thompson's Columbus-America Discovery Group located the *Central America* with side-scan sonar. Sonar images of a salt-encrusted tower of double eagle coins, a sprinkling of gold dust, amorphous unassayed nuggets, and ingots stacked tidily on the sea's floor overwhelmed Thompson. Setting out from the *Arctic Discoverer*, the crew maneuvered the remote operated vehicle *Nemo* to the bottom to locate the ship. Gary Kinder's book *Ship of Gold in the Deep Blue Sea* (1998) stated the salvor's exact response:

> The bottom was carpeted with gold. Gold everywhere, like a garden. The more you looked, the more you saw gold growing out of everything, embedded in all the wood and beams.... Some of the bars formed a bridge, all gold bars spanning one area of treasure over here and another area over there, water underneath, and the decks collapsed through on both sides [Kinder 1998, p. 452].

In proof of finder's rights, his team salvaged the ship's bell, a sealed trunk, uncirculated gold pieces, and ingots from the wreckage, which lay too deep to be disturbed by tides or storms. In June 1991, a court of appeals in Richmond, Virginia, awarded a small amount of the treasure to the 35 insurance companies that had settled claims on the lost gold; the rest went to Thompson.

The cache, a time capsule of America's West Coast mining and minting, glinted orange, brown, and yellow through the silt and the rusted remains of the hull. Piled like poker chips, one coin castle of eight columns seemed frozen together. Thompson filmed the scene, covering collapsed circlets, mounds of gold dust, dotted nuggets, and gold bars, which capped the heap. When numismatist James Lamb, coin appraiser for Christie's auction house, examined the trove on its arrival to docks in Wilmington, North Carolina, he appraised them as the finest of their type and age in existence, most with mint luster and no wear.

Scientific observers poured in from Woods Hole, the Smithsonian Institution, the

University of North Carolina, Texas A & M, the Field Museum of Natural History, the U.S. Geological Survey, Oak Ridge National Laboratory, Harvard, Yale, Columbia, the U.S. Navy, and the California Academy of Sciences. Thompson was the subject of articles in the British journal the *Economist* and the *Washington Post* and gave interviews on the *Today Show* and *Prime Time Live*. In 1997, science reporter William Broad summarized the salvage operation in *The Universe Below: Discovering the Secrets of the Deep Sea*. The *Central America*'s treasure, worth a billion dollars, went on public display at the Long Beach Convention Center in California in February 2000.

In November 2001, the auction of a huge ingot from the *Central America*'s trove brought eight million dollars. Called the Eureka from the Greek exclamation "I found it!" the 80-pound bar was the size of a bread loaf. It was the work of assayers Augustus Humbert and John Kellogg, who formed it out of ore from the strikes of California's '49ers. They melted and cast the mass in 1857 and stamped it with a currency value of $17,433.57. The Eureka bar traveled by ship from San Francisco to Panama City to be portaged on a four-hour overland rail trek to the Gulf of Mexico for shipping to New York. A small piece of history, the Eureka symbolized for historians the raw and unrefined quality of life and fortune in the West Coast goldfields.

SOURCES: "America's Lost Treasure: The S. S. *Central America*." http://www.sscentralamerica.com/. • Basbanes, Nicholas A. "Talk about Books 'Ship of Gold' Is Tale of History." *Patriot Ledger*, July 25, 1998. • Kinder, Gary. *Ship of Gold in the Deep Blue Sea*. New York: Atlantic Monthly Press, 1998. • Klare, Normand E. *The Final Voyage of the "Central America," 1857*. Spokane, Wash.: Arthur H. Clark Company, 1992. • Sandz, Victoria. *Encyclopedia of Western Atlantic Shipwrecks and Sunken Treasure*. Jefferson, N.C.: McFarland, 2001. • "Ship of Gold." http://www.shipofgoldinfo.com/. • Steelman, Ben. "Author Strikes 'Gold' with New Book." Wilmington, N.C., *Star-News*, August 8, 1999.

Chinese money

Trade and barter dominated the Chinese commercial transaction from early times in such common commodities as gold ingots, porcelain, rhubarb, silk, cowrie shells, salt cakes, and opium. Early Chinese coins give a glimpse of the beliefs, customs, and interests of the peasantry. They spent fish coins for a curative, the water in which the dead were bathed. At Abor near Tibet, *danki* (ritual bowls) decorated with geometric designs served as ritual presentation gifts. For marketing, shoppers easily strung bronze *chung ch'ien* (clapperless bells), a charming folk cash, on thongs for hands-free transportation. In Tibet, a variant, the *deogonta* bell, was an ornate shape with pierced handle.

Around 1000 B.C., a common exchange medium was leather money made from one-foot squares of white stag pelts and worth 40,000 *cash*, a standard metal coin used for small change. Mintmasters replaced the crude hide rectangles with bronze and copper coins. The metal circlets gave the state control over currency and greater protection from counterfeiting. Unlike the coins of Greece, Rome, Persia, India, and Islamic strongholds that pictured monarchs, religious symbols, and pious mottoes, these practical trade moneys were plain, but functional. Only the temple coins distributed by Buddhist and Taoist priests served religious purposes, including amulet coins inscribed with signs of the zodiac for bearers to wear as good-luck medallions and talismans. Another popular coin image, the peach, was an emblem of long life.

Coin designers inscribed different denominations, which they shaped to resemble cowries, hoes, and *huo-pu* (shovels). One widely accepted shape, *tao* (knives), circulated from merchant guilds throughout the state of Ch'i in the Yen principality, which reached north toward Mongolia. The bladed shape may have derived from the bronze knives used like currency by traders from the Indian Ocean who settled at Shantung after 670 B.C. Research corroborated the history of bladed shapes as "Chinese knife money, pieces of razor-shaped iron, six inches long, current in the first century of the Christian era, before which date knives were actually used as money" (Bancroft). Because of the fragility and artistry of Chinese shell and tool coins, these bronze shapes were useful only for their abstract value as money.

Like later wheel coins, knife and spade money contained round or square piercing for stringing. The maker of the spade coin struck in the state of Liang in the Chou Dynasty from 362 to 344 B.C. stated the value in *lieh* and *chin*, different denominations issued in two areas. The shape recurred in Persia during the 1500s, when the *larin* coin, twisted from silver wire, replicated the long blade, angled handle, and punctured end of China's knife money. The long bladed shapes gradually receded until only the ring in the handle survived.

In the seventh century B.C., mints also produced ingots and *yüan* ("wheels"), round *cash* coins with square holes in the center for stringing on cords. During minting, the coiner could align ring money on a dowel and file edges into a standard shape. Typical of square-holed disks are the Tang dynasty's round coins from A.D. 621 cast with Chinese characters marking its four quadrants and the coins from the state of Wei struck in Yüan City late in the Chou Dynasty from 250 to 221 B.C. Because the coins had no intrinsic value, they could be counted rather than weighed on a scale like gold nuggets. Because of their convenience, they remained in use until 1912. They influenced the Korean treasury's issuance of *chon*, round coinage with square holes or enameled designs at center that imitated almost exactly the shape of the rim and square hole in the Chinese coins and the placement of four characters marking each quadrant.

In 221 B.C., the innovative emperor Ch'in Shihuangdi (also Qin Shiuangdi or Huang-ti) raised the Great Wall of China against Mongol insurgents. His metrologists established uniform weights and measures for precious metals based on human body parts:

Chinese Measure	*Current Equivalent*
shih or tan	132 pounds
chih	9.8 inches
chang	9.8 feet

To advance trade and commerce further, the emperor replaced the awkward spade and knife coins with round pieces. For the convenience of ordinary citizens, he commissioned small copper change, the *pan liang*.

From A.D. 7 to 14, Hsin Wang Mang, the power behind puppet emperor P'ing Ti, produced round as well as knife and spade money during four coinage reforms. Within six centuries of Asian trade, eastern Chinese coins in silver and bronze were plentiful as far west as Khotan north of Kashmir. The wide variety of punch and stamped coins indicates a healthy commerce in the interior as well as sophistication with banking and commerce.

By the 1000s, larger transactions required more complex coinage, including the *sycee*, thick uniface ingots shaped like boats or shoes and weighing as much as 3,000 grams each. To make them, coiners filled a mold with melted silver, then struck only the top surface with a square die. The chunky coins were still in production in 1911. During the Northern Sung Dynasty, the round ten-*cash* coins of Hui Tsung, who ruled from 1101 to 1125, were easily copied for their simple arrangement of four pictographs around a square hole. In the 1800s, this distinctive round coin with wide solid rim and square hole at center evolved into elaborate silver good luck pieces.

Metal coinage attested to the monetary sophistication and technological advancement of East Asians. In the 1100s, Tibetans living far from eastern Chinese culture used thin bamboo strips in lieu of coins. To the east, the Chien Lung dynasty made small change from bamboo sticks, which were common markers for gamblers.

In the 13th century, West conquered East. The successful sweep of Mongol warlord Kublai Khan's armies over China resulted in the Yüan dynasty, begun in 1280. When Marco Polo arrived with his brother Niccolò in 1275, he observed shoppers using paper bills, which he called "flying money" in his journal, *The Travels of Marco Polo* (1299). The downfall of Mongol control in 1368 restored China to its cultural roots. Because of a resurgence of national concerns, during the reign of the first post–Mongol emperor Hung-wu, moneyers of the Ming dynasty issued a one-*kwan* paper note to replace the badly inflated paper "flying money" printed by the khans. In relief at the departure of the bellicose Mongols, mintmasters stamped new coinage with mottoes extolling serenity.

The expansionist emperor Kangxi (or K'ang-hsi), who annexed parts of Russia, Tibet, and Outer Mongolia to China after his enthroning in 1661, ordered a coin series with mythic healing properties. Laced vertically to a wood hilt and bearing the characters for well-being and wealth, the metal circlets formed a symbolic sword shape. Peasants valued the symbolic weapon as a dispeller of illness, evil spirits, and demons when held over the bed of an invalid. Another protective token, the exorcism charm, mimicked a minted coin, but displayed images and words driving off fever.

In the mid–1700s during the Ching Dynasty, Chinese coiners designed oval, cup-shaped pieces called "boat money." Unlike the thin cup-shaped scyphate coin of the Byzantine era, the Chinese version was flat on one side and as thick as an ingot. Produced until 1911, the heavy, scooped-out pieces bore a square stamp at center marked with Chinese characters. Boat money circulated until 1933, when Chiang Kai-Shek, head of the Nationalist government in China from 1928 to 1949, demonetized the economy and modernized specie. Coinsmithies melted down most of the boat coins for flat coins or other silver products.

The growth of modern Chinese currency set the Asian standard in Hong Kong, Japan, Korea, Macao, Mongolia, Singapore, Taiwan, and Vietnam. In the 1800s, the weight of heavy coins caused local bankers in Shanghai to issue sticks of bamboo money as Tibetans had done in the twelfth century. In Kiangsu and Chekiang, merchants and moneyers used the sticks during coin shortages.

In the final years of the Ch'ing dynasty, China updated obsolete coinage in 1889 with an advanced minting operation at Canton and additional branch mints at twelve provincial sites. Generating decimal-based dollars and small change in five-, ten-, 20-, and 50-cent gradations, designers added English legends, but retained the imperial image of the flying dragon on paper dollars. Commemorating the Chinese Revolution of 1911 were silver pieces picturing a spare likeness of Dr. Sun Yat-sen, father of the Chinese republic. Sixteen years later, Chinese moneyers commissioned the Austrian mint to produce a portrait piece, which backed the founder's likeness with an appropriate bas-relief of his tomb at Nanking.

In this same era, Chinese tea blocks, a stackable commodity compressed into bricks, sufficed for currency in the hinterlands. The blocks circulated as far from the mainland as Burma, Mongolia, Russia, and Tibet and served as a monetary standard. According to Hubert Howe Bancroft's *The Book of the Fair* (1893), a summary of exhibits at the World's Columbian Exhibition, the Chinese as far north as Siberia used bricks of tea as a medium of exchange and a standard by which the government regulated the price of camels, sheep, bullocks, and other commodities.

Traveler Henri D'Orleans Price, author of *From Tonkin to India* (1898), observed tea bricks weighing from 2.5 to five pounds. They were appropriate payment for daily market purchases, livestock, pipes and tobacco, even soldiers' pay and a new house. Formation of tea into blocks required the gluing of tea leaves and herbs with the blood of bullocks. Although tea graders kept the best quality leaves for consumption and jettisoned the worst for bricks, owners of the blocks could shred them to mix with rye meal, sheep fat, and salt to steep as a hearty beverage.

When Marxism swept eastern Asia, the Chinese Communists realized the value of currency as a vehicle for propaganda. In 1967, during a devaluation of the pound, they promoted social unrest in the British colony of Hong Kong by printing inflammatory, anti-government mottoes on paper notes. One paper bill discredited the English by caricaturing them as a buccaneer. Marxist messages urged a Communist brotherhood to throw off British overlords. As they planned, the slogans charging greed, imperialism, theft, and deception churned up anti–British feeling.

See also **Japanese money; leather and hide money; money laundering; paper money; salt money; spirit money; world money; Wu-Ti.**

SOURCES: Allen, Larry. *Encyclopedia of Money.* New York: Checkmark Books, 2001. • Angell, Norman. *The Story of Money.* Garden City, N.Y.: Garden City Publishing, 1929. • Bancroft, Hubert Howe. *The Book of the Fair.* Chicago: The Bancroft Company, 1893. • Clain-Stefanelli, Elvira, and Vladimir Clain-Stefanelli. *The Beauty and Lore of Coins, Currency, and Medals.* Croton-on-Hudson, N.Y.: Riverwood Publishers, 1974. • Cribb, Joe. *Money.* Toronto: Stoddart, 1990. • Cribb, Joe, Barrie Cook, and Ian Carradice. *The Coin Atlas.* London: Little, Brown and Co., 1999. • Davies, Glyn. *A History of Money from Ancient Times to the Present Day.* Cardiff: University of Wales Press, 1994. • Einzig, Paul. *Primitive Money.* Oxford: Pergamon Press, 1966. • Grierson, Philip. *Numismatics.* London: Oxford University Press, 1975. • Hastings, James, ed. *Encyclopedia of Religion and Ethics.* New York: Charles Scribner's Sons, 1951. • James, Peter, and Nick Thorpe. *Ancient Inventions.* New York: Ballantine, 1994. • Kiernan, Philip. "Alfred Petrie Leaves His Coins to the National Currency Collection." *Canadian Numismatic Association Journal,* October 2001, 389–395. • Lewis, Brenda Ralph. *Coins & Currency.* New York: Random House, 1993. • Opitz, Charles J. *Odd and Curious Money.* Ocala, Fla.: First Impressions, 1986. • "Over 10,000 Han Dynasty Coins Found in Central China." *Xinhua News Agency,* August 23, 2001. • Rust, William, and Amy Cushing. "Buried Cities of Khotan." *Athena Review,* Vol. 3, 2001, 78–88. • Stapleton, Cy. "Small Talk." *Southern Graphics,* January 2001. • Starr, Chester G. *A History of the Ancient World.* New York: Oxford University Press, 1991. • Weatherford, Jack. *The History of Money: From Sandstone to Cyberspace.* Pittsburgh, Pa.: Three Rivers Press, 1998.

Clark, S. M.

The first superintendent of the National Currency Bureau, forerunner of the U.S. Bureau of Engraving and Printing, Spencer M. Clark, an appointee of Abraham Lincoln, stamped his own likeness on a five-cent note. A money innovator, he experimented with dry printing and a range of security documents. According to legend, he took the liberty of placing on the half-dollar note the image of U.S. Treasurer Francis Elias Spinner, a war hero who introduced fractional currency and hired the first female employees at the Treasury Department. During a free-handed selection of portraits, Spinner returned the favor by agreeing to print Clark's picture on the lesser note, but actually misunderstood the request, thinking that the chief engraver was referring to explorer William Clark of the Lewis and Clark expedition.

The uproar in Congress over the engraver's high-handedness resulted in a law, passed on April 7, 1866, banning the likeness of living persons from U.S. currency. The stringent action prohibited the circulation of notes picturing Civil War generals Ulysses S. Grant and William T. Sherman, which were already printed and awaiting release. To replace the five-cent notes, on May 16, 1866, Congress okayed the nickel, the first use of the metal as a monetary standard, and prohibited the printing of paper money valued at less than ten cents.

SOURCES: "The Bureau of Engraving and Printing." http://www.bep.treas.gov/. • "Cecilia Wertheimer, Curator of the Bureau of Engraving and Printing." *Montgomery Coin Club Bulletin,* October 1997. • "The Gift of History." http://www.scripophily.net/mohvalban.html./

cloth and fiber money

Woven mats and fabric in designated lengths have served as money in pre-industrialized countries where coinage and printing of paper bills were unknown. Cloth equated with legal tender in Bohemia, Scandinavia, Borneo, and the Philippines. Icelandic trade and taxation, according to medieval sagas, were standardized in lengths of *wadmal,* a hand-loomed wool fabric, and in silver rings. In the A.D. 960s, Jewish-Arab merchant-traveler Ibrahim ibn Jakub, an ambassador to Prague from Tolosa, Spain, witnessed Bohemians using linen scraps as money for the purchase of precious metal, horses, and slaves. A medieval forerunner of the *Deutschemark,* the *Reilmark* or *Gewandmark* ("cloth coin") of Norway and Germany consisted of strips of cloth valued as currency. During a serious inflationary period following World War I, German treasuries returned to fiber money of burlap, canvas, felt, and silk as well as compressed coal, linoleum, and aluminum foil as well as porcelain coins molded at Meissen.

Fiber money also permeated European exchange with native Americans. During Pontiac's War, from 1763 to 1764, Ottawa Chief Pontiac produced bark token notes consisting of pictures of individual supply items drawn on birch bark strips alongside his personal glyph. By the time that whites were trading regularly with Pacific coast and Pueblo Indians, blankets had superseded bark, wampum, and furs as legal tender. To the north in Vancouver, Canada, the Kwakiutl prized a white wool blanket as a medium of exchange and a unit of value, particularly during extreme forms of gift-giving at potlatch ceremonies, which could bankrupt the host after marathon exchanges lasting for weeks. Because the Canadian government banned potlatches, Indians ceased holding the events, denying tribes a central social institution and medium of displaying status and prestige.

Other examples of cloth money occurred in the Pacific. In the Alu Islands near Sumatra, eyewitness Cheng-lo attested that scraps of cotton fabric were in use as early as 1415. In Indonesia during the 1800s, state looms on Button Island wove *kampuna* (king's head cloth). To differentiate individual specie, sultans demanded that their own currency bear unique designs. On Tikopia, the durability and ease of storage of bark cloth and sinnet, a form of braided cording, increased their value.

In Samoa, the weaving of *ie toga* (artisanal mats) produced a currency that served as money into the 1940s. Woven of native bark by female islanders over a period of months or years, the mats ranged from two to three yards square and acquired worth according to size and fineness of thread. The exchange of mats worth up to 40 shillings each satisfied the need for peace initiatives, guest gifts, bribes for votes, fines, wedding presents, requital of injured parties in a love triangle, and blood money to compensate families of murder victims. The mats also served as legal tender for the purchase of homes, boats, tattooing, and the services of a shaman. Revered as sacred objects or as heirlooms with sentimental value, stores of mats, even though old and worn, passed from parent to child.

In Africa, the use of fiber for money applied natural resources to daily use. In Zambia, calico served consumers engaged in local commerce. Nigerians reserved cloth bundles, raffia mats, and woven *gabanga* (cotton strips), either natural or dyed, for special occasions, particularly ritual gifts marking childbirth, funerals, coming of age, gifts, tribute, court fines, and wartime restitution. Because of variances in weave and width, from four to six inches, the owner could negotiate worth. The seller had additional leverage based on demand for fiber money.

See also **African money; fur money; leather money.**

SOURCES: Allen, Larry. *Encyclopedia of Money*. New York: Checkmark Books, 2001. • Clain-Stefanelli, Elvira. "Donors and Donations: The Smithsonian's National Numismatic Collection." *Perspectives in Numismatics*, 1986. • Cribb, Joe. *Money*. Toronto: Stoddart, 1990. • Davies, Glyn. *A History of Money from Ancient Times to the Present Day*. Cardiff: University of Wales Press, 1994. • Durant, Will. *Our Oriental Heritage*. New York: Simon and Schuster, 1942. • Einzig, Paul. *Primitive Money*. Oxford: Pergamon Press, 1966. • Lewis, Brenda Ralph. *Coins & Currency*. New York: Random House, 1993. • Opitz, Charles J. *Odd and Curious Money*. Ocala, Fla.: First Impressions, 1986.

cobs

When Spain's colonial bureaucrats ran mining operations in Bolivia, Colombia, Mexico, and Peru, they produced makeshift Spanish *real* coins called cobs. The silver pieces take their slang name, meaning "end," from the Spanish *cabo de barra* because they were struck from the "end of the bar." From 1556 to 1621 under Philip II and Philip III of Spain, *reales* hastily minted in denominations of pieces of one, pieces of two, pieces of four, and pieces of eight underwrote the cost of a huge army and navy. Their combined power on land and sea enabled Spain to assume ascendancy in the New World and to threaten the economies of their chief rivals, England and Holland. Under Philip IV, the half-*real* cob further simplified commerce by supplying small change.

Cobs were shapeless blobs of high-grade silver that had no standard shape or dimension and only a perfunctorily hammered die stamp. They bore the haphazard mint marks of the Indian slave operation. Processors cut strips of molded silver into crudely flattened planchets, which required placement over a die and topping with a second die for a one-stroke impression. Processing concluded with the assayer's estimation of weight and the clipping of excess silver, leaving a ragged edge and large cracks. Cobs required frequent reweighing to determine if they were full weight or had been shaved or clipped. For their South American provenance and irregularity, they earned from American colonials the slang name "Peruvians." The hand-striking method remained in use until the invention of the weighted screw press, first installed at Mexico City in 1732. Old-style cobs continued to circulate from Bolivia's Potosí mint until 1773.

Identification of cobs is possible from an assessment of the types of crosses incised on the face and the positioning of the lions of Leon opposite the castles of Castile on the Hapsburg shield. Mints at Bogotá, Cartagena, La Plata, Lima, and Potosí applied the *cruz Griega* ("Greek Cross"), a simple right-angle cross with arms of equal length. In 1652, Potosí mintmasters introduced the Jerusalem cross, the Greek cross with bars added across the ends of the four arms. In 1684, the Lima mint also began striking cobs with the Jerusalem cross. The Mexican mint was the only colonial coin operation applying the *cruz Florenzado*, an ornate cross with tripartite detailing at the ends of the arms.

Sizeable treasures in cobs survived on the wrecks of the *Nuestra Senora de Atocha* and sister ship *Santa Margarita* of the Tierra Firme fleet, which sank in a hurricane on a reef 35 miles off Key West, Florida, on September 6, 1622. A lesser find by Kip Wagner in 1959 from the wreckage of a flotilla sunk off Florida in 1715 produced a valuable cache of pieces of eight. Another trove of 140 tons of silver from the *Nuestra Senora de la Pura y Limpia Concepción*, flagship of Admiral Don Juan de Villavicencio, brought cobs to light upon its recovery by salvor Burt Webber in 1978. The ship, wrecked 70 miles off the Dominican Republic in September 1641, carried more Colombian minting and a large number of cobs from the Cartagena, Mexico City, and Potosí operations.

See also Atocha; **colonial coins; Mel Fisher; pieces of eight; Spanish coins.**

SOURCES: "Atocha Dive Expeditions." *Skin Diver*, December 1999, 96. • Bowden, Tracy. "Gleaning Treasure from the Silver Bank." *National Geographic*, July 1996, 90–105. • Jordan, Louis. "The Coins of Colonial and Early America." http://www.coins.nd.edu/ColCoin/ColCoinContents/Introduction.html. • Lewis, Brenda Ralph. *Coins & Currency*. New York: Random House, 1993. • Sandz, Victoria. *Encyclopedia of Western Atlantic Shipwrecks and Sunken Treasure*. Jefferson, N.C.: McFarland, 2001. • Trupp, Philip. "Ancient Shipwrecks Yield Both Prizes and Bitter Conflict." *Smithsonian*, October 1983, 79–89.

cocoa bean money

When European *conquistadores* first arrived in Central America, they found a stable monetary system based on the cocoa bean. Cacao originated on the banks of the Amazon and Orinoco rivers. After 1000 B.C., the Olmec cultivated it as food and a symbol of life. Myth extolled cocoa in creation lore contained in the *Popol Vuh,* the Quichéan scripture composed in the Mayan hierglyphic language of the Sierra Los Cuchematanesa Mountains in north-central Guatemala and written down by historian Diego Reynos, a proselytized Indian, between 1554 and 1558.

From around A.D. 100 throughout Mesoamerica, the Maya and Aztec revered cacao for ritual, food, and currency. Counterfeiters increased their investment in fresh beans by weighting bags of beans with sand and grit. The cocoa-rich stored their hoards of chocolate patties in screw-top stuccoed canisters like pennies in a piggy bank. A tomb at Río Azul, Guatemala, from A.D. 500 contained a cocoa urn etched with its own glyph. After the crowning of Montezuma II in 1502, Central and South Americans sanctified the bitter, foaming *chocólatl* or *cacahuatl* beverage as a stimulant valued for aphrodisiac and healing powers.

Numerous accounts of cocoa bean money reached Europe from the Americas. In the 1400s, the emperor Nazahualcoyotl, who traveled in disguise to observe his subjects in their daily milieu, recognized the extent of poverty. He uplifted the poor by sending royal agents to trade cloth and cocoa beans in depressed markets. When Spanish explorer Hérnan Cortés traveled to Mesoamerica in 1519, he observed the bean-based economy still flourishing along with government restrictions on planting and harvesting to control inflation.

Nearly a half century later, Milanese trader Girolamo Benzoni, author of *Historia del Mondo Nuovo* (*History of the New World*) (1565), wrote of a similar trade in beans in Guatemala. In 1572, Henry Hawks found Aztec Guatemalan shoppers using the beans for purchases of meat, cheese, and bread. Suffolk-born navigator Thomas Cavendish, the third man to sail around the world, reached Aguadulce, Panama, in 1587 and noted that the customs house guarded sacks of cocoa beans valued at 4,000 crowns. An aide to Sir Francis Drake, Francis Petty, concurred with earlier commentary on the use of cocoa beans for money in Central America.

The circulation of minted silver coins did not supplant cocoa beans as money. Even though the beans were bulky, unstackable, and highly perishable, by 1712, Brazilians valued the beans as well as cloves, sugar, and tobacco as currency and paid their soldiers in a set number of beans. In the 1800s, when cocoa beans served Mesoamerican Indians as pocket change worth 1/40 of a silver coin, Nicaraguans estimated the worth of a slave at 100 beans. In Guatemala, where eggs replaced the beans as small change, gifts of cocoa beans among the Chorti retained ritual significance.

***See also* Spanish coins.**

SOURCES: Allen, Larry. *Encyclopedia of Money.* New York: Checkmark Books, 2001. • Andrews, Tamra. *Nectar and Ambrosia: An Encyclopedia of Food in World Mythology.* Santa Barbara, Calif.: ABC-Clio, 2000. • Brothwell, Don and Patricia. *Food in Antiquity: A Survey of the Diet of Early Peoples.* New York: Frederick A. Praeger, 1969. • Coe, Sophie D., and Michael D. Coe. *The True History of Chocolate.* London: Thames & Hudson Ltd., 1996. • Einzig, Paul. *Primitive Money.* Oxford: Pergamon Press, 1966. • "Mexican Cocoa Bean Money." *Money Talks,* 1972. • Opitz, Charles J. *Odd and Curious Money.* Ocala, Fla.: First Impressions, 1986. • Patterson, Lotsee, and Mary Ellen Snodgrass. *Indian Terms of the Americas.* Englewood, Colo.: Libraries Unlimited, 1994. • Römer, Joachim, and Michael Ditter, chief eds. *Culinaria: European Specialties.* Cologne, Ger.: Könemann, 1995. • Romey, Kristin M. "Canned Remains." *Archaeology,* May/June 2001, 25. • Schärer, Martin, and Alexander Fenton, eds. *Food and Material Culture.* East Lothian, Scotland: Tuckwell Press, 1998. • Yzábal, María Dolores, and Shelton Wiseman. *The Mexican Gourmet.* McMahons Point, Australia: Thunder Bay, 1995.

coconut money

In the tropics, the long-lived coconut palm, *Cocos nucifera,* is valuable for its grace and as a source of nutrition, rehydrating fluids, fuel, cooking oil, kitchen canisters, and building and craft material as well as a form of currency. The tree originated in Indo-Malaya and migrated throughout the southern Pacific to South America. Traders brought it to Egypt and the rest of the Mediterranean around A.D. 500, Polynesian immigrants ferried the palm to Kaho'Olawe, the smallest of Hawaii's eight major land masses. For those who planted the palm as an investment, retrieval of the coconuts required climbing the ringed trunks to the feathery fronds while the fruits were green or waiting until they ripened and collecting the tough, fibrous husks that tumbled to the ground and floated on seawater.

On the Nicobar Islands in the Bay of Bengal northwest of Sumatra, inhabitants treasured coconuts as currency as late as the 1950s. The perishable palm fruit suited local merchants, who amassed coconuts in storage courts fenced with palm fronds to keep out foraging pigs. The cumbrous fruit, counted in twenties, paid for a fleet of ships that Chowra islanders sold at Car Nicobar Island for 5,000 score. As of 1896, a Chowran canoe was worth 1,750 score. In 1885, Indian merchants established an exchange rate between coconuts and *rupees* at 500 to one. Within 16 years, the rate had fallen to 100 to one, a ratio that was still viable in 1917.

SOURCES: Allen, Larry. *Encyclopedia of Money.* New York: Checkmark Books, 2001. • Andrews, Tamra. *Nectar and Ambrosia: An Encyclopedia of Food in World Mythology.* Santa Barbara, Calif.: ABC-Clio, 2000. • Brothwell, Don and Patricia. *Food in Antiquity: A Survey of the Diet of Early Peoples.* New York: Frederick A. Praeger, 1969. • Davidson, Alan. *The Oxford Companion to Food.* Oxford: Oxford University Press, 1999. • Doren, Eugene T. "Vegetable Ivory and Other Palm Nuts." *Principes,* Vol. 41, No. 4, 1997. • Frawley-Holler, Janis. "The Coconut Palm." *Islands,* November 2000, 28. • Opitz, Charles J. *Odd and Curious Money.* Ocala, Fla.: First Impressions, 1986. • Schuiling, M., and H. C. Harries. "The Coconut Palm in East Africa." *Principes,* Vol. 38, No. 1, 1994.

coin clipping and shaving

For two millennia, clipping was a common method of stretching the value of coins by striking or shaving off bits of metal for sale and passing off the remaining piece as full value coinage. A less obvious variant on scraping off valuable metal was sweating, the tumbling of coins in a skin pouch to jostle off bits of gold and silver while imitating normal wear. These shady abuses of coins were not easily detected on hammered coins, which lacked the standardization of size and shape found on machine-milled coins of later centuries. Despite a death penalty for defacing legal tender, merchants, loan sharks, and money changers considered the proceeds worth the risk.

After Henry II, the first Plantagenet, came to the English throne in 1154, he minted the short-cross penny, his first coin. Because clipping of silver for melting down into saleable bullion was widespread, his designer replaced the coin with a long-cross penny, with arms extended to the edge to discourage shaving and cutting off metal slivers. The next "Henry," Henry III, crowned in 1216, continued the practice of striking coins with long crosses. In the mid–1300s, Edward III added pious New Testament phrases to the edge to discourage shaving, a scheme that also served Henry VII.

In Florence, pre–Renaissance moneyers producing the first *florin* in 1252 made technologically advanced efforts to defeat coin defacers. Long before machinery milled serrulated edges, the *florin* bore a corrugated rim to display authenticity and full weight. The coins left the mint in sealed, tamper-free leather pouches, which attested to newness and value.

The 17th century produced heavy assaults on coin clipping on several fronts. Oliver Cromwell, the Puritan rebel who ruled the English Commonwealth after the beheading of Charles I in 1649, initiated sweeping changes to coinage. He attempted to end the age-old problem with coin clipping by incising an edge that established that a coin bore full weight and value. His coiners stamped in Latin on the rims, "*Has nisi periturus mihi adimat nemo*" ("Let no one remove these [letters] from me under penalty of death") (Clain and Clain 1974, p. 215). After years among the French, Charles II, on his return to power in 1660, initiated their technologically advanced system of graining, milling, ribbing, or serrulating coin edges produced by machine. In 1662, Charles II installed ingenious coining mills that added to the edges of new money the phrase "*Decus et Tutamen*" ("Ornament and Safeguard"). The edging established at a glance whether coins held their full value. In 1696, an unlikely detective of clipping, physicist and mathematician Sir Isaac Newton, resigned the Lucasian Chair of Mathemat-

The lobed edge of this East Caribbean five-cent piece prevents shaving, a method of filing off bits of metal for sale and passing off the remaining piece as full value coinage.

ics at Cambridge to accept appointment as the warden of the mint at the Tower of London under William III. Within three years, Newton completed a thorough recoinage of old pieces dating to Elizabeth I and remained at his task of halting coin thievery until his death in 1727.

During the colonial era, petty thievery through coin skimming was easy to arrange with Portuguese *moidores*, which circulated widely among world traders, and New World cobs, the sloppily stamped Spanish silver from Bolivia, Mexico, or Peru. Because the amorphous coins lacked a standardized shape and edging, they were not easily comparable unless weighed. The "NE" piece, the first coin minted in the New England colonies, was so simple in design that it also was the target of coin clippers. Clever metalsmiths could blend the clipped or shaved silver with base metals and pass off their alloys as pure silver. To assure full value, the Massachusetts court ordered a counterstamp to establish the true weight, but the ineffective ordinance did not stop further clipping and shaving or debasing with alloys.

The Church of England had its say on the matter of draining worth from the nation's coins. On December 16, 1694, Royal Chaplain William Fleetwood, later bishop of Ely and author of *Chronicon Preciosum: or, An Account of English Money* (1707), delivered a sermon at Guildhall before the lord mayor and aldermen on the subject of coin clipping. Citing as examples of commerce the actions of Abraham as described in Genesis 23, Fleetwood explained that coins stamped with their weight and value provided humanity with a portable trade token that ended dependence on scales to determine worth. He inveighed against thievery and stressed that clipping was not a victimless crime. His text, which justified capital punishment for coin clippers, preceded the government plan to mill coin rims to make them less subject to shaving and clipping.

Fleetwood's harsh condemnation bore fruit in multiple criminal investigations. The members of an English clipping ring, led by John Moore, were hanged on July 12, 1695. A famous purveyor of clipping operations, "King" David Hartley led the Cragg Vale Coiners in skimming gold from coins. After his capture, in 1770, he went to the gallows in York. His clipping equipment remains on display at Hinchcliffe Arms, Cragg Vale, England. In 1772, Thomas Bacchus, who learned clipping and coining from his father, William Bacchus, joined Samuel Roberts in counterfeiting coins from the metal shaved from legal tender. Both men died at Tyburn by hanging.

See also **cobs; English money; Alexander Hamilton; mint mark; Sir Isaac Newton; Patching hoard; scyphate coins.**

SOURCES: Allen, Larry. *Encyclopedia of Money*. New York: Checkmark Books, 2001. • Clain-Stefanelli, Elvira, and Vladimir Clain-Stefanelli. *The Beauty and Lore of Coins, Currency, and Medals*. Croton-on-Hudson, N.Y.: Riverwood Publishers, 1974. • Jordan, Louis, "The Coins of Colonial and Early America," http://www.coins.nd.edu/ColCoin/ColCoinContents/Introduction.html. • Nash, Jay Robert. *Encyclopedia of World Crime*. 6 vols. Wilmette, Ill.: CrimeBooks Inc., 1990. • Reinfeld, Fred. *Treasury of the World's Coins*. New York: Sterling Publishing, 1953. • Sinclair, David. *The Pound*. London: Century Books, 2000. • Weatherford, Jack. *The History of Money: From Sandstone to Cyberspace*. Pittsburgh, Pa.: Three Rivers Press, 1998.

coin collectors

The science of numismatics encompasses the cultural, economic, and political conditions under which coins were minted, a study advanced by such scholars as Petrarch and Thomas Aquinas. The hobby of coin collecting and display, a layperson's entry into numismatics, began in Renaissance Italy. For medieval numismatists, the study of coins and their legends offered glimpses of ancient times, rulers, beliefs, and philosophies. At the end of the Crusades, Europeans touring the eastern Mediterrean perused old buildings, manuscripts, and coins for background material. Private agencies bought antiquities and coins for patrons, religious houses, or governments. Working through consulates or embassies, they inquired into the provenance of their purchases and sometimes petitioned for permission to excavate antique sites to turn up new finds.

During the Italian Renaissance, magnate and merchant banker Cosimo de' Medici, who became Florence's ruler in 1434, treasured classical coinage as art, which he acquired through constant inquiry. Acting as his agents, his son and grandson, Pietro de' Medici and Lorenzo the Magnificent, located new finds for his collection, which grew in beauty, fineness, and monetary value. By 1465, the de' Medici trove contained 503 silver pieces and 100 in gold.

According to historians, to those who could afford collecting as a hobby, the amassing, cataloguing, and display of unique, rare, or artful coins and medals became serious business. Prize collections adorned the homes of the d'Estes near Padua, and added to the wealth of the Farnese and Barberini, the Bavarian emperor Maximilian I, the Hungarian king Matthias I Corvinus, Joachim II of Brandenburg, Frederick II of Saxe-Coburg, and the wealthy art connoisseur Jean, Duc de Berry. The German Hapsburgs considered portrait coins essential additions to a portrait gallery of Holy Roman emperors. France's Sun King, Louis XIV, worked daily over a coin collection. His successor, Louis XV, housed the royal trove in a grand cabinet decorated with coins. In Holland, painter Peter Paul Rubens invested in some 18,000 coins.

In England, Henry IV used coin displays to beautify his home and as a means of instructing his children in history. Diarist Samuel Pepys, a navy official during the restoration of Charles II to the monarchy in 1660, fretted that he could not obtain for his collection a coronation medal of Charles II, whom he saw restored to the English throne. Easing the problem of locating prize pieces were the first coin catalogues, first compiled in the late 17th century.

One astute collector, German financier Hans Jakob Fugger "the Rich" of Augsburg, pursued a methodical style of collection until his death in 1469. The family banker with branches in Innsbruck, Rome, and Vienna, he was skilled at monopolies and ruthless at acquiring his heart's desire as far afield as Britain, Hungary, Portugal, and Spain. He purchased huge arrays of books and art. To locate the best in coins, he commissioned Jacob Strada, a Mantuan antiquary, to purchase rare Italian pieces.

Austrian monarch Francis I, the Holy Roman Emperor from 1700 to 1740, was fanatical about his collection of *Monnoyes en Or* (gold coins) and *Monnoyes en Argent* (silver coins). After the death of his wife in 1780, he commissioned the *Maria-Theresien-Taler* (Maria Theresa *thaler*), one of Europe's most popular and long-lived portrait coins. During the War of the Spanish succession, which ended in 1714, the war with Turkey in 1716, and the War of the Polish Succession, which began in 1733, Francis took his prize coins with him into the field. To organize and protect them, he transported them in a special case.

Confusing collectors were spurious drawings and woodcuts inserted within numismatic handbooks by such phony specialists as Salomon Franck, who claimed to have line drawings of Saxon *thalers*. Hubertus Goltzius surveyed some 950 European collections, but his *Les Images presque de tous les empereurs depuis C. Iulius Caesar iusques a Charles V* (*Nearly all the portraits of the emperors from Gaius Julius Caesar up to Charles V*) (1559) presented as authentic coins the drawings of fictitious Roman specie. Nicolaus Seeländer, coin artist from Erfurt, Germany, perpetrated a similar fraud with *Ten Works on German Coins* (1743), in which he made up concave *pfennigs* that never existed. The work of true aficionados like Louis Jobert of Nuremberg, author of *An Introduction to the Science of Medals and Coins* (1738), and Joseph Hilarius Eckhel, compiler of the comprehensive eight-volume set *Doctrina Nummorum Veterum* (*Knowledge of Ancient Coins*) (1792–1798), helped to clear up mistakes and expose fantasy coins.

New World coin collections date to the early 1790s, when New York's Tammany Society, a Democratic party organization in New York county, began acquiring classic coins. In the 1850s, collecting became a popular U.S. endeavor, resulting in the formation of the American Numismatic Society in 1858 as a forum for coin lore. After the long period of hoarding begun during the Civil War, coin collecting burgeoned in 1876. A second collectors' group, the American Numismatic Association, begun in 1891 and headquartered in Colorado Springs, Colorado, initiated a monthly journal, the *Numismatist*.

Notable American collectors have located prize and rare pieces for historical specialties:

collector	*place*	*specialty*
William S. Appleton	Boston	classical and American coins
Colonel E. H. R. Green	Massachusetts	U.S. quarters
Reed Hawn	Texas	U.S. coins
Josiah K. Lilly, Jr.	Indianapolis	world gold coins
Max Mehl	Texas	U.S. coins
Joseph J. Mickley	Philadelphia	variety
J. P. Morgan	New York	antique Greek coins
Matthew A. Stickney	Boston	tokens

For the public's edification, the Smithsonian Institution in Washington, D.C., acquired the Philadelphia Mint Collection. Known as the National Coin Collection, it features significant additions to U.S. specie.

Encouraging serious students of specie were articles and guidance published in *The American Journal of Numismatics* and *The Coin Collector's Journal*. Students well versed in world medals and coins selected sub-specialties, for example, Bavarian crowns, coins of ancient Greece or Rome, American coins picturing George Washington or Abraham Lincoln, Miss Liberty coins, or English commemoratives and medals. In the 1890s, artist Augustus Heaton, a member of the Philadelphia Sketch Club, added a new twist to collecting with his treatise on mint marks. Currently, the best collections reside at the Cabinet des Médailles of the Bibliothèque Nationale in Paris, London's British Museum, the Staatliche Museen in Berlin, Oxford's Ashmolean Museum, and the Museum of the American Numismatic Society in New York City.

See also **Joseph Hilarius Eckhel; Hubertus Goltzius; numismatics; *pfennig;* Jean Varin.**

SOURCES: Allen, Larry. *Encyclopedia of Money*. New York: Checkmark Books, 2001. • "Aspects de la naissance d'une monnaie nouvelle à la Renaissance." http://www.i-numis.com/europe/articles/moderne/moderne2-fr.html. • Bowers, Q. David. *Adventures with Rare Coins*. Los Angeles: Bowers & Ruddy Galleries, Inc., 1979. • Clain-Stefanelli, Elvira, and Vladimir Clain-Stefanelli. *The Beauty and Lore of Coins, Currency, and Medals*. Croton-on-Hudson, N.Y.: Riverwood Publishers, 1974. • Cribb, Joe. *Money*. Toronto: Stoddart, 1990. • Davies, Glyn. *A History of Money from Ancient Times to the Present Day*. Cardiff: University of Wales Press, 1994. • *Encyclopedia of Art*. New York: McGraw-Hill Book Co., 1968. • Freeman, Anthony. *The Moneyer and the Mint in the Reign of Edward the Confessor*. Oxford: B. A. R. British Series 145, 1985. • Grierson, Philip. *Numismatics*. London: Oxford University Press, 1975. • *Handbook to Life in Ancient Egypt*. New York: Facts On File, Inc., 1998. • Hipkiss, Edwin J. "A Florentine Coin of the Sixteenth Century." *Bulletin of the Museum of Fine Arts*, February 1937. • Pollak, Henry. *Coinage & Conflict*. Clifton, N.J.: Coin & Currency Institute, 2001. • Sardin, Frédérique. "Les légendes en creux fautées sur les tranches des monnaies françaises en or et en argent du XIXe siècle." http://www. amisdufranc.org/articles/varietes/tranches_fautees.html. • Stephen, Sir Leslie, and Sir Sidney Lee, eds. *Dictionary of National Biography*. London: Oxford University Press, 1922. • Van Ryzin, Robert R. *Twisted Tails: Sifted Fact, Fantasy and Fiction from U.S. Coin History*. Iola, Wisc.: Krause Publications, 1995.

coinage

A nation's coins are a people's most immediate and tangible representation of culture, history, and identity. Valid currency ranges from the finger ring-coins of Thailand, copper bar coins of Ceylon, and nested hat-shaped coins and cast tin elephants and crocodiles of Malaysia to the feather coils of the island of Santa Cruz and fringed stag hide and silk scraps in China. The Yap of Micronesia

A naton's coins, like this nationalistic piece minted in Germany in 1975, are a people's most immediate and tangible representation of culture, history, and identity.

developed a form of stone money with their huge wheels of limestone quarried on coral reefs; on the island of Alor, the *moko,* a token shaped like an hourglass, carried the value of 3,000 *rupiahs* while *Piki fe* (pig money), was worth only five *rupiahs* each. Imported from Java by Makassarese traders, the *moko* gained more value after islanders stopped importing them. A more usable coin-like currency, the Aztec cocoa bean, was serving as valuable, easily traded tokens when Europeans first reached Mesoamerica. To govern the monetary structure, finance ministers restricted the planting and cultivation of cacao.

The forerunners of true coinage date to 9,000 B.C. in the neolithic era, when residents of Palestine used plain clay tokens as symbols of value. Located during Dame Kathleen Mary Kenyon's archeological dig in the 1950s, these artifacts were the first of a series of symbolic money found in the Near East. The hollow clay variants called envelopes, which were in use at Susa around 3300 B.C., bore tallies that preceded a written number system or alphabet. As inventories and bookkeeping grew more complex, differentiated symbols quantified cattle, sheep, and grain as well as tools, utensils, and fiberwork.

True coins in the modern sense appeared simultaneously in three locales. In the same period as the rise of the Lydian monetary system, the first in the Middle East, around 600 B.C., the Chinese generated hammered coins from base metal, which rendered them virtually useless and too heavy to carry except for small purchases. Around 595 B.C., metal coins reached Greece from Lydia. About the same time, Indian merchants and shoppers in the Magadha empire used silver bars bent at one end. The government bureaus, banks, or traders who issued them punched each with certification of weight and purity. True silver coins replaced the bent bars around 600 B.C.

The Greeks and Romans of classical times turned coins into works of art. To produce these coins, Greek moneyers at Acarnia, Athens, Corinth, Macedonia, Magna Graecia, and Sicily molded flans for striking into flat disks. Manufacture began with the casting of ball-shaped ingots in sand molds. Coiners then heated individual metal pieces for hammering, trimming, weighing, and evening into rounds for stamping with pattern dies. Greek and Roman minting based coin values on silver with copper serving as a convenient material for small change.

Roman coinage established its own denominations, notably the *aes* or *as, denarius, aureus,* and *sestertius,* and created the base of the word "coin" from *cuneus,* meaning "die or stamp." As Roman territorial governments emulated the mother state with similar bureaucracies, they set up independent mints and coins that circulated wherever trade extended. Because of this multi-faceted global economy, the *argentarius* (money changer) took on major importance to city ports and marketplaces. In the most cosmopolitan, shoppers could change the *obol* for Persian *darics,* Greek *tetradrachms,* or Lydian *staters.*

With the waning of the Roman Empire to the west, Byzantine minting began a separate coinage in A.D. 491, but emulated the self-glorifying portraiture of Roman emperors. Also imitating Roman coinage were the Lombards, Ostrogoths, Vandals, and Visigoths, who maintained the principles of die-stamping, but with less attention to artistry and fine quality. Under the Danelaw of the A.D. 880s, Scandinavians settling East Anglia copied the pennies of Alfred the Great and circulated their own coins. Poorly incised and underweight, they failed in comparison with the York mintmasters, who created more original designs that blended pagan motifs with Christian symbolism.

The English maintained high standards of coinage by confiscating incoming specie at their ports and restriking them. Government officials scrutinized the moneyers at Canterbury and London and punished those who debased coins by shaving, clipping, recasting, or debasing alloys. The demand for coins after A.D. 924 under the rule of Athelstan, the warrior-prince who became *Rex Totius Britannia* ("King of All Britain"), required six facilites at Winchester, seven at Canterbury, and eight in London. Following the Norman takeover in 1066, the numbers increased, with twelve coinsmithies in York and twenty in London.

The first original medieval European coiner was Charlemagne, King of the Franks, who issued a silver *denarius* in A.D. 800. With the stimulus of trans–European banking that accompanied the Crusades, which began in 1095, demand for coins rose significantly as trade increased. Under Henry I, the quality of silver coins rose, then fell from adulterated alloys. Their appearance suffered from consumers hacking into them to determine the quality of their content. On December 25, 1124, the lopping off of right hands among the mint staff at the assize of Winchester resulted in a temporary rise in standards.

Coins came into their own on the Continent in 1252, when Florence led the continent by imitating English coinage. Production of the *florin* and *ducat* attested to the rise of Italian city-states through improved marketing and banking methods. In the mid–15th century, the artistic design of coins drew on the skilled engravings of medalist Benvenuto Cellini, portraitist Antonio "Pisanello" Pisano of Pisa, and Matteo de' Pasti, a Veronese miniaturist who, around 1450, modeled a coin on the likeness of Leon Battista Alberti and, in 1446, captured the feminine grace of Isotta degli Atti. Pisanello's coins profiled the powerful figures of his day — Alfonso V, Lionello d'Este, Sigismondo Malatesta, Niccolò V, Francesco Sforza, and Filippo Visconti. Simultaneously, other powers struck elegant celebratory coins in classic style, notably the silver *gros* issued by Adolph, Bishop of Liège; the stylized lion of Philip le Bon of Burgundy; and the gold *ducat* of Rudolph, Bishop of Utrecht.

Marking coins by place of origin were mint marks, such as the Roman aqueduct stamped at the top of the face of coins from the mint in Segovia, Spain. For Christian IV, King of Denmark and Norway from 1588 to 1648 and founder of Christiana, now Oslo, the establishment of mercantile policy, import duties, and subsidized trading monopolies preceded the updating of coins. Mintage for his two realms required silver pieces in separate designs and languages. Such skilled marking demanded a metalsmith's experience with a tool collection of hammer and mallet, tongs, dies, files, and shears. In 1484, English coinmaster Robert Hart passed to his apprentice just such an array of specialty tools.

Late in the 15th century, inventor Leonardo da Vinci, while working at the papal mint, came to the conclusion that coins had to be perfectly round and finished with a rim. His notebooks delineated a labor-saving method of placing uniform metal plates under a stamping device and winnowing the finished planchets through a sorting sieve. He explained:

> The hollow of the die must be uniformly wider than the lower, but imperceptibly. This cuts the coins perfectly round and the exact thickness, and weight; and saves the man who cuts and weighs, and the man who makes the coins round [Allen 2001, p. 89].

To that end, Leonardo adapted the printing press into a rapid money-stamping drop-hammer machine that standardized the shape and size of each coin. Powered by water, the mill's drive shaft operated seven hammers simultaneously, creating a fierce noise, the standard atmosphere of the coinsmithy.

The 16th and 17th centuries saw the end of hand-hammering and the beginning of coin machines, beginning with horse-powered devices pioneered by French pioneer Eloye Mestrell (also Eloi or Eloy Meystrell or Mestrelle), an engineer who came to work at the English royal mint in 1553. By 1561, his mechanism rolled metals, sliced blank disks uniformly, pressed dies into the surfaces above and below, and inscribed, beaded, or engrained the edges to prevent shaving, clipping, and counterfeiting. After Mestrell fell from favor in 1572 and went to the gallows at Tyburn in 1578 for producing counterfeit coins, the English mint staff gave up the screw press and returned to old-fashioned hand-striking.

The first half of the 17th century was a low point in European coinage. After the onset of the Thirty Years' War in 1618, provoked by religious, dynastic, territorial, and trade rivalries, individual nations combatted inflation with a huge meltdown and recoinage of *thalers* and *ducats*. A flurry of new mint operations accepted water tanks, pipe, even church roofing and the lining of baptismal fonts to turn into money. Mintmasters cranked out base coins of copper, which they bleached white. With a few weeks' use, the coins mellowed into an unsettling coppery red.

A subsequent French transplant to the London operation, Nicholas Briot, a portraitist and skilled mechanic who was once the head engraver at the Paris mint, experimented with screw presses, advanced coinage methods he implemented with the aid of colleague Jean Varin (or Warin), one of Europe's most famous coin artists. Briot took his innovative concepts to England in 1625, where the king's chief engraver, Thomas Rawlins, supervised production of the Oxford crown, most regal coin of the era. After overcoming initial hostility to milled coinage, Briot advanced to chief engraver within three years and worked at the Oxford and York operations. In 1631, in competition with traditional hammered coins, he manufactured silver coins in London and Edinburgh by machine. At the Scottish coronation of Charles I, a contingent of Scottish lords preceded the king and his attendants, who threw to the cheering throngs Briot's medals and coins bearing the king's likeness. The king's agent, William Drummond of Hawthornden, orchestrated displays of largess by sounding trumpets echoed by trumpeters at Edinburgh Castle.

Outstanding in Briot's work was a handsome sixpence featuring the likeness of Charles I, which is preserved in the Tregwynt hoard discovered in Pembrokeshire, Wales, in 1996. Briot's control of the operation ended in 1642 with the overthrow of the monarchy and the installation of the Puritan Commonwealth under Oliver Cromwell. His bureaucrats returned coinage to the hand-made system of old. Conservative in all phases of their operation, they rid coins of Latin mottoes and inscribed such Christian sentiments as "God with Us" and "Faith and Truth I will Bear unto You." The tenuous relationship between England and France affected coinage. With the English out of competition for the most technologically advanced coinage, it was the French who produced the first completely mechanized milled coins in 1645. The Puritans imported engineer Jean-Pierre (or Peter) Blondeau, another expatriate from the Paris mint, to mill silver captured from Spanish galleons.

Undervalued by the hard-handed Commonwealth minting staff, Briot lost heart and returned to Paris, where he remained until the glorious restoration of Charles II to the English throne in 1660. A fan of technology, the king gradually replaced hand-hammering with milling machines. Assisting Briot was Blondeau, his countryman, whom Charles summoned to perfect milled edging and create dies for new coppers, and Flemish silversmiths John, Joseph, Norbert, and Philip Roettiers, members of a family of goldsmiths from Antwerp, assigned in 1662 to cut planchets and mechanize stamping. John Roettiers, a renowned, Paris-trained medallist and chief engraver at the Tower mint, struck a valued medal, the first of the baroque era, and accepted commissions to incise original dies for the American colonies from Richard Holt, who obtained the patent to create tokens.

The result of the synergy at the coinworks was England's first machine-milled pound coin, which profited from the technology introduced by French engineer Jean Castaing, whose roll press also added the edge lettering and devices to early U.S. coins. In

1665, Philip Roettiers incised a new image of a seated Britannia for the halfpenny and other coppers. For James II, John Roettiers sculpted the coronation medal, with the coiner's initial below the inscription, "*Iacobus II D. G. Ang. Sco. Rex*" ("James II by the Grace of God King of England and Scotland"). Roettiers included the legend "*A Militari ad Regiam*" ("From the Military to the Kingdom").

In the late 1700s, mints in undeveloped countries like Burma and Tibet continued to press out precious metals in appropriate weights. The Tibetan mint, opened in 1791 for a two-year operation, issued attractive coins featuring geometric religious designs called mandalas, an element of tantric mysticism. Within a holy space, designers depicted the elements of the universe. The resulting ritual diagrams, used as meditation circles or sacred polygons, symbolized cosmic and spiritual relationships in perfect order. By concentrating on these and other geometric emblems, seekers escaped mortality as they found their way to communion with the divine.

Meanwhile, coins in the Western world ceased to represent the actual value of the metal in their makeup. With the loss of intrinsic value, coins no longer had to be weighed and assessed in banks, changing houses, or mercantile establishments. The flat rate or face value stamped on the coin also simplified evaluation from the more tedious establishment of value based on the fluxuating value of metal.

In France, the end to two-stage coinage presaged more efficiency and standardization for coiners. Swiss inventor and engraver Jean Pierre Droz (also Drost) set up an exhibition at the Paris mint in 1786 to demonstrate how his segmented coin press made Louis XVI *écus*. An improvement on the old press, it held a planchet in a six-part collar to prevent uneven spreading during the single operation that stamped top, bottom, and sides with one blow. Because the machine opened and closed the collar automatically, the blanks could feed and drop without aid from the operator. The show impressed the U.S. ambassador, Thomas Jefferson, and engineer Matthew Boulton.

By the 19th century, gold was the most common standard for monetary systems worldwide, but other forms of currency met particular needs. Some experimentation with platinum in Russia, Africa, and the United States as well as testing of zinc, lead, and aluminum produced insubstantial disks for daily circulation. In the early 1800s, the Imperial Russian-American Company, operating in Siberia, the Aleutian Islands, and Alaska, traded via seal skin money, parchment notes printed at St. Petersburg in green ink on the hide wrappings of fur bales. Briefly, porcelain, compressed fiber, plastic, and blocks of tea leaves served as national monetary units.

During gold strikes, private coinage offered security for raw gold or silver, which could be banked and spent when stamped into legal tender. The convenience of the system spurred trade in such out-of-the-way gold fields as the Yukon and Sutter's Mill, California. In the 1900s, coinage passed from private hands to governments, which set value systems and regulated minting equipment and circulation. At the outbreak of World War I, disruptions in standard metal used for coinage resulted from the redirection of copper from minting to manufacture of shell casings. Without the appropriate metal for their coinsmithies, Danish mints struck coins from iron, Norwegian mints used aluminum and zinc. In the United States, wartime minting returned military scrap metal to peaceful use by recycling copper shell casings into pennies.

In the 1900s, coinage passed from private hands to governments, which set values and symbols, as with the privy marks count on this 25-cent piece from Holland.

In mid century, Malacca on the Malay archipelago, a leading tin producer, simplified the problem of carrying small change by issuing tin coin trees. The coins were made from molten metal poured into a branching mold. A frond of 13 coins attached to the central stem with small connectors. The user could carry a single frond and snap off coins as needed for small change.

Into the 21st century, as paper money gradually supplanted metal for daily commerce, coins and currency continued to make news, notably Europe's creation of the euro as the standard issue for twelve united nations. On the Isle of Man, the striking of an updated one-crown piece in 2001 presented a new reverse to the portrait of Elizabeth II — a whimsical image of Harry Potter, fictional wonderboy of a young adult fantasy series written by J. K. Rowling. Private systems struck commemorative coins, plaques, and medals; gambling casinos created their own tokens as media of exchange within the limited field of related gambling houses. Other coins limited in use included *jetons* or *gettone* for operating pay telephones; tokens for rail, bus, and subway travel; religious medals and communion tokens; and military scrip, used only at military trading centers.

See also **bracteates; Canadian coins; cocoa bean money; counterfeiting; gold standard; Greek coins; Lydian coins; Macedonian coins; John Roettiers; Roman coins; stone money.**

SOURCES: Allen, Larry. *Encyclopedia of Money.* New York: Checkmark Books, 2001. • "Aspects de la naissance d'une monnaie nouvelle à la Renaissance." http://www.i-numis.com/europe/articles/moderne/moderne2-fr.html. • Clain-Stefanelli, Elvira, and Vladimir Clain-Stefanelli. *The Beauty and Lore of Coins, Currency, and Medals.* Croton-on-Hudson, N.Y.: Riverwood Publishers, 1974. • Cribb, Joe. *Money.* Toronto: Stoddart, 1990. • Davies, Glyn. *A History of Money from Ancient Times to the Present Day.* Cardiff: University of Wales Press, 1994. • da Vinci, Leonardo. *The Codex Leicester, Notebook of a Genius.* Sydney, Aust.: Powerhouse Publishing, 2000. • *Encyclopedia of Art.* New York: McGraw-Hill Book Co., 1968. • Freeman, Anthony. *The Moneyer and the Mint in the Reign of Edward the Confessor.* Oxford: B. A. R. British Series 145, 1985. • Grimbley, Shona, ed. *Encyclopedia of the Ancient World.* London: Fitzroy Dearborn, 2000. • Grosvenor, Melville Bell, ed. in chief. *Everyday Life in Bible Times.* Washington, D.C.: National Geographic Society, 1967. • Howatson, M. C., ed. *The Oxford Companion to Classical Literature.* Oxford: Oxford University Press, 1991. • James, Peter, and Nick Thorpe. *Ancient Inventions.* New York: Ballantine, 1994. • Laing, Lloyd R. *Coins and Archaeology.* New York: Schocken Books, 1969. Pollak, Henry. *Coinage & Conflict.* Clifton, N.J.: Coin & Currency Institute, 2001. • Reinfeld, Fred. *Treasury of the World's Coins.* New York: Sterling Publishing, 1953. • Sardin, Frédérique. "Les légendes en creux fautées sur les tranches des monnaies françaises en or et en argent du XIXe siècle." http://www. amisdufranc.org/articles/varietes/tranches_fautees.html. • Snodgrass, Mary Ellen. *Encyclopedia of World Scripture.* Jefferson, N.C.: McFarland, 2001. • Stephen, Sir Leslie, and Sir Sidney Lee, eds. *Dictionary of National Biography.* London: Oxford University Press, 1922. • "The Story of the Sixpence." http://www.24carat.co.uk/sixpencesstory.html. • Taxay, Don. *The U.S. Mint and Coinage.* New York: Arco Publishing, 1966. • Vaughan, Rice. *A Discourse of Coin and Coinage.* London: Th. Dawks, 1675.

coins and currency in art

Art depicts coins and currency as integral elements of human activity. Images of marketing, banking, hoarding, and thieving characterize money as the means to an end as well as an end in itself. Coin art sometimes provides the only source of historical figures and events. In the ancient world, depictions on coins of events, daily commerce, and rulers substantiate surmises about the government and finances of early peoples. One example is the portrait coinage of Marcus Aurelius Mausaeus Carausius, an egotistical Roman naval pilot from the Belgae who, in A.D. 286, forged an independent British state. In imitation of Roman emperors, he pictured himself in glory on gold, silver, and bronze specie. On a double *denarius*, he appears with crown and laurel wreath; on the *antoninianus*, his likeness accompanies his self-styled title "*Imp Carausius Tr Pf Aug*" ("Emperor Carausius Tribune Pontifex Augustus").

In the Middle Ages, anecdotal art depicted religious scenes as well as current events. A 12th-century mural painted at a church in Zwillis, Switzerland, features a dramatic moment in the New Testament — Christ gesturing toward the coins that his disciple Judas received for betraying his master. Two centuries later, manuscript illuminations show monetary security measures by picturing Florentine bankers at work counting handfuls of coins and securing leather moneybags in ironbound chests. Depictions of tellers jotting figures in account books while throngs of customers wait for banking services attest to the importance of currency to a city-state that became the financial heart of the Mediterranean world.

From the late 1490s to mid–1500s, Flemish Calvinist Marinus van Reymerswaele of Antwerp chose themes of ugliness and covetousness for caricatures. He painted *Tax Gatherers*, *The Lawyer's Office*, and *A Banker and His Wife* to epitomize a Dutch proverb claiming that a banker, moneylender, tax collector, and miller were the devil's four evangelists. *Tax Gatherers* examines the gloating of grotesque bureaucrats with deformed souls who delight in squeezing money from peasants. The latter vignette captures the tedium of the moneyer's job in the long, thin fingers holding up a balance beam scale to weigh coins as a test for clipping.

In the mid seventeenth century, Dutch painter, Jan Vermeer of Delft stressed the seedy side of the exchange of coins in *The Procuress* (1656), an anecdotal glimpse of a libidinous rake paying the keeper of a *Bordeeltje* ("brothel") with one hand while groping her breast with the other. Vermeer subtly plays the light gold, coin-colored dress and hood on the madam against dark-figured drapery and an even darker female observer and male companion of the rake, who lift their glasses in a toast to debauchery. Provocative and mercenary, the scene damns the principle figures for their venality and for reducing human sexuality to a cheap financial arrangement. Vermeer derived the composition from common images of the Prodigal Son wasting money on whoring and other pleasures, perhaps building on Dirck van Baburen's *The Procuress*, a painting that Vermeer's mother-in-law owned. Vermeer inserted van Baburen's picture as a backdrop to two seemingly innocent poses, *The Concert* (ca. 1665) and *Lady Seated at the Virginals* (1673).

Dutch painters maintained coins as evidence of wickedness and wasted lives. *The Miser's Dream*, an unsigned Flemish oil painting of the 1600s, depicts a table heaped with beautifully worked containers in precious metals, a stack of IOUs, rings, and gold *florins* heaped in jars. Alongside the hoard, a scrap shows the miser's tally of his amassed wealth. An inset picture of the man on his deathbed presents his final moments facing two winged demons and a third pointing to the heaped table.

For the Emperor Maximilian's autobiographical novel *Weisskunig* (*White Knight*) (ca. 1506), German painter Hans Burgkmaier (or Burgkmair) of Augsburg engraved a woodcut showing a workshop view of coinsmiths turning out baskets of specie. The tutorial pictures a mintmaster taking charge of a balance-beam scale suspended from the wall. In a wall furnace, beakers of bullion melt at high flame. In the foreground, a craftsman trims planchets that another staff member strikes from sheet metal on an anvil. To the right, the coiner places a die over the planchets one by one as the minter's boy hands them to him. As Burgkmaier indicates, the organization of the 16th-century mint was neat and well supervised, but the operation was tediously slow.

As coin technology and banking fueled the financial dealings of the Renaissance, the jobs of metalsmith and money changer appeared more frequently as a subject of art. In 1531, an unsigned anecdotal woodcut pictured a German peasant soliciting a loan from a Jewish moneylender. Picturing the client armed with a knife standing with hand outstretched over the counter, the scenario contrasts the threat of the virile young bargainer against the passivity of an aged, bearded broker. In a menacing atmosphere, the moneylender sits at a tabbed abacus and stretches his right hand toward coins, which he appears to be counting. In 1582, a stained-glass window at Strasbourg presented a coinsmithy similar to that in Burgkmaier's painting. In orderly fashion, laborers hammered flat a sheet of metal, cut blanks with shears, filed and hammered them to a suitable thickness, and positioned each piece over a fixed die for striking with a handheld mobile die.

In the early 20th century, Frank Stewart commissioned New York artist John Ward Dunsmore, famed for his depictions of historic scenarios, to paint *Inspection of the First Coins of the First United States Mint*. In a horizontal grouping, Dunsmore pictured Secretary of the Treasury Alexander Hamilton and Elizabeth Schuyler Hamilton, first secretary of state and U.S. Mint supervisor Thomas Jefferson, engineer David Rittenhouse, General George Washington and Martha Washington, presidential secretary Tobias Lear, chief coin designer Henry Voigt, and mint officer Adam Eckfeldt inspecting the first coins, reputedly struck from dies engraved by British medalist William Russell Birch and struck by Eckfeldt and machinist John Harper. The scene pictures Eckfeldt turning the crank on a screw press while six standing figures examine a tray of new half-*dismes*. The first lady holds glasses to her eyes to get a better view. The period fashions and grooming portray the principal figures as refined and serious about the business of creating coins for U.S. citizens, who had suffered shortages of small change throughout the colonial period.

See also **Greek coins; paper money; Royal Exchange; South Sea Bubble.**

SOURCES: Ausubel, Nathan. *The Book of Jewish Knowledge*. New York: Crown, 1964. • Clain-Stefanelli, Elvira, and Vladimir Clain-Stefanelli. *The Beauty and Lore of Coins, Currency, and Medals*. Croton-on-Hudson, N.Y.: Riverwood Publishers, 1974. • Crain, Stephen A. "Half Dimes Inspection of the First Coins of the United States Mint." *John Reich Journal*, January 1907. • Cribb, Joe. *Money*. Toronto: Stoddart, 1990. • Cribb, Joe, Barrie Cook, and Ian Carradice. *The Coin Atlas*. London: Little, Brown and Co., 1999. • Grierson, Philip. *Numismatics*. London: Oxford University Press, 1975. • Van Ryzin, Robert R. *Twisted Tails: Sifted Fact, Fantasy and Fiction from U.S. Coin History*. Iola, Wisc.: Krause Publications, 1995.

coins and currency in drama and film

Stage and screen often enhance the abstract concepts of bribery, piracy, and miserliness by picturing characters coveting, handling, counting, or distributing money. Productions of William Shakespeare's *The Merchant of Venice* (ca. 1596) transform the image of the crabbed Jewish moneylender Shylock from realism into caricature by enhancing his appearance in Act I, Scene iii with lurid strokings of *ducats*, bagged and naked, winking in the footlights. The extremes of miserliness draw on classic examples in Greek and Roman drama, notably, Plautus's pinchpenny Euclio in *Aulularia* (*The Pot of Gold*) (ca. 200 B.C.), a seedy, money-obsessed no-good reprised in the *commedia dell' arte* and Italian opera. Shakespeare's original name for his creepy miser may derive from *shallach*, Hebrew for "cormorant," a raspy-voiced scavenger bird known for greed in devouring the flesh of fish. By extension, "fish" conjures the Greek fish symbol of Christ, a common bakery and confectionary shape in Renaissance England.

To explain the Jewish philosophy of usury, Shylock instructs Antonio on the story in Genesis of Jacob, the clever Bible patriarch who outsmarted his father-in-law Laban by breeding multi-colored lambs. Cautious of his inventory, Shylock nervously remarks, "I will go and purse the ducats straight, see to my house, left in the fearful guard of an unthrifty knave, and presently I'll be with you" (ll. 173–176).

As tension mounts, in Act III, Scene i, Shylock pours out his concerns as well as outrage at indignities heaped on his race by Christians. He complains of Antonio:

> He hath disgraced me and hind'red me half a million, laughed at my losses, mocked at my gains, scorned my nation, thwarted my bargains, cooled my friends, heated mine enemies — and what's his reason? I am a Jew [ll. 54–58].

Brimming with hostility at centuries of anti–Semitism, Shylock quivers for a chance at revenge. When he encounters Antonio in Act III, Scene iii, he intends to call in the loan. Shylock sputters, "I'll not be made a soft and dull-eyed fool, to shake the head, relent, and sigh, and yield to Christian Intercessors ... I will have my bond." (ll. 14–17)

The threat to wealth is the mechanism by which the play brings Shylock to heel. When the tables turn in Act IV and Portia outwits him, the crafty moneylender is so distraught at the thought of confiscation of half his wealth that he cries disconsolately, "You take my life when you do take the means whereby I live" (IV, i, 375–376). Notable actors who have reveled in the meaty stage stereotype of Shylock include Edmund Kean, Edwin Booth, John Gielgud, and Laurence Olivier, who starred in the 1973 film version opposite his wife, Joan Plowright.

For human reasons, money on stage and in film pairs naturally with piracy, criminal acts, and fights to the death. The classic Robert Louis Stevenson adventure tale *Treasure Island* (1883) first appeared on screen in 1934 with Wallace Beery playing the old salt Long John Silver against the vulnerability and enthusiasm of the barkeep's boy Jim Hawkins, played by Jackie Cooper. In subsequent presentations of Silver — acted by Jack Hawkins in 1950, Orson Welles in 1972, and Charlton Heston in 1989 — the race for the pirate stash focuses more on coming of age on a far South American shore than on enrichment through a chance discovery of a map to buried treasure.

Enhancing the search for the money are romantic window dressings — a tall pine tangled with green liana near a skeleton clad in shreds of clothing. In Stevenson's original, Jim enjoys the tactile pleasure of sorting

> English, French, Spanish, Portuguese, Georges, and Louises, doubloons and double guineas and moidores and sequins, the pictures of all the kings of Europe for the last hundred years, strange Oriental pieces stamped with what looked like whisps of string or bits of spider's web, round pieces and square pieces and pieces bored through the middle, as if to wear them round your neck — nearly every variety of money in the world [Stevenson 1962, p. 219].

Confronting a boy inexperienced with the worst of human character is the image of Silver, who would gladly seize the bounty, board the *Hispaniola* at night to "cut every honest throat about that island, and sail away as he had at first intended, laden with crimes and riches" (*ibid.*, p. 212). In the aftermath, when Silver is long gone, Jim's dreams boom with the pounding surf and the parrot's brittle cry of "Pieces of eight! pieces of eight!" (*ibid.*, p. 224).

Greed and piracy also serve as lessons in human avarice. A 1965 Columbia Pictures version of Joseph Conrad's allegorical novel *Lord Jim* (1900) combined a star cast, featuring Peter O'Toole as the naive, guilt-ridden sailor Jim against seedy pirates acted by James Mason and Eli Wallach. A literary stab at English colonialism, the plot advances to a face-off between the primitive Far Easterners of Patusan and villainous exploiters. The comeuppance is poetic justice at its best — a cannon blast of the gold coins that fuel their greed.

In comedy, the theft of money is a source of humor and entertainment in fast-paced robbery plots. A classic, *Butch Cassidy and the Sundance Kid* (1969), paired Paul Newman and Robert Redford with Katharine Ross in a cinematic reprise of crime in the Old West. Picturing the dim-witted Hole in the Wall Gang plotting a train robbery, the action moves to the cash transported by boxcar and protected by a willowy employee of Mr. E. H. Harriman, the railroad robber baron who intended to secure shipments on the Union Pacific "Katy Flier." By allotting too much dynamite to open the safe, the hapless Butch blows paper money skyward, forcing the thieves to dismount and grab for cash before riding away to the memorable strains of music by Burt Bacharach. For its balance of comedy with greed and daring, the picture swept Academy Awards for best film, actor and actress, George Roy Hill's direction, and a score lightened with "Raindrops Keep Fallin' on My Head."

In 1979, *The Great Train Robbery* pictured Sean Connery as the dapper thief stealing from the Folkestone bullion express. Set in 1855, the story presents the Victorian caper as the first moving train robbery; it is based on a 1975 novel by Michael Crichton in which the thieves replace gold with cloth packets of lead shot. In the screen version, above money in theme and action stands the good breeding of the master criminal, red-bearded Edward Pierce, who masterminds the heist of sealed, iron-bound strongboxes holding £25,000 pounds in gold while they are under guard of ten security agents on their way to the Crimea. Central to the tedious disclosure of gold is the luggage van with its two impregnable, 550-pound Chubb safes built of three-quarter inch tempered steel and equipped with two locks, requiring a total of four keys, which Pierce must commandeer while scrambling atop a steam train traveling at 55 miles per hour. Just as Stevenson laces *Treasure Island* with the lore of piracy, Crichton overheaps greed with the meticulous plotting of athletic thieves intent on outwitting the protectors of the gold.

Following the fictional convention of the burial of cash in a desolate spot, the reality-based movie *Fargo* (1996), produced by Ethan and Joel Coen, intrigued viewers with the image of one million dollars in ransom money buried in an undisclosed snowbank in North Dakota. In the plot, car salesman Jerry Lundegaard hires two criminals to kidnap his own wife so he can collect a cash ransom from her wealthy father to satisfy creditors. Dark crime drama emerges after the thugs shoot a state patrolman and two bystanders.

Nominated for seven Academy Awards, the heavily nuanced story was an original screenplay that seemed authentic enough to spark interest in the missing ransom money and calls to police asking directions. On November 9, 2001, 28-year-old Takako Konishi of Tokyo, Japan, flew to Minneapolis and took a bus to Bismarck, North Dakota, to locate the money. Local police found her walking roadways as though searching for a lost item. She showed officers a hand-drawn map and explained in broken English that she intended to find the lost cache pictured in the movie.

Confusing the woman was a claim on the movie trailer that the plot recreated an actual burial of banknotes in Minnesota in 1987. From Bismarck, she boarded a bus for Fargo; on November 12, she journeyed on by cab from Fargo to Detroit Lakes, Minnesota, ostensibly to view the Leonid meteor showers. A bowhunter discovered her body on November 15. Police deduced that she died of exposure to sub-freezing temperatures while searching for treasure.

***See also* coins and currency in literature; Fort Knox; Knights Templar; Mel Fisher; moneylending; ring and bullet money; Roman coins — Empire.**

SOURCES: Boyce, Charles. *Shakespeare A to Z.* New York: Facts on File, 1990. • Connors, Martin, and Jim Craddock, eds. *Video Hound's Golden Movie Retriever.* Detroit: Visible Ink, 1999. • Conrad, Joseph. *Lord Jim.* London: Penguin, 1989. • Crichton, Michael. *The Great Train Robbery.* New York: Ballantine Books, 1995. • Gardner, Bill. "Futile Hunt for Film Loot Turns Fatal." *Charlotte Observer,* December 9, 2001, 18A. • McMurtry, Jo. *Understanding Shakespeare's England.* Hamden, Conn.: Archon Books, 1989. • Shakespeare, William. *The Riverside Shakespeare.* Boston: Houghton-Mifflin, 1974. • Stevenson, Robert Louis. *Treasure Island.* New York: Airmont, 1962. • Walker, John, ed. *Halliwell's Film & Video Guide.* New York: HarperPerennial, 1999.

coins and currency in literature

Coins and currency in the arts and literature typically depict daily commerce and the underlying morality and emotion arising from the passage of money from hand to hand. From "Sing a Song of Sixpence" and "A dillar a dollar a ten o'clock scholar" to the murdered pawnbroker in Fyodor Dostoyevsky's *Crime and Punishment* (1866) and Mark Twain's "The Man That Corrupted Hadleyburg" (1900), money is a common theme in nursery rhyme, parable, scripture, and morality tale. Unlike implied worth in Lillian Hellman's *The Little Foxes* (1939), a tragedy of greed, actual cash serves the writer as more palpable evidence of ambition and thrift as well as covetousness, venality, and profligacy.

Geoffrey Chaucer, the master storyteller of 14th-century England, depicted in "The Shipman's Tale" (ca. 1385) the self-exile implicit in the typical arrangement of a merchant's counter:

> His bookes and his bagges many oon
> He leith biforn hym on his countyng-bord.
> Ful riche was his tresor and his hord,

For which ful faste his countour-dore he shette;
And eek he nolde that no man sholde hym lette
Of his acountes. (Chaucer 1961, p. 157)
[His books and his many bags
He lays before him on his counting board.
Rich was his treasury and hoard
Rapidly he shut the counting-room door;
And he also kept secret his accounts.]

Obviously, hoarding bears its own punishment: those who confine themselves during the constant counting and retabulation of wealth grow paranoid and shut out the world. In so doing, they become prisoners of money.

More ominous is Chaucer's "The Pardoner's Tale," the morality tale of a Flemish youth wasting money in dicing, drinking, and wenching. For his edification, the pardoner presents in pulpit form the parable of the three rioters and the search for death. The discovery of eight bushels of gold *florins* distracts them from the trail. One rioter develops such a lust for the entire trove that he searches out an apothecary, who provides him with poison to kill the two companions who remain behind to guard the gold. The irony is lethal and direct: the two keepers of the treasure kill the would-be poisoner, drink from the tainted bottles, and die. Thus, greed for gold lures all three to death, the figure they had been seeking.

The more fanciful, ornate Victorian morality tale reaches its height in Charles Dickens's immortal *A Christmas Carol* (1843), one of five yuletide books he published to awaken the English to a growing hard-heartedness in the moneyed class. The image of accountant Ebenezer Scrooge shut into his cheerless apartment develops complacency into terror with the clanking and ghostly footfalls progressing up the stairs. When the phantasm of Jacob Marley, Scrooge's deceased partner, appears, the obvious reason for Marley's punishment in the afterlife is a chain fastened to his middle. In one sentence, Dickens summarizes the years of avarice that weighted Marley down to hell: "[The chain] was long, and wound about him like a tail; and it was made ... of cash-boxes, keys, padlocks, ledgers, deeds, and heavy purses wrought in steel" (Dickens 1963, p. 26). In explanation of his torment, Marley confesses, "I wear the chain I forged in life" (*ibid.*, p. 30). Marley warns that Scrooge is elongating his own "ponderous chain," which he will have to drag throughout eternity. Marley ruefully returns to his own sin of greed: "My spirit never walked beyond our counting-house — mark me! — in life my spirit never roved beyond the narrow limits of our money-changing hole; and weary journeys lie before me!" (*ibid.*).

Dickens reprises the anguish that Scrooge faces with images presented by the Ghost of Christmas Future: by magic, Scrooge witnesses the heart of the City and stands among his peers "on 'Change, among the merchants, who hurried up and down, and chinked the money in their pockets, and conversed in groups, and looked at their watches, and trifled thoughtfully with their great gold seals" (*ibid.*, p. 99). To Scrooge's horror, he hears his colleagues gossiping cynically about his death. One chortles, "Old Scratch has got him at last, hey?" (*ibid.*, p. 101). In 1861, Dickens reprised the characterization of a doomed moneyer in *Great Expectations* with the Colonel, a pale inmate in greasy hat confined in Newgate for crimes committed while he served as a royal coiner. More realistic than Marley's symbolic fate is the Colonel's sentence to death by hanging.

The same year that Dickens wrote *Great Expectations*, George Eliot produced an English morality masterpiece, *Silas Marner*. Carefully nuanced with allegorical names for characters and places, the text pictures the myopic weaver named Marner, a suggestion of "mourner," in the town of Raveloe, where his hoarded fortune indeed ravels, shredding to nothing. Like the accountant in Chaucer's "Shipman's Tale," Silas has withdrawn from society to gloat over his coins. As a result, "His gold, as he hung over it and saw it grow, gathered his power of loving together into a hard isolation like its own" (Eliot 1981, p. 44).

After Dunstan Cass steals the weaver's coins from Silas's hiding place, the crazed weaver recedes into monomania, hoping to recover his treasure by wheedling and by charging neighbors at random of robbing him. Suitably, he receives a replacement on New Year's Eve, the symbolic night that renews his lapsed humanity. On the hearth, he spies gold that seems to expand as he reaches out to grasp hard coin. Because of his limited vision, he mistakenly identifies as round gold pieces the soft, springy gold curls on a sleeping little girl.

At a spiritual epiphany, Marner refuses to give up the foundling to local families. His reasons are justified: "It's a lone thing—and I'm a lone thing. My money's gone, I don't know where—and this is come from I don't know where. I know nothing—I'm partly 'mazed" (*ibid.*, p. 123). When the stolen money returns 16 years later, Silas's use of it for a visit to Lantern Yard, the town that originally drove him out, rounds out the tag ends of the past. To Dolly Winthrop, a loving Christian neighbor, Silas declares that, despite the loss of his savings, his religious faith is firm since the child came to him. He adds, "I think I'll trusten till I die" (*ibid.*, p. 182).

An unusual application of coins in Victorian literature occurs in Thomas Hardy's *Far from the Madding Crowd* (1874), a novel blending tragedy with agriculture and pastoral settings in Wessex, the author's fictional shire. Laden with melodrama, the plot pictures Bathsheba Everdene setting herself up as lady of the manor she inherits from a relative. At the homestead, Hardy describes her at the task of paying her laborers. She sits at her desk in a pose usually struck by a male head of household, opens the time book, and reaches for the canvas money bag, from which she extracts half-sovereigns that she doles out in workers' pay. The bold act suggests that Bathsheba has unwisely advanced far beyond the ambitions of womenkind.

One totemic example from American literature, the gold doubloon that Captain Ahab nails to the mainmast in Herman Melville's *Moby Dick* (1851), takes on significance in a novel laden with symbols. Just as Ahab fixates on the white whale, he allows the coin to capture his attention as he paces the deck. The text enlarges on its provenance:

> Now this doubloon was of purest, virgin gold, raked somewhere out of the heart of gorgeous hills, whence, east and west over golden sands, the head-waters of many a Pactolus flows. And though now nailed amidst all the rustiness of iron bolts and the verdigris of copper spikes, yet, untouchable and immaculate to any foulness, it still preserved its Quito glow. (Melville 1961, p. 409)

It becomes the ship's navel, a sanctified amulet graced by the light of the setting sun that the sailors revere as "the White Whale's talisman" (*ibid.*). Melville remarks on the legend, "Republica del Ecuador: Quito," and on Ahab's mad mutterings about the gold disk, which he compares to a magician's glass. First Mate Starbuck, striking a note of sanity, warns, "No fairy fingers can have pressed the gold, but devil's claws must have left their mouldings." (*ibid.*, p. 410)

Unlike the straightforward presentation of monetary transactions in Hardy's early novel and the weighty symbolism in Melville's *Moby Dick*, Mark Twain's *A Connecticut Yankee in King Arthur's Court* (1886) creates a new economy and a complex currency system as parts of the armorer Hank Morgan's tinkering with the English society of the Middle Ages. Forced back in time by a blow on the head, he attempts to introduce U.S. conveniences of the year 1879 at Camelot in A.D. 528 With pride in accomplishment, he crows:

> A thing that gratified me a good deal was to find our new coins in circulation—lots of milrays, lots of mills, lots of cents, a good many nickels, and some silver; all this among the artisans and commonalty generally; yes, and even some gold—but that was at the bank, that is to say, the goldsmith's [Twain 1963, p. 220].

He takes a dig at a leery shopkeeper who changes a 20-dollar bill "after they had chewed the piece, and rung it on the counter, and tried acid on it, and asked me where I got it, and who I was, and where I was from, and where I was going to, and when I expected to get there" (*ibid.*). Although the English appear slow to give up long-held suspicions, they take to Hank's new money. He exults that "People had dropped the names of the former moneys, and spoke of things as being worth so many dollars or cents or mills or milrays" (*ibid.*, p. 221). For Hank, the shift in coinage is proof that he is on the right track to retrieve England from its backward medievalism.

See also **Anglo-Saxon coins; bible currency; coins and currency in drama and film; fur money; Greek coins; Hibernia coppers; Captain William Kidd; paper money; piracy; ring and bullet money; Russian money; Scottish coins; Spanish coins; spirit money; Jean Varin; *Wizard of Oz*.**

SOURCES: Chaucer, Geoffrey. *The Works of Geoffrey Chaucer*. Boston: Houghton Mifflin, 1961. • Chute, Marchette. *Geoffrey Chaucer of England*. New York: E. P. Dutton, 1946. • Dickens, Charles. *A Christmas Carol*. New York: Airmont, 1963. • Eliot, George. *Silas Marner*. New York: Signet, 1981. • Gardner, John. *The Life and Times of Chaucer*. New York: Alfred A. Knopf, 1977. • Hardy, Thomas. *The Thomas Hardy Omnibus*. New York: St. Martin's Press, 1979. • Melville, Herman. *Moby Dick*. New York: New American Library, 1961. • Scott, A. F. *Who's Who in Chaucer*. New York: Hawthorn Books, 1974. • Twain, Mark. *A Connecticut Yankee in King Arthur's Court*. New York: Signet, 1963.

Colonial coins

New World colonies survived in wild, undeveloped lands lacking contemporary conveniences, including currency. The first European arrivals to New England relied on swapping and barter as a means of conducting the business of the Massachusetts Bay Colony. Accepted as commodity money were lumber, corn and wheat, butter, sides of beef and pork, fish, sugar, and leaf tobacco. In Barbados and Antigua, commerce relied on sugar as currency; in Australia, rum served as money; in Bermuda, leaf tobacco paid for rent and groceries. British Hondurans relied on unchipped mahogany logs. In South Carolina, rice became legal tender at tax offices and in contract negotiations in 1739. In all locales, the cumbrous nature of trying to even out a bushel of rice, cord of wood, noggin of rum, or bale of pelts with the price of cattle, tallow, or herbal preparations inhibited trade. The lack of coins also confused community issues, such as a clergyman's salary or court judgments calling for fines in lieu of jail time or pillorying.

Because colonists survived on imported goods, they rapidly paid out to traders the little cash on hand. Governor John Winthrop's *Journal of the Transactions and Occurrences in the Settlement of Massachusetts and the Other New England Colonies* noted in October 1640 that the scarcity of coins imported from England, France, Holland, Mexico, Peru, Portugal, Spain, and the West Indies hampered not only buying and selling, but the settling of debts. As a result cattle and real estate prices fell dramatically by half. Adding to the problem of a coinless society was the inability of employers to pay servants, artisans, and tradesmen and the need to convert livestock into cash to facilitate everyday purchases for items as small as a candle, spool of thread, or bar of soap.

On March 4, 1635, New England authorities established a money substitute — a relationship between musket balls and farthings. Thus, they converted a common commodity into a set trade value known as country pay, which was legal tender for paying taxes. Seven years later, the arbitrary conversion of commodity to cash set a bushel of wheat at four shillings, the same amount of peas or rye at three shillings four pence, and corn at two shillings and sixpence. By the 1690s, the addition of pork at three pounds sterling per barrel, butter at six pence per pound, and tobacco at half the price of butter increased the number of options for exchange, thereby bringing more people into the country pay system. In 1707, a cord of pine lumber entered the monetary conversion chart at the rate of 25 shillings.

Commodity exchange had its faults. At issue in these exchanges were problems of convenience — the housing and feeding of livestock and cartage of bales of tobacco, barrels of sugar, bushels of barley, and cords of oak slats to the payee. More serious were questions of quality, especially for items that deteriorated in storage, or of deliberate interspersal of low-grade produce, a common problem with leaf tobacco. For this reason, the wary receiver did well to sample pork ribs from the center of the load, check for discoloration in a firkin of butter, search out wet spots in sheaved oats, and sniff monkfish on the bottom of the basket as well as the top. In 1674, the Connecticut colony named an adjudicator to settle squabbles over evaluating commodities offered as pay. The commodity system remained in use on the frontier and in rural areas after the coining of money and returned to metropolitan areas during shortages of currency, which struck Massachusetts in 1727 and in all thirteen colonies at the height of the American Revolution.

When trade stabilized between colonists and with settlers in the West Indies in the 1640s, a limited number of silver coins came into use in Massachusetts, notably French *écus*; Dutch *daalders*, *doits*, and *guilders*; Rix dollars and *stuivers*; the less common Portuguese *johannes* and *moidores*; Irish St. Patrick coppers called "Patrick's pence"; and the widely circulated Spanish doubloons and *pistoles*, which European overlords minted near slave-operated mines in Bolivia, Mexico, and Peru. The least standardized were Spanish cob dollars, hastily minted blobs of silver that had no standard shape or dimension and required reweighing to determine if they were full weight or had been shaved or clipped.

The first indigenous New England coinage began in May 26, 1652, after a Massachusetts General Court okayed the melting of silver cobs, bars, dishes, and jewelry into New England's own shillings and pence. As might be expected, the new pieces reflected the denominations and motifs of the motherland. The new round coins were the work of Boston goldsmith John Hull, a native of Leicestershire, England, and his assistant Robert Sanderson and supervisors Richard Bellingham, Thomas Clark, William Hibbins, John Leveritt, and Edward Rawson. Although nothing of the mint house remains, such an operation would have required a stone hearth and bellows, assaying equipment, and a roller or rocker press, later replaced by the more accurate screw press.

The original New England coins began as blank circular planchets cut from silver strips, then die punched with NE for "New England' on the face and the Roman numerals denoting the denomination on the reverse. To deter counterfeiters, who cranked out pewter copies, the operation shifted to die stamping rather than punching. For a later pattern, ironsmith Joseph Jenks, Sr., of Hammersmith carved an elaborate willow tree on sturdy dies. The minter placed each blank between a pair of dies and struck them to impress the design front and back with a single hammer blow. Within months of the original state order, laws to halt clipping provided for a beaded border and date center and the inscriptions "Masathuset In" on the face and "New England *An Dom*" ("New England in the Year of Our Lord") on the reverse.

Trees dominated colonial American coinage. In 1662, the Boston mint was producing a more sophisticated Oak Tree twopence, which probably derived from a lever-operated roller or rocker press. In 1667, the pine tree replaced the oak as the official motif for the shilling, sixpence, and threepence and remained in circulation for 30 years, all with 1652 as the minting date. The familiar silver piece roused a folk myth that coiner John Hull pledged his daughter Hannah Hull to jurist Samuel Sewall along with her weight in the attractive coins. The marriage, contracted on February 28, 1675, was successful and produced 14 children. When Judge Sewall came to fame during the Salem witch trials of summer 1692, superstitious colonists carried bent coins on their persons as a deterrent to witches.

Smaller than English coins, the Massachusetts coins were not intended for export. Because they solved daily problems of trade, they were immensely popular as far away as Virginia, Quebec, and the West Indies. In 1984, a salvage operation retrieved coins from the English frigate *Feversham*, which sank in a storm on October 7, 1711, in the Laurentian Gulf off Scatari Island, Nova Scotia. A team of Canadian-American divers recovered evidence of a shipment of food for the Royal Navy's galleys and much of the fleet payroll.

Among the hoard were colonial Massachusetts pine tree coins from 1652 as well as Dutch, English, and Spanish cobs and pesos in circulation during the period. Most common were the British regal copper, tin halfpence, and copper halfpenny.

Curtailing the export of colonial coins was a law of August 22, 1654, appointing nine searchers at Boston, Charlestown, Ipswich, Isle of Shoals, Piscataqua, Salem, and Sudbury to examine trunks and boxes, vessels, and persons to determine whether anyone carried out of the country more than twenty shillings. Continued problems with lost coins required more appointments of searchers for Braintree, Dedham, Marblehead, Marlboro, and Springfield. As is generally true of border and harbor patrols, these searches proved inadequate to stop large-scale smuggling of coins from New England.

In 1658, Cecil Calvert, Lord Baltimore, one of the eight lords proprietors of the Carolinas, resorted to private minting of copper *denarii*, groats, shillings, and sixpence to facilitate repayment of soldiers. At a location in London, perhaps the Tower Mint, his coinsmith began operations in 1659, making silver coins worth four, six, and twelve pence. The design featured Lord Baltimore's profile and the Latin inscription "Caecilius DNS Terrae-Mariae & Ct." On the opposite side, the minter incised the family crest and the motto "*Crescite Et Multiplicamini*" ("Increase and Multiply"). He shipped the finished specie to Lord Baltimore's half-brother, Philip Calvert, the colonial governor of Maryland. In October, the English coiner was arrested for minting money that deviated by 30 percent from the British standard weight and for exporting silver illegally to the colonies. Because of the uproar he caused on both sides of the Atlantic, he ceased producing coins.

The Crown interfered further in proposals to supply the colonies with coins. In 1665, Charles II sent inspectors to New England smithies to determine the legality of colonial coinage. To keep their mints in operation and promote commerce and growth, local authorities bribed the king with a shipment of masts and warned that their annual payment of custom would decrease if colonists had no coins to support the economy. Coinage at Boston continued until the mid–1680s, but without an official minting license from the king. In 1690, colonists took a new tack by issuing the first paper money, which effectively replaced coins, which were more expensive to produce.

Paper notes did not end colonial currency problems. During a scarcity of small change in the late 1690s, which inhibited small purchases, private minting concerns began producing brass and tin pence worth one cent to supplement circulation of Spanish *pistareens*, a debased coinage minted in Iberia and valued in the American South for minor transactions. Desperate colonists altered commemorative tokens of the London plague of 1665 and the great London fire of 1666 by changing the legend from "Preserve London" to "Carolina and the Lord Protector" and "Preserve New England." Quickly, Massachusetts authorities moved to halt circulation of counterfeit tokens and unofficial coinage, which was below standard weight. The law allowed any possessor of the coins to demand exchange for legal tender, notably British coppers.

The subject of small change coins surfaced repeatedly in colonial assemblies, where the need for metal money as a medium of trade became a serious issue. State mints issued coins in Connecticut, Vermont, Massachusetts, New Hampshire, New Jersey, and New York. William Penn, founder and governor of Pennsylvania, noted that Bostonians were so bereft of coins that the authorities had proposed issuing monetary tickets. Circulation of the Dutch *leeuwendaalder* (lion dollar), named for its image of a lion in heraldic pose, humbled a noble coin with the slang phrase the "dog dollar," a term legitimized by the Maryland Act of 1708. In 1737, in Granby, Connecticut, Yale-trained metallurgist Samuel Higley began manufacturing the Higley or Granby copper with pure ore extracted from his mine at Simsbury. The coin took shape in four motifs by the outmoded hammer process and bore the legend "Value of Threepence."

To facilitate the coin's acceptance at the local pub, he inscribed the reassuring motto "Value Me as You Please — I Am Good Copper" along with wheel designs. Historian Hubert Howe Bancroft, author of *The Book of the Fair* (1893), marvelled at their excellence during his visit to the World's Columbian Exhibition in Chicago.

Many mid- to late-colonial coppers were minted abroad, notably the Irish St. Patrick halfpence and farthing. They were transported aboard the Dublin ship *Ye Owners Adventurer*, which arrived in the Americas on September 19, 1681, and circulated in New Jersey by English Quaker merchant Mark Newby (or Newbie), who left Ireland to escape religious persecution. His purchase of £30 in coppers — around 14,400 coins — replaced wampum as legal tender. He died within the year, but the "Newby coppers" remained in circulation for a century.

In 1722, English metalworker and copper miner William Wood circulated the Hibernia halfpence and farthing denominations, both rejects from Ireland minted from a cheap bronze alloy called bath metal, which contained minute quantities of silver added to copper and zinc. Under contract from George I, Wood also produced the Rosa Americana halfcent, penny, and twopence as well as the silver Lord Baltimore fourpence, sixpence, and shilling for use in Maryland. In circulation in this same era were the Carolina and New England tokens, a Virginia halfpenny authorized by George III, and copper and brass tokens issued by companies and advertisers.

In 1773, Richard Yeo, royal medalist of George III, received a commission to supply the American colonies with coppers. On February 14, 1774, he shipped to New York harbor aboard the *Virginia* five tons of coins amounting to 670,000 halfpence. Virginia treasurer Robert Nicholas publicized the welcome arrival in a March edition of the *Virginia Gazette*. When war between patriots and redcoats broke out at Lexington and Concord, Massachusetts, on April 19, 1775, colonists hoarded the new coin among their other coppers even though Yeo's design pictured the hated Hanoverian king. After the Civil War, Colonel Medes Cohen of Baltimore located a hoard of Yeo's halfpennies in a keg.

Following the printing of Continental paper money in June 1775, the chancy backing of bills by a nascent government left many colonials with qualms. By the next January, patriots were obliged to accept unbacked paper currency or else be labeled traitors. Nonetheless, the *Pennsylvania Evening Post* printed a word to the wise on February 17, warning that the outbreak of war could force investors to negotiate loans from foreign sources, even from English banks. The author urged "the procurement of ... precious metals" as a backing for colonial paper money (Taxay 1966, p. 3). Within weeks, patriots were demanding an official mint operation fed with colonial plate as its bullion. After the American Revolution, Thomas Jefferson took up the call for an official coinage.

Until the U.S. Mint in Philadelphia took charge of official coinage on April 2, 1792, state coining enabled local commerce to thrive. From 1785 to 1788, Connecticut's operation turned out the largest number of coins, striking 1,800 pounds of pennies featuring the allegorical figure of Liberty, the new nation's symbol. In 1786, Massachusetts set up coinage picturing an Indian holding a bow and arrow and the legend "Commonwealth." The reverse pictured an eagle, the image that eventually dominated the nation's coin art.

The following year, Ephraim Brasher, a member of New York's silversmiths' society, partnered with John Bailey in petitioning for the lucrative state coin franchise. He struck the first gold coins in U.S. history, a doubloon picturing a bird motif that was the forerunner of the U.S. seal. In 1790, Baltimore silversmith Standish Barry, head of a watchmaker's guild, crafted a silver threepence commemorative token in tribute to the events of July 4, 1776. It was not until 1795 that the Philadelphia mint got down to the job of striking gold eagles, half-eagles, and quarter-eagles.

***See also* Ephraim Brasher; Abel Buell; Canadian money; continental currency; counterfeiting; elephant token; *escudo*;**

Alexander Hamilton; hogge money; John Hull; Thomas Jefferson; Thomas Machin; paper money; penny; Jacob Perkins; pieces of eight; piracy; pistareen; Rix dollars; John Roettiers; Russian money; Spanish coins; St. Patrick coppers; U.S. coins; U.S. Mint; U.S. Treasury; wampum.

SOURCES: Allen, Larry. *Encyclopedia of Money.* New York: Checkmark Books, 2001. • Babbitt, John S. "Coins and Currency on U.S. Stamps." *Stamps,* January 21, 1995. • Bancroft, Hubert Howe. *The Works of Hubert Howe Bancroft.* San Francisco: The History Company, 1887. • Bowers, Q. David. *Adventures with Rare Coins.* Los Angeles: Bowers & Ruddy Galleries, Inc., 1979. • Bowers, Q. David. "American Gold." *American Heritage,* December 1984, 43–49. • "The Bureau of Engraving and Printing." http://www.bep.treas.gov/. • Clain-Stefanelli, Elvira, and Vladimir Clain-Stefanelli. *The Beauty and Lore of Coins, Currency, and Medals.* Croton-on-Hudson, N.Y.: Riverwood Publishers, 1974. • Davies, Glyn. *A History of Money from Ancient Times to the Present Day.* Cardiff: University of Wales Press, 1994. • Davis, Andrew McFarland. *Colonial Currency Reprints, 1682–1751.* Boston: The Prince Society, 1911. • Einzig, Paul. *Primitive Money.* Oxford: Pergamon Press, 1966. • Jordan, Louis. "The Coins of Colonial and Early America." http://www.coins.nd.edu/ColCoin/ColCoinContents/Introduction.html. • Kleeberg, John, ed. *The Money of Pre-Federal America.* New York: American Numismatic Society, 1992. • Lewis, Brenda Ralph. *Coins & Currency.* New York: Random House, 1993. • McCusker, John J. *How Much Is That in Real Money?* Worcester, Mass.: American Antiquarian Society, 2001. • Mossman, Philip L. "The Circulation of Irish Coinage in Pre-Federal America." *The Colonial Newsletter,* April 1999, pp. 1899–1917. • Newman, Eric. "Coinage for Colonial Virginia." *Numismatic Notes and Monographs,* no. 135, 1956. • Newman, Eric. *The Early Paper Money of America.* Iola, Wisc: Krause, 1997. • Opitz, Charles J. *Odd and Curious Money.* Ocala, Fla.: First Impressions, 1986. • Pollak, Henry. *Coinage & Conflict.* Clifton, N.J.: Coin & Currency Institute, 2001. • Reiter, Ed. "A Quick Sale for Yale's Brasher Doubloon." *New York Times,* January 18, 1981, p. D32. • Sinclair, David. *The Pound.* London: Century Books, 2000. • Schwarz, Ted. *Coins as Living History.* New York: Arco Publishing, 1976. • Standish, David. *The Art of Money.* San Francisco: Chronicle Books, 2000. • "Tales from the Crypt." *Time,* April 18, 1994, p. 67. • Taxay, Don. *The U.S. Mint and Coinage.* New York: Arco Publishing, 1966. • Van Ryzin, Robert R. *Twisted Tails: Sifted Fact, Fantasy and Fiction from U.S. Coin History.* Iola, Wisc.: Krause Publications, 1995.

commemorative issue

Commemorative coins, sometimes called presentation pieces, have turned money into markers of historic occasions. The concept began with the Syracusan *decadrachms* honoring the tyrant Gelon, a renowned cavalry commander, who halted the Carthaginian invasion of Sicily in 480 B.C. The coin pictures the nymph Arethusa on front; on the reverse, a charioteer and two horses trample a lion. Overhead, Nike, the flying deity of victory, leads the way. Syracuse remained victorious over the Carthaginians, who once more assaulted Sicily in 400 B.C. A third victory against Athens resulted in the most elegant coin of ancient times — the head of Arethusa or Artemis on front with a figure on the back driving a chariot with four rearing horses. Decorating the coin are good-luck dolphins on the obverse and Nike on the back.

After 294 B.C., Demetrius, king of Macedonia and admirer of Alexander III the Great, commissioned a grand scenic *tetradrachm* to recall the glories of the past. Called "Poliorcetes" ("the Besieger"), Demetrius allowed the coin to advertise his ambitions. The *tetradrachm* pictured Nike flying above the prow of a warship, a reminder of the overwhelming sea victory at the battle of Salamis. The first naval conquest recorded in history, in 480 B.C., it matched Themistocles at the head of the Greek fleet against Xerxes's invasive Persian navy. The Greeks sank 300 Persian ships while losing only 40 of their own.

With a 20-*excelentes de la Granada,* a rare and artistically pleasing coin, Ferdinand II of Aragon and Isabella I of Castile, joint monarchs of Spain in the 1490s, lauded the reclamation of Granada and of the sunny, fruitful Costal del Sol from the Moors in January 1492. The royal couple ordered the broad-rimmed piece, featuring their crowned likenesses looking at each other, in 1497, the year they reformed Spanish coinage. Exquisitely proportioned with two inner circles of beading, the gold disk features a double X above the portrait to indicate the amount. The popular coin yielded a dynasty of moneys, each bearing the couple's portraits. The *excelente* remained in mintage through Spain and the Spanish Netherlands for many years.

In the German states, gold and silver commemorative issue for marriages, coronations, births, and the death of royalty was dramatic and artistic. In 1699, Prince Augustus of Saxe-Weissenfels ordered a *thaler* to honor his wife Anna Maria. The coin pictured an angel carrying her toward a setting sun and the pious motto, "*Habet Deum Qui Habet Omnia*" ("He Who Has God Has Everything"). An unusual commemorative, the Saxon "butterfly *thaler*," notes the death of Frederick Augustus I in 1733. The smooth coin with deeply rimmed frame pictures a butterly with multiple spotted wings, but no motto.

The U.S. Mint began issuing special coins in the 1890s. The first coincided with Chicago's 1893 Columbian Exposition, marking four centuries since Christopher Columbus's discovery of America. To capture the provenance of his command of a Spanish expedition, coiners struck quarters and half-dollars picturing both him and Queen Isabella, the Spanish monarch who bankrolled his three ships, the *Pinta, Niña*, and *Santa María*. For the Panama Pacific Exposition, held in San Francisco in 1915, the U.S. Mint issued one-, 2.5-, and 50-dollar gold coins and a silver half-dollar.

This ten-dollar note depicts mulatto freedom fighter, George William Gordon, an island assemblyman and national hero who went to the gallows for his alleged role in the Morant Bay Rebellion in 1865, during the Dark Age of Jamaica.

This one-dollar portrait note from Jamaica honors its first prime minister, Sir Alexander Bustamante, founder of the Jamaica Labour Party and, in 1938, of the Bustamante Industrial Trade Union, the island's largest workers' cooperative.

This 100-*baht* paper currency from Thailand pictures King Bhumibol, the longest reigning Thai monarch.

Commemorative issues tend to honor positive events and optimism. In Canada, a 1958 dollar honored the centennial of British Columbia's status as a colony with the image of a totem pole, the artistry of the Salish and Haida. A 1973 gold dollar celebrated 100 years of lawful control with the figure of a member of the Royal Canadian Mounted Police. In Oceania, Samoans honored Robert Louis Stevenson, the famed Scottish fiction writer, who settled on Upolu Island in 1889. A 1969 coin picturing him at work with pen and paper notes his birth in Edinburgh and death in Vailima and the islanders' nickname for him, Tusitala ("Teller of tales"). In France in 1988, the Paris mint struck a silver *franc* noting the 30th anniversary of Charles de Gaulle's first presidency. The familiar likeness in profile recalled his stoic expression, a face that sparked courage during World War II.

A favorite subject of commemorative issues are human activities expressing character, courage, and victory. Olympic Games challenge coin designers to visualize the excitement of physical contests held in historic cities. In 1968, a coin lauding the games in Mexico pictured a dancing Aztec chief surrounded by the legend "*Juegos de La XIX Olimpiada Mexico*" ("Games of the 19th Olympiad in Mexico"). Four years later, German coiners sculpted a stylized image of a blazing fire and sun symbol encircled by the legend "*Spiele Der XX Olympiade München*" "(Games of the 20th Olympiad in Munich"). For the Soviet games of 1980, Polish artists conceived a vivid image of a runner at the 22nd Olympiad. The U.S. version, commissioned after the 1988 games in Los Angeles, stressed cooperation in the lighting of the Olympic torch. In 1990, Spain illustrated the exertion of the Olympic athletes with a muscular discus thrower straining to make the goal. Usually positioned on the exergue is the symbol that most Olympic coins have in common, the interlinking five rings, representing cooperation among nations and people of divergent cultures and ethnicity.

***See also* U.S. Mint.**

SOURCES: Clain-Stefanelli, Elvira, and Vladimir Clain-Stefanelli. *The Beauty and Lore of Coins, Currency, and Medals*. Croton-on-Hudson, N.Y.: Riverwood Publishers, 1974. • Cribb, Joe. *Money*. Toronto: Stoddart, 1990. • Cribb, Joe, Barrie Cook, and Ian Carradice. *The Coin Atlas*. London: Little, Brown and Co., 1999. • Davies, Glyn. *A History of Money from Ancient Times to the Present Day*. Cardiff: University of Wales Press, 1994. • Lewis, Brenda Ralph. *Coins & Currency*. New York: Random House, 1993. • Pollak, Henry. *Coinage & Conflict*. Clifton, N.J.: Coin & Currency Institute, 2001. • Reinfeld, Fred. *Treasury of the World's Coins*. New York: Sterling Publishing, 1953. • Taxay, Don. *An Illustrated History of U.S. Commemorative Coinage*. New York: Arco Publishing, 1967.

Confederate money

Three decades before the American Civil War, bilingual Southern currency printed by the Bank of Louisiana influenced the region. A ten-dollar paper bill, which bore the French *dix* for "ten," introduced the term "dixie." After 1860, Northern minstrel singer Dan Emmett popularized the term, which was the title of the South's unofficial anthem and a slang term for the land and its culture and citizens.

After the internal conflict began with the firing on Fort Sumter on April 12, 1861, the U.S. Treasury was forced to print the first paper greenbacks, a siege issue that Secretary of the Treasury Salmon Portland Chase commissioned to cover the lack of reserves of precious metals. Also basing its currency on trust, the Treasurer of the newly formed Confederacy, Gustavas Mem-

A favorite subject of commemorative issues is human activities expressing character, courage, and victory. Spain's 100-*peseta* note displays the bust of Manuel de Falla, a distinguished and influential early twentieth-century composer.

minger, distributed paper notes backed by coin to be redeemed within two years of war's end. Elegantly scrolled, signed by H. Morse, and illustrated with gallant cavalrymen and flags, the paper bills were worthless by the fourth year of combat, when the South had little hope of winning and maintaining sovereignty.

Confederate specie got its start after a treasury official commissioned a Philadelphia jewelry die-cutter, Bailey & Company, to incise designs for a penny. Sculptor Robert Lovett, Jr., of Philadelphia, who had designed the Washington Medal, created the first coin. He featured the bust of Minerva, the Roman goddess of wisdom, a pattern he had first incised on tokens the previous year. He established a link to the Southern agrarian economy and slavery by picturing a cotton bale, an innocuous image that belied the hardship and toil of the blacks who grew, harvested, cleaned, and shipped the South's prime product. After completing the first issue, struck on a cupronickel alloy, Lovett hid the coins and pattern dies out of fear of confiscation by federal authorities and punishment for aiding a rebel government. Legend describes Lovett's reverence of the penny as a good luck charm and commiserates with his unintentional circulation of the coin in 1873 at a Philadelphia tavern.

After rebel forces took possession of the U.S. Mint in New Orleans in late February 1861, B. F. Taylor became chief coiner of Confederate specie. The Confederate dollar, a reprise of the seated figure of Liberty engraved by die-sinker A. H. M. Patterson, went into production in New Orleans within the year. Because of difficulties fitting the dies to the press, foreman Conrad Schmidt stopped the manufacture of coins. Laborers returned to a screw press and produced only four coins when the mint ran out of bullion. In April, the mint staff halted operation. Simultaneously, most banks held their cash in vaults and ceased printing banknotes.

The Confederate printing department began producing notes on March 9, 1861, and continued until its fourth and last printing in 1864, issuing $200 million in paper money. A ten-dollar bill from February 17, 1864, presented a false bravado with the image of four war steeds pulling a cannon into position. As supplies fell from blockaded ports and failed factory and farm output, inflation rose. In Alabama, state officials printed dollar bills in 1863 claiming that they were "receivable in payment of all public dues." Elegantly scrolled, signed, and countersigned and picturing an engraving of the state capitol, they rivaled a note designed the previous year for the state of Georgia featuring General James Oglethorpe, Georgia's colonial founder, and printed at the Milledgeville operation.

Confederate paper quickly became a joke to all but those subsisting on it. In Mark Twain's *A Connecticut Yankee in King Arthur's Court* (1886), his Yankee character, Hank Morgan, reflects,

> In the North a carpenter got three dollars a day, gold valuation; in the South he got fifty — payable in Confederate shinplaster worth a dollar a bushel. In the North a suit of overalls cost three dollars — a day's wages; in the South it cost seventy-five — which was two days' wages [Twain 1963, p. 220].

The diminution of buying power and resulting bloating of prices sent mobs of housewives charging against the speculators who stockpiled sugar, coffee, tea, and flour in anticipation of even higher yield. Flailing female arms rummaged barrels and bags for foodstuffs to load waiting wagons. In March 1863, ax-wielding women in Salisbury, North Carolina, attacked the price-gougers who flouted government cost controls. In support of hungry citizens, Governor Zebulon B. Vance warned that "broken laws will give you no bread, but much sorrow; and when forcible seizures have to be made to avert starvation, let it be done by your county or state agents" [Smith and Wilson 1999, 127].

A political cartoonist for the *Pictorial War Record* ridiculed petticoated rioters ravaging Mobile, Alabama, in September 1863. Without cash to stock their pantries, grim-visaged housewives armed with rakes and staves stormed Dauphine Street and looted grocers' shelves and back rooms. The cartoonist depicted soldiers brandishing bayoneted rifles in a face-off with belligerent Southern women waving signs labeled "Bread or Peace" and "Food or Death" [Simmons 2001, 10]. One aproned reb cowed a peace officer with her bare fists.

At the height of inflation in the South, Mary Jackson of Richmond, Virginia, headed a raiding party from the Belvidere Hill Baptist Church to Capital Square. During a two-hour bread riot, cashless women terrorized shopkeepers with cleavers, hatchets, and pistols. Undaunted by Virginia governor John Letcher, they ceased their display only after Confederate President Jefferson Davis called out the guard. The court convicted Mary Jackson of felonious assault; the 16 women who were tried for disorderly conduct and theft received fines for misdemeanor affray.

For the military, camp life required its own version of stretching inflated dollars for food and necessities. For anything beyond army issue clothing, bedding, and equipment, Union soldiers garnered monthly salaries of thirteen dollars to buy goods sold at profiteering commissaries and sutleries. Although not government-approved, wagonloads of stores tempted men who quickly tired of camp kitchen hardtack and salt pork. Displays of overpriced liquor and tobacco, moldy pies and molasses candy, raisins, sugar, stale crackers, flour, butter and cheese, eggs, rancid bacon, salt mackerel, apples and oranges, and soft drinks brought complaints, but men had little choice but to hand over their coins for small extras. When price-gouging ranged out of hand, compassionate officers looked the other way as angry rebs and yanks set torches to sutlers, their wagons and tents, and goods.

On April 4, 1865, when Federal authorities overran Chimborazo Hospital, a 150-building complex in Richmond, Virginia, they relieved chief matron Phoebe Yates Pember of her duties, which had encompassed the care of a total of 76,000 Confederate casualties. She refused to leave and remained in charge of patients until they were well enough to transfer to other facilities or return to their families. As told in her memoirs, *A Southern Woman's Story* (1879), after two years without pay, she found herself unemployed in Union-occupied territory with just a silver 10-cent piece and a box of worthless Confederate money.

At war's end, rumors of lost Confederate treasure permeated the wealth of lore that romanticized a lost cause. In one version, during the evacuation of Richmond, Southern officials amassed for transport gold ingots and double eagle coins, silver coins and bricks, thick Mexican silver dollars, U.S. paper currency, copper coins, and jewels. Bank officers John M. Goddin, R. T. Reynolds, William F. Taylor, and J. H. Weisiger left on April 28, 1865, trailing the gold train that President Jefferson Davis supposedly rode south. On May 8, Captain William H. Parker, the four bankers, and an escort of U.S. soldiers from Iowa crossed trails with the shipment in Washington, Georgia. They loaded ammunition boxes, flour kegs, sugar sacks, and chests into five wagons, and, on May 24, hauled the aggregate to a rail depot in Abbeville, South Carolina. Ostensibly, Davis, who had guaranteed he would repay loans from France, intended the treasure to travel to a ship at Savannah harbor. Another version of the flight from the fallen capital named the destination as the U.S. Mint at Charlotte, North Carolina.

Supposedly, a spy dispatched some East Tennessee cavalrymen to seize the treasure. Near a pontoon bridge over the Savannah River at the Chennault home in Chennault County, Georgia, the raiders waylaid the convoy, transferred $251,029.90 in coin to sacks, and departed, scattering coins in their wake. Goddin transported the remaining $159,929.90 to Richmond. By offering a $5,000 reward and a ten percent recovery fee, General Edward Porter Alexander recovered $111,000 of the stolen cash. Former Confederate Secretary of State Robert Toombs found $5,000 that the raiders may have left in his yard. The rest probably accompanied the thieves as they fled West.

Federal troops searched for the stolen coins. They tortured ex-slaves and removed the Chennault family to Washington, D.C., to question them further about the heist. Agents recovered some of the loot at the capture of Jefferson Davis in Irwinsville, Georgia, and confiscated another $100,000 from a Washington bank. The remainder became the stuff of fiction.

Legends maintain that the raiders buried the unfound portion — around $100,000 — in Wilkes County east of Athens, Georgia, in one of three places — at the Chennault residence, at the Sutherlin mansion in Danville, or perhaps at the confluence of the Apalachee and Oconee rivers. Some contend that the gold is buried in Florida or that it journeyed by false-bottomed wagon to vessels moored at Charleston, South Carolina, and bound for Europe or the Bahamas. A more fanciful strand asserts that, after the treasure arrived by train on April 3, 1865, staff at the Confederate Treasury at Danville, Virginia, buried in kegs a fortune as large as $75 million in foreign gold and silver coins weighing five tons. In all, some 21 locations carry the mystique of the burial site of the Confederate cache.

***See also* Anthony C. Paquet; scrip; tokens; U.S. Mint.**

SOURCES: Allen, Larry. *Encyclopedia of Money*. New York: Checkmark Books, 2001. • Allen Larry. "American Gold." *American Heritage*, December 1984, 43–49. • Ashby, Thomas A. *The Valley Campaigns*. New York: Neale Publishing Co., 1914. • Avary, Myrta Lockett. *A Virginia Girl in the Civil War*. New York: D. Appleton & Co., 1903. • Avirett, James Battle. *The Old Plantation: How We Lived in Great House and Cabin Before the War*. New York: F. Tennyson Neely Co., 1901. • Baker, Bernard. "Confederate Gold." *Danville Register & Bee*, June 29, 1996. • Balch, T. B. *My Manse, During the War*. Baltimore: Sherwood & Co., 1866. • Betts, A. D. *Experience of a Confederate Chaplain, 1861–1864*. Greenville, S. C.: n.p., 190?. • Boggs, William Robertson. *Military Reminiscences of Gen. Wm. R. Boggs, C.S.A.* Durham, N.C.: Seeman Printery, 1913. • Bowers, Q. David. *Adventures with Rare Coins*. Los Angeles: Bowers & Ruddy Galleries, Inc., 1979. • Burge, Dolly Sumner. *A Woman's Wartime Journal: An Account of the Passage over a Georgia Plantation of Sherman's Army on the March to the Sea*. New York: The Century Co., 1918. • Chesnut, Mary Boykin. *A Diary from Dixie*. New York: D. Appleton and C., 1905. • Cribb, Joe. *Money*. Toronto: Stoddart, 1990. • Curry, J. L. M. *The South in the Olden Time*. Harrisburg, Pa.: Harrisburg Publishing Co., 1901. • Fearn, Frances. *Diary of a Refugee*. New York: Moffatt, Yard & Co., 1910. • Hermann, Captain I. *Memoirs of a Veteran*. Atlanta, Ga.: Byrd Printing Company, 1911. • Lee, J. Edward, and Ron Chepesiuk. *South Carolina in the Civil War*. Jefferson, N.C.: McFarland, 2000. • Lewis, Brenda Ralph. *Coins & Currency*. New York: Random House, 1993. • McCarthy, Carlton. *Detailed Minutiae of Soldier Life*. New York: Time-Life Books, 1982. • Newsom, John. "Legendary Treasure Beckons." *Greensboro News & Record*, August 12, 1996. • Simmons, Donald C. *Confederate Settlements in British Honduras*. Jefferson, N.C.: McFarland, 2001. • Smith, Margaret Supplee, and Emily Herring Wilson. *North Carolina Women: Making History*. Chapel Hill: University of North Carolina Press, 1999. • Standish, David. *The Art of Money*. San Francisco: Chronicle Books, 2000. • "The Strange Tale of the Iowa Soldiers Who Guarded Confederate Gold." http://www.iowa-counties.com/civilwar/gold.htm. • Taylor, Richard. *Destruction and Reconstruction: Personal Experiences of the Late War*. New York: D. Appleton & Co., 1879. • Twain, Mark. *A Connecticut Yankee in King Arthur's Court*. New York: Signet, 1963. • Volo, Dorothy Denneen, and James M. Volo. "Daily Life in Civil War America." *Daily Life Through History* (database), http://greenwood.scbbs.com:8080. • Weatherford, Jack. *The History of Money: From Sandstone to Cyberspace*. Pittsburgh, Pa.: Three Rivers Press, 1998.

continental currency

With the beginning of a successful rebellion against the British in spring 1775, on May 10, American colonial authorities backed the continental note or bill, a local currency advocated by statesman Benjamin Franklin to pay for the American Revolution. The note was the first official paper currency issued in the Western World. Printed in black on homely dun-colored paper, each bore a scrolled border. On the three-dollar bill, an image of two warring birds, an eagle and heron, is ringed by the legend "*Exitus in Dubio Est*" ("The Outcome Is in Doubt"). The text promised to exchange the paper for milled Spanish dollars "or the Value thereof in Gold or Silver, according to the Resolutions of the Congress, held at Philadelphia, the 10th of May, 1775" (Standish 2000, 0. 117).

For good reason, patriots took as their

watchword "United we stand, divided we fall." Because the Continental Congress collected no taxes, the notes stood on shaky ground — the faith of colonists in their union and its future. On June 29, 1776, the *Constitutional Gazette* commented that delegates in Philadelphia were proposing a recall of poorly struck copper coins. The author added that, if there is still a need of coins for ordinary use, "a new impression struck of Continental Copper Coin, of a larger size; twelve of which is to pass for an eighth of a dollar, after which no other Coppers are to pass current" (Taxay 1966, p. 8).

Originating as a pewter coin minted in New Haven, Connecticut, the subsequent paper note stamped by Hall & Sellers of Philadelphia in 1776 was worth 1/6 of a dollar. In addition to a scrolled border, it featured 13 interlacing circlets, each bearing the name of one of the 13 original colonies. On the face flashed a sunburst around a ring proclaiming at center "American Congress" with "We Are One." The same optimistic styling marked a tin coin.

Printers produced continental bills for five years in 42 runs amounting to $210 million. The notes, picturing a phoenix encircled by 13 stars, circulated simultaneously with competing state notes and Spanish coin. In ornate script and bounded by scrolled borders, the 40-dollar note read: "This Bill entitles the *Bearer* to receive *Forty Spanish milled Dollars*, or the *Value* thereof in *Gold* or *Silver*, according to a *Resolution*, passed by *Congress at Philadelphia* Sept. *26th*, 1778" (Clain and Clain 1974, p. 220).

Quickly depreciated and widely counterfeited by the British in 1778 from copper plates, colonial notes earned the epithet "not worth a continental" (Davies 1994, p. 465). On January 6, 1777, the *New York Gazette* sneered at "the vile continental currency, a cartload of which ... in a little time would not purchase a single dollar" (Taxay 1966, p. 9). An advertisement in the same paper that year offered confiscated forged notes by the ream, available at the Coffee House from 11 P.M. to 4 A.M. As of 1783, the government's presses issued no more continentals. Five states halted production, Rhode Island being the major holdout.

So serious did the problem of legal tender become that Massachusetts farmers launched Shays' Rebellion, a revolt named for Daniel Shays. Begun in Massachusetts in 1786, the uprising erupted after five years of growing agricultural debt, high taxes, and shrinking commodity prices. The legislature's repeal of the continental and its rejection of goods to satisfy debts exacerbated the shortage of coins. Farmers and homeowners who were in arrears faced jailing and protracted trials while their creditors auctioned off their property.

Rebels demanded an amended state constitution to lessen government cost. Angry citizens prohibited county courts and the Massachusetts Supreme Court from hearing cases. The legislature took stop-gap action. The aggrieved, including veteran Daniel Shays, led armed regiments toward the federal arsenal at Springfield on January 25, 1787, and on skirmishes in Berkshire county and border raids. Major General Benjamin Lincoln put down insurgents at Petersham on February 4, 1787.

At the next session of the legislature, lawmakers raised private funds to pay the army and reduced court costs, but refused to issue paper notes. When John Hancock was elected governor, he guided the Massachusetts authorities toward aiding rebel farmers by lessening poll and estate taxes and by halting the jailing of debtors. Condemned to hang, Shays and 13 others gained pardons. An end to difficulties did not appear until the seating of Congress, the creation of a federal treasury department and mint, and the coining of official U.S. moneys.

***See also* colonial money; Alexander Hamilton; Thomas Jefferson; U.S. coins; U.S. Mint.**

SOURCES: Clain-Stefanelli, Elvira, and Vladimir Clain-Stefanelli. *The Beauty and Lore of Coins, Currency, and Medals.* Croton-on-Hudson, N.Y.: Riverwood Publishers, 1974. • Cribb, Joe. *Money.* Toronto: Stoddart, 1990. • Davies, Glyn. *A History of Money from Ancient Times to the Present Day.* Cardiff: University of Wales Press, 1994. • Grierson, Philip. *Numismatics.* London: Oxford University Press, 1975. • Pollak, Henry. *Coinage & Conflict*. Clifton, N.J.: Coin & Currency Institute, 2001. • Standish, David. *The Art of Money*. San Francisco: Chronicle Books, 2000. • Taxay, Don. *The U.S. Mint and Coinage*. New York: Arco Publishing, 1966. • Weatherford, Jack. *The History of Money: From Sandstone to Cyberspace*. Pittsburgh, Pa.: Three Rivers Press, 1998.

counterfeiting

Counterfeit issue — whether coin, banknotes, postage stamps, bonds, stock certificates, airline tickets, travelers' checks, credit cards, food stamps, or grocery store coupons — vary from the authorized method of printing, stamping, or striking. Every national currency has been copied, from the earliest coins and the first paper money in China to the dog-tooth bracelets of the Solomon Islands, which German counterfeiters reproduced in porcelain in the 1890s. Severe penalties have ranged from pillorying to lopping off of hands and hanging. The Chinese exacted a capital penalty on an industrious printer, who, in 1183, passed 2,600 forged paper bills within six months.

To guard coins against forgery, Greek, Roman, and Islamic die-cutters incised microlettering too small to be detected by the naked eye. The earliest extant forgeries appeared on the Greek isle of Aegina, where, in the sixth century B.C., copiers duplicated silver coins by stamping planches comprised of copper cores washed with silver. Under the monetary reforms of Solon, the archon of Athens during the economic chaos of 594 B.C., the temporary government issued penalties against counterfeiting. During the reign of Nikokles of Cyprus around 330 B.C., his coiner at Paphos concealed microencryption in a bas-relief of Alexander the Great dressed in the lion head of Hercules. The minute letters spelling "Nikokles" blended into the lion's mane. Historians deduce that the king also intended his name to indicate his independence of Greek rule.

Roman mint officials introduced punch marks to denote purity and added dentate or serrate rims to halt clipping and counterfeiting. According to Roman encyclopedist Pliny the Elder's *Natural History* (A.D. 77), during the last years of the Roman Republic, the crime of forgery sullied the reputation of Mark Antony, one of the triumvirs who ruled Rome in 40 B.C. after the assassination of Julius Caesar. Antony altered the silver *denarius* and the brass small change piece by tempering their metals with iron.

To outflank less noteworthy counterfeiters in the Roman Empire, who used clay molds to cast ersatz coins, Marcus Marius Gratidianus, who was praetor in 85 B.C., issued a law requiring testing of silver *denarii*. The refinement of public moneys earned him a hero's reputation and public statues to the glory of his name. Pliny fumed that Gratidianus's test was "the only means to teach deceit and wickedness, for many a man will give too much for false money: yea, and many silver deniers for one counterfeit, well and cleanly made; to take forsooth a pattern thereby, and learn to deceive others" (Pliny 1962, 369).

The production of phony currency in the ancient world required numerous skills, including engraving and molding. Counterfeiters' molds date to the creation of coins. Usually formed of clay or terra cotta, molds that produced either blank planchets or finished coins survive from Egyptian, Greek, Roman, Celt, German, Syrian, Lebanese, Israeli, and Tunisian mint operations as well as from the workshops of counterfeiters. Of the two methods, finished coins were the most cost effective. Blanks required a second stage of stamping with an engraved die. A serious offense in the Byzantine empire, counterfeiting resulted in legislation preserved in the Codex Theodosianus, which was firm, yet did not suppress criminal efforts.

In England, counterfeiting, clipping, shaving, and other forms of specie skimming threatened the late-tenth century peace that King Ethelred bought at the rate of 40 million pennies a year in tribute to Danish occupation forces. To assure quality and keep the Danes satisfied, the king issued a firm law in 978 against false or "light" money by calling for trial by ordeal. The guilty lost their hands, which were hacked off and nailed above the moneyer's bench. Furthermore, he warned:

> Concerning merchants who bring false or chipped money to our port, we have said that they shall defend themselves if they are able; if they cannot, let them incur the penalty of their *wer* [man-price] or of their life just as the king wishes; or, as we have said, let them prove themselves innocent in this ordeal that they knew there was nothing wrong with the money itself with which they carried on their business; and afterwards let him suffer the loss due to his carelessness, so that he exchange it with the decreed moneyers for money pure and of correct weight ["Aethelred II the Unready"].

Ethelred spelled out to post customs agents, estate managers, clerics, aldermen, and citizens of all types, whether Dane or English, that he would not tolerate false coinage.

Over a century later, King Henry I, who came to power in 1100, faced serious problems with debasement and counterfeiting. After the monetary reform of 1125, his mintmaster reduced counterfeiting by striking a nick in the edge of each legal coin. The king also issued a threat of serious punishment — blinding, lopped limbs, or death — to any who in any way copied or altered legal tender. Henry III carried out that threat in 1224 between Christmas and Twelfth Night, when he maimed 94 coiners at Winchester for forgery by hacking off their testicles and right hands. The crippling of the nation's experts forced the king to close 19 branch mints for lack of staff. As the *Anglo-Saxon Chronicle* explained, "And that was all in perfect justice, because that they had undone all the land with the great quantity of base coin that they all bought" ("Anglo-Saxon Chronicle").

In the American colonies, counterfeiters could expect flogging, hanging, or sale into slavery, the punishment suffered by a surgeon found counterfeiting in Canada in 1690. In 1773, stamped warnings on Virginia's official paper money declared "Death to Counterfeit." Printer Harry Ashby altered the next run of paper notes with a variant phrase, "To Counterfeit Is Death." Colonial printer Benjamin Franklin of Philadelphia made copying difficult by stamping the imprints of real leaves from plaster casts on banknotes. Nonetheless, the crime proliferated, especially during the American Revolution, when British forgers produced copper plates of paper continentals dated September 26, 1778.

In England, one of the outstanding counterfeiters in national history thrived around 1800. William Booth, a Warwickshire farmer, lived far from town in a hideout equipped with rope ladders and trapdoors. He used fake Bank of England plates and those of local banks to make high-quality tokens and halfcrowns. Living close to Birmingham gave him an added advantage of accessing bullion from factories. He thrived until 1812, when a family servant passed a phony two-pound note and was arrested. When constables searched the premises, they caught Booth printing notes and sentenced him to hang.

The harshness of anti-forgery laws outraged the populace. From 1805 to 1818, courts convicted 501 perpetrators and hanged 207. The weight of the law fell on too many innocent citizens, who could be charged with merely possessing counterfeit money. In protest, the Society of the Arts issued *Report on the Mode of Preventing the Forgery of Bank Notes* (1819), which shifted blame for runaway counterfeiting to the Bank of England's slipshod note production. Contributing authors T. C. Hansard, T. Ransom, R. H. Sully, and Richard Williamson recommended four remedies — the use of diamond type, copper plate engraving from a composite note incised by three different engravers, a new copper plate printing machine, and fine steel engraved plates. Satirical caricaturist George Cruikshank lambasted the policy of capital punishment for forgers by sketching the allegorical likeness of Britannia, England's female symbol, topped by a bare skull. In the cartoon, she singles out Jack Ketch, the 17th-century executioner at Tyburn Prison who was the original of a nickname for all hangmen and a comic figure in Punch and Judy shows and barroom ditties.

After three study commissions and a riot caused by Cruikshank's cartoon, the English government hired Murray, Draper, Fairman & Company, a Philadelphia-based firm organized in 1810, to install a siderographic or steel-plated transfer printing process that could produce a complex note background. The pioneering equipment, invented by Jacob Perkins of Newburyport, Massachusetts, operated hard and soft steel cylinders to duplicate imprints. Perkins and his partner, Gideon Fairman, journeyed to England in 1818 and equipped a factory to make plates and to print banknotes and the nation's first penny postage stamps.

To suppress forgers and combat bogus money by domestic and foreign criminals, on July 5, 1865, U.S. Secretary of the Treasury Hugh McCullough organized the Secret Service. The agency monitored U.S. currency and coins, treasury checks, food coupons, and postage stamps. In 1883, Bostonian Josh Tatum created a new wrinkle in fraud. A familiar deaf-mute among local merchants, he circulated 1,000 Liberty Head nickels that he had plated with gold to look like five-dollar gold pieces. After snagging a neat profit of $4.95 per coin, he made a run of gilded nickels five times the initial platage and spread 2,000 of them as far away as New York. After his arrest by Treasury agents, his attorney successfully pled an unusual defense — the counterfeiter never demanded change. Thus, the error was the fault of cashiers who assumed the gold-hued coins were worth 100 times their actual value. The trick gave new meaning to the phrase "You're joshing."

The seriousness of counterfeiting to national security involves the destabilization of treasuries, the intent of Prince Ludwig Windisch-Graetz of Hungary, who mastermined copying of the French 1,000-*franc* note in 1925 to ruin the Bank of France and enable his party to seize Hungary. In Nazi Germany during World War II, Heinrich Himmler conceived the counterfeiting of 8,965,080 banknotes in five-, ten-, 20-, and 50-pound denominations during Operation Bernhard, a military scheme intended to drain the British treasury and bankrupt the Allies. The U.S. Office of Strategic Services attempted a similar weakening of the Japanese yen by circulating bogus bills in Asia.

After World War II, counterfeiters in Communist China enjoyed a heyday because of the ease with which they carried off their crime. During high inflation, they targeted greedy hoarders with U.S. bills, particularly the dollar. Few criminals faced penalties because the purchasers had to remain silent to conceal their own felony of possessing foreign currency. A similar plot against Cuban money in 1959 set Florida-based anti–Castroites to the task of duplicating *pesos* to flood the market and undermine the island's Communist regime.

Like wartime plots, domestic counterfeiting follows a pattern of rising crime during hard times. In the 1930s, Depression-era printers tended to pass fake one- and five-dollar bills. During World War II, the denomination rose to ten dollars, a shift necessitated by the high cost of creating dummy plates and purchasing quality offset presses, ink, and paper. By the 1960s, inflation had driven counterfeiters to up the denomination to 20 dollars. At the end of the 20th century, counterfeiters of U.S. currency made up to $11 million worth of fake money per year.

The most copied world money is U.S. currency, which is frequently duplicated in Colombia. The present law covers counterfeiting or altering paper currency, counterfeiting coins, and the possession of counterfeit with intent to defraud. All three crimes carry a 15-year sentence and fine up to $5,000 or both. Altering coins for the purpose of defrauding carries a five-year sentence and $2,000 fine or both. For forging or trafficking in bogus bonds and checks, criminals face ten years in prison, a $10,000 fine, or both. Additional punishments attach to mutilating, cutting, disfiguring, perforating, uniting, or reproducing bills, checks, bonds, postage or revenue stamps, and securities of the United States or foreign governments.

Since 1996, the U.S. Bureau of Engraving and Printing has advanced security features on paper money, the first alteration in 68 years. Changes involved enlargement of por-

This five-*gulden* note from Holland presents an interlinking series of patterns to challenge the counterfeiter.

This 50-*escudo* bill from Portugal exhibits the fine webbing that designers employ to foil counterfeiters.

traits and setting them off-center, more life-like details on presidential portraits, a watermark visible on both sides, colored polyester security threads, flag and denomination visible on both sides, ink that appears to shift from green to black, microprinting of "United States of America," and fine parallel lines in the background. These alterations combat technical criminal methods involving lithographics and reprographics by color copiers, ink jet printing, electronic digital scanners, color workstations, and computer software interface to generate fake paper money.

In the United States, numerous details of coinage increase the cost of minting, but protect the public from counterfeit. Real coins above five cents in value receive a corrugation on the rim called reeding that machines stamp in place. To copy the three-dimensional coinage, criminals have to do more than impress fake planchets top and bottom. To duplicate the rim, they must pour molten metal into dies or molds to make bogus coins. Their methods leave tell-tale cracks, die marks, uneven reeding, crooked or missing edging, and pimples that are visible to the eye or under a microscope. Another scam involves the alteration of dates and mint marks on genuine coins to make them attractive to collectors.

Fake bills also vary from the standard method of manufacture. To deter counterfeiters, U.S. notes pass through a high-speed rotary press that sinks imagery below the surface. To create a three-dimensional effect, printers ink the plates, then wipe residue from the surface. Transfer results from the wells of ink in the design and letter grooves. The use of twenty tons of pressure on each sheet of 32 uncut bills produces finely recessed lines, which are difficult to duplicate by lesser plates and presses. The most difficult elements to simulate are the minute blue and red fibers that paper-makers embed in the surface. In England and 48 other countries, treasuries add a thin metallic security thread to the paper as an anti-crime device.

Obvious signs of counterfeiting are low-grade ink and paper, imperfect printing, and variations in quality. On U.S. currency, Federal Reserve and Treasury seals should be sharply detailed down to the sawtooth edging. Suspicious bank officials and police check the portrait, which should be distinct and realistic. They also determine whether the background is clear and unspotted and screen for blunt or misshapen points on seals, fine lines that are smudged or irregular, and blurred scrollwork and margins. Another giveaway is uneven serial numbers, which should be distinctly printed in the same color as the Treasury Seal.

Other methods of establishing authenticity include boosting the durability of currency. Recent manufacturing techniques have increased the life-span of bills by making paper money stand up to crumpling, folding, washing, soiling, and soaking in such solvents as acid, gasoline, and laundry detergent. To aid people with impaired vision, the U.S. Bureau of Engraving and Printing produces 20-dollar and 50-dollar notes with a large dark numeral visible on the lower righthand corner of the reverse side. These counter-measures to counterfeiting increase print costs by two cents per bill.

The people who have attempted to foil anti-counterfeiting measures extend across much of world and United States history; they had a variety of fates:

counterfeiter	*nationality*	*dates*	*product*	*fate*
Sulejman Asanoski	Yugoslavian	1995	U.S. bills	disappeared
John the Blind	Bohemian	1309	English sterlings	died in battle at Crecy
Ackerman	U.S.	1840s	unknown	natural death
Charles Adams	U.S.	1860s	$10	arrested
David L. Anderson	U.S.	1880–1918	unknown	shot
Thomas Bacchus	English	1772	coins from clippings	hanged
Ebenezer Ball	U.S.	1811	unknown	executed
José Bandiera	Portuguese	1953	banknote	natural death
Thomas Barber	English	1798	pennies	acquitted
Carl Wilhelm Becker	German	1790–1800s	antique coins	famed copier
Charles "Dutchman" Becker	German	1929	$10, £100, £500	convicted
Edward P. Bennett	U.S.	1880–1890	silver dollars	imprisoned
Frederick Biebusch	German	1860–1870	unknown	arrested
Joseph Blandchard	U.S.	1674	base coin	arrested
Giangiacomo Bonzagna	Parmesan	ca. 1560	Roman bronzes	famed copier
William Booth	English	1812	tokens	hanged
Charles Brancati	Italian	1920s	unknown	shot
Baldwin S. Brendell	U.S.	1897–1899	$100 silver certificates	convicted
William "Long Bill" Brockway	U.S.	1850–1890	U.S. bonds	imprisoned; paroled at 82
Abel Buell	U.S.	1764	notes	branded, imprisoned, lost property
Adolf Burger	German	1945	$100; British bank notes	liberated
Stephen Burroughs	U.S.	1780–1800	coins	became a teacher
Jack Canter	U.S.	1873	railroad stock	imprisoned
Ann Carson	U.S.	1816	unknown	natural death
James Colbert	English	1860s	$10	jailed
Giovanni Covino	Paduan	ca. 1560	Roman bronzes	famed copier
William Challoner	English	1696	coins	executed
Arthur Chambers	English	1706	coins	hanged
Austin M. Clark	U.S.	1860–1863	gold coins	unknown
John L. T. Cooper	U.S.	1905	$10 gold coins	imprisoned
Anna Corne	English	1954	stamps	suspended
Thomas H. Daniels	U.S.	1819	unknown	hanged himself
Govind Davria	Indian	1800s	paper money	set himself on fire
Pedro de Moreno	French	1901–1904	railroad tickets	sentenced
Thomas Denton	English	1789	coins	hanged
Ricardo de Requesans	Costa Rican	1897	*pesos*	imprisoned
Giovanni de Sperati	Italian	1954	stamps	suspended
Jean de Sperati	French	1954	stamps	suspended sentence

counterfeiter	*nationality*	*dates*	*product*	*fate*
Raul de Thuin	Mexican	1966	stamps	natural death
Alfredo-Hecktor Donadieu	French	1918–1948	100-*franc* notes	imprisoned
Robert Douglass	U.S.	1825	unknown	hanged
Samuel B. Downey	U.S.	1897–1899	$100 silver certificates	convicted
John du Plisse	U.S.	1674	colonial coins	convicted
Belle Freeland	U.S.	1893	paper money	arrested
Judson Freeland	U.S.	1893	paper money	imprisoned
William Grey	English	1818	base coins	hanged
George Grimes	U.S.	1674	base coins	arrested
Emanuel Henry Gruber	U.S.	1860–1863	gold coin	unknown
Phoebe Harris	English	1786	unknown	strangled
Hartley gang	English	1780s	coppers	hanged
Gustav Hennies	Portuguese	1953	banknotes	imprisoned
Thomas Houghton	English	1697	sixpenny stamps	sentenced to death
John Howell	English	1790–1806	shillings, sixpences	imprisoned
Ellert P. Ingham	U.S.	1897–1899	$100 silver certificates	convicted
William Jacobs	U.S.	1897–1899	$100 silver certificates	convicted
Edwin Johnson	Canadian	1880	paper money	suspended
John Jones	English	1789	coin	hanged
William L. Kendig	U.S.	1897–1899	$100 silver certificates	convicted
Ryan Kore	Canadian	2001	$10, $20	arrested
Walter Koslov	U.S.	1930–1940	50¢ coins	sentenced
Friedrich Krüger	German	1941	pound notes	disappeared
Victor Lustig	U.S.	1935	$100	convicted
Karel Marang	Portuguese	1953	banknotes	escaped
Louis R. Martin	English	1875–1883	$500	imprisoned
James Mattiazzo	Canadian	2001	$10, $20	arrested
Will Maw	English	1705–1711	coins	convicted
Ivan Miassojedoff	Russian	1953	£50 notes	natural death
Frederico Mora	Costa Rican	1897	pesos	imprisoned
Giuseppe Morello	Sicilian	1903	$5 bills	imprisoned
Edward Mueller	U.S.	1938–1949	$1 bills	released
Christian Murphy	English	1789	coins	hanged
Francis Naylor	U.S.	1938	$10 bills	tortured
Frederick Neilson	Australian	1954	gold sovereigns	exonerated
Harvey K. Newitt	U.S.	1897–1899	$100 silver certificates	convicted
Emanuel Ninger	German	1890–1896	$20, $50, $100	paroled
Charles Nissen	English	1879	stamps	became the king's stamp dealer
Phil Oster	U.S.	1872	unknown	imprisoned
Patrick O'Sullivan	U.S.	1755	£2	hanged
William Parsons	English	1740s	unknown	hanged
Daniel Perreau	English	1775	bonds	hanged
Robert Perreau	English	1775	bonds	hanged
Elmar Raamat	U.S.	1930–1940	50¢ coins	sentenced
Arthur Reis	Portuguese	1953	banknotes	freed
Maria Reis	Portuguese	1953	banknotes	freed
Samuel Roberts	English	1772	coins from clippings	hanged
William Roberts	English	1944–1948	coupons	imprisoned

counterfeiter	*nationality*	*dates*	*product*	*fate*
John Roettiers	English	1696	guineas	fired
Francis Salisbury	English	1697	sixpenny stamps	sentenced to death
Hans Schmidt	U.S.	1913	diplomas	electrocuted
Nicolaus Seeländer	German	1740s	medieval coins	famed copier
Duke Galeazzo Sforza	Milanese	1470	Venetian currency	assassinated
Thomas Sharp	English	1704	coins	hanged
Sing Lee	Chinese	1910	gold coins	assassinated with a hatchet
John Albert Skog	Swedish	1904	100 *kroner* notes	shot himself
Solomon Smolianoff	Russian	1928	£50 notes	imprisoned
Barbara Spencer	English	1721	unknown	hanged
Jacob Sprinkle	U.S.	1850s	silver	natural death
Nancy Sprinkle	U.S.	1850s	silver	natural death
Thomas Stucley	English	1578	—	killed in battle
Arthur Taylor	U.S.	1897–1899	$100 silver certificates	convicted
John Taylor	English	1800	documents	released
Charles Ulrich	Prussian	1860s	$10	imprisoned
William Watts	U.S.	1935	$100	convicted
Edward John Wellman	U.S.	1930–1940	50¢ coins	sentenced
Ludwig Windisch-Graetz	Hungarian	1920s	*francs*	freed

At present, agencies worldwide — Europol, Interpol, Scotland Yard, and the U.S. Secret Service — track counterfeit coins and bills. In Canada, the Royal Canadian Mounted Police, headquartered in Edmonton, Halifax, Vancouver, and Regina, operates a forensic laboratory that backs investigation of counterfeiting. Through examination and analysis of physical evidence, a staff of 300 forensic scientists, technologists, and administrators provide data and expert court testimony on bogus foreign and domestic currency, bonds, credit cards, licenses, passorts, travelers checks, and visas. Equipment studies chemical alteration, handwriting, photocopying, stamping, typing, and printing as a means of apprehending counterfeiters.

See also **Matthew Boulton; Baldwin Brendell; William E. Brockway; Abel Buell; Adolf Burger; colonial coins; continental currency; Joseph Hilarius Eckhel; English money; euro; Mel Fisher; fishhook money; greenbacks; hallmark; incuse; Interpol; Irish money; Knights Hospitallers; John Law; *markka;* Hugh McCulloch; Muhammad ibn Tughluq; Sir Isaac Newton; Emanuel Ninger; paper money; penny; Jacob Perkins; pieces of eight; John Roettiers; Spanish coins; U.S. Bureau of Engraving and Printing; U.S. Secret Service.**

SOURCES: "Aethelred II the Unready: The Laws of London 978." http://www.britannia.com/history/docs/unready.html. • Allen, Larry. *Encyclopedia of Money.* New York: Checkmark Books, 2001. • "The Anglo-Saxon Chronicle." http://sunsite.berkeley.edu/OMACL/Anglo/. • Bowers, Q. David. "Jacob Perkins, Early Die Cutter." *Hobbies,* July 1981, p. 123–124. • "The Bureau of Engraving and Printing." http://www.bep.treas.gov/. • Clain-Stefanelli, Elvira, and Vladimir Clain-Stefanelli. *The Beauty and Lore of Coins, Currency, and Medals.* Croton-on-Hudson, N.Y.: Riverwood Publishers, 1974. • Cribb, Joe. *Money.* Toronto: Stoddart, 1990. • Cribb, Joe, Barrie Cook, and Ian Carradice. *The Coin Atlas.* London: Little, Brown and Co., 1999. • Davis, Curtis Carroll. "The Craftiest of Men: William P. Wood and the Establishment of the United States Secret Service." *Maryland Historical Magazine,* Summer 1988, pp. 111–126. • "Forensic Laboratory," *Royal Canadian Mounted Police,* http://www.rcmp-grc.gc.ca/html/labs.htm. • Gilbert, Martin. *Atlas of the Holocaust.* New York: William Morrow and Co., 1993. • Grierson, Philip. *Numismatics.* London: Oxford University Press, 1975. • James, Michael. "Counterfeiters Using Desktop Printers to Churn Out a Cascade of High-Quality Bogus Cash." *Buffalo News,* July 12, 1998. • James, Peter, and Nick Thorpe. *Ancient Inventions.* New York: Ballantine, 1994. • Kumpikevicius, Gordon. "The Art of the Coin Forger." *Canadian Coin News,* May 27, 2000.

• "Lake Search Yields Counterfeit Bills, but No Nazi Gold." Bergen, N.J., *Record,* November 23, 2000. • Levy, Alan. "Adolf Burger: The Forger as a Work of Art." *Prague Post,* November 1, 2000. • Laing, Lloyd R. *Coins and Archaeology.* New York: Schocken Books, 1969. • Nash, Jay Robert. *Encyclopedia of World Crime.* 6 vols. Wilmette, Ill.: CrimeBooks Inc., 1990. • Pliny. *The Natural History.* New York: McGraw-Hill, 1962. • Powell, John. "The Birmingham Coiners, 1770–1816." *History Today,* July 1993, p. 49–55. • Reed, Mort. *Cowles Complete Encyclopedia of U.S. Coins.* New York: Cowles Book Company, 1969. • "The Search for Answers." *CBS News,* November 21, 2001. • Sinclair, David. *The Pound.* London: Century Books, 2000. • Stone, Alexander. "Illegal Tender." *Harvard International Review,* Summer 2001, p. 7. • "United States Secret Service," http://www.treas.gov/usss. • Wheal, Elizabeth-Anne, Stephen Pope, and James Taylor. *Encyclopedia of the Second World War.* New York: Castle Books, 1989.

counterstamp

As an expedient method of coining new specie, governments have typically counterstamped or countermarked foreign moneys with a small figure or symbol establishing the validity of the coin as legal tender, as occurred in the Mediterranean when the treasury of the island of Thasos legitimized coins of their Ottoman Turk overlords in 1893 with a countermark.

Counterstamping helped to spread early Greek coins to neighboring realms. As slaves dug silver from the Athenian mines at Laurion, the city-state produced elegant coins in large number. Other regions, lacking raw material, found it easier and cheaper to overstrike the Athenian coins than to mint their own. Careless use of the punch often left exposed the outer edges of an original design.

The Greek system of overstamping had several practical functions. It allowed mints to withdraw and recycle outdated or worn specie. Counterstamping served the colonies of ancient Corinth, a city-state that rivaled Athens for its quality coinage, as well as victorious cities that remarked the coins of their defeated rivals. In turn, mintmasters in rival cities stamped unique images over the likenesses of Aphrodite and winged Pegasus that characterized Corinth's *stater* and *drachma.*

During the second century of the Roman Empire, turmoil in Jewish Palestine caused the Roman conquerors to expunge the name "Judaea" from local coins and replace it with Syria-Palaestina. Devout Hebrews fought back with a counterstamp. After the destruction of the temple at Jerusalem, Rome intended to rename the city Colonia Aelia Capitolina, to raise a temple of Jupiter Capitolinus above the temple ruins, and to force Judeans to accept Roman customs. According to Eusebius, author of *Historia Ecclesiastica* (*Ecclesiastical History*) (A.D. 324), the Romans kept so tight a control that they forbade Jews to approach Jerusalem even on foot.

Against heavy odds, Jews refused assimilation that required them to abandon all aspects of their worship and lifestyle, including issuing coins, keeping the Sabbath and marking the Jewish calendar, teaching the Torah, and the customary *berit milah* ("ritual circumcision"), a symbol of God's covenant with Abraham, which Domitian made a capital crime before A.D. 86. A half century later around Hebron, Rabbi Akiva chose as Jewish champion Simon (or Shimon) Bar Kochba, literally "Son of the Star," a descendant of King David. Akiva proclaimed Bar Kochba the messiah — the "star out of Jacob" foretold by the Old Testament prophet Isaiah. The rising hero incited the militant band of nearly 600,000 to three years of guerrilla warfare known as the "circumcision war" (Pollak 1990, 46).

To demonstrate his disrespect for Rome and the new Emperor Hadrian, in 132 B.C., Bar Kochba seized tax revenues and stole strongboxes from Roman outposts. Until 134 B.C., he overstruck imperial coins as quarter shekels picturing Simon's name within triumphal palm fronds. On the reverse, he pictured a palm and urn and the legend "Year one of Jerusalem's freedom." Other of Bar Kochba's shekel coins pictured the Torah within the holy of holies at the temple, the *kinor* ("harp") of David, and the trumpets by which Aaron's sons called the Hebrews to the tabernacle to worship or to war.

The resulting war brought Commander

Gaius Julius Severus from Britannia with the Tenth Legion and the Emperor Hadrian from Rome to oversee the situation. Combat ground on, costing the Jews 580,000 casualties, 985 villages, and 50 fortresses, according to the Roman historian Dio Cassius. The rebels relented shortly after their hero died in battle at Betar in A.D. 135. Rome rebuilt Jerusalem and named it Aelia Capitolina, but Hadrian took no joy in the victory and conquests. His only reply upon return to Rome was the customary phrase "I and the Army are well." The Roman treasury commemorated the hard fighting with a coin inscribed "*Exercitus Judaicus*" ("the Judaean army"). A coin pictured the temple at Aelia Capitolina housing Jupiter Capitolinus, a pagan deity who was anathema to the Jews.

Other examples of overstamping coins permeate history.

- England's treasury made use of the gold *pesos* captured from treasure ships from New World minting sites by restamping the plunder with GR, the royal cipher of Georgius Rex, George III. At first unwelcome to English citizens, the coins eventually recycled through the Bank of England for converting to bullion for recoinage in more familiar form.
- In Barbados, Grenada, Jamaica, and Montserrat during the resettlement of the New World, local coinages overstamped Spain's *reales* and crudely struck cob coins with their own dies to create a form of quasi-official island coinage.
- In 1573, William of Orange impressed the Spanish *pesos* of Philip II on the front with Holland's lion and on the back with the arrow bundle symbolizing the united provinces of Holland. Circulating simultaneously with coins struck at the Duchy of Gelderland, the hastily remarked coins increased Dutch buying power.
- In 1663, during the reign of Dom João IV of Portugal, overstamping of Portuguese silver coins elevated their value 25 percent as a boost to the economy during a war with Spain.

The switching of nationalities continued with a fury in the 18th century. The Hanoverian kings sullied their monetary history with overstrikes. Jamaican moneyers made use of the Spanish eight-*escudo* piece in 1758 by overstamping the image of Ferdinand VI with GR, two letters representing George II, King of England. Treasuries in Martinique and Guadeloupe applied the same method of legitimizing Spanish coins for island use. The custom continued into the 1770s on coins restamped for George III. The imprint of his face on the portrait pieces of eight of Charles IV of Spain prompted the composition of an unflattering barroom ditty:

> The Bank, to make
> their Spanish dollar pass,
> Stamped the head of a fool
> on the head of an ass [Reinfeld 1953, p. 90].

One of the most ridiculed counterstamps of the period was the 1804 Bank of England dollar. To halt counterfeiters, who were undeterred by threats of beheading or transportation to Australia, the Tower Mint issued a coin with the background covered with a stone wall, perhaps suggesting the strength of the Bank of England.

On Prince Edward Island, moneyers simplified the problem of restamping by punching out the central dump of six-shilling coins, reducing them in value to one shilling coins called "holey dollars" (Jacobs 2001, 434). Contributing to the legend of P. E. I.'s dollars was the disappearance of the dumps, which should have returned to the mint for melting. One possibility is collusion between the minter and George Birnie, an importer of West Indian rum, sugar, and liqueurs who may have made a profitable under-the-table trade.

The flawed system of making doughnut dollars also suited the mint of New South Wales, Australia, from 1813 to 1822. The "holey dollar," which the moneyer had counterstamped with a circlet marked "New South Wales 1813," was worth five shillings. The plug punched free of the circle was valued at only one shilling and threepence. Circulation of the altered ring reduced the coins to the level of counterfeit.

See also **elephant token; English money; Islamic money; Knights Hospitallers; Sir Isaac Newton; pieces of eight; Russian money; scrip; tokens; treasure ships.**

SOURCES: Bass, George F., ed. *Ships and Shipwrecks of the Americas: A History Based on Underwater Archaeology*. London: Thames and Hudson, 1996. • Cribb, Joe. *Money*. Toronto: Stoddart, 1990. • *Handbook to Life in Ancient Greece*. New York: Facts on File, Inc., 1997. • Jacobs, Wayne L. "The Mystery of the Disappearing P. E. I. 'Dumps.'" *Canadian Numismatic Association Journal*, November 2001, 433–438. • Lewis, Brenda Ralph. *Coins & Currency*. New York: Random House, 1993. • Meshorer, Ya'akov. *Coins of the Ancient World*. Jerusalem: Jerusalem Publishing House, 1974. • Pollak, Henry. *Coinage & Conflict*. Clifton, N.J.: Coin & Currency Institute, 2001. • Reed, Mort. *Cowles Complete Encyclopedia of U.S. Coins*. New York: Cowles Book Company, 1969. • Reinfeld, Fred. *Treasury of the World's Coins*. New York: Sterling Publishing, 1953. • "Unlocking the Secrets of the Kinor and the bar Kochba Coins." http://www.harpofdavid.com/barkochba.htm. • Wigoder, Geoffrey. *The Encyclopedia of Judaism*. New York: Macmillan, 1989.

cowrie

The cowrie, a small humped or olive-shaped snail shell known as the *Cypraea moneta*, is the most widely used primitive currency in world history. It was a common form of money in China from 1500 B.C., in Pacific rim countries before 1000 B.C., and in India into the late A.D. 1800s. The wide-ranging cowrie, which takes its name from the Sanskrit *kauri*, is easily located in crevices and under stones in shallow tropical lagoons. Naturally polished and often freckled a deep golden brown or yellow or ringed with gold, the one- to three-inch oblong shell has a dentate labial opening into the inner chamber. The ubiquitous olive-shaped shell carried a wide-ranging significance. Governments valued the cowrie as coin because it was tough, easy to locate and clean, and impossible to counterfeit. Individuals collected cowries because they increased human fertility. As money, it survived longer than any other currency, reaching people in Asia, Africa, and the Pacific.

From early times, the cowrie has been valued as money among Asians, Pacific islanders, and West Africans and as royal insignia among Fijian chieftains. In the Solomon Islands, artisans fashioned shells into both money and personal adornments, which found their way into sailors' curios. In the description of Venetian traveler Marco Polo, who visited in China in 1275 and compiled *The Travels of Marco Polo* (1299), the cowrie was "white porcelain found in the sea" (Clain-Stefanelli and Clain-Stefanelli 1974, p. 15). The shell was so common to the Chinese that the ideograph for "shell" evolved into synonyms for merchandising and shopping, price, and wealth.

During the Shang dynasty, which began in 1500 B.C., Chinese bronze workers inscribed drinking cups with records of strings of cowries given as gifts. Numerous incidents of hoarding shells in Anyang, the Shang capital, in 1375 B.C. prompted Emperor P'an Keng to scold his ministers for their greed. Far from the Pacific Ocean at Anyang, in 1200 B.C., tomb attendants buried Queen Fu Hao, consort of Wu Ding and the first female general in Chinese history, in a lacquered coffin along with three ivory goblets, 200 bronze vessels, 700 jade sculptures, and 7,000 cowries, proof of her wealth and prestige.

At the order of the prime minister, around 600 B.C., mintmasters of the Ch'u (or Tsu) kingdom shaped turtle-back coins like tiny gold cowries. Beginning around 400 B.C., bronze workers in Yunnan Province fashioned cowrie containers for shell storage. Families paid the toll for entrance to the afterlife by placing cowries on the tongues of the deceased.

Modernization introduced European coinage, which eclipsed the primitive cowrie. To simplify regional finance, Chinese treasury officials outlawed the shells in 221 B.C. in favor of stackable coins. As a tie to early Chinese tradition, in A.D. 10, Hsin Wang Mang, an energetic reformer of the Han Dynasty, briefly restored the cowrie as legal tender. As colonists migrated from mainland China to the Ryukyu

Islands to search for cowries, they spread Chinese culture throughout Japan.

In the late Middle Ages, Islamic Africans traded in cowries, brass rings and rods, and iron bars, a fact observed by mid–14th century Muslim traveler ibn Battuta, author of *Tuhfat al-Nuzzar fi Ghara'ib al-Amsar wa'Ajaib al'Asfar* (*On Curiosities of Cities and Wonders of Travel*) (1354), one of the earliest descriptions of the peoples of Ceylon, Sudan, and the Maldives. He witnessed the use of cowries in Mali and Sudan and commented specifically on relative value in the Maldives. After falling ill with fever, he determined to sell some of the jewels his hosts had given him. In exchange, he hoped to get enough cowries to pay passage to Bengal. The Wazír, who had given him the gold, demanded its return, but forbade the exchange of cowries for gold to keep the traveler on his island. Other reports explain how Islamic merchants to Gao and the Sahelian kingdoms used as currency gold ore, salt, slaves, ivory, kola nuts, and cowrie shells, bringing with them their religious faith, which Africans rapidly adopted. In 1526, Leo Africanus of Granada, author of *The Description of Africa* (1550), quantified Persian cowries in monetary terms, with 400 shells equaling a *ducat*.

According to a three-volume travelogue, *The Voyage of François Pyrard of Laval to the East Indies, the Maladives, the Molucas and Brazil* (early 1600s), the Bengali maintained a dual monetary standard comprised of cowries and precious metals. The financial system standardized cowrie trade in lots, 12,000 shells per basket. The shells were the sole currency of the queen of the Maldives in A.D. 916. Cowries were so valuable to traders with the Maldives that they readily traded luxury goods, rice, and spices for them. Nigerians rolled beads from cowries purchased from as far away as the Maldives and exchanged necklaces like native American wampum. In exchange for ivory, palm oil, pepper, and slaves, exploiters of Nigeria from Denmark, Great Britain, Holland, and Portugal reimbursed naive natives with bags of cowries and cases of gin.

Throughout Africa, cowries carried predetermined valuation, for example, 25 for a chicken, 500 for a goat, and 2,500 for a beef. The shells could be grouped and evaluated in various combinations. One simple method of accounting was to string 32 cowries into a *rotl* (necklace). The next denomination was the bunch, consisting of five strings or 160 shells. Ten bunches or 1,600 shells constituted a head of cowries. In Timbuktu, where cowries had served for cash since the A.D. 500s, fixed rates pegged the French *franc* at 1,000 shells. After the French colonized the Sudan, they controlled cowrie circulation to boost the economy of lesser villages.

For commercial convenience, European explorers of the colonial period rapidly replaced the cowrie by introducing minted coins for international trade. Uganda was one of the nations to make the switch from primitive money, yet retained shells for local buying and selling. In 1860, Ugandan males could purchase wives at the rate of 1,000 shells per woman. In 1911, regional values were set on the cowrie:

purchase	*cost in cowries*
cow	2,500 shells
ivory tusk	1,000 shells
goat	500 shells
chicken	25 shells

The medium of exchange remained viable until the laying of railroad tracks after World War I, which brought European coinage to isolated areas above and below the Equator. As coined money supplanted shells, the French *sou* replaced the cowrie in Mali for payment of taxes. To end the dual monetary system, government agents burned state stockpiles of cowries for lime. The only cowries still circulating were legal tender only for limited folk trade.

***See also* African money; blood money; fishhook money; India, money of; piracy; ring and bullet money.**

SOURCES: Akimichi, Tomoya. "Okinawa and the Sea Roads of East Asia." *Japan Echo*, August 2000. • Allen, Larry. *Encyclopedia of Money*. New

York: Checkmark Books, 2001. • "The Artistry of African Currency." http://www.nmafa.si.edu/exhibits/site/manillas.htm. • Bloch, David. "Salt and the Evolution of Mone." *Journal of Salt History*, Vol. 7, 1999. • "The British Royal Mint." http://www.royalmint.com. • Clain-Stefanelli, Elvira, and Vladimir Clain-Stefanelli. *The Beauty and Lore of Coins, Currency, and Medals*. Croton-on-Hudson, N.Y.: Riverwood Publishers, 1974. • Davies, Glyn. *A History of Money from Ancient Times to the Present Day*. Cardiff: University of Wales Press, 1994. • Einzig, Paul. *Primitive Money*. Oxford: Pergamon Press, 1966. • Ibn Battuta. *The Travels of Ibn Battuta*. Cambridge: Cambridge University Press, 1971. • James, Peter, and Nick Thorpe. *Ancient Inventions*. New York: Ballantine, 1994. • "Leo Africanus: Description of Timbuktu." *The Description of Africa*, http://www.wsu.edu:8080/~wldciv/world_civ_reader/world_civ_reader_2/leo_africanus.html. • "Nigeria: The Free Giant." *Time Europe*, October 10, 1960. • Opitz, Charles J. *Odd and Curious Money*. Ocala, Fla.: First Impressions, 1986. • Weatherford, Jack. *The History of Money: From Sandstone to Cyberspace*. Pittsburgh, Pa.: Three Rivers Press, 1998. • Xu, Jay. "The Enigmatic Art of Sanxingdui." *Natural History*, November 1, 2001, 72–79.

credit card fraud

The use of plastic cards to obtain cash, goods, or services is a 20th-century phenomenon that spawned its own excesses and crimes, including manipulating cards to acquire cash. Chicago bankers at First National and Continental of Illinois incriminated themselves in December 1966 by competing unfairly with Bank of America through postal delivery of unsolicited credit cards to local bank clients. Receivers abused and duplicated the cards, forged cards, and obtained goods fraudulently, costing the banks up to three million dollars. Because of the costly experiment in mass distribution of cards, the U.S. Congress outlawed mailing unsolicited cards; the Illinois legislature tightened laws on credit card misuse. A similar case of ill-advised distribution of cards occurred in 1967 in New York after the First National City Bank distributed to its depositors the Everything Charge Credit Card. Some 1,700 counts of abuse, fraud, and forgery to obtain cash and goods bilked the bank of $100,000 until District Attorney Burton Roberts worked through an extensive paper trail to halt the operation.

In 1967, Alfonse Confessore used his skills as a manufacturer of Diners' Club cards to print bogus plates during his lunch break. Instead of using them himself, he made a deal with the Mafia to sell them 1,500 cards for $40,000. A crime squad uncovered his operation and charged him with aiding the crime family to cheat the credit company of $621,000. In the 1970s, Dorothy Woods organized a complex social services scam and credit card swindle that allowed her to live in luxury in Pasadena, California, and to drive a Rolls-Royce. After making restitution and serving prison time, she and husband John Woods resumed their criminal activities.

SOURCES: "The Chinese Connection." *Banker*, October 1994, pp. 14–15. • Nash, Jay Robert. *Encyclopedia of World Crime*. 6 vols. Wilmette, Ill.: CrimeBooks Inc., 1990.

daric

After the fall of the Lydian King Croesus to the Persian Cyrus II the Great in 550 B.C., the *daric*, the world's first internationally known coin, characterized the greatness of the Achaemenid dynasty and its notable administrator. The standardization of the coin, which may derive from an Elamite model, was a pet project of Cyrus's successor, Darius I the Great (or Darius Hystaspis), after 522 B.C. However, the coin appears to have taken its name from the Persian *zariq* ("gold piece") rather than from the king's name.

As intent on proper coinage, weights and measures, and trade routes as on his other civic projects, Darius considered quality specie an asset to commerce and the imperial economy. In the estimation of the Greek historian Herodotus in the mid-fifth century B.C., "Darius was a tradesman ... being out for profit wherever he could get it." (1954, p. 214) For metal, Darius demanded 95 percent gold, with only a small percentage of copper and silver. According to 19th-century antiquarian George Rawlinson, author of *The History of Phoenicia* (1889):

> Darius must have coined [*darics*] in vast abundance, since early in the reign of his successor a single individual of no great eminence had accumulated as many as 3,993,000 of them.... The establishment of this excellent circulating medium, and the wide extension which it almost immediately attained, must have given an enormous stimulus to trade, and have been found of the greatest convenience by the Phoenician merchants, who had no longer to carry with them the precious metal in bars or ingots, and to weigh their gold and silver in the balance in connection with every purchase that they made, but could effect both sales and purchases in the simple and commodious manner [Rawlinson 1889].

In Chapter IV of *The Histories* (ca. 440 B.C.), Herodotus characterizes Darius's pride at his coinage and describes the anger that caused him to execute Aryandes, governor of Egypt, for competing against the gold *daric* with equally pure silver coinage.

Probably minted at the capital city of Sardis, the *daric* was called in Hebrew *darkemon* and in Greek *dareikos*. Darius's treasury subdivided the dominant denomination on a base-twelve system, which produced small change in thirds, sixths, and twelfths of a coin. The coin must have followed the Persian army, for it paid the fleet and soldiers in 480 B.C., when 1,000 ships supplied an invasion of Thrace, Macedonia, and Thessaly. At a canal that Xerxes sliced across the peninsula at Mount Athos, a hoard of 300 gold *darics* attested to the demand on Persian specie. The *daric* was also the original monthly salary for a soldier under Cyrus, who promised his men a 50 percent raise to 1.5 *darics*. The gold piece remained unaltered until the emergence of the panhellenic currency of Philip the Great of Macedon and of his son, Alexander III the Great.

From the picture of an active monarch on the face — the running figure of a crowned king armed with bow and a sheaf of arrows at his back — the *daric* earned a slang name, the "archer." The reverse featured a crude rectangle. When the Spartan king Agesilaus II set out to loot Persian provinces in 395 B.C., the Persians bribed his neighbors to attack his kingdom while the army was out of residence. Agesilaus complained, "I have been conquered by thirty thousand Persian archers," a cynical reference to the coin's nickname (Draper 1897). The monetary unit was valued in a proportion of gold to silver, the first of the modern world's bimetallic ratios.

For two centuries, the Persians circulated the famed gold coin contemporaneously with the Greek *drachma* and *obol*, both coined from native silver. Among Hebrews during a quarter century after their release from the Babylonian captivity in 548 B.C., the *daric* was the daily medium of commercial exchange. In *The History of the Jews* (A.D. 94), the Romanized Hebrew historian Flavius Josephus used the *daric* in assigning value to a spoonful of incense in the tabernacle. When Islamic rule overran the Middle East, Muslim moneyers based the *dinar* on the historic *daric*.

SOURCES: Allen, Larry. *Encyclopedia of Money*. New York: Checkmark Books, 2001. • Draper, John William. *History of the Conflict Between Religion and Science*. New York: D. Appleton, 1897. • Durant, Will. *Our Oriental Heritage*. New York: Simon and Schuster, 1942. • Herodotus. *The Histories*. London: Penguin Books, 1954. • Hill, G. F. *Historical Greek Coins*. Chicago: Argonaut, Inc., 1966. • Josephus. *Complete Works*. Grand Rapids, Mich.: Kregel Publications, 1960. • *New Catholic Encyclopedia*. San Francisco: Catholic University of America, 1967. • Paunov, Evgeni I. "Ancient Treasures from Thracian Tombs." *Athena Review*, 1998, pp. 76–82. • Rawlinson, George. *History of Phoenicia*. London: Longmans, Green, and Company, 1889. • Severy, Merle, ed. *Greece & Rome*. Washington, D.C.: National Geographic Society, 1977.

de Francisci, Anthony

Italian-born sculptor and medalist Anthony de Francisci (or da Francisci) made his mark on American coinage by designing a beloved Liberty dollar. Born to Benedict and Maria Liberante de Francisci on June 13, 1887, he immigrated to New York City with his parents at age seven. After studying at the Cooper Institute and the Academy of Design, he became a naturalized citizen and married Mary Teresa Cafarelli, mother of their daughter Gilda. He apprenticed in sculpture under George T. Brewster, Philip Martiny, Hermon

Atkins MacNeil, and A. A. Weinman for ten years before establishing his independence. In addition to studio work, he taught at Columbia University in 1917 and returned to teaching at age 72 at the National Academy of Fine Arts.

De Francisci first earned renown as a designer of coins and medals in 1920, when the Commission of Fine Arts petitioned the War Department for a Militia Bureau insignia. He complied by allying the Roman fasces with the citizen soldier and an eagle, a union of the people and the federal government. For its Hall of Fame, he executed the Lincoln medal and the Benjamin Fairless medal for the Iron and Steel Institute. Subsequent commissions for Eli Lilly, Ford Motor Company, United Parcel Service, and the veterans bureau display his skill and attention to detail. At his death on October 20, 1964, he had earned a host of medals, including those of the Pennsylvania Academy of Fine Arts, National Academy, Allied Artists of America, and National Art Club.

In 1921, when the U.S. Mint determined to replace the Morgan dollar with the Peace dollar, de Francisci won a competition against the talent of his day: Robert Aitken, Chester Beach, Victor David Brenner, John Flanagan, Henry Hering, Hermon MacNeil, Robert Tait McKenzie, and Adolph Alexander Weinman. In art deco style, de Francisci created a Liberty coin in silver stengthened with ten percent copper. President Warren G. Harding made the final choice, requiring one change, the removal of a dimple from Liberty's chin. Minted until 1935 in Denver, Philadelphia, and San Francisco, de Francisci's coin featured the pose of the Statue of Liberty, which was modeled on Auguste-Charlotte Bartholdi. For his own vision of Miss Liberty, de Francisci superimposed on the model the profile of his wife, Teresa Cafarelli de Francisci. He sculpted the face in high relief with his glylph, the initial A superimposed over F, near the figure's neck.

The honor of being Miss Liberty on a coin thrilled Teresa, who had come to the United States at age five, when she first saw the Statue of Liberty. In a letter to her brother Rocco, she exulted:

> You remember how I was always posing as Liberty, and how broken-hearted I was when some other little girl was selected to play the role in the patriotic exercises in school? I thought of those days often while sitting as a model for Tony's design, and now seeing myself as Miss Liberty on the coin, it seems like the realization of my finest childhood dream [Bowers 1979, p. 106].

The Peace coin featured the female likeness with a corona of rays about her head. To enhance and enliven her embodiment of liberty, the sculptor opened the studio window to let wind muss her hair. In a letter to a newspaper columnist, he explained, "I wanted Liberty to express something of the spirit of the country — the intellectual speed and vigor and virility America has, as well as its youth" (Rochette 1985, 88).

The highly stylized design commemorated the end of World War I at the Paris armistice of November 1918. To perpetuate a war theme, de Francisci designed an eagle holding a broken sword, a symbol of the end of the Great War. The mint had George T. Morgan replace the reverse with an eagle atop a pinnacle with furled wings and an olive branch clutched in its talons. The Peace dollar earned its share of notoriety. Hawks proclaimed the shattered sword a sign of disgrace in combat or surrender; wags at the *Wall Street Journal* dubbed the coin the "flapper dollar" for Teresa's vibrant, mildly sexy profile. More practical critics complained that the coin was too lumpy to stack evenly. The Peace dollar succumbed in large numbers to meltdown during World War II and again in the 1980s, when the value of pure silver outpaced the value of the coin as a collector's item.

For all its controversial history, De Francisci's design remained fresh in the eyes of Americans. In 1964, President Lyndon Baines Johnson reissued the silver dollar after three decades of its absence from U.S. currency. For a figure of Liberty, he revived the profile of the sculptor's wife. An outcry in Congress caused the Denver mintmaster to retain the run of

316,076 coins and melt them. In 1973, after de Francisci's death, Teresa received the adulation of the American Numismatic Association.

See also **Peace dollar.**

SOURCES: Bowers, Q. David. *Adventures with Rare Coins*. Los Angeles: Bowers & Ruddy Galleries, Inc., 1979. • Howe, Marvine, "Teresa Da Francisci, Miss Liberty Model for Coin, Dies at 92," *New York Times*, October 21, 1990, p. 38. • Law, Steven, "Sculptors of Cape Ann," *American Art Review*, October 1997. • Reed, Mort. *Cowles Complete Encyclopedia of U.S. Coins*. New York: Cowles Book Company, 1969. • Rochette, Ed, "A Flip Over a Flapper," *Hobbies*, May 1985, pp. 88–89. • Taxay, Don. *The U.S. Mint and Coinage*. New York: Arco Publishing, 1966. • Van Ryzin, Robert R. *Twisted Tails: Sifted Fact, Fantasy and Fiction from U.S. Coin History*. Iola, Wisc.: Krause Publications, 1995. • *Who Was Who in America*. Chicago: Marquis Who's Who, Inc., 1968.

denga

The small change of Russia, the *denga*—plural *dengi*—appeared after the area's coinless period, which coincided with invasions of Mongol and Turk invaders, called the Ulus Juchi or Golden Horde, from the western half of the Mongol Empire, which arose in the mid–13th century and flourished until the late 1300s. First minted in Moscow, the silver coin, worth 1/200 of a *ruble*, took its name from the *tanka* or *tenga*, an Iranian silver piece circulating in the late 1300s.

The early models minted in multiple principalities bore Mongol detailing and crude legends and symbols in Russian and Arabic. Moscow moneyers issued the silver *moskovka denga* with an equestrian image and the *polushka* half-*denga*, a coin so small that merchants issued them by the handful. Novgorod struck the *chetvertsa* half-*denga* and its own *novgorodka denga*, picturing a cavalryman with spear and bearing the legend "Likago Novagoroda" ("From the Great Novgorod"). Others bore fantastic birds, dragons, lions, and bowmen.

The word *denga* came to mean "money," much like the general application of the Chinese character for "cowrie," the Hebrew word "shekel," and the English "dollar." Some *dengi* were so small that merchants could hold them in their mouths to keep them safe and handy for transactions. After 1470, the latest *denga*, inscribed in both languages at Novgorod, carried the name Ivan, which reflected the ruthless consolidation wrought by Ivan III, who came to power in 1462. Through a policy of conquest known as the "gathering of the Russian lands," he placed Moscow at the center of power and annexed East Slavic territory, Belorus, the Ukraine, Novgorod, and the upper Volga. After Ivan's consolidation of smaller powers, the purification of Russian coinage was not complete until the rise of Peter I the Great, who, after 1705, halted bilingual coinage.

SOURCES: Clain-Stefanelli, Elvira, and Vladimir Clain-Stefanelli. *The Beauty and Lore of Coins, Currency, and Medals*. Croton-on-Hudson, N.Y.: Riverwood Publishers, 1974. • "Metallic Analysis of the 1730–1754 Polushka." *Journal of the Russian Numismatic Society*, Winter 1991-1992, p. 45. • Schena, Eric R. "The Influence of Islamic Coins on the Russian Monetary System." *Journal of the Islamic Coins Group*, Winter 1999/2000.

denier

The *denier*, first struck by Frankish monarchs, was the first truly French coin. Its development and modification paralleled the political expansions and contractions of power. Several undistinguished and anonymous versions of the *denier* circulated in the low countries from as early as A.D. 670. The real introduction of the coin accompanied the accession of Pepin the Short (also Pepin III), founder of the Carolingian dynasty and preserver of Clovis's empire

In A.D. 752, the period that saw the dominance of the *bezant* and *dinar* farther south along the Mediterranean and into southern India, Pepin made up for a lack of gold by concentrating on the production of a silver *denarius novus* (new *denarius*), the first true medieval money, which circulated throughout the Middle Ages. As he reformed mint procedures, he introduced the wide, thin *denier argenteus* (silver *denier*), the foundation of the

Italian *denaro,* Portuguese *dinheiro*, and Spanish *dinero*. His designs were small geometric emblems, namely battleaxes, crosiers, crosses, and stars; the inscriptions were also uncomplicated: "*R P*" (*Rex Pepinus*) with "*R F*" (*Rex Francorum*) on the back.

At the high point of the Frankish empire, Pepin's son Charlemagne strengthened northwestern European currency. He coined his first metal specie with a simple Latin "*Carolus R F*" ("Charles King of the Franks"). After his victory in Lombardy in 774, Charlemagne broadened and thickened the denier and increased its efficiency by introducing the *obole* or half-denier. He continued to mark them with "*Carolus*" and added a temple or portal and the legend "*Xristiana Religio*" ("Christian Faith"). On some, he named the city of minting and occasionally applied his image.

Charlemagne's far-flung coin artisans struck *deniers* in France, Germany, north Italy, and Spain. When Pope Leo III awarded him a royal crown at Rome on December 25, 800, the new king added Roman emperor to his original title and acknowledged the elevation in power with a coin stamped "*Karolus Imp Aug*" ("Charles August Emperor") and "*Rex F et L*" ("King of the Franks and Lombards"). To produce enough coins to meet his subjects' expanded trade, he set up mints at Cologne, Metz, Strasbourg, and Trier.

At his death, Charlemagne left lesser men to rule the Franks. From A.D. 850 under Louis IV d'Outremer and the archbishop of Rheims, feudal coins replaced the *denier*. Shape and thickness altered in the tenth century at mints in Milan and Pavia. Parallel to these developments in the north, the Venetian doge produced his own *deniers*, but dropped the imperial title under Lothair I. The papal coins struck during the reign of Adrian I late in the A.D. 700s added the papal initials to Charlemagne's name and title. By A.D. 904, the name of Pope Sergius III supplanted that of the emperor.

In the late A.D. 900s, Hugh Capet, founder of the Capetian dynasty of 14 monarchs, continued the tradition of simplicity begun by Pepin. The front of Capet's coins listed his title; the back placed a cross at center and identified the mint. After 1012, Odalricus of Bohemia issued a crude *denier* with typical naive medieval styling and broad band. In the 12th century, the coin shrank in size. Near the end of the 1100s, Philip II Augustus, a hero of the Third Crusade, expanded his kingdom and its commerce by reshaping the basic coin into the *denier parisis* (Parisian *denier*) and the *denier tournois* (*denier* of Tours), which spread in ever-widening circles of trade into the outlands.

The *denier* remained strong until the end of the 13th century. It has the distinction of being the only coin displaying "Ricardus," the Latin name of Richard the Lion-Hearted, the Count of Poitou and hero of the Third Crusade. Seventeen years before his crowning as king of England, he commissioned a silver piece struck in 1172 at Poitou. Because he chose warfare over the inglorious duties of governance, he spent all but a half year of his nearly ten years on the throne either on campaign or in the prison of Duke Leopold and died childless in 1199. In 1191, an era when Italian cities were minting their own coinage as elements of their economic growth, Bologna struck a variation on the *denier* called the *bolognino*. During numerous changes in size and surface treatment, the *denier* served France as its only coin until the saintly Louis IX created the silver *gros* in 1266.

See also **medieval coins; Offa of Mercia; penny; Renaissance coins; *sou*.**

SOURCES: Balzaretti, Ross. "Charlemagne in Italy." *History Today*, February 1996, 28–35. • Clain-Stefanelli, Elvira, and Vladimir Clain-Stefanelli. *The Beauty and Lore of Coins, Currency, and Medals*. Croton-on-Hudson, N.Y.: Riverwood Publishers, 1974. • Cohn-Sherbok, Lavinia. *Who's Who in Christianity*. London: Routledge, 1998. • Cribb, Joe. *Money*. Toronto: Stoddart, 1990. • Cribb, Joe, Barrie Cook, and Ian Carradice. *The Coin Atlas*. London: Little, Brown and Co., 1999. • Hastings, James, ed. *Encyclopedia of Religion and Ethics*. New York: Charles Scribner's Sons, 1951. • Holmes, George, ed. *The Oxford Illustrated History of Medieval Europe*. Oxford: Oxford University Press, 1988. • Lewis, Brenda Ralph. *Coins & Currency*. New York: Random House, 1993. • Rice, David Talbot, ed. *The Dawn of European Civilization: The Dark Ages*. New York: McGraw-Hill,

1965. • Sinclair, David. *The Pound.* London: Century Books, 2000. • Webster, Hutton. *Early European History.* New York: D.C. Heath, 1924.

dinar

A uniquely Arab coin common to Algeria, Bahrain, Iraq, Jordan, Kuwait, Libya, Serbia, Tunisia, Yemen, and Yugoslavia, the *dinar* emulated the *denara* of India and the Persian *daric*, but took its name from the Roman *denarius*, a long-lived coin throughout the Mediterranean world. After the rise of the 'Umayyad rulers in A.D. 661, Muslims overran the Byzantine power structure and took over imperial coinage. In A.D. 696, Caliph Abd al-Malik deliberately undermined the old monetary system by engineering a true Arabic coinage that asserted the supremacy of Allah. His coins expressed the oneness of God as a slur at the Christian concept of a triune god, comprised of God the father, the son Jesus, and the Holy Ghost.

In A.D. 703, the mechanics of the campaign, left to Governor al-Hajjaj bin Yusuf, demanded the establishment of an Islamic mint, which he built at Wasit. He hired impeccably honest staff and cowed them with threats of chopping off the hands of anyone violating strict monetary law. Working virtually under the scimitar, artisans melted down currency and struck new Muslim coins, which the peasantry accepted under threats of death to any hoarding the old money.

The Islamic mint at Damascus expanded coinage to a full range of denominations—whole silver *dinars* equal in weight to the Byzantine *solidus*, half-*dinars*, one-third *dinars*, and small change consisting of *dirhans* (or *dirhems)* and copper *fals* (or *fulus)*. Following the Damascan style of coinage were operations at Baghdad and Misr, Egypt, and at the far western edge of the Mediterranean in the Muslim conquest cities of Córdoba, Granada, Málaga, and Seville, Spain. From 800 to 1100, the Arab *dinar* thrived under laws standardizing size and weight.

During the Islamic push into Europe, Muslim specie denominations influenced central European coin design. A Polish silver *denar*, a version of the Arab *dinar*, copied the workmanship of the Regensburg penny. In the late 1000s and 1100s, Bohemian coin makers refined a *denar* into a tiny silver penny popularized by its artistry. Local legend permeated design, including hunts for wild animals, human figures, and an angel rescuing a baby.

For the next two centuries, changes under the 'Abbasid dynasty, which crushed its Umayyad predecessors in A.D. 750 and ruled from 751 to 1258, altered the uniformity that had linked the entire Arab world. Similar to the Umayyad coinage, the script exaggerated horizontal letters and reduced others to a blur. The caliph's name, which was absent on early coins, gradually became a standard feature. With the rise of the Italian city-states during the Renaissance, the *ducat* and *florin* infiltrated coins along the established Arabic trade routes. By 1300, just as Islam lost out to Christianity at the beginning of the Renaissance, the *dinar* surrendered its dominance of Eastern Mediterrannean markets and banking.

***See also bezant*; *daric;* India, money of; Islamic money; Medieval coins; Muhammad ibn Tughluq; Offa of Mercia; paper money; Spanish coins.**

SOURCES: Allen, Larry. *Encyclopedia of Money.* New York: Checkmark Books, 2001. • Clain-Stefanelli, Elvira, and Vladimir Clain-Stefanelli. *The Beauty and Lore of Coins, Currency, and Medals.* Croton-on-Hudson, N.Y.: Riverwood Publishers, 1974. • Grierson, Philip. *Numismatics.* London: Oxford University Press, 1975. • Lewis, Brenda Ralph. *Coins & Currency.* New York: Random House, 1993. • Standish, David. *The Art of Money.* San Francisco: Chronicle Books, 2000.

dirhan

The Muslim *dirhan* (or *dirhem* or *dirham)* derived from Parthian coinage from before 200 B.C. Like Persian and Macedonian prototypes, the pieces featured a monarch's portrait on the obverse and a deity or seated figure on the back. From A.D. 227 over the next four and a half centuries, the Sassanian dynasty produced *dirhans* from large, thin silver flans on which design typically exalted the

Zoroastrian fire altar. One piece produced at Herat in northwestern Afghanistan in A.D. 686 pictured the last Sassanian king, Yezdigird III, who witnessed the destruction of the Persian army at Nehawand. Opposite the king, a polite grouping of handmaidens tends the sacred flame.

Around A.D. 945, officials of the Sallarid dynasty near the Black Sea ordered a silver *dirhan* in Islamic style, featuring no religious image out of respect for Allah. To create an artistic effect, the Persian designer created complex calligraphy at center within a wide circlet of Arabic writing. The motto, the Islamic *Kalima* (creed), reads, "There is no God but God, Mohammed is the Prophet of God" (Clain and Clain 1974, p. 175). By A.D. 1000, the ornate Islamic writing style reached an art form through refinements by calligrapher Ibn al-Bawwab of Baghdad, who hand-lettered 64 copies of the Koran. He taught calligraphy in his hometown and in Shiraz, emphasizing the harmonic beauty of rounded *nakshi* letters.

In the 13th century, the horoscope *dirhans* of Rum, a series of the Seljuk Turks, broke the austere Islamic tradition that rejected human likenesses on coin art. Struck by Sultan Kay Khusro II after 1236, the set pictured the zodiacal image of Leo, the lion sun sign of his Georgian consort. In the late Middle Ages, the invasive Mongols, who took no interest in coinage, copied Muslim *dirhans* without achieving the graceful arabesques of previous coin calligraphy. Beginning with the Mongol invasions after 1237, markets in Kiev relied on the *dirhan* struck from the pure silver ores of central Asia. In turn, Russia, lacking its own specie, circulated Islamic money. Thus, pious Muslim coin style survived among Eurasian people who had no interest in mottoes praising Allah.

***See also bezant*; Islamic money; Muhammad ibn Tughluq; paper money; Russian money; world money.**

SOURCES: Bond, Constance. "Islamic Metalwork at Freer Gallery." *Smithsonian*, October 1985, p. 225. • Clain-Stefanelli, Elvira, and Vladimir Clain-Stefanelli. *The Beauty and Lore of Coins, Currency, and Medals*. Croton-on-Hudson, N.Y.: Riverwood Publishers, 1974. • Glueck, Grace. "The Nature of Islamic Ornament, Part 1: Calligraphy." *New York Times*, April 24, 1998, p. B32. • Grierson, Philip. *Numismatics*. London: Oxford University Press, 1975. • Reif, Rita. "Islamic Calligraphy Makes a Statement." *New York Times*, December 16, 1990 , p. H48. • Standish, David. *The Art of Money*. San Francisco: Chronicle Books, 2000. • Weatherford, Jack. *The History of Money: From Sandstone to Cyberspace*. Pittsburgh, Pa.: Three Rivers Press, 1998.

dollar

The dollar is the standard monetary unit of 52 countries or distinct geographic entities — American Samoa, Anguilla, Antigua, Australia, Barbuda, Bahamas, Barbados, Belize, Bermuda, British Virgin Islands, Brunei, Caicos Islands, Canada, Cayman Islands, Dominica, Fiji, Grenada, Grenadines, Guam, Guyana, Hong Kong, Jamaica, Kiribati, Liberia, Malaysia, Marshall Islands, Micronesia, Montserrat, Namibia, Naura, Nevis, New Zealand, Norfolk Island, Northern Mariana Islands, Palau, Panama, Pitcairn Island, Puerto Rico, St. Christopher, St. Lucia, St. Vincent, Singapore, Solomon Islands, Taiwan, Tobago, Trinidad, Turks, Tuvalu, United States of America, U.S. Virgin Islands, and Zimbabwe. Ranging over the Danish and Norwegian silver *daler* and the long-lived German *thaler*, the dollar has existed in numerous forms. Sweden had few native coins until Sten Sture the Younger, who ruled from 1513 to 1520, began to upgrade national specie and introduced a third Scandinavian version of the *thaler*. In 1534, Sweden's King Gustav I, first of the Vasa dynasty and a conservative fiscal manager, created the first silver *daler*, an ornate coin traded into Finland, a Swedish possession. The founder of modern Sweden, Gustav II Adolf, who came to power in 1611, ordered a decorative issue of the silver *daler* featuring a portrait of his daughter Kristina standing in ornate gown, full sleeves, and ruff.

The spelling of "dollar" got its start in Scotland. Proud Scots, who had initiated a dollar coin in the 1500s, adopted a new name for their monetary unit to differentiate it from English money. After 1567, they popularized the English word "dollar" in reference to a ten-shilling piece commissioned by the Scottish king James VI, who became England's James I. Peasants called the coin a "sword dollar" and added the term "thistle dollar" for a two-*merk* coin struck in 1578. In colonial North America, Scottish immigrants brought along their dollars, the first in the United States. New Englanders, who had no coinage of their own, applied the term generically to Mexican *pesos* and Spanish pieces of eight. For those still dealing in kind, the use of buckskin preceded the slang term "buck" for the dollar.

The first official colonial dollar denomination circulated from the Maryland state treasury in 1767. It earned national acceptance after Thomas Jefferson acknowledged that it was "a known coin and the most familiar of all to the mind of the people. It is already adopted from south to north" (Weatherford 1998, p. 118). By July 6, 1785, when the new republic set up its own financial system, the United States treasury chose the dollar as the nation's official monetary unit, even though it would be seven years before the U.S. Mint struck authentic national coins. Canada also chose the dollar in 1858, when it installed a decimal system; Australia followed the pattern in 1966 and New Zealand the next year. In China, Taiwanese moneyers copied the denomination in the 1840s as the Taiwan dollar, followed in 1890 with the Imperial Dragon dollar and in 1934 with a dollar struck by the Communist army bearing a citation from Karl Marx and Friedrich Engels's *Communist Manifesto* (1848) exhorting the proletariat to unite.

Beginning in 1861, the United States Printing Office issued paper notes in dollars. For portraits, designers chose these historic figures:

portrait	*amount*
George Washington, the first president	$1 bill
Thomas Jefferson, the third president	$2 bill
Abraham Lincoln, the 16th president	$3 bill
Alexander Hamilton, first secretary of the treasury	$10 bill
Andrew Jackson, the 7th president	$20 bill
Ulysses S. Grant, the 18th president	$50 bill
Benjamin Franklin, spokesman for the colonies	$100 bill
William McKinley, the 25th president	$500 bill
Grover Cleveland, the 22nd and 24th president	$1000 bill
James Madison, the fourth president	$5000 bill
Salmon P. Chase, sixth chief justice	$10,000 bill

The ham-handed dispersal of dollars to solve world problems resulted in a cynical pejorative, dollar diplomacy, implying the attempt to settle complex human issues with cash. After 1909, President William Howard Taft and Secretary of State Philander C. Knox established the dollar-based fiscal policy to secure economies of foreign lands while furthering American profits. Pioneered by Theodore Roosevelt in the Dominican Republic, the concept affected Nicaragua during the unseating of José Santos Zelaya and the installation of Adolfo Díaz, the leader most favored by the United States. In exchange for guaranteed loans, Díaz allowed the U.S. government to micromanage the collection of customs, which boosted faith in the Panama Canal and in U.S. investment in Latin America. When Taft applied dollar diplomacy to China, negative reaction worldwide forced abandonment of the policy in 1912.

From 1945 to 1971, the world monetary system was based on a dollar standard in place of the former gold standard, which had required gold bullion on hand to back paper dollars. The dollar came to dominate exchange rates and international trade and to back foreign currency as a primary treasury reserve. The last nations to adopt the dollar as a standard were Slovenia and Zimbabwe. Because of global dependence on the dollar, U.S. fiscal health affected all the world's economy; however, after Europe's switchover to a shared monetary unit on January 1, 2002, the power of the euro threatened to make inroads into dollar dominance. Nonetheless, when Iraq fell to U.S.–led forces in 2003 its traditional *dinar* gave plce to the dollar as an interim currency.

See also **Continental currency; Anthony de Francisci; Thomas Jefferson; lion dollar; James Barton Longacre; George T. Morgan; Robert Maskell Patterson; Peace dollar; pieces of eight; plate money; Sacagawea coin; Sigismund, Archduke of Tyrol; *thaler;* U.S. coins; Adolph A. Weinman; world money.**

SOURCES: Allen, Larry. *Encyclopedia of Money.* New York: Checkmark Books, 2001. • Cribb, Joe. *Money.* Toronto: Stoddart, 1990. • Newman, Eric. *The Early Paper Money of America.* Iola, Wisc: Krause, 1997. • Pollak, Henry. *Coinage & Conflict.* Clifton, N.J.: Coin & Currency Institute, 2001. • Reed, Mort. *Cowles Complete Encyclopedia of U.S. Coins.* New York: Cowles Book Company, 1969. • Velasco, Andres. "Dollar Diplomacy." *Time,* February 8, 1999. • Weatherford, Jack. *The History of Money: From Sandstone to Cyberspace.* Pittsburgh, Pa.: Three Rivers Press, 1998.

drachma

The basic monetary unit of ancient Greece, the *drachma* originated on the island of Aegina and derives from the Greek for "handful," referring to its value as six *obols.* The *drachma* figures frequently in classical history. During the building of the Erechtheum outside the temple of Athena on the Acropolis, begun in 421 B.C., the architect earned one *drachma* per day, which was three times the wage of a common laborer. At the rise of Alexander to the throne of Macedon in 336 B.C., he paid his men on a sliding scale based on skill and experience:

soldier	*daily wage*
mercenary	⅔ *drachma*
foot soldier	one *drachma*
cavalryman	two *drachmas*

After launching his conquests to the east, Alexander budgeted 120,000 *drachmas* daily, which amounted to 20 talents or a half ton of silver to be secured and dispersed. Thus, he found it expedient and economical to capture treasuries of Persian cities and to issue coins struck on the spot from looted precious metals rather than haul a huge treasury over Asia Minor.

From the fall of Damascus alone in 330 B.C., Alexander acquired 2,600 talents in coin and 50,000 silver talents from Susa, a pittance compared to the vast plunder in moneys and bullion his wars produced. Out of generosity and a sincere love of his soldiers, he offered bonuses, for example, an additional 50 *drachmas* to mercenaries and 600 *drachmas* to his horsemen after the surrender of Susa in July 331 B.C. To the soldiers opting to return home to Macedonia, at Ecbatana in 323 B.C., he distributed a mustering-out bonus of 2,000 talents.

Emulating the *drachma* were numerous moneys of the Middle East, including the Iranian silver *drachm.* After 123 B.C., the expansive Mithradates II the Great of Parthia pictured his profile with long beard and diadem on a silver *drachma.* He spread his power and money so far into Mesopotamia and Babylonia that he rightly claimed the title "king of kings." After the rise of the Sassanian dynasty east of Byzantium in A.D. 226, Persian monarchs struck artistic *drachmas.* The most artistic of their designs featured King Shapur I, consolidator and expander of the empire, who, like the vainglorious Mithradates, set the standard for subsequent royal coinage. A tradition of crowned portraits challenged Shapur's followers to create diadems and headpieces identifying their uniqueness.

To picture the re-emergence of Zoroas-

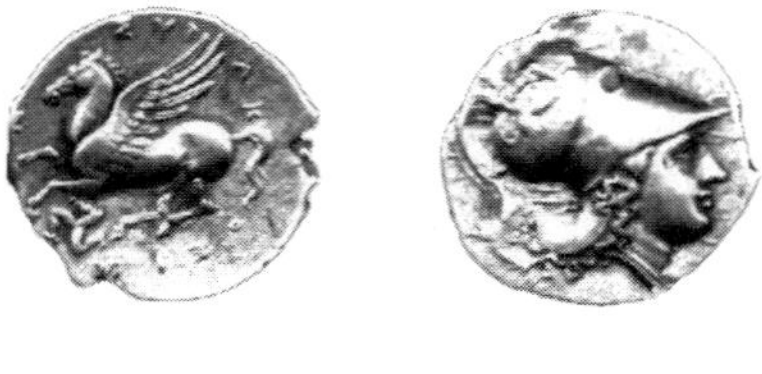

In 310 B.C., the Corinthian mint struck a *drachma* with the shape of winged Pegasus, the magical flying horse of the mythic hero Bellerophon, opposite a profile of Athena, goddess of war. (Guy Clark, Ancient Coins and Antiquities, Norfolk, Virginia)

trianism, artistic coiners under Shapur II, Shapur III, Varhan II, Varhan IV, and Khusroe II incised silver *drachmas* with images of the god Ahuramazda and the fire cult. The designs personified the fire altar as a ritual center where worshippers offered gifts. The rich pageantry of Sassanian coins reached a height under Khusroe II, who extended his rule and trade as far west as Jerusalem and Alexandria, Egypt. His reign preceded a violent end to royal posturing and privilege and the rise of calligraphied Islamic *drachmas* featuring phrases from the Koran, but no human image.

In 1905, U.S. President Theodore Roosevelt chose the Greek *tetradrachm* as the epitome of coin esthetics. To reproduce classic style, he cultivated a friendship with sculptor and portrait artist Augustus Saint-Gaudens, an Irish immigrant, and commissioned him to sketch an eagle and double-eagle. The artist satisfied the president's desire for worthy coinage by envisioning the allegorical figure of Liberty in mid-stride. The initial contour failed the test of pragmatism because of its height, and would soon wear down from constant use. A flattened version lost the original immediacy and vigor of the pose.

The modern *drachma* dates to the 1830s, when Greece won its independence from the Ottoman Turks. The Greek monarchy chose the unit and its classical designs as a boost to pride and patriotism. Manipulation of the *drachma* saved the Greek treasury in 1915, when slicing 100-*drachma* notes produced small change in the amounts of 25 and 75 *drachmas*. A decade later, bisection of paper *drachmas* allowed the treasury to circulate half the bill at half the original value. The remaining half provided the government with a temporary loan. Colombia applied the same logic to the withdrawal of *pesos* in 1944, when the Banco de la República de Colombia sliced and overstamped bills as half *pesos*. After 1945, Finland implemented similar halved *markkas* as a means of shoring up shaky finances. On January 1, 2002, Greece ceased striking its *drachmas* when it joined the twelve European nations basing their monetary system on the euro.

See also **bas-relief; euro; Greek coins; Islamic money; world money.**

SOURCES: Allen, Larry. *Encyclopedia of Money.* New York: Checkmark Books, 2001. • Clain-Stefanelli, Elvira, and Vladimir Clain-Stefanelli. *The Beauty and Lore of Coins, Currency, and Medals.* Croton-on-Hudson, N.Y.: Riverwood Publishers, 1974. • Davies, Glyn. *A History of Money from Ancient Times to the Present Day.* Cardiff: University of Wales Press, 1994. • Henneberger, Melinda. "Reluctance in Greece to Let Go of the Coin of History." *New York Times*, December 31, 2001, p. A4. • Johnston, Megan. "Death of the Drachma." *Money*, March 1, 2001, p. 28.

Drake, Sir Francis

An English privateer, Sir Francis Drake captained vessels for the Crown during the rise of piracy in the Caribbean Sea and Atlantic. In addition to circumnavigating the globe, from 1567 to 1596, he made seven voyages seeking Spanish treasure in the West Indies and off South America's northwestern coast. As the commissioned sea agent of Elizabeth I, he earned the nickname "the Queen's pirate." His trove of coins, jeweled ornaments, images of pagan gods, and gold nuggets placed him at the height of English sea marauding and boosted England's navy to the greatest fleet of the era.

An English farm boy from Tavistock, Devonshire, Drake was born around 1541 into a Calvinist household of twelve children, of which he was the oldest. Because his father, Edmund Drake, was accused of stealing horses, the family left their tenant farm, moved to Kent, and resided in a ship's hull on the River Medway. He disdained the work and faith of his father, a lay preacher to sailors, and studied navigation before apprenticing in the Thames coastal trade. Around age 25, he shipped out for the Cape Verde cluster aboard John Lovell's slaver. The next year, Drake took a post as officer on John Hawkins's 50-ton *Judith* for a doomed slaving voyage to Africa. Apprehended by a Spanish patrol, he and Hawkins managed to elude their captors, who destroyed the fleet.

After a brief adjustment to married life, Drake set out on the *Susan* with a specific goal — to intercept Peruvian and Chilean gold that expeditioners transported from the New World to Spain. He rightly chose the Panamanian port of Nombre de Dios, Central America's treasure house, lavished by slave labor with the area's precious stones and ores. A local minting operation began with smelting, shaping, and stamping coins with the carat weight and Philip II's royal seal. Silver required cords of wood and charcoal for the hot fires that purified the ore. While slaves pumped bellows to stoke the flame, metalsmiths shaped the flow of pure metal in clay forms to turn out ingots, bars, and plaques.

In 1572, Drake intercepted the Spanish mule trains hauling 15 tons of silver over the Isthmus of Panama. To load the immense treasure onto his own vessels, he hired *cimarrones*, escaped black slaves living in the jungle. He had to bury his cache in the sand until he could connect with English ships, which had moved down the coast out of range of a Spanish convoy. He retrieved the coins, set sail, and arrived home in England in 1573. The fleet's ample cargo of loot made him a hero, but Queen Elizabeth I urged him to cease outraging the Spanish, with whom she had arranged an uneasy truce before the final ousting of Catholicism from England.

When *detente* soured between England and Spain after the execution of the Catholic pretender Mary Queen of Scots, in 1587, Elizabeth secretly bankrolled subsequent voyages to rob Spain of its gold hoard. Drake once more sailed west aboard the 100-ton *Golden Hind* (originallly called the *Pelican)* to the Strait of Magellan, then ventured south of Patagonia, around Cape Horn, and into the Pacific. His lust for gold produced new knowledge of the globe and the oceans by which England could reach other nations. Traveling the west coast of South America, on March 1, 1579, he awarded a gold coin to his nephew, the first of his crew to spy a Spanish ship, the fabulously wealthy *Nuestra Señora de la Concepción*. From its hold, he looted a huge bounty in gemstones, gilded silver bottles, and 13 chests of silver *rials* plus 80 pounds of raw gold and 26 tons of uncoined silver. Seamen joked that he ballasted his ship with coins and ingots.

In his journal, Drake exulted over the capture of the ship, which sailors called the *Cacafuego* ("*Shitfire*") for its outpouring of shot from cannon. For his daring raid, Drake stirred hatred among Spain's naval officers. The Spanish hissed a new pronunciation of his name, "*El Draque*" ("the Dragon"), and dispatched a convoy of battleships to hunt him down. To elude them, he headed west to the Pacific, choosing a direction based on oral advice from captains who had attempted the same chancy route.

On his lengthy reconnaissance of the Western Hemisphere's Pacific coast, Drake made a five-week stop at Marin County, California, on June 17, 1579, at a spot known as Drake's *Estero* (estuary), where his men fraternized with the Miwok. He countersank a sixpenny coin in a brass plate as a formal claim of England's ownership of New Albion. His return to Plymouth, England, on September 26, 1580, brought him historic notoriety, dinner with the queen, and a knighthood, which she conferred publicly aboard the *Golden Hind* to sanction his sea piracy on the nation's behalf. He earned for himself Buckland Abbey outside Plymouth, a seat in Parliament, and the mayor's office in Plymouth. The reward for England was immeasurable. John Maynard Keynes called the Inca and Aztec plunder aboard the *Golden Hind* the foundation of England's foreign investment, valued at between £300,000 and £1,500,000.

When war with Spain seemed imminent, Drake received the queen's commission to intervene in the Spanish seizure of English ships. After an astonishingly bold raid on 39 Spanish ships at anchor in Cadiz harbor in 1587, he left the port aflame. He later boasted of his feat as "singeing the beard of the King of Spain" (Reinfeld 1953, p. 83). Drake further abased King Philip by seizing the *San Felipe*, the king's own galleon, which was nearing home with holds filled with cottons and silks, spices, cannons, and gold and silver. It also carried prominent passengers whose ransom upped the value of the cargo considerably.

In July 1588, Drake, aboard the *Revenge*, joined with Hawkins and Martin Frobisher in facing the Spanish Armada, which Philip had christened his "*Felicissima Armada*" ("Most Lucky Fleet"). Economic warfare advanced the English cause, which was severely compromised by Spain's intent to control the seas. Because the English cornered the market on credit from Genoan financiers, the Spanish Armada was delayed, missing the best weather for their endeavor. Philip's navy met multiple disasters and lost all. In typical fashion, at Dartmouth, Drake managed to seize a disabled vessel, the *Nuestra Señora del Rosario*, a treasure ship that enriched the queen's military budget. With the nation safe, Drake could return to his primary goal of stemming the flow of gold from the Western Hemisphere into Spain.

One choice spot for Drake's sea piracy was Terceira in the Azores, where Philip II set up naval headquarters and a mint at Angra do Heroísmo to turn Mexican and Peruvian wealth into coin. The island became a port of call for traders from India and a clearinghouse for the Spanish treasure fleet. Like vultures on hens, Dutch, English, and French corsairs regularly preyed on sea traffic off Terceira. Drake attempted to sack the city in 1589, but failed to breach the stronghold at São Filipe Castle.

Shortly before his death from dysentery on January 28, 1596, off Puerto Bello, Honduras, Drake returned to the Queen's employ to halt the transfer of coin from Panama to Spain by commanding 27 ships and 2,500 sailors. The resentful Spanish cheered his demise from bloody flux, which may have been a symptom of yellow fever. Lope de Vega immortalized the doughty navigator as a subhuman dragon in a historical epic, *La Dragontea* ("*The Dragon Monster*") (1598). Toasted in verse, biography, spectacle, and opera in his homeland, Drake earned the nation's respect for his acumen at sailing and destroying Spain's coastal outposts and for cinching England's place as maritime ruler and heir to the New World.

SOURCES: Cordingly, David. *Under the Black Flag*. San Diego, Calif.: Harvest Books, 1995. • Cummins, John. "'That Golden Knight' Drake and His Reputation." *History Today*, January 1996, 14–22. • *Encyclopedia of World Biography*. Detroit: Gale Research, 1998. • *Explorers and Discoverers of the World*. Detroit: Gale Research, 1993. • *Historic World Leaders*. Detroit: Gale Research, 1994. • Klinkenborg, Verlyn. "The West Indies as Freshly Seen in the 16th Century." *Smithsonian*, January 1988, 89–98. • Reinfeld, Fred. *Treasury of the World's Coins*. New York: Sterling Publishing, 1953. • Schwarz, Frederic D. "Drake Sees the Pacific." *American Heritage*, February-March 1998, 94–95. • "Sir Francis Drake's Secret Voyage to the North Coast of America, A.D. 1579." *Mercator's World*, September 2001, 17. • Winchester, Simon. "Sir Francis Drake Is Still Capable of Kicking Up a Fuss." *Smithsonian*, January 1997, 82–91.

drum money

Located between the Flores and Savu seas, the Alor Islands, an Indonesian cluster in Timur province, was home to an unusual folk money based on pigs, goats, chickens, and brass drums and gongs. Central to Alorese celebrations and livestock exchanges were the gong and the *moko*, a bronze kettledrum shaped like an hourglass and bearing a Malaysian name. The *moko*, also called a Dongson (or Dông Son) drum, entered the islands through trade with the Dongson people of Vietnam, metalworkers who migrated south from southern China and Annam in 700 B.C. and who began making sacred ritual drums late in the century. Metalsmiths decorated tympanum and sides with low-relief figures and geometric shapes. Skilled drum makers traded the bronze pieces in South China, Thailand, Laos, West Malaysia, Java, Borneo, and New Guinea.

Like money in systematized denominations, *moko* drums varied in shape and ranged in value from one to 3,000 *rupiahs*, the monetary unit of the Dutch East Indies. Each style had a set worth:

moko	*value in* rupiahs
Lasingtafa	1
Salaka	2
Fatafa	2.5
Kabali	3

moko	*value in* rupiahs
Piki or Tawantama	5
Hiekbui	6
Tamamia	8
Maningmauk	10
Kalmale	13
Hawataka	15
Yekasing	25
Fehawa	30
Aimala	65
Afuipe	70
Makassar	130
Djawa	500
Itkira	1,000

The inhabitants of the Alor Islands elevated the ordinary or non-ceremonial drums along with gongs, livestock, and arrows above ordinary barter to official monetary units. They prized small drums only as good luck pieces or tokens of exchange; broken gongs served as small change worth up to a few *rupiahs*. Upon the arrival of the costliest drum money to a village, people danced a welcome and processed with it to its stopping place.

In the 1850s, islanders established drum money as an integral part of dowry arrangements and exchanges of gifts. Purchase of a wife required a complex set of negotiations between extended family. The deal making began with an engagement gift of an inexpensive *moko* and a shawl and continued throughout the nuptials. Before consummation of the marriage, the groom had to produce the engagement gift along with the highest-priced *moko*. If a young girl lived in the home of her future in-laws, she increased the likelihood of a wedding. According to an island adage, "if she cooks for the man, his heart will remember *mokos* and he will want to pay her family" (Du Bois 1960, p. 86). Similarly, arranging for the building of a dwelling or ritual burial feasts required more tedious discussions of value and costs.

Around 1915, Dutch colonizers introduced modern currency and halted trade in drums, which authorities reduced to scrap metal. By 1940, according to a government census reported in Dora Du Bois's *The People of Alor*, only 20,000 *mokos* remained in use. Consequently, the surviving *mokos* attained greater value as they became more scarce.

SOURCES: Allen, Larry. *Encyclopedia of Money*. New York: Checkmark Books, 2001. • Du Bois, Cora. *The People of Alor*. Cambridge, Mass.: Harvard University Press, 1960. • Einzig, Paul. *Primitive Money*. Oxford: Pergamon Press, 1966. • "Folk Art." http://www.shalimar.co.id/folk%20art.htm. • Kumar, Bachchan. "Dongson Culture of Vietnam." http://www.ignca.nic.in/nl_00404.htm. • McKinnon, E. Edwards. "The Sambas Hoard: Bronze Drums, and Gold Ornaments Found in Kalimantan in 1991." *Journal of the Malaysian Branch of the Royal Asiatic Society*,1994, pp. 9–28. • Miksic, John N. "Evolving Archaeological Perspectives on Southeast Asia, 1970–95." *Journal of Southeast Asian Studies, March 1995*, pp. 46–62. • Opitz, Charles J. *Odd and Curious Money*. Ocala, Fla.: First Impressions, 1986.

ducat

An artful Venetian coin common to Renaissance Mediterranean trade, the *ducat* became the world's most popular gold piece. Issued by Doge Giovanni Dandolo on October 31, 1284, and approved by Venice's Great Council, the coin earned the folk name *zecchino* or *sequin* from La Zecca, the Venetian mint in Piazza San Marco, which Jacopo Sansovino adorned with an imposing façade. Each ducat featured a lengthy motto: "*Sit Tibi Christe datus quem tu regis iste ducatus*" ("To thee, Christ, be dedicated this kingdom, which you rule"). One of the most graceful and balanced Italian *ducats* was the Milanese *ducato doppio d'oro* (double gold ducat) of 1481, which presented the profile of Giovanni Galeazzo Maria Sforza opposite the family blazon, designed by Leonardo da Vinci.

At a time of phenomenal growth in trade, the ducat shared commercial preference with the Florentine *florin*. For their grand portraits, pious symbolism, and tidy edgings, both coins influenced the engravings on moneys throughout Europe, notably, a widely circulated Hungarian gold *ducat* struck from locally mined ores during the reign of Bela IV. Until the late 1400s, the Ottoman Turks used the Venetian *ducat* in lieu of their own monetary anchor. The coin augmented two Turkish coins — the *akche* (also *akce* or *aqche*), a small silver piece that Europeans called the *asper*, and the *ashrafi altin*, modeled on Venice's *ducat* and manufactured at Al-Ruha, Amasya, Amid, Basra, Cezayir, Edirne, and Siruz and at territorial mints as far away as Russia and Tunisia. Drawing on its success, Turks created the *altun*; the Spanish made their own version, the *ducado*, commissioned by Juan II of Aragon after 1458.

In circulation until World War I in denominations as great as 105 *ducats*, the coin served Christian and Islamic countries bordering the Mediterranean Sea as a monetary standard. It figured heavily in history and literature about the corsairs, Barbary pirates who infested the waters of north Africa at Algiers, Bône, Salli, Tripoli, and Tunis. Named for Berber tribesmen, the Barbary pirates plundered, enslaved, and kidnapped at large after the decline of the Roman Empire left a naval vacuum in the Mediterranean. In 1550, 17 Spanish treasure ships circumvented pirates to relieve the debt-ridden Holy Roman Emperor Charles V in the form of 3,000,000 *ducats* minted in the silver mines of Potosí, Bolivia.

In the 1600s, Gustav II Adolf of Sweden minted gold ducats in imitation of Italian coinage. In this same period, the Transylvanian treasury issued a hexagonal 10-*ducat* piece featuring the profiled monarch at center and a circlet bearing the standard royal title and Latin "*Dei Gratia*" ("By the grace of God"). In Hungary, issuance of a 100-*ducat* denomination resulted in the world's largest gold coin. It pictured Ferdinand III of Bohemia and Hungary in armor and ruff softened in tone by an encircling leafy border. Before 1740, the *ducats*, *thalers*, *groshcen*, *guilders*, and *tympfes* produced for Frederick William I, second king of Prussia, earned the joking name *Schwanzdukaten* (pigtail *ducats*) because the artist completed the portrait bust with braided hair.

***See also* amulet coins; banking; Byzantine coins; coinage; coins and currency in drama and film; écu; Islamic money; papal coins; pirary; Renaissance coins; Russian money; U.S. Mint.**

SOURCES: Clain-Stefanelli, Elvira, and Vladimir Clain-Stefanelli. *The Beauty and Lore of Coins, Currency, and Medals*. Croton-on-Hudson, N.Y.: Riverwood Publishers, 1974. • Cordingly, David. *Under the Black Flag*. San Diego, Calif.: Harvest Books, 1995. • Cribb, Joe. *Money*. Toronto: Stoddart, 1990. • Lewis, Brenda Ralph. *Coins & Currency*. New York: Random House, 1993. • Reinfeld, Fred. *Treasury of the World's Coins*. New York: Sterling Publishing, 1953. • Weatherford, Jack. *The History of Money: From Sandstone to Cyberspace*. Pittsburgh, Pa.: Three Rivers Press, 1998.

E Pluribus Unum

The first U.S. usage of the motto "*E Pluribus Unum*" ["Out of Many, One" or "One [nation] Out of Many [States]") adorned pennies manufactured in New Jersey following the Revolutionary War. A reflection of the egalitarianism and human diversity forming the thirteen original colonies, in 1776, the phrase struck the fancy of the committee designing the national seal. With a British fleet of 400 already looming off New England's shores, committeemen Benjamin Franklin, Thomas Jefferson, and John Adams went to work on selecting a national motto. Aided by Swiss portrait and silhouette artist Pierre Eugène Du Simitière, seal designer for the states of Delaware, Georgia, and Virginia, and founder of American numismatics, the committee continued for four years, concluding in 1780. The careful combing of possible mottoes moved far afield from the New World. Benjamin Franklin pictured Moses, the Hebrew patriarch, and the phrase "Rebellion to Tyrants Is Obedience to God." Du Simitière suggested "E Pluribus Unum," a motto he saw on the title page of the *Gentleman's Journal*.

A second committee, empaneled on March 25, 1780, placed James Lovell of Massachusetts as chair over members William Churchill Houston of New Jersey and John Morin Scott of New York and *ad hoc* member Francis Hopkinson, a Philadelphian who had designed a flag adopted three years before. Within seven weeks, the panel chose "*Bello vel Paci*" ("[Let There Be] War or Peace"). On May 14, 1782, a third committee began studying the issue. Chaired by Arthur Middleton of South Carolina, members John Rutledge of South Carolina and Elias Boudinot of New Jersey worked with coin and heraldry expert William Barton, who designed complex motifs. Marking the seal were three legends: "*In Vindiciam Libertatis*" ("In Defense of Liberty"), "*Virtus Sola Invicta*" ("Only Strength Unconquered"), and "*Deo Favente*" ("God Favoring") along with "*Perennis*" ("Forever").

On June 13, 1782, Charles Thomson, secretary of the Continental Congress, made the final decision with input from the three committees. A former Latin teacher in Philadelphia, he studied the phrases and blended elements of all the designs. He chose the eagle holding arrows and olive branch of peace. In the beak, he placed a scroll with a motto proposed by the first committee, "*E Pluribus Unum*," symbolically split with the first two words to the left and "*unum*" standing majestically alone at the right. Above it, he inscribed a dawn and constellation of silver stars, one for each of the 13 original colonies. He noted the newness of American democracy on the reverse, where two inscriptions—"*Annuit Coeptis*" ("[Providence] Favored the Beginnings") and "*Novus Ordo Seclorum*" ("The New Order of the Ages"). Proposed on June 20, 1782, the final design and motto passed that same day.

See also **Great Seal of the United States; Thomas Jefferson; Augustus Saint-Gaudens.**

SOURCES: "The Bureau of Engraving and Printing." http://www.bep.treas.gov/. • Clain-Stefanelli, Elvira, and Vladimir Clain-Stefanelli. *The Beauty and Lore of Coins, Currency, and Medals*. Croton-on-Hudson, N.Y.: Riverwood Publishers, 1974. • "The Great Seal of the United States." http://greatseal.com/. • "The Great Seal of the United States." Washington, D.C.: U.S. Department of State Dispatch, 1996. • Reed, Mort. *Cowles Complete Encyclopedia of U.S. Coins*. New York: Cowles Book Company, 1969.

Eckhel, Joseph Hilarius

An Austrian coin specialist, Joseph Hilarius Eckhel systematized the classification of moneys by date, region, and type. A native of Enzersfeld near Pottenstein, Austria, he was born on January 13, 1737, to Johann Anton Eckhel, steward of the Prince of Montecucul. Eckhel studied in Vienna at a Jesuit school, where he first came in contact with a sizeable assortment of Greek coins. He completed coursework in humanities, math, Greek, Hebrew, and philosophy at Leoben and Graz. At age 14, he took vows in the Jesuit order. He was ordained into the priesthood and taught school until his retirement. A semi-invalid, until his death in Vienna on May 16, 1798, he absorbed himself in numismatics.

At age 35, Eckhel journeyed to Italy to study coin collections at Bologna, Florence, and Rome, in particular, those amassed by Cosimo de' Medici and his family. Three years later, Eckhel held the chair of antiquities and numismatics at the University of Vienna and supervised the coin collection of Austria's Empress Maria Theresa, which was enlarged with additions from the estate of Francis I. Among Eckhel's greatest achievements was the chronology of Roman coinage as well as that of Persia and Parthia. He also removed counterfeit coins and corrected errors in classification, in particular, the inaccuracies and forgeries of Dutch engraver Hubertus Goltzius. In 1789, Eckhel advanced to dean of the university.

From years of experience in classical studies, archeology, and cataloguing, Eckhel wrote extensively, but simply. Over decades, he compiled his life's work in the eight-volume set *Doctrina Nummorum Veterum* [*Knowledge of Ancient Coins*] (1792–1798). In his honor, the sculptor Manfredini designed a medal featuring the legend "*Systematis Rei Numariae Antiquae Conditori*" ("To the Founder of the Cataloguing of Ancient Coins").

See also **Hubertus Goltzius.**

SOURCES: Cribb, Joe. *Money*. Toronto: Stoddart, 1990. • Cribb, Joe, Barrie Cook, and Ian Carradice. *The Coin Atlas*. London: Little, Brown and Co., 1999.• MacDonnell, Joseph F. *The Jesuit Family Album*. Fairfield, Conn.: The Clavius Mathematics Group, 1997.• *Merriam-Webster's Biographical Dictionary*. Springfield, Mass.: Merriam-Webster, 1995.• New Catholic Encyclopedia. San Francisco: Catholic University of America, 1967.

écu

The French *écu* or *denier d'or*, a gold or silver coin named for the French for "shield," was the concept of Louis IX, saintly warrior-king and hero of the Seventh Crusade. Introduced in the late Middle Ages, it originally presented the royal triad of *fleurs-de-lis* on a shield and carried a three- or four-*franc* value in a money system newly advanced to bimetallism. In 1328, Philippe VI de Valois issued the *chaise écu*, a regal piece ornately incised front and back with royal cyphers. From the reign of Francis I, beginning in 1515, these esthetically pleasing moneys bore royal portraits, crowns, and blazons and a stylized lettering on the rim that denoted the high artistic flair of the Renaissance. One commanding profile, that of Louis XIV the Sun King in full curled wig, graced a silver *écu* that court sculptor Jean Varin designed along with the legend "*Lud XIIII D. G. Fr. et Navarre Rex*" ("Louis XIV by the grace of God king of France and Navarre").

Under the ruinous counsel of Scots financier John Law, author of *Money and Trade Considered with a Proposal for Supplying the Nation with Money* (1705), Louis XV, an underage monarch represented by acting regent Philippe II, the Duc d'Orléans, undermined the French treasury, which was already burdened with debts dating to the extravagant Louis XIV. In an era of heightened international trade, the new boy-king's wreathed *écu* circulated in western Europe and the Americas after Law's company, the *Banque Générale*, merged with the French East India Company as the *Compagnie des Indes* (Company of the Indies). The king's successor, Louis XVI, followed the dynastic coinage tradition with the grand *écu constitutionnel* of 1791. Curiously, the coin still circulated a year after the guillotine silenced Louis at *la Place de la Révolution* in Paris on January 21, 1793.

Replacing the coinage of the decapitated king was a new *écu*, designed by French medalist Augustin Dupré. In the egalitarian spirit of the French Revolution, it pictured an abstract peasant figure in Phrygian slave cap symbolizing the nation's new-found freedom from monarchy. The legend restructured national priorities: "*La Nation, la Loi, le Roi*" ("Nation, Law, King"). Dupré adapted traditional emblems with new images of a vivacious French socialite, Julie Récamier, wearing the cap of freedom. The soft, amorphous cap remained influential in coin design and appeared on numerous U.S. coins.

During the six years preceding the release of the euro in 2000, member states discussed the shape, size, color, and name that would suit a common European currency. The frontrunner in the naming contest was ECU because the term had named a medieval French coin and because the letters formed an acronym standing for European Currency Unit. In 1995, German Chancellor Helmut Kohl opposed the name because it reminded the Germans of *kuh* ("cow"). Proposals for the Renaissance terms *ducat* and *florin* received mention, but the winning suggestion of "euro" was that of Felipe González Marquez, Spain's prime minister.

***See also* coinage; *franc*; John the Good; John Law; medieval coins; U.S. Mint; Jean Varin.**

SOURCES: Cribb, Joe. *Money*. Toronto: Stoddart, 1990. • Cribb, Joe, Barrie Cook, and Ian Carradice. *The Coin Atlas*. London: Little, Brown and Co., 1999. • *Encyclopedia of World Biography*. Detroit: Gale Group, 1998. • Fry, Maxwell J. "Choosing a Money for Europe." *Journal of Common Market Studies*, September 1991, pp. 481–527. • Kunzig, Robert. "Euroland or Bust." *Discover*, October 1998. • Reinfeld, Fred. *Treasury of the World's Coins*. New York: Sterling Publishing, 1953.

Edward the Confessor

The establisher of Norman custom and rule in England, Edward the Confessor was the nation's first monarch of the House of Wessex and the employer of over 500 moneyers. He was born around 1002 to Emma of Normandy and Ethelred II (also Aethelred or Ethelred the Unready) and came under a murderous regime eager to kill him and his brother. Safely reared in Hungary and educated at Ely, Edward became a soulful visionary, scholar, and philanthropist. He was crowned in 1042. Nine years later, he relieved his overburdened people by abolishing the *heregeld* (soldier debt), the tax levied in four previous decades to hire mercenaries and support a fleet of battleships against Scandinavian insurgents. Instead of heavy taxation, Edward relied on the nation's commerce.

After remodeling Westminster Abbey in 1065, Edward set up a regular program of hands-on healing for victims of scrofula, a tubercular swelling of lymph glands in the neck. He learned about the faith-healing treatment from a woman's dream that the king could cure the "King's Evil" with one touch. Among his gifts to the poor in addition to the royal touch were coins, which he dispensed in person. In the time of Henry VII, the ceremonial touch plus the recitation of prayers and passages of scripture expanded to dispersal of special coins that were said to bear the king's curative magic. The respected ritual appeared in Act IV, Scene iii, ll. 140–159 of William Shakespeare's *Macbeth* (ca. 1603–1606) and continued into the time of Queen Anne, England's last Stuart monarch.

After 1065, Edward the Confessor set up a regular program of hands-on healing for victims of scrofula and dispensed to each a royal coin marked with his image and a Christian cross. (Guy Clark, Ancient Coins and Antiquities, Norfolk, Virginia)

Venerated, yet failing to establish a dynasty, Edward attended to the shoring up of abbeys and enjoyed hunting and the arts. He paid a monthly salary in coin to the royal *huscarls*, a home guard of mercenaries who collected taxes from the peasantry. To strengthen the economy, he weakened the alloy of silver in pennies with copper and zinc and cut to three years the established cycle of recoinage, a method of building up the national treasury.

Edward's demands on 76 mints included issuance of ten new coins by mint workers who identified their artistry with individual ciphers. The size of operations varied widely, from one mintmaster each at Bedwyn, Berkeley, Bury St. Edmunds, Chichester, and Droitwich to 36 at Lincoln, 25 in London, and 24 at York. At his death on January 5, 1066, his heirless family lost control of the throne, which passed to Harold, the weak king who lost Anglo-Saxon England to William the Conqueror and the invading Normans at the battle of Hastings on October 14, 1066. Nonetheless, Edward received a place of honor in the burial vault of Westminster Abbey and sainthood, conferred by Pope Alexander III in 1161.

***See also* Anglo-Saxon coins; Appledore hoard.**

SOURCES: Cannon, John, and Ralph Griffiths. *Oxford Illustrated History of the British Monarchy*. Oxford: Oxford University Press, 1988. • Cavendish, Richard, ed. *Man, Myth & Magic*. New York: Marshall Cavendish, 1970. • Clain-Stefanelli, Elvira, and Vladimir Clain-Stefanelli. *The Beauty and Lore of Coins, Currency, and Medals*. Croton-on-Hudson, N.Y.: Riverwood Publishers, 1974. • Cribb, Joe. *Money*. Toronto: Stoddart, 1990. • Cribb, Joe, Barrie Cook, and Ian Carradice. *The Coin Atlas*. London: Little, Brown and Co., 1999. • *Encyclopedia of World Biography*. Detroit: Gale Group, 1998. • Farmer, David Hugh. *The Oxford Dictionary of Saints*. Oxford: Oxford University Press, 1992. • Freeman, Anthony. *The Moneyer and the Mint in the Reign of Edward the Confessor*. Oxford: B. A. R. British Series 145, 1985. • Hastings, James, ed. *Encyclopedia of Religion and Ethics*. New York: Charles Scribner's Sons, 1951. • "The Life of King Edward the Confessor." http://www.lib.cam.ac.uk/cgi-bin/Ee.3.59/bytext. • Magnusson, Magnus. *Cambridge Biographical Dictionary*. Cambridge: University of Cambridge, 1990. • *New Catholic Encyclopedia*. San Francisco: Catholic University of America, 1967. • Parker, Michael St. John. *Britain's Kings and Queens*. Andover, Hants: Pitkin, 1994. • Pollak, Henry. *Coinage & Conflict*. Clifton, N.J.: Coin & Currency Institute, 2001. • Snodgrass, Mary Ellen. *Who's Who in the Middle Ages*. Jefferson, N.C.: McFarland, 2001.

Egbert

The warrior-king Egbert (or Ecbert, Ecgberht, or Ecgbryht), the longest-ruling monarch of the Cerdic dynasty, was the first *Rex Anglorum* ("King of the Angles") and coiner of money at a series of mints. Born about A.D. 784 to Ealhmund, he was descended from Ine and added the Franks to his bloodline by marrying Redburh. Banished by Offa of Mercia and Beorhtric of Wessex, around age eighteen, Egbert returned to West Saxony to accept the throne. In A.D. 829, Northumbrians accepted his overlordship and proclaimed him "Bretwalda," Britain's only ruler. At Dore, he completed the conquest of Essex, Mercia, North Wales, and West Wales by overthrowing Aenred. Egbert's control of these realms plus West Saxony, Sussex, Surrey, Essex, and Kent produced a united Saxon kingdom.

Egbert balanced the powers of the council and see of his shire, established a standing home guard, and at Sheppey, warded off Norse pirates. He coined money at East Anglia, Mercia, and Wessex and issued coins marked with "Rex Egbert" and the mint marks "Saxo," "M," or "A" denoting the royal coinsmithies he established in Wessex, Mercia, and East Anglia. After ruling his vast kingdom for 37 years, he died on November 19, A.D. 839, leaving his throne to his son Ethelwulf and ultimately to his grandsons Ethelbald, Ethelbert, Ethelred I, and Alfred the Great.

SOURCES: *Encyclopedia of World Biography*. Detroit: Gale Group, 1998. • Hastings, James, ed. *Encyclopedia of Religion and Ethics*. New York: Charles Scribner's Sons, 1951. • Llewellin, Philip, and Ann Saunders. *Book of British Towns*. London: Drive Publications, Ltd., 1979. • Magnusson, Magnus. *Cambridge Biographical Dictionary*. Cambridge: University of Cambridge, 1990. • Montague-Smith, Patrick W. *The Royal Line of Succession: The British Monarchy from Cerdic to Queen Elizabeth II*. Andover, England: Pitkin, 1986. • *New Catholic Encyclopedia*. San Francisco: Catholic University of America, 1967. • Parker, Michael St. John. *Britain's Kings and Queens*. Andover, Hants: Pitkin, 1994. • Snodgrass, Mary Ellen. *Who's Who in the Middle Ages*. Jefferson, N.C.: McFarland, 2001.

Egyptian coins

Egyptian moneys began with trade items, including strings of amber beads. Around 1300 B.C., some five centuries after the Babylonians created a money system based on the shekel, Egyptian financiers determined their own coin standards by weight of copper, silver, and gold rather than by coins stamped with a set value. The use of bent wire precipitated a standard hieroglyph that equated with "money." The *deben* (also called *tabnu*, *uten*, and *utnu*) coin, derived from the term "circular," set a standard of value, as with the price of an ox or knife or the wage of a temple laborer. A smaller denomination called the *kit* (also *chat* or *kedet*) served as small change for peasant marketing.

Merchants used the balance beam scale to determine the value of gold rings, metal circlets that the owner could carry as body adornment or as a line of monetary units collected on a rod or cord or gathered into a basket. Because weight was the main criterion rather than shape, other forms of legal tender ranged from bars and coils to flattened metal sheets and amorphous lumps. In 1200 B.C., traders accepted gold and silver along with apes, animal hides, linen, and cedar planks.

During the period of Persian domination in the fourth century B.C., Egyptians coined no money of their own. Instead, they continued exchanging silver by weight as well as snipped pieces and whole coins from Greece and Persia. Proof of Egypt's crude media of exchange exists in the silversmith's hoard found at Naucratis, in which the owner accumulated 15 archaic coins from Greek cities along with lumps sliced from silver bullion. The first genuine in-country coinage dates to the time of Macedonian conqueror Alexander the Great, who built the city of Alexandria in 331 B.C. At local mints, his coinmasters began stamping *staters* and *tetradrachms*. These bronze coins, which Egyptians dubbed "Alexanders," bore the conqueror's picture.

When Egypt passed to the Greek dynasty begun by Ptolemy I Soter and ending with Cleopatra VII, local *tetradrachms* generated by the Alexandrian mint in silver and gold were unremarkable and few in number, perhaps because peasants preferred the nation's excellent grain banks for commerce. The landmark

This portrait piece is a domestic coin struck by Ptolemy II Philadelphus ("Brother-lover"), builder of the grat lighthouse at Alexandria. The Egyptian treasury reserved such coins mainly for purchasing foreign goods and services and for funding the military. (Guy Clark, Ancient Coins and Antiquities, Norfolk, Virginia)

coin, featuring a portrait bust of Ptolemy, introduced the custom of self-adulation of living monarchs. Imports from Athens and Rhodes blended with local coppers and some gold and silver pieces. The Egyptian treasury reserved domestic coins mainly for purchasing foreign goods and services and for funding the military. Authorities favored gold coins for foreign trade.

Rome's emperors perpetuated the style of Egypt's coinage. Most notable of the historic models was a coin struck at Cyprus depicting Cleopatra with son Caesarion, sired by Julius Caesar. The pair posed as Aphrodite carrying the infant Eros. The loss of Caesar as her lover and promoter preceded the portrait *tetradrachm* of Cleopatra in the headdress of Isis, her patron goddess, struck at Ascalon after her sexual and military alliance with Mark Antony. After A.D. 296, production of base billon and bronze sufficed for small change along with Roman *solidi*. The invasion of Islamic conquerors after A.D. 690 ended circulation of Christian coins from Rome and Byzantium, both of which offended Muslims. By A.D. 711, Islamic coiners at Alexandria, al-Fayyum, Atrib, and Cairo were producing bronze, copper, silver, and gold pieces.

See also **giro system; Islamic money; portrait coins; ring and bullet money; Roman coins; world money.**

SOURCES: Allen, Larry. *Encyclopedia of Money*. New York: Checkmark Books, 2001. • Angell, Norman. *The Story of Money*. Garden City, N.Y.: Garden City Publishing, 1929. • Clain-Stefanelli, Elvira, and Vladimir Clain-Stefanelli. *The Beauty and Lore of Coins, Currency, and Medals*. Croton-on-Hudson, N.Y.: Riverwood Publishers, 1974. • Cribb, Joe. *Money*. Toronto: Stoddart, 1990. • Einzig, Paul. *Primitive Money*. Oxford: Pergamon Press, 1966. • *Encyclopedia of African History and Culture*. New York: Facts on File, Inc., 2001. • Head, Barclay V. *A Guide to the Principal Coins of the Greeks*. London: British Museum, 1959. • Head, Barclay V. *Historia Numorum*. Chicago: Argonaut, 1911. • Opitz, Charles J. *Odd and Curious Money*. Ocala, Fla.: First Impressions, 1986.

elephant token

Minted in London after the fire of 1666, possibly in 1672, the elephant token was an intriguing coin commissioned by English nobles. Of uncertain origin, the coin, featuring a sturdy tusked animal with the shield of London and picturing a cross and sword on the reverse, may have been the design of French diecutter John Roettiers. The piece was the issue of the British East India Company and the Royal African Company, a slaving business that the Duke of York formed in 1622. Incised in copper at the Tower Mint, the elephant token bore the legend, "God Preserve London." Some models of the thin elephant token were counterstamps of common half-pence coins issued by Charles I.

Unlike merchant tokens, the elephant token appears to have functioned as an advertisement. Various surmises about other uses include lottery tickets and promotional pieces supporting colonization of the Carolinas, which Charles II chartered in 1663. Although the animal was an anomaly in the New World, the image may have been a curiosity or a pragmatic use of handy coin dies. In 1694, variations appeared with the mottoes "God Preserve Carolina and the Lords Proprietors" and "God Preserve New England." In the American colonies, where coins were always in short supply, the disks circulated as half-pennies. The tokens also followed slavers and traders to Africa, Asia, and Europe.

SOURCES: Geiger, Rusty. "Elephant Tokens One Legacy of N.C. Colony." *Coin World*, February 25, 1987, p. 38. • Jordan, Louis. "The Coins of Colonial and Early America." http://www.coins.

nd.edu/ColCoin/ColCoinContents/Introduction.html. • "1694 Elephant Token." http://www.lib.unc.edu/ncc/gallery/elephant.html. • Yeoman, R. S. *A Guide Book of United States Coins*. Racine, Wisc.: Western Publishing, 1993.

Eligius, St.

A goldsmith, engraver, and coin master during the Merovingian dynasty in the era preceding the emergence of a true French coinage, St. Eligius of Noyon (also St. Éloi, Eloy, or Loy) was an artisan at the Paris mint. The son of Terrigia and Eucherius, a metalsmith, according to Bishop Dado's *Vita S. Eligius* (*The Life of Saint Eligius*) (A.D. 742), he was born around A.D. 588 at Chaptelet outside Limoges, France, and apprenticed under mintmaster Abbo. As a staff worker under Bobon, the royal treasurer, Eligius crafted King Clotaire's throne before initiating a career as coinsmith, worker in religious artifacts, and decorator of a monument for Clotaire and Dagobert I.

After his ordination, Eligius became a missionary and fought pagan Roman worship. He financed the ransom of slaves and built feeding centers, shrines, and monasteries. Under this influence, Bathild, widow of Clovis II, studied the slave trade and guaranteed rest for servants on the Sabbath and Catholic holidays. Eligius became patron of goldsmiths, moneyers, and coin collectors. He is identifiable in art and stained glass by the mint worker's hammer, anvil, and pincers. His craft survives in Paris among Merovingian coins at the National Library.

SOURCES: Brown, R. Allen. *The Origins of Modern Europe: The Medieval Heritage of Western Civilization*. New York: Barnes & Noble, 1972. • Butler, Alban. *Lives of the Saints*. New York: Barnes & Noble, 1997. • Englebert, Omer. *The Lives of the Saints*. New York: Barnes & Noble, 1994. • Farmer, David Hugh. *The Oxford Dictionary of Saints*. Oxford: Oxford University Press, 1992. • Hallam, Elizabeth, gen. ed. Saints: *Who They Are and How They Help You*. New York: Simon & Schuster, 1994. • Hollister, C. Warren. *Medieval Europe: A Short History*. New York: McGraw-Hill, 1994. • Holmes, George, ed. *The Oxford Illustrated History of Medieval Europe*. Oxford: Oxford University Press, 1988. • Lopez, Robert S. *The Birth of Europe*. New York: M. Evans & Co., 1967.

English money

The first British coinage involved the casting of speculum, an alloy of bronze and tin, in the style of money minted on the French Mediterranean coast at Massilia before 100 B.C. These coins encouraged trade among the Celts in southeastern England. Also available were plain gold coins entering the country from trade in Beauvais, the capital of the Bellovaci, a Gallic people living in Picardy. For size and design, metalworkers copied a Macedonian *stater* minted under King Philip II, father of Alexander III the Great. Incursions of Belgic forces around 75 B.C. further mixed British coins with Gallic gold pieces, the source of numerous crude Celtic imitations.

The seizure of Britannia by Julius Caesar's forces in 55 B.C. provided the first true model of a formal monetary system, which stabilized on the island during the Pax Romana of Augustus, Rome's first emperor. When Claudius came to power, Roman coinage supplanted local mintage after A.D. 43 except for the gold disks of the Brigantes of Yorkshire and billons, a low-grade coinage of silver alloyed with equal parts of base metal and cast in Dorset and Hampshire. When Roman money ran short, British mints generated unofficial imitations of the *as*, a small bronze Roman coin valued at 1/10 of a Greek *drachma*.

A hoard that archaeologist Joe Severn discovered in a leather bag in January 2001 at a palatial villa in London produced remarkable coinage dating from A.D. 60 to A.D. 174. Stashed during an ominous period of uprisings in Wales and Scotland around A.D. 180, the gold *aurei*, unearthed by Trevor Brigham, an archaeologist at the Museum of London on Fenchurch Street, survived in good condition in an underground chamber. Historians surmise that the owners placed their life savings in the basement of the new townhouse during its construction as a religious "foundation offering" (Keys 2001). According to period superstition, the coins would have conferred prosperity, health, and happiness on the homeowner and his household. Fine mosaic flooring, classic columns, bone game pieces, beads and bracelets, lamps, tableware, and storage jars attest to the wealth of the family.

Curiously, of the people who settled the British Isles, the Anglo-Saxons were the only nation to coin their own original money, except for a small issue of Welsh pennies by the great lawgiver King Hywel Dda (Hywel the Good) of Wales, master of Dinefwr Castle overlooking the Twyi Valley, from A.D. 920 to 950. The mint at Londinium continued output under the Roman Emperor Constantine I the Great until A.D. 324. Reopened by Magnus Maximus after A.D. 383, the site functioned only five years. During the lapse of local mintage, Britons relied heavily on Continental issue. With gold from Merovingian Gaul, Anglo-Saxon mints produced ecclesiastical coinage in the seventh century in the area between Kent and London and possibly also in Mercia and York. Church specie gave place to coppers from Northumbria, minted into the mid-ninth century.

The silver penny, a holdover from Roman influence that Penda issued in the mid-seventh century, was the mainstay of the English merchant class. Under Penda and his son Peada, silver *sceats* circulated among traders from operations in Frisia. A useful coin for the poorest people was the farthing, which equalled one-quarter cent. It replaced the custom of quartering pennies manually, a time-consuming task at weekly markets.

At a time when minting and taxing were interlinking royal prerogatives, the first official English coins were silver pennies struck after A.D. 757 during the reign of Offa of Mercia at Canterbury. They displayed a true Anglo-Saxon artistry rather than an emulation of Roman bas-relief. When Ethelwulf came to power in A.D. 838, he standardized coins over most of southern England. A year later, Archbishop Wigmund of York struck ceremonial gold coins to pay the Romescot or Peter's pence, the tax levied by the pope at Rome for lighting the church and succoring the poor. Patterned after the wreathed pieces of the Emperor Louis I, these coins bore the legend "*Munus Divinum*" ("Sacred Gift"). Moneys altered once more after A.D. 870 under the Vikings, who founded mints at Lincoln and York.

After A.D. 871, the initiator of an Anglo-Saxon renaissance, Alfred the Great, Ethelwulf's son, became England's energetic coiner. He hired quality metalsmiths and launched coinsmithies at Canterbury, Exeter, Gloucester, London, Oxford, and Winchester. Because of Alfred's high standards, attention to quality and artistry survived in subsequent years under his son, Edward the Elder, minter of a silver penny picturing new fortifications built under the direction of the king and his sister Ethelflaed. After A.D. 924, Alfred's grandson Athelstan (also Aethelstan or Ethelstane), the first *Rex Totius Britanniae* ("King of All Britain"), managed 30 mints, reaching to Chester. Edgar, who was crowned king of Wessex in A.D. 959, set up mints that produced standardized coins. Under Ethelred II (also Aethelred or Ethelred the Unready), who was crowned in A.D. 978, the number of sites grew to 70, with Lincoln, London, and Winchester generating the largest number of specie.

Following the Norman Conquest, England's monetary system profited from the redistribution of property under a feudal system of noble landownership and tenant labor. William I the Conqueror, England's first Norman king, employed the same moneyers as his Anglo-Saxon predecessors and added his own coinmakers, including Otto the Goldsmith, an honored artisan who is listed along with his wife Leofgiva in the *Domesday Book* (1086). A landholder at Essex, Otto obtained the honor of erecting the king's tomb at Caen, France. After supervising some 50 provincial operations through the reigns of William's two sons, William Rufus and Henry I, Otto prepared his sons to continue the family trade of engraving, thus establishing "Goldsmith" as a respected family surname. In all, William's staff drafted thirteen coins minted at 57 sites, where laborers worked steadily to keep up his high standards of workmanship.

Despite William's interest in quality control, the design of his silver penny was primitive. Struck between 1077 and 1080, it pictures him face-front and grasping in his right hand a sword rather than a scepter. The pose speaks to all who handle the coin of the nature of the king's power over England. Historically, however, the full-face pose was unflattering and quickly wore down the king's features, leaving a blur. To end the peasant habit of further defacing coins by hacking into the surface to determine if it was solid or a layered counterfeit, the king ordered his coins pre-cut.

Under Henry I, after 1100, the English treasury produced a grand silver coin featuring the king's portrait under the legend "*Heinricus Leo Dux*" ("Henry the Lion Leader") and introduced the halfpence, which ended the need to halve pennies. He denied mintmasters the option of coining silver bullion from outside the shire and reduced counterfeiting by striking a nick in the edge of each legal coin. The ploy failed to reassure consumers. Suspicious citizens so chopped and battered Henry's pennies to determine the purity of silver that, by 1112, English money was a mess. In 1124, a year of crop failure and hopelessness, Chapter 15 of the *Anglo-Saxon Chronicle* remarked that "The penny was so adulterated, that a man who had a pound at a market could not exchange twelve pence thereof for anything" ("Anglo-Saxon Chronicle").

A smooth royal system of coinage foundered during civil war from 1138 to 1153, when Stephen de Blois, Henry's nephew, came to the throne after battling Matilda, Henry's daughter, for power. Amid bureaucratic chaos and rebel mints releasing coins deliberately marred with strikes across Stephen's portrait, England's nobles had to issue their own coins. Contributing to low quality money from mints at Carlisle, Derby, Lincoln, and Nottingham was the irregular supply of silver and lack of refinement of ores from the Bakewell and Alston mines. In view of failing specie, peasants had little choice but to return to a barter system.

When England most needed able leadership, it came under the control of Henry II, one of the royal figures most suited to rule during the entire Middle Ages. He hired Philip Emery, mintmaster in Tours, France, to fill English coffers with new coins. Money in hand, Henry revamped traditional feudal military duty owed by tenants by converting days of service into a scutage or soldier tax payable in cash. Instead of pleading for volunteers, he had the funds to hire professionals named "soldiers" because they worked for the king's *solidi*.

Henry's overreaching created one of the scandals of the era, the murder of Thomas à Becket, whom he made archbishop of Canterbury. Henry's intent to manipulate Becket to open the church coffers for military support resulted in a contretemps. In the face of Becket's six-year withdrawal to France, on Christmas in 1170, Henry dispatched four assassins — Hugh de Morville, Reginald Fitznurse, Richard le Breton, and William de Tracy — to murder the archbishop. The brutal slaying while Becket said prayers before Canon Grim at Canterbury Cathedral obliged Henry to undergo public whipping at the martyr's tomb and to accept a 14-year penance in the Holy Land.

To restore the money system to its prewar status, Henry II called a council at Oxford at Christmas in 1179. He placed in charge of finance his accountant, Bishop Richard FitzNigel, who reduced the work of England's mints by ending the custom of removing from circulation or restriking coins of previous monarchs. This revised policy allowed the king to close superfluous mints and still produce high quality coins at an even rate. FitzNigel hired artist Philip Aymer of Tours to design a new coin issued in 1180 and featuring the king's face and his right hand clutching a scepter.

Managing the technicalities were 11 of the king's best mintmasters, including Isaac of York, whom Sir Walter Scott depicted in his popular historical romance *Ivanhoe* (1819). Consequently, the coins of Henry II remained the mint standard after Henry's death in 1189 and through the reigns of his two sons, the crusader Richard the Lion-Hearted and his inept brother John, who struck no English coins of their own. In 1247, Henry III replaced the short-cross penny with the long-cross piece, which extended the perpendiculars to the edge to prevent coin clipping. Because the ploy failed to deter coin defacers, blame shifted to Jewish moneylenders, whom English authorities persecuted in 1278 and expelled from the country in 1290.

On English pennies, the cross became commonplace and rapidly lost its significance as a Christian symbol. Because it resembled a star, it earned the coin the name "starling," forerunner of "sterling," which moneyers in Belgium and Luxembourg reprised as *esterling*. The four arms of the cross served makers of small change as scoring lines. When split into four pieces, a single penny produced "fourthlings," the basis of the term "farthing." In 1807, the discovery of a cache of 6,000 coins featuring Henry II's distinctive crossbar markings earned for the mintage the name "Tealby pennies" for the village in Lincolnshire where they were unearthed. Coins marked with "Henricus," the king's name in Latin, remained the standard through the reigns of six Norman kings. The addition of the moneyer's mark assured quality control.

A major reaction against the rapacity of the crown was the compromising of Henry's weak-willed youngest son John, ridiculed as John Lackland and Softsword. The least promising of successors to Henry II, John paid the price for his father's strength. On June 15, 1215, at Runnymede, a faction of nobles obliged John to redress wrongs against all English barons by signing the Magna Carta. The cornerstone of English liberties, the document declared:

> Omnes mercatores habeant salvum et securum exire ab Anglia, et venire in Anglia, morari et ire per Angliam, tam per terram quam per aquam, ad emendum et venendendum. [Let all merchants have safe and secure exit from England, and passage into and out of England, both on land and water, for the purpose of buying and selling] ["Magna Carta"].

In addition to supporting free trade, the Magna Carta limited the king's power to levy a scutage tax, the drain on the nobles' moneys that had supported the Crusades. With their newly gained power over absolute monarchy, the barons prevented the king from issuing debased coins.

A similar crushing of Henry III, John's son, resulted from his Continental taste in coinage and his disdain for English folk tradition. One of Henry's failures was the circulation of a gold *florin* modeled on that of Florence, Italy. Considered effete by the English, it met with immediate rejection. The concept of the *florin* did not return for consideration until the reign of Edward III two generations later.

After service in the Eighth Crusade, King Edward I, called Longshanks, returned home to take charge of England's muddled monetary matters. A pragmatist, he accepted as rent for the Scilly Islands 50 puffins per year, the equivalent of six shillings and eight pence. A sound economist, he minted the first farthing or quarter penny coins and promoted circulation of halfpence. He banned the cutting of pennies, a makeshift method of producing small change from a coin worth a day's pay for a laborer. Gradually, the number of mints decreased as the authority of the London coinage headquarters increased, especially under mintmaster William de Turnmire of Marseilles, whom Edward appointed on December 8, 1279.

It was Turnmire who struck the first *grossus sterling* (groat), worth four pence, the first coin in English history worth more than one cent. Issued at the London mint in 1279, the large coin, featuring the king's bust and a cross on the reverse side, influenced the styling of coins until the time of Henry VII. It was frequently copied by foreign mints, namely, Dutch, French, and German operations and that of Robert I the Bruce of Scotland. In 1299, Edward halted the circulation of imitation groats with a grand recoinage. A year later, he further centralized coinage and monetary circulation by moving the Royal Mint and Exchequer to the Tower, thus putting it within his household and offices.

The next innovative coiner was Edward III, a valiant king who modelled his reign on that of King Arthur and remained on the throne for five decades. After the failure of his plan for bimetallism, in 1346, he created the gold noble. The front image of Edward on board a twin-castled ship with a sword and a shield bearing crests of England and France symbolized his naval victory off Sluis (or Sluys) in 1340, when the Flemish reversed their loyalty from France to England. The presumptuous legend identified him as "*Rex Maris*" ("King of the Sea"). A splendid reverse interwove English lions and crowns around a crusader's cross. About the edge, workers inscribed phrases from the New Testament, a scheme that was both pious and canny as a means of halting clipping. The grand coin inspired Philippe le Hardi of Flanders to create his own version.

The final years of Edward's promising reign sank into ignominy as bubonic plague killed off half the populace, sapping England of labor and professional skills. Although he authorized a national mint on the north shore of France at Calais in 1347, money hoarding and trade with weaker, more debased currencies from France, Milan, and Venice increased inflation and bled England of coins. The crown devalued currency, stabilized prices and wages, and turned to the people for poll taxes, generating anger that erupted into the Peasants Revolt of 1381.

Contemplating the results of the bubonic plague on money and finance, political economist and mathematician Nicolas Oresme (also Nicole d'Oresme or Nicole Oresme) of Allemagne composed *Tractatus de Origine, Nature, Jure, et Mutationibus Monetarum* (*Treatise on the Origin, Nature, Law and Alterations of Money*) (ca. 1355), in which he anticipated Gresham's Law. The reformer of the French treasury, minting, and tax codes and author of *Traité de la Premiere Invention des Monnaies* (*Treatise of the Invention of Coins*) (ca. 1360), he was already familiar with the basics of coinage and money circulation. He concluded that the quantity of precious metal in circulation determines the value of currency and added to his theories additional speculation on inflation and the hoarding of coins.

The invention of the pound established Henry VII's place in monetary history. The creation of the gold crown or sovereign in 1489 presented to citizens the "King's coin" (Martinez 2002, p. C11). An emblem of wealth and power equal to five shillings, it pictured Henry along with his crest and the Tudor rose, a reminder that he ended the Wars of the Roses. The flower earned the pound coin the name "rose noble"; its value in the 19th century boosted it to the world's most secure trading currency. The surface, engraved by Antwerp artist Alexander von Brugsal (also Alexandre or Sanders van Bruchsal or Bruchsaal), featured the king in full-front pose enthroned between columns and holding his staff of office and orb. Von Brugsal also created the inscription "*Posui Deum Adiutorem Meum*" ("I Have Made God My Aide"). When the king died in 1509, he left to his heir a full chest of gold bullion and regular revenue from his estates. Historians muse that his success at money and finance set England on the path to becoming a world economic power.

Henry VIII, aided by mintmaster Sir William Sharington, continued the tinkering with coin design by adding a royal crest held up by the dragon and lion and by initiating the George noble, featuring St. George, England's patron, slaying the dragon. In 1498, Henry began clearing the nation's tills of substandard Irish pennies and groats issued by the Holy Roman empire. He followed his specie housecleaning with smaller coins, notably the shilling or teston, a debased metal disk worth 12 pence, which was designed by engraver John Sharp and minted in 1504. Muddling issues of coinage was the addition of a cardinal's hat to coins by the king's councillor, Thomas Wolsey, who came before a tribunal under the Statute of Praemunire in 1529 for treason. In William Shakespeare's version, found in Act III, Scene ii of *Henry VIII* (ca. 1612), Suffolk blasts the cardinal with charges, including carrying the Great Seal to Flanders and "[causing] your holy hat to be stamp'd on the King's coin" (III, ii, 324–325). Found guilty, Wolsey forfeited his property to the crown and surrendered all his titles as well as possession of the Great Seal of England.

As a result of Tudor fiscal policies, the two Henrys earned credit for upgrading coinage to the best that England had produced. However, because of extravagant harbor-building projects and an expanded navy, Henry VIII was unable to maintain a high level of coinage and produced adulterated gold and silver coins on a ratio of half precious metal and half base metal. The shiny surface quickly wore thin, exposing the cheap base underneath. For his blatant debasement, peasants dubbed him "Old Coppernose" because of the dull shine that peeked through worn silver-washed coins. The epithet derived from the angry retort of Sir John Rainsford, a loyalist who met the adviser who instigated debasement of the silver shilling. Raising his fists, Rainsford charged the coiner with depicting "his Soveraigne Lord, the most beautiful Prince, King Henry, with a redde and copper nose" (Reinfeld 1953, p. 81).

In 1534, Henry VIII hit on an audacious plan of raiding friaries and monasteries of their altar plate and candelabra, religious medals, bells, and *objets d'art*. Within six years, he had seized church properties, imposed heavy taxes on the Catholic hierarchy, and ransacked English Christendom to the tune of some 75,000 pounds in pelf. To thwart the Henrician reforms, wily abbots schemed to conceal church treasure. Faithful parishioners hid priests and objects in niches, walls, and chimney nooks called "priest holes." Meanwhile, Henry's goldsmiths stripped the collected treasury of jewels, silver plate, and precious metals for immediate meltdown and use in coinage. Henry's son, the boy-king Edward VI, continued pillaging any religious houses that his father had missed. After 1551, he furthered the dynastic bent for portrait coinage with silver shillings, sixpence, and a crown, England's first dollar-sized piece and its first dated coin.

Secure on the seas and in the New World, England profited from Sir Francis Drake's pirating of Spanish coins and ores, which enabled the Royal Mint to double its output during the reign of Henry VIII's daughter, Elizabeth I. She revitalized fine silver coins, streamlined manufacture of coins by introducing new striking devices, and reduced the number of denominations by withdrawing the groat. To assist illiterate consumers and shopkeepers, she had her moneyers add a rose behind her portrait bust to distinguish the sixpence from the groat and shilling.

Always on the political edge, Elizabeth managed to outflank the undercurrent of papist support for the pious Mary, Queen of Scots, who designed her own coinage bearing the self-ennobling motto "*Ecce Ancilla Domini*" ("*Behold, the Lord's Handmaiden*") and "*Quae Deus Conjunxit Nemo Separet*" ("*What God Has Joined, Let No One Part*"), a galling reference to Elizabeth's quasi-legitimate birth to Henry VIII's second wife, Anne Boleyn, following his divorce from Catharine of Aragon. For the East India Company, Elizabeth's new colonial trading alliance exploiting commerce with India and the Orient, she issued the portcullis token in 1600, intended to aid her seizure of Spanish and Portuguese monopolies in Eastern spice markets. A boon to common trade, these inferior tokens, bearing the likeness of the drop grating at the gate of the Tower Mint and valued at eight, four, two, and one *reales*, were common in the tills of vintners and barkeeps.

Elizabeth's circulation of "mixt monies" in 1601 spawned a unique legal case (Allen 2001, p. 51). Elizabeth Brett incurred debt to a London shopkeeper on April 23 and agreed to pay him £100 the following September. A month after the transaction, the queen's agents shipped the mongrel specie from the Tower Mint to Dublin, where Brett intended to make the final payment. When she tendered the new coins to quit her debt, the merchant rejected the payment and demanded the quality coins in use the previous April. Because subjects had no control over the legal tender issued by the crown, English courts found Brett in compliance with the verbal contract.

James I, the first king of the United Kingdom of England and Scotland, was obliged to mint the first gold union coin, a lighter ten-shilling piece stamped "*Henricus Rosas Regna Jacobus*" ("Henry [United] the Roses, James the Kingdoms"). The motto reminded citizens of the heavy cost of the Wars of the Roses and was a tribute to Henry VII. James also contracted out-of-house coinage of the first English coppers, called Harrington farthings after the private moneyer whom the king licensed to produce them in 1613. The use of entrepreneurial mintage continued until 1672, when the job returned to the Royal Mint. During this period, the people of the united kingdom adopted the Union Jack, a flag comprised of the crosses of St. George and St. Andrew. Under Charles II, the flag appeared on coins in the hand of Britannia, the female emblem of England who is the equivalent of Marianne in France, Hibernia in Ireland, and Lady Liberty and Uncle Sam in the United States.

To his credit, in 1604, James I ordered the "unite" sovereign, worth 20 shillings, and incised a motto calling for the merger of two nations into one people: "*Tueatur Unita Deus*" ("May God Guard These United [Kingdoms]"). The coin that the people called the unite bore a statement from the Old Testament prophet Ezekiel: "*Faciam eos in gentem unam*" ("I will make them into one nation"). For the first time in English coinage, the mintmaster altered the legends to include values stated in Roman numerals:

coin	*marking*	*value*
angel	X	10 shillings
spur ryal	XV	15 shillings
laurel	XX	20 shillings

Overall, James left English specie strong, historically accurate, and appealingly designed.

The ill-destined Charles I added more coins, including the poorly struck Oxford silver crown, and presented himself in an equestrian pose sculpted by medalist and engraver Thomas Rawlins. The king supported coinsmithies at Chester, Colchester, Cork, Dublin, Edinburgh, Exeter, London, Salisbury, Truro, Weymouth, Worcester, and York and, in 1638, added a new facility at Aberystwyth, run by Thomas Bushell to strike coins from native Welsh silver. Lesser operations functioned at Carlisle, Newark, Pontefract, and Scarborough. To maintain high quality coins when bullion was scarce, the royal council, led by Sir Thomas Roe, prevented the king from instituting a scheme to turn out £300,000 in shillings reduced to only one-quarter silver.

As the demand for precious metals rose, the king's quality coins rapidly disappeared from circulation when goldsmiths began hoarding them for export or melting into ingots. One violator, Thomas Violet, plea-bargained his case in 1634 by naming other transgressors of the law; nonetheless, silver thievery continued into mid-century. In another incident, Violet went to prison on January 6, 1643, for passing a letter from the king to the mayor and council. Violet joined other inmates at the Tower of London on June 16, 1647, in signing a grievance, "A True Relation of the Cruell and Unparallel'd Oppression which hath been illegally imposed upon the Gentlemen Prisoners in the Tower of London," a general complaint followed by two personal addresses to Charles II in 1661. The next September, mockers skewered Violet in a cavalier ballad, Sir Francis Wortley's "The Royal Feast," which snickered,

> Tom Violet swears his injuries
> Are scarcely to be numb'red;
> He was close prisoner to the State
> These score dayes and nine hundred ["The Royal Feast"].

The verse fit the tune "Chevy Chase."

In 1640, Charles I instigated another quick-cash solution to his perennial fiscal shortage by halting the outflow of minted coins to royal creditors and by diverting all new moneys to his hoard in the Tower mint. To the merchants and goldworkers to whom he owed money, he allotted a meager 8 percent of his cash to satisfy their claims. The blatant confiscation of England's coins ruined the king's credit, thus fueling the demand for a national bank outside the whims of self-enriching royalty. In 1642, he set up an emergency mint at Shrewsbury to melt plate into coins to pay his new army. To boost loyalty to the monarchy, he had the pieces stamped in English, for the commoner to read, "Let God arise, let his enemies be scattered."

With civil war foiling the king's plans to enrich his treasury, he established minting wherever he could to keep his court afloat. In 1643, after the capture of Exeter, he opened an operation run by a Cornish soldier, Sir Richard Vyvyan. At Dublin in July 1643, Irish coiners led by James Butler, Earl of Ormonde, stamped "Ormonde money," which reimbursed badly needed Irish troops who joined the king's forces.

A year later, Charles I hastily opened another mint at Oxford, his military headquarters, where he relied on stolen plate from the university for bullion. Again, he turned to the faithful Thomas Bushell and Sir William Parkhurst for management. The building narrowly escaped burning to the ground when a soldier tried to conceal the roasting of a purloined pig. In May 1644, the king appointed Sir Thomas Cary to open mints in the marches at Cheshire, Herefordshire, Shropshire, and Worcestershire. In a patriotic pose, Charles issued the "declaration" shilling, an inelegant coin featuring three royal ciphers and the legend "*Relig. Pro. Leg. Ang. Lib. Par.*" ("Protestant Faith, English Law, Freedom of Parliament"). His plan to heighten the enmity between England and Scotland failed. Both nations agreed to turn the recalcitrant king over to a parliamentary commission.

After the English Revolution and the unprecedented execution of an English monarch — Charles I — on January 30, 1649, Oliver Cromwell's commonwealth reduced the affectations of coinage to align with his prim Puritan notions. One hastily minted coin in 1651 earned Royalist scorn as "breeches money," a reference to elongated oval shields that overlapped like a baggy pair of pants. Overall, his specie was simpler and less royal, with some mottoes rendered in English. The administration's fiscal restraint figures in a nursery rhyme, "I Had a Little Nut Tree," collected in C. D. Piguenit's *Tom Tit's Song Book: being a Collection of Old Songs, with which most Young Wits have been delighted* (ca. 1790):

> I had a little nut tree, nothing would it bear
> But a silver nutmeg and a golden pear.
> The King of Spain's daughter came to visit me,
> And all for the sake of my little nut tree.
> I skipped over water, I danced over sea,
> And all the birds in the air couldn't catch me
> ["I Had Little Nut Tree"].

The "silver nutmeg" and "golden pear" in line two may refer to English coins, which made Cromwell a prize catch for "the King of Spain's daughter."

The superstitious believed that English coins predicted the end of the Commonwealth and prophesied the return of the thwarted Stuart dynasty. When Cromwell's portrait crown appear in 1658, the year of his death, it developed a flaw at the throat. The rift pointed to the Latin *nemo* ("no man"), which, when read in reverse, spelled "omen." Three years after his death from natural causes, a macabre discovery proved the folk belief true: an autopsy of his exhumed remains found that his skull had detached from the skeleton.

With the restoration of the crown in 1660, the English had reason for celebration. Diarist Samuel Pepys observed the newly restored Charles II on June 23, when the poor stood in the rain in the garden awaiting his arrival. Freed from the hard hand of religious fanatics, England entered a modern era of coinage and a return to the touch and coin distribution ceremony to ease scrofula. The

In the 1670s under King Charles II, the English flag appeared on coins in the hand of Britannia, the female emblem of England who is the equivalent of Marianne in France, Hibernia in Ireland, and Lady Liberty and Uncle Sam in the United States. (Guy Clark, Ancient Coins and Antiquities, Norfolk, Virginia)

sumptuous petition crown that Thomas Simon designed in 1663 acknowledged the people's will that Charles II return from France to a royal throne left empty through eleven years of Puritan control. Drawing on Lysimachus's elegant commemorative piece of 297 B.C. picturing Alexander III the Great, Charles II introduced the long-lived golden guinea displaying the filleted head of the king and a tiny elephant at bottom to indicate that England acquired gold from Guinea in Africa.

As an impetus to quality English coinage, Charles II upgraded the minting process. On a technologically advanced mill, coinsmiths produced a series of silver crowns, half-crowns, and shillings from the Tower Mint. To encourage commerce, a new law allowed trade in foreign currency and bullion. Another statute abolished the customary levy that mint clients paid for the coinage of their private stock of precious metals.

In 1665, Charles introduced the Britannia symbol, the design of one of the Flemish Roettiers (also Roettier or Rotier) family, John, Joseph, Norbert, and Philip. The graceful emblem, which became the hallmark of English moneys, appeared on a pattern in 1665 encircled by the motto "*Quattuor Maria Vindico*" ("I Claim the Four Seas"). For small change, Charles added a copper half-cent and a Britannia farthing, struck in 1672. The workmanship on his specie was so fine that filmmakers shooting *Forever Amber* (1947) outfitted star George Sanders with wigs modeled from the era's portrait coins.

Charles's successor, James II, introduced a form of recycling with gun money, a coinage stamped on the meltdown of various metals from plate, bells, brass cannon, and scrap and marked with the pious legend "*Christo Victore Triumpho*" ("Through Christ the Victor I Triumph"). During the Glorious Revolution, James used the cash in June 1689 to pay the mercenaries who helped him fight for the English throne against William and Mary. After a disreputable season of debased brass and white metal coins churned out from the Dublin mint, by 1698, less than 44 percent of English business was conducted in coin. The rest relied on bills, banknotes, and tallies.

New coins entered the English treasury under William III, who called in hand-hammered specie from circulation in 1695 and absorbed the loss by issuing new for old. After melting down old, worn, and clipped coins, the king furthered recycling operations at Bristol, Chester, Exeter, Norwich, and York. Represented by Charles Montagu, the Earl of Halifax and Chancellor of the Exchequer, the crown solicited advice from John Locke, author of *Further Considerations concerning Raising the Value of Money* (1695). Locke, a proponent of halting devaluation, clashed with the Secretary of the Treasury, William Lowndes, who preferred cheapening coinage as a way to cut minting costs. To recoup the health of his treasury, William chose a unique fiscal dodge, a tax on windows. The unfair basis caused builders to reduce the number of windows in new buildings. Loss of sunlight and fresh air threatened health as well as the education of the young, who had to study by fireside and candlelight.

As the treasury floundered, royal authorities sought further consultation with former Lord Mayor of London Sir John Houblon, physicist and mathematician Sir Isaac Newton, architect Sir Christopher Wren, and mathematician Edmond Halley, discoverer of Halley's comet. Montagu established the English national debt and founded the Bank of England, with Houblon as its first governor. Because Montagu initiated an affair with Catherine Barton, Newton's niece, Montagu named Newton warden of the Tower Mint to superintend a three-year, general recoinage, completed in 1699 from mints at Bristol, Chester, Exeter, London, Norwich, and York. Newton advanced to mintmaster, a responsibility he aptly discharged until his death in 1727.

When England reached the breaking point from shortages of small change, the Bank of England circulated foreign silver and restruck Spanish pesos captured from treasure ships, covering the likeness of Charles IV of Spain with the queen's profile in 1703, with that of George II after 1744, and in the 1770s, with the bull-necked profile of George III. The inaccurate restrike caused the English to ridicule the overstamping and lose respect for the English mint. The era saw additions to coded indications of the metal's provenance:

date	*coin*	*symbol*	*origin*
1603	crown	plume	Wales
1663	guinea	elephant	Africa Company
1702–1703	crown	"Vigo"	Spanish gold guineas and silver pieces of eight seized from a fleet in Vigo Bay, Spain
1745	half-crown	"Lima"	Spanish treasure seized in Lima, Peru

England reached the breaking point during the American Revolution, an expensive war that soaked up available cash. The shortages fueled a demand for token money, private-issue disks exchanged within towns or between workers and the employers who issued them.

The application of steam to coin presses in the 1790s simplified and improved the stamping of planchets by passing metal strips into the device and completing coinage in one operation. Developed and refined by Matthew Boulton, partner of James Watt, the Scottish inventor of the steam engine, the new press rapidly improved the shape and quality of English coinage with grained and lettered edging, a method of preventing counterfeiting, clipping, and shaving. The thick-rimmed Britannia penny and twopence coins steam-pressed in 1797 and featuring Britannia with trident and shield earned the nickname "cartwheels." A more attractive gold coin of the era was the gold sovereign that George III modeled on the original sovereign of Henry VII.

In the early 1800s at the height of the Industrial Revolution, England began solving its coinage problems, in part by the Bank of England's boost of reserves by some three million pounds in coin and bullion. In 1816, the year that the treasury adopted a gold standard, the money system regained integrity with an elegant recoinage featuring St. George and the dragon, incised by Benedetto Pistrucci, Italian cameo engraver and medalist who was trained by Niccolò Morelli of the Accademia San Luca in Rome. By 1821, small silver replaced the ubiquitous token. Coin sizes began shrinking after the public rejected the double *florin*, a large coin issued in 1887.

The late 19th and early 20th centuries saw the stabilization of the British monetary system, based primarily on the steady trading value of the gold sovereign. In the words of Michael Sedgwick, the North American representative for the Royal Mint, "At the height of the Victorian era, when the sun never set on the British Empire, it never set on the gold sovereign either" (Martinez 2002, C11). Until the coin went out of circulation in World War I, royal moneyers kept it in constant production.

Victoria's accession ushered in England's most prosperous era since the time of Elizabeth I. During Victoria's reign, from 1837 to 1901, over two billion United Kingdom coins bore her changing portraits, depicting her at age 18, as the mother of nine royal children, and, in 1861, as the widow who mourned the death of her beloved consort and helpmeet, Prince Albert of Saxe-Coburg-Gotha. The use of Victoria's portrait aided her rule of a vast empire, where subjects knew her only as the bust on coins. In May 2001, a new likeness based on the Penny Black postage stamp by artist Mary Milner Dickens, featured the iron-framed Crystal Palace, which Albert designed as the site of the Great Exhibition of 1851. A merger of railway lines into a V, the queen's initial, recalled the steam age and greater travel opportunities.

George VI introduced an unusual polygonal coin in 1938. The nickel-brass threepence, bounded by twelve sides, pictured his profile. The threepence duplicated the short-lived issue of Edward VIII, George's brother, who, after eleven months on the throne, abdicated on December 11, 1936, in George's favor. Edward chose self-exile and ignominy in order to marry a divorced American, Wallis Warfield Simpson, who earned the opprobrium of Parliament and the royal family. Sculpted by Thomas H. Paget, coiner at London's Tower Mint, the threepence pictured three thistle heads on the reverse.

The most commonly reproduced face on late 20th-century money was Queen Elizabeth II, whose head, crowned and uncrowned, adorned money in Australia, the Bahamas, Belize, Canada, Fiji, Gibraltar, Guernsey, and Jamaica. In 1952, 70-year-old sculptor Mary Gillick designed the first of the four royal portraits. She pictured a youthful pose with ribboned fillet, the initials MG, and the inscription "*Regina Elizabeth II Dei Gratia*" ("*Queen Elizabeth II by the Grace of God*"). The image, which served projects at several Commonwealth mints, was the first of an English sovereign on British paper money. The serene gaze of the queen sent a steadying vision of the government's control of specie and the newly nationalized Bank of England. Two more royal portraits were the work of Arnold Machin in 1966 and of Raphael Maklouf in 1985.

When the United Kingdom changed to decimal currency on February 15, 1971, the Royal Mint began striking coins valued at a half-pence, and one, two, two and a half, five, ten, and fifty pence. Two years before the new millennium, sculptor and medalist Ian Rank-Broadley, creator of the 1994 Royal Mint Centenary Medal, designed a new royal portrait for the one-pound coin and returned the Royal Arms to the reverse. He placed Queen Elizabeth II in profile facing right in the tiara that her grandmother, Queen Mary, gave her as a wedding present.

In 2000, the Royal mint broke tradition to consult with citizens on design of a Marconi coin, which commemorates the 100th anniversary of the first wireless transmission over the Atlantic. The royal mintmaster issued through the Royal Mint, post offices, and banks a motif selected through consultation with over 13,000 citizens. Designed by Welsh artist Robert Evans, senior engraver at the Royal Mint, the bi-color coin pictured radio waves of the first wireless signal of the modern communications system from Poldhu, Cornwall, to St. John's, Newfoundland, in December 1901. Evans captured the event's impact on 20th century communication. Lettering on the edge exults, "Wireless bridges the Atlantic. Marconi 1901" ("Royal Mint Unveils" 2000). Special guest Princess Elettrat, daughter of Guglielmo Marconi, observed the unveiling at the BBC Broadcasting House in London.

Twenty-first-century British coinage maintained traditional symbols and dignity. A 2001 Britannia bullion coin crafted by sculptor and coin artist Philip Nathan, designer of the Prince Charles and Princess Diana Royal Wedding Crown, featured a standing figure of Britannia and a British lion, which recall the Una and Lion five-pound piece of 1839, during the second year of Queen Victoria's long reign. Thus, the coin also honored the centenary of Victoria's death.

In 2002, the British Royal Mint in Llantrisant, Wales, dusted off the image of the gold sovereign with a makeover. A unique part of England's history, the sovereign has traditionally served soldiers in a pinch for bribery and for bartering in foreign markets, during World War II, the Persian Gulf War, and the 2001-2002 war on terrorism in Afghanistan. U.S. soldiers also carried British sovereigns and gold rings in their survival packets. The new design, featuring the Royal Arms encircled by a laurel wreath, honored the 50th anniversary of Queen Elizabeth II.

***See also Admiral Gardner*; Anglo-Saxon coins; Athelstan; Bank of England; bimetallism; Matthew Boulton; Nicholas Briot; Canadian Coins; Canute I; Carausius; colonial coins; Edward the Confessor; Egbert; euro; Exchequer; florin; gold standard; Sir Thomas Gresham; Gresham's Law; groat; guinea; hallmark; Irish coins; *lira*; moneylending; Offa of Mercia; penny; William Paterson; Sir William Petty; Benedetto Pistrucci; John Roettiers; Royal Exchange; screw press; shilling; Thomas Simon; sterling; tally; Johann Sigismund Tanner; tokens; touch coin; treasure ships; Tregwynt**

hoard; trial of the pyx; William the Conqueror; world money; Wyon family.

SOURCES: Allen, Larry. *Encyclopedia of Money.* New York: Checkmark Books, 2001. • "The Anglo-Saxon Chronicle." http://sunsite.berkeley.edu/OMACL/Anglo/. • Bevan, Wilson Lloyd. "Sir William Petty: A Study in English Economic Literature" (monograph). Publications of the American Economic Association, 1894. • "The British Royal Mint." http://www.royalmint.com. • Burke, James. "On Track." *Scientific American*, November 23, 2001. • Cannon, John, and Ralph Griffiths. *Oxford Illustrated History of the British Monarchy.* Oxford: Oxford University Press, 1988. • Clain-Stefanelli, Elvira, and Vladimir Clain-Stefanelli. *The Beauty and Lore of Coins, Currency, and Medals.* Croton-on-Hudson, N.Y.: Riverwood Publishers, 1974. • Cribb, Joe. *Money.* Toronto: Stoddart, 1990. • Cribb, Joe, Barrie Cook, and Ian Carradice. *The Coin Atlas.* London: Little, Brown and Co., 1999. • Davies, Glyn. *A History of Money from Ancient Times to the Present Day.* Cardiff: University of Wales Press, 1994. • Einzig, Paul. *Primitive Money.* Oxford: Pergamon Press, 1966. • *Encyclopedia of Art.* New York: McGraw-Hill Book Co., 1968. • Freeman, Anthony. *The Moneyer and the Mint in the Reign of Edward the Confessor.* Oxford: B. A. R. British Series 145, 1985. • "Gold Coin Hoard Unveiled." *BBC News*, January 10, 2001. • "I Had a Little Nut Tree." http://www.zelo.com/family/nursery/nuttree.asp. • Keys, David. "Buried 1,800 Years Ago, 43 Coins Offer Clues to High-Society Roman London." *Independent*, January 10, 2001. • Laing, Lloyd R. *Coins and Archaeology.* New York: Schocken Books, 1969. • "Late Victorian Coinage." *Studium Magazine*, November 23, 2001. • "Magna Carta." http://www.fh-augsburg.de/~harsch/Chronologia/Lspost13/MagnaCarta/mag_cart.html. • Magnusson, Magnus. *Cambridge Biographical Dictionary.* Cambridge: University of Cambridge, 1990. • Martinez, Alejandro J. "U.K.'s Mint Molds New Image for Sovereign Coins." *Wall Street Journal*, January 14, 2002, p. C11. • Pepys, Samuel. *The Dairy of Samuel Pepys.* New York: Harper Torchbooks, 1960. • Petty, William. *Quantulumcunque concerning Money.* http://socserv2.socsci.mcmaster.ca/~econ/ugcm/3ll3/petty/money.txt. • Petty, William. *A Treatise of Taxes & Contributions.* London: N. Brooke, 1662. • Reinfeld, Fred. *Treasury of the World's Coins.* New York: Sterling Publishing, 1953. • "The Royal Feast," http://www.acronet.net/~robokopp/english/godsavet.htm. • "Royal Mint Unveils Results of First Ever Public Consultation on New Coin Design." *PR Newswire*, October 24, 2000. • Schwarz, Ted. *Coins as Living History.* New York: Arco Publishing, 1976. • Shakespeare, William. *The Riverside Shakespeare.* Boston: Houghton-Mifflin, 1974. • Sinclair, David. *The Pound.* London: Century Books, 2000. • Smith, Aquila. "On the Ormonde Money." *Journal of the Kilkenny and Southeast of Ireland Archaeological Society*, 1854. • Snodgrass, Mary Ellen. *Who's Who in the Middle Ages.* Jefferson, N.C.: McFarland, 2001. • Standish, David. *The Art of Money.* San Francisco: Chronicle Books, 2000. • Stephen, Sir Leslie, and Sir Sidney Lee, eds. *Dictionary of National Biography.* London: Oxford University Press, 1922. • "Tradesmen's Tokens." http://www.ee.surrey.ac.uk/Contrib/manx/manxsoc/msvol17/ch05.htm.

escudo

A common gold coinage from the 1600s to the 1800s, the *escudo* (shield) became a global currency produced from New World treasure. Minted after 1675 in the New World in the half *escudo* or *escudito*, one-, two-, four-, and eight-*escudo* denominations and in Spain in an additional one-half coin, the coin was the standard gold piece circulated in Latin America, the Caribbean, and the American colonies. Among non–Latinos, it filled a need in areas that had not established minting operations. The popular language of the day named the two-*escudo* piece a *pistole*. The four-*escudo* coin became a "double *pistole*" or doubloon. The eight-*escudo* coin was the "quadruple *pistole*" or "double *doblon,*" which American settlers named the "Spanish doubloon."

One large cache of *escudos* resulted from the bullion that *conquistador* Francisco Pizarro looted in Cuzco, Peru, in November 1533. From his plunder, the ransom in gold ornaments and jewelry for Atahualpa, the Incan king, Pizarro's coiners melted down rough bars and ingots to pay the troops. To facilitate transportation to the Spanish strongholds at Cartagena and Portobello, they turned gold into *escudos*. The coin became the currency of colonial Angola and Mozambique, the independent states of Latin America, and Cape Verde as well as modern Portugal, which created an upgraded *escudo* in 1915.

See also **Leone Leoni; Spanish coins.**

SOURCES: "The Bureau of Engraving and Printing." http://www.bep.treas.gov/. • Burgan, Michael. "Lost and Found Treasure." *National Geographic World*, April 2000, 19. • Cordingly, David.

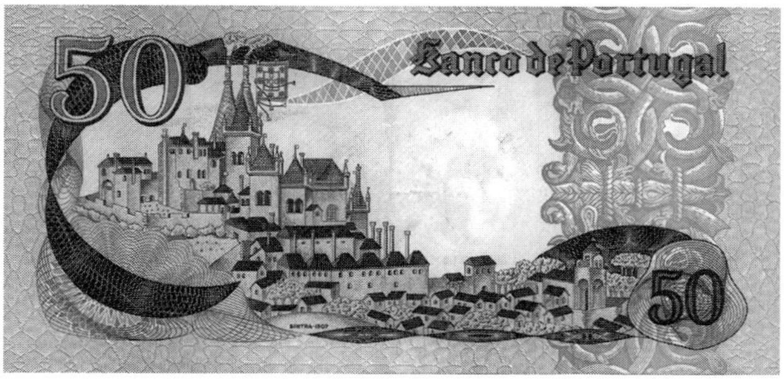

Top: **This 20-*escudo* note from Portugal commemorates the heroism of aviator Gago Coutinho, who was the first to fly across the Southern Atlantic in 1922 from Lisbon to Rio de Janeiro; *middle:* This 50-*escudo* note pictures the Moorish castle of Sintra, a town in west Portugal; *bottom:* This 100-*escudo* commemorative note from Portugal honors late eighteenth-century lyric sonneteer Manual Maria Barbosa du Bocage.**

This Dutch ten-cent piece picturing Queen Beatrix became obsolete on E-day (euro day), January 1, 2002, when Holland joined eleven other countries in adopting the euro.

Under the Black Flag. San Diego, Calif.: Harvest Books, 1995. • Kemp, Peter, ed. *The Oxford Companion to Ships and the Sea*. Oxford: Oxford University Press, 1988. • Skerry, Brian. "Pirates of the *Whydah*." *National Geographic*, May 1999, 64.

euro

On E-day (or euro day), January 1, 2002, 370 million Europeans in twelve countries — Austria, Belgium, Finland, France, Germany, Greece, Ireland, Italy, Luxembourg, the Netherlands, Portugal, and Spain plus Monaco, San Marino, and the Vatican — began using the euro, a common currency abbreviated EUR. The dramatic shift from many national money systems to one replicated the European economy during the Roman Empire, when Rome's *sestertius* and gold *solidus* were acceptable over all the known world. A forerunner of a standardized global money occurred in 1865, when parties promoting the idea formed the Latin Monetary Union. Member nations included Belgium, Bulgaria, France, Greece, Italy, Switzerland, and the Vatican, all of whom supported the pragmatic advantages of one world money system. The grand scheme collapsed with a drop in the price of silver after World War II.

Prefacing the 21st-century advance to a uniform and fully convertible currency, the gradual unification of European peoples began in 1957 with the Treaty of Rome, which promoted a common European market as a means toward greater economic prosperity and political union. Introducing the notion of a single monetary unit in 1970 was Pierre Werner, minister of the Grand Duchy of Luxembourg and initiator of a groundbreaking fiscal plan. He proposed the free movement of capital, permanent exchange rates, and replacement of existing currencies by a single currency.

Voices lined up yea against nay on the issue of one money system overleaping the boundaries of nations. Battling a strong tide of unification, a xenophobic political force, the National Front, mounted a virulent campaign against the euro and globalized trade and currency. One optimistic proponent of the change, Robert Boursault, executive vice president of Credit Agricole of France, predicted that the euro would force American financiers into second place globally. In his words, "This is an economic bloc that is being created. It is not just a technical change of currency" (Kunzig 1998).

Another yea vote came from Alsatian economist Francis Woehrling, who predicted that Europeans would identify with the currency itself, just as Americans think of national security in terms of the dollar and the U.S. Federal Reserve.

In 1986 and 1992, the Single European Act and the Treaty on European Union enhanced international bonding by introducing the Economic and Monetary Union (EMU), the basis of a single currency to move people, services, capital, and goods more freely. Another plus for the unified currency was an uncomplicated statement of prices and wages across Europe and a spur to competition and trade. During a 1995 session to discuss the type of currency, its size and color, and a name acceptable to all member states, a committee discussed three historic denominations — the *écu, ducat*, and *florin* — before settling on the euro. The one holdout was a Greek representative, who commented that the word sounded like the Greek for "urine."

As talks progressed toward minting, planners began to solve logistical problems with ores and mechanical style and method of coinage. The Swedish delegate opposed a preponderance of nickel in the alloys. Because of their strong antipathy to nickel, moneyers made the three lowest coins from copper-plated steel. The next three they struck from a Finnish alloy called Nordic gold, a blend of copper with aluminum, tin, and zinc.

Designers fashioned the system's most common coins, the euro1 and euro2, from a tri-level stack of copper alloy with nickel in the middle. To make them copy-proof, the French took charge of fabrication. According to Emmanuel Constant, director of the Paris mint, the two coins "will be among the most secure in the world" (Kunzig 1998). The logic undergirding a reduction of coin types is to fight counterfeiters by establishing the familiarity of only eight coins throughout Europe, where there were once hundreds of types, shapes, alloys, and motifs.

To stabilize prices and to unify monetary policy, on June 1, 1998, the EMU created the European Central Bank in Frankfurt am

Germany, along with eleven other European nations, did away with distinctive coins, such as this coin struck in 1970, when the euro was introduced January 1, 2002.

Main, Germany, headed by Wim Duisenberg of Holland. American sources supported the move, claiming that one currency lowered the costs and risks of transactions with the European market. Seven months later, the original eleven states of the EMU set exchange rates of the participating currencies and implemented a common monetary policy. On January 1, 2001, Greece joined as the twelfth member state. The EMU engineered the currency conversion, the largest in the world's monetary history. Three states — Denmark, Sweden, and the United Kingdom — chose to support the union, but to retain their native currencies.

The new moneys rapidly filled Europe's tills, edging out the familiar Spanish *peso,* Italian *lira,* Irish *punt,* and French *franc.* National banknotes and coins ceased to be legal tender after a dual circulation period ranging in each member country from four to eight weeks, except in Spain, where the Madrid European Council decided in 1995 to extend the time limit to six months. The widespread changeover caused headaches for vending machines and clerks, especially at one-operator newsstands, where conversion of moneys is calculated in the head rather than by a cash register or computer. For all its headaches, in the estimation of Smain Laacher, a French sociologist, the new money is "an element of social cohesion" (Kunzig 1998). Because it identifies users as Europeans, the loss of national identity shifted the way people think of themselves and their loyalties.

To establish the new money among global currencies, the European Commission created a universal euro typographical symbol — € — which Belgian designer Alain Billiet based on the Greek epsilon, to symbolize Europe. He intended the emblem to make money highly recognizable, to be easy to write by hand, and to provide an aesthetically pleasing design. Of the shape, Billiet said, "A round symbol gives the idea of an expectation, and the ideal form is open, not a closed sphere. It gives expectations of what the euro has to be in the future — it's unlimited, a circle without limits" (Pruzan 1999).

After over thirty drafts of emblems, European citizens assessed them and left a choice between the final two to the President of the Commission, Jacques Santer, and the European Commissioner of the euro, Yves-Thibault de Silguy, who rejected portraits of historic figures to maintain international consensus. His selection of bridges and gates assured reasonable anonymity to the moneys flowing throughout Europe, particularly in winter, when Scandinavians and the British tend to vacation along the Riviera and in Spain. A pool of too many bills with distinct national markings would require southern European bankers to single out crumpled and frayed northern bills to return to the home bank for shredding and reprinting.

Coins, on the other hand, have a longer life span. Therefore, national markings are less of a problem and also an opportunity for member states to express their heritage. National designs also help bankers establish a pattern of tourism and trade as a means of studying economic factors and demand for commodities.

There were a number of complaints about currency design that included charges of corny, bland, and blurred motifs. Milanese designer Massimo Vignelli of Vignelli Associates in New York, winner of the Gran Premio Triennale di Milano and the prestigious Compasso d'Oro, protested: "It's a great opportunity gone down the drain, as usual. People without knowledge of design, and having done no homework, were in charge of doing a job they're no good at" (Pruzan 1999). He proposed an orderly process of surveying Europe's best currency and commissioning one designer, either Dutch money artist R. D. E. Oxenaar of Holland or Jorg Zintzmeyer, specie designer for Switzerland.

On E-day (euro day), January 1, 2002, Italy joined eleven other European nations in abandoning distinctive money, such as this *lira* coin struck in 1977.

Replacing the *escudo, franc, guilder, lira, mark, markka, peseta, punt,* and *schilling* notes, the finished designs went into production in July 1999 at 12 printing houses — two in Germany and one in each of the other euro countries except Luxembourg. On the initial run, the countries produced a varied number of bills:

nation	*number of EUR banknotes*
Ireland	180,000
Luxembourg	45,000,000
Finland	170,000,000
Portugal	450,000,000
Austria	520,000,000
Belgium	530,000,000
Netherlands	605,000,000
Spain	1,925,000,000
Italy	1,950,000,000
France	2,585,000,000
Germany	4,030,000,000

The presses rolled out a total of 14.5 billion banknotes, valued at € 600 billion and paid for by individual national banks. Late in 2001, tellers, post offices, cash-in-transit companies, vending machine operators, parking meter designers, and retailers introduced the new money to clerks and issued starter kits to individuals. The commission circulated ten billion banknotes in January 2002 and reserved 4.5 billion to accommodate fluctuations in demand, a factor determined by electronic and credit spending.

Accepted for electronic monetary transactions by banks and global businesses since January 1999, the euro advanced to banknotes and coins negotiable across national lines without the need for exchange. Available in seven denominations, the bills are large and easily recognized by their size, design, and dominant colors:

value	*size*	*color*	*design*
5 EUR	120 × 62 mm	gray	classical
10 EUR	127 × 67 mm	red	Romanesque
20 EUR	133 × 72 mm	blue	Gothic
50 EUR	140 × 77 mm	orange	Renaissance
100 EUR	147 × 82 mm	green	baroque and rococo
200 EUR	153 × 82 mm	yellow	iron and glass architecture
500 EUR	160 × 82 mm	purple	modern architecture

(Duisenberg 2001, 1)

The commission announced the winner of the design competiton, Robert Kalina of the Oesterreichische Nationalbank, in December 1996 at the Dublin European Council. He sketched his motifs from seven major architectural periods in Europe's cultural history — classical, Romanesque, Gothic, Renaissance, Baroque and Rococo, iron and glass, and modern. Variant sizing chosen in co-operation with the European Blind Union made the notes user-friendly, especially for the partially sighted.

Applying one or both of two themes — "Ages and styles of Europe" and an abstract modern theme — designers of the notes chose two dominant symbols: a series of portals — doors, archways, and gates — represents open dealings among nations. The obverses display hypothetical bridges, tokens of cooperation between Europe's nations and the rest of the world as well as signs of dynamism and optimism. Each bill shows the flag of the European Union, the name of the currency in Latin (EURO) and Greek (EYPO) alphabets, and the initials of the European Central Bank in five linguistic variants that cover the 11 official languages of member nations.

Securing the notes are a series of precautions that raised the cost of production above that of old European currencies. Authenticity is obvious to ordinary citizens in the feel of raised print and the look of the watermark and security thread as well as a see-through register visible on both sides. By tilting a banknote, the examiner can see the shifted imagery on the hologram foil stripe or patch. On the back, a tilt reveals a bright iridescent stripe or color-shifting ink. To assure honest exchange in euros, the European Police Office (Europol) combats counterfeiting with the aid of the Eurosystem and national police forces.

Euro coins display two vital pieces of information — the value and heads of state. The advanced technology of euro coins varies composition and feel of each denomination, which increases in weight and thickness to denote a higher value:

coin	*metallic composition*	*outer rim*
EUR2	three layers of copper-nickel, nickel, copper-nickel and clad in nickel brass	edged with lettering

coin	*metallic composition*	*outer rim*
EUR1	three layers of copper-nickel, nickel, copper-nickel and clad in nickel brass	edged with sporadic milling
50 cent	Nordic gold	fine scallops
20 cent	Nordic gold	plain
10 cent	Nordic gold	fine scallops
5 cent	copper-coated steel	smooth
2 cent	copper-coated steel	smooth with a groove
1 cent	copper-coated steel	smooth

Striation and edgings make counterfeiting extremely difficult and easy to detect. All euro coins incorporate machine-readable characteristics for use in member state vending machines.

The mastermind behind the euro coin was computer engineer Luc Luycx of Dendermonde, Belgium, a coin designer for the Monnaie Royale de Belgique (the Belgian Mint), winner of a European competition among artists, medalists, and sculptors from the European Union begun in February 1996 by the Council of the European Monetary Institute (EMI), the forerunner of the ECB. Using a scanner and CorelDraw software, he created a non-partisan image of Europe that won the votes of 64 percent of the 1,900 judges. He placed one of three common designs on all 12 coins. The motif shows a series of maps encircled by the European Union's 12 stars.

The reverse of each coin pictures individual country-specific motifs created by national artists:

nation	*coin designs*
Austria	radical pacifist and Nobel-prize winner Bertha von Suttner, author of *Die Waffen Nieder* (*Lay Down Your Arms*) (1889); composer Wolfgang Amadeus Mozart; the secession building in Vienna; the baroque Belvedere Palace, where a treaty re-establishied the sovereignty of Austria in 1955; the Viennese Gothic St. Stephen's Cathedral; a flower series depicting alpine primroses, edelweiss, and gentian, all by artist Josef Kaiser
Belgium	King Albert II and a monogram with crown among 12 stars, designed by Jan Alfons Keustermans, Director of the Municipal Academy of Fine Arts of Turnhout
Finland	cloudberries and cloudberry flowers, designed by Raimo Heino; two flying swans created by Pertti Maekinen to commemorate the nation's 80th year of independence; the heraldic lion by sculptor Heikki Häiväoja
France	a tree in a hexagon surrounded by the motto of the Republic "Liberté, Egalité, Fraternité," the design of artist Joaquim Jiminez; the semeuse ("sower") designed by Laurent Jorlo as a celebration of life; a young, feminine Marianne, the symbol of France, designed by Fabienne Courtiade, an engraver at the Paris Mint
Germany	an eagle incised by Heinz and Sneschana Russewa-Hoyer; the Brandenburg Gate, a triumphal arch modeled on the Propylaea in Athens and built in 1791 by Carl G. Langhans, designed by Reinhard Heinsdorff; an oak twig designed by Professor Rolf Lederbogen
Greece	a scene from a mosaic in Sparta (third century A.D.), showing Europa being abducted by Zeus; an ancient Athenian four-*drachma* coin (fifth century B.C.); diplomat Eleftherios Venizelos, a pioneer of social reform; diplomat Ioannis Capodistrias, the first Governor of Greece; Rigas-Fereos, a visionary of Balkan liberation from Ottoman rule; a modern sea-going tanker; a corvette, a ship used during the Greek War of Independence, all by sculptor Georges Stamatopoulos
Holland	two views of Queen Beatrix in profile, revisions of Bruno Ninaber van Eyben's previous Dutch coin design
Ireland	a Celtic harp, designed by Jarlath Hayes
Italy	Raphaël's portrait of Dante Alighieri; Leonardo da Vinci's view of the ideal proportions of the

nation	*coin designs*
	human body; the equestrian statue of the philosopher-emperor Marcus Aurelius; a futuristic figure sculpted by Umberto Boccioni, creator of *Unique Forms of Continuity in Space* (1913); Sandro Botticelli's *The Birth of Venus*; the Flavian amphitheatre, begun by Emperor Vespasian in A.D. 75 and inaugurated by the Emperor Titus in A.D. 80 ; the Mole Antonelliana tower designed in 1863 by Alessandro Antonelli; the Castel del Monte, which Frederick II built in the 1240s
Luxembourg	three views of Grand Duke Henri designed by Yvette Gastauer-Claire, designer of a 1995 silver coin featuring the effigy of Grand Duke Jean and marking Luxembourg's year as a European city of culture
Portugal	castles and coats of arms encircled by European stars, the royal seal of 1142, and the first royal seal of 1134, all by designer Vítor Manuel Fernandes dos Santos
Spain	King Carlos I, author Miguel de Cervantes, the facade of the cathedral of Santiago de Compostela, begun in 1667 by Jose del Toro and Domingo de Andrade and completed by Fernando Casas y Novoa

The milled edges of these coins aid people with impaired sight to recognize coin values.

Distributed at the rate of 50 billion for the first minting, begun in May 1998, the coins were completed well before the deadline under strict quality control. In France alone, 14 million bank customers exchanged their francs for euros, enough to fill 800 Brinks trucks. On December 14, 2001, banks in France, Holland, and Ireland began selling 200 million currency packets to individuals. Financial advisers hoped to see kits distributed according to the demands of each country's economy:

number of kits	*country*
53,500,000	Germany
53,000,000	France
30,000,000	Italy
24,800,000	Holland
23,000,000	Spain
6,000,000	Austria
5,500,000	Belgium
3,000,000	Greece
1,000,000	Ireland
1,000,000	Portugal
600,000	Luxembourg
500,000	Finland

(Sims and Woodruff 2001, A10)

The purpose of the kits was to increase awareness of the change that the euro made in everyday transactions. Consumers derived additional information from televised ads on BBC World, CNBC, CNN, and TV5. A tutorial website and an Internet game, the "Be a Euro SuperStar" competition, encouraged children to familiarize themselves with the new moneys.

The tedious replacement of old currencies with shipments of euros was not without problems. Although cautious treasury agents rifled Europe for all available armored cars, thefts marred the first distribution. Italian thieves stole $900,000 worth of specie at bank robberies in Bologna and Milan. German bandits made off with 1.2 milllion euros after commandeering an armored car. A more insidious theft was a rise in prices, an opportunity seized by the Vatican, which boosted the cost of gate fees to the Sistine Chapel and Vatican Museum and for saying a mass for the dead.

On the stroke of the New Year, 2002, nations experienced more than the usual "out with the old, in with the new." While a small percentage of world citizens retained obsolete currency as souvenirs or to donate to charity, most embraced the euro by taking advantage of commission-free bank swaps of a "household amount" equal to about $500. Some 140,000 tons of old coins left circulation for meltdown and resale in small batches to prevent a glut on the market and reduced metal prices. Worth $15 billion, the aggregate of obsolete specie weighed 240,000 tons, enough to fill two acres of storage space or 10,000 truck trailers.

***See also écu*; *franc*; *gulden*; U.S. Mint.**

SOURCES: Allen, Larry. *Encyclopedia of Money*. New York: Checkmark Books, 2001. • "Among Our Key People." *The Key Reporter*, Winter 2002, 8–9. • Bauman, Richard. "The Lady and the Peace Prize." *Modern Maturity*, January 1984, p. 89. • Becatoros, Elena. "Greece Bids Farewell to Link with Ancient Past." *Bergen County Record*, December 31, 2000. • "Belgian Graphic Designer Creates Euro Coins." *Newsbytes*, January 17, 1999. • Duisenberg, Willem F. "European Central Bank." *Journal of the European Communities*, August 31, 2001. • "The Euro." http://www.euro.ecb.int. • "Euro: Printing of 13 Billion Euro Banknotes Gets Under Way." *Europe Information Service*, July 17, 1999. • "Germany Reviews Design of Its Euro Coins." *Europe Information Service*, October 7, 1998. • Hale, Ellen. "Europeans Make Change to Euro." *USA Today*, December 26, 2001, 3B. • Hale, Ellen. "Europe Makes Switch to Euro." *USA Today*, December 31, 2001, 1A. • Kummer, Corby. "The Pull of Puglia." *Atlantic Monthly*, April 1994, p. 54–58. • Kunzig, Robert. "Euroland or Bust." *Discover*, October 1998. • Loesch, Robert K. "Seven Nobel Women." *Christian Century*, November 17, 1982, p. 1158–1159. • Parker, John. "Happy E-Day, Europe." *Traffic World*, September 10, 2001. • Pruzan, Todd. "The Almighty Euro." *Print*, March-April 1999, pp. 138–143. • Reid, T. R. "The New Europe." *National Geographic*, January 2002, 32–47. • Sims, G. Thomas, and David Woodruff. "Distribution of Euros to Start Tomorrow." *Wall Street Journal*, December 13, 2001, A10. • Standish, David. *The Art of Money*. San Francisco: Chronicle Books, 2000. • Steinmetz, Greg. "The Euro Designer's Art Is Sure to Have Wide Currency." *Wall Street Journal*, July 7, 1998, p. B1. • Vigdor, Irving. "The Euro, a New Profit Engine." *Bobbin Group*, September 1999. • "Yvette Gastauer-Claire," British Art Medal Society. http://www.bams.org.uk/artists/gast_claire.htm.

Exchequer

The English Exchequer or treasury, once called "the tallies," is a government bureaucracy that receives and disperses public revenue. Derived from the Latin *scaccarium* meaning "chessboard," the word "exchequer" refers to the checkered cloth on which the principal parties reckoned the nation's revenues. Formalized by Henry I in the early 1100s, the treasury dates to the coming of his father, William I the Conqueror, to England in 1066, when Norman-style monetary accounting replaced Anglo-Saxon methods. A bicameral department, the Exchequer consisted of the lower exchequer, which received coins and paid out amounts, and the upper exchequer or *scaccarium* proper, the auditing board that twice annually regulated accounts. Supervising the books of Henry II was the aged Bishop Nigel of Ely, whose son Richard followed him as royal accountant.

The nature and function of the Exchequer was defined and characterized in the works of Bishop Richard FitzNigel (also Son of Nigel or Fitzneale), a pioneering accounting text entitled *Dialogus de Scaccario* (*Discourse on the Exchequer*) (1179), a Latin treatise on biennial treasury sessions. Using the familiar literary device of master-to-student question and answer, he expressed the importance of a ruling board of cautious accountants in assuring the rights of all citizens. He credited William I with importing the system from northwestern Europe, but admitted that some believed that the Anglo-Saxons employed their own version.

Of the function of the Exchequer, Bishop FitzNigel explained the physical layout of its accounting system:

> The exchequer is a quadrangular surface about ten feet in length, five in breadth, placed before those who sit around it in the manner of a table, and all around it it has an edge about the height of one's four fingers, lest any thing placed upon it should fall off. There is placed over the top of the exchequer, moreover, a cloth bought at the Easter term, not an ordinary one but a black one marked with stripes, the stripes being distant from each other the space of a foot or the breadth of a hand. In the spaces moreover are counters placed according to their values ["Medieval Sourcebook: The Dialogue"].

The court sitting with the Exchequer was also called the Exchequer and was named for the year of each session "at the tallies" (*ibid.*). The bishop viewed the fairness and simplicity of the accounting system as a "superior science" (*ibid.*). In 1300, Edward I centralized coinage and monetary circulation by moving the Royal Mint and Exchequer to the Tower of London to be a part of the royal household and offices.

See also **English money; moneylending; tally; trial of the pyx.**

SOURCES: Cannon, John, and Ralph Griffiths. *Oxford Illustrated History of the British Monarchy*. Oxford: Oxford University Press, 1988. • Davies, Glyn. *A History of Money from Ancient Times to the Present Day*. Cardiff: University of Wales Press, 1994. • "Medieval Sourcebook: The Dialogue concerning the Exchequer." http://www.medievalhistory.net/excheq1.htm. • Probert Encyclopedia. http://www.probertencyclopaedia.com/money.htm. • Sinclair, David. *The Pound*. London: Century Books, 2000. • *66 Centuries of Measurement*. Dayton, Ohio: Sheffield Measurement Division, 1984.

feather money

Among the world's primitive currencies, one of the most bizarre is the feather money circulated into the late 1940s in the Santa Cruz Islands, a volcanic chain of the Solomons. At one time, islanders also relied on shell disks, but they eventually reduced the strings of shell pieces to jewelry and relied solely on feathered strips. Luring and entrapping the *Trichoglossus massena*, a curved-billed lorikeet, or the honey-eating *Mzeomela cardinalis* found in the rain forest presented difficulties to the stalker, who attracted the species with favorite flowers and with chirps he delivered on a tree-bud whistle from behind a blind of betal palm leaves. He then gathered birds whose feet stuck to a latex spread on portable perches. After plucking the choice feathers, he packed them in a coconut shell. He then released the denuded birds, which usually died.

The money artisan collected sap from the paper mulberry (*Broussonetia papyrifera*) for glue for feathering strips of fiber cording ranging up to 3 by 15 feet. Each feathered length required 1,500 platelets topped with plumage from 300 birds. To adorn the strip, he stuck feathers to 2.25 × 1.25-inch wood disks, which he decorated with gray plumage of the Pacific pigeon (*Ducula Pacifica*). During up to 600 hours of intense labor, the worker completed the strip by conjoining the platelets to parallel cording of three-ply fiber and appended the wood amulets plus pig teeth, charm stones, and shells expressing the coil's monetary denomination.

The binder polished off the artisan's work with braid woven out of fiber from the rainforest tree *(Gnetum gnemon)*. During the edging process, he stretched the cords between trees five feet apart and held lengths in place at the center with a notched bat-bone spacer bar. Application of the platelets to the belt began at the center and worked outward in both directions like overlapping shingles. He rounded off the strip with sheathing and plaiting on the ends with his version of a mint mark before he attached the cords to a bark ring.

Possessors of feather money accumulated the coils in stacks wrapped in bark cloth as conspicuous evidence of esteem, political authority, and net worth and used them to buy canoes, pigs, concubines, and food for feasts and to pay compensatory blood money, bride price, labor costs, ransoms, and fines. As an indigenous Melanesian currency based on a living animal, feather money was perishable, particularly from excess handling. It required careful storage in warm, dry sheds to maintain the integrity of the fiber and the scarlet hue of its surface. Owners placed coins above the smoke of a ground fire to discourage mold and insect infestations. The skill of the artisan and the depletion of the native bird population increased the value of feathered strips.

Over time, feather currency held its worth, even after Australian traders introduced coins and paper money to the islands. The highest grade, valued in the number of pigs it could buy, was called a "porker." Lesser grades were called "sucklings" because they were equal in value to piglets too small to be eaten. Professional money evaluators determined the value. Like Muslim prayers to Mecca, they draped pieces under scrutiny in the direction of the Nembo River, a stream that islanders associated with money deities. Par value ranged downward from a "crown piece," the highest grade, with scarcity determining market value. Only after the natural color faded was feather money discarded.

Fully interchangeable for cash, feather money was true currency. It was not worn or displayed as household adornment and had no other purpose than a store of wealth. When traded to outer islanders at Utupua or Vanikoro, the people outside the feather-money district reciprocated with packets of red feathers for the woven cloth and shell disks that they valued as currency. The trade of two money systems interlocked them into a fiscal interdependence. At one time, Santa Cruz islanders also traded women for concubinage at ten times the price of a bride, but British colonizers ended the practice.

Into the last half of the 20th century, feather money waned as island currency. Extensive circulation of cash from Australia for native tobacco and copra lessened the demand for feathered coils, thus enabling the bird population to increase. Only the traditional pledge of lengths of feathers for marital arrangements perpetuated the system. In 1993, a cyclone destroyed some rare coils of feather money; six years later during a civil war, thieves stole a model roll from the National Museum at Honiara. These events helped raise the value of the feathered rolls as they became more scarce. Even on the Santa Cruz islands, Gresham's law applied as second-rate Australian cash drove out the admirable red-feather money, improving its exchange rate.

A variant of Santa Cruz feather money were the feather *bilum* (string bags) of Papua New Guinea. Netted by women, they passed to male artisans, who interwove the mesh with bird feathers, cowries, and the tails of wild pigs. On the mainland in Wosera, the bags requited in-laws for the bride price at betrothals. At Irian Jaya, members of the Dani tribe exchanged *bilum* as cash. To display wealth, men slung the bags conspicuously over their shoulders. A more ostentatious display was the wearing of a mask, headdress, or head band holding cassowary or bird of paradise feathers, which rose well over two feet high above the owner's head.

SOURCES: Allen, Larry. *Encyclopedia of Money*. New York: Checkmark Books, 2001. • Davenport, William. "Red-Feather Money." *Scientific American*, March 1962, pp. 94–104. • Davies, Glyn. *A History of Money from Ancient Times to the Present Day*. Cardiff: University of Wales Press, 1994. • Einzig, Paul. *Primitive Money*. Oxford: Pergamon Press, 1966. • Opitz, Charles J. *Odd and Curious Money*. Ocala, Fla.: First Impressions, 1986. • "Shell and Feather Money of the Solomons." http://www.melanesianhandcraft.com/The_Shell_Money.htm.

fiat money

Fiat money or inconvertible money issued by government decree depends on the citizens' faith in a treasury that issues coins with a trace or less of precious metals in their alloys. Because the currency lacks the backing of gold, silver, or platinum coin or specie, like that printed to pay for the American Revolution and the Civil War, the money bears no written guarantee that it can be exchanged. Since the United States and other major world states abandoned the gold standard, which offered conversion of paper money for treasury stores of gold, its paper currency became fiat money. Its value, especially during peacetime, is the acceptance of its convenience for trade.

When governments lose the confidence of citizens by over-issuing fiat money and causing inflation, they risk the collapse of a monetary system based on mutual respect between citizens and their elected officials. In 1866, during a period of expansion, Italy began a 15-year trend in issuing inconvertible paper money called *il corso forzoso* ("forced currency"), but kept a close watch on inflation and over-printing. By 1881, the treasury was able to pledge convertibility of their paper notes.

***See also* gold standard; greenbacks; Knights Hospitaller; John Law; leather and hide money; James Barton Longacre; paper money; Russian money; siege money.**

SOURCES: Allen, Larry. *Encyclopedia of Money*. New York: Checkmark Books, 2001. • Davies, Glyn. *A History of Money from Ancient Times to the Present Day*. Cardiff: University of Wales Press, 1994. • Paul, Ron. "Greenspan Go Home." *Liberty*, March 2000. • "The Power of Gold: The History of an Obsession." *Traders*, December 1, 2001.

Fibonacci, Leonardo

A boon to the counting of coins and changing one currency into another was the work of mathematician and merchant Leonardo Fibonacci of Pisa (also Leonardo Pisano), who revolutionized accounting in coins and currency. Education under Moorish teachers and an apprenticeship in trade with Algeria in his youth helped him master both classic and Arabian number theory. As assistant to his father, Gulielmo Bonacci, a customs officer, Fibonacci traveled Provence, Greece, and Sicily as well as the Islamic nations of Egypt and Syria. His fluency in two number systems allowed him to count money and figure costs and profits in both Roman and Arabic numerals.

At age 32, Fibonacci democratized math by reconciling Greek and Arabic arithmetic in *Liber Abaci* (*Book of the Abacus*) (ca. 1202). The introduction of the place-value decimal system rid bookkeeping of cumbrous Roman numerals and the need to use an abacus in business dealings. While the clergy, government officials and university dons sniffed at a number system invented by infidels, merchants readily embraced Arabic numerals and quick calculations that could be done in the head by tens. Even uneducated supply clerks, money changers, and shopkeepers could understand the new arithmetic and number notation.

Over the next three centuries, the study of math reached the peasantry, who could at last figure their own earnings and business transactions without guessing or relying on awkward tallies. In 1478, publication of *Treviso Arithmetic,* an anonymous math handbook, educated traders on adding and subtracting, multiplying and dividing, calculating interest and fractions, and applying arithmetic and geometric progressions. Aiding bank clerks and budget ministers in keeping track of long strings of zeroes was a physician, Nicolás Chuquet of Paris, who composed *Triparty en la Science des Nombres* (*Three-part Treatise on the Science of Numbers*) (1484), which explained how to figure square roots and proposed a method of grouping numbers in sets of three by marking off triads with separators. He also took Fibonacci's number system into the extremes by inventing the terms million, billion, trillion, quadrillion, all the way to nonillion, a number followed by 30 zeroes.

More advances on Fibonacci's work extended the simplification of higher mathematics. Belgian windmill engineer and surveyor Simon Steven of Bruges compiled in Flemish *De Thiende* (*The Tenth*) (1585), a math text that proposed a decimal system of units and money. More popular was the French version, *La Disme* (1634), which added the word "decimal" to English. From Steven's work as a cashier in Antwerp, he knew the difficulties of computing money for loans. For loan officers, bankers, and creditors, he issued the first tables of interest. Out of this growing interest in money and arithmetic came the sciences of mathematics and economics.

See also **Al-Khwarizmi.**

SOURCES: Allen, Larry. *Encyclopedia of Money.* New York: Checkmark Books, 2001. • Crombie, A. C. *Medieval and Early Modern Science.* Cambridge, Mass.: Harvard University Press, 1967. • Snodgrass, Mary Ellen. *Who's Who in the Middle Ages.* Jefferson, N.C.: McFarland, 2001. • Wasilewska, Ewa. "On the Money." *The World & I,* November 1, 1998, 222. • Weatherford, Jack. *The History of Money: From Sandstone to Cyberspace.* Pittsburgh, Pa.: Three Rivers Press, 1998.

50 state quarters

The U.S. Mint initiative producing new designer quarters at the rate of five per year from 1999 to 2008 launched an unprecedented artisanal program. Generating public interest in history and coin design, the plan derived from the U.S. Commemorative Coin Act of 1996 superintended by the Secretary of the Treasury. Under authorization of President Bill Clinton on August 1, 1997, Congress began the Circulating Commemorative Coin Program, which called for the initial issue of five coins on January 1, 1999, and proceeding through all fifty states in the order of entry into the Union.

The new coins encouraged states to identify sources of state pride. Each new coin would replace the eagle on the standard quarter with a dignified motif honoring some aspect of the state's history rather than the bust or portrait of a person or a flag or state seal. The guidelines required an inscription, date of entry into the union, and some universally recognized landmark, landscape, building, industrial symbol, flora and fauna, state icon, or physical outline. Managed by the state governor, each design proposal would receive review by the Citizens Commemorative Coin Advisory Committee and the Secretary of the Treasury and promotion through the U.S. Mint as collectibles and historic souvenirs.

The designs produced a stir of recognition and comment as each took its place in the lineup of new quarters, made from a trilevel stack of a copper-nickel alloy sandwiching a copper core:

date	*state*	*design*
January 1999	Delaware	Caesar Rodney astride a galloping horse on the way to cast his vote for indendence from England, executed by mint sculptor-engraver William Cousins; inscription, "The First State"
March 1999	Pennsylvania	"Commonwealth" statue, keystone, and an outline of the state; inscription, "Virtue, Liberty and Independence"
May 1999	New Jersey	George Washington crossing the Delaware on December 18, 1787, from an 1851 painting by Emmanuel Leutze; inscription, "Crossroads of the Revolution"
July 1999	Georgia	peach and live oak branches superimposed on the outline of the state with a motto on a streamer; inscription, "Wisdom, Justice, Moderation"
October 1999	Connecticut	Charter Oak, in which Joseph Wadsworth hid the state charter from agents of James II in 1687; inscription, "Charter Oak"
January 2000	Massachusetts	"The Minuteman," superimposed over the state's outline with a star designating Boston as the capital; inscription, "The Bay State"
March 2000	Maryland	Maryland State House dome and oak leaf clusters; inscription, "The Old Line State"
May 2000	South Carolina	Carolina wren, yellow jessamine, and palmetto tree, the state bird, flower, and tree; inscription, "The Palmetto State"
August 2000	New Hampshire	"The Old Man of the Mountain" on Mt. Cannon at Franconia Notch, with nine stars indicating the state's place among the 13 original colonies; inscription, "Live Free or Die"
October 2000	Virginia	Jamestown quadricentennial honoring the arrival of the *Susan Constant*, *Godspeed*, and *Discovery* on April 10, 1606; inscription, "Jamestown, 1607–2007" and "quadricentennial"
January 2001	New York	Statue of Liberty over the outline of the state, Hudson River, and Erie Canal and flanked by eleven stars indicating the state's place among the 13 original colonies, designed by Daniel Carr; inscription, "Gateway to Freedom"
March 2001	North Carolina	Wilbur Wright watching his brother Orville launching their "Flyer" at Kitty Hawk on December 17, 1903; inscription, "First Flight"
May 2001	Rhode Island	sailboat on Narragansett Bay with the Pell Bridge in the background, designed by Daniel Carr; inscription, "The Ocean State"
August 2001	Vermont	tapping of two maple trees and Camel's Hump Mountain in the background; inscription, "Freedom and Unity"
October 2001	Kentucky	horse, fence, and Federal Hill, Stephen Foster's Bardstown home, incised by mint engraver Jim Ferrell; inscription, "My Old Kentucky Home"
January 2002	Tennessee	fiddle, trumpet, and guitar and musical score representing the state's contribution to music; inscription, "Musical Heritage"
March 2002	Ohio	the Wright brothers' plane and a space suit superimposed over the state outline; inscription, "Birthplace of Aviation Pioneers"
May 2002	Louisiana	a map displaying the Louisiana Purchase plus a pelican and a trumpet playing jazz; inscription, "Louisiana Purchase"

August 2002	Indiana	19 stars signifying Indiana as the 19th state to ratify the Constitution, topped with a formula racer, signifying the Indianapolis Motor Speedway, built in 1909; inscription, "Crossroads America"
October 2002	Mississippi	a Magnolia grandiflora, named for French botanist Pierre Magnol and adopted as the state flower in 1952; inscription, "The Magnolia State"

Following in prescribed order are the state quarters of Illinois, Alabama, Maine, Missouri, and Arkansas in 2003; Michigan, Florida, Iowa, Texas and Wisconsin in 2004; California, Minnesota, Oregon, Kansas, and West Virginia in 2005; Nevada, Nebraska, Colorado, North Dakota, and South Dakota in 2006; Montana, Washington, Idaho, Wyoming, and Utah in 2007; and Oklahoma, New Mexico, Arizona, Alaska, and Hawaii in 2008.

SOURCES: "Anchors Aweigh for Rhode Island's New Quarter — Last of the Original 13 Colonies." *PR Newswire,* May 21, 2001. • "Banking on Children." *Chicago Sun-Times,* April 7, 2000. • "Change Is Exciting." *Kipling's Personal Finance Magazine,* October 1, 2000. • "50 State Quarters." http://catalog.usmint.gov/ • "Finally — A New Design for Quarters." *America's Community Banker,* February 1, 1999. • "State Quarters." http://www.statequarters.com. • "There's a New Flip Side to Quarters." *Omaha World Herald,* February 1, 1999.

Fisher, Mel

An optimist searching for Spanish gold at the bottom of the ocean, Melvin A. "Mel" Fisher kept the faith that his crew would make the world's largest undersea discovery. His goal was not just any find. For 17 years, he combed the reefs off the Florida keys for the remains of the *Nuestra Señora de Atocha,* a Spanish gunship loaded with the output of Caribbean mints for transport to Spain. After its loss in a hurricane on a reef 35 miles off Key West, Florida, on September 6, 1622, the ship remained out of reach until Fisher's discovery on July 20, 1985. The search cost his operation lawsuits, near bankruptcy, and the deaths of two family members, but yielded $400 million in precious metals, gems, and newly minted coins, the bulk from Spanish operations in Potosí, Bolivia.

Born on a chicken farm on August 21, 1922, in Hobart, Indiana, Fisher loved romantic buccaneer lore about Blackbeard, Jean Lafitte, and the treasure troves of the Spanish Main, especially Robert Louis Stevenson's *Treasure Island* (1883). After three semesters in engineering at Purdue University, Fisher began drafting bridges as his life's work and joined the D-Day landing with the army during World War II. At war's end, he completed his college degree.

Fisher tried chicken farming and steel work at Gary, Indiana, plants before opening Mel's Aqua Shop, a diving emporium at a shed on Redondo Beach near his chicken ranch in Torrance, California. The concept preceded the popularity of skin diving and spear fishing. A pioneer of underwater sport and movies, he scripted a TV show about sea dives and trained other enthusiasts in the use of scuba equipment and underwater cameras. He also invented and marketed at portable dredge that sifted gold from currents of water.

Influenced by successful diver Kip Wagner, at age 39, Fisher and his second wife, diver Dolores "Deo" Fisher, abandoned their California home and business and resettled in a houseboat anchored off Key West. He pursued his dream of locating historic wrecks, which he studied in a compendium, John S. Potter's *The Treasure Diver's Guide: Including Locations of Sunken Treasures, Techniques of Research, Search, and Salvage* (1960), a classic on underwater exploration. In 1968, Fisher's company, Treasure Salvors, launched a hunt for the Spanish galleon *Atocha,* which earned four stars on Potter's rankings.

To facilitate filtering, Fisher applied technical equipment — air hoses, magnetometers, side-scan sonar, sub-bottom profilers, pulse-detection sleigh, and atomic-absorption photospectrometers — and invented the mailbox, a clearing device attached to the stern of his boat that churned up water and silt by directing his wake toward the sea floor. He intended the mechanism to scatter the sand that had covered the *Atocha* in the 363 years since its sinking. On its maiden voyage, Fisher's mailbox improved visibility in the murky depths, disclosing doubloons from a flotilla of Spanish treasure vessels that capsized in 1715. Fisher's clever invention secured treasure worth several hundred thousand dollars, which bankrolled the rest of his operation.

Spurring Fisher's interest in 1970 was historian Eugene Lyon's disclosure of the original salvor's 1641 memorandum at Seville's Archive of the Indies. The text pinpointed the sinking at the Marquesas Keys, named for the Marquis Francisco Nuñez Melian, who had tried to recover the lost treasure in 1624. In 1973, the recovery of the *Atocha*'s anchor confirmed the location, yet proved to be a false lead. Repeated dives produced tempting finds, but not the hull and huge cargo of precious metals in the hold, which the second storm had scattered. While continuing the search, Fisher had to fight the state of Florida, which demanded one-quarter of the salvage, and the U.S. Department of the Interior, which claimed all of it as a national heritage. In 1982, the Supreme Court awarded Fisher ownership of the treasure, setting a precedent that cost states the rights to underwater relics.

Fisher survived legal fees, media skepticism, charges of environmental rape, and criticism of his archeological methods. Adding to emotional stress was the drowning of his 22-year-old son Dirk, Dirk's wife Angel, and crew member Rick Gage when a salvage tug overturned in a late-night squall on July 20, 1975. The first stroke of luck for the dogged head diver was his sighting of the *Santa Margarita* in 1980 and the recovery of $20 million in swords, communion plate, rosaries, jewelry, and precious metals. Five years later, Fisher knew that he was nearing the *Atocha* after diver Greg Wareham located the hull. The team retrieved 13 gold ingots, a gold chain, twelve emeralds, and 400 silver pieces of eight, the most common coin in circulation during the period from the Caribbean north to Canada. To preserve vulnerable wood and metal, he set up a preservation laboratory where teams cleaned brass with acid baths, tapped calcification from bronze with rubber mallets, and protected artifacts with such additives as polyethylene glycol, which halted wood shrinkage as it dried.

After the sweeping of 120,000 linear miles of ocean floor, Fisher's discovery of the *Atocha*'s hull stunned the media, which had tweaked him repeatedly for pursuing a pipedream. From 54 feet down, his company of 70 divers hauled to surface a bank of eleven bronze cannon, 1,000 silver bars, silver ewers and candlesticks, gold bangles and cups, uncut emeralds, and mahogany chests of gold blocks and silver pesos. Twelve programmers worked at evaluating and cataloguing each item to assure fair shares to Fisher and his crew. The find resulted in Fisher's being named on *Life* magazine's list of newsmakers of the year 1985.

Aided by archeologist R. Duncan Mathewson, Fisher gloried in the historic value of the hull as well as in the five percent of loot that was his to keep after he paid the rest to investors holding 1,016,000 shares of stock in the venture. One quarter of the cache went to the Florida state archives, where some $100,000 worth of items including a chalice, huge emerald, and 500 coins, disappeared over a three-year period. He launched a sale of Spanish cobs assessed as high as $1,200 each for top quality and displayed 70 items from the *Atocha*'s hulk at the Indianapolis Children's Museum. He also began sorting through book offers and contracts from movie and television producers, including a TV documentary and a film, *Dreams of Gold* (1986), starring Cliff Robertson as Fisher and Loretta Swit as Deo.

Eight months before Mel Fisher's death on December 19, 1998, disclosure of irregularities tarnished his legend after numismatists charged him with selling counterfeit *reales.* On April 22, 1998, Florida State agents raided his operation and seized 25 suspect coins of the 130,000 he retained as his share. Fisher, ill with bladder cancer for 20 years, refuted claims that he swindled the public with bogus coins and traveled to Mexico to locate the original dies on which some coins were struck. He lodged his own charges that environmentalists were eager to wreak vengeance on him for disturbing the ocean floor with blowers, which swept sand away from the *Atocha*'s hull.

***See also Atocha;* cobs; underwater archeology.**

SOURCES: "Atocha Dive Expeditions." *Skin Diver*. December 1999, 96. • Banks, William C. "The Curious Deals Behind the Key West Treasure." *Money*, September 1985, 46–50. • Bass, George F., ed. *Ships and Shipwrecks of the Americas: A History Based on Underwater Archaeology*. London: Thames and Hudson, 1996. • Bowden, Tracy. "Gleaning Treasure from the Silver Bank." *National Geographic*, July 1996, 90–105. • Cockburn, Alexander. "Beat the Devil: Imperial Addictions." *The Nation*, August 3, 1985, 70–71. • *Contemporary Newsmakers 1985*. Detroit: Gale Research, 1986. • Cordone, Bonnie J. "In Memoriam: Mel Fisher 1922–1998." *Skin Diver*, March 1999, 42–44. • "Finally, the Payoff." *Life*, September 1985, 47. • Frankel, Bruce, and Tim Roche. "Good As Gold?" *People Weekly*, June 15, 1998, p. 89. • "Mel Fisher's Payoff: Sinkin' Treasurre." *Money*, November 1986, 15. • Monroe, Sylvester. "The Trouble with Treasure." *Time*, May 11, 1998, 30. • Murphy, Jamie. "Down into the Deep." *Time*, August 11, 1986, 48–54. • "Newsmakers." *Life*, January 1986, 26. • O'Reilly, Jane. "From Davy Jones, a Tax Shelter." *Time*, April 11, 1983, 77. • Sandz, Victoria. *Encyclopedia of Western Atlantic Shipwrecks and Sunken Treasure*. Jefferson, N.C.: McFarland, 2001. • Stall, Sam. "Treasures of the 'Atocha.'" *Saturday Evening Post*, November 1986, 50–56. • "Treasure Hunter Who Went for the Gold." *U.S. News & World Report*, August 5, 1985, 13. • Trupp, Philip. "Ancient Shipwrecks Yield Both Prizes and Bitter Conflict." *Smithsonian*, October 1983, 79–89. • Wilentz, Amy. "We Found It! We Found It!" *Time*, August 5, 1985, 21–22.

fishhook money

Fishhook currency, similar in shape and convenience to Scottish nail money or needle change in India, was valued as cash in the Gilbert Islands in the central Pacific, as trade tokens among Alaskan Eskimo, and for African commerce in the Cameroon and Nigeria. The hooks possessed some of the conveniences of modern coins. They were small enough to fit into change bags and were easily produced by handcrafters. On the Gilberts, moneyers cut pearl shells into hooks and added them to a monetary system based on coconut shell disks, whale teeth, and other local shells. In colonial Africa, Cameroonians exchanged hooks along with cowries, gunpowder, and soap.

Micronesian trade in the Maldives was once based on fishhooks as currency. Traditionally, Maldivians exchanged bundles of cowries, a system in force in the 1500s when silver fishhook money was devised. In the 1800s, Maldivians living southwest of India created the *larin*, a silver coin shaped like a hook. Approved by the monarchy and stamped with a state cipher, the hook money anchored the island treasury. For small change, islanders broke them into pieces. As explained in W. S. W. Vaux's *On Coins of Ceylon* (1853) and English orientalist Thomas William Rhys Davids's *The International Numismata Orientalia: On the Ancient Coins and Measures of Ceylon* (1877), hook money, called *tangas de prata* or *kokku kasi*, also comprised trade tokens in Ceylon in the early 1500s, when Portuguese traders introduced European currency. According to English numismatist Colonel B. Lowsley, who visited Colombo, Ceylon, in 1890, the hooks, which circulated in both silver and gold, underwent a period of counterfeiting problems in the 1670s.

See also larin.

SOURCES: Allen, Larry. *Encyclopedia of Money*. New York: Checkmark Books, 2001. • Dewaraja, Lorna S. "Rhys Davids: His contribution to Pali and Buddhist Studies." (Sri Lanka) *Daily News*, July 15, 1998. • "Early Monetary Systems of Lanka." http://lakdiva.com/coins/lanka_monetary.html. • Einzig, Paul. *Primitive Money*. Oxford: Pergamon Press, 1966. • "Exploring Ethnomathematics in the Maldives." http://www.mcst.gov.mv/sitefiles/science-tech/research/counting.htm. • Lowsley, Colonel B. "Coins of Lanka." *Numismatic Chronicle Series*, 1895, pp. 211–223. • Opitz, Charles J. *Odd and Curious Money*. Ocala, Fla.: First Impressions, 1986.

florin

The elegant coinage of Renaissance Florence, the gold *florin* developed into a global currency. Originally called *fiorino d'argento* ("little silver flower") for the depiction of the lily, the city's chosen flower, the silver coin appeared in the mid–1200s with a likeness of John the Baptist, forerunner and baptizer of Christ. By 1252, the city's mint followed with the *fiorino d'oro* ("little gold flower"), a coin named for its incised iris, a stylized flower on the reverse created with a central stalk and two arabesque petals flanking the slender column.

The popular *florin*, which equaled 20 shillings or 250 pennies, was first limited in use to multinational banking and trade in cloth, silks, wool, furs, and foodstuffs. Because of its wide circulation, bookkeepers noted debit and credit and stated wholesale prices in *florins*, which coinsmiths struck of purer ore than the silver used for peasant transactions. The disparity between quality coins for rich and poor raised an outcry from San Antonino, who became archbishop of Florence in 1445 during the rise of the Renaissance powermonger Cosimo de' Medici.

In the 1330s, to finance trans–European trade, the mint at Florence produced 350,000 gold *florins* annually. According to the *Florentine Chronicle* (ca. 1348), a history written by Giovanni Villani, a banking merchant and shareholder in the Peruzzi company, the *florin* also figured in the hiring of mercenaries and in the bribery of officials and political parties. Following his description of one grim set-to between Siena and Florence:

> When the Sienese and Florentine exiles saw what a poor showing the Florentines had made against so few German knights, they decided they could win the war with more troops. They immediately provided themselves with twenty thousand gold *florins* from the company of the Salimbeni, who were merchants at that time. As security, they put up the fortress at Tentennana and other castles belonging to the commune. Then they sent their ambassadors off to Apulia again bearing the money and a message to Manfred that his few German knights, by great vigor and valor, had engaged the entire Florentine army, put much of it to flight, and would have beaten it if the German forces had been bigger [Villani].

The padding of the military with German mercenaries, however, turned into a debacle. Villani noted that, because the additional German troops were inadequate, "all lay dead on the field and [Manfred's] standard had been dragged in disgrace through the camp, then in and about Florence" (*ibid.*).

Along with the *ducat* of Venice, the *florins* of Florence and Milan fueled transactions of the Medici bank and its many European branches. The design influenced the style of European moneys, including the gold models from Brabant and Hainault; the English *florin*, which Edward III issued in 1344; and the German *gulden*, picturing mounted knights, St. John, St. Lambert, and St. Peter. Hungarian coin designers produced their own stylish *florin*, which pictured the national crest. By 1458, diemasters under King Matthias Corvinus were producing the longest-lived national coin, a *florin* picturing the Virgin Mary and Child Jesus.

Single *florins* preceded the double *florin*, which coiners first struck in 1504. Into the Renaissance, the original coin played a significant part in political and economic history. At Augsburg in 1519, Jakob II Fugger the Rich handed over a cache of around two million *florins* to Charles I of Spain, who needed the money to bribe electors. For such a treasure, the Spanish king acquired the title Charles V, Holy Roman Emperor.

In the 1840s, Sir John Bowring, a member of Parliament from Exeter, Devonshire, England, advocated that Britain's treasury adopt the *florin* as the first stage in establishment of a decimal system of currency. The production of a two-shilling *florin* in 1849 replicated coins that were popular in the United States and France. The beauty of the English *florin* did not relieve the designer's chagrin at charges of godlessness for omitting the customary D. G., standing for "*Dei Gratia*" ("By the Grace of God"). The "godless *florin*" circulated only two years before moneyers produced a corrected piece.

The Irish mint revived the *florin* in 1939. One of the island's most attractive coin motifs, the silver piece presented the traditional Irish harp on the face with the date and "Eire," the country's name in Gaelic. Balancing the surface design was an obverse picturing the curved body of a salmon and the Gaelic word *floirin*.

See also **amulet coins; banking; *ducat*; *écu*; English money; *gulden*; papal coins; Renaissance coins; U.S. coins; U.S. Mint.**

SOURCES: Allen, Larry. *Encyclopedia of Money*. New York: Checkmark Books, 2001. • Clain-Stefanelli, Elvira, and Vladimir Clain-Stefanelli. *The Beauty and Lore of Coins, Currency, and Medals*. Croton-on-Hudson, N.Y.: Riverwood Publishers, 1974. • Cribb, Joe. *Money*. Toronto: Stoddart, 1990. • Davies, Glyn. *A History of Money from Ancient Times to the Present Day*. Cardiff: University of Wales Press, 1994. • "Giovanni Villani: Florentine Chronicle." http://www.fordham.edu/halsall/source/villani.html. • Hastings, James, ed. *Encyclopedia of Religion and Ethics*. New York: Charles Scribner's Sons, 1951. • Reinfeld, Fred. *Treasury of the World's Coins*. New York: Sterling Publishing, 1953. • Weatherford, Jack. *The History of Money: From Sandstone to Cyberspace*. Pittsburgh, Pa.: Three Rivers Press, 1998.

food stamps

Used like money, food stamps consist of grocery coupons exchanged only for food in approved stores. The original purpose of the U.S. Department of Agriculture–issue stamps was the eradication of malnutrition among the poor, whom individual states identified as truly needy. Begun in 1939 during the Great Depression to lessen the interlinking problems of hunger and farm surplus, the program extended into 1943, the middle of World War II, when service in the military and a boom in factory-made goods for the military curtailed unemployment and boosted the national standard of living.

In the 1960s, in response to the plight of West Virginians, President John F. Kennedy called for a return to limited food stamp programs in depressed areas. Congress re-initiated Food and Nutrition Service food stamps in 1964, and required recipients to buy the coupons with cash. Kennedy's successor, President Lyndon B. Johnson, creator of the Great Society program of domestic reform, expanded the reach of free groceries by increasing allotments per household and broadening eligibility to include the elderly and disabled. Revisions in 1980 eliminated fees for stamps. Social service agencies gauged family need based on the number of dependent children, cost of living, and annual family income. To the program's detriment, dishonest recipients extended the purchasing power by trading stamps for cash and using the money to buy cigarettes, beer and wine, drugs, and other non-food items disallowed by the original token system.

Under the hard-edged policies of the Reagan era, the food stamp program came under intense congressional scrutiny, ostensibly to end fraud and misuse, particularly by illegal immigrants, alcoholics, and drug addicts. Fueling concern among conservative taxpayers was the phenomenal growth of enrollment of low-income recipients from 4.3 million in 1970 to 21.4 million a decade later. Despite congressional tinkering, the coupon system survived, reaching 7.3 million households in 2000. Of the total funds distributed, 91 percent went to homes containing either a child or an elderly or disabled person. Electronic debit cards began replacing paper vouchers, which were often lost or stolen. Standardized across the nation, the bank card credit system called EBT (electronic benefit transfer) cards eased the stigma of purchasing with stamps and helped to assure that federal dollars paid only for food and didn't circulate on ghetto streets as a folk currency.

SOURCES: Allen, Larry. *Encyclopedia of Money*. New York: Checkmark Books, 2001. • "Characteristics of Food Stamp Households." http://www.fns. usda.gov/OANE/MENU/Published/FSP/FILES/Participation/2000Characteristics.htm. • Gunderson, Craig, and Victor Oliveira. "The Food Stamp Program and Food Insufficiency." *American Journal of Agricultural Economics*, November 1, 2001. • "States Must Standardize Food Stamp Systems." *Government Computer News*, April 2000, p. 16. • "Who Can Get Food Stamps?" http://www.ssa. gov/pubs/10100.html.

forint

The *forint*, a new Hungarian currency introduced in the months following World War II, saved the country from huge inflation and monetary chaos. While Hungarians relied on the *pengo*, its previous monetary standard, paper money quickly outpaced control of the economy. To keep up, the treasury issued a *milpengo* or million *pengos*, followed in three months by a *bilpengo*, equal to a billion *pengos*. The next paper money was so large that it had no name, only the number 10,000,000,000,000,000,000,000,000,000 *pengos*.

In July 1946, the government suspended plans to circulate the new nameless bill. Instead, it created the *forint*, a new denomination abbreviated as HUF and worth 400,000,000,000,000,000,000,000 *pengos*. The shift halted the post-war inflation. As of June 2001, the *forint* became a fully convertible currency.

SOURCES: Clain-Stefanelli, Elvira, and Vladimir Clain-Stefanelli. *The Beauty and Lore of Coins, Currency, and Medals*. Croton-on-Hudson, N.Y.: Riverwood Publishers, 1974. • "Hungary: Government Grants 55 Billion Forints for Projects Boosting Economy." *BBC Monitoring European Economic*, October 25, 2001. • Platt, Gordon. "Europe/Africa: Hungary Widens Band for Forint." *Global Finance*, June 1, 2001.

Fort Knox

Legendary for its security and impregnability, Fort Knox, Kentucky, has a long military background. In 1862 during the Civil War, the Union army stationed the 6th Michigan Infantry there to erect bridges and fortifications and bridges. In 1902, the army staged maneuvers in an area of the fort under consideration as a permanent military post. After the outbreak of World War I, Congress leased 10,000 acres near Stithton for a field artillery training center and named it after a hero of the American Revolution, Major General Henry Knox, the Continental Army's artillery chief and the first U.S. Secretary of War.

In June 1918, Congress began building a permanent facility at Fort Knox on 40,000 acres, but shelved the original plans in the 1920s. A more conservative proposal in 1932 conceived a training center for reserve officer training and the National Guard. Additional uses as an infantry base and armored car and tank training ground preceded formation of a mechanized force in 1930. On January 1, 1932, the installation took the name Fort Knox to indicate placement of a permanent garrison, the 1st Cavalry Regiment.

The 1930s placed serious burdens on the nation. During the Great Depression, the fort supported the Civilian Conservation Crops, one of President Franklin D. Roosevelt's New Deal programs that relieved unemployment from 1933 to 1942. The labor agency hired teams of unemployed men to perform such national conservation work as tree planting, dam building, forest fire prevention, and maintaining forest roads, trails, and bridges. Living in work camps, a total of three million men received food, housing, medical care, and necessities plus $30 a month in cash, which some sent home to destitute families.

In 1936, the staff at Fort Knox took on a different task—guarding the nation's gold, which had risen to over 50 percent of the world's supply. Advisers chose Fort Knox because it was inland and less vulnerable to attack than treasury buildings in Washington, D.C., near the Atlantic coast. To lessen the chance of seizure of all the nation's bullion, treasury officials also dispersed some of the cache at sites in Denver, West Point, and the Federal Reserve Bank in Manhattan. Government officials fortified the Fort Knox site with concrete, granite, and steel and equipped it with guard boxes on the corners, fencing, security devices, and sentry boxes at the gate. A gold Treasury seal capped the entrance.

In January 1937, the U.S. Treasury made its first bullion deposit at the fort, where agents stacked gold supplies in a bomb-proof vault. Some of the nation's reserve had remained undisturbed from Thomas Jefferson's presidency. A large portion consisted of bullion paid to foreign governments, but retained at the fort for safe-keeping and to reduce the cost and danger of shipping out of the country. To assure the security Fort Knox vaults, civil service guards practiced marksmanship on a firing range in the basement.

The U.S. Treasury stocked the vault with

large amounts of the nation's bullion during World War II as well as England's crown jewels and the Magna Carta. The site also accumulated the gold of other European nations occupied by the Nazis. After the Japanese bombing of Pearl Harbor on December 7, 1941, U.S. archivists secured in the vaults along with gold the original drafts of the Constitution, Declaration of Independence, and Abraham Lincoln's Gettysburg Address. In October 1944, the historic statements of U.S. freedoms returned to Washington, D.C.

The Fort Knox gold vault continues to store gold in unwrapped standard mint bars or bricks in either fine gold or coin quality, the result of melting gold coins. Each fine gold bar is worth $16,888.00. The officer in charge and a guardian force secure the gold against theft, either internal or external. They allow no media photographers or tourists.

The U.S. Mint Police, established in 1792, is one of the nation's oldest federal law enforcement agencies in the nation. They secure the money and the printing plates stored in Washington, D.C., and the 4,600 tons of gold at Fort Knox as well as another 3,400 tons of gold and the national interests at Treasury installations in Philadelphia, San Francisco, Denver, and West Point. In addition to guarding staff and property, they prevent, detect, and investigate crimes involving the theft of money. To assure internal security, the Treasury Department audits deposits on a regular schedule.

In 1964, United Artists filmed an amusing Ian Fleming spy novel, *Goldfinger*, which novelist Anthony Burgess called "one of the 99 best novels in English since 1939" (Weller 1993). The plot is a tense, complex caper that puts international gold smugglers inside Fort Knox. The villain, wittily named Auric Goldfinger, schemes to detonate a nuclear bomb in the bullion depository to create economic upheaval and boost the worth of his own hoard of gold. The screen version pictured stacks of gold bricks in a cage made of steel pipes and enclosed with high-tech security devices that instantly electrocuted intruders. A big-budget film starring Sean Connery as British secret service agent 007, the movie contributed to the mystique of Fort Knox.

***See also* world money.**

SOURCES: Allen, Larry. *Encyclopedia of Money*. New York: Checkmark Books, 2001. • Aven, Paula. "Mint Guards Gold Bullion Worth Billions." *Denver Business Journal*, February 9, 1996, p. 16A. • Brookhiser, Richard. "A Founding Father's Return to Grace." *U.S. News & World Report*, November 10, 1997, pp. 71–72. • *Encyclopedia of World Biography*. Detroit: Gale Group, 1998. • "Fort Knox." http://library.louisville.edu/ekstrom/govpubs/states/kentucky/ftknox.html. • Lind, Michael. "Hamilton's Legacy." *Wilson Quarterly*, Summer 1994, 40–52. • Reed, Mort. *Cowles Complete Encyclopedia of U.S. Coins*. New York: Cowles Book Company, 1969. • Weatherford, Jack. *The History of Money: From Sandstone to Cyberspace*. Pittsburgh, Pa.: Three Rivers Press, 1998. • Weller, Anthony. "Bond at 40." *Forbes*, November 22, 1993, pp. 133–143.

franc

The French *franc* has been a significant monetary unit in the global economy since John II the Good de Valois (also Jean le Bon) struck the first coins in 1360. The first franc, minted from gold, bore a name that equated with freedom. The design depicted the hapless John, a triumphant king on horseback, after the battle of Poitiers. His liberty was short-lived, for he died in captivity in London four years later. The coin bore on the standard pious Latin legend "*Johannes Dei Gratia Francorum Rex*" (*John, by the Grace of God, King of the Franks*). Called the *franc à cheval* ("equestrian franc") because of the mounted pose, it circulated simultaneously with the *franc à pied* ("franc on foot"), issued by Charles V of France with a likeness of the king standing under a canopy. It became the coin of the nobility, but seldom passed through the purses of peasants, who relied on the *denier* or *gros blanc*.

The French augmented the gold coin with silver *francs* in 1577, then stopped minting gold francs altogether during the 1600s, yet kept the name for new units of exchange. After the unfortunate demise of the *assignat*, a failed paper currency, the mint issued stan-

The octagonal two-*franc* coin made of nickel depicts the female sower and a rising sun, French symbols of hope.

dard French *francs* and *livres* in coin, but varied the likenesses to display a shift of power from monarchy to a republic. Among the new specie was a five-*livre* disk picturing Louis XVI shortly before he was guillotined at *la Place de la Révolution* in Paris on January 21, 1793. His queen, Marie Antoinette, survived until her own execution the following October 16. Her likeness gave place to the French female emblem, Marianne, the equivalent of Britannia on British coins, Hibernia in Ireland, and Lady Liberty on U.S. coins. Various models provided profile busts for coins; some poses emulated the helmeted Athena and filleted maidens; a bold art deco face with streaming hair adorned coins during the Fifth Republic, which began in 1958.

In 1795, the republican government introduced a new *franc* coin commemorating the French Revolution of 1789. Emulating the U.S. decimal system created by Thomas Jefferson and colonial financier Robert Morris, coiners established decimal currency with the *franc* as the nation's basic monetary unit. For bullion, the treasury commissioned Napoleon Bonaparte to scour Italy for silver and gold plate and coins. He returned with goods worth 53,000,000 *francs*, some of which he rifled from the Vatican's art galleries and coin and medal collections.

The first piece the French treasury staff minted was the five-*franc* silver coin picturing Hercules flanked by the human representations of Liberty and Equality. In 1799, the government formally established the division of the *franc* into 10 *decimos* and 100 *centimes*, a system that remained in use until the emergence of the euro 2000. In like loyalty to the *franc*, the Swiss Helvetian Republic adopted the coin in 1799; Belgium also adopted a *franc* unit after separating from Holland in 1830. Luxembourg established its own *franc* in 1848.

Napoleon strengthened the French monetary system and established decimal coinage. In 1802, the mint supplanted the war-era coins with Napoleons, gold pieces worth 20 *francs*. As Napoleon's regime grew in opulence and majesty, the concepts of liberty and equality shrank to nothing. Nonetheless, the *franc* flourished across Europe. A portrait coin issued in 1804, the year Napoleon was made Premier Consul of the republic, pictured him in profile with short wavy hair combed forward around his face. The reverse still honored republicanism. Subsequent coins displayed his head filleted Roman style along with the title *Empereur* and legend *Empire Français*. By 1809, the republic and its dreams of liberty had withered away, leaving only an egotistical emperor. Gold replaced silver on large coins, which the treasury produced at French mints and at subject cities of Genoa, Rome, Turin, and Utrecht.

When Napoleon III succeeded Louis XVIII, *francs* grew larger, to denominations of 50 and 100. Members of the Latin Monetary Union accepted the *franc* as their monetary unit after Belgium, Greece, Italy, and Switzerland allied with France in December 23, 1865, and adopted a common coinage and weights and measures as means of promoting commerce. Following the model were Rumania and Spain, but the United States declined to give up the dollar. When the Franco-Prussian War deposed Napoleon III, the Paris mint revived Augustin Dupré's noble Liberty and Equality on 600,000 silver five-*franc* coins struck from confiscated royal silver and from reserves at the French central bank. The motto harked back to a statement of faith: "*Dieu Protége la France*" ("God Protects France").

While France was involved in the trench warfare of World War I, private banks and mercantile concerns issued paper bills for small change. From the Grenoble chamber of commerce came a 50-*centime* note dated November 8, 1917. The small print promised that

"*Cette coupure échangeable contre des billets de la Banque de France*" ("This bill exchangeable for notes drawn on the Bank of France"). A disclaimer warned that bearers should demand reimbursement during the immediate post-war period, no later than November 9, 1922.

Because of the importance of France to world power, the franc is also the monetary unit of Andorra, Belgium, Benin, Burkina Faso, Burundi, Cameroon, Central African Republic, Chad, Comoros, Congo, Côte d'Ivoire, Djibouti, Equatorial Guinea, French Guiana, French Polynesia, Futuna Islands, Gabon, Guadeloupe, Guinea, Guinea-Bissau, Liechtenstein, Luxembourg, Mali, Martinique, Mayotte, Miquelon, Monaco, New Caledonia, Niger, Réunion, Rwanda, St. Pierre, Senegal, Switzerland, Togo, and Wallis. In 1999, France joined 11 other European countries — Austria, Belgium, Finland, Germany, Greece, Ireland, Italy, Luxembourg, the Netherlands, Portugal, and Spain — in accepting the euro, a common currency abbreviated EUR. The French proposed calling the new currency the *écu*, the name of a medieval French coin. By a slim vote of 51 percent to 49 percent, the treasury determined that the Paris mint would cease producing francs, a currency that had served them for over six centuries. The mint director, Emmanuel Constant, senior officer of the French Ministry of Economics, Finance, and Industry, looked forward to the Brussels-based euro currency, of which his own mint was producing 2,585,000,000 new banknotes, the first printed on the continent.

This Monacan *franc*, struck in 1943 on aluminum bronze, is minted from a makeshift alloy because of metal shortages created by World War II. (Vic Gardner, Lion Coins, Cheshire, England)

***See also assignat*; commemorative coins; Thomas Jefferson; John the Good; Robert Morris; U.S. coins; world money; Wyon family.**

SOURCES: Allen, Larry. *Encyclopedia of Money*. New York: Checkmark Books, 2001. • Castle, Stephen. "Last Rites of the French Franc Marked by Confident Display of Gallic Indifference." *London Independent*, February 18, 2002. • Clain-Stefanelli, Elvira, and Vladimir Clain-Stefanelli. *The Beauty and Lore of Coins, Currency, and Medals*. Croton-on-Hudson, N.Y.: Riverwood Publishers, 1974. • Cribb, Joe. *Money*. Toronto: Stoddart, 1990. • Cribb, Joe, Barrie Cook, and Ian Carradice. *The Coin Atlas*. London: Little, Brown and Co., 1999. • Davies, Glyn. *A History of Money from Ancient Times to the Present Day*. Cardiff: University of Wales Press, 1994. • Given-Wilson, Chris, and Francois Beriac. "Edward III's Prisoners of War: The Battle of Poitiers and Its Context." *English Historical Review*, September 1, 2001. • Kunzig, Robert. "Euroland or Bust." *Discover*, October 1998. • Weatherford, Jack. *The History of Money: From Sandstone to Cyberspace*. Pittsburgh, Pa.: Three Rivers Press, 1998.

Franklin, Benjamin

During a six-year furor over the need for a simplified currency in the American colonies, Benjamin Franklin, a printer, pragmatic scientist, political consultant, and publisher of the *Pennsylvania Gazette*, concurred with the clamoring merchants of Pennsylvania that the new nation needed its own money. He made public his belief in a paper currency system with an upbeat letter printed in the *American Weekly Mercury* on March 27, 1729. The following April 3, he issued a more scholarly, detailed study of paper money in "A Modest Enquiry into the Nature and Necessity of a Paper Currency," an unsigned monograph encouraging acceptance of paper notes as legal tender.

Franklin based his commentary on a belief that the interest rate was anchored to the money supply and, thus, influenced domestic and foreign trade, investments, and real estate values. He also surmised that paper money increased community through the immigration of skilled artisans and workers and encouraged them to buy local goods. He explained, "A Plentiful Currency will encourage great Numbers of Labouring and Handicrafts Men to come and Settle in the Country, by the same Reason that a Want of it will discourage and drive them out" (Franklin). By welcoming newcomers as producers as well as consumers of domestic products, the nation and its economy were certain to thrive.

The Pennsylvania Land Bank reciprocated Franklin's support by hiring him to produce their paper currency, forcing him to suspend issuance of the *Pennsylvania Gazette* until after the bills came off the press. In his autobiography, first published in 1868, Franklin confided, "My friends [in the Pennsylvania assembly], who consider I had been of some service, thought fit to reward me by employing me in printing the money; a very profitable job, and a great help to me" *(ibid.)*. Critics questioned his assumption that control by a land bank secured values and prevented depreciation. Most vocal was John Webbe, who riposted with "A Discourse Concerning Paper Money" (1743), a rebuttal claiming that Franklin had miscalculated the effect of land-based mortgaging.

The success of paper money proved Webbe wrong and Franklin right. At the same time, homeland currency angered the British, who banned colonial paper bills in New England in 1751 and, 13 years later, throughout the North American colonies. In 1766, Franklin accepted appointment to an embassy to England and pled in person in Parliament for the colonies' right to print their own money. His crisp aphorisms about money permeated his writings, particularly *Poor Richard's Alamanack* (1733–1758), in which he collected pithy reminders that "time is money" and that ready money is as faithful as old wives and old dogs. In his honor, the U.S. treasury issued 100-dollar bills displaying his picture.

***See also* continental currency; Great Seal of the United States; paper money; Joseph Wright.**

SOURCES: Allen, Larry. *Encyclopedia of Money.* New York: Checkmark Books, 2001. • Cribb, Joe. *Money.* Toronto: Stoddart, 1990. • Davis, Andrew McFarland. *Colonial Currency Reprints, 1682–1751.* Boston: The Prince Society, 1911. • Davies, Glyn. *A History of Money from Ancient Times to the Present Day.* Cardiff: University of Wales Press, 1994. • Franklin, Benjamin. "A Modest Enquiry into the Nature and Necessity of a Paper Currency." http://www.people.virginia.edu/~rwm3n/webdoc6.html. • Franklin, Benjamin. "The Writings of Benjamin Franklin." http://www.historycarper.com/resources/twobf2/paper1.htm. • Grierson, Philip. *Numismatics.* London: Oxford University Press, 1975. • Lewis, Brenda Ralph. *Coins & Currency.* New York: Random House, 1993. • Newman, Eric. *The Early Paper Money of America.* Iola, Wisc: Krause, 1997. • Weatherford, Jack. *The History of Money: From Sandstone to Cyberspace.* Pittsburgh, Pa.: Three Rivers Press, 1998.

Fraser, James Earle

James Earle Fraser asserted his influence on U.S. coinage with the initial F on the Indian Head or buffalo nickel, a coin that captured the native roots of America. A student of Augustus Saint-Gaudens, he began specie sculpture already with a background in classical art and developed one of the favorite U.S. coins with a native American theme. Born to Carolina West Fraser in Winona, Minnesota, on November 4, 1876, he learned about mechanics from his father, Thomas Alexander Fraser, a railroad engineer. Fraser lived on a ranch in South Dakota and attended school in the town of Mitchell. Much of his childhood brought him in contact with Sioux and other Indians of the Great Plains. In his mid-fifties, he reflected, "I have seen the Indian in his natural habitat, with his finest costumes being worn" (Van Ryzin 1995, p. 13).

Fraser developed a love of sculpture and carved stone figures in boyhood and learned his trade from watching the blade control of a town whittler. In 1890, Fraser entered the Chicago Art Institute in his mid-teens and completed a masterwork, "End of the Trail," three years later. His subject was a mounted Indian seemingly broken in spirit by the genocidal mistreatment of European settlers. While Fraser studied at L'École des Beaux-Arts in Paris, his Indian sculpture won a $1,000 award at the American Association of Paris. A bronze enlargement later stood at a cemetery in Waupun, Wisconsin.

Mentored by famed sculptor Augustus Saint-Gaudens, Fraser learned medal art and assisted his teacher in sculpting a mounted likeness of General William Tecumseh Sherman, famed Union army commander during the American Civil War. On return to the United States, the sculptor opened a studio in New York City and contributed his medallion of Horatio H. Brewster to the National Gallery in Washington, D.C. Fraser earned acclaim for his busts of Thomas Edison, Alexander Hamilton, John Hay, and Elihu Root and for a seated pose of Thomas Jefferson, displayed in St. Louis in 1904 at the Louisiana Purchase Exposition. A rapid rise in commissions brought business from the Belgian government and three commissions to sculpt images of Theodore Roosevelt.

In 1913, in the last months of office for one-term Secretary of the Treasury Franklin MacVeagh under President William Howard Taft, Fraser accepted a commission to design the buffalo nickel, a uniquely North American coin that popularized his art. For the Indian profile on the reverse, he made a composite sketch from the sittings of three Indians:

- Northern Cheyenne tribesman Two Moons (or Ishi'eyo Nissi), a warrior from the Black Hills who had fought along with Crazy Horse and Sitting Bull at the Powder River and at Little Bighorn engagements in the 1870s and had published "General Custer's Last Fight as Seen by Two Moons" (1898) in *McClure's magazine*
- Iron Tail (or Sinte Maza), an Oglala Sioux war chief who had fought in the Black Hills and at the Little Bighorn and traveled to Europe in 1889 as a performer in Buffalo Bill Cody's Wild West Show.
- Fraser and his wife, coin designer Laura Gardin Fraser, tentatively identified a third model as movie star Chief John Big Tree of the Onondaga (sometimes given as Seneca), born at Glacier National Park, Montana, in 1865. He starred in 100 films, including *The Iron Horse* (1924) and in two popular John Wayne vehicles, *Stagecoach* (1939) and *She Wore a Yellow Ribbon* (1949), as well as in Tim McCoy westerns. Big Tree died in Syracuse, New York, in 1967 at age 102.

In a letter to the Bureau of Indian Affairs in June 1931, Fraser was unclear on how many models he actually posed for the composite profile. He did deny any dealings with Chief Two Guns White Calf, a Blackfoot who claimed to have been a third model for the coin and who wore an oversized medallion of the famed nickel to advertise his connection with it.

For the buffalo, Fraser studied Black Diamond (also called Toby), a 20-year-old male American bison housed at the Bronx Park Zoo. Fraser declared that he spent hours observing the animal's shape, mood, and movements before making a clay model. He described Black Diamond as

> less conscious of the honor being conferred on him than of the annoyance which he suffered from insistent gazing upon him. He refused point blank to permit me to get side views of him, and stubbornly show his front face most of the time [*ibid.*, p. 38].

A veteran of both Fraser's nickel and the ten-dollar bill, Black Diamond was euthanized on November 17, 1915. His image required touch-ups because Fraser had elevated the bas-relief of his head and hump, making them subject to rapid wear. The animal became a national icon of the free range once found in the American West.

Fraser's interest in native Americans intrigued the public, who admired the Indian head nickel and came to San Francisco to see his exhibit of "End of the Trail" at the 1915 Panama-Pacific International Exposition. His later works were primarily governmental and military — symbolic figures for the U.S. Supreme Court Building and the World War I Navy Cross and victory medal — along with some portraits of children. In 1951, the American Academy of Arts and Letters presented him a gold medal. In 2001, U.S. Mint Director Jay W. Johnson announced the reissue of the Buffalo nickel, a special one-dollar, 90 percent pure silver commemorative coin. A portion of the proceeds helped to fund the Smithsonian National Museum of the American Indian.

See also **Augustus Saint-Gaudens; U.S. coins.**

SOURCES: *Biography Resource Center.* Farmington Hills, Mich.: Gale Group, 2001. • Clain-Stefanelli, Elvira, and Vladimir Clain-Stefanelli. *The Beauty and Lore of Coins, Currency, and Medals.* Croton-on-Hudson, N.Y.: Riverwood Publishers, 1974. • Kageleiry, Jamie. "The Other Side of the Coin." Yankee, September 1993, p. 58. • Reed, Mort. *Cowles Complete Encyclopedia of U.S. Coins.* New York: Cowles Book Company, 1969. • Rochette, Ed. "Meeting the Man with the Five-cent Profile." *Hobbies,* January 1984, pp. 82–83. • Taxay, Don. *The U.S. Mint and Coinage.* New York: Arco Publishing, 1966. • Van Ryzin, Robert R. *Twisted Tails: Sifted Fact, Fantasy and Fiction from U.S. Coin History.* Iola, Wisc.: Krause Publications, 1995. • Waldman, Carl. *Who Was Who in Native American History.* New York: Facts on File, 1990.

Frederick the Great

The renowned philosopher king of Prussia, Frederick II the Great (also Friedrich der Grosse) strengthened German money with a coinage founded on *thalers* and *pfennigs*. Born in Berlin in 1712, he came to power at age 28 and amazed Europe with his military and diplomatic acumen and an innate ability to govern with taste and prudence. As an enlightened monarch, he enhanced Prussia's prestige on multiple levels — through combat strength as well as artistry and productivity in factories and competence in agriculture. In 1750, he ordered the first ten-*thaler* piece minted at Berlin. Its legend, surrounding a noble profile, stated simply "*Fredericus Borussorum Rex*" ("Frederick King of the Prussians").

Well disciplined citizens accepted Frederick's exploitation of the textile and porcelain industries and his demands for a large cash reserve from excise taxes on food and property taxes to bolster the army in case of war. However, laws preventing the export of over 300 *thalers* per person and the amassing of a substantial treasury restricted fiscal flexibility and removed from circulation too much cash. Thus, he turned his people into cowed paupers.

As Prussia engaged in combat year after year, costs took a serious toll on national economic health. Frederick debased currency, suspended salaries owed to government workers and judges, and sought financial aid from England. At the beginning of the Seven Years War in 1756, he confiscated silver plate to be melted down and stamped into *thalers* featuring cannon, military banners, and an eagle. After two heavy defeats in 1758 and 1759, he faced the fury of Brandenburg's landowners, who rebelled against taxation to support the army. In 1767, he commissioned a Levantine *thaler*, a silver portrait coin intended to boost the nation's treasury through trade with the Turks. Before his death in Potsdam on August 17, 1768, he enjoyed the rewards of duty, conservatism, and responsible despotism. His civil servants at the Royal Bank of Berlin and in commerce, mining, and metallurgy performed like well-oiled machines.

See also **Rix dollars; *thaler*.**

SOURCES: Cribb, Joe. *Money.* Toronto: Stoddart, 1990. • Cribb, Joe, Barrie Cook, and Ian Carradice. *The Coin Atlas.* London: Little, Brown and Co., 1999. • "The Deserter." *Freemasons Monthly Magazine,* 1842. • *The Harper Encyclopedia of Military Biography.* New York: HarperCollins, 1992. • "Old Fritz Returns to Prussia." *Economist,* July 27, 1991, p. 44. • Reinfeld, Fred. *Treasury of the World's Coins.* New York: Sterling Publishing, 1953.

fur money

In the economic era preceding coinage and paper currency, traders and individuals have valued animal pelts as easily obtainable, storeable, and portable money. Among the Lapps of northern Norway, the standard trade was either furs or reindeer. In Mongolia, according to Henning Haslund, member of Sven Hedin's Sino-Swedish expedition to Central Asia from 1927 to 1930 and author of *Tents in Mongolia* (1934), nomadic shoppers paid merchants with squirrel skins. Hedin also observed that a wealthy Buddhist lama collected debts from peasants in the form of pelts. The Kirghiz traded in horses and sheep with lamb and wolf pelts as small change.

Fur money was also legal tender in Oceania. In New Caledonia, islanders treasured both shell money and pelts of the flying fox as well as bead necklaces. An offshoot of fur money were fur pieces and belts woven of flying fox hair. On the Loyalty Islands, just the red hair under the ears of the flying fox served as currency.

In Russia, where silver had to be imported and the only metal coinage was Middle Eastern *dirhans*, fur served as domestic money from the 700s and maintained a constant value within regions throughout the Middle Ages. *Kunitza*, the term for marten pelt, evolved into *kuna* ("money"); *polushka* coins took their name from rabbit pelts. The monetary relationship of fur to cash equalled 2.5 *kuna* per sable skin. The need for lesser denominations produced small change from claws, ears, noses, and small circlets of dried pelt.

Visitors recorded incidents of payment in fur currency into the late Middle Ages. Around A.D. 950, Ibn Dasta from Arabia saw Volga Bulgars using marten skin as small change. In 1253, an eyewitness to Russian fur money, William of Rubruck (also Guillaume de Rubruquis), a Franciscan friar and ambassador to China from Louis IX of France, arrived at the court of Mangu Khan at Karakoram. He confirmed that the Russians circulated scraps of fur. In 1514, Grand Duke Ivan Vasilyovich of Moscow — later Ivan the Terrible — arranged a wedding on payments of marten hides. This nature-based money, like shell and feather tokens, remained the standard until the rise of metal coinage when Muscovite princes centralized power.

In the New World, fur money got its start in the 1500s in the Mississippi Valley and Canada, where French-Canadian *coureurs de bois* (woodsmen) and agents of the Hudson Bay Company traded with the handiest commodity, usually pelts of beaver, bear, moose, wildcat, and wolf. In Quebec in 1673 and 1674, council decrees insisted that bear and moose pelts were valid currencies and ordered all citizens to accept them as legal tender. In the Canadian and Alaskan outbacks, reliance on marten, fox, sable, and lynx served an area where coins were rare. Alaskan Eskimo prized furs as well as beads and clothing as exchange media.

Easterners had to establish exchange ranges for fur money, one of many forms of "country pay." In 1703, New York financiers and merchants relied on a standard pelt evaluation, which equated it with other animal skins and equivalent commodities. The beaver hide, the most valuable of all forest animals, was worth one-half of a moose hide, one bear or otter, one pint of shot, two foxes or woodchucks, four raccoons, five pecks of corn or five pounds of feathers, six knives, or ten pounds of pork.

Lee Merrithew noted in an article for the November 1899 issue of *Cosmopolitan* that whites dealt unfairly with native Americans by devaluing furs. He explained, "In olden times when an Indian wanted a rifle, the rifle was stood on end and the Indian laid furs flat on the ground till they were heaped to the top of the gun barrel" (Einzig 1966, p. 167). The Indian walked away with a gun worth $50; the Hudson Bay Company sold the pile of furs for 20 times that amount. The decline in value of beaver pelts in New England caused a parallel slump in the value of wampum. Until around 1850, when a more sophisticated monetary system replaced the remnants of barter, acceptance of furs as legal tender supported commerce among whites and with Indians as far to the northwest as the Yukon.

Historic mountaineers like Jim Beckwourth, Daniel Boone, Joe Meek, Davy Crockett, Jim Bridger, Manuel Lisa, John C. Frémont, Kit Carson, and Milton and William Sublette wore their wealth in fur hats and jackets, stored their water and pemmican in skins, slept in buffalo bedrolls, and seated their saddles on their sturdiest pelts. When the need arose, these items could be transformed into monetary units at trading posts for purchase of pistols, knives, ammunition, and provisions to see them through the winter. On July 31, 1834, in his instructions to Robert Evans, a partner of the Columbia River Fishing and Trading Company at Fort Hall, Oregon, contractor Nathaniel Jarvis Wyeth stated: "You will say to every white man and Indian that visits the fort that we shall continue to trade new clean robes, [muskrats] and beaver, deer, elk and antelope skins dressed, at the prices established in the tariff" ("Instructions"). The formal declaration of trade policy stated that beaver was worth six dollars per skin or five dollars per pound of pelts. Muskrats and minks were valued at five dollars per pelt or $3.50 per pound.

In 1914, Osborne Russell, another employee of Nathaniel Wyeth, recorded in *Journal of a Trapper* the annual meeting of his peers at a traditional wilderness rendezvous, where furs served the settling of debts, purchase of the blacksmith's skills, and gambling for a blend of American, French Canadian, Dutch, English, Indian, Irish, and Scottish trappers. When William H. Ashley, a fur trader based in St. Louis, arrived at the 1825 rendezvous on Henry's Fork of the Green River, Missouri, he listed in his personal accounts three packs of beaver pelts, 50 to the pack, as spendable currency along with tobacco, knives, and Indian trinkets. In 1974, novelist James Michener reprised the days of fur money in the opening chapters of *Centennial*, which described the fictive frontiersman Pasquinel trading beads, silver, cloth, and blanket to Indians along the Missouri River in exchange for valuable furs.

Blankets woven in red and white replaced fur and wampum as frontier currency, particularly for loans. At potlatches or giveaways, wealthy Pacific Coast tribe members flaunted the huge number of copper shields and blankets that they could afford to give as gifts. Around 1850, blankets were so valuable to Indians that the Hudson Bay Company traded the indigenous people of Vancouver Island 950 blankets in exchange for 200 square miles of property.

See also **Canadian money; Peter I; Russian money; trade and barter.**

SOURCES: Allen, Larry. *Encyclopedia of Money*. New York: Checkmark Books, 2001. • Collins, Miki. "Fierce and Beautiful World — Life on an Alaskan Trapline." *Pacific News Service*, April 22, 1997. • Cribb, Joe. *Money*. Toronto: Stoddart, 1990. • Davies, Glyn. *A History of Money from Ancient Times to the Present Day*. Cardiff: University of Wales Press, 1994. • Einzig, Paul. *Primitive Money*. Oxford: Pergamon Press, 1966. • "Instructions to Robert Evans." http://www.xmission.com/~drudy/mtman/html/fthall/instruct.html. • Labbé, Dominic. "The Hudson [*sic*] Bay Company Tokens." *Tasmanian Numismatist*, July 1999. • Michener, James. *Centennial*. New York: Random House, 1974. • *New Catholic Encyclopedia*. San Francisco: Catholic University of America, 1967. • Opitz, Charles J. *Odd and Curious Money*. Ocala, Fla.: First Impressions, 1986. • Russell, Osborne. *Journal of a Trapper*. Lincoln: University of Nebraska Press, 1965. • Snodgrass, Mary Ellen. *Who's Who in the Middle Ages*. Jefferson, N.C.: McFarland, 2001. • Standish, David. *The Art of Money*. San Francisco: Chronicle Books, 2000.

Gardner, Percy

Antiquities expert Percy Gardner, was a giant of the science of numismatics. The first editor of the *Journal of Hellenic Studies*, published by the Society for the Promotion of Hellenic Studies, he made a comprehensive study of Greek international currencies, ancient minting, and coin engraving. On location at Naucritus, a Greek colony in Egypt, he assisted archeologist W. M. Flinders Petrie. Gardner's analysis and interpretation of a coin he found at ancient Mesembria, a colony in Samothrace, resulted in identification of the swastika as a sun symbol and the emblem of the city, whose name translates into "noon sun."

Born in 1847, Gardner taught archeology at Cambridge and Oxford for a total of 45 years while building up the university's holdings and library works on antiquities. Simultaneous with his classroom work and encouragement of budding antiquarians, he produce massive amounts of scholarly reference material on the Hellenic world and edited a Macmillan series, *Handbooks of Archaeology and Antiquities*. His books include *The Coinage of Parthia* (1877), *Samos and Samian Coins*

(1882), *Types of Greek Coins* (1883), *Catalogue of the Coins of Greek and Scythic Kings of Bactria and India in the British Museum* (1886), and *History of Ancient Coinage* (1918). His brother, Ernest Arthur Percy, was also a field archeologist, teacher, and writer of books on early Athens and the Aegean milieu.

Percy Gardner earned accolades for publishing illustrious, clearly arranged texts accompanied by excellent plates. Colleagues lauded his sober judgment of numismatic evidence as data reflecting on history. He publicly lauded the English system of logic and analysis at prominent digs and castigated German control of ancient sites. He vocalized complaints against German-style archeology, in particular, the suspect methods of Heinrich Schliemann. Gardner formally charged German scholars with tedious fact collecting as an end in itself. In 1889, Gardner's distinguished service to numismatic science earned him the medal of the Royal Numismatic Society. He died in 1937.

See also **George Hill.**

SOURCES: Calder, William M. "Is the Mask a Hoax?" *Archaeology*, July/August 1999. • *Columbia Encyclopedia*, Edition 6. Farmington, Mich.: Gale Group, 2000. • Marr, John. "The Death of Themistocles." *Greece & Rome*, October 1995. • *Merriam-Webster's Biographical Dictionary*. Springfield, Mass.: Merriam-Webster, 1995.

Gasparro, Frank

The chief sculptor and engraver for the U.S. Mint, Frank Gasparro applied his classical training to coins from 1965 to 1981. His art on commemoratives and American coins include the John F. Kennedy half-dollar reverse, Eisenhower dollar, Congressional Medal of Honor, a World War II Victory Anniversary medal, George Washington bicentennial medal, Statue of Liberty Commemorative medal, Pearl Harbor 50th Anniversary medal, American Numismatic Association Centennial piece, Olympic U.S. five-dollar gold coin, and the K. K. Mikveh Israel Synagogue medal. He also designed coins for Guatemala, the Philippine Islands, Panama, Liberia, and the Bahamas.

A native of Philadelphia, Gasparro was born August 26, 1909, to Bernard and Rosa Gasparro. He studied at Philadelphia Industrial Arts and the Pennsylvania Academy of Fine Arts and apprenticed at the Samuel S. Fleisher Art Memorial school as a headstone carver under Giuseppe Donato, a student of Auguste Rodin. For the Federal Art Administration, Gasparro completed sculpture for Philadelphia pools and playgrounds. He went to work at the U.S. Mint in Philadelphia at age 33, leaving as evidence the initials FG on the Lincoln penny and Kennedy half-dollar. On retiring from government service, he continued to consult on coin design and taught sculpting at the Philadelphia Academy of Fine Arts. Of his work, he stated that he considered each day a challenge to work toward achievement and enjoyment.

Gasparro's most famous motif was the Lincoln Memorial penny reverse. Based on the tradition of classical Greek coinage, it featured a deity and a temple on the reverse. His was the winning suggestion out of 20 to replace the wheat sheaves on the reverse of the Lincoln penny when it came up for a 50-year replacement in 1959. He also suggested a log cabin and an ax head protruding from a tree. The final penny pleased him greatly, especially the circulation of 100 billion copies for daily use. It was the first U.S. coin to feature a double likeness on front and back because Gasparro revealed the seated statue of Abraham Lincoln within the memorial.

Gasparro involved himself personally in projects and enjoyed the Kennedy half-dollar in 1964, the Eisenhower dollar in 1971, and a commemorative issue featuring Western film star John Wayne. Despite acclaim for design, Gasparro was keenly disappointed by negative response to the Susan B. Anthony dollar, which the mint circulated in 1979. The choice replaced his original sketch of Lady Liberty with cap and streaming hair.

After Congress settled on suffragist Anthony, Gasparro labored under constant observation and criticism. He abandoned the original image of Anthony in her youth and developed a more sober, mature face — the likeness of a woman who had traveled by steamer, buggy, stage, and horseback over the nation urging women to demand full citizenship. He retired two years after the coin's failure to win public approval. His awards include the Order of Merit of the Italian Republic, the Outstanding Achievement award of the Da Vinci Art Alliance, and American Numismatic Association sculptor of the year in 1968. He died in October 2001 from complications of a fall in his hometown, Havertown, Pennsylvania.

See also **U.S. coins; U.S. Mint.**

SOURCES: "Americans for Common Cents." http://www.pennies.org/. • Clain-Stefanelli, Elvira, and Vladimir Clain-Stefanelli. *The Beauty and Lore of Coins, Currency, and Medals*. Croton-on-Hudson, N.Y.: Riverwood Publishers, 1974. • Greene, Bob. "Heads You Lose, Tails You Lose." *Esquire*, April 1981. • "Lincoln Bicentennial Commission Asked to Consider Minting New Penny." *PR Newswire*, April 7, 2000. • Martin, Douglas. "Frank Gasparro, 92, of Mint [obituary]." *New York Times*, October 3, 2001. • Reed, Mort. *Cowles Complete Encyclopedia of U.S. Coins*. New York: Cowles Book Company, 1969. • Reiter, Ed. "Circulated Coins." *New York Times*, November 4, 1984. • Reiter, Ed. "New Coin May Place Washington on Horseback." *New York Times*, February 21, 1982. • Taxay, Don. *The U.S. Mint and Coinage*. New York: Arco Publishing, 1966. • Zielinski, Graeme. "Frank Gasparro Dies [obituary]." *Washington Post*, October 4, 2001.

Gibbs, Charles

Pirate, kidnapper, and murderer Charles Gibbs established his illicit career long after the golden age of Captain Kidd and Blackbeard. From his Caribbean headquarters in Cuba, he became famous for blatant murders and the theft of thousands of dollars. In quiet times, he withdrew to New York City until the next buccaneer foray.

Born in Rhode Island in 1800, Gibbs went to sea in boyhood and sailed with privateers during the War of 1812. He established a name for belligerence and for plundering ships and, by age 21, was a full-fledged pirate. As a crewman on a pirate ship out of Argentina, he targeted vessels in the Caribbean Sea. He also mutinied aboard vessels on which he served, slew the officers, then appropriated the cash and cargo. His criminal acts included burning crews alive, dismembering his enemies, and killing 400 victims.

Wanted by the U.S. Navy, Gibbs was a prize quarry for Lieutenant Commander Lawrence Kearney, captain of the *Enterprise*, who stopped four pirate vessels in his search. After eluding Kearney for a decade, Gibbs was at last careless. The end came after he signed on with the crew of the *Vineyard* on November 1, 1830. Sailing from New Orleans through the Gulf of Mexico and the Caribbean Sea up the coast of North America, he overthrew the officers off North Carolina's Cape Hatteras on the Outer Banks, the famous graveyard of the Atlantic. After killing Captain William Thornby and Mate William Roberts and tossing their remains into the sea, Gibbs and his assistant, ship's cook Thomas G. Wansley, stole goods worth $50,000.

Gibbs sailed for Long Island, sank the *Vineyard*, and traveled toward New York City. Three of his confederates turned him in to authorities. While in custody, he bragged about his amassed fortune in plunder, embroidering fact with creative boast. A charge of murder and piracy in November 1831 preceded Gibbs's hanging on April 22, 1831, on Ellis Island, New York.

SOURCES: *Biography Resource Center*. Farmington Hills, Mich.: Gale, 2001. • Nash, Jay Robert. *Encyclopedia of World Crime*. 6 vols. Wilmette, Ill.: CrimeBooks Inc., 1990. • *Outlaws, Mobsters & Crooks: From the Old West to the Internet*. Farmington Hills, Mich.: U*X*L, 1998. • Roberts, Nancy. *Blackbeard and Other Pirates of the Atlantic Coast*. New York: John F. Blair, Publisher, 1993.

giro system

Developed before coins and currency, the giro system was the first business exchange based on abstract values. Instead of commodities, livestock, precious metals, or gems passing from buyer to seller, the parties agreed to a transfer of holdings in a palace bank, storehouse, or private institution, such as that first instituted by Yacob Egibi in Babylon 648 B.C. A subsequent setup at Alexandria in

Egypt's Ptolemaic period demonstrated the efficiency of grain banks, a warehouse depository for wealth that allowed transfer of credit from one account to the other without any physical transfer of commodities.

Around 200 B.C., banking transactions by pre-arranged agreement or by credit enriched the Greek financiers on the Greek island of Delos, the heart of the eastern Mediterranean banking world. Enriched by Macedon's trade in silver, tar, and timber, Delian financial institutions also dealt in Asian wares and slaves. They stored clients' chests of wealth at Apollo's temple, the most prominent architectural feature of the island and a secure storehouse for valuables. The abstract system of credit payment and receipt superseded direct barter or trade in convenience and security and provided a third-party record admissible in court.

SOURCES: Clain-Stefanelli, Elvira, and Vladimir Clain-Stefanelli. *The Beauty and Lore of Coins, Currency, and Medals.* Croton-on-Hudson, N.Y.: Riverwood Publishers, 1974. • Davies, Glyn. *A History of Money from Ancient Times to the Present Day.* Cardiff: University of Wales Press, 1994. • Weatherford, Jack. *The History of Money: From Sandstone to Cyberspace.* Pittsburgh, Pa.: Three Rivers Press, 1998.

Gobrecht, Christian

The third head of engraving in the history of the U.S. Mint in Philadelphia, Christian Gobrecht, a largely self-trained sculptor and diemaker, earned a place for himself in coin art for his numerous creations, including the 1836 Seated Liberty dollar and smaller denominations. His perched and flying eagles remained standard poses that influenced American sculptor Augustus Saint-Gaudens and later mintmasters J. A. Bailly, James Barton Longacre, William Barber, and Charles Barber. A native of Hanover, Pennsylvania, Gobrecht, one of seven children, was born on December 23, 1785, to the Reverend John C. Gobrecht, a German immigrant and pastor of the German Reformed Church, and Elizabeth Sands Gobrecht, member of a respected early American family that settled at the Plymouth Colony. Gobrecht apprenticed in banknote engraving at Manheim, Pennsylvania, at the firm of Murray, Draper, Fairman & Company, the pioneer of a type of steel-plate printing used on government bonds. After his employer died, vacating the indenture, Gobrecht joined the staff of a Baltimore clockmaker crafting watches, mantle clocks, type faces, newspaper logos, and name plates. While in Maryland, he married Mary Hamilton Hewes.

At age 26, Gobrecht perfected techniques of bas-relief on seals and dies while engraving banknote plates and improved on his invention of a reverse pantograph — a medal-ruling device that reduced three-dimensional carving to a two-dimensional illustration, which he used to make a portrait of Russian Tsar Alexander I. Gobrecht also invented a reed organ, camera, and talking doll and made dies for bookbinders and calico prints. He engraved the Charles Willson Peale and Massachusetts Charitable Mechanic Association medals and, in 1824, increased his fame after executing dies for the Franklin Institute.

At age 39, Gobrecht began working for the U.S. Mint and applied for the post of chief engraver following the death of Robert Scot. Mint authorities denied Gobrecht the position primarily because he was an outsider. Despite his lack of connections to staff members, in 1835, he advanced on merit alone to assistant to chief engraver William Kneass. Because Kneass suffered a stroke, Gobrecht began producing dollars and half dollars that the mint ascribed to Kneass.

Gobrecht based his 1836 Seated Liberty dollar on the line drawings by portrait artist Thomas Sully and the eagle on the reverse of the dollar from a sketch by naturalist Titian Ramsay Peale, the manager of the Philadelphia Museum. The figure of Liberty sits at ease with right hand supporting a shield displaying "Liberty" on the diagonal. Her left hand holds a stick uplifting the Phrygian cap of liberty, a standard icon in coin art. The field is plain except for "1836" at the bottom and a circle of raised dots framing the pose.

Despite charges of conceit, the coiner placed his mark with the Romanized abbreviation "C. Gobrecht F." (Christian Gobrecht *fecit* ["made it"]) on the stone beneath the figure's sandaled feet. Engraver Charles E. Barber preferred the signature to the plain initial C. Because he disliked the image, he feared that the letter would imply that he was the designer.

The Seated Liberty design faced the 1873 half-dime and silver dollar and the 1891 half-dime, dime, and quarter. Also popular was Gobrecht's Coronet Liberty Head, which graced the 1840 half-cent, cent, $2.50, five-dollar, and ten-dollar gold coins. For his 1838 Eagle, he patterned the fluid female form on the Venus with tiara pose from Benjamin West's painting *Love Conquers All* (1811). At Gobrecht's succession to the position of chief, he worked from 1840 to his death on July 23, 1844, in the production of U.S. coins.

***See also* James Barton Longacre; Robert Maskell Patterson.**

SOURCES: *Biography Resource Center*. Farmington Hills, Mich.: Gale, 2001. • Bowers, Q. David. *Adventures with Rare Coins*. Los Angeles: Bowers & Ruddy Galleries, Inc., 1979. • Bowers, Q. David. "Christian Gobrecht: American Coin Die Engraver Extraordinaire." *Rare Coin Review*, November/December 1998. • Clain-Stefanelli, Elvira, and Vladimir Clain-Stefanelli. *The Beauty and Lore of Coins, Currency, and Medals*. Croton-on-Hudson, N.Y.: Riverwood Publishers, 1974. • Johnson, Allen, ed. *Dictionary of American Biography*. New York: Charles Scribner's Sons, 1928. • Reed, Mort. *Cowles Complete Encyclopedia of U.S. Coins*. New York: Cowles Book Company, 1969. • Taxay, Don. *The U.S. Mint and Coinage*. New York: Arco Publishing, 1966. • Van Ryzin, Robert R. *Twisted Tails: Sifted Fact, Fantasy and Fiction from U.S. Coin History*. Iola, Wisc.: Krause Publications, 1995.

gold dust

Unlike nuggets, bars, and ingots, gold dust provided ease of dividing wealth into portions. In early Mesoamerica, however, the Inca of Peru had not discovered the use of metal for commerce. Instead, they traded in coca leaves and saved silver and gold for personal adornment. Father Joseph de Acosta described in *The Natural and Moral History of the Indies* (1880) a coinless monetary system akin to that of Homer and Pliny's writings. In the opinion of historian William Hinkling Prescott's *The Conquest of Mexico* (1909), it was traders from the outside world who filled quills with gold dust as a form of money.

In Japan after 900 A.D., the transportation of packets of gold dust in varied units encouraged mercantilism more easily than unwieldy bars. In the 1600s and 1700s, Filipinos and Indonesians also established a system of gold dust currency based on fluid amounts. After 1800, Tibetans founded their own system of gold dust currency evaluated by weight at the time of each transaction. Siamese traders used a similar currency consisting of standardized tubes of gold dust, according to Étienne Aymonier, author of *Voyage en Laos* (*Journey to Laos*) (1895), who witnessed the exchange of a single tube to buy a water buffalo. In Malaya, travel writer Sir R. C. Temple, author of *Notes on Currency and Coinage among the Burmese* (1919), observed that the uniform packet of gold dust was wrapped in scraps of cloth. In the same era, Ghanians assessed both weight and volume to determine the worth of gold dust. For a base measure, they calculated the amount picked up on the point of a knife. Under a ban on coinage in 1808, Brazilian miners at Mato Grosso, Rio das Mortes, Serro Frio, and Villa Rica had to carry on commerce with either gold dust or bars. They entrusted bags of precious dust to foundrymen for casting into bars and retrieved only 80 percent after authorities reserved a fifth of their take for the treasury.

When the California Gold Rush of 1848 began, a similar system served the "forty-niners," who had to evolve a method of currency on the frontier. Over $200 million in gold dust enriched the mass of newcomers, who swelled the non-native population of California in four years almost 18 times its original size of 14,000 to 250,000. In 1855 alone, some 31,000 people and 1,150 vessels reached San Francisco. In a booming economy, sacks of gold dust and unrefined gold nuggets served in the place of legal tender until prospectors could arrange for coinage. As described in Gary Kinder's *Ship of Gold in the Deep Blue*

Sea (1998), a history of the loss of the mail ship *Central America* in a hurricane off Wilmington, North Carolina, in September 1857 and its subsequent salvaging, "Business often was conducted with a 'pinch'— two pinches of dust for a sack of flour, one pinch for a shot of whiskey" (p. 480). The pinches earned the name "pioneer gold."

Sometimes purchasers had to sacrifice accuracy and value for expediency, especially when the commodity being purchased was food, ammunition, or other contributors to comfort and safety. Because amounts were irregular in shape and value like the early Roman *aes rude* ("crude bronze"), buyers and sellers had to renegotiate at each transaction. As Kinder explains, "Since miners in from the hills often hit the saloons first and had no way to pay except with gold dust, saloon owners hired bartenders with big thumbs" (*ibid.*, p. 480).

The prospector's only recourse was to entrust the precious dust to an assayer and have the gold melted and shaped into bars, octagonal slugs, or coins of equivalent value. These finished solids returned to the owner stamped with a company seal, estimate of fineness or purity, their weight in ounces, and serial numbers for identification, e. g. Justh & Hunter, 900 fine, 754.95 ounces, no. 4051. When recovered from the wreckage of the *Central America* at the end of the 20th century, this bar, formed of one miner's gold dust and worth $14,045 in 1857, was worth a quarter million dollars.

In Alaska, gold dust functioned like currency by circulating in small sealed paper packets marked with the weight of the contents. One traveler, Hudson Stuck, author of *Ten Thousand Miles with a Dog Sledge: A Narrative of Winter Travel in Interior Alaska* (1914), described packaging gold dust in vellum to resemble headache powder, writing the weight on the front, and trading the packets for fish. The envelopes, available on dollar denominations, remained in circulation for up to two years as far away as the Kobuk Valley of the Baird Mountains in Alaska's extreme northwest.

***See also Central America;* J. J. Conway; Japanese money; Captain William Kidd; piracy; Templeton Reid; Heinrich Schliemann; Wells Fargo.**

SOURCES: Allen, Larry. *Encyclopedia of Money*. New York: Checkmark Books, 2001. • Bowers, Q. David. *Adventures with Rare Coins*. Los Angeles: Bowers & Ruddy Galleries, Inc., 1979. • Bowers, Q. David. "American Gold." *American Heritage*, December 1984, 43–49. • Clain-Stefanelli, Elvira, and Vladimir Clain-Stefanelli. *The Beauty and Lore of Coins, Currency, and Medals*. Croton-on-Hudson, N.Y.: Riverwood Publishers, 1974. • Einzig, Paul. *Primitive Money*. Oxford: Pergamon Press, 1966. • Kinder, Gary. *Ship of Gold in the Deep Blue Sea*. New York: Atlantic Monthly Press, 1998. • Klare, Normand E. *The Final Voyage of the "Central America," 1857*. Spokane, Wash.: Arthur H. Clark Company, 1992. • Moorehead, Caroline. *Lost and Found: The 9,000 Treasures of Troy*. London: Penguin Books, 1994.

gold rush

Western gold rushes actualized a dream that dated to the Spanish expeditions of the late 1400s. Seeking the fabled El Dorado, *conquistadores* and their contemporaries filled journals, fiction, and poetry with pipe dreams of instant wealth in cities of gold. Following carpenter James Wilson Marshall's discovery of gold at Sutter's Mill, California, on January 24, 1848, Swiss sawyer John A. Sutter negotiated a three-year lease on twelve square miles of land from the Columa Indians. His diary entry for March 3 notes mounting exasperation with emerging gold fever:

> The first party of Mormons, employed by me left for washing and digging Gold and very soon all followed, and left me only the sick and the lame behind. And at this time I could say that everybody left me from the Clerk to the Cook. What for great Damages I had to suffer in my tannery which was just doing a profitable and extensive business, and the Vatts was left filled and a quantity of half finished leather was spoiled, likewise a large quantity of raw hides [Sutter 1932].

While the discovery was still a secret, Marshall trekked up the American River and collected a pint of nuggets. That same month, 35 percent of San Francisco's male citizens headed out for the goldfields. In France, a broadside announced, "*Mines d'Or de la Californía*" ("California Gold Mines"). Clipper ships and steamers overran the city's harbor as crews left them at anchor to trade sailing for panning.

Expert and amateur prospectors inundated the area, where gold lay in visible specks in streambeds. To separate gold from gravel, the prospector sloshed it about in a pan to extract the heaviest particles, then advanced to a more efficient system of rocking the slurry in a cradle that handled more shovelfuls of dirt at one time. By 1850, the innovative had moved on to a "long tom," a 30-foot wood sluice box that contained baffles to trap gold as a stream of water passed through. An advanced long tom, which cost $55,000 to build, stretched for over a mile.

By 1855, many miners had traded pan, cradle, and sluice box for hydraulic devices called monitors, high pressure hoses that eroded hillsides. The task was tedious and the weather in the Sierras unforgiving. At work throughout daylight hours at panning and sluicing and at rest each night in tents and hastily hammered-together shanties, many died of pneumonia, cholera, exposure, malnutrition, and knife and gunshot wounds after gamblers accused them of cheating at cards or claim jumpers stole their stash.

Eyewitness journals and articles filled in the heady emotions and gritty, sometimes deadly details, as did that of Catherine Haun, a bride who traveled the Oregon Trail and kept her observations in *A Woman's Trip Across the Plains in 1849* (1992), which noted the disparity between people's hopes and the reality of living in boom times. Another journal, Sarah Eleanor Bayliss Royce's *A Frontier Lady: Recollections of the Gold Rush and Early California* (1932), describes "chronic prospectors" (Royce 1977, 87). She tells of buying a scale and weights to measure gold dust in lieu of coins minted in standard amounts. From experience with a variety of newcomers, she commiserates with the bitter failures, who abandoned business and homes in the East and Europe to live the violence and uncertainty of the American west coast. In 1853, Southern humorist Joseph Glover Baldwin wrote about Asian adventurers in *The Flush Times of California*, published in *The Southern Literary Messenger,* and about veterans of the Mexican War in *Ebb Tide* (1864). He satirized the American bumpkins and woodsmen and an onslaught of starry-eyed Europeans, all bent on loosening "yellow-boys" from the California landscape. (Baldwin 1966, 46)

The eruption of gold bullion on the market from strikes in California, Colorado, and Oregon boosted supplies from one million to fifty million dollars. Ironically, the huge reserve contrasted a lack of usable specie for daily transactions for meals, a haircut and bath, hands of poker, and the occasional trip to a frontier bordello. To handle the onslaught of gold nuggets and dust, private companies opened assay and minting operations, beginning in 1849 with the emergence of 18 minting offices in San Francisco to pump out gold rush coins and ingots in a variety of sizes and weights. The first to offer services was the firm of Norris, Gregg, & Norris at Benicia City, a trio of Brooklyn plumbers who went West to strike pieces resembling U.S. legal tender. The firm relocated in Stockton in 1850. Others thrived in various locations:

date	*place*	*firm*	*owners*
1849	Benicia City	Norris, Gregg & Norris	Thomas H. Norris Hiram A. Norris Charles Gregg
1849	Columbus, Ohio	Columbus and California Industrial Association	John Walton J. G. Canfield
1849	Oregon City	Oregon Exchange Company	unknown
1849	Sacramento	J. S. Ormsby	J. S. Ormsby

date	*place*	*firm*	*owners*
1849	San Francisco	Cincinnati Mining & Trading Company	unknown
1849	San Francisco	Miners' Bank	unknown
1849	San Francisco	Moffat & Co.	John Little Moffat
1849	San Francisco	Pacific Company	John W. Cartwright
1849	San Francisco	Templeton Reid	Templeton Reid
1850	San Francisco	Baldwin & Company	George C. Baldwin Thomas S. Holman
1850	San Francisco	Dubosq and Company	unknown
1850	San Francisco	F. D. Kohler	F. D. Kohler
1851	San Francisco	Dunbar and Company	unknown
1851	San Francisco	Wass, Molitor & Company	Samuel Wass Agoston Molitor
1851	San Francisco	Schultz and Company	unknown
1852	San Francisco	Kellogg & Humbert	Augustus Humbert John Glover Kellogg
1853	San Francisco	Moffat & Co.	G. F. Richter
1854	San Francisco	Kellogg & Hewston	John Glover Kellogg John Hewston
1855	Sacramento	Blake & Agrell	Gorham Blake
1855	Sacramento Marysville	Harris, Marchand & Co.	Harvey Harris Desiré C. Marchand
1855	San Francisco Marysville	Justh & Hunter	Emanuel Justh Solomon Hunter
1855	San Francisco	Kellogg & Humbert	John Glover Kellogg Augustus Humbert
1856	San Francisco Marysville	Henry Hentsch Assay Office	Henry Hentsch Francis Berton S. C. Wass
1859	Park County, Colorado	John Parsons & Co.	Dr. John Parsons
1860	San Francisco	Kellogg, Hewston & Co.	John Glover Kellogg J. H. Stearns
1861	Georgia Gulch, Colorado	J. J. Conway & Company	J. J. Conway
1861	Tarryall Mines, Colorado	John Parsons & Company	John Parsons
1866	San Francisco	San Francisco Assaying & Refining Works	John Glover Kellogg

Until the establishment of the San Francisco Mint in 1854, government regulation was the work of the State Assay Office of California and the United States Assay Office, a makeshift frontier operation.

Under contract from the U.S. Treasury in 1851, Moffat & Company, headed by assayer John Little Moffat, and agent Augustus (or August) Humbert, a watchmaker from New York, founded the U.S. Assay Office of Gold, a provisional office contracted by the U.S. Treasury. The minting operation turned out convenient octagonal gold slugs, nicknamed "bricks" or "adobes." These coins were official, but not enough to meet the need of everyday business.

Demand kept moneyers in business and created peripheral commissions for medals and engraving. Baldwin & Company sold balances, magnets, and magnifying lenses in addition to producing huge numbers of low coin denominations — five, ten, and twenty dollars — bearing the designs of engraver Albert Kuner. Justh, a Hungarian immigrant, enticed business his way by circulating newly struck gold eagles.

The unforeseen collapse of Baldwin & Company was the work of James King, a political muckraker writing for the *Daily Globe* in Washington, D.C. Arriving in San Francisco in late 1848, he determined that he would rather buy, sell, or lend cash than dig for gold. As a partner in Samuel J. Hensley's bank and other firms, King came to grief after his manager embezzled his savings. To recoup his losses, King created a get-rich-quick scam by informing Augustus Humbert that Baldwin & Company was short-weighting coins. In 1851, King circulated the facts to newspapers, creating a rush to buy the suspect coins at a 20 percent discount.

Readers expressed outrage at private moneyers who struck underweight coins and named Baldwin as one source to avoid. The outcry forced merchants to stop honoring the coins at full value. A follow-up in the *Pacific News* noted that Baldwin's employees departed by the steamer *Panama* in April 1851 and implied that their pockets bulged with profit. The luckless had two choices — sell their fraudulent Baldwin coins at a discount or melt them down for bullion. By the end of the year, few of Baldwin's coins circulated on the West Coast.

In Colorado, one newly minted coin preserved for history the mechanics of changing nuggets to coin. In 1861, John Parsons & Company struck a five-dollar coin picturing an ore crusher. The rectangular frame housed five arms that the operator lowered by turning a crank to smash ores from the nearby Tarryall mines. Colorado mintmaster J. J. Conway joined Clark, Gruber & Company and John Parsons & Company in turning ore from the Pike's Peak Gold Rush into coin. Issued in the denominations of $2.50, five-, ten-, and 20-dollars, Conway's coins were crude attempts to standardize the exchange of raw gold from local strikes for goods and services.

An 1896 strike at the Klondike on the western Canadian frontier buoyed another rush along the Yukon river. Some 30,000 newcomers scrambled over the frozen terrain, spawning Dawson City and raising Canada to third place among the world's goldfields. In 1898, Jasper N. "Jap" Wyman described the events he witnessed while traveling for the Galesburg-Alaska Mining and Developing Company in *Gold Dust*, published in 1988 as *Journey to the Koyukuk*. As his expedition were ending a harrowing journey, they passed 25 newcomers in mid–May leaving Arctic City to push upland to prospect for gold. With some bitterness and much disillusion at failed get-rich-quick schemes, Wyman wrote, "I am not afraid, but it is not pleasant, see?" (p. 124).

***See also Central America;* J. J. Conway; James Barton Longacre; *manilla;* Templeton Reid; Heinrich Schliemann; Charles Cushing Wright.**

SOURCES: Allen, Larry. *Encyclopedia of Money*. New York: Checkmark Books, 2001. • Baldwin, Joseph Glover. *The Flush Times of California*. Athens: University of Georgia Press, 1966. • Bowers, Q. David. *Adventures with Rare Coins*. Los Angeles: Bowers & Ruddy Galleries, Inc., 1979. • Bowers, Q. David. "American Gold." *American Heritage*, December 1984, 43–49. • Clain-Stefanelli, Elvira, and Vladimir Clain-Stefanelli. *The Beauty and Lore of Coins, Currency, and Medals*. Croton-on-Hudson, N.Y.: Riverwood Publishers, 1974. • Haun, Catherine. *A Woman's Trip across the Plains in 1849*. In *Women's Diaries of the Westward Journey*. New York: Schocken, 1992. • Kagin, Donald H. *Private Gold Coins and Patterns of the United States*. New York: Arco Publishing, 1981. • Royce, Sarah. *A Frontier lady: Recollections of the Gold Rush and Early California*. Lincoln: University of Nebraska Press, 1977. • Snodgrass, Mary Ellen. *Encyclopedia of Frontier Literature*. Santa Barbara, Calif.: ABC-Clio, 1997. • Sutter, John August. *The Diary of Johann August Sutter*. San Francisco: Grabhorn Press, 1932. • Tebben, Gerald. "On My Way to California." *Coin World*, July 19, 1999, pp. 74–76. • Wyman, J. N. *Journey to the Koyukuk*. Missoula, Mont.: Pictorial Histories Publishing, 1988.

gold standard

From the beginning of coinage in 700 B.C., governments used gold as the traditional standard of value. They based their choice on a bright, workable mineral that was free of decay and corrosion. From mines in Lydia, Mexico, Nubia, Peru, South Africa, and the Yukon, the flow of ore fueled intense scrambles to unearth the valuable ores that artisans altered into coins. Minted in Rome and the Byzantine Empire into the Middle Ages, gold was the metal of choice in Florence for the *florin*, the most popular coin of the Renaissance. England emulated the *florin* with its own version, the guinea, which Charles II introduced in 1663.

Silver lost its hold in 1821, when Great Britain chose gold over silver as its monetary standard. The royal treasury set a model of monometallism on which Austria-Hungary, France, Germany, Holland, Russia, and Scandinavia based their national money. As paper money gained popularity, it carried the promise that it was convertible to gold on demand from gold reserves that backed central banking systems. Supporting the conversion to the gold standard were mid–19th century gold strikes in California, Australia, and the Canadian Yukon. In 1871, Wilhelm I of Prussia, regulated the value of the true *mark*, worth 100 *pfennige* with the Prussian gold standard, which ended a fragmented Germany system of seven currencies serving 30 independent states.

The drift from the gold standard began during the Napoleonic era, when French banks ceased redeeming paper notes with gold. The eventual lapse in all countries coincided with the outbreak of World War I. As nations reverted to inconvertible paper money and battled restrictions on gold export, adherence to a gold standard was an unrealistic burden. By 1928, gold returned to its former status, but foundered because of the scarcity of ore. Most nations altered policies to a gold-exchange standard supplemented with U.S. dollars and British pounds.

Gold continued to rule U.S. finance, primarily because of gold strikes in Africa, Alaska, and Australia. During World War I, the gold standard foundered as nations printed more paper bills to finance their involvement, but failed to meet obligations of deposit in gold. England's difficulties in importing gold reduced the gold standard to only five percent reserves. After the armistice, nations battled fluctuating exchange rates as they attempted to maintain a gold standard. England hung on to gold from its adoption as a standard in 1816 until 1931, when its treasurers abandoned the standard of redemption.

As a result of the Great Depression, in 1934, the U.S. Congress revoked the gold standard, which the Coinage Act of 1873 had established. Authorities reclaimed all of the nation's monetary gold, including bullion and coins held by Federal Reserve banks. The Bureau of Engraving and Printing released the largest unit of money in 1934 with the $100,000 Gold Certificate. Issued for three weeks, from mid–December until January 9, 1935, the certificates, circulated from the Treasurer of the United States to Federal Reserve Banks as abstract representations of gold bullion on hand. Unavailable to individual citizens, the notes served only banks.

Globally, central banks stopped issuing gold coins in exchange for bank notes and ceased redeeming notes in gold bullion. Britain, Canada, and other governments suspended requirements that the central bank match its note and deposit liabilities with gold. By 1937, no nation remained on a full gold standard. From 1945 to 1971, the world monetary system was based on a dollar standard in place of the former gold standard, which had required gold bullion on hand to back paper dollars. In 1971, the United States halted the conversion of paper bills to gold, a move that fueled inflation. Gradually, treasury experience with control of prices and wages increased national confidence that the gold standard had outlived its usefulness.

See also* William Jennings Bryan; *Wizard of Oz.

SOURCES: Allen, Larry. *Encyclopedia of Money*. New York: Checkmark Books, 2001. • Davies, Glyn. *A History of Money from Ancient Times to the Present Day*. Cardiff: University of Wales Press, 1994. • Hallwood, Paul, Ronald MacDonald, and Ian W. Marsh, "An Assessment of the Causes of the Abandonment of the Gold Standard by the U.S. in 1933," *Southern Economic Journal*, October 2000, p. 448. • Weatherford, Jack. *The History of Money: From Sandstone to Cyberspace*. Pittsburgh, Pa.: Three Rivers Press, 1998.

Goltzius, Hubertus

Dutch artist, printer, and coin engraver Hubertus Goltzius, the father of ancient numismatics, enhanced his knowledge of coins by traveling Europe to examine 950 collections. Born in 1526, he learned the basics of art, copper engraving, and woodcut. An early numismatist later associated with his nephew, Dutch artist Hendrik Goltzius, he applied duo-tone illustrations of coins to books describing specie from the Roman Empire. In one portrait book, *Les Images presque de tous les empereurs depuis C. Iulius Caesar jusques à Charles V* (*Nearly All the Portraits of the Emperors from Gaius Julius Caesar Up to Charles V*), published at Antwerp in 1559, he featured chiaroscuro prints. He followed at Bruges from 1563 to 1579 with a print survey of ancient coins, a handbook treasured by numismatists. Two centuries later, he earned the scorn of antique coin expert Joseph Hilarius Eckhel of Vienna for careless histories, inconsistency, and outright forgery and fraud.

See also **Joseph Hilarius Eckhel.**

SOURCES: *New Catholic Encyclopedia.* San Francisco: Catholic University of America, 1967. • "Numismatics in the Age of Grolier," http://www.grolierclub.org/ExNumismatics.htm.

Görtz, Georg Heinrich, Baron von

A martyr to financial innovation, Georg Heinrich, Baron von Görtz (also von Freiherr) of Franconia introduced a promissory currency backed by the royal treasury of Sweden, a forerunner of modern money systems. An economist and ambassador, he served Frederick V by negotiating an alliance between Holstein-Gottorp and Sweden. As a consultant to King Charles XII of Sweden, in 1714, during peace initiatives to Peter I the Great of Russia, von Görtz advanced to chief minister. In 1715, he issued siege money — 20 million fiduciary copper tokens dubbed "Görtz *dalers*," which coiners stamped with mythic and symbolic figures. They were redeemable for precious metals at the end of the conflict.

Because the king refused to moderate his military stance, he shifted blame for the protracted Northern War and depreciation of Swedish currency onto von Görtz. When the king was shot through the head during an invasion of Norway in 1718, his sister, reigning Queen Ulrica Eleanora, had von Görtz decapitated at Stockholm as a traitor. Her decision rid her of a supporter of her rival, the duke of Holstein-Gottorp. At the same time, the execution negated past financial arrangements without maligning the dead monarch. Left unsecured were the promissory coppers that had financed the king's army of 60,000.

SOURCES: Clain-Stefanelli, Elvira, and Vladimir Clain-Stefanelli. *The Beauty and Lore of Coins, Currency, and Medals.* Croton-on-Hudson, N.Y.: Riverwood Publishers, 1974. • Simpson, John. "Arresting a Diplomat." *History Today,* January 1985, pp. 32–37.

Great Seal of the United States

First displayed on the back of a 1935 one-dollar Federal Reserve note, the Great Seal of the United States resides at the Department of State in Washington, D.C. For citizens and nations trading with Americans, the seal symbolizes national beliefs in democracy. A five-member committee was assigned on July 4, 1776, to design a suitable symbol of sovereignty for the new nation. Contributing to the debate over an appropriate symbol were John Adams, Benjamin Franklin, and Thomas Jefferson.

The commission pictured Lady Liberty holding a staff topped with a Phrygian slave's cap, a Roman symbol of the freedman shaped like a turban. Opposite Liberty, blindfolded Justice held a balance-beam scale. Between them stood a heraldic shield beneath the eye of God, a symbol common to the French *sou* and the German *thaler,* and above a banner reading "*E Pluribus Unum.*" A double circle surrounded them: the inner circle held the shields of the thirteen colonies in order of their settlement with their names abbreviated as D, C, G, M, MR, NC, NH, NJ, NY, P, RI, SC, and V for Delaware, Connecticut, Georgia, Massachusetts, Maryland, New Hampshire, New Jersey, New York, Pennsylvania, Rhode Island, South Carolina, and Virginia. The outer circle contained the bold legend "Seal of the United States of America" and the date, MDCCLXXVI. On the back, the shield pictured a crowned pharaoh in his chariot raising his sword toward the Red Sea, where a pillar of fire guided Moses and the Israelites out of bondage in Egypt. The motto proclaimed, "Rebellion to Tyrants Is Obedience to God."

A second committee tackled problems with design on March 25, 1780. The combined labors of William Churchill Houston of New Jersey, James Lovell of Massachusetts, and John Morin Scott of Virginia produced a flaming shield held by a Roman soldier and Liberty, who bore an olive branch. A constellation of thirteen stars represented the original colonies above a scroll exclaiming "*Bello Vel Paci*" ("[Let There Be] Peace or War). Surrounding the scenario was the legend "The Great Seal of the United States" without a date. On the reverse, Liberty sat on a high-backed chair and held a staff topped with the Phrygian slave's cap. Above, the word "*Semper*" ("Always") balanced the date below, MDCCLXXVI.

The third committee went to work on May 14, 1782, chaired by Arthur Middleton of South Carolina, members John Rutledge of South Carolina and Elias Boudinot of New Jersey plus William Barton, who had experience in numismatic heraldry. They proposed the female figure of Liberty and the male figure in colonial dress flanking a shield topped with an eagle and flag. Marking the seal was a low banner reading "*Virtus Sola Invicta*" ("Only Strength Unconquered") and an upper banner marked "*In Vindiciam Libertatis*" ("In Defense of Liberty"). The reverse, picturing an unfinished pyramid topped with the eye of God was encircled with two legends: "*Deo Favente*" ("God favoring") along with "*Perennis*" ("Forever").

On June 20, 1782, the final drawing took shape. Secretary of Congress Charles Thomson, another heraldry expert, visualized the face of the seal with red and white bands representing the 13 original colonies. To unite the image, he added an expanse of blue representing Congress.

In the seal's present state, the colors duplicate the American flag, which displays white for purity, red for courage, and blue for justice and vigilance. The national shield or escutcheon is displayed on the chest of the American eagle. Clutched in its talons are 13 arrows, one for each of the colonies. An olive branch balances the warlike talons with a symbol of peace. The heavenly constellation represents the new nation taking its place in a formation of world states. A streamer scrolling from the eagle's beak contains the Latin motto "*E Pluribus Unum*," meaning "Out of Many, One" or "One (Nation) Out of Many (States)." As featured on the title page of the *Gentleman's Magazine*, published in London after 1732, the motto may have caught the attention of readers in the colonies, including the seal's creators.

The reverse side of the seal continues the symbolism of nationhood. An unfinished 13-step pyramid bears the Roman number MDCCLXXVI, the year of the nation's founding. The peak at top takes the shape of God's eye, a mythic glance radiating glory. Above the pyramid appears the Latin inscription "*Annuit Coeptis*" ("[Providence] Favored the Beginnings"); on the banner below, "*Novus Ordo Seclorum*" ("A New Order of the Ages"). The finished seal resembles the presidential seal, which features the eagle within a circlet of stars and the legend in bold capitals "Seal of the President of the United States." Added to the original eagle are thirteen rays and thirteen stars.

The Great Seal has impacted national money. In 1798, U.S. sculptor Gilbert Stuart applied a modified version of the Great Seal to the back of the dollar coin. In 1804, U.S. Mint engraver John Reich graced the back of the quarter with a motif based on the seal. He deviated from the standard arrangement with the 1815 quarter, which displayed the eagle in an asymmetric pose. The first paper money to incorporate the Great Seal of the United States was the one-dollar Silver Certificate, which the treasury issued in 1935. The bill also featured Martha Washington in the only female portrait used on a U.S. currency note.

***See also E Pluribus Unum;* Thomas Jefferson; paper money; *sou;* U.S. Bureau of Engraving and Printing; U.S. Treasury.**

SOURCES: "The Bureau of Engraving and Printing." http://www.bep.treas.gov/. • Clain-Stefanelli, Elvira, and Vladimir Clain-Stefanelli. *The Beauty and Lore of Coins, Currency, and Medals.* Croton-on-Hudson, N.Y.: Riverwood Publishers, 1974. • "France, 1793." http://www.napoleonicmedals.org/coins/fran93-2.htm. • "The Great Seal of the United States." http://greatseal.com/. • "The Great Seal of the United States." Washington, D.C.: U.S. Department of State Dispatch, 1996. • Reed, Mort. *Cowles Complete Encyclopedia of U.S. Coins.* New York: Cowles Book Company, 1969. • Reinfeld, Fred. *Treasury of the World's Coins.* New York: Sterling Publishing, 1953.

Greek coins

The use of precious metals in Greece as monetary units dates into prehistory and appears in Homer's *Iliad* (ca. 850 B.C.) alongside

This Ionian coin from 650 B.C. was a boon to traders between Mesopotamia and the coastal cities of Greece and formed the basis of city-state financial systems. (Guy Clark, Ancient Coins and Antiquities, Norfolk, Virginia)

In 370 B.C., the obverse of a Greek *stater* minted in southern Turkey pictured two wrestlers locked in an arm-to-arm struggle; the opposite displays a slinger. (Guy Clark, Ancient Coins and Antiquities, Norfolk, Virginia)

an exchange system based on the value of oxen. In discussion of wealth, the poet names the *talanta*, the two-panned balance beam scale, as a synonym for units of gold. Before

The profiles of gods and goddesses bore distinct Greek features, like this coin from 317 B.C. bearing the image of Persephone, goddess of the Underworld. (Guy Clark, Ancient Coins and Antiquities, Norfolk, Virginia)

This Ionian *stater*, stamped in 650 B.C., features the geometric style that dominated monetary design before the Greeks valued coins for art as well as for commerce. (Guy Clark, Ancient Coins and Antiquities, Norfolk, Virginia)

formal coinage, the inconvenient, amorphous ore had to be weighed during each transaction to determine value. In Chapter XVIII, Homer refers to the *talanta* on Achilles's shield as a prize, perhaps in reference to earlier gold ingots or silver lumps found at Knossos, Crete, or to the iron meat-grilling spits on which sheep and oxen were roasted. These culinary tools were useful both as raw material and as currency. The spits recur in references to gifts donated to the gods at temples.

In the early years of authorized currency, the Greeks valued coins for art as well as for commerce, portable wealth for the paying of

A Greek coin from Boeotia, 371 B.C., features the Boeotian oxhide shield indented with two handholds and, on the reverse, a tall double-handled urn, a symbol of plenty. (Guy Clark, Ancient Coins and Antiquities, Norfolk, Virginia)

Tarentine silver coins like this one struck in southern Italy in 272 B.C. reached a height of beauty with images of the mythic founder Taras astride a dolphin, which bore him safely to shore after a shipwreck. (Guy Clark, Ancient Coins and Antiquities, Norfolk, Virginia)

the bride price and other monetary obligations, political propaganda, and elements of superstition and veneration of Greek gods. Those seekers visiting the oracle of Hermes at Pharae in Achaea placed their bronze coin to the statue's right. At Paphos, those seeking the assistance of the love goddess Aphrodite tossed money to her statue in more casual fashion, as though rewarding a prostitute. An additional festival issue promoted a gathering at Pompeiopolis in 163 A.D. and throughout Asia Minor during Roman rule.

The accumulation of treasuries at temples was beneficial to the budgeting of general upkeep and repairs, such as the remodeling of

Because coins lacked dating and mint marks, archeologists deduced their origin from symbols. This coin from 390 B.C. bears a honeybee, the symbol of Ephesus. (Guy Clark, Ancient Coins and Antiquities, Norfolk, Virginia)

Amphiaraus's shrine at the holy well of Oropus in the third century B.C. from the meltdown of personalized gold and silver, to which suppliants had attached labels listing their names. Additional proof of mintage for religious or semi-religious purposes derives from the bronze coins at Eleusis in the 300s B.C., Olympian coins struck at Elis for the Hellenic games, and a special issue of the Delphic Amphictyonic Council, a confederacy of twelve tribes sending two deputies each to promote peace at a spring session at Delphi and a fall meeting at Thermopylae. The innovative coiner Philip II of Macedon became a member of the council in 346 B.C.

The art of die carving grew directly out of the making of sealstones and signet rings, carved either into or above the plane surface of bone, ivory, or wood with a drill and picks and used to mark a personal cipher on the hot wax that closed a scrolled letter, will, or other official document. A model coin die stamped on the island of Peparethus around 500 B.C. bears a graceful winged god in mid-stride with laurel wreaths in each hand. Set in a square frame with beaded edging, the coin was the work of an artisan who stamped a die into

In 445 B.C., an artisanal coin struck on the island of Aegina bore the likeness of the sea turtle, an image that took on national significance. (Guy Clark, Ancient Coins and Antiquities, Norfolk, Virginia)

amorphous metal disks. The Greeks initiated the custom of tossing these elegant coins into fountains to propitiate divinities of sacred waters. Another of their symbolic gestures was the positioning of a coin in the cornerstone of architectural sites, a carryover from human and animal sacrifice to assure the builder that the structure would last.

One coin, the silver *dimareteion*, preserved as a mode of propaganda the victory at Himera, a Greek frontier town in Sicily. When Hamilcar, the Carthaginian commander, sailed north from the African coast to menace the Greek tyrant Theron in late summer of 480 B.C., the invasion threatened Himera. Island colonists defeated the insurgents by allying with Gelon, the tyrant of Syracuse. As a

This coin struck on the island of Lesbos in 100 B.C. exhibits an emerging realism that replaced the more stylized features on earlier portrait pieces. (Guy Clark, Ancient Coins and Antiquities, Norfolk, Virginia)

token of thanksgiving and self-congratulation, Gelon commissioned the lovely *decadrachm*. Ironically, the Carthaginians held a grudge against Himera and returned in 409 B.C. to obliterate it utterly.

Another commemorative scene depicted the erection of the Colossus at Rhodes, a victory symbol marking the defeat of the Macedonian invader Demetrius Poliorcetes in 305–304 B.C. To express civic pride, in 290 B.C., the Rhodians engineered a titanic bronze-plated statue of the sun god arrayed in glory and lifting a torch. Designed by Chares of Lindus, the 90-foot statue, which towered over Rhodes harbor, was listed among the Seven Wonders of the World. Toppled by an earthquake around 225 B.C., the statue survives only in ancient coins, the descriptions of a few eyewitnesses, and the design of the Statue of Liberty, modeled in France on a pose by Auguste-Charlotte Bartholdi and shipped to New York Harbor in 1886.

The evolution of coins as standardized exchange tokens paralleled a similar concept in Asia Minor. At Knossos before 1000 B.C., merchants and customers exchanged unminted silver pellets called "dumps." The first real coins derived from the island of Aegina south of Piraeus harbor after 750 B.C. The uniface coins, Europe's first specie, varied in size to represent different denominations. Unlike coinage of Asia Minor, Aeginetan coiners struck money from pure silver, which they acquired from the nearby isles and from the Laurion mine south of Athens. In addition to the island's silver standard, the money system produced two more firsts, the *obeliskoi* (iron meat spits) and *drachma*, the backbone of Greek coinage.

Minted by abundant slave labor, the first hammered disks replaced the *obeliskoi* when the tyrant Pheidon of Argos standardized weights and measures and initiated rudimentary coinage in the mid-seventh century B.C. His *obeliskoi* became state gifts to the goddess Hera at her temple, a common storehouse for valuables and holy vessels. Whether he circulated these metal bars as a true currency is unclear. His government-guaranteed coins served as models for Athens, Chalcis, Corinth, and Eritrea.

The Athenians minted the gold *drachma*, derived from the Greek *drax* ("handful"), in the mid–600s B.C. At Athens, where the state held a monopoly on coinage, a furnace and water tank in the Agora accommodated workers hammering bronze disks. Artisans enhanced metal money by striking both sides, the world's first examples of obverse/reverse coins. The coin remained the Greek monetary standard for 2,650 years. During its long life, it circulated as far east as Afghanistan and influenced the design of the Arabic *dirhan*. The Greek *drachma* became more convenient after the famed Attic lawgiver Solon studied the gold money of Croesus of Lydia and reduced coin weight in Athens around 575 B.C. to make the *drachma* less cumbrous and more practical for commerce. From this specie derived another first, the origination of fixed relationships among denominations.

Greek city-states emulated the original coins almost immediately. Introduced to coinage during the reign of Periander, Corinth began rivaling Aeginetan and Attic coinage in 655 B.C. and introduced double-sided coins and denominations marked by individual designs. The Corinthian mint struck a *drachma* with the shape of winged Pegasus, the magical flying horse of the mythic hero Bellerophon, and a *stater* picturing Aphrodite, goddess of love and beauty. According to Barclay V. Head's landmark handbook, *A Guide to the Principal Coins of the Greeks* (1959), coin art evolved from extreme crudeness in form and expression of action to a clear definition of body, which was angular and stiff. He adds:

> The eye of the human face is always drawn, even when in profile, as if seen from the front, the hair is generally represented by lines of minute dots, the mouth wears a fixed and formal smile [p. 2].

For all its anatomical shortcomings, the design presented both strength and delicate touch, virtues that were the hallmarks of Greek sculpture during the Golden Age, the fifth century B.C.

After 650 B.C., artisanal coins struck at Aegina, Chalcis, and Eritrea bore likenesses of deer, lions, sea turtles, and tortoises stamped on one side only. The choice of image took on national meanings, as with the Carian lion, Andrean vase, squid of Ceos, Athenian beetle, and Aeginetan turtle. In contrast, the Spartans under Lycurgus ceased shopping with precious metals in 600 B.C. to forestall the evils of greed and thwart robbers. According to the biographer Plutarch, Lycurgus replaced gold and silver coins with heavy iron bars or disks. In the ruler's opinion, any would-be thief would need a yoke of oxen to remove any chest of iron worth stealing. The establishment of iron money also discouraged trade with neighbor city-states and assured Sparta's cultural isolation.

Throughout Greece, coins became the lifeblood of taxation and the source of funds, commodities, and forced labor for the state treasury. The advance from barter to metal coinage encouraged levies, particularly those that underwrote equipment and soldier pay during wars. The enactment of a *metoikion* (poll tax) of six *drachmas* for a woman and twelve for a male citizen plus an *eisphora* (property tax), *eponia* (excise tax) on local commerce transacted at the agora and at city docks and gates, and *leitourgia* ("public duty") to underwrite public amusements and festivals attests to the complexity of city finance and the constant need for currency. In addition, the wealthy contributed the *epidosis*, a voluntary payment to the state coffers during war. Collecting these moneys and valuables were tax farmers, private contractors who bid for the privilege. Their corrupt dealing earned the hatred and loathing of honest citizens.

Around 595 B.C., an artful metal coinage bearing the double-struck imprint of royal lion and bull heads reached Greece from Lydia and Ionia, where coins had flourished from about 680 B.C. as a boon to traders between Mesopotamia and the coastal cities of Greece. The coins that formed the basis of city-state financial systems came in several denominations based on the *obol*, which was worth one iron meat spit and compensated a worker for a half day's labor:

name	*type*	*value*
hemitartemorion	silver	¼ *obol*
chalkoi	copper	1/12 *obol*
trihemitartemorion	silver	⅜ *obol*
hemioboloon	silver	½ *obol*
obol	silver	1 iron spit
triobol	silver	3 *obols*
drachma	silver	6 *obols* or 6 spits
didrachma	silver	12 *obols*
tetradrachma	silver	24 *obols*
stater	silver, gold, electrum	2–3 *drachmas* or 12–18 *obols*
mina		600 *obols* or 100 *drachmas*
talent		60 minas or 3,600 *obols*

Coins made from silver, gold, or electrum, a blend of the two metals, were handy substitutes for trade in kind, except for large purchases, which were calculated in silver weighed in *talents*. Because coins lacked dating and mint marks, archeologists deduced their chronology from clues such as the location of coins buried in the foundation of the Temple of Artemis at Ephesus in 560 B.C. and the beetle of the Athenian rule of 540 B.C.

One area where moneys were essential to prosperity was the colony of Tarentum in southern Italy. The local economy thrived from the profits on the fluid of marine snails called *Murex brandaris*, which occupy rocky shallows and feed on other mollusks through long snouts. Tarentines collected the yellow exudate, the source of royal Tyrian purple, a valued dye for ceremonial robes and drapings. Furthering trade from 500 B.C., Tarentine silver coins reached a height of beauty with images of the mythic founder Taras astride a dolphin, which bore him safely to shore after a shipwreck. By 425 B.C., the motif had shifted to equestrian scenes.

By the Greek Golden Age, the prevailing love of beauty in all phases of life marked native coinage. Specie bore the high relief markings and exterior framing incised by professional engravers and cameo makers, as found in the flying pig on silver struck at Ialysus on the island of Rhodes and the serpent on a silver *tetradrachm* from Pergamum. The sea turtle and subsequent tortoise that faced silver *staters* from Aegina demonstrated the shift in island powers after the decline of the Aeginetan navy. The profiles of gods and goddesses bore distinct Greek features and mythological trappings, including ivy leaves, grape clusters, *amphorae* (storage jars), weapons, monarchs' faces in the poses of deities, and appropriate inscriptions.

For Attic bullion, the tyrant Peisistratus mined silver ore from the Laurion quarries 65 miles south of Athens overlooking the Aegean Sea and manufactured the first Greek owl coins, which bore the sacred symbol of Athena, the maiden-goddess of wisdom and protector and patroness of the city. The symbol derived from a divine omen, an owl flying over Marathon at the great battle of 490 B.C., when the Greeks overcame the invasion force of Darius, king of Persia. The comic playwright Aristophanes reprised the event in *The Birds* (414 B.C.) with the exultation: "How we drove the ranks before us ere the close of eventide as we closed an owl flew o'er us and the gods were on our side" [Pollak 2001, p. 34]. The owl coins set a fashion in money art of adorning only one face with the silhouette of a divine or notable person.

A rich seam of around 160 million ounces of silver enabled Athens to rise to unprecedented power and wealth. When enslaved miners unearthed a richer lode seven years after the victory at Marathon, Themistocles directed state riches toward a new concept in civic readiness — a standing navy of 200 battleships manned by professional sailors at the harbor of Piraeus. Organized primarily as a defense against Aegina, the armada preserved Athenians from a Persian invasion in 480 B.C. at the battle of Salamis. After the defeat of the Persian king Xerxes and his navy, Athenians flourished from a boost to state pride and from the capture of Persian coins, which advanced the city to a cultural mecca. In 478 B.C., officials drew neighboring city-states into the Delian League, a confederacy led by Cimon, a statesman and empire builder. League officials collected dues in cash, ships, or guaranteed military service.

A Greek coin from 214 B.C. exhibits two views of Artemis, the goddess of chastity and the hunt. The reverse depicts her in short tunic, field gear, and drawn bow with a hunting hound springing toward the kill. (Guy Clark, Ancient Coins and Antiquities, Norfolk, Virginia)

The collection of customs and tolls on exported and imported goods generated additional wealth for Athens as well as Corinth, the city rising on the narrow neck of land separating Greece from the Peloponnesus. The standard two to five percent of assessed value made harbor control lucrative. At the Hellespont, Athenian civil servants began collecting ten percent in duties after 410 B.C. and continued for a quarter century.

To simplify these complex financial dealings, the Greeks needed portable wealth. Over the next quarter century, two-sided *tetradrachm* coins marked with Athena and the trusty Greek owl dominated mint design on the island of Aegina and in Athens and Corinth. The owl coin was so common that Greeks popularized a cynical saying about "taking owls to Athens," indicating a futile duplication of efforts similar to "coals to Newcastle" [Durant 1939, p. 273]. The Athenian treasury could not vary the owl because of its acceptance as an international medium of ex-

In the fifth century B.C., Greek owl coins bore the sacred symbol of Athena, the maiden-goddess of wisdom and protector and patroness of Athens. The coins set a fashion in money art of adorning only one surface with a human silhouette. This model was minted in 449 B.C. (Guy Clark, Ancient Coins and Antiquities, Norfolk, Virginia)

change as far away as Sicily, Spain, Syria, and Egypt, where a hoard of 10,000 owl coins was unearthed in 1946.

Engravers pictured a number of variations on Athena's big-eyed likeness, including the unadorned helmet the goddess wore on the coinage following the first Persian invasion of 490 B.C., and the wreath of victory commemorating the Athenian win over the Persians at the battle of Salamis, a massive coinage that supported trade of the growing Athenian state. While the fusty Spartans continued to circulate only their original *obeloi*, Athenian *trapezitai* (money changers) did a swift business in world coinage, thriving from April into October, when the season of safe sailing ended. At the first fall wind, the market quieted, then closed altogether as porters, lenders, and speculators retreated to their homes to wait out the winter in comfort.

The popularity of Athenian coins is obvious in copies of the famous owl by Arabian, Egyptian, Judean, Mesopotamian, Parthian, and Turkish mints and even by the crude Celtic workshops of Britain. Adding to the world's knowledge of Greek coins of this era was a hoard of 1,661 coins that treasure hunters excavated in 1984 in Elmali, Turkey. Of the cache, 14 rare Athenian *decadrachms* appeared to be commemoratives commissioned in honor of the Athenian victory over the Persians around 468 B.C. This period, according to Barclay V. Head of the British Museum, produced the high art of numismatic history marked by drama, pathos, charm, rich ornamentation, and refined execution.

A second wave of Greek coins emerged from colonial mints, beginning at Naxos with grape-decked coins and a seated image of a bearded, rotund Silenus with wine crater in hand, struck around 460 B.C. The designer scattered letters over the face spelling "Naxion." An innovation in coinage was the result of experimentation by Pythagoras, the Samian philosopher and educator who had founded an academy at Croton in 532 B.C. His contribution was the incuse die, a striking face that produced a bas-relief or raised image on the face and the same pattern in reverse sunk into the metal on the back side.

An innovation in coinage was the work of Pythagoras, the Samian philosopher and educator who invented the incuse die. When applied to the back of a coin blank, the striking face produced a bas-relief or raised image like the grain head on the front of this coin minted in 510 B.C. at Lucania, a Greek settlement in southern Italy. (Guy Clark, Ancient Coins and Antiquities, Norfolk, Virginia)

The concept of uniform coinage spread to additional symbolic designs — Messina's dolphins, Akragas's crab, Croton's tripod of Apollo and Zeus's eagle, Stiela's man-faced bull, Metapontum's grainhead, and the racing chariots and three-legged triskelion of Syracusa, where coiners boasted of their rule of the three-cornered island of Sicily. After 480 B.C., Gelon reportedly coined a winning team of four chariot steeds from gold that his wife Demarete collected from the jewelry of her handmaidens. Their donation was a generous act intended to fund a military campaign to halt the advance of Carthage to Sicily. In Catana around 415 B.C., an artful full-face image of Apollo with leafy hair projected precision with its realistic emotion in eyes and jowls. Other pictorial coinage emulated Corinth's *stater*, notably at Ambrakia, Amphilochicum, Argos, Corcyra, Leucas, Locri, and Syracusa. In 1925, during the rise of the second Greek republic, coinsmiths revived an *art deco* version of Athena's helmeted profile from a Corinthian coin for a new two-*drachma* coin.

Sports victories were the source of numerous active coin scenarios, particularly the four-horse racing chariots of Gela rounding the field. On a half *stater* struck in 420 B.C., the placement of the flying eagle, symbol of Zeus, celebrated the Olympic games at Elis in the northwest of the Peloponnesus, where the event was founded in 776 B.C. The year was momentous in Greek history for the defection of Elis from alliance with Sparta to support Athens. According to the histories of Thucydides, by marching in 1,000 *hoplites* (infantry), the Spartans violated the *ekecheiria* (sacred truce) established in the 800s B.C. by King

A Greek colony on the island of Sicily struck a portrait coin in 317 B.C. featuring the lyre, a symbol of the arts, on the obverse. (Guy Clark, Ancient Coins and Antiquities, Norfolk, Virginia)

In 300 B.C., a Greek colony on the island of Sicily chose as coin art the rugged profile of Alexander III the Great of Macedon and, on the reverse, a spirited steed, perhaps his legendary horse Bucephalus. (Guy Clark, Ancient Coins and Antiquities, Norfolk, Virginia)

Iphitos of Elis and supported by kings Cleosthenes of Pisa and Lycurgus of Sparta. For the infringement of an international agreement, the Olympic committee fined the Spartan team 200 *drachmai* per man. The haughty Spartans sneered at a 200,000 *drachmai* penalty with bogus claims that they had initiated military maneuvers before the official beginning of the games. Ignoring Spartan posturing, the committee barred the nation's athletes from participating in that year's games.

The finest coins of the classical era were the signed *decadrachms* minted in 413 B.C. at Syracusa, the first colony to turn gold into money. The coinage, which the magistrate Silanos ordered, commemorated a victory over Athens on dainty disks. The master die engravers of the era, Cimon (or Kimon), Evainetos (or Euainetos), Eukleidas, Eumenes, and Phrygillos, preserved for posterity their identity by adding their names to the design. Cimon incised the most beautiful full-face view of Arethusa, patron of Syracusa, and made commemorative pieces celebrating military might. About 400 B.C., Eukleidas pioneered three-dimensional portraiture of Athena, whom he ornamented richly.

By the end of the fifth century B.C., local minters added bronze to the types of ore turned into money. The proof of the era's genius lies in the Carthaginian and Tunisian imitations that followed Evainetos's skilled creation of the head of the naiad Arethusa, and a charioteer in a quadriga, which he designed at Catana for the tyrant Gelon. It was the minting of Syracusa and colonies at Catana, Croton, Massilia, Rhegium, Taormina, and Tarentum during the fourth century B.C. that influenced the Roman monetary system. One of the outstanding artistic contributions to Greek coinage was the Tarentine gold *stater* displaying Taras appealing to Poseidon, god of the sea. Farther north, Massilia, the prosperous colony that became the French seaport Marseilles, struck engaging silver coins in small denominations that influenced trade with northern Italy and Celtic Gaul.

The wealth of the Laurion mines fell into the hands of Sparta, Athens's chief rival, in

407 B.C. During the Peloponnesian War, the Spartans disabled future production by dispersing the enslaved miners, who had crawled the subterranean ledges of Laurion in heavy shackles under appalling conditions of filth, disease, and accidents. From 406 to 405 B.C., as silver coins grew scarce, widespread hoarding forced the populace to resort to silver-washed bronze coins, a monetary impasse that the comic playwright Aristophanes satirized in *The Frogs* (405 B.C.) as trash specie. He lauded ancient coins for being well struck, giving a pure ring in proof of their fineness. He then groused that people resorted to cheap copper "baubs, base metal, struck awry, and scarcely yet in circulation upwards of a day," which lacked the bravura for which Athenian mintmasters were known (Aristophanes 1952, p. 207).

The Athenian *tetradrachm* altered to a classical profile and ornate helmet for the goddess after Athens lost the Peloponnesian War of 404 B.C. By 393 B.C., the decommissioning of coppers restored high quality coins to circulation. The period also saw the first inscriptions on coins, for example, the Ephesian coin marked in Greek "I Am the Badge of Phanes." In the same era, minting spread to the Greek colonies as far east as Lampsacus on the Sea of Marmora and Panticapaeum on the Black Sea. Decorating official coins were the predictable profile of Athena backed by an owl and olive sprig plus an abbreviation of the city's name. Individual motifs and/or deities characterized each mint site:

This Larissan coin minted in 395 B.C. in eastern Thessaly displays the head of Medusa, the mythic female gorgon whose glance turned her victims to stone. The obverse presents a realistic image of a horse and the Greek letters "LARIS" as the only marking. (Guy Clark, Ancient Coins and Antiquities, Norfolk, Virginia)

city-state	*emblem*	*deity*
Abdera	griffin, grain of wheat	
Aegina	land tortoise, sea turtle	
Aenus		Hermes, messenger of the gods and god of commerce
Amphipolis		Apollo, god of light, healing, and creativity
Arcadia		the hero Hercules
Argoswolf		Hera, consort of Zeus
Athens	owl	Athena, goddess of wisdom
Chalcis	wheel; gorgon's head	
Cnidus		Aphrodite
Corinth	winged Pegasus	Aphrodite
Cydonia	Cydon, suckled by a dog	
Cyrene	silphium stalk	
Cyzicus	tuna	
Delphi		Apollo and Demeter
Elis	eagle	Zeus, chief Olympian god; his consort, Hera
Emisa	sacred stone	
Ephesus	bee; temple	Artemis
Ioni	the admiral Themistocles	
Mende	wine cup	Dionysus, god of wine
Metapontum	barley head	
Olympia	winged Victory	Zeus, his eagle, his thunderbolt
Paphos	cones; temple	Aphrodite
Perga		Artemis
Pheneus	caduceus	Hermes carrying baby Arcas
Phocaea	state seal	
Populonia	seahorses	
Poseidonia		Poseidon, god of the sea
Rhegium	lion head; Jokastos, the city's founder	
Rhodes	rose	
Selinus		Selinus, the river god
Sicyon	chimera	

city-state	*emblem*	*deity*
Syracusa	owl; nymph; triskeleon	Athena
Tarentum	dolphin; horse and rider; bull	
Teos	griffin	
Terina	the nymph Terina	
Thebes		Hercules's exploits;
	Boeotian oxhide shield	
Thurium	Scylla, a sea monster	Athena
Velia	lion	

Aeginetan specie became so familiar that "turtle" doubled as a synonym for "coin," as found in the cynical adage, "Turtles overcome the principles of right and virtue" (Hopper 1976, p. 113). By 400 B.C., the moneys of individual city-states were so numerous and confusing that mints added letters to identify the source, for example AI for Aegina.

After 308 B.C., coiners in Cyrene on the North African coast pictured an endangered species long gone from their soil. Around 630 B.C., when Theran settlers had established the colony, they grew and exported the sticky, resinous silphium plant, the sap of which some people chewed like gum. The demand for the stalk as cattle fodder and for the clear, pine-scented juice, which was an effective suppressant of ovulation in women, depleted the plant entirely. By the time that the stalk appeared on the coin, it had long since disappeared from Cyrenian fields.

After Macedonia spread coin usage around the eastern Mediterranean and into lands conquered by Alexander III the Great, other kingdoms developed unique motifs to distinguish their coins. Macedon selected images of farming and hunting. Fourth-century B.C. Spartans gave up their earlier objections to coinage and produced heavy iron disks. In Crete, citizens abandoned trade in bronze *lebetes* (bowls), but retained the shape of the dish on their coins as a statement that each coin was worth one bowl. At Olbia, a Greek colony on the Black Sea, fisherfolk produced bronze fish-shaped coins to proclaim their trade.

The production of silver *tetradrachms* flourished from 196 to 187 B.C., when the Athenian mint struck millions of coins comprising 110 separate issues. A Boeotian hoard, buried during the invasion of Euboea by Antiochus II of Syria in 192 B.C., preserved coins that exhibit the fineness of late Greek mint craft. Among the most elegantly detailed is the *tetradrachm* struck in a new style at Athens before 100 B.C. It depicts the profile of the goddess Athena with realistic features and wearing a scrolled helmet with horsehair crest. On the reverse, her owl stands on an overturned amphora, a symbol of local trade in olive oil.

As more eastern countries emulated Greek coinage, they recorded for history elements of individual reigns. One ruler, Azes II of Bactria, issued a silver *tetradrachm* picturing a mounted monarch opposite an image of Athena. Historians suggest that this king, who ruled the Scytho-Parthian realm from 35 B.C. until 10 A.D., may have been one of the magi mention in the book of Matthew as following a star to Bethlehem to worship the newborn Christ child.

See also **banking; *daric;* euro; Percy Gardner; giro; Sir George Hill; Lydian coins; Macedonian coins; medieval coins; *obolus;* Pasion of Archarnae; Heinrich Schliemann; world money.**

SOURCES: Allen, Larry. *Encyclopedia of Money*. New York: Checkmark Books, 2001. • Aristophanes. *Frogs* in *Classics in Translation*, ed. Paul MacKendrick and Herbert M. Howe, Vol. I. Madison: University of Wisconsin Press, 1952. • Becatoros, Elena. "Greece Bids Farewell to Link with Ancient Past." *Bergen County Record*, December 31, 2000. • Clain-Stefanelli, Elvira, and Vladimir Clain-Stefanelli. *The Beauty and Lore of Coins, Currency, and Medals*. Croton-on-Hudson, N.Y.: Riverwood Publishers, 1974. • Cribb, Joe. *Money*. Toronto: Stoddart, 1990. • Davies, Glyn. *A History of Money from Ancient Times to the Present Day*. Cardiff: University of Wales Press, 1994. • Durant, Will. *The Life of Greece*. New York: Simon and Schuster, 1939. • Einzig, Paul. *Primitive Money*. Oxford: Pergamon Press, 1966. • *Encyclopedia of the Ancient Greek World*. New York: Facts on File, Inc., 1995. • Galbraith, John Kenneth. *Money: Whence*

It Came, Where It Went. Boston: Houghton Mifflin, 1975. • Grierson, Philip. *Numismatics.* London: Oxford University Press, 1975. • Grosvenor, Melville Bell, ed. in chief. *Everyday Life in Bible Times.* Washington, D.C.: National Geographic Society, 1967. • *Handbook to Life in Ancient Greece.* New York: Facts on File, Inc., 1997. • Hastings, James, ed. *Encyclopedia of Religion and Ethics.* New York: Charles Scribner's Sons, 1951. • Head, Barclay V. *A Guide to the Principal Coins of the Greeks.* London: British Museum, 1959. • Hastings, James, ed. *Historia Numorum.* Chicago: Argonaut, 1911. • Hill, G. F. *Historical Greek Coins.* Chicago: Argonaut, Inc., 1966. • "Hoard Returned." *Archaeology,* May/June 1999. • Hopper, R. J. *The Early Greeks.* New York: Harper & Row, 1976. • Howatson, M. C., ed. *The Oxford Companion to Classical Literature.* Oxford: Oxford University Press, 1991. • James, Peter, and Nick Thorpe. *Ancient Inventions.* New York: Ballantine, 1994. • Jansen, H. W., and Anthony F. Janson. *History of Art.* New York: Harry N. Abrams, Incorporated, 1997. • Kiernan, Philip. "Alfred Petrie Leaves His Coins to the National Currency Collection." *Canadian Numismatic Association Journal,* October 2001, 389–395. • Laing, Lloyd R. *Coins and Archaeology.* New York: Schocken Books, 1969. • Meshorer, Ya'akov. *Coins of the Ancient World.* Jerusalem: Jerusalem Publishing House, 1974. • Moorehead, Caroline. *Lost and Found: The 9,000 Treasures of Troy.* London: Penguin Books, 1994. • Pliny. *The Natural History.* New York: McGraw-Hill, 1962. • Pollak, Henry. *Coinage & Conflict.* Clifton, N.J.: Coin & Currency Institute, 2001. • Reinfeld, Fred. *Treasury of the World's Coins.* New York: Sterling Publishing, 1953. • Severy, Merle, ed. *Greece & Rome.* Washington, D.C.: National Geographic Society, 1977. • Starr, Chester G. *A History of the Ancient World.* New York: Oxford University Press, 1991. • Williams, Trevor. *The History of Invention.* New York: Facts on File, 1987.

greenbacks

From the outbreak of the American Civil War in 1861 to its end in 1865, the U.S. Bureau of Engraving and Printing financed combat with the rebellious South by producing paper money worth $450,000,000 to cover a shortage of reserves. The idea took shape on December 30, 1860, raising an outcry among financiers against the first U.S. demand notes. Salmon Portland Chase, Secretary of the Treasury under President Abraham Lincoln, had to make the decision to issue wartime money, a paper currency lacking the promise of convertibility to precious metals.

On February 25, 1862, under the initial Legal Tender Act, the U.S. Treasury issued the first fiat money, an inconvertible paper note backed only by trust in the government. The front bore red seals and an eagle with wings outstretched as though taking flight in the Union cause; the reverse side pictured intricate designs to foil counterfeiters. A statement in ornate script read, "This note is a legal tender for all debts public and private except duties and imports and interest on public debt and is receivable in payment of all loans made to the United States" (Davis 1988, p. 115).

Federal moneyers printed the paper money in green, source of the name "greenbacks." The liquid ink remained the color of choice because it resisted chemical change. Less easily counterfeited than black, the ink also generated a psychological factor, an optimism in the treasury implied by the color green, a symbol of hope and regeneration. Because the system of printed money met with popular support, two more legal tender acts — July 11, 1862, and March 3, 1863 — put more of the bills in circulation. By 1865, three-quarters of the nation's money was comprised of greenbacks.

When the surrender of Confederate general Robert E. Lee to Union general Ulysses S. Grant ended the war on April 9, 1865, U.S. party politics dominated the question of the greenback's future. A year later, Hugh McCulloch, U.S. Secretary of State under President Andrew Johnson, began retiring the outstanding notes, but ceased the recovery with 79 percent of them still unaccounted for. After the Panic of 1873, Midwestern farmers who demanded additional greenbacks in circulation formed the Greenback-Labor Party, which had limited success in forcing the Treasury to continue issuing paper money not backed by specie.

As the Treasury's gold reserve began to build, fewer people surrendered greenbacks for gold. In 1878, Congress agreed to leave in circulation $346,681,000 in greenbacks as part of the nation's legal tender. It was not until

January 2, 1879, when gold reserves mounted upward once more to a comfortable level, that the Treasury could offer gold coins in exchange for greenbacks. The flow of green bills over the years presaged modern reliance on paper money.

In July 1994, for the first time since 1929, U.S. Treasury officials began restyling the familiar green bills as a means of outwitting counterfeiters using personal computers, scanners, ink-jet printers, and other electronic duplicating systems. To make forging more difficult, staff artists enlarged and offset portraits that once occupied the center of each bill's face. The addition of watermarks and color-shifting ink protected currency while preserving the shape and texture of the greenback. Within two years, production of 100-dollar bills, the denomination of choice among frauds, entered service. In 1997, the 20- and 50-dollar bills, featuring larger numerals on the back, began circulating. The protective measures paralleled similar redesigns by moneyers in Australia, Belgium, Canada, France, Great Britain, Japan, and Switzerland and the work of the designers of the euro.

***See also* Hugh McCulloch; money slang.**

SOURCES: Allen, Larry. *Encyclopedia of Money*. New York: Checkmark Books, 2001. • Bowers, Q. David. *Adventures with Rare Coins*. Los Angeles: Bowers & Ruddy Galleries, Inc., 1979. • Bowers, Q. David. "American Gold." *American Heritage*, December 1984, 43–49. • "The Bureau of Engraving and Printing." http://www.bep.treas.gov/. • Davis, Curtis Carroll. "The Craftiest of Men: William P. Wood and the Establishment of the United States Secret Service." *Maryland Historical Magazine*, Summer 1988, pp. 111–126. • *Encyclopedia of World Biography*. Detroit: Gale Group, 1998. • Weatherford, Jack. *The History of Money: From Sandstone to Cyberspace*. Pittsburgh, Pa.: Three Rivers Press, 1998.

Gresham, Thomas

London-born financier and royal adviser Thomas Gresham, called the "prince of London merchants," was a commoner risen to greatness. He is best known for building for the merchants of his native city the Royal Exchange, an attractive and convenient hall of commerce. Born around 1518 and educated in law at Gonville and Caius College, Cambridge, he apprenticed under Sir John Gresham, his uncle, and, at age 25, joined the mercers' guild. Gresham's business acumen and daring, acquired over 23 years of studying foreign trade at the bourse in Antwerp, made him one of England's wealthiest men.

Gresham served in the first of many royal appointments as factor or manager of foreign debts for Edward VI and triumphed at manipulating moneys through Antwerp's bourse. He spied for the crown, smuggled bullion and war materiel, and negotiated business in foreign countries. After Henry VIII devalued English coins below the level of other European currencies by minting them from base metals, Gresham suggested that the crown could raise the value of the pound by trading through English banks rather than with foreign moneylenders.

Under Elizabeth I, Gresham urged that the royal treasury restore coinage and boost the crown's coffers by halving the face value of silver coins. The strategy impacted commerce, but stabilized the queen's treasury. He also cornered so much of the currency financing the Spanish Armada of Philip II that he delayed the launch and possibly contributed to England's salvation. When Gresham died in London on November 21, 1579, he retained a reputation for philanthropy with the building of Gresham College and for financial vision through the formulation of Gresham's Law, a theory that bad money drives out good, giving rise to hoarding of coins.

***See also* English coins; Gresham's Law; Medieval coins; Royal Exchange.**

SOURCES: Allen, Larry. *Encyclopedia of Money*. New York: Checkmark Books, 2001. • Davies, Glyn. *A History of Money from Ancient Times to the Present Day*. Cardiff: University of Wales Press, 1994. • "Les Dernières Volontés de Sir Thomas Gresham." http://u2.u-strasbg.fr/lexis/a992000/frame_txt_fichiers/F3_fichiers/gresham/lwill_ward_ok.html. • Galbraith, John Kenneth. *Money: Whence It Came, Where It Went*. Boston: Houghton Mifflin, 1975. • "Gresham College." http://www.gresham.ac.uk/special/history.html. • Laing, Lloyd R. *Coins and Archaeology*. New York:

Schocken Books, 1969. • Magnusson, Magnus. *Cambridge Biographical Dictionary.* Cambridge: University of Cambridge, 1990. • Nicholls, C. S., ed. *Encyclopedia of Biography.* Oxford, Eng.: Helicon Publishing Ltd., 1996.

Gresham's Law

Gresham's Law, a theory that bad money drives out good, correctly describes a sequence of events that follows a rise in the value of coins as sources of precious metal rather than as exchange media. The first statement of the law occurred in Greek theater after the Greek comic playwright Aristophanes mentions the hoarding of silver and increased circulation of bronze coins in *The Frogs* (405 B.C.). Although French economist and mathematician Nicolas Oresme (also Nicole d'Oresme), treasurer of the Collège de Navarre at the University of Paris and author of *Traité de la Première des Monnaies* (*Treatise on the Invention of Coins*) (ca. 1360) clarified the concept and Nicholas Copernicus stated the idea outright in *De Monetae Cudendae* (*On Coinage*) (1526), Tudor financier and government agent Sir Thomas Gresham received the credit.

Gresham maintained that issuance of high-grade gold, silver, and copper coinage causes collectors and speculators to hoard specie or melt it down, thus leaving only lighter, poorer quality coins in circulation. For this phenomenon, Scottish economist Henry Dunning Macleod, author of *The Theory and Practice of Banking* (1856) and *Elements of Political Economy* (1858), proposed the erroneous term "Gresham's Law." In the opinion of French financier Charles Gide, economics professor at the universities of Bordeaux, Montpellier, and Paris and author of *Consumers' Co-operative Societies* (1904), two other stimuli exacerbate the disappearance of specie — sales by weight and payment of out-of-country debt.

Historical periods proving Gresham's law occur with regularity, for example, during the Roman retreat from Britannia and in Europe during World War I, when people held their silver coins because the price of silver boosted their value as bullion. In Burma, a rice currency encouraged peasants to cook the best grains and save the broken and stunted grains for money. Similarly, unattractive blocks of tea served Mongols and Burmese as cash, while the superior grade of tea went into the pot. In the Commonwealth of Virginia, tobacco used as a medium of exchange tended to be the lowest grade from the bottom of the barrel. Other examples of hoarding and culling coincide with the failure of banks or loss of trust in financial institutions, such as the uncertainty aroused by the French Revolution and the loss of faith that Southerners experienced at the decline of the Confederacy during the U.S. Civil War. When hoarding became a problem during the Great Depression, President Franklin Roosevelt forbade the stockpiling of gold coins and, in 1933, ordered them returned to the Treasury.

See also **English coins; feather money; Thomas Gresham; hoarding; Samuel Pepys; Royal Exchange.**

SOURCES: Allen, Larry. *Encyclopedia of Money.* New York: Checkmark Books, 2001. • Davies, Glyn. *A History of Money from Ancient Times to the Present Day.* Cardiff: University of Wales Press, 1994. • "Gresham College." http://www.gresham.ac.uk/special/history.html. • Grierson, Philip. *Numismatics.* London: Oxford University Press, 1975. • Laing, Lloyd R. *Coins and Archaeology.* New York: Schocken Books, 1969. • Magnusson, Magnus. *Cambridge Biographical Dictionary.* Cambridge: University of Cambridge, 1990. • Nicholls, C. S., ed. *Encyclopedia of Biography.* Oxford, Eng.: Helicon Publishing Ltd., 1996. • Snodgrass, Mary Ellen. *Who's Who in the Middle Ages.* Jefferson, N.C.: McFarland, 2001.

groat

A common European penny in the 1200s, the groat took its name from middle Latin for "fat" or "thick." Called the *croat* by Spaniards, *gros* by the French, and *groschen* by Bohemians, Germans, and Poles, it spawned a family of European coins and flourished over time as a useful form of silver change:

- Venetian moneyers placed Christ in glory at the center of an Italian groat, the *grosso matapan* introduced by Doge Giovanni Dandalo after 1280 in the style of a Byzantine *nomisma.*

- Following the same model, in the mid-1200s, Tsar Ivan II Asen, a stalwart soldier and state manager, copied eastern Mediterranean coinage for a silver groat essential to the commerce of Serbs and Bulgars.
- In 1300, Wenceslaus II, who boosted Bohemian wealth, introduced a groat that he based on the shape and style of the French *gros tournois*, which Louis IX originated in 1266. Called the Prague groat, the long-lived coin with its diadem, Bohemian lion, and tri-level rim remained in use throughout the late Middle Ages.
- Hungarian diemakers imitated Italian coins in 1329 with a groat that emulated the *grosso* of Naples.
- In 1339, coiners in Brabant and Flanders issued a *Leeuwengroot* (lion groat) in imitation of the French *gros tournois.* For the castle of Tours, designers substituted the Flanders lion.
- In the early 1400s, Mantua issued a *grosso* featuring a pious illustration of the local shrine of a prized relic, the sponge that had absorbed Christ's blood at the crucifixion.
- After 1471, Sixtus IV, a great-hearted restorer of churches, founder of the Vatican library, and builder of the Sistine Chapel and a foundling hospital, commissioned single and double groats in silver, the first portrait coins to bear the image of a pope. They expressed his enthusiasm for philanthropy with the legend "*Publicae Utilitati*" ("For Public Use").

The groat issued around 1485 by moneyers of James III of Scotland, the Stuart monarch known as the "commoner's king," characterized his Renaissance style and multiple interests in art, music, ships, firepower, commerce, and currency. The coin featured a realistic Renaissance portrait bust of him wearing a domed crown topped with a cross. The introduction of realism to coin art influenced the silver groat of Henry VII at the end of the 1500s. The first English king to alter motifs since Edward III, he pictured himself much like James III in a closed crown and natural bust pose.

See also **amulet coins; *gros*; *gros tournois*; Irish money; medieval coins; paper money.**

SOURCES: Cannon, John, and Ralph Griffiths. *Oxford Illustrated History of the British Monarchy.* Oxford: Oxford University Press, 1988. • Cribb, Joe. *Money.* Toronto: Stoddart, 1990. • Davies, Glyn. *A History of Money from Ancient Times to the Present Day.* Cardiff: University of Wales Press, 1994. • Grierson, Philip. *Numismatics.* London: Oxford University Press, 1975.

gros

A thick French or German penny also called the "groat" in English, the *gros* took its name from the Latin *denarius grossus* ("thick penny"). The silver *gros—groschen* in the plural—was the issue of Adolph, Bishop of Liège, after 1313 and displayed the Prussian eagle in a heavy circular frame. The coin's popularity inspired Charles Robert, King of Hungary, to commission a silver *grosz* and Bogdan I of Moldavia to order a half *groszy.* In Poland, Casimir II the Great added to the *denar* a Polish *grosz,* which he produced at the Cracow mint. After 1394, Ladislas Jagiello II increased denominations by introducing the *polgrosz* or half-*grosz.*

A common coin among the peasantry, the gros reached a height of design in 1357 with the *gros blanc à la couronne*, a silver *denier* minted in France by John II the Good (Jean le Bon de Valois). Grandly decorated with an ornate crown and ringed by twelve *fleurs-de-lis,* it celebrated the return of the king after his capture by Edward the Black Prince at the battle of Poitiers in 1356. In the early 1500s, the warrior king Francis I, Renaissance arbiter of art and learning, emulated the successful coinage of John II by placing his own profile on a gros *blanc* in classic style.

Influenced by the French *gros tournois,* the popular German *groschen* served the growing economic climate of the Rhineland and Westphalia. A repository of the era's self-confidence and unique style, the coin developed in Meissen, Prague, and Saxony. One type, the *Judenkopfgroschen* ("Jew's head groat"), acquired its unusual name from the image of a man in pointed cap, reminiscent of standard Jewish attire. The three-*groschen* piece minted in Prussia in the 1500s earned the name *duettchen*, a humorous reference to the two-headed imperial eagle.

***See also* denier; groat; *gros tournois*; Islamic money; Knights Hospitallers.**

SOURCES: Clain-Stefanelli, Elvira, and Vladimir Clain-Stefanelli. *The Beauty and Lore of Coins, Currency, and Medals.* Croton-on-Hudson, N.Y.: Riverwood Publishers, 1974. • Cribb, Joe. *Money.* Toronto: Stoddart, 1990. • Davies, Glyn. *A History of Money from Ancient Times to the Present Day.* Cardiff: University of Wales Press, 1994. • Grierson, Philip. *Numismatics.* London: Oxford University Press, 1975. • Reinfeld, Fred. *Treasury of the World's Coins.* New York: Sterling Publishing, 1953.

gros tournois

A medieval coin minted in high-grade silver, the *gros tournois*, the groat of Tours, France, originated in 1266. The prototype emerged from wrought-iron dies by the moneyers of the beloved Louis IX, warrior king and hero of the Seventh Crusade. The design featured an ornate cross and "Ludovicus Rex" ("King Louis") on front with a circlet of *fleurs-de-lis* on the back. A pious legend read "Benedictus Sit Nomen Domini Dei Jesus Christi" ("Blessed Be the Name of the Lord Jesus Christ"). For a name, the king reshuffled the Roman *denarius grossus* into *gros tournois*, which acknowledged the outline of the castle of Tours on the back. Louis intended the coin to be royal money to serve his entire realm, as opposed to local coins that served towns and districts only.

Anticipating the flair and grace of the Renaissance, the *gros tournois* influenced the groat of Charles II of Provence, Walram of Jülich at Cologne, and additional town coins struck at Basel and Metz. Almost simultaneous with the French version was the Dutch *gros tournois* commissioned by Florenz V von Graf of Westfriesland. From the last years of the 13th century, Brabant, Flanders, Hainault, and Liège generated additional copies of the *gros tournois*. In 1320, the Belgians of Brabant produced a unique touch, the likeness of St. Peter, Louvain's patron saint. In subsequent years, Liège struck its *gros tournois* with the griffin image. Count Louis de Mâle ordered a Flemish two-groat *botdragers* featuring a mailed lion, a common image of strength in the post–Crusades years.

At its high point, the *gros tournois* of the handsome French king Philip IV (also Philippe le Bel or Philip the Fair), grandson of Louis IX, featured "*Philippus Rex*" ("King Philip") on the face along with a pious blessing on his reign. On the reverse appears the Latin "*Turonus Civis*" ("City of Tours"), which echoes the coin's name. A subsequent coinage was the work of the ill-starred John II the Good (Jean le Bon de Valois), who struck an imitative *gros tournois* in 1359, a year before he introduced the *franc*. The coin influenced the German *Groschen*, which mints in various parts of central Europe produced.

***See also* groat; Philip IV of France.**

SOURCES: Clain-Stefanelli, Elvira, and Vladimir Clain-Stefanelli. *The Beauty and Lore of Coins, Currency, and Medals.* Croton-on-Hudson, N.Y.: Riverwood Publishers, 1974. • Cribb, Joe. *Money.* Toronto: Stoddart, 1990. • Cribb, Joe, Barrie Cook, and Ian Carradice. *The Coin Atlas.* London: Little, Brown and Co., 1999. • Grierson, Philip. *Numismatics.* London: Oxford University Press, 1975. • Reinfeld, Fred. *Treasury of the World's Coins.* New York: Sterling Publishing, 1953.

guinea

Great Britain's first machine-milled coin, the one-pound gold guinea, was the work of five imported experts to London's Tower Mint — French engraver Nicholas Briot, engineer Pierre Blondeau from the Paris mint, and three Flemish brothers, John, Joseph, and Phillip Roettiers. In 1663, on behalf of Charles II, the assembled staff restored quality coinage in England, in part to replace the hastily designed coins of the Commonwealth. With "guinea gold" from West Africa's Gold Coast, the staff fully mechanized England's coinage.

The portrait of Dutch playwright Joost van den Vondel adorns this commemortive five-*gulden* note.

After Charles returned from 11 years of exile in France, the guinea featured him newly restored and officially crowned with a fillet, perhaps as a gesture of humility from a king whose father brought dishonor to the Stuart line through profligacy and mismanagement. The coin carried the name "guinea" as well as the likeness of the elephant, symbol of the Africa Company, to acknowledge its provenance from English colonies. The Latin motto "*Decus et Tutamen*" ("An Ornament and Safeguard") replicated an inscription on the purse of Armand Jean Duplessis, Cardinal Richelieu. Under Queen Anne, a gold guinea bore her dignified profile and a grand foursome of shields. In the 1770s, engraver Richard Yeo honored George III with portrait guineas that pictured the Hanoverian king in the haughty guise of a Roman emperor crowned with a laurel wreath.

The coin's long life paralleled an era of dubious slang usage of its name as "guinea" permeated the English language. The word served as a synonym for an African slave, more pointedly in the fuller phrase a "guinea nigger." The slaving trade's unliked vessels were dubbed "guineamen." African pheasants acquired the slang names "guinea fowl" or "guinea hen." Grains of paradise, an African spice, passed as "guinea pepper"; African grain and grass became "guinea corn" and "guinea grass." An infective African nematode was called a "guinea worm." Unpromising naval enlistees earned the pejorative "guinea pigs."

***See also* Sir Isaac Newton; John Roettiers.**

SOURCES: Cribb, Joe. *Money*. Toronto: Stoddart, 1990. • Cribb, Joe, Barrie Cook, and Ian Carradice. The Coin Atlas. London: Little, Brown and Co., 1999. • Davies, Glyn. A History of Money from Ancient Times to the Present Day. Cardiff: University of Wales Press, 1994. • Sinclair, David. The Pound. London: Century Books, 2000.

gulden

The northern European *gulden*, a name derived from "guilder" or "gilden," was a popular gold coin in Holland and Germany. Comparable in size and worth to the *florin* of Florence, on which it was modeled, the coin first flooded the market in the 1300s. After Sigismund, the wealthy Archduke of Tyrol, invented the dollar-sized *apfelgulden* around 1410, Frederick III the Wise, elector Palatine of the Rhine and champion of Lutheranism, emulated it in 1500 with stamps incised at Sigismund's mint at Halle.

Gulden figure heavily in the declining years of the Holy Roman Empire. They served the political ends of Frederick and the archbishops of Cologne, Mainz, and Trier. At Lübeck, new gold *gulden* minted in the 1400s promoted trade in the Baltic among members of the Hanseatic League. At Nordlingen, Frederick IV, a lover of luxury who promoted the Union of Evangelical Estates in 1608, released a version of the coin depicting him as a nimbate Holy Roman Emperor.

In 1521, the Emperor Charles V, who inherited a Spanish-Habsburg empire stretching from Spain and Naples to the Netherlands and Austria and reaching over the Atlantic to Spanish America, attempted to standardize the disparate coins of his massive realm with a unified silver *guldiner* as the imperial coin. His grandiose plan failed, but prefaced similar proposals in the late 20th century with the euro. When Danzig, Poland, earned temporary freedom in 1920, it returned to the *pfennig* and *gulden* as historic memorials to past central European coinage.

***See also* klippe; Samuel Pepys; Sigismund, Archduke of Tyrol.**

SOURCES: Clain-Stefanelli, Elvira, and Vladimir Clain-Stefanelli. *The Beauty and Lore of Coins, Currency, and Medals.* Croton-on-Hudson, N.Y.: Riverwood Publishers, 1974. • Cribb, Joe. *Money.* Toronto: Stoddart, 1990. • Cribb, Joe, Barrie Cook, and Ian Carradice. *The Coin Atlas.* London: Little, Brown and Co., 1999. • Davies, Glyn. *A History of Money from Ancient Times to the Present Day.* Cardiff: University of Wales Press, 1994. • *New Catholic Encyclopedia.* San Francisco: Catholic University of America, 1967.

hallmark

A medieval form of consumer protection, the hallmark was the distinctive device of England's Worshipful Company of Goldsmiths or Goldsmiths' Company. Initiated in 1300 and chartered by the Crown in 1327, the consortium was a trade guild that became one of London's twelve great livery companies and issuers of hallmarks. After paying a subscription, members received a clothing and food allowance and a badge. In return for honorary emblems, the company assembled at Goldsmiths' Hall and marked all gold and silver items as a promotion of standards in precious metals. From their symbolic stamp of the what, where, and when of metals came the term "hallmark," a guarantee issued at centers in Birmingham, Chester, Edinburgh, and Exeter. The guild also conducted touchstone tests of metal purity and the trial of the pyx, a formal ceremony overseeing the integrity of coinage at the Royal Mint.

On September 20, 1773, over opposition from the London Goldsmiths' Company, the town of Sheffield received its own assay office and acquired a crown as its municipal symbol. More strictly supervised than the London office, the non-profit Sheffield operation organized as supervisors Thomas, Earl of Effingham, and 29 other local men called "Guardians of the Standard of Wrought Plate within the Town of Sheffield." As the only office income, the assay master, bonded for £500, collected hallmarking charges from manufacturers in a 20-mile radius of the city. Because of the success of the Sheffield assay office, after 1903, the company began to scrutinize and evaluate gold, which staff marked with the Yorkshire rose. After the Hallmarking Act of 1973, assayers examined international goods and foreign gold, silver, and platinum. With the emergence of the European Union, in 1999, Parliament amended the act to conform to continental standards, thus rendering Sheffield's fineness symbol and date letter voluntary criteria of quality.

The goldsmiths' guild survived into the 21st century as assayers and supervisors of purity in gold, silver, and platinum crafts and jewelry. The office also assesses antique silver for unauthorized marks and locates forgeries. Among the services of the company are seminars on counterfeiting and forgery and public exhibits of coins, medals, and plate.

See also **assay marks; touchstone; trial of the pyx.**

SOURCES: "Eight Centuries of Sampling Inspection: The Trial of the Pyx." *Journal of the American Statistical Association*, September 1977, 493–500. • "Sheffield Assay Office — A History." http://www.assayoffice.co.uk/history.htm. • Stigler, Stephen. "Stephen Stigler's New Book Challenges Researchers to Show Him the Numbers." *University of Chicago Magazine*, December 1999. • "The Trial by Pyx Order 1998," http://www.hmso.gov.uk/si/si1998/ 19980264.htm.

Hamilton, Alexander

The first Treasury Secretary of the United States, Alexander Hamilton was a pragmatic visionary who supported a strong central government, opposed slavery, and conceived a bimetallic currency system based on gold and silver. Born on the leeward isle of Nevis on January 11, 1757, Hamilton came of sturdy, proud Scots stock. His father, James Hamilton was a St. Kitts businessman; his mother, French Huguenot Rachel Fawcett (or Faucette), divorced an unpleasant first husband to marry for love. When Hamilton was 11 year old, his mother died, leaving him virtually untended. From his scourings of island neighborhoods, he grew up bilingual in French and English and clerked at Christianstadt in Nicholas Cruger's mercantile office until his aunts sent him to grammar school in New Jersey when he was 15.

Educated at King's College, Hamilton displayed astonishing scholarship and, abandoning royalist loyalties, developed a resilient patriotism. While still in his teens, he issued opinions in worthy pamphlets. Because of his loss of family support in childhood, he established a loving relationship with his wife, Elizabeth Schuyler, mother of their eight children.

Commissioned as a musketeer in 1776, Hamilton fought under General George Washington in New York and New Jersey and advanced to the rank of lieutenant colonel. Washington was impressed by Hamilton's writing skills and offered him opportunities to expand his knowledge of the military and government through a wide correspondence with colonial leadership. Hamilton used his rising fame as a wedge against slavery by proposing the manumission and arming of black African patriots during the Revolutionary War.

While serving in the Continental Congress, Hamilton despaired of a workable plan for financing colonial government. After practicing law privately in New York, he took an active role in the Constitutional Convention of 1787, where his keen-edged oratory bore weight with financiers and merchants. In favor of a firm central government, he debated persistently and well and earned appointment to the new government as finance manager. A brilliant money manager, he advocated that the federal government shoulder war debts, to be retired through disbursals of annuities and real estate and through excise taxes and import duties. More important to fiscal health, he surmised that regular attention to a national debt would promote regular payments to strengthen credit and that federal securities would feed cash into the economy.

After haggles with James Madison, Thomas Jefferson, and Robert Morris, Hamilton proposed plans for a mint and national bank, the forerunner of the Federal Reserve, and advised on stimuli to trade and investments. The bank, modeled after the Bank of England and chartered for 20 years, went into operation in 1791. His initial administration of federal and state certificates of debt precipitated speculation, manic growth, panic, and depression. In time, however, his farsighted financial concepts proved worthy, as did stable banking procedures and currency, based on the Spanish dollar and regulated by the Coinage Act of 1792. The legislation established the U.S. Mint as the responsibility of the secretary of state and named as the official currency dollars, *dismes*, half-*dismes*, copper pennies and half-pennies, and milles. Mint staff began planning a series of larger denominations valued at $2.50, $5, and $10. Anyone clipping or stealing coins from the mint faced the hangman.

The differences of opinion generated by the mint's fiscal control and establishment of a fixed-rate bimetallic monetary system alienated Hamilton from strong conservative John Witherspoon, a Scotch Presbyterian minister, and even further from Jefferson, creating two bitterly warring camps known as Hamiltonians and Jeffersonians. After the airing of charges and suspicions in Congress, in 1793, Hamilton vindicated his fiscal philosophy. By 1794, the new nation's high credit rating in Europe proved the feasibility of his grand financial plan.

In 1795, Hamilton resigned his cabinet office to return to more lucrative work at a New York office, but continued to influence the Treasury Department and to write critical essays for the newspapers under the pen names "Camillus" and "Philo-Camillus." He remained popular among merchants and insurance brokers. In 1798, he served Washington as military inspector-general. When the federalist coalition crumbled, Hamilton lashed out angrily at John Adams with public diatribes. To continue expressing his opinions on finance and the value of a centralized government, he co-founded the New York *Evening Post*. In 1804, a duel at Weehawken against Vice President Aaron Burr, whom Hamilton helped defeat in a state gubernatorial election, ended Hamilton's life with a single shot. The Treasury Department honored him by placing his likeness on the ten-dollar bill.

***See also* coins in art; Thomas Jefferson; U.S. coins; U.S. Mint; U.S. Treasury.**

SOURCES: Allen, Larry. *Encyclopedia of Money*. New York: Checkmark Books, 2001. • Brookhiser, Richard. "A Founding Father's Return to Grace." *U.S. News & World Report*, November 10, 1997, pp. 71–72. • *Encyclopedia of World Biography*. Detroit: Gale Group, 1998. • Lind, Michael. "Hamilton's Legacy." *Wilson Quarterly*, Summer 1994, 40–52. • Reed, Mort. *Cowles Complete Encyclopedia of U.S. Coins*. New York: Cowles Book Company, 1969. • Taxay, Don. *The U.S. Mint and Coinage*. New York: Arco Publishing, 1966.

Heyn, Piet

Unlike ordinary privateers who followed lone Spanish treasure ships separated from *flotas* ("convoys"), Piet Heyn (or Hein) made history as the merchant captain who captured a whole flotilla known as the *Zilvervloot* ("silver fleet"). A national hero to the Dutch, he garnered more treasure from Iberian ships than the total stolen by other pirates and privateers in the 1500s and 1600s. He was born Pieter Pieterszoon in the Delfshaven of Rotterdam on November 15, 1577. At age 20, he was captured by the Spanish and forced to row a galley for four years. After gaining his freedom through an exchange for a Spanish prisoner, he rose to admiral in the Dutch navy and enriched himself as a privateer while directing the Dutch West India Company.

Fueling Heyn's seagoing zeal was a lust for vengeance. In December 1623, he began making his reputation aboard the *Hollandia* by bombarding and capturing Bahía, Brazil. With a band of 60, he seized 38 Portuguese vessels in the harbor, then took the walled city. His occupation force also apprehended galleons arriving at the harbor without knowledge of the Dutch seizure. Heyn returned home with four shiploads of pelts, sugar, and tobacco. His next assignment to wrest the slaving center of São Paulo de Loanda, Angola, from the Portuguese failed, as did an encounter with Don Fadrique de Toledo, who retook Bahía on April 30, 1625.

Still vigorously pursuing plunder, Heyn looted the port of Matanzas Bay, 50 miles east of the heavily fortified Caribbean harbor of Havana, Cuba, and seized Spanish ships. In 1627, he waylaid 22 Portuguese galleons off Havana, where citizens quaked at his reputation for bold attack. After losing the *Hollandia* to cannon fire, he left it to sink in Bahía harbor along with treasure and swag. On August 4, 1628, he toyed with the Spanish by anchoring off Cuba to size up the formation of the annual convoy. Sea scouts reported his presence to Admiral Juan de Benavides, an inept captain general of a 20-ship treasure convoy from Vera Cruz, who returned to port on the excuse that his ship had lost its mast.

Leading 30 warships, Heyn chased Benavides's ship into the bay, where Benavides unintentionally grounded it. Before the flagship or its companion could fire one of its 51 cannon, Heyn and a fighting force of musketeers boarded tenders and nabbed the ships of Benavides and his second in command, Admiral Don Juan de Leoz. The treasure was so massive that Heyn added two Spanish ships to his fleet of 28 to haul the money to Holland. On his way east during a storm, he lost two of the Spanish galleons and much treasure in silver coins at Golden Rock south of Lucaya Beach in the Bahamas.

In all Heyn seized six galleons loaded with 46 tons of silver pieces of eight and bars, which he added to the plunder from nine other seizures. The total, worth 12 million guilders, was sufficient to finance Holland's war with Spain. For a triumphant parade in Amsterdam, laborers worked for five days loading Heyn's haul on 1,000 mule carts. The wealth of the silver fleet enabled the West India Company to declare a 50 percent dividend and plunged the Spanish economy into deficit.

Heyn spared his victims, Benavides and Leoz. In disgrace, they returned to Spain, where Philip IV charged Benavides with cowardice and decreed his public humiliation and decapitation. Leoz received a sentence of life in prison. Commissioned lieutenant-admiral by Frederick Hendrik, Prince of Oranje, Count of Nassau, in 1629, Heyn died in action by cannon fire while he pursued 10 Dunkirk privateers from Oostende on a raid of the Schelde Canal. A statue depicting the privateer adorns his birthplace; a tunnel and a Dutch naval frigate bear his name. Biographer Robert F. Marx summarized his heroism in *The Capture of the Treasure Fleet: The Story of Piet Heyn* (1977). In 1995, the republic of Cuba issued a brass *peso* picturing Heyn's assault on Spanish sailors.

SOURCES: Allen, Thomas B. "Cuba's Golden Past." *National Geographic*, July 2001, 74–91. • "Atocha Dive Expeditions." *Skin Diver*, December 1999, 96. • Bowden, Tracy. "Gleaning Treasure from the Silver Bank." *National Geographic*, July 1996, 90–105. • Cockburn, Alexander. "Beat the Devil: Imperial Addictions." *The Nation*, August 3, 1985, 70–71. • *Contemporary Newsmakers 1985*. Detroit: Gale Research, 1986. • Cribb, Joe. *Money*. Toronto: Stoddart, 1990. • Kemp, Peter, ed. *The Oxford Companion to Ships and the Sea*. Oxford: Oxford University Press, 1988. • Marx, Robert F. "Discovery of the Admiral's Flagship." *Sea Frontiers*, March-April 1982, 80–86. • Pickford, Nigel. *The Atlas of Ship Wrecks & Treasure*. New York: Dorling Kindersley, 1994. • Sandz, Victoria. *Encyclopedia of Western Atlantic Shipwrecks and Sunken Treasure*. Jefferson, N.C.: McFarland, 2001.

Hibernia coppers

Contributing to colonial currency during widespread scarcity of small change were Hibernia coppers, the product of English copper and tin miner William Wood. In 1722, he supplied ores for coinage of pennies for circulation in Ireland and America. With a patent from the Duchess of Kendal, which he bought for £10,000, he monopolized Irish coinage and generated 360 tons of Irish half-cent coins and farthings called Hibernia coins from the Latin name for the island. On them he pictured the king, George I, and, on the reverse, the personified Hibernia plucking a harp. The pieces, called "Wood's halfpence," were better than Ireland's native coins, but were so debased and heavy that the coiner lost on his investment.

Because of their origin outside Ireland by the hated English exploiters, the coins did not please peasants, but they remained in use for 15 years because they supplied a need. In 1723, Ireland's Houses of Parliament protested Wood's patent as anti–Irish. Dublin-born satirist and pamphleteer Jonathan Swift spoke for nationalists through "The Drapier's Letter" (1725), an epistle from a fictitious M. B. Drapier to shopkeepers that savaged Wood as a profiteer on Irish poverty. Intent on Irish fiscal independence, Drapier pointed out that Charles II and James II licensed Ireland to coin its own money and retain the profits. Skating close to defaming the crown, Drapier charged:

> Now, here you may see that the vile Accusation of Wood and his Accomplices, charging us with disputing the King's Prerogatives, by refusing his Brass, can have no Place; because compelling the Subject to take any Coin, which is not Sterling, is no Part of the King's Prerogative [Swift 1958, 463].

Swift, speaking through the thin mask of Drapier, thundered, "We should only give our manufactures in Exchange, and keep our Gold and Silver at home" (*ibid.*, p. 467).

To Wood himself, whose action Drapier characterized as "the insupportable Villainy and Impudence of that incorrigible Wretch," the letter summoned visions of the "Hanging, Beheading, Quartering, Emboweling, and the like" of the traitor William Wallace and warned "here is a Dinner getting ready for us" (*ibid.*, p. 471). Swift demanded that officials melt down the Hibernia coins and cast the metal into copper balls for Wood to swallow. The bold confrontation of Wood's monopoly earned Swift the admiration of his fellow Irish and the support of English poet Alexander Pope, who wrote in *Imitations of Horace* (1737):

> Let Ireland tell, how Wit upheld her cause,
> Her Trade supported, and supply'd her laws;
> And leave on Swift this grateful verse ingrav'd,
> The Rights a Court attack'd, a Poet sav'd
> [Baugh 1948, p. 864].

Simultaneous with Swift's rise to heroism, Wood, who was three years into his copper coinage, wisely abandoned the project and transferred some of his coins to the American colonies, where, in lieu of a national monetary system, citizens welcomed foreign coins and immigrants' money. In 1737, the production of regal Irish coppers ended the circulation of Hibernian pennies. Wood's coppers returned to favor in Georgia during the specie shortage during the American Civil War.

SOURCES: Baugh, Albert C. *A Literary History of England.* New York: Appleton-Century-Crofts, 1948. • Drabble, Margaret, ed. *The Oxford Companion to English Literature.* Oxford: Oxford University Press, 1985. • Jordan, Louis, "The Coins of Colonial and Early America." http://www.coins.nd.edu/ColCoin/ColCoinContents/Introduction.html. • Mossman, Philip L. "The Circulation of Irish Coinage in Pre-Federal America." *Colonial Newsletter,* April 1999, pp. 1899–1917. • Mossman, Philip L. *Money of the American Colonies and Confederation.* New York: American Numismatic Society, 1993. • Swift, Jonathan. *Gulliver's Travels and Other Writings.* New York: Modern Library, 1958.

Hill, Sir George

Numismatist and archeologist Sir George Francis Hill elevated the importance of coin lore as a source of history and culture. Born to a missionary family in Bengal in 1867, he was educated in London and at University College, where he studied Greek art in sculpture, pottery, and coins. After completing graduate training on scholarship at Merton College, Oxford, he took up numismatics as a career. Influenced by antiquities expert Percy Gardner, author of *Types of Greek Coins* (1883), Hill obtained a position at the British Museum, a national repository of ethnology, as a specialist in Greek and Renaissance art. In April 1893, he began cataloguing Greek coins for the Department of Coins and Medals.

Hill's prolific writings particularize much of the art and coinage of the Mediterranean. His articles and many illustrated titles advanced knowledge of ancient coinage and their legends: *Lycia, Pamphylia, and Pisidia* (1897), *Handbook of Greek and Roman Coins* (1899), *Lycaonia, Isauria, and Cilicia* (1900), *A Manual of Greek Historical Inscriptions* (1901), *Coins of Ancient Sicily* (1903), *Cyprus* (1904), *Historical Greek Coins* (1906), *Historical Roman Coins* (1909), *Phoenicia* (1910), *Palestine* (1914), *Arabia, Mesopotamia, and Persia* (1922), *L'Art dans les Monnaies Grecques and Select Greek Coins* (1927), *The Coins of Narbonensis with Iberian Inscriptions* (1930), *Notes on the Ancient Coinage of Hispania Citerior* (1931), and *A Guide to the Principal Coins of the Greeks* (1932). In addition, his intense scholarship on coins on the museum's behalf included the editing of *Historia Nummorum* (1911), a classic to coin experts.

Hill became more than a collector of memorabilia. His interest in treasure troves influenced laws governing rewards to the finder. During World War I, as keeper of coins and medals at the British Museum, he labeled, packed, and hid the contents of 500 cabinets in subterranean vaults to protect precious antiquities from possible seizure. At age 64, he became the first archeologist to direct the museum. During debate of the Elgin marbles, he actively defended its holdings and oversaw remodeling and acquisitions, including the *Codex Sinaiticus,* the earliest extant biblical manuscript. His dedication earned him a knighthood, honorary degrees, medals, and fellowship in the British Academy.

SOURCES: "George Hill." http://www.amnumsoc.org/inc/hillbio.html. • Hill, G. F. *The Ancient Coinage of Southern Arabia.* Chicago: Ares Publishers, 1969. • Hill, G. F. *Historical Greek Coins.* Chicago: Argonaut, Inc., 1966. • Hill, G. F. *Historical Roman Coins.* Chicago: Argonaut, Inc., 1966. • "The Law of Treasure Trove in England and Wales." http://www.amnumsoc.org/inc/treasur2.htm. • "The Parthenon Sculptures." *The British Museum,* http://www.thebritishmuseum.ac.uk/parthenon/7.html.

hoarding

Sizeable caches of coins, paper notes, and plate provide valuble information about coinage and offer a glimpse into the behaviors of people during war or in social situations where they chose to secure coins in a secret stash. As described by Philip Grierson's *Numismatics* (1975), coin finds fall into identifiable categories — casual finds, savings caches, emergency caching, abandoned hoards, accidental loss, and excavation finds. For studies of history, money troves like those unearthed by archeologist Heinrich Schliemann are useful to research, particularly the study of the emergence of money as a medium of exchange. In the 1930s, for example, London-born classicist and numismatist Michael Grant, author of *The Climax of Rome: The Final Achievements of the Ancient World, A.D. 161–337* (1968), applied microchemical analysis to brass and bronze Roman pieces to determine how much lead, tin, and zinc impurities adulterated the coins of the early empire.

For historians, casual finds like the coins that collected in the stairwell of the Campanile that collapsed at St. Mark's Piazza in Venice in 1902, those from ritual burials, and those from requests for healing through being tossed into St. Querdon's well at Kirkcudbrightshire in Scotland are less useful than sizeable accumulations of one person. These include robber and pirate hoards, quick burials of coins during Viking invasions and raids, and the stash found at the Old Customs House at Bristol, England, in 1923, which provide samples and proportions of circulating specie. Numismatic analysis provided a valuable cross-section of history from examination of the 13,000 good luck coins that Romans tossed into the Celtic goddess Coventina's well at Procolitia (or Brocolitia) on Hadrian's Wall at Carrowburgh, England, from A.D. 130 until A.D. 407. Studies of such archeological digs offer a stratified sample of coin populations by period.

One class of coin hoard consists of specially minted ritual money similar in nature and manufacture to Chinese spirit money. Coins retrieved from the shrine of Zeus Kasios at Corcyra and the temple of Apollo at Didyma in Miletus revealed a special class of priest-made dedicated pieces. At a fountain at Nîmes, France, temple staff struck normal round coins with official Roman dies and added an appendage to resemble hams, perhaps convenient substitutes for sacrifice of living pigs. The *denarii* that seekers cast into a well at Bar Hill, Scotland, were counterfeit pieces made from copper alloy, tin, and silver from a limited number of molds. These finds generate clues to culture and religious custom and to the government and politics of the monarchs pictured on each coin.

Underground hoards, oftentimes secreted far from towns, present unique qualities, for example the international collection of Byzantine, English, German, Muslim, and Roman coins found in the Oxarve hoard on the island of Gotland off Sweden in 1920. A worthy example of a personal stash is the Johann Lohe hoard of 18,000 pieces of silver dating from the late 1600s to 1741. Numismatist Bengt Thordeman summarized the output of Swedish mints after the discovery of the cache in 1937 at a residential cellar vault in Stockholm. The largest classical hoard, which was unearthed near Modena, Italy, in 1714, contained 80,000 *aurei* from the Roman Republic. The owner probably buried them in 37 B.C. during the upheaval that followed the assassination of Julius Caear and the subsequent rise of the Roman Empire. Another stash, the Demanhur hoard of 8,000 *tetradrachms* of Alexander the Great found in Lower Egypt in 1905, attests to an annual tribute that Theodosius II paid to Attila the Hun in the A.D. 440s. The money appears to have passed to one of Attila's retainers.

The more personal savings hoards date to times and places where the banking of personal wealth was either unavailable or unsafe. Characterizing personal stashes was a French saying, "*Le sol était le coffre-fort de nos ancêtres*" ("The *sol* was the strongbox of our forebears") (Grierson 1975, p. 135). Families found unusual places to secure their savings, for example, in hollowed out spots in walls and overhead beams or behind loose stones in chimneys and hearths. These hoards often proved Gresham's law in that they comprised high-quality, high-value coins, often newly minted and uncirculated. To cull the least valuable, owners tossed out or spent for everyday purchases the underweight or clipped coins and kept the best specimens.

In November 2001, when allied forces besieged the Taliban government in Afghanistan, historians speculated on a 20,000-coin hoard rumored to lie in a vault at the presidential palace in Kabul. Amassed in six burial mounds called Tillya-tepe around 100 B.C., the "Golden Hoard of Bactria" collected ornaments, dragon figurines, winged goddesses, pendants and necklaces, a pearl-and-turquoise crown, and 600 gold pieces from Kunduz dating to the third and second centuries B.C. Among them were the largest Greek coins ever unearthed. Among the glorious hoard were an Indian coin in Kharoshthi script picturing a human form steadying the eight-spoked *dharmachakra* (wheel of truth), a symbol of the multiple views of a human dilemma and the eightfold path of Buddhism.

The treasure went into the ground during a period of regular treks along the Silk Road, a trade route carrying Central Asian goods to Persia, Byzantium, and Republican Rome. The first to unearth the trove was Greek-Russian archaeologist Viktor Ivanovich Sarianidi (or Sariyiannidis) of the Institute of Archaeology in Moscow in 1978, at a time when civil war threatened Afghanistan. He summarized the hoard in *Bactrian Gold: From the Excavations of the Tillya-tepe Necropolis in Northern Afghanistan* (1985). Most exciting of the coins he unearthed was a gold Parthian portrait coin, the first of its kind in numismatic history.

The riches passed to the Kabul Museum and remained there until 1991, when President Najibullah retrieved them from a rock vault to exhibit them to ambassadors and the media. Since that time, the hoard may have been purloined, distributed to other countries, or melted down to fund the Taliban war against Russia. Ahmed Shah Massoud, an anti–Taliban warrior, confirmed that the trove remained under the presidential palace.

***See also Admiral Gardner;* Anglo-Saxon coins; Appledore hoard; *Atocha;* Canute I; *La Capitana;* Celtic coins; *Central America; daric;* English money; Mel Fisher; Thomas Gresham; Gresham's Law; India, money of; Islamicmoney; *klippe; mark; Palemón;* paper money; Patching hoard; Samuel Pepys; Peter's pence; plate money; postage currency; Redfield hoard; Heinrich Schliemann; Scottish coins; shekel; shipwrecks; Peter Throckmorton; tokens; Tregwynt hoard; underwater archeology; U.S. Bureau of Engraving and Printing; U.S. Mint.**

SOURCES: Baronowski, Donald Walter. "Review: From Rome to Byzantium: The Fifth Century A.D." *Canadian Journal of History*, August 1999, p. 265. • Dupree, Nancy Hatch. "Museum Under Siege." *Archaeology*, April 20, 1998. • Grierson, Philip. *Numismatics*. London: Oxford University Press, 1975. • Hastings, James, ed. *Encyclopedia of Religion and Ethics*. New York: Charles Scribner's Sons, 1951. • Keys, David. "Buried 1,800 Years Ago, 43 Coins Offer Clues to High-Society Roman London." *Independent*, January 10, 2001. • Sarianidi, Viktor Ivanovich. "The Golden Hoard of Bactria." *National Geographic*, March 1990, pp. 50–75. • "Treasure News." http://www.treasurelore.com/florida/treasure_news.htm.

hogge money

The copper shillings of Bermuda, which English mints produced from 1615 to 1616, earned the name "hogge money" because they presented the likeness of a wild boar on the back of a dignified surface image of a three-masted ship. Historians assume that the vessel was the *Sea Venture* (or *Sea Adventurer*), which carried the first island settlers from Plymouth, England, in 1609. The shilling symbolized the swine that Juan de Bermudez introduced to local fauna when he sailed to Bermuda on the Spanish galleon *La Garza* in 1503. The image also commemorated the foraging of the first 150 settlers for food after their shipwreck on "Somers Islands," which they named for Admiral Sir George Somers. The coins were the first struck in the Western Hemisphere's English colonies.

Like other English colonies, the islands lacked currency for daily commerce. After a year of the exchange of leaf tobacco in lieu of legal tender, King James I licensed island planters to mint coins. Arranged by Governor Richard Tucker through a London mint, the first pieces were deliberately poor quality copper or mixed metal *subaerati* (coated coins) washed in a silver glaze. The four known denominations — twopence, threepence, sixpence, and twelvepence — displayed the inscription "Sommer Islands" and the value in Roman numerals.

In summer 1994, Dr. Edward Harris, director of the Bermuda Maritime Museum, and Norman Barka from the College of William and Mary in Williamsburg, Virginia, led a dig of Castle Island, a three-acre cay at the mouth of Castle Harbour. The site of the remains of King's Castle, the island fort, revealed a ditch dug after 1612 and a midden. Among the left-overs from island trash were 13 coins, the hogge money of the first settlers. Because only 19 examples survive, historians surmise that the first batch, shipped from England in February 1616, was small.

SOURCES: "The British Royal Mint." http://www.royalmint.com. • "Hog Money Discovery at Castle Island." http://www.insiders.com/bermuda/sb-history.htm. • Jordan, Louis. "The Coins of Colonial and Early America." http://www.coins.nd.edu/ColCoin/ColCoinContents/Introduction.html. • "Sommer Islands 'Hogge Money' the First Coinage in the English-Speaking New World." *Money Talks*, American Numismatic Association, December 1996.

Hull, John

Puritan silversmith John Hull struck the first coins produced by the Massachusetts Bay Colony and kept a ledger, the first record of an American mint. A native of England born on December 18, 1624, at age 11, he emigrated from Harborough, Leicestershire, to Boston on the ship *George* with his parents, Elizabeth Storer and Robert Hull, a farmer and blacksmith. The family settled on a plot on the Muddy River. After brief studies under Philemon Pormort, Hull aided his father on the farm while learning goldsmithing from his stepbrother Richard, who had apprenticed for ten years under London goldsmith James Fearne. In 1647, a few months after his mother's death, John married Judith Quincy and built a house on land given him by his father.

A worthy treasurer for the Massachusetts colony, Hull was a pious churchman, corporal in the militia, and cautious businessman. Because the shortage of coins stymied commerce, the colony set up minting in 1652 and hired Hull to strike the first issue at a profit of five percent. At a mint house erected on his property, he incised dies with the willow, oak, and pine, the symbols of the colonies' first shillings, along with his mint mark and the legend "Masathusets." He was aided by a partner, Robert Sanderson, who produced twopence, threepence, and sixpence pieces while Hull made necessary trips to England.

In 1658, Hull was elected Boston's treasurer and rose to ensign of its musketeers. His other accomplishments — co-founder of South Church and deputy to the general court — indicate the high trust citizens placed in him. In 1675, he kept the war treasury and, five years later, joined the governor's cabinet. With his accumulated lands and wealth, he became the colony's unofficial financier. According to legend, when his daughter, Hannah Hull, his only living child and heir, wed American jurist Samuel Sewall, John Hull posted a dowry of colonial pine tree shillings equal to her weight in coin.

***See also* colonial coins.**

SOURCES: *Biography Resource Center*. Farmington Hills, Mich.: Gale Group, 2001. • Davies, Glyn. *A History of Money from Ancient Times to the Present Day*. Cardiff: University of Wales Press, 1994. • Jordan, Louis. "The Coins of Colonial and Early America." http://www.coins.nd.edu/ColCoin/ColCoinContents/Introduction.html. • Pollak, Henry. *Coinage & Conflict*. Clifton, N.J.: Coin & Currency Institute, 2001. • Van Ryzin, Robert R. *Twisted Tails: Sifted Fact, Fantasy and Fiction from U.S. Coin History*. Iola, Wisc.: Krause Publications, 1995.

Hunley

The world's first submarine and the first to sink a battleship, the C.S.S.H.L. *Hunley*, built from a recycled iron steam boiler in 1863 at Mobile, Alabama, served the Confederacy in the defense of the harbor in Charleston, South Carolina. Measuring 39.5 by 5 by 4 feet, the cucumber-shaped sub was called a "David Board" after submarine inventor David Bushnell. Traveling up to four knots, the short-range craft functioned by an eight-person crank shaft and a rudder steered by the captain. Its only fittings included a snorkel for drawing air from the surface and a candle to light the interior.

On February 17, 1864, the *Hunley*'s crew sank the U.S.S. *Housatonic*, a Union gunship, with a 135-pound spar topedo attached to the sub's bow. The enemy ironclad erupted from an explosive charge thrust into its side. The *Hunley* crew signaled success, but sank before reaching shore, killing engineer Lieutenant George E. Dixon, the sub's commander, and his crew. It was the third sinking of the *Hunley*; two previous crews had drowned.

After a 14-year search at a cost of $130,000, in May 1995, a salvage operation led by author Clive Cussler and a search team from the National Underwater and Marine Agency, supported by the National Geographic Society, located the wreckage of the *Hunley*. Using several slings and trusses, salvors raised the hulk in August 2000 at a cost of $17 million. In remains of clothing, searchers found a 20-dollar double eagle gold piece minted in 1860 that Dixon received from his fiancée, Queenie Bennet of Mobile, Alabama. Because he carried the coin in his pants pocket, it had saved his leg from a Minié ball at Shiloh, Tennessee, where he had fought for the 21st Alabama Infantry.

The coin took on a new life as an amulet. Dixon engraved it in script with "Shiloh/April 6, 1862/My Life Preserver/G. E. D." He treasured the dented, bell-shaped piece and frequently rubbed and gripped it as a good-luck charm. During Dixon's convalescence from the war injury, which left him with a limp, he helped Horace Lawson Hunley and James McClintock, two New Orleans designers, build and test submarines.

Archeologist Maria Jacobsen's recovery of the amulet coin ends supposition that Dixon may not have been aboard the night the Hunley sank. Another crew member, Union soldier Ezra Chamberlin, left his calling card in the hulk. Salvors located his medallion, which opened to question whether he was a spy, changed sides to fight for the Confederacy, or lost his medal in combat, perhaps to a Rebel looter searching his corpse after his death at Fort Wagner at Morris Island, South Carolina, on July 11, 1863. Although one tall human skeleton clutched a candle, nothing linked the remains to a specific crew member. The remains of the *Hunley* lie at the Warren Lasch Conservation Center at the Charleston Navy Base, where restorers study early submarine operation and history. The coin resides in an undisclosed safe.

SOURCES: "Forget the Titanic: Everyone Really Wants a Piece of the Hunley." *Wall Street Journal*, March 23, 2001. • Hicks, Brian. "Hunley Team Hoping to Find Fabled Coin." (Charleston, S.C.) *Post and Courier*, May 24, 2001. • Hicks, Brian. "Union Private's Tale adds to Hunley Lore," (Charleston, S.C.) *Post and Courier*, May 1, 2001. • "The Hunley.com." http://www.thehunley.com/coinfound.htm. • Kropf, Schuyler, and Brian Hicks. "Dixon's Coin Found." (Charleston, S.C.) *Post and Courier*, May 25, 2001. • Sandz, Victoria. *Encyclopedia of Western Atlantic Shipwrecks and Sunken Treasure*. Jefferson, N.C.: McFarland, 2001. • "A Submarine Sinks Myths About the Confederacy." *Christian Science Monitor*, July 25, 2001.

Ieyasu

The organizer of Japan's first money system, Tokugawa Ieyasu excelled at governance. Born to the warrior class in Okazaki, Japan, on January 31, 1543, he lived east of Nagoya and came of age during the Tokugawa or Edo shogunate. While his father engaged in combat, in 1549, the boy's mother left home, giving the father no choice but to pledge his son as a hostage. Residing with the Imagawas at Sumpu without knowledge that his father had fallen in battle in 1560, Ieyasu studied warfare, falconry, and political science. In his mid-teens, he made his first venture into combat.

With no family to claim him, after 12 years under virtual house arrest in Sumpu, Ieyasu returned to the family home, retrieved his wife and son Hidetada, and headed a family comprised of his relatives and their clients. An admirable warrior and leader, he worked toward developing a stable government and court system. After winning the Sekigahara War in 1600, he set up a capital at Hamamatsu. He encouraged coastal trade by establishing Kinza gold mints at Tokyo and the Ginza silver mints at Tokyo with branches at Kyoto, Obanza, and Sado to strike coins, particularly the oblong pieces called *oban* and *koban*. Financial success boosted him to the status of *daimyo* (feudal lord) and from there to Japan's master.

A qualified governor, Ieyasu pacified his people by disarming them and supplied water to their hamlets. To promote commerce, he ordered artisans to hammer or mold gold and silver into oval *cho-gin* (bean cake ingots) and square *mameita-gin* (bean ingots). His system of fixed values simplified valuation of money for peasants:

coin	*value*
ichibuban	one *shu*
isshuban	one *shu*
bu	four *shu* or four *ichibuban* or four *isshuban*
ryo	four *bu* or 16 *shu* or one *koban*
koban	four *bu* or 16 *shu* or one *ryo*
oban	10 *ryo* or 10 *koban* or 40 *bu* or 160 *shu*

The coins fueled foreign trade with China, the Philippines, Mexico, and Europe. In the three years preceding his death from a lingering illness on June 1, 1616, he joined his son in building an impressive moated castle.

***See also* oban.**

SOURCES: Clain-Stefanelli, Elvira, and Vladimir Clain-Stefanelli. *The Beauty and Lore of Coins, Currency, and Medals.* Croton-on-Hudson, N.Y.: Riverwood Publishers, 1974. • Cribb, Joe. *Money.* Toronto: Stoddart, 1990. • *The Harper Encyclopedia of Military Biography.* New York: HarperCollins, 1992. • Lubarsky, Jared, "Showcase of the Shoguns," *National Geographic Traveler*, March 2001, pp. 50–57. • Shappell, Chris, "Y Notes and Y News," *American Numismatic Association Newsletter*, November 14, 2001.

incuse

Incuse or intaglio style coinage and signet rings, adorned with a design struck into a plane, is the opposite of bas-relief, which emerges from a field or background, and derives its name from the Latin for "beat in." In the late 600s B.C., coinsmiths of Ardys, King of Lydia, struck electrum disks with incuse punches, sinking a design into each coin surface. The technician left the reverse blank. One example of a *stater* from Croton, a city-state of Magna Graecia in southern Italy, around 530 B.C., pictured the tripod of Apollo stamped into the coin; a contemporary, the stater of Sybaris, displayed a horned ox. On the other side, the images were evident in reverse.

From around 530 B.C., a *stater* of Sybaris, a Greek colony in southern Italy, displays a horned ox. On the back side, the images are evident in reverse. (Guy Clark, Ancient Coins and Antiquities, Norfolk, Virginia)

A silver *drachma* from Sinope, Paphlagonia, from around 480 B.C. revealed a crudely stamped eagle head opposite a nondescript square punch mark. For all its crudeness, the coin serves as one of the earliest examples of silver coinage. A more artistic coin, a *stater* struck at nearby Caulonia, featured Apollo standing alongside an antlered stag. Around 450 B.C., in the time of Xerxes of Persia, a silver *siglos* pictured the king holding bow and arrow in a recessed image.

In 1772, English engineer Matthew Boulton applied steam-powered coinage to the problem of counterfeit coppers. To make the coins difficult to copy, he created a heavy, efficient machining system that impressed incuse lettering into the edge with a retaining collar to protect the coin from wear. The heavy striking mechanism, which few counterfeiters would attempt to copy, turned out 150 small coins per minute. In 1786, the East India Company commissioned 100 tons of his copper pennies. Two years later, the Royal Mint invited him to submit motifs for the halfpence, but gave Boulton no contract until 1797, when he began cranking out the popular cartwheel coins.

***See also* Matthew Boulton; Greek**

coins; medieval coins; penny; Benedetto Pistrucci; Bela Lyon Pratt.

SOURCES: Clain-Stefanelli, Elvira, and Vladimir Clain-Stefanelli. *The Beauty and Lore of Coins, Currency, and Medals.* Croton-on-Hudson, N.Y.: Riverwood Publishers, 1974. • Cribb, Joe. *Money.* Toronto: Stoddart, 1990. • Cribb, Joe, Barrie Cook, and Ian Carradice. *The Coin Atlas.* London: Little, Brown and Co., 1999. • Davies, Glyn. *A History of Money from Ancient Times to the Present Day.* Cardiff: University of Wales Press, 1994. • Reinfeld, Fred. *Treasury of the World's Coins.* New York: Sterling Publishing, 1953. • Van Ryzin, Robert R. *Twisted Tails: Sifted Fact, Fantasy and Fiction from U.S. Coin History.* Iola, Wisc.: Krause Publications, 1995. • *World of Invention,* 2nd ed. Farmington Hills, Mich.: Gale Group, 1999.

India, money of

From early times, India's economy got by on primitive moneys — conch shells and iron in Angami Nagas, salt cakes and knife blades in Sema Nagas, brass disks in Ao Nagas, iron hoes in Manipur, gongs among the Chan, and rice seed in Malabar. Based on fragmentary evidence, historians deduce that the concept of money derived from Roman spice traders and Asokan missionaries. As described in the undated *Mahawamsa* (also *Maha Vamsa* or *Mahavamsa),* the great island chronicle of the Sinhalese compiled by Mahanama Maha Thera, the Indian subcontinent and neighboring Ceylon produced *kahapana* ("money") as early as the sixth century B.C.

The first true coins followed models made by the Persians who dominated northern India from 500 to 331 B.C. Although no descriptions survive, both *puranas* ("coins") and pearls served as negotiable funds for trade at Salgahawatta and Gedige in Anuradhapura. The rule of Greek princes in the Punjab and Kabul Valley coincided with mintages featuring the standard Greek pantheon of gods, primarily Zeus, Athena, Apollo, Artemis, Hercules, and the Dioscuri, the twins Castor and Pollux. Gradually, these deities gave place to distinctive Indian imagery, notably the Buddhist god Siva (also Siwa or Shiva) and the eight-spoked *dharmachakra* (wheel of truth), a symbol of the multiple views of a human dilemma and the eightfold path of Buddhism.

The first true coins in India followed models made by the Persians who dominated northern India after 500 B.C. (Guy Clark, Ancient Coins and Antiquities, Norfolk, Virginia)

According to Buddhist records, Ceylon developed a coin system of exchange in Lanka separate from mainland India around 400 B.C. Punched rather than hammered or stamped, the coins were small metal bars or strips sliced from hammered metal sheets and bearing a royal cipher. By clipping corners, the coinsmith adjusted each finished piece to suit its value. More artistic were the coins originating after 210 B.C., which bore the auspicious Pandyan fish symbol on the back. After 177 B.C., the elephant symbol supplanted the fish. In 28 B.C., Lanka acquired independence and circulated copper specie, some marked with goddess figures, perhaps indicating a single purpose for the coins for temple tithes. After the lapse of the dominant dynasty in A.D. 297, Lanka coins were mixed with lion-wheel coins from India.

The Greek territory south of Kush created its own *drachmas* after Eucratides, the king of Bactria, settled the region in 171 B.C. He appointed local monarchs and allowed them to coin their own money. One of the most historic of these satrapies was the Bactrian-Greek trade center at Sagara, ruled by King Menander or Milinda, a convert to Buddhism and author of *The Questions of King Milinda* (ca. 160 B.C.). He issued a silver *tetradrachma* in high relief picturing a standing figure of Athena with thunderbolt and standard. On the back is a more realistic image of the king himself on horseback. After Menander, Apollodotus II, who ruled the eastern bank of the Indus River, improved coinage with a realistic profile and a much

A gold *stater* minted in the Kushan kingdom of northern India and Afghanistan after A.D. 300 pictures King Shaka standing with a trident and banner in his hands and, on the reverse, the goddess Ardoksho enthroned. (Guy Clark, Ancient Coins and Antiquities, Norfolk, Virginia)

finer depiction of Athena in combat with upraised shield and lightning bolt.

The Gupta dynasty, northern monarchs who came to power in the late A.D. 200s, produced a renaissance of the arts marked by over three centuries of elegant coinage in bronze, silver, and gold. At the forefront were likenesses of Hindu deities, including the graceful Lakshmi, often depicted holding a lotus or riding a lion. Balancing her role as an emblem of beauty were the death god Siva on the bull Nandi and the likeness of Karttikeye the warrior. After the rise of the military conqueror Samudra Gupta in A.D. 330, like Rome's emperors, he used high-quality gold specie as propaganda to alter his bellicose reputation. The coins balanced his image as a warlord with humanistic endeavors by featuring his devotion to Vishnu and picturing Samudra playing the lyre.

From around A.D. 350, Indian mintmasters hired prime metalsmiths and sculptors to strike the gold *denara*. The coin, which influenced the Arab *dinar*, pictured Brahmanic design — graceful human shapes and valiant horses with oversized head and neck to suggest pride. Hindu symbology diversified into numerous emblems — a trident for empire, bull or elephant for power, umbrella for royal presence, crescent for a lunar dynasty, and spear or thunderbolt for might. Indian coiners acquired a new source of models from Arab invaders, who founded a dynasty in Sind in the A.D. 700s. After A.D. 998, the Muslim warrior-king Mahmud, sultan of Ghazna, pressed east from Afghanistan and became the first conqueror to carry Islam to central India. His method of spreading the faith included coining coins with tutorial messages in Nagari, the local language, to introduce pagans to the Koran and for the deification of Mohammed.

One of the influences on quality Indian coins was Iltutmish, the third and greatest of the Delhi sultans. After unseating the son and heir of Aibak in A.D. 1210, Iltutmish inaugurated his monarchy in the Rajput states at the new state capital, Delhi, which he protected from Mongol insurgents. Until the coinage of money, he signed over to his soldiers and clients the *Iqta*, the territorial revenue owed to the state. Eventually, he introduced copper *jitals* and silver *tanka*. In 1336, Vijayanagar of southern India, another influential financier, issued *pagodas* picturing the triune sacred pantheon of Laskhmi, Siva, and Vishnu.

Buddhist symbols declined on coins as Islam crept into the Indian subcontinent. The Islamic *kalima* ("creed") — "There is no God but God, Mohammed is the Prophet of God" — came to dominate specie legends both in Arabic and Sanskrit and bore Islamic dating rather than that of the Roman calendar (Clain and Clain 1974, p. 175). Apart from the religious fervor of the mainland, the Ceylonese, who escaped Muslim oppression, used lumps of antimony to shape bullet coins.

Into the late 1500s, as described by a French traveler in *The Voyage of François Pyrard of Laval to the East Indies, the Maladives, the Molucas, and Brazil* (ca. 1610), cowries remained the cash of the peasant for trade in northeastern Indian around Bengal and required transport in baskets and bales of 12,000 shells each. Even lords and royalty built storehouses to hold shells. As India profited from trade with the Middle East, coiners acquired copper, silver, and gold and struck their own *dinars* and *adli* of pure metal. From billon, a cupro-silver alloy, they produced small change.

From the 1500s, the *rupee*, named for the Sanskrit for "silver" or "cow," became the predominant monetary unit in India, Pakistan, and Sri Lanka. 'Umayyad silver made a major contribution to the monetary system into the reign of Afghan emperor Sher Shah of Sur in northwestern India. A devout Muslim, he established a model of Islamic coinage with the silver *rupiya*, featuring the emperor's title opposite identification of four caliphs and the Islamic profession of the faith in calligraphy. The shah assured the services of a *shroff* ("money changer") during transactions to establish legitimate value based on quality of coinage and subsequent wear.

The emperors Akbar the Great, ruler of Hindustan from 1556 to 1606, and his son and heir Jahangir (or Jehangir), the Mughal king of India from 1605 to 1627, also beautified Indian money. Outstanding elements include the Muslim scrollery on the square and round silver *rupees* of Akbar and portraits and signs of the zodiac on the gold coins that Jahangir's coinsmiths minted at Dacca. More eclectic than Mohammedan fanatics, Akbar ended Islamic calendar notation by renumbering years according to the *ilahi* ("divine era") formula to date from his accession to the throne. As a token of his religious tolerance, he further altered coinage by removing the Islamic creed and replaced it with the generic legend, "*Allahu Akbar Jalla Jalala*" ("God Is Most Great, Eminent Is His Glory") (Clain and Clain 1974, p. 184.) The dual meaning of "Akbar" heaped praise on both God and the emperor.

As Islam gained strength over India, Akbar's liberal and self-serving innovations disappeared. Less liberal than his father, Jahangir returned the Islamic creed to his coins. He also added lyrical compliments to his wife, Nur Jahan Badshah Beghum. For all his piety, his coiners boldly pictured Jahangir bearing the Koran in one hand and a wine goblet in the other in defiance of Mohammed's injunctions against alcohol. Because of Jahangir's inclusion of mythological figures and signs of the zodiac on his early coins and his impious portrait coins, his intensely Islamic son and successor, Shah Jahan, builder of the Taj Mahal, outlawed money minted during the previous reign and sentenced bearers to death.

The self-promoting monarchical style continued from 1658 to 1707 with the coinage of Jahan's successor, Aurangzeb, India's last great Mughal emperor. He identified pieces by mint and added a series of inscriptions in Persian honoring his name. Like Akbar, he also secularized coins, but for a pious reason. To keep sacred phrases from being desecrated in "unworthy places and [falling] under the feet of infidels," he abolished the minting of coins displaying Islam's holy creed (Hastings 1951, III, p. 709).

In 1658, Aurangzeb, India's last great Mughal emperor, introduced a self-promoting monarchical style of coinage. After abolishing the minting of coins displaying Islam's holy creed, he added Persian inscriptions honoring his name. (Guy Clark, Ancient Coins and Antiquities, Norfolk, Virginia)

Indian mintmasters produced noteworthy artistry on the square gold *mohur* of the 1600s and on the circular *pagoda*, an incised coin in circulation from the 1600s to the 1800s, but made no improvements on early models. During this era, French merchant Jean-Baptiste Tavernier, author of *Voyage en Perse, et Description de Ce Royaume* (*Journey to Persia, and a Description of Its Realm*) (1637), reported the use of bitter almonds for small change in Gujarat, a commercial center bordering the Arabian Sea. Merchants distributed them at the rate of 32 to 40 nuts to the *pice*.

Coinage in southern India was enumerated in *kasu* or cash, the Tamil term for "coin." As early as 1660, currency in Madras, as recorded by the East India Company, rated 80 cash as one gold *fanam*, a trading coin that had thrived in Ceylon since the 1300s. The cash became so common a unit in the English colonies that it could refer to any copper piece. Subsequent coinage produced multiple denominations. In 1691, a ten-cash coin or *dudu* appeared along with the half *dudu*, worth five cash. By 1803, trade required a 20-cash coin, called a *pice* or *pysa*, and advanced in 1807 to a 40-cash denomination as well as a 2.5-cash coin. The domination of the cash ended in 1818.

The *rupee* gained further acceptance after 1671, when the British East India Company struck copies of native coins; this set the *rupee* as the basic monetary unit. The value fluctuated until 1835, when Britain colonized India and issued laws standardizing the *rupee's* worth. Until 1893, any citizen could coin silver in either the *rupee* or half-*rupee* denomination. For its East African holdings in 1916, Germany altered the standard metal and minted gold *rupees* picturing Mount Kilimanjaro in Kenya and a New Guinean coin featuring a bird of paradise.

In addition to functional round coins, Indian mintmasters produced some of the world's most elegant scalloped coins. In 1915, the stamping of a one-*anna* piece contrasted a 12-lobed edging with an inset diamond shape formed of curved arches. In 1971, the style of a ten-*paise* piece displayed the modern version of the scalloped edge, which paired twelve doves with an elaborate flower circlet centered with a circle of small dogs. The next year, the treasury commissioned a two-*paise* coin with only eight lobes surrounding the lions that comprise the national blazon. Parallel to artful coinage thrived the traditional grain standard of villagers, who hoarded coins rather than spend them. According to author Radhakakmal Mukerjee's *The Foundation of Indian Economics* (1916), villagers used coins either as a means of storing value and or for wearing as jewelry or both.

Strongly influenced by Western colonizers, 20th-century coins and banknotes took on the designs common to northwestern Europe. For example, a ten-cent note issued on July 14, 1942, in Ceylon pictured the youthful face of George VI in typically British scrolled framing. Repetition of necessary data appeared near the bottom in native alphabet for the benefit of users who didn't read English. As colonialism crumbled, native mintmasters regained control of moneys after 1948 in Ceylon, India, and Pakistan. The Muslim state of Bangladesh began producing its unique money in 1972, a year after gaining its independence.

***See also* amulet coins; cowrie; fishhook money; Islamic money; world money.**

SOURCES: Allen, Larry. *Encyclopedia of Money*. New York: Checkmark Books, 2001. • "Beginnings of the Bhikkuni Sasanaya." *London Times*, October 2, 2001. • Clain-Stefanelli, Elvira, and Vladimir Clain-Stefanelli. *The Beauty and Lore of Coins, Currency, and Medals*. Croton-on-Hudson, N.Y.: Riverwood Publishers, 1974. • Cribb, Joe. *Money*. Toronto: Stoddart, 1990. • Cribb, Joe, Barrie Cook, and Ian Carradice. *The Coin Atlas*. London: Little, Brown and Co., 1999. • Einzig, Paul. *Primitive Money*. Oxford: Pergamon Press, 1966. • Grierson, Philip. *Numismatics*. London: Oxford University Press, 1975. • Hastings, James, ed. *Encyclopedia of Religion and Ethics*. New York: Charles Scribner's Sons, 1951. • Lewis, Brenda Ralph. *Coins & Currency*. New York: Random House, 1993. • Mitchiner, Michael. *Oriental Coins*. London: Hawkins, 1978. • Opitz, Charles J. *Odd and Curious Money*. Ocala, Fla.: First Impressions, 1986. • Starr, Chester G. *A History of the Ancient World*. New York: Oxford University Press, 1991. • Thomas, Edward. *Numismata Orientalia*. London: Trübner & Co., 1874. • Wickramasinhe, Rajah M. "Minted Legacy." *Sunday Observer*, June 10, 2001.

In God We Trust

The Christian tradition, established in the English colonies of North America by the Puritans, remained alive after Thomas Jefferson insisted on the separation of church and state with the First Amendment to the Constitution. Stated as the first law of the Bill of Rights, the First Amendment requires that Congress "make no law respecting an establishment of religion" (Pollak 2001, 32). The non-religious status quo in coinage shifted permanently in 1863 after James Barton Longacre, chief engraver ot the U.S. Mint, struck a two-penny coin featuring a national shield and banner bearing the legend "In God We Trust." It was the third attempt at producing the right tone and phrase, following "Our Trust Is in God" on the 1862 half-dollar, and "God Our Trust" on the same denomination the following year.

The phrase reflected the hardships the nation weathered at the height of the Civil War, as described in a letter dated November 13, 1861, from the Reverend M. R. Watkinson (also cited as N. R. or W. R. Watkinson) of Ridleyville, Pennsylvania, to Salmon P. Chase, Secretary of the Treasury. Watkinson, who called himself a "minister of the gospel," spoke passionately of fears for America's reputation in ages to come:

> What if our Republic were now shattered beyond reconstruction. Would not the antiquaries of succeeding centuries rightly reason from our past that we were a heathen nation. What I propose is that instead of the goddess of Liberty we shall have next inside the 13 stars a ring inscribed with the words "perpetual union"; within this ring the allseeing eye, crowned with a halo; beneath this eye the American flag, bearing in its field stars equal to the number of the States united; in the folds of the bars the words "God, liberty, law" ["In God We Trust on U.S. Coinage"].

As though the nation were already condemned for godlessness, Watkinson asserted that such a shift in coinage would free the United States "from the ignominy of heathenism" (*ibid.*).

Chase pondered a suitable phrase and instructed mint engraver James Pollock to add suitable wording to coin dies for a new coin, the two-center. The proposed wording varied from "Our Trust Is in God" to "God Our Trust," the exact phrase stamped in 1861 on copper, silver, and gold half dollars and gold and copper eagles. In 1863, more experimentation produced "God and Our Country" and "In God We Trust." The final phrase, "In God We Trust," earned Secretary Chase's approval for the two-cent piece produced in 1864. The coin, minted at the rate of two million the first year, became the first circulating U.S. specie bearing the new national motto.

Public and clerical response to the phrase "In God We Trust" was mixed. In 1907, President Theodore Roosevelt reputedly banned the godly phrase from gold eagles because he thought the words cheapened piety and promoted ridicule and disrespect for God. Enlarging his point, he said that the phrase "not only does no good but does positive harm, and is in effect irreverence which comes dangerously close to sacrilege" (Van Ryzin 1995, p. 142). A letter to *Century Illustrated Monthly Magazine* from Homer Saint-Gaudens, son of coiner Augustus Saint-Gaudens, in 1920, clarified that the artist discarded the phrase as "an inartistic intrusion" (*ibid.*, p. 138). To public approbation, Roosevelt left the matter up to Congress. On May 18, 1908, Congress made the phrase mandatory on gold and silver U.S. coins. It first appeared on paper notes in 1947.

An act passed by the 84th Congress and signed by President Dwight D. Eisenhower on July 30, 1956, made the phrase the national motto and required U.S. coins to bear the motto. When a court suit challenging the appearance of "In God We Trust" on national money reached the federal courts, it carried the frustration of citizens seeking the separation between church and state prescribed by the founding fathers, who feared establishment of a state church. The challenge, argued by the American Civil Liberties Union, was rejected by the lower federal courts. On appeal, the Supreme Court of the United States declined to review the case. In a preliminary trial in Topeka, Kansas, in October 2000, the American Center for Law and Justice, an international public interest law firm, asked the high court to dismiss the suit.

After the World Trade Center disaster on September 11, 2001, school districts and conservative religious groups pressed for leeway to display the motto in classrooms. In Tupelo, Mississippi, the 200,000-member American Family Association successfully pushed for a legislated requirement that each classroom post "In God We Trust" for student edification. Michigan passed a similar law in December 2001. While Indiana legislators rejected the idea, citizens in six states — Arizona, Florida, Louisiana, New Jersey, Utah, and Virginia — sought their own version of the motto-posting law. Opponents feared that the demand for display of the phrase as a support of patriotism disguised a push to put religion in school curricula.

See also **Thomas Jefferson; James Barton Longacre; paper money; Peace dollar; U.S. Bureau of Engraving and Printing; U.S. coins.**

SOURCES: "ACLU Asks Federal Court to Dismiss 'In God We Trust' Lawsuit Filed Against

Kansas County." *Business Wire*, October 3, 2000. • "Florida County Rejects 'In God We Trust' Posters." *Church & State*, October 1, 2001. • "History of the Motto 'In God We Trust.'" http://www.ustreas.gov/opc/opc0011.html. • "'In God We Trust' Motto for Mississippi Schools." *New York Times*, March 25, 2001. • "In God We Trust on U.S. Coinage." http://www.coinlibrary.com/info/ingodwetrust.html. • Pollak, Henry. *Coinage & Conflict*. Clifton, N.J.: Coin & Currency Institute, 2001. • Reed, Mort. *Cowles Complete Encyclopedia of U.S. Coins*. New York: Cowles Book Company, 1969. • Van Ryzin, Robert R. *Twisted Tails: Sifted Fact, Fantasy and Fiction from U.S. Coin History*. Iola, Wisc.: Krause Publications, 1995.

inscriptions

Coin and currency inscriptions offer a glimpse into the political, economic, and religious bias of the issuing country. Usually composed in elevated language, mottoes on coins and paper money often repeat a philosophical sentiment found in scripture or on district shields or family blazons. Models exist from the early history of coinage in a blend of Greek and Roman alphabets:

coin motto	*language*	*place/source*
A Deo et Caesare [From God and the Emperor]	Latin	Frankfurt, Germany
A Domino Factum est Istud et est Mirabile in Oculis Nostris [This Is the Work of the Lord and It Is Wondrous in Our Eyes.]	Latin	England
Ab Inimicis Meis Libera Me Deus [God, Free Me from My Enemies]	Latin	Burgundy
Adiuva Nos Deus Salutaris Noster [Help Us, Our God of Salvation]	Latin	Lorraine
Ad Legem Conventionis [According to the Law of Conventions]	Latin	Furstenberg
Ad Normam Conventionis [According to the Standard of Conventions]	Latin	Prussia
Ad Palmam Pressa Laeturo Resurgo [Pressed to the Palm I Joyfully Rise]	Latin	Wittgenstein
Ad Usam Luxemburgi CC Vallati [For the Use of the 200 Besieged of Luxemburg]	Latin	Luxemburg
Adventu Aug. Iudaea [On the Arrival of the August (Emperor) to Judea]	Latin	Rome
Adventus Optimi Principis [The Coming of the Chief Prince]	Latin	Vatican
Aes Usibus Aptius Auro [Bronze in Its Uses (Is) More Fitting Than Gold]	Latin	Brazil
Aeternum Meditans Decus [An Ornament Intended for All Time]	Latin	Alençone
Aliis Inserviendo Consumor [I Am Employed in Serving Others]	Latin	Brunswick-Wolfenbuttel
Allahu Akbar Jalla Jalala [God Is Most Great, Eminent Is His Glory]	Arabic	India
Alles Mit Bedacht [All with Reflection]	German	Brunswick
A Militari ad Regiam [From the Military to the Kingdom]	Latin	Britain
Amor Populi Praesidium Regis [The People's Love (Is) the King's Protection]	English	Charles I

coin motto	*language*	*place/source*
Ang Fra Dom Hib & Aquit [(King) of England and France, Lord of Ireland and Aquitaine]	Latin	Edward II
Anna Dei Gratia [Anne (Queen) by the Grace of God]	Latin	Britain
Anno Regni Primo [In the First Year of the Reign]	Latin	Britain
Apres les Tenebres la Lumiere [After the Shadows, the Light]	French	Geneva
Archangelus Michael [Archangel Michael]	Latin	Grimoald IV of Italy
Ardua ad Gloriam Via [Struggles (Are) the Path to Glory]	Latin	Waldeck
Arte Mea Bis Iustus Moneta Lud Iust [By My Art (I Am) Twice the Just Coin of Louis (XIII)]	Latin	France
A Solo lehova Sapientia [From Jehovah Alone (Comes) Wisdom]	Latin	Wittgenstein
Aspera Oblectant [Difficulties Please (Me)]	Latin	Nassau-Weilburg
Aspice Pisas Sup Omnes Specio [Behold This Coin, Superior to All (Other) Pisan (Coins)]	Latin	Pisa
Audiatur Altera Pars [Let the Other Party Be Heard]	Latin	Stavelot Monastery
Auf Gott Trawe Ich [In God I Trust]	German	Brunswick
Ausen Gefaesen der Kirchen und Burger [From the Vessels of the Church and Citizens]	German	Frankfurt
Auspicio Regis et Senatus Angliae [By Authority of the King and English Parliament]	Latin	East India Company
Auxilio fortissimo Dei [With the Mightiest Help of God]	Latin	Mecklenburg
Auxilium de Sanctio [Aid from the Sanctuary]	Latin	Vatican
Auxilium Meum a Duo Qui Fecit Celum e Terram [My Help (Comes) from God Who Made Heaven and Earth]	Latin	Portugal
Basileos Antiochou Theou Epiphanous Nikephorou [King Antiochus, God Manifest, Victory Bearing]	Greek	Syria
Basileus Romaion [King of the Romans]	Greek	Byzantium
Beata Tranquillatis [Blessed Tranquillity]	Latin	Licinius II of Rome
Beatus Qui Speravit in Dom [Blessed Is He Who Has Hoped in the Lord]	Latin	Mansfield
Benedic Haereditati Tuae [Blessings on Your Inheritance]	Latin	Savoy
Benedicta Sit Sancta Trinitas [Blessed Be the Holy Trinity]	Latin	Albon
Benedictio Domini Divites Facit [The Lord's Blessing Makes Riches]	Latin	Teschen
Benedictus Sit Nomen Domini Dei Jesus Christi [Blessed Be the Name of the Lord Jesus Christ]	Latin	France

coin motto	*language*	*place/source*
Benedictus Qui Venit in Nomine Domini [Blessed (Is) He Who Comes in the Name of the Lord]	Latin	Flanders
Beschaw das Ziel Sage Nicht Viel [Consider the Matter but Say Little]	German	Quedlinburg
Besser Land und Lud Verloren als ein Falscher Aid Geschworn [(It Is) Better to Lose Land and Wealth Than to Swear a False Oath]	German	Hesse
Bononia docet [Bologna teaches]	Latin	Bologna
Britanniarum Regina [Queen of the Britains]	Latin	England
Britt Omn Rex [King of all the Britains]	Latin	Britain
Caesar Dict Per Petuo [Caesar, dictator for life]	Latin	Rome
Cal et Car Com de Fugger in Zin et Norn Sen & Adm Fam [Cajetan and Carl, Counts of Fugger in Zinnenberg and Nordendorf, Lords and Family Administrators]	German	Fugger
Calumnia Sublata Fisc. Judaici [The Insult of the Jewish Tax Rescinded]	Latin	Rome
Candide et Constanter [Sincerely and steadfastly]	Latin	Hesse-Cassel
Candide sed Provide [Clearly but Cautiously]	Latin	Osterwitz
Candore et Amore [With Sincerity and Love]	Latin	Fulda
Candore et Constantia [With Sincerity and Constancy]	Latin	Bavaria
Capit Cath Ecclesia Monasteriensis [Chapter of the Cathedral Church of Munster]	Latin	Munster
Capit Eccle Metropolit Colon [Chapter of the Metropolitan Church of Cologne]	Latin	Cologne
Capitulum Regnans Sede Vacante [Chapter Governing While the See Is Vacant]	Latin	Eichstadt
Carola Magna Ducissa Feliciter Regnante [Grand Duchess Charlotte, Happily Reigning]	Latin	Luxembourg
Carolus a Carolo [Charles (I) to Charles (II)]	Latin	England
Cedunt Prementi Fata [The Fates Yield to Him Who Presses]	Latin	Ploen, Hesse-Cassel
Charta Magna Bavariae [The Great Charter of Bavaria]	Latin	Bavaria
Charitate et Candore [With Generosity and Sincerity]	Latin	East Frisia
Xpc Vincit Xpc Regnat [Christ Conquers, Christ Reigns]	Latin	Scotland, Spain
XPC Vincit XPC Regnat XPC Imperat [Christ Conquers, Christ Reigns, Christ Commands]	Latin	France
Xpc Vivet Xpc Regnat Xpc Impat [Christ Lives, Christ Reigns, Christ Commands]	Latin	Cambrai

coin motto	*language*	*place/source*
Xpe Resurescit [Christ Lives Again]	Latin	Venice
Xpistiana Religio [The Christian Faith]	Latin	Carolingian Empire
Xps Ihs Elegit Me Regem Populo [Jesus Christ Chose Me as King to the People]	Latin	Norway
Xristiana Religio [Christian Faith]	Latin	France
Christo Auspice Regno [I Reign with Christ's Guidance]	Latin	England
Christo Victore Triumpho [Through Christ the Victor I Triumph]	Latin	Britain
Christus Spes Una Salutis LatinCleve [Christ (Is) the Only Hope of Salvation]		
Chur Mainz [Principality of Mainz]	German	Mainz
Circumeundo Servat et Ornat [In Circulating, It Serves and Adorns]	Latin	Sweden
Civibus Quorum Pietas Coniuratione Die III Mai MDCCXCI Obrutam et Deletam Libertate Polona Tueri Conabatur Respublica Resurgens [To the Citizens Whose Piety the Resurgent Polish Republic Tried to Protect During the Conspiracy of May 3, 1791, Which Overturned and Destroyed Liberty]	Latin	Poland
Civitas Lucemborgiensis Millesimum Ovans Expletannum [Fulfilling the Celebration of a Thousand Years of the city of Luxembourg]	Latin	Luxembourg
Civium Industria Floret Civitas [By the People's Industry the State Flourishes]	Latin	Great Britain
Cluniaco Cenobio Petrus et Paulus [Peter and Paul from the Abbey of Cluny]	Latin	Cluny
Cnut Rex Cunnetti [Cnut, King of Cnut's People]	Latin	England
Comes Provincie Fili Regis Francie [Court of Provence of the Son of the French King]	Latin	Provence
Communitas et Senatus Bonon [Citizenry and Senate of Bologna]	Latin	Bologna
Concordia Fratrum [The Harmony of the Brothers]	Latin	Anholt-Zerbst
Concordia Patriae Nutrix [Harmony, the Fatherland's Nurse]	Latin	Waldeck
Concordia Res Parvae Crescunt [Little Things Increase Through Harmony]	Latin	Batavia, Holland
Concordia Res Parvae Crescunt, Discordia Dilabuntur [By Harmony Little Things Increase, by Discord They Will Fall Apart]	Latin	Lowenstein-Wertheim-Virneburg
Concordia Stabili [With lasting peace]	Latin	Hildesheim
Confidens Deo Non Movetur [He Who Trusts in God Is Unmoved]	Latin	Spanish Netherlands

coin motto	*language*	*place/source*
Confidentia in Deo et Vigilantia [Trust in God and Vigilance]	Latin	Prussia
Confoederato Helvetica [Helvetian Confederation]	Latin	Switzerland
Conjuncto Felix [Fortunate in Connections]	Latin	Solms
Conservator Urbis Suae [Saviour of His City]	Latin	Rome
Consilio et Aequitate [With Deliberation and Justice]	Latin	Fulda
Consilio et Virtutis [With Deliberation and Valor]	Latin	Hesse-Cassel
Constanter et Sincere [Steadfastly and Sincerely]	Latin	Lautern
Crescite et Multiplicamini [Increase and Multiply]	Latin	Maryland
Cristiana Religio [Christian Religion]	Latin	Germany
Crux Benedicat [May the Cross Bless (You)]	Latin	Oldenburg
Cuius Cruore Sanati Sumus [By His Martyrdom Are We Healed]	Latin	Reggio
Cultores Sui Deus Protegit [God Protects His Followers]	Latin	England
Cum Deo et Die [With God and the Day]	Latin	Württemberg
Cum Deo et Jure [With God and the Law]	Latin	Württemberg
Cum Deo et Labore [With God and Work]	Latin	Wittgenstein
Cum His Qui Orderant Pacem Eram Pacificus [With Those Who Order Peace I Have Been Peaceful]	Latin	Zug
Curie Bonthon to so Doulo [Protect His Servant, O Lord]	Italian	Byzantium
Custos Regni Deus [God (Is) the Kingdom's Guardian]	Latin	Naples and Sicily
Da Gloriam Deo et Eius Genitrici Marie [Give Glory to God and His Mother Mary]	Latin	Württemberg
Da Mihi Virtutem Contra Hostes Tuos [Give Me Strength Against My Enemies]	Latin	Netherlands
Date Caesaris Caesari et Quae Sunt Dei Deo [Render to Caesar (the Things That Are) Caesar's and to God (the Things That Are) God's]	Latin	Stralsund
Dat Wort Is Fleis Gworden [The Word Is Made Flesh]	German	Münster
Decreto Reipublicae Nexu Confoederationis Iunctae Die V Xbris MDCCXCII Stanislao Augusto Regnante [By Decree of the State in Conjunction with the Joint Confederation on December 5, 1792, Stanislaus Augustus Ruling]	Latin	Poland

coin motto	*language*	*place/source*
Decus et Tutamen [Ornament and Safeguard]	Latin	Britain
Deducet Nos Mirabiliter Dextera Tua [Your Right Hand Will Guide Us Miraculously]	Latin	Savoy
Dei Gratia [Thanks (Be) to God]	Latin	England
Dei Gratia Regina Fidei Defensor [By the Grace of God Queen and Defender of the Faith]	Latin	Great Britain
Denarium Terrae Mariae [Penny of Maryland]	Latin	Maryland
Deo Conservatori Pacis [To God, Preserver of Peace]	Latin	Brandenburg-Ansbach
Deo lhs Chs Rex Regnantium [Lord Jesus Christ, King of Kings]	Latin	Rome
De Oficina [From the Mint]	Latin	France
Deo OM Auspice Suaviter et Fortiter sed Iuste nec Sibi sed Suis [Under the Auspices of God, Greatest and Best, Pleasantly and Bravely but Justly, not For Himself but For His People]	Latin	Speyer
Deo Patriae et Subditio [For God, Country, and Territory]	Latin	Mainz
Der Recht Glaubt In Ewig Lebt [Who Believes in Right Will Live in Eternity]	German	Linange-Westerburg
Der Rhein Ist Deutschlands Strom Nicht Deutschlands Grenze [The Rhine Is Germany's River Not Germany's Frontier]	German	Germany
Deum Solum Adorabis [You Will Worship Only God]	Latin	Hesse
Deus Constituit Regna [God Establishes Kingdoms]	Latin	Nijmegen
Deus Dat Qui Vult [God Gives (to Him) Who Wishes]	Latin	Hanau-Munzenberg
Deus et Dominus [God and Lord]	Latin	Rome
Deus in Adiutorium Meum Intende [God, Reach Out in My Aid]	Latin	France
Deus Providebit [God Will Provide]	Latin	Lowenstein-Wertheim-Virneburg
Deus Ptetor Ms Z Lib'ator Ms [The Lord (Is) My Protector and Liberator]	Latin	Scotland
Deus Refugium Meum [God (Is) My Refuge]	Latin	Cleves
Deus Solatium Meum [God (Is) My Comfort]	Latin	Sweden
Dextera Domini Exaltavit Me [The Right Hand of God Has Raised Me Up]	Latin	Modena, Spain
Dextra Dei Exalta Me [Right Hand of God, Uplift Me]	Latin	Denmark

coin motto	*language*	*place/source*
Dieu et Mon Droit [God and My Right Hand]	French	Great Britain
Dieu Protege la France [God Protects France]	French	France
Dilectus Filius Meus [My Beloved Son]	Latin	Tuscany
Dilexit Deus Andream [The Lord Chose Andrew]	Latin	Holstein
Dilexit Dominus Decorem lustitiae [The Lord Loved the Grace of Justice]	Latin	Unterwalden
Dirige Deus Gressus Meos [O God, Direct My Steps]	Latin	Tuscany, Britain
Discerne Causam Meam [Decide My Cause]	Latin	Savoy
Divina Benedictiae et Caesarea lustitia [Divine of Blessings and Justice of the Empire]	Latin	Coblenz
Divus Augustus Pater [Holy August Father]	Latin	Rome
Dominabitur Gentium et lpse [Nations Will Be Ruled by the People and the Lord Himself]	Latin	Austrian Netherlands
Domine Conserva Nos in Pace [Lord, Preserve Us in Peace]	Latin	Basle, Mulhausen
Domine Elegisti Lilium Tibi [Lord, You Have Chosen the Lily for Yourself]	Latin	France
Domine ne in Furore Tuo Arguas Me [Lord, Rebuke Me Not in Your Anger]	Latin	England
Domine Probasti Me et Cognovisti Me [Lord, You Have Tested Me and Recognized Me]	Latin	Mantua
Domini est Regnum [The Kingdom Is the Lord's]	Latin	Austrian Netherlands
Dominus Deus Omnipotens Rex [Lord God, Almighty King]	Latin	Vikings
Dominus Mihi Adiutor [The Lord (Is) My Helper]	Latin	Spanish Netherlands
Dominus Providebit [The Lord Will Provide]	Latin	Berne
Dominus Spes Populi Sui [The Lord (Is) the People's Hope]	Latin	Lucerne
Donum Dei ex Fodinis Vilmariens [A Gift of God from the Vilmar Mines]	Latin	Coblena
Duce Deo Fide et Justicia [By Faith and Justice Lead (Us) to God]	Latin	Ragusa
Dum Praemor Amplior [While I Die Prematurely, I Increase]	Latin	Savoy
Dum Spiro Spero [While I Breathe, I Hope]	Latin	Pontefract
Dum Totum Compleat Orbem [Until it Fills the World]	Latin	France
Durae Necessitatis [Through Force of Necessity]	Latin	Bommel

coin motto	*language*	*place/source*
Dura Pati Virtus [Valor to Endure Hardships]	Latin	Saxe-Lauenburg
Durum Telum Necessitas [Necessity (Is) a Hard Weapon]	Latin	Minden
Dux et Gubernatores Reip Genu [Duke and Governors of the Republic of Genoa]	Latin	Genoa
Eadgar Rex Anglorum [Edgar King of the English]	Latin	England
Ecce Ancilla Domini [Behold, the Lord's Handmaiden]	Latin	Scotland
Ecce Grex [Behold the Flock]	Latin	Ireland
Eccl S. Barbarae Patronae Fodin Kuttenbergensium Duo Flor Arg Puri [The Church of St. Barbara, Patron of the Kuttensberg Mines, Two Florins of Pure Silver]	Latin	Hungary
Een en Ondelbaer Sterk [One and Indivisible]	Dutch	Batavia
Eendracht Mag Macht [Unity Makes Strength]	German	Belgium, South Africa
Eid Mar [The Ides of March]	Latin	Rome
Einigkeit Rechtund Freiheit [Union, Right, and Freedom]	German	Germany
Electorus Saxoniae Administrator [Elector (and) Administrator of Saxony]	Latin	Saxony
Elimosina [Alms]	Latin	France
Ep Fris & Ratisb Ad Prum Pp Coad Aug [Bishop of Freising and Regensburg, Administrator of Pruem, Prince Provost, Co-adjutant Bishop of Augsburg]	Latin	Trier
E Pluribus Unum [Out of Many, One; One (Nation) Out of Many (States)]	Latin	United States
Equa Libertas Deo Gratia Frat Pax in Virtute Tua et in Domino Confido [I Trust in Equal Liberty by the Grace of God, Brotherly Love in Your Strength and Trust in the Lord]	Latin	Burgundy
Equitas Iudicia Tua Dom [Equity and Your Judgments, Lord]	Latin	Gelderland
Espoir Me Conforte [Hope Comforts Me]	French	Mansfeld
Espreuve Faicto Par L'expres Commandement du Roy Louis XIII [Proof Rendered by the Express Command of King Louis XIII]	French	France
Et in Minimis Integer [Blameless Even in the Smallest Things]	Latin	Olmutz
Exaltabitur in Gloria [He Shall Be Exalted in Glory]	Latin	England

coin motto	*language*	*place/source*
Ex A. P. [Ex Argento Publico] [From the Public Treasury]	Latin	Rome
Ex Auro Argentes Resurgit [From Gold, It Arises Silver Again]	Latin	Sicily
Ex Auro Sinico [From Chinese Gold]	Latin	Denmark
Excelsior, Nova Eboraca Columbia [Loftier, New York, Columbia]	Latin	New York
Exemplum Probati Numismatis [An Example of a Proof Coin]	Latin	France
Exemtae Eccle Passau Episc et SRI Princ [Prince Bishop of the Freed Church of Passau and the Holy Roman Empire]	Latin	Passau
Ex Flammis Orior [I Rise from the Flames]	Latin	Hohenlohe-Neuenstein-Ohringen
Ex Fodinis Bipontio Seelbergensibus [From the Seelberg mines of Zweibrucken]	Latin	Pfalz-Birkenfeld
Exitus in Dubio Est [The Outcome Is in Doubt]	Latin	American colonies
Ex Metallo Novo [From New Metal]	Latin	Spain
Expectate Veni [Come, Expected One]	Latin	Britannia
Ex S. C. [Ex Senatus Consulto] [Authorized by the Senate]	Latin	Rome
Extremum Subidium Campen [Kampen Under Extreme Siege]	Latin	Kampen
Ex Uno Omnis Nostra Salus [From One (Is) All Our Salvation]	Latin	Eichstadt, Mulhouse
Exurgat Deus et Dissipentur Inimici Eius [Let God Arise and Let His Enemies Be Scattered]	Latin	England
Ex Vasis Argent Cleri Mogunt Pro Aris et Focis [From the Silver Vessels of the Mainz Clergy for Altars and for Hearths]	Latin	Mainz
Ex Visceribus Fodinse Bieber [From the Depths of the Bieber Mine]	Latin	Hanau-Munzenberg
Faciam Eos in Gentem Unam [I Will Make Them Into One Nation]	Latin	Britain
Faith and Truth I Will Bear unto You	English	Britain
Fata Consiliis Potiora [Destiny (Us) More Powerful Than Councils]	Latin	Hesse-Cassel
Fata Viam Invenient [Destiny Will Find a Way]	Latin	Gelderland
Fecit Potentiam in Brachio Suo [He Put Power in His Own Arm]	Latin	Lorraine
Fecunditas [Fruitfulness]	Latin	Naples and Sicily
Feliciter Nubtiis [Luck to the Newlyweds]	Latin	Byzantium

coin motto	*language*	*place/source*
Felicitas Perpetua [Unending Good Fortune]	Latin	Rome
Felix Coniunctio [Fortunate Union]	Latin	Brandenburg-Ansbach
Fel Temp Reparatio [The Restoration of Favorable Times]	Latin	Rome
Fiat Misericordia Tua Dne [Let Thy Mercy Be Fulfilled, Lord]	Latin	Gelderland
Fiat Voluntas Domini Perpetuo [May the Lord's Goodwill Last Forever]	Latin	Fulda
Fidei Defensor [Defender of the Faith]	Latin	Great Britain
Fidelitate et Fortitudine [With Trustworthiness and Courage]	Latin	Batthanyi
Fideliter et Constanter [Faithfully and Steadfastly]	Latin	Saxe-Coburg-Gotha
Fidem Servando Patriam Tuendo [By Keeping Faith and Protecting the Fatherland]	Latin	Savoy
Filius Augustorum [Son of Emperors]	Latin	Rome
Firme por la Union [Steadfast for the Union]	Spanish	Peru
Fisci Iudaici Calumnia Sublata [The Oppression of the Jewish Tax Lifted]	Latin	Rome
Floreat Rex [May the King Flourish]	Latin	Ireland
Floreat Terra Nova [May the New Land Flourish]	Latin	Canada
Florent Concordia Regna [Through Harmony Kingdoms Flourish]	Latin	England
Fortitudo et Laus Mea Dominu [Courage and Praise to My Lord]	Latin	Sardinia
4th Centenario do Descobrimento do Brasil [400th Anniversary of the Discovery of Brazil]	Portuguese	Brazil
Frat. et. Duces. Saxon [Brothers and Saxon Leaders]	Latin	Saxony
Fredericus Borussorum Rex [Frederick, King of the Prussians]	Latin	Prussia
Free Trade to Africa by Act of Parliment [*sic*]	English	Gold Coast
Friedt Ernehrt Unfriedt Verzehrt [Peace Nourishes, Unrest Wastes]	German	Brunswick
Fugio [I Fly]	Latin	United States
Fulgent Sic Littora Rheni [Thus Shine the Rhine's Banks]	Latin	Mannheim
Fundator Pacis [Founder of Peace]	Latin	Rome
Gaudium Populi Romani [The Joy of the Roman People]	Latin	Rome

coin motto	*language*	*place/source*
Genannt Braunschweigische Julius Loeser [Named the Redeemable of Julius of Brunswick]	German	Brunswick
Gen C Mar Vl Dim Col USC & RAMAI Cons & S Conf M [General Field Marshal, Colonel of the Only Dragoon Regiment, Present Privy Councillor of Both Their Sacred Imperial and Royal Apostolic Majesties, and State Conference Minister]	Latin	Batthanyi
Gerecht und Beharrlich [Just and Steadfast]	German	Bavaria
Germania Voti Compos [Germany Sharing the Vows]	Latin	Brandenburg-Ansbach
Germ Hun Boh Rex AAD Loth Ven Sal [King of Germany, Hungary, and Bohemia, Archduke of Austria, Duke of Lorraine, Venice, and Salzburg]	Latin	Austria
Germ Jero Rex Loth Bar Mag Het Dux [King of Germany, Jerusalem, Lorraine, and Bar, Grand Duke of Tuscany]	Latin	Austrian Netherlands
Gloria ex Amore Patriae [Glory from Love of Country]	Latin	Denmark
Gloria in Excelsis Deo [Glory to God in the Highest]	Latin	France, Sweden
Gloriam Regni Tui Dicent [They Will Speak the Glory of Your Reign]	Latin	France
Gloria Novi Saeculi [The Glory of a New Century]	Latin	Rome
God Preserve London	English	Britain
Godt Behofde Leyden [God Save Leiden]	Dutch	Leiden
Godt Met Ons [God with Us]	Dutch	Oudewater
God with Us	English	England
Gottes Freundt der Pfaffen Feindt [God's Friend, the Priest's Enemy]	German	Brunswick
Gratia Dei Sum Id Quod Sum [By the Grace of God, I Am What I Am]	Latin	Navarre
Gratia Di Rex [By the Grace of God, King]	Latin	France
Gratitudo Convibus Exemplum Posteritati [Thanks to Fellow Citizens, an Example to Posterity]	Latin	Poland
Gud och Folket [God and the People]	Swedish	Sweden
Habet Deum Qui Habet Omnia [He Who Has God Has Everything]	Latin	Saxe-Weissenfels
Hac Nitimur Hanc Tuemur [With This We Strive, This We Shall Defend]	Latin	Batavia
Hac Sub Tutela [Under This Protection]	Latin	Eichstadt
Haec Sunt Munera Minerae S Antony Eremitae [These Are the Gifts of the Mine of St. Antony the Hermit.]	Latin	Hildesheim

coin motto	*language*	*place/source*
Hanc Deus Dedit [God Has Given This]	Latin	Pontefract
Hanc Tuemur Hac Nitimur [This We Defend, by This We Strive]	Latin	Batavia
Has Nisi Periturus Mihi Adimat Nemo [Let No One Remove These (Letters) from Me Commonwealth Unless He Die]	Latin	English
Henricus Dei Gra Francoru et Anglie Rex [Henry by the Grace of God King of the Franks and the English]	Latin	France
Heinricus Leo Dux [Henry the Lion Leader]	Latin	England
Henricus Rosas Regna Jacobus [Henry (United) the Roses, James the Kingdoms]	Latin	England, Scotland
Herculeo Vincta Nodo [Bound by a Herculean Knot]	Latin	Savoy
Herre Gott Verleich Uns Gnade [Lord God, Grant Us Grace]	German	Brunswick
Herr Nach Deinem Willen [Lord, Thy Will Be Done]	German	Palatinate Erbach
Hic Est Qui Multum Orat Pro Populo [Here Is He Who Prays Long for the People]	Latin	Paderborn
Hir Steid te Biscop [Here Is Represented the Bishop]	German	Gittelde
Hispaniarum Infans [Prince of Spain's Lands]	Latin	Spain
Hispaniarum et Ind Rex [King of Spanish Lands and the Indies]	Latin	Spain
Hispaniarum Rex [King of Spain]	Latin	Spain
His Ventis Vela Levantur [By These Winds the Sails Are Lifted]	Latin	Hesse-Cassel
Hoc Signo Victor Eris [With This Sign You Will Be a Victor]	Latin	Rome
Honeste et Decenter [Honestly and Decently]	Latin	Nassau-Idstein
Honi Soit Qui Mal y Pense [Shame to Him Who Thinks Evil of It]	French	Great Britain, Hesse-Cassel
Hospitalis et S Sepul Hierusal [Hospital and Holy Sepulchre of Jerusalem]	Latin	Malta
Hun Boh Gal Rex AA Lo Wi et in Fr Dux [King of Hungary, Bohemia, and Galicia, Archduke of Austria, Dalmatia, Lodomeria, Wurzburg and Duke in Franconia]	Latin	Austria
Hung Boh Lomb et Ven Gal Lod Ill Rex Aa [King of Hungary, Bohemia, Lombardo-Venezia, Galicia, Lodomeria, and Illyria, Archduke of Austria]	Latin	Austria
Iacobus II D. G. Ang. Sco. Fr. Hi. Rex [James II by the Grace of God King of England, Scotland, France, and Ireland]	Latin	Britain

coin motto	*language*	*place/source*
Iacobus II D. G. Mag. Bri. Fran. et Hib. Rex [James II by the Grace of God King of Great Britain, France and Ireland]	Latin	Britain
Iam Nova Progenies Caelo Demittitur Alto [Now a New Generation Is Sent from on High]	Latin	Roman Britain
Ich Dien [I Serve]	German	Aberystwyth
Ich Getrawe Gotin Aller Noth [I Trust in God in All My Needs]	German	Hesse-Marburg
Ich Habe Nur Ein Vaterland und das Heisst Deutschland [I Have but One Fatherland and That Is Called Germany]	German	Germany
Ielithes Penniae [Penny of Gittelde]	Latin	Gittelde
Iesus Christos, Theou Uios Soter [Jesus Christ, Son of God, Savior]	Greek	Vatican
Iesus Autem Transiens Per Medium Illorum Ibat [But Jesus, Passing Through the Midst of Them, Went His Way]	Latin	England, Scotland, Anglo-Gallia
Iesus Rex Noster et Deus Noster [Jesus (Is) Our King and Our God]	Latin	Florence
Ihs Xs Rex Regnantium [Jesus Christ, King of Kings]	Latin	Byzantium
Ihsus Xristus Basileu Baslie [Jesus Christ, King of Kings]	Greek	Byzantium
Imago Sanch Regis Illustris Castelle Legionis e Toleto [Likeness of Sancho the Illustrious King of Castile, Leon and Toledo]	Latin	Spain
Immunis Columbia [Unfettered Columbia]	Latin	New York
Imperat aut Servit [It Either Rules or Serves]	Latin	Vatican
In Casus Per Vigil Omnes [Through Caution in All Happenings]	Latin	Wertheim
Incorrupta Fides Veritasque [Unsullied Faith and Truth]	Latin	Britain
In Deo Meo Transgrediar Murum [In My God I Shall Pass Through the Wall]	Latin	Teschen
In Deo Spes Mea [In God (Is) My Hope]	Latin	Gelderland
Ind Imp [Empress of India]	Latin	Great Britain
India Tibi Cessit [India Has Yielded to You]	Latin	Portuguese India
Insignia Capituli Brixensis [Badge of the Chapter of Brixen]	Latin	Brixen
In Domino Fiducia Nostra [In the Lord (Is) Our Trust]	Latin	Scotland
In Equitate Tua Vivificasti Me [In Your Fairness You Have Given Me Life]	Latin	Gelderland

coin motto	*language*	*place/source*
Infestus Infestis [Hostile to the Troublesome]	Latin	Savoy
In God We Trust	English	United States
In Hoc Signo Vinces [In This Sign Will You Conquer]	Latin	Portugal
In Honore Sci Mavrici Marti [In Honour of the Martyr St. Maurice]	Latin	St. Maurice
In Manibus Domini Sortes Meae [In the Hands of the Lord (Is) My Destiny]	Latin	Mainz
In Memoriam Conjunctionis Utriusque Burgraviatus Norice [In Memory of the Union of Both Burgraviates in Noricum]	Latin	Brandenburg-Ansbach
In Memoriam Connub Feliciaes Inter Princ Her Frider Carol et Dub Sax August Louis Frider 28 Nov 1780 Celebrati [In Memory of the Happy Marriage Between the Hereditary Prince Friedrich Karl and the Duchess of Saxony Augusta Louisa Frederika, Celebrated on November 28, 1780]	Latin	Swarzburg-Rudolstadt
In Memoriam Felicisssimi Matrimonii [In Memory of the Most Happy Marriage]	Latin	Wied
In Memoriam Pacis Teschinensis [Commemorating the Peace of Teschen]	Latin	Brandenburg-Ansbach
In Memor Vindicatae Libere ac Relig [In Memory of Vindicated Freedom and Religion]	Latin	Sweden
In Nomine Domini Amen [In the Name of the Lord Amen]	Latin	Zaltbommel
In Omnem Terram Sonus Eorum [Into All the Land (Shall Go) Their Sound]	Latin	Chateau Renault
In Silencio et Spe Fortitudo Mea [In Silence and Hope (Is) My Strength]	Latin	Brandenburg-Kustrin
In Spe et Silentio Fortitudo Mea [In Hope and Silence (Is) My Strength]	Latin	Viana
In Te Domine Confido [In You, Lord, I Trust]	Latin	Hesse
In Te Domine Speravi [In You, Lord, I Have Hoped]	Latin	Gurk
In Terra Pax [(Let There Be) Peace in the Land]	Latin	Vatican
In Via Virtuti Nulla Via [There Is No Way for Strength on the Way]	Latin	Veldenz
Isti Sunt Patres Tui Verique Pastores [These Are Your Fathers and True Shepherds]	Latin	Vatican
Iudicium Melius Posteritatis Erit [Posterity's Judgment Will Be Better]	Latin	Paderborn
Iure et Tempore [By Law and Occasion]	Latin	Groningen
Iusque a Sa Plenitude [Law and Your Plenitude]	Latin	France
Iuste et Constanter [Justly and Constantly]	Latin	Paderborn

coin motto	*language*	*place/source*
Iustitia et Concordia [Justice and Harmony]	Latin	Zurich
Iustitia et Mansuetudine [By Justice and Clemency]	Latin	Bavaria, Cologne
Iustitia Regnorum Fundamentum [Justice (Is) the Foundation of Kingdoms]	Latin	Austria
Iustitia Thronum Firmat [Justice Strengthens the Throne]	Latin	England
Iustus Non Derelinquitur [The Just Person Is Not Deserted]	Latin	Brandenburg-Calenberg
Iustus Ut Palma Florebit [The Just Will Flourish Like the Palm]	Latin	Portugal
Johannes Dei Gratia Francorum rex [John, by the Grace of God, King of the Franks]	Latin	France
Karolus Imp Aug [Charles August Emperor]	Latin	France
Landgrin Cleggov Com in Sulz Dux Crum [Landgrave of Klettgau, Count of Sulz, Duke of Krumlau]	Latin	Schwarzburg-Sonderhausen
Latin a Emeri Munita [Latin Money of Merida]	Latin	Suevi
Lege et Fide [By Law and Faith]	Latin	Austria
Let God Arise, Let His Enemies Be Scattered	English	Britain
Lex Veritas [Law (Is) Truth]	Latin	Tuscany
Libertad en la Ley [Freedom Within the Law]	Spanish	Mexico
Liberta Eguaglianza [Freedom and Equality]	Italian	Venice
Libertas Carior Auro [Freedom (Is) More Precious Than Gold]	Latin	St. Gall
Libertas Vita Carior [Freedom Is More Precious Than Life]	Latin	Kulenberg
Libertas Xpo Firmata [Freedom Strengthened by Christ]	Latin	Genoa
Liberté, Egalité, Fraternité [Freedom, Equality, Brotherhood]	French	France
Likago Novagoroda [From the Great Novogorod]	Russian	Novogorod
L Mun Planco Rauracorum Illustratori Vetustissimo [To L Municius Plancus the Illustrious and Most Ancient of the Rauraci]	Latin	Basle
L. Sulla feli. dic. [Lucius Sulla, the Blessed Dictator]	Latin	Rome
L. Sulla/imper. iterum [Lucius Sulla, General a Second Time]	Latin	Rome
Lucerna Pedibus Meis Verbum Est [The Word Is a Lamp to My Feet]	Latin	England
Lud XIIII D. G. Fr. et Navarre Rex [Louis XIV by the Grace of God King of France and Navarre]	Latin	France

coin motto	*language*	*place/source*
Lumen ad Revelationem Gentium [Light to Enlighten the Nations]	Latin	Vatican
L'Union Fait la Force [The Union Makes Strength]	French	Belgium
Macula Non Est in Te [There Is No Fault on You]	Latin	Essen
Magnus ab Integro Saeculorum Nascitur Ordo [The Great Order of the Centuries Is Born Entire]	Latin	Bavaria
Mandavit Dominus Palatie Hanc Monetam Fiert [The Lord of the Palatine Ordained This Coin]	Latin	Balath
Manibus Ne Laedar Avaris [May I Not Be Harmed by Greedy Hands]	Latin	Sweden
Mar Bran Sac Rom Imp Arcam et Elec Sup Dux Siles [Margrave of Brandenburg, Archchamberlain of the Holy Roman Empire and Elector, Senior Duke of Silesia]	Latin	Prussia
Maria Mater Domini Xpi [Mary Mother of Christ the Lord]	Latin	Teutonic order
Maria Regina i Romanilor [Queen Mary of Romania]	Romanian	Romania
Maria Unxit Pedes Xpisti [Mary Washes the Feet of Christ]	Latin	France
Masathusets	English	Massachusetts Bay Colony
Mater Castrorum [Mother of the Camp]	Latin	Rome
Mater Studiorum [Mother of Studies]	Latin	Bologna
Matrimonio Conjuncti [Joined in Wedlock]	Latin	Austria
M B F et H Rex F D B et L D S R I A T et E [Magnae Britanniae, Franciae Et Hiberniae Rex Fidei Defensor, Brunsviciensis Et Luneburgensis Dux, Sacri Romani Archi-Thesaurarius Et Elector or King of Great Britain France & Ireland, Defender of the Faith, Duke of Brunswick & Luneburg, High Treasurer and Elector of the Holy Roman Empire]	Latin	Britain
Me Coniunctio Servat Dum Frangor [Union Serves Me While I Am Being Broken]	Latin	Lowenstein-Wertheim
Mediolani Dux [Duke of Milan]	Latin	Milan
Mediolani et Man [Milan and Mantua]	Latin	Milan
Melius Est Dare Quam Accipere [It Is Better to Give Than to Receive]	Latin	Vatican
Memor Ero Tui Iustina Virgo [I Shall Remember You, Lady Justina]	Latin	Venice
Merces Laborum [Wages of Work]	Latin	Wurzburg
Mirabilia Fecit [He Made Wonders]	Latin	Vikings

coin motto	*language*	*place/source*
Misericordia Di Rex [King by the Mercy of God]	Latin	France
Mo Arg Ord Foe Belg D Gel & CZ [Silver Coin of the Order of the Belgian Federation, Duchy of Guelderland, County of Zutphen]	Latin	Guelderland
Moneta Abbatis [Coin of the Abbey]	Latin	Germany
Moneta Argentiae Ord Foed Belgii Holl [Silver Coin of the Federated Union of Belgium and Holland]	Latin	Batavia
Moneta Bipont [Coin of Zweibrucken]	Latin	Pfalz-Birkenfeld-Zweibrucken
Monet Capit Cathedr Fuld Sede Vacante [Coin of the Cathedral Chapter of Fulda, the See Being Vacant]	Latin	Fulda
Moneta in Obsidione Tomacensi Cusa [Coin Struck During the Siege of Tournai]	Latin	Tournai
Moneta Livosesthonica [Coin of Livonia]	Latin	Estonia
Moneta Nova Ad Normam Conventionis [New Coin According to Conventional Standard]	Latin	Orsini-Rosenberg
Moneta Nova Domini Imperatoris [New Coin of the Lord Emperor]	Latin	Brunswick
Moneta Nova Lubecensis [New Coin of Lubeck]	Latin	Lubeck
Moneta Nova Reipublicae Halae Suevicae [New Coin of the Republic of Hall in Swabia]	Latin	Swabia
Moneta Nov Arg Regis Daniae [New Silver Coin of the King of Denmark]	Latin	Denmark
Moneta Reipublicae Ratisbonensis [Coin of the Republic of Regensburg]	Latin	Regensburg
Mon Lib Reip Bremens [Coin of the Free State of Bremen]	Latin	Bremen
Mon Nova Arg Duc Curl Ad Norma Tal Alb [New Silver Coin of the Duchy of Courland, According to the Standard of the Albert Thaler]	Latin	Courland
Mon Nov Castri Imp [New Coin of the Imperial Free City]	Latin	Friedberg
Mo No Arg Con Foe Belg Pro Hol [New Silver Coin of the Belgian Federation, Province of Holland]	Latin	Holland
Mo No Arg Pro Confoe Belg Trai Holl [New Silver Coin of the Confederated Belgian Provinces, Utrecht and Holland]	Latin	Batavia
Munus Divinum [Sacred Gift]	Latin	France, York
Nach Alt Reichs Schrot und Korn [According to the Old Empire's Grits and Grain]	German	Hesse
Nach dem Conventions Fusse [According to the Convention's Basis]	German	Germany
Nach dem Frankf Schlus [According to the Frankfurt Standard]	German	Solms

coin motto	*language*	*place/source*
Nach dem Schlus der V Staend [According to the Standard of the Union]	German	Hesse
La Nation, la Loi, le Roi [Nation, Law, King]	French	France
Navigare Necesse Est [It Is Necessary to Navigate]	Latin	Germany
Nec Aspera Terrent [Nor Do Difficulties Frighten (Us)]	Latin	Brunswick
Nec Cito Nec Temere [Neither Hastily Nor Rashly]	Latin	Cambrai
Necessitas Legem Non Habet [Necessity Has No Law]	Latin	Magdeburg
Nec Numina Desunt [Nor Is Divinity Lacking]	Latin	Savoy
Nec Temere Nec Timide [Neither Rashly Nor Timidly]	Latin	Danzig, Lippe
Nemo Me Impune Lacessit [No One Touches Me with Impunity]	Latin	United Kingdom
Nihil Restat Reliqui [No Relic Survives]	Latin	Ypres
Nil Sine Numme [Nothing Without God]	Latin	Denver, Colorado
Nil Ultra Aras [Nothing Beyond the Rocks]	Latin	Franquemont
Nobilissimum Dom Ac Com in Lipp & St [Most Noble Lord and Count in Lippe and Sternberg]	Latin	Schaumburg-Lippe
Nomen Domini Turris Fortissima [The Name of the Lord Is the Strongest Tower]	Latin	Frankfurt
Non Aes Sed Fides [Not Bronze (Money) but Trust]	Latin	Malta
Non Est Mortale Quod Opto [What I Desire Is Not Mortal]	Latin	Mecklenburg
Non Mihi Sed Populo [Not to Me but to the People]	Latin	Bavaria
No Nobis Dne Sed Noi Tuo Da Gloriam [Not to Us, Lord, but to Thy Name Give Glory]	Latin	France
Non Relinquam Vos Orphanos [I Shall Not Leave You as Orphans]	Latin	Vatican
Non Surrexit Major [None Greater Has Arisen]	Latin	Genoa, Malta
Nullum Simulatum Diuturnum Tandem [Nothing Pretended (Lasts) Long]	Latin	Wittgenstein
Nummorum Famulus [Servant of Coins]	Latin	England
Numquam Retrorsum [Never in Retreat]	Latin	Brunswick-Wolfenbuttel
Nunquam Arescare [(It) Never Dries Up]	Latin	Scotland
Ob Cives Servatos [On Behalf of the Citizens]	Latin	Rome

coin motto	*language*	*place/source*
O Crux Ave Spes Unica [Hail, O Cross, Our Only Hope]	Latin	England, France
Oculi Domini Super Iustos [The Eyes of the Lord Over the Just]	Latin	Neufchatel
O Maria Ora Pro Me [O Mary, Pray for Me]	Latin	Bavaria
Omnia Auxiliante Maria [Mary Helping Everything]	Latin	Schwyz
Omnia Cum Deo [Everything with God]	Latin	Reuss-Greiz
Omnia cum Deo et Nihil Sine Eo [All with God and Nothing Without Him]	Latin	Erbach
Omnis Potestas a Deo Est [All Power Is from God]	Latin	Sweden
Opp & Carn Aur Velleris Eques [Duke of Troppau, Knight of the Golden Fleece]	Latin	Liechtenstein
Opp & Carn Dux Comm Rittb SCI Cons Int & Compi Mareschal [Duke of Troppau and Carniola, Count of Rietberg, Privy Councillor to His Sacred Imperial Majesty, and Field Marshal]	Latin	Liechtenstein
Opportune [Conveniently]	Latin	Savoy
Optimus Princeps [Best Prince]	Latin	Rome
Opulentia Salerno [Wealth to Salerno]	Latin	Italy
Pacator Orbis [Pacifier of the World]	Latin	Rome
Pace et Iustitia [With Peace and Justice]	Latin	Spanish Netherlands
Palma Sub Pondere Crescit [The Palm Grows Under Its Weight]	Latin	Waldeck
Parate Viam Domini [Prepare the Way of the Lord]	Latin	Vatican
Pater Noster [Our Father]	Latin	Flanders
Pater Patriae [Father of the Country]	Latin	Rome
Patria Si Dreptul Meu [The Country and My Right]	Romanian	Romania
Patrimon Henr Frid Sorte Divisum [The Heritage of Heinrich Friedrich Divided by Lot]	Latin	Hohenlohe-Langenberg
Patrimonia Beati Petri [The Inheritance of Blessed Peter]	Latin	Vatican
Patrona Franconiae [Patron of Franconia]	Latin	Wurzburg
Pax Aeterna [Eternal Peace]	Latin	Rome

coin motto	*language*	*place/source*
Pax et Abundantia [Peace and Plenty]	Latin	Burgundy, Gelderland
Pax Missa Per Orbem [Peace Sent Throughout the World]	Latin	England
Pax Petrus [Peace of Peter]	Latin	Trier
Pax Praevalet Armis [Peace Prevails Through Arms]	Latin	Mainz
Pax Quaeritur Bello [Peace Is Sought by War]	Latin	English Commonwealth
Pecunia Totum Circumit Orbem [Money Goes Round the Whole World]	Latin	Brazil
Per Aspera Ad Astra [Through Hardships to the Stars]	Latin	Mecklenburg-Schwerin
Per Angusta ad Augusta [Through Precarious Times to the Majestic]	Latin	Solms-Roedelheim
Per Crucem Tuam Salva Nos Christe Redemptor [By Your Cross Save Us, Christ the Redeemer]	Latin	England
Per Crucem Tuam Salva Nos Xpe Redemt [By Your Cross Save Us, Christ the Redeemer]	Latin	Portugal
Perdam Babillonis Nomen [I Shall Destroy the Name of Babylon]	Latin	Naples
Perennitati Iustissimi Regis [To an Eternity of the Most Just King]	Latin	France
Perennitati Principis Galliae Restitutionis [To an Eternity of the Restoration of the Prince of the Gauls]	Latin	France
Perfer et Obdura Bruxella [Carry On and Endure, Brussels]	Latin	Brussels
Perpetuus in Nemet Vivar [Always in Nemt-Ujvar]	Latin	Batthanyi
Pietate et Constantia [By Piety and Constancy]	Latin	Fulda
Pietate et Iustitia [By Piety and Justice]	Latin	Denmark
Plebei Urbanae Frumento Constituto [Grain to the Urban Peasantry Established]	Latin	Rome
Pleidio Wyf I'm Gwlad [I Am True to My Country]	Welsh	United Kingdom
Plus Ultra [More Beyond]	Latin	Spanish America
Point du Couronne sans Peine [Point of the Crown Without Penalty]	French	Coburg
Pons Civit Castellana [The Bridge of the Town of Castellana]	Latin	Vatican
Populus et Senatus Bonon [The People and Senate of Bologna]	Latin	Bologna
Post Mortem Patris Pro Filio [For the Son After His Father's Death]	Latin	Pontefract

coin motto	*language*	*place/source*
Post Tenebras Lux [After Darkness, Light]	Latin	Geneva
Post Tenebras Spero Lucem [After Darkness I Hope for Light]	Latin	Geneva
Posui Deum Adiutorem Meum [I Have Made God My Aide]	Latin	England, Ireland
Praesidium et Decus [Protection and Ornament]	Latin	Bologna
Prima Sedes Galliorum [First See of the Gauls]	Latin	Lyons
Princeps Iuventutis [Prince of Youth]	Latin	Rome
Pro Defensione Urbis et Patriae [For the Defense of City and Country]	Latin	France
Pro Deo et Patria [For God and Country]	Latin	Fulda
Pro Deo et Populo [For God and the People]	Latin	Bavaria
Pro Ecclesia et Pro Patria [For Church and for Country]	Latin	Constance
Pro Lege et Grege [For Law and the Flock]	Latin	Fulda
Pro Maxima Dei Gloria et Bono Publico [For the Greatest Glory of God and Public Good]	Latin	Württemberg
Pro Patria [For Country]	Latin	Würzburg
Propitio Deo Secura Ago [With God's Favor I Live Securely]	Latin	Saxe-Lauenburg
Protege Virgo Pisas [Protect Pisa, Virgin (Mary)]	Latin	Pisa
Provide et Constanter [Cautiously and Dependably]	Latin	Württemberg
Providentia et Pactis [Through Foresight and Agreements]	Latin	Brandenburg-Ansbach
Providentia Optimi Principis [With the Foresight of the Best Prince]	Latin	Naples and Sicily
Proxima Soli [Nearest to the Sun]	Latin	Modena
Publicae Utilitati [For Public Use]	Latin	Vatican
Pugno pro Patria [I Fight for My Country]	Latin	Holland
Pulcra Virtutis Imago [A Beautiful Likeness of Strength]	Latin	Genoa
Pulo Moscovskoye [Pulo of Moscow]	Russian	Moscow
Pupillum et Viduam Suscipiat [Let Him Support the Orphan and the Widow]	Latin	Savoy
Quae Deus Conjunxit Nemo Separet [What God Has Joined Let No One Part]	Latin	Scotland

coin motto	*language*	*place/source*
Quattuor Maria Vindico [I Claim the Four Seas]	Latin	Britain
Quem Quadragesies et Semel Patriae Natum Esse Gratulamur [Whom We Congratulate for the Forty-first Time for Being Born of the Country]	Latin	Lippe-Detmold
Qui Dat Pauperi Non Indigebit [Who Gives to the Poor Will Never Be in Need]	Latin	Münster
Quid Non Cogit Necessitas [What Does Necessity Not Drive]	Latin	Ypres
Quiescat Plebs [Let Commoners Be at Ease]	Latin	Ireland
Quin Matrimonii Lustrum Celebrant [They Celebrate Their Silver Anniversary]	Latin	Austria
Quocunque Jeceris Stabit [Whichever Way You Throw It, It Will Stand]	Latin	Isle of Man
Quod Deus Vult Hoc Semper Fit [What God Wishes Always Happens]	Latin	Saxe-Weimar
Quod Habeo Tibi Do [What I Have I Give to You]	Latin	Vatican
Reconduntur non Retonduntur [They Are Laid Up in Store, Not Thundered Back]	Latin	Savoy
Recta Tueri [Defend the Right]	Latin	Austria
Recte Constanter et Fortiter [Rightly, Constantly, and Bravely]	Latin	Bavaria
Recte Faciendo Neminem Timeas [In Doing Right, Let You Fear No One]	Latin	Solms-Laubach
Rector Orbis [Master of the World]	Latin	Rome
Rectus et Immotus [Right and Immovable]	Latin	Hesse
Redde Cuique Quod Suum Est [Return to Each That Which Is His]	Latin	England
Redeunt antiqui Gaudia Moris [The Joys of Ancient Custom Return]	Latin	Regensburg
Regier Mich Her Nach Deinen Wort [Govern Me Here According to Your Word]	German	Palatinate
Regnans Capitulum Ecclesiae Cathedralis Ratisbonensis Sede Vacante [Administering the Chapter of the Cathedral Church at Regensburg, the See Being Vacant]	Latin	Regensburg
Regni Utr Sic et Hier [Of the Kingdom of the Two Sicilies and of Jerusalem]	Latin	Naples and Sicily
Reg Pr Pol et Lith Saxon Dux [Royal Prince of Poland and Lithuania and Duke of Saxony]	Latin	Trier
Religio Protestantium Leges Angliae Libertas Parliamenti [The Protestant Faith, Laws of England, and Freedom of Parliament]	Latin	England
Relinquo Vos Liberos ab Utroque Homine [I Leave You as Children of Each Man]	Latin	San Marino

coin motto	*language*	*place/source*
Restauracao da Independencia [Restoration of Independence]	Portuguese	Portugal
Restitutor Exercitus [Restorer of the Army]	Latin	Rome
Restitutor Galliarum [Restorer of the Gauls]	Latin	Rome
Restitutor Generis Humani [Restorer of Humankind]	Latin	Rome
Restitutor Libertatis [Restorer of Freedom]	Latin	Rome
Restitutor Orbis [Restorer of the World]	Latin	Rome
Restitutor Orientis [Restorer of the East]	Latin	Rome
Restitutor Saeculi [Restorer of the Century]	Latin	Rome
Restitutor Urbis [Restorer of the City]	Latin	Rome
Rex F et L [King of the Franks and Lombards]	Latin	France
Rosa Americana Utile Dulci [The American Rose, Useful (and) Sweet]	Latin	American colonies
Rosa Sine Spina [A Rose Without a Thorn]	Latin	England
Rutilans Rosa Sine Spina [A Dazzling Rose Without a Thorn]	Latin	England
Sac Nupt Celeb Berol [For the Holy Matrimony Celebrated at Berlin]	Latin	Brandenburg-Ansbach
Sac Rom Imp [Holy Roman Empire]	Latin	Germany
Sac Rom Imp Provisor Iterum [Administrator of the Holy Roman Empire for the Second Time]	Latin	Saxony
Salus et Gloria Romanorum [Safety and Glory of the Romans]	Latin	Byzantium
Salus Generis Humani [Well-being of Humankind]	Latin	Rome
Salus Patriae [Health of the Country]	Latin	Italy
Salus Populi [Well-being of the People]	Latin	Spain
Salus Provinciarum [Well-being of the Provinces]	Latin	Rome
Salus Publica Salus Mea [Public Safety (Is) My Safety]	Latin	Sweden
Salus Reipublicae [The Health of the Republic]	Latin	Rome
Salus Reipublicae Suprema Lex [The Well-being of the Republic is the Highest Law]	Latin	Poland

coin motto	*language*	*place/source*
Salvam Fac Rempublicam Tuam [Make Your State Safe]	Latin	San Marino
Sanctus Iohannes Innocens [St. John the Harmless]	Latin	Gandersheim
Sans Changer [Without Changing]	French	Isle of Man
Sans Eclat [Without Pomp]	French	Bouchain
Sapiente Diffidentia [Wisdom Doubting]	Latin	Teschen
S Ap S Leg Nat Germ Primas [Legate of the Holy Apostolic See, Born Primate of Germany]	Latin	Salzburg
S Carolus Magnus Fundator [Holy Charlemagne, Founder]	Latin	Munster
Scutum Fidei Proteget Eum/Eam [The Shield of Faith Will Protect Him/Her]	Latin	England
Secundum Voluntatem Tuam Domine [According to Your Will, Lord]	Latin	Hesse
Securitati Publicae [For the Public Safety]	Latin	Brandenburg-Ansbach
Sede Vacante [The See Being Vacant]	Latin	Vatican
Sena Vetus Alpha et W Principum et Finis [Old Siena Alpha and Omega, the Beginning and the End]	Latin	Siena
Senatus Populus QR [Senate and People of Rome]	Latin	Rome
S. Gertrudis Virgo Prudens Niviella [St. Gertrude the Wise Maiden of Nivelles]	Latin	Nivelles
S. Ian Bapt F. Zachari [St. John the Baptist, Son of Zacharias]	Latin	Florence
Sic Vos Non Vobis [Thus You (Work) Not for Yourself]	Latin	Britain
Si Deus Nobis cum Quis Contra Nos [If God (Is) with Us Who (Can) Oppose Us]	Latin	Hesse
Si Deus Pro Nobis Quis Contra Nos [If God (Is) for Us Who (Can) Oppose Us]	Latin	Roemhild
Sieh Deine Seeligkeit Steht Fest Ins Vaters Liebe [Behold Your Salvation Stands Surely in Your Father's Love]	German	Gotha
Signis Receptis [When the Standards Were Recovered]	Latin	Rome
Signum Crucis [The Sign of the Cross]	Latin	Groningen
Sincere et Constanter [Genuinely and Steadfastly]	Latin	Hesse-Darmstadt
Sit Nomen Domini Benedictum [Blessed Be the Name of the Lord]	Latin	Burgundy, Strasbourg
Sit Tibi Christe datus quem tu regis iste ducatus [To Thee, Christ, Be Dedicated This Kingdom, Which You Rule]	Latin	Venice

coin motto	*language*	*place/source*
Sit Unio Haec Perennis [Let This Union Last Forever]	Latin	Hohenlohe-Langenberg
S. Kilianus Cum Sociis Francorum Apostoli [St. Kilian and His Companions, Apostles to the Franks]	Latin	Wunburg
S. Lambertus Patronus Leodiensis [St. Lambert, Patron of Liege]	Latin	Liege
Sola Bona Quae Honesta [The Only Good (Is) That Which (Is) Honest]	Latin	Brunswick
Soli Deo Honor et Gloria [To God Alone (Be) Honor and Glory]	Latin	Nassau
Soli Reduci [To Be Restored to Him Alone]	Latin	Naples and Sicily
Solius Virtutis Flos Perpetuus [The Flower of Virtue Alone (Is) Eternal]	Latin	Strasbourg
Spes Confisa Deo Numquam Confusa Recedit [Hope Entrusted to God Never Retreats in Disorder]	Latin	Lippe
Spes Nr Deus [God (Is) Our Hope]	Latin	Oudenarde
Spes Rei Publicae [The Hope of the Republic]	Latin	Rome
Stella Quarta Decima [14th Star]	Latin	Vermont
Subditorum Salus Felicitas Summa [Safety of the Subjects (Is) the Highest Happiness]	Latin	Lubeck
Sub Pondere [Under Weight]	Latin	Fulda
Sub Protectione Caesarea [Under Imperial Protection]	Latin	Soragna
Sub Tuum Praesidium Confug [We Take Refuge Under Your Protection]	Latin	Salzburg
Sub Umbra Alarum Tuarum [Under the Shadow of Your Wings]	Latin	Scotland
Sufficit Mihi Gratia Tua Domine [Sufficient to Me (Is) Your Grace, Lord]	Latin	Ploen
Supra Firmam Petram [Upon a Firm Rock]	Latin	Vatican
Susceptor Noster Deus [God (Is) Our Defense]	Latin	Tuscany
Sydera Favent Industriae [The Stars Favor Work]	Latin	Furstenberg
Tali Dicata Signo Mens Fluctuari Nequit [Consecrated by Such a Sign, the Mind Cannot Waver]	Latin	England
Tandem Bona Causa Triumphat [A Good Cause Eventually Triumphs]	Latin	Dillenburg
Tandem Fortuna Obstetrice [With Good Luck Ultimately as the Midwife]	Latin	Wittgenstein
Tene Mensuram et Respice Finem [Hold the Measure and Look to the End]	Latin	Burgundy
Tert Ducat Secular [Let Him Lead into the Third Century]	Latin	Württemberg

coin motto	*language*	*place/source*
Te Stante Virebo [With You Standing (at My Side) I Shall Blossom]	Latin	Moravia
Thu Recht Schev Niemand [Go with Right and Fear No One]	German	Saxe-Lauenburg
Tibi Laus et Gloria [To You Be Praise and Glory]	Latin	Venice
Timor Domini Fons Vitae [Fear of the Lord Is a Source of Life]	Latin	England
Tout Avec Dieu [Everything with God]	French	Brunswick
Travail, Famille, Patrie [Work, Family, Country]	French	Vichy
Triumphator Gent Barb [Victor Over a Barbarian People]	Latin	Byzantium, Arcadius
Tueatur Unita Deus [May God Guard These United (Kingdoms)]	Latin	Britain
Turck Blegert Wien [Vienna Besieged by the Turks]	German	Vienna
Turonus Civis [City of Tours]	Latin	Tours
Tut Mar Gab Pr Vid de Lobk Nat Pr Sab Car et Aug Pr de Lobk [Regency of Maria Gabriela, Widow of the Prince of Lobkowitz, Born Princess of Savoy-Carignan, and August Prince of Lobkowitz]	Latin	Lobkowitz
Tutela Italiae [The Guardianship of Italy]	Latin	Rome
Ubique Pax [Peace Everywhere]	Latin	Rome
Ubi Vult Spirat [He Breathes Where He Wants]	Latin	Vatican
Union et Force [Union and Strength]	French	France
Unus non Sufficit [One (World) Is Not Enough]	Latin	Naples
Urbe Obsessa [City Under Siege]	Latin	Maastricht
Urbem Virgo Tuam Serva [Protect Your City, Virgin (Mary)]	Latin	Strasbourg
Veni Lumen Cordium [Come, Light of Hearts]	Latin	Vatican
Veni Sancte Spiritus [Come, Holy Ghost]	Latin	Vatican
Verbum Domini Manet in Aeternum [The Word of the Lord Abides Forever]	Latin	Hesse-Darmstadt, Veldenz
Veritas Lex Tua [The Truth Is Your Law]	Latin	Salzburg
Veritas Temporis Filia [Truth (Is) the Daughter of Time]	Latin	England, Ireland
Veritate et Iustitia [By Truth and Justice]	Latin	Germany

coin motto	*language*	*place/source*
Veritate et Labore [By Truth and Work]	Latin	Wittgenstein
Victoriae Laetae Princ Perp [Joyful Victories of the Everlasting Ruler]	Latin	Rome
Victoria Principum [Victory of Princes]	Latin	Ostrogoths
Videant Pauperes et Laetentur [Let the Poor See and Rejoice]	Latin	Tuscany
Virgo Maria Protege Civitatem Savonae [Virgin Mary, Protect the City of Savona]	Latin	Savona
Viribus Unitis [United in Strength]	Latin	Austria
Virtute et Fidelitate [By Strength and Loyalty]	Latin	Hesse-Cassel
Virtute et Prudentia [With Strength and Caution]	Latin	Auersperg
Virtute Viam Dimetiar [I Shall Measure the Way with Strength]	Latin	Waldeck
Virtutis Gloria Merces [Glory Is the Reward of Strength]	Latin	Holstlein-Gottorp
Visitavit Nos Oriens ex Alto [He Has Visited Us Arising on High]	Latin	Luneburg
Vis Unita Concordia Fratrum Fortior [Power United (Is) the Stronger Harmony of Brothers]	Latin	Mansfeld
Vivit Post Funera [He Lives After Death]	Latin	Bremen
Von Gottes Gnaden [At God's Mercy]	German	Germany
Vota Optata Romae Fel [Vows Pledged for the Luck of Rome]	Latin	Rome
Vox de Throno [The Voice from the Throne]	Latin	Vatican
Was Got Beschert Bleibet Unerwert [What God Hath Endowed Leave Undisturbed]	German	Hesse-Cassel
We are one.	English	U.S. colonies
Wider macht und List Mein Fels Gott Ist [Against Might and Trickery God Is My Rock]	German	Hesse-Cassel
Zelator Fidei Usque ad Montem [An Upholder of the Faith All the Way to the Mountain]	Latin	Portugal
Zu Gott Allein Mein Hoffnung [To God Alone My Hope]	German	Mansfeld
Zum Besten des Vaterlands [To the Best of the Fatherland]	German	Bamberg

***See also* Knights Hospitallers; paper money.**

SOURCES: "The British Royal Mint." http://www.royalmint.com. • Clain-Stefanelli, Elvira, and Vladimir Clain-Stefanelli. *The Beauty and Lore of Coins, Currency, and Medals.* Croton-on-Hudson, N.Y.: Riverwood Publishers, 1974. • Cribb, Joe. *Money.* Toronto: Stoddart, 1990. • *New Catholic Encyclopedia.* San Francisco: Catholic University of America, 1967. • Pollak, Henry. *Coinage & Conflict.* Clifton, N.J.: Coin & Currency Institute, 2001. • Reinfeld, Fred. *Treasury of the World's Coins.* New York: Sterling Publishing, 1953.

Left: **This twentiety-century Swiss coin bears classic styling and the word "Helvetica," which is a shortened form of the nation's name in latin, "Confoederatio Helvetica."** ***Right:*** **This twentieth-century Swiss coin bears classic styling and the nation's name in Latin, "Confoederatio Helvetica."**

The reverse of the French two-*franc* coin cites the motto of the French Revolution: "Liberté, Egalité, Fraternité" ("Freedom, Equality, Brotherhood").

Interpol

The International Criminal Police Organization (Interpol), founded in 1914, is a global information center aiding law enforcement agencies in the apprehension of criminals who typically evade capture by fleeing beyond national boundaries. Shortly before World War I, the first meeting of interested police chiefs, judges, and magistrates convened in Monaco at the request of Prince Albert I. The participants established a method of sharing identification methods and tracking information to assist member nations in arresting counterfeiters, forgers, con artists, pirates, smugglers, drug dealers, embezzlers, slavers, and notorious fugitives. The outbreak of war ended implementation of the cooperative.

Johann Schober, Vienna's police chief and two-time Austrian legate, revived the concept in 1923 with a meeting of representatives from 20 nations. An Amsterdam division, the Keesing Reference Systems B. V., established in the Netherlands in 1923, began publishing materials concerning the verification of banknotes, passports, driver's licenses and other forms of identification, security documents, and vehicle registration documents and plates. The consortium launched the International Criminal Police Commission (ICPC) in Vienna, where it compiled essential indexes and files until the Nazi seizure of the country in 1938. Subverted by S.S. chief Reinhard Heydrich, the agency targeted victims of the Third Reich. By the end of the war, German mishandling had destroyed fundamental police documents.

Belgian police inspector F. E. Louwage revived the Interpol concept in 1946. Delegates of 19 nations met in Brussels to establish a high command, with Louwage presiding first at the Paris headquarters. From its beginning, Interpol received strong backing from Britain, France, and Germany, but lost U.S. support temporarily in 1950 after FBI director J. Edgar Hoover began doubting the system. Upgrading of the Interpol charter in 1956 further unified the work of 55 national police agencies, altered the name to the present Interpol, and banned the use of the agency for military, political, racial, or religious persecutions.

Headquartered in Lyons, France, Interpol is a strong alliance of 178 nations. Currently, each member pursues domestic law enforcement through an individual clearinghouse, the National Central Bureau (NCB). It requires that members uphold civil rights and respect the agency's constitution, which forbids political manipulation of data and disregard of national laws. By sharing descriptions of missing persons, aliases, photos, fingerprints, and voice analysis through the Interpol telecommunications network, member enforcers back international police work and speed extradition to bring criminals to justice. Among its contributions to law are seminars on cybercrime, computer viruses, and forensic crime detection, including identification of bodies.

In an age of rapid travel, Interpol's 21st century cooperative has boosted arrests of criminals worldwide. A regular newsletter, *Counterfeits & Forgeries*, available in Arabic, English, French, German, and Spanish, explains methods of authentication and lists alterations to the watermark, intaglio and micro printing, and security threading of world currencies. A monthly listing of forged bills along with color reproduction and description of dimensions, geometric symbols, date of validation, serial numbers, print defects, ultraviolet reaction, and print method enables Interpol to track and thwart counterfeiters. In 2001, Interpol president Ronald K. Noble of Fort Dix, New Jersey, the first non–European and first American chief, orchestrated a hunt for financial and physical clues to the terrorists who destroyed the World Trade Center. At a September meeting in Budapest, Interpol pledged to fight global terrorism through joint efforts to halt money laundering, weapons smuggling, conspiracy, and organized crime.

SOURCES: "The Chinese Connection." *Banker*. October 1994, pp. 14–15. • Goldstein, Steve. "Early Casualty of War on Terrorism Is Easy Sharing of Information." Knight-Ridder/Tribune News Service, November 4, 2001 p. 453. • Jones, Peter M. "Fighting World Crime." *Scholastic Update*, December 4, 1987, pp. 22–23. • McLeod, Marcia. "Crime Watch." *Computer Weekly*, February 27, 1997, p. 48. • Nash, Jay Robert. *Encyclopedia of World Crime*. 6 vols. Wilmette, Ill.: CrimeBooks Inc., 1990. • Nuthall, Keith. "Interpol Most-Wanted Goes Online." *Computer Weekly*, November 23, 2000, p. 20. • *Outlaws, Mobsters & Crooks: From the Old West to the Internet*. Farmington Hills, Mich.: U*X*L, 1998. • "Ronald Noble Picked to Head Interpol; First American to Hold Post." *Jet*, July 26, 1999, p. 4. • "Terrorism Added to Interpol Agenda." *Washington Post*, September 23, 2001, p. 36.

Irish money

Like the rest of the world, the Irish survived on a barter system in prehistory. After A.D. 100, Fergus, king of Uldah, established human females as part of the acceptable payment of blood money. In the 400s B.C., St. Patrick, a former slave, fumed in his autobiographical *Confessio* that the *ancilla* (handmaiden) or *kumal* (slave girl), a monetary unit by which people valued commodities and fixed court fines, was primitive and uncivilized, but the treatment of females as commodities continued. In the *Book of Acaill*, a law book written in the third century A.D. by King Cormac McAirt, and the *Senchus Mor*, a law code compiled before A.D. 465 by St. Benignus, tables of value equated a slave woman punctiliously at three cows, 18 heifers, 72 sheep, or 5,184 grains of wheat.

From the A.D. 700s to the 900s, Ireland began following medieval European trade customs and managed its commerce on Anglo-Saxon, Arabic, French, and Scandinavian coins. The first Hiberno-Norse silver pennies were struck in A.D. 995 in imitation of Saxon and Norse models under Dublin's Norse monarch Sihtric Silkenbeard. Norse influence ended around 1150, by which time coinage had degenerated to poorly designed uniface bracteates struck on base metal.

Under England's King John Lackland, after 1207, Dublin mints struck the first Anglo-Irish issue. His designer, Richard Olof, a one-term mayor of Dublin, faced these silver pennies with a triangle that Edward I perpetuated after 1279. Production of denominations from farthing to groat remained in operation at Cork, Dublin, Limerick, Trim, and Waterford and continued for two centuries. In 1536, the nation's coinage acquired its distinctive harp groat under Henry VIII, who initialed the piece on opposite sides of the harp with H and I to stand for Henry and Jane Seymour, his third and most loved wife. From 1689 to 1691 during the Irish campaigns of James II, Irish minters coined gun money, a series of brass coins stamped out of the meltdown of cannon, bells, and scrap silver, brass, and iron. After William III overthrew James, the coins were worthless.

The Irish rebelled against English contractor William Wood, who, in 1723, gained sole rights to strike a debased coin called Wood's halfpence or Hibernia coppers. In his pro–Irish period, Dublin-born satirist Jonathan Swift skewered Wood in the *Drapier's Letters* (1724–1725), which attacked the English for their intent to supply Ireland with devalued farthings and half cents. Swift demanded to know why Ireland couldn't operate its own mint and why a monopoly favored an Englishman. Wood ceased production in 1725.

Because money was scarce and people illiterate, counterfeit halfpence circulated widely. Particularly vulnerable were canal laborers, who moved frequently among work sites. In 1784, the mayor of Newcastle-upon-Tyne wrote to the Royal Mintmaster in London to complain that shopkeepers were accepting counterfeit coins in lieu of genuine specie. Three years later, an investigation countered the mayor's charge of insufficient coinage. In 1822, Ireland ceased coining its own money and relied solely on British issue, tokens, and promissory cards, which numismatic historian Glyn Davies compared to an "anachronistic, involuntary, reverse credit card" (Davies 1994, 247).

Left: **Like modern Canadian moneyers, Irish mints chose unadorned animal symbols like this bull.** ***Right:*** **This Irish coin shows a trout, a popular fish on restaurant and inn menus.**

In recent times, a popular ten-pound note honored Dublin-born novelist James Joyce, author of *Ulysses* (1922). The circuitous journey of the Homeric Ulysses prompted the designer to pair Joyce with an image of the original fictional character, on which the author based his work. On the banknote's face, Joyce strikes a mild-mannered pose. On the obverse, a Greek bust appears over a map of the heart of Dublin, accompanied by the author's signature and a line from his book.

Alongside the Gaelic "éire," the name of the Irish Free State since 1937, the Irish harp is a long-lived image on Irish coins reflecting the beauty of native poetry and the oral tradition of storytelling.

See also **colonial coins; English money; *florin;* Hibernia coppers; plate money; ring money; St. Patrick coppers; Tregwynt hoard; world money.**

SOURCES: Allen, Larry. *Encyclopedia of Money.* New York: Checkmark Books, 2001. • Cribb, Joe. *Money.* Toronto: Stoddart, 1990. • Cribb, Joe, Barrie Cook, and Ian Carradice. *The Coin Atlas.* London: Little, Brown and Co., 1999. • Davies, Glyn. *A History of Money from Ancient Times to the Present Day.* Cardiff: University of Wales Press, 1994. • Einzig, Paul. *Primitive Money.* Oxford: Pergamon Press, 1966. • *New Catholic Encyclopedia.* San Francisco: Catholic University of America, 1967. • Opitz, Charles J. *Odd and Curious Money.* Ocala, Fla.: First Impressions, 1986. • Petterwood, Graeme. "The Shamrock and the Harp." *Tasmanian Numismatist,* July 1999. • Powell, John. "The Birmingham Coiners, 1770–1816." *History Today,* July 1993, p. 49–55. • Snodgrass, Mary Ellen. *Who's Who in the Middle Ages.* Jefferson, N.C.: McFarland, 2001. • Standish, David. *The Art of Money.* San Francisco: Chronicle Books, 2000.

Islamic money

Islamic money is a marvel of propaganda that replaced such pagan currencies as the Berber leather belt studded with agates on brass bezels and Buddhist images of Siva and Lakshmi on Indian coins. Like most of the mideastern Mediterranean world, the Ottoman Turks designed true coins based on Greek and Parthian models and named their monetary standard, the *dirhan,* after the *drachma,* which the Greeks began minting in 650 B.C. For centuries, these coins honored monarchs, dynasties, the gods, the sacred altar, and fire symbols of Zoroastrianism.

After Mohammed's death on June 8, A.D. 632, over some four decades, Islam became the first philosophy to abolish paganism and unite Arabs into one civilization. Wisely, proselytizers moved gradually toward abolishing paganism and establishing Islam as the state religion. A universal embrace of the Islamic faith produced transitional pieces that hinted at a dramatic, often violent abandonment of worldliness as decor shifted to worship of Allah and the strictures of the Koran. Nationalistic pieces bore the crescent and star and the Arabic motto "In the name of God." In North Africa, converted Carthaginian coinsmiths attempted to render the Arabic *kalima* (profession of faith) from the Koran, Chapter XLVII, verse 21 in fractured Latin, "*Non est Deus nisi Deus, et alius non est*" ("There is no God but God, and there is no other") (Hastings 1951, III, p. 709).

The early Islamic *drahm*, the first true Muslim money, dated to the A.D. 600s and characterized the shift of Arabic people from Hellenism and Zoroastrian influence to a Muslim theocracy. At Tunisia after A.D. 610, the Emperor Heraclius of Byzantium produced thick coins inscribed with the Islamic creed written in Latin as a challenge to pervasive Christianity. By A.D. 715, the same types of coins bore Arabic phrases, e.g. "There is no God but God, who has no associate," "Mohammed is the messenger of God," and "God is one, God is eternal; he begetteth not, nor is begotten" (Grierson 1975, p. 41). Islamic dating methods abandoned the Gregorian calendar and counted years from the Hijra, Mohammed's flight to Mecca, in A.D. 622. The bold Shi'ite rulers added personal professions of faith, as with "Ali is the friend of God" (*ibid.*).

Ridding themselves of the likenesses of Sassanian kings and the Persian fire altar, after the Islamic religious reforms of A.D. 700, moneyers began creating Muslim motifs at some 40 mints. Predominating were Koranic slogans extolling Mohammed on front or back as well as political sentiments, some counterstamped to express opposing views. Rapidly, memories of Greek owls and Judean, Roman, and Persian coinage lapsed as specie presented modest, sober expressions of Islamic piety.

After A.D. 711, when a Moorish army ousted Visigoths from Spain, mints issued epigraphic coins — copper *fals*, silver *dirhems*, and gold *dinars*—with Islamic designs and lettering. When Islamic workers erected the series of ramparts that formed the Alhambra, a Moorish fort-palace in Granada, they received their pay in Islamic silver *dirhems*, including those minted at the Al-Andalus mint in southern Iberia under a series of 'Umayyad caliphs dating from Abd ar-Rahman, who ruled from A.D. 756 to 788, to Muhammed I, whose reign ended in 1055. Found at the base of the Alhambra, a casual hoard of silver coins struck during the reign of Caliph Abd ar-Rahman II carried no picture, but a typical pious phrase from the Koran in elaborate calligraphy: "There is only one god and Mohammed is the messenger of that god." In this same period, Caliph Al Mansur's gold *dinar* circulated as far north as the kingdom of Offa of Mercia, influencing the design of his gold coins.

After A.D. 998, the Muslim warrior king Mahmud, sultan of Ghazna, pressed east from Afghanistan and became the first conqueror to carry Islam to central India. He expressed Muslim faith in Islamic coins and commissioned one piece solely for commerce in areas he seized by *jihad* (holy war). As a tutorial device, he added Islamic slogans and Koranic verses to coins translated from Arabic to Nagari, a local language. The method set the standard for subsequent Islamic invaders, who scripted their coins with godly phrases in Nagari and Persian.

The late Middle Ages produced similar designs wherever Islamic people lived. In Castile, a commemorative gold piece called a *morabitino* harked back to the Almoravides, a Berber people, and replicated the beauty of the Islamic *dinar*. The designer maintained Arabic calligraphy, which spelled out Christian tenets. One of the grandest of Islamic coins was the silver piece of the Kurdish warrior king Salah al-Din (Saladin). He distinguished himself by ending the Third Crusade in 1187 through the seizure of Jerusalem from Christian hands.

A strict but fair-minded Muslim, Saladin limited Christian propaganda by halting production of Christian motifs on coins, but countenanced Christian pilgrimages to the Holy Land. Struck at Aleppo, Saladin's artful coin featured a six-pointed star edged in raised dots and centered with praise for Allah, giver of victories. At Saladin's death from exhaustion on March 4, 1193, a grand funeral copper issued by Juluk-Arslan, prince of Diarbekir, presented a clutch of four women grieving for Saladin.

The Muslim world emulated Saladin's religious fervor. In the 1200s, Algeria's mints got a late start in disseminating Islamic coins. Likewise, the Muwahhid Berber of Morocco minted gold ore from south-central African mines into coins scripted with Arabic lettering. In the void created by uninspired Ottoman currency after the fall of Constantinople in 1453, the first hint of originality came from the *altun*, which Western Europeans called the *sequin*. A patterned gold piece struck in 1478, it emulated the *zecchino* of Venice. In 1512, an *ashrafi altin* featured a stream of hyperbole: "Sultan Selim Khan, son of Bayazid Khan, may his victory be glorious: striker of bright coins and lord of might and victory by land and sea, struck at Amid" (Cribb 1999, p. 137).

In 1520, Suleiman the Magnificent, chief sultan of the Ottoman Empire, issued the gold *altin*, an ornate coin featuring scrolled calligraphy minted at Istanbul. More essential to daily commerce was the silver *akche* (also *akce* or *aqche)*, a small silver coin that Europeans called the *asper*, and the gold *ashrafit*, modeled on Venice's *ducat*. Akbar the Great, ruler of Hindustan from 1556 to 1606, who conquered India in 1556 and set up the Mughal dynasty, produced Afghani-style specie and flattered himself with an Islamic pun, "Allah Akbar" ("Allah is great"). In the late 1600s, Suleiman III challenged the strength of the Austrian *thaler* with the silver *qurush*, the Islamic version of the *gros*. The beauty of Arabic calligraphy influenced other world coin design, including a Swedish coin.

Islamic money production remained an artisanal skill in the 1700s, when Iranian traders exchanged blue-glazed earthen donkey beads on a leather thong as small change. Around 1850, Turkish mints replaced folk moneys and hand-stamping with their first coining machines. It was another quarter century before mechanized coinage reached Tehran. In Ethiopia, coinage of brass in the mid–1880s involved the melting of Egyptian brass shell casings into planchets and the application of Islamic texts.

In 1908, 'Ali Dinar, sultan of Darfur, Sudan, cast about for a better source of coins than those he imported from Egypt. After he located Hamid Muhammad, a silversmith who made dies for forging piastres, the sultan determined to set up his own coinage operation. The former forger, with the aid of the chief armorer, began sculpting dies and struck coins in the palace courtyard. The method was simple: five metalsmiths received four rials of copper and one rial of silver each morning to melt into bars, hammer into sheets, and cut into 70 planchets per sheet.

Security was tight. Under guard, one metalsmith struck each blank between paired dies. After the pieces passed inspection, they reached the desk of the royal supervisor. When the noisy operation moved outside the palace, quality diminished, but the sultan's subjects had to accept them in trade on pain of beheading on the spot. In 1912, the Ali Dinar Museum honored the sultan's contribution to Sudanese culture.

To the north, the Ottoman Turks printed paper notes ahead of the Iranian treasury, which issued its first paper bills in the 1880s. In 1930, Turkey began issuing a pound note called the *lira* or *livre*, while other countries of the region continued to commission paper money from European printshops. Until the Persian Gulf War in 1990, Iraq ordered its paper bills from De La Rue, a British security paper and print company in Basingstoke producing vouchers, stamps, passports and visas, security labels, checks, and currencies for 150 nations.

In 1991, the Islamic Republic of Iran issued a gold *azadi* celebrating the 1979 overthrow of Mohammad Reza Pahlavi, the former shah. A polished, worldly monarch, he had produced gold coins he named *pahlavis* and that pictured the lion uplifting a sword, symbol of his power. The success of the Ayatollah Khomeini in ousting Pahlavi marked the new design, a return to religious emblems. Backing the image of a mosque, the moneyer produced a tripartite statement of Ali, the name of Mohammad's son-in-law and Islam's fourth caliph, whom the Shi'ite Muslims revere.

In 1997, the American Numismatic Society received from donor Olivia Garvey Lincoln 7,000 coins of India and the Jem Sultan Collection of Turkish coins, originally acquired by William D. Holberton, author of the two-volume *The Ever Victorious: A Beginner's Guide to Ottoman Empire Numismatics*, which he published in 1971 under the pseudonym "Jem Sultan." Comprised of 5,601 coins, seals, and medals, the gift nearly doubled the society's holdings, making the total hoard the largest and most representative coin collection outside Turkey. A source of history, art, and culture, the coins reside at society headquarters in New York City.

In his last series of articles on the war in Afghanistan in 2001, *Wall Street Journal* writer Daniel Pearl, whom Islamic extremists kidnapped and murdered in Pakistan near the end of January 2002, described the state of printed money under the conservative Taliban. Speculation on currency continued in a primitive trading pit even as demonstrators lobbed tear gas canisters over the wall. Contributing to the uncertainty of the money market was the fact that the Taliban shut down their print operation in 1996. The split in loyalties resulted in popular bills printed by the Northern Alliance under Tajik commander Ahmed Shaw Masood and the less welcome bills printed by Uzbek commander Abdul Rashid Dostum. One of the upshots of uneven values was frequent fistfights and brawling in the bazaar.

***See also bezant; dinar; dirhan;* coins of India; Egyptian coins; *larin;* Muhammad ibn Tughluq; Offa of Mercia; penny; Peter I; tughra.**

SOURCES: Allen, Larry. *Encyclopedia of Money*. New York: Checkmark Books, 2001. • "ATS Money Systems." http://www.atsmoney.com/index.asp. • Becatoros, Elena. "Greece Bids Farewell to Link with Ancient Past." *Bergen County Record*, December 31, 2000. • Clain-Stefanelli, Elvira, and Vladimir Clain-Stefanelli. *The Beauty and Lore of Coins, Currency, and Medals*. Croton-on-Hudson, N.Y.: Riverwood Publishers, 1974. • Cribb, Joe. *Money*. Toronto: Stoddart, 1990. • Cribb, Joe, Barrie Cook, and Ian Carradice. *The Coin Atlas*. London: Little, Brown and Co., 1999. • Grierson, Philip. *Numismatics*. London: Oxford University Press, 1975. • Hastings, James, ed. *Encyclopedia of Religion and Ethics*. New York: Charles Scribner's Sons, 1951. • Hill, G. F. *The Ancient Coinage of Southern Arabia*. Chicago: Ares Publishers, 1969. • "Islamic Coins." http://www.islamiccoinsgroup.50g.com/jims.htm. • "Jem Sultan Collection Donated to ANS." *American Numismatic Society Newsletter*, Winter 1997. • Laing, Lloyd R. *Coins and Archaeology*. New York: Schocken Books, 1969. • Lewis, Brenda Ralph. *Coins & Currency*. New York: Random House, 1993. • Meshorer, Ya'akov. *Coins of the Ancient World*. Jerusalem: Jerusalem Publishing House, 1974. • Opitz, Charles J. *Odd and Curious Money*. Ocala, Fla.: First Impressions, 1986. • Pearl, Daniel. "Amid Global Turmoil, Wild Times in Trading Afghanis." *Wall Street Journal*, November 14, 2001, C1, C13. • Sears, Stuart D. "An Introduction to Early Muslim Drahms." *As-Sikka*, Winter 2000. • "Treasure Found in Southern Kyrgyzstan." *BBC Monitoring Service*, June 1, 2001.

Japanese money

Japan retained a barter system until the A.D. 600s, based largely on rice and including copper rings, jade, beads, and agate and semiprecious stones carved into talons and arrowheads. Influenced by circulation of Chinese cash coppers, the island nation first produced extensive coinage after A.D. 708, when the Empress Genmyo turned new strikes of copper ore into coins. Within five years, tax collectors accepted copper coins as legal tender. At the imperial Nara mint, imported Chinese mint workers struck their own native motifs on small coppers, which supplied the country until 1000.

Silver and gold coinage in Japan was extremely rare. By the A.D. 900s, packets of gold dust served Japanese shoppers as media of exchange in units of *ryo, bu,* and *shu*. In place of the messy chore of sealing dust in envelopes, owners of gold dust melted it into bars, which required cutting and weighing in the appropriate amount. They also carried silver to market in lumps and slabs for hacking into small amounts. For blood money, convicted killers requited family and clan loss only with horses and swords. Eventually, copper coins fell from use and didn't return to circulation until the 1200s.

Importation of obsolete bronze coins from China in the tenth century rekindled a national interest in metal media of exchange. The earliest mass production required pouring melted copper into segmented molds attached to a single shaft. After the coins hardened, workers snapped them free from the shaft like leaves from a tree branch. Because the process resembled nature, the poured coins earned the name *tane sen* ("seed money"). The concept of government coinage degenerated for 250 years. Operations halted in 958 and remained dormant for six centuries.

In the monetary vacuum, Japanese merchants had to rely heavily on Chinese *eiraku sen* ("imported coins)) as well as other moneys from outside the island nation. The first official Japanese coinage derived from reforms of Toyotomi Hideyoshi, a *daimyo* (feudal lord) of the mid–1500s who nationalized mining and standardized the money system. Furthering reform around 1600, Tokugawa Ieyasu, the warlord who succeeded Toyotomi, established state mints and set up a balanced system of coins with fixed values.

Early in the 1600s, the Japanese added paper money to their monetary system in the form of silver receipts, which took the place of silver shards snipped from whole coins. The paper notes, called *yamada hagahi*, were the brain-child of a Yamada merchant. Emulating his simple solution to the need for small change, temple and town officials and feudal barons extended the system of paper change. Rice notes issued by land barons offered to redeem paper money with grain from storehouses. These convenient notes survived until the early 1940s.

Perhaps out of Confucian conservatism, the Japanese were more willing to deal in paper money than in metal coins, which they considered immoral. From the 17th century, they issued silver *cho gin* beans indented at the center; a century later, they traded in bronze, gold, and silver bars, which remained in circulation until 1850. After 1837, the rectangular *ichibu gin* (1-*bu* coins) presented a vertical silver piece resembling a shield and was edged in raised dots, stars, or florettes. The *cho gin* of the 1800s was a cast silver ovule counterstamped at each end with small circles. In 1860, the casting of the gold *koban* produced a long oval coin with a striped background and chop marks or stamps at center and on top, bottom, and both sides. Over the surface, the moneyer brushed the mint mark in Japanese characters with black india ink.

At the end of the shogunate period, the restoration of an emperor in 1868 placed Matsuhito in charge of Japan's monetary system. He ordered a coining machine from Birmingham, England, and installed it at the Osaka mint. The issuance of round coins spelled the end of Japan's distinctive rectangles. To upgrade currency, under the 1871 *Shinka Jorei* (New Currency Regulations), Matsuhito produced round coins pegged to a decimal system based on the *yen* ("round coin"), a term derived from the Chinese *yüan* ("wheels"). For a decimalized currency, he divided each *yen* into 100 *sen* and the *sen* into 10 *rin*. In the Edo period, late 19th-century metalsmith and coin artist Kano Natsuo modeled attractive coins with sunbursts, dragons, and chrysanthemum motifs at Osaka on European minting equipment obtained in Hong Kong. In 1945, Japan established the *yen* as its national unit of currency.

See also **Ieyasu; *oban*; *obolus*; paper money; world money.**

SOURCES: Allen, Larry. *Encyclopedia of Money*. New York: Checkmark Books, 2001. • Clain-Stefanelli, Elvira, and Vladimir Clain-Stefanelli. *The Beauty and Lore of Coins, Currency, and Medals*. Croton-on-Hudson, N.Y.: Riverwood Publishers, 1974. • Cribb, Joe. *Money*. Toronto: Stoddart, 1990. • Cribb, Joe, Barrie Cook, and Ian Carradice. *The Coin Atlas*. London: Little, Brown and Co., 1999.

• Einzig, Paul. *Primitive Money.* Oxford: Pergamon Press, 1966. • Hastings, James, ed. *Encyclopedia of Religion and Ethics.* New York: Charles Scribner's Sons, 1951. • Lewis, Brenda Ralph. *Coins & Currency.* New York: Random House, 1993. • Opitz, Charles J. *Odd and Curious Money.* Ocala, Fla.: First Impressions, 1986.

Jefferson, Thomas

America's prized colonial statesman, Thomas Jefferson served in numerous capacities during the momentous shift from English colonies to an independent union of states. Appointed to a committee to design the Great Seal of the United States, he proved himself worthy by suggesting elements of history, language, and heraldry to represent national themes. In debate with Robert Morris, the chairman of finance for the Continental Congress, Jefferson worked out a national currency based on a decimal system. As Secretary of State in the first cabinet from 1790 to 1793, he served President George Washington by supervising the first U.S. Mint in Philadelphia. Jefferson intended to import Jean-Pierre Droz, a Swiss engraver and inventor of the six-part coin collar, to produce the first dies, but opposition forced him to accept an American, David Rittenhouse.

It was Jefferson who recommended a bimetallic currency based on silver and gold. On the issue of a decimal system, he and Morris approved the concept, but differed in particulars. Morris proposed a system based on the *mark* and divisible in 1,000 units. Jefferson countered with a unit modeled on the Spanish dollar, a currency that served the new colonies in lieu of a national monetary system. Already familiar to citizens, the dollar required no great shift in commercial value. He based the standard American dollar on 100 units called "cents" for the Latin for "hundred." Because few of the 1794 U.S. silver dollars entered circulation, Jefferson president 1801 to 1809, ended their production.

The array of moneys for the new decimal system was pragmatic. Suited to the demands of everyday shopping, dollar coins ranged in amounts from ten, two, and one to a small coin valued at one-tenth of a dollar. The tiniest coin, the *disme,* took its name from the French *dixième* ("tenth"), a monetary denomination drawn from Jefferson's considerable command of French developed during his tenure in Paris as the U.S. ambassador to France. Thus, American currency became the world's first fully decimal system and served as a model for the French republic, which jettisoned the Bourbon coinage for its own *franc* composed of 100 *centimes.*

In 1938, U.S. Mint sculptor Felix O. Schlag honored Jefferson with a five-cent portrait piece. Schlag competed against 390 other artists for the honor, which carried a $1,000 purse. Drawing on a magazine photo he located in a secondhand bookshop in Chicago, he encircled the president's profile on the obverse with "In God We Trust" and the date. On the reverse, Schlag took the suggestion of President Franklin D. Roosevelt and incised a front-facing view of Monticello, Jefferson's Virginia estate, along with the motto "*E Pluribus Unum*" ("Out of Many, One" or "One (Nation) out of many (states)].

***See also* banking; coinage; coins in art; *E Pluribus Unum*; Fort Knox; *franc*; Great Seal of the United States; Alexander Hamilton; In God We Trust; pistareen; U.S. coins; U.S. Mint; U.S. Treasury.**

SOURCES: Allen, Larry. *Encyclopedia of Money.* New York: Checkmark Books, 2001. • Clain-Stefanelli, Elvira, and Vladimir Clain-Stefanelli. *The Beauty and Lore of Coins, Currency, and Medals.* Croton-on-Hudson, N.Y.: Riverwood Publishers, 1974. • *Encyclopedia of World Biography.* Detroit: Gale Group, 1998. • *Gale Encyclopedia of U.S. Economic History.* Farmington Hills, Mich.: Gale Group, 1999. • Johnson, Allen, ed. *Dictionary of American Biography.* New York: Charles Scribner's Sons, 1928. • Pollak, Henry. *Coinage & Conflict.* Clifton, N.J.: Coin & Currency Institute, 2001. • Reed, Mort. *Cowles Complete Encyclopedia of U.S. Coins.* New York: Cowles Book Company, 1969. • Taxay, Don. *The U.S. Mint and Coinage.* New York: Arco Publishing, 1966. • Van Ryzin, Robert R. *Twisted Tails: Sifted Fact, Fantasy and Fiction from U.S. Coin History.* Iola, Wisc.: Krause Publications, 1995. • Willoughby, Jack. "What Your Country Can Do for You." *Forbes,* October 23, 1989, pp. 104–106.

John the Good

The first *franc*, struck in 1360, depicted John II the Good (Jean le Bon de Valois), a triumphant king on horseback. He came to power on September 26, 1350, at age 31 and fathered Charles the Wise, Louis I, and Philip the Bold by his first wife, Bonne of Luxembourg, and art connoisseur Jean Duc de Berry by his second wife, Jeanne of Boulogne. A hapless monarch, John attempted to rally the French barons' compromised loyalties. In 1355, France went to war with the English, who met the French army near Poitiers on September 19, 1356, and captured Jean. Ruling during his five-year jailing was the dauphin Charles, who was unable to face mounting national crises. In 1356, when the Estates-General discussed the king's ransom, they negotiated for reforms. The dauphin called his own assembly at Compiègne and allied with Charles the Bad, initiating rebellion in Picardy in May 1358.

On May 8, 1360, the kidnappers set John's ransom at three million gold *écus* (crowns) in an initial pledge of 600,000 *écus d'or* and annual payments of 400,000 *écus d'or* over a six-year span plus the transfer to Edward III of Angoumois, Aunis, Calais, Gascony, Guienne, Poitou, and Saintonge. On payment of the first installment, the king returned to Calais in early July, when the coins changed hands, a burden of gold weighing 12.5 tons. To aid his people, the king agreed to set up a stable currency.

In his honor, John the Good is pictured in equestrian glory on a gold *franc d'or à cheval* (gold equestrian franc), featuring the legend "*Johannes Dei Gratia Francorum Rex*" ("John, King of the Francs by the Grace of God"). Despite high hopes of redemption from the English, he died ignobly. Because the nobles refused to sign the Treaty of Calais, in October 1360, the English once more incarcerated John in London, where he died on April 8, 1364.

***See also* leather and hide money; medieval coins.**

SOURCES: Castle, Stephen. "Last Rites of the French Franc Marked by Confident Display of Gallic Indifference." *London Independent*, February 18, 2002. • Given-Wilson, Chris, and Francois Beriac. "Edward III's Prisoners of War: The Battle of Poitiers and Its Context." *English Historical Review*, September 1, 2001. • Kunzig, Robert. "Euroland or Bust." *Discover*, October 1998. • *New Catholic Encyclopedia*. San Francisco: Catholic University of America, 1967.

Kidd, Captain William

The West Indies pirate connected with buried treasure, Captain William Kidd turned a legitimate job as privateer into the lucrative career of pirate. A native of the port town of Greenock, Scotland, Kidd was born around 1645. Legend claims that his father was a Calvinist preacher. Kidd worked in trade and became a ship builder. By age 45, he was living in the English colony of New York and sailing aboard his own vessel.

In his heyday, Kidd sailed the Atlantic seaboard, the West Indies, and the Indian Ocean in search of likely merchant vessels to seize and loot. In 1689, he belonged to a crew of French and English brigands who had stolen a ship from their captain, renamed it the *Blessed William*, and sailed to Nevis to join the pirate armada of Governor Christopher Codrington. Kidd earned his way by robbing £2,000 from the French isle of Mariegalante off Martinique.

For a brief period, even though the crew grumbled, Kidd aided the British Royal navy in assailing French battleships. While he went ashore on Nevis, his men stole both his stash of coins and the *Blessed William*. Codrington supplied a replacement vessel and sanctioned the hunting of Kidd's disloyal crew, but Kidd chose to ferry guns and powder to the British colony of New York. For his heroic intervention in a dangerous rebellion, the colonial assembly awarded him £150. After meeting Sarah Bradley Oort, whom he helped to make a widow, he married her and took charge of the fortune left by her recently deceased husband. Among the goods was a townhouse on Wall Street, a pew at Trinity Church, a country estate, and a brigantine, the *Antigua*.

Bankrolled by King William III during a territorial war with the French, Kidd left his wife and two stepdaughters in 1695 to join Robert Livingston and Captain Thomas Hewetson in waylaying French, Portuguese, and Spanish pirates at the request of the East India Company. He hired model seamen, but had to pad the original 70 with louts and cutthroats from poorhouses and prisoners. Aboard the 110-foot, 287-ton *Adventure Galley*, fitted with 30 cannon, he sailed from Plymouth, England, toward Madagascar with 80 mariners.

An act of violence ended Kidd's model citizenship. A greedy crewman, gunner Robert Moore, complained that Kidd was keeping his word not to attack English vessels. When the two men fought, Kidd killed Moore with one blow from a bucket over the head. The upshot of the killing was Kidd's return to freewheeling piracy in the Red Sea and Indian Ocean rather than hang for murder. When he wore out his ship, he loaded accumulated swag on the newly captured *Quedah Merchant*, a 500-ton Armenian merchant ship laden with gold, calico, silk, opium, sugar, and iron from Bengal.

It was not until Kidd's return to Anguilla in 1699 that he learned of a price on his head. He rid himself of the logy merchantman and purchased a sloop, the sleek trader *Antonio.* On the homeward sail, he appears to have buried coin, gold dust and bars, silver plate, and precious jewels at Oyster Bay on Gardiner's Island. Historians also have pondered possible calls at Block Island, Rhode Island, and at Fisher's Island and Rhy Beach in New York.

After Kidd's capture in Boston by the royal pursuers, Kidd brazened out his last days with eloquence and an appropriate bribe to the governor, to whom he sent gold bars wrapped in silk. In the meantime, the governor organized a search party to recover Kidd's loot. For the royal treasury, the governor managed to restore silver, gold, precious stones, and 100 sacks of trade goods.

From his cell, Kidd protested his innocence and produced proof that he had a commission from the king sanctioning the privateering operation. Nonetheless, a Massachusetts court found him guilty of piracy and murder and extradited him to England on February 6, 1700, aboard the H.M.S. *Advice*. From two months of cabin confinement, he entered a solitary cell at London's Newgate Prison. A year later, he pled his case with a lengthy oration. Found guilty of murdering Moore and of committing acts of piracy, he tried to arrange a pardon through Robert Harley, speaker of the House of Commons, in exchange for buried treasure that Kidd valued at £100,000.

Draped in black on a tumbrel, Kidd was mercifully dead drunk when he rode to the gallows at Execution Dock in Wapping on May 23, 1701. After the rope broke and dropped the captive into the mud, the hangman strung Kidd up a second time, breaking his neck. The tar-coated body hung in a cage at Tilbury Point on the River Thames as a lesson to would-be criminals.

Kidd's forfeited goods were valued beyond £16,000, a small total for so many piracies. One theory concerning his treasure of some 4,200 pieces of eight and 4,000 more in gold dust and ingots surmises that he presented some of his profits to his wife and partner. A more romantic possibility is that he escaped hanging by bribing the hangman with a gold coin, reunited with his wife, and took the identity of Christopher Rousby, her supposed third husband. The couple lived out their lives in Rahway, New Jersey, where the husband died in 1728.

Kidd's story intrigued the imagination of fortune hunters. Because he had sailed the Caribbean, New York's Hudson Valley, New England, and the Indian Ocean, searchers were forced to follow his legendary trail around the globe. Some began at Gardiners Island near the tip of Long Island, the last place he visited before his arrest. John Gardiner, Kidd's friend, forfeited to authorities eleven sacks of gold and silver, part of the chests and bales of goods that Kidd left with him. The rest of Kidd's treasure never surfaced.

The romance of the Kidd legend inflamed the imagination of Edgar Allan Poe, who served with the army at Sullivan's Island near Charleston, South Carolina, at age 18. In 1843, he won a prize from the Philadelphia

Dollar Newspaper for "The Gold Bug," a short story set on the island. The tale of William Legrand, a penniless Huguenot aristocrat, and his old black retainer Jupiter is a macabre plot involving a scarab beetle and Captain Kidd's treasure map, which the pirate encrypted and signed with drawings of a death's head and a young goat. By dropping a plumb line through the eye of a skull impaled to the limb of a tree and digging at the spot on the ground below, Legrand unearths skeletons and a cask containing a huge treasure in precious stones, jewelry, and "gold of antique date and of great variety — French, Spanish, and German money, with a few English guineas, and some counters" (Poe 1962, p. 189).

Another Kidd admirer, Barry Clifford, the undersea adventurer who located the treasure-laden *Whydah* off Wellfleet, Massachusetts, was intrigued by a sworn statement from pirate Theophilus Turner concerning the spot where the *Adventure Galley* ran aground in Ile Sainte Marie, Madagascar. Clifford corroborated the site with a map found in Paris at the Bibliotheque Nationale. In 20 feet of water, he used magnetometers to locate a likely stash of ballast stones, an oarlock, and porcelain Ming vases dating to 1666–1722. Other links to Kidd included rum bottles, naval fittings, cannon, an Islamic coin, and Ottoman coins, which may have been remnants of the trove transferred to the *Quedah Merchant*. Before historical archaeologists in Melbourne, Florida, could substantiate his belief that he had found Kidd's ship, the Malagasy government forced Clifford to end the search.

***See also* money pit.**

SOURCES: Bordsen, John. "Prowling with Pirates." *Charlotte Observer*, August 12, 2001, 1G, 8G. • Cordingly, David. *Under the Black Flag*. San Diego, Calif.: Harvest Books, 1995. • *Encyclopedia of World Biography*. Detroit: Gale Group, 1998. • Foege, Alec. "Sunken Dream: Barry Clifford Has Found Captain Kidd's Long-Lost Pirate Ship — Maybe." *People Weekly*, May 22, 2000, 169. • Ho, Erling. "The Things Kidds Do." *Geographical*, February 2001, 61. • Johnson, Allen, ed. *Dictionary of American Biography*. New York: Charles Scribner's Sons, 1928. • Kelleher, Terry. "Pirate Tales." *People Weekly*, August 25, 1997, 18. • Poe, Edgar Allan. *Selected Stories and Poems*. New York: Airmont, 1962. • Pomerleau, Charlie. "Tall Tales of Buried Treasures Run Deep." *Bangor Daily News*, August 27, 1998.

klippe

From the late 1500s into the next century, Danish mintmasters issued the diamond-shaped *klippe*, named for its square planchet. An emergency or famine currency more easily struck during wartime than round coins, the *klippe* evolved from siege coinage into fashionable money. For the latter, coiners presented noble images of royalty, for example, the elephant coin of Christian V, marked with his initial C. Monarchs favored the *klippe* as a gift to visitors, especially the elegant ¼-*ducat* minted in France in 1700 featuring a crowned city logo and globe.

From the late 1620s, the Dutch *Geoctroyeerde Westindische Compagnie* ("Chartered West-Indian Company") grabbed land along the Amazon in the Portuguese colony of Brazil and named it "New Holland." Under the leadership of Prince John Maurice of Orange-Nassau, founder of a capital at Recife, coiners struck uniface *klippe* siege money in the diamond shape to pay mercenaries and to underwrite equipment, munitions, and supplies. For bullion, their ships imported Guinea gold from west Africa.

According to historian Gerard van Loon's four-volume *Beschryving der Nederlandsche Historipenningen* (*Description of the Dutch Historical Coins/Medals*) (1732), in January 1654 only days before the Dutch surrendered to the Portuguese, they used gold plate from two aristocrats to strike badly needed currency in three-, six-, and 12-*gulden* denominations. Although the company forbade the coinage, each piece bore the official logo, "GWC" encircled with raised beads, and the legend Anno Brasil and either 1645 or 1646, also in a beaded circle.

In 1967, a collection known as the Rio Formoso hoard returned these *klippes* to history. The cache of around one thousand of these *klippes* along with stamped bars and copper, silver, and gold coins appeared after a state highway grader unearthed a clay *olla* near Rio Formoso, some 25 miles from Recife. At first, excavators thought the pieces were sugar mill tokens, but numismatists identified them as siege pieces.

Another dire situation at Artois, France, in 1641, forced Louis XIII to issue *klippes.* As the Spanish twice laid siege of the fortress of Aire-sur-la-Lys in May and August, coiners struck a uniface silver diamond. For bullion, the mint staff used the governor's personal silver plate as well as church altar pieces. Artless by necessity, the coins, which became soldier pay, bore in crudely lettered Latin "*Lud XIII Rex Pius Iustus Invictus Arianoa Bis Obses 1641*" ("Louis XIII, a Righteous, Just, and Unconquered King, Twice Besieged at Artois, 1641"). Ironically, when the French held the fort in 1710, they had to strike their own siege coins while they fought off allied forces.

As the French forces of Louis XIV assaulted Amsterdam in 1672, desperate officials called in silver plate from the rich to mint into cash to arm and fortify the city. For this special issue, coiners in an abandoned tower struck an emergency four-*thaler klippe* in medieval style. The obverse pictured an armed, mounted knight raising his sword. To affirm state pride, an official logo on the reverse featured two lions holding the United Provinces' crowned shield. Within ten months, the makeshift operation had stamped five million *klippes.*

The *klippe* flourished in the German states at mints in Salzburg, Nuremberg, and Leipzig. The latter city produced a diamond shape with a loop for hanging on a chain for a medallion. The obverse bears a wide-angle view of the business district. In the late 1600s, the Saxon prince John George II issued even-sided pieces honoring his daughter and commemorating another daughter's marriage and the birth of a male heir. Into the 20th century, imitations of the *klippe* shape have suited designers of commemorative coins, for example, a 1929 five-*pengo* silver piece from Hungary featuring Ladislaus on horseback and a token two-*écu* piece struck in France in 1995 featuring a mounted figure.

SOURCES: "The British Royal Mint." http://www.royalmint.com. • Clain-Stefanelli, Elvira, and Vladimir Clain-Stefanelli. *The Beauty and Lore of Coins, Currency, and Medals.* Croton-on-Hudson, N.Y.: Riverwood Publishers, 1974. • Cribb, Joe. *Money.* Toronto: Stoddart, 1990. • "Treasure of Rio Formoso." http://www.heraldstar.u-net.com/botija.htm.

Knights Hospitallers

A medical corps established during the Crusades, the Knights Hospitallers, also called the Order of St. John of Jerusalem and the Poor Knights of Christ and Solomon's Temple, worked as the Holy Land's main battlefield nurse corps. As the area's only militia, the knights organized in 1050 at Amalfi hospital, erected by Latin merchants of Amalfi near the Holy Sepulcher consecrated to the Virgin, to treat the poor and succor male combatants of any faith or nationality. Protected by the papacy, from their headquarters at Felixkirk, England, they recruited Christian laymen to their company. The knights' black vestments, worn over armor, bore the white Maltese cross as a symbol of altruism and protection to the wounded.

The knights set up shelters in Cyprus, England, and Malta. In Palestine, they opened a 1,000-bed hospital, St. John of Jerusalem, superintended by Peter Gerhard. In combat, the garrison joined the crusades to halt insurgent Ottoman Turks. Heavily supported by Henry II and his crusader son Richard the Lion-Hearted, the knights became financiers through pawning warriors' goods, issuing bills of exchange, and collecting funds to ransom captive crusaders.

At their height, throughout the Crusader states, the Knights Hospitallers owned 140 manors and seven forts, notably, Crac des Chevaliers. At Rhodes, they minted their own *gros d'argent* coins under Foulques de Villaret, who was grand master from 1307 until 1319. Rich in humility and service, the coins show the grand master barefoot and kneeling at a cross marked with the Greek alpha and omega, the first and last letters of the Greek alphabet. He wears the Maltese cross on the left sleeve of his uniform. The legend states "*Fratri Fulcho de Villerto Dei Gratia Ierosolymae*" ("Brother Foulques de Villaret of Jerusalem by the Grace of God"). The reverse also depicts a cross encircled by "*Magistro Hospitalis Conventus Sancti Johannis Hierosolimitani Rodi*" ("Master of the Hospital of the Convent of St. John of Jerusalem, at Rhodes").

Subsequent coinage altered the mottoes under a series of grand masters:

grand master	*date*	*legend*
Antonine Fluvian	1421–1437	Sit tibi, Christe, datus, Quia to Regis iste ducatus [Let this ducat be given to You, Christ, because you rule]
Pierre D'Aubusson	ca. 1476–1503	Behold the Lamb of God, which taketh away the sins of the World
Guy de Blanchefort	1513	In Hoc Signo Vinces [In this sign will you conquer]
Fabrice de Carretto	1513–1521	To God and the Blessed Virgin
Philippe Villiers de L'Isle Adam	1521–1534	Give me courage against your enemies.
Claude de La Sengle	ca. 1553–1557	Prepare ye the way of the Lord
Jean de la Vallette-Parisot	1557–1568	It is not money we want, but faithful service
Pierre de Monte	1568–1572	Propter Veritatem et Justitiam [For Truth and Justice]
John Levesque de la Cassiere	1572–1581	Give me valor against Thine Enemies
Hugo de Loubena de Verdalle	1582–1595	Not Money but Fidelity
Alofio de Wignacourt	1601–1622	Not Money but Fidelity
Raymond Perellos	1697–1720	Conquer by Devotion

The list of coin legends summarizes the pious nature of the knights' organization into the last years of the 18th century.

After the Muslims gained Jerusalem, the knights' property receded rapidly into Arab hands. As the Knights of Rhodes, they amassed their own fleet on the island in 1310. In 1530, they headquartered on Malta as the Knights of Malta. To support the order and its military objectives, they minted gold, silver and copper coins, which they adapted to the monetary standards of Sicily. Local citizens supplemented the knights' specie with French *Louis d'Ors*, Venetian *zecchini*, and Spanish doubloons. Meanwhile, Edward VI confiscated their English property, forcing the knights to rely on their Mediterranean holdings.

As described in C. G. Addison's *Temple Church* (1843) and the Reverend George Fyler Townsend's *The Sea-Kings of the Mediterranean* (1872), in 1565, under Grand Master Jean de la Vallette-Parisot, the building of the city of Valletta on Mt. Sceberras, formation of a 9,000-man army, and siege preparations for an attack by the Ottoman sultan Sulieman I required the knights to strike emergency fiduciary coppers, a fiat money that bore the legend "*Non aes sed fides*" (Not money but faith). The onslaught, which lasted nearly four months, left 38,400 dead. Vallette returned to the construction site and completed his fortified city with the aid of newly minted *tari* coppers, which were easily counterfeited.

After 1636, during heightened hostilities between France and Spain, Grand Master Jean-Paul Lascaris Castellar, exceeded economic standards by overproduction of fiduciary coins in brass. Grand Master Lascaris battled the pervasive counterfeiting problem in 1646 by calling in all coppers for counterstamping with symbolic stars, crescents, crowns, *fleurs-de-lis*, and eagles or religious emblems, including John the Baptist and paschal lambs. He demanded fines, imprisonment, and exile of counterfeiters, but could not halt the creation of fraudulent coins. Counterstamping at frequent intervals produced coins with up to six separate stamps. After 1722, the knights produced their finest coinage under Grand Master Antonio Manoel de Vilhena, who introduced a 12-*zecchini* gold piece, the order's largest denomination. Additional seizures in France further impoverished the order in 1792. In 1827, the British retired the knights' coins.

***See also bezant*; medieval coins; Renaissance coins.**

SOURCES: Cantor, Norman F., ed. *The Civilization of the Middle Ages*. New York: HarperPerennial, 1993. • Cavendish, Richard, ed. *Man, Myth & Magic*. New York: Marshall Cavendish, 1970. • Grotz, Alfred Fisk. "Notes on the Coins of the Grand Masters of the Knights of Malta." http://users.bigpond.net.au/jagatt/notes_on_the_coins_of_the_grand_.htm. • Hallam, Elizabeth, gen. ed. *Saints: Who They Are and How They Help You*. New York: Simon & Schuster, 1994. • Hastings, James, ed. *Encyclopedia of Religion and Ethics*. New York: Charles Scribner's Sons, 1951. • Hollister, C. Warren. *Medieval Europe: A Short History*. New York: McGraw-Hill, 1994. • Milton, Joyce, et al. *The Cross and the Crescent*. Boston: Boston Publishing Co., 1987. • "The Order of St. John of Jerusalem, Knights Hospitaller." http://www2.prestel.co.uk/church/oosj/history.htm. • Setton, Kenneth M., ed. *The Middle Ages*. Washington, D.C.: National Geographic, 1977. • Sinclair, David. *The Pound*. London: Century Books, 2000. • Snodgrass, Mary Ellen. *Who's Who in the Middle Ages*. Jefferson, N.C.: McFarland, 2001. • Tuchman, Barbara W. *A Distant Mirror: The Calamitous 14th Century*. New York: Alfred A. Knopf, 1978.

Knights Templar

The Knights Templar, also called the Poor Brothers of the Temple of Jerusalem, merged monastic and chivalric principles to create a protective brotherhood of 200,000 religious warriors drawn from all nations. Founded in 1118 as guardians of pilgrims by Godfrey of St.-Omer and Sir Hugues de Payens under the charter of Pope Innocent II, the company headquartered on the side of Solomon's Temple at Jerusalem, the source of their name. In addition, they operated ships, depots, and warehouses from England west to Iberia, south to Egypt, and east to Syria. Marked by a red cross on their white capes, on land and sea they guarded the wealth of Christian journeymen and protected merchants from Saracen attack.

Despite the vow of poverty described in crusader and historian William of Tyre's "The Foundation of the Order of Knights Templar" in *Gesta Orientalium Principum* (*Deeds of the Eastern Kingdoms*) (ca. 1180), within a century, the order acquired a fortune in unclaimed treasure in coin, jewels, and plunder and evolved into moneylenders to crusaders, kings, and popes throughout France, Germany, Iberia, and Turkey. At their numerous castles, they stored treasure, wills, and other valuables securely and transported large sums from site to site, using fortified strongholds as way stations on the route from Europe to Jerusalem. Individual knights remained chaste and free of greed and kept no individual funds. Any knight violating vows of poverty was denied holy burial in hallowed ground.

The Templars' wealth and power proved their undoing. They profited from an alliance with the French in 1190, when they provided banking service to Philip II, leader of the Third Crusade and fellow warrior with Richard the Lion-Hearted. The relationship altered in 1307, when Philip IV of France (also Philippe le Bel or Philip the Fair) seized the Templars and their treasury, which he coveted. Philip had attempted to enrich himself by debasing French currency, reminting coins, confiscating the goods of Lombard merchants, taxing the church, and robbing the Jews. When nothing worked, he turned to the knights, falsely accusing them of

> a bitter thing, a lamentable thing, a thing which is horrible to contemplate, terrible to hear, a detestable crime, an execrable evil, an abominable work, a detestable disgrace, a thing almost inhuman, indeed set apart from all humanity [Weatherford 1998, p. 69].

After their torture, Master William of Paris, Philip's juror, convicted them of an embroidered list of crimes — heresy, sodomy, despoiling virgins, necrophilia, idolatry, satanism, alliance with Muslims, and witchcraft — and blamed them for the loss of Jerusalem to the infidels. Sixty Templars burned at the stake in Paris and Sens.

In 1312, on flimsy rumors of sexual perversion and heresy in the ranks, Pope Clement V dissolved the rest of the order and plotted the seizure and disbursal of its goods. On March 18, 1314, a further roundup of Templars sent the aged grand master Jacques De Molay into the hands of inquisitor Guillaume Imbert, who forced the head knight to reenact Jesus's crucifixion. Before the arrest, De Molay destroyed coded lists of funds and property and shipped treasure out of France. Along with officers Geoffroy de Charnay, Geoffroy de Gondeville, and Hughes de Pairaud, De Molay died at the stake in Paris on an isle of the Seine River in sight of Notre Dame Cathedral. Supplanting the Templars as multinational bankers were Italy's finance centers.

Although King Philip and Edward II apparently impounded the remains of the Templars' goods, both men died within months of De Molay's execution. Legends arose that more chests of coins and plate and possibly the Holy Grail escaped the search for Templar treasure. Some pictured the grail as the cup from which Christ and his disciples drank at the Last Supper; others described it as the bowl that caught Christ's blood at the cross. In 1989, a spy-adventure film, *Indiana Jones and the Last Crusade*, starring Harrison Ford and Sean Connery, reprised the grail myth with emphasis on healing powers rather than riches.

A third interpretation of Templar lore claims that the grail is actually the children of Jesus and Mary Magdalene, whom protectors spirited away to protect them from harm. Whether sacred object or kin of Christ, it may have been the grail that the Sinclair clan safeguarded at Rosslyn Chapel in Midlothian near Edinburgh, Scotland. Jarl Henry St. Clair of Roslin (also Prince Henry Sinclair or Sinkler) is thought to have later secured the grail in Nova Scotia after leading 12 ships on an expedition there in 1398 to establish a new Jerusalem called Arcadia.

See also **money pit; Philip IV of France.**

SOURCES: Allen, Larry. *Encyclopedia of Money*. New York: Checkmark Books, 2001. • Cantor, Norman F., ed. *The Civilization of the Middle Ages*. New York: HarperPerennial, 1993. • Cavendish, Richard, ed. *Man, Myth & Magic*. New York: Marshall Cavendish, 1970. • Cooper, J. C., ed. *Dictionary of Christianity*. Chicago: Fitzroy Dearborn, 1996. • Hastings, James, ed. *Encyclopedia of Religion and Ethics*. New York: Charles Scribner's Sons, 1951. • Hollister, C. Warren. *Medieval Europe: A Short History*. New York: McGraw-Hill, 1994. • McCall, Andrew. *The Medieval Underworld*. New York: Dorset Press, 1979. • Rowley, Trevor. *The Norman Heritage, 1066–1200*. London: Routledge & Kegan Paul, 1983. • Setton, Kenneth M., ed. *The Middle Ages*. Washington, D.C.: National Geographic, 1977. • Sinclair, David. *The Pound*. London: Century Books, 2000. • Snodgrass, Mary Ellen. *Who's Who in the Middle Ages*. Jefferson, N.C.: McFarland, 2001. • Tuchman, Barbara W. *A Distant Mirror: The Calamitous 14th Century*. New York: Alfred A. Knopf, 1978. • Weatherford, Jack. *The History of Money: From Sandstone to Cyberspace*. Pittsburgh, Pa.: Three Rivers Press, 1998.

krugerrand

A valuable gold coin minted in South Africa, the largest gold producing nation on the globe, the krugerrand displays fine gold from the Pretoria mines. The Chamber of Mines of South Africa turned the krugerrand into a commodity by exporting it in demonetized bullion coins for sale to investors. Less cumbersome than gold bars and bearing no face value, the coin derived worth from the fluctuating price of gold. The first on the market were proof coins issued in July 1967 in tradeable quantities.

In April 1970, uncirculated, mass-produced one-ounce coins made their first appearance, picturing the bearded profile of Dutch-African statesman Paul Kruger, president of the original South African Republic from 1883 to 1902. The coin, designed by Otto Schultz, displayed the legend "Suid-Afrika" ("South Africa"). On the reverse, designer Coert Steynberg reverenced nature with the springbok or gazelle, the national animal of South Africa. A decade later, South Africa marketed smaller coins in ½-, ¼-, and ⅒-ounce sizes, which suited the buying needs of small investors. By the mid–1980s, krugerrands were the world's most widely held gold bullion coins, symbols of prosperity and prestige. A millennium issue in 2000 pictured the springbok as a symbol of freedom.

At Christmas 2001, a donor to the Salvation Army kettle stirred interest in Mason City, Iowa, in krugerrands by dropping one anonymously in the charity collection. Discovered in a clear plastic sleeve by Lieutenant Kris Augenstein, the anonymous Friday-night donation at a Kmart site consisted of one ounce of pure gold valued at around $350. The gift continued a tradition that started in suburban Chicago in 1982, when five gold krugerrands appeared in a kettle. Over the years, more coins enriched the Illinois charity drive in Bloomington, Michigan City, Shelby, and Chicago. In 2000, the number rose to 40 gold pieces in the Chicago area, where collectors submitted sealed bids to exchange cash for the valuable coins.

SOURCES: Baskins, Kevin. "It's a Krugerrand Christmas in Mason City, Too." *North Iowa Globe-Gazette*, January 23, 2001. • Cribb, Joe. *Money*. Toronto: Stoddart, 1990. • "Krugerrands." http://www.krugerrand.org/. • "New Krugerrand 2000 Coin Issued in South Africa." *African Mining Monitor*, October 25, 1999. • Nicholas, John. "Gold Coin Appears in Salvation Army Kettle." *South Bend Tribune*, December 13, 1998. • Savaiko, Bernard C. "The International Glitter in the World of Gold Coins." *Barron's*, December 15, 1986, p. 36. • Storey, Sallie L. "Understanding the Market for Gold Bullion Coins." *Barron's*, January 26, 1987, p. 56. • Tarpley, Cassie. "A Golden Touch." *Shelby* [Illinois] *Star*, December 10, 2001.

larin

The *larin*, a hook-shaped, uninscripted Persian coin, bore the name of the Iranian city of Lar (or Larr), a Persian Gulf trading center on established caravan routes. The inventor of the coin, Safavid Shah Tahmasp (or Tahmasb) of Hormuz, a vigorous builder and patron of Iranian arts, first bent silver wire into an open loop and stamped it with geometric dies around 1550. Also called *koku ridi*, these thick silver question marks may model Arabic lettering.

Larins remained in circulation for two centuries. Imported from Arab states in the Persian Gulf to Sri Lanka during heavy trade with Portugal throughout the 1600s, the *larin* displayed a unique coin artistry. To maintain the high standard of specie, Persian law required recipients of alien coins to present them for melting and reshaping into *larins*.

The *larin* received mention in traveler Robert Knox's *Historical Relation of Ceylon* (1659–1679), an account of his 20 years in a Ceylonese prison along with his father, a commander of the British East India Company, after a storm drove their ship into port at Cottier Bay. The text describes Knox as a prisoner at large for 19 years, supporting himself as an itinerant merchant, knitter of caps, and lender of corn and rice. In his commercial enterprises, he witnessed use of the *larin* as folk currency. Some bore the hatchmarks of the doubtful, who tested their purity by slicing into them. The truly skeptical heated the metal and dropped it into water to produce the stark white that proved the silver pure.

Around 1789, Carmelite Father Paolino da San Bartolomeo, professor of Oriental language at Rome University, witnessed the *larin* in use, as described in his *A Voyage to the East Indies* (trans. 1800). He claimed that the king of Kandy, a Sri Lankan town, initiated the odd coinage from rolled silver wire twisted into the shape of a wax taper. Making change required hacking off a portion of the hook that equalled the amount of the transaction. Toward the end of the 19th century, a translation of *The Voyage of François Pyrard de Laval* (1890) reported that shoppers snipped small change from *larins*, a sacrifice that cost the whole piece 8 percent of its original value.

***See also* Chinese coins.**

SOURCES: Allen, Larry. *Encyclopedia of Money*. New York: Checkmark Books, 2001. • Cribb, Joe. *Money*. Toronto: Stoddart, 1990. • Cribb, Joe, Barrie Cook, and Ian Carradice. *The Coin Atlas*. London: Little, Brown and Co., 1999. • Einzig, Paul. *Primitive Money*. Oxford: Pergamon Press, 1966. • Opitz, Charles J. *Odd and Curious Money*. Ocala,

Fla.: First Impressions, 1986. • "Shah Tahmasb." http://isfahan.anglia.ac.uk/oldsite/glossary/tahmasb.html. • Thomas, Edward. *Numismata Orientalia*. London: Trübner & Co., 1874.

Law, John

A genius who sired paper currency, John Law, a suave salesman and gambler, tested his theories on national economy with disastrous results. Born to an Edinburgh financier and goldsmith in 1671, Law showed talent in mathematics and exploited his good looks by ingratiating himself with the privileged and elite. After squandering his inheritance, he popularized the theory of probability as a means of predicting shifts in the economy. An unfortunate love triangle and duel that killed Beau Wilson forced Law to flee to Amsterdam to escape hanging for murder. During his self-exile, he studied banking.

In his text, *Money and Trade Considered with a Proposal for Supplying the Nation with Money* (1705), Law stressed the importance of a growing economy to national governments and advised treasurers to increase the specie in circulation by supplementing coins with paper money. To stretch limited supplies of gold and silver coins, he recommended to Britain's Queen Anne that she print paper money in amounts far greater than the reserves of precious metals on hand. When she rebuffed him and his ideas, he took his radical financial notions to France.

On December 14, 1718, under Law's influence, Philippe II, the Duc d'Orléans, spokesman and regent for the underage Louis XV, founded the private *Banque Générale*, the first French bank, which Law surmised would revive the flagging French economy. Newly printed *cent livres tournois* ("100 *livres tournois*") notes carried a simple statement:

> La Banque promet payer au Porteur à vue Cent livres Tournois en especes d'Argent, valeur reçue. À Paris le premier Janvier mille sept cents vingt [The bank promises to pay the bearer on sight 100 *livres Tournois* in silver coin of stated worth. At Paris, January 1, 1720] [Clain and Clain 1974, p. 196].

With an audacious pyramid scheme, Law used public funds to buy shares in his *Compagnie d'Occident* or Mississippi Company, which monopolized Mississippi Valley commerce in tobacco and furs from Louisiana north to Canada. Law, dubbed the "Duc d'Arkansas," dramatized the riches of the New World by paying out-of-work men to pose as emigrant miners carrying pickaxes and shovels on their way to the harbor to set sail for America. In 1719, his company merged with the French East India Company as the *Compagnie des Indes* (Company of the Indies). So many people thronged his office at Quincampoix and bought into the oversold stock scheme that the term "millionaire" entered the French language.

Law's scheme tottered from two blows to public confidence—first, the Mississippi Company failed to locate gold or silver; then, the predicted surge in immigration fizzled. Even though the state guaranteed the numbered and signed paper notes, the shareholders' loss of faith in frivolous paper money and wariness at widespread counterfeit issue precipitated a mass sell-off in 1720. A horde of angry investors demanded bullion to back the 200,000 shares Law issued in his company. American fiction writer Washington Irving described throngs of people banging on bank doors seeking coins for worthless paper money. The mob trampled some of the investors to death. Investors, who lost 90 percent of their outlay, blamed John Law.

Terrified of the consequences of the "Mississippi bubble," but still convinced of his theory, Law, the controller general of finance, hurriedly left France with only a few coins to his name. In the streets, he could hear lurid ditties suggesting that his paper notes should be used for toilet tissue. Still on the run, he supported himself by gambling and died in disgrace in Venice eight years later. Also moribund were joint-stock companies and paper moneys, which people no longer trusted.

***See also* paper money.**

SOURCES: Allen, Larry. *Encyclopedia of Money*. New York: Checkmark Books, 2001. • Clain-Stefanelli, Elvira, and Vladimir Clain-Stefanelli. *The Beauty and Lore of Coins, Currency, and Medals.* Croton-on-Hudson, N.Y.: Riverwood Publishers, 1974. • *Columbia Encyclopedia*, Edition 6. Farmington, Mich.: Gale Group, 2000. • Crossen, Cynthia. "Progenitor of the Paper Millionaires; John Law's Currency System Devastated Royal France, Transformed World Trade." *Wall Street Journal*, July 19, 2000, p. B1. • *Encyclopedia of World Biography.* Detroit: Gale Group, 1998. • Kaiser, Thomas E. "Money, Despotism, and Public Opinion." *Journal of Modern History*, March 1991, p. 1–28. • Murphy, Antoin E. "The Evolution of John Law's Theories and Policies, 1707–1715." *European Economic Review*, July 1991, pp. 1109–1126. • Sinclair, David. *The Pound.* London: Century Books, 2000. • Weatherford, Jack. *The History of Money: From Sandstone to Cyberspace.* Pittsburgh, Pa.: Three Rivers Press, 1998. • Wenick, Robert. "When the Bubble Burst." *Smithsonian*, December 1989, p. 155–165.

leather and hide money

Leather, hide, and parchment, like cloth and pelts, served communities as legal tender long before the printing of paper notes, as witnessed by observers on Tappanuli in Indonesia, where commerce involved exchange of benzoe cakes or buffalo hides, and in the Great Basin of North America, where Southwestern Indians used doeskin as money. In ancient Carthage, Rome's dogged North African competitor, moneyers issued rolled leather and sealed its exterior to preserve the unidentified contents. Described in the *Dialogues of Socrates* (ca. 320 B.C.), composed by the Athenian philosopher and orator Aeschines, the leather cover was the size of a *tetradrachm* and contained a filler known only to the coiner. Historians surmise that the makeshift wrapped coins may have been tin or copper slugs enfolded in parchment made from sheepskin.

In China, an unusual moneyer, Wu-ti (also Wudi or Wu-di), the greatest Han emperor, who reformed trade, monetary exchange, and prices, introduced another type of non-metal fiber money around 115 B.C. His intent was to generate funds to ward off the Mongolian Huns, whose constant battering of Chinese borders depleted the royal treasury. To rid the economy of debased coins, he withdrew them from circulation and replaced metal with official notes on squares of stag's hide equal in buying power to 400,000 coppers.

For a pelt, Wu-ti used the rare white stag from his own park at Ch'ang Ngan and had his moneyers fringe and decorate each piece with intricate designs. By limiting the new currency to an unusual animal, the emperor hoped to foil would-be forgers. The intent of the leather money was to extort payment from princes visiting the palace. Each was obligated to buy one of the squares, thus enriching the treasury with his payment. The clever scheme ended after Wu-ti had distributed the last of his leather money.

Medieval applications of leather and hide to currency occurred in Europe. Near the end of the 11th century, Philippe I of Normandy issued leather money studded with silver nails. Doge Domenico Michiel (or Michaele) of Venice equipped a regiment of troops and ships in 1122, financing the venture with leather bills bearing his stamp, a forerunner of paper notes. Frederick II, the emperor of Sicily, used leather as convertible funding in 1237 during the sieges of Faventia and Milan. During a specie famine in the 13th and 14th centuries, Louis IX, John the Good, and Charles V the Wise also employed leather as a substitute for metal coins.

The concept of leather money resurfaced during the Renaissance. Nostradamus, a French physician and astrologer, commented on the need to coin leather with reflective quatrains about the seventh century that he composed in 1557:

> Par guerre longue tout l'exercite expuiser,
> Que pour souldartz ne trouveront pecune:
> Lieu d'or d'argent, cuir on viendra cuser,
> Gualois aerain, signe croissant de Lune
> [Through long war all the army exhausted,
> so that they do not find money for the soldiers;
> instead of gold or silver, they will come to coin leather,
> Gallic brass, and the crescent sign of the Moon] [Nostradamus].

His verse may refer to the creation of leather fiat money in 1532, when English politician

Thomas Cromwell proposed that England create a state church free of Roman Catholicism. To raise funds for the military, Cromwell advised Parliament to stamp leather squares to pay 40,000 soldiers during the English army's drive into France. He feared, however, that if King Henry VIII should be captured, the French would not accept leather coins as ransom.

Leather and skin money remained in use in Russia, Canada, Alaska, and parts of the British Isles for at least two more centuries. In 1799, Tsar Paul I, son of Catherine the Great, chartered the Russian American Company, a monopoly that made parchment notes from walrus hides for commerce in the Aleutian Islands and along North America's west coast. In Quebec after 1673, bear skins were legal tender; in Southern Alaska, the Tlingit relied on caribou and otter skins around 1885. On the Isle of Man, people coined their own leather currency and stamped it with the maker's name and date. A severe inflationary period following World War I caused German moneyers to craft currency from linen, burlap, chamois, even aluminum foil.

See also **Canadian money; Chinese money; Egyptian coins; fur money; Russian money; scrip; trade and barter.**

SOURCES: Allen, Larry. *Encyclopedia of Money*. New York: Checkmark Books, 2001. • Angell, Norman. *The Story of Money*. Garden City, N.Y.: Garden City Publishing, 1929. • Clain-Stefanelli, Elvira. "Donors and Donations: The Smithsonian's National Numismatic Collection." *Perspectives in Numismatics*, 1986. • Cribb, Joe. *Money*. Toronto: Stoddart, 1990. • Davies, Glyn. *A History of Money from Ancient Times to the Present Day*. Cardiff: University of Wales Press, 1994. • Durant, Will. *Our Oriental Heritage*. New York: Simon and Schuster, 1942. • Einzig, Paul. *Primitive Money*. Oxford: Pergamon Press, 1966. • Lewis, Brenda Ralph. *Coins & Currency*. New York: Random House, 1993. • Nostradamus, "Centurie VII," http://was.kewlhair.com/nostra/cent7.html. • Opitz, Charles J. *Odd and Curious Money*. Ocala, Fla.: First Impressions, 1986. • Weatherford, Jack. *The History of Money: From Sandstone to Cyberspace*. Pittsburgh, Pa.: Three Rivers Press, 1998.

Leoni, Leone

Goldsmith, sculptor, and pictorial medalist Leone Leoni (also Leone Aretino), served Emperor Charles V of Germany and Holland as court sculptor by carving statuary and bas-reliefs featuring his household. Born in 1509 and apprenticed to a goldsmith in his youth, Leoni engraved the coinage of Pope Paul III until the artist's arrest and imprisonment in 1540 for plotting to murder the papal jeweler. Released at age 32, Leoni settled in Milan at the sumptuous Casa Degli Omenoni and devoted the rest of his career to supervising the Hapsburg mint.

A rival of sculptor Benvenuto Cellini and an influence on Spanish art, Leoni produced bronze busts of Philip II of Spain, carved art for the tomb of the Marquis of Marignano in the Milan Cathedral, and cast medals of the bearded profile of Admiral Andrea Doria, Michelangelo, and numerous Genoese statesmen. Leoni lived in splendor at Brussels while sketching the Holy Roman Emperor Charles V, who observed the progress of the portrait. When the emperor struck *testons* and introduced the *scudo d'argento* at Milan, Leoni provided surface art. Leoni also apprenticed his son, Pompeo Leoni, in bas-relief and sent raw sculptures to his workshop in Spain for refinement, including 27 pieces for the altar of El Escorial in Madrid.

SOURCES: Chilvers, Ian. *The Concise Oxford Dictionary of Art and Artists*. Oxford: Oxford University Press, 1996. • Clain-Stefanelli, Elvira, and Vladimir Clain-Stefanelli. *The Beauty and Lore of Coins, Currency, and Medals*. Croton-on-Hudson, N.Y.: Riverwood Publishers, 1974. • *Columbia Encyclopedia*, Edition 6. Farmington, Mich.: Gale Group, 2000. • *Merriam-Webster's Biographical Dictionary*. Springfield, Mass.: Merriam-Webster, 1995.

Lesher, Joseph

A Rocky Mountain pioneer, Joseph Lesher rose from a silver mine laborer to minter of silver coins. A native of Fremont, Ohio, he was born on July 12, 1838, and served in the Union army during the Civil War. Afterward, he clerked in retail, then moved west to Georgetown, Colorado, to mine precious metals. He quit briefly and returned east to run a livery before journeying west once more to the Rockies to mine at Georgetown, Leadville, and Silver San Juan, Colorado. His mine at Central City, Colorado, turned a profit until 1892. He abandoned it during the Panic of 1893, kept his realty holdings, and resettled in Victor, Colorado, during a severe slump in silver prices that idled operations in Cripple Creek, Georgetown, Idaho Springs, and Silver Plume.

An innovative thinker, Lesher pressed Coloradans to coin the state's low-profit silver to simplify exchange and promote business. He discovered that there was no law prohibiting private coinage so long as he refrained from counterfeiting U.S. legal tender. He had a Denver die-maker produce dies and bought bullion for striking from a smelter. From 1900 to 1901 at his operation on West Victor Avenue in Victor, he oversaw the rolling out of silver sheets to be cut into octagonal planchets weighing one ounce each. Stamping 100 dollar coins daily and numbering them serially, he bought materials for 65 cents each and manufactured coins for an additional 15 cents each. His sale price of $1.25 earned him a profit of 45 cents each.

Called "referendum dollars," the coins left up to the parties exchanging and receiving them whether they were acceptable as money. The silver pieces varied from standard U.S. silver dollars by being the same diameter, but heavier and thicker. They bore the legend "Joseph Lesher's Referendum Souvenir, one ounce of pure silver, price $1.25 Mf'd. Victor, Colo., 1900" ("Victor Man" 1998). The back side described each coin as "A commodity, will give in exchange currency, coin or merchandise at face value" (*ibid.*).

Lesher intended his coins to circulate locally in payment for labor, groceries, rent, and ordinary expenses. His coinage brought a query from the Associated Press and stirred interest among investors, bankers, and mine owners, who demanded more of the dollars than Lesher had minted. The first businessman to agree to circulate the coins as currency was A. B. Bumstead, who wanted to use them for commerce at his grocery store on North Street.

The transfer of 10,012 referendum dollars to the grocer saved Lesher from operating a private treasury. He stamped on the private minting, "Pikes Peak Silver Mine" and "A Commodity will give in exchange merchandise A. B. Bumstead" (*ibid.*). His motto declared "*Nil Sine Numme*" ("Nothing Without God"). Soon, other merchants asked to follow Bumstead's example. Lesher began supplying trade tokens and novelty coins to grocer J. M. Slusher at Cripple Creek, jeweler Sam Cohen at Victor, the D. W. Klein liquor dealership, and two private individuals, George Mullen and J. E. Nelson.

When Bumstead reordered, Lesher promised a new striking of 500 more pieces by November 14, but appears to have produced only 210 of the order. Meanwhile, locals continued to debate the feasibility of a private local coinage and its benefit to state industries. The rare Colorado coinage of about 1,900 silver pieces ended a few days later when U.S. Treasury agents confiscated Lesher's dies and claimed that he had issued illegal coins.

SOURCES: Bowers, Q. David. *Adventures with Rare Coins*. Los Angeles: Bowers & Ruddy Galleries, Inc., 1979. • "Lesher Dollars in Demand," *Victor Daily Record,* November 14, 1900. • Reiter, Ed, "Historic Lesher House Recalls a Bygone Era," *New York Times*, June 16, 1985, p. H35. • "Victor Man Starts a Mint," *American Numismatic Association Newsletter,* September 1998. • Wilde, Adna G., "Lesher Referendum Medals," *The Numismatist,* November 1978.

lion dollar

To facilitate international commerce during a struggle for independence from Spain, in 1574, the Dutch in six of seven estates produced the silver *Leeuwendaalder* ("lion or lyon dollar"), the original silver dollar. The coin saved merchants from requiting foreign debt in costly *rijksdaalders*. To promote pride, the designer pictured a knight behind a shield displaying a rampant lion, an emblem of the Dutch and Belgian blazons. The legend read

"*Mo. Arg. Pro. Confoe. Belg. Wes.*" ("Silver money of the Province of the Belgian Confederation Westfriedland"). For a motto, the coiner added on the reverse "*Confidens Dno non Movetur*" ("Who trusts in the Lord is unmoved"). The inspiration was the *Leeuwengroot* ("lion groat"), struck in 1339 in Brabant and Flanders and featuring the Flanders lion.

The lion dollar circulated in the Middle East, Dutch East Indies, and colonies of Maryland, Massachusetts, New Jersey, New York, Pennsylvania, and Virginia and inspired German and Italian imitations. Because of heavy trafficking in specie, the New York lion dollar earned the nicknamd "dog dollar" because of its worn surface. When the H.M.S. *Feversham* sank off Scatari Island, Nova Scotia, in 1711 on its way to Quebec, it carried to the sea bottom a hoard of Spanish cobs, Massachusetts silver pieces, and lion dollars. By 1713, the Austrian *thaler* and Spanish milled dollar replaced the lion dollar.

SOURCES: Codrington, H. W. *Ceylon Coins and Currency*. Colombo, 1924. • Jordan, Louis, "The Coins of Colonial and Early America," http://www.coins.nd.edu/ColCoin/ColCoinContents/Introduction.html. • Newman, Eric P., "The Earliest Money Using the Dollar as a Unit of Value," Perspectives in Numismatics, 1996.

lira

The Italian *lira*, spelled *lire* in the plural, is the monetary unit of Italy, Malta, San Marino, Turkey, and the Vatican City State. Divisible into 100 *centesimi*, the lira was the creation of Charlemagne, who chose a name based on the Latin *libra*, the balance beam scale that was standard equipment for merchants, money changers, and moneylenders. The letter L evolved into the English symbol £ for the pound sterling.

After years of use as a standard of account, the phantom medium developed into the first *lira* coin, the work of Renaissance Italian mintmasters. In 1472, Venetian coiners produced the *liria tron*, named for Doge Nicolo Tron and used in trade and banking. Unlike traditional design, the surface featured his likeness wearing the *corno ducale* ("duke's horn"), and, on the back, the lion, symbol of St. Mark, the city's patron. The broad coin, also called a *testone*, set a trend in portrait coinage by leaving enough space for the incising of a human face, called in Italian a *testa*. Emulating the style were the French *teston*, Portuguese *testaos*, Swiss *Dicken*, and the British testoon of Henry VII, first minted in 1504. Later in the 16th century, sculptor Benvenuto Cellini designed some of the most beautiful *testoni* honoring the egotistical de' Medici clan.

The *lira* figured heavily in Tuscan mathematician Fra Luca Bartolomes Pacioli's ingenious double-entry bookkeeping system, which he explained in *Summa de Arithmetica, Geometria, Proportioni, et Proportionalità* (*On Arithmetic, Geometry, Ratios, and Proportionality*) (1494). He adapted his treatise from an earlier work, Benedetto Cotrugli's *Delia Mercatura et del Mercante Perfetto* (*On Trading and the Perfect Trader*) (1458). The method enabled Pacioli to keep track of expenses and income in *lire*, which broke down into smaller denominations:

coin	*value*
lira	20 *soldi* or 10 *ducati*
ducato	2 *soldi* or 24 *grossi*
soldo	12 *grossi*
grosso	32 *piccioli*
picciolo	1/32 *grosso*

The beauty of the system, set up on the *deve dare* [left side] and *deve avere* [right side], was Pacioli's replacement of cumbrous Roman numerals with Arabic numbers.

A 500-*lire* Italian note depicts a classic image of Mercury, the winged messenger of the Roman gods.

Victor Emmanuel II, the first king of a unified Italy, made the lira Italy's national currency in 1860, when the coin replaced the *grana, ducat, zecchino, florin,* and *giulio. Lire* coins served as legal tender in all states as well as the islands of Sicily and Sardinia. Italian money became so inflated under the dictator Benito Mussolini in the late 1930s that he begged patriotic Italians to surrender their gold plate, even their wedding bands, to support the fascist cause. The plea brought in 400 million *lire.*

As inflation spiraled, Mussolini's trust in the lira was badly shaken. He put into currency in the conquered state of Abyssinia the Austrian Maria Theresa silver *thaler,* which he began producing in Italy. During World War II, Allied forces engaged in war in the former Italian colony of Libya received their pay in *lire* banknotes featuring the mythic *lupa* ("wolf") suckling Romulus and Remus, the founders of Rome. The wartime currency earned the nickname "desert rat money" (Cribb 1990, p. 23).

After the war, the *lira* took on new meaning in July 1948 in the new state of Israel, where Eliezer Kaplan, the first Finance Minister in David Ben Gurion's cabinet, proclaimed the Israeli *lira* (IL) the national currency; he had had it printed in New York. The shaky monetary standard survived numerous devaluations until 1980, when Israel instituted the *shekel.* On January 1, 2002, the Italian *lira* met its own demise as one of 12 European currencies replaced by the euro.

See also **euro; paper money; portrait coins; world money.**

SOURCES: Clain-Stefanelli, Elvira, and Vladimir Clain-Stefanelli. *The Beauty and Lore of Coins, Currency, and Medals.* Croton-on-Hudson, N.Y.: Riverwood Publishers, 1974. • Cribb, Joe. *Money.* Toronto: Stoddart, 1990. • Davies, Glyn. *A History of Money from Ancient Times to the Present Day.* Cardiff: University of Wales Press, 1994. • "So Long to the Lira." BBC News, October 31, 2001.

Longacre, James Barton

Over a quarter century, James Barton Longacre, the fourth chief engraver of the U.S. Mint, designed the Indian head penny, shield nickel, liberty head dollar, 20-dollar piece, Indian princess dollar, three-dollar coin, and flying eagle half-dollar as well as coins for the government of Chile. A native of Delaware County, Pennsylvania, born on August 11, 1794, he was the son of Peter Longacre and learned commerce while apprenticing in the book business under John F. Watson of Philadelphia. Shifted to the tutelage of engraver George Murray, Longacre mastered the production of banknotes.

At age 25, Longacre worked at illustrating encyclopedias and biographies and at incising metal plates for banknotes and the portraits of John Hancock, Thomas Jefferson, and George Washington for a facsimile edition of the Declaration of Independence. Senator John C. Calhoun aided Longacre's quest for the job of chief engraver of the U.S. Mint, where he succeeded Christian Gobrecht on September 16, 1844. Assisting him in mastering national coinage were William Barber, P. F. Cross, William H. Key, and Anthony C. Paquet. Longacre's first original contribution, a Liberty head dollar, required some reduction of relief, but produced a coin that circulated from 1849 to 1907. As the supply of gold burgeoned from one million dollars to 50 million, he suppressed silver coinage and introduced the first gold double eagle, the nation's smallest coin shape. Because it was the product of gold from the 1848 California strike at Sutter's Mill, it bore the mintmark "Cal."

At the proposal of Senator Stevens Dickinson of New York, in 1851, Longacre's staff produced a three-cent coin, which increased the amount of small change in circulation and suited the price of U.S. postage stamps. A tiny cupro-silver coin, the silver three-center, a fiduciary coin called a "trime," was the first U.S. coin produced with less intrinsic worth than the stated value. Artistically, it required careful incision within limited space. Longacre designed a six-pointed star and shield for the face with the Roman "III" indicating value on the back. Because of the darkening of the alloy, called "billon" from the French for "ingot," the trime fell into disfavor, earned the dubious nickname "fish scale," and went out of circulation in 1873.

Longacre remained busy after 1853 reducing other coins. He re-engineered the shape of the half-dime, dime, quarter, and half-dollar. In 1854, he created a three-dollar gold piece picturing corn, cotton, tobacco, and wheat. Marring his tenure were a series of in-house squabbles, notably with head coiner Franklin Peale, whom President Franklin Pierce fired to end Peale's moonlighting on outside jobs on U.S. Mint equipment. Longacre produced the flying eagle cent in 1856, expressing the concept of liberty in the form of the noble bird with wings upraised in flight.

In 1858, Longacre created dies for the Indian head penny, choosing as his model a classic Roman statue rather than a real native American model and adding a feathered war bonnet bearing the legend "Liberty." According to a questionable legend, he posed his daughter Sarah as a model because of her classic features and topped her hair with a headdress showing nine feathers. Between hair and bottom feather, he incised the initial L. To qualms about the acceptance of a native American image, he stated, "We have only to determine that it shall be appropriate and all the world cannot wrest it from us" (Reed 1969, p. 95).

The mint ran more smoothly in 1863, when Longacre struck in French bronze the two-center, the first U.S. coin to bear the motto "In God We Trust." The coin served commerce well until the introduction of the nickel in 1866. As inflation rose, the two-center became obsolete in 1873, four years after Longacre's death, when the mint destroyed a variety of pennies, half-cents, and two-centers to apply the metals to smaller pennies.

See also **Anthony C. Paquet; Charles Cushing Wright.**

SOURCES: Akers, David W. *United States Gold Coins*. Englewood, Ohio: Paramount Publications, Englewood, Ohio, 1975. • *Biography Resource Center*. Farmington Hills, Mich.: Gale, 2001. • Blythe, Al. *The Complete Guide to Liberty Seated Half Dimes*. Virginia Beach, Va.: DLRC Press, 1992. • Breen, Walter. *Walter Breen's Complete Encyclopedia of U.S. and Colonial Coins*. New York: F. C. I. Press/Doubleday, 1988. • Briggs, Larry. *The Comprehensive Encyclopedia of United States Liberty Seated Quarters*. Lima, Ohio: Larry Briggs Rare Coins, 1991. • Clain-Stefanelli, Elvira, and Vladimir Clain-Stefanelli. *The Beauty and Lore of Coins, Currency, and Medals*. Croton-on-Hudson, N.Y.: Riverwood Publishers, 1974. • De Lorey, Thomas. "Longacre, Unsung Engraver of the U.S. Mint." *The Numismatist*, October 1985. • *Merriam-Webster's Biographical Dictionary*. Springfield, Mass.: Merriam-Webster, 1995. • Morris, Richard B. *Encyclopedia of American History*. New York: Harper & Row, 1976. • Reed, Mort. *Cowles Complete Encyclopedia of U.S. Coins*. New York: Cowles Book Company, 1969. • Taxay, Don. *The U.S. Mint and Coinage*. New York: Arco Publishing, 1966. • Van Ryzin, Robert R. *Twisted Tails: Sifted Fact, Fantasy and Fiction from U.S. Coin History*. Iola, Wisc.: Krause Publications, 1995. • Yeoman, R. S. *A Guide Book of United States Coins*. Racine, Wisc.: Western Publishing, 1993.

Lydian coins

Lydia, a powerful and cultured kingdom of Asia Minor and home of the rich king Midas, was the fount of the Western world's true coinage, perhaps as early as 800 B.C. The supplanting of herds of cattle, grain, shells, feathers, salt bars, weapons, tools, nails, and pre-coin ingots of precious metal with true bean-shaped coins occurred in Lydia in 687 B.C., a few decades before the Argives coined their precious metal. Historians surmised that, because Lydians were pastoral, rural people, they probably adopted the concept of coins from Ionian tokens to make use of an ample supply of silver-specked gold that washed up from river beds.

The Lydian method of striking was complex, but endured for 1,500 years: The designer carved an intaglio motif on a bronze disk for the obverse pattern. The die fit into a recessed circle in an anvil. With a punch carved with a second pattern, the striker lifted heated metal disks with tongs, placed them one by one into the pit on the anvil, fitted the intaglio pattern of the punch against the disk, and struck the top of the punch with a hammer. Formed of a pale yellow blend of gold and silver called electrum or white gold, the Lydian slugs bore King Gyges's lion insignia backed with punch marks assuring citizens that the metal was pure and coined in a valid amount.

According to Book I of the Greek traveler Herodotus's *Histories* (ca. 450 B.C.), the Lydians developed not only coinage, but also retail merchandising. Under King Gyges, the founder of the Mermnadae dynasty, who ruled Assyria from 687 to 652 B.C., Lydian coiners made solid money out of naturally occurring electrum found along the Pactolus River. The coins took the shape of river pebbles and bore a stamp guaranteeing quality and weight. Wealth from trade in electrum prompted Gyges to hire mercenaries and attempt to spread his rule over Ionia and Aeolia. Over the next half century, Lydians profited further by learning methods of separating the gold from electrum.

Croesus, the reformer of Lydian money, learned about gold coins during military expeditions to the coast of Asia Minor and from the coinage of his father, King Alyattes, the fourth Lydian monarch after Gyges. After Croesus's crowning in 570 B.C. at age 35, he halted the striking of coins from electrum and upgraded Lydian money to the world's first bimetallic system by inventing *staters* in silver and gold. Enhancing the design of his oval coins was a dramatic face-off between a lion and bull. His coiners shaped flans or blank circlets of electrum for the stamping of Croesean *staters*, which he used as a bonus to Delphians when he sought a prophesy from the Pythia, Apollo's spokeswoman. According to Herodotus, Croesus rashly interpreted as favorable her ambiguous prediction that, if he attacked Persia, "he would destroy a great empire" (Herodotus 1954, p. 32). Overjoyed, he allotted each male Delphian two gold staters. He failed to consider the possibility that the empire he destroyed would be his own.

Croesus replaced the old punch-and-die coinage with a two-die method. The creation of a coin required the metalworker to lift the heated circlet with tongs, place it between two dies, then strike the upper die with a hammer, thus impressing both sides with one blow. This innovation of two-sided coinage in silver and gold constituted the first bimetal coinage in the Western world. After the Persians captured the king in 546 B.C., the concept of pure metal coinage spread north to Greece and southeast to Persia, where coiners and merchants preferred gold over silver.

***See also* incuse.**

SOURCES: Allen, Larry. *Encyclopedia of Money*. New York: Checkmark Books, 2001. • Becatoros, Elena. "Greece Bids Farewell to Link with Ancient Past." *Bergen County Record*, December 31, 2000. • Clain-Stefanelli, Elvira, and Vladimir Clain-Stefanelli. *The Beauty and Lore of Coins, Currency, and Medals*. Croton-on-Hudson, N.Y.: Riverwood Publishers, 1974. • Cribb, Joe. *Money*. Toronto: Stoddart, 1990. • Davies, Glyn. *A History of Money from Ancient Times to the Present Day*. Cardiff: University of Wales Press, 1994. • Durant, Will. *The Life of Greece*. New York: Simon and Schuster, 1939. • Einzig, Paul. *Primitive Money*. Oxford: Pergamon Press, 1966. • *Encyclopedia of the Ancient Greek World*. New York: Facts on File, Inc., 1995. • Galbraith, John Kenneth. *Money: Whence It Came, Where It Went*. Boston: Houghton Mifflin, 1975. • Grosvenor, Melville Bell, ed. in chief. *Everyday Life in Bible Times*. Washington, D.C.: National Geographic Society, 1967. • Herodotus. *The Histories*. London: Penguin Books, 1954. • Hopper, R. J. *The Early Greeks*. New York: Harper & Row, 1976. • Howatson, M. C., ed. *The Oxford Companion to Classical Literature*. Oxford: Oxford University Press, 1991. • James, Peter, and Nick Thorpe. *Ancient Inventions*. New York: Ballantine, 1994. • Jansen, H. W., and Anthony F. Janson. *History of Art*. New York: Harry N. Abrams, Incorporated, 1997. • Kiernan, Philip. "Alfred Petrie Leaves His Coins to the National Currency Collection." *Canadian Numismatic Association Journal*, October 2001, 389–395. • Moorehead, Caroline. *Lost and Found: The 9,000 Treasures of Troy*. London: Penguin Books, 1994. • Pliny. *The Natural History*. New York: McGraw-Hill, 1962. • Pollak, Henry. *Coinage & Conflict*. Clifton, N.J.: Coin & Currency Institute, 2001. • Reinfeld, Fred. *Treasury of the World's Coins*. New York: Sterling Publishing, 1953. • Severy, Merle, ed. *Greece & Rome*. Washington, D.C.: National Geographic Society, 1977. • Starr, Chester G. *A History of the Ancient World*. New York: Oxford University Press, 1991. • Thomas, Edward. *Numismata Orientalia*. London: Trübner & Co., 1874. • Williams, Trevor. *The History of Invention*. New York: Facts on File, 1987.

Macedonian coins

Fourth-century B.C. Macedonia was heir to Lydian and Greek monetary innovations,

Lydian and Greek monetary motifs influenced this early Macedonian coin struck in 500 B.C. (Guy Clark, Ancient Coins and Antiquities, Norfolk, Virginia)

In 465 B.C., when this coin was designed, Macedonian coin art relied heavily on Lydian and Greek originals. (Guy Clark, Ancient Coins and Antiquities, Norfolk, Virginia)

In 336 B.C., Macedonia produced an artful gold coin featuring the image of the goddess Athena displaying a decidedly Greek profile and wearing a war helmet. The obverse depicts Nike, the winged goddess of victory, with whom artists often paired Athena. (Guy Clark, Ancient Coins and Antiquities, Norfolk, Virginia)

particularly the famed Athenian owls, which pictured Athena, goddess of wisdom, on the obverse. In a shift from the mythic past to human dynamism, the era's coins downplayed divine motifs and honored great people and events. One notable coiner, the admiral Demetrius I Poliorcetes (the Besieger) of Macedon, depicted the ramming prow of a warship, emblem of his brilliance as a naval commander over Ptolemy in 306 B.C. at Salamis, Cyprus. He also ordered a silver *tetradrachm* picturing Nike, later known as the Winged Victory of Samothrace, posed like a figurehead on a ship, and, on the back, Poseidon lifting his trident. A Peloponnesian engraver from Polycleitus's school, sometime after 371 B.C., incised Arcadian Pan seated on a rock, the first depiction of a complete figure and another landmark. The people of Lamia in Thessaly honored Demetrius by striking a portrait coin of Lamia, the flute player and *hetaira* ("courtesan") who, according to Plutarch's biography *Demetrius* (A.D. 75), passed as his wife and, after 294 B.C., ruled Athens by influencing his political decisions.

Under Philip II of Macedon, royal coins like this one, struck in 359 B.C., moved beyond utilitarian state coinage to attractive international moneys suited to commerce over the whole eastern Mediterranean. (Guy Clark, Ancient Coins and Antiquities, Norfolk, Virginia)

Under Philip II of Macedon, who mined gold from Mount Pangaeus and copper, iron, and silver from other state-owned mines, royal coins moved beyond limited state use to attractive international moneys suited to commerce over the whole eastern Mediterranean. The king kept mintmasters busy striking extra silver *tetradrachms* and gold *philippeioi* (philippics) to underwrite Greek forays into Persia. From Pangaeus alone, he achieved 1,000 talents a year. The Roman odist Horace so admired Philip's gold *staters* that he referred to them as *regale numisma Philippos* ("*Philip's royal coins*").

Philip used coins for political gain and bragged that he could bribe satraps anywhere he could lead an ass train of gold. He elevated coin art with an artful *tetradrachm* picturing a mounted jockey and also bolstered his image by commissioning a gold *stater* that glimpsed his win in chariot racing at the Olympic games of 356 B.C. His *tetradrachm* featuring the bold bust of Hercules implied strength and greatness, perhaps even suggesting that the king's lineage sprang from that of the god-like hero. Of Philip's obsession with coins, Pliny the Elder, a critic of greed in *Natural History* (77 A.D.), smirked that "King Philip of Macedon was never wont to go to bed and sleep without a standing cup of gold under his pillow" (Pliny 1962, 357). Whatever his faults, Philip circulated silver *tetradrachms* far from the source, influencing the Celtic coiners of Britain around 325 B.C. The same pieces from the Tarsus mint filled a hoard of 8,000 coins at Demanhur, Egypt, in 318 B.C.

Philip's famous son, Alexander III the Great, put a greater stress on the Macedonian monetary system from 336 to 323 B.C. Spending a half ton of silver daily, he depended on captured Persian wealth from palaces and temple treasuries as the bullion needed to supply his mints. His manipulation of coins for political ends was ingenious: He had no dies incised with a royal portrait, but gradually humanized representations of Hercules to resemble his own silhouette.

After the death of Darius in 330 B.C., Alexander harnessed the Babylonian mint, the most productive of the Persian empire, to strike new silver. He also activated operations at Accho, Alexandria, Amphipolis, Ardaus, Citium, Ecbatana, Lampsacus, Miletus, Sardis, Sicyon, Sidea, Sydon, and Tarsus to transform his plunder into coins, which his men rapidly spent. His conquests introduced peoples as far away as India to Greek-style coinage, deities, and art.

From conquest in Persia, Macedonian coinage added gold pieces to local silver. To standardize the exchange rate, Alexander set the ratio of silver to gold at ten to one and left to quibblers the odd change. Alexandrine coins paid to his soldiers, engineers, retainers, and spies buoyed trade throughout the new cities they founded in the eastern Mediterranean from Egypt to Samarkand. Alexander valued trade as a Hellenizing force to bring Greek principles and values to the Persian masses.

One of Alexander's successors, Lysimachus, commander of the royal bodyguard and satrap of Macedonia, issued a massive coinage around 297 B.C. picturing the profile of Alexander decked in corona and the ram's horn of Zeus Ammon, the Greek embodiment of the Egyptian god Amun. The upswept eyes, open lips, and tousled, serpentine hair idealized the conqueror as an engaging young man turned into a god. The majesty of the coin influenced the moneys issued by the Roman Emperor Hadrian in A.D. 130 and by his successor, Antoninus Pius.

After Alexander's death in 323 B.C., the Egyptian ruler Ptolemy I, one of his favorite generals, retained Alexander's strongly Greek profile with elephant pelt headdress on a coin struck around 310 B.C. A decade later, Ptolemy set a world record for being the first living man pictured on a coin. To the Jews of Judea, these coins were abominations. The sight of Alexander's boyish portrait with flowing hair and masterful gaze, Alexander overcoming the Indian king riding an elephant in 326 B.C., and the likenesses of Olympian Zeus and of Hermes in a *kausia* (broad-brimmed hat) insulted them and their god-fearing principles. Whatever the coins' value as trade tokens in Palestine, the Jews despised them as reminders of widespread Hellenism, pagan gods, and the vitiation of Hebrew modesty and conservative religious practice.

Hellenistic coinage dominated Mediterranean trade and influenced the development of sophisticated finance in Bactria, Mauretania, Parthia, and other regions that Alexander's troops crossed. Slave-run factories mass-produced goods such as *amphorae* (storage jars) and tableware for general markets. As ships introduced foreigners to Greek goods, expanded commerce placed demands on Egypt, Pergamum, Rhodes, and Seleucia to develop their own treasuries and money systems, which emulated the success of Greek coinage.

The post–Alexandrine era flooded eastern Mediterranean tills with attractive historically accurate coins. Seleucus, another of Alexander's former generals, struck grand disks at Pergamum picturing a horse and elephant. In 250 B.C., Bactria's mint turned out a biographical series of coins picturing the six successors of Alexander's generals. The proud Pontine king Mithradates IV presented his portrait opposite a wreathed stag or Pegasus, the winged horse of the mythic hero Bellerophon. Parthians exalted their first king, Arsaces I, founder of the Arsacid dynasty which survived until A.D. 224, as well as the murderous Queen Musa, who slew her husband and elevated her son Phraates V to the throne that the two shared from 2 B.C. to A.D 4.

After 260 A.D., the Roman usurpers, Titus Fulvius Macrianus Senior and his sons Macrianus the Younger and Quietus, known collectively as the Macriani, used Alexander's coins as protective amulets. The elder Macrianus, as *procurator arcae* ("master of the treasury"), controlled the Emperor Valerian's purse and minted his coins. When Macrianus usurped imperial power, he began commissioning coinage honoring himself and his sons. As characterized by the historian Trebellius Pollio, author of the undated biography *Vita Valeriani I* (*The Life of Valerian I*), the Macriani "dicuntur iuvari in omni actu suo, qui Alexandrum expressum vel auro gestant vel argento" ("were said to have been aided in all acts by wearing the likeness of Alexander, either in gold or silver) (Hastings 1951, III, p. 703). The amulets failed to protect them from the retribution of the real emperor, Gallienus, who crushed their forces.

SOURCES: Allen, Larry. *Encyclopedia of Money*. New York: Checkmark Books, 2001. • Becatoros, Elena. "Greece Bids Farewell to Link with Ancient Past." *Bergen County Record*, December 31, 2000. • Clain-Stefanelli, Elvira, and Vladimir Clain-Stefanelli. *The Beauty and Lore of Coins, Currency, and Medals*. Croton-on-Hudson, N.Y.: Riverwood Publishers, 1974. • Cribb, Joe. *Money*. Toronto: Stoddart, 1990. • Davies, Glyn. *A History of Money from Ancient Times to the Present Day*. Cardiff: University of Wales Press, 1994. • Durant, Will. *The Life of Greece*. New York: Simon and Schuster, 1939. • *Encyclopedia of the Ancient Greek World*. New York: Facts on File, Inc., 1995. • Grosvenor, Melville Bell, ed. in chief. *Everyday Life in Bible Times*. Washington, D.C.: National Geographic Society, 1967. • *Handbook to Life in Ancient Greece*. New York: Facts on File, Inc., 1997. • Hastings, James, ed. *Encyclopedia of Religion and Ethics*. New York: Charles Scribner's Sons, 1951. • Head, Barclay V. *A Guide to the Principal Coins of the Greeks*. London: British Museum, 1959. • Head, Barclay V. *Historia Numorum*. Chicago: Argonaut, 1911. • Hill, G. F. *Historical Greek Coins*. Chicago: Argonaut, Inc., 1966. • Howatson, M. C., ed. *The Oxford Companion to Classical Literature*. Oxford: Oxford University Press, 1991. • James, Peter, and Nick Thorpe. *Ancient Inventions*. New York: Ballantine, 1994. • Jansen, H. W., and Anthony F. Janson. *History of Art*. New York: Harry N. Abrams, Incorporated, 1997. • Kiernan, Philip. "Alfred Petrie Leaves His Coins to the National Currency Collection." *Canadian Numismatic Association Journal*, October 2001, 389–395. • Meshorer, Ya'akov. *Coins of the Ancient World*. Jerusalem: Jerusalem Publishing House, 1974. • Moorehead, Caroline. *Lost and Found: The 9,000 Treasures of Troy*. London: Penguin Books, 1994. • *New Catholic Encyclopedia*. San Francisco: Catholic University of America, 1967. • Pliny. *The Natural History*. New York: McGraw-Hill, 1962. • Pollak, Henry. *Coinage & Conflict*. Clifton, N.J.: Coin & Currency Institute, 2001. • Starr, Chester G. *A History of the Ancient World*. New York: Oxford University Press, 1991. • Williams, Trevor. *The History of Invention*. New York: Facts on File, 1987.

Machin, Thomas

A war hero and private producer of coins, Bostonian metalsmith Thomas Machin turned out some of the first U.S. specie. Born in Staffordshire, England, on March 20, 1744, he was the son of mathematician John Machin and apprenticed in ironworking under inventor James Brindley. After earning a reputation for civil engineering feats, Machin emigrated to New England at age 28 to study the New Jersey copperworks.

Quickly won to the patriot cause, Machin participated in the Boston Tea Party and served as an artillery officer in the Continental Army under General George Washington. Machin sustained an arm wound at the battle of Bunker Hill before becoming involved in building defenses for the patriots. South of West Point, the army corps of engineers stretched an iron chain, a frail and poorly designed obstacle that the British quickly dismantled. In 1776, Washington appointed engineers to forge a more rugged underwater defense on the Hudson River between Plum Point and Pollepel Island consisting of stone caissons bristling with *chevaux-de-frise*— tree trunks tipped with iron points. To halt battleships from sailing upriver, Washington chose Machin to devise a sturdier obstruction spanning the river. The intent was to prevent a fleet from menacing Albany and the upper Hudson Valley.

With a deadline of winter 1778, Machin forged a flexible linkage nicknamed "General Washington's Watch Chain." At forges in the Ramapo Mountains, Machin crafted 750 two-foot iron links, each weighing 125 pounds. He strung them into a 1,500-foot chain, supervised hand-hammered chamfering, and fitted the finished links with swivels, shackles, and anchors. To position the whole across an S curve near West Point, his staff built log rafts. Associates of the Sterling Iron Works labored in teams day and night without a break for six weeks and winched the chain into place on April 30, 1778. The English, wary of a trap, wisely turned their manpower south.

At war's end, in May 1783, Captain Machin built a home on Great Pond near Newburgh, New York, and upgraded boggy land with a canal, grist mill, and sawmill and began turning out hardware. In 1785, he subcontracted with Vermont metalsmith Reuben Harmon, a minter at Hagar's Brook in Bennington, to strike state coppers, the first minted after the Revolutionary War. When New York legislators began coining coppers in 1787, Machin applied for the franchise and planned a conversion of his mills to minting. To educate himself in an unfamiliar craft, he readied pattern coins with a number of designs, notably, a silhouette of Governor George Clinton on the front and the New York state seal on the reverse.

SOURCES: Diamant, Lincoln. *Yankee Doodle Days*. Fleischmanns, N.Y.: Purple Mountain Press, 1996. • Kleeberg, John, ed. *The Money of Pre-Federal America*. New York: American Numismatic Society, 1992. • McGuire, Bill. "The Man Who Chained the Hudson." *Townline*, Fall 2000. • Simms, Jeptha R. *History of Schoharie County, and Border Wars of New York*. Albany, N.Y.: Munsell & Tanner, Printers, 1845.

MacNeil, Hermon Atkins

In the early years of the 20th century, when American sculpture came into its own as a recognized art form, Hermon Atkins MacNeil contributed to the era's most attractive and nationalistic coin designs. A native of Chelsea, Massachusetts, he was born on February 27, 1866, to Mary Lash Pratt and John Clinton MacNeil, an Irish-American horticulturist and nurseryman. At the urging of his cousin, Jeanette Mitchell, MacNeil enrolled at Boston's Massachusetts Normal Art School and won honors during the four-year art course. At age 20, he began a three-year stint teaching modeling at Sibley College, forerunner of the school of engineering at Cornell University.

With a loan of $500, in 1888, MacNeil mastered impressionistic styling in Paris while training at the Académie Julian under Henri Chap, designer of a contemplative statue of Joan of Arc, and at the École des Beaux-Arts with Jean Falguière, who contributed to the monument to the Marquis de Lafayette in Washington, D.C. Amply educated in forthright modeling of figures in motion, at age 26, MacNeil refined the architectural pieces sculpted by Philip Martiny for the 1893 World's Columbian Exposition in Chicago, earning for himself a designer's medal for two statues at the Electricity Building. Until age 30, he taught at Chicago's Art Institute while privately learning the primitive styles of the Moqui and Zuñi in Arizona, Colorado, and New Mexico.

As a Roman Rinehart Scholar, MacNeil and his bride, sculptor Carol L. Brooks, made an extensive study of the plastic arts at the American Academy in Rome. At his studio at the Villa dell' Aurora, he applied his knowledge of Indian lore to notable poses, including *A Primitive Chant*, *Moqui Runner*, and *From Chaos Came Light*. His most successful work, *Sun Vow*, paired a male figure mentoring a young Sioux, who aims an arrow skyward as a coming-of-age ritual. The piece earned a silver medal at the 1900 Paris Salon and preceded a bronze pairing of a young Indian with Chief Multnomah in *The Coming of the White Man*, commissioned by the city of Portland, Oregon. After settling at College Point, Queens, New York, MacNeil pursued his art and entered more competitions, winning a first-place medal at the Pan-American Exposition in Buffalo in 1901 and a silver medal at the 1902 Exposition in Charleston, South Carolina. Success at sculpture exhibits at the 1904 Louisiana Purchase Exposition in St. Louis and the 1915 Panama Pacific Exposition in San Francisco established his fame. MacNeil ventured into life-size portraiture with a bronze likeness of President William McKinley for his memorial in Columbus, Ohio, and a bronze image of Ezra Cornell, founder of Cornell University. Additional portraits of explorer George Rogers Clark, Colonel David Humphrey, presidents George Washington and James Monroe, historian Francis Parkman, and colonial leader Roger Williams as well as military monuments contributed to the artist's growing canon of nationalistic subjects.

The submission of MacNeil's "Standing Liberty" to the U.S. Mint in 1916 added his name to the list of major American sculptors contributing to popular coinage. He based the icon on the likeness of Irene MacDowell, wife of his tennis partner, who sat for him over a period of ten days. Selected from some fifty candidates, the pose ennobled a U.S. quarter with a classic female figure bearing a round shield and olive branch. According to a U.S. Mint spokesman, the Standing Liberty coin "[typified] in a measure the awakening interest of the country to its own protection" (Van Ryzin 1995, p. 83). The reverse pictured a majestic eagle with upraised wings dominant.

Problems with the coin necessitated alterations, which incorporated MacNeil's input. Legend provides two views of the new design: that the public was outraged at the female figure's bare right breast and demanded modest covering and that the addition of chain mail to the torso reflected a militant mood in the country at the oubreak of World War I. Whatever the reason for the alteration, in August 1917, after a halt in production, the pose returned to production with dimpled chain mail cloaking the torso. The coin remained prominent in everyday commerce until the creation of the Washington quarter in 1932.

MacNeil garnered numerous prestigious commissions and awards, including an honor from the Architectural League of New York and a visiting professorship at the American Academy in Rome. He spent years in the classrooms of the national Academy of Design, Pratt Institute, and New York's Art Students League. In 1929, a film, *The Medal Maker*, featured his coin artistry along with that of James Earle Fraser and Adolph A. Weinman. MacNeil died on February 2, 1946. Treasured for enhancing America's image of its past, his canon of work contributed to American art, among other things, a Connecticut scenario of the pilgrims, a pony express rider, a pediment of the U.S. Supreme Court Building in Washington, D.C., a frieze for the Missouri State Capitol, a memorial to Jesuit pioneer Père Marquette, and a Civil War memorial to defenders of Fort Sumter, South Carolina.

See also **Peace dollar; Augustus Saint-Gaudens; U.S. coins.**

SOURCES: Johnson, Allen, ed. *Dictionary of American Biography*. New York: Charles Scribner's Sons, 1928. • Reed, Mort. *Cowles Complete Encyclopedia of U.S. Coins*. New York: Cowles Book Company, 1969. • Taxay, Don. *The U.S. Mint and Coinage*. New York: Arco Publishing, 1966. • "The U.S. Mint." http://www.usmint.gov. • Van Ryzin, Robert R. *Twisted Tails: Sifted Fact, Fantasy and Fiction from U.S. Coin History*. Iola, Wisc.: Krause Publications, 1995.

Mammon

A mythic figure of ill-gotten wealth, Mammon is a pervasive symbol of money in writing and speech. The icon often appears in cartoons alongside a chest of coins and plate or as a bloated, greedy human caricature grasping wads of cash or stuffing money into pockets. Taking the word from the Chaldean or Syriac language, the Greeks hellenized Mammon or Mamona into *mamonas*, an illusive figure in scripture and subsequent literature personifying the abstract term "greed" as well as the concrete image of coins, ore, and stored-up valuables.

In the New Testament, the word occurs in Matthew 6:24 and in Luke 16:9, 11, and 13, the parable of the unjust steward. The moral of Jesus's illustrative story comes down to a single warning, "No servant can serve two masters: for either he will hate the one, and love the other; or else he will hold to the one, and despise the other. Ye cannot serve God and mammon" (Luke 16:13). The intent of the injunction is to turn humans from materialism to spirituality. To the apostle Paul, Mammon was an idol, a goal that lured humankind from the love of God to the acquisition of treasure. As such, the figure represented a violation of the first of the Ten Commandments, which declares, "Thou shalt have no other gods before me" (Exodus 20:3).

During the era before Alexander III the Great, Arameans and Phoenicians dominated Mediterranean trade. In both their tongues, "mammon" meant "money" or "cash." In explaining their usage, St. Jerome, the father of the church and translator of the Vulgate bible into Latin around 400 A.D., declared that, in the Syriac language, "mammon" equated with personal enrichment. In the Jewish Talmud, a story about 300 poor Nazirites seeking purification corroborates Jerome's thinking. The Talmud account concludes with the reminder that "There are men whose *mammon* is dearer to them than their own body" (Hastings, 1951, VIII, p. 375).

In the Middle Ages, Mammon advanced from an abstract evil mentioned in the Roman poet Ovid's story of the Age of Gold in the *Metamorphoses* (8 A.D.) to the prince of the bottom nine orders of demons. Around 520 A.D., the Roman philosopher Boethius, author of *De Consolatione Philosophiae* (*On the Consolation of Philosophy*), pictured Mammon as a grubby miner, an image that Chaucer restated:

> But cursed was the tyme, I dar wel seye,
> That men first dide hir swety bysinesse,
> To grobbe up metal, lurkinge in derknesse
> [But cursed was the time, I dare well say,
> That men first did their sweaty business,
> To grub up metal, lurking in darkness]
> [Hughes 1957, p. 229].

In Christian terms, the chief fault that condemns Mammon to hell is his willingness to look down for tangible wealth rather than upward to God.

In the 12th century, Italian theologian Peter Lombard, a respected compiler of aphorisms, typified mammon in his text *Liber Sententiarum* (*Book of Mottoes*) (ca. 1155). Lombard turned Mammon into a demon prince of greed representing cupidity, worldliness, and wealth unjustly obtained. Later, the term gave difficulty to bible translator John Wyclif, whose 14th-century scripture chose "riches" as a synonym, implying absorption in money getting as opposed to preparation of the soul for the hereafter. English allegorist William Langland's *The Vision of William Concerning Piers the Plowman* (ca. 1395) transformed Mammon into a god of material wealth and possessions.

John Milton, the English epic poet who wrote *Paradise Lost* (1667), further clarified the concept of Mammon by turning him into a fallen angel, a devil of covetousness, "the least erected Spirit that fell from heaven," who leads the doomed in the pit of hell (*ibid.*, pp. 228–229). In Book I, lines 678–681, the poet pictures Mammon admiring the gold pavement of heaven as more precious than anything divine or sacred. A deluder of earthlings, Mammon teaches the unwary to mine earth for "treasures better hid" (*ibid.*, p. 229). Milton pictures the figure instructing his crew to hack a gaping wound in a hill and pluck out "ribs of gold" (*ibid.*).

In Book II, Mammon, who instigated the building of Pandemonium, further dooms himself by arguing that the demons should stay in their new underworld kingdom and exploit its gold rather than warble hymns or lift alleluias to God. He concludes, "How wearisome eternity so spent in worship paid to whom we hate" (*ibid.*, p. 238). He points to the soil and lures his company with reminders that beneath the surface gold and gems await. He tempts them away from warring against God with a question, "What can Heav'n show more?" (*ibid.*). They reward his twisted logic with applause.

***See also* paper money.**

SOURCES: Crystal, David, ed. *The Cambridge Biographical Dictionary*. Cambridge: University of Cambridge, 1996. • Hastings, James, ed. *Encyclopedia of Religion and Ethics*. New York: Charles Scribner's Sons, 1951. • Hughes, Merritt Y., ed. *John Milton: Complete Poems and Major Prose*. New York: Odyssey Press, 1957. • Lacroix, Paul. *Science and Literature in the Middle Ages*. New York: Frederick Ungar, 1964. • Mantinband, James H. *Dictionary of Latin Literature*. New York: Philosophical Library, 1956. • *New Catholic Encyclopedia*. San Francisco: Catholic University of America, 1967.

manilla

The anklet, bangle, or torque money of the West African equatorial coast, the *manilla* applied iron, brass, or copper to a common form of personal adornment that doubled as currency. From prehistoric times, natives of Zaire north to Senegal collected portable wealth in heavy anklets, bracelets, and collars that served as highly visible savings accounts rather than everyday shopping cash. The Ekonda poured melted metal into a clay or mud cast called a puddle mold to shape the item, then wrapped the cooling piece around the body for a perfect fit. The body-hugging bangles took their name from the Portuguese for "little hand."

The beginnings of metal trade goods date to the salvage of iron bolts, oarlocks, brads, and other metal bits from the wreckage of trading vessels. In the early 1500s, Bini trade with the Portuguese along the Guinea coast encouraged the fashioning of C-shaped bangle money as a convenient way of carrying, displaying, and securing heavy accumulations of metal. The exchange rate was simple: consumers could buy an ivory tusk for one *manilla* or a slave for eight to ten *manillas*. The newcomers also brought brass ingots for purchasing gold dust at Akan trading forts. Because the Akan had no use for the brass bars, they melted and recast them into more familiar objects.

After the first wave of Portuguese merchant vessels, Africans established trade with the Dutch, Scandinavians, French, and English. English traders began stocking *popo manillas*, a miniature version too small for wearing on the body. The bangles were designed especially for the African slave trade in Birmingham, England, where counterfeiters produced fake bronze collars. Significantly, the shape replicated the Roman slave torque, a circlet for the neck that symbolized ownership of the human wearer as well as the master's dominance. In the English market, a male enslaved in the 1400s and 1500s sold for two to ten *manillas*.

In Nigeria and Ghana, skilled artisans forged wide-spread arcs or horseshoes from thick bars of copper alloy. They decorated the arcs with metal coils, end knobs, or engraved patterns. The buyer assessed the worth of each piece according to its metal extrusions, metallic brilliance, or ringing sound. The wearing of a *manilla* produced an overt boast of wealth, especially when placed around the neck. To enhance social prestige, the owner of smaller circlets might have all of them melted down into one stunning torque. Metalsmiths in Benin often collected trade-quality *manillas* for melting down into artistic medallions or statuettes.

In 1942, Sir William Nevill M. Geary reported in *Nigeria under British Rule* (1927) that natives had an eye for counterfeit and underweight *manillas*. He remarked that the visitor saw no differences, but locals noticed at a glance. Geary commented on the circulation of types of *manillas*:

> The Antony *Manilla* is good in all interior markets; the *Congo Simgolo* or *bottle necked* is good only at Opungo market; the *Onadoo* is best for the Ibo country between Bony and New Calabar; the *Finniman Fawfinna* is passable in Juju Town and Qua market; but it is only half the worth of the *Antony*; and the *Cutta Antony* is valued by the people at Umballa [Einzig, 1966, p. 141].

Still flourishing among the Ibo and at Wukai, the *manilla* enjoyed a wide market resurgence shortly after World War II.

Trade with *manillas* ceased around 1948, when the Ibo of eastern Nigeria were still shaping copper into rings and arcs. When Biafra formed as a country in 1967, its treasury managed to issue aluminum coins and paper currency during a two-year struggle against Nigeria. One-pound notes carried the emblem of a palm tree with sunrise in the background. The three-pence coin showed the traditional *manilla* of slave times, an emblem heavy with historic significance.

SOURCES: Allen, Larry. *Encyclopedia of Money*. New York: Checkmark Books, 2001. • "The Artistry of African Currency." http://www.nmafa.si.edu/exhibits/site/manillas.htm. • Clain-Stefanelli, Elvira, and Vladimir Clain-Stefanelli. *The Beauty and Lore of Coins, Currency, and Medals*. Croton-on-Hudson, N.Y.: Riverwood Publishers, 1974. • Cribb, Joe. *Money*. Toronto: Stoddart, 1990. • Davidson, Basil. *African Kingdoms*. New York: Time, Inc., 1966. • Davies, Glyn. *A History of Money from Ancient Times to the Present Day*. Cardiff: University of Wales Press, 1994. • Einzig, Paul. *Primitive Money*. Oxford: Pergamon Press, 1966. • Opitz, Charles J. *Odd and Curious Money*. Ocala, Fla.: First Impressions, 1986. • Tibbles, Anthony. "TransAtlantic Slavery." *Antiques*, June 1999. • "Trading with Europeans." http://educate.si.edu/resources/lessons/siyc/currency/essay5.html.

March of Dimes

The U.S. dime carries the distinction of launching a populist drive against poliomyelitis. In January 1938, the National Foundation for Infantile Paralysis (NFIP), a forerunner to the March of Dimes, was the brain-child of President Franklin Delano Roosevelt, a victim of polio at age 39 while vacationing at his family's vacation home on Campobello Island, New Brunswick, Canada. To fight the disease, he had initiated the Warm Springs Foundation earlier in the 1930s.

Fund-raisers held "Birthday Balls" to honor Roosevelt's 52nd birthday in 1934, raising over one million dollars through the assistance of radio celebrities and movie stars like Eddie Cantor, who named the March of Dimes charity. The unusual phrase pictured round coins on a legless march against a paralytic disease. He suggested that people send coins directly to the White House, where the President maneuvered daily with the aid of a wheelchair and braces. The first research grant went to Yale University. In 1939, citizens of Coshocton, Ohio, opened the first local March of Dimes chapter.

Subsequent campaigns for the NFIP held from October through January amassed stacks of letters and some 2,680,000 dimes in the first year alone. From 1939 through 1942, planners buttonholed potential donors at home, in offices and taverns, at clubs and sports events, and in theaters and bowling alleys. Children held out collection canisters on the street and filled individual folders slotted to hold dimes. Honoring President Roosevelt was the Roosevelt Dime, designed by Dr. Selma H. Burke, the first black coiner of U.S. specie, which was introduced in 1946.

From 1949, the March of Dimes sponsored development of the Salk and Sabin vaccines as well as research into phenylketonuria or PKU, a disease of newborns that causes mental retardation. The health agency first selected Dr. Jonas Salk to lead research into infective viruses. Within four years, he had produced a workable vaccine from killed virus, which he tested on 1,830,000 school-age children. By 1962, Dr. Albert Sabin replaced the needle with an oral vaccine delivered in one pink drop on a sugar cube. By 1968, research into bone marrow transplants spent donors' coins on a medical breakthrough in treatment of numerous blood diseases.

Methods of canvassing altered. In 1950, parents in Phoenix, Arizona, launched the Mother's March on Polio, which targeted houses where supporters left their porchlights on. In 1958, the name of the parent agency changed to National Foundation — March of Dimes; in 1979, it altered again to March of Dimes Birth Defects Foundation, with headquarters in White Plains, New York. Within 20 years, the March of Dimes had raised $551.8 million and permeated the American mind with positive thoughts about donating dimes for a cure to the dread crippler. The image of a small, thin coin fighting paralysis helped citizens to envision themselves as champions of wellness, regardless of their income or ability to donate.

In 1984, gene study enhanced the role of

the March of Dimes in preventing inherited disease. Sponsored by the March of Dimes Birth Defects Foundation, genetic research linked abnormalities to cancer cycles in children, notably retinoblastoma, a deadly eye tumor. Another anomaly, Wilms's tumor of the kidney, seemed to predict the onset of liver cancer in later years. A reproduction of abnormal genes appeared to foster these two cancers. Examination of amniotic fluid from the placenta allowed physicians to warn pregnant mothers accurately in 90 percent of cases. Preventive measures included a diet rich in fiber and screening as early as the eighth week of gestation or in the 16th week by chorion villus biopsy performed with a syringe through the cervix. Another advance, surgery for a genetic cardiac disease called Marfan's syndrome, prevented the rupture of the aorta by bolstering it with dacron tubing.

As advancements in prevention and correction relieved more children of paralysis, the March of Dimes moved far beyond wheel chairs, iron lungs, and leg braces to combat preterm birth, low birth weight, birth defects, maternal alcohol and drug abuse, and infant mortality. Genetic diagnostics and technology also accounted for human reaction to chemicals. With gene splicing, doctors identified over 200 genetic abnormalities and alerted parents to such disorders as xeroderma pigmentosa or pockmarked skin. Cloning identified the gene responsible for X-linked adrenoleukodystrophy, the cause of paralysis and adrenal failure. Other direct treatment combatted Lesch-Nyhan syndrome, a form of mental retardation and physical handicap.

To the credit of donors, the March of Dimes supported outstanding Nobel laureate researchers:

year	*researcher*	*discovery*
1954	Dr. Linus Pauling	molecular structure newborn screening
1954	Dr. John F. Enders Dr. Thomas Weller Dr. Frederick Robbins	growth of polio virus in tissue culture
1962	Dr. James D. Watson	double helix structure of DNA.
1969	Dr. Max Delbruck	gene direction of normal development and mutations causing abnormal development
1976	Dr. D. Carleton Gajdusekun	conventional infectious agents in degenerative brain disorders
1985	Dr. Joseph L. Goldstein	cellular cause of familial hypercholesterolemia
1995	Dr. Edward B. Lewis Dr. Eric F. Wieschaus	master gene theory

The combined efforts of these discoveries rapidly reduced the chances of abnormality in human births.

In 2000, the 30th anniversary of the March of Dimes WalkAmerica campaign targeted infants and toddlers by collecting cash in 1,400 communities in the 50 states and Puerto Rico. The anniversary marked the charity's arrival at the one billion-dollar mark after three decades of canvassing for dimes. The money supported research into *in utero* fetal surgery, fetal ultrasound monitoring, development of vaccines, and intensive care nurseries for the 150,000 infants born each year with severe disabilities and diminished life spans. The March of Dimes staff distributed brochures warning women about the dangers of inadequate intake of folic acid, a cause of malformations of brain and spine.

Leading some of the 20,000 teams of canvassers were sports and film stars Kathy Ireland, Howie Mandel, Joe Namath, Jerry Rice, and Kathy Smith. On Mustela Baby Day on April 21, 2002, Mustela, a French pharmaceutical house producing hair- and skin-care products for children, joined the Wisconsin chapter of the March of Dimes to promote prenatal monitoring. The outreach urged mothers to donate duplicate shower gifts and nursery items to the March of Dimes for presentation to poor women. To assist the 500,000 expectant mothers who received in adequate care each year, the company sold specially marketed baby sets and donated a dollar from each to the March of Dimes.

See also **Dr. Selma Burke.**

SOURCES: Carey, Joseph. "New Insight into Genes: Now the Payoff." *U.S. News & World Report*, August 6, 1984, p. 57. • "Infant Well Being," *Soap & Cosmetics*, November 2001, p. 9–10. • "March of Dimes." http://www.modimes.org/. • "March of Dimes Holds WalkAmerica 30th Anniversary Continuing the Fight to Save Babies' Lives." *Fund Raising Management*, June 2000 , p. 30. • Olcott, William. "The Roots of Fund Raising." *Fund Raising Management*, April 1989, pp. 25–30. • Sheets, Tara E., ed. *Encyclopedia of Associations*. Farmington Hills, Mich.: Gale Group, 1999. • Smith, Jane S., and Paul Wagner. *A Paralyzing Fear: The Triumph over Polio in America*. New York: TV Books Inc., 1998.

mark

The long-lived *mark* appears to have originated in the Middle Ages from the Old Norse term "mork," a unit of value establishing the ratio of silver to gold. The term "mark" occurs in the Anglo-Dane peace treaties negotiated in the time of Alfred the Great with Guthrum (also Godrum, or Guthorm), who invaded England in A.D. 865. A medieval forerunner of the *Deutschemark*, the *Reilmark* or *Gewandmark* (cloth coin) of Norway and Germany pressed into service strips of cloth as currency. Created by Wilhelm I of Prussia in 1871, the true *mark*, worth 100 *pfennige*, was both unit of weight and of currency. It replaced the *ducat*, *gulden*, and *thaler* and ended a fragmented German system of seven currencies serving 30 independent states.

The *mark* characterized Germany's greatness until the end of World War I, when defeat reduced banknotes in worth. Banks responded to the devalued *mark* by producing higher denominations. From Cologne came a banknote worth 200 million *marks*, issued in 1923. Discouraged citizens turned the valueless bills into wallpaper and play money for their children. During these hard times, local governments printed notes and coined from iron small change like the *frankenthal*, a ten-*thaler* piece struck in 1918. Pride in the *Graf Zeppelin*, designed by Ferdinand Graf von Zeppelin in 1900, resulted in attractive designs for a *Reichsmark* minted in 1930. Opposite the German eagle were Art Deco views of the sleek airship superimposed over a globe.

After 1939, the *Reichkreditstrassen* (State Credit Treasury) printed notes with images of churches, the Brandenburg Gate, and other architectural landmarks as well as innocent white edelweiss, female images, and reproductions of artist Albrecht Dürer's *The Architect*. Validating these paper bills was the blind embossing or inkless seal of the Nazi war eagle bearing a wreath encircling a swastika, a geometric icon that dates far back into symbology. Until 1945, the treasury produced legal tender for local needs and those of German-occupied nations and territories.

At the fall of Hitler's reich in 1945, when a beaten nation was reduced to barter in cigarettes and lumps of coal, the *Deutschemark* replaced the Nazi *Reichsmark*. A disagreement arose among Britain, France, and the United States fearing to trust print plates to the Soviet Union, their wartime ally. Under the hush-hush name Operation Bird Dog, the dominant allied nations transferred responsibility for a new money system to England and set up a central bank, the *Bank of Deutscher Länder* (Bank of German States).

At the Konklave of 1948, founders of the new German currency convened at Haus Poser in Frankfurt, Germany. A consortium of eleven experts—financiers, economists, teachers—met with the U.S. Army occupation force to formulate a new monetary system. For a model, they chose the U.S. Federal Reserve. Dr. Gerhard Colm, the "Father of the German Currency Reform," worked out methods of lowering inflation and circumventing the black market that thrived from May 1945 after the German surrender ("Among" 2002, p. 8). His plan met with the approval of the Allied Control Council, comprised of representatives from France, Great Britain, the U.S., and the U.S.S.R. Edward Tenenbaum arranged printing of the German bills in the United States. Stymying the plan was the division of Germany, which required a separate currency for the eastern sector.

By June, citizens of West Germany made the trade of old *Reichsmarks* for new *Deutschemarks* on a one-to-one basis. The monetary unit of Bosnia-Hercegovina and Germany, the *Deutschemark* developed into a strong international currency. Simultaneously, Soviet financiers produced the *Deutschemark East*, which fell in value to half that of the *Reichsmark*. Abbreviated DM and divisible into 100 *pfennigs*, the *Deutschemark* eventually served both East and West Germany and the reunited nation, which reformed in 1990.

The re-engineering of Germany's money system was a study in cooperative effort. Almost immediately after the exchange of old money for new, hoarded commodities returned to markets as commerce produced signs of health. Issued and managed by the *Deutsche Bundesbank* in Frankfurt am Main, Germany's financial center, the *Deutschemark* circulated as one of the success stories of the 20th century until January 1, 2002, when it gave place to the euro. In 1990, a meeting of interested parties opened the Museum Währungsreform (Currency Reform Museum), which housed a tribute to the Haus Posen consortium and the post-war German *Deutschemark*, the *Reichsmark*, east *Deutschemark*, German currency union, and the euro.

See also **euro; Frederick the Great; *pfennig*; scrip; *thaler*; William the Conqueror; world money.**

SOURCES: Allen, Larry. *Encyclopedia of Money*. New York: Checkmark Books, 2001. • "Among Our Key People." *The Key Reporter*, Winter 2002, 8–9. • Berger, Stefan. "Historians and Nation-building in Germany after Reunification." *Past & Present*, August 1995. • Cribb, Joe. *Money*. Toronto: Stoddart, 1990. • Grumbacher, Armin. "The Early Years of a German Institution: The Kreditanstalt fur Wiederaufbau in the 1950s." *Business History*, October 1, 2001. • Sinclair, David. *The Pound*. London: Century Books, 2000.

markka

The national currency of Finland, the *markka*, introduced by Russia in 1859, replaced the Russian *ruble* and *kopek*, which had supplanted the Swedish crown in 1809, when the country passed to Russian rule. The *markka* coin was decimal-based on 100 *pennia*. In 1906, a historic example pictured the imperial eagle, official crest of Nicholas II, whose execution in 1918 ended the Romanov line. After his demise, the Finnish mint chose not to follow the example of Denmark, Faroe Islands, Greenland, Norway, Sweden, who chose the *krona*—plural, *krone*—which was divisible into 100 *öre*. Instead, the Finns replaced the Romanov blazon with an uncrowned double-headed eagle on the *markka*, an event that preceded increased trade and internal development.

Subsequent *markka* have displayed the innovative use of metals, as with the aluminum-bronze 10-*markka* piece coined in 1931 and, in 1973, a cupro-nickel *markka* struck with modern sword-wielding lion standing on a second sword, the emblem of Finland since its independence on December 6, 1917. In 1952, Finland became the first nation to circulate an Olympic commemorative coin, a *markka* piece struck in honor of the Helsinki games. In 1997, the Finnish treasury modernized currency and foiled counterfeiters by placing a hologram on its 20-*markka* note. On January 1, 2002, a sweeping change in Europe replaced twelve currencies, including the Finnish *markka*, made obsolete by the euro.

See also **euro; world currency.**

SOURCES: Cribb, Joe. *Money*. Toronto: Stoddart, 1990.• Cribb, Joe, Barrie Cook, and Ian Carradice. *The Coin Atlas*. London: Little, Brown and Co., 1999.• Duisenberg, Willem F. "European Central Bank." *Journal of the European Communities*, August 31, 2001.• "The Euro." http://www.euro.ecb.int.• "Euro: Printing of 13 Billion Euro Banknotes Gets Under Way." *Europe Information Service*, July 17, 1999. • Kunzig, Robert. "Euroland or Bust." *Discover*, October 1998.

maundy money

Maundy money derives from the Latin translation of Christ's crucifixion-eve commandment, or *mandatum*, to his disciples: "*Mandatum novum do vobis*" ("A new commandment I give you — that ye love one another) (John 13:34). The interpersonal responsibility resulted in a series of rituals based on voluntary servitude that included gifts of maundy money. Monarchs participating in Good Friday ceremonies that preceded Easter Sunday observed the Royal Maundy, which included self-abasement by washing the feet of the needy and distributing food, clothing, and cash.

Begun in the Mediterranean world in the fourth century among ordinary Christians, the maundy money tradition reached England by 600 and extended to royalty in the 1200s. The first recorded ceremony was conducted by King John Lackland in 1210 at Knaresborough, Yorkshire. According to period text, the ritual allowed for the "robing of garments of poor men, sewing of garments 2s 2d, for 13 girdles, 13 knives, 13 breeches for the same poor men; the king fed 1,000 poor men, paid £4 13s 9d for food, 9s 4d for fish" ("The Maundy Tradition").

The Royal Maundy became an annual custom with Edward I, a just and peaceloving king crowned in 1272 while he was fighting in the Eighth Crusade. The monetary gifts of specially minted silver pennies was a Tudor custom that originated with Henry IV of England, who gave silver pennies numbering the years of his age. During Henry VIII's debasement of coinage, the mint cheapened gifts by making them of base metal.

The maundy gifts altered further after the English Commonwealth. In 1662, Charles II gave out hammered coins valued at one, two, three, or four pennies. In 1670, the English treasury collected maundy money into dated sets of all four coins. Until the 1700s, recipients were all male. By the 1800s, a monarch's contact with the poor shrank to a ritual robing of the king or queen in linen robe and towel at Westminster Abbey for the symbolic bestowal of money to selected Londoners.

In 1932, for the first time since the 1600s, George V initiated the custom of presenting the coins personally into the hands of each recipient. After his son, Edward VIII, replaced him in 1936, he chose not to carry out the traditional Maundy service on the following April 9. He offered coins, food, and clothing to the needy, but did not distribute his own portrait coins. His negotiations with Thomas H. Paget and Percy Metcalfe of the London Tower Mint staff dragged on as the king quibbled over the appearance of his hairline beneath a crown. Vanity held up the molding of a final plaster cast until, on December 11, 1936, Edward abdicated in favor of his younger brother, George VI. The abdication rested on Edward's decision to defy royal custom and marry a divorced American, Wallis Warfield Simpson.

In the 21st century, Queen Elizabeth II, daughter of George VI, continued the Royal Maundy by bestowing on a number of elderly Christian pensioners of modest means, male and female, leather string bags of maundy coins equal in number to her own age. She began the custom after her coronation in 1953 at age 27 by offering 27 men and 27 women 27 pennies each. The coins, prepared for the ceremony by the Secretary of the Royal Almonry, displayed the royal portrait that Mary Gillick completed at the time of the queen's coronation.

The queen made the presentation at a different cathedral each year in the presence of representatives of local church denominations, children and men of Her Majesty's Chapel Royal, and 22 Yeomen of the Guard carrying the alms dishes stored with the crown jewels in the Tower of London. The entourage had as its special guests the dean, provost, and senior staff of the cathedral. Each person received ordinary coins in a red purse and silver maundy coins in a white purse totaling the queen's age in years. In 2000, coins totaling five pounds commemorated the centenary year of Queen Elizabeth the Queen Mother; the remaining 50 pence celebrated public libraries.

SOURCES: "The British Royal Mint." http://www.royalmint.com. • "Maundy Money." *Royal Report*, May 2000. • "Maundy Money for Pensioners." *Coventry Evening Telegraph*, April 13, 2001. • "The Maundy Tradition." http://www.royalinsight.gov.uk/200004/focus/index.html. • Reinfeld, Fred.

Treasury of the World's Coins. New York: Sterling Publishing, 1953. • Schwarz, Ted. *Coins as Living History*. New York: Arco Publishing, 1976.

McCulloch, Hugh

A manager of U.S. currency during and after the Civil War, Hugh McCulloch battled the issue of greenbacks and established the forerunner of the current national banking system. The son of a shipwright and importer from the West Indies, he was born in Kennebunk, Maine, on December 7, 1808. He studied at Bowdoin College and completed law training in Boston. After conducting private law practice in Fort Wayne, Indiana, he shifted into banking in 1835 as head teller and supervisor of the local branch of the state bank and, in 1863, was elected bank president of the parent institution in Indianapolis. During his on-the-job training in finance, he co-leased the Wabash-Erie Canal in Ohio, a major Midwestern shipper and transporter.

After lobbying in Washington, D.C., for the independence of state banks, McCulloch won the confidence of Salmon P. Chase, Secretary of the Treasury, and became the nation's first currency supervisor. At first, according to historian Henry Adams in *The Education of Henry Adams* (1907), McCulloch seemed out of place with his caution, selflessness, and lack of party loyalty or drive for power. Won over to the federal banking system, he began enticing state banks to seek federal charters. In 1865, President Abraham Lincoln, only weeks before his assassination, named McCulloch as the nation's 27th Secretary of the Treasury to replace Chase, who resigned to head the Supreme Court. On July 5, 1865, McCulloch began the suppression of rampant counterfeiting and inaugurated the U.S. Secret Service by swearing in its first chief, William P. Wood.

In the monetary chaos following the end of the Civil War, McCulloch distributed greenbacks as temporary currency. Without backing in gold and silver, the paper money helped to control inflation and curtail gold speculation. McCulloch urged Congress to return to the gold standard and managed to retire over 30 percent of the greenbacks before leaving office to return to banking for Jay Cooke, McCulloch, & Company in London. At age 67, McCulloch accepted a brief reappointment from President Chester A. Arthur as Secretary of the Treasury. After a brief stint as president of the International Chemical Company in New York, he retired to an estate in Maryland to compile his memoirs, *Men and Measures of Half a Century* (1888). He died in 1895.

See also **greenbacks; U.S. Secret Service.**

SOURCES: Adams, Henry. *The Education of Henry Adams*. Boston: Houghton-Mifflin, 1961. • Allen, Larry. *Encyclopedia of Money*. New York: Checkmark Books, 2001. • "The Bureau of Engraving and Printing." http://www.bep.treas.gov/. • *Encyclopedia of World Biography*. Detroit: Gale Group, 1998. • Johnson, Allen, ed. *Dictionary of American Biography*. New York: Charles Scribner's Sons, 1928. • Taxay, Don. *The U.S. Mint and Coinage*. New York: Arco Publishing, 1966. • "United States Secret Service." http://www.treas.gov/usss. • Weida, Lorraine. "The Bankers Magazine Bankers Hall of Fame." *Bankers Magazine*, September-October 1982, pp. 58–67.

medieval coins

After the fall of the Roman Empire, medieval coins mirrored the beauty of Alexandrian Greek coins as well as the rise of Catholicism through deities, saints, and holy objects. Among the outstanding Christian pieces were the *obols* of William of Petersheim, struck in 1310 featuring a cross and the words "*Signum Crucis*" ("Sign of the Cross"). To adorn the era's specie, die-makers punched in the shape of annulets, crescents, dots, periods, and wedges. Some of the most appealing results were the Lombard *tremiss* picturing a winged saint and a coin icon of the Virgin Mary produced at Trier, a mint established by the Romans.

Because of the religious significance of motifs, bearers revered them, wore them as amulets, applied them over aching bodies as curatives, and carried them into battle to ward off harm. The first mention of coppers used as devotional medals occurs in the biography of

St. Geneviève, the fifth-century patron warrior saint and savior of Paris, who received from St. Germain a coin that he found on the ground. Because the piece bore the sign of the cross, she wore it constantly as a holy medallion.

At Rome, barbaric invaders with no artistic background thoughtlessly mimicked the portrait coinage of the emperors. At Ravenna, Italy, after 489 A.D., Theoderic, the first true Germanic king, paid his standing armies in Ostrogothic coins picturing him balancing a globe on his hand. Athalaric, the boy-king of the Ostrogoths who co-ruled with his mother Amalasuntha, produced imitations of gold coins after A.D. 526. Theodebert I of Rheims, a just Merovingian king, outraged the historian Procopius of Caesarea, author of the eight-volume *De Bellis* (*On the Wars*) (A.D. 552), by placing himself on the Roman *solidus* after the fashion of Justinian I and adding the legend "*Victor*." A century and a half later, Perctarit, the Lombard monarch, began to create his own style, picturing a standing likeness of himself with robe and scepter. In Iberia, Leovigild, the Visigoth king enthroned in 568 A.D., produced stylized self-portraits on the gold *tremiss*.

In A.D. 526, Athalaric, the boy-king of the Ostrogoths who co-ruled with his mother Amalasuntha, produced a poor imitation of Greek portrait coins. (Guy Clark, Ancient Coins and Antiquities, Norfolk, Virginia)

Other artistic traditions flourished as moneyers broke ties with Roman coinage. To the north, Baltic Slavs issued money strips of *platni* (linen), forerunner of the verb *platiti* (pay). Another version, Swedish and Icelandic *wadmal* (wool cloth), flourished in the 1300s in place of metal coins. In Gaul, Charlemagne issued coins with his highly stylized Latin monogram "*Carolus*" within a scalloped border. To the south, Gunderic and his brother Gaiseric, Vandal kings who overran Carthage, pictured noble horses on their bronze coinage, a vigorous motif also preferred by the Franks. In Bohemia, Odalricus, who came to the throne in 1012, issued *deniers* and *dinars* in heavily stylized design featuring broad-stroke portraiture and his name taking up a quarter of the face.

In the 1100s, burgeoning Italian cities began designing their own self-promoting coinage. The silver pieces of Bologna, Lucca, Genoa, Pavia, and Milan tended to reflect piety by complementing the title of the Holy Roman Emperor with a cross.

- Bologna lauded its university, founded in 1158, with the pro-education mottoes "*Bononia* docet" ("Bologne teaches") and "*Mater studiorum*" ("mother of studies").
- Genoa maintained the architectural sketch of the city gate and the name of Conrad III, who sanctioned the Genoese mint.
- The Luccan design featured St. Veronica, the legendary contemporary of Christ who assisted him in lifting the cross and received his image on her veil.
- Mantua elevated a pivotal figure, the Roman poet Virgil, Augustus's epicist and author of the *Aeneid* (ca. 30 B.C.), whom medieval prelates esteemed as an enlightened pagan.
- In 1202, Doge Enrico Dandolo of Venice struck the *grossus Venetianus*, a popular medium-sized silver piece called the *matapan*, which influenced design and coin size in the Balkans and Byzantium. He ennobled himself by picturing his likeness receiving the banner of St. Mark opposite Christ enthroned in glory.
- Neapolitan mintmasters of Charles II d'Anjou introduced the *gigliato*, a medium-sized silver piece, in 1304. Later in the 14th century, the *gigliato* became a popular coin minted by the Knights Hospitallers at Malta to display the Maltese Cross.

In a period marked by religious fervor, the connection between saints and their patron cities produced instant recognition of the origins of certain coins on whose faces the images of saints appeared. Following are some of the saints who adorned medieval coins and their patron cities:

saint	*city or region*
Geminiano	Modena
George	Britannia
Mark	Venice
Peter	Rome
Petronio	Bologna
Ursus	Solothun
Volto	Lucca
Wenceslas	Bohemia

As modernity crept into medieval coinage, the faces of saints gave way to the images of allegorical figures, notably Ireland's Hibernia, the *Semeuse* ("sower") of France, and Britannia, female emblem of England.

The refinement of coinage rapidly moved European mintmasters from the heavier pieces issued by the Roman Empire to a new look and lighter feel. As the right to coin money slipped away from monarchs to churchmen and nobles during the Merovingian era, competition for artists put diemakers and engravers at a premium. Working for personal enrichment, they strayed from dynastic loyalty to work for the highest bidder at commercial centers, tax offices, abbeys, and courthouses. A total of 2,000 coin crafters of Frankish kings found work at 900 mints, which shifted from gold to silver coinage after the rich silver strike at Melle, Poitou, in the fifth century A.D.

To the east at a mint at Kurzuwan, a trade center of the Khwarezm Empire in northern Afghanistan, Genghis Khan employed private coiners to strike a bronze *jital*, a piece unknown to numismatists until discoverers unearthed a trove of 800 coins in the area in 1992. The siege piece fell short of the beauty and stylistic grace of European coins, but made up in audacity what it lacked in esthetics. Inscribed in Arabic with his title, *al-Malik*, the *jital* noted his valor in personally leading a Mongol invasion force into northern Afghanistan in 1221 to avenge the murder of a merchant train traveling under his protection. He left no one alive in the area. His bloody campaigns solidified the world's most expansive empire, reaching from the Baltic east to China and south to the Persian Gulf.

The coins of crusaders captured the spirit of the era. To support military efforts, minting of *deniers* and *obols* began at Antioch, Edessa, Jerusalem, and Tripoli. From the latter in the late 1200s came silver groats marked by ornate crosses in a roseate frame. Some of the grandest mintage of the era came from private operations under the command of the Order of St. John of Rhodes, a medical corps comprised of combat nurses who doubled as warriors known as the Knights Hospitallers. They instituted a *denier de Sainte Hèlene* ("St. Helena's coin") extolling Helena, mother of Constantine I the Great and discoverer of the true cross and founder of churches on the sites of Christ's Nativity and Ascension. The pious made wax casts of the coin on Good Friday. Pilgrims locating coins of the same mintage bore them home, revered them as amulets, and enshrined them in churches at Rome, Oviedo, Catalonia, Paris, and Vincennes, where they proclaimed them true relics of the crucifixion.

By 1413, the Knights Hospitallers had replaced the revered St. Helena coin with a Rhodian piece minted in the 300s B.C., which they proclaimed was one of Judas's thirty pieces of silver. Wax impressions of the amulet piece supposedly had the power to revive failing health, ease the labor of parturient women, and guard sailors from peril at sea. After the knights moved the coin to Malta in 1530, it continued to bless and assure the well-being of the devout.

Crusaders produced *bezants* (or *besants*) inscribed at first in Arabic calligraphy, then with Christian phrases written in Arabic and surrounding the crusader's cross. Pictorial coins focused on Christ's tomb, David's tower, and the Temple at Jerusalem. During the Seventh Crusade, which began in 1248, the saintly Louis IX introduced a new coin, the *gros tournois*, worth 12 *deniers*. It bore an ornate cross and "*Ludovicus Rex*" ("King Louis") on front with a circlet of *fleurs-de-lis* on the back. A pious legend read "*Benedictus Sit Nomen*

Domini Dei Jesus Christi" ("Blessed be the name of the Lord Jesus Christ").

In Europe, Frankish and Germanic designers pictured architectural landmarks, notably, the churches of Cologne and Münster. After his crowning in 1215, Frederick I, the Holy Roman Emperor, decked with classic detailing a popular gold coin he called the *augustalis,* which carried his portrait in the style of Rome's emperors and the legend "*Caesar Augustus Imperator Romanorum*" ("Augustus Caesar, Commander in Chief of the Romans"). Accommodating more ornate scenarios were the wide uniface bracteate and *Dunnpfennige* (thin pennies) of the era that displayed the surface design in reverse on the back incuse style. A practical German coin designed in the mid-thirteenth century, the *Kreuzer* was a silver fourpence that suited an economy needing more than the common penny. Minted in the silver-rich Tyrol with Christian icons, the coin took its name from the *Kreuz* (cross) depicted on it.

After 1285, Philip IV the Handsome (also Philippe le Bel, Philip the Fair, Philip I of Navarre), the French crusader king, caught the spirit of the Sixth Crusade, from which his mother, Isabella of Aragon, never returned. He designed the *masse d'or* ("gold mace"), a straightforward, yet attractive coin named for the ceremonial club that the king holds in his portrait. Ringing the reverse is the feudal era inscription "*XPC Vincit XPC Regnat XPC Imperat*" (Christ Conquers, Christ Rules, Christ Reigns), a stirring motto that remained in use until the French Revolution. Common to the era was the abbreviation of "Christ" with the Greek monogram "*XPC.*"

To the south, Philip of Taranto, despot of Epirus, revived the moribund Greek coinage after his accession in 1294. At new mints he founded on the northwestern coast of Greece and Albania, the westernmost reaches of the Byzantine Empire, he improved production methods. A neat, attractive silver *denier* designed in crusader style pictured the Christian cross opposite a stylized castle, an architectural symbol of the ongoing security needs of lands of the eastern Mediterranean under Arab menace.

By the 1300s and 1400s, some of the world's most elegant coins emerged from medieval mints. Among the innovative additions to French moneys were the French *agnel d'or* ("gold lamb"), *ange d'or* ("gold angel"), *chaise d'or* ("gold throne"), *mouton d'or* (gold sheep"), and *pavillon d'or* ("gold canopy"). Connected with the lives of familiar figures of the era were the leopard coin of Edward the Black Prince, hero at Poitiers, and the *franc d'or à cheval* ("equestrian franc"), part of the ransom money of the ill-fated John II the Good (Jean le Bon de Valois). A separate class of religious coins, the French ecclesiastical *méreaux* ("earned tokens") or *jetons de présence* ("tokens of admission"), appeared in the 1400s and 1500s as rewards for the pious entitling them to special favors.

On the cusp of the Renaissance, one notable coiner, Jacques Coeur, a social climber and former worker at the Royal Mint at Bourges, accompanied Charles VII of France and his dignitaries on a triumphal chariot procession through Rouen on November 10, 1449. Celebrating the ouster of the English from Normandy, Coeur, treasurer of the king's household, enriched himself as mintmaster, alchemist, arms dealer to Muslims in the Levant, and investor in French mines and merchant ships sailing from Turkey to the North Sea.

History records in verse the rise of the ambitious merchant and money man, an icon of the rising middle class: "Jacques Coeur indeed was there, the man of pounds and pence,/Who had, with heartfelt care, showed utter diligence" (Severy 1977, p. 299). Coeur was arrested and tried in 1452 for debasing coins, forgery, and poisoning the king's mistress, Agnes Sorel. The court fined him 400,000 crowns and exiled him. He spent the last 18 years of his life as a grandee on the island of Cyprus.

See also **Alexius I Comnenus; amulet coins; Anglo-Saxon coins; *bezant*; blood money; bracteates; Byzantine coins; Celtic Coins; coinage; coin clipping and shaving; *denier*; ducat; Edward the Confessor; St. Eligius; franc; fur money; groat; *gros*; *gros***

***tournois*; *gulden*; hallmark; Islamic money; John the Good; Knights Hospitallers; Knights Templar; maundy money; Offa; Papal coins; penny; *pfennig*; Philip IV of France; Roman coins — Empire; Spanish coins; *thaler*; touch coins; trial by the pyx.**

SOURCES: Allen, Larry. *Encyclopedia of Money*. New York: Checkmark Books, 2001. • Clain-Stefanelli, Elvira, and Vladimir Clain-Stefanelli. *The Beauty and Lore of Coins, Currency, and Medals*. Croton-on-Hudson, N.Y.: Riverwood Publishers, 1974. • Cribb, Joe. *Money*. Toronto: Stoddart, 1990. • Davies, Glyn. *A History of Money from Ancient Times to the Present Day*. Cardiff: University of Wales Press, 1994. • Grierson, Philip. *Numismatics*. London: Oxford University Press, 1975. • Hastings, James, ed. *Encyclopedia of Religion and Ethics*. New York: Charles Scribner's Sons, 1951. • Pollak, Henry. *Coinage & Conflict*. Clifton, N.J.: Coin & Currency Institute, 2001. • Severy, Merle, ed. *The Middle Ages*. Washington, D.C.: National Geographic Society, 1977. • Snodgrass, Mary Ellen. *Who's Who in the Middle Ages*. Jefferson, N.C.: McFarland, 2001.

Mercury dime

A model of balanced views, the two sides of the Mercury dime, engraved by German immigrant Adolph Alexander Weinman, came into circulation in 1916 and remained a standard for three decades. It offers the yin and yang of government. The uplifting vision of the winged figure on the front celebrates the liberties promised by the Bill of Rights, particularly free thought. The opposite side, which pictures the Roman fasces tied with a classic fillet, symbolizes absolute power. Combined on a shiny disc, the coin demonstrates a neo-classic beauty and economy of figure.

Popular from its inception, the thin silver coin surged to greater importance during the Great Depression as an artistic representation of American principles available in a small denomination for everyday use. The coin passed through new mintings in 1931 and 1932. After the bombing of Pearl Harbor, the U.S. Mint struck large quantities of the total 2.7 billion Mercury dimes — 250 million coins from 1941 to 1943 and in 1945, as the war came to a close. In 1944 alone, the mint generated 33,333,000 of the coins.

***See also* Augustus Saint-Gaudens; U.S. coins; Adolph A. Weinman.**

SOURCES: "Adolph Weinman." http://www.kargesfineart.com/links2/Adolph-Weinman.htm. • *Almanac of Famous People*. 6th ed. Farmington Hills, Mich.: Gale Group, 1998. • Gohmann, Stephan F. "The End of Liberty." *The Freeman*, November 1999. • "Looking at Art: Arts Community Reflects on Significant 20th Century Artists." *Baton Rouge Advocate*, January 9, 2000. • Marotta, Michael E. "The Mercury Dime." *The Shinplaster*, March 1994. • Olert, Chris. "Buried Treasure Faceless Statue Gets a Name and a Rich History." *Fort Worth Star-Telegram*, April 5, 1998. • Reiter, Ed. "The Silver Bullion." *New York Times*, December 14, 1986, p. H43. • Silver, Constance S., et al. "U.S. Custom House, New York City: Overview of Analyses and Interpretation of Altered Architectural Finishes." *Journal of the American Institute of Conservation*, Vol. 32, No. 2, 141–152. • Soderberg, Susan C. "Maryland's Civil War Monuments." *The Historian*, Spring 1996. • Starita, Angela. "On the Map: From the Ruins, a Granite Couple Will Stand Over Newark." *New York Times*, December 24, 2000. • "Visual Thinking: Sketchbooks from the Archives of American Art." http://artarchives.si.edu/exhibits/sketchbk/weinman.htm. • Vitello, Barbara. "Undiscovered Gems: The Epitome of Modernism." *Daily Herald*, April 23, 1999.

mint mark

As a control of corrupt moneys, mints began marking issue with mint marks, official stamps in abbreviated form during the first years of the Roman Empire. Some examples of European markings became almost as famous as the coiners themselves, for example, the B and anchor or flower of Nicholas Briot, designer under Charles I of England of the crown and half-crown, and the bold EB set in an oval of American colonial assayer and metalsmith Ephraim Brasher, designer for George Washington. The Roman emperor Diocletian, who reformed coinage in 284 A.D., replaced inefficient and unreliable operations of the Senate and provinces with fifteen imperial mints. Each identified legal tender with a stamp of origin:

mint mark	*significance*
A or Alpha	*prima officina* [first workshop]
B or Beta	*secunda officina* [second workshop]
C or Gamma	*tertia officina* [third workshop]
L or LN	Londinium
M	the goddess Moneta
P	*pecunia* [money]
R	Roma
SM	*sacra Moneta*, the emblem of imperial moneys

A combination such as PR for "*Prima Roma*" translated as "the first workshop at Rome."

With this codification, the imperial treasurer could monitor sources of underweight or clipped coinage and punish those responsible for criminal mishandling of the emperor's coinage. The team of coin casters, trimmers, and hammerers usually applied the mark on the back side at the exergue or bottom of the coin and topped it with a line to set it apart from the artistic motif. Variant placements included strikings made within the design and, less frequently, on the obverse or front surface.

At New World mints, markings determined which of the Spanish operations had produced copper, silver, or gold coins. The listings paralleled the simplicity of the system used in Rome:

mint mark	*significance*
C	Cartagena, Colombia
G	Guatemala
L	Lima, Peru
M	Mexico City
NR	Bogotá, Colombia
P	Potosí, Bolivia
S	Santiago, Brazil

Contributing to the identification of Spanish specie were unique cross styles, for example, the Jerusalem cross on coins from Bogotá, Cartagena, and Mexico City and the unadorned cross used in Lima and Potosí.

The stamping of mint marks in U.S. coinage aided staff in quality control. The list covers eight locations:

mint mark	*city*	*dates*
C	Charlotte, North Carolina	1838–1861
CC	Carson City, Nevada	1870–1893
D	Dahlonega, Georgia	1838–1861
D	Denver, Colorado	1906–present
O	New Orleans, Louisiana	1838–1861, 1879–1909
P	Philadelphia, Pennsylania	1793–present
S	San Francisco, California	1854–1955, 1968–present
W	West Point, New York	1976–present

The D, which went out of use in 1861 when the Dahlonega operation closed, passed to Denver in 1906 for a second period of use.

An unusual version was the A-over-W of coiner Adolph A. Weinman, which produced numerous misreadings of the emblem as "Woodrow Wilson" and the rumored "watchful waiting" in the months preceding World War I. During coin shortages in the early 1960s, mint officials presumed that unusual mint marks caused collectors to amass pieces that might one day be valuable. After removing all mint marks in 1965, the U.S. Mint received such a deluge of complaints that the mintmaster rescinded the order in 1968.

See also **assay mark; cobs; coinage; feather money; hallmark; John Hull; Japanese money; George T. Morgan; Offa of Mercia; Thomas Simon; Spanish coins; Johann Sigismund Tanner; *thaler*; Tregwynt hoard; U.S. coins; U.S. Mint; Adolph A. Weinman; *Whydah*.**

SOURCES: Clain-Stefanelli, Elvira, and Vladimir Clain-Stefanelli. *The Beauty and Lore of Coins, Currency, and Medals*. Croton-on-Hudson, N.Y.: Riverwood Publishers, 1974. • Sandz, Victoria. *Encyclopedia of Western Atlantic Shipwrecks and Sunken Treasure*. Jefferson, N.C.: McFarland, 2001. • Spadone, Frank G. *Major Variety and Oddity Guide of United States Coins*. Wisconsin: Krause Publications, 1967. • Van Ryzin, Robert R. *Twisted Tails: Sifted Fact, Fantasy and Fiction from U.S. Coin History*. Iola, Wisc.: Krause Publications, 1995.

Molo, Gaspare

Engraver and goldsmith Gaspare Molo (or Gasparo Moli), designer of coins for Pope Urban VIII, enlarged papal dignity and majesty with dignified *scudi* bearing the papal silhouette. A native of Como or Lugano, Molo, called the "Lombard Cellini," gained a reputation for precision medals. He flourished in the early 1600s at Milan, Mantua, and Florence, where he was *maestro delle stampe della monete* ("master of the coin stamp").

After incising wedding medals for Duke Cosimo II, Molo began designing *thalers* and badges for Italian nobility before becoming the die-cutter for the *Zecca* (papal mint) in 1623. Urban VIII kept him busy creating self-ennobling pieces. The job extended through the terms of two successors, Innocent X and Alexander VII. Molo appears to have trained a namesake, either a son or nephew, who extended Molo's standards of bas-relief. Also succeeding the original Molo was one of his pupils, Hamerani, the first of a dynasty of coin engravers.

See also **papal coins.**

SOURCES: Allen, Larry. *Encyclopedia of Money.* New York: Checkmark Books, 2001. • Clain-Stefanelli, Elvira. "Donors and Donations: The Smithsonian's National Numismatic Collection." *Perspectives in Numismatics*, 1986. • *New Catholic Encyclopedia.* San Francisco: Catholic University of America, 1967.

Moneta

Moneta, the remembrancer or adviser, bore a title accorded to the Roman goddess Juno, queen of the gods. The surname characterizes her as the Roman deity of warning, the ever-observant guardian spirit celebrated each June 1 and October 10. She became the Roman watch god and counselor in early history after her voice issued from her temple following an earthquake. After demanding the slaughter of a pregnant sow, she became Rome's fiscal adviser; her temple served as a treasury. As described by the historian Livy, the original mint of the Roman Senate, managed by *tresviri monetales* ("three moneymasters"), stood next door to the *Arx* ("citadel") atop the Capitoline Hill. It was the trio's job to head the *aerarium Saturni* ("state treasury"), comprised of *tributa* ("taxes") from outlying tribes, internal taxes, and other forms of toll, harbor duty, and regulatory fees.

According to Cicero's *On Divination* (ca. 45 B.C.), Moneta earned the gratitude of Republican Rome in 390 B.C., when the sacred geese at the *Arx* cackled and alerted the hero Manlius and his guards to lurking invaders. When Pyrrhus menaced the city during a time when the treasury ran low, the goddess promised that the people would remain solvent if they waged war ethically. When Roman defenders defeated Pyrrhus in 275 B.C., the treasury began minting coins under Moneta's patronage. The citizenry raised a shrine to the goddess, whose name, which derives from *monere* ("to remind") became the root for "money" and "mint." In 269 B.C., Roman coiners propitiated Juno Moneta with her likeness on the first *denarius*. Four years later, Roman officials erected a mint on the temple grounds, the location of the current church of Santa Maria in Aracoeli and the Capitoline Museum.

See also **mint mark.**

SOURCES: Allen, Larry. *Encyclopedia of Money.* New York: Checkmark Books, 2001. • Bell, Robert E. *Women of Classical Mythology: A Biographical Dictionary.* Santa Barbara, Calif.: ABC-Clio, 1991. • Bunson, Matthew. *A Dictionary of the Roman Empire.* New York: Oxford University Press, 1991. • Davies, Glyn. *A History of Money from Ancient Times to the Present Day.* Cardiff: University of Wales Press, 1994. • *Dictionary of Roman Religion.* New York: Facts on File, Inc., 1996. • *Encyclopedia of the Roman Empire.* New York: Facts on File, Inc., 1994. • Hammond, N. G. L., and H. H. Scullard, eds. *The Oxford Classical Dictionary.* Oxford: Clarendon Press, 1992. • Howatson, M. C., ed. *The Oxford Companion to Classical Literature.* Oxford: Oxford University Press, 1991. • Reinfeld, Fred. *Treasury of the World's Coins.* New York: Sterling Publishing, 1953. • Warmington, E. H. *Remains of Old Latin: Volume IV, Archaic Inscriptions.* Cambridge, Mass.: Harvard University Press, 1967.

money laundering

The passing of illicit funds through legitimate businesses and banks enables criminals to turn cash into investments, lines of credit, and foreign bank deposits. The method is three-stage: place the cash in a cash-rich business, conceal or disguise it under complex layers of transactions such as stock or electronic transfer to bank accounts out of the country, and turn the cash into other assets, such as jewelry or antiques, to make it appear legitimate. One purpose of clandestine money operations is to hide cash or assets from the state to prevent confiscation or taxation or to avoid thievery by despots or criminal regimes, such as the Nazis in the late 1930s, who helped themselves to the assets accrued by Jews and other "non-desirables." Methods of hiding wealth include parallel bank accounts, operation of legitimate businesses with the proceeds of crime, and conversion of hot cash into diamonds and gold specie for hoarding.

The crime of money laundering began with the emergence of trade and banking, when entrepreneurs and criminals sought to hide the source, ownership, and full amount of their money. Around 2000 B.C., crafty Chinese merchants concealed their profits from monarchs to prevent seizure. The best way to hide the cash was to invest it in commerce in distant provinces or offshore. Similar assimilations of money outside the city of Rome occurred after the emperor Diocletian issued an edict of A.D. 301 raising taxes to all but the senatorial class. Various bogus bookkeeping, hiding of assets, and tax evasion schemes helped the middle-income Roman citizen avoid poll and property taxes by reducing the stated amount of taxable holdings. For this reason, the clever property owner during the Roman Empire tended to cultivate land and plantations in the provinces.

The term "money laundering" has its roots in the crime-ridden United States during the 1920s, when gangsters and the Mafia cycled huge profits from prostitution, drugs, liquor, numbers running, and gambling through legitimate transactions, such as laundries, florists, and other neighborhood cash-based businesses. Against detection by the federal government's "Untouchables," headed by Eliot Ness, cautious Mafia chiefs cloaked their operations behind Mafia-run banks and accounting firms, corrupt lawyers and judges, and other forms of bribery of government officials. Rather than prove a connection to crime, in June 1931, a federal court convicted Al Capone, a noted Chicago crime kingpin, on tax evasion. His accountant, Meyer Lansky, avoided the same fate by shuttling criminal proceeds to Swiss bank accounts, which he accessed through loans.

In the 20th century, money laundering became a global phenomenon, particularly among smugglers, arms dealers, terrorists, extortionists, scam artists, black marketeers, bootleggers, drug cartels, and white-collar criminals. A Mexican operation headed by Emilio Quintero Payán and his brother, Juan José Quintero Payán, enabled their nephew, drug lord Rafael Cáro Quintero, to legitimize $33 million. Working from a ranch near Guadalajara, the coterie distributed cocaine and marijuana and cycled cash receipts through banks in California, the Cayman Islands, New York, and Texas. A Houston federal court indicted the brothers, who eluded capture and continued their operation.

From 1979 to 1987, Mafia-owned cheese distributors, bakeries, restaurants, and pizza parlors on the Atlantic seaboard and Midwest recycled $60 million in dirty money, the proceeds of the sale of cocaine and heroin. Heading the illegal operation were Gaetano Badalamenti, a Cosa Nostran, and Salvatore Catalano of the Bonanno family. One of the most protracted U.S. federal court cases, the trial of 38 organized crime members opened in Manhattan in October 1985 and lasted until March 2, 1987. A sordid affair marked by jury tampering and the murder of Carmine Galante, head of the Bonanno clan, the legal action netted 17 convictions and $2.5 million in fines. Badalamenti and Catalano each received 45-year sentences. The outcome, which resulted in 100 additional convictions, split a Sicilian alliance dating back centuries.

In the 1990s, money laundering was rampant in the drug-dealing underworld in El Salvador, casinos of the French Riviera, and throughout the Caribbean. Prince Rainier of

Monaco heard hints of money laundering at the Monte Carlo casino. He launched an internal audit to determine if organized crime had acquired large quantities of chips for cash as a means of recycling dirty money. The scheme required individuals to spend the cash on chips, play some of the tokens, then redeem the rest in the form of a check. Jean Pastorelli, the state finance councillor, determined that the rumors were untrue. The charge returned in 1998, when Monaco was the chosen money laundering area for Latin American drug runners and the Russian mafia. A similar situation arose at St. Lucia in March 1993. Officials ousted criminal elements and frauds, tightened security against offshore money recycling, and upped fines and prison sentences. On St. Kitts and Nevis, island authorities instituted a system of property forfeiture for those found guilty of money laundering.

See also **Roman coins — Empire; U.S. Secret Service.**

SOURCES: Bartlett, Sarah, et. al. "Money Laundering; Who's Involved, How It Works, and Where It's Spreading." *Business Week*, March 18, 1985, pp. 74–80. • Bunson, Matthew. *A Dictionary of the Roman Empire*. New York: Oxford University Press, 1991. • Burke, Daniel. "Questions behind Locked Doors." *Maclean's*, February 11, 1985, p. 12. • Nash, Jay Robert. *Encyclopedia of World Crime*. 6 vols. Wilmette, Ill.: CrimeBooks Inc., 1990. • Scheibla, Shirley Hobbs. "Where Hot Money Hides." *Barron's*, July 11, 1983, pp. 16–18. • Varchaver, Nicholas. "Hiding Dirty Money." *Fortune*, March 4, 2002, p. 44.

money pit

The site of the world's longest and costliest treasure hunt, Oak Island, 70 kilometers south of Halifax, Nova Scotia, holds a mysterious subterranean shaft that has been connected to the lost continent of Atlantis, the Knights Templar and the Holy Grail, Aztec and Mayan gold, Freemasons, and pirates of the Spanish Main. Discovered by young Daniel McGinnis (or McInnis) at Mahone Bay in 1795, a depression 13 feet in diameter lay beneath a tree limb holding the remains of a block and tackle. The setting inspired him and two teenage friends, John Smith and Anthony Vaughn, to dig down two feet, where they found flagstone. They continued their excavating another 28 feet. In 1825, Smith bought the property and lived there for the remainder of his life, but he made no further finds.

In 1803, a Nova Scotian, Simeon Lynds, and the Onslow Company secured excavation rights and tripled the depth of the hole. They located an inscribed stone before flooding stopped the endeavor. The next year, the company dug a parallel hole 110 feet deep and again were flooded out. In 1849, the Truro Company drilled through two oak barrels or chests and took core samples containing scrap metal and three gold chain links. A year later, discovery of an underground waterway and artificial beach at Smith's Cove suggested that a clever prankster may have engineered the mythic money pit.

In 1861, the year that the money pit claimed the life of an explorer, the bottom fell out of the hole as cross tunneling weakened the shaft. In 1897, discovery of a triangular rock formation, parchment, and cement vault whetted interest in the money pit. That same year, the pit took a second life when a digger fell to the bottom of the shaft. In 1899, the Oak Island Treasure Company's discovery of the south shore "pirate tunnel" contributed to the mystery of the unidentified engineer. Workers dynamited the tunnel, but made little headway in solving the mystery. In 1909, Franklin D. Roosevelt directed his company, Old Gold Salvage, to search the pit, and he maintained his interest in the pit throughout his presidency. Two years after Roosevelt entered the treasure hunt, a skeptic questioned the findings of early searchers and proposed that the money pit was nothing more than one of many natural sinkholes on the island filled in with fallen timber, natural marl, and debris.

In 1936, explorers found a second inscribed stone and traces of a cofferdam. Errol Flynn, athletic star of Hollywood adventure flicks, showed interest in the money pit in 1940, but learned that the search rights already belonged to actor John Wayne. In 1965, four more diggers died in their investigation of the pit, perhaps overcome by naturally occurring methane. The total digging and earth removal changed the terrain irretrievably from its late 18th-century contours:

10-foot increments	*alterations to the surface since 1792*
• 0	depression and flagstone 2 feet down in 1792
• 10	rotted oak; top ten feet of surface area removed in 1932
• 20	current level of surface removal
• 30	Daniel McGinnis digs down 30 feet in 1792
• 40	oak platform above high tide level
• 50	charcoal, oak platform
• 60	putty above oak platform
• 70	coconut fiber above oak platform
• 80	oak platform
• 90	oak platform, 1803, Simeon Lynds & the Onslow Co.
• 100	oak platform above inscribed stone at 108 feet
• 110	oak platform; flood in parallel hole in 1804
• 120	oak platform below oak chests at 114 feet in 1849
• 130	cofferdam at flood tunnel from Smith's Cove in 1850
• 140	thick oak platform at 132 feet
• 150	
• 160	cofferdam at flood tunnel from south cove in 1899
• 170	
• 180	
• 190	bedrock
• 200	brass, charcoal; underground channels to Atlantic Ocean
• 210	
• 220	
• 230	cement vault at 225 feet; cavity at 232 feet

By the 21st century, joint efforts had extended excavation to 200 feet and unearthed underground channels directing rising Atlantic tides from the beach some 500 feet away.

The fame of the money pit grew to such lengths that the term became an English idiom for wasted effort and money, a fool's errand, the epic boondoggle. The legends linked to Oak Island are numerous. Among the suppositions are:

- that Sir Francis Bacon concealed William Shakespeare's works early in the 17th century and left in the shaft a scrap of an original play
- that Sir Francis Drake dug the pit to conceal treasure from Queen Elizabeth I
- that Captain William Kidd, a privateer who lived from 1645 to 1701, buried a hoard of pilfered gold and silver coins there while his crew reconditioned his ship, the *Queen's Revenge*
- that the pit contains the crown jewels of the executed French Queen Marie Antoinette, which disappeared after the French Revolution in 1791.

Certainly, cofferdams, flagstones, oak log platforms, oak chests that may contain pieces of eight, 30 feet of clay, layers of iron, a cement vault, a megalithic cross, and strata of charcoal, putty, and some coconut husks used as cargo packing on ships were found in the hole, but no one has come up with an explanation of who went to the trouble of devising it and why it was worth sabotaging with booby traps. Proposals to mount a ten million dollar expedition supervised by scientists at the Woods Hole Oceanographic Institution in Massachusetts continue the quest.

SOURCES: Daly, John. "Solving Old Mysteries." *Maclean's*, March 20, 1989, p. 45. • Fanthorpe, Lionel, and Patricia Fanthorpe. *The Oak Island Mystery: The Secret of the World's Greatest Treasure.* Toronto: Hounslow Press, 1995. • Harris, Graham, et al. *Oak Island and Its Lost Treasure.* Victoria, B.C.: Formac, 2000. • Nickell, Joe. "The Secrets of Oak Island." *Skeptical Inquirer*, March 2000, p. 14. • Preston, Douglas. "Death Trap Defies Treasure Seekers." *Smithsonian*, June 1988, pp. 52–61. • Preston, Douglas. "Is Oak Island Ready to Yield Its Treasure?" *Reader's Digest* (Canadian), October 1988, pp. 58–62. • Proctor, Steve. "Island of Controversy." *Maclean's*, August 21, 1995, p. 54. • Taylor, Michael. "Yep, They're Still Digging." *Forbes*, September 25, 1995, pp. 138–142.

money slang

Money slang, like other elements of folk culture, often reduces the cumbrous to the simple and memorable, as with the English "bob" for "shilling" and the rhymes sky diver/Pam Shriver/fiver for £5 and nifty/fifty for £50. The reduction of dignified coinage and paper notes to common slang and nicknames indicates human affection and sometimes contempt for government or nobility, for example, the "pony" of ancient Corinth, which distinguished its coin with the image of winged Pegasus; the Roman *nummus* ("the coin") for the *sestertius*, the nation's workhorse coin; and the British term "archer" for the £2,000 note, the amount a Lord Archer offered a strumpet. One branch of money slang consists of puns and word games, as with "poorly fish" for "six quid" (sick squid) and "Pavarotti" for "tenner" (tenor). Street argot is sometimes temporal, as with a "Bernie" for £1,000,000, the amount that formula-one driver Bernard Ecclestone donated to the Labour Party.

The following list captures an element of popular idiom and of contempt as they apply to money:

term	*source*	*meaning*
Alan	British	£1
'alf an Oxford	British	2 shillings & 6 pence; half a crown
archer	British	£2,000
Aryton Senna	British	£10
assignat	French	worthless paper money
B. A. F. note	British	military scrip
bag of sand	British	£1000
bar	British	£1,000,000
beer token	British	£2 coin
Bernie	British	£1,000,000
big one	American	$1,000 bill
bin lid	British	£1
bit	American	*real*
bob	Australian, British	shilling
Bobby Moore	British	£20
bon pour	French	monetary token
boodle	American	money
bottle	British	£2 or £200
brass	American	money
bread	American	money
browny	British	£10
buck	American	$1
bulls-eye	British	£50
cabbage	American	money
canary	British	£1
capital	American	money

term	*source*	*meaning*
carpet	British	£3 or £300
cartwheel	American	silver dollar
cartwheel	British	penny and twopence
century or cenny	British	£100
ching	British	£5
chips	American	money
C note	American	$100
coachwheel	British	5 shillings; a crown
cock and hen	British	£10
cockle	British	£10
cold cash or cold hard cash	American	money
colt	Corinthian	coin
commodore	British	£15
Continental	American	Continental currency
copper	American, British	penny
Dead Brazilian	British	£10
dead octopus	British	6 quid
dead presidents	American	paper money
deener or deenah	Australian	shilling
deep sea diver	British	£5 note
dinero	American	money
dirty	British	£30
dosh	British	cash
double sawbuck	American	$20 bill
dough	American	money
eagle	American	paycheck
edge pence	British	20 pence
eight bits	American	4 quarters; $1
Elsie	British	sixpence
filthy lucre	American	money
fin	American	$5
five spot	American	$5 bill
flag	British	£5
folding money	American	paper money
four bits	American	50¢
G or G note	American	$1,000
garden gate	British	£8
gelt	American	money
ging	Australian	money
grand	American	$1,000
grand	British	£1,000
grease	American	money used as a bribe
green or green stuff	American	money
greenbacks	American	paper money
green goods	American	counterfeit bills
gringo money	American	American cash
half a C	American	$50 bill
half grand or half G	American	$500
Hampden Roar	British	£20
Hell money	Chinese	funeral scrip
IGWT	Australian	U.S. dollar
jack	American	money
Jacks alive	British	£5
Jackson	British	£5
J. I. M. note	Japanese	Japanese invasion money
joey	British	groat
kale	American	money

term	*source*	*meaning*
lady or Lady Godiva	British	£5
lettuce	American	money
lolly	British	cash
long green	American	paper money
long 'un	British	£100
loonie	Canadian	$1
louis	French	Louis d'or
Louise Wener	British	£10
macaroni	British	£25
Maggie	British	£1 coin
marigold	British	£1,000,000
mazuma	American	money
McGarret	British	£50
McGiver	British	£5
means	American	cash
Melvin	British	£5
money pit	Canadian	ghost treasure
monkey	British	£500
moolah	American, Australian	money
mother hen	British	£10
Nelsons	British	money
nevis	British	£7
new pee	British	penny
nicker	British	£1
nifty	British	£50
Notgeld	German	emergency issue
nugget	British	£1
oil of palms	American	money for bribes
one-er	British	£100
owl	Athenian	coin
Oxford or Oxford scholar	British	5 shillings; a crown
P	British	penny
Pam Shriver	British	£5 note
Paul McKenna	British	£10
Pavarotti	British	£10
pelf	American	money
petty cash	American	small amount of money
pin money	American	small amount of money
pistareen	English, Canadian, American	two-*real* piece
plum	British	£100,000
pocket money	American	small amount of money
pony	British	£25
pony	Corinthian	coin
poorly fish	British	6 quid
queer money	American	counterfeit bills
quid	Australian, British	£1
rake-off	American	cash
reddie	British	£50
rocket	British	£5
rocks	American	money
rofe	British	£4 or £400
roll	American	money
sawbuck	American	$10
score	British	£20
scratch	American	cash
shekels	American	money
shinplaster	American	worthless small denomination paper money

term	*source*	*meaning*
simoleons	American	money
six bits	American	75¢
skin diver	British	£5 note
skins	American	money
sky diver	British	£5 note
smackers	American	paper money
small change	American	small amount of money
spanner	British	50 pence
spinach	American	paper money
spirit money	Chinese	funeral scrip
spondulicks or spondulix	American	cash
sprarsy Anna	British	tanner; sixpence
squid	British	£100,000
stake	American	money
stash	American	money
tanner	British	sixpence
tenner	British	£10
ten-spot	American	$10
threepenny bit	British	threepence
thrifty	British	£50
tilbury	British	sixpence
tin	American	money
Tom Mix	British	£6
ton	British	£100
tortoise	Aeginetan	coin
trey	Australian	three pence
two bits	American	25¢
two bob	Australian	two shilling; a florin
two spot	American	$2 bill
wad	American	money
wampum	American	money
wedge	British	small change
wheaty	American	penny
wherewithal	American	money
wicker basket	British	£15
wooden nickel	American	counterfeit coin
yard	American	$100
yellow boy	British	guinea
zack	Australian	sixpence

Numerous slang phrases reveal aspects of currency history. The term "to pay on the nail," similar to the American "cash on the barrelhead," appears to describe an actual transaction site dating to a time when promoters of medieval fairs carried portable nails, flat-topped stools on which they conducted business and counted cash. There is another possibility. The Limerick Stock Exchange contains a pillar with a circular plate of copper three feet in diameter. Called the Nail, this disk symbolizes sincere intent to pay all stock-exchange offers. Two more sites may be the source of the phrase: one at the open-air market at the Bristol Corn Exchange, which has displayed four brass pillars called nails since 1552, where captains received pay for shipping, and the other, a copper plate at the Liverpool Exchange where bargainers settle deals.

***See also* greenbacks.**

SOURCES: Beavis, Bill, and Richard G. McCloskey. *Salty Dog Talk: The Nautical Origins of Everyday Expressions.* Dobbs Ferry, N.Y.: Sheridan House, 1995. • "Goodbye Faraday, Hello Elgar." *London Daily Mail,* February 24, 2001. • Head, Barclay V. *A Guide to the Principal Coins of the Greeks.* London: British Museum, 1959. • Langly, Mike. "Sir Stanley's Famous Fivers." *Johannesburg*

Mail and Guardian, March 3, 2000. • Lewis, Brenda Ralph. *Coins & Currency*. New York: Random House, 1993. • Reinfeld, Fred. *Treasury of the World's Coins*. New York: Sterling Publishing, 1953.

moneylending

From ancient times moneylending got a bad name for charging interest, a form of profiteering banned by biblical and Koranic tradition. The book of Leviticus commands, "Take thou no interest of [the borrower] or increase" (25:36). In Chapter 5 of Nehemiah's book, written around A.D. 250, the devout reformer and builder grieves over the outcome of mortgaging lands, homes, and vineyards. He declares in verse 5, "Lo, we bring into bondage our sons and our daughters to be servants." The grim-voiced Ecclesiasticus warns the manipulative usurer of the bottomless pit of greed: "He that loveth silver shall not be satisfied with silver; nor he that loveth abundance with increase" (Ecclesiastes 5:10). Just as the Bible blamed the usurer for taking advantage of those in need, the Koran, the supreme source of moral instruction for Muslims and a guide to legal, historical, polemical, and religious issues which was compiled in A.D. 635, inveighed against earning interest on money and goods. In Surah 2:275, the Prophet proclaims, "Those who charge usury are in the same position as those controlled by the devil's influence.... For those who persist in usury, they incur Hell, wherein they abide forever."

The Talmud — particularly the *Seder Neziqin* (or *Nezikin*) (*Damages*) also called *Seder Yeshuot* (*yeshuot* means "rescues") — a ten-part civil and criminal law code, denounces profiteering and compares usurers to those who shed blood. The *Bava Mets'ia* ("Middle gate") deals specifically with business ethics, contracts, and usury; in the *Bava Batra* ("last gate"), the writer reasons: "Come and let us take stock of the accounts of the world: the loss caused through a Mitzvah [blessing] versus the gain, and the gain through a sin versus the loss" (Newman & Spitz 1945, 137). In spite of clear biblical and Talmudic injunctions, Jewish sages countenanced usury and exploitation as long as it victimized the non–Jewish *goyim*.

For those who lent cash as a form of neighborliness, the act expressed love or concern for people in difficult financial straits. In *Moreh Nevukhim* (*The Guide for the Puzzled*) (1190), Rabbi Moses ben Maimon, a Cordoban court physician also known as Maimonides or Rambam, stated the "Eight Degrees of Charity," which he called a golden ladder. He advised:

> Anticipate charity by preventing poverty; assist the reduced fellowman, either by a considerable gift, or a sum of money, or by teaching him a trade, or by putting him in the way of business, so that he may earn an honest livelihood, and not be forced to the dreadful alternative of holding out his hand for charity [Bartlett 1992, 122].

The *Horayot* commented, "He who loves his neighbors and lends money to the needy in his need, concerning him it is written: 'Thou shalt call and I shall answer'" (Newman & Spitz 1945,p. 240). In addition to encouraging acts of charity, Rabbinic tradition placed an additional moral burden on the borrower to repay every cent.

On this tenuous ground, Jewish usury flourished from ancient Judea to modern times. Among professional moneylenders, the worst of the lot charged exorbitant interest and targeted the poor. In regard to the apostates who violated both biblical and Talmudic tenets, patriarchs thundered that the writing of a loan was the same as the usurer publicly admitting that he was a reprobate and blasphemer.

Historically, the early Jews and Muslims were the holdouts in a field of world religions that did not condemn lending. Confucius's *Analects*, composed after 483 B.C., urged serenity of mind and harmony with the universe. For behavior, the text describes the best choice of action toward fellow humans as avoiding actions that individuals would not want done to them, but Confucius does not mention moneylending as one of those actions. In the *Dhammapada* (*Words of Doctrine or Way of Truth*) (first century B.C.), the scripture for Buddhists of Sri Lanka and Southeast Asia, the Buddha urges freeing the soul of desire for prestige, power, money, and "the dark places of the heart," but does not specify moneylending as a sin (Byrom 1976, p. 35).

During the rise of Catholicism, moneylending became a major source of rancor between Christians and Jews. The Jewish skill at pawnbroking, money-changing, and loansharking gave Christians an excuse for anti–Semitism and persecutions that often resulted in confiscation of goods and property or worse. To Jews in the money trade, Christians were fond of citing St. Paul, who stated, "For the love of money is the root of all evil" (I Timothy 6:10), an adage often erroneously cited as "Money is the root of all evil."

Into the Middle Ages, the image of the greedy Jew permeated biased literature written by Gentiles. As Nathan Ausubel summarizes in *The Book of Jewish Knowledge* (1964), the Hebrew moneylender became "a kind of human spider who deviously spun his web of greed, in which he caught his Christian victims, wringing from them a conscienceless rate of interest" (p. 296). In 1170, *The Dialogue of the Exchequer*, probably composed by Richard FitzNeal, treasurer to King Henry II of England, lambasted public and common usury. The text characterizes lending

> in the manner of the Jews, [as] anyone [taking] more by agreement of the same species of money than he lent: as a pound for a mark, or twopence for a pound of silver, for a week's interest besides the principal. We do not call that public, but damnable usury ["Dialogue concerning the Exchequer"].

In art as in literature, the long, narrow fingers of the usurer totted up amounts on the abacus, weighed bullion on scales, and fingered bright circlets of gold and silver as though fondling a beloved artifact.

Based on prejudice against Jewish moneylenders, Henry II of England set up a system of recording loans and contracts on paper and declared,

> Every Jew shall swear upon his roll that all his debts, pledges, rents, goods, and possessions have been written down by him, and that he has hidden nothing, as we have said. And if any one learn that some one has hidden something, let him reveal it secretly to the judges sent to him, and let them detect and expose forgers of charters, and clippers of coins, and likewise concerning false charters ["Henry II of England"].

At the heart of Henry's decree is the common slander that Jews are not to be trusted, particularly in matters concerning cash loans.

In 1173, the situation worsened after an unpleasant incident involving the debts of the Abbey of Bury St. Edmunds. Abbey historian Jocelin de Brakelond wrote,

> I saw another bond made to Isaac, the son of Rabbi Joce, for 400 pounds, but I do not know why. And I saw a third bond made to Benedict the Jew of Norwich, for 880 pounds; and this was the origin and cause of this debt. Our buttery was destroyed and William the sacristan undertook willy-nilly to restore it and he secretly borrowed from Benedict the Jew 40 marks at usury ["Jocelin de Brakelond"].

The scandal broke when the outstanding amount rose to £100. The lender publicized the sacristan's shameful debt to the Jew, a secret negotiation of which the abbot and monks were unaware.

Until the Third Lateran Council of 1179, the Catholic church maintained its own lending institutions. When canon law made an unprecedented shift and forbade usury on pain of banning from the sacraments and from sanctified burial, the task passed from Christians to Jews, who financed growth within the Catholic realm. One example, Aaron of Lincoln, who was active in the 1180s, headed a consortium to help build Cistercian monasteries, St. Albans abbey, and the cathedrals of Lincoln and Peterborough. Out of respect for medieval relics, he claimed that "when a Christian saint went homeless, he, Aaron the Jew, built a home for him" (Ausubel 1964, p. 408). When Aaron died in 1186, King Stephen felt justified in confiscating Aaron's savings and used the cash to pay English soldiers fighting in France.

In 1194, Richard I, who raged when his finances dwindled, created a registration of

Jewish moneylenders and their outstanding debts called the *Scaccarium Judaeorum* [*Exchequer of the Jews*]. With this accounting, his tax collectors could more easily levy a 10 percent tax against the Jews' cash on hand, pledges of armor and castles, promised crop yields, church plate and vestments, revenues, even holy relics, which Bishop Nigel of Ely pledged in the 1100s in exchange for a cash advance. Under Richard and subsequent monarchs, Jews who failed to satisfy the tax audit faced torture, prison terms, and property loss. To safeguard earnings, the era's moneylenders had no choice but to raise interest rates. The uptick in the cost of borrowing caused Christians to revile Jews even more as heartless bloodsuckers.

As the situation worsened between borrower and lender, statements of blame grew more direct. St. Bernard of Clairvaux, a 12th-century theologian from Dijon, France, and founder of the religious house of Clairvaux in Langres, Champagne, earned a reputation for being an opinionated zealot. He turned the word "Jew" into a synonym for "loan-shark" and added to the French language the *judaizare*, meaning "to profiteer from making loans." Offsetting blatant anti–Semitism was English chronicler Matthew of Paris, author of *Usury of the Cahorsins* (1235), who charged that the Christian moneylenders of Cahors, who financed papal projects, "circumvented the needy in their necessities, cloaking their usury under the show of trade, and pretending not to know that whatever is added to the principal is usury, under whatever name it may be called" ("Matthew of Paris").

In an era that saw increased denunciation, assault, imprisonment, and murder of Jewish moneylenders, one of the most cruel comeuppances to the financier occurred during the Crusades, when governments and the Catholic hierarchy excused the "soldiers of Christ" from repaying the Jews who financed their holy mission against the pagan Saracens (Ausubel 1964, p. 299). Resulting from an era that thoroughly discounted Jews as human beings was the Jew-baiting of Franciscan John of Capistrano and papal inquisitors, who found cunning methods of disinheriting, torturing, and slaying their religious adversaries, particularly in Iberia.

Late in the 13th century, the heyday of the Jewish moneylender came to an abrupt end. In 1275, the church softened its condemnation of Christian money changers and moneylenders. The financial tide swept beyond Jews after Pope Leo X nullified decrees against usury. Soon, Jewish lenders had to compete with the rich Corsini, the *popolo grasso* (rich merchants) who ruled Florence. Competitors for the money trade included the pushy Lombards and the church itself, which established *monti di pietá* ("mounts of piety"), a new name for the old games of money changing, pawnbroking, and loan-sharking. In 1290, when Gentiles no longer depended on the Jewish money market, England expelled 16,000 Jews and entered a period of 400 years in which their sole contact with Judaism came from myth and biased literature such as Christopher Marlowe's *The Jew of Malta* (ca. 1589), a popular stage success featuring a power-mad financier.

The Renaissance did not ameliorate the Jewish-Christian contretemps. Fresh from a break with Catholicism, reformer Martin Luther, author of *The Jews and Their Lies* (1543), denounced Jews for greed and claimed "They are nothing but thieves and robbers who daily eat no morsel and wear no thread of clothing which they have not stolen and pilfered from us by means of their accursed usury" ("Martin Luther"). Siding with Luther's point of view, Sir Francis Bacon enlarged on mounting public scorn of Jewish moneymen in *Of Usury* (1597), an essay that condemned the taking of profits on the Sabbath and the turning of money into a god in defiance of the First Commandment, "Thou shalt have no other gods before me" (Exodus 20:3). Bacon caricatured profit-mongers, pawnbrokers, money changers, and mortgagees as lazy and hard-hearted. To identify them to the unwary, he proposed that "usurers should have orange-tawny bonnets, because they do judaize" (Bacon). The bright headgear was the standard color that Jews had to wear before the English expelled them in 1290. On the pragmatic side, Bacon proposed that usurers be tolerated, licensed, and carefully monitored to prevent over-charging.

One of the ironies of monetary history is the position that Jews occupied in the late Middle Ages and Renaissance during the rise of modern banking. The Jewish moneylender was indispensable to the economy and hobnobbed with barons, lords, bishops, popes, kings, and emperors. Through centuries of refining lending techniques and standards, money marketers managed to bankroll wars and religious crusades to retake the Holy Land from the Saracens and to elevate the *nouveau riche*, who jockeyed to acquire the good life whatever the cost. Because of dependence on the outcast Jew, Christians stoked a vicious hatred of the lender and compounded mental images of moral turpitude that led to centuries of social, economic, and religious scapegoating and genocide. Evidence of unfair treatment were the levies, fines, and confiscation of moneys by legal and quasi-legal maneuverings.

Living the life of the social and religious outcast, out of necessity, Jews accepted the medieval stereotype of conniving profiteer because they had no way to escape it. As landless chattels of kings, barons, and church prelates, they were virtual slaves to usury with little opportunity to follow any other trade, even farming. In competition with Christian money marketers, Jews fought glaring inequities. Queen Elizabeth I's diplomat and councillor Thomas Wilson, the author of "Discourse on Usury" (1572), noted that in Venice, Christian financiers could charge up to 40 percent interest. He declared, "Go where you will through Christendom and you shall have of the Jews under ten percent in the hundred, yea, sometimes for five, whereas our English usurers exceed all God's mercy" (Ausubel 1964, p. 298).

Jews who dared charge more than five percent risked fines, prison sentences, or banishment. Elderly and handicapped ghetto dwellers no longer able to pursue the hard work of commerce, pawnbroking, and mortgaging developed a variety of lowly trades dealing in the resale of rags, old clothes, junk, and bones. Adding to the traditional burden of scorn, Jewish moneylenders suffered permanent castigation from William Shakespeare's *The Merchant of Venice* (ca. 1596). The popular comedy skewered all professional Jewish moneylenders in the caricature of the villain Shylock, whose name became a synonym for the greedy Jew. The bloated Shylock myth added elements of vengefulness, treachery, and gloating, thus exacerbating the denigration of Jews as Christ-killers, Judas Iscariots, and Wandering Jews, and the people who bore the eternal punishment of roving the earth until Jesus's return.

***See also* coins and currency in drama and film; Knights Templar; Roman coins — Monarchy and republic; Spanish coins.**

SOURCES: Ausubel, Nathan. *The Book of Jewish Knowledge*. New York: Crown, 1964. • Bacon, Francis. "Of Usury." http://www.orst.edu/instruct/phl302/texts/bacon/bacon_essays.html#OF USURY. • Bartlett, John. *Familiar Quotations*. Boston: Little, Brown & Co., 1992. • Brand, Paul. "Jews and the Law in England, 1275–1290." *English Historical Review*, November 2000. • Byrom, Thomas. *The Dhammapada: The Sayings of the Buddha*. New York: Alfred A. Knopf, 1976. • Cantor, Norman F., ed. *The Civilization of the Middle Ages*. New York: HarperPerennial, 1993. • Cantor, Norman F., ed. *The Jewish Experience*. New York: HarperCollins, 1996. • Cohn-Sherbok, Lavinia. *Who's Who in Christianity*. London: Routledge, 1998. • Hastings, James, ed. *Encyclopedia of Religion and Ethics*. New York: Charles Scribner's Sons, 1951. • Holmes, George, ed. *The Oxford Illustrated History of Medieval Europe*. Oxford: Oxford University Press, 1988. • Lopez, Robert S. *The Birth of Europe*. New York: M. Evans & Co., 1967. • McMurtry, Jo. *Understanding Shakespeare's England*. Hamden, Conn.: Archon Books, 1989. • "Medieval Sourcebook: The Dialogue Concerning the Exchequer." http://www.medievalhistory.net/excheq1.htm. • "Medieval Sourcebook: Henry II of England: Concerning Loans from the Jews." http:// www.fordham.edu/halsall/source/hen2-jewsloans. html. • "Medieval Sourcebook: Jocelin de Brakelond: Concerning Loans to the Abbey of Bury St. Edmunds, 1173." http://www.fordham.edu/halsall/source/1173badloans.html. • "Medieval Sourcebook: Martin Luther (1483–1546): The Jews and Their Lies, excerpts (1543)." http://www.fordham.edu/halsall/

source/luther-jews.html. • "Medieval Sourcebook: Matthew of Paris: The Usury of the Cahorsins, 1235." http://www.fordham.edu/halsall/source/1235cahorsins.html. • Newman, Louis I., and Samuel Spitz, eds. *The Talmudic Anthology.* West Orange, N.J.: Behrman House, 1945. • Snodgrass, Mary Ellen. *Who's Who in the Middle Ages.* Jefferson, N.C.: McFarland, 2001.

moneyless societies

Either voluntarily or under duress, primitive societies remained virtually cashless well into the 20th century. In South America, the hardships of daily barter impeded the commerce of Paraguayan Indians before their contact with Europeans. From the early 1600s to the 1750s, Jesuit missionaries controlled 150,000 Indians in 30 *reducciones* (settlements). The church conspired to suppress more sophisticated money systems as a means of keeping the people dependent on an idealized collectivism. Even in this oppressive theocracy, the Paraguayans managed to transform tea and tiny disks cut from snail shells into currency for making change, buying livestock, and paying taxes.

Nineteenth-century utopian schemes often proposed a perfect world that needed no money for its operation. In 1832, Welsh socialist Robert Owen, boy wonder of the textile industry and founder of British socialism, proposed a moneyless world where people functioned by exchanging equal amounts of labor and goods. On September 3, 1832, a model of Owen's plan opened at Gray's Inn Road in London. Called a bazaar, the planned workers' community presented labor notes to be swapped for goods. His exchange media, designed like banknotes, were ornate slips of paper issued from the Birmingham branch of the National Equitable Labour Exchange in denominations equivalent to hours of labor.

People who accepted Owen's notion supported the bazaar and set up a second model in Birmingham, but the concept did not survive long because of obstacles imposed by labor unions, legislation, squabbles among the planners, and strikes. For a brief time, parallel Owenite communes at New Lanark, England; New Harmony, Indiana; Kendall and Yellow Springs, Ohio; Nashoba, Tennessee; and Coxsackie and Haverstraw, New York, imitated the London experiment. At their demise, Owen's concepts survived in the Fabian Society, led by George Bernard Shaw and H. G. Wells, and in the British Labour Party, a less radical approach to social betterment.

A second utopist, French economist Charles Fourier, a traveler and socialist from Besançon, attempted a more complex utopian concept, which his follower, Albert Brisbane, brought to America. Championed by editor Horace Greeley and by clergyman and reformer George Ripley, Fourier's idea produced a commune, the North American Phalanx, New Jersey, in 1843, with alternative forms of the concept developed at Oneida, New Icaria, and Trumbull. Integral to Fourier's idea of a moneyless society was a public treasury that maintained equal portions of proceeds from common endeavors. The original community survived for 12 years; Brook Farm, begun in 1844, lasted only three years.

The cooperative system of French visionary Étienne Cabet, a teacher and attorney from Dijon, took shape on paper in *Voyage en Icarie* (*The Journey to Icaria*) (1840), a trek to an imaginary realm. On the advice of Robert Owen, Cabet tried to install a moneyless society in Red River, Texas, in 1848, which functioned via the sharing of work, land, and profits. After the loss of 65 percent of his settlers, Cabet moved a small company to Nauvoo, Illinois. A split in philosophies sent another splinter group to Cheltenham, Missouri, in 1856, followed by new attempts at Corning, Iowa, and Cloverdale, California. Cabet's idea foundered in 1895, largely because his experimental moneyless society lacked leadership.

SOURCES: Angell, Norman. *The Story of Money.* Garden City, N.Y.: Garden City Publishing, 1929. • Cabet, Étienne. *Voyage en Icarie.* New York: Kelley, 1973. • Einzig, Paul. *Primitive Money.* Oxford: Pergamon Press, 1966 • Fourier, Charles. *Selections from the Works of Fourier.* New York: Gordon Press, 1972. • Heilbroner, Robert L. *Behind the Veil of Economics: Essays in the World Philosophy.*

New York: W. W. Norton & Co., 1989. • Mumford, Lewis. *The Story of Utopias*. Gloucester, Mass.: Peter Smith, 1959.

Morgan, George T.

Creator of the Morgan dollar, engraver George T. Morgan incised U.S. coins for 48 years. He apprenticed at his trade in Birmingham, England, and learned design and modeling of bronze medals at the South Kensington Art School. To enter the coin art trade, he assisted the Wyons family of engravers at the British Royal Mint. A U.S. immigrant at age 31, Morgan enrolled at the Academy of Fine Arts and found work under Henry R. Linderman, director of the Philadelphia Mint, assisting Charles and William Barber. From 1872, Morgan's simple M identified his work on the dollar. He also made pattern coins, notably, the attractive 1877 half dollar, 1879 "Schoolgirl" dollar, 1880 Stella coin, and 1882 "Shield Earring" coin. He also sculpted numerous presidential medals, including that of Rutherford B. Hayes, and collaborated with designers of postage stamps.

In 1878, the U.S. Mint set its staff to the task of hurrying production of tons of silver dollars. At his quarters in a rooming house, Morgan crafted the classic Liberty dollar, based on a sketch of 19-year-old kindergarten teacher Anna Willess Williams, whom he met through artist Thomas Eakins. Morgan persuaded her to pose and finished the initial sculpture in five sittings. He featured a classic face with cap bearing the word "liberty" and the 13 stars of the original colonies joining the legend "*E Pluribus Unum*" ("Out of Many, One" or "One [nation] out of many [states]"). He backed it with a heraldic eagle.

Critiques of the Liberty dollar were mixed. In Philadelphia, the coin earned slurs for its stiff, ungainly eagle. Charges that Morgan had sketched a turkey prompted Linderman to assign him to sculpting a new bird. The flip side was different, though; because of the portrait's realistic presentation of Williams, she gained instant fame. From anonymous teacher, she became the equivalent of a World War II pinup girl—the recipient of sackfuls of mail and unexpected visits from admirers. Linderman's sharp criticism and hurry-up work on a replacement coin ended abruptly with his illness in 1878 and death in 1879.

The mint struck the original Morgan piece from silver mined from Nevada's Comstock Lode and produced it in Philadelphia, San Francisco, and the small mint at Carson City, Nevada. Remaining in production until 1904 and revived in 1921, the silver dollar earned its highest praise in the West, which felt an affinity for native silver, and in the South, especially among former slaves who preferred dollars in coin rather than paper. The production staff put 22 million of the coins in circulation by the end of the year.

Because William Barber and his son Charles Barber received preferment at the mint, Morgan remained an assistant until 1917, when he was named chief engraver, a title he held until his death from a sudden illness on January 4, 1925, at age 79. In 1918, the U.S. government recalled 270 million Morgan dollars to melt down for the aid of Great Britain during World War I. The coin went back into production in 1921. The Peace dollar replaced it in 1922.

***See also* Charles Edward Barber; Anthony C. Paquet; Peace dollar; Redfield hoard; U.S. coins.**

SOURCES: Ahwash, Kamal M. *Encyclopedia of United States Liberty Seated Dimes 1837–1891.* Wallingford, Pa.: Kamal Press, 1974. • Bowers, Q. David. *Adventures with Rare Coins.* Los Angeles: Bowers & Ruddy Galleries, Inc., 1979. • Breen, Walter. *Walter Breen's Complete Encyclopedia of U.S. and Colonial Coins.* New York: F. C. I. Press/Doubleday, 1988. • De Lorey, Thomas. "George T. Morgan Remembered." *COINage*, September, 1996. • Pollak, Henry. *Coinage & Conflict.* Clifton, N.J.: Coin & Currency Institute, 2001. • Reiter, Ed. "Numismatics: The Roman Touch." *New York Times*, January 16, 1983, p. H40. • Rochette, Ed. "Four Hundred Cents to the Stella Dollar!" *Antiques & Collecting Hobbies*, December 1986, p. 72. • Taxay, Don. *The U.S. Mint and Coinage.* New York: Arco Publishing, 1966.

Morgan, Sir Henry

One of the most notorious and brutal pirates headquartering in Port Royal, Jamaica, Sir Henry Morgan enjoyed the height of Caribbean plunder. He was born to farmer Robert Morgan in rural Llanrhymney outside Cardiff, Wales, in 1635 and went to sea from Bristol in boyhood to escape a life of plowing, harvesting, and livestock management. At age 20, he apprenticed under Sir Christopher Myngs, who acquired a phenomenal plunder of 1.5 million pieces of eight. Morgan's share of the coins bought him his own vessel.

Under General Venables, Morgan accepted a staff position in Oliver Cromwell's army and arrived in Barbados in the heyday of piracy on the Spanish Main. At age 28, Morgan replaced Edward Mansfield as captain of a crew of privateers in Myngs's armada. While making his fortune, he partnered with the thieving team known as Jackman & Morris in looting the Central American coast. After the death of his uncle, Edward Morgan, lieutenant governor of Jamaica, Henry married Edward's daughter, Mary Elizabeth.

Morgan's career thrived from a license to prey on the enemies of the British Royal Navy during the Second Anglo-Dutch War, from 1665 to 1667. He sacked Puerto Príncipe, Cuba, gaining 50,000 pieces of eight, which became so common in pirate commerce that they were legal tender in Jamaica along with English coins. In the coup of the century, he plundered Puerto Bello, Panama, for a month and departed the area after Indians warned him that the Spanish intended to wreak vengeance on his crew. His haul amounted 250 million coins as well as spices, silks, jewels, ale and rum, weapons, and slaves. The massive haul earned him a hero's welcome in Jamaica.

Aboard the *Oxford*, Morgan once more set out and seized the *Cour Volant*, a French galleon he renamed the *Satisfaction*. He made a successful raid on Maracaibo, Venezuela, where he overran the fort and again filled the ship's hold with coins and gemstones. A hunted man, he stayed ahead of pursuers as he pillaged additional settlements and, in 1668, fought off Captain Manuel Pardal, who attempted a raid on Jamaica. Morgan chased Pardal northwest to Cuba and shot him dead. As Morgan's reward for saving Jamaica, the island authority set him in command over the island fleet of 35 ships and 2,000 sailors.

As a civil servant, in 1668, Morgan spied for Sir Thomas Modyford, Governor of Jamaica, to determine Spanish plans for a military mission. In 1669, as Admiral Alonso de Espinosa and three Spanish frigates of the Windward Armada pursued Morgan, his flagship *Oxford* exploded and sank off the French island of St. Domingue as he was planning an assault on settlements at lake Maracaibo near Cartagena, Colombia. His ship *Magdalena* sank off Venezuela in 1669, losing 40,000 pieces of eight, silver ingots, and swords. His men recovered 15,000 pieces of eight.

Although Morgan exceeded his authority, he managed to stay on the right side of the law. At his best, in 1671, he captured the wealthy colony of Panama, thus robbing the Spanish of a major monetary stronghold. He and 460 crewmen took the Castle of San Lorenzo at the mouth of the Chagres River and, on January 9, pressed upriver in a fleet of 23 canoes.

After Morgan's hard-fought victory, he left the way he came — traveling downriver escorting a train of 175 mules bearing gold doubloons, 750,000 pieces of eight, and 600 Spanish prisoners. However, he failed to secure the entire Spanish treasure, much of which local officials carried with them as they fled the burning city. Nonetheless, Morgan earned around £1,000 and his men received 200 pieces of eight each. On May 31, Jamaicans expressed formal thanks for his daring in the era's most daring raid.

When Morgan's friends fell from power, he was arrested and sent to England in 1672 to set an example of appeasement to Spain, where the monarchy seethed over the sacking of Panama City. As a long-time friend of the crown, Morgan exonerated himself before Charles II, advised the military on how to fortify Jamaica, and earned a knighthood two years later. An English seagoing hero credited with establishing English supremacy in the Caribbean, in 1674, he commanded the Jamaican navy and was elevated to deputy governor of Jamaica. He remained a comrade of other buccaneers and steady customer at Port Royal pubs and spent his retirement as planter, military captain, and opponent to piracy.

In old age, Morgan lost his position in the assembly for cursing it. Shortly before he died of alcoholism and dropsy on August 25, 1688, in Lawrencefield, Jamaica, the king overrode Governor Thomas Lynch's denunciation and reinstated Morgan. The famed buccaneer received a royal send-off, including cannon salute from the island's forts and a patriot's burial at the palisades.

Working from eyewitness accounts by Henri Esquemelin, Morgan's shipboard surgeon, and other Jamaicans, undersea adventurers recovered Morgan's ship *Oxford* on Haiti's south shore. They deduce that Morgan lured the officers of a French vessel onto his ship to avenge their passing of worthless notes in payment for supplies. The celebrating that followed resulted in gunfire that set off a powder magazine, destroying the ship and killing 300. Morgan and his staff survived. Aboard the *Jamaica Merchant*, Morgan returned to the site to retrieve his loot, but wrecked the second ship as well off Isla Vaca. His efforts led historians to believe that the *Oxford* went down with a sizeable treasure when it sank in 1669 after the looting of Puerto Bello, where he added to his treasure with ransom totalling 4,000 gold *pesos*, ten times that amount in silver, chests of silver plate, and silver bars. The wreck also offered salvors opportunities to excavate and identify artifacts from the only active pirate ship located in Caribbean waters.

SOURCES: *Almanac of Famous People*. 6th ed. Farmington Hills, Mich.: Gale Group, 1998. • Cordingly, David. *Under the Black Flag*. San Diego, Calif.: Harvest Books, 1995. • Kelleher, Terry. "Pirate Tales." *People Weekly*, August 25, 1997, 18. • *Merriam-Webster's Biographical Dictionary*. Springfield, Mass.: Merriam-Webster, 1995. • Nash, Jay Robert. *Encyclopedia of World Crime*. 6 vols. Wilmette, Ill.: CrimeBooks Inc., 1990. • Paris, Sheldon. "Sir Henry Morgan: Pirate or Patriot?" *Stamps*, June 17, 1995, 3. • Pickford, Nigel. *The Atlas of Ship Wrecks & Treasure*. New York: Dorling Kindersley, 1994. • Sandz, Victoria. *Encyclopedia of Western Atlantic Shipwrecks and Sunken Treasure*. Jefferson, N.C.: McFarland, 2001. • "Subsea Recovery." http://www.subsearecovery.com/ssr.html. • Weston, John. "Sir Henry Morgan." http://www.datawales.co.uk/morgan.htm.

Morris, Robert

The Colonies' richest man and financier of the American Revolution, Robert Morris encouraged the establishment of the U.S. mint and the placement of monetary values on a decimal system. An Englishman born near Liverpool on January 31, 1734, he immigrated to America at age 12 with his father, the elder Robert Morris, a tobacco exporter killed aboard ship when a cannon misfired. The younger Robert Morris, heir to an estate of $7,000, briefly attended school in Philadelphia and worked in Charles Willing's mercantile trade of tobacco, wheat, and flour. Morris's skill at money marketing and buying earned him a partnership with the import house Willing, Morris & Company, to the affairs of which he added shipping, exchange, and banking.

A committed patriot, Morris rose in importance as harbor warden for Philadelphia and member of the Council of Safety. During the Revolutionary War, he negotiated banking arrangements for the assembly and worked in secret to procure munitions and fortify ports. He mounted his own blockade running with a privateering fleet headed by Captain George Ord, who seized British cargo ships from Haiti and slavers from Africa. Investing through Amsterdam, Morris boosted his cash holdings by speculating on the British stock exchange. After signing the Declaration of Independence, he backed General George Washington and the Continental Army, managed finance for the Continental Congress, and won a seat on the Pennsylvania Assembly.

When the outlook for the colonists ebbed along with their credit in 1780, Morris took over colonial finance with the stipulation that he be able to remain in private business while negotiating military contracts. He was elected unanimously. In a formal report to Congress on May 17, 1781, he insisted that a national bank be separate from the federal mint. He proposed collecting taxes in coin to pay outstanding interest on the colonial debt and, to avoid military commissaries, he personally outfitted the navy. By maintaining multi-national connections and negotiating a loan of $250,000 in silver bullion from France, in 1782, he created the Bank of North America, underwritten with his personal credit. Citizens dubbed the notes he circulated "Morris notes." Frustrated that the states did not pay their debts, he resigned his office in 1783, but remained in office until he had reimbursed the scrip that paid the army for their services at Yorktown.

Returned to the General Assembly of Pennsylvania in 1785, Morris studied the commercial future of the colonies. By monopolizing the tobacco trade with France, he assured his financial success. He observed debate during the framing of the Constitution and declined the post of President George Washington's first Secretary of the Treasury in favor of a Senate seat. He also helped to negotiate the move of the capital from New York City to Washington, D.C.

Burdened by his land-rich investments in New York, Virginia, and Washington, D.C., during the monetary depression caused by the Napoleonic wars, Morris found himself irreversibly strapped for cash to pay three million dollars in taxes and interest on loans. At age 63, he was arrested for non-payment of debt and incarcerated in Philadelphia's debtors' prison. Upon his release in 1801, he lived out his last five years on handouts from friends and the annuity of his wife, Ann White Morris. Historians debate whether Morris preserved the new union by lending his personal wealth and influential connections or bankrolled himself by monopolizing the deal-making that accompanied the American Revolution.

***See also* Alexander Hamilton; Thomas Jefferson; U.S. coins; U.S. Treasury.**

SOURCES: Clain-Stefanelli, Elvira, and Vladimir Clain-Stefanelli. *The Beauty and Lore of Coins, Currency, and Medals.* Croton-on-Hudson, N.Y.: Riverwood Publishers, 1974. • *Encyclopedia of World Biography.* Detroit: Gale Group, 1998. • *Gale Encyclopedia of U.S. Economic History.* Farmington Hills, Mich.: Gale Group, 1999. • Johnson, Allen, ed. *Dictionary of American Biography.* New York: Charles Scribner's Sons, 1928. • Taxay, Don. *The U.S. Mint and Coinage.* New York: Arco Publishing, 1966. • Willoughby, Jack. "What Your Country Can Do for You." Forbes, October 23, 1989, pp. 104–106.

Muhammad ibn Tughluq

A Turco-Afghan sultan of Delhi, the second of the Tughluq dynasty, Muhammad ibn Tughluq established a multi-layered bureaucracy of Mamluk Turks, Hindus, and lower cast functionaries and manipulated coinage as a means of political control. Born around 1290 to Sultan Ghiyas-ud-Din Tughluq, he studied Islamic law, logic, philosophy, rhetoric, astronomy, and medicine and memorized much of the Koran. Before he came to power at age 35, he had already established a military career with the siege of Warangal and legitimized his rule through the imprimitur of a Cairo caliph. For over a quarter century, Muhammad controlled Hindu rajas, but failed to subdue the Sufis, a company of ascetic Muslim mystics who influenced the pious. He expanded his power over much of the Indian subcontinent, but lost control of southern India through mismanagement.

According to a brief autobiography, Muhammad influenced Indian culture in 1327 by the transfer of the capital from Delhi to Deogir near the Qutab Minar complex and Siri Fort, a combination defense and administration center. The move spread Urdu as a native language into the Deccan. He reformed finance according to his interpretation of Chinese financial texts and ordered the most attractive coins of the era. His monetary policies called for the coining of base metal into nearly worthless small change made of copper and for the introduction of tokens. The faulty coins were easily counterfeited. Copies bled the treasury, which backed them with the sultan's stash of gold.

Around 1333, Muhammad mended a misunderstanding with the famous travel writer ibn Battuta, author of *Tuhfat al-Nuzzar fi Ghara'ib al-Amsar wa'Ajaib al'Asfar* (*On Curiosities of Cities and Wonders of Travel*) (1354), by sending him on a royal embassy to China. To set up an audience with the sultan, ibn Battuta engineered a silent partnership with a merchant who staked him to *dinars*, treasure, and camels as a suitable bribe. Muhammad appointed ibn Battuta as *qadi* (judge) of Delhi at the annual salary of 12,000 silver *dinars* with one year's signing bonus in advance.

At the beginning of World War I, the Bank of England became the nation's only source of paper money, such as this one-pound note picturing physicist and mathematician Sir Isaac Newton, a key player in the 17th-century scientific revolution.

Muhammad developed a reputation for grandstanding. One of his publicity stunts involved the positioning of miniature catapults mounted on elephants for projecting *dinars* and *dirhams* to the people during royal processions. In his travelogue, ibn Battuta characterized the munificent Muhammad as "addicted to the making of gifts and the shedding of blood," mainly the result of persistent revolts of taxpayers forced to underwrite the sultan's largesse (Bullis 2000, 23). Muhammad's other contributions to Indian history included crop rotation, state farms, famine relief, and an agricultural bureaucracy controlling irrigation. He died at Sonda on March 20, 1351, during a war against Taghi's rebel faction.

SOURCES: Bullis, Douglas. "The Longest Hajj: The Journeys of Ibn Battuta." *Aramco World*, July/August 2000, pp. 2–39. • Ibn Battuta. *The Travels of Ibn Battuta*. Cambridge: Cambridge University Press, 1971. • "Islamization of Central Asia." http://baskurt.homestead.com/Islamization.html. • *Merriam-Webster's Biographical Dictionary*. Springfield, Mass.: Merriam-Webster, 1995.

Newton, Sir Isaac

To recoup the health of his treasury, William III of England appointed physicist Isaac Newton warden of the Tower Mint to superintend a three-year, general recoinage, completed in 1699 from mints at Bristol, Chester, Exeter, London, Norwich, and York. Newton advanced to master of the mint and remained dedicated to the post until his death in 1727. For 30 years, Newton was an able administrator pursuing counterfeiters and shavers of royal coinage, thus enriching himself and earning knighthood, conferred in 1705 by Queen Anne.

Newton's post required production of coronation coins for Queen Anne in 1702 and the counterstamping of coins confiscated during an English-Dutch assault on Vigo Bay, Spain, in 1703. In 1707, the union of England and Scotland demanded the recoinage of old Scottish money and the upgrading of the Scottish mint to meet English standards. He introduced new coppers and, in 1714, initiated the Hanoverian coinage for George I. In the 1720s, he contracted the production of Ireland's coppers.

Newton was a scientist of impecable skill, knowledge, and judgment who took the king's business seriously. He performed meticulous assays of precious metals and personally wrote reports on quality. To learn more about monetary skimming, he grilled informers, coin shavers, and counterfeiters. In 1717, he supervised the devaluation of the guinea to 21 shillings. Despite grumblings from old-timers at the mint, he managed the Tower's business without scandal or public squabbling from assay master Hopton Haynes, deputy Francis Fauquier, or warden Sir John Stanley.

Newton was primarily responsible for an increase in mint accuracy. He did not hesitate to withdraw a series of gold coins and a half-ton of coppers from circulation because of their poor quality. Scrupulous in matters of weight and fineness, he rejected the bribe of a contractor for £6,000 and took pride in saving the treasury money. Because of his pride in service, he was outraged in 1710 when the trial by the pyx mistakenly found his coinage wanting. Owing to his integrity and management of minutiae, he raised the reputation of English coinage at home and abroad.

SOURCES: Allen, Larry. *Encyclopedia of Money*. New York: Checkmark Books, 2001. • Clain-Stefanelli, Elvira, and Vladimir Clain-Stefanelli. *The Beauty and Lore of Coins, Currency, and Medals*. Croton-on-Hudson, N.Y.: Riverwood Publishers, 1974. • Jordan, Louis, "The Coins of Colonial and Early America." http://www.coins.nd.edu/ColCoin/ColCoinContents/Introduction.html. • Reinfeld, Fred. *Treasury of the World's Coins*. New York: Sterling Publishing, 1953. • Sinclair, David. *The Pound*. London: Century Books, 2000. • Weatherford, Jack. *The History of Money: From Sandstone to Cyberspace*. Pittsburgh, Pa.: Three Rivers Press, 1998.

Ninger, Emanuel

In 1882, a Flagtown, New Jersey, farm sheltered a secret forger, retired sign artist Emanuel Ninger, an immigrant from Holland living with a wife and four children. Dubbed "Jim the Penman" by authorities for his expertise, he made hand-drawn pen-and-ink bank notes in ten-, 20-, and 50-dollar denominations on bond paper from Crane and Company, the Dalton, Massachusetts, firm that produced the premium stock permeated with colored threads for the U.S. Bureau of Engraving and Printing. Ninger's output reached 70 realistic bills a year, a phenomenal achievement in counterfeiting in that he drew freehand without magnifying glass or special equipment.

A meticulous artist, Ninger improved on designs that didn't meet with his approval. To age his forgeries, he soaked them in diluted coffee and sketched in additional threads with blue and red ink. Each bore the legal imprimatur "Act of March 3, 1863." He was unable to duplicate the fine lines created by repeating lathes. Nonetheless, he successfully circulated forged bills in limited quantities from 1890 to 1896. He easily fooled bank and treasury officials and enriched himself by $40,000, which he spent on annual jaunts to buy supplies in New York City.

On March 27, 1896, police arrested Ninger in the act of fleeing toward a ferry after he bought a cigar and plopped a bogus bill in a puddle of alcohol on a Manhattan tavern bar. The runny ink gave away his fakery to the bartender. Ninger offered a five-dollar bribe, but the bartender rejected it and summoned the U.S. Secret Service. In custody, Ninger offered two stories to cover his trail. He claimed to be Joseph Gilbert, an innocent victim of a confidence man; then he claimed to be the "boodle" carrier for Emanuel Ninger, entrusted with seven fake bills to pass in New York for small purchases.

At first, Chief William P. Hazen of the New York Bureau of the Secret Service doubted that the suspect was the forger. By tracing the other six bills he had passed in New York and having witnesses identify the forger, Hazen was convinced. Ninger finally confessed, then gave a demonstration of his skills at forgery. Sentenced to six years in prison and fined one dollar, Ninger was paroled at the end of four years and two months, in part because admirers bombarded the prison board with letters and media articles begging for clemency. He returned to farming in Reading, Pennsylvania. Followers of his crime combed his former home for stashes of phony cash.

SOURCES: James, Michael. "Counterfeiters Using Desktop Printers to Churn Out a Cascade of High-Quality Bogus Cash." *Buffalo News*, July 12, 1998. • McLaughlin, Abraham. "20 Ways to Foil Forgers." *Christian Science Monitor*, September 24, 1998. • Nash, Jay Robert. *Encyclopedia of World Crime*. 6 vols. Wilmette, Ill.: CrimeBooks Inc., 1990.

numismatics

Numismatics is the branch of history dealing with types of money, scrip, tokens, medals, and other media of exchange. The world's first book on coins came from China — Hung Tsun's *Chhuan Chih* (*A Treatise on Coinage*) (1149). The formalized study of coin history began in the Italian Renaissance, and included among the aficionados was the Italian poet Petrarch, who specialized in ancient classical coins. Nobles and princes of the era preferred Greco-Roman specie along with the literature and art of Greece and Rome. Counterfeiters preyed on unsuspecting collectors by feeding their coin cabinets with cast copies and fantasy coins.

In the 1600s, numismatists advanced from coins for art's sake to coins as testimonies to rulers, governments, religions, and philosophies. The first coin auction was held in 1598 at Leiden, when a French aristocrat had to liquidate his collection of rare Greco-Roman portrait pieces. Through systematic analysis, European scholars compared collections, rooted out false assumptions, and published catalogs of extant specie. By the 1800s, the production of lists and handbooks had become an essential part of the study of history, notably from the scholarly dating and cataloging of coins in the British Museum's collection. Aiding private and public collectors were London's Numismatic Society, formed in 1836, which evolved into the Royal Numismatic Society.

The 1900s brought more collectors to the study of numisimatics and added to the coin displays at museums in Berlin, Boston, Cambridge, Glasgow, London, Munich, New York City, Oxford, Paris, and Vienna. Numismatists cleaned coins with sophisticated chemical and physical treatments and protected their investments in rare and unusual finds with vaults and complex security systems. Supporting the burgeoning interest in world coinage were the International Numismatic Commission, established in 1936, quality numismatic journals, and photographic and electronic methods of sharing coin facts and hoard discoveries via newsletters and the Internet. One non-profit agency, the American Numismatic Association, received a charter from the U.S. Congress to promote the study, research, interpretation, and preservation of history and culture from ancient times to the present through numismatics.

***See also* coin collectors; Joseph Hilarius Eckhel; fishhook money; Percy Gardner; Hubertus Goltzius; Sir George Hill; hoarding; Redfield hoard; Franz Seraph Streber.**

SOURCES: Allen, Larry. *Encyclopedia of Money*. New York: Checkmark Books, 2001. • Clain-Stefanelli, Elvira, and Vladimir Clain-Stefanelli. *The Beauty and Lore of Coins, Currency, and Medals*. Croton-on-Hudson, N.Y.: Riverwood Publishers, 1974. • Davies, Glyn. *A History of Money from Ancient Times to the Present Day*. Cardiff: University of Wales Press, 1994. • Reinfeld, Fred. *Treasury of the World's Coins*. New York: Sterling Publishing, 1953. • Sinclair, David. *The Pound*. London: Century Books, 2000. • Weatherford, Jack. *The History of Money: From Sandstone to Cyberspace*. Pittsburgh, Pa.: Three Rivers Press, 1998.

oban

The Japanese *oban* ("big piece"), modeled on Chinese money, was an oversized rectangular gold coin with rounded edges and ornate Japanese lettering on the obverse. It was prized for its value in gold and artistry. The *tensho oban*, crafted from native gold and silver ores by the goldsmith Goto in the late 1500s, was the creation of Toyotomi Hideyoshi, a *daimyo* (feudal lord). He originated the oblong coin as a gift to the Muromachi shogunate in the Tensho Era, which began in 1573. Each bore Goto's signature on the back in india ink.

Too precious for ordinary commerce, the coin became a treasured reward or gift to retainers, officials, embassies, and nobles. Peasants rarely saw the *oban* and used for daily exchange Chinese coins. Typical of the Tokugawa shogunate from 1603 to 1868 during the Edo period, the *oban*, inscribed with the name of the mintmaster, was gaudy and awkward. Smaller versions of the *oban* were called *ichibu-ban* and *koban*, the first of which Ieyasu minted in 1601.

At the end of the Edo period, the *oban* and *koban* depreciated during successive recoinages, which devalued them. The coins went out of production in 1862 and ceased to circulate in 1869, when the Tokyo mint began coining silver *yen* as well as nickel, copper, and gold coins, modeled after European money. The Hiroshima branch of the Mint Bureau of the Ministry of Finance maintains an exhibit of the *oban* and subsequent Japanese coins.

See also **Ieyasu; Japanese money.**

SOURCES: Clain-Stefanelli, Elvira, and Vladimir Clain-Stefanelli. *The Beauty and Lore of Coins, Currency, and Medals.* Croton-on-Hudson, N.Y.: Riverwood Publishers, 1974. • Cribb, Joe. *Money.* Toronto: Stoddart, 1990. • Shappell, Chris. "Y Notes and Y News." *American Numismatic Association Newsletter,* November 14, 2001.

obolus

The Greek *obolus* (also *obol, obelos, obolos,* or *odelos*), which originated on the island of Aegina, bore religious significance for the pious in ancient times. At Aropus, visitors to the shrine of seer Amphiaraus in Attica presented nine *obols* before asking the god to treat illness. Patients dropped the coins in a chest in sight of a sacristan before bedding down on hides to await an oracle in their dreams. Those seekers who achieved a cure tossed either gold or silver into the god's fountain. The ritual differed at Corinth. In the words of the Greek satirist Lucian, author of *Dialogues of the Gods* and *Dialogues of the Dead* (ca. A.D. 180), those suppliants seeking miraculous cures for fever from the statue of the Corinthian military hero Pelichos left *obols* at its feet or affixed them to the statue's thigh with wax.

The *obolus* was the culture's choice of money to place under the tongue or between the teeth of corpses that had been properly anointed with oil and wine or prepared for cremation. The source of this custom may be the belief that, after death, the spirit exits through the mouth. Roman families altered the custom by covering the eyes with coins. The paired grave gifts became common finds at exhumations at archeological sites throughout the Roman world, including Egypt and Gaul. The money accompanied the corpse to the tomb to pay the miserly ferryman Charon for passage over the river Styx into Tartarus, the dreary underworld. Mythology singles out characters who cross without paying "Charon's obol," notably, citizens of Hermione, who, according to the first-century B.C. historian Strabo of Pontus, had access to a shortcut to the afterlife.

In myth, the superhero Hercules and singer Orpheus made their way to the land of the dead by sway of their unique personalities. On completing the twelfth of a series of labors, Hercules glowered so frighteningly at the boatman that Charon began rowing without a word. For the irregularity of forgoing the fare, the god Hades kept Charon chained for a year. Orpheus, a musician and recently bereaved husband, sang so sweetly about the boats of his childhood that he caused Charon to weep and allow passage without the customary *obolus.*

The serious obligation of sending a relative's body into the next world with a coin lies at the heart of the tragedy of Antigone, the daughter of doomed king Oedipus of Thebes, who slew his father Laius, married his mother Jocasta, and fathered two daughters and two sons in an incestuous relationship unknown to him. In her last act, Antigone faces her proud uncle Creon, the king of Thebes, who refuses burial to her rebellious brother Polynieces, and disobeys his edict that the corpse must lie unsanctified as an example against future anarchists. In Sophocles's version of the tragic face-off, written in 441 B.C., Antigone boldly performs burial purification, then admits her guilt of a capital crime. She rebukes Creon for violating laws of burial established by God. The confrontation between niece and uncle ends with Antigone's immurement in a cave, where she hangs herself with a linen noose. The additional deaths of Antigone's fiancé Haemon and the suicide of Creon's wife Eurydice disorients the king, leaving local citizens to obey ritual laws and prepare the corpses for burial.

The Trojan hero Aeneas managed to evade the required payment by carrying the golden bough of the sibyl Deiphobe, whom he sought at a cave near Cumae in Italy to direct him toward his father's spirit in Hades. According to Virgil's *Aeneid* (ca. 30 B.C.), once among the dead, Aeneas encounters Palinurus, the hapless helmsman who fell overboard on depature from the Trojan War as the surviving band of Trojans passed the island of Cythera. Aeneas assumed that he drowned in the Tyrrhenian Sea and washed ashore to lie unburied at Velia. On encountering him in Hades, Aeneas learns that the pilot swam to southern Italy, where Lucanians murdered him. At Aeneas's request, the sybil promises to locate the sailor's remains, pay the *obolus*, and send his soul on its final journey.

The ritual coin in the mouth or in the coffin permeated cultures outside the Greco-Roman world — the Hindus of India, Slavs, Tankinese, and Teutons. A Japanese version of the classic burial *obolus* became a ritual element of dressing the corpse. According to Buddhist custom, the dead went their way dressed in socks and straw sandals. Into a *dzudabukuro* (ritual pilgrim's bag), the priest placed prayer beads, a change of clothes, tobacco, comb, needles and pins, thread, a towel, and hair and nail parings of mourners along with *rokumonsen*, six coins that paid the ferryman's fee for bearing the spirit across the Sandzunogawa River. The custom declined from real money to paper coins stamped to look like actual specie, later replaced by one sheet picturing six coins.

See also **Greek coins; medieval coins.**

SOURCES: Allen, Larry. *Encyclopedia of Money*. New York: Checkmark Books, 2001. • Clain-Stefanelli, Elvira, and Vladimir Clain-Stefanelli. *The Beauty and Lore of Coins, Currency, and Medals*. Croton-on-Hudson, N.Y.: Riverwood Publishers, 1974. • Cribb, Joe. *Money*. Toronto: Stoddart, 1990. • *Dictionary of Roman Religion*. New York: Facts on File, Inc., 1996. • Graves, Robert. *The Greek Myths*. London: Penguin Books, 1955. • Hastings, James, ed. *Encyclopedia of Religion and Ethics*. New York: Charles Scribner's Sons, 1951. • Hopper, R. J. *The Early Greeks*. New York: Harper & Row, 1976. • Meshorer, Ya'akov. *Coins of the Ancient World*. Jerusalem: Jerusalem Publishing House, 1974. • Severy, Merle, ed. *Greece & Rome*. Washington, D.C.: *National Geographic Society*, 1977. • Snodgrass, Mary Ellen. *Voyages in Classical Mythology*. Santa Barbara, Calif.: ABC-Clio, 1994. • Sophocles. *Antigone*. New York: Longman, 1962. • Virgil. *The Aeneid*. New York: Mentor Classic, 1961.

Offa of Mercia

The first British king to circulate coins, Offa of Mercia set the style of minting and monetary art in Europe from Ireland to Poland. An ambitious man hoping to outclass the Frankish king Charlemagne, Offa established an Anglo-Saxon coinage at Canterbury featuring the royal name, "*Offa Rex*" ("King Offa"), surrounded by laurel leaves. England's most progressive monarch before the Norman Conquest, he united fractious groups and established an embassy to continental Europe, where he entered into trade agreements with Charlemagne and dispatched agents as far as the Islamic realm. Significant to Offa's fiscal responsibility was careful budgeting, a restraint that did not carry over to subsequent royal treasuries.

Offa, whom the Venerable Bede describes as the son of Sighere, was born around 730 and died on July 29, 796. At age 27, he succeeded his cousin Ethelbald to the throne. He wisely pledged his daughters to Ethelred of Northumbria and Boerhtric of Wessex, warded off attacks by the Welsh on the western border, and negotiated trade agreements with nearby powers. To support commerce beyond the borders of Mercia, in 785, he hired skilled portrait artists trained in classic traditions, who began minting quality silver pennies similar to Charlemagne's *deniers*. The Anglo-Saxon penny continued until the end of his reign and circulated in significant numbers throughout the region for five centuries.

Contributing to Offa's economic success were Babba, Eoba, and Udd, three mintmasters from Kent who superintended production. Demand for Offa's penny required the boost of staff to 21 moneyers, who struck thick blank discs and incised framed portrait heads, the name "Offa," and the artisan's name. The output of a total of 30 moneyers challenged the insubstantial Mercian *sceats* by turning 30 tons of silver into nearly 40 million sturdy coins of an artistic quality unknown in previous centuries. From trade with Arabs, he also struck a gold coin similar to the Caliph Al Mansur's *dinar*, which influenced the silver coinage of Ethelbert II, the East Anglian king. The coin bore in Arabic the pious mottoes: "There is no God but Allah who has no associate" and "Mohammed is the Apostle of Allah, who sent him with the doctrine and true faith to prevail over every religion."

Offa's popular portrait coinage, which pictured his uncrowned head in profile, set a new style in Anglo-Saxon silver pennies by also picturing his wife Cynethryth as the classically draped "*Regina M[erciorum]*" ("Mercian queen"), the first Englishwoman so honored. The presentation of a consort attests to the Christian stress on holy wedlock and the rights of legitimate royal offspring. Because Offa's familiar penny was roughly equal to a day's wages for a laborer, it became a synonym for "money." The coin was so influential that it served as the model for others made by Boguslav the Mighty of Poland and by moneyers in Denmark, Germany, Holland, Ireland, Norway, and Sweden.

In addition to establishing England's first money economy, in A.D. 788, Offa tapped into church power by convincing Pope Adrian I to establish a see at Lichfield. Offa supported monasticism as centers of faith and education by founding abbeys at Bath and St. Albans. To assure monetary ties with the Catholic church, he appears to have initiated Peter's pence, an annual stipend or tithe to the church, which survived as a traditional tax until Henry VIII abolished it in 1534 and created a separate Church of England.

In Kent in A.D. 796, Heaberht, Offa's client king in Kent, emulated the successfull Anglian penny by minting his own version. At the command of Offa, Heaberht produced a flatter, broader coin that influenced subsequent English pennies. Heabehrt's moneyers at the Canterbury mint initiated an amazing standardization and quality control nearly nine centuries before milled coinage simplified the process.

See also **Islamic money; penny; Peter's pence.**

SOURCES: Allen, Larry. *Encyclopedia of Money*. New York: Checkmark Books, 2001. • Bryant, Arthur. *The Medieval Foundation of England*. Garden City, N.Y.: Doubleday & Co., 1967. • Cannon, John, and Ralph Griffiths. *Oxford Illustrated History of the British Monarchy*. Oxford: Oxford University Press, 1988. • Cribb, Joe. *Money*. Toronto: Stoddart, 1990. • Cribb, Joe, Barrie Cook, and Ian Carradice. *The Coin Atlas*. London: Little, Brown and Co., 1999. • Davies, Glyn. *A History of Money from Ancient Times to the Present Day*. Cardiff: University of Wales Press, 1994. • Grierson, Philip. *Numismatics*. London: Oxford University Press, 1975. • Mackay, Angus, and David Ditchburn, eds. *Atlas of Medieval Europe*. London: Routledge, 1997. • Rowley, Trevor. *The Norman Heritage, 1066–1200*. London: Routledge & Kegan Paul, 1983. • Sinclair, David. *The Pound*. London: Century Books, 2000. • Snodgrass, Mary Ellen. *Who's Who in the Middle Ages*. Jefferson, N.C.: McFarland, 2001.

Oresme, Nicolas

A medieval giant among mathematicians, geometers, and scientists, economist Nicolas Oresme (also Nicole d'Oresme or Nicole Oresme) challenged schemes to debase coinage by asserting that precious metals in specie determine value. Born in Allemagne, France, around 1320, he completed training in liberal arts and theology before becoming a teacher and treasurer of the Collège de Navarre of the University of Paris. From canon to dean of Rouen Cathedral and archdean of Bayeux, he advanced to the post of confessor and ambassador for Charles V (or Charles the Wise), whom he knew in his youth. To summarize the evolution of period coinage, he compiled *Traité de la Première Invention des Monaies* (*Treatise on the Invention of Coins*) (ca. 1360), also available in Latin translation as *De Moneta* (*On Money*) or *De Re Monetaria* (*On Monetary Matters*).

It was Oresme who placed French minting and collections on a system that remained in use until the French Revolution in 1789. He insisted that currency belongs to the people and, like treasured icons, must remain pure and undefiled as a means of upholding the public trust. In his words, integrity in coinage was an element of *noblesse oblige*, the duty a monarch owed to subjects:

> I am of opinion that the main and final cause why the prince pretends to the power of al-

> tering the coinage is the profit or gain which he can get from it. Therefore, from the moment when the prince unjustly usurps this essentially unjust privilege, it is impossible that he can justly take profit from it [von Nothaus].

In addition to championing fair coinage, standardizing tax codes, distinguishing between astrology and scientific star lore, and writing about the earth, skies, motion, and divination, Oresme translated into French Aristotle's *Economics, Ethics, and Politics* (ca. 350 B.C.). In 1377, Oresme became bishop of Lisieux and died there on July 11, 1382. His encyclopedia of coinage was still an authoritative source in the 1600s.

See also **Gresham's law.**

SOURCES: Cooper, J. C., ed. *Dictionary of Christianity*. Chicago: Fitzroy Dearborn, 1996. • Crombie, A. C. *Medieval and Early Modern Science*. Cambridge, Mass.: Harvard University Press, 1967. • *Encyclopedia of Occultism and Parapsychology*, 5th ed. Farmington Hills, Mich.: Gale Group, 2001. • Galbraith, John Kenneth. *Money: Whence It Came, Where It Went*. Boston: Houghton Mifflin, 1975. • Hicks, Michael. *Who's Who in Late Medieval England*. London: Shepheard-Walwyn, 1991. • Kline, Morris. *Mathematical Thought from Ancient to ModernTimes*. New York: Oxford University Press, 1972. • Lacroix, Paul. *Science and Literature in the Middle Ages*. New York: Frederick Ungar, 1964. • *Notable Mathematicians*. Detroit: Gale Research, 1998. • Snodgrass, Mary Ellen. *Who's Who in the Middle Ages*. Jefferson, N.C.: McFarland, 2001. • von Nothaus, Bernard. "Pre-Constitutional Concept of Money." *Norfed Report*, August 2000.

Palemón

In November 2000, a Toronto salvor, Visa Gold Explorations, Incorporated, located 7,000 artifacts from the *Palemón*, a 100-foot Spanish brigantine from the 1800's. The ship, captained by José Antonio de Ageo, foundered at 3:30 A.M., on April 25, 1839. After eighteen months' exploration of the Caribbean off Cuba, with the aid of the Cuban government, the firm located a graveyard of 1,600 sinkings, including shipwrecks of colonial galleons from the 1600s.

Operating out of a Havana marina in conjunction with the Museum of Sub-Aquatic Archaeology, the crew worked off a small island from the port of La Isabela. They perused near-virgin territory cut off from American treasure hunters because of the U.S. embargo of Cuba after the failed Bay of Pigs invasion of 1961. Because Fidel Castro was a skin diver keen on recovering Spanish treasure, the Canadian firm found an eager supporter of their venture.

To the delight of the treasure-hunting world, Paul Frustaglio, Visa Gold's president, announced that the company's team of 14 divers located the *Palemón* with a magnetometer, a metal detector with a range of eight feet. Scattered over an area the size of a football field, the galleon had lain undisturbed since it hit a reef and sank off Cuba's northern coast on its way to the Caribbean from Le Havre, France. Finds, which are the largest to date for the area, include cash, jewels, diamonds, crystal, cannon, pistols, ballast stones, anchors, saddles, cutlery, ivory dominoes, and billiard balls. The items went on public display at the 18th Annual Havana International Fair 2000.

See also **shipwrecks.**

SOURCES: Cawthorne, Andrew. "Cuban Sea Treasures Surface." *Toronto Star*, November 30, 2000. • Nickerson, Colin. "Canadian Divers Agree to Share Their Undersea Finds with Cuba." *Boston Globe*, March 9, 2001. • "Visa Gold Announces Patrimony Evaluations of 'Palemon Artifacts' to Be Completed by August 8th 2001." *Business Wire*, July 24, 2001. • Wilson, Scott. "Castro Forms a New Alliance — With Treasure Hunters." *Washington Post*, December 27, 2000, p. A16.

pantograph

A pantograph is a precise instrument that duplicates a geometric shape to a modified scale, such as a map, an engineer's drawing, an architectural draft, or the sketch of one face of a coin reduced to the exact measurements of the minted version of the piece. Pantography facilitates die-sinking, the application of a cutter to a die block to produce the shape of a model in soft metal, plaster of paris, or wood. By tracing the contours of the original or of a template, the die-maker transmits to the cutter the surface details of the sunken die at a predetermined size and quality. The machine, called a transfer lathe, uses scrapers, files, and grinders to refine the shape.

First applied to die-sinking at the U.S. Mint in 1907, coin pantography derived from the sensitive transmission of intricate design by the Janvier lathe. To make the reduction, the user assembled bars joined with pins and traced the outline, depressions, and elevations of the original, which was attached to a rotating disc. The turning disc moved the bars in such a way as to make a three-dimensional copy to scale with a stationary stylus attached to the tracer arm.

According to Gilroy Roberts, chief engraver at the U.S. Mint in 1967 during the creation of dies for the Kennedy half-dollar, the reproduction of a sculpted bas-relief began with flattening of the curves to suit the demands of coins. The staff cast a mold out of plastilene and prepared a galvano, a brass model that replaced the original art to protect it from possible damage during die-making. The Janvier lathe then completed the die in the exact measurements of the finished coin.

See also **Charles Edward Barber; Christian Gobrecht; Benedetto Pistrucci.**

SOURCES: "Celebrating the American Medal." *American Numismatic Society Newsletter*, Fall 1997. • Clain-Stefanelli, Elvira, and Vladimir Clain-Stefanelli. *The Beauty and Lore of Coins, Currency, and Medals*. Croton-on-Hudson, N.Y.: Riverwood Publishers, 1974. • Lewis, Brenda Ralph. *Coins & Currency*. New York: Random House, 1993. • Reed, Mort. *Cowles Complete Encyclopedia of U.S. Coins*. New York: Cowles Book Company, 1969.

papal coins

In the Middle Ages, when governments, duchies, towns, and individuals struck their own specie, the Catholic Church added its tokens and money to a complex world monetary system. After Adrian I was crowned pope in A.D. 772, he requested permission from Charlemagne to commission the first papal coinage, which circulated in the surrounding Papal States. Before the creation of an official mint, Adrian's moneyer used the facilities on the Campidoglio in Rome.

As the tradition of papal money grew, popes hired the best in medalists and sculptors to create religious images and portraits on *ducats* and *sequins*. Common iconography ranged from the stylized fish, an image reflecting the Greek anagram of "*Iesous Christos, Theou Uios Soter*" ("Jesus Christ, son of God, Savior"), to the lion of St. Mark, keys of St. Peter, papal crown, and ship and anchor, emblems of Christianity and faith. Around 1450, medalist Matteo de Pasti of Verona pioneered the medal of Christ, which influenced subsequent amulet pieces made by Zurich-based sculptor Peter Flötner, who introduced Renaissance motifs to northern Europe a century later. Flötner created reversible images that resembled pious figures until turned upside down to present visages of demons and fools.

During the Renaissance, the popularity of *testoni* ("head coins") among egotistic self-made men found favor with popes who were no less eager to build their reputations. A splendid likeness of Sixtus IV, crowned in 1471, introduced the portrait coin along with the standard Latin legend proclaiming him *pontifex maximus* ("chief priest"). In the early 1500s, Pope Julius II commissioned architect Donato Bramante to erect a new *Zecca* (papal mint), which Florentine ecclesiastical architect Antonio da Sangallo il Giovane (the Younger), designer of the Farnese Palace, reshaped with an imposing façade. Julius further ennobled himself by commissioning a portrait silver *giulio*. The ornate coinage of the world's Catholic center so enraged reformer Martin Luther that, on December 10, 1520, he burned papal coins along with books, volumes of canon law, and reminders of papal extravagance and vanity on a symbolic bonfire at Worms.

Coinage kept pace with Milan and Florence with the popular chamber *ducat* and chamber *florin* In 1530, the *Zecca* introduced the *scudo d'oro in oro* ("gold shield on gold"), followed by the *carlina* and additional *giulii*. After the slaughter of Huguenots in Paris on St. Bartholomew's Day, 1572, Pope Gregory

XIII assigned the papal mint to strike a commemorative coin, a propaganda image picturing an angel clasping cross and sword over a huddled Protestant band in flight from retribution. The outpouring of sumptuous coinage from the Vatican upgraded European iconography standards for beauty and quality artisanship, as found in the full-face image of Clement VI with hand uplifted in papal benediction and the profile of Clement VIII in robe and stole in a ritual pose sculpted after 1592. For the outpouring of papal coins and medals during the High Renaissance, popes hired the best in designers, notably Bolognese artist Francesco Francia and the era's masterworker, Florentine goldsmith Benvenuto Cellini, author of *Trattato della Scultura* (*Treatise on Sculpture*) (1568) and a text on metalwork, *Trattato dell' Oreficeria* (Treatise on Goldsmithing) (1568). Aiding later mintmasters was the hydraulic coin press that the sculptor and papal architect Gianlorenzo Bernini of Naples invented for Pope Urban VIII in the mid-17th century.

Graceful monetary art of the period announced the accomplishments of individuals holding St. Peter's chair. The pope's designer, Gaspare Molo (or Gasparo Moli) of Como, created *scudi* bearing the papal silhouette. After Alexander VII re-established the *Zecca* at the rear of St. Peter's Basilica in 1665 and equipped it with balancing equipment engineered by Francesco Girardini, the artist's nephew, Gaspare Morone Molo, used the precise instrumentation to strike a detailed profile of the pope in full mitre and robe. On the reverse, Molo broadened the scope of the papacy with a grand procession that surrounds Alexander on his throne under the bronze *baldachino* (ceremonial canopy), the focal point of the chancel of St. Peter's. The second Molo also skimped on dies by restriking various surfaces with used images.

A less imaginative coiner, Clement X, who was crowned in 1670, introduced at the papal mint the Bavarian Hamerani clan of engravers, students of Gaspare Molo. Through 13 popes, family artisans, beginning with Alberto, created Vatican money. Another contributor to the late 17th-century papal coins was French engraver Ferdinand Saint-Urbain, who created a bas-relief for Pope Innocent XII in 1699 featuring the children of Israel gathering manna from heaven. In 1703, Clement XI's mintmaster, Ermenegildo Hamerani, pictured the pope's preservation of Roman architecture, including the restored Pantheon and a bridge. Ermenegildo also addressed the issue of greed with a *testone* picturing coins heaped on a table and the brief homily "*Imperat aut Servit*" ("It Either Rules or Serves"). In 1719, Ottone Hamerani struck a pictorial medal of the Princess Clementina guiding a two-horse chariot past the Roman coliseum. He inscribed a three-word motto, "*Fortunam Causamque Sequor*" ("I Follow Fortune and [Just] Cause").

In 1869, Ignazio Bianchi, engraver at the papal mint, attained a height of perspective art with a masterly medal. Picturing the sweep of St. Peter's Basilica in Rome, he incorporated the patterned marble floor, piers, and barrel vault. Sight lines lead the eye to the lofty canopy under which the pope conducts the ritual of Vatican ceremonies. The encircling legend explains in Latin that the view is of the sanctuary's interior "*in Honorem Beati Petr I*" ("Honoring the Blessed Peter I"). In bold script at the bottom of the image, Bianchi identified himself as artist and sculptor.

***See also* Benvenuto Cellini; euro; Leone Leoni; Gaspare Molo; paper money.**

SOURCES: Allen, Larry. *Encyclopedia of Money*. New York: Checkmark Books, 2001. • Chilvers, Ian. *The Concise Oxford Dictionary of Art and Artists*. Oxford: Oxford University Press, 1996. • Clain-Stefanelli, Elvira. "Donors and Donations: The Smithsonian's National Numismatic Collection." *Perspectives in Numismatics*, 1986. • Clain-Stefanelli, Elvira, and Vladimir Clain-Stefanelli. *The Beauty and Lore of Coins, Currency, and Medals*. Croton-on-Hudson, N.Y.: Riverwood Publishers, 1974. • Lewis, Brenda Ralph. *Coins & Currency*. New York: Random House, 1993. • *New Catholic Encyclopedia*. San Francisco: Catholic University of America, 1967. • Reinfeld, Fred. *Treasury of the World's Coins*. New York: Sterling Publishing, 1953. • Weatherford, Jack. *The History of Money: From Sandstone to Cyberspace*. Pittsburgh, Pa.: Three Rivers Press, 1998.

paper money

Paper currency replaced a series of other non-metallic moneys, including cotton cloth, leather, pelts, and silk. In 460 B.C., Chinese authorities authorized money in four forms — coins, gems, gold, and silk. Around A.D. 100, Ts'ai Lun reputedly turned mulberry bark into paper money. During the T'ang dynasty, paper money called *balisht* replaced coins in A.D. 806 under the Chinese Emperor Hien Tsung. Lacking copper for coins and eager to curtail highway robbery of merchants laden with cash, he issued paper notes by default and acknowledged delivery of goods to government warehouses and receiving centers. The paper bills were negotiable only within a single city or district. A second replacement of metal coins with paper currency occurred in A.D. 910. Within a half century, distribution of paper money became established state policy.

The system grew unwieldy around 1020, when the Chinese government had to pay huge quantities of cash to bribe northern insurgents and to buy imported goods. Exacerbating the deflation of paper currency were frivolous notes issued by 16 private banks. Although the government curtailed the issuance of notes from banks and perfumed bills in circulation to make them pleasing to users, the result among Chinese citizens was a loss of faith in paper currency and a return of fiscal conservatism and trust in coins alone.

In 1236, the Mongols imported the concept of paper notes, which they circulated as far east as the Danube River. The use of printed currency allowed them to standardize money. In 1260, under Kublai Khan, the empire generated a large issue of paper currency, a flurry of bills that caught the attention of Venetian traveler Marco Polo, who arrived in China with his brother Niccolò in 1275. During a 17-year sojourn, Marco took notes on China's "flying money," so named because a breeze could blow it off counters if it were not weighted down. He observed the methods of Peking money printers, who steeped and pounded the inner bark of the mulberry into pulp for paper and stamped the notes in red. With no basis for comparison from his experience in Venice, he valued paper bills in amounts equal to the coins of his own day — the Venetian *groat* and *bezant*.

On the return of Marco Polo in 1295 from his 20-year sojourn in the Orient, he brought back knowledge of paper currency, a new concept in Europe. Around 1299, a year after his capture by the Genoese at the battle of Curzola, he dictated to Rusticiano of Pisa, his cellmate, *The Travels of Marco Polo*, which circulated particulars of the famed traveler's firsthand study of Chinese governmental operations. In his estimation, the khan's mint in

The reverse of the Thai 100-*baht* note depicts the elephant, a symbol of majesty and military might.

Kanbalu produced near magic in printing paper money in varied sizes authenticated as though it were precious metal.

Marco Polo explained the concept of backing paper with gold and silver reserves. Assuring value were official red stamps and a death penalty to anyone counterfeiting imperial paper notes. The mintmaster accepted damaged and worn bills and replaced them with newly printed notes for a premium of three percent. The notes also bought bullion for the making of cups and other articles. Because the great khan paid his army in lightweight paper money, Marco Polo concluded that the Mongol leader was the world's best treasury manager.

In 1292, the Mongols spread the concept of printed notes southwest to Iran. On September 12, 1294, the Persian treasury experimented with paper money, the first experiment in block printing west of China. Citizens of Tabriz in eastern Azerbaijan were forced to comply on pain of death with the paper bills as legal tender. Within two months, the hamfisted circulation failed when the paper money system faltered, halting commerce at local markets. In time, the idea returned for consideration. To the Western world, Persian physician and statesman Rashid al-Din corroborated the memoirs of Marco Polo concerning the value of paper notes in a universal history, *Jami' at-tawarikh* (*Collector of Chronicles*) (ca. 1310). By 1331, the concept of paper money had passed to Annam, Burma, India, Japan, and Thailand.

While journeying through east Asia as ambassador for Muhammad ibn Tughluq, sultan of Delhi, mid–14th-century travel writer ibn Battuta of Tangiers, author of *Tuhfat al-Nuzzar fi Ghara'ib al-Amsar wa'Ajaib al'Asfar* (*On Curiosities of Cities and Wonders of Travel*) (1354), observed paper money for the first time in the hands of money changers. He commented, "If anyone goes to the bazaar with a silver *dirham* or *dinar*, no one will accept it from him until he changes it into *balisht*" (Bullis 2000, 31). The Chinese moneyers of the period produced the world's largest note, a paper poster measuring 9 × 13 inches, which pictured at center the 1,000 coins it replaced. Validating each paper strip was the sultan's seal. To assure the dominance of China's paper money, embassies required that foreign merchants surrender alien cash on entering the country and exchange it for Chinese paper bills. On departing the borders, visitors could reverse the process. Ibn Battuta noted that some merchants who distrusted paper money got around the law by melting their coins into ingots.

During this same period, paper money flourished in Europe under the Florentine de' Medici family of bankers and their German counterparts, the Fuggers. The receipts that bank clerks issued for deposits of money or valuables were legal tender exchanged like coin. Within a century, the stable system of bank receipts preceded the printing of banknotes.

By the 1600s, paper money had proven its worth. The Japanese added paper money to their monetary system and issued money from monarchs as well as extended clans and temples. Under the imprimatur of the king, Johann Palmstruck of the Swedish Stockholm Bank printed numbered paper *Kreditivsedlar* (credit notes) on watermarked stock in 1661 during a shortage of coins, thus making Sweden the first European nation to circulate paper money. To assure their validity, he required eight corroborating signatures on each note. The failure of Palmstruck's resources ended in great loss and his imprisonment.

The English, still hand-writing monetary transfers on paper in the 1660s, had yet to print banknotes. Late in the 17th century, the Bank of Scotland issued paper money, as did a Norwegian merchant, Jorgen Thor Mohlen. Printed paper money took on a professional look in the 1700s after John Law, a Scot living in France, set up an account trading the notes of King Louis XV for coins. Because of poor control of issuance, the notes lost value. In 1786, the Vatican *Banco di Santo Spirito di Roma* ("Bank of the Holy Spirit of Rome") issued paper notes from Pope Pius VI to papal states. The venture was so successful that Pope

Paul V was able to open the continent's first national bank in 1605.

In New World colonies, paper currency called into play the talents of financiers, politicians, and specie designers from states and territories. The first paper notes were promissory IOUs, legal agreements or contracts negotiated between two private parties. A folk version of bank notes appeared in Canada in 1685, after the French army paymaster quartered playing cards. On each piece, he wrote amounts owed to individual soldiers. The card pieces, called "bearer instruments," were legal tender only within the garrison.

At the Massachusetts Bay Colony, Sir William Phips gave his soldiers part of a loan guarantee plus a portion of loot taken during King William's War, fought in Acadia, Nova Scotia, in April 1690. When a summer siege against Quebec's fort failed, Phips returned to Boston. He faced 2,000 mutinous troops demanding pay in lieu of booty. On December 10, the Massachusetts General Court hastily issued £7,000 worth of paper currency, the Western world's first public paper money. The official explanation was somewhat convoluted: "Withal considering the present poverty and calamities of the country, and (through scarcity of money) the want of adequate measure of Commerce whereby they are disadvantaged in making present payment as desired" ["The First Printed Currency"].

The new paper money required a print staff. The first engraver of copperplates, Boston silversmith John Coney (also Conney or Conny), a student of silversmith Jeremiah Dummer, the colonial agent for Massachusetts and Connecticut, incorporated both the official seal and official signatures as proofs of validity. Authorized to oversee the treasury books and Dummer's use of plates for printing the bills were three colonial supervisors, John Foster, Captain Joseph Lynde, and Captain Samuel Ruggles. The system worked so well that, by 1692, colonial paper currency was acceptable legal tender.

The combined efforts of colonial treasuries produced a long history of paper moneys, ranging from simple, unadorned statements of amounts with authorized signatures to ornate bills artfully designed and supplied with Latin legends. South Carolina issued its first notes in 1703, followed six years later by Connecticut, New Jersey, and New York. In 1713, Virginia established tobacco notes, a paper money based on tobacco that planters stored in the commonwealth's warehouses. Tobacco served as a medium of exchange for paying taxes and for the salaries of the clergy and government offices.

An unusual opportunity for businesswoman Ann Smith Franklin, of Newport, Rhode Island, occurred in 1735. After her husband, colonial printer James Franklin, died of a lingering illness, the "Widow Franklin" and her two daughters operated the printshop in Washington Square. Under the pseudonym Poor Robin, she compiled and edited the *Rhode Island Almanack*. In addition to publishing the assembly's laws and the weekly *Rhode Island Gazette*, the three women turned out colonial documents, ballots, and paper money. In 1762, after her son and partner James Franklin died, she worked alone to publish the *Newport Mercury*.

Throughout the colonies, the printing of paper notes took on the trappings of modern paper money, including artful design and calligraphy, year of issuance, and legend:

year	*state*	*designer/printer*	*motto*
1710	Massachusetts	John Coney (or Conny)	none
1717	Louisiana	unknown	none
1724	Connecticut	Jeremiah Dummer	Sustinet Qui Transtulit [What Is Transplanted Survives]
1733	Connecticut	Nathaniel Mors	Qui Transtulit Sustinet [What Is Transplanted Survives]

year	*state*	*designer/printer*	*motto*
1733	Maryland	unknown	none
1737	Massachusetts	John Draper	none
1742	New Hampshire	Thomas Johnston	none
1746	Delaware	Thomas Leech	none
1748	North Carolina	unknown	none
1755	New York	James Parker	none
1756	New Jersey	James Parker	none
1756	Pennsylvania	Benjamin Franklin; David Hall	none
1759	New York	William Weyman	none
1760	Pennsylvania	Benjamin Franklin; David Hall	To Counterfeit Is Death
1761	North Carolina	James Davis	none
1766	Georgia	unknown	none
1769	Pennsylvania	David Hall; William Sellers	Mercy Justice
1770	Connecticut	Timothy Green	Qui Tran Sust [What Is Transplanted Survives]
1770	Maryland	Anne Catherine Green; William Green	'Tis Death to Counterfeit
1771	New York	Elisha Gallaudet	none
1771	North Carolina	unknown	Magna Charta [The Great Charter]
1772	Pennsylvania	James Smithers	Mercy Justice
1773	Pennsylvania	David Hall; William Sellers	To Counterfeit Is Death
1773	Virginia	Harry Ashby	none
1773	Virginia	Harry Ashby	To Counterfeit Is Death
1774	Maryland	unknown	Crescite et Multiplicamini [Increase and Multiply]
1775	Maryland	Frederick Green	Sub Clypeo [Under the Shield]
1775	Maryland	Thomas Sparrow	Pro Aris et Focis [For Altars and Hearths] Pax Triumphis Potior [Peace (Is) Preferable to Triumphs]
1775	Massachusetts	Paul Revere	Issued in defence of American Liberty Ense petit placidam sub Libertate Quietem [By the Sword One Seeks Tranquil Peace Under Liberty]
1775	Massachusetts	Samuel Willard	none
1775	New Hampshire	Daniel Fowle	none
1775	New York	J. C. Weigels	Acervus e Parvis Grandis [A Heap Enlarged by Small Things]
1775	Rhode Island	unknown	none
1775	South Carolina	James Oliphant	Auspicium Salutis [A Sign of Health] Et Deus Omnipotens [And God Almighty]

year	*state*	*designer/printer*	*motto*
			Fides Publica [Public Trust]
1775	Virginia	Harry Ashby	To Counterfeit Is Death
1776	Massachusetts	Nathaniel Hurd	Omne tulit punctum qui miscuit utile dulci [He Has Won Universal Approval Who Has Blended the Useful with the Sweet]
1776	New Jersey	Isaac Collins	To Counterfeit Is Death
1776	New York	J. C. Weigles	His Ornari aut Mori [To Be Adorned with These or Die]
1776	Rhode Island	John Carter	none
1776	South Carolina	unknown	Meliorem Lapsa Locavit [The Fallen Found Better] Animis Opisbusque Parati [Prepared in Spirit and Might] Deus Pugnavit et Dissipantur [God Fought and They Were Scattered] Turbat sed Extollit [It Roils but Lifts]
1776	South Carolina	J. C. Weigels; Nicholas Verien; Joachim Camerarius	Per Ardua Surgo [Through Hardships I Rise] Et Soli et Marti [For the Sun and Mars] Fata Viam Invenient [Fate Will Find a Way] The Actaeon Iram Prudentia Vincit [Actaeon Wisdom Conquers Anger] Multorum Spes [The Hope of Many] Aut Mors ut Victoria [Either Death or Victory]
1776	Virginia	unknown	Sic Semper Tyrannis [Thus Always to Tyrants]
1777	Pennsylvania	John Dunlap	Agriculture Commerce
1777	Pennsylvania	Joseph Ogden	Work and Be Rich
1777	South Carolina	unknown	Ubi Libertas ibi Patria [Where There Is Liberty, There Is a Homeland] Misera Servitus Omnis [All Slavery Is Wretched.]
1778	North Carolina	James Davis	Virtuous Councils the Cement of States
	Virginia	unknown	Sic Sempter Tyrannis [Thus Always to Tyrants]
1779	North Carolina	Hugh Walker	Peace on Honourable Terms
1779	South Carolina	Thomas Coram	Providentia Nostris Praesideat [Let Foresight Guard Us] Mutua Defensio Tutissima [Mutual Defense (Is) Safest] Spes Mentis Solatio [Hope Is the Mind's Comfort] Constantia Durissima Vincit [The Firmest Consistency Conquers] Armis Concurrite Campo [With Arms Run Together into Combat]

year	*state*	*designer/printer*	*motto*
1780	Massachusetts	Henry Dawkins	Depressa Resurgit [The Oppressed Rises Again]
1780	New Hampshire	Henry Dawkins	Aut Mors aut Vita decora [Either Death or an Honorable Life]
1780	North Carolina	James Davis	Mutare vel Timere Sperno [I Refuse to Change or to Fear]
1780	Rhode Island	Henry Dawkins	Tribulatio Ditat [Affliction Enriches] Exitus in Dubio [The Outcome Is in Doubt] Sustine vel Abstine [Persist or Refrain] Majora Minoribus Consonant [Great Things Harmonize in Small Things] Vi Concitatae [With Rapid Force]
1780	Virginia	Henry Dawkins	Si Recte Facies [If You Will Act Rightly]
1781	Vermont	Judah P. Spooner; Timothy Green III	Vermont Calls for Justice
1781	Virginia	John Dunlap	In Hoc Signo Vinces [In This Sign You Will Conquer]
1785	North Carolina	Thomas Davis	Justitiae [For Justice]
1785	Pennsylvania	Francis Bailey	Commerce and Agriculture
1786	Georgia	John E. Smith	Pro bono publico [For the Public Good]
1786	Rhode Island	Solomon Southwich; Henry Barber	In Te Domine Speramus [In Thee, Lord, We Hope]
1789	Pennsylvania	Benjamin Bache	none
1789	South Carolina	Abernethie	Abernethie Fecit [Abernethie Made It]
1790	New Jersey	S. Kollock	none
1799	Connecticut	Thomas Doolittle	none

To validate early notes and protect them from counterfeit, printers edged them with borders around the wording and encompassing a stub and serial number. When the issuer sliced the bill from the stub, the separation of a wavy or curved edging produced a cut called the "indent." The uniqueness of the cut assured that the user could line up the redeemed note with the stub. The system worked until around 1775, when excessive handling wore the notes beyond hope of matching edges.

England differed with colonists like Benjamin Franklin on the matter of fiat money. In 1751, a currency act restricted the issuance of fiduciary paper bills and halted their use for paying private debt in Connecticut, Massachusetts, New Hampshire, and Rhode Island. In 1764, a similar law curtailed issuance of paper money in the middle Atlantic and Southern states. A subsequent money-hobbling act in 1773 sanctioned government circulation of fiat money but limited its use to payment of taxes. These bills increased the mother country's stranglehold on the colonies, where raw materials and opportunity were manifold, but currency for trade and investment always departed colonial coffers much faster than it arrived. Without gold or silver to mine and stamp, settlers along the Atlantic seaboard continued to trade in commodities and Spanish dollars. What little coined specie importers gained from trade had to be returned to England for future purchases of goods.

By 1787, the U.S. Constitution ended makeshift printing of state and colonial moneys. Laws rejected anything but coins of intrinsic worth in payment of debt. During a widespread shortage of coins, institutions printed paper notes in place of small change ranging from one dollar to 12.5¢. Dubbed "shinplasters" by wags, these small bills carried little validity beyond the companies and institutions that issued them. Some financial institutions, including the State Bank of New Brunswick, issued three-dollar bills, fine banknotes printed in black ink with artistic designs and ornate calligraphy.

An unusual closed-circuit paper money scheme emerged from Guernsey, one of the Channel Islands, in 1815. To underwrite a public construction project, the treasury issued paper bills and redeemed them in payment for rent in the new buildings, which included parochial schools and Elizabeth College. Thus, the limited circulation from treasury to backer completed its loop with return of the notes to satisfy the demands of the lease. Within a decade, the notes had recycled back to the treasury for cancellation.

An ominous side of paper money figured in English romantic poet Percy Bysshe Shelley's *Oedipus Tyrannus; or, Swellfoot the Tyrant* (1820), a satirical drama reflecting on the public calumny of Caroline of Brunswick, estranged wife of King George IV, for adultery. Rapidly suppressed for its effrontery to the monarchy, the drama depicts the god Mammon as a cynic calling for the printing of paper money if the treasury fails. Shelley swells his assault on baseless paper money with references to rulers who rely on paper notes and words and to Banknotina, the daughter who inherits Mammon's estate of bonds and paper bills. The poet implies that the downfall of a monetary system based on worthless paper is a preface to revolution.

Likewise scathing, German poet Johann Wolfgang von Goethe's prophetic *Faust* (1832) foretold Europe's monetary conversion from coins to inconvertible paper notes. At the height of his country's intellectual golden age, Goethe studied astrology, mysticism, alchemy, and the occult, dwelling on the scientist's mania to turn base metal into gold. In Goethe's opinion, basing paper money on future earnings was a new form of alchemy. The human failing for greed colored his great tragic drama about the necromancer Faust. Goethe based the stage figure on the physician Johann Faustus of Württemberg, who lived between 1480 and 1540 and practiced medical alchemy. In Goethe's tragic version, the relentless striving for pleasure and riches pictures the evil side of technology.

Accompanied by the demon Mephistopheles, in Act I, Scene ii, Faust visits the throne room of the Holy Roman Emperor, who struggles to pay his troops and lenders. In despair at empty coffers, his treasurer complains:

> Who is there now who'll help his neighbour?
> Each has enough to help himself.
> Barred are the gates where gold is stored,
> And all men scratch and scrape and hoard,
> And empty all our coffers stay [Goethe].

To Mephistopheles's proposal of issuing paper notes, the emperor warns:

> If you're not lying, I will lend
> My own exalted hands, this work to end,
> But if you're lying, I'll send you to hell! [*ibid.*].

The illusion of quick solutions to monetary problems soon woos the emperor from wisdom to folly.

In Italy, the enaction of *Corso Forzoso* ("forced circulation"), on May 1, 1866, removed the nation from a bimetallic standard for a span of fifteen years. The result of the unification war of 1859 and the consolidation of individual state financial systems in 1861 was a gold shortage. To halt runs on the national bank, the treasury ceased to back paper *lire* with gold and forced citizens to build up their own currency and internal markets. When stability returned to the budget and debts declined, the government rescinded the decree.

Top: **Jamaica's five-dollar note bears the portrait of Norman Washington Manley, organizer of the People's Party and arranger of the island's orderly withdrawal from the United Kingdom. The island's international airport also bears his name.** ***Bottom:*** **The reverse of the Jamaican five-dollar note depicts the Old Parliament Building, which remained in service from 1872 to 1960.**

The United States developed paper money for multiple reasons — as a cultural and historical token as well as currency. The first paper money to feature the Great Seal of the United States, the one-dollar silver certificate, was issued in 1935. It also pictured Martha Washington, the only female portrait used on a U.S. currency note. In 1947, Congress extended the use of "In God We Trust" as a national motto from coins to paper bills.

Globally, the processing of banknotes involved nations in more complicated protection of value than did coinage. To secure the money system from counterfeiters, money designers began with detailed sketches and incised motifs with sharp tools on intaglio plates, which resemble a photographic negative in form and purpose. Before the plates went to the presses, banks chose fibrous paper, watermarks, colored security threads, implanted mica flakes, complicated inks, and numbering devices to keep count of the individual notes. To create fine colorations, each bill printed by lithography required breaking the image down into primary colors for individual contact with an inked plate. The cost of the system became onerous in view of the brief life span of a paper note.

In calculating intrinsic worth and inflation, people often overlook the artistic and historical value of paper money. More than other forms of popular culture, paper bills frequently display a height of design and style unlike other artistic media. Human achievements tend to dominate designs. In 1996, Thailand designed a commemorative note honoring King Bhumibol Adulyadej on the 50th year of his reign. Another current note featuring a bold ruler is Israel's bill picturing Prime Minister Golda Meir. Artistic birds and animals are also common, for example Denmark's sparrows, Estonia's swallows, Finland's gulls, Guatemala's quetzel, the New Guinea bird of paradise, South Africa's zebra, Sri Lanka's fish and lizards, Suriname's toucan, Sweden's geese, and Zambia's aardvark.

The following examples from Elvira Clain-Stefanelli and Vladimir Clain-Stefanelli's *The Beauty and Lore of Coins, Currency, and Medals* (1974) and from David Standish's *The Art of Money* (2000) demonstrate the achievement of money designers in extolling the best in art, architecture, landmarks, transportation, manufacture, government, history, biography, national aspirations, and flora and fauna.

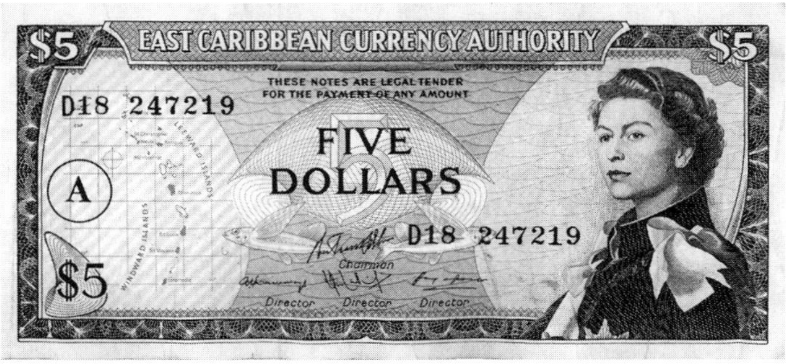

Top: **This East Caribbean five-dollar bill combines a map of the islands and the flying fish emblem with a romanticized pose of Elizabeth II of England in military dress.** ***Bottom:*** **The reverse of this five-dollar bill from the East Caribbean names nine member islands alongside a postcard image of an island bay.**

country	*money*	*date*	*illustration*
Afghanistan	500 *Afghanis*	1939	athletes on horseback
Australia	10 dollars	1988	aboriginal boy in body paint
	20 dollars	undated	Mary Reibey, who rose from convict and indentured servant to wealthy shipper
Bahamas	3 dollars	1960s	beach scene
Belgium	200 *franken*	undated	Adolphe Sax, inventor of the saxophone
Benin	500 *francs*	undated	agricultural worker on a primitive tractor
Bolivia	100,000 *pesos*	undated	workers plowing and harvesting grain with a combine
Bulgaria	50 *lev*	1950s	Balkan peasant woman gathering flowers in baskets
Cameroon	1,000 *francs*	undated	loggers moving wood down a river
Canada	5 dollars	1986	Sir Wilfred Laurier, the first French-Canadian prime minister
	10 dollars	1989	Sir John Macdonald, Canada's first prime minister
Cayman Islands	1 dollar	late 1990s	Queen Elizabeth II; pirate chest of gold coins
Central African Republic	10,000 *francs*	undated	native female and green fronds
China	10 *fen*	1950s	waterfall
	1 *yuan*	1960	agricultural workers
Cook Islands	3 dollars	undated	swimmer and shark
Costa Rica	5 *colónes*	1989	reproduction of an 1857 painting of marketers in San José

country	*money*	*date*	*illustration*
Cyprus	20 pounds	undated	reconstructionn of a vessel that sank in 300 B.C.
Ecuador	1,000 *sucre*	1986	Ruminhaui, an Inca official who rebelled against the insurgent Spanish
	5,000 *sucre*	undated	the Galapagos tortoise that Darwin observed in 1835
Egypt	10 pounds	undated	Ramses II and three pyramids
Eritrea	10 *nakfa*	1997	railway bridge spanning the Dogali River
Ethiopia	10 *birr*	undated	farmer plowing
Fiji	5 dollars	undated	circle of men netting fish
France	20 *francs*	undated	composer Claude Debussy
	50 *francs*	1997	essayist Antoine de Saint-Exupéry, author of *The Little Prince*
	100 *francs*	undated	impressionist Paul Cézanne
	100 *francs*	1984	Eugène Delacroix and Marianne, the French symbol of liberty
	200 *francs*	1996	architect Gustave Eiffel, designer of the Eiffel Tower and engineer of the Statue of Liberty
	500 *francs*	undated	physicists Marie and Pierre Curie
French Polynesia	10,000 *francs*	1985	female profiles, grass huts, fish
Gambia	10 *dalasis*	1991	Abuko earth satellite station
Ghana	1,000 *cedis*	1991	cacao harvesters
	2,500 *cedis*	1991	worker spraying cacao grove with pesticide
Guatemala	50 *centavos*	1992	Tecun Uman warrior; quetzal
Guinea	50 *francs*	1985	plowing with water buffalo
	100 *francs*	undated	workers harvesting bananas
Holland	50 *guilden*	undated	sunflower
Iceland	10 *króna*	undated	listeners enjoying the reading of a saga
Ireland	10 pounds	undated	James Joyce, author of *Ulysses*
Isle of Man	10 pence	undated	Viking ship
Italy	1000 *lire*	undated	educator Maria Montessori
Jamaica	2 dollars	1980	Paul Bogle, leader of the Morant Bay Rebellion of 1865, for which he was executed
	10 dollars	undated	George William Gordon, chief of the rebellion, also executed; earth-moving equipment
Kuwait	¼ *dinar*	undated	oil refinery
Laos	100 *kip*	1950s	native woman and Laotian temple
Luxembourg	20 *frang*	1943	harvesters and field of wheat
Macedonia	10 *dinar*	undated	mosaic of a peacock laid in the basilica at Stobi in the fifth century A.D.
Madagascar	500 *malgache*	undated	blue heron
Malaysia	2 dollars	1996	Kuala Lumpur telecommunications tower
Mexico	100 *pesos*	undated	Netzahualcóyotl, Aztec ruler
Mongolia	500 *tugrik*	undated	22 oxen moving a yurt (tent)
Morocco	5 *dirhams*	1966	workers harvesting wheat with modern combines
New Zealand	5 dollars	undated	Sir Edmund Hillary, scaler of Mount Everest in 1953
	10 dollars	undated	feminist Kate Sheppard
North Korea	10 *won*	1978	factory overlooking a harbor
Norway	100 *kroner*	undated	soprano Kirsten Flagstad
	500 *kroner*	undated	Nobelist Sigrid Undset, author of the medieval epic *Kristin Lavransdatter*

country	*money*	*date*	*illustration*
Peru	10 *sol*	1997	J. Abelardo Quiñones, an aviator killed in battle in 1941
Réunion	500 *francs*	1967	harvesters hauling sugar cane in ox carts
Romania	10 *leu*	1966	large factory
Rwanda	100 *francs*	undated	zebras in Akagera National Park
Saint Pierre et Miquelon	50 *francs*	1960	island woman and native hut
Senegal	500 *francs*	1959	ancient and modern methods of agriculture
South Africa	5 *rand*	undated	mining operation
Suriname	5 *guilden*	undated	logger operating a chainsaw
Swaziland	1 *lilangeni*	undated	row of female dancers honoring the Queen Mother
Sweden	20 *kronor*	undated	novelist Selma lagerlof, the first female writer to win the Nobel Prize
Switzerland	10 *francs*	undated	modern architect Charles Le Corbusier
Tunisia	10 *dinar*	1994	turbaned official watching a deserted street
Uganda	5 shillings	undated	female coffee picker
Vietnam	500 *dông*	undated	rice harvesters and tractor
Zaire	50,000 *francs*	1991	gorillas at Lake Kivu

See also **cloth money; confederate money; continental currency; counterfeiting; euro; Benjamin Franklin; gold certificates; greenbacks; John Law; leather money; James Barton Longacre; Hugh McCulloch; Jacob Perkins; plate money; Russian money; scrip; U.S. Bureau of Engraving and Printing; U.S. Mint.**

SOURCES: "Advanced Encryption Technology." *Business Wire*, September 28, 1998. • Allen, Larry. *Encyclopedia of Money*. New York: Checkmark Books, 2001. • Bullis, Douglas. "The Longest Hajj: The Journeys of Ibn Battuta." *Aramco World*, July/August 2000, 2–39. • "The Bureau of Engraving and Printing." http://www.bep.treas.gov/. • Clain-Stefanelli, Elvira. "Donors and Donations: The Smithsonian's National Numismatic Collection." *Perspectives in Numismatics*, 1986. • Cribb, Joe. *Money*. Toronto: Stoddart, 1990. • Davies, Glyn. *A History of Money from Ancient Times to the Present Day*. Cardiff: University of Wales Press, 1994. • Davis, Andrew McFarland. *Colonial Currency Reprints, 1682–1751*. Boston: The Prince Society, 1911. • Durant, Will. *Our Oriental Heritage*. New York: Simon and Schuster, 1942. • Erkelenz, Michael. "The Genre and Politics of Shelley's 'Swellfoot the Tyrant.'" *Review of English Studies*, November 1996. • "The First Printed Currency." http://www.coins.nd.edu/ColCurrency/CurrencyIntros/IntroEarliest.html. • Franklin, Benjamin. "A Modest Enquiry into the Nature and Necessity of a Paper Currency." http://www.people.virginia.edu/~rwm3n/webdoc6.html. • Franklin, Benjamin. "The Writings of Benjamin Franklin." http://www.historycarper.com/resources/twobf2/paper1.htm. • Goethe. *Faust*. http://www.levity.com/alchemy/faustidx.html. • Ibn Battuta. *The Travels of Ibn Battuta*. Cambridge: Cambridge University Press, 1971. • James, Peter, and Nick Thorpe. *Ancient Inventions*. New York: Ballantine, 1994. • Lewis, Brenda Ralph. *Coins & Currency*. New York: Random House, 1993. • Newman, Eric. *The Early Paper Money of America*. Iola, Wisc: Krause, 1997. • Opitz, Charles J. *Odd and Curious Money*. Ocala, Fla.: First Impressions, 1986. • Sinclair, David. *The Pound*. London: Century Books, 2000. • Snodgrass, Mary Ellen. *Encyclopedia of Fable*. Santa Barbara, Calif.: ABC-Clio, 1998. • Snodgrass, Mary Ellen. *Who's Who in the Middle Ages*. Jefferson, N.C.: McFarland, 2001. • Standish, David. *The Art of Money*. San Francisco: Chronicle Books, 2000. • Weatherford, Jack. *The History of Money: From Sandstone to Cyberspace*. Pittsburgh, Pa.: Three Rivers Press, 1998.

Paquet, Anthony C.

A major player at the U.S. Bureau of Engraving and Printing, Anthony C. Paquet produced coin art decorating much late 19th-century American money. He was best known in his own time for sculpting medals at the Philadelphia Mint, in particular, the 1860 Washington Cabinet Medal, the Crystal Palace Medal, and the gold and silver U.S. Coast Guard Lifesaving medals. He refined the seated Liberty figure on the dime and surfaced a one-cent coin in 1858, half-dollars in 1859 and 1877, a ten-dollar gold piece, and 20-dollar coins in 1859 and 1861.

The son of bronzesmith Toussaint François Paquet, the diemaker was born in Hamburg, Germany, in 1814. After emigrating to the United States at age 34, he opened a workshop in New York City and turned out the John C. Frémont campaign medal. By 1857, he was accepting engraving commissions from the U.S. mint and was a full-time employee that same year under chief engraver James Barton Longacre. One of Paquet's noteworthy details was the "wreath of cereals," a balanced spray of corn, wheat, and maple and oak leaves that adorned dimes until 1916. For seven years, he worked at his trade, earning acclaim for a bust of George Washington, which he drew from the 1785 sculpture of Jean-Antoine Houdon, and for an 1867 Chilean *peso*, for which he sculpted a condor and wreath. The image remained the standard for a quarter century, which saw the production of 20 million coins circulated throughout Latin America.

In 1877, Paquet joined William Barber and George T. Morgan as the producers of the most esthetically appealing half-dollar pieces. During the year, the U.S. Mint saw production of more patterns than any other year and the elevation of national coinage in popular and esthetic appeal. After Paquet's death in 1882, he left a collection of Civil War–era medals and coin dies, notably, the Congressional Medal of Honor that Abraham Lincoln commissioned on July 12, 1861.

***See also* James Barton Longacre.**

SOURCES: "Anthony C. Paquet." http://www.uspatterns.com/uspatterns/anthonycpaquet.html. • Bowers, Q. David. *Adventures with Rare Coins.* Los Angeles: Bowers & Ruddy Galleries, Inc., 1979. • Clain-Stefanelli, Elvira. "Donors and Donations: The Smithsonian's National Numismatic Collection." *Perspectives in Numismatics*, 1986. • Taxay, Don. *The U.S. Mint and Coinage.* New York: Arco Publishing, 1966.

Pasion of Acharnae

At Athens in 394 B.C., after establishing a bank and acquiring his freedom, the foreign-born slave Pasion of Acharnae rose to fame as the city's richest financier. He began as a servant of financiers Antisthenes and Archestratus and porter of coins. Under their mentorship, he advanced to clerk to the money changer. By keeping an ear to local and foreign trade, he could offer advice and judge the integrity of potential associates. His system of monetary transactions allowed people to bank in cash both in the city and at the port of Piraeus five miles south. He named among his clientele the military and political elite, who depended on his integrity and meticulous accounting.

Headquartered in Piraeus, Pasion joined the coterie of Green *trapezitai* (bankers), named for the tables on which they counted coins. According to historian Will Durant,

> Pasion's bank had many departments and employees, mostly slaves; it kept a complex set of books, in which every transaction was so carefully recorded that these accounts were usually accepted in court as indisputable evidence [Durant 1939, p. 464].

Pasion developed a guaranteed deposit system for valuables and an early form of city-to-city checking accounts. His depositors were happy to use his bank rather than risk robbery or loss from carrying large bags of coins on their persons or in saddlebags. From secured loans, he advanced to speculative insurance on shipping and chartering. Eventually, he acquired a furniture shop and an armament factory making swords and shields.

By paying his personal and professional debts to the city of Athens, Pasion acquired citizenship. As a free Athenian, he was able to expand into real estate. He kept the good will flowing by making a gift of 1,000 shields to the Athenian army and by outfitting five triremes for the Athenian navy. He settled the estate of one of his mentors and married the deceased man's widow. Pasion's second marriage, to fifteen-year-old Archippe, produced two free-born sons, Apollodorus and Pasicles.

Pasion survived a lawsuit against a prince of Bosporus, who claimed that Pasion spent money held in trust. In old age, he instructed Apollodorus on paying off debts. The father cringed at the thought of turning his office over to his sons — one too young and one too eager to gamble and carouse. Instead, Pasion gave the bank to Phormio, his manager, a former slave Pasion had bought, groomed for banking, and manumitted. To keep the assets in the family, he stated in his will that Phormio should marry his widow. In time, Phormio enriched himself just as his former master had done.

SOURCES: Casson, Lionel. *The Ancient Mariners.* Princeton, N.J.: Princeton University Press, 1991. • Davies, Glyn. *A History of Money from Ancient Times to the Present Day.* Cardiff: University of Wales Press, 1994. • Durant, Will. *The Life of Greece.* New York: Simon and Schuster, 1939. • *Handbook to Life in Ancient Greece.* New York: Facts on File, Inc., 1997. • Reden, Sita von. "The Piraeus — A World Apart." *Greece & Rome,* April 1995, pp. 24–39.

Patching hoard

Increasing the knowledge of Roman mintage and circulation was the Patching hoard, a trove of 47 gold and silver coins produced from A.D. 333 to 470. Discovered in April 1997 west of Brighton on England's south shore, the complete stash was excavated by John Manley and Richard Jones of the Sussex Archaeological Society. Dating from at least 60 years after Roman forces left England in A.D. 410, the money was a valuable collection of coins, bullion, and rings.

When the imperial mint at Londinium closed in A.D. 325, mints in Gaul served Britannia's needs. When those closed, Romans in Britain relied on coinage from Italy and the East. Therefore, most of the coins in the Patching hoard bore stamps of the Ravenna and Treveri mints; one-third were Visigothic moneys issued between 430 and 470 at Ravenna under the emperors Valentinian III, Majorian, and Libius Severus. Much of the trove, derived from the years A.D. 367 to 455, consisted of the latest Roman money found in Britain and derived from trade and soldiers' pay.

Historians surmise that the valuables were buried after 475, the beginning of the Dark Ages. Commerce and travel still flourished under the Romano-British administration, but the regular flow of money from Rome ceased. The clipping of 13 of the coins illustrates the shortage of small cash for change. The high quality of the Visigothic coins suggests that they were new when the owner added them to the collection.

The loss of Roman garrisons, the invasion of Picts, and the summoning of Teutonic merecenaries may have exacerbated local strife, forcing locals to hide their valuables. An alternative interpretation suggests that a Teuton may have captured the goods and buried them for safekeeping. The *Anglo-Saxon Chronicle* notes that, in 477, Aelle and his sons Cissa, Cymen, and Wlencing landed at Cymenesora ("Cymen's Shore"), Britain, in three ships and slew Welshmen at a wooded area some 25 miles west of the location of the cache. Continued warfare in 485 shows Aelle still battling the Welsh in Kent, completing the extermination of Britons in 491.

SOURCES: "Archaeological Resource Guide for Europe." http://odur.let.rug.nl/arge/General/oldlinks.html. • Grierson, Philip. *Numismatics.* London: Oxford University Press, 1975. • "The Patching Hoard." http://www-wrds.uwyo.edu/coinnet/hoards/Britain/Patching/release.html. • Snyder, Christopher. "The Age of Arthur: Some Historical and Archaeological Background." *Heroic Age,* Spring/Summer 1999.

Paterson, William

Scottish financier and investor William Paterson offered the English treasury enough cash to set up the Bank of England. Born around 1658 at Trailflat, Dumfriesshire, he was the son of Bertha and John Paterson, tenants on Skipmyre farm. He left rural life to travel to England, America, the West Indies, and Holland. At age 23, he joined the Merchant Taylors Company and invested in the Hampstead Water Works.

In 1694, Paterson advanced the concept of a national bank for England, a method of easing the financial shortfall of William and Mary, who were engaged in a lengthy war with the French holdings of Louis XIV in Holland. He loaned the government £1,200,000 and became one of its original bank directors. For the bank's governor and company, subscribers formed a corporation based on the concept of a "Fund of Perpetual Interest," a permanent national debt. Staffing required 17 tellers and two janizaries. Paterson, who turned his attention to New World ventures, resigned as a bank director after a year's service, primarily because he quarreled with other bank backers over the Orphans' Fund, a London corporation administering the inheritance of parentless children. On March 19, 1695, he sold his bank stock.

Paterson tarnished his reputation with involvement in the Darien scheme to establish an entrepot on the Isthmus of Darien, a pre–Panama Canal trading shortcut. The Scottish trading colony at New Edinburgh, Panama, proposed in 1693, took the name Company of Scotland Trading to Africa. The colony began with five ships — the *Caledonia*, *Dolphin*, *Endeavour*, *St Andrew*, and *Unicorn*— which set out from Leith, Scotland, on July 12, 1698. Under sealed orders, they did not learn their destination until they opened the envelope at Madeira. After three months at sea, they arrived at Panama and staked out the territory of Caledon on November 3.

The venture set up an open harbor welcoming cargo vessels from the Atlantic and Pacific. Officials portaged freight over the mosquito-infested isthmus, thus ending the dangerous sea-to-sea journey around Cape Horn. Rather than the huge profits Paterson envisioned, the risk from hardships cost him his wife, Hannah Kemp, and their son, who died of hunger, fever, and dysentery. His countrymen, who pledged £400,000, half of Scotland's capital, lost their investment when squabbles reduced the colony's efficiency. English competitors scuttled the project to protect the interests of the East India Company.

Poor planning and naivete destroyed Paterson's dream. He didn't take into account Spanish settlements or the English refusal to offer help. Although a ship left Scotland with needed medicines and supplies, it never arrived. When the colony broke up in November, Paterson was too weak and sick to persuade settlers to try harder. The colonists signed over their territory and Caledonia Bay to Spain. The total loss amounted to half the initial capital and 2,000 lives. From the nation's consequent monetary turmoil grew the Royal Bank of Scotland, chartered on May 31, 1727.

Paterson, who died in January 1719, reclaimed some of his integrity in 1707 by setting up financial backing for the union of England and Scotland. Encouraging the merger were the bitter Scottish memories of New Edinburgh's failure and the lack of support from established English colonies. In 1994, at the tercentenary of the Bank of England, the Royal Mint struck a £2 coin bearing Paterson's motto, "*Sic Vos Non Vobis*" ("Thus You [Work] Not for Yourself").

SOURCES: Davies, Glyn. *A History of Money from Ancient Times to the Present Day*. Cardiff: University of Wales Press, 1994. • Magnusson, Magnus. *Cambridge Biographical Dictionary*. Cambridge: University of Cambridge, 1990. • "William Paterson." *Significant Scots*. http://www.electricscotland.com/history/other/paterson.htm.

patio process

The patio process refined raw copper, gold, and silver ore, which contained too many impurities for coinage. Before ores could be shaped, they had to be cleansed. The prevailing method of removing usable metal from raw ore was the labor-intensive patio process, a late medieval method of chloride leaching. It was first recorded in 1540 in an Italian publication, the *De la Pyrotechnia* (*On Working with Fire*), a posthumous treatise on gunpowder, fireworks, smelting and foundries, and the use of furnaces to refine metals for the making of coins, by Siennese metallurgist and arms maker Vannucio Beringuccio (or Vannoccio Biringuccio). Introduced at Pachuca, Mexico, in 1554 by a German engineer called Lomann and by Spanish trader Bartolomé de Medina, the method applied mercury amalgamation as a means of purifying ores of precious metals. Mercury deposits discovered at Huancavelica, Peru, in 1563, increased the production schedule, but exposed conscript Indian workers to hazardous metal poisoning.

The process required the grinding of even low-grade ore in an arrastra, a circular bed centered with a shaft that held a heavy iron wheel pulled around the edge by a mule or horse. Workers and dray animals continued pulverizing the ore on stone patios, where they reduced it to a watered slurry. To complete the reduction of particles, they spread it thin and sprinkled on plain and ferric ion salt, copper sulfate, and mercury, called "quicksilver." Complete powdering required treading for days or weeks until the wet ore and water formed a paste. After a rinse, pressure and heat evaporated the mercury, thus producing pure metal for coinage. The heating of the stone grinding floor with subterranean flues developed the patio method into the Buytron process at Potosí, Bolivia, in 1590.

The damage to human health and the environment from the patio process was considerable. After a silver strike at Virginia City in the late 1850s, the Washoe pan process replaced the patio method. Silver workers worked at iron tanks rather than patios, replaced the arrastra with a stamp mill, and crushed ore with iron mallets instead of horses. To speed the refining process from weeks to a few hours, they steam-heated the lime, salt, copper sulfate, and mercury mixture. Between 1860 and 1890, Nevada's mercury-based extraction released 7,500 tons of mercury, dumps, and tailings into the Carson River Basin. By the early 1900s, mills replaced the patio process with a more efficient cyanidation method used in refining copper, gold, and silver ore.

See also **shipwrecks; Spanish coins.**

SOURCES: Allen, Larry. *Encyclopedia of Money*. New York: Checkmark Books, 2001. • Bowers, Q. David. *Adventures with Rare Coins*. Los Angeles: Bowers & Ruddy Galleries, Inc., 1979. • Crozier, Ronald. "A History of the Chloride Leach Process." *Bulletin of the Canadian Institute of Mining and Metallurgy*, July 1993. • Tingley, J. V. "Salt and Silver." *Nevada Geology*, Summer 1990. • "Virginia City in Ruins." *Territorial Enterprise*, October 27, 1875.

Patterson, Robert Maskell

A director of the U.S. Mint from 1835 to 1851, Robert Maskell Patterson commissioned the operation's first steam-powered coining press, which went into production on March 23, 1836. After observing steam milling machines in France and Germany, he looked for ways of replacing the awkward screw press with new technology, which would reduce labor costs by half. For a model, he asked engineer Franklin Peale to create a workable mockup of a machine that would reduce staff from three men per press to one.

In his second year as director, Patterson imported a belt-driven lever press from France that churned out 100 coins per minute with only one operator. In triumph, he reported to President Andrew Jackson on the savings to taxpayers:

> On the 23rd of March last [1836], the first steam coinage in America was executed at this Mint; and the performance of the press, in which the power of the lever is substituted for that of the screw, has answered all our expectations. Since that time, all the copper coins have been struck by this press, and it has been lately used with success for coining half dollars. The workmen are now engaged in making other steam presses; and as these are completed, the coining by human labor [will] be abandoned, and the work that can be executed in ... the Mint will be greatly increased ["Powered Coining Press"].

The link-operated mechanism remained in service until 1875.

During shaky times for paper currency, Jackson and Patterson agreed on the value of metal coins. To replace the dollar coin, which dated to 1804, Patterson set his sights on a new silver dollar. Basing his design on England's seated Britannia, he chose a seated Lady Liberty and hired portraitist Thomas Sully to submit sketches, which assistant engraver Christian Gobrecht adapted into bas-relief. Over the next 55 years, the resulting figure adorned coins valued at five, ten, 20, 25, and 50 cents, and one dollar.

See also **Charles Cushing Wright.**

SOURCES: Alexander, David T., Thomas K. DeLorey, and P. Bradley Reed. *Coin World Com-*

prehensive Catalog & Encyclopedia of United States Coins. New York: World Almanac-Pharos Books, 1990. • Bowers, Q. David. *The History of United States Coinage as Illustrated by the Garrett Collection.* Wolfeboro, N. H.: Bowers & Merena Galleries, 1979. • Breen, Walter. *Walter Breen's Complete Encyclopedia of U.S. and Colonial Coins.* New York: F. C. I. Press/Doubleday, 1988. • "Powered Coining Press." *Inquiry Attic,* February 2000. • "Pressing—Full Steam Ahead." *Franklin Institute,* http://fi.edu/qa00/attic2/index.html. • Taxay, Don. *The U.S. Mint and Coinage.* New York: Arco Publishing, 1966. • Vermeule, Cornelius. *Numismatic Art in America.* Cambridge, Mass.: Harvard University Press, 1971. • White, Weimar W. *The Liberty Seated Dollar 1840–1873.* New York: Sanford J. Durst, 1985.

Peace dollar

An outgrowth of post–World War I emotion, the Peace dollar was the idea of Editor Frank G. Duffield in his November 1918 column in *The Numismatist.* He had intended a pre-armistice push for the coin at the American Numismatic Association (ANA) convention in Philadelphia, which was cancelled because of the influenza outbreak that eventually killed 100,000 U.S. citizens. Two years later, Farran Zerbe, founder of the Pacific Coast Numismatic Society, took up Duffield's crusade in a letter that ANA president Moritz Wormser read aloud at the convention in Chicago, held at the Art Institute. The text declared that democracy had won the hearts of those engaged in a war against Germany and Austria.

The specific name "Peace dollar" was the proposal of Congressman Albert H. Vestal, chairman of the House Committee on Coinage, Weights, and Measures, on May 9, 1921. The coin commemorated the end of hostilities between the United States and Germany and Austria as stated in the Berlin peace treaty ratified the following November. Conditions required German troop withdrawal in Belgium, France, Alsace-Lorraine, and the west bank of the Rhine.

The return of peace to Europe concluded the world's first taste of a mechanized trench warfare, where casualties reached 8,500,000 soldiers lost to wounds, poison gas, and disease, especially influenza. The greatest number died on July 1, 1916, at the battle of the Somme. At the battle of Verdun, carnage wrought by cannon shells left the unidentifiable remains of 150,000. The machine gun increased the number of men losing lower limbs and surviving as single and double amputees. Of the total 13,000,000 dead, most succumbed to artillery, disease, exposure, and starvation.

The artistic Peace coin, comprised of 90 percent silver and ten percent copper, replaced the Morgan dollar, which was struck in 1878. The *art deco* design, chosen in December 1921 from submissions by Robert Aitkin, Chester Beach, Anthony De Francisci (or da Francisci), John Flanagan, Henry Hering, Hermon A. MacNeil, Robert Tait McKenzie, George T. Morgan, and Adolph A . Weinman to the Fine Arts Commission of the U.S. Mint, was the sketch of Teresa de Francisci, the wife of Italian-born coin modeler de Francisci. He pictured a bust of a young, vulnerable Lady Liberty arrayed in light like the Statue of Liberty. The accompanying legend, "In God We Trust," was spelled with the classical V in place of the U, thus breaking the designer's custom of modern spelling.

Repeating the motif of a vigorous burst of light, the reverse depicted the dawn of peace with an eagle clasping an olive branch on a mountain peak, the design of George T. Morgan. Although the coin earned the approval of President Warren G. Harding, Anthony de Francisci and Farran Zerbe were among many who expressed disappointment in the imagery and the interpretation of the allegory, particularly the direction of the timid rays shining on the eagle. Da Francisci preferred his own proposal for a reverse showing an eagle with a broken sword clutched in its talons. Because the artist depicted Liberty with a loose, sensual mouth, some critics declared her a mouth-breather. The *Wall Street Journal* called her a flapper, a slang term for the high-living, amoral women of the roaring '20s.

The high relief and shiny surface of the Peace dollar, a reflection of an infectious optimism, paralleled the era's enthusiasm for industry, particularly Henry Ford's automobiles. To increase the life span of the coin and its dies, George T. Morgan, chief engraver of the mint, reduced the relief in 1922 and flattened the concave background to facilitate mass production and storage. To introduce the public to the coin, in summer 1924, the Treasury Department paid 5,000 employees in Peace dollars. The distribution set an example for other government paymasters. The coin gradually gained approval and found champions among immigrant populations on the Atlantic seaboard and in the Western states of Colorado, Montana, and Nevada.

Altogether, at Denver, Philadelphia, and San Francisco in four production years —1921, 1928, 1934, 1935 — the mint issued over 190 million of the silver dollars. The coin fell victim to a silver meltdown during World War II. It returned to production in 1964, but was immediately shelved because the rise in silver prices encouraged coin holders to melt it for the resale value. It was again produced in 1971, when the U.S. Mint replaced the image of Liberty with a portrait of President Dwight D. Eisenhower, hero of World War II and commander of the European theater.

See also **Anthony de Francisci; Redfield hoard.**

SOURCES: Cribb, Joe. *Money*. Toronto: Stoddart, 1990. • Howe, Marvine. "Teresa Da Francisci, Miss Liberty Model for Coin, Dies at 92." *New York Times*, October 21, 1990, p. 38. • Law, Steven. "Sculptors of Cape Ann." *American Art Review*, October 1997. • Pollak, Henry. *Coinage & Conflict*. Clifton, N.J.: Coin & Currency Institute, 2001. • Rochette, Ed. "A Flip Over a Flapper." *Hobbies*, May 1985, pp. 88–89. • *Who Was Who in America*. Chicago: Marquis Who's Who, Inc., 1968.

penny

The Roman occupation of Britain introduced residents to the convenience of coins. Anglo-Saxon traders not only kept the concept of the silver penny, but also retained the Roman abbreviation of "d" for *denarius*, a basic Roman monetary denomination. When the Romans decamped in A.D. 411, the tribes who returned to control of their land resumed trade and barter and struck few coins, except for the rare issue of imitations of the conqueror's money.

A term in use from Anglo-Saxon times, the *penig* (penny) dates to Penda, who ruled west Mercia from A.D. 632 to 654. Renowned as a warrior king who invaded East Anglia, he appointed Pada of Kent as moneyer. Pada incised Anglo-Saxon pennies with runes, which contributed to the mystical history of the penny and its origins. One theory claims that the term "penny" came from the Old English *pennig* and derives from Penda's name. Another links the coin to "pan," the containers in which coiners poured molten copper into disc shapes. The world's longest circulating specie, the denomination remained in use for over 600 years in England as the only royal coin, until 1280.

Between A.D. 688 and 726, Ine, king of the West Saxons, or Wessex, codified laws that structured English society. Bound with the laws of Alfred the Great, these statutes established court proceedings along with specified crimes and penalties. Among the details of his laws was the first mention of *sceattas*, lightweight Anglo-Saxon coins that Ine commissioned in A.D. 694. He called them "pennies," a term that may have meant "bond."

The eighth century introduced more coins to England, notably the silver *deniers* that the Frankish King Pepin the Short, founder of the Carolingian dynasty, commissioned in A.D. 755, and similar English pennies initiated by the Anglo-Saxon king Offa of Mercia. The resilient silver coin remained standard legal tender into the late Middle Ages. The esthetic appeal of Anglo-Saxon coinage influenced Viking coin designers, notably that of Raienalt, the Norse monarch at York. His silver penny, struck around A.D. 920, pictures a bearded profile, and on the reverse, a bow with a fletched arrow nocked and ready to shoot. The obvious militant motif suggests the tenor of his rule to all who did business in the coin of York.

After A.D. 852, Burgred, king of Mercia, issued a silver penny that captured the spirit of a time known as the Dark Ages. His coiner's artless workmanship paired a stylized portrait bust with a reverse completely filled with the moneyer's name. Simple, yet functional, the coin characterized the decline of the arts among a people who devalued beauty and cultural appeal in favor of pragmatism at a time when the ouster of insurgent Danes from Nottingham dominated their lives.

King Edgar, a beloved peacemaker who came to the throne in A.D. 955 at age 14, established a uniform die for the English penny and called in old coins for restriking with the new motif. In A.D. 978, Edgar emulated Roman style coins by having his portrait bust placed on pennies. The inclusion of a cross on the reverse eased their acceptance by peasants, who were dubious about new coinage, but open to Christian symbols. As a result of his careful plan, the penny made itself welcome over largely Christian northwestern Europe.

In the latter quarter of the tenth century, coins began replacing the more cumbrous payment in kind. The toll chart for the Billingsgate port on the Thames River stated:

> If a small ship arrives at Billingsgate it will give one *obole* as thelony [custom]; if a larger ship, and if it has a sail, one *denarius*. If it is a long ship, or a barge, and if it stays there, one *denarius* as thelony. From a ship full of timber, one log as thelony. A freight ship gives thelony on three days a week, namely, Sunday, Tuesday, and Thursday. If any one comes to the bridge with a boat full of fish, he will give one *obole* as thelony in order to sell the fish; from a larger ship he will pay one *denarius* ["List of Tolls"].

The intrusion of Scandinavians into England brought new coins, but also substantiated the dominance of the silver penny.

Under the Danelaw, the settling of northern, central, and eastern England colonized by invading Danish forces in the late 800s, the *penge* ("penny") became the prevailing monetary unit to both Anglo-Saxons and Danes. The coin was the standard for heavy court fines for breaking the peace and for dunning criminals for felonies. It also paid tribute to the Danish occupation force. Increased demand required that 75 mints work constantly to issue around 40 million coins just to keep the Viking wolves from devouring the English sheep. The style spread to Ireland and Holland, where the Dutch penny was called the *esterlin anglais*. German states produced the Wendish and Otto-Adelheid pennies, minted from rich veins of silver from the Harz Mountains and incised with coarsely designed images.

In Sweden, the penny proved a workable solution to the need for native coinage. One coin, the eight-penny *ortug*, denoted the amount of business a slave was able to conduct on his own behalf. Magnus I the Great gained popular support by reducing taxes, bolstering commerce, codifying laws, and improving governmental administration. One of his innovations was a single-face silver penny. He stamped one with M for Magnus. Later, Swedish mintmasters produced copies of Islamic coins and English pennies. In 1625, the productivity of Swedish copper mines, Europe's largest, established copper coins as the national standard. Because of the weight of copper pennies, the Swedish *Riksbank* (state bank) began issuing paper notes.

The Danes and Norwegians copied English moneys during the 11th-century rule of the Danish king Canute I, who came to power in 1016, and of his brother-in-law, Olaf Kyrre of Norway, one of the nation's last Viking kings, who replaced his brother Magnus in 1069. Because Olaf was gracious to his people, disbursals of money figure in the conclusion to his saga *Heimskringla* (ca. 1225):

> The man-at-arms a golden ring
> Boasts as the present of his king;
> At the king's table sits the guest,
> By the king's bounty richly drest.
> King Olaf, Norway's royal son,
> Who from the English glory won,
> Pours out with ready-giving hand
> His wealth on children of the land [Sturluson].

As religious conversion preceded coinage, most pennies pictured churches and Christian emblems. One unusual coinage, the *Satansmuenze* ("Satan's pieces") of the early 1100s, earned their nickname because Duke Vladislaw I of Bohemia pictured the demon during a time when superstitions about hellish beings circulated among the peasants.

To foil counterfeiters, early in the 11th century under Ethelred II, mintmasters extended the cross to the coin's edge to prevent clipping or filing bits of metal. This clever deterrent survived to the seventeenth century in the doomed reign of Charles I, when the royal mint incised the first beaded and milled edging. The copper lost face in 1751 when the chief assayer of the London mint, Joseph Harris, ceased to classify coins stamped from copper as money. He labeled them tokens, useful only for making small change.

The era of Central European history impacted by the Hohenstaufen dynasty, from 1138 to 1254, wrought great changes in medieval coinage. In Austria, Bohemia, Germany, Hungary, and Poland, the newly introduced *Hohlpfennig* ("hollow penny") or bracteate coin was larger in diameter, but thinner than early medieval moneys. The widening of the coin enable artists to increase depictions of the family crests, scenarios, and architecture; for example, a multi-towered Brunswick castle or the Duke of Saxony's lion monument. Another coin variety of Bavaria, Franconia, Hesse, and Lower Saxony, called *Dunnpfennige* ("thin pennies"), revealed detailed surface imagery that, like the negative of a photograph, penetrated to the back in incuse or intaglio. Imaginative and artistic, the pennies pictured hunting scenes and fantastic animals that ranged from lions to centaurs and dragons.

German pennies, the currency of the peasantry, spawned their share of folk humor. After 1670, the two-*pfennig* piece minted for three decades at Brandenburg earned the name *Hahnekaemme* ("cockscomb") for the ruffed palm tree on the back. Similarly, the hollow pennies minted by the See of Halberstadt acquired the nickname *Sargnaegel* ("coffin nails") because the likeness of St. Stephen, the first Christian martyr, pictures his head like a corpse's skull and his torso in the shape of a coffin. In 1701, the six-*pfennig* piece of Frederick William I the Strong of Saxony lost value because his mint alloyed the silver with copper. The unease of the peasantry resulted in the nickname *Seufzer* ("sigh") for a coin that caused them to despair over the era's financial troubles. A *pfennig* from Bayreuth minted mostly from copper in 1772 earned the name *Wanzen* ("bedbugs") because of the coppery glow.

The English first struck copper pennies in 1613. Despite prejudice against copper as the metal of debased specie, the pragmatic use of copper for one-cent pieces suited the needs of commerce at weekly markets, country fairs, inns, and taverns. A reference to small change in nursery rhyme appears in "Simple Simon," the narrative of a transaction with a pie-seller collected in Cluer Dicey and Richard Marshall's chapbook of 1764 and reprised in *Nancy Cock's* (or Cook's) *Pretty Song Book for All Little Misses and Masters*, published in London by John Marshall around 1780. The four-verse jingle, which bounces along in alternating tetrameter/trimeter, inspired literary analyst Katherine Elwes Thomas to connect the simple scenario with a royal contretemps. Simon, the English simpleton under James I, England's first Scottish monarch, lives at "the fair," the rich pickings of England. The wares that the venal king sells are titles and honors, for which he demands "your penny," i. e., cash. Simon, who eats no pie and catches no whale, finds no plums on the thistle, the national symbol of Scotland. Instead, the stereotyped witless Englishman gets only a pricked finger for his trouble.

In 1797, England shifted all penny production from silver to copper. The first were the work of Matthew Boulton, partner of James Watt, inventor of the steam engine. The duo pressed out pennies and tuppences on powerful machinery at their Soho factory in Birmingham. These uniform coins earned the name "cartwheel" pennies, and featured the allegorical figure of Britannia. In 1860, the metal shifted again to bronze, but pennies were still known as "coppers."

Perhaps because of its humble spot at the lower end of the monetary scale, the penny permeates history. In 1882, Michael Marks, a Polish-Russian refugee from Bialystock, entered trade in Leeds, England, with a tray of clothing items strapped to his neck. Two years later, he purchased a trestle table with a loan of £5, stocked it, and set up shop in Leeds Market. At his Penny Bazaar, he operated a one-price trade under the slogan, "Don't ask the price — it's a penny" ("Leeds"). After expanding to seven other locations, he formed a partnership with a cashier, Tom Spencer, and expanded the business into an English department store institution, Marks & Spencer.

Perhaps because of their use by the lowest and least educated social class, pennies have often suffered castigation and outright rejection. An unpopular small coin, the dodecagonal threepence struck in 1937, earned the public's immediate disapproval. Dubbed the "threepenny bit," the coin replaced a slender silver threepence. When England's treasury circulated the new penny in 1971, wags referred to it as the "new pee." The ribald term denigrated a noble design featuring the crowned portcullis, ensign of Henry VII, founder of the Tudor dynasty. After 11 years of newness, the mint dropped the word "new" from its pennies.

In the United States, the indigenous penny, first minted in Massachusetts in 1786, soon edged out foreign coppers, which the Coinage Act of 1792 outlawed. That same year, Newburyport inventor Jacob Perkins devised an all-in-one machine to mill blanks and stamp the edges to prevent counterfeiting. The first cents, which pictured a flowing-haired Liberty and a thirteen-link chain in the coins stamped 1793, eventually mirrored heroes and losses shared by all citizens.

In 1837, New York coiner Lewis Feuchtwanger proposed an original penny design. For metal, he used German silver, a blend of copper, nickel, and zinc. The suggested alloy did not come into service until 1857, when the U.S. Mint struck flying eagle dimes. The "wheat-ear penny," lovingly treasured as the "wheaty," pictured Abraham Lincoln's profile on the coin closest to the common people, the ones he admired and supported during the hardships of the Civil War.

According to Edwin H. Dressel, Philadelphia mint superintendent, during World War II, pennies suffered the same privations as the rest of the nation. In 1943, after using up all the copper planchets left in storage, the mint struck three million of the short-term steel penny, a coin made from steel plated with rust-proof zinc, to spare copper for the war effort. From 1944 to 1946, the "shell-case penny" recycled spent cartridge cases from the battlefields of Europe and the Pacific into new pennies.

An unusual World War II penny coinage appeared in Germany in 1939 under Adolf Hitler. Commissioned by the National Socialist Party, the *Reichspfennig*, available in 1-, 2-, 5-, and 10-penny denominations, pictured the Nazi emblem, an eagle with spread wings with talons gripping a wreath encircling a swastika. A simple reverse presented the name of the coin and an oak cluster. Minted of aluminum, aluminum-bronze, bronze, silver, or zinc, this coinage helped to demean the ancient swastika from a symbol of fortune and wealth to a reminder of racial hatred and genocide.

By the 21st century, the U.S. Mint was turning out 13 billion pennies per year. Their coinage accounted for ⅔ of the staff output. However, an undercurrent of political and economic debate presaged calls to retire the one-center as obsolete. Still popular as a family coin and as the price of a gum ball from vending bubbles, it occupies an important place in the training of young children in thrift and dominates home change hoards and children's piggy banks. It also permeates folk idiom and literature in the phrases "penny for your thoughts," "in for a penny, in for a pound," "pennies from heaven," and "penny wise pound foolish."

See also **amulet coins; Victor D. Brenner; Canute I; Confederate money; Edward the Confessor; Indian head cent; James Barton Longacre; maundy money; medieval coins; Offa of Mercia; Jacob Perkins; Peter's pence; pfennig; Roman coins — Monarchy and republic; Scottish coins; St. Patrick coppers; U.S. coins; U.S. Mint; Joseph Wright; Wyon family.**

SOURCES: Allen, Larry. *Encyclopedia of Money*. New York: Checkmark Books, 2001. • Baring-Gould, William S., intro. and notes. *The Annotated Mother Goose*. New York: Clarkson N. Potter, 1962. • Bristow, Sallie. "Penny That Ended Up Jewelry." *Hobbies*, July 1981, p. 124. • Cannon, John, and Ralph Griffiths. *Oxford Illustrated History of the British Monarchy*. Oxford: Oxford University Press, 1988. • Clain-Stefanelli, Elvira, and Vladimir Clain-Stefanelli. *The Beauty and Lore of Coins, Currency, and Medals*. Croton-on-Hudson, N.Y.: Riverwood Publishers, 1974. • Cribb, Joe. *Money*. Toronto: Stoddart, 1990. • "Curious Names." http://www.moneymuseum.ch/standard_english/raeume/geld–lieben/ueberlieferung/sprachliches/ • Davies, Glyn. *A History of Money from Ancient Times to the Present Day*. Cardiff: University of Wales Press, 1994. • Grierson, Philip. *Numismatics*. London: Oxford University Press, 1975. • "Leeds Junior Chamber." http://www.cjirish.demon.co.uk/cityofleeds.htm. • Lewis, Brenda Ralph. *Coins & Currency*. New York: Random House, 1993. • Sinclair, David. *The Pound*. London: Century Books, 2000. • Snodgrass, Mary Ellen. *Who's Who in the Middle Ages*. Jefferson, N.C.: McFarland, 2001. • Sturluson, Snorri. "Heimskringla or the Chronicle of the Kings of Norway Saga of Olaf Kyrre." http://sunsite.berkeley.edu/OMACL/Heimskringla/kyrre.html.

Pepys, Samuel

One of the most famous hoarders, London diarist Samuel Pepys, England's first secretary of the admiralty, proved Gresham's law during a serious panic in London. During the Second Anglo-Dutch War of 1665–1667, as enemy warships approached the Thames River, penetrated the trans-river chain at Chatham, and set fire to the ship *The Royal Charles*, Pepys recorded in his diary, "I do this night resolve to study with my father and wife what to do with the little that I have in money by me" (Pepys 1960, p. 399). On his orders, on June 13, 1667, his wife and father traveled swiftly by coach to his Huntingdonshire country estate. There his servants dug holes to bury £1,300 in gold coins. The site is an example of a refugee hoard, a collection of coins secured at the place where the Pepys family took refuge from the turmoil in London.

Pepys learned that a fellow Londoner discovered a run on Blackwell's bank, where clerks declined to empty its vault. The bank staff explained, "It is payable at twenty days: when the days are out we will pay you" (*ibid.*). The next day, panic sent Pepys back to his reserves to consider the options. He dispatched his man, Mr. Gibson, with 1,000 guineas to bury in the same spot. For himself, he kept £300 in gold coins in a lumpy money belt, "that I may not be without something in case I should be surprised" (*ibid.*, p. 400). His instincts were correct, for the enemy continued firing English ships, destroying the *London*, *Oake*, and *The Royal James*.

Recovery was an equally harrowing task. Pepys discovered that the bags holding his original cache of coins had burst on the road to his estate. His wife reported that she and his father had carried out the burying of funds in the garden by daylight in view of nearby houses in the belief that neighbors and servants were gone to church. When he returned for the bags of money by lantern light on October 10, he filled his journal with the anguish of looking for gold pieces that had leaked from the rotted pouches.

After collecting the coins, dirt and all, Pepys ate dinner and waited for the family to retire before he began reclaiming the cache. With water and pails, he and his clerk, William Hewer, did "at last wash the dirt off of the pieces, and part the pieces and the dirt, and then begun to tell [count]; and by a note which I had of the value of the whole in my pocket, do find that there was short about a hundred pieces, which did make me mad" (*ibid.*, p. 432). He went out at midnight and found 45 more coins by candlelight. After cleaning them, he was able to retire at 2:00 A.M.

The following morning, Pepys and Hewer locked themselves in the garden and began sifting dirt with a sieve, "Just as they do for dyamonds in other parts of the world" (*ibid.*, p. 433). The ordeal produced 34 more coins. Content that the loss was small, Pepys ordered a guard to accompany him and the hoard in a coach for a two-day journey back to London. Naturally nervous after the frantic hunt for coins, he placed the coins in a basket and secured it under his seat. To avoid another coin loss, he checked every 15 minutes that his savings were safe. In 1842, subsequent owners of Pepys's country property located an iron pot containing coins from the era and earlier. The dates suggest that Pepsy may have overlooked one coin receptacle.

SOURCES: Allen, Larry. *Encyclopedia of Money*. New York: Checkmark Books, 2001. • Davies, Glyn. *A History of Money from Ancient Times to the Present Day*. Cardiff: University of Wales Press, 1994. • "Gresham College." http://www.gresham.ac.uk/special/history.html. • Grierson, Philip. *Numismatics*. London: Oxford University Press, 1975. • Laing, Lloyd R. *Coins and Archaeology*. New York: Schocken Books, 1969. • Magnusson, Magnus. *Cambridge Biographical Dictionary*. Cambridge: University of Cambridge, 1990. • Nicholls, C. S., ed. *Encyclopedia of Biography*. Oxford, Eng.: Helicon Publishing Ltd., 1996. • Pepys, Samuel. *The Diary of Samuel Pepys*. New York: Harper Torchbooks, 1960.

Perkins, Jacob

Colonial inventor and metalsmith Jacob Perkins, dubbed "the American inventor," earned renown for incising a medal picturing George Washington and for improving coinmaking. Born on July 9, 1766, in Newburyport, Massachusetts, Perkins was the son of tailor Matthew and Jane Dole Perkins and apprenticed with a goldsmith, who taught him how to make gold and silver buckles and beads. In 1787, he designed a nail-making machine. After learning the carving of coin dies, he worked for the Massachusetts commonwealth treasury as engraver of the cent and half-cent.

Perkins's contributions to coinage continued in 1792 with the creation of devices that cut and stamped planchets and lettered coin edges. The New Hampshire Packet described the value of his engineering:

> He has invented a new machine which cuts the metal into such circular pieces as are wanted and gives the impression at the same time — its motion is accelerated by a balance wheel, and more than one-third of the time and labor thereby saved. He has also constructed another machine of his own invention for milling or lettering the edge by which a boy can mill 60 each minute [Bowers 1981, p. 123].

The newspaper article lauded Perkins's coining machine for lessening problems with counterfeit coins.

Around this same time, Perkins engraved a memorial military portrait of George Washington for a ten-dollar pattern piece. It featured a sentimental legend, "He Is in Glory, the World in Tears." Advertised in 1800 in an article by *J. Russell's Gazette*, the Washington medal was available from two Newburyport dealers in white metal, silver, or gold.

Perkins continued concentrating on refining the manufacture of money. In 1799, he devised a method of microprinting to prevent the counterfeiting of paper banknotes. The method required multiple printings of the bill's denomination in tiny type across the background. Five years later, he formulated a process for hardening steel plates, which enhanced his reputation in the field of moneying. The Massachusetts legislature required state banks to employ the plates for printing all banknotes.

At age 50, Perkins moved to Philadelphia and traveled in England. He invented a bathometer for measuring ocean depths in mild and windy weather and also devised a rapid-fire steam-powered gun, which he demonstrated for the Duke of Wellington. Before Perkins's death on July 30, 1849, he added to his list of inventions a steam rocket engine and a propeller for steamships.

***See also* counterfeiting; penny.**

SOURCES: Bowers, Q. David. "Jacob Perkins, Early Die Cutter." *Hobbies*, July 1981, pp. 123–124. • Clain-Stefanelli, Elvira, and Vladimir Clain-Stefanelli. *The Beauty and Lore of Coins, Currency, and Medals*. Croton-on-Hudson, N.Y.: Riverwood Publishers, 1974. • Davis, Andrew McFarland. *Colonial Currency Reprints, 1682–1751*. Boston: The Prince Society, 1911. • Jordan, Louis. "The Coins of Colonial and Early America." http://www.coins.nd.edu/ColCoin/ColCoinContents/Introduction.html. • Kleeberg, John, ed. *The Money of Pre-Federal America*. New York: American Numismatic Society, 1992.

peso

The *peso*, the modern currency of Argentina, Chile, Colombia, Cuba, the Dominican Republic, Mexico, the Philippines, and Uruguay, was born of strife. The creation of the Emperor Maximilian, it went into production after Napoleon III dispatched the Hapsburg archduke of Austria to replace Benito Juárez. A paternal, benevolent ruler, Maximilian imagined himself as the protector of peasants against the former regime and the Roman Catholic hierarchy. Napoleon, who easily manipulated his naive puppet, intended the new emperor to restore money owed the French government.

After assuming the throne of Mexico on June 10, 1864, Maximilian went to work on fiscal matters. He accepted Juárez's monetary reforms calling for an end to Spanish *reales* and establishment of a decimal coinage of 100 *centavos* to the *peso*. The imperial treasury was so bereft of bullion, that he had to spend his own inheritance. For only two years, coiners struck the *peso*, picturing the balding emperor with long pointed beard. In 1867, Juárez overthrew the interloper and had him shot outside Querétaro.

In 1917, Mexico's mints generated richly detailed, highly artistic coinage picturing the nation's past. A historically accurate 20-*peso* coin detailed the Aztec calendar or Sun Stone, a pair of circular matrices that the Aztecs called the *cuauhxicalli* ("eagle bowl"), which pre–Columbian artisans carved on a 25-ton stone slab in 1479. In the astrological calendar, 20 divisions of 13 days each noted lucky days. In the solar calendar, 18 periods of 20 days each specified the best times for ceremonies and agricultural plantings. In 1948, Mexico's moneyers added to the nation's species with a five-*peso* piece picturing the Aztec emperor Cuauhtémoc. His featured headdress and stoic profile belie his execution by Spanish conquistador Hernán Cortés, who hanged the emperor for refusing to disclose the location of hidden treasure.

This Mexican 50-*centavo* coin, worth one-half a *peso*, displays finely incised native artistry. The choice of decimal coinage of 100 *centavos* to the *peso* was the decision of the Emperor Maximilian.

See also **Spanish coins; trade and barter; world money.**

SOURCES: Allen, Larry. *Encyclopedia of Money*. New York: Checkmark Books, 2001. • Clain-Stefanelli, Elvira, and Vladimir Clain-Stefanelli. *The Beauty and Lore of Coins, Currency, and Medals*. Croton-on-Hudson, N.Y.: Riverwood Publishers, 1974. • Cribb, Joe. *Money*. Toronto: Stoddart, 1990. • Davies, Glyn. *A History of Money from Ancient Times to the Present Day*. Cardiff: University of Wales Press, 1994. • Pollak, Henry. *Coinage & Conflict*. Clifton, N.J.: Coin & Currency Institute, 2001. • Reinfeld, Fred. *Treasury of the World's Coins*. New York: Sterling Publishing, 1953.

Peter I

Until the rise of Peter I the Great, an energetic progressive and reformer, Russian coinage was a slipshod flow of Scandinavian coins from the northwest along European trade routes and Islamic and Byzantine pieces from the south. With a *ukase* ("edict"), he halted the use of pelts, beads, metal weights, and other goods money as monetary units in 1700. To support national currency, he set up a central minting operation at St. Petersburg and established branches at Ekaterinburg and Moscow along with temporary auxiliary workshops. For artistic die-cutters, he imported experienced carvers from western Europe to grace silver pieces with his likeness.

As a boost to national pride, Peter ended the circulation of bilingual *denga*, small change inscribed with Arabic and Russian lettering and crude designs. He also halted the snipping of wire money in lieu of small change. As a means of Westernizing his subjects, he taxed those who insisted on wearing beards and awarded them beard money, a token minted in 1705. The tax-paid coin proved they had complied with his levy.

From the upgraded national monetary system of Peter I came the Romanovs' tsarist coinage based on a decimal system and minted from copper, gold, silver, and platinum, a metal pioneered for minting by Russian moneyers. On March 15, 1719, Peter commissioned an imperial portrait *ruble*, to be printed at the St. Petersburg mint, which he had established in an army barracks with equipment transferred from Moscow. From his introduction of Russia's first gold coin came the popular *chervonet*, a customary Boyar gift at Easter or military award. Soldiers earning *chervonets* often pierced them to wear on lanyards as good luck tokens.

See also denga*; Russian money; *tympf.

SOURCES: Clain-Stefanelli, Elvira, and Vladimir Clain-Stefanelli. *The Beauty and Lore of Coins, Currency, and Medals*. Croton-on-Hudson, N.Y.: Riverwood Publishers, 1974. • Einzig, Paul. *Primitive Money*. Oxford: Pergamon Press, 1966. • Opitz, Charles J. *Odd and Curious Money*. Ocala, Fla.: First Impressions, 1986. • Reinfeld, Fred. *Treasury of the World's Coins*. New York: Sterling Publishing, 1953. • Weatherford, Jack. *The History of Money: From Sandstone to Cyberspace*. Pittsburgh, Pa.: Three Rivers Press, 1998.

Peter's pence

The Vatican's Peter's pence survives in history under several terms—*census s. petri* ("St. Peter's census"), *denarius*, hearth-money or hearth-penny, *heordpaenning* ("penny hoard"), Peterspence, Romesceat, or Romescot. An annual levy or feudal tribute to the Holy See at Rome of one pence per Christian household, it was imposed by the holy exchequer. The tax was most onerous in northwestern Europe and England but extended south to Dalmatia, Hungary, Istria, and Poland. The levy may have originated in A.D. 727 under Ine (or Ina), King of Wessex; it is clearly indicated during the reign of Offa of Mercia at the rate of 365 *mancuses* or 30 pence yearly. He pledged the amount to papal legates as a tribute confirmed with Pope Adrian I at the Synod of Chelsea in A.D. 787, when Offa joined Beorhtric of Wessex in requesting a see at Lichfield, England's third archbishopric.

The momentous gathering before the pope included numerous ships and an entourage of Offa, two archbishops, nine bishops, six abbots, and eight Mercian officials. The promise of the annual pledge rid Offa of allegiance to the see at Canterbury and brought Mercia control of Dunwich, Elmham, Hereford, Leicester, Lindsey, and Worcester under Bishop Hygeberht. He held the see from A.D. 779 to 787 until his advancement to archbishop. Included in the arrangement was the bishop's legitimizing of Offa's dynasty by crowning Offa's son Ecgfrith while Offa was still alive and actively ruling. As part of his share of the *quid pro quo*, Offa reciprocated by establishing Winchcombe Abbey in the central town in the Cotswolds, which also was the location of one of Offa's mints. The abbey did not enter service until its completion in A.D. 811.

The collection of the annual tithe recurred in a letter from Pope Leo III to Kenulf, Offa's successor, who set aside the pence for charity and for lighting Rome's churches, an expensive task requiring near round-the-clock burning of candles and lamps. Around A.D. 855, Ethelwulf, father of Alfred the Great, journeyed to Rome and upped the annual pledge by 300 *mancuses*, which nearly doubled the original amount. History does not record whether he intended to pay the amount from his treasury or from pennies collected from citizens. According to the *Anglo-Saxon Chronicle*, Alfred dutifully collected from Wessex folk and remitted the tax to Rome.

As mentioned in the *Dooms of Edward and Guthrum*, the tax was known as the *romfeoh*. After King Edmund I assembled the London synod in A.D. 941, including archbishops Oda and Wulfstan, the king prioritized in importance after chastity the laws of tithes and churchscots. His decree stated: "A tithe we enjoin to every Christian man by his Christendom and churchscot [church payment], and Rome-feoh [Peter's pence], and plough-alms. And if any one will not do so, let him be excommunicated" ("Anglo-Saxon Dooms"). Thus, failure to pay the tax resulted in an irrevocable expulsion from society and the hereafter, excluded citizens in arrears from burial in hallowed ground, and made their property subject to seizure.

Under Edgar the Peaceful after A.D. 959, the peasant tax was called a "hearth-penny," indicating one per dwelling. The sum was due each August 1 at Lammastide, the feast of St. Peter's Chains. Collections required the transport of bulky small change to Rome. Affirming the difficulty of packing and shipping the coins was a hoard located in a papal palace at Rome in 1883, which consisted of Anglo-Saxon silver pennies minted before A.D. 947.

King Canute I, England's first Scandinavian monarch, reaffirmed the necessity for tribute to Rome in 1027. Nonetheless, subsequent collections were irregular into the time of William I, the first Norman king of England, who arrived in 1066. In 1074, Pope Gregory VII commanded William to consider his contribution to the church treasury with the same concern he would value his own purse. Although William renewed royal promise of the tribute, the papacy regularly found fault with the consistency of tax collection. On January 28, 1214, Pope Innocent III declared his annoyance to his English bishops that they appeared to be keeping most of Peter's pence collections for themselves. Payment continued until 1534 when Henry VIII ousted papal control from England and set up his own state church. After the Reformation, the concept of a Peter's pence died out entirely in Europe.

***See also* Canute I; English coins; Offa of Mercia; *pfennig*; William the Conqueror.**

SOURCES: "Medieval Sourcebook: The Anglo-Saxon Dooms, 560–975." http://www.fordham.edu/halsall/source/560-975dooms.html. • "Medieval Sourcebook: List of Tolls Exacted at Billingsgate, c. 978–1016." http://www.fordham.edu/halsall/source/billingsgate-tolls.html. • *New Catholic Encyclopedia*. San Francisco: Catholic University of America, 1967. • Sinclair, David. *The Pound*. London: Century Books, 2000. • "Waterfront Used at Synod of Chelsea." *British Archaeology*, September 1997.

Petty, Sir William

Economist and statistician Sir William Petty from Romsey, Hampshire, was army physician for Irish forces. As commissioner of military land grants, he mapped Ireland for Oliver Cromwell, head of the English Commonwealth. In 1654, Petty distributed the confiscated lands to England's creditors, earning a knighthood for completing the "Down Survey" in 13 months. A subsequent favorite of Charles II and one of the founders of the Royal Society, Petty also set up quarries, mines, and ironworks.

Petty was a multifaceted scholar who taught anatomy at Oxford and music at Gresham College, invented a twin-hulled ship, and dabbled in political economics. He published *A Treatise of Taxes and Contributions* (1662), which claimed that land and labor were more significant indicators of national wealth than stores of precious metals. Subtitled "Shewing the Nature and Measures of Crown Lands, Assessments, Customs, Poll-Money, Lotteries, Benevolence, Penalties, Monopolies, Offices, Tythes, Raising of Coins, Harth-Money, Excize, etc.," the text states a truism on the importance of ready cash to tax collection:

> Scarcity of money, is another cause of the bad payment of Taxes; for if we consider, that of all the wealth of this Nation, viz. Lands, Housing, Shipping, Commodities, Furniture, Plate, and Money, that scarce one part of an hundred is Coin; and that perhaps there is scarce six millions of Pounds now in England, that is but twenty shillings a head for every head in the Nation. We may easily judge, how difficult it is for men of competent estates, to pay a Summe of money on a sudden [Petty, 1662].

For the crown's benefit, Petty suggested that tax collectors accept livestock and grain in lieu of coin and turn a better profit from wise sale or conversion of goods into cash. He developed the notions that the supply of farthings per commercial exchange increased trade and the financial health of the country and that the flow of moneys impacted much of England's daily life, from benevolence to crime.

Petty further reordered thinking on coins and banking in *Quantulumcunque concerning Money* (1682), an oddly titled treatise urging the foundation of a national bank to make better use of coined money. Composed in question-and-answer format, the text proceeded with reason and pragmatism toward useful conclusions. For example, Questions 29: "What is Exchange? Answer. Local Interest, or a Reward given for having your Money as such in a Place where you need the use of it" (Petty, *Quantulumcunque*).

On the question of how many farthings the Royal Mint should generate, he quantified the amount according to the census at the rate of 12 pence per family for one million English households. He continued his musings on supplying enough coins in *Politic Arithmetic* (1690), perhaps his most influential work.

SOURCES: Allen, Larry. *Encyclopedia of Money*. New York: Checkmark Books, 2001. • Bevan, Wilson Lloyd. "Sir William Petty: A Study in English Economic Literature" (monograph). Publications of the American Economic Association, 1894. • Clain-Stefanelli, Elvira, and Vladimir Clain-Stefanelli. *The Beauty and Lore of Coins, Currency, and Medals*. Croton-on-Hudson, N.Y.: Riverwood Publishers, 1974. • Cribb, Joe. *Money*. Toronto: Stoddart, 1990. • Cribb, Joe, Barrie Cook, and Ian Carradice. *The Coin Atlas*. London: Little, Brown and Co., 1999. • Davies, Glyn. *A History of Money from Ancient Times to the Present Day*. Cardiff: University of Wales Press, 1994. • Fritz, David. "Who's the Real Father of Economics?" *Across the Board*, January 1988, pp. 62–63. • Magnusson, Magnus. *Cambridge Biographical Dictionary*. Cambridge: University of Cambridge, 1990. • Petty, William. *Quantulumcunque concerning Money*. http://socserv2.socsci.mcmaster.ca/~econ/ugcm/3ll3/petty/money.txt. • Petty, William. *A Treatise of Taxes & Contributions*. London: N. Brooke, 1662. • Reinfeld, Fred. *Treasury of the World's Coins*. New York: Sterling Publishing, 1953. • Stephen, Sir Leslie, and Sir Sidney Lee, eds. *Dictionary of National Biography*. London: Oxford University Press, 1922.

pfennig

A long-lived German coin introduced in the 1000s, the *pfennig* was 1/100 of a *Deutschemark*. Patterned after English and French royal portrait coinage, it served as a unit of weight for measuring gold and silver during the Middle Ages, particularly during the reign of 12th-century rulers Frederick I and Otto I of Brandenburg. To pay large sums, citizens collected the small silver disks, melted them, and cast them into *usualmarks*, amorphous shapes that minters stamped with their value by weight.

Around 1750, Frederick II the Great of Prussia established the *thaler* and *pfennig* as the foundations of his realm's monetary system. He employed at Leipzig the coiner Veitel Ephraim and set him the task of systematic devaluation of silver coinage. Frederick's fiscal philosophy remained in power until the rise of Kaiser Wilhelm I, who reduced the *thaler* and *pfennig* in 1871 to place the *Deutschemark* in a prominent position. In private, he pursued coin collecting, extending the display in the Berlin coin cabinet set up by the Elector Joachim II after 1535.

When Germany split into eastern and western entities at the end of World War II, after 1948, their mints issued separate *pfennigs* until the countries' reunion in 1990. The pro-labor ten-*pfennig* piece of the *Deutsche Demokratische Republik* (German Democratic Republic) pictured a simple face naming the country and denomination. The reverse exalted manufacturing and agriculture by placing a grain head before a gear wheel. Post-reunion coins featured the Prussian eagle, a long-lived symbol of national pride.

***See also* Frederick the Great; *mark*; *thaler*; world currency.**

SOURCES: Cribb, Joe. *Money*. Toronto: Stoddart, 1990. • Davies, Glyn. *A History of Money from Ancient Times to the Present Day*. Cardiff: University of Wales Press, 1994. • Kiernan, Philip. "Alfred Petrie Leaves His Coins to the National Currency Collection." *Canadian Numismatic Association Journal*, October 2001, 389–395. • Sinclair, David. *The Pound*. London: Century Books, 2000.

Philip IV of France

An arbiter of good taste and showmanship, the handsome French king Philip IV (also Philippe le Bel or Philip the Fair) infused the nation's monetary system with gorgeous gold coins, the most appealing and valuable of the late 13th and early 14th centuries. He was born in 1268 at the beginning of the Sixth Crusade, in which his mother, Isabella of Aragon, died during her return from the Holy Land. The son of Philip III, he took for a role model his grandfather, Louis IX. Energetic and self-sufficient, Philip established the Rouen naval base from which Admiral Michel du Mons led a flotilla of 300 ships in 1297.

A warrior king during the eighth and last crusade, Philip had a stone statue carved in 1304 picturing himself and his horse in royal military regalia. His attractive *gros tournois* coin, the innovation of his grandfather Louis, featured Philip in scalloped inset full-face on the throne wearing flowing draped robe and crown. After war with England extended for a decade after its outbreak in 1294, Philip failed to revitalize his treasury when he debased French currency, reminted coins, confiscated the goods of Lombard merchants, taxed the church, and robbed the Jews, whom he expelled from France. Another ploy, the abolition of property tax, paired with his decree that all must join the war effort or buy dispensation with cash, also proved a failure.

In open conflict with Pope Boniface I on the right to tax French church property, Philip rebelled against Rome's authority by burning a papal bull as a gesture of defiance. Dramatizing the act was his curse on his sons if any valued God over France. He tarnished his reputation in 1307 by arresting and torturing the Knights Templar, charging them with heresy and sodomy, and seizing their treasure, which he coveted as a means of ridding his treasury of its shortfall. Seven years later, he assigned William of Paris the grisly task of executing grand master Jacques De Molay and his officers Geoffroy de Charnay, Geoffroy de Gondeville, and Hughes de Pairaud at the stake before Notre Dame Cathedral in Paris.

***See also gros tournois*; Renaissance coins.**

SOURCES: Cantor, Norman F., ed. *The Civilization of the Middle Ages.* New York: HarperPerennial, 1993. • Cavendish, Richard, ed. *Man, Myth & Magic.* New York: Marshall Cavendish, 1970. • Cooper, J. C., ed. *Dictionary of Christianity.* Chicago: Fitzroy Dearborn, 1996. • Cribb, Joe. *Money.* Toronto: Stoddart, 1990. • Hastings, James, ed. *Encyclopedia of Religion and Ethics.* New York: Charles Scribner's Sons, 1951. • Hollister, C. Warren. *Medieval Europe: A Short History.* New York: McGraw-Hill, 1994. • McCall, Andrew. *The Medieval Underworld.* New York: Dorset Press, 1979. • Rowley, Trevor. *The Norman Heritage, 1066–1200.* London: Routledge & Kegan Paul, 1983. • Setton, Kenneth M., ed. *The Middle Ages.* Washington, D.C.: National Geographic, 1977. • Snodgrass, Mary Ellen. *Who's Who in the Middle Ages.* Jefferson, N.C.: McFarland, 2001. • Tuchman, Barbara W. *A Distant Mirror: The Calamitous 14th Century.* New York: Alfred A. Knopf, 1978.

pieces of eight

The stereotypical pirate cache, silver pieces of eight, properly known as *de a ocho reales* ("eight royals"), were Spanish milled *pesos*, a high silver content coin worth one Spanish dollar. Widely circulated from the early 1500s to the 1800s, they became a global currency and the model for numerous coins in many countries, including the New England colonies and Latin America, the Irani and Omani *ria*, and the Qatari, Saudi Arabian, and Yemeni *riyal.* In 1777, the Danish Asiatic Society struck a silver piece of eight for circulation in China, complete with standard pillars and globe motif and the noble Latin motto "*Gloria ex Amore Patriae*" ("Glory from Love of Country").

The first pieces of eight resulted from an era of gold and silver hunting unparalleled in world history. After Francisco Pizarro pillaged the Inca stronghold of Cuzco, Peru, in November 1533, he acquired a vault of gold ornaments and jewelry in payment of ransom for Atahualpa, the Incan king. Pizarro had the king murdered, then melted the precious metal for distribution among his men. The original piece of eight derived after 1536 during the reign of Charles I of Spain and Juana, the queen mother and daughter of Ferdinand and Isabella, who had bankrolled Columbus's voyages to the New World. The royal couple commissioned the coin in 1497 to be struck in Mexico from Central American ore, most of which enslaved Indians mined for Spanish *conquistadores*. Each coin bore the legend "*Plus Ultra*" ("More Beyond"), the ideal of limitless expansion in the Western Hemisphere. A rich find in the mountain village of Potosí, Bolivia, in 1545 added silver from a warren of tunnels, mined at high level with considerable danger to Indian laborers.

To facilitate the packing, overland shipping, and unloading of specie at the treasure houses at Cartagena and Portobello, Panama's major ports, the Spanish treasure seekers palisaded their hoards and fortified them with batteries and ramparts. Initially, they melted the metal and molded it into bars and ingots before establishing minting operations. From mints at Mexico City, Mexico; Lima, Peru; and Potosí, Bolivia, they shaped their ores into pieces of eight. Armed flotillas bore payloads east to Havana, the primary naval base of the Caribbean, which was guarded by the fort called Castillo de los Tres Reyes del Morro and by a chain stretched across the harbor's entrance. From there, ships logy and awkward with full loads of coin and gold bars sailed across the Atlantic to the military treasury of Seville. The wealth helped Philip II pursue Catholic dominance of Europe, a failed vision that ended in July 1588 with the defeat of the Spanish Armada.

From 1596 to 1600, mintmasters shipped coins worth $774 million to Spain and its colonies in the West Indies and Central and South America. The coins passed into the hands of New England traders, who had relied on country pay or equivalent amounts of commodities to substitute for coin. Unrefined in appearance, the coin, called a "cob," bore an irregular round shape. Because it displayed a gaudy engraving of the Spanish coat of arms opposite Gibraltar's pillars of Hercules, the Mediterranean gateway to the Western Hemisphere, it was dubbed a "pillar dollar."

The popularity of pieces of eight influenced the *thaler* of Charles V, a multinational political figure who was Holy Roman Emperor, king of Spain, and archduke of Austria. The identification of pieces of eight with a P^8 and the uprights of the pillars gradually acquired an overlay in the shape of an S, which evolved into the "$" symbol, a monogram used by the government coiners at the U.S. Bureau of Engraving and Printing. Because the *real* was nicknamed the "bit," the quartered parts of a dollar earned the common slang tag "two bits" for one, "four bits" for two and "six bits" for three.

When New World colonists broke up coins to make small change, they produced irregular halves of a quarter called long and short bits, worth 15 cents and 10 cents. Alteration of the whole *real* varied with the place:

place	*alteration*
Curaçao	Authorities sliced each coin into five pie wedges and applied the rose stamp to each.
Grenada	Island treasury officials discouraged the export of milled pieces of eight by lopping them into 11 segments, each stamped with a G.
Madagascar	Slivers of the original coin as small as 1⁄72 of a coin required weighing to substantiate value.
New Orleans	Quartered coins were counterstamped for use as trade tokens.
Australia	In 1813, the treasury punched out the center of the coins and stamped on the inner edge the date and country. In the colonies of Demerara and Essequibo, a serrated portion punched off center produced two coins, the remaining portion and the small, jagged-edged piece, each bearing the colonial stamp E & D.
Saint Lucia	Moneyers chose to make three parallel cuts across the

place	*alteration*
	surface. The center piece, stamped "St. Lucie 1807," was worth 60 percent of the original coin's value; side slices were each worth 20 percent.

Pirate swag, often accounted in pieces of eight, provides historians with accurate amounts earned by privateers. One pirate, Basil Ringrose, noted that the men who seized the Spanish ship *San Pedro* off Chile in July 1681 received 234 pieces of eight per crewman. Alexandre Exquemelin's *The Buccaneers of America* (1678) summarizes the plunder of French privateer Francis L'Ollonais as 40,000 pieces of eight and jewelry worth a quarter that amount, all seized from a Spanish ship. Exquemelin's text describes the shipboard gambling of 260,000 pieces of eight in a three-week period of marathon dicing and card playing. Such high stakes caused some captains to rule out gambling in the code of conduct.

Exquemelin also recorded the boarding agreements that pirates signed. The standard sharing of loot followed the payment of 100 to 150 pieces of eight to the shipwright for carpentry and 200 to 250 pieces of eight for the ship's doctor. In addition to a portion of the loot, the captain agreed to reimburse injured parties on a sliding scale:

loss	*compensation*
right arm	600 pieces of eight or six slaves
left arm	500 pieces of eight or five slaves
right leg	500 pieces of eight or five slaves
left leg	400 pieces of eight or four slaves
eye	100 pieces of eight or one slave
finger	100 pieces of eight or one slave

What was left of the plunder the men divided equally, giving a double portion to the captain and first mate, one and a half or one and one quarter to botswains and gunners, and half share to ship's boy.

Emulating the popular Spanish coin were other European pieces called *piastra*, *piastre*, or *piaster*. In 1684 at age 23, Charles II the Mad of Spain, an arrogant Hapsburg monarch, issued a *piastra* gloating "*Unus non Sufficit*" ("One [World] Is Not Enough"). Ironically, he died childless, leaving an unsecured throne as the prize to be had at the end of the 14-year War of Spanish Secession, an international melee of claims and counterclaims.

Another emulator, Father Miguel Hidalgo y Costilla of Dolores, who led a fight for Mexican independence, attempted to advance parishioners economically through modern farming methods. In 1810 during the uproar following the accession of Joseph Bonaparte, Father Miguel led a folk revolt of Indians and Mestizos at San Miguel to overthrow the oligarchy. Under the banner of the Virgin of Guadalupe, his followers seized Valladolid and Guanajuato, where, with the aid of counterfeiters, he issued needed currency. His diecutters based their coinage on standard Spanish pieces of eight.

Father Miguel's band marched on Mexico City before losing their nerve near Guadalajara. General Félix Calleja del Rey seized the priest and defrocked, tortured, and executed him at Chihuahua before a firing squad. The workmanship on the rebel coins was so fine that government agents preserved the dies and transported them to Mexico City for use at the royal mint. At the centenary of Father Miguel's revolt, Mexico circulated a silver coin featuring the allegorical figure of Victory on horseback.

See also **dollar; doubloon; Sir Francis Drake; ducat; Piet Heyn; Henry Morgan; pieces of eight; piracy; Spanish coins; *thaler*; treasure ships; U.S. coins; U.S. Mint; *Whydah*.**

SOURCES: Allen, Larry. *Encyclopedia of Money*. New York: Checkmark Books, 2001. • Allen, Thomas B. "Cuba's Golden Past." National Geographic, July 2001, 74–91. • "The Bureau of Engraving and Printing." http://www.bep.treas.gov/. • Burgan, Michael. "Lost and Found Treasure." *National Geographic World*, April 2000, 19. • Clain-Stefanelli, Elvira, and Vladimir Clain-Stefanelli. *The Beauty and Lore of Coins, Currency, and Medals*. Croton-on-Hudson, N.Y.: Riverwood Publishers, 1974. • Cordingly, David. *Under the Black Flag*. San Diego, Calif.: Harvest Books, 1995. • Cribb, Joe. *Money*. Toronto: Stoddart, 1990. • Jordan, Louis.

"The Coins of Colonial and Early America." http://www.coins.nd.edu/ColCoin/ColCoinContents/Introduction.html. • Kemp, Peter, ed. *The Oxford Companion to Ships and the Sea.* Oxford: Oxford University Press, 1988. • Reed, Mort. *Cowles Complete Encyclopedia of U.S. Coins.* New York: Cowles Book Company, 1969. • Skerry, Brian. "Pirates of the *Whydah.*" *National Geographic*, May 1999, 64.

piracy

The robbing of vessels at sea has long filled romantic stories of sea rovers with detailed accounts of treasure chests brimming with jewels and gold and silver coins, notably silver pieces of eight and gold doubloons. According to 18th-century legend, the ubiquitous Spanish coins were a substantial cargo aboard the privateer *Prince Eugene*, which crept up the Atlantic seaboard. At Yorktown, authorities arrested the captain and seized the coins from pits that the pirate crew had dug in the sand along the York River. These familiar coins also figure in such stage romances as Edward Fitzball's *The Red Rover, or The Mutiny of the Dolphin* (1829), Scottish novelist Robert Louis Stevenson's classic *Treasure Island* (1883), and Gilbert and Sullivan's popular parody *The Pirates of Penzance* (1879). Although much of the connection between pirates and coins is driven by legend and fantasy, the history of thievery from sailing vessels has a basis in fact.

The first pirates in history were the Phoenicians, who menaced ships and coastal areas from 2000 B.C. The pattern of jeopardizing lives and fortunes along the Mediterranean continued into the second century B.C., when the Cilician pirates of southern Turkey intervened in grain shipments to Rome. Julius Caesar fell into the hands of pirates and enjoyed their company until a large ransom arrived in cash. The fun ended when he returned to their lair and slew them all. For the sake of safe sea lanes and the coastlines of Rome and its territories, it took a concerted effort to subdue pirate bands and liberate traders.

After 38 B.C., coiner Quintus Nasidius, a naval officer under the command of Sextus Pompeius, commissioned a silver-plated *denarius* in honor of Sextus's father, Pompey the Great, the Roman general who cleared the Roman coastline of pirates. In 44 B.C., Pompey, son-in-law of the recently assassinated statesman Julius Caesar, began curtailing piracy along trade routes. The coin pictures Pompey's handsome profile on the obverse. On the back, a galley plies the waters under sail and by power of enslaved rowers below deck. Because the coin derives from a decade of political and economic turmoil as young Octavian shored up power before establishing the Roman Empire, Sextus may have issued the coin as an expedient means of paying his soldiers.

The most romantic era of sea rovers began in 1520, when the Spanish grew rich transporting metal ingots, which they refined from Aztec silver and gold bullion and Inca jewelry to pay to soldiers. In fully armed flotillas, pirates crossed the Atlantic to Europe from their strongholds around the Caribbean Sea, which acquired the name "the Spanish lake" *(Historic World Leaders*, 1994). One of the largest thefts was the work of French buccaneer Jean Florin, who, in 1523, seized three chests of gold ingots plus gold dust, emeralds, and pearls in a daring raid of three Spanish galleons off Cape Saint Vincent, Portugal. Such easy pickings stirred the dishonest to acts of piracy. Over 170 years, the rise in confiscation of ships and chests of coins and treasure endangered national economies, creating outrage among shippers and governments along with folk legend in song and verse.

History records the wealth of Port Royal, Jamaica, where pirates like Henry Morgan freely drank, gambled, chased prostitutes, and decked themselves in finery purchased from local merchants with *pistoles* and pieces of eight, bullion, silver ingots, jewels, and exotica from around the globe. From home base in the harbor, pirates looted some 60 settlements and towns between 1655 and 1661, an average of ten per year. The buccaneer homeland came to grief with an earthquake on July 7, 1692, which slid most of the buildings and streets into the harbor. Undersea archeology has turned up whole blocks still intact and located evidence of a glittering lifestyle generated by pirate treasure.

During piracy's golden age, the ungoverned and ungovernable Caribbean Sea hosted so many plundering rogues that they endangered the treasuries of Europe's great nations. To lure unsuspecting pilots into their lair, pirates often pretended to have a leaking hull or broken mast. When rescuers drew within range, brigands hidden below or in the shrouds sprang into action, often killing the innocent sailors and rifling the ship or stealing it outright. As crime burgeoned between 1716 and 1718 and the number of free agents rose to 2,400, some freebooters controlled whole islands, harbors, and sea lanes. Until the drop in number in 1723, the situation remained perilous for shippers and travelers. Writers and artists enhanced the images of desperadoes with the stereotypical cutlass and bandolier, purloined scarves and shirts, watches and earrings, and chests heaped with doubloons and *piastres*.

In part, the figure bore some resemblance to real people, but omitted the poorly groomed and uneducated cutthroats and navy deserters who found a way of preying on their betters. They formed crews under discipline of the pistol and lash and performed normal duties at sea:

position	*job*
sailor	rig sails, steer, interpret weather weather and wind
cook	superintend provisions and meals, perform minor surgery and treatment of wounds
carpenter	plug leaks and maintain hull, masts, yards, tenders, machines
gunner	supervise ammunition and artillery, prevent accidents from overheated cannon
boatswain	supervise work crews, maintain rigging and anchors
quartermaster	elected to keep order, distribute rations and supplies, punish minor infractions, lead attacks, board and captain any ships seized, divide loot
captain	make decisions

In addition to scurvy, yellow fever, dysentery, malaria, syphilis, and near starvation, the cost of signing on was usually heavy scars, blindness, and body parts amputated in the thick of hand-to-hand combat. Alexandre Exquemelin's *The Buccaneers of America* (1678) recorded the *chasse-partie* ("charter-party") that men signed, which stipulated pay for lost limbs at 600 pieces of eight or six slaves for a right arm, 500 or five slaves for a left arm or right leg, 400 or four slaves for a left leg, and 100 or one slave for an eye or finger.

The stereotype also omitted international piracy, such as that of Henry III's freebooters Adam Robernolt and William le Sauvage in 1213 and of privateer Jean Fleury, attacker of Spanish transport galleons in 1523, who gained the backing of King Frances I of France in robbing foreign vessels, particularly those of Spain, and turning over the spoils to the French treasury. Fleury's greatest haul was a trio of Spanish caravels from Mexico anchored off Cape St. Vincent, Portugal, where he seized 500 pounds of gold dust, three chests of gold ingots, pearls, emeralds, jeweled gold masks, and ritual regalia. His success inspired Francis I of France to license privateers who scouted Spanish treasure ships for the next four decades.

State-supported sea thieves carried letters of marque (or *mark*) and reprisal (also called *lettres de represailles* or privateering commissions), licenses that exonerated the bearers of acts against ships belonging to enemy nations. The only requirement was that privateers share the plunder with the monarch who dispatched them. The remaining portion of coins and swag the privateers counted out before their crew as a means of keeping down mutinies and bloody fights over who received the richest pile. In 1506, the Bahamian mint designed a copper halfpenny with a motto exclaiming the islanders' delight in restoring trade by expelling such disruptive and dangerous pirates. In 1953, the Bank of Nassau reprised the motto on a four-shilling banknote.

One of the prime thieves of coin, Murat Rais, a North African sea dog, raided Italian and Spanish shipping lanes as well as Christian strongholds along the Mediterranean Sea as far west as the Canary Islands. He became a pirate after his kidnap in boyhood by Kari Ali Rais. Choosing to become a corsair, he sailed small galiots that he easily concealed. After stealing from Philip II of Spain and the papacy, he nabbed a larger haul of a million *ducats*. He died in glory in 1635 at the siege of Vlorë.

Aided by John Hinson and Lionel Wafer, around 1688, Edward Davis, called the greatest buccaneer, acquired chests of gold weighing up to 500 pounds each. Inside were silver plate and gold coins worth up to £6,000. King William III pardoned the trio and returned the swag on condition that they underwrite the founding of William and Mary College. A 16th-century British pirate, Thomas Cavendish, collected so many spoils that he used the gold to adorn the deck and masts of his ship, the *Santa Ana*. One prize for swag probably belongs to American privateer Thomas Tew, who stole so much ivory, gold, and silver from Arab ships seized on the Red Sea that he brought down a Pennsylvania governor, Benjamin Fletcher, for collusion in dividing the haul. Another from the late 1690s, Antonio Fuet of Narbonne, France, earned the nickname "Captain Moidore" because he substituted gold Portuguese or Brazilian *moidores* in his six-pounders when he ran out of cannon balls.

According to Indian chronicler Khafi Kahn, a fortuitous heist in the Red Sea made Henry "Long Ben" Avery one of the wealthiest 17th-century pirates. Aboard the *Fancy*, armed with 46 cannon, he and a crew of 150 and a fleet of associates easily outgunned and outmanned merchant vessels, which were slow and bulky from heavy loads. The prize catch was the *Ganj-i-Sawai*, a large vessel owned by the Great Mogul of India. By shooting down the mainmast, Avery crippled the ship. Avery's men swarmed aboard, raping and torturing the Mogul's daughter and her handmaids and slaves. Avery seized gold and silver bars and 500,000 *rials*. Each pirate was richer by £1,000.

Avery retired to the Caribbean, paying his way with a gift of the *Fancy* and ivory tusks to the governor of New Providence. Officials hanged six pirates for the crime, but Avery went unpunished. Playgoers at the Theatre Royal in Drury Lane recognized the outrageous brigandry of Avery in Charles Johnson's stage melodrama *The Life and Adventures of Captain John Avery, the Successful Pirate* (ca. 1709), the story of the fictional Arviragus, King of Madagascar.

In 1718, during the golden age of pirates, Thomas Anstis, an English brigand, seized the *Buck Sloop*, a brigantine shipping out of Providence, Rhode Island. Sailing it under the Jolly Roger, he boarded and ransacked the *Morning Star* out of Bermuda on its way from Africa's Guinea coast to the Carolinas. A second capture, of the Irish sloop *Antelope*, furthered Anstis's career in the Bahamas. The arrival of the man-of-war *Winchelsea* stopped further plunder. British naval agents shot Anstis as he lolled in his hammock. A more fortunate contemporary, Howell Davis, reached Gambia and, while posing as a Liverpool merchant, looted a warehouse stacked with gold and ivory. The richest of the era, Bartholomew "Black Bart" Roberts, English captain of the *Royal Rover* from 1719–1722, may have stolen a fortune in diamonds and as many as 90,000 gold *moidores* from the *Sagrada Familia* ("holy family"), a Portuguese merchant ship departing Brazil.

Another successful contemporary looter of coins, Edward "Ned" Low worked at a Boston rigging house before going to sea. After being forced to chop wood in hostile territory on the Gulf of Honduras, he mutinied, hoisted a Jolly Roger, and sailed for the Cayman Islands. In 1722, he seized the *Nostre Signiora de Victoria* ("our lady of victory"), a Portuguese ship, and forced the crew to point out a bag of cash lowered by rope out a window in the ship's bow. The captain slashed the rope, causing 11,000 gold coins to tumble into the water. Low was so angry at his loss that he sliced off the captain's lips and burned them.

In August 1766, Joseph Andrews, a sailor aboard the schooner *Polly*, joined two crewmates in overthrowing and axing the captain and other officers and men on the way to St. Kitts in the Caribbean. After jettisoning their remains in the sea, the three mutineers were unable to profit from the theft because of their reputation as murderers. When Andrews was captured and tried in New York in 1769, he was hanged and his body chained up on Bedloe's Island to decay as a warning to other seamen.

In 1832, a foiled pirate, Pedro Gibert, sailed the schooner *Panda* toward the brigantine *Mexican,* which was carrying $20,000 in silver from Salem, Massachusetts, to Rio de Janeiro. After overtaking his quarry, he set his henchmen to plundering. The pirates immured the original crew in the forecastle, slit the rigging and sails, and set fire to the galley. Leaving the brig to burn and sink, Gibert sailed away. When the crew of the *Mexican* escaped and put out the fire, they were able to sail back to New England. Extradited from Africa to a Boston jurisdiction, Gibert went to the gallows for his crimes.

Captain Henry "Bully" Hayes, who was an active U.S. smuggler and pirate in 1857, stole from pirate Eli Boggs two chests of silver coins. Hayes used the cache to bankroll a South Seas operation in robbing traders, slaving, and gun-running. When his free hand in the area came to an end in the 1870s with the establishment of a Christian mission and the British navy, he fled a charge of piracy and transportation to Australia. His lucrative career ended with flight from a Manila jail and murder on the seas by a shipmate.

Abokka, the self-styled "Superintendent of River Traffic" along the Niger Delta in the 1860s, collected ransom for kidnap victims. His boldest caper was the capture of Bishop Samuel Crowther, the first prelate dispatched by the Anglican Church Missionary Society. In exchange for his prey, Abokka received thousands of sacks of cowrie shells and beads, both viable currency on Africa's west coast. His predations ended late in the decade when the British navy sent gunboats to destroy the pirate's lair along the Congo River.

The list of world pirates bears many names of thieves and killers and privateers. They were responsible more for sordid deaths and other depredations than for treasure carted away or hidden on sandy shores. The following are prime examples of such individuals:

pirate	*nationality*	*dates*	*ship(s)*	*fate*
Carausius	Belgian	A.D. 285	—	murdered
Alwilda	Swedish	A.D. 400s	—	captured at sea
Kanhoji Angria	Indian	1710–1729	—	natural death
Sumbhajee Angria	Indian	1736	*Derby*	natural death
Thomas Anstis	English	1718–1723	*Good Fortune*	murdered
Henry "Long Ben" Avery	English	1690s	*Fancy*	natural death
Joseph Boulanger Baker	Canadian	1800	*Eliza*	hanged
Adam Baldridge	Madagascan	1685	—	unknown
Aruj Barbarossa I (Redbeard)	Turkish	1504	Vatican ship	slaughtered
Kheir-ed-din Barbarossa II (Redbeard)	Turkish	1516–1546	—	retired
Felix Barbeito	U.S.	1827	*Crawford*	hanged
Joseph Barss	English	1812	*Liverpool Packet*	freed
Jean Bart	French	1651–1697	—	rewarded by Louis XIV
Bartolomeo "El Portugues"	Portuguese	1660–1670	—	shipwrecked
Andrew Barton	Scottish	1511	—	killed in battle

pirate	*nationality*	*dates*	*ship(s)*	*fate*
Charles Bellamy	British	1717–1718	*Whydah*	fled
Samuel "Black" Bellamy	British	1717–1718	*Whydah*	hanged
Don Benito	Spanish	1724	*Francis de la Vega*	unknown
Baron Maurice de Benyowski	Polish	1768	—	unknown
Lancelot Blackburne	English	1681	—	became an archbishop
Abraham Blauvelt	Dutch	1650	*La Garse*	unknown
Eli Boggs	Hong Kongese	1857	—	captured
Benito Bonito	Portuguese	1820	—	unknown
Stede Bonnet	English	1718	*Revenge, Royal James*	hanged
Anne Bonny	English	1718–1720	*Queen Royal; William*	natural death
George Booth	English	1696	*Pelican*	killed in battle
Pierre Bousquet	French	1716	—	unknown
John Bowen	Bermudan	1700–1702	*Speaker; Speedy Return*	died of disease
Roche Brasiliano	Dutch	1670s	—	unknown
George Brown	U.S.	1819	*Retrieve*	hanged
Nicholas Brown	British	1720s	—	beheaded
Dixie Bull	American	1632	—	disappeared
Samuel Burgess	English	1690	*Blessed William*	poisoned
John Callice	English	1580	*Golden Chalice*	killed
Jose Hilario Casares	U.S.	1827	*Crawford*	hanged
Thomas Cavendish	English	1570–1591	*Santa Ana; Desire*	died at sea
Cheng Chih-lung	Chinese	1628	—	beheaded
Ching Yih	Chinese	1806	—	drowned
Madame Ching Yih	Chinese	1807–1810	—	thrived
Dirk Chivers	Dutch	1695	*Resolution; Soldado*	pardoned
George Clifford	English	1592–1594	*Las Cinque Chagas*	honored by the queen
Edward Coates	U.S.	1680s	—	imprisoned
Thomas Cocklyn	English	1719	*Bird Galley*	unknown
Edward Collier	English	1668	*Satisfaction*	retired
John Baptist Collins	U.S.	1794	*Betsy*	hanged
Christopher Condent	British	1781–1720	—	retired
Richard Coote	English	1697–1701	—	became governor of New York
John Coxon	English	1680	—	unknown
Cui Apu	Chinese	1850–1851	—	out of business
Robert Culliford	English	1698	*Blessed William Mocha*	disappeared
Alexander Dalzeel	Scottish	1685	—	hanged
William Dampier	English	1680–1691	*Cygnet; Bachelor's Delight*	commissioned; wrote a book
Simon Danziger (or Dansker)	Dutch	1600–1611	—	hanged
Edward Davis	U.S.	1688–1692	*Quaker*	exonerated
George James Davis	English	1830	—	hanged
Howell Davis	Welsh	1720	*Bird Galley; Buck*	shot at ambush
Stephen Decatur	U.S.	1779–1820	*Philadelphia*	killed in a duel
Michiel de Ruyter	Dutch	1665	—	—
Benito de Soto	Spanish	1827	*Black Jack*	hanged

pirate	*nationality*	*dates*	*ship(s)*	*fate*
Thomas Dover	unknown	1709	—	became a doctor
Sir Francis Drake	English	1567	*Golden Hind*	died at sea
Philip Drake	U.S.	1800s	—	unknown
Rene Duguay-Trouin	French	1730s	—	honored
Peter Easton	English	1610	—	retired
Edward England	English	1720	*Pearl; Royal James*	marooned; died poor
Eustace the Black Monk	Flemish	1217	—	beheaded
John Evans	Welsh	1722	*Scowerer*	disappeared
Alexandre Exquemelin	French	1670–1690s	—	published *Buccaneers of America* (1678)
John Fenn	English	1717–1722	*Morning Star*	hanged
Manuel Fernandez	U.S.	1835	—	hanged
Jean Fleury (or Florin)	French	1523	*Dieppe*	rewarded
William Fly	U.S.	1726	*Fame's Revenge*	hanged
Josiah Forbes	U.S.	1716	*John and Mary*	arrested
Elliot Forrest	French	1924	—	imprisoned
Joseph Freeman	English	1798–1800	*Wentworth*	unknown
Antonio Fuet	French	1660–1690s	—	unknown
Fujiwara Sumitomo	Japanese	A.D. 941	—	defeated
Emanuel Furtado	U.S.	1794	*Betsy*	hanged
Vincent Gambi	U.S.	1819	—	murdered with an ax
Arthur Gautschi	German	1933	—	condemned to death
Michael Geare	English	1586–1603	*Michael and John*	retired rich
Charles Gibbs	U.S.	1831	*Vineyard*	hanged
Pedro Gibert	U.S.	1832	*Panda*	hanged
Alex Godfrey	Canadian	1800–1804	*Rover*	unknown
Nathaniel Gordon	U.S.	1832–1862	*Erie*	hanged
John Gow	English	1724	*Revenge*	executed
Sir Richard Grenville	English	1585	*Revenge; Tiger*	died at sea
Lewis Guittar	U.S.	1700	*La Paix*	hanged
John Halsey	U.S.	1705	*Charles*	died of fever
Israel Hands	English	1715–1718	*Queen Anne's Revenge*	died a beggar
Klaus "Little Jack" Hanslein	Dutch	1570–1573	—	beheaded
Sir John Hawkins	English	1563–1564	*Jesus of Lubeck*	died at sea
Richard Hawkins	English	1593–1594	—	imprisoned and released
Henry Hayes	U.S.	1857–1870s	—	murdered at sea
Klein Henszlein	German	1573	—	beheaded
James Hepburn	English	1567–1578	—	died in prison
Piet Heyn (or Hein)	Dutch	1624–1627	*Hollandia*	killed by pirates
Albert E. Hicks	U.S.	1860	*A. E. Johnson*	hanged
William Hill	U.S.	1826	*Decatur*	hanged
John Hinson	U.S.	1688–1692	*Quaker*	exonerated
John Hoar	U.S.	1695	*John and Rebecca*	killed by Indians
William Holmes	U.S.	1818	*Buenos Ayres*	hanged
Benjamin Hornigold	English	1717–1718	*Whydah*	died at sea
Thomas Howard	English	1702–1703	*Prosperous*	retired rich
Victor Hugues	French	1790s	—	thrived
Rahmah ibn Jabr	Arabian	1800–1826	*Ghatrusha*	committed suicide
John James	Welsh	1700	*Alexander*	unknown
Henry Jennings	Bahamian	1718	*Bathsheba*	pardoned
Joasmi tribe	Arabian	1804–1816	—	quelled
John Paul Jones	Scottish	1770s–1792	*Bonhomme Richard*	natural death

pirate	*nationality*	*dates*	*ship(s)*	*fate*
James Kelley	English	1684–1688	*Bachelor's Delight*	hanged
Walter Kennedy	Bahamian	1718–1720	*Rover*	hanged
William Kidd	Scottish	1695–1701	*Adventure Galley*; *New York Revenge*	hanged
Lady Mary Killigrew	English	1580s	—	reprieved
Oliver la Buze (or la Bouche)	English	1719	*Bird Galley*; *Victory*	unknown
Jean Lafitte	French	1808–1815	—	disappeared
Captain Lamprier	American	1740s	—	unknown
Sir James Lancaster	English	1595	*Edward Bonaventure*	knighted
Francois le Clerc (Jambe de Bois) ("pegleg")	French	1553–1554	—	successful
Louis le Golif	French	1780s	—	unknown
Pierre le Grand	French	1665	—	unknown
William le Sauvage	English	1213	—	exonerated
Guillaume le Testu	French	1570s	—	beheaded
Robert Livingston	English	1695	*Antigua*	unknown
Edward "Ned" Low	English	1722–1724	*Fancy*; *Fortune*	disappeared
George Will Lowther	English	1721–1724	*Happy Delivery*; *Ranger*	shot himself
Hendrick Lucifer	Dutch	1628	—	—
Henry Mainwaring	English	1612	*Resistance*	died in poverty
Pierre Maisonnate	French	1692	—	exchanged
Henry Mann	U.S.	1718	*Providence*	exonerated
Edward Mansfield	Dutch	1665	—	executed
William Marsh (or deMorisco)	English	1235–1242	—	hanged
William Mason	U.S.	1680s	—	disappeared
William Maurice	Scottish	1241	—	hanged, drawn, and quartered
William May	U.S.	1690	—	escaped
Roger McKeel	U.S.	1680s	*Quaker*	unknown
Suds Merrick	U.S.	1860–1870s	—	murdered
Robert Moore	English	1695	*Adventure Galley*	unknown
Jose Morando	U.S.	1827	*Crawford*	hanged
Henry Morgan	Welsh	1667–1670	*Oxford*	natural death
John Morris	English	1663–1672	—	commissioned to hunt pirates
Zachary Moulton	English	1608	—	hanged
Walter Müller	German	1933	—	condemned to death
Sir Christopher Myngs	English	1658	*Marston Moor*	promoted
Jean-David Nau (Francois l'Ollonois)	French	1667	—	dismembered and burned
Nathaniel North	English	1707	*Dolphin*	murdered
John Nutt	Canadian	1620	—	freed
Grace O'Malley	Irish	1550s	—	unknown
John Oxenham	English	1577	—	hanged
Augustus Palacha	U.S.	1794	*Betsy*	hanged
Thomas Parker	English	1798–1800	*Wentworth*	unknown
William Parker	English	1590s	—	made vice admiral
Matthew Pennell	English	1756–1758	*Musketo*	unknown
John Phillips	English	1723–1725	—	imprisoned
John Plantain	Madagascan	1720s	—	escaped and lived well
Plug	U.S.	1820	—	drowned

pirate	*nationality*	*dates*	*ship(s)*	*fate*
Thomas Pound	U.S.	1689–1691	*Mary*	commissioned
John Power	English	1768	*Bravo*	hanged
Lawrence Prince	Dutch	1670	—	promoted
John Quelch	U.S.	1704	*Charles*	hanged
John Rackham (Calico Jack)	English	1718–1720	*Vane*	hanged
Raga	Malaysian	1920s	—	suppressed
Rahmah bin Jabr	Arabian	1820–1826	—	suicide
Murat (or Murad) Rais (Jan Jansz)	Dutch	1600–1635	—	died in battle
Sir Walter Raleigh	English	1616–1618	—	beheaded
Mary Read	English	1718–1720	*Vane*	died in prison
John Richardson	U.S.	1738	—	hanged
Basil Ringrose	English	1686	—	killed
Manuel Pardal Rivero	Spanish	1670	*San Pedro*	shot
Adam Robernolt	English	1213	—	exonerated
Bartholomew Roberts (Black Bart)	English	1719–1722	*Royal Rover*; *Good Fortune*; *Little Ranger*; *Loyal Fortune*; *Rover*; *Royal Fortune* *Sea King*	killed in battle
Philip Roche	Irish	1721–1723	*Mary Snow*	hanged
Edward Rosewaine	U.S.	1818	*Buenos Ayres*	hanged
Abraham Samuel	Jamaican	1690s	—	unknown
Richard Sawkins	English	1670s	—	killed
Shap-'ng-tsai	Chinese	1849	—	escaped
Sir Anthony Sherley	English	1596	—	died poor
Simon Simonson	Dutch	1609–1616	—	executed
William Stoke	U.S.	1718	*Providence*	exonerated
Stortebeker	Dutch	1390s	—	executed
Ralph Stout	English	1690s	*Mocha*	murdered
Thomas Stucley	English	1578	—	killed in battle
Robert Surcouf	French	1820s	*Triton*; *Kent*	successful
Sweyn Forkbeard	Danish	1010s	—	became king
Hugo Taudien	German	1933	—	condemned to death
John Taylor	English	1720	*Victory*; *Cassandra*	escaped
Edward "Blackbeard" Teach	English	1715–1718	*Queen Anne's Revenge*	killed in battle
Thomas Tew	U.S.	1694	*Liberty*; *Amity*	killed in battle
Samuel Tully	English	1812	—	hanged
Uskok band	Italian	1600s	—	beheaded
Charles Vane	English	1719	*Ranger*	hanged
Aure Van Pelt	U.S.	1718	*Providence*	exonerated
Francis Verney	English	1600s	—	enslaved; died in a hospital
Lionel Wafer	U.S.	1688–1692	*Quaker*	exonerated
Thomas G. Wansley	U.S.	1831	*Vineyard*	hanged
John Ward	English	1615	*Little John*; *Gift*	retired, died of plague
Thomas Warrington	U.S.	1818	*Buenos Ayres*	hanged
William Watts	English	1830	—	hanged
Butcher Westermann	German	1933	—	condemned to death
Alexander White	U.S.	1784	—	hanged
Thomas White	English	1698–1703	*Prosperous*	died of drink

pirate	*nationality*	*dates*	*ship(s)*	*fate*
Captain Worley	U.S.	1719	—	hanged
Richard Worley	U.S.	1718	*Eagle*	killed in battle

The actual historic ties with pirate swag are limited to eyewitness reports, letters and handbills, and such scraps as a 1775 chart of the Virgin Islands noting, "On Anegada is Ye Treasure Point, so called by ye freebooters from the gold and silver supposed to have been buried there about after the wreck of a Spanish galleon" (Sandz 2001, p. 224). Glamorizing piracy and life at sea were numerous popular works of fiction and questionable research, including a New England legend preserving the brigandage of Dixie Bull, the notorious "Pirate of Pemaquid," who farmed the area at Agamenticus, Maine, in 1632 and operated a trading post specializing in beaver pelts. After seizure by the French, he became a pirate and scuttled French ships in retaliation. When Bull's predations turned inland, Governor Winthrop of Massachusetts dispatched authorities to find him, but Bull dropped out of sight. More lasting than oral tales are published descriptions in Douglas Botting's *The Pirates* (1699), Charles Johnson's two-volume *A General History of the Robberies and Murders of the Most Notorious Pyrates* (1724, 1728), Lord Byron's *The Corsair* (1814), Captain Marryat's *The Pirate* (1836), Charles Elms's *The Pirates' Own Book* (1837), J. M. Barrie's *Peter Pan* (1904), and Rafael Sabatini's *Captain Blood* (1922).

See also **Blackbeard; Anne Bonny; Carausius; Sir Francis Drake; Charles Gibbs; Piet Heyn; Captain William Kidd; Sir Henry Morgan; money pit; Mary Read; pieces of eight; Roman coins — Monarchy and republic; Roman coins — Empire; Scottish coins; sixpence; treasure ships; *Whydah.***

SOURCES: Bordsen, John. "Prowling with Pirates." *Charlotte Observer*, August 12, 2001, 1G, 8G. • Burgan, Michael. "Lost and Found Treasure." *National Geographic World*, April 2000, 19. • Cordingly, David. *Under the Black Flag*. San Diego, Calif.: Harvest Books, 1995. • *Historic World Leaders*. Detroit: Gale Research, 1994. • Lewis, Brenda Ralph. *Coins & Currency*. New York: Random House, 1993. • Link, Marion Clayton. "Exploring the Drowned City of Port Royal." *National Geographic*, February 1960, 151, 158–182. • Nash, Jay Robert. *Encyclopedia of World Crime*. 6 vols. Wilmette, Ill.: CrimeBooks Inc., 1990. • *Outlaws, Mobsters & Crooks: From the Old West to the Internet*. Farmington Hills, Mich.: U*X*L, 1998. • Pickford, Nigel. *The Atlas of Ship Wrecks & Treasure*. New York: Dorling Kindersley, 1994. • Pomerleau, Charlie. "Tall Tales of Buried Treasures Run Deep." *Bangor Daily News*, August 27, 1998. • Rediker, Marcus. *Between the Devil and the Deep Blue Sea*. Cambridge: Cambridge University Press, 1987. • Rediker, Marcus. "When Women Pirates Sailed the Seas." *Wilson Quarterly*, Autumn 1993, 102–111. • Sandz, Victoria. *Encyclopedia of Western Atlantic Shipwrecks and Sunken Treasure*. Jefferson, N.C.: McFarland, 2001. • Skerry, Brian. "Pirates of the *Whydah*," *National Geographic*, May 1999, 64 • Snodgrass, Mary Ellen. "Grace O'Malley: Pirate Extraordinaire." *Islands*, July/August 1986, 18–21. • Wheeler, Richard. *In Pirate Waters*. New York: Thomas Y. Crowell, 1969.

pistareen

During the era when heavy gold and silver coins were being manufactured in the New World, Iberian Spain produced coinage that was 20 percent lighter than colonial issue after the removal of one-fifth of the value for the enrichment of Charles III of Spain and Naples. The two-*real* portrait piece, which English colonists called the "pistareen," earned its nickname from an alteration of "peseta." Of suspect value in Europe, the new Spanish money was easily identified in the American colonies because it bore the Hapsburg crest opposite the Castilian cross and shield of Leon.

Valued as small change, the pistareen remained in circulation into the 1830s in Central and South America, the Caribbean, Florida, New Orleans, the British colonies, and Canada. The coin was debased in Spain, but popular in the American colonies. It appears in *Journals of the Continental Congress* on October 7, 1775, when General Washington paid half a pistareen a day to laborers at Cambridge, Massachusetts. Three months later, when Congress debated the advantages of paper and silver money, a proposal by Governor Morris called for an American pistareen. According to a summary by Samuel Osgood and Walter Livingston, Thomas Jefferson's "Notes on the Establishment of a Money Unit and on a Coinage for the United States" (1784) promoted coinage of a double dime, which he called a pistareen. He valued the coin for its convenience, familiarity, and simple, decimal-based denomination.

***See also* portrait coins.**

SOURCES: Cordingly, David. *Under the Black Flag*. San Diego, Calif.: Harvest Books, 1995. • Jordan, Louis. "The Coins of Colonial and Early America." http://www.coins.nd.edu/ColCoin/ColCoinContents/Introduction.html. • Reinfeld, Fred. *Treasury of the World's Coins*. New York: Sterling Publishing, 1953. • Stanton, Lucia C. "Realms of a Coin." *Monticello Newsletter*, Summer 1994.

Pistrucci, Benedetto

The English recoinage of 1816 featured a significant national icon, St. George and the dragon, the work of Benedetto Pistrucci, Italian cameo engraver and medalist. Born in Rome on May 29, 1784, he was the son of Antonia Greco and Judge Federico Pistrucci of the city's high criminal court. After studying at Bologna, Naples, and Rome, he showed no interest in classical education. An inveterate tinkerer in toy cannon and vehicles, he put manual dexterity to use as apprentice to Signor Mango, a Roman cameo carver. From elemental tasks at shaping flint, Pistrucci progressed beyond his teacher's expectations.

In his early teens, Pistrucci got his break into fine engraving after executing a tri-level stone for Domenico Desalief, a jewel merchant commissioned by the empress of Russia. Pistrucci trained under Niccolò Morelli of the Accademia San Luca in Rome's Campidoglio. Despite a skin condition that hardened the flesh of his hands, he earned a prize for fine sculpture. By age 16, he had left his master and begun earning his own commissions. He married and worked for Count Demidoff of Russia, General Bale, Vescovali, Queen Maria Carolina of Naples, the Princess Borghese, and a seller of fraudulent antiques, Anigolo Bonelli. After besting rivals Girometti and Santarelli, Pistrucci completed a portrait cameo of Napoleon's sister, the Princess Bacciochi. She rewarded him by setting up classes at court in Florence and Pisa, where he taught modelling to nobles.

After a sojourn in Paris making a wax model of Napoleon, Pistrucci migrated to London in 1815. While completing a portrait of botanist Sir Joseph Banks, he encountered one of his marked originals of Flora that the fraud Bonelli had passed off to Richard Payne Knight as an antique. Knight refused to admit that he had been duped and wrote in a catalog of his gem collection that Pistrucci was equally stupid and impudent. The incident earned the sculptor the patronage of William Richard Hamilton, an officer of the Society of Antiquaries.

At the instruction of Banks, Pistrucci sculpted a test profile of George III in jasper. In 1816, London mintmaster Wellesley Pole accepted the cameo and had engraver Thomas Wyon the Younger make a royal portrait die for the half crown, which Pistrucci touched up with a diamond point. For a new gold sovereign, Pistrucci offered a wax pose of St. George, a Byzantine soldier executed in A.D. 304 during Diocletian's persecution of Christians. The sculptor pictured the saint mounted on a horse that trampled a dragon, a scene Pistrucci copied from a shell cameo belonging to the duke of Orléans.

Pistrucci replaced the original figure with the likeness of an Italian servant at Brunet's Hotel in Leicester Square and intended the model for the Earl of Spencer. Surrounding the dramatic pose, Pistrucci placed the French motto of the Order of the Garter, "*Honi Soit Qui Mal Y Pense*" (Shamed Be the Person Who Thinks Evil of It"). He engineered the design with a pantograph, a cast-iron reducing machine with paired arms that traced the large original with the pointer arm and reproduced it to smaller scale on a die. The St. George appeared during the reign of George IV on a gold crown, which the director of the French mint considered Europe's finest coin.

After Thomas Wyon's death, on September 22, 1817, Pistrucci became chief engraver of the London mint, an appointment that brought criticism for advancing a foreign artist. To end the outcries in the *Times*, in 1828, William Wyon took the top post, with Pistrucci assigned as chief medalist. In addition to upgrading the mint's punches and matrices of silver coins and replacing heraldic devices with human subjects, in 1821, he designed the George IV coronation medal from live sittings and created a bas-relief still in use on British coins and medals and on the rix dollar of Ceylon. On his own time, Pistrucci continued earning handsome sums by carving cameos and intaglios and by sculpting busts of engineer Matthew Boulton, Pozzo di Borgo, the Duke of York, and the helmeted Duke of Wellington and by completing the Blane naval medical medal, the Fothergillian medal of the Royal Humane Society, and military medals of William IV and Victoria.

A stubborn man, Pistrucci refused to make copies of royal busts executed by English sculptor Sir Francis Chantrey. He is also known for honoring the British victory over Napoleon Bonaparte with dramatic and intricately carved battle scenes in classic pose on the Waterloo Medal and for carving the silver seal of the duchy of Lancaster. Pistrucci earned membership in the Athenaeum Club and honoraria from Rome's Academy of St. Luke, the Institute of France, and the Royal Academy of Arts at Copenhagen. He ended his contributions to England's coins in 1824, but continued to live at the mint for another quarter century before retiring to Windsor, where he died of respiratory arrest on September 16, 1855.

Pistrucci's contribution to coinage and cameo art was considerable. His son Camillo and daughters Elena and Maria perpetuated the family reputation for fine sculpture. The mint reprised the famous pictures of St. George trampling the dragon for the 1887 double sovereign honoring Queen Victoria's half-century of rule. Canada's first gold sovereign, minted in 1908, pictured the raised image, made by an incuse die. It was also the featured design on the centenary sovereign of 1999 from the Royal Australian Mint. In 2002, England's Royal Mint replaced Pistrucci's St. George with the commemorative sovereign to mark the 50th year of the reign of Elizabeth II. At the end of a year's circulation, the Pistrucci design returned to its familiar place on England's most popular and successful coin.

See also **Canadian money; Rix dollars; Wyon family.**

SOURCES: Burke, James. "On Track." *Scientific American*, November 23, 2001. • Clain-Stefanelli, Elvira, and Vladimir Clain-Stefanelli. *The Beauty and Lore of Coins, Currency, and Medals*. Croton-on-Hudson, N.Y.: Riverwood Publishers, 1974. • Davies, Glyn. *A History of Money from Ancient Times to the Present Day*. Cardiff: University of Wales Press, 1994. • "Late Victorian Coinage." *Studium Magazine*, November 23, 2001. • Martinez, Alejandro J. "U.K.'s Mint Molds New Image for Sovereign Coins." *Wall Street Journal*, January 14, 2002, C11. • Reinfeld, Fred. *Treasury of the World's Coins*. New York: Sterling Publishing, 1953. • Stephen, Sir Leslie, and Sir Sidney Lee, eds. *Dictionary of National Biography*. London: Oxford University Press, 1922.

plate money

Plate money consists of rectangles or unusual cuts of unadorned plate metal bearing the authenticating stamp of the coiner. This spare form of coinage served the Irish in 1642, when the mint struck silver Inchiquin money on irregular polygons and authenticated them with the stamp of the nation's lord justice. Subsequent groats, crowns, half-crowns, and sixpence pieces were no more artful. Such hastily produced siege coinage was common to the era that saw the beheading of Charles I of England and the installation of the Commonwealth under Puritan warrior Oliver Cromwell.

Sweden experimented with *plattmynt* or plate money in the mid–17th century. Under Queen Kristina, called the "Minerva of the North," the nation profited from its first newspaper, compulsory school attendance, and advances in commerce and copper mining at Avesta that undergirded new coinage. To replace silver, mintmasters created massive copper plate coins worth one, two, four, eight, and ten *dalers*. They hammered each piece from four pounds of ore mined at Avesta near Falun. The awkward square plates contained official stamps but were otherwise plain. Mint workers applied the circular seal with drop hammers operated by a capstan, the design of engineer Marcus Koch and sons in 1644. Within the year, they increased the size of currency with a ten-*daler* copper, weighing 43 pounds. For convenience, merchants preferred paper substitutes for the bulky plate coins.

Kristina's plate *dalers* helped to control the price of copper by using up the ore before it could be exported. In 1717, when Sweden's war with Russia depleted the treasury, the Swedish crown issued copper *dalers* as well as paper notes until the mint returned to stamping plate coins. In the next decade, when Russia ruled Finland, the imperial treasury mimicked Swedish plate money with its own venture into square copper disks, notably a *hryvnia* stamped five times — at the four corners and in the middle.

One-*daler* plates issued in 1768 by Adolphus Frederick, the Swedish king, bore his initials topped with a crown. During the years 1777–1811, Danish shippers carried both minted and unminted copper plates and plate money to India. In 1782, the three-masted *Nicobar* departed Copenhagen for Tranquebar, India, carrying eight tons of Swedish plate coins from the *Riksbank* (state bank) for trade in new ships, cast guns, or Indian goods. Wrecked off Quoin Point, South Africa, it lay undisturbed until 1987, when local divers recovered the world's largest plate money hoard — 5,183 pieces of Swedish plate money, lost at sea for over two centuries. Two writers, Jimmy Herbert and coin expert Bertel Tingström, described the unusual hoard of square coins in an English-Swedish volume, *The Plate Money Treasure of Nicobar* (1999).

SOURCES: Clain-Stefanelli, Elvira, and Vladimir Clain-Stefanelli. *The Beauty and Lore of Coins, Currency, and Medals*. Croton-on-Hudson, N.Y.: Riverwood Publishers, 1974. • Cribb, Joe. *Money*. Toronto: Stoddart, 1990. • Cribb, Joe, Barrie Cook, and Ian Carradice. *The Coin Atlas*. London: Little, Brown and Co., 1999. • Grierson, Philip. *Numismatics*. London: Oxford University Press, 1975. • Herbert, Jimmy, and Bertel Tingström. *The Plate Money Treasure of Nicobar*. Stockholm: Royal Coin Cabinet, 1999. • "Plate Money from the *Nicobar*." http://www.tranquebar.dk/nicobar.htm#Plate Money from the Nicobar. • Weatherford, Jack. *The History of Money: From Sandstone to Cyberspace*. Pittsburgh, Pa.: Three Rivers Press, 1998.

portrait coins

The placement of human figures on coins figured in the careers and histories of a range of world notables — Offa of Mercia, Maria Theresa of Austria, Franklin Delano Roosevelt, and Sacagawea. The concept was essentially the innovation of Alexander III the Great of Macedon in the fourth century B.C., whose father, Philip II, minted silver coins picturing himself on horseback. Alexander backed gold coins with the likeness of Athena,

Top: **This portrait piece bears a militaristic image of Mithradates II, conqueror of Mesopotamia, who began ruling Parthia in 123 B.C.** ***Bottom:*** **This portrait coin featuring Lysimachus, one of the bodyguards of Alexander III the Great, was commissioned in 323 B.C., the year after Alexander's death from fever, when Lysimachus inherited Thrace. (Guy Clark, Ancient Coins and Antiquities, Norfolk, Virginia)**

A flattering Hellenized profile of Antiochus IV Epiphanes of Syria with a fillet among his curls appears opposite his name in Greek, "ANTIOXOV." (Guy Clark, Ancient Coins and Antiquities, Norfolk, Virginia)

the goddess of land victories, and placed Nike, goddess of sea victory, on the reverse of silver coins. At a height in Greek coin sculpting, these images displayed deep-set eyes, strong brow lines, and expressive features, the introit to portrait coins.

From the wide trading of Greek money throughout Europe and the Mideast into the Indian subcontinent, the stylish placement of monarchs on the obverse became standard procedure for engravers and mintmasters. In 412 B.C., the Miletus mint struck the first picture of a living subject, the satrap Tissaphernes, incised by a skilled Greek artist. The first true portrait coin displayed the bust of Ptolemy I Soter of Egypt, a former general of Alexander III the Great, in crown and aegis around 304 B.C. He furthered coinage not only in his homeland, but also in Cyprus and Cyrenaica. In addition to generating fine portrait coins of Alexander, he compiled a biography of his hero from Alexander's journals and official military documents. Two of Ptol-

A portrait coin picturing Alexander III the Great of Macedon in profile and a crab on the reverse was minted in 336 B.C. in Caria, a Greek colony on the Aegean coast of Asia Minor. (Guy Clark, Ancient Coins and Antiquities, Norfolk, Virginia)

emy's coins honored Alexander IV, the young son of Alexander III the Great and Roxana.

A marvel of balance and proportion was the romanticized filleted head of Antiochus I of Syria after 281 B.C. on a coin minted in southern Turkey. Farther east at Bactria, the

The placement of a human figure on coins figured in the career of Narseh, who began his reign over the Sassanian kingdom in Armenia in A.D. 293, the year this piece was struck. The reverse features a Zoroastrian fire altar. (Guy Clark, Ancient Coins and Antiquities, Norfolk, Virginia)

silver portrait coin of Antimachus in flat headgear produced a penetrating study of upturned lips and keen eyes, the face of an attentive, intelligent ruler. At Antioch around 78 B.C., after annexing Syria, Tigranes II the Great of Armenia, who called himself "king of kings," ennobled his rule with a sober profile and majestic headpiece. To the southwest, coastal Egypt produced *tetradrachms* with sculptural detailing and anatomical modeling derived from Greek artistry.

In addition to rulers, portrait coins featured other notables living and dead. In Italy, where Renaissance art moved beyond Roman self-adulation to religious scenarios, portrait coins raised an issue of taste. Whereas rulers of Florence, Genoa, and Venice tended to avoid portraits, the self-made men indulged their egos with portraits grandly displayed on *testoni* ("head coins"). The coin was the invention of the Milanese *condottiero* Francesco Sforza after 1450 and recurred in the mint designs of Ludovico "il Moro" Sforza, Duke of Milan, engraved by medalist Cristoforo "Caradosso" Foppa, and in the specie of Francesco's son, Galeazzo Maria Sforza, a generation later. A gold coin pictured Galeazzo's contemporary, the extravagant arts patron Pope Leo X, a member of the prominent de' Medici family, who enriched themselves through commerce and banking. After 1471, Venetian doge Niccolo Tron commissioned the first portrait *testone* called the *lira.* In the late 1500s, Cosimo de' Medici, a Florentine duke, adorned a silver coin that honored the extensive clan of Italian magnates. Ferrara's portrait coins pictured the noble d'Este family; Mantuan coin art honored the Gonzagas.

Similar forms of *testoni* appeared in England as the shilling and throughout southwestern Europe under varied names: the French *testons,* Portuguese *testaos,* and Swiss *Dicken.* The French *teston,* such as that of Louis XII of France, emulated Italian elegance, but lacked the skill of fine sculpture. To make up for lapses in Gallic bas-relief, during the Renaissance, Francis I, a warrior king and arbiter of culture, assembled at his court master sculptors Benvenuto Cellini and Leonardo da Vinci, and Andrea del Sarto, admired as the "faultless painter." Through these masters, Francis was able to generate a series of *testons* depicting him at important periods of his rise to be the nation's *grand roi.*

In 1771, Charles III, king of Spain and Naples, altered the standardized pillars of Hercules by issuing silver portrait pistareens minted in the Spanish colonies. The tradition governed coinage through the rest of his line until the loss of Spain's New World colonies. Another example of symbolic portrait busts in Europe was the coining of individual Dutch and Belgian royal pieces in 1830 after the Kingdom of the United Netherlands ended 16 years of union. Representing Belgium was a gold coin featuring Leopold I; his counterpart, Willem III, adorned a Dutch coin.

New World coinage dropped earlier Spanish denominations and royal portraits in favor of more recent historic names and images. In Bolivia, the coining of the *boliviano* commemorated the heroism of Simón Bolívar, Venezuelan liberator of South America. Upon taking Upper Peru in April 1825, at the height of his popularity, he created the state of Bolivia and authored a constitution. The *boliviano* coin, worth a *peso,* circulated his likeness throughout northern South America and influenced portrait coinage in other Hispanic nations. In 1965, the *peso boliviano* replaced the *boliviano* as the nation's official currency.

In China, the influence of British coins followed the opening of Asian markets to European trade. After 1875, the Emperor Kuang Hsu emulated the Indian *rupees* honoring Queen Victoria. His austere portrait pieces featured a silhouette with graceful queue falling straight from the brim of his hat. A circlet of raised dots provided the only other adornment to the legendless coin.

Hawaiian coin artists also created portrait coins in the 1880s and 1890s to extol royalty. A silver piece struck in 1883 pictured King Kalakaua with unadorned head, curly beard, and thick mustache. A decade later, a gold coin depicted Queen Liliuokalani in Victorian splendor, with square-necked gown, cameo on a ribbon at her neck, and upswept hairstyle topped with a dainty tiara. Like the pattern image of Queen Victoria, the legend followed Latinate form: "*Lilivocalania Dei Gratia*" ("Liliuokalani by the Grace of God").

See also **African money; Athelstan; bas-relief;** ***bezant*****; bible currency; Victor D. Brenner; Dr. Selma Burke; Byzantine coins; Canadian coins; Caradosso; Carausius; Benvenuto Cellini; Celtic coins; coinage; coin collections; coins and currency in art;** ***dirhan;*** **dollar;** ***drachma; ducat; écu;*** **Egyptian money; English money; euro;** ***franc;*** **Frederick the Great;** ***florin;*** **Christian Gobrecht; Hubertus Goltzius; guinea; India, money of; Islamic coins; Thomas Jefferson;** ***lira;*** **Macedonian coins; maundy money; medieval money; George T. Morgan; numismatics; Offa of Mercia; papal coins; paper money; Peace dollar; pistareen; John Roettiers; Roman coins; Renaissance coins; Roman coins — Monarchy and republic; Scottish coins; shilling; tughra; U.S. coins; Jean Varin; Wyon family.**

SOURCES: Clain-Stefanelli, Elvira, and Vladimir Clain-Stefanelli. *The Beauty and Lore of Coins, Currency, and Medals.* Croton-on-Hudson, N.Y.:

Riverwood Publishers, 1974. • Cribb, Joe. *Money*. Toronto: Stoddart, 1990. • Cribb, Joe, Barrie Cook, and Ian Carradice. *The Coin Atlas*. London: Little, Brown and Co., 1999. • Davies, Glyn. *A History of Money from Ancient Times to the Present Day*. Cardiff: University of Wales Press, 1994. • Head, Barclay V. *A Guide to the Principal Coins of the Greeks*. London: British Museum, 1959. • Head, Barclay V. *Historia Numorum*. Chicago: Argonaut, 1911. • Jansen, H. W., and Anthony F. Janson. *History of Art*. New York: Harry N. Abrams, Incorporated, 1997. • Lewis, Brenda Ralph. *Coins & Currency*. New York: Random House, 1993. • Reinfeld, Fred. *Treasury of the World's Coins*. New York: Sterling Publishing, 1953. • Thorncroft, Tony. "The Great Charms of Old Money." *Financial Times*, January 20, 2001.

postage currency

In the absence of small change, postage stamps have served as makeshift coins. The use of stamp currency for small commercial transactions was common in the United States during the Civil War, when coin shortages were common. On July 11, 1862, President Abraham Lincoln agreed to the proposal of Secretary of the Treasury Salmon Portland Chase to accept postage stamp notes in lieu of coins. Approval of the Postage Currency Act six days later authorized notes in five-, ten-, 25-, and 50-cent denominations known as postage stamp currency. The face of each note bore a copy of the era's postal stamps made with genuine stamp dies. A block of the notes separated at the perforations that outlined each pane, which measured around 2½ by 1⅝ inches. Unlike legal tender, the stamp notes were negotiable for up to five dollars.

Another variety of postage currency, token money, consisted of metal discs to which the user affixed postage stamps. This type had its faults, depending on the strength of the glue or fixative and the cleanliness of the hands that exchanged the tokens. In 1862, Bostonian sewing machine merchant John Gault of Kirkpatrick & Gault in New York City, invented and patented a small brass case with a transparent isinglass (mica) cover that kept a single stamp clean and secure, yet visible. Like coins, the "money stamps" remained whole and clearly marked for numerous exchanges.

Available in denominations of one, two, three, five, ten, 12, 24, 30, and 90 cents, the encased stamps, made by Scovill Company of Waterbury, Connecticut, replaced small coins at a time when hoarders were removing silver from circulation. Most popular were the one-cent, three-cent, and five-cent stamps. Paying for the process of wrapping the coins were individual merchants seeking publicity for their goods and services. Gault advertised his firm as did patent medicine manufacturer S. Steinfeld's Cognac Bitters, Drake's Plantation Bitters, Tremont House in Chicago, North America Life Insurance Company, Brown's Bronchial Troches, Irving House in New York City, Lord & Taylor, Verdon Liqueur, John Shillito of Cincinnati, Mencum's Family Wine Emporium, Boston stereopticon seller Joseph L. Bates, White the Hatter of New York, Weir and Larminie of Montreal, and Dr. J. C. Ayer of Lowell, Massachusetts, maker of Cathartic Pills and sarsaparilla.

Encased postage stamps continued to serve commercial needs during the 20th century. South Africans accepted the stamped cards of the British South Africa Company in 1900. In Russia during World War I, the treasury emulated the postage stamps on thick cardboard as monetary tokens worth one, two, ten, 15, and 20 *kopecks*. In Denmark, a coin shortage caused by World War II encouraged private businesses to wrap regular postage stamps in small cardboard holders, apply an advertisement on the back, and top with cellophane. The English used a similar stamp-for-coin system, but without the paper envelopes. Similar postal coinage emerged in Argentina, Austria, Belgium, France, Germany, and Greece.

Mail order business later in the 20th century also relied on postage stamps to pay for the return of merchandise through the mails. Light and safer than coins in envelopes, the stamps were worth the same as coins without the weight and bulk. The substitution of stamps for coins discouraged mail pilferage and surreptitious rifling of the post.

SOURCES: Allen, Larry. *Encyclopedia of Money.* New York: Checkmark Books, 2001. • Bowers, Q. David. *Adventures with Rare Coins.* Los Angeles: Bowers & Ruddy Galleries, Inc., 1979. • Clain-Stefanelli, Elvira, and Vladimir Clain-Stefanelli. *The Beauty and Lore of Coins, Currency, and Medals.* Croton-on-Hudson, N.Y.: Riverwood Publishers, 1974. • Lewis, Brenda Ralph. *Coins & Currency.* New York: Random House, 1993. • Opitz, Charles J. *Odd and Curious Money.* Ocala, Fla.: First Impressions, 1986. • Weatherford, Jack. *The History of Money: From Sandstone to Cyberspace.* Pittsburgh, Pa.: Three Rivers Press, 1998.

potin

An alloy of copper, lead, and zinc with a high tin content, potin was a common coin metal among Celtic moneyers in France and Belgium from 100 B.C. to around A.D. 30. An unattractive grey or black metal that was also called white bronze, potin produced a smooth, durable, and slightly lustrous surface, but crude, indistinct detailing. The first coins in Britain were the potins cast by the Belgae of Kent. The term "potin" also applies to coins of Alexander III the Great, which are also known as "AE" *tetradrachms.*

As the Celts developed complex communities and commerce, they began producing non-standardized metal money modeled on Greek *staters, drachms,* and *tetradrachms.* Their coinsmiths relied on alluvial tin from France's Atlantic coast or imported from across the English Channel from southwestern England. The addition of tin to bronze alloy reduced the melting temperature and simplified casting in molds.

The process began with a coin or pattern, which the shaper sandwiched between two slices of clay. After removal of the master shape, the two sides of the mold required a thin channel from the hollow to the outside and repositioning one atop the other for the pouring of molten metal down the groove and into the center. After trimming the cooling flan, the worker could remelt the scraps to make the most of an investment in base metal. Recyling of molds produced blurred images that made coins look used.

Less valuable than the gold and silver exchange gifts between chieftains, potin tokens served daily buying and selling in a limited area. They featured spoked wheels as sun symbols and wild boars and horses as emblems of valor and equestrian skill. To denote nobility in human figures, coin designers incised a torque about the neck and added a spear to represent military acumen.

See also **Celtic coins; tokens.**

SOURCES: Cribb, Joe. *Money.* Toronto: Stoddart, 1990. • Cribb, Joe, Barrie Cook, and Ian Carradice. *The Coin Atlas.* London: Little, Brown and Co., 1999. • Laing, Lloyd R. *Coins and Archaeology.* New York: Schocken Books, 1969. • "The Significance of Celtic Coinage." http://www.ex.ac.uk/~RDavies/ arian/ celtic.html.

Pratt, Bela Lyon

Innovative coin sculptor Bela Lyon Pratt popularized incuse styling on $2.50 and five-dollar gold pieces, the only ones of their type in U.S. monetary history. The son of Sarah Victoria Whittlesey and attorney George Pratt, he was born in Norwich, Connecticut, on December 11, 1867. He grew up in New England religious austerity and studied under John Henry Niemeyer and John Ferguson Weir at the Yale School of Fine Arts.

At age 20, Pratt began learning modeling, drawing, and painting at the Art Students' League of New York City, where he was mentored by sculptor Augustus Saint-Gaudens, who influenced his style. Pratt studied in Paris and won prizes as the star pupil of l'École des Beaux-Arts. He polished his Water Gate sculpture for the 1893 World's Columbian Exposition in Chicago, the impetus to the offer of a life-long teaching job at the Boston Museum School of Fine Arts. In addition to family groupings, Pratt produced a medal for Harvard alumni and the Yale bicentennial medal as well as huge entranceway sculptures for the Library of Congress in Washington, D.C. and a bronze *Victory* for the battleship *Massachusetts.* In 1901, he won a medal for *Fountain of Youth* at the Buffalo Pan-American Exposition.

In 1907, during the height of artistic U.S. coin design, Pratt, on the recommendation of

Dr. William Sturgis Bigelow, a prominent Boston physician, collaborated with President Theodore Roosevelt on an upgrade to specie. Mint chief Charles E. Barber approved Pratt's sculpture of a true native American profile for the half eagle and the quarter in the style of ancient Greek and Egyptian coins. Issued the following year with sunken outlines rather than protruding bas-relief, his intaglio coins earned admiration for picturing a real Plains Indian in feathered headdress. On the practical side, the incuse styling received criticism for harboring dirt and germs. Rumors made the sunken design a health issue. The U.S. Mint continued circulating the incuse coins for 22 years, yet never produced another piece with recessed image.

Later, Pratt sculpted a Spanish War infantryman, likenesses of Nathan Hale and John Winthrop, and a Civil War memorial, the *Andersonville Prisoner Boy*. Additional male figures include a whaler grasping a harpoon, a likeness of novelist Nathaniel Hawthorne, *Barefoot Boy*, and the popular Soldiers' and Sailors' Monument. In 1915, he surpassed his earlier awards with a gold medal from the Panama-Pacific International Exposition in San Francisco, where he displayed 17 statues. He died on May 18, 1917, in Jamaica Plain, Massachusetts.

***See also* Augustus Saint-Gaudens.**

SOURCES: *Almanac of Famous People*. 6th ed. Farmington Hills, Mich.: Gale Group, 1998. *Biography Resource Center*. Farmington Hills, Mich.: Gale Group, 2001. • Clain-Stefanelli, Elvira, and Vladimir Clain-Stefanelli. *The Beauty and Lore of Coins, Currency, and Medals*. Cfoton-on-Hudson, N.Y.: Riverwood Publishers, 1974. • Johnson, Allen, ed. *Dictionary of American Biography*. New York: Charles Scribner's Sons, 1928. • Van Ryzin, Robert R. *Twisted Tails: Sifted Fact, Fantasy and Fiction from U.S. Coin History*. Iola, Wisc.: Krause Publications, 1995.

quetzal

Following the dissolution of the United Provinces of Central America in 1839, the resulting five independent nations — Costa Rica, El Salvador, Guatemala, Honduras, and Nicaragua — coined their own moneys. After 1920, Guatemala's specie revived the Maya and Aztec mythology of a young man who was slain and turned into a sacred bird called the quetzal. The monetary unit *quetzal*, therefore, was named for a rare, iridescent gold-green mountain bird, the *Pharomachrus mocino*, which flourishes from southern Mexico to Bolivia. In addition to being the state emblem, the bird is an element of the Guatemalan coat of arms and of the highest national award, the Order of the Quetzal. First given in 1936, the award honors international, civic, scientific, literary, or artistic service to the nation. In 1998, the award committee selected Mayanist and hieroglyphics expert Dr. Linda Schele, a scholar specializing in Mesoamerican culture, to receive the honor.

The male bird's two three-foot tail feathers, a feature of the ritual Mexican *quetzales* dance, adorned only nobility. The plumes called to mind the ancient god Quetzalcóatl, the feathered serpent of the Teotihuacán civilization from A.D. 200 to 700. An agrarian god controlling earth and water, he also represented the morning and evening star, emblems of mortality, energy, and rebirth. A patron of shamans and creator of human life, the god also devised the Aztec calendar and agriculture, invented literacy and bookbinding, and fostered goldsmiths.

In 1991, Guatemala's treasury struck a 25-*centavo* coin picturing the quetzal perched above a scroll announcing the date the country gained independence. Symbolizing "libertad" ("freedom") to the "Republica de Guatemala," the graceful bird embodies the ability to fly as well as natural beauty. The surrounding greenery and the reverse image of a somber, dignified native in traditional dress link the images on the coin to Guatemala's roots and to its future.

***See also* paper money.**

SOURCES: Clain-Stefanelli, Elvira, and Vladimir Clain-Stefanelli. *The Beauty and Lore of Coins, Currency, and Medals*. Croton-on-Hudson, N.Y.: Riverwood Publishers, 1974. • "Guatemalan Government Honors Renowned UT Austin Scholar for Her Work in Deciphering Hieroglyphics." *University of Texas at Austin News*, March 18, 1998. • Harnik, Eva. "The Land of Eternal Spring." *World*

& I, August 1, 2001. • Lewis, Brenda Ralph. *Coins & Currency*. New York: Random House, 1993. • Opitz, Charles J. *Odd and Curious Money*. Ocala, Fla.: First Impressions, 1986.

Read, Mary

A notorious cross-dressing pirate and soldier, Mary Read, garbed like other seagoing thieves and swearing and swaggering like men, established a career at sea. In league with Anne Bonny aboard the ship of John "Calico Jack" Rackham (or Rackam), Read figured in the first major reference source on pirates, Captain Charles Johnson's two-volume *A General History of the Robberies and Murders of the Most Notorious Pyrates* (1724, 1728), a sourcebook for Robert Louis Stevenson's *Treasure Island* (1883). Born in London at the end of the 1680s to Polly Read, the widow of Alfred Read, a sailor who died at sea, Read was an illegitimate child. She conspired with her mother to claim she was the man's son, who had died.

By dressing like a boy to fool her supposed paternal grandparents in Devon, Read developed a knack for fraud and adventure. The disguise concealed her gender after her grandmother's death, when Read took a post as a Frenchwoman's page. Around age sixteen, to escape poverty, Read served as a seaman aboard an English man-of-war and fought as an infantryman and horse soldier. While in service, she revealed her identity to a handsome comrade, Corporal Jules Vosquon. They married and, after mustering out, ran the Three Horseshoes Inn near Breda castle in the south of Holland.

Widowed in 1716, Read lost her trade after the Peace of Ryswick ended brisk business with occupation forces. She journeyed to Flanders once more in the guise of a male soldier. When her military service ended, she sailed for the Caribbean on a Dutch ship, which pirates captured. She joined their crew, led by Captain Jennings, who headquartered in New Providence in the Bahamas, and took a new lover, whom she defended in a duel.

Upon meeting Anne Bonny, a fellow transdressing pirate of similar humble origin, Read became her lover and remained in Rackam's company of freebooters, who shared in the cash and plunder of the Spanish Main. An eyewitness, kidnap victim Dorothy Thomas, described the two women's dress as jacket, pants, and kerchief with pistols and machetes for arms. For a time, Read and 600 other pirates accepted a general amnesty offered by King George I. She worked for Woodes Rogers, the Bahamian governor, as a privateer fighting the Spanish, but once more lapsed into piracy.

After the crew seized the English ship *William*, Rogers declared Rackham, Read, and Bonny outlaws. The pirates kept the *William* and used it to victimize more merchant vessels and fishing trawlers. In Jamaica's Negril Bay, Captain Jonathon Barnet and a troop of British law enforcers destroyed the rigging of the pirate ship and boarded it in summer 1720. According to reports, as a British sloop drew alongside, Read displayed more courage than her fellow pirates, whom she shot at in exasperation at their cowardice.

Brought to justice on November 28, 1720, Read appeared before Governor Nicholas Lawes at the Grand Court at St. Jaco de la Vega (now Spanish Town), Jamaica. Facing authorities at the end of their patience with murder and thievery in the Caribbean, Read claimed that she became a pirate solely out of penury. She and Bonny used their pregnancies to elude hanging and rotting in chains, the fate of Rackham and other fellow crew members, who went to the gallows on Deadman's Cay. Read died in prison of fever on December 4. Translations of Johnson's work from English into major European languages spread Read's notoriety globally.

See also **Anne Bonny.**

SOURCES: Cordingly, David. *Under the Black Flag*. San Diego, Calif.: Harvest Books, 1995. • *Gay & Lesbian Biography*. Detroit: St. James Press, 1997. • Nash, Jay Robert. *Encyclopedia of World Crime*. 6 vols. Wilmette, Ill.: CrimeBooks Inc., 1990. • *Outlaws, Mobsters & Crooks: From the Old West to the Internet*. Farmington Hills, Mich.: U*X*L, 1998. • Rediker, Marcus. "When Women Pirates Sailed the Seas." *Wilson Quarterly*, Autumn 1993, 102–111.

Redfield hoard

One of history's most famous caches of silver pieces, the Redfield hoard contained mint-quality Morgan and Peace silver dollars. The coins belonged to eccentric investment banker LaVere (or Lavere) Redfield of Los Angeles, California. During the Great Depression, he developed a distrust of banks, paper money, and government bureaucracy. He withdrew from finance and farmed in Reno, Nevada. When pressed to pay property tax, he chose jail rather than to give money to the government. He also hoarded canned goods, especially peaches.

In later years, paranoia caused Redfield to convert his wealth into silver dollars in $1,000 amounts. On tips from friendly bank tellers, he learned when shipments were arriving and bought up new coins in bulk quantities, which he brought home in his battered farm truck. After each conversion, he tossed bank bags of coins down his coal chute. Over 35 years, he accumulated 600 bags containing a total of 600,000 silver dollars. Some bore the acid etching of spewed peaches, which burst from rusted cans. In the 1960s, robbers stole 100 bags of coins, apparently for the purpose of gambling in Nevada casinos. A decade later, Redfield sold some of his coins.

At Redfield's death in 1974, his net worth in land and stock was valued at over $100 million. When the authorities who conducted the appraisal of his property discovered the 11-ton basement cache, they spied a note asking that the finder not report him to the Internal Revenue Service. Numismatists placed high value on rare, uncirculated, and high quality coinage. At auction, Redfield dollars brought the highest price paid for a hoard—$7,300,000 for 407,000 U.S. silver dollars

SOURCES: "Hoards of Coins." *Coins and Currency Weekly*, December 6, 1998. • "LaVere Redfield and His Dollars." http://coin-shop.com/gold26.htm. • Highfill, John W., and Walter H. Breen. *The Comprehensive U.S. Silver Dollar Encyclopedia.* Broken Arrow, Okla.: Highfill Press, Inc., 1992. • Young, Douglas. "Local Coin Collector Builds $1 Billion Firm." *Los Angeles Business Journal*, August 21, 1995, pp. 45–46.

Reid, Templeton

Goldsmith Templeton Reid from Milledgeville, Georgia, preceded other U.S. engravers and private mintmasters in converting raw gold into coins. Before the founding of the federal branch mint in Dahlonega, Georgia, he solved the problem of creating uniform currency from gold dust and nuggets, which were too cumbrous for ordinary commerce. He opened an assay office and workshop in Milledgeville and moved to mining operations in northern Georgia at Gainesville. His advertisements appeared in a hometown paper and in those of Athens, Augusta, Columbus, and Macon.

From July through October 1830, Reid converted $1,500 in gold into high quality coins worth $2.50, five dollars, and ten dollars. According to the *Southern Recorder* article of July 24, 1830, he incised on the dies "Georgia Gold," the year, and "Templeton Reid, Assayer" and stamped 1,000 quarter eagles, 300 half eagles, and 250 eagles. Assays of his coins revealed that he made seven percent on each. Because of the high cost of machinery, loss of gold in fluxing, and complaints of devalued coins, he closed his operation within a year and began manufacturing guns and an improved cotton gin, which he patented. When he died in August 1851, the *Columbus Times* called him a genius at invention and mechanics for operating the first private U.S. mint.

SOURCES: Bowers, Q. David. *Adventures with Rare Coins.* Los Angeles: Bowers & Ruddy Galleries, Inc., 1979. • Bowers, Q. David. "American Gold." *American Heritage*, December 1984, 43–49. • Clain-Stefanelli, Elvira, and Vladimir Clain-Stefanelli. *The Beauty and Lore of Coins, Currency, and Medals.* Croton-on-Hudson, N.Y.: Riverwood Publishers, 1974. • Hammett, A. B. J. *The History of Gold.* Kerriville, Tex.: Braswell Printing, Co., 1966. • Stevenson, Jed. "A Bite of Gold." *New York Times*, September 1, 1991, p. 57.

Renaissance coins

Buoyed by trade derived from the Crusades, Italy's Renaissance city-states of Florence, Genoa, Siena, and Venice produced great art, culture, and coins. After the low quality stamping and imitative art of the Middle Ages, designers escaped the classical detailing and rigid portraiture of Greek, Roman, and Byzantine minting for the style and flair of their own time. In place of predictable portraits of emperors, die-makers incised religious art rich with symbolism. Some of the most treasured coins of the era derive from England, France, and Italy, among them the *salut d'or* ("gold medal").

At the demise of the French *denier*, the Duke of Bedford commissioned the first *saluts d'or* for his nephew. One example designed for Charles I of Anjou and struck after 1277 offers the shield of Jerusalem sharing a blazon with the French royal symbol. The back features the annunciation of the angel to the Virgin Mary. In 1422, the Anglo-Gallic *salut d'or* of Henry VI, struck at St. Lô, pictured the Virgin Mary receiving a one-word message — "*Ave*" ("hail") — from the archangel Gabriel and the legend "*Henricus Dei Gra Fracoru Z Aglie Rex*" ("Henry by the Grace of God King of the Franks and the English"). A pious reverse motto in blended Greco-Roman alphabets exults "*XPC Vincit XPC Regnat XPC Imperat*" ("Christ Conquers, Christ Reigns, Christ Commands") around the blazons of France and England side by side with the nimbate head of the Virgin Mary facing the angel Gabriel in the background. In 1423, the striking of a *salut d'or* preserved the Christian cross within deep scallops and a circlet of *fleurs-de-lis*.

In this same period, other refined coin styles emerged. The fine Gothic style of the moneyers of Philip IV of France produced the portrait of a seated king with scepter within a scalloped frame on a coin dalled a *masse d'or* ("gold mace" or "scepter"). The meticulous *écu* or French shield coin displayed royal self-importance in the three *fleurs-de-lis* on the shield beneath a crown. The wide border, containing ornate lettering and enhanced with beaded edge, produced a wheel effect that the English dubbed "cartwheels."

At a height of humanistic endeavors, Henri II of France introduced the theme of medieval chivalry on his *Henri d'or* ("golden Henry"), a coin in half, single, and double denominations that revived the best in classicism. As depicted by his chief moneyer Marc Béchot for the mint at La Rochelle, the more ornate laurel-crowned profile is both grave and noble with its carefully clipped beard and braided stand-up collar. To issue the coins evenly and efficiently, the king imported a rolling mill, punch, and an innovation, the *balancer* or screw press invented by German goldsmith Marx Schwab of Augsburg. Up to a dozen coinsmiths took turns rotating the arms of the heavy device to press out specie. Use of the press outraged coinsmiths who hammered out coins medieval style — one by one on paired dies.

In Valletta, Malta, the Knights of Malta, formerly called the Poor Knights of Christ and Solomon's Temple or the Knights Hospitallers, extended their philanthropy in the tradition of their seventh-century patron John the Almsgiver. As patriarch of Alexandria, he lived on a small stipend and dispensed the rest of his wealth to the poor. He protected the underclass from the frauds and cheating of merchants by demanding that trade be conducted with fair weights and measures. The 80,000 gold pieces that accrued in the church treasury he alloted to abbeys and hospitals. He used some coin to ransom captives and to bankroll Rome after the Persian invasion.

John's example encouraged altruism during the Crusades, when Grand Master Elion de Villeneuve of the Knights of St. John set an example of benevolent coinage with the striking of silver *gigliati* after 1319. In 1530, the Holy Roman Emperor Charles V sanctioned a resettlement of the Knights Hospitallers at Malta, where they altered their name to reflect the location. Just as they had in the past, the brothers minted their own silver *zecchini*. Initiating the operation was Grand Master Philippe Villiers de L'isle Adam, who erected Malta's mint. After 1557, Grand Master John de la Vallette commissioned token coppers to pay for labor at public works. Until the 1770s, the knights produced a range of denominations and affixed to each coin the profile of the ruling grand master and an appropriately pious motto.

Coinage extending from the late Renaissance into the baroque period resulted in some of Europe's most artistic issue. From Tuscany came a dramatic baptism of Christ by John the Baptist surrounded by the legend "*Dilectus Filius Meus*" ("My Beloved Son"); a Mantuan *ducatone* pictured a fierce guard dog with curled tail, emblem of the Gonzagas. The Genoese produced a richly incised gold coin picturing the Virgin Mary on a cloud holding a scepter and the child Jesus under a crown of stars raised by two cherubs. At the height of the era's decorative coinage, the papal *Zecca* ("mint") generated a shower of pictorial showpieces displaying Vatican scenarios — a conclave of cardinals around the pope under the canopy of St. Peter's Basilica, pilgrims to Rome, the blessing of St. Anthony, St. Peter's generosity to the handicapped with the legend "*Quod Habeo Tibi Do*" ("What I Have I Give to You"), an eight-sided shield proclaiming "*Melius Est Dare Quam Accipere*" ("It Is Better to Give Than to Receive"), and St. John the Baptist under the biblical citation "*Parate Viam Domini*" ("Prepare the Way of the Lord").

See also **banking; Donato Bramante; Caradosso; *ducat; écu;* English money; *florin;* groat; *gros;* Leone Leoni; *lira;* papal coins; screw press; shilling; Sigismund, Archduke of Tyrol; *thaler;* Jean Varin.**

SOURCES: Acar, Ozgen, "Mammoth Ottoman Hoard," *Archaeology*, January/February 2002, p. 8. • Clain-Stefanelli, Elvira, and Vladimir Clain-Stefanelli. *The Beauty and Lore of Coins, Currency, and Medals*. Croton-on-Hudson, N.Y.: Riverwood Publishers, 1974. • Cribb, Joe. *Money*. Toronto: Stoddart, 1990. • Cribb, Barry, Barrie Cook, and Ian Carradice. *The Coin Atlas*. London: Little, Brown and Co., 1999. • Grierson, Philip. *Numismatics*. London: Oxford University Press, 1975. • Hallam, Elizabeth, ed. *Chronicles of the Crusades*. Wayne, N.J.: CLB, 1997. • Hallam, Elizabeth, gen. ed. *Saints: Who They Are and How They Help You*. New York: Simon & Schuster, 1994. • Hastings, James, ed. *Encyclopedia of Religion and Ethics*. New York: Charles Scribner's Sons, 1951. • Hollister, C. Warren. *Medieval Europe: A Short History*. New York: McGraw-Hill, 1994. • Laing, Lloyd R. *Coins and Archaeology*. New York: Schocken Books, 1969. • Severy, Merle, ed. *The Renaissance*. Washington, D.C.: National Geographic Society, 1977. • Tuchman, Barbara W. *A Distant Mirror: The Calamitous 14th Century*. New York: Alfred A. Knopf, 1978.

ring and bullet money

Rings have served as personal adornment and a convenient and transportable form of currency from ancient times. As early as 2500 B.C., Mesopotamians simplified the carrying of wealth by producing coils and metal bangles or circles called *hat* that fit easily around the wrist or arm. The practical styling contrasted the awkward metal rods or spit money of the Greeks and the hoarding of grain at Egyptian banks. For small change, Mesopotamian consumers could easily break off pieces and retain the rest.

To farm folk far from harbor trading centers or from crossroads emporia, the emergence of ring money allowed growers to limit the types of crops they planted and to cultivate only one specialty, which they swapped for tradeable metal. When metal adornments became more popular than trading in other commodities or when merchants began demanding rings above other forms of payment, ring money advanced from one choice of commercial medium to the dominant medium of exchange, a forerunner of coins. The main differences between authentic coins and ring money were standardization and a validating stamp of worth.

Around 1300 B.C., the Egyptians produced bent wire specie that was uniform in weight of copper, silver, and gold. Its success resulted in a pervasive hieroglyph that equated with "money." The *deben* ring coin, derived from the term "circular," set a recognized unit of value, as with the price of an ox or knife or the wage of a temple laborer. For ease of transportation, buyers aligned metal circlets on rods or cords or bore them to market in baskets. During transactions, merchants weighed ring money on a balance beam scale to determine its value.

In northwestern Europe from around 500 B.C. until the Roman invasions of the 50s

B.C., Celts in England, the Danube territory, France, Ireland, and Scotland created a form of ring money resembling the *manillas* of Africa. Cherished as religious votive emblems as well as currency, the gold, silver, and bronze rings came in a variety of thicknesses and diameters. Some contained two, three, or four metal ears or knobs spaced evenly over the outer edge; others were interlocking or strung on rope or copper wire to disencumber the bearer. More ornate ring proto-coins bore overlapped edges or the shapes of stars or wheels. In 1893, traveler and historian Hubert Howe Bancroft described the practicality of ancient ring coins in *The Book of the Fair*, a summary of exhibits of ancient items at the World's Columbian Exhibition.

Use of open-ended ring money to pay the *wergild* (also *weregild* or *wergeld)* ("blood money"), a Germanic form of compensation paid by an offender to an injured party or to the victim's survivors, accounts for accumulations of rings and bracelets among the medieval Danes. Specific terms described the monetary worth of a victim: for example, a *twelfhyndeman*, one evaluated at 1,200 shillings of compensation; the *syxhyndeman*, worth half the value of a *twelfhyndeman*; and the least valuable, a *twyhyndeman*, evaluated at 200 shillings. The killing of an outlaw, the felon who operated outside the bounds of law, was unregulated and required no compensatory payment of *wergild*. The system of fines and forfeits paid in metal rings remained in effect until the reign of Swend Tweskideg (or Sweyn Forkbeard), king of Denmark and father of Canute I, around A.D. 1000.

In Thailand, shoppers also preferred the portability of rings and bracelets for cash. In the A.D. 1200s, a formal coinage emulated the successful metal ring as money. At Sukhothai Kingdom, King Ramkamhaeng appears to have invented a hybrid, called a *pot duang* ("curled worm") or bullet money. In Chiengmai, coinsmiths stamped weight and mint location on bars, then used tongs to bend each into a circle suggesting the shape of a cowrie. Completing the ring money was a slash of the chisel demonstrating that the metal was solid silver rather than layered metal or a silver wash. Small round stamps established authenticity with symbols from nature or wheels.

A century later, coiners hammered the bars into a tight configuration, which looked to Westerners like a spent bullet. Examples struck at Ayutthaya between 1350 and 1767 were of high quality. One type bore the lotus mark, symbol of Narai, the king from 1656 to 1688. In 1687, their distinctive shape caught the attention of a French ambassador, Monsieur de la Loubère, who drew pictures preserving bullet coins.

The manufacture of bullet coins was tedious. Four coiners divided the chores. One pumped the bellows, another stoked the furnace, a third dispensed silver in measured amounts into a crucible, and the fourth slid the container into the furnace. When the silver liquefied, the coinsmith poured it from the crucible to a grooved wood block for shaping into a bar that was round on one side and flat on the other. The fourth worker cut the bar twice on the flat side, positioned it on an iron anvil, and hammered the flat piece into a rounded lump. After sliding the slug into an elephant bone to steady it, the coiner applied a stamp.

The slug-shaped bullet coins served Malaccans into the 19th century and remained in circulation into the time of Maha Mongkut, known as Rama IV, the monarch in Margaret Landon's biography *Anna and the King of Siam* (1944), drawn on two memoirs of Welsh schoolteacher Anna Harriette Leonowens, *The English Governess at the Siamese Court* (1870) and *The Romance of the Harem* (1872). Landon's book was the basis for the long-running hit Broadway play and film *The King and I*, written in 1951 by Rodgers and Hammerstein. A progressive king, Mongkut hired Leonowens to enable his dynasty and nation to abandon primitive ways, and emulated European culture by producing flat coins stamped with his symbol, a crown.

In 1857, Queen Victoria supplied Mongkut with a minting machine like the one that King Ang Duong set up in Cambodia. Mongkut's staff struck the first modern Thai coins, called *bannakarn* ("royal gift coins"). In 1860, the Thai treasury imported a steam-driven machine, operated by a Thai coiner, Nai Moed. On Mongkut's 60th birthday in 1863, the chief coiner created a presentation set of silver and gold coins. By 1886, the striking of bullet coins ceased as flat coins of tin, copper, and glass took their place in a modern Siam. The glass pieces were legal tender valued as gambling tokens at casinos.

Chulalongkorn, the boy whom Anna Leonowens had taught about the industrialized world, took his father's place as Chulalongkorn the Great and completed Mongkut's plans for modernizing Siam. From studying Europe, which he traveled incognito, he encouraged the arts and folkways, built railroads, improved roads and bridges, set up mail and telegraph offices, installed public water and electricity, and initiated a Thai Red Cross. His interest in the abolition of slavery and kowtowing and the introduction of new cash crops, religious tolerance, education, modern irrigation, hospitals, birthing centers, and orphanages attest to his interest in the people's welfare. He standardized taxation, set up the Siam Commercial Bank, introduced decimal currency, formed a ministry of the treasury, and established a mint to produce paper bills and flat coins to replace bullet money.

***See also* African money; Anglo-Saxon coins; Egyptian coins; Russian money.**

SOURCES: "Celtic Gold 'Ring Money' Sells for (Pounds) 2,800." *Irish Times*, February 28, 1998. • Cribb, Joe. *Money*. Toronto: Stoddart, 1990. • Cribb, Joe, Barrie Cook, and Ian Carradice. *The Coin Atlas*. London: Little, Brown and Co., 1999. • Cristal, Ronald J. *Siamese Coins from Funan to the Fifth Reign*. Bangkok: National Museum, 1996. • Einzig, Paul. *Primitive Money*. Oxford: Pergamon Press, 1966. • Opitz, Charles J. *Odd and Curious Money*. Ocala, Fla.: First Impressions, 1986. • Pringle, Heather. "The Cradle of Cash." *Discover*, October 1998. • Sheehan, John, "The Viking-Age Gold and Silver of Scotland: A.D. 850–1100," *Antiquity*, December 1995. • Yoffee, Norman. "Sippar-Amnanum: The Ur-Utu Archive." *Journal of the American Oriental Society*, October 12, 1997.

Rix dollars

Common colonial coins of the Dutch West Indies and New Amsterdam, New York, were *ducatoons* (or *ducatones* or *dukatons)*, called "silver riders," and Rix dollars, a trade medium legitimized in Massachusetts General Court in September 27, 1642, and in 1686 by the Maryland colony. The term "Rix dollar" evolved from the colonial English pronunciation of *Nederlandse Rijksdaalder* ("Dutch state dollar"), modeled on German *thalers* and minted by cities and provinces in the Netherlands. Similar coins flourished in Scandinavia as the Swedish *riksdaler* and Danish *rigsdaler*. In 1644, Dutch missionary Johannes Megapolensis reported a native American encounter with the Rix dollar in "A Short Account of the Mohawk Indians." Accustomed to trade in pelts and wampum, made from small shells threaded on a string, a chief examined a Rix dollar and asked its worth. On learning the value of the silver coin, he laughed exceedingly at Christians, "saying we were fools to value a piece of iron so highly; and if he had such money, he would throw it into the river" (Megapolensis 1909).

To replace earlier unartistic efforts at minting Rix dollars, George III of England commissioned new versions, but his plan never moved beyond proof coins. After 1820, George IV commissioned the Royal Mint to strike silver Rix dollars for Ceylon. A winsome, attractive coin, the silver dollar pictured his likeness, designed by Benedetto Pistrucci, backed by an enwreathed elephant, the motif of William Wyon, the Hanoverian king's chief engraver. The coin circulated on the island in 1822.

Rix dollars were integral to American immigration history, according to a report issued in 1870 by A. Lewenhaupt, the chargé d'affaires of the Swedish-Norwegian legation in Washington, D.C. Emigrants departing Copenhagen on American steamships tolerated inadequate and unpalatable food. Then, on arrival at a New York escarpment called "Castle Garden," passengers paid immigration officials seven Rix dollars and 50 *øre* per person, a head tax that amounted to an annual collection of three million Rix dollars. The funds underwrote the maintenance of the immigration bureau and paid for transporting newcomers to New York poorhouses for temporary accommodation until they could join local relatives.

A growing population of a half-million Scandinavians included 60 percent Norwegians, 35 percent Swedes, and the rest Danes. At Swedish enclaves in Illinois, incoming Rix dollars built a Lutheran church. In Illinois, Minnesota, and Kansas, Rix dollars paid for land, carpentry tools, furniture, farm implements, and livestock that started the holdings of Scandinavian settlers. Workers valued their toil and savings in Rix dollars and indentured their youth in the same coin.

Rix dollars were also elements of the Freemasons' charter. When Frederick II the Great (Friedrich der Grosse) of Prussia, the famed philosopher king, was initiated at age 26 on August 15, 1738, at Brunswick, he resolved to form a German lodge at Berlin. He set up regulations for membership, which required that each applicant be of high character. Upon entry into the fellowship, each man paid 25 Rix dollars for a first degree, 50 for second degree, and 100 for achievement of master mason. The amounts maintained the lodge, supported brothers in need, and relieved the poor.

In South Africa, the Rix dollar became the standard monetary unit of the Cape, where many units of world currency passed from sailors, slavers, and traders through local banks. Rix dollars bankrolled the Dutch East India Company, which sanctioned a garrison and homesteading into Khoikhoi territory on the Liesbeek River in 1657 for the planting of wheat and vineyards, building of livestock *kraals* ("corrals"), and pasturage of sheep and cattle. For dealings with natives, Dutch Trekboers traded in alcohol, tobacco, and trinkets, the same barter money American settlers had used to wheedle land from New England Indians. After Cape Town grew into a trade and financial center, in 1781, the Cape mint issued its first paper Rix dollars, abbreviated "Rd," which remained in circulation until the pound supplanted them after British seizure of control in 1806.

See also **Benedetto Pistrucci; wampum.**

SOURCES: "The Deserter." *Freemasons Monthly Magazine*, 1842. • Jordan, Louis. "The Coins of Colonial and Early America." http://www.coins.nd.edu/ColCoin/ColCoinContents/Introduction.html. • Megapolensis, Johannes. "A Short Account of the Mohawk Indians." in J. Franklin Jameson's *Narratives of New Netherland, 1609–1664*. N.Y.: Charles Scribner's Sons, 1909. • "An Official Report on Swedish and Norwegian Immigration, 1870." *Norwegian-American Studies*, Vol. 13, 1943.

Roettiers, John

When England's Charles II sought methods of streamlining minting and standardizing coins, he imported French medalist Nicholas Briot and Flemish silversmiths John, Joseph, and Philip Roettiers (also Roettier or Rotier), sons of an Antwerp goldsmith. The eldest, John Roettiers, a renowned, Paris-trained medallist and chief engraver at London's Tower mint, was the firstborn of Philip and Elizabeth Thermés Roettiers of Antwerp on July 4, 1631. His two brothers, Joseph and Philip, were also natives of Antwerp. John got his start in sculpting as a stone- and gemcutter and produced his first medals around age 25. After the trio of brothers went to England in 1661, they gained employment from the king, who owed their father a debt of gratitude for lending him cash during the long exile during the English Commonwealth.

In 1662, John Roettiers began cutting planchets and mechanizing stamping. He joined medalist and seal-engraver Thomas Simon in perfecting a new process of milling gold and silver into coins. The preferment process chose Roettiers's new dies over those of Simon, who had sculpted a majestic "petition crown" engraved with a tiny plea to the king: "Thomas Simon most humbly prays Your Majesty to compare this his tryal piece with the Dutch and if more truly drawn & embossed more gracefuly order'd and more accurately engraved to relieve him" (Clain-Stefanelli and Clain-Stefanelli 1974, p. 132). On May 19, the petition proved prophetic when John Roettiers assumed the title of chief engraver. While incising the first of a series of medals commemorating Charles's restoration, in 1666, Roettiers also designed Britain's great seal.

In 1680, John's brother, Joseph Roettiers, who had served as his assistant, returned to Paris to accept the post of engraver-general. In his place, John's son James took the post of assistant at the Tower mint. John's brother Philip, who had also worked there, left for Holland around 1684 and moved up to the position of engraver for the King of Spain in Holland. Philip's work included medals picturing Charles II and Catharine, the State of Britain, and Liberty of Conscience. Replacing Philip at the Tower mint was John's third son Norbert.

In addition to accepting commissions from Richard Holt to cut original dies for the American colonies, John Roettiers struck a valued likeness of Charles I. The surface depicted the king in profile and the inscription "*Carlos II. Dei Gra*" ("Charles II by the Grace of God"). The reverse linked shields of England, Scotland, Ireland, and France centered by St. George, England's patron saint, and the inscription "*Mag Bri Fr et Hib Rex 1662*" ("King of Great Britain, France, and Ireland 1662"). John also produced quality portraits of James II and William and Mary.

In 1697, John Roettiers's reputation was ruined by an incident involving the unlawful use of Tower dies after prisoners began striking counterfeit guineas of James II on copper planchets painted gold. Because Roettiers had full custody of official dies, he was suspected of gross negligence leading to the counterfeiting. Sullying his name further was his Catholic faith, which brought him under suspicion of blatant papist disloyalty to William III. Relieved from his post, he moved to Red Lion Square and lived an invalid from kidney stones and a crippled right hand. At his death in 1703, he was interred in the Tower.

Among John Roettiers's treasured works are a medal featuring Charles II landing at Dover in 1660, his restoration to the throne and marriage, the Duke of York, the Peace of Breda, and a silver set from Louis XVI exhibited at Berkeley Castle. In 1694, John's son Norbert, a strong Jacobite, appears to have incised a minute satyr's head on the profile of William III. The following year, Norbert withdrew to St. Germain to serve the Stuart faction, for whom he made medals for the elder pretender. Norbert succeeded his uncle Joseph Roettiers to the post of head engraver at the Paris mint in 1703. His chief works include medals of Queen Mary, Charles I, Prince James, James II, William III, and Queen Anne.

James Roettiers, Norbert's son and John Roettiers's grandson, worked at engraving, then returned to goldsmithing for the crown until Norbert's death in 1727, when James became chief engraver of the Paris mint. In 1731, he took up his grandfather's dies in London and struck new medals, signing himself Jac Roettiers. Like his father Norbert, James was elected to the French Academy of Painting and Sculpture.

***See also* elephant token; Thomas Simon.**

SOURCES: Allen, Larry. *Encyclopedia of Money*. New York: Checkmark Books, 2001. • Clain-Stefanelli, Elvira, and Vladimir Clain-Stefanelli. *The Beauty and Lore of Coins, Currency, and Medals*. Croton-on-Hudson, N.Y.: Riverwood Publishers, 1974. • Davies, Glyn. *A History of Money from Ancient Times to the Present Day*. Cardiff: University of Wales Press, 1994. • *Encyclopedia of Art*. New York: McGraw-Hill Book Co., 1968. • "Late Victorian Coinage." *Studium Magazine*, November 23, 2001. • Magnusson, Magnus. *Cambridge Biographical Dictionary*. Cambridge: University of Cambridge, 1990. • Mehl, B. Max. "The Petition Crown of Thomas Simon." *The Star Rare Coin Encyclopedia and Premium Catalog: An Elaborate Encyclopedia of the Coins of the World*. Fort Worth: The Numismatic Company of Texas, 1923. • Petty, William. *Quantulumcunque concerning Money*, http://socserv2.socsci.mcmaster.ca/~econ/ugcm/3ll3/petty/money.txt. • Petty, William. *A Treatise of Taxes & Contributions*. London: N. Brooke, 1662. • Snodgrass, Mary Ellen. *Who's Who in the Middle Ages*. Jefferson, N.C.: McFarland, 2001. • Stephen, Sir Leslie, and Sir Sidney Lee, eds. *Dictionary of National Biography*. London: Oxford University Press, 1922.

Roman coins

Monarchy and republic

Roman coinage emulated systems of the Eastern Mediterranean, which got their start in Lydia and spread west to city-states and island nations. Closer to home, the Greek bronze monetary system impacted Magna Graecia, the name given to colonies of Sicily and southern Italy, which influenced the monetary system of Etruria, forerunner of ancient Rome. In the days of the Roman monarchy, Servius Tullius, who ruled from 578 to 534 B.C., was the first to impress copper-based billon with symbols on proto-coins. For each citizen added to his realm, he had quasi-coins deposited in the temple of Juno Lucina, the goddess of childbirth worshipped at the Matronalia ceremony each March 1. The growing heap tallied increases in the population. A complementary ceremony involved dropping a coin offering to Libitina, goddess of funerals, at her temple following each death.

Votive coins figured in the spiritual life of Romans, including soldiers and travelers far from home who communed with the gods through gifts. Coins presented to Juventas, goddess of youth, protected the young. At *asclepieia*, shrines of the healing god Aesculapius, particularly the Roman sanctuary on Tiber Island, patients cured of illness presented offerings of thanks of food, animals, garlands, molded images of diseased limbs, and coins. At sacred springs, money along with bronze, pewter, or tin tablets and inscriptions on lead strips stated in tangible form a sincere oath, curse, or presentation to the gods or request for blessing. Some Romans bent or damaged their gifts or marred, scored, or nicked coins as though slaughtering a live bird for sacrifice. To assist in the changing of alien coins, licensed money changers operated stalls at temples and throughout the *forum*, Rome's great marketplace and business center.

Incubation, a form of divination, required that the sick deck themselves in garlands and sleep at special chambers in the *aesclepieium*. Dreams arising during rest at a sanctuary required interpretation by professional dream analysts, who suggested treatment or improvements to diet and hygiene. Miraculous cures sometimes resulted from these visions. To prepare for incubation, patients purified their bodies with a three-day regimen and presented gifts of cakes to the priests as well as coins.

The bribing of Roman *haruspices* (soothsayers) was endemic, but constituted sacrilege. Under the nation's last king, Tarquinius Superbus or Tarquin the Proud, diviners who served the state and individual seekers derived their art from Etruscan superstitions. The chief responsibility of the soothsayers was to interpret prodigies or omens, such as the appearance of birds singly or in flocks in unusual settings. Contrary to logic, people wishing a favorable forecast for a journey, wedding, or business proposition believed that the proffering of a few coins earned them a better fate.

One peculiar family, the Servilii, set up a bronze four-*triens* as a god. As described in Book 34 of Pliny the Elder's encyclopedia *Natural History* (A.D. 77), which covers the role of copper and brass in culture, the household made annual sacrifices to the coin and left it feasts of gold and silver. Pliny adds that family members performed these rituals "with great devotion and solemnity, omitting no magnificence nor ceremonies thereto belonging" (Pliny 1962, p. 390). The encyclopedist quotes Messala, an eyewitness to the fact that, as the coin's shape altered over time from fat to thin, it predicted shifts in the family's fortune.

The earliest official coinage, the *aes rude* ("crude bronze") or *infectum* ("unmarked"), Rome's first coin, required a punch, hammer, anvil, and tongs for the hammerings of an irregular shape chipped off cast metal sheets. The production of coins was a necessity for Rome's expansionary policies. Where the army trudged, their pay had to follow, along with native customs, diet, values, and language. Romans on the move carried along miniature images and scenes on coins that illustrated greatness, for example, the replendent likenesses of its lighthouses, engineering feats that survive at Ostia, Puteoli, and Ravenna, in the west in Coruña, Spain, north at Boulogne, France, and Dover, England, and south at Leptis Magna, Caesarea Maritima, and the island of Delos.

After the government imposed the *Lex Aeterna Tarpeia* (Tarpeian law) in 454 B.C., Roman officials ceased accepting fines and fees in kind and demanded only bronze or copper coins. To supplant primitive trade goods and livestock with coin, they applied a typically Roman method — appoint a commission to study Athenian monetary standards and adopt a Roman copy. A fixed ratio of sheep or oxen to copper coins influenced the system of fines established in the *Lex XII Tabularum* (Laws of the Twelve Tables), a prime legal source codified in 450 B.C. Under Table XII, "Torts and Delicts," the law states blood money in terms of coin: "If he has broken or bruised a freemen's bone with his hand or a club, he shall undergo a penalty of 300 pieces [coins]; if a slave's, 150" ("Laws of the Twelve Tables"). Addenda extended the listings of fines payable in coin.

Until the end of the copper standard in 30 B.C., officers of the *aerarium Saturni*, the Roman treasury, imported copper for coins from Cyprus, the root of their term *aes cyprium* ("Cyprus copper") and of the English "copper" and cu, the chemical abbreviation for the element. Retaining the connection with the former barter economy was the term *pecunia* ("money"), derived from the Latin *pecus* ("cow"). In a move toward artistic money, the coiner stamped bronze disks with a leaf motif from around 400 B.C. Unlike genuine coins, these monetary tokens had no uniform weight or value and thus had to be renegotiated for each transaction. From the Latin *aestimare* ("to value in bronze") came the verbs "estimate" and "esteem."

Early coins preserved for history events that contributed to the growth of Rome into a mighty Mediterranean power. In 338 B.C., the Romans overthrew the rebellious Latin League, including the town of Lanuvium. To establish a working relationship with Lanuvians, the two cities shared culture and religious figures. From Lanuvium, the Romans adopted Juno Sispes, the savior deity to whom they made an annual tribute. To demonstrate sincere sharing of the cult, the Romans erected temples to the protective goddess at Rome. On coins, they depicted her likeness decked in horned goathead and skin and the shield, spear, and chariot of a warrior. Sometimes she is portrayed with a snake, and sometimes with a crow or raven. Some coins bear her initials, ISMR, standing for *Juno Sispes Mater Regina* ("Juno, savior, queen mother").

Replacing cattle and the lumpy, amorphous *aes rude* around 300 B.C., the *aes signatum* ("signed bronze money") offered uniform, but heavy bars or bricks struck with a bovine or leaf shape, the ship of state, trophies, the god Zeus, the mythic Romulus and Remus, or the allegorical figures of Victoria or the goddess Roma, patron of the Eternal City, wearing a helmet in the style of the Greek Athena. The use of livestock images connected in peasants' minds bronze money with barter in sheep or oxen. Rapidly competing were die-struck trade coins, the work of Greek engravers, and the popular *aes grave* ("heavy bronze"), a rectangular ingot cast around 269 B.C. with raised pattern and portrait. This coinage served Romans for some 70 years in payment for imported goods from Africa, Afghanistan, India, and Indochina. In trade, Roman merchants exported gems and jewelry, amber, coral, glassware, pottery, wine, and purple dye.

Named to take charge of early Roman coins around 289 B.C. were *tresviri monetales* ("three moneymasters"), who headed the state treasury, comprised of *tributa* ("taxes") from outlying tribes, internal taxes, and other forms of toll, harbor duty, and regulatory fees. These conservative fiscal guardians worked under the direction of the Senate and ran the first mint, which stood at the top of the Capitoline Hill next to the *Arx* (citadel) and the temple of Juno Moneta, Rome's patron adviser on treasury matters. Die-cutters trained in Greek methods produced the stamps and applied suitable *tituli* ("legends" or "mottoes"). The actual labor was performed by slaves under the direction of freedmen.

The type, quality, and style of coins grew from the incised ingots featuring an elephant used in the Greek invasion of Italy in 280 B.C. to the first real minting around 269 B.C., beginning with the lowly *aes* or *as*, backbone of republican commerce until its replacement by the *sestertius*. The *aes* bore the abbreviation S. C. for "Senatus Consultum," a symbol of authority, and the *quadrigatus*, a chariot motif. The rest pictured individual deities and ranged upward in value:

name	*deity*	*type*	*mark*	*value*
aes or *as grave* (pl. *asses*)	Janus	bronze or copper	I	one pound or 1/10 of a Greek *drachma*
semi or *semis*	Jupiter	brass	S	1/2 *as* or 6 ounces
triens	Minerva, Virtus, or Roma	bronze	••••	1/3 *as* or 4 ounces
quadrans	Hercules	bronze	•••	1/4 *as* or 3 ounces
sextans	Mercury	bronze	••	1/6 *as* or 2 ounces
uncia	Bellona	bronze	•	1/12 *as* or 1 ounce

Symbolic of the Roman yen for greatness was the cast bronze likeness of Janus bifrons, the two-faced god of past and future and beginnings and endings, whose two visages looked back to Rome's humble beginnings on the Tiber's banks and ahead to future conquests and the establishment of just laws.

Significant to the mythos of the early Roman republic were the *Pii Fratelli* ("Pious Brothers"), heroes elevated to gods at Catania, Sicily. Legend declares that they threw themselves in the path of their parents to save them from lava flowing from Mount Etna. The gods acknowledged their devotion by dividing the flames to allow them safe passage, much as Yahweh divided the Red Sea for Moses and the fleeing Hebrew slaves. The Roman mint pictured this mystical experience for over four centuries. Less pictorial abstracts took priority during the republic, which valued *Libertas* ("Freedom"), *Victoria* ("Victory"), *Aeternitas* ("Eternity"), *Fecunditas* ("Fertility"), *Fides* ("Faith"), *Pudicitia* ("Modesty"), and *Securitas* ("Security"). The Roman mints in Alexandria added Egyptian abstracts *Dynamis* ("Dominion"), *Kratesis* ("Valor"), and *Semasia* ("Victory").

Early in the Punic Wars, which raged from 218 to 201 B.C., Barcid coiners in Spain produced a silver quarter shekel picturing Herakles opposite a walking elephant. The image dominated coinage about the time that the Carthaginian general Hannibal maneuvered 36 big-eared African elephants and one Indian variety, his pet named Syrus, over the Alps in 217 B.C. on his way to attack Rome. Coin historians surmise that the thick neck and strongly Greek nose and jawline may be a portrait of Hannibal himself. After his legionaries rifled the temple of the goddess Feronia in 211 B.C., the superstitious returned to drop a store of *rudera* ("bronze ingots"), probably part of the temple treasure.

Heightened demand for soldiers' pay during the war with Hannibal caused the Roman mintmaster to devalue coins in weight and purity to a third their initial worth. After 155 B.C., value fell to 1/12 the original value. Near the end of the third century B.C., silver replaced the cumbersome bronze specie. Coiners used the style of minting common to Magna Graecia, notably Tarentum in southern Italy, and originally struck at mints in Campania.

The units reflect Greek influence:

name and date issued	*type*	*mark*	*value*
quadrigatus (225 B.C.)	silver		2 drachmas
denarius (268 B.C.)	silver	X	ten *asses* or a Greek *drachma*
victoriatus (211 B.C.)	silver		valued only as trade coins
quinarius (Republican Era) (also *quinquarius*)	silver	V	five *asses* or ½ *drachma*
sestertius (296 B.C.) (or *nummus* ["the coin"])	silver or bronze	I•IS	2.5 *asses* or ¼ *drachma*

The *denarius* or tenpiece, one day's wages for a skilled laborer, became the standard unit of monetary measure and the forerunner of the modern penny. To test its authenticity, wary citizens and merchants nicked and grooved each with a testmark. After 206 B.C., Romans elected moneyers to superintend coinage and allowed them to sign the pieces they minted or to adorn them with family symbols or crests, which gave rise to the term consular or "family" coins.

Within the environs of Rome, coin purses were a necessity for the daily tasks of buying a bird to sacrifice at the temple or pass to a slave for purchase of necessities at the market. For those plebeians worming their way into the good graces of aristocrats, the patron-client relation attached to the powerful or rich a bevy of hangers-on seeking preferment, loans, or civil service appointments. Roll-call of clients was an everyday affair, beginning with the *salutatio* ("greeting") at the patron's foyer, rewarded with a kind word, useful introduction, assignment, or *sportula* (monetary gift or tip). In exchange, patrons surrounded themselves with fawning flatterers, factotums, and outright parasites, standard figures in classic stage comedy.

Increased circulation of coins beyond the city of Rome called for additional minting at Capua and Lugdunum (later called Lyons) on the Rhone River, the seat of administration of the legate, which specialized in designs picturing divinities. Designers produced richly pictorial storytelling coins showing Roman mythology and commemorated military campaigns against the Carthaginians along with glimpses of collected armaments and *tubae* (war trumpets), voting and grain distribution, passage of laws, athletic contests, and public works. Coin views of notable structures — aqueducts, law courts, temples, villas, a lighthouse, and roadways — characterized Roman engineering and architecture. Marking these coins were phrases like "*Ex Argentio Publico*" ("From the Public Treasury") and primitive statements of value: "*I Roma*" (one-piece Rome), "*S Roma*" (half-piece Rome), "*XXXX Roma*" (forty-piece Rome), and "*IIS Roma*" (two-and-a-half-piece Rome) (Warmington 1967, pp. 224–227).

During wars, generals and territorial governors established private mints to strike imperatorial coins, a sub-species used to buy armaments and pay troops. Pompey appeared on coins depicting the region and victories in Europe, Asia, and Africa. Commanders found opportunities to enrich themselves with treasuries belonging to captive peoples. In Judea, Lucius Flaccus confiscated *fiscus Judaicus,* the annual half-shekel dues that each male Jew paid to the temple for its operation. The 75,000 *didrachms* he stole amounted to 75 pounds of gold. After placing the cache in the Roman treasury, Flaccus came before the courts to defend his action against a religious minority. Ably defended by Marcus Cicero, Flaccus was exonerated. The gold remained in Rome's custody.

In 90 B.C., a silver *denarius* commemorated the generosity of Lucius Calpurnius Piso, founder during the Second Punic War in 212 B.C. of the *Ludi Apollinares* (Apollinarian games), one of six major annual celebrations. To capture the glories of athleticism, the coiner honored Apollo, god of light and excellence, on the obverse. Four variations of reverses portrayed action in the arena: horses galloping while the riders held a torch, whip, or palm branch. These views appear to represent equestrian events in the Circus Maximus held annually by senate decree during the week of July 6. The celebration also featured theatrical performances, mimes, fairs, and markets.

The following year, the Tituria clan commissioned a silver *denarius* depicting a rougher side of Roman history, the rape of the Sabine women. To advertise Roman descent from the first kings of Rome, designers chose the figure of the Sabine king Tatius and of Roman soldiers abducting women. The event occurred during the rule of Romulus, Rome's legendary founder and first king. To assure a future for the rowdy settlement on the Tiber River, he invited the Sabines to a festival. The unarmed male guests were unprepared for the true purpose of the stage show — the capture of young Sabine women to serve Roman males as wives and producers of the next generation of citizens.

Near the end of the republic, Sulla, Pompey the Great, and Julius Caesar began minting private stocks of a gold piece called the *aureus* (pl. *aurei)*. Around 85 B.C., Sulla, then an outlaw warring against Mithradates VI Eupator, ordered the coining of an *aureus* on the Peloponnesus from talents levied from Asia Minor. His quaestor Lucullus ordered on each the trophies of victories at Chaeroneia and Orchomenos and the markings "*L. Sulla/ imper. iterum*" ("Lucius Sulla/general a second time"). As his self-confidence grew, Sulla struck another round of triumph coins around 81 B.C. proclaiming himself "*L. Sulla feli. dic.*" ("Lucius Sulla, the blessed dictator").

From the early 70s to 44 B.C., coins commemorated history, featuring a series of events that Romans valued as rudiments of their culture. Around 65 B.C., Marcus Aemilius Lepidus issued a *denarius* picturing Aemilia the vestal virgin and a view of the Basilica Aemilia decorated with shields and ancestral portraits by his father, Marcus Aemilius Leppicus. About two years later, Gaius Servilius circulated a coin featuring the head of the goddess Flora and the inscription "*Floral Primus*," commemorating the establishment of games at the *Ludi Florales* (spring games) around 240 B.C. These games took place between April 28 and May 3 to ensure good crops and ample harvest. The six-day bash began with theatrical performances and offered wild spectacles in the circus involving the release of goats and the showering of the crowd with lentils, symbols of good luck. The exuberance, like Christian pre–Lenten carnivals, drew a riotous crowd and improved traffic at brothels.

In 67 B.C., the tribune Aulus Gabinius enacted the Gabiniae, laws controlling banking and the exportation of Roman coins. He curtailed the freedom of licensed moneylenders to loan Roman specie to provincial and foreign legates and intervened in favor-buying. The *Lex Gabinia de piratis persequendis* (Gabinian law on apprehending pirates) helped stem the outflow of Roman money to pirates, a pervasive threat to shipping and deterrent to the transfer of funds to outlying commercial centers badly in need of change.

In 56 B.C., Faustus Cornelius Sulla ordered a coin thanking his famous father, Lucius Cornelius Sulla Felix (the Lucky), a Roman statesman and general who overcame Bocchus I of Mauritania and Jugurtha of Numidia during the Jugurthine War. The silver *denarius* presented on its face Diana, goddess of chastity and the hunt. On the back, the three-man pose pictures both conquered kings kneeling before Sulla. The real scenario was less bright. In 107 B.C. at the height of the North African war, young Sulla manipulated Bocchus to ensnare Jugurtha, whom the Romans later executed.

Another proud Roman, Quintus Cassius Longinus, extolled his ancestry with a silver *denarius* struck in 55 B.C. depicting Libertas and the official chair in the Temple of Vesta, Rome's ritual hearth from the seventh century B.C. The primly Roman coin refers to a terrifying scandal among the vestal virgins, attendants at the city's sacred flame. On charges that the temple's priest had failed to punish young priestesses who had compromised their purity, Lucius Cassius Longinus Ravilla conducted an investigation. Symbolizing the casting of votes for a verdict were an urn and a table on which jurors wrote either A for *absolvo* ("I acquit") or C for *condemno* ("I condemn"). The matter was serious — any young vestal who even flirted with a male could be flogged and buried alive.

That same year, Aulus Plautius commissioned a superbly styled and executed silver *denarius* featuring Cybele, the mother goddess, on the obverse. On the back, a male kneels alongside a camel and faces the word "*Iudaeus.*" The scenario represents the conquest of Judah Aristobulus II, last of the Hasmonean warriors, in 56 B.C. by Pompey the Great, one of Rome's greatest generals. The catastrophic event precipitated the total subjugation of Judea, the southern portion of Palestine. Aristobulus remained in a Roman prison until his death seven years later.

A noble Roman *praetor* (judge), Marcus Junius Brutus, minted an intriguing coin around 54 B.C. A proud scion of Lucius Junius Brutus, the republican hero who expelled the last tyrannic king, Tarquinius Superbus (or Tarquin the Proud), Marcus took pride in his family's founding of the republican form of government. The reverse of the two-headed coin pictured Caius Servilius Ahala, another ancestor, who executed Spurius Maelius, a rising tyrant, by stabbing him to death. The arrangement of these two freedom fighters back to back may have been intended as a warning to Caius Julius Caesar, Rome's ambitious general and statesman whom Brutus helped to assassinate with one of multiple stab wounds a decade after the coinage.

That same Julius Caesar, a scion of the powerful Julian clan, made significant innovations in numismatics and coinage. He added to general knowledge of world coinage with his *Gallic Commentaries* (58 B.C.), a compressed series of war notes on the subjugation of Celtic tribes in Gallia and Britannia. He noted that Britons, in lieu of coins, completed transactions with the presentation of sword blades. As a civic reformer, he reshaped state fiscal policy in 49 B.C. by seizing the state treasury and replacing the *quaestors* (administrators) with a pair of professional *aediles* (civic supervisors).

After 49 B.C., Julius Caesar commissioned a symbolic silver *denarius* picturing an elephant trumpeting as it trampled a serpent. The back of the coin pictured the ritual implements of the *pontifex maximus* ("chief priest"), a state title that Caesar attained in 63 B.C. The silver piece captures the two sides of Caesar's ambitions — a crusher of Rome's enemies and a civil servant ambitious to rise through a sequence of offices to the top position. Around 48 B.C., Caesar ordered additional coins commemorating his conquests in Gaul and had his moneyer inscribe his age, LII (52). A year later, he ennobled himself further with a classic coin featuring Venus, the goddess of romantic love, opposite the Trojan hero Aeneas bearing his father Anchises from the ruined city of Troy. Because Caesar claimed descent from Venus, he publicly worshipped her and centered her temple in a new forum as thanksgiving for his brilliant defeat of Pompey at Pharsalus in 48 B.C.

When Caesar advanced from commander in chief to dictator, in February 44 B.C., he exalted himself as the first living Roman pictured on a state coin, a dangerous precedent in the minds of king-hating citizens. He expressed a mounting egotism that caused a conspiracy to plot murder against him in the Senate foyer before he could overthrow the republic. The issue earned the darkly humorous title of the *denarius* that killed Caesar. The legend "*Caesar Dict Per Petuo*" ("Caesar — Dictator for Life") so angered senators that they shunned the coin. Within weeks of stamping the image of his cowled head on the silver *denarius*, he lay dead in the Senate of 42 stab wounds made by envious politicians eager to end his climb to tyrant and possibly hereditary monarch. Despite the violent end of his life, the concept of portrait coinage flourished throughout the Empire.

The noble Marcus Brutus, one of the conspirators, marked the shocking assassination as the necessary removal of a dangerous despot by ordering a silver *denarius* stamped with a cap of liberty, two daggers, and the fateful date, "*Eid Mar*" ("the Ides of March"), the Roman denotation of March 15. His intent was to justify the audacity and cruelty by which the cabal dispatched the chief threat to Roman freedoms. Within two years, Brutus had committed suicide at the battle of Philippi, leaving his own portrait coins in circulation.

The military coin became standard treasury issue during the empire, founded in place of the Roman Republic at Caesar's death by his nephew, Octavian, the first of five Julio-Claudian emperors. The Roman mint closed permanently in 40 B.C. during the turmoil that followed the assassination of Julius Caesar and the installation of his nephew as the first emperor. Mark Antony, one of the triumvirs, had a somber image struck on a coin depicting him with veiled head in mourning for Caesar. A generation later, Antony earned the spite of Pliny the Elder, who claimed that Antony "mixed iron with the Roman silver denier. He tempered it also with the brass coin, and so sent abroad false and counterfeit money" (Pliny 1962, p. 368).

As a free agent rebelling against Octavian, Antony had to have ready cash. In 42 and 41 B.C., he struck birthday coins marked XL and XLI denoting his 40th and 41st years. Upon realizing that his career in Rome was finished, he ordered the production of an Antony and Cleopatra VII coin, a monetary challenge to Octavian that circulated among client states in Asia Minor and North Africa. Antony had to search Greece for a goldsmith to issue his series of 18 battleship *denarii* recognizing each of his legions and picturing the galleys at important sea battles. One series served as pay for his legions and bore Roman numerals from I to XXIII. In Roman fashion, in 32 B.C., he had the designer incise a war galley and legionary *aquila* ("eagle"), the military emblem.

Historians have matched some of Antony's military coins with army service records. The III Gallica coin praised men stationed in Gaul; the V Alaudae appears to acknowledge Gallic recruits. The XVII Libyca lauds veterans of service in Libya; the III Cyrenaica praises veterans of war in Cyrenaica after 31 B.C. under Lucius Pinarius Scarpus, who fought with Antony as commander of four legions at the battle of Actium. To recall a Scythian conflict, Antony himself may have drafted the IV Scythica. In anticipation of victory, he commissioned a huge quantity of the commemoratives before the decisive battle of Actium in 31 B.C., when he chose to desert his forces and follow Queen Cleopatra's barge out of the fray and back to Egypt. In defeat, he, like Brutus, killed himself Roman style by falling on a sword.

See also **Byzantine coins; Carausius; counterfeiting; counterstamp; Moneta; Patching hoard; salt money; scrip; tokens.**

Empire

Under the name Augustus Caesar, Rome's first emperor took charge of a precarious political and economic situation. He levied a sales tax, land tax, and poll tax and reopened Rome's mint, which returned to the Capitol the operations of teams of coin casters, trimmers, and hammerers, many of whom were hereditary moneyers trained by their fathers. One of his early issues was a silver *denarius* picturing his boyish profile opposite the temple he was erecting in the Forum at the spot where state officers cremated the remains of his assassinated uncle, Julius Caesar. A sober coin, it reminded citizens of his connection with the glories of the recent past and the high price Caesar paid for ambition. In 27 B.C., Augustus ordered another *denarius* depicting a brilliant comet that appeared before Caesar's death. In time, Augustus advanced the metaphysical event to deification of his uncle.

Along with managers of the *fiscus* (emperor's treasury), the new emperor controlled precious metals from raw ores and the meltdown of obsolete coins, which he processed at a separate mint that may have stood near the baths later erected by Trajan. Augustus produced coins bearing the motto "*Ob Cives Servatos*" ("On Behalf of the Citizens"). Bronze coinage — actually made of *orichalcum* (brass) — he left to the Senate, who entrusted management to *praefecti aerarii* (money chiefs) at the original mint on the Capitoline Hill. Distribution was the job of *nummularii* (state financiers), who saw to the recycling of old coins into new moneys.

Augustus's reforms fine-tuned the changes that his uncle had begun shortly before his assassination. In place of *quaestors*,

Augustus placed *praefecti* (appointed officials) in charge of money matters, then rescinded his original plan in 23 B.C. by advancing two *praetores* (magistrates or minor judges) over the treasury. The most common coins of the era were the gold *aureus* and the silver *denarius*, brass *sestertius* and *dupondius*, and the copper *as* and *semis* or *quadrans*. For paying soldiers, in A.D. 6, the new emperor set up an *aerarium militare* (military treasury) and three *praefecti aerarii militaris* (military pay chiefs), who superintended transfer of moneys owed to legions in the field and dispensed *praemia militiae* (military retirement funds) to soldiers at all points in the empire. During this period, the typical Roman dogface earned 18.75 *denarii* per month for an annual salary of 225 *denarii*.

Augustus introduced the *donativum* (bonus), a presentation of coins or valuables to legionaries and to the Praetorian Guard, the emperor's private body guard and palace security force. The cash served as bribes as well as rewards for good service or special favors. As the empire grew more corrupt, paying off the guard with *donativa* kept individual emperors on the throne and prevented disgruntled security officers from plotting assassinations. In A.D. 41, the guard turned against the emperor Caligula, slew him, and elevated Claudius to the throne.

Augustus's system established satellite mints throughout the provinces, primarily to issue money at distant points without risking large treasury convoys through sea lanes plagued by pirates. Imperial mints ranged over a wide territory:

mint	*mint mark*	*province*	*empire*
Alexandria	ALE	Aegyptus	eastern
Antioch	A or ANT	Syria	eastern
Aquileia	AQ or AQR or AQS	Italia	western
Arles (Constantia)	AR or ARL, CON or CONST	Gallia	eastern
Caesarea	—	Cappadocia	eastern
Carthago	—	Africa	eastern
Cologne	—	Germania	western
Cyzicus	KV or KA or SMK	Bithynia	eastern
Emesa	—	Syria	eastern
Heracleia	HA or HTA	Thrace	western
Hispania	—	Hispania	western
Laodicea	—	Syria	eastern
Londinium (Augusta)	L or LN or LON, AVG, also PLN or PLON	Britannia	eastern
Lugdunum (Lyons)	L or LG or LVG or LVGD	Gallia	western
Maroneia	—	Thrace	eastern
Mediolanum (Milan)	—	Italia	western
Nicomedia	SMN or SMNA	Bithynia	eastern
Rome	R or RM or ROM	Italia	western
Serdica	SD or SM	Illyricum	western
Siscia	S or SIS or SISC or SISA or ASIS	Illyricum	western
Thasos	—	Thrace	eastern
Thessalonica	TES	Macedonia	western
Ticinum	T	Italia	western
Treveri (Trier)	TR or TRR or ATR or PTR	Gallia Belgica	western

For legends, coin designers established a typically terse system of abbreviation to extend the amount of information. For example:

full term	*abbreviation*	*meaning*
Augustus	Aug	senior emperor
Caesar	C or Caes	junior emperor
Consul	Cos	consul
Deo Gratia	D G	thanks [be] to God
Divus	Div	divine
Dominus Noster	DN	Our lord
Ex Argento Publico	Ex A. P.	from the public treasury
Felix	F	lucky
Imperator	Imp	military commander
Pater Patriae	PP	father of the country
Pius	PF	dutiful
Pontifex Maximus	PM or Pon Max	chief priest
Senatus Consultum	SC	decreed by the Senate
Senatus Populusque Romanus	SPQR	Senate and the Roman people
Tribunicia Potestas	Tr P or Trib Pota	tribune's power
Vota	Vot	pledge

Much of the money pouring out of these sites presented images of rulers rather than the scenarios of gods and goddesses that once dominated Greek *staters* and *drachmas.*

One function of portrait coinage was the connection in the minds of citizens between rulers and divinity, a designation that Augustus and subsequent emperors claimed for themselves with the addition of *divus* ("divine") to inscriptions. Monetary depiction of the Lugdunum Altar of *Tres Galliae* (tripartite Gaul) raised in 12 B.C. at Lyons at the confluence of the Rhone and Saône rivers reminded Romans of the emperor's victory over 60 tribes. The altar introduced the imperial cult, which raised Augustus from human ruler to deity. Maintaining admiration for him was the priest Gaius Julius Rufus, who erected an amphitheater around A.D. 19 as the site of several weeks of ceremonial games begun each August 1. Gradually, addition of a temple implied godhood for Augustus.

To justify the overthrow of the republic, Augustus also spread propaganda to celebrate his empire's *Pax Romana* ("Roman Peace") through special coin dies that pictured him as a generous, benevolent ruler under the phrase "*Caesar Augustus Divi F. Pater Patriae*" ("Augustus Caesar, Favored of the Gods, Father of the Country), set off by pairs of shields and spears. The title was so awe-inspiring that his successor, Tiberius Claudius Nero, opted not to use it. Less scrupulous were Caligula, Claudius, Nero, Vespasian, Nerva, Trajan, and Hadrian, all of whom thought themselves worthy enough to issue specie proclaiming them the nation's founts.

Augustus publicized two of his honors — the *clipeus virtutis* ("shield of virtue") and *corona civica* ("state crown") — with special coins and ennobled himself with a *dupondius* inscribed "*Divus Augustus Pater*" ("Holy Augustus Father"). His stepson and heir, Tiberius, who ruled during Christ's ministry, issued the tribute penny mentioned in Matthew 22:17–21, which popularized the command, "Render unto Caesar [the things that are Caesar's]." Tiberius featured his own profile on a portrait *denarius* with his mother, Livia Drusilla, on the reverse in the womanly pose of spinner of thread.

Another special class of Roman coins was the commemorative issue marking the emperor's sacred vow at a particular event, such as the new year or a royal wedding, or an oath creating good public relations. In 27 B.C., votive coins marked Augustus's pledge to citizens that he would pacify Rome and its tributaries in one decade. He swore additional oaths at increments during his reign. Following his example were coins marking public oaths taken by Antoninus Pius, Marcus Aurelius, and Commodus.

After Tiberius's 24-year reign, Caligula restored the Roman Senate to complete control of the mint and issued money under Augustus's self-aggrandizing phrase "Pater Patriae" ("Father of the Country"). Caligula cheated the citizens by ordering silver-plated *denarii* to replace pure silver coins. With the proceeds, he indulged bizarre tastes and lived lavishly. He was so despised and feared that, after his death, the Senate recalled his coins and melted them for recoinage as a gesture to Romans who no longer trusted state specie.

The empire's fourth emperor, Claudius Drusus Nero Germanicus, a brilliant but handicapped ruler who stammered and may have suffered paralytic polio in childhood, came to power precipitately. Either by choice or under extortion from the power-mad palace guard, the new emperor awarded each man $3,500 in coin. Officials doubted his strength and will power, but he surprised them by ruling wisely and, in A.D. 43, by joining the Roman army invading Britannia. A dramatic coin celebrated his victory over the barbarous British Celts by depicting Nemesis pointing her scepter at a snake. To emphasize her loathing for the serpent, she lifts the hem of her robe out of its way and spits.

Claudius quickly wearied of administrative matters. He set powerful freedmen — Gaius Julius Callistus, Narcissus, and Marcus Antonius Pallas — over his monetary control, but remained actively involved in designing specie. About A.D. 44, he chose a surface design to honor the Praetorian Guard, the king-making security force that formed a buffer between the emperor and his people. A commemorative issued by Nero, Claudius's successor, depicted the completion of Rome's artificial harbor and warehouse center west of town at Ostia, which Julius Caesar's corps of engineers had designed and Claudius completed.

The business of managing the funds of a far-flung empire increased fears of embezzling, graft, and mismanagement. To allay the worries of his ministers, Nero further altered the Roman monetary system in A.D. 56 by appointing two cabinet ministers called *praefecti aerarii* (treasury chiefs). As a means of introducing himself to the citizenry, he kept his coin art close to home with a *tetradrachm* struck in Alexandria and marked by his profiles in classic pose on front and back. He also chose likenesses of his mother, Julia Agrippina, as well as those of his spouse Poppaea and other kin and placed on the reverse Fecunditas Augusta, the imperial female nursing infants. When relatives fell from favor, their coins ceased to circulate, as was the case with Agrippina, whom he had murdered. For the Roman colony in Egypt, he chose the hippopotamus as an appropriate symbol. Nero was also the source of the Roman Empire's painful, protracted inflation, which he initiated by debasing silver and gold coins.

New coins carried the "*Ex S. C.*" ("by order of the senate") stamp of authority, which remained the standard until A.D. 64, when the Lugdunum mint reopened and, within the year, burned. After Nero's staff disclosed the plot of Gaius Calpurnius Piso to kill the emperor and seize the throne, the main conspirators committed suicide rather than face trial and public execution. Of the remaining cabal, 19 were beheaded and 13 exiled. Nero celebrated his delivery by raising a temple to Salus, goddess of health and well being, and minted a coin in A.D. 65 picturing himself on the front and the goddess on the obverse.

Vespasian, Nero's top general and the founder of the Flavian dynasty, succeeded three failed emperors in the year A.D. 69. To secure control during precarious times, he followed Claudius's example of making Rome the supreme authority over imperial coinage. He implied an intent to restore order by placing Salus, allegorical female representing health and well being, on the reverse side of his portrait *denarii.*

Vespasian followed the imperial perquisite of placing his filleted portrait on a *cistophorus* or four-*drachma* piece. Two coins display the contrasting views of his career. He commissioned coins honoring the Tenth Legion, a crack troop that inflicted the most damage on the Jews during the first Jewish War of A.D. 70. To carry out his crushing of Galilee, Vespasian sent his son Titus, who stifled the Jews in Jerusalem and Masada, site of a mass suicide of Jews who chose death over

After the First Jewish War of A.D. 70, the victor, the Roman Emperor Titus, commissioned a bronze *sestertius* picturing himself opposite a sobbing Jewess seated under a palm tree beside a male captive in chains. (Guy Clark, Ancient Coins and Antiquities, Norfolk, Virginia)

enslavement. Roman coins struck in Jerusalem dramatized the victor's pride — a war galley, a wild boar, and the legion's insignia, marked "*L X F*" for "*Legio Decima Fretensis*" ("Tenth Legion").

After the war, a *denarius* designed in A.D. 73 featured Pax, an idealized female symbol of peace extending a cornucopia in the left hand and an olive branch or staff in her right. A bronze *sestertius* struck in remembrance of the Judean wars paired a sobbing Jewess seated under a palm tree beside a male captive in chains. The legend summarizing the conquest of the Jews proclaims "*Iudaea Capta*" ("Judea Captured"). Thousands of Jews enslaved on the battlefield journeyed in chains to Rome through the port of Apulia. Their use to Romans was limited because they followed dietary laws outlined in the Torah and refused to work on the Sabbath. Most either passed to Jewish masters or bought their freedom. Two years later, coins depicted Vespasian's dedication of the Temple and Forum of Peace and his portrait opposite the Roman *aquila* ("eagle") or *Pax* extending an olive branch. Before the end of his reign in A.D. 79, he issued a coin featuring yoked oxen, a symbol of agriculture recalling the home- and work-centered lives of the first Romans.

The year that Vespasian died, Rome survived a fire, an eruption of Mt. Vesuvius, and plague. Titus issued coins denoting the epidemic that threatened the city's survival. To appease the gods, the Senate arranged a *sellisternium* (formal feast) set before a row of thrones on which attendants placed images of deities, including Minerva, goddess of wisdom, and the thunderbolt of Jupiter. In A.D. 80, Titus's coins featured the newly completed Colosseum, the empire's most acclaimed architectural landmark. The work of gangs of Jewish slaves, it seated 50,000 for some of the empire's bloodiest and most spectacular amusements, including mock sea battles. Titus himself died of a fever the next year.

The mint motif of enthroned gods survived into the reign of Domitian, who ruled until A.D. 86 and who expressed particular devotion to Minerva as a patron of national victory. Coins in her honor depict her Greek style — a martial goddess with helmet, shield, and spear and an owl at her feet. Other issues present Domitian on the face of a copper coin with the allegorical *Virtus* (Strength) in a dominant stance. His strength overcame wisdom after he demanded that Jews begin paying the *fiscus Judaicus* to Rome rather than to the temple.

A series of "five good emperors" — Nerva, Trajan, Hadrian, Antoninus Pius, and Marcus Aurelius — revived Rome's earlier civic virtues. The first, an attorney, showcased *Justitia* ("Justice") on coins as a token of his concern for citizens of all classes, whom he aided with a grain dole, low-interest loans, and welfare payments for indigent children. Nerva dealt with the uproar in Judea among Jews, whom Domitian's sacrilege had outraged, by reversing the imperial order to seize temple coffers and return the annual dues to the presiding priests. To congratulate himself for smoothing out an international scandal, Nerva coined a *sestertius* picturing himself opposite the palm, symbol of Palestine, alongside the legend "*Calumnia Sublata Fisc. Judaici*" ("The Insult of the Jewish Tax Rescinded").

Under the ambitious warrior builder Marcus Ulpius Trajan, the imperial engineers erected aqueducts and bridges while the military extended the empire's frontiers. Imperial minting passed to a single facility in Cappadocia, Rome's eastern satellite capital. Trajan's innovative coinage featured the allegorical *Roma, Virtus, Pax, Victoria, Vesta* ("the Hearth"), *Fortuna* ("Luck"), *Arabia*, and *Aeternitas* ("Eternity") along with the motto

"*Optimus Princeps*" ("The Best Prince"). A silver *drachm* presented a two-humped camel in profile, a common sight in Roman Jordan. Numerous architectural coins lauded his construction of the Forum of Trajan, Circus Maximus, and Basilica Ulpia and his triumph over Dacia, including captured arms and the celebratory column raised in Rome. At Segovia in Hispania, the hammering of local coins after A.D. 98 honored Trajan's grand Roman aqueduct, a symbol of civic pride that returned to architectural coinage in the 1500s and remained a part of the civic water system for two centuries.

In A.D. 130, Hadrian, Trajan's successor and a noted admirer of all things Greek, restored the high classicism of Roman coinage. He used as a model Lysimachus's commemorative of Alexander III the Great, issued in 297 B.C. and ordered coins picturing *Disciplina*, the personification of a well regulated civic order. From his travels in Egypt, he minted a silver piece picturing the personified Aegyptus lifting a *sistrum*, a musical rattle sounded during rituals of Isis. The scenario acknowledged the cult of Isis that had begun around 50 B.C. and flourished in harmony with the traditional Roman gods.

A humanitarian in an age of brutality and usurpation, Hadrian made peaceful overtures to the Jews and commemorated his visit to Judea with a coin depicting a woman and her children welcoming him with palm fronds and the legend "*Adventu Aug Iudaea*" ("Arrival of the August [Emperor] to Judea"). Before the coin could circulate to the ends of the empire, Rome had put down another Jewish revolt so harshly that Rome expunged the country's name and replaced it with Syria-Palaestina.

Antoninus Pius followed Trajan's mindset with artistic coins of similar beauty minted in Alexandra, Antioch, Caesarea, and Judea. Some displayed the Temple of Augustus, a symbol of peace; others featured the river god Nilus and victory wreaths. Like the allegorical coins of his predecessors, Trajan's symbolic series focused on emblematic female figures — Clementia (lenience), Felicitas (happiness), Indulgentia (mercy), and Liberalitas (generosity). He also honored his wife, Faustina the Elder, before and after her death, with serene portraits of the empress opposite Juno with her peacock, a scenario contrasting his wife's humility with the godess's pride. In Faustina's honor, he established a charity, *Puellae Faustinianae* ("Faustina's little daughters"), to aid young girls in poor families.

The last of Rome's good emperors, Marcus Aurelius, continued the female series with portrait coins of his wife, Faustina the Younger, daughter of Antoninus Pius and Faustina the Elder. Additions to the family poses featured Annia Lucilla, Marcus Aurelius's daughter and wife of his foster brother and co-emperor, Lucius Verus. For state reasons, Aurelius also issued money picturing Honos (Honor) and the ancient temple of Mercury, which he rebuilt, and ordered coins bearing the phrase "*Pax Aeterna*" ("Eternal Peace"), a vain wish during his 17 years fighting uprisings on the German front. The films *The Fall of the Roman Empire* (1964), starring Sir Alec Guinness as the emperor, and *Gladiator* (2001), an Academy Award–winner casting Richard Harris as Marcus Aurelius, reprise the hardships of the imperial staff and Roman legionaries weathering Danube winters during protracted combat with the barbarous Germani.

The reign of good emperors ended after Marcus Aurelius died in A.D. 180, leaving the empire to his only surviving son, the paranoid, murderous Lucius Commodus. After twelve years of Commodus's destructive rule, in A.D. 192, his advisers paid an assassin, reputedly the champion wrestler Narcissus, to throttle the emperor. In exchange for 12,000 *sestertii* each in coin, the powerful Praetorian Guard selected the next emperor, Publius Helvius Pertinax, and gave him ten weeks to reform Rome and restore strength to the treasury. Because he refused to pay extravagant amounts to the guard, they tore him apart and paraded with his head. The vending of power continued with Marcus Didius Julianus, who offered 6,200 *denarii* for the throne, which he held for nine weeks. He managed to strike 31 portrait coins of himself, his wife Manlia Scantilla, and their daughter Didia Clara. For a legend, he chose the pathetically presumptuous "*Rector Orbis*" ("Master of the world").

It was not until A.D. 197 that prostitution of the emperor's throne and civil wars ended. Lucius Septimius Severus, who established the Severan dynasty, first had to trounce the upstart Gaius Pescennius Niger and unseat the venal Didius Julianus, who bid 25,000 *sestertii* to each guard for the throne. Severus took charge of eastern money centers, set up coinage at Laodicea, and probably founded the mints at Emesa and Antioch. Out of spite that the Samaritans in Neapolis, a city north of Jerusalem, supported Pescennius's bid for the empire, Severus shut down their thriving mint, leaving it idle for 17 years. To exalt himself and his policies, he decked coins with the delicate Dea Caelestis ("heavenly goddess") seated on a lion and chose for his personal motto "*Fundator Pacis*" ("Founder of Peace").

As Rome declined, so did coinage, particularly in the colonies of the eastern Mediterranean. The production of beautiful pieces in Caesarea, Jaffa, and Jerusalem came to a halt as the Roman treasury standardized money and issued it from centralized operations in Egypt, Gaul, North Africa, Syria, and the mother mint in Rome. The empire's slide from greatness is evident in the debasement of precious metals with copper, a commonly added adulterant during the financial crises that followed. By A.D. 250, formerly solid silver coins were no more than 40 percent pure; two decades later, when the silver layers topped a copper core, coins were only 4 percent pure. In the words of historian Chester G. Starr, "Prices rose, and after 250, soared; many economic sectors turned to barter" (Starr 1991, 653). While tributaries in Gaul and Egypt rebelled and the common people groaned under fiscal indignities, the empire ran on spirit and the capital amassed over two centuries of conquest.

In the third century A.D., Severus's eldest son, Caracalla, who never trusted the Senate or its fiscal management, faced a monetary crisis. He increased revenues by conferring citizenship on much of the outer empire's male population. The honor of becoming voting Romans also carried the obligation to pay inheritance taxes, which fattened the imperial coffers. With some of the money, he restored the Circus Maximus and once more sent Roman troops to halt insurgent barbarians from the north.

Caracalla struck coins at mints in Turkey and issued from his Syrian operation an oddly stiff-necked portrait in profile, featuring low beard and filleted head. To relieve dependence on the heavy *aureus*, he replaced it with the lightweight *solidus*, forerunner of the modern shilling, valued at 25 *denarii*. In A.D. 215, he renamed the silver double *denarius* the *antoninianus* after his real name, Marcus Aurelius Antonianus. His *solidus* survived for seven centuries and became the touchstone for moneyers in Byzantium, Denmark, England, France, Italy, Spain, and Sweden.

Following his forced obsolescence of the *denarius*, Caracalla set up a new system of coin values, which the emperors Lucius Domitius Aurelian and Gaius Aurelius Valerius Diocletian augmented:

name and date issued	*type*	*value*
solidus (ca. A.D. 348)	gold	one *pecunia* or 2,000 *denarii*
pecunia	silver and bronze	one *solidus* or 2,000 *denarii*
aureus (49 B.C.)	gold	25 *denarii* or 100 *sestertii* or 400 *asses*
quinarius (late A.D. 200s)	silver	12.5 *denarii* or 50 *sestertii* or 200 *asses*
denarius	silver	4 *sestertii* or 16 *asses*
antoninianus (A.D. 211)	silver and bronze	1.5–2 *denarii*
argentius (A.D. 296)	silver	10 *asses* or 5 *dupondii* or 2.5 *sestertii*
sestertius (296 B.C.)	brass	4 *asses*
dupondius (Republican Era)	brass	2 *asses* or ½ *sestertius*
aes (Republican Era)	bronze	¼ *sestertius*

One of Caracalla's more traditional *denarii* pictured him opposite Serapis, an Egyptian god whose cult he sponsored.

After A.D. 251, the emperor Trebonianus Gallus chose for his coins the image of Juno Martialis, the enthroned goddess honored with ritual each March 7. The image also recognized his home town, Perugia, and its patron, Juno Perusina, another incarnation of the same deity. In contrast, the emperor Egnatius Gallienus's chintzy copper coins, produced from A.D. 260 to 268, were so thin that banks refused to honor them. Vying for power, Gallienus's cavalry commander, Marcus Aureolus, who rebelled against the emperor and set up a rogue rule at Milan, struck a bronze *antoninianus*. Gallienus quickly trounced Aureolus, executed him, and put so rapid and thorough an end to his coins that they remained unknown until a late discovery and identification. In their place, Gallienus commissioned coins grandly stamped "*Ubique Pax*" ("Peace Everywhere"). Another loss to the Roman coinage system was the demise of the *sestertius*, which was last minted under the usurper Postumus in A.D. 267. He generated his own coinage bearing the claim that he was "*Restitutor Galliarum*" ("Restorer of the Gauls").

From A.D. 270 to 275, as barbarian insurgents raided borders, Aurelian took a soldier's approach in manhandling the monetary system, canceling debts, controlling prices, and rationing grain to halt peasant riots. The silver *antoninianus* had devolved into a mere scrap of base metal. The two small billon coins that he introduced failed because they were copper-cored with a silver wash on top. He issued a pure gold coinage, financed by his wars in the eastern Mediterranean, but inflated their value more than twice.

For his apt administration and imposition of order, Aurelian glorified himself with the coin mottoes "*Pacator Orbis*" ("Pacifier of the World") and "*Restitutor Exercitus*" ("Restorer of the Army"). The uprising of mintmaster and secret forger Felicissimus and the mint staff on the Mons Caelius at Rome produced 7,000 military casualties and subsequent executions of senators. It was an event that historian Edward Gibbon examined in *The Decline and Fall of the Roman Empire* (1788). The mint operation closed while the treasury exported its work to Antioch, Cyzicus, Lugdunum, Mediolanum, Phoenicia, Serdica, Siscia, Ticinum, and Tripolis, all locations that were handy to military pay centers. Aurelian was good for Rome, but a murder plot between his secretary Eros and the Praetorian Guard ended Aurelian's reign after five years of sincere reform.

To put Rome on its first comprehensive budget, Diocletian, the first emperor in the past 100 years to survive two decades in office, took charge of the muddled system in A.D. 284. For the sake of commerce, he turned out light, usable tokens in gold, silver, copper, and other metals, including the unalloyed silver *argentius* or *siliqua* and a bronze *follis* bearing the motto "*Genio Populi Romani*" ("To the Spirit of the Roman People"). At the fifteen imperial mints that replaced Senate and provincial coinage, legal tender carried a stamp of origin, e. g., L for Londinium and R for Roma. To protect valuable coins, moneyers issued sealed purses containing up to 2,000 pieces, which bankers often stamped with an official cipher. Diocletian closed small territorial operations, controlled wages and prices, called for a new census, and taxed officially enrolled citizens with a heavy hand.

Diocletian's levy exempted the senatorial class, Rome's wealthiest and most privileged denizens. Hardest hit were farmers, artisans, and mid-level businessmen, whom his edict of A.D. 301 obliged to pay a poll tax and *annona* (property tax) in gold ore or coin rather than in kind. The burden encouraged numerous methods of money laundering to reduce taxable properties. To avoid confiscation and enslavement, those lacking cash to pay the tax awarded to senators their properties and themselves and took the official status of *coloni* (tenant farmers). Diocletian's economic plan backfired, producing an era of falsified bookkeeping, hidden assets, and tax evasion. His requirement that peasant *coloni* accompany the sale of villas initiated a binding of the worker to the land that evolved into Europe's feudal system.

The era's most trustworthy coin was the gold *solidus* struck by Constantius I Chlorus, a great general and deputy emperor whom Diocletian groomed as a successor. The gold piece was the basis of tax collection, mainstay of the imperial economy, and the world's longest-lived coin, surviving into the Middle Ages. One issue, distributed to his faithful soldiers, derived from the Roman mint at Trier and pictured the emperor receiving his crown from the figure of Victory while Britannia kneels in fealty. The personified Britannia gave the coin its common name.

After A.D. 306, Constantius's son, Constantine I the Great, Rome's first Christian emperor, issued a popular gold *solidus*. Bearing the self-congratulatory motto "*Restitutor Libertatis*" ("Restorer of Freedom"), the coin served his treasury primarily for government purchases. Mooting the issue of his true religious leanings were his replacement of the Hebrew Sabbath with Sunday as the first day of the week, and his choice of the likeness of Sol Invictus, the sun god, on his coins. By A.D. 314, the first Christian cross marked a coin minted at Terraco, six years later came the *chi-rho*, the monogram of "Christ," which looks like an X superimposed on a P. These pieces were forerunners of medieval ritual tokens and Renaissance religious medals.

Constantine adapted into a Christian standard the image of the *labarum* (emperor's standard), which the army displayed from the time of Hadrian only when the emperor accompanied them. Topped with the *chi-rho*, the emblem inset the Greek cipher in the first and last letters of the Greek alphabet, *alpha* and *omega*, reminders of the end-time prophecy of St. John the Divine in Revelation 22: 13, "I am the Alpha and Omega, the beginning and the end, the first and the last." After the Council of Nicea in A.D. 326, these monograms became common. Amply fortified with a bulging treasury, Constantine could support gold coinage, but chose to use cheaper copper and silver coins, which burdened the underclass with continued inflation. During his reign, the imperial mints at Londinium closed and remained defunct except for a five-year return to operation from A.D. 383 to 388 under Magnus Maximus.

Constantius II, the third son of Constantine the Great, introduced two new coins — the *centenionalis* and the *miliarense*— around A.D. 348 and added to currency the hopeful, but unlikely motto "*Felicitas Perpetua*" ("Unending Good Fortune"). Late imperial coins included these values:

name	*date issued*	*type*	*value*
siliqua	(late Empire)	silver	approximately one *denarius* or three *tremisses*
tremissis	(post–Empire)	gold	1/3 *solidus*
centenionalis (or *pecunia maiorina*)	(A.D. 348)		12,000 *sesterti* or 1/24 *solidus*
miliarense	(early A.D. 300s)	silver	1/12 *solidus* or two *centenionales* or 24,000 *sesterti*
follis	(ca. A.D. 305)	bronze	a pittance

He introduced a coin picturing the personified female forms of Roma and Constantinopolis, a sign that the empire was already beginning to feel a midline severance that would divide it in halves, east and west. Struck at Antioch, the coin was exceptionally fine in execution and detail worthy of Constantius's long and prosperous reign.

On Rome's 1,100th anniversary, around A.D. 350, Constans, youngest son of Constantine the Great, ordered the mint at Siscia to conceive a historic bronze *centenionalis*.

Featuring his portrait bust opposite another pose of him standing on a galley prow, the reverse produces a symbolic pairing. In his right hand, he grasps the phoenix, the legendary bird that regenerates itself from ash every millennium. In his left, he raises the Roman military *signum* ("standard") topped with two Greek letters, *chi* and *rho*, the abbreviation of "Christ." The two-letter emblem characterized the latter portion of Roman dominance much as the SPQR had in earlier times. The two letters also honored his father's influence in Christianizing Rome.

A successor, Flavius Claudius Julian II the Apostate, attempted more reform in A.D. 361 by curbing inflation and spending. Despite his good intentions, the Roman system continued to revert to the fiscal policies of Diocletian and Constantius I, who placed all money matters, from minting to tax collection, in the hands of bureaucrats who added to the cadres of officialdom and secured the state's troubled financial situation. Most important was the *comes sacrarum largitionum* (manager of the sacred funds), who replaced the *rationales* (state treasurer) and collected taxes and tolls, set fees and customs, supervised mining, examined banks, compiled a civic budget, purchased military supplies, and administered local and territorial minting. The *comes privatae largitionis* (commissioner of the privy purse), kept an account of all assets in property, commodities, and cash. A third, the *comes rerum privatarum* (commissioner of the emperor's stores), supervised the accounting of properties, rent collection in crops and coin, and placement of cash in the public treasury.

See also **Bible coins; Byzantine coins; Carausius; counterfeiting; counterstamp; Hubertus Goltzius; Moneta; Patching hoard; Roman coins — Monarchy and republic; salt money; *sou;* tokens.**

SOURCES, *Monarchy and republic*: Allen, Larry. *Encyclopedia of Money*. New York: Checkmark Books, 2001. • "The British Royal Mint." http://www.royalmint.com. • Bunson, Matthew. *A Dictionary of the Roman Empire*. New York: Oxford University Press, 1991. • Clain-Stefanelli, Elvira, and Vladimir Clain-Stefanelli. *The Beauty and Lore of Coins, Currency, and Medals*. Croton-on-Hudson, N.Y.: Riverwood Publishers, 1974. • Cribb, Joe. *Money*. Toronto: Stoddart, 1990. • Cribb, Joe, Barrie Cook, and Ian Carradice. *The Coin Atlas*. London: Little, Brown and Co., 1999. • Davies, Glyn. *A History of Money from Ancient Times to the Present Day*. Cardiff: University of Wales Press, 1994. • *Dictionary of Roman Religion*. New York: Facts on File, Inc., 1996. • *Encyclopedia of the Roman Empire*. New York: Facts on File, Inc., 1994. • Friedenberg, Daniel M. "Early Jewish History in Italy." *Judaism: A Quarterly Journal of Jewish Life and Thought*, Winter 2000. • Grierson, Philip. *Numismatics*. London: Oxford University Press, 1975. • *Handbook to Life in Ancient Rome*. New York: Facts on File, Inc., 1994. • Hastings, James, ed. *Encyclopedia of Religion and Ethics*. New York: Charles Scribner's Sons, 1951. • Head, Barclay V. *Historia Numorum*. Chicago: Argonaut, 1911. • Hill, G. F. *Historical Roman Coins*. Chicago: Argonaut, Inc., 1966. • Howatson, M. C., ed. *The Oxford Companion to Classical Literature*. Oxford: Oxford University Press, 1991. • Laing, Lloyd R. *Coins and Archaeology*. New York: Schocken Books, 1969. • "The Law of the Twelve Tables." http://members.aol.com/pilgrimjon/private/LEX/12tables.html. • Lewis, Brenda Ralph. *Coins & Currency*. New York: Random House, 1993. • Lyttelton, Margaret, and Werner Forman. *The Romans: Their Gods and Their Beliefs*. London: Orbis Publishing, 1984. • Meshorer, Ya'akov. *Coins of the Ancient World*. Jerusalem: Jerusalem Publishing House, 1974. • Pliny. *The Natural History*. New York: McGraw-Hill, 1962. • Pollak, Henry. *Coinage & Conflict*. Clifton, N.J.: Coin & Currency Institute, 2001. • Reinfeld, Fred. *Treasury of the World's Coins*. New York: Sterling Publishing, 1953. • Severy, Merle, ed. *Greece & Rome*. Washington, D.C.: National Geographic Society, 1977. • Starr, Chester G. *A History of the Ancient World*. New York: Oxford University Press, 1991. • Tatum, W. Jeffrey, "The Lex Papiria de Dedicationibus: A Clarification," *Ancient History Bulletin*, 1997. • Warmington, E. H. *Remains of Old Latin: Volume IV, Archaic Inscriptions*. Cambridge, Mass.: Harvard University Press, 1967.

SOURCES, *Empire*: Allen, Larry. *Encyclopedia of Money*. New York: Checkmark Books, 2001. • "The British Royal Mint." http://www.royalmint.com. • Bunson, Matthew. *A Dictionary of the Roman Empire*. New York: Oxford University Press, 1991. • Clain-Stefanelli, Elvira, and Vladimir Clain-Stefanelli. *The Beauty and Lore of Coins, Currency, and Medals*. Croton-on-Hudson, N.Y.: Riverwood Publishers, 1974. • Cribb, Joe. *Money*. Toronto: Stoddart, 1990. • Cribb, Joe, Barrie Cook, and Ian Carradice. *The Coin Atlas*. London: Little, Brown and Co., 1999. • Davies, Glyn. *A History of*

Money from Ancient Times to the Present Day. Cardiff: University of Wales Press, 1994. • *Dictionary of Roman Religion.* New York: Facts on File, Inc., 1996. • *Encyclopedia of the Roman Empire.* New York: Facts on File, Inc., 1994. • Friedenberg, Daniel M. "Early Jewish History in Italy." *Judaism: A Quarterly Journal of Jewish Life and Thought,* Winter 2000. • Grierson, Philip. *Numismatics.* London: Oxford University Press, 1975. • *Handbook to Life in Ancient Rome.* New York: Facts on File, Inc., 1994. • Hastings, James, ed. *Encyclopedia of Religion and Ethics.* New York: Charles Scribner's Sons, 1951. • Head, Barclay V. *Historia Numorum.* Chicago: Argonaut, 1911. • Hill, G. F. *Historical Roman Coins.* Chicago: Argonaut, Inc., 1966. • Howatson, M. C., ed. *The Oxford Companion to Classical Literature.* Oxford: Oxford University Press, 1991. • Laing, Lloyd R. *Coins and Archaeology.* New York: Schocken Books, 1969. • "The Law of the Twelve Tables." http://members.aol.com/pilgrimjon/private/LEX/12tables.html. • Lewis, Brenda Ralph. *Coins & Currency.* New York: Random House, 1993. • Lyttelton, Margaret, and Werner Forman. *The Romans: Their Gods and Their Beliefs.* London: Orbis Publishing, 1984. • Meshorer, Ya'akov. *Coins of the Ancient World.* Jerusalem: Jerusalem Publishing House, 1974. • Pliny. *The Natural History.* New York: McGraw-Hill, 1962. • Pollak, Henry. *Coinage & Conflict.* Clifton, N.J.: Coin & Currency Institute, 2001. • Reinfeld, Fred. *Treasury of the World's Coins.* New York: Sterling Publishing, 1953. • Starr, Chester G. *A History of the Ancient World.* New York: Oxford University Press, 1991. • Tatum, W. Jeffrey, "The Lex Papiria de Dedicationibus: A Clarification," *Ancient History Bulletin,* 1997. • Warmington, E. H. *Remains of Old Latin: Volume IV, Archaic Inscriptions.* Cambridge, Mass.: Harvard University Press, 1967.

Royal Exchange

The Royal Exchange was a symbol of the strength of England's financial institutions. Begun on June 7, 1566, on a plot of land on Threadneedle Street purchased by London merchants for £3,532, it was built under the direction and philanthropy of financier Sir Thomas Gresham, former Lord Mayor of London and financial adviser to Elizabeth I, who presided over the building's opening in 1571. On the day workers initiated the building, one by one, aldermen laid the first bricks and left gold pieces as bonuses for the Flemish bricklayers.

On November 26, 1579, Gresham presented the finished stone and glass structure to London and the mercers' guild. In exchange, he accepted the city's promise that it would endow Gresham College, an independent institution and home of the Royal Society at Gresham's estate at Bishopsgate, the location it occupied until the construction of a new campus on Gresham Street. Sweetening the arrangement was the queen's extension of the term "royal" to the name of the exchange in 1571.

Each day at noon, London businessmen, insurers, auctioneers, officers of the merchant marine, and traders gathered at the 'Change for three hours to confer and transact business. During a period that saw the rise of the London financial market and the decline of the Antwerp bourse, the Royal Exchange flourished in importance throughout Europe. The original building remained in service until the Great Fire of 1666, when Sir Christopher Wren, England's notable architect, replaced it with a grand, double-fronted structure at the current location.

In 1760, the ejection of 150 rowdy brokers forced them to seek a new gathering spot. They chose Jonathan's Coffee House, where they relaxed for conversation and refreshments while trading shares. The London Metal Exchange had a similar beginning at a separate locale, the Jerusalem Coffeehouse. In 1808, lithographer Rudolf Ackermann of Saxony pictured the more sedate all-male assemblage at the Royal Exhchange in indoor and courtyard sketches entitled "Microcosm of London," an erroneous title that failed to note the absence of women and lower-class people.

In 1715, Scotland acquired its own exchange on Queen Street in Glasgow, which bore the name the Glasgow Royal Exchange. It faced disaster after the Napoleonic War, when bankruptcies reached a level of two million pounds. In 1817, the Royal Bank of Scotland bought and remodeled the building by adding a telling-room for counting cash, a cashier's reception room, and cashier's residence. James Ewing of Strathleven and other Glasgow merchants opened a new exchange designed by David Hamilton on December 18, 1827. Completed on September 3, 1829, the Glasgow Royal Exchange offered 1177 shares at £50 each to subscribers for use of the building for daily trade.

Over Scottish history, distinguished visitors and important events marked the financial history of Glasgow. In 1848, the Bread Riots required quartering of troops in the exchange and the stacking of muskets around the pillars to protect cash reserves and members. The building remains a monument to enterprise and business in the United Kingdom.

***See also* Thomas Gresham; Gresham's Law; South Sea Bubble.**

SOURCES: Davies, Glyn. *A History of Money from Ancient Times to the Present Day*. Cardiff: University of Wales Press, 1994. • "Gresham College." http://www.gresham.ac.uk/special/history.html. • Magnusson, Magnus. *Cambridge Biographical Dictionary*. Cambridge: University of Cambridge, 1990. • Nicholls, C. S., ed. *Encyclopedia of Biography*. Oxford, Eng.: Helicon Publishing Ltd., 1996. • "The Royal Exchange." *Scottish Country Life*, July 1917.

Russian money

In the neolithic era, Russians hoarded flint arrowheads as caches of tradeable wealth. The primitive money of early Siberia was a blend of furs, skins, and reindeer, which served for paying taxes or bride price. The Ossetes and Chefsurs of the Caucasus evolved a cattle currency; the Tcherkess chose oxen as money. In Caucasia and Armenia in prehistory, bronze rings accompanied the dead to their graves as emblems of wealth. Peasants in Darwaz conducted business in dried mulberry cakes. Adding to the commodity base were trade goods — vodka, tea bricks, leaf tobacco, sugar, tools, and weapons. As late as the 1930s, according to Hindu representative to London Leonard Warburton Matters, who visited Russia shortly after the 1917 revolution and wrote *Through the Kara Sea: The Narrative of a Voyage in the Tramp Steamer through Arctic Waters to the Yenisei River* (1932), the isolated tribes lacking coins pressed into service containers of jam.

Based on Byzantine issue, the first true Russian coinage dates to A.D. 988, when a gold coin and smaller silver pieces circulated alongside Scandinavian and western European coins and Arabic *dirhans*. Like the coins of the eastern Mediterranean, the early coins of Olbia or Astacus, a city in northwestern Turkey on the Black Sea, were cast ingots shaped like dolphins, a good luck symbol. After the coinless, Mongol-dominated era from the 1100s to the 1300s, the revival of trade and commerce demanded coins. At Saratov in the 1200s, the Bulgars stamped the amorphous Ukrainian *hryvnia* (also *hryvna* or *grivna)*, a deeply incised ingot resembling unrefined silver ore. Kiev and Tchernigov produced their own unique *hryvnia* ingots in a lozenge shape that emulated the grain bags used by transporters along the Volga River. A century later, the Tatar's oblong *hryvnia* from Old Qrim (Crimea) exemplified the hasty, artless coinage commissioned by Uzbek and Toktamish khans.

Following the defeat of the Mongols' Golden Horde at the Don River in 1380 by Dmitri Ivanovich Donskoi, Grand Prince of Moscow, and building of a stone fort at the Kremlin, moneyers counterstamped foreign coins and introduced local minting. As the fur trade flourished, they initiated a controlled operation in Moscow, Novgorod, and Ryazan and, in 1400, in Tver. Much of the design, which featured Mongol motifs and ornately scrolled Arabic lettering, lacked truly Russian style.

Dimitri's son and heir, Vasily I Dmitrievich, bolstered the monetary system of greater Moscow to underwrite his military expeditions. He applied to himself the over-blown title "Grand Prince of All Russia" on coin inscriptions, but still paid homage to the khan Timur (or Tamerlane), who defeated the Golden Horde in 1395. After a hard-fought succession, Vasily's son, Vasily II the Dark, who came to power at age ten in 1425, enlarged his majesty with coin inscriptions boasting to "Lord of all the Russian Lands."

Around 1484, the warrior king Ivan III of Moscow, the son of Vasily II, ushered in an era of building and codification of law. He created a rare *ducat* from gold and circulated it alongside nondescript copper *pul* pieces marked "Pulo Moscovskoye" ("Pulo of Moscow"). Under Ivan IV the Terrible, and the first Russian monarch to call himself the tsar, who came to power in 1547, coinage was as uncouth and artless as his methods of subduing unruly subjects. Nonetheless, he succeeded in forming the nucleus of the Russian state.

For peasants, a common form of change was wire money, metal strips stamped with proof of authenticity. Rather than cut metal circlets from sheets by the European method,

A five-*kopek* piece depicts the royal emblem of Russia, a two-headed phoenix clutching a scepter above the Greek letters alpha and omega, Christian symbols of the beginning and end of time. (Russian Coin World)

Russian coinsmiths cut copper and silver wire rolls to a size suiting the desired weight. After annealing, the pieces required hasty hammering over dies. When the coin size shrank in the 1500s, artisans flattened each wire piece, producing off-strikes and irregular shapes.

The bar money of Kiev and Novgorod required cutting or chopping, the root of the Russian word *ruble*, the national monetary standard based on 100 *denga*. The *ruble* coin carried folk significance, for example, as a good luck piece buried in the foundation of a new house or sewn into a coat, both as an amulet and to put added weight in the hem. When tossing for "heads or tails," the bearer of good fortune was the reverse, which displayed the Russian eagle crest over the face, in one of the vivid designs randomly chosen.

In 1700, the reformer Peter I the Great of Russia ended the use of pelts, beads, metal weights, and other goods as money as well as the snipping of wire money for small change. After halting the circulation of bilingual *denga* inscribed with Arabic and Russian lettering, he set up a central minting operation at St. Petersburg with branches at Ekaterinburg and Moscow and imported artistic die-cutters from western Europe. From the upgraded national monetary system of Peter I came the Romanovs' tsarist coinage based on a decimal system.

A high point in the development of Russian currency resulted from the pragmatism of Catherine II the Great. Influenced by the writings of enlightened British economist Adam Smith, in 1766, she set up a new coinage and encouraged a free flow of European monies; two years later, she introduced the *rouble-assignat*, an inconvertible paper money. At the Sestoretsk arms factory, in 1770, she minted copper *rubles*. She founded a Siberian mint to make *kopeks* and staffed and equipped the operation from the royal coinworks at Ekaterinburg.

The innovative Catherine II the Great of Russia found a Siberian mint to make *kopeks* and staffed and equipped the operation from the royal coinworks at Ekaterinburg. (Russian Coin World)

Catherine II the Great of Russia modernized coinage and issued 10-*kopek* pieces featuring her coat of arms and, on the reverse, the royal cipher. (Russian Coin World)

Under Tsar Nicholas I Romanov, Russian coins displayed scrollery, crowns, and laurel wreaths that echoed the grandeur of his dynasty. (Russian Coin World)

In 1836, during Russia's literary and cultural flowering, Tsar Nicholas I Romanov issued a remarkably innovative *ruble* picturing the profile of his consort Alexandra, the former Princess Charlotte of Prussia, at center surrounded by silhouettes of their seven children. Among them stood the future Tsar Alexander II. Nicholas reformed Russian money and added silver notes, a stronger currency than the inconvertible *rouble-assignat* introduced by Catherine the Great in 1768. While Russia battled England in the Crimea in 1854 and Turkey in 1877, Nicholas's paper money supplanted convertible silver notes.

The last twelve years of Imperial Russia saw the design of spectacular banknotes. One 7 × 4-inch ten-*ruble* bill from 1909 displayed vertical imagery and crowned the text with the double-headed Romanov eagle. The following year, a grand 100-*ruble* note over ten inches long grandly pictured Catherine the Great twice — in a portrait oval and on the watermark. A 500-*ruble* note printed in 1912 pictured Peter the Great alongside the stylized form of "Mother Russia," a symbolic female benefactor equal to England's Britannia, France's Marianne, Ireland's Hibernia, and Lady Liberty in the U.S. The commemorative *ruble* of 1913, printed four years before the Russian Revolution, pictured Nicholas II alongside the Romanov founder, Tsar Michael — ironically, the first and last of the dynasty, and of the Russian tsars. As conditions reached starvation levels during World War I, Russian peasants were forced to use cakes of cheese bearing official stamps as trade media.

Under Communist rule, the Soviet Union used coins as a billboard for Marxist propaganda. Designs featured a hammer and sickle atop a globe, indicating the Communist intent to spread their philosophy around the world. Heavy sprinklings of grains of wheat suggested that agrarian prosperity undergirded Soviet success. Marx's rallying cry, "Workers of the world unite," marked banknotes, which the Soviet print press stamped in seven languages. An anti-capitalism poster pictured the bloated figure of a male plutocrat in top hat, tails, and gold rings and a watch chain on which dangled a gold heart as proof that he had abdicated compassion for profits. Above him, an encircling net of spider web satirized the ensnaring powers of greed. Flowing out from the figure from the waist down were a deluge of gold coins.

Paper money retained some of the glamour and romanticism of tsarist Russia. In 1919, 1000- and 5000-*ruble* notes bore scrollery, banners, and portrait ovals. General Anton Deniken, leader of the Army of the South during the power struggle between the Reds and the Whites, produced emergency money centered with a large engaging portrait of an unsmiling Mother Russia. In place of her usual scepter of state, she held sword and buckler. The White Russians issued their own banknote decked with victory wreath, medal, eagle clutching a lightning bolt, St. George and the Dragon, and the Kremlin bell, which, like the American Liberty Bell, cracked immediately after it was hung. A finer St. George, which adorned a 5000-*ruble* note, gazed out with stalwart posture as though unaware of the serpent writhing at his feet. The mix of images in this era's paper money characterized a clash of ideologies that remained in flux until the final triumph of Communism.

In 1949, the Russian mint eulogized Josef Stalin on his 70th birthday with 50- and 100-*korun* commemorative coins. Struck in silver, they pictured his spartan uniform and steely profile, noting his pseudonym, which he adopted from the Russian *stal* ("steel"). A master at making troublesome citizens disappear, over a six-year period, his staff arrested 20 million suspects. Most served time in gulags; some seven million he ordered shot. By the

This Russian *ruble* coin from 1829 features the royal emblem of Russia, a two-headed phoenix clutching a scepter. (Exhibitions, Georgia-Gateway)

This Russian *ruble* coin from 1820 features the royal emblem of Russia, a two-headed phoenix clutching a scepter and orb in its talons. (Exhibitions, Georgia-Gateway)

end of his regime in 1953, his sadistic rule had cost Russia a tenth of its population. Author and patriot Alexander Solzhenitsyn captured the grim survivalism of the era in the novel *One Day in the Life of Ivan Denisovich* (1962), which helped to win him the 1970 Nobel Prize for literature.

In 1967, the 50th anniversary of the Russian Revolution, the U.S.S.R. issued a cupronickel *ruble* featuring the standing figure of Vladimir Ilyich Lenin, the revolutionary writer who, in November 1917, joined Leon Trotsky in leading a revolt against the government that overthrew the Romanov dynasty. The combined efforts of Lenin and Trotsky brought down the Kerensky government and empowered the Bolsheviks. The coin's raised hand above the star symbol and the cyrillic letters CCCP symbolized his importance to the new Communist confederacy.

***See also* Catherine II; *denga*; fur money; Peter I; plate money; salt money; Heinrich Schliemann; scrip; *tympf*; world money.**

SOURCES: Allen, Larry. *Encyclopedia of Money*. New York: Checkmark Books, 2001. • Clain-Stefanelli, Elvira, and Vladimir Clain-Stefanelli. *The Beauty and Lore of Coins, Currency, and Medals*. Croton-on-Hudson, N.Y.: Riverwood Publishers, 1974. • Cribb, Joe. *Money*. Toronto: Stoddart, 1990. • Cribb, Joe, Barrie Cook, and Ian Carradice. *The Coin Atlas*. London: Little, Brown and Co., 1999. • Davies, Glyn. *A History of Money from Ancient Times to the Present Day*. Cardiff: University of Wales Press, 1994. • Einzig, Paul. *Primitive Money*. Oxford: Pergamon Press, 1966. • Opitz, Charles J. *Odd and Curious Money*. Ocala, Fla.: First Impressions, 1986. • "Tribute to Leonard Matters Miscellaneous." *The Hindu*, November 2, 1951. • Weatherford, Jack. *The History of Money: From Sandstone to Cyberspace*. Pittsburgh, Pa.: Three Rivers Press, 1998.

Sacagawea coin

Introduced 21 years after the failed Susan B. Anthony dollar, the Sacagawea dollar coin was the 12th U.S. coin to feature a native American likeness, the last being the 1938 Indian head nickel. When stock of the unpopular Susan B. Anthony dollar ran out in the late 1990s during the first term of President Bill Clinton, senators Barbara Boxer and Carol Moseley-Braun led a Democrat initiative voting down a symbolic Statue of Liberty coin and supporting currency that recognized in-the-flesh women's citizenship. Robert Rubin, Secretary of the Treasury, distinguished his term of office by choosing to depict a real woman.

After perusing proposals for images of Elizabeth Cady Stanton, abolitionists Harriet Beecher Stowe and Harriet Tubman, and activist-diplomat Eleanor Roosevelt, the commission looked elsewhere. Influenced by Stephen Ambrose's *Undaunted Courage* (1996) and the 1997 Ken Burns PBS-TV documentary on the Lewis and Clark expedition, members chose Sacagawea (also Bird-woman, Sacajawea, or Sakakagawea), a Lemhi Shoshone or Bannock translator and guide for the 1804–1806 westward expedition of George Rogers

Clark and Meriwether Lewis. Although she is a historic figure enhanced by the mystique of legend and the absence of documentation, she suited the nation's need for a female portrait coin.

Before paying tribute to Sacagawea, the U.S. Mint solicited suggested subjects from the public, who responded with letters, faxes, and email. In June 1998, a reviewing commission chose the Shoshone woman and invited 23 designers to propose sketches. The final selection from 121 submissions fell to prolific New Mexican sculptor Glenna Goodacre, realistic designer of works featuring an inclusive array of American subjects — survivors of the Irish potato famine, the Vietnam Women's Memorial, a life-size bronze of Ronald Reagan, and portrait busts of General Dwight D. Eisenhower, actress Greer Garson, author Katherine Anne Porter, and musician Scott Joplin, the father of American ragtime. Strongly humanistic, the image of Sacagawea, which pictures authentic shell earrings and blanket, acknowledges all native American women, a population largely ignored by historians. The coin, stamped with the initials G. G., earned the artist 5,000 Sacagawea dollars as commission.

On May 4, 2000, at the White House, the U.S. Mint unveiled the new gold-toned dollar coin featuring the likeness of Sacagawea. Because there is no surviving portrait of her, the image is speculative. Legend weakens much of her personal history, offering conflicting dates of her death. Born around 1784 or 1787, she was 12 years old when Hidatsa captors took her from camp at Three Forks, Montana, east to present-day Mandan, South Dakota.

The Hidatsa either sold or gambled away Sacagawea and her companion, Otter Woman, to French-Canadian fur trader Toussaint Charbonneau as slave wives. On February 17, 1805, Sacagawea gave birth to Jean-Baptiste Charbonneau about the time that she joined her husband in guiding the Lewis and Clark "Corps of Discovery" — 28 white men and one black male slave named York — west to survey 7,689 miles of unmapped territory between the Mississippi and Missouri rivers and the Pacific Ocean (Lewis 1999). Sacagawea's duties ranged from translating and guiding to standard female endeavors — gathering edible plants, cooking, sewing, and treating minor ailments.

Because of her knowledge of sign language and Shoshone and Sioux dialects, Sacagawea was a valuable liaison to explorers in horse trades with native tribes along the way. Still recovering from childbirth when the company set out, she retraced familiar Shoshone trails and assisted with portage at falls and cataracts along the watery route. The presence of a mother and infant helped the explorers make peaceful contact with native Americans. The men enjoyed having a youngster with them and nicknamed Sacagawea's baby Pompey or Pomp. When a canoe overturned, she dived into the swift current to recover lost journals and provisions from the Yellowstone River.

Along the route up the Clearwater, Snake, and Columbia rivers, after a separation of around nine years, Sacagawea reunited with her brother Cameahwait at Three Forks, Montana, in August 1805. The expedition ended near present-day Astoria, Oregon. Upon the group's return in 1806, Lewis and Clark paid Charbonneau in currency and land for the couple's work. Sacagawea received no money or property of her own. After returning to St. Louis with Charbonneau, she bore a daughter, Lisette, and appears to have died in 1812 of disease, rather than among the Comanche in Wind River, Wyoming, in 1884, as an alternative story suggests. Pompey Charbonneau, whom Clark adopted, studied in Missouri and Europe and returned to the West as a mountain guide, trapper, prospector, and hunter.

Sacagawea's picture bore Goodacre's vision of a bright, youthful young woman peering over her shoulder at her infant son, "Pompey" Charbonneau, asleep Indian style in a skin carrier and snuggled against his mother's neck. For a model, Goodacre chose Randy'L Teton, a 22-year-old Shoshone-Bannock student at the University of New Mexico, and posed her in an antique beaded doeskin dress from Morning Star Gallery. Mint engraver Thomas D. Rogers, Sr., sculpted the eagle for the reverse side. To gain public approval, the mint distributed the first 500 million coins through Wal-Mart and launched an advertising campaign to prepare citizens for the new addition to U.S. coins.

The coin, as lustrous as 14-carat gold, was made of a new alloy produced by Olin Brass of East Alton, Illinois. The disk, a blend of manganese and zinc with nickel centered with copper, required casting in 10-ton ingots for compressing through rollers to the proper thickness. The finished coin bore a wide border and smooth edge to enable users, both sighted and visually impaired, to recognize it by touch.

The third annual Coinstar National Currency Poll disclosed a 79 percent approval rating for the Sacagawea coin. Not surprising was a greater approval among females, who welcomed the first coin featuring the likeness of a madonna and child — an ingenuous mother in fluid, casual pose with eyes turned toward the viewer. John M. Kleebert, curator of modern coins at the American Numismatic Society in New York, acknowledged, "The modeling of Sacagawea is nicely done, and the pose is an unusual one" (Wu 2000). Despite the coin's welcome, citizens still preferred paper notes to coins for daily transactions and apparently chose merely to collect Sacagawea dollars.

See also **U.S. coins; U.S. Mint.**

SOURCES: Cantor, George. *North American Indian Landmarks.* Detroit: Gale Research, 1993. • Champagne, Duane, ed. *Chronology of Native North American History.* Detroit: Gale Research, 1994. • "How Popular Will Sacagawea Be?" *USA Today Magazine,* November 2000. • Johansen, Bruce E., and Donald A. Grinde. *The Encyclopedia of Native American Biography.* New York: Da Capo Press, 1998. • Lewis, Michael J. "Of Kitsch and Coins." *Commentary,* October 1999. • Patterson, Lotsee, and Mary Ellen Snodgrass. *Indian Terms of the Americas.* Englewood, Colo.: Libraries Unlimited, 1994. • Pritzker, Barry M. *A Native American Encyclopedia: History, Culture, and Peoples.* Oxford: Oxford University Press, 2000. • "Renowned Artist Glenna Goodacre Creates Sculpture for New Gold-Colored Dollar Coin for Year 2000." *People Weekly,* June 14, 1999. • Waldman, Carl. *Who Was Who in Native American History.* New York: Facts on File, 1990. • Wilfong, Tara N. "Coining a New Era." *Arts and Antiques,* September 1999. • Wu, Corinna. "The Buck Starts Here." *Science News,* April 1, 2000.

Saint-Gaudens, Augustus

The 19th century's prize sculptor, Augustus Saint-Gaudens modeled neo-classic statues and low relief on medals and coins. A native of Dublin born on March 1, 1848, he was the son of an Irish mother, Mary McGuiness, and French father, shoemaker Bernard Paul Ernest Saint-Gaudens. Within the year, the family emigrated to Boston with several sons. Saint-Gaudens grew up in New York City and apprenticed to cameo-cutter Louis Avet and, in 1861, to shell cameo artist Jules Le Brethon. Wretched at his day work, which he called slavery, Saint-Gaudens took night courses at the Cooper Union and the National Academy of Design. In 1867, on a journey to the Paris Exposition, he learned to model nudes and entered l'École des Beaux-Arts to study with François Jouffroy.

When the Franco-Prussian War made France an unsafe place to work, at age 22, Saint-Gaudens moved to Rome and set up as a cameo maker for a jeweler named Lupi. While seeking additional training at l'École Gratuite de Dessin, Saint-Gaudens completed a statue of the Iroquois chief Hiawatha, which hinted at the sculptor's future greatness. To earn money to fight illness and poverty, for two years, he sought commissions to copy antique statues. On return to New York in 1875, he opened his own atelier in Cornish, New Hampshire, and made friends with painter John La Farge and architects Charles Follen McKim, Henry Hobson Richardson, and Stanford White.

Saint-Gaudens's first original contribution to sculpture was a life-size portrait monument to Admiral David Farragut, located at Madison Square Park in New York City. By 1880, Saint-Gaudens was the most respected sculptor, portraitist, and medalist in the United States. He produced pieces for Cornelius Vanderbilt, completed the draped Adams Memorial honoring Mrs. Henry Adams, and sculpted his most lasting works — the *Puritan* for Springfield, Massachusetts; the beloved Boston monument to Colonel Robert Gould Shaw, leader of the first black regiment in the Civil War; an equestrian likeness of General William Tecumseh Sherman for New York's Central Park; and adornment for Boston's Trinity Church.

Saint-Gaudens came late to coin design with his creation of ten-dollar and 20-dollar gold pieces. He modeled a magnificent double eagle on classic art in response to a dinner conversation with President Theodore Roosevelt, a fellow fan of Greco-Roman style. The famed double eagle symbolized for the United States the optimism and exuberance of Teddy Roosevelt's progressivism. Born in 1905, the idea derived from the president's admiration of the high relief and grace of Hellenistic coins struck under Alexander the Great. Roosevelt prodded Saint-Gaudens to emulate them on a U.S. coin and agreed to help him sell the idea to Charles Barber, head engraver at the U.S. Mint, who feared that deep bas-relief would not hold up to heavy wear.

From the synergy of artist with president grew plans for the double eagle, which numismatists have lauded as America's finest coin. The sculptor, infused with the president's enthusiasm, proposed merging a realistic image of Liberty with the drapings of Athena and the winged figure of Nike, the goddess of victory that Athena traditionally held in outstretched hand. In a subsequent letter to Roosevelt, Saint-Gaudens developed the billowy abstract figure into a living female form who would symbolize progress. Picturing an eagle in flight against the rays of a sunrise on the reverse, the coin, completed in 1907, featured a starred edge bearing the motto "*E Pluribus Unum.*"

For the face of Liberty, who wears an eagle-feather bonnet, his assistant, Henry Hering, posed an Irish model, Hettie Anderson, the model Saint-Gaudens had chosen for the figure of Victory on his Sherman monument. Other models rumored to have provided the coin's face were Vermont waitress Mary Cunningham, model Alice Butler, and the sculptor's mistress, Davida Clark. Subsequent research into Saint-Gaudens's personal papers disclosed a statement of his regard for Anderson, the true model. In addition to her "goddess-like" beauty, he admired "a power of posing patiently, steadily and thoroughly in the spirit one wished. She could be depended on" (Van Ryzin, 1995, p. 129, 132).

After influencing a generation of sculptors and medalists to escape convention, Saint-Gaudens died of cancer on August 3, 1907, before the release of his gold coin and before completion of a proposed series of smaller coins. His students Adolph Alexander Weinman and James Earle Fraser perpetuated Saint-Gaudens's neo-classic designs with the Mercury dime and Indian head nickel; a protégé, Hermon A. MacNeil, produced the Standing Liberty Quarter. Two others, John Flanagan and Bela Lyon Pratt, incised famous pieces — Flanagan completed the Washington quarter, Pratt, two Indian Head gold coins. Through the work of Saint-Gaudens's wife Augusta and son Homer, his studio was renamed the Saint-Gaudens National Historic Site.

***See also* Charles Edward Barber; *drachma;* Bela Lyon Pratt; U.S. coins; Adolph A. Weinman.**

SOURCES: "Augustus Saint-Gaudens," http://www.sgnhs.org/Augustus.html. • Bowers, Q. David. *Adventures with Rare Coins.* Los Angeles: Bowers & Ruddy Galleries, Inc., 1979. • Bowers, Q. David. "American Gold." *American Heritage,* December 1984, 43–49. • *Encyclopedia of World Biography.* Detroit: Gale Group, 1998. • Gustaitis, Joseph. "The Lady of the Tower." *American History,* June 1999, 44–60. • Howarth, William. "The Work of Augustus Saint-Gaudens." *Smithsonian,* June 1983, 124–125. • Johnson, Allen, ed. *Dictionary of American Biography.* New York: Charles Scribner's Sons, 1928. • Lewis, Michael J. "Of Kitsch and Coins." *Commentary,* October 1999. • Reed, Mort. *Cowles Complete Encyclopedia of U.S. Coins.* New York: Cowles Book Company, 1969. • Snodgrass, Mary Ellen. *Religious Sites in America.* Santa Barbara, Calif.: ABC-Clio, 2000. • "Saint-Gaudens National Historic Site," http://www.nps.gov/saga/. • Taxay, Don. *The U.S. Mint and Coinage.* New York: Arco Publishing, 1966. • Van Ryzin, Robert R. *Twisted Tails: Sifted Fact, Fantasy and Fiction from U.S. Coin History.* Iola, Wisc.: Krause Publications, 1995.

St. Patrick coppers

Minted in Ireland, St. Patrick Coppers, briefly produced in 1674 and 1675, were makeshirt currency during the shortage of coins that plagued colonial North America. They picture a kneeling King David in eastern crown plucking the harp as he gazes at the English crown. The back displays the Dublin shield behind Saint Patrick with miter and crozier blessing a congregation with a shamrock. The motto reads "*Ecce Grex*" ("Behold the Flock"). The smaller version shows him banishing serpents from the island with an inscription "*Quiescat Plebs*" ("Let Commoners Be at Ease").

The choice of St. Patrick on coin art was propitious for Ireland, where people revered the early fifth-century saint as their patron. Born at Bannavem Taburniae around A.D. 395, he was an Irish or Welsh grandson of a priest and the child of Calpurnius, a town assemblyman and deacon. After his enslavement by Irish pirates, Patrick herded their sheep. On gaining his liberty around 411, he came under the influence of St. Caranoc at Straford Lough and took the name Patrick to indicate conversion to Christianity. He taught Gaelic and catechized Irish youngsters. Elevated to Bishop of Tara in 432, he lived at the see of Armagh, preached, baptized lepers, and converted the Celts. As bishop of Ireland, he became the most influential Christian of his era.

The St. Patrick coppers appear to have been the issue of Arthur, Earl of Essex, who was lord lieutenant of Ireland from 1672 to 1677. Struck from a copper planchet clad in brass, they possessed a golden sheen like that of English coins and bore the royalist motto "*Floreat Rex*" ("May the King Flourish"). They circulated on the Isle of Man during the minority of the Earl of Derby, hereditary lord of the island.

Imported by Quaker merchant Mark Newby (or Newbie), St. Patrick coppers arrived in New Jersey with the docking of the *Owners Adventurer* on September 19, 1681. On May 18, 1682, the state assembly proclaimed the coins legal tender valued at a halfpenny, replacing strings of shell wampum. To circulate his coins, Newby placed 300 acres of land as his bond. At his death in 1682, the estate contained around 10,800 coppers valued at £30 in coppers. The coins continued to supply Americans in the colonial and early federal periods.

SOURCES: Davies, Glyn. *A History of Money from Ancient Times to the Present Day.* Cardiff: University of Wales Press, 1994. • Jordan, Louis. "The Coins of Colonial and Early America." http://www.coins.nd.edu/ColCoin/ColCoinContents/Introduction.html. • Lewis, Brenda Ralph. *Coins & Currency.* New York: Random House, 1993. • Snodgrass, Mary Ellen. *Who's Who in the Middle Ages.* Jefferson, N.C.: McFarland, 2001. • Weatherford, Jack. *The History of Money: From Sandstone to Cyberspace.* Pittsburgh, Pa.: Three Rivers Press, 1998.

salt money

A valued commodity once associated with the tables of the rich and the altars of gods, salt passed from sack to hand as a form of money. As currency, Africans of Ethiopia and Mali exchanged salt cakes and salt cylinders mined in the Sahara; this was a monetary system also in use in Tibet. In the mid-fifth century B.C., the Greek historian Herodotus described passage of salt over a caravan route linking the oases of Libya. From the Greek isles to Russia's Black Sea coast, people traded in salt that a low-caste or slave population evaporated from ocean water in artificial ponds at the Dnieper River delta. In the Iron Age, salt-makers flourished in England at Cheshire, East Anglia, Teeside, Tyneside, and Worcestershire.

The Romans extended Britannia's dominance of the salt market with a pan-and-kiln operation at an appropriately named settlement at Salinae, now Middlewich, Cheshire. On the frontier, Roman soldiers and civil servants collected their *salarium* (salt allotment), an allowance for purchasing salt. In Italy during the early empire, the Romans transferred sacks of salt over the Via Salaria (or Salarian Way) from the harbor city of Ostia east to Rome for dispersal to Reate and Castrum Novum on the east coast and throughout Roman territories. The value to life was so crucial that satirist Gaius Petronius Arbiter, author of the *Satyricon* (A.D. 60), coined the phrase "not worth his salt," which originated as an insult to imply that a slave was not worth the salt he received.

In 1275, Marco Polo and his brother Niccolò observed Chinese salt money, which Marco described in his journal, *The Travels of Marco Polo* (1299). At Kaun-Du, Marco witnessed the manufacture of salt in boiling pans at saline springs. When the evaporation was complete, the salt moneyer shaped the goo into hollowed cakes, which dried on tiles at a hearth. The official stamp of the khan attested to the value of each cake, worth twopence.

The salt trade figures in the works of mid–14th century travel writer ibn Battuta of Tangiers, author of *Tuhfat al-Nuzzar fi Ghara'ib al-Amsar wa'Ajaib al'Asfar* (*On Curiosities of Cities and Wonders of Travel*) (1354). While journeying from Taghaza to Walata in the kingdom of Mali in west Africa, he observed a salt mine in the Sahara Desert of *bilad al-sudan* (black Africa). Workers removed layers of natural sand crystals in thick slabs and stacked them two per camel. He commented,

> A load of it is sold at [Walata] for eight to ten *mithqals*, and in the city of Malli for 20 to 30, sometimes 40. The blacks trade with salt as others trade with gold and silver; they cut it in pieces and buy and sell with these. For all its squalor *qintars* and *qintars* of gold dust are traded there [Bullis 2000, 37].

In an atmosphere booming with profits, Battuta was glad to depart after spending ten days in an atmosphere of flies and brackish water.

Salt money cropped up frequently in other 19th-century travel writing. British travel writer Sir Richard Francis Burton, author of *Pilgrimage to El Medinah and Meccah* (1855) and *The Gold-Mines of Midian and the Ruined Midianite Cities* (1878), discovered salt money in use at Harar, Ethiopia. At the going rate, a slave cost as much in salt slabs as a donkey could carry. At Zimmé between Siam and Burma, British imperial publicist Holt S. Hallett, author of *A Thousand Miles on an Elephant in the Shan States* (1890), witnessed the exchange of salt as market currency in 1874.

Salt was still in use in Abyssinia in brick form in the last years of the 19th century, according to historian and traveler Hubert Howe Bancroft, author of *The Book of the Fair* (1893) concerning his visit to a numismatic exhibit at the 1893 World Columbian Exhibition. Hoarded by the Amole tribe of Irianjaya province, Papua New Guinea, in the 1920s, the salt bar was a long slice of rock salt valued as currency and in cooking. To preserve the shape, users bound the outer edges in reeds. The culture singled out for admiration anyone rich enough to eat salt.

***See also* trade and barter.**

SOURCES: Allen, Larry. *Encyclopedia of Money*. New York: Checkmark Books, 2001. • Bancroft, Hubert Howe. *The Book of the Fair*. Chicago: The Bancroft Company, 1893. • Bullis, Douglas. "The Longest Hajj: The Journeys of Ibn Battuta." *Aramco World*, July/August 2000, 2–39. • Bunson, Matthew. *A Dictionary of the Roman Empire*. New York: Oxford University Press, 1991. • Clain-Stefanelli, Elvira, and Vladimir Clain-Stefanelli. *The Beauty and Lore of Coins, Currency, and Medals*. Croton-on-Hudson, N.Y.: Riverwood Publishers, 1974. • Cribb, Joe. *Money*. Toronto: Stoddart, 1990. • Davies, Glyn. *A History of Money from Ancient Times to the Present Day*. Cardiff: University of Wales Press, 1994. • Einzig, Paul. *Primitive Money*. Oxford: Pergamon Press, 1966. • Ibn Battuta. *The Travels of Ibn Battuta*. Cambridge: Cambridge University Press, 1971.

Schliemann, Heinrich

German linguist and archeologist Heinrich Schliemann exhibited to an unbelieving world caches of artifacts and disks and roundels resembling money, all proving that the heroes and cities of ancient Greek poetry really existed. In addition to gates and graves, he found hammered gold and the beginnings of a monetary system based on coins. When he dug into Troy at Hissarlik, Turkey, he uncovered silver bars from the 1300s B.C. shaped like tongues. At Mycenae, he located metal platelets that resembled modern tokens or coins. His recovered treasures enriched the world's knowledge of ancient eastern Mediterranean culture and boosted the writings of Homer from fantasy to history.

A native of Neubukow, Mecklenburg,

Schlieman was born on January 6, 1822, the fifth of the nine children of Ernst and Sophie Schliemann. After his mother died, in 1831, his father, a humble parson who had an affair with a housemaid, was publicly shamed and had to split up the children. Schliemann lived with his uncle and attended the university-preparatory Carolinum Gymnasium until his father's humiliation and resignation from the ministry. Schliemann entered a Realschüle, from which he graduated at age 14 with preparation in trades. He worked at Ernst Holtz's food market at Fürstenberg, a lackluster job for an intelligent, imaginative youth.

To rid his life of tedium, Schliemann embarked on the *Dorothea* for a voyage to Venezuela. After the ship foundered off the Dutch shore, he was destitute. He worked for an Amsterdam merchant and mastered Dutch, English, French, Italian, Portuguese, and Spanish. At age 22, he kept accounts for B. H. Schröder and Company. After Schliemann learned Russian to aid in translating import documents, he traveled to St. Petersburg as company agent. By 1847, he opened his own trading firm and, as business in saltpeter and indigo increased during the Crimean War, expanded to include a Moscow outlet.

At age 41, Schliemann had accumulated enough wealth to support an immersion in classical Greek history and archeology. He traveled Carthage, India, China, Japan, and the Americas and gained a U.S. citizenship after opening a bank at Sacramento during the California Gold Rush of 1849. During an era when coinage had not caught up with rich strikes in nuggets and gold dust, he dealt in as much as 150 pounds of dust daily, which he shipped to San Francisco in return for coins. Aiding him in his dealings with immigrant prospectors and speculators were the eight languages he had learned. From October 19, 1851, to April 5, 1852, he and two clerks managed $1,350,000 in gold dust. In his diary, he recorded that "All is based here on swindling ... abominable falsehood, fraud and humbug" (Moorehead 1994, p. 39).

Schliemann left California abruptly, apparently for having shorted the agent who converted the gold dust into coin. With a fortune entrusted to him by depositors, Schliemann fled by steamer to New York. He returned to his beloved Russia and courted Ekaterina, a young Russian woman eager to marry a rich man. Their brittle, loveless marriage produced three children, but no lasting relationship. To occupy his restless mind, he retired from business and traveled.

In 1868, Schliemann completed an advanced degree from the University of Rostock and launched a dig at Troy. From his discoveries, he published *Antiquités Troyennes* (*Trojan Antiquities*) (1874). In August 1876, he moved on to Mycenae, Agamemnon's capital on the Peloponnesus, and excavated the Dome Tombs of the ancient kings, which contained the world's greatest cache of precious metals and art objects. Inside the citadel walls, he unearthed a two-stage ring of slabs enclosing five shaft graves and a king's ransom in gold, silver, bronze, and ivory. The treasure consisted of gold battleaxes, diadems, goblets, jewelry, 150 disks, and 400 proto-coins, which he summarized in *Mykenä* (1878).

Vigorous and absorbed in antiquities until his death on Christmas day, 1890, in Naples, Italy, Schliemann enjoyed a happy married life with a second wife, a Greek schoolgirl named Sophia Engastromenos. He sired a son and daughter, Agamemnon and Andromache, traveled widely, wrote in numerous languages about his theories and discoveries, and made further studies of Tiryns, Orchomenos, Cythera, and Pylos. After a lifetime of successful digs, in 1881 he donated to Berlin's State Museum the Homeric trove that he smuggled out of Asian Turkey. In 1996, Moscow's Pushkin Museum exhibited Trojan art treasures called "Priam's Gold," which Russian allies stole from Berlin at the end of World War II. In addition to gold coins, the display featured perfume cruets, delicately hand-molded jewelry, buttons, and belts.

***See also* Percy Gardner.**

SOURCES: Clain-Stefanelli, Elvira, and Vladimir Clain-Stefanelli. *The Beauty and Lore of Coins, Currency, and Medals*. Croton-on-Hudson, N.Y.: Riverwood Publishers, 1974. • Einzig, Paul. *Primitive Money*. Oxford: Pergamon Press, 1966. •

Encyclopedia of World Biography. Detroit: Gale Group, 1998. • Glasgow, Eric. "The Gold of Troy Emerges from the Cold War." *Contemporary Review*, June 1996, pp. 312–314. • Lemonick, Michael D. "Troy's Lost Treasure." *Time*, April 22, 1996 , pp. 78–80. • Moorehead, Caroline. *Lost and Found: The 9,000 Treasures of Troy*. London: Penguin Books, 1994. • Plagens, Peter, "The Golden Hoard," *Newsweek*, April 8, 1996, pp. 72–73. • Traill, David A., and Paul C. Appleton, "Letters from Troy," *Archaeology*, January/February 2002, 54.

Scottish coins

The Scots were late to produce their own money and used in the interim a variety of Roman, Anglo-Saxon, and English coins. After his crowning in 1124, David I MacMalcolm (also Canmore or Dunkeld), Scotland's revered ruler and saint, improved the standard of government for his people. He strengthened the established church and founded royal burghs at Dunfermline, Perth, and Stirling. To advance commerce in peasant communities and encourage sale of local goods, the able administrator and reformer introduced an authorized system of weights and measures and circulated the nation's first silver pennies, a copy of those minted by his rival, Stephen I.

David issued uniform coinage from his mints at Berwick and Roxburgh. A portrait coin featured his crowned profile in classic style alongside a sword. His ambitions for the Scots were short-lived, ending with the accession of his grandson Malcolm IV, a tender youth nicknamed "the Maiden." David's brother, Henry, Earl of Northumberland, struck his own series of coins at Bamburgh, Carlisle, and Corbridge.

A coin from difficult times in Scotland pictured William I the Lion opposite a cross highlighted with stars. It was struck at a royal mint in Roxburgh, a city that he surrendered to the English in 1174 along with Berwick and Edinburgh. To restore the latter city to the Scots, William married Ermengarde, cousin of Henry II. With the bride came the city as dowry. A Scottish renaissance after 1249 under Alexander III, the last of the line from Malcolm III Canmore, restored coinage to esthetic beauty. The prosperous Alexander issued a long-cross silver penny that served an era of progress and balanced trade that lasted until 1275.

In its relatively short era of production, the Scottish mint issued unique coins, notably the elegant gold St. Andrews crown of Robert III, struck after 1390. Small change for the Scots consisted of the "hard-head" twopence, the "turner" penny, and the fourpence billon and copper piece called a "plack," source of the Scot retort "I don't care a plack" and the adjective "plackless" for "penniless." A casual find of some of these pennies came to light at Crossraguel Abbey in Ayrshire in 1919 during the cleaning of a latrine drain. Larger units included the threepence "half-bawbee" and the sixpence "bawbee," a slang truncation of the name of Alexander Orrok, the Laird of Sillebawby, James V's mintmaster after 1538. In his second year on the job, Sillebawby produced the Bonnet piece, a gold *ducat* made from gold mined by imported German laborers at Crawford Muir and the first Scottish specie to be dated. At the king's request, the job of mintmaster passed to James Gunyear Aitcheson in 1558. Sir Walter Scott lauded the quality bonnet coins in *Tales of a Grandfather* (1828). After James VI was crowned James I of England at the death of the childless Queen Elizabeth I, the union of England and Scotland decreased circulation of native Scottish coins as a separate indigenous currency.

The Scottish mint shut down from 1649 to 1664, a period encompassing the Commonwealth and the first two years after the restoration of Charles II. Local coinage supplied Scots with silver and copper change, including James III's production of "blak pennyis," an insubstantial copper suited to peasant commerce. The country's mint ceased production with the Act of Union of 1707, the year that England's parliament merged with Scotland's. Ostensibly, the Articles of Union preserved national coinage in the same standard and value as English coins, but the reality was the loss of Scottish specie, a source of contention among rabid Jacobites.

The penny proved the savior of an English soldier challenging the Scots. On April 16, 1746, a gallant Jacobite troop of 5,000 highlanders fighting the 40-minute battle of Culloden (or Drummossie) at Inverness to boost the pretender Charles Edward "Bonnie Prince Charlie" Stuart to the throne of England faced 9,000 English, led by the duke of Cumberland. In a lopsided victory that killed 1,000 Scots and only 50 British, one Englishman took a bullet that glanced off a copper half-pence, sparing his life.

See also **groat; paper money; sixpence; touch coins; trade and barter.**

SOURCES: Cannon, John, and Ralph Griffiths. *Oxford Illustrated History of the British Monarchy.* Oxford: Oxford University Press, 1988. • Cribb, Joe. *Money.* Toronto: Stoddart, 1990. • Cribb, Joe, Barrie Cook, and Ian Carradice. *The Coin Atlas.* London: Little, Brown and Co., 1999. • Pomerleau, Charlie. "Tall Tales of Buried Treasures Run Deep." *Bangor Daily News,* August 27, 1998. • Snodgrass, Mary Ellen. *Who's Who in the Middle Ages.* Jefferson, N.C.: McFarland, 2001.

screw press

One of the controversial changes in world coinage was the shift from hand-striking with a hammer, dies, and anvil to machining. The idea took shape in Italy to hold a lower die in place while raising and lowering the upper die on a screw shaft through guide plates to impact the face below. The operation, requiring two operators and a coiner's boy to place blanks on the lower surface, produced up to 25 coins per minute. The first screw-press coinage dates to 1514, when Renaissance architect Donato Bramante, master designer for the Vatican, applied the principle to the pressing of money. By 1538, goldsmith Benvenuto Cellini, author of *Trattato della Scultura* ("*Treatise on Sculpture*") (1568) and a text on metalwork, *Trattato dell' Oreficeria* ("*Treatise on Goldsmithing*"), had tinkered with a similar method of shaping small coins.

Around 1550, silversmith Marx Schwab originated a factory-style device in Augsburg, Germany, as a tool for the printing industry. The technology that produced milled coins was called in French the *balancer* or screw press, a simple forcing device operated by turns on a capstan. The press was applicable to numerous industries, including wine, oil, and paper. The use of a screw mechanism to increase the force exerted between opposing arms required one worker to load planchets and move them from the base and a team of strong laborers to turn the crank. The press enabled moneyers to incise patterns and motifs from a pair of dies applied to opposite sides of a planchet or blank metal disk. Iron worker Aubin Olivier upgraded Schwab's press with a collar that held blanks in place for an even strike and the incision of milling or lettering on the edge.

In 1551, French moneyers assembled the Schwab press. It was operated by engineer Aubin Olivier at *Du Moulin des Étuves* in the royal gardens at the site of any old gem-polishing mill on l'Île de la Cité of Paris. Among the oglers who watched the crew stamp coins was Charles IX, who took turns on the machine to tighten the vise action. The French government, faced with complaints from hand strikers of coins, opted not to replace medieval minting methods on the basis of cost and loss of jobs to artisans. The *Cour de Monnaies* forced the millmaster to produce only tokens and medals. In this same era, medalists at Nantes, directed by Étienne Bergeron, cranked out copper pieces on a *monnaie du moulin* (money mill), a water-powered screw press.

In England, the new press technology caused a serious rift between coin artisans still producing coins one at a time by the method introduced during the Roman occupation. Eloy (or Eloi) Mestrell, the mintmaster of Elizabeth I, tested the new equipment in 1566 by stamping a silver sixpence featuring the profile of "Regina Elizabeth I" in crown and ruff (Cribb 1990, p. 46). The vise-style system, applied to three farthing pieces, threepences, and sixpences until 1571, produced quality coinage that was neater, sharper, and less wasteful of time and planchets than hammering by hand. Because the pieces never earned popular respect, the technology lapsed and gave place in 1628 to the roller mill, an idea invented during the Italian Renaissance by Leonardo da Vinci and perfected in Germany under Archduke Ferdinand in 1566.

In France, the insistence of engraver and machinist Nicholas Briot that the Paris Mint replace hand-striking with mechanized coinage earned him death threats. Persecution forced him to leave the country and seek employment under Charles I of England in 1625. At London's Tower Mint, Briot was able to convince mintmaster Thomas Rawlins of the value of a machine that turned out uniform coins.

The technology spread south and west. Salvors located silver *Dos Mundos* ("two worlds") pillar dollars dated 1732 and 1733 in the wreckage of the *Nuestra Señora de Balvaneda*, which sank near the Florida Keys in a hurricane in 1733 along with all but one of a Spanish fleet of 22 ships. The coins were the first manufactured by screw press in the Western Hemisphere. One version of the screw press installed at the Madrid Mint in 1700, at the Seville Mint in 1735, and at the Segovia Mint in 1772 survived until the refinement of roller mill pressing.

As presented in engravings in French compiler Denis Diderot's *Encyclopédie* (1772), the technology of the screw press and the hand-cranked edger was tedious, but more precise than medieval methods. The press served moneyers at the U.S. Mint in Philadelphia until later time- and work-savers replaced it. In 1830, German mechanic Dietrich Uhlhorn devised a coin press that supplanted the screw mechanism with lever operation. In 1845, the steam-operated Thonnelier press relieved the labor of Paris coinsmiths.

***See also* Nicholas Briot; Benvenuto Cellini; cobs; coinage; English coins; Robert Maskell Patterson; Renaissance coins.**

SOURCES: "Aspects de la naissance d'une monnaie nouvelle à la Renaissance." http://www.i-numis.com/europe/articles/moderne/moderne2-fr.html. • Bass, George F., ed. *Ships and Shipwrecks of the Americas: A History Based on Underwater Archaeology*. London: Thames and Hudson, 1996. • "CGB.Fr Numismatiques." http://www.ordonnances.org/regnes/louis13/1622_1632.html. • "Coins of the Louis Kings." http://www.cgb.fr/monnaies/articles/monnaiesfrance/roislouisgb.html. • Cribb, Joe. *Money*. Toronto: Stoddart, 1990. • Davies, Glyn. *A History of Money from Ancient Times to the Present Day*. Cardiff: University of Wales Press, 1994. • *Encyclopedia of Art*. New York: McGraw-Hill Book Co., 1968. • Laing, Lloyd R. *Coins and Archaeology*. New York: Schocken Books, 1969. • "Louis XIII Le Juste." http://www.cgb.fr/monnaies/vso/v12/fr/monnaies8287.html. • *Merriam-Webster's Biographical Dictionary*. Springfield, Mass.: Merriam-Webster, 1995. • "Monnaies Royales Françaises." http://www.epromat.com/poindessault/ve26/p2605.htm. • Reinfeld, Fred. *Treasury of the World's Coins*. New York: Sterling Publishing, 1953. • Sardin, Frédérique. "Les légendes en creux fautées sur les tranches des monnaies françaises en or et en argent du XIXe siècle." http://www. amisdufranc.org/articles/varietes/tranches_fautees.html. • Sargent, Thomas J., and Francois R. Velde. *The Evolution of Small Change*. Chicago: Federal Reserve Bank, 1997. • Stephen, Sir Leslie, and Sir Sidney Lee, eds. *Dictionary of National Biography*. London: Oxford University Press, 1922. • "The Story of the Sixpence." http://www.24carat.co.uk/sixpencesstory.html.

scrip

Scrip is a scrap of paper, playing card, wood, silk, buckskin, leather, aluminum foil, or other flimsy material substituted for legal tender. As currency, scrip has short-term value, as illustrated by the cutting of playing cards into paper tokens in Nova Scotia in 1685 to supply emergency pay for soldiers. In 1916, issuance of square cardboard coins served Algerians in the period preceding World War I. A post-war inflationary period necessitated the bright-colored emergency issue of *Notgeld* (temporary currency) in the 1920s by Austria and Germany.

The Romans originated scrip with the *nummus castrensis* ("camp coin"), an artless, temporary specie that generals commissioned to pay soldiers in the field. Later versions were less spartan. The siege money issued by French invaders of Mainz, Germany, in 1793, was a red-bordered sheet bearing a number, signature, and official stamp of the French Republic. One historic example, the paper promissory notes distributed to General George Washington's army before the siege at Yorktown in 1781, moved soldiers to mutiny until congressional financier Robert Morris personally underwrote the military payroll from his own funds. Another type, a numbered series of Alaskan notes printed on both sides of seal skin in 1820, served the Russian-American Company in lieu of small change.

When the Confederacy developed its treasury, the new Southern government experienced demands for currency to maintain a viable economy. Until officials in Richmond, Virginia, could establish a money system, they issued short-term promissory notes. Meanwhile, individuals, companies, cities, and states hastily printed scrip, which quickly lost its value. The situation grew so desperate that buyers battled rapidly spiraling inflation with food riots and, in some agrarian areas, initiated a barter system.

Twentieth-century wars raised additional need for short-term paper money. In 1919, scrip issued at Russian prisoner of war camps supplied Czechoslovakian inmates with viable cash. The Uzbekistanis printed *rubles* on fringed silk in 1921. Chinese Communists stamped linen scrip with a star and fist in 1933. In the United States, when the Great Depression stymied American communities and businesses, private issuance of wooden nickels, buckskin notes, and scrip eased a difficult coin shortage. One version, a five-cent piece stamped on wood, featured the Peace Arch of Blaine, Washington, a landmark erected in 1914 between Blaine, Washington, and Douglas, British Columbia, to commemorate the centennial of the Treaty of Ghent, which ended the War of 1812 between the United States and Great Britain.

In the 1940s, camp scrip, the earnings of inmates under Nazi guard, circulated in German concentration camps at Buchenwald, Oranienburg, Sachsenhausen, and Theresienstadt and in the Warsaw ghetto. Cruel camp bosses awarded "special privilege" funds ostensibly as a bonus to belabored inmates so they could redeem them for extra rations. In reality, the amount of food went unchanged, with camp favorites receiving a greater share while the weak, sick, or rebellious starved.

Buchenwald's contribution to Holocaust money was a quality paper scrip printed with a flower design, military symbol and RM for *Reichsmark*, and the location, *Standort-Kantine* (mobile canteen). Camp staff at Theresienstadt printed an internal camp scrip to convince Red Cross inspectors that inmates enjoyed a normal life. At Oranienburg, an inmate, Jewish graphic artist Horst-Willi Lippert, designed a plate for paper scrip worth 50 *pfennigs* with a hidden letter "G" in the word *Konzentrationslager* (concentration slayer). His gesture of rebellion preserved for history an attempt to fight back against Nazi genocide.

See also **Canadian money; Robert Morris; siege money; stone money.**

SOURCES: Clain-Stefanelli, Elvira, and Vladimir Clain-Stefanelli. *The Beauty and Lore of Coins, Currency, and Medals*. Croton-on-Hudson, N.Y.: Riverwood Publishers, 1974. • Cribb, Joe. *Money*. Toronto: Stoddart, 1990. • *Encyclopedia of the Roman Empire*. New York: Facts on File, Inc., 1994. • Levy, Alan. "Adolf Burger: The Forger as a Work of Art." *Prague Post*, November 1, 2000. • Medovoy, George. "Merchant Runs Holocaust Museum with Price Tags." *Jewish Bulletin of Northern California*, October 27, 1995. • Opitz, Charles J. *Odd and Curious Money*. Ocala, Fla.: First Impressions, 1986. • Reinfeld, Fred. *Treasury of the World's Coins*. New York: Sterling Publishing, 1953.

scyphate coins

The Byzantine scyphate (cup-shaped) coin, also called a *nomisma* (or *noumisma)*, the twin of the Roman *solidus*, was a thin, concave disk with ragged edge similar in style to the nested hat money of Malaysia. Introduced after A.D. 811, the coin appeared under the name *michalatus* after its initiator, Michael I Rhangabe, who pictured himself on the front with a Greek cross and a religious inscription on the reverse. Byzantine coinsmiths struck each coin on a curved flan to make it easier to stack, at least in small numbers.

Scyphates flourished during the imperial fight against the Seljuk Turks. A half century before the First Crusade, Constantine IX, who ruled from A.D. 1042 to 1055, minted scyphate *trachea* coins picturing a portrait of Christ. At the start of the First Crusade in 1096, the warrior-emperor Alexius I Comnenus perpetuated the scooped-out coin by debasing gold *nomismata* and restriking them with his likeness stamped in the curve. A blend of imperial, divine, and hagiographic imagery marked subsequent scyphate coins of John II, Manuel I, Isaac II Angelus, Andronicus I, and Andronicus II Palaeologus, who chose for himself a humble pose at the feet of Christ. The coins lost favor because they were easily debased by clipping. Nonetheless, in 1130, when Roger II came to the throne of Naples and Sicily, a silver scyphate depicted him and his son and heir in Byzantine design.

***See also* Alexius I Comnenus; Byzantine coins.**

SOURCES: Clain-Stefanelli, Elvira, and Vladimir Clain-Stefanelli. *The Beauty and Lore of Coins, Currency, and Medals.* Croton-on-Hudson, N.Y.: Riverwood Publishers, 1974. • Cribb, Joe. *Money.* Toronto: Stoddart, 1990. • Davies, Glyn. *A History of Money from Ancient Times to the Present Day.* Cardiff: University of Wales Press, 1994. • Pollak, Henry. *Coinage & Conflict.* Clifton, N.J.: Coin & Currency Institute, 2001.

shekel

The shekel is one of the world's most stable and long-lived currencies. The word "shekel" is derived from the Hebrew *seqel* ("weight") and names a silver coin worth 1/60 of a *mina*. An obsolete form of the word *shekel* is *sicle*, from the Greek *siklos* and the Latin *siclus.* From modern use of the term *shekel* came the slang expression "rake in the shekels," meaning to gain a great amount of money in a short time.

The use of a stamped ingot valued in shekels in Cappadocia after 2250 B.C. produced a proto-coinage, the forerunner of a money economy. The Talmud, particularly the twelve-part *Seder Mo'ed* (Season or Festival), comments on ceremony, sacred holidays, and temple offerings. The text particularizes the shekel in numerous instances — annual temple dues, the ceremony of presenting the tribute, substituting gold coins for silver, purchasing temple offerings, surplus funds, officers overseeing the temple and its coins, and disposal of meat or coins found in the temple or on temple grounds.

The shekel originated in Babylon as a commercial weight equal to 180 barley heads. Adopted by Hittites, Assyrians, Phoenicians, and Hebrews, it was recognized throughout the Middle East. The Mesopotamians carved stones and stamped them with a government insignia to authenticate weights for use in the marketplace, for example, a graceful 60-shekel ovule incised to represent a goose with long curving neck. In Assyria after 705 B.C., Sennacherib commissioned a silver piece carrying the likeness of the mother goddess Ishtar. Worth a half-shekel, the coin earned the folk name "Ishtar head." The Phoenicians minted their own distinctive silver coins featuring Melqart (or Melkarth), the god of death and the underworld who was the major deity of Tyre, Carthage, and Gadir, Spain.

The shekel became an essential unit of weight and price in the stabilization of the economy. After 1865 B.C., according to a clay tablet inscribed in cuneiform, Sin-Kasid of Uruk established price controls by defining the shekel as the equal of three measures of barley or sesame oil, twelve mina of wool, ten mina of bronze, or three measures of sesame oil. A century later, Hammurabi, the lawgiver of Babylon's first dynasty, established legal fines based on minas and shekels. The Code of Hammurabi, inscribed on a 7'4" stela that French Orientalist Jean-Vincent Scheil discovered at Susa in 1901, specified fines and penalties for crimes, for example, hanging for burglars, enslavement of a careless farmer who flooded a neighbor's property, blinding for those prying into state secrets, and the loss of fingers for the thief who stole seeds, rations, or fodder. Other misdeeds carried monetary penalties:

infraction	*monetary settlement*
striking in the face	10 shekels to the victim
causing the death of a fetus	10 shekels to the woman
theft of a plow or shadduf (an irrigation device)	3 shekels

infraction	*monetary settlement*
causing the death of a slave's fetus	2 shekels to the master
runaway slave	2 shekels to the captor
kidnap	1 mina to the victim's family
blinding or breaking a bone	1 mina to the victim
hewing down a neighbor's tree	½ mina to the owner
rape	½ mina to the victim
murdering a woman	½ mina to the family
unintentional manslaughter	½ mina to the family
murdering a slavewoman	⅓ mina to the master
killing a slave	⅓ mina to the owner
knocking out a tooth	⅓ mina to the victim
extortion of money or grain	⅓ mina to the victim

Also stated in minas and shekels were fees to a home builder, shipwright, boat captain, physician, surgeon, veterinarian, and owner of breeding stock or dray animals.

The early Hebrews employed the shekel as a unit of weight that developed into an Israelite silver coin, thus simplifying conversion of value from raw ore to currency. Ezekiel 45:10–12, written in the early sixth century B.C., quantifies the ephah, bath, homer, shekel, gerah, and mina; the prophet Amos a generation later quotes dishonest merchants who skimp on weights to cheat the poor and needy. Varying from 11.42 grams in the beginning, by A.D. 70, the shekel weighed 14.27 grams. In 110 B.C., when the Israelites began coining money, they issued a shekel piece and, for small change, a half, quarter, and 1/20th shekel denominations.

The shekel earned frequent mention in the Bible. The term occurs notably in Genesis 37–43, during Jacob's revenge against his 11 brothers for selling him to Egyptian traders arriving at Dothan around 1800 B.C. In I Samuel 17:4–7, the weight of Goliath's bronze helmet and coat of mail and in his iron spear head were calculated in shekels. Similarly, in I Kings 10:16, Solomon measured in shekels the gold he beat to form 200 shields, the value of a chariot imported from Egypt for 600 shekels, and a horse worth 150 shekels. The book of Nehemiah, a state history of a priestly builder and governor drawn from archival works around 424 B.C., characterized the bribery of King Artaxerxes with 40 silver shekels per person. Likewise punctilious about monetary amounts is Jeremiah, who stated in Jeremiah 32:9 the cost of a field purchased from his cousin Hanamel at 17 silver shekels.

In Exodus 30, the Law of the Shekel revealed the fine of a *bekah* (half-shekel) from each male citizen. As explained in scripture:

> Each who is numbered in the census shall give this: half a shekel according to the shekel of the sanctuary, half a shekel as an offering to the Lord. Every one who is numbered in the census, from twenty years old and upward, shall give the Lord's offering [Exodus 30: 13–14].

The reward ransomed the soul, a custom also of soldiers before combat to atone for taking human life. The collected funds supported the temple, Israel's holy shrine. Later, the sanctuary staff imposed an annual tax of a half-shekel in place of the ransom. In Palestine, where the shekel is still the standard unit of money, rabbinical schools collect the shekels. So, too, the World Zionist Organization amasses shekels as membership tokens for Jews aiding the state of Israel.

Leviticus, the legalistic text or rulebook once called *Torath Kohanim* ("The Law of the Priests"), continued the discussion of priestly tradition begun in Exodus with laws governing sacrifice and personal religiosity. For sin offerings, Leviticus 5:15 commanded:

> If a soul commit a trespass, and sin through ignorance, in the holy things of the Lord; then he shall bring for his trespass unto the Lord a ram without blemish out of the flocks, with thy estimation by shekels of silver, after the shekel of the sanctuary, for a trespass offering.

The stiff penalty accompanied personal atonement plus a monetary gesture to the priest. In Leviticus 27:35, the text established the centrality of the coin in assessing values: "And all thy estimations shall be according to the shekel of the sanctuary: twenty gerahs shall be the shekel." The clarification recurs in Numbers 3:47.

Similar laws governing the maligning of a virgin by her husband appear in chapter 22 of Deuteronomy, a temple scroll from Jerusalem dating to 621 B.C. The law, which Moses gave the Hebrews, declared that the parents of the bride "shall amerce him in an hundred shekels of silver, and give them unto the father of the damsel, because he hath brought up an evil name upon a virgin of Israel: And she shall be his wife; he may not put her away all his days" (Deuteronomy 22:19). For compromising a virgin, the cost in coin was half that for slighting a bride. According to Moses's statute, a man fornicating with a virgin "shall give unto the damsel's father fifty shekels of silver, and she shall be his wife; because he hath humbled her, he may not put her away all his days" (Deuteronomy 22:29). As was standard in patriarchal societies, the defiler owed recompense to the girl's father rather than to her because she was considered property exchanged between two males.

In the book of Joshua, a work of conquest literature compiling invasion details dating to 1440–1200 B.C., the sacking of the town of Ai tempted Achan to conceal spoils. When Joshua's forces apprehend Achan, the villain summarizes his temptation to pillage in terms of goods and coin:

> When I saw among the spoils a goodly Babylonish garment, and two hundred shekels of silver, and a wedge of gold of fifty shekels weight, then I coveted them, and took them; and, behold, they are hid in the earth in the midst of my tent, and the silver under it [Joshua 7:21].

When Joshua's men corroborated Achan's crime, they convened his family and stoned him in the valley they called Achor, meaning "trouble."

Other stories of sin and crime, particularly Samson's temptation and fall and Micah's idolatry, take up the last chapter of the book of Judges, which was part of the *Nevi'im* or Prophets canonized around 200 B.C. and revered second only to the Pentateuch. After falling in love with the Philistine woman named Delilah, a worshiper of the pagon god Dagon, Samson fell into her plot to learn the secret of his might, which she revealed to his enemies in exchange for 1,100 shekels. In Chapter 17, the same amount of money appeared in the story of Micah and the making of a pagan idol. After he restored 1,100 silver shekels that he stole from his mother, she violated the first of the Ten Commandments by making a silver idol from the coins and placed it in a shrine in Micah's house. Worsening the crime was Micah's installation of a priest, a Levite from Bethlehem, as family chaplain of the shrine.

The two books of Samuel, a court document drawn from archival material and divided in 1516, record events between 1050 and 960 B.C. In II Samuel 14:26, the author estimated the weight of Absalom's gorgeous head of hair at 200 shekels. Ironically, when he rebelled against his father, King David, and fled Joab, the commander of the army, Absalom became entangled by his hair in an overhanging branch. Joab offered a man ten shekels to slay Absalom, but the man demurred—"Even if I felt in my hand the weight of a thousand pieces of silver, I would not put forth my hand against the king's son" (II Samuel 18:12).

Significant to Jewish history is the final chapter of II Samuel 24, in which David obeyed God's command to build an altar on the threshing floor of Araunah the Jebusite. To avert the plague, David complied and negotiated with Araunah, pledging oxen for a burnt offering plus threshing sledges and wood yokes. David insisted on adding fifty silver shekels, lest he purchase an offering that cost him nothing. Dramatically, the book concludes with God's acceptance: "So the Lord heeded supplications for the land, and the plague was averted from Israel" (II Samuel 24:25).

The two-part book of Kings, set about 970–586 B.C. and completed by an unknown author before 536 B.C., draws details from two lost histories, *The Book of the Acts of Solomon* and *The Book of Chronicles of the Kings of Judah*. In the summary of Solomon's reign and the split of the united kingdom into Israel to the north and Judah to the south, according to II Kings 15:20, the bribery of the Assyrian king Pul (Tiglath-Pileser III) cost 1,000 silver talents and 50 shekels per male citizen, which Menahem collected. The heavy penalty represented a godly punishment against the whole Hebrew nation, which had fallen into idolatry in violation of the first commandment.

In the two-part book of Chronicles, compiled around 300 B.C. in Hebrew as *Dibre Hayammim* (*Events of the Times*), the writer reprises David's illustrious dynasty from details drawn from *The Book of the Kings of Israel and Judah, Chronicles of Samuel the Seer, Chronicles of Nathan the Prophet, Commentary on the Book of Kings*, and *Chronicles of Gad the Seer.* Chapter 1 repeats the cost of Solomon's chariot and horse. The shekel standard clarified the outlay for building materials used in the construction of the temple at Jerusalem, which required fifty shekels of gold nails. Extending the evidence of Solomon's wealth were the construction of targets and shields from gold shekels.

In 1968, a Samarian hoard of hundreds of silver shekels and jewelry found in a cave at Wadi Daliyeh surfaced in Jerusalem's antiquities shops. The original owners apparently fled the advance of Alexander the Great some time around 333 B.C. The cache preserved unknown varieties, including Phoenician, Tyrian, and Sidonian mintage as well as Arabian coins. As historical treasures and views of the past, they corroborated some of the questionable assertions of the Romanized Hebrew historian Flavius Josephus, author of *The History of the Jews* (A.D. 94) and clarified the sequence of Palestinian rulers.

During the decline of the Seleucid kings, local mints went back into operation under the aegis of Antiochus VII and produced coins based on the Greek silver *obol* and bronze *chalkoi*. The values of the shekel were thus calculated:

coin	*worth*
prutah	2 *leptons* or 1 *dilepton*
chalkos	7 *leptons* or 3.5 *prutot*
obol	8 *chalkoi* or 28 *prutot* or 56 *leptons*
drachm	6 *obols* or 48 *chalkoi* or 168 *prutot* or 336 *leptons*
Tyrian *shekel*	4 *drachmas* or 24 *obols* or 192 *chalkoi* or 672 *prutot* or 1344 *leptons*

John Hyrcanus I produced impressive pictorial shekels after 135 B.C. In this period, depiction of stars associated the image with luck and destiny. At synagogues and the Jewish catacombs of Italy, mosaics depicted the signs of the zodiac, which established a common interest in astrology.

Alexander Jannaeus, a Hasmonean ruler from 103 B.C., produced less attractive coinage. He had his star coins encircled by a diadem, proof of his majesty as well as affirmation of the prediction in Numbers 24: 17, "There shall a star come out of Jacob and a scepter shall rise out of Israel," which Christian hymnologists later applied to the promise of Advent and the birth of Christ. Additional symbols of Jannaeus's coinage were the anchor, lily, and ivy wreath, a garland worn by temple priests.

In 47 B.C., Julius Caesar selected John Hyrcanus II as ruler of Judea. According to Josephus's wording of the honor, Caesar stated that Hyrcanus, for his loyalty to Rome during the Alexandrian war, was a hero for aiding 1,500 Roman soldiers during Caesar's victory over Pompey the Great at the battle of Pharsalus. As a reward, Caesar stated that "Hyrcanus, son of Alexander, and his children shall be ethnarchs of the Jews and shall hold the office of high priest of the Jews for all time in accordance with their national customs and that he and his sons shall be our allies" (Josephus 1960, p. 299).

The grand gesture survived on an engraved bronze tablet at Rome and at provincial capitals and in coins that Hyrcanus commissioned to publicize his elevation. However, Caesar's preference did not save Hyrcanus from Mark Antony's demotion of the ethnarth in 42 B.C. at the rise of Herod and Phasael as tetrarchs of Judea. In 40 B.C., Hyrcanus's fate worsened during the Parthian invasion, when his nephew Antigonus lopped off Hyrcanus's ears to make him ineligible for the priesthood.

After four years of exile in Babylon, Hyrcanus returned to Jerusalem, where Herod ended any threat he might offer to the throne by executing Hyrcanus.

In the short reign of Mattathias Antigonus, who began a three-year rule in 40 B.C., the constant struggle of Jews against enemies resulted in one of the most precious and long-lasting of Jewish emblems. The menorah coin, depicting a seven-branched candelabrum, replicated a symbol of faith carved on gems, charms, glass, pottery, lintels, and synagogue decoration. In the estimation of coin expert Ya'akov Meshorer, author of *Ancient Jewish Coinage* (1982), the image was the earliest dateable menorah in Jewish art. He further deduced that the introduction of the menorah into Hebrew iconography encouraged Antigonus's supporters and reminded the faithful that they were responsible for preserving temple sanctity during an era that threatened Judaism with extinction.

Edging out indigenous shekels were the Roman coins of Herod the Great, who came to the throne of Palestine in 37 B.C. His coins countered the menorah with Roman lamps and other ceremonial objects. The onerous rule of Rome suppressed the Jewish shekel until the resurgence of Syro-Palestinian coinage from A.D. 50 to 250. The two-century period saw increased productivity at Judean operations at Ascalon, Gaza, and Jerusalem and some issues from Anthedon, Caesarea, Eboda, Eleutheropolis, and Nicopolis.

See also **bible currency; blood money; counterstamp; *lira;* talent; trade and barter; world currency.**

The onerous rule of the Roman Empire suppressed circulation of the Jewish shekel until the resurgence of Syro-Palestinian coinage from A.D. 50 to 250. This was minted in A.D. 66. (Guy Clark, Ancient Coins and Antiquities, Norfolk, Virginia)

SOURCES: Abbott, Walter M., et al. *The Bible Reader*. New York: Bruce Publishing Co., 1969. • Alexander, David, and Pat Alexander, eds. *Eerdmans' Handbook to the World's Religions*. Grand Rapids, Mich.: William B. Eerdmans Publishing Co., 1982. • Allen, Larry. *Encyclopedia of Money*. New York: Checkmark Books, 2001. • Anderson, Bernhard W. *Understanding the Old Testament*. Englewood Cliffs, N.J.: Prentice-Hall, Inc., 1966. • Clain-Stefanelli, Elvira, and Vladimir Clain-Stefanelli. *The Beauty and Lore of Coins, Currency, and Medals*. Croton-on-Hudson, N.Y.: Riverwood Publishers, 1974. • Cribb, Joe. *Money*. Toronto: Stoddart, 1990. • Davies, Glyn. *A History of Money from Ancient Times to the Present Day*. Cardiff: University of Wales Press, 1994. • Einzig, Paul. *Primitive Money.* Oxford: Pergamon Press, 1966. • James, Peter, and Nick Thorpe. *Ancient Inventions*. New York: Ballantine, 1994. • Jeffrey, David Lyle, gen. ed. *A Dictionary of Biblical Tradition in English Literature*. Grand Rapids, Mich.: William B. Eerdmans Publishing Co., 1992. • Josephus. *Complete Works*. Grand Rapids, Mich.: Kregel Publications, 1960. • Kee, Howard Clark, Franklin W. Young, and Karlfried Froehlich. *Understanding the New Testament*. Englewood Cliffs, N.J.: Prentice-Hall, 1965. • Lockyer, Herbert. *All the Women of the Bible*. Grand Rapids, Mich.: Zondervan Publishing, 1988. • Maxey, Al. "The Lord's Supper: A Historical Overview." http://www.zianet.com/maxey/Supper5. htm. • May, Herbert G., and Bruce M. Metzger, eds. *The Oxford Annotated Bible*. New York: Oxford University Press, 1962. • Meshorer, Ya'akov. *Ancient Jewish Coinage*. New York: Amphora Books, 1982. • May, Herbert G., and Bruce M. Metzger. *Coins of the Ancient World*. Jerusalem: Jerusalem Publishing House, 1974. • Pollak, Henry. *Coinage & Conflict*. Clifton, N.J.: Coin & Currency Institute, 2001. • Snodgrass, Mary Ellen. *Encyclopedia of World Scripture*. Jefferson, N.C.: McFarland, 2001. • Starr, Chester G. *A History of the Ancient World*. New York: Oxford University Press, 1991. • Thomas, Edward. *Numismata Orientalia*. London: Trübner & Co., 1874.

shell money

Perhaps the oldest circulating currency in global history, shell money has flourished in the Middle East, Oceania, coastal Asian nations, and the Americas from prehistory. From 3500 B.C. Sumerians coined shell money by polishing rings of seashells and stringing them onto necklaces for use in daily purchases. Because of their common use, they fueled commerce along trade routes from Mesopotamia to Assyria.

Other nations developed seashells as specie. On the Trobriand Islands, strings of shell money and miniature shell armbands suited a ceremonial system of exchange and barter. The exchange of shells in China was so entwined in daily life that it became a symbolic part of the writing system. Around 1200 B.C., Chinese writers developed a character for money based on the shape of the cowrie, a shell that served as a coin in many parts of the world. To the north, Eskimo on the Alaskan coast transacted with European visitors and fur traders and used *dentalia* shells as money. In Paraguay, a poor, moneyless land where Indians relied almost entirely on the barter of commodities, buttons snipped from snail shells and strung on long cords served as money.

In the Solomon chain, islanders traded in both teeth and whole shells as well as disks, strings, and rings made of shells. On Choiseul Island, artisans valued *kesa*, the fragile shell cylinders that are sea worm husks or fossilized giant clam shells. The pieces are so old and revered that, currently, they exchange hands only on the most solemn occasions. Malaitans strung disks carved from mollusks and mussels. Called *tafuliaé*, the money required extensive shaping with stone hammers, heating with hot stones to deepen the color, and smoothing and flattening with grinding stones. After artisans pierced the disks with a pump drill, the pieces were suitable for such serious transactions as blood money or court fines for slander, trespassing, or defiling a cemetery.

On Santa Cruz, traders relied on *kapkap*, a two-part currency made from an intricately carved tortoise shell mounted on a shell base. Another form, *abaquaro*, consisted of armbands formed of black, red, or white shell disks set at an angle. The decorative strips could be worn as anklets, belts, bracelets, or necklaces at feasts and other dress-up occasions or as bride price.

Shell money users throughout Melanesia set monetary worth according to color, with red being the most *rongo* (sacred) and valuable. In one study conducted in 1883, a male slave of medium worth carried a value of a high quality pig, a human head, or a marble shell ring. Islanders valued a wife at 500 porpoise teeth, 100 strings of red money or dog teeth, 1,000 strings of white money or sticks of tobacco, or 10,000 coconuts. Based on this carefully delineated value chart, Solomon islanders used shells and lesser moneys to buy canoes, negotiate bride price or blood money, placate spirits, and pay fines and fees.

A folk ballad retained the poignance of love gone wrong in terms of shells: "I broke off a long string of small shell beards and gave it to you, but you refused ... Therefore I am dissolved in tears. Surely your heart is longing for shell money" (Einzig, 1966, pp. 57–58). In addition to winning maidens, shell currency paid for livestock and food.

In the New Hebrides, shell money, a decorative artisanal currency strung on a lanyard, was both specie and jewelry. Called *birok* or pig money, the strands were ceremonial cash displayed at pig-killing rituals. Pierced at center and strung edge to edge, the shell circlets were often topped by pig tails and other natural ornamentation.

On the York Islands in the Bismarck Archepelago, *diwara* was the name of sacred shell tokens carried on strings and spent at the rate of 50 strings for one wife. For small change to buy tobacco or food, owners removed a few shells from a string. The value equated with island commodities:

diwara	*worth*
¼ to ½ string	one chicken
1 string	50–80 taro roots
6–40 strings	a pig
20–30 strings	an older woman
20–50 strings	blood price for murder
50–200 strings	a young girl

Gathered by divers in Blanche Bay, *diwara* shells were scarce enough to attain high value and influence trade with New Britain.

Owners stored the strings in coils ranging from 50 to 200 hand spans in length. Kept in money houses, they went on display on certain occasions as symbols of wealth and prestige. During enemy attacks, islanders carried packets of shell coins to hiding places. The *diwara* currency continued in use into the 1890s, when German colonists set legal fines in shell money.

The introduction of European paper money and coins did not deter the exchange of shells as money. In 1896, traders in British New Guinea exchanged shell specie for gold dust. Eventually, British authorities seeking to civilize and modernize natives limited these trades to commerce between indigenous tribes and banned them among European colonists. When old strings depreciated, owners exchanged them for newer strings. Shell bankers restrung the old pieces for storage or recirculation.

On Rossel Island off Papua New Guinea, a complicated system of exchange valued two kinds of currency — the *ndap* or *Spondylus* shell and the *nko* or sets of ten disks from the giant clam shell. Under gender strictures, the former was limited to male use and the latter to female. A religion-based specie, the system reflected propitiation of Wonajo, a serpent god. Various taboos and intricacies governed commerce and appropriate payment for rituals, weddings, pig slaughter, and human sacrifice. The convoluted exchange rates were so overlaid with social implications that they required the services of a loan broker, a professional money assessor who determined fair market value.

Additional New Guinean shell currency involved the stringing of conus shell beads on a lanyard. These strands formed necklaces that the Melawea of the Sepik River region valued as money. In the highlands, a variant form of necklace money aligned parallel bamboo sticks on cords to make *omak* money.

See also **cowries; stone money; tooth money; trade and barter; wampum.**

SOURCES: Allen, Larry. *Encyclopedia of Money*. New York: Checkmark Books, 2001. • Clain-Stefanelli, Elvira, and Vladimir Clain-Stefanelli. *The Beauty and Lore of Coins, Currency, and Medals*. Croton-on-Hudson, N.Y.: Riverwood Publishers, 1974. • Davies, Glyn. *A History of Money from Ancient Times to the Present Day*. Cardiff: University of Wales Press, 1994. • Einzig, Paul. *Primitive Money*. Oxford: Pergamon Press, 1966. • Opitz, Charles J. *Odd and Curious Money*. Ocala, Fla.: First Impressions, 1986. • Weatherford, Jack. *The History of Money: From Sandstone to Cyberspace*. Pittsburgh, Pa.: Three Rivers Press, 1998.

shilling

The shilling, introduced by Henry VII during his housecleaning of English moneys in 1498, emulated the success of the Roman *solidus*, which the emperor Caracalla had created in the third century B.C. and moneyers in Byzantium, Denmark, France, Italy, Spain, and Sweden copied. The shilling carried the nickname "teston" or "testoon" from the Latin *testa* ("head"). The first *teston* was a silver coin that Galeazzo Maria Sforza, Duke of Milan, minted with his own portrait after 1468. Manuel I of Portugal coined a version of the *teston* in 1500. In Italy, artists Benvenuto Cellini, Andrea del Sarto, and Leonardo da Vinci created artistic copies of the shilling. In 1500, Mantuan moneyers featured a flattering image of Francesco II Gonzaga opposite a melting pot engulfed in flame.

The devalued English version of the shilling carried a monarch's image, the first such use in three centuries and a precedent followed by subsequent coin designers. In Mecklenburg, issuance of a four-shilling piece in the 1600s received sneers because the imperial eagle looked more like a parrot. Commoners called it the *papphahn* ("parrot"), a nickname that also clung to an official, the Schreckenberger of Saxony, Hesse, and Brunswick.

The shilling figures in children's verse, such as "A Cow and a Calf" from *The Comic Adventures of Old Mother Hubbard and Her Dog* (1805), supposedly compiled by an English belle, Sarah Catherine Martin. In the six-line nursery rhyme, the suitor asks whether livestock and "forty good shillings and three" is "enough tocher," the Scottish term for dowry. The courtship theme reprises a longer poem, *The Lad They Ca' Jumpin John*, written by Scottish poet Robert Burns in 1788 on the theme of evaluating potential brides in equivalent commodites and coin of the realm.

A three-verse nursery rhyme anthologized in antiquarian Joseph Ritson's *Gammer Gurton's Garland: Or, the Nursery Parnassus; A Choice Collection of Pretty Songs and Verses* (1784) entitled "The Jolly Tester," speaks of the sixpence and penny. The coin, a debased metal disk worth 12 pence, replaced devalued Irish pennies and groats issued by mints of the Holy Roman Empire. England's smaller coin, designed by engraver John Sharp and minted in 1504, ennobled English coinage.

See also **Colonial coins; English money; Sir William Petty; Roman coins — Empire; Joseph Sigismund Tanner; touch coins.**

SOURCES: Baring-Gould, William S., intro. and notes. *The Annotated Mother Goose*. New York: Clarkson N. Potter, 1962. • Davies, Glyn. *A History of Money from Ancient Times to the Present Day*. Cardiff: University of Wales Press, 1994. • Lewis, Brenda Ralph. *Coins & Currency*. New York: Random House, 1993. • Reinfeld, Fred. *Treasury of the World's Coins*. New York: Sterling Publishing, 1953. • Sinclair, David. *The Pound*. London: Century Books, 2000.

shipwrecks

Shipwreck is one of the acknowledged dangers of sea travel. During the 1700s and 1800s, in the opinion of Willard Bascom's *Deep Water, Ancient Ships: The Treasure Vault of the Mediterranean* (1976), of the active wood sailing vessels, up to 20 percent disappeared in deep water; 40 percent sank closer inland on reefs, rocks, or beaches. Valued for precious metals were the famed Spanish treasure fleets bound from the New World laden with ore, coins, enslaved Indians, and curiosities unseen in Europe. From 1492, the year that Christopher Columbus lost his 100-ton flagship *Santa Maria*, to 1520, about 50 sailing vessels capsized in the Caribbean. The high price of ocean voyages pervaded the 19th century, when English insurers cataloged 10,000 lost vessels, many carrying valuable trade goods and bullion.

After the invention of the aqualung by French naval diver Jacques Cousteau in 1943, many wreck sites became hunting grounds for salvors seeking riches. Unfortunately for historians and archeologists, the plunder of remains became a modern form of piracy, a scourge that left valuable historic scenarios in shambles across the French Riviera, off the coasts of Florida and Texas, and throughout the Caribbean.

For the adventuresome willing to risk life and a considerable investment in time, labor, and money, sunken treasure vessels have yielded trade goods, art works, and the fabled coin hoards that reveal the commerce of an era. The earliest major loss occurred in 1554, when three merchant ships in a four-ship convoy — the *Espíritu Santo, San Estebán*, and *Santa Maria de Yciar*— capsized in a storm near Padre Island, Texas. The fourth, the *San Andres*, escaped. The second of the shipwrecked trio survived four centuries undersea to be examined by the Texas Archeological Research Laboratory. A catalogue of cargo recorded gold ingots and silver bullion and newly minted *reales*.

The most famous treasure ships, the *Nuestra Señora de Atocha* and sister ship *Santa Margarita*, part of a 28-ship convoy, left Havana harbor and went down in a hurricane on September 6, 1622, 35 miles out to sea at a reef off Upper Matecumbe and Lower Matecumbe, two islands near Key West, Florida. The haul recovered in 1985 by diver Mel Fisher was the world's largest treasure, totaling over $400 million.

Nineteen years later, another fabled galleon departing Havana, the aged *Nuestra Señora de la Pura y Limpia Concepción*, newly repaired, headed for Spain as *almiranta* (rear guard) of a fleet. Captained by Juan de Villavicencio, it lacked hull upkeep, caulking, and resheathing with lead and had to return to Havana for replacement of stern planking. Departing dangerously late in the season with 60,000 coins, it sank on October 31, 1641, north of Hispaniola after being blown north up the Atlantic seaboard by a hurricane. Fewer than a third of the 600 on board survived.

Thirty men who tossed treasure chests onto the reef gave it the name Silver Bank.

Heavy storms impeded immediate salvage of the galleon. Official recovery expeditions set out in 1650, 1652, 1667, 1673, and 1687. On the last, Captain William Phips of Boston sailed the *Henry* to the site and retrieved 32 tons of silver, coins, gold, pearls, and leather pouches of gems. It was enough treasure to earn him knighthood from James II, the king of England, who also appointed Phips governor of Massachusetts. The treasure made the salvor one of America's richest men.

In 1978, historian Peter Earle backed up salvor Burt Webber with enough information about the Silver Bank to guide a crew to the *Concepción*. Webber used a cesium magnetometer to locate silver, pottery, marble statuary, and gold chains. Recovery by Victor Santos, Francis Soto, Tracy Bowen, and Tomás Guerrero aboard the *Dolphin* produced 3,000 silver coins, ingots, astrolabes, plate and cutlery, Ming porcelain, a pewter box filled with ambergris, gold dust, and gold and diamond jewelry. A false bottom in a trunk revealed 1,440 contraband coins not listed on ship manifests. The final count of over 60,000 coins earned the site the name "money hole." Most recovered specie came from Mexico City with sprinklings of coins from Santa Fé de Bogotá, Cartagena, Cuenca, Madrid, Seville, and Valladolid. The dated pieces from Cartagena and Bogotá established that minting began as early as 1621, two years before the date historians had assumed.

Weather like that prohibiting the first salvors from reaching the *Concepción* was often deadlier than pirate sloops to treasure ships. On July 24, 1715, 11 galleons, protected by the French sloop *El Grifon* and carrying 56 million *reales*, gold doubloons, contraband bullion, and gold and silver bars, set out from Havana for Spain. Seven days later, the fleet drifted north on the Gulf Stream. All but the guardian sloop succumbed to a hurricane at the delta of the Saint Sebastian River near Vero Beach and Cape Kennedy, Florida. The violent sinking killed almost half of the 2,500 people aboard and scattered timbers and coins over a wide expanse of sea floor.

In 1716, while Spain bankrolled salvors to retrieve the treasure, Captain Henry Jennings, a British privateer, conceived a get-rich-quick scheme. He rapidly provisioned a fleet of five ships at Barbados and Jamaica. His crew of 300 dispersed 60 Spaniards diving into the wreck. The British salvors lost one of their ships, the *Jesus María*, but their take of 350,000 pieces of eight returned with them to Jamaica.

Scavenging of the legendary Spanish fleet continued through the centuries. Cartographer Bernard Romans returned in 1773 to the reef, where masts still protruded above the water line. Without diving for treasure, his staff collected coins washed up from the deep. In the late 1950s, carpenter Kip Wagner, afloat on an inner tube, located the wreckage and found more uncirculated Spanish coins borne up onto the beach by a hurricane. After researching the source at the Archives of the Indies in Seville, Spain, he started the Real Eight Corporation and began salvage operations. Using metal detectors and a primitive scoop and dump method, his divers located 20 cannon and clumps of silver coins and 1,000 gold doubloons. In 1974, another haul of 1,000 doubloons brought to the surface the bulk of a treasure lost nearly 260 years before. Because Wagner failed to keep archival documents or to catalog artifacts, historians were unable to make positive identifications of the five wrecks.

On August 24, 1724, the 1,500-ton *Conde de Tolosa* and the 1,000-ton *Nuestra Señora de Guadalupe* sank in 40 feet of water off Samaná Bay, Hispaniola. The two were sailing from Cádiz, Spain, to the frontier town of Veracruz, Mexico, via Aguada, Puerto Rico. In the last port of call, the crew loaded provisions for a short trans-Caribbean leg to Havana, Cuba, Spain's naval clearinghouse. Constructed of massive timbers, the duo transported European trade goods and 400 tons of mercury, a year's supply of the essential element that minters mixed with salt to refine pure gold and silver from raw ore by the patio process. Packagers sealed the liquid metal in half-quintal lots in sheepskin bags and secured them in wood casks for storage low in the hold.

After anchor lines snapped, the *Tolosa*, caroming about the bay at dawn, carried around 560 of the original 600 aboard to their deaths. Eight of the survivors climbed the mast and clung to the rigging, where all but one survived for 32 days on rainwater collected in the sails while they kept a close watch on the sharks that fed on floating corpses below. Saved from the *Guadalupe* some 7.5 miles away was silvermaster Don Francisco Barrero y Palaez along with 550 of the 650 aboard. Some swam to shore and walked 220 miles to Santo Domingo; others rowed the lifeboat 240 miles to Cap Haïtien.

In 1976, salvors of the *Guadalupe* boarded the *Hickory*, captained by Tracy Bowden with a license from the government of the Dominican Republic. Divers began combing the remains with a magnetometer, a sensitive metal detector that reported masses of iron. Fighting off nurse sharks and a barracuda, the men probed the sandy shoals for the 144 cannons ripped out of their moorings in the soughing winds. They found gold doubloons and 400 religious medals, flatware and jewelry, smuggled luxuries like a London-made brass clock, grenades and pistols, and iron fittings for a new ship to be built of New World lumber.

With data from historian Jack Haskins, divers identified the crushed remains of the *Tolosa* in June 1977. Wreckage yielded musket balls, cobalt glassware, a filigreed gold cross and reliquary, papal bulls from Pope Innocent XIII, 1,000 pearls, and a bronze church or ship's bell cast in 1710 in Amsterdam. Eluding the dive crew was the most promising treasure, pure mercury, the loss of which to the coin-producing mints of Mesoamerica had endangered Spain's imperial treasury. Nonetheless, the diving operation provided the Museo de las Casas Reales with 400 coins minted under King Philip V of Spain.

In 1733, the same pattern of ill luck and harsh weather sank a Spanish flotilla of four galleons and 18 merchant *naos* (ships) leaving Havana and traveling north to the Florida Keys. The convoy spread over an 80-mile area before sinking, with only the *Nuestra Señora de Rosario* reaching harbor intact. In the 1930s, fisherman and diver Arthur McKee located the flagship, *El Rubi Segundo*, captained by Rodrigo de Torres. Dating the undersea remains was a gold *escudo* struck in 1721. Salvors grabbed 20 cannon and small arms, religious statues and medals, ingots, 1,000 silver coins, and gold bars from the wreckage, but destroyed the archeological and historical value of the wrecks through blatant treasure hunting. In 1949, McKee opened the first marine shipwreck museum in the United States, at Tavernier, Florida.

Two years after the loss of the Spanish fleet, the Dutch East Indiaman *Vliegenthart* ("Flying Hart") capsized off the south coast of Holland due to a pilot miscalculation. The trading vessel bore goods as well as contraband coins and a legitimate stash of silver cobs and silver ducatoons called *rijders* because they pictured a mounted cavalryman at full gallop. All 256 aboard the vessel sank to the sea bottom along with the loot. Twentieth-century divers were able to salvage some of the finely crafted silver coins that bore the ironic legend "*Concordia Res Parvae Crescunt*" ("Little Things Increase Through Harmony").

A summary of wrecked treasure ships and their locations suggests the value of cargoes and the difficulties of transporting goods by sea:

ship	*place*	*date*	*destination*	*cargo*
Roman merchant vessel	Anticythera	70–80 B.C.	Italy	bronze statues
Serce Limani	south Turkey	A.D. 1000	unknown	Islamic coins; glass
Arnbjorn	Greenland	1125	Greenland	money
Stangarfoli	Greenland	1189	Greenland	money

ship	*place*	*date*	*destination*	*cargo*
Mandarin's Cap junk	Philippines	1200	unknown	silver ingots
Chinese junk	Burma	1300s	unknown	porcelain
Sinan ship	Korea	1323	Japan	porcelain, copper coins
Tu Yuan's ship	Sumatra	1400	unknown	treasure
Ulbo Island wreck	Ulbo Island, Italy	1417	Venice	coins, bullion, glass
Abu Qir wreck	Darnah, Libya	1418	Egypt	spice, oil, cloth, coral, almonds
Venetian ship	Istanbul, Turkey	1452	Venice	valuables
San Michele	Alexandria, Egypt	1479	Naples	valuables
unidentified pair of *naos*	Puerto Principe, Hispaniola	1501	unknown	gold dust and nuggets
26 unidentified Spanish caravels	Hispaniola	1502	Spain	gold nuggets
unidentified flagship	Punta de Canoas, Colombia	1504	South America	gold nuggets, emeralds
Flor de la Mar	Sumatra	1511	India	gold, tin coins
Serrao's ship	Spice Islands	1512	Spice Islands	Malaccan coins
unidentified Spanish caravel	Pedro Shoals, Jamaica	1512	Hispaniola	treasure
Santa Catalina	Havana, Cuba	1537	Spain	gold and silver
San Miguel	Cape Cabrón, Hispaniola	1542	Spain	gold and silver
Santa María de Jesús	Puerto Rico	1550	Mexico	gold, pearls, jewelry
San Miguel	Cape Francés, Hispaniola	1551	Spain	gold and silver coin and bullion
Santa Barbola	Bermuda	1551	Spain	gold *ducats*
unidentified pair of Spanish galleons	Silver Shoals, Bahamas	1551	Spain	150,000 *ducats*
La Salvadora	Monte Cristo, Hispaniola	1553	Spain	gold and silver
San Estéban, Espíritu Santo, Santa María de Yciar	Padre Island, Texas	1554	Spain	gold bar, silver coins and bullion
unidentified pair of ships	Bahama Channel	1554	unknown	treasure in silver
Santa María de Villacelan	Matanzas Bay, Cuba	1555	Spain	treasure in coin
unidentified pair of Spanish caravels plus *La Magdalena La Concepción*	Cape San Anton, Cuba	1556	Spain	treasure
unidentified Spanish galleon	Lake Maracaibo, Colombia	1559	Cartagena, Venezuela	900,000 *pesos*
São Paulo	Sumatra	1560	India	cloth, tapestry
Nuestra Señora de la Concepción, Nuestra Señora de laConsolación, San Juan, San Juan Bautista, Santa Margarita	Jardines Reef, Cuba	1563	Mexico	church treasure, mercury
unidentified flagship	Bermuda	1563	Spain	silver coins
Santa Clara	El Mime, Bahamas	1564	Spain	gold and silver
unidentified Spanish galleon	Cartagena, Colombia	1564	Spain	treasure

ship	*place*	*date*	*destination*	*cargo*
Josva	Baltic Sea	1566	Visby, Gotland	German coins
El Espíritu Santo, San Felipe, San Juan, Santa Barbola, two *naos*	Dominica	1567	Spain	3 million *pesos*
La Girona	Ireland	1588	England	405 gold *escudos*, jewelry, bronze
Florenzia	North Sea	1588	England	$15,000,000 in gold
Tobermory	Scotland	1588	England	gold, jewels
Als Efferne	Cornwall, England	1589	unknown	treasure
Nuestra Señora del Rosario	Florida	1590	Spain	gold chains, jewelry, silver coin
Vidalia	Dalmatia	1592	Asia	130,000 *ducats*
Nuestra Señora del Rosario, Santa María de San Vicente	Havana, Cuba	1593	Spain	treasure
Santo Alberto	Cochin, India	1593	Cochin, India	gold, silver, crystal
Tobie	Gibraltar	1593	Livorno, Italy	coins, tin, wool
Las Cinque Chagas	Azores	1594	unknown	jewelry
San Gabriel	Havana, Cuba	1595	Spain	silver
San Felipe	Japan	1596	Acapulco, Mexico	gold, porcelain
San Pedro	Bermuda	1596	Spain	emeralds, bars and cubes of gold
San Agustin	San Francisco	1599	unknown	gold, porcelain
Treasure	Bahamas	1599	Havana, Cuba	gold and silver bars
Royal Captain junk	Borneo	1600	Borneo	ceramics, beads, bronze
Kuantung wreck	Philippines	1601	unknown	silver coins
La Rosa, San Juan Bautista, Capitana, one unidentified ship	Guadeloupe	1603	Spain	one million *pesos*
Seranillas wrecks (4)	Cuba	1605	Spain	silver, gold, emeralds
Reinera e Soderina	Kithira, Greece	1609	Venice	unknown
Madre de Deus	Nagasaki, Japan	1609	Nagasaki, Japan	silk, silver bars
unidentified English privateer	Isle of Pines, Cuba	1610	unknown	captured Spanish coins
Chinese junk	Macao	1611	Japan	porcelain
Guidotta e Simona	Zakinthos, Greece	1613	Venice	gold, jewelry
Witte Leeuw	southwest Africa	1613	Holland	diamonds, pottery, spices
Bacaim wreck	India	1618	Persia	gold, perfume
San Antonio	Bermuda	1621	unknown	hides, wood, indigo, tobacco, gold and silver English coins, cowries
La Margarita	Key West, Florida	1622	Spain	500,000 *pesos*, gold bars and chain, jewelry, silver ingots
Nuestra Señora de Atocha	Key West, Florida	1622	Spain	21,323 pieces of eight
Nuestra Señora del Rosario	Key West, Florida	1622	Spain	500,000 silver *pesos*
Tortugas wreck	Florida	1622	Spain	gold bars
Santa Margarita	Key West, Florida	1622	Spain	34 gold bars, silver ingots, 118,000 *reales*

ship	*place*	*date*	*destination*	*cargo*
Espíritu Santa el	Bahama Channel	1623	Spain	one million *pesos*
Mayor Hollandia	Bahía, Brazil	1627	unknown	pirate treasure, gold and silver coins, nuggets
Nuestra Señora de la Concepcion	Saipan	1628	Acapulco, Mexico	gold chain, silver plate, copper, iron
24 unidentified Spanish ships	Matanzas Bay, Cuba	1628	Holland	15 million *guilders*
unidentified Honduran galleon	Cape San Anton, Cuba	1628	unknown	silver specie
unidentified pair of Spanish galleons	Lucaya Beach, Bahamas	1628	Spain	silver coins
Vasa	Stockholm harbor	1628	Poland	barrels and chests holding 4,000 coins
Batavia	Wallibi Island, Australia	1629	unknown	silver, jewels, lead
unidentified Spanish ship	Florida	1634	Spain	100,000 *pesos*
La Viga	Bermuda	1639	unknown	silver
Nuestra Señora de la Pura y Limpa Concepción	Silver Shoals, Hispaniola	1641	unknown	silver, jewels, gold dust, thousands of silver *pesos*
Stellingwerf junk	Java	1643	Java	porcelain
La Capitana Jesus Jesus Maria de la Limpia Concepción	Ecuador	1654	Panama	silver coins, ingots
Nuestra Señora de las Maravillas	Bahamas	1656	Bahamas	salvage from the *Capitana*; 1.5 million coins
Vergulde Draeck	East Indies	1656	Australia	eight chests of 10,000 silver *guilders*
Chanduy Reef wrecks (3)	Peru	1659	Spain	silver, 12 million gold pieces
Santo Cristo de Castello	Cornwall	1666	England	silver coins
Santíssimo Sacramento	Bahia, Brazil	1668	Bahia, Brazil	Portuguese silver coins
Magdalena	Venezuela	1669	unknown	40,000 *pesos*, silver, swords
Oxford	St. Domingue	1669	Cartagena, Colombia	silver, gold
Jules	Lisbon, Portugal	1673	Lisbon, Portugal	amber, pearls
Nuestra Señora de la Encarnación, Santa Teresa, Nuestra Señora de la Soledad, Nuestra Señora de la Asunción	Cartagena, Colombia	1681	Panama	treasure
Rosario	Peru	1681	Panama	silver
Anna Maria	Portland, England	1682	Holland	silver, rice, sulfur
Sacramento	Brazil	1688	East Indies	brass, majolica
Herbert	Comoros Islands	1689	unknown	silver coins and bars

ship	*place*	*date*	*destination*	*cargo*
Vung Tau wreck	Hon Bay Cahn, Vietnam	1690	Jakarta	porcelain
Nuestra Señora de la Concepción, Santa Cruz	Pedro Shoals, Jamaica	1691	Havana	chests of coins
Jufron Gertrud	Little Bahama bank	1694	Holland	74,000 pieces of eight
Sussex	Gibraltar	1694	Savoy	gold and silver coins
Almiranta Nuestra Señora de las Mercedes	Simarana, Cuba	1695	Spain	treasure
Nuestra Señora de la Soledad y San Ignacio de Loyola	Havana, Cuba	1695	Spain	treasure
Henry	Ireland	1695	England	diamonds
Vigo Bay wrecks	Vigo, Spain	1702	Cadiz, Spain	silver *pesos*
San José	Baru Island, Colombia	1708	Spain	11 million *pesos*
Feversham	Scatari Island, Nova Scotia	1711	Quebec	varied colonial and European coins and cobs
Nuestra Señora del Rosario, San José y Las Animas, Santisima Trinidad	Havana, Cuba	1711	Spain	1,700,000 *pesos*
Zuytdorp	Batavia	1712	Australia	7,000 coins
San Juan Evangelista	Grand Bahama Island	1714	Puerto Rico	300,000 *pesos*
11 Spanish galleons	Vero Beach, Florida	1715	Spain	6,466,066 *pesos*, 955 *castellanos*, contraband gold
Nuestra Señora del Carmen, Nuestra Señora de Concepción, Refuerzo	Matecumbe Key, Florida	1715	Cadiz, Spain	15,000 silver *pesos*, 350 silver *marcos*, goldbars; sacks of passengers' cash
Whydah	Cape Cod, Massachusetts	1717	New England	silver, gold
Conde de Tolosa	Hispaniola	1724	Veracruz, Mexico	mercury for minting
Nuestra Señora de Guadalupe	Hispaniola	1724	Veracruz, Mexico	mercury for minting
Le Chameau	Cape Lorenbad, Nova Scotia	1725	Quebec	30,000 *livres* in gold and silver
Santa Rosa	Recife, Brazil	1726	Lisbon, Portugal	gold
Genovesa	Pedro Shoals, Jamaica	1730	Portugal	silver bars, three million *pesos*
Nuestra Señora de Lorento y San Francisco Xavier	Anegada, Virgin Islands	1730	Cartagena, Colombia	treasure
Señor San Miguel	Cayman Islands	1730	Vera Cruz, Mexico	mercury used in refinement of ore for coinage
unidentified Spanish galleon	Anegada, Virgin Islands	1731	Mexico	mercury
El Rubi Segundo,	Florida Keys	1733	Havana	6 million *pesos* from Mexico

ship	*place*	*date*	*destination*	*cargo*
Nuestra Señora de Balvaneda, San Francisco de Asís (?), *El Sueco de Arizón* (?), *San José de las Animas, Nuestra Señora de las Angustias y San Rafael, San Fernando,* and 14 other ships in one fleet				including rare silver *Dos Mundos* pillar dollars
Vliegenthart	Holland	1735	Dutch East Indies	*ducats*, silver cobs
Vendela	Shetland Islands	1737	unknown	silver coins and bullion
Princess Augusta	Sandy Point, Rhode Island	1738	New York	personal treasure
Saint Geron	Port Louis, Mauritius	1744	unknown	money barrel
unidentified Spanish merchantman	Sugar Cay, Bahamas	1744	Mexico	300,000 pounds sterling
Prince de Conty	Belle Île, France	1746	unknown	gold ingots, porcelain
unidentified Spanish merchantman	Ensenada de Vixiras, Cuba	1748	Spain	ten million *pesos*
Nuestra Señora de la Soledad	Ocracoke, North Carolina	1750	Spain	treasure
unidentified Spanish *nao*	Drum Inlet, North Carolina	1750	Spain	treasure
San Antonio y San Felix	Cape San Anton, Cuba	1751	Spain	400,000 *pesos*
Geldermalsen	Indonesia	1752	Holland	porcelain, gold ingots, bronze
Duke Compagni	St. Eustatius	1758	Amsterdam	silver coins
unidentified Spanish merchantman	Port Morant, Mexico	1762	Vera Cruz, Mexico	coins
Grandy	Halifax, Nova Scotia	1771	Halifax	3,000 pounds sterling in coin
Vrouw Maria	Baltic Sea	1771	Russia	art treasures
Rynsburgh	China	1772	unknown	silver
Mercedes	Spain	ca. 1775	Spain	silver, gold
unidentified Spanish galleon	Beak Cay, Bahamas	1775	Spain	treasure
H.M.S. *Hussar*	Hell's Gate, New York	1779	England	treasure
General Barker	Holland	1781	Holland	money chests
Grosvenor	South Africa	1782	unknown	diamonds
Nicobar	South Africa	1782	Tranquebar, India	Swedish plate money
Samson	Norway	1786	Norway	*skillings*
Hartwell	Cape Verde Islands	1787	England	silver *pesos*, cloth, clocks, jewelry, lead
Telemaque	Quillebeuf, France	1790	unknown	treasure
H.M.S. *DeBraak*	Lewes, Delaware	1798	England	copper ingots, and silver coins, gold bullion
H.M.S. *Colossus*	Scilly	1798	London, England	Greek vases

ship	*place*	*date*	*destination*	*cargo*
Lynx	Halifax, Nova Scotia	1798	England	100,000 pounds sterling
Penelope	Halifax, Nova Scotia	1798	America	100,000 pounds sterling
unidentified fleet of eight merchant vessels	Great Inagua Island, Bahamas	1800	unknown	600,000 pounds of silver
Ferrolena	China	1802	Manila, Philippines	1 million *pesos*
Mentor	Kithira, Greece	1802	England	Greek art
Arles wreck	Rhone River	1805	Paris, France	Roman statues
Pelluce	Elba	1806	unknown	treasure
Portuguese wreck	Mangalore, India	1808	Portugal	600,000 *rupees*
Admiral Gardner	English Channel	1809	Madras, India	54 tons of 110 and 20 cash coins
Barbados	Sable Island, Canada	1812	England	gold and silver coin and bullion
Tamerlane	Cape Henry, Virginia	1813	France	silver and gold specie
San Pedro Alcantara	Caracas, Venezuela	1815	Venezuela	800,000 silver *pesos*
Sir John Sherbroke	Dry Tortugas, Florida	1816	New York	$60,000 in coin
L'Américaine	Sable Island, Canada	1822	France	$1 million in gold and silver bullion
Fame	Sumatra	1824	England	jewelry, documents
Dourado	Singapore	1829	India	medals, cameos, antiquities, books
Thetis	Cape Frio, Brazil	1830	England	gold and silver bars
Palemón	Spain	1839	Cuba	treasure
Vietnamese junk	Madagascar	1850s	Gulf of Tonkin	treasure
Madagascar	Cape Horn, South America	1853	London, England	gold
Yankee Blade	Baja, Mexico	1854	Panama	gold
Central America	North Carolina	1857	New York	gold
Royal Charter	Llanallgo, Wales	1859	Plymouth, England	gold
Malabar	Ceylon	1860	Bombay, India	bullion
Cleopatra	Sierra Leone	1862	unknown	gold dust, silver coins
Golden Gate	Manzanillo, Mexico	1862	New York	treasure
Brother Jonathan	Oregon	1865	Vancouver, Canada	gold
Baltic	Bahamas	1866	United States	trade goods
General Grant	New Zealand	1866	England	gold, zinc
Carnatia	Red Sea	1869	Bombay, India	money
Queen of the Thames	South Africa	1871	London, England	gold dust
American paddlesteamer	Yokohama, Japan	1872	Japan	gold, Mexican *pesos*
Prins Frederik	Ushant Island	1890	Java	400,000 silver *rijksdaalders*
John Elder	Cape Carranza, Chile	1892	Liverpool, England	gold, silver

ship	*place*	*date*	*destination*	*cargo*
Cattherthun	eastern Australia	1895	Hong Kong	gold sovereigns
Titanic	Atlantic Ocean	1912	New York	diamonds, jewels
Empress of Ireland	Gulf of St. Lawrence, Canada	1914	Liverpool, England	purser's safe
Egypt	Brittany, France	1922	Bombay, India	gold and silver bullion, ingots, gold sovereigns
Asiatic Prince	unknown	1928	Yokohama, Japan	two tons of gold
Niagara	New Zealand	1940	Canada	gold
American minelayer	Manila Bay, Philippines	1942	unknown	silver *pesos*
City of Cairo	Atlantic Ocean	1942	England	silver coins
Edinburgh	Norway	1942	England	gold bars
Empire Manor	Nova Scotia	1944	England	gold bars
I-52	Pacific Ocean	1944	Germany	gold ingots
Itsukishima	East Indies	1944	Japan	gold
John Barry	Persian Gulf	1944	Russia	silver Saudi *riyals*
Awa Maru	China	1945	Japan	gold, platinum, diamonds, tin
Andrea Doria	Sandy Hook, New Jersey	1956	New York	paper money, jewels, art, mosaics

Recent use of the magnetometer and other imaging devices increased the chances of relocating shipwrecks. In November 2000, a Toronto salvor, Visa Gold Explorations, Incorporated, recovered 7,000 artifacts from the *Palemón*. The 100-foot Spanish brigantine, captained by José Antonio de Ageo, foundered off Cuba at 3:30 A.M., on April 25, 1839.

Later, the Visa Gold crew justified the more than $1 million invested in deep-water exploration with its discovery of the remains of the historic battleship U.S.S. *Maine*. The warship exploded in Havana Bay on February 15, 1898, killing 266 U.S. sailors, touching off the Spanish-American War and leading to the end of Spanish colonial rule. Raised in 1912 by the U.S. Army Corps of Engineers, the *Maine* was towed to sea and scuttled in an undisclosed location. Of historic value only, its remains are of minimal monetary worth to the divers. Other targets of the Visa consortium include the wreck of the *Atocha y San Jose*, which sank near Havana in January 1642, and, at 2,200 feet, a submerged city that some link with the fabled Atlantis and which has left an undersea plateau with urban development resembling roads, buildings, and pyramids.

Shipwrecks also permeate adventure lore, including Daniel Defoe's *Robinson Crusoe* (1719), the story of a lone survivor on a desert isle off Brazil. Defoe based the plot on the adventures of Alexander Selkirk, sailing master for buccaneer William Dampier. On the fictional Crusoe's first return to the hull for cargo, he retrieves "some pieces of eight, some gold, some silver" (Defoe 1963, p. 64). Realizing the worthlessness of coins to a lone islander, he smiles and speaks aloud to himself, "O drug! … what art thou good for? Thou are not worth to me, no not the taking off of the ground" (*ibid.*). On his departure with rescuers on December 19, 1686, he retrieves the silver, which has rusted and tarnished from disuse on an island where money has no meaning.

See also Admiral Gardner; Atocha;* George Bass; Samuel Bellamy; *La Capitana; Central America;* counterstamp; Mel Fisher; Sir Henry Morgan; *Palemón;* piracy; plate money; screw press; Peter Throckmorton; tokens; treasure ships; underwater archeology; *Whydah.

SOURCES: Allen, Thomas B. "Cuba's Golden Past." *National Geographic*, July 2001, 74–91. •

"Atocha Dive Expeditions." *Skin Diver*, December 1999, 96. • Bascom, Willard. *Deep Water, Ancient Ships: The Treasure Vault of the Mediterranean*. Garden City, N.Y.: Doublday and Co., 1976. • Bass, George F., ed. *Ships and Shipwrecks of the Americas: A History Based on Underwater Archaeology*. London: Thames and Hudson, 1996. • Bowden, Tracy. "Gleaning Treasure from the Silver Bank." *National Geographic*, July 1996, 90–105. • Bowers, Q. David. *Adventures with Rare Coins*. Los Angeles: Bowers & Ruddy Galleries, Inc., 1979. • Cockburn, Alexander. "Beat the Devil: Imperial Addictions." *Nation*, August 3, 1985, 70–71. • *Contemporary Newsmakers 1985*. Detroit: Gale Research, 1986. • Cribb, Joe. *Money*. Toronto: Stoddart, 1990. • Crittenden, Jules. "Treasure Island: Explorers May Have Located Sunken Pirate Ships." *Boston Herald*, January 19, 2001. • Defoe, Daniel. *Robinson Crusoe*. New York: Airmont Books, 1963. • Jones, Bart. "Modern Day Pirates?" *Hannibal Post-Courier*, June 27, 1998. • Laing, Lloyd R. *Coins and Archaeology*. New York: Schocken Books, 1969. • Lewis, Brenda Ralph. *Coins & Currency*. New York: Random House, 1993. • Peterson, Mendel. "Graveyard of the Quicksilver Galleons." *National Geographic*, December 1979, 850–876. • Pickford, Nigel. *The Atlas of Ship Wrecks & Treasure*. New York: Dorling Kindersley, 1994. • Randall, Lorelei. "Our Marine Heritage." *Nordic Underwater Archaeology*, May 1999. • Reinfeld, Fred. *Treasury of the World's Coins*. New York: Sterling Publishing, 1953. • Ritchie, David. *Shipwrecks: An Encyclopedia of the World's Worst Disasters at Sea*. New York: Checkmark Books, 1996. • Sandz, Victoria. *Encyclopedia of Western Atlantic Shipwrecks and Sunken Treasure*. Jefferson, N.C.: McFarland, 2001. • Schemo, Diana Jean. "Recovery of Spanish Galleon off Ecuador's Coast Raises Controversy and Romance." *New York Times*, April 14, 1997. • Stemm, Greg. "Thirty-First Annual Law of the Sea Institute." *Odyssey News*, March 30, 1998. • "Treasure Hunter Who Went for the Gold." *U.S. News & World Report*, August 5, 1985, 13. • Velazquez, José. "Salvagers Recover Thousands of Coins from Galleon Sunk off Ecuador." *News Times*, April 4, 1997. • Wilson, Scott. "Castro Forms a New Alliance — With Treasure Hunters." *Washington Post*, December 27, 2000, p. A16.

siege money

Like scrip, siege money has short-term value determined by state emergencies, including wars and invasions, such as the period of crisis in Aragon and Catalonia in 1250, when Jaime I of Aragon authorized paper bills. One of the most poignant examples of siege money financed the Dutch after Spanish king Philip II sent the Duke of Alva to blockade access to the Dutch dikes at Leiden in 1574. Prince William of Orange (also William the Silent), the father of his country, held out against the Inquisition and hard-line Catholicism. From spring to fall, the starving people, lacking imported goods, ate dray horses, cats, dogs, rats, and the leaves from the trees.

The mayor, Pieter Andriaanszoon, gathered all coins and other metals for making guns and ammunition. As receipts, he had Dutch minters turn to emergency cardboard coinage struck on 25 leaves torn from hymnals, prayer books, and the bible, which they pasted together into a solid board. Using circular cutters, workers sliced out disks featuring the cap of freedom at the top of a pike held by the Dutch lion. For legends, they stamped "*Godt Behofde Leyden*" ("God Save Leiden") and, in elementary Latin, "*Pugno pro Patria*" ("I Fight for My Country").

As Zeelander Admiral Boisot approached the dikes, he sent a message by carrier pigeon that his fleet was bringing provisions. The Dutch gamely hacked into the Meuse and Isle dikes in 16 locations to allow the fleet enough depth to enter. Fortunately, a hurricane raised the water level on October 1, when Boisot's rescue ships sailed in. Crew tossed loaves to the townspeople, who cheered from the docks. The people lit bonfires and rang church bells in thanks to God for deliverance. Four years later, as the Dutch retaliated, the Spanish governor struck a square silver coin at the trading port of Amsterdam featuring a noble shield and the date, 1578.

Other examples of siege money relieved similar monetary crises, notably, Inchiquin money during the civil war of 1642 to 1649, the amorphous metal polygons that the Confederate Catholic moneyers of Ireland stamped on both sides to record the weight. A siege at Carlisle, Scotland, from 1644 to 1645 resulted in the impromptu use of silver dinner plates for the minting of octagonal coins. Another siege currency was "Görtz *dalers*," the wartime fiduciary copper coinage of Charles XII of Sweden, initiated by his financier George

Heinrich, Baron von Görtz, in 1715, during war with Peter I the Great of Russia. In 1793, while invading Mayence (Mainz), Germany, the French army issued a numbered series of paper siege money. It featured a red-bordered sheet and bore a number, signature, and official stamp of the French Republic. The inscription stated, "*Monnoye de Siège à échanger contre Billon ou monnoye de métal de siège*" ("Siege money to be exchanged for billon or siege coins").

In 1814, a similar siege coinage in Belgium resulted in copper disks stamped with the grand N for Napoleon Bonaparte and the encircling laurel wreath of the conqueror. Additional siege moneys eased desperate situations from 1884 to 1885 at Khartoum, Sudan, where British colonial official Charles George Gordon held out during an attack by the local Mahdi, Muhammad Ahmad, and signed promissory notes by hand. A tiny emergency one-*peso* note, the issuance of José de San Martín, Argentina's liberator, gave little more than series number, value, and the date, May 1822.

***See also* Confederate money; Frederick the Great; Georg Heinrich, Baron von Görtz; *klippe;* leather and hide money; medieval coins; plate money; scrip; tokens; Tregwynt hoard.**

SOURCES: Allen, Larry. *Encyclopedia of Money.* New York: Checkmark Books, 2001. • Clain-Stefanelli, Elvira, and Vladimir Clain-Stefanelli. *The Beauty and Lore of Coins, Currency, and Medals.* Croton-on-Hudson, N.Y.: Riverwood Publishers, 1974. • Cribb, Joe. *Money.* Toronto: Stoddart, 1990. • Lewis, Brenda Ralph. *Coins & Currency.* New York: Random House, 1993. • Magnusson, Magnus. *Cambridge Biographical Dictionary.* Cambridge: University of Cambridge, 1990. • Pollak, Henry. *Coinage & Conflict.* Clifton, N.J.: Coin & Currency Institute, 2001. • Weatherford, Jack. *The History of Money: From Sandstone to Cyberspace.* Pittsburgh, Pa.: Three Rivers Press, 1998.

Sigismund, Archduke of Tyrol

In the 1480s, Harnich Erzherzog Sigismund, the wealthy Archduke of Tyrol, invented the dollar-sized coin. The son of penurious Duke Frederik IV, he was born in Innsbruck in 1427. Claiming private coinage rights, he commissioned *Guldiners* and *halbguldiners* picturing his crowned image with staff in hand. At the closure of the Merano mint, he introduced state-of-the-art coinage equipment at a new operation in Hall, Europe's most efficient mint. In 1476, he accessed recent silver strikes in Schwarz for dime-sized *Kreuzers* and also produced heavy silver *Pfunder* and restruck the *ducats* of Hungary and Italy. In 1486, his mintmaster, Giovanni Antonio de Cavalli (also Antonio de Caballis or Anthonis von Ross), superintended the production of silver half-dollars dubbed *unciales* (or *unziales*), a dated coin that was the first dollar-sized piece in history. Other European facilities quickly followed his example.

On a coin engraved by Christof Loch and struck from South American silver bullion, the narcissistic Sigismund placed around the reverse picture fifteen shields, the combined arms of Alsace, Austria on Enns and Burgau, Carinthia, Feldkirch, Hohenberg, Habsburg, Krain, Kyburg, Nellenburg, Pfirt, Portenau, Styria, Tyrol, and Windisch-Mark. He so enjoyed seeing his armored likeness as a tournament knight standing on the front surface and astride a galloping horse on the reverse that he kept buckets of coins to fondle at his home at Castello Principesco. His subjects called him *Sigismund der Munzreiche* ("Sigismund the coin-rich"). The dollar coin, one of the most treasured of the Renaissance, found favor as presentation pieces between noblemen, but failed to replace gold coins for everyday commerce.

See also thaler.

SOURCES: Clain-Stefanelli, Elvira, and Vladimir Clain-Stefanelli. *The Beauty and Lore of Coins, Currency, and Medals.* Croton-on-Hudson, N.Y.: Riverwood Publishers, 1974. • Cribb, Joe. *Money.* Toronto: Stoddart, 1990. • Davies, Glyn. *A History of Money from Ancient Times to the Present Day.* Cardiff: University of Wales Press, 1994. • *New Catholic Encyclopedia.* San Francisco: Catholic University of America, 1967.

silver strikes

In the United States, silver mining followed the rich strikes of Harry T. P. Comstock and James Fennimore, who began their careers prospecting for gold deep in the Virginia Range, Nevada. After Nevadans B. A. Harrison and J. F. Stone had their blue-gray ore assayed, the news spread, drawing some 5,000 diggers and panners from the gold sluices of California. By 1860, they converged on Virginia City to be near a legendary bonanza, the Comstock Lode.

The Yellow Jacket Silver Mining Company was one of many extraction sites stripping the lode of its silver. One triad — the Mexican, Sierra Nevada, and Union mining companies — shared a joint shaft, the descent site for hundreds of miners who chipped away at "stopes" or veins that spread underground at odd angles. Within four years, combined efforts from large operations and one-man pick-and-shovel efforts had removed nearly $40 million in ore. The amount stabilized, then decreased as veins played out. A new burst of activity in 1889 kept the Nevada bonanza going until 1893.

To turn ore into specie, Congress established a Nevada branch mint at Carson City in 1863. By 1870, the coining facility was assaying, refining, and stamping coins. In 1873, new strikes by the Consolidated Virginia Mine and additional production from the Comstock Lode renewed excitement and greater demand for silver dollars. Additional half-dollars from the San Francisco Mint increased the amount of silver specie in circulation.

A city newspaper promoted doubts about local coinage in June 1876 by spreading scandalous rumors that a U.S. Treasury agent had found the mint dollars underweight by as much as two cents per coin. The author of the article surmised that skimpy coins were the reason that Chinese financiers spurned Carson City money. The next October, the *American Journal of Numismatics* announced that the so-called scandal was actually a fiction cooked up by the San Francisco reporter to further a coin war waging between the U.S. mints in Nevada and California. To prove allegations that the story was deliberately erroneous, a San Francisco silver broker weighed some 600 Carson City coins to prove their integrity. To promote circulation of silver, New York City's sub-treasury began exchanging paper change for dimes, quarters, and half dollars.

The work of silver mining and processing was hot, dusty, poorly lighted, and dangerous, both from industrial accidents and from ingestion of the mercury used to leach pure silver from raw ore. Into the 1920s, the Gould and Curry Mill, one of 70 Nevada processing plants, refined ore for coinage despite a disastrous shaft fire in 1875 that engulfed much of central Virginia City. Undeterred, workers rebuilt the charred remains the next year. Beginning in 1865, Adolph Sutro, a German immigrant living in San Francisco, lessened problems with flooding by digging the Sutro Tunnel, completed in 1878, which drained two billion gallons of groundwater per year to expedite mining. Completed ingots bore the company stamp along with weight, fineness, value, serial number, and date of processing.

***See also* Greek coins; Joseph Lesher; patio process.**

SOURCES: Bowers, Q. David. *Adventures with Rare Coins.* Los Angeles: Bowers & Ruddy Galleries, Inc., 1979. • Crozier, Ronald. "A History of the Chloride Leach Process." *Bulletin of the Canadian Institute of Mining and Metallurgy*, July 1993. • "The Sutro Tunnel Company." http://www.library.unr.edu/specoll/mss/NC7.html. • "Virginia City in Ruins." *Territorial Enterprise*, October 27, 1875.

Simon, Thomas

As England's Tower Mint advanced from medieval hand-struck coinage to milling, it was medalist and seal-engraver Thomas Simon (or Simmonds) who provided dies. Born in Yorkshire around 1623 to Guernsey native Anne Germain and Pierre (Peter) Simon of London, he served under engineer Nicholas Briot, who introduced modern minting in France and England. Supported by Sir Edward Harley, Simon also established a career in goldsmithing and portrait medals, which he may have learned from his older brother, medalist Abraham Simon.

In 1639, Thomas Simon began earning his reputation as the finest medalist of his time by producing the Scottish Rebellion medal. As co-chief engraver with Edward Wade, he struck some of the crowns of Charles I that were minted at the Tower. Simon brought attention to his art for incising the great seal of the Commonwealth in 1649. The success of his work earned him the title of chief engraver to the mint and seals.

Simon succeeded under Oliver Cromwell as die engraver for proposed coins and traveled to Edinburgh to engrave the Dunbar medal. He prepared privy seals, the great seals of Ireland and Jamaica, and seals of the Order of the Garter, Royal Society, Admiralty, and Council of Wales. With the aid of engineer Jean-Pierre (or Peter) Blondeau, Simon completed an unusual 50-shilling coin marked with frosting. Although he had to petition the privy council for back pay, he modeled a portrait of Cromwell that staff carried in the lord protector's funeral cortege on November 23, 1658.

After the restoration of the monarchy in 1660, under Charles II, Simon returned to minting and hammering coins as an underling of chief engraver Thomas Rawlins. Simon rose once more to favor as engraver of the king's armaments, stamps, seals, and dies. In 1662, when French engraver John Roettiers began cutting planchets and mechanizing stamping, he joined Simon in perfecting a new process of milling gold and silver into coins. Under the preferment process, officials chose Roettiers's new dies for the Petition Crown over those of Simon, who lost his job.

Greatly diminished in prestige, Simon worked for two more years on royal commissions and died of plague in June 1665. He willed to William Simon, son of his brother Nathaniel, a collection of incising tools and punches. Simon's mastery of the flan marks his most beautiful coins and medals, which carry the initials T. S. Some name him England's finest medalist.

***See also* John Roettiers; Johann Sigismund Tanner.**

SOURCES: Clain-Stefanelli, Elvira, and Vladimir Clain-Stefanelli. *The Beauty and Lore of Coins, Currency, and Medals*. Croton-on-Hudson, N.Y.: Riverwood Publishers, 1974. • Davies, Glyn. *A History of Money from Ancient Times to the Present Day*. Cardiff: University of Wales Press, 1994. • Stephen, Sir Leslie, and Sir Sidney Lee, eds. *Dictionary of National Biography*. London: Oxford University Press, 1922.

sixpence

The sixpence appears in the first line of a nursery rhyme, "Sing a Song of Sixpence," collected around 1744 in Mary Cooper's three-volume *Tommy Thumb's Pretty Song Book*. Volume II, the only survivor from the set, resides in the British Museum as a major source of children's jingles. Illustrated with unrefined woodcuts, the poems appear to have circulated long before Cooper's collection. The four-verse narrative relates the baking of a pie stuffed with "four-and-twenty" blackbirds. While the unnamed king counts money in his counting house, the queen dines on honeyed bread. The maid, the loser in the scenario, is hanging clothes on the line when a blackbird snips off her nose.

Interpretations of the rhyme range far, including the allegorical vision of a king sun and queen moon superintending the 24 hours of the day. Another explanation pictures the 24 blackbirds as the letters of the alphabet baked into the first printing of the King James Bible, published in 1611. A third identifies the monarchs as Henry VIII and Catherine of Aragon and the maid as Anne Boleyn, for whom Henry divorced his wife, overthrew the Catholic church, and instituted the Church of England.

A connection between the rhyme and greed proposes that it dates to the golden era of piracy, when privateers waylaid and ransacked treasure ships passing between the gold and silver mints of the New World and Spain. The implications of a coded hiring message from sea dogs to potential crew rings true. For captains who ran through a long list of hirelings, it was necessary to replace those lost at sea, killed, lost to alcoholism or disease, or absconding with their share of the coins and loot. To conceal illicit privateering, the ship's agent may have created a harmless jingle about a sixpence and a leather canteen of rye whiskey, the typical daily pay earned by Blackbeard's crew. The "four-and-twenty blackbirds baked in a pie" could refer to the trickery of pirates, who pretended to be in distress at sea awaiting rescue. When rescuers arrived to help, the 24 leaped out of hiding from their trap "when the pie was opened."

The sweet reward became the subject for the next verses. The successful buccaneers sang for their own king, Blackbeard, and set before him a "dainty dish," a new ship to plunder. After the pillage, the king retired to his counting house to tabulate his money and make the standard division of spoils for the crew. The queen in the parlor refers to Blackbeard's possession of the 26-gun slaver called the *Concorde de Nantes*, a merchant vessel from Nantes, France, bound for Martinique in 1717. Blackbeard chose to make it his own queen and named it *Queen Anne's Revenge*. Upon return to port, he loaded it with "bread and honey," provisions for the next cruise. The clothes that the maid hangs may refer to sails or flags, which the crew of pursuit vessels suspended from the rigging on return to "the garden," a slang name for the easy pickings of the Caribbean Sea. Blackbeard then "snapped off her nose," a jolly euphemism for the mayhem that resulted from clashes with government sloops attempting to end piracy on the Spanish Main.

Another representation of the sixpence in nursery rhymes occurs in "There Was a Crooked Man," anthologized in James O. Halliwell's *The Nursery Rhymes of England* (1842). The familiar crooked fellow who finds a "crooked sixpence against a crooked stile" may refer to General Sir Alexander Leslie, Earl of Leven, one of Scotland's chief Covenanters. On the crooked border separating northern England and Scotland, Leven survived on the edge opposite his adversary Charles I. Distrusting permanent detente, he offered half pay to his men to keep them active. The measure proved canny after Charles mustered his forces, a move that provoked Leven to gallop north to storm Newcastle. At the king's surrender in 1647 at Newark, Nottinghamshire, Leven turned him in to parliament.

SOURCES: Baring-Gould, William S., intro. and notes. *The Annotated Mother Goose*. New York: Clarkson N. Potter, 1962. • Magnusson, Magnus. *Cambridge Biographical Dictionary*. Cambridge: University of Cambridge, 1990. • Myers, John. "Priest Cracks Carol's Secret Code." Evening Standard, December 23, 2000.

sou

The *sou* is a French coin named from a shortening of the Latin *solidus*, a long-lived Roman coin introduced by Constantine, the first Christian emperor. From the French coin's name came the phrase "not a sou," an expression of poverty or lack of coins. Under Charlemagne, king of the Franks, the *sou* was a phantom coin used only as a measure of worth. It figured in a set table of coin values based on the *livre* (pound):

coin	*value*
livre	20 *sous* or 240 *deniers* or 480 *obols*
sou	12 *deniers* or 24 *obols*
denier	2 *obols*

Similar to the French term is the Italian *soldo*, the name of a small coin. It remained in use in Corfu, an Ionian island that escaped control by the Ottoman Turks and passed into nearly 400 years' rule of Venice in 1402.

Following his father's currency policies, Louis I of France fought infringement of his minting at the port of Frisian Duurstede. Northern coin crafters copied his gold portrait *sous* and half-*sous*, which were designed for disbursal to the pope in Rome. Characterizing the sacred tithe was a cross encircled by the letters "*Munus Divinum*" ("Divine gift").

The French disliked copper *sous*, but accepted them in lieu of better quality small change. In 1719, the copper *sou* circulated widely in tandem with American dollars and Spanish pesos or pieces of eight in the commerce of Quebec. French-Canadians depended on the low-denomination *sou* to nourish local economy. The least valuable was made of billon, a cheap silver mixed with base metal. The most common after 1738 was the *sou marque*, which French moneyers shipped in large quantity to New France and the French Caribbean isles. When the coins turned black from oxidation, colonists dubbed them "black dogs," a similar name to "black money," nickname of the copper Spanish *vellón*.

Following the French Revolution, the humble *sou*, struck from copper or bell metal, carried a heavy weight of propaganda. Named the "*Sol à la Table de Loi*" ("Sol of the Table of the Law"), it presented a balance beam scale enwreathed in oak leaves and topped with the Phrygian cap of liberty and the inscription "*Liberté Egalité*" ("Freedom, Equality"). The motto, framed beneath an all-seeing eye, reminded the bearer that "*Les Hommes Sont Egaux Devant la Loi*" ("Men Are Equal Before the Law"). The iconography influenced a five-member committee of American colonists assigned on July 4, 1776, to design a national seal. The debate of John Adams, Benjamin Franklin, and Thomas Jefferson leaned toward a depiction of Lady Liberty holding a staff topped with a Phrygian slave's cap opposite blindfolded Justice. Between them stood a heraldic shield beneath the eye of God, a symbol common to both the *sou* and the German *thaler*.

***See also* Matthew Boulton; Canadian money; Great Seal of the United States; touch coins.**

SOURCES: Allen, Larry. *Encyclopedia of Money*. New York: Checkmark Books, 2001. • Clain-Stefanelli, Elvira, and Vladimir Clain-Stefanelli. *The Beauty and Lore of Coins, Currency, and Medals*. Croton-on-Hudson, N.Y.: Riverwood Publishers, 1974. • "France, 1793." http://www.napoleonicmedals.org/coins/fran93-2.htm. • Reed, Mort. *Cowles Complete Encyclopedia of U.S. Coins*. New York: Cowles Book Company, 1969. • Reinfeld, Fred. *Treasury of the World's Coins*. New York: Sterling Publishing, 1953.

South Sea bubble

An investment madness among British financiers, the South Sea bubble began in 1711 when statesman Robert Harley, first Earl of Oxford, founded the South Sea Company, a trading cartel that secured backing from the government and a commercial monopoly in Latin America and the Pacific. Assuming that the War of the Spanish Succession would conclude in favor of free trade, investors traded cash for stock. In 1713, the Treaty of Utrecht was less generous than bankers assumed. As a result, it limited the number of trading vessels per year and imposed a head tax on imported slaves.

The first company expedition, which set sail in 1717, was moderately remunerative. Confidence in speculation rose after George I became company governor the next year. By 1720, stock boomed at an outrageous rate at a time when the company proposed to assume ten million pounds of England's national debt at six percent interest. Swindlers and frauds lured the unwary into side deals as the stock price rose from 128.5 to 1,000. When money-waving investors flocked to pubs, shops, coffeehouses, and bordellos to buy stock and blocked the street alongside the Exchange, wags composed a scurrilous ballad of the frenzy:

> Then stars and garters did appear
> Among the meaner rabble;
> To buy and sell, to see and hear
> The Jews and Gentiles squabble.
>
> The greatest ladies thither came,
> And plied in chariots daily,
> Or pawned their jewels for a sum
> To venture in the Alley [Jackson 1999].

In September, the market caved in, lowering stock prices to 124. Knight, the company treasurer, fled to Brussels. Analysts compared the fiasco to the mythic flight of Icarus, the son of Daedalus the inventor, who flew too near the sun, melted the wax that held the feathers on his wings, and crashed into the Mediterranean Sea. In 1721, William Hogarth satirized the madness of crowds with a riotous narrative print entitled *An Emblematic Print on the South Sea Scheme*, which pictured the middle class abandoning honesty for speculation and tittered at the sudden disillusion in "mony's magick power" (Krasner-Khait 2002, p. 51).

He ridiculed wild dreams of wealth as a ride on a merry-go-round.

Because the bursting of the bubble ruined many financiers and banks and generated public panic, the House of Commons initiated an investigation. Their inquiry disclosed the bribery and speculation of three ministers and several courtiers. Humiliated board directors had to forfeit their holdings, but Sir Robert Walpole, whom some labeled a Cassandra for warning of the crash, was able to extricate the government from the scandal without serious loss. Parliament outlawed future unincorporated joint-stock enterprises. In 1750, the surviving owners sold rights to the South Sea Company to Spain, which maintained it until 1853. The effect on normal investment was significant for decades because the public feared trickery and overstated promises of profit.

SOURCES: Clain-Stefanelli, Elvira, and Vladimir Clain-Stefanelli. *The Beauty and Lore of Coins, Currency, and Medals*. Croton-on-Hudson, N.Y.: Riverwood Publishers, 1974. • Cordingly, David. *Under the Black Flag*. San Diego, Calif.: Harvest Books, 1995. • Cribb, Joe. *Money*. Toronto: Stoddart, 1990. • Harrison, Paul. "Rational Equity Valuation at the Time of the South Sea Bubble." *History of Political Economy*, July 1, 2001, pp. 269–281. • Jackson, Gerard. "Net Stocks and the South Sea Bubble." *New Australian*, February 21–27, 1999. • Krasner-Khait, Barbara. "The South Sea Bubble." *History*, March 2002, pp. 47–51. • Lewis, Brenda Ralph. *Coins & Currency*. New York: Random House, 1993.

Spanish coins

Spain's coins reflect the mixed cultural heritage and vast history that carried Spanish colonists to greatness in the New World and Pacific rim. When Spain belonged to the Roman Empire, soldiers' pay and trading moneys spread the coinage of Rome as well as that of Celtica and Greece, which introduced coins to Iberia in the fourth century B.C. In the Middle Ages, rule of the Moors and the Christian monarchs in Aragon, Castile, and Leon produced a varied coinage based on western Muslim coinage. Some replicated the style of Charlemagne's issue; others retained the florid calligraphy of Arabic lettering.

Castile's earliest coins, which Alfonso VIII minted at Toledo late in the 1100s, equaled the *dinars* of the Almoravid kings. Called *morabitinos* and later *maravedís*, they echoed the dynasty's Arabic name. Ferdinand III, Spain's beloved warrior-saint who came to the throne in 1217, issued the *masmudina* or half-*dinar*, which also carried the name *maravedí*. In the late 1200s, the *dobla*, a *dinar* called the "double *maravedí*," bore Castilian and Leonian crests. The popular coin circulated in numerous denominations, including the 10-*dobla* portrait coin of Pedro the Cruel and the cross-bearing *dobla cruzada*. The boy king John II of Castile, who defeated the Muslims at the battle of Higueruela in 1431, minted the *dobla de la banda* ("bordered *dobla*") from the meltdown of coins from Muslim Málaga.

In 1471, John's son Henry IV, a monetary reformer under the influence of a greedy constable, Álvaro de Luna, replaced John's coins with the massive Gothic 60-*enrique* coin, also called by the patriotic nickname *castellano* ("Castilian") or *dobla castellana*, and later called the *excelente*. Henry reduced the one hundred royal mints to six — Burgos, La Coruña, Cuenca, Segovia, Seville, and Toledo. The strong duo of Ferdinand and Isabella reaffirmed Henry's ordinances fixing the values of the four main coins, the *dobla*, *excelente*, *reale*, and the *vellón*, the common copper piece among the peasantry similar to the French *sou*, nicknamed the "black dog." Because of the *vellón's* darkened color in the presence of silver coins, the Spanish called it "black money." A shortage of *vellóns* at Toledo in 1480 worsened poverty, forcing commoners to rely on the French *tarja* and Flemish *placa*. In 1497, the royal couple chose the *ducado de oro* ("gold *ducat*") as the monetary standard.

As Spain's *conquistadores* seized lands in the Western Hemisphere, their concept of money supplanted the primitive Mexican system of paying with cocoa beans or miniature copper axes. The first authentic coins, featuring the pillars of Hercules and royal blazon, were commissioned by Charles I of Spain and Juana, the queen mother. Bearing the motto

"*Plus Ultra*" ("More Beyond"), the imagery summarized Spain's attitude toward exploitation of New World wealth to make it even richer and grander. In 1851, Herman Melville remarked in his novel *Moby Dick* on the accomplishment of Spanish coinage:

> Now those noble golden coins of South America are as medals of the sun and tropic token-pieces. Here palms, alpacas, and volcanoes; sun's disks and stars; ecliptics, horns-of-plenty, and rich banners waving, are in luxuriant profusion stamped; so that the precious gold seems almost to derive an added preciousness and enhancing glories, by passing through those fancy mints, to Spanishly poetic [Melville, 1961, p. 410].

As the fictional Captain Ahab examines the gold doubloon he has fastened to the mainmast of the *Pequod* as a promised bonus to the sailor locating the great white whale, he notes that the coin was cast in the Andes and pictures a crowing rooster, flame, tower, and signs of the zodiac. For its beauty and promise, the coin becomes the ship's navel.

The outpouring of gold and silver from the New World's mines was presaged in an early incident marked by greed and self-aggrandizement. Bartolomé de las Casas (or Casaus), the Dominican missionary who wrote *Historia de las Indias* (*History of the Indies*), first printed in 1875 by the Royal Academy of Madrid, chronicled the decline in Spain's economic and political morality as the power-crazed, gold-hungry adventurers pillaged and raped the Indies. He surmised that Columbus borrowed his own share of the costs from Martín Alonso, a silent partner. De las Casas noted that Columbus ended his extraordinary expeditions a poor man and concluded, "since the cost of the expedition was recorded at 1,500,000 *maravedís*, it is likely that Martín Alonso supplied [Columbus's share]" (de las Casas 1971, p. 33). Columbus's obsession with riches is apparent in journal entries that mention God 26 times and gold 114 times.

Spain's treasury profited directly from Columbus's discoveries, beginning with the unpolished gold nuggets he presented to Ferdinand and Isabella on arrival in Barcelona in mid–April 1493. Before leaving for a second voyage, Columbus explained to the impatient King Ferdinand that his crew brought no gold because it lay in underground veins. Historian de las Casas observed caustically that removal from the veins would require heavy labor because "nowhere in the world has gold ever been extracted without toil unless it be stolen from someone else's chests" (de las Casas 197, p. 56). The egg-sized nuggets that arrived in Spain with Columbus's third voyage proved beneficial in persuading the royal couple to continue bankrolling expeditions. In a letter to Isabella, Columbus boasted, "I have opened the doors to great quantities of gold, pearls, precious stones, spices and a thousand other things" (*ibid.*, p. 75).

Spain enriched itself from New World plunder with a three-stage system of grab, stamp, and ship. Around 1500, artist Albrecht Dürer witnessed a display at Brussels of New World treasure and described it as "a sun all of gold a whole fathom broad, and a moon all of silver of the same size" (Weatherford 1998, p. 95). After seizing Cuba in 1511, Diego Velázquez de Cuéllar demanded that natives provide gold in increasing amounts. A priest characterized his rapacity as the cause of overworking laborers and killing or helping to kill them in the process. To speed up the process of self-enrichment, de Cuéllar sent his relative, Hernán Cortés, northwest to Mexico to apply the same pressure on local people, who also had to raise food and dray animals, weave cloth for sacks, and cut wood to supply the mining operation.

The first official New World Spanish coinage, under the direction of Viceroy Antonio de Mendoza, was produced in Mexico City in 1535 in quarters belonging to Cortés. Additional operations produced silver *reales* at Zacatecas; Santo Domingo's coiners minted the first copper *maravedís*, which were each worth 1⁄34 of a *real*. The patio process, a new technology introduced at Pachuca in 1554 by a German engineer called Lomann and by Spanish trader Bartolomé de Medina, applied mercury amalgamation as a means of purifying ore. It required the grinding of even low-grade ore into a watered slurry to be spread thin and sprinkled with salt, copper sulfate, and mercury for treading into a paste by workers and their mules. After a rinse, pressure and heat evaporated the mercury, thus producing pure metal for coinage. The local mints, bolstered by importation of African slaves, expanded to become the world's largest. By 1832 they had produced ore worth 667 million *pesos*.

Although the Spanish crown dispensed parcels of land to adventurers, it retained mineral rights as well as half rights to all plunder from native temples, pyramids, and burial grounds. To those contractors to whom the Spanish king sold mining rights, the return of a *quinto real* ("royal fifth") retained for the Spanish treasury 20 percent of proceeds. The king also extorted more wealth from New World mining by exacting a two to six percent *alcabala* ("sales tax") and 7.5 percent *almojarifazgo* ("import tax"), by collecting a *diezmo* ("tithe") for the church, and by monopolizing supplies of mercury, salt, gunpowder, and leaf tobacco, which served the colonists as a form of money for trade with Indians.

Over four decades, native slaves operated the silver mints established in Lima, Peru, in 1565. At the behest of Philip II, Andean workers produced 300 million coins, ranging from pieces of eight down to the *cuartilla* or one-quarter *real*. So fiendish was their work that they erected altars to *El Tío* ("the uncle"), an underworld deity with bulbous eyes, mulish ears, tusks, and curled horns. To their devil god they lit candles and left coca leaves and alcohol to stave off accidents with tools, cave-ins, and rock slides, three curses associated with mining silver and minting coins. Additional Spanish minting by Quechuan Indians in the high mountains of Potosí, Bolivia, in 1575 and in Santa Fé de Bogotá, Columbia, in 1620 flooded the world's markets with eight billion coins struck from Spanish ore to pay soldiers of a farflung empire. The region was so blessed with precious metal that the Spanish labeled any source of great wealth as *vale un Potosí* ("worth a Potosí") (Clain and Clain 1974, p. 148).

In Spain and Portugal, money brought out the worst in human character. The flow of coins enriched royalty and their relatives and retainers at an unprecedented rate. Contraband gold and silver diverted from the glittering stream fell to the devious, who siphoned off some 165,000 tons. Additional under-the-table dealings put graft into the pockets of unscrupulous priests and government officials. After the Portuguese settlers of Brazil found gold in 1695, they paralleled Spanish greed with their own mining operations, which they worked with African slave labor.

An excess of gold presented complex problems for the Spanish economy. Throughout Iberia and the Indies, the glut of gold and silver coins quadrupled prices, especially for imported luxuries — glass, jewelry, weapons, porcelain, silk, and fine foods. During the *Siglo de Oro* ("Century of Gold"), the rich decked their walls in gilt hangings and frames, coated doors and coaches in gold, embroidered gold thread into chair and bed fabrics, gilded their books and the livery of servants, and decked cabinetry, knives, belts and buckles, and snuffboxes in more glitter. The church also entered an era of conspicuous display of precious metals on altarpieces, ceilings, statuary, and ceremonial regalia.

As a result of burgeoning grandeur, inflation plunged the underclass into worsening poverty and forced grandees into spiraling debt, which enriched Dutch and German moneylenders and Italian bankers. The failure of Philip II to pay his troops in 1575 led to rebellion and the sacking of Antwerp. Thus, the lopsided enrichment of a few generated resentment against the self-centered rich as well as corruption, crime, and wars.

The unspoken result of too much wealth to too few was the rise in slavery and human misery. Mine work demanded increasing numbers of workers conscripted from Indian villages by an infamous quota system. Eyewitness accounts of whippings, clubbings, humiliations, and verbal abuse attest to the near enslavement of miners. In the words of de las Casas, "Indian gold is what prevails on the market all over the world (this is not the place to speak of the disorder and accidental abuses of how it gets there)" (de las Casas 1971, p. 36).

Unknown to the workers was the poisonous effect of the patio process — the constant trampling through salt and mercury from Huancavelica, Peru, to extract pure silver from raw ore. The Andean city, founded in 1571 by Francisco de Angulo, became a base for the nearby Santa Bárbara mercury mines, where locals toiled in unspeakable conditions and faced constant danger of work injuries and falls. Ignoring the cost in suffering, Viceroy Teodoro La Croix labeled the rich mercury deposits a world marvel. Mercifully, landslides ended easy access to the mines and spared the Indians more bondage to the Spanish.

In 1675, when Spain lifted the ban on minting gold in the Spanish colonies, Mexico became the first New World producer of gold *escudos*. For manufacturing gold ingots, goldsmiths shaped holes in a wood box filled with wet sand. Into the depressions, they poured melted gold ore. When the ingots cooled, they required an inspection, weighing, and stamp with a mint mark and royal seal to attest to the paying of the king's portion, the *quinto* or ⅕ of the value. In Potosí, the silver mining operation derived from ores removed through underground passages and carried to a compound, where enslaved Indians purified and smelted ores for striking into coins.

The fresh coinage and other treasure went directly to Spain, stopping briefly at Cuba for captains to maneuver fleets into position and add fresh crew. In 1583, an official letter noted that ships overburdened with new coins commissioned by Philip II had to halt in Havana harbor to remove excess crates for a later convoy. At first, the king demanded half. Gradually, the crown dropped its demand to 30 percent, 20 percent, and, in some cases, ten percent. Other gold coinage enriched religious houses and churches, which grew as greedy and self-glorying with New World gold as Spanish grandees.

Constant transport of coins gave rise to piracy on the routes the treasure ships took on their way to the Caribbean and Europe. By 1571, Spain had set up a colonial outpost at Manila in the Philippines to funnel South American silver *pesos* into lucrative trade for silk and porcelain. Essential to purification of ores was mercury, the purifying agent that had to be shipped in. Two supply ships, the tender *Conde de Tolosa* and the *Nuestra Señora de Guadalupe* were bound from Cadiz, Spain, to Havana, Cuba, and Veracruz, Mexico, in 1724. The heavy mercury loads plus iron fittings, English clocks, and German glass sank with the ships off Samaná Bay, Hispaniola, in a hurrcane on August 24. In 1977, Captain Tracy Bowden of Caribe Salvage recovered mercury from the *Tolosa*, which foundered in deep water at a reef that sheltered its cargo.

In 1728, Spain outlawed the crudely stamped cobs and required modern milling of coins. In 1732, the mint in Mexico City gave up hammer striking and installed a screw press, which stamped images on milled planchets. Operated with a weighted lever, the device pressed both sides of the blank with images incised on dies above and below it. The application of controlled pressure produced uniform coins of equal weight and shape with a corded edge to prevent clipping, filing, or shaving and to deter counterfeiters. The screw press ended Spain's reputation for cracked, lopsided coins with uneven edges and blurred images by turning out quality coins in denominations of one-half, one, two, four, and eight *reales*. Old-style cobs continued to circulate from Bolivia's Potosí mint until 1773.

Spain's coins had global influence. *Reales* were the originals for European copies, notably, the Dutch *daalder*, which was modeled on the *peso* and traded to Asia from 1601. Islamic companies incorporated the *real* into their monetary system as the Irani and Omani *rial* and the Qatari, Saudi, and Yemeni *riyal*. Of less value were the "new plate" or "plata provincial" ("provincial silver") coins minted in Spain, which were lighter than colonial coins.

More directly, Spanish coinage supplied the markets of American, Canadian, and Caribbean colonies, which had not evolved a standard currency, and served as a monetary standard by which other coins were valued. The U.S. Coinage Act of 1793 declared the Spanish dollar legal tender and continued to recognize the coin as official money for the next 64 years. Into American English came the terms "two bits" for a Spanish coin broken into quarters, "pieces of eight" for eight-*real* coins, and "picayune," the name for a small coin worth a half *real*.

See also **Atocha; *La Capitana*; cobs; coins and currency in literature; colonial coins; commemorative issue; counterstamp; *escudo*; Mel Fisher; Piet Heyn; Thomas Jefferson; patio process; *peso*; pieces of eight; piracy; *pistareen*; screw press; treasure ships.**

SOURCES: Allen, Larry. *Encyclopedia of Money*. New York: Checkmark Books, 2001. • Allen, Thomas B. "Cuba's Golden Past." *National Geographic*, July 2001, 74–91. • Bowden, Tracy. "Gleaning Treasure from the Silver Bank." *National Geographic*, July 1996, 90–105. • Clain-Stefanelli, Elvira, and Vladimir Clain-Stefanelli. *The Beauty and Lore of Coins, Currency, and Medals*. Croton-on-Hudson, N.Y.: Riverwood Publishers, 1974. • Cordingly, David. *Under the Black Flag*. San Diego, Calif.: Harvest Books, 1995. • de las Casas, Bartolomé. *History of the Indies*. New York: Harper & Row, 1971. • Cribb, Joe. *Money*. Toronto: Stoddart, 1990. • Dunn, Oliver, and James Kelley, eds. *The Diario of Christopher Columbus' First Voyage, 1492–1493*. Norman: University of Oklahoma Press, 1989. • Galbraith, John Kenneth. *Money: Whence It Came, Where It Went*. Boston: Houghton Mifflin, 1975. • Jordan, Louis. "The Coins of Colonial and Early America." http://www.coins.nd.edu/ColCoin/ColCoinContents/Introduction.html. • Lewis, Brenda Ralph. *Coins & Currency*. New York: Random House, 1993. • Link, Marion Clayton. "Exploring the Drowned City of Port Royal." *National Geographic*, February 1960, 151, 158–182. • Melville, Herman. *Moby Dick*. New York: New American Library, 1961. • Pickford, Nigel. *The Atlas of Ship Wrecks & Treasure*. New York: Dorling Kindersley, 1994. • Reed, Mort. *Cowles Complete Encyclopedia of U.S. Coins*. New York: Cowles Book Company, 1969. • Sandz, Victoria. *Encyclopedia of Western Atlantic Shipwrecks and Sunken Treasure*. Jefferson, N.C.: McFarland, 2001. • Weatherford, Jack. *The History of Money: From Sandstone to Cyberspace*. Pittsburgh, Pa.: Three Rivers Press, 1998.

spirit money

For their dead relatives, mourners in Burma, China, Korea, Taiwan, and Vietnam sent to the underworld high denominations of spirit coins and paper money or Hell notes, ersatz paper or silk banknotes printed just for Buddhist funerals. These richly designed notes contained gold and silver foil seals and pictured clouds, pagodas, dragons, musicians, and symbols of good luck as well as the underworld Keeper of the Gate and Judge alongside the Buddhist money deity. To assure that the dead received the bills, their mourners burned the money on a funeral pyre, at a temple, or in a household shrine along with food and images of cars, servants, and houses. For accident victims, the burning took place at the site alongside the corpse. The devout sent the amenities into the afterlife for deceased loved ones to absorb their essence as a guarantee that they could live in comfort. By honoring dead ancestors, the living assured themselves blessings on earth.

Spirit money had other ritual applications. It was integral in healing ceremonies of the *tang-ki* ("spirit medium"), who pricked his tongue and dripped blood onto spirit money to turn it into a blood charm for carrying next to the body to ward off harm. Spirit money opened the doors to the spirit world for commemoration of ancestors, propitiating malicious deities that tortured the dead, and summoning the god of wealth during celebrations of the Chinese New Year, when the devout Buddhist also placed coins on the altar. For the construction of a new building, spirit money was the appropriate offering to bury in the foundation.

At the spring Ching Ming Festival, a time to remember ancestors, the living cleaned graves, touched up markers, and made burned offerings of meals, rice wine, paper clothing, and spirit money. A demanding rite observed during the seventh month of the lunar year, the religious holiday was rightly named the Festival of the Hungry Ghost. On this occasion, the gates of hell opened so spirits of the dead could visit earth temporarily. To ease the passage and comfort the travelers, ancestors offered prayers at the household shrine, where they lighted incense and burned hell money.

In 1991, Asian-American novelist Amy Tan's *The Kitchen God's Wife* described the role of spirit money in the Buddhist funeral of Auntie Du Ching, a fictional refugee from Peking who died in a bus accident in 1990 at age 97. Tan explains that the mother figure, Winnie, purchased "a dozen or so bundles of spirit money, money Grand Auntie can supposedly use to bribe her way along to Chinese heaven" (Tan 1991, p. 20). Also integral to tradition were foil-wrapped candies and red envelopes of lucky money distributed to mourners.

A similar system of bankrolling the dead existed in ancient Afghanistan. In November 2001, historians speculated on the survival of a treasure hoard, the "Golden Hoard of Bactria," unearthed from six burial mounds called Tillya-tepe dug around 100 B.C. Afghan authorities reportedly secured the collection in a vault at the presidential palace in Kabul. The original owner buried the tiaras, mirrors and plaques, coins from Kunduz, and jewelry dating to the third and second centuries B.C. during regular passage along the Silk Road, a trade route carrying Central Asian goods to Byzantium, Persia, and republican Rome. The first to unearth the trove was Greek-Russian archaeologist Viktor Ivanovich Sarianidi (or Sariyiannidis) of the Institute of Archaeology in Moscow in 1978. Among the goods Sarianidi summarized in *Bactrian Gold: From the Excavations of the Tillya-tepe Necropolis in Northern Afghanistan* (1985) was a shower of burial spangles, tiny gold squares stamped with a four-leafed clover set in a frame. The coin-platelets, a form of ritual confetti, accompanied the dead to their graves to serve as pocket change for spirits in the afterlife.

The riches passed to the Kabul Museum and remained until 1991, when President Najibullah retrieved them from a rock vault to exhibit to ambassadors and the media. In 1992, the rogue Taliban government murdered the president and seized his residence. After that time, the hoard may have been purloined, distributed to other countries, or melted down to fund Taliban wars. One insider, Ahmed Shah Massoud, an anti–Taliban warrior, confirmed that the trove remained under the presidential palace.

***See also* obolus.**

SOURCES: Eastman, Lloyd. *Gods, Ghosts and Ancestors: The Popular Religion*. New York: Oxford, 1988. • Hastings, James, ed. *Encyclopedia of Religion and Ethics*. New York: Charles Scribner's Sons, 1951. • Lewis, Brenda Ralph. *Coins & Currency*. New York: Random House, 1993. • Opitz, Charles J. *Odd and Curious Money*. Ocala, Fla.: First Impressions, 1986. • Sarianidi, Viktor Ivanovich. "The Golden Hoard of Bactria." *National Geographic*, March 1990, pp. 50–75. • Tan, Amy. *The Kitchen God's Wife*. New York: Ivy Books, 1991.

sterling

The origin of the medieval term "pound sterling" leaves to conjecture its historical source and meaning. The word itself derives from "sterilensis," a medieval Latin or Norman-French term that occurs in oral interviews and written source material that Benedictine historian Ordericus Vitalis amassed at Saint-Evroult-d'Ouche Abbey in Normandy before compiling the 13-book *Historia Ecclesiastica* (*Church History*) (1141). The word appears without clarification or comment in the abbreviated Latinate phrase "*XVlibr sterilensium*" ("15 pounds of sterling"), the first record of a long-lived term that eventually attached to the English pound.

If the term is a Latinization of Norman-French, it may derive from *esterlin* ("little star"), a reference to emblems on Frankish coins. A possible source from Great Britain is the Old English *steorra* ("star") combined with the diminutive suffix -ling. If the term came from the Rhineland Franks, it might derive from *Iesterling*, a descriptive of money. Another possibility is *easterling*, a generic term for money changers and merchants. An alternative explanation is the Germanic root *ster*, meaning "sturdy," a direct reference to genuine, stable, and unvarying coinage from pure ore. After Henry II refined coinage after 1154, the term "sterling" took on an implication of quality. Mintmasters began striking silver pennies and placed within the quadrants formed by the arms of crosses four stars and starlings, which could have been the source of the term.

SOURCES: Davies, Glyn. *A History of Money from Ancient Times to the Present Day*. Cardiff: University of Wales Press, 1994. • *New Catholic Encyclopedia*. San Francisco: Catholic University of America, 1967. • Sinclair, David. *The Pound*. London: Century Books, 2000.

stone money

One unusual currency that stirs curiosity is Pacific Yap stone money. The Yap migrated from the Philippines or eastern Indonesia to Micronesia, a string of 15 islands spread over 600 miles of ocean. They maintained a five-part currency — they paid in *reng* or turmeric root dye compressed into a ball, *yar* or shell money, *mmbul* or betel nut sheaths, *jar* or pearl shells, and *gaw*, necklaces strung with scrimshaw carved onto Chama Pacifica shells and whale teeth. Additional currencies ranged from baskets of taro root to syrup, tobacco, coconuts, and hibiscus fiber mats, an inter-island money throughout Oceania. The most unusual method was *ray* (or *rai*), round aragonite or limestone money formed from volcanic stone lifted from coral reefs and perilously ferried home to Palau by outrigger canoe.

The *Yap* stone coin, pierced at center with a stone adze, was a huge, thick, and cumbrous disk that could equal the size of a dinner plate or wagon wheel and extend to a circle over three times taller than the islanders themselves. Assessors used the hand span from thumb to little finger to measure the smallest stones and applied the outstretched arms to measure the largest stones in fathom units. According to folklore, the mythic hero Fathaan discovered glistening crystalline limestone in Palau's caves. With a stone ax, he cut pieces into fish shapes, but found them too awkward to manage. Subsequent quarrying shaped pieces like the full moon.

Like whale tooth money, stone money conferred not only wealth, but also power and prestige to the bearer. The highest quality was a streaky, chocolate-hued aragonite or milk-hued crystalline stone. The stone wheels carried value in pigs, fish, yams, taro, and coconuts and required mother-of-pearl shells as change. Stone pieces were legal tender for paying debts and taxes, trade, and political bribes. When European museums negotiated for models of the wheels, a stone twice the height of an adult was too expensive for curators to buy.

Quarried in Guam and Palau as *fé* or *fei*, stone currency required tedious transport to the Caroline Island cluster some 260 miles by pirogue or by canoe towing a bamboo raft. Because some voyagers died making the return trip, pieces of stone money honored the quarrier by carrying his name and the names of subsequent owners. Those stones lost at sea still conferred honor on the quarrier, even though islanders never saw the piece or marveled at its size and shape. To increase mobility, islanders thrust timbers into the center and hoisted the stone money over their shoulders or rolled their coins like wheels on an axle. When sellers completed transactions, they typically did not disturb the giant wheel cash, but instead left it at the buyers' residences and identified the change of ownership through word of mouth, an opportunity to boost the recipients' prestige.

Oddly, unlike other primitive cultures, the Yap did not abandon non-uniform, barely portable stone money after they came in contact with more convenient minted moneys of the western Hemisphere, Europe, and Japan. Reports of the island currency reached Europe after Portuguese adventurer Diego da Rocha sailed to Ulithi island on October 1, 1525, and remained for four months. Into the early 1700s, some 20 American, British, Dutch, and Spanish explorers and traders enountered the Yap Islands. The arrival of Andrew Cheyene, a British trader sailing the brig *Naiad*, in the early 1800s encouraged the Yapese to establish trade routes to Guam and the Marianas and to colonize Saipan.

After sailing on a pearl diving expedition to Manila aboard the *Belvedere* in 1871, Irish-born naval captain David Dean O'Keefe of Savannah, Georgia, was shipwrecked and rescued by the Yapese. Aboard a German trader, he reached Hong Kong and returned the next year as captain of a Chinese junk, the *Katherine*, while working for Webster and Cook of the Celebes Sea Trading Company. He expanded the Yap islanders' copra trade and devised a simpler method of quarrying and making stone money with iron pick, chisels, crowbars, and mallets. As the biggest merchant in the Carolines, he became the King of Yap, Monarch of Mapia, and Sovereign of Sonsorol. Perhaps because he went to less trouble to shape stone wheels, his coins, called "O'Keefe's money," were less valuable than older versions.

O'Keefe occupied his island throne for 30 years, aiding the island poor and increasing trade with mainland Asia in copra and trepang, also called *bêche-de-mer* (sea cucumbers). In May 1901, he disappeared at sea during a typhoon. According to the Savannah *Morning News* on June 11, 1903, his will left a half-million dollars to be divided between his legitimate daughter, Louisa Veronica O'Keefe, in Georgia and his island family. The article surmised that O'Keefe died along with his sons, leaving only a wife and daughter on Mapia Island.

Writers Lawrence Klingman and Gerald Green reprised O'Keefe's adventures in a colorful fictionalized biography, *His Majesty O'Keefe* (1950). Along with descriptions of sailing and fraternizing with natives is a description of stone money and its manufacture:

> The natives refer to [Yap stones] as *fei*. They're by far the most important kinds of money. These shell necklaces you see are of lesser value. They also use large single pearl shells, which they call *kau*, and which are also unavailable here for coins. Further to confuse the system, there's a kind of mat made of beaten lemon hibiscus fiber, which they use only in very special trades.... Everyone knows his own particular pieces of *fei*. It just sits here like a bank deposit. When they trade, there's just a verbal agreement, and the money itself isn't even moved [Klingman and Green 1950, p. 49].

When the fictional O'Keefe formulates his grand plan, he meets with the village headmen to explain how his sailboat, the *Katherine*, will save them "the labor of hewing the stone from the steep cliffs and the long, weary trips in our canoes, loaded down with the giant wheels and of our many brothers who have died at sea" (*ibid.*, p. 166).

The plan goes into action. By the second week of concerted labor, they derive a rhythm to their organization. "It took five men working one week at top-speed to hew a stone disk from the cliff, shape it and polish it to perfection" (*ibid.*, p. 172). O'Keefe manages to ferry 50 tons of stones per trip, with one huge Yap disk weighing as much as a quarter ton. Villagers move the *fei* down winding trails on chestnut saplings thrust through center holes and laid across their shoulders.

In the novel, the work is not without mishap. Some wheels break on the descent from the escarpment to the sea. Another sinks when the raft transporting it to the ship overturns. To secure the finished wheels, the natives lash them to the deck with whale warp or stow them in the hold for the journey to Tomil Harbor. To establish an exchange rate in copra and trepang, O'Keefe works out an arbitrary scale:

stone size	*value*
3 handspans	5 sacks of trepang or 35 reed sacks of copra
6 handspans	130 sacks of copra
18 handspans	650 sacks of copra

The receipts from the first week's stone money making results in a profit of two tons of trepang and 15 tons of copra, a source of soap, livestock feed, and oil for cosmetics and cooking. The work of harvesting and sacking coconut meat for copra falls to women and children. When O'Keefe inquires about work habits, the supervisor grins, "No one dares be lazy. The god Legerim who first ordered man to quarry *fei* for his glory would strike him dead who dared shirk his share of the work" (*ibid.*, p. 178). In 1954, a film version of *His Majesty O'Keefe*, shot on Fiji and starring Burt

Lancaster, publicized the historic rise of the plucky Irishman.

After Germany took possession of Yap territory in 1898, the new bureaucracy had difficulty improving the land. Orders to upgrade roads failed to stir the Yapese. German agents resorted to seizing ownership of stone money and marked their possession by painting black crossmarks on valuable wheels. The threat to islanders' prestige and public standing brought immediate results. After locals straightened and smoothed roads, German agents cleaned the crosses from the stone money. When the Japanese acquired rule of the Yap after World War I, they banned German coins and imposed circulation of the yen.

A survey of stone money in 1929 disclosed that 13,281 coins survived. The predations of another world war in the 1940s cost islanders many of their stone pieces, which Japanese invaders destroyed or used in sea walls or as anchors or pavers on airstrips. Surviving stone money dates from 1700 to 1931. When American soldiers occupied the island at the end of World War II, islanders embraced military scrip in exchange for goods and services. Natives found that spending American paper money at U.S. government stores was less trouble and more convenient than purchasing with traditional stone wheels.

A less conspicuous type of stone money, the Irian Jayan *je* stones, promote serious transactions in Papua New Guinea. A flattened oval, each stone must be imported from the Balim Valley. Whether black or green, the surface requires adornment at center with braided bark or orchid fiber, fur, or cloth. Consumers in the Dani tribe exchange them like currency at betrothals and funerals and for extensive commercial trade.

***See also* wampum.**

SOURCES: Allen, Larry. *Encyclopedia of Money.* New York: Checkmark Books, 2001. • Clain-Stefanelli, Elvira, and Vladimir Clain-Stefanelli. *The Beauty and Lore of Coins, Currency, and Medals.* Croton-on-Hudson, N.Y.: Riverwood Publishers, 1974. • Cribb, Joe. *Money.* Toronto: Stoddart, 1990. • Du Bois, Cora. *The People of Alor.* Cambridge, Mass.: Harvard University Press, 1960. • Davies, Glyn. *A History of Money from Ancient Times to the Present Day.* Cardiff: University of Wales Press, 1994. • Einzig, Paul. *Primitive Money.* Oxford: Pergamon Press, 1966. • Hezel, Francis X. "A Yankee Trader in Yap: Crayton Philo Holcomb." Journal of Pacific History, 1975, pp. 3–19. • Jordan, Louis. "The Coins of Colonial and Early America." http://www.coins.nd.edu/ColCoin/ColCoin Contents/Introduction.html. • Klingman, Lawrence, and Gerald Green. *His Majesty O'Keefe.* New York: Charles Scribner's Sons, 1950. • Lewis, Brenda Ralph. *Coins & Currency.* New York: Random House, 1993. • Opitz, Charles J. *Odd and Curious Money.* Ocala, Fla.: First Impressions, 1986. • Orr, Francine, and Tim Engle. "Yap Facts: A Primer of Yapese Culture." *Kansas City Star*, 1998. • Scarr, Deryck, ed. *More Pacific Island Portraits.* Canberra: ANU Press, 1979. • Weatherford, Jack. *The History of Money: From Sandstone to Cyberspace.* Pittsburgh, Pa.: Three Rivers Press, 1998.

Streber, Franz Seraph

Numismatist Franz Seraph Streber clarified many historical misconceptions about money. Born at Deutenkofen, Lower Bavaria, on February 26, 1805, he studied philosophy, theology, and archeology at Erlangen. In 1854, he gained membership in the Academy of Munich. At age 30, he joined the faculty of the University of Munich as professor of archeology and campus rector. In 1827, he began a career as numismatist for the royal treasury of coins, first as clerk, then assistant, and, in 1841, curator. He superintended Vienna's coin collection and catalogued 18,000 Greek coins while compiling a lexicon illustrated with line drawings of 6,000 examples.

Streber's work *Numismata Nonnulla Græca* (*Some Greek Coins*) (1834) corrected erroneous information, particularly the placement of moneys on a time line. Awarded a prize from the Academy of Paris, he also published the first explanation of the rainbow patina on Celtic coins and treatises on Celtic, Greek, and medieval coins as well as archæology, mythology, and art history. His writings enlarged by half the research of Austrian coin specialist Joseph Hilarius Eckhel. Streber died at Munich on November 21, 1864.

SOURCES: *New Catholic Encyclopedia.* San Francisco: Catholic University of America, 1967.

Susan B. Anthony dollar

Introduced in 1979, the Susan B. Anthony dollar was a worthwhile investment for the U.S. Mint, which sought a coin to replace easily frayed dollars, the soul of daily monetary transactions. For the good of the nation, she was a long-overlooked heroine who deserved acclaim. The mother of the women's rights movement, Susan Brownell Anthony was the spokeswoman for millions of suffragists. A Quaker born on February 15, 1820, in Adams, Massachusetts, she earned respect in meetinghouse gatherings and came of age in an era that saw the growth of demand for female independence from husbands and fathers.

Like other women of the period, Anthony chose teaching as the only profession that welcomed her and joined the faculty of a seminary in New Rochelle, New York. She allied herself with abolitionists William Lloyd Garrison and orator Frederick Douglass, a former slave who fled servitude in Maryland and became an adviser to presidents and publisher of the *North Star*. With their encouragement, in 1856, she headed the New York branch of the American Anti-Slavery Society and formed the Women's Loyal National League, a society of female patriots backing President Abraham Lincoln and the Union during the Civil War.

After the Worcester, Massachusetts, women's rights convention of 1850, Anthony read Lucy Stone's convention speech in the Rochester, New York, newspaper and joined writer-activist Elizabeth Cady Stanton in a half-century campaign for gender equality. In a well-balanced synergy, Stanton compiled data and wrote the speeches that Anthony delivered across the country on street corners and in lyceums and assembly halls. In an era when polite women never traveled without a male chaperone, she journeyed alone by coach, paddlewheeler, and carriage along the Eastern seaboard and as far west as California and Wyoming to win support for women's rights and to organize cells of activists to expand the grassroots effort.

Assertive in the public rostrum, Anthony demanded a new interpretation of the Fourteenth Amendment to the Constitution to acclaim that all citizens were entitled to voting rights. Of the Preamble to the Constitution, she said:

> It is we, the people, not we, the white male citizens, nor we, the male citizens; but we, the whole people, who formed this Union. We formed it not to give the blessings of liberty but to secure them; not to the half of ourselves and the half of our posterity, but to the whole people — women as well as men [Anthony 1990, p. 161].

She joined Stanton and Matilda Joslyn Gage in compiling the first three volumes of the six-volume *History of Woman Suffrage* (1902) from a morass of clippings, documents and historic data. In 1867, she crusaded for state enfranchisement of women in Kansas.

At age 52, Anthony made her most public stand by casting a vote for the presidency in the November election. After her arrest by a U.S. marshal in Rochester, New York, she used the pre-sentencing hearing at a Canandaigua courthouse as a public opportunity to rail at the judge, jury, and media. When the judge fined her $100, she refused to pay it and continued on her way to Michigan, Utah, the Dakotas, and Colorado to make speeches. When Congress passed the Nineteenth Amendment to the Constitution long after her death, the media called it the "Anthony amendment." Around 118 years after her face-off against the judge, the courthouse exhibited an oil painting of Anthony above a bronze bust that occupied a place of honor.

The U.S. dollar coin pictured Anthony with scalloped collar and cameo. Situated in an 11-sided frame, the portrait of the suffragist in a humorless, iconic pose was more suited to hatchet-bearing temperance leader Carrie Nation than the famed Quaker orator. Characterizing Anthony as a prim, pious spinster with stereotypical bony features and hair in a tight bun, the coin provoked ridicule rather than respect. The reverse pictured the Eagle, the Apollo 11 spacecraft. Banks received little call for the coin, which was the same size and weight as a quarter. In 1981, the mint stopped striking them and began gathering in some 441 million Susan B. Anthony dollars. In 1997, Congress planned the Sacagawea dollar coin to succeed the Anthony dollar.

See also **Frank Gasparro; U.S. coins.**

SOURCES: Anthony, Susan B. "Women's Right to Vote." The American Reader. New York: HarperCollins, 1990. • Clarke, Mary Stetson, comp. *Women's Rights in the United States* (poster packet). Amawalk, N.Y.: Jackdaw, 1974. • Davidson, Cathy N., and Linda Wagner-Martin, eds-in-chief. *The Oxford Companion to Women's Writing in the United States.* New York: Oxford University Press, 1995. • Faderman, Lillian. *To Believe in Women: What Lesbians Have Done for America.* Boston: Houghton Mifflin, 1999. • Lewis, Michael J. "Of Kitsch and Coins." *Commentary,* October 1999. • Maggio, Rosalie. *The New Beacon Book of Quotations by Women.* Boston: Beacon Press, 1996. • National Women's Hall of Fame, http://www.greatwomen.org. • Sherr, Lynn, and Jurate Kazickas. *Susan B. Anthony Slept Here: A Guide to American Women's Landmarks.* New York: Times Books, 1976. • *Webster's Dictionary of American Women.* New York: Merriam-Webster Incorporated, 1996. • "Woman's Suffrage: Women's History Month." The Voter, March 2001. • *Women and Social Movements in the United States, 1830–1930,* http://womhist.binghamton.edu/index.html. • "Women's History," *The History Net,* http://womenshistory.about.com/mbody.htm.

talent

A unit of weight and monetary value, the talent, from the Greek *talanton* ("weight"), evolved in Babylon before the eighth century B.C. and remained in use by Hebrews, Egyptians, Greeks, and Romans. In ancient Greece, the talent equaled 60 *minas* or 6,000 *drachmas.* Adding to its convenience as a measure of worth was the ease of its conversion to its weight in silver, whether in rings, bracelets, bars, or ingots. In Athenian reckoning, one talent equalled 57 pounds; on the island of Aegina, it equalled 83 pounds. In the history of currency, these indexes of worth and weight preceded true coinage.

In his *Histories* (ca. 450 B.C.), the Greek historian Herodotus quantified in talents the tribute owed to the Persian kings Cyrus and Darius by their 20 provinces:

amount	*peoples in each province*
400	Aeolia, Caria, Ionia, Lycia, Magnesia, Milya, Pamphylia
500	Cabalia, Hytenia, Lasonia, Lydia, Mysia
360	Mariandynia, Paphlagonia, Phrygia, Syria, Thrace
500	Cilicia
360	Phoenicia, Syria
700	Egypt, Libya
170	Aparyta, Dadica, Gandaria, Sattagydia
300	Cissia, Susa
1000	Assyria, Babylon
450	Ecbatana, Media, Orthocorybantes, Paricania
200	Caspia, Darita, Pantimathus, Pausica
360	Bactria
400	Armenia, Pactyica
600	Mycius, Sagartia, Sarangia, Thamana, Utia
250	Caspia, Saca
300	Aria, Chorasmia, Parthia, Sogdia
400	Ethiopia, Paricania
200	Alarodia, Matienia, Saspires
300	Macrones, Mares, Moschus, Mosynoecus, Tibarenus
360	India

Of this cumbrous accounting of duties on client nations, Herodotus specified that "those who paid in silver were instructed to use the Babylonian talent as the measure of weight, while the Euboean talent was the standard for gold — the Babylonian being worth 1⅙ of the Euboean" (Herodotus 1954, p. 214). He totaled the combined talents as 14,560 in Euboean values. To manage so hefty a sum, he added that provincial treasurers melted the metal and poured it into earthenware jars. When it cooled, they chipped away the pottery, leaving a series of oversized solid metal coins in the shape of the interiors.

In 432 B.C., the sculptor Phidias and architects Callicrates and Ictinus worked within a tight budget that Pericles allotted for the completion of exterior decoration to the Parthenon, the focal point of the city of Athens. For the purchase of bronze, cypress, gold, ivory, and marble, Phidias made the most of 24 silver talents per year for the 15-year project, begun in 447 B.C. The coins also paid carters to haul marble blocks ten miles from the Pentelicus quarries and for salaries to subcontract carpenters, goldsmiths, painters, quarriers, and stonecutters. The most skilled laborers earned up to two *drachmas* daily. To assure honesty, city inspectors audited the accounts, checked payrolls for padding, and rebuked suppliers for bilking the city.

The talent was an exact measure and monetary value in numerous books of the Bible. It was the weight of David's crown in II Samuel 12:30; David's charge from God to Solomon, his son and heir, concerning the erection of the temple at Jerusalem in I Chronicles 22:14 and 29:4, 7; and the Tyrian King Hiram's gift, 120 and 420 gold talents, to Solomon to adorn the new temple in I Kings 9:14, 28. Talents quantified the military salaries of men serving Amaziah in II Chronicles 25:6, 100 talents per 100,000 men, as well as the huge treasury that Ezra entrusted to priests in Ezra 8:26–27. The talent also characterized the conniving of the hatemongering villain Haman, minister of King Ahasuerus, who plotted in Esther 3:8–9 to wipe out the Jews through hired killers, whom he paid 10,000 silver talents, and to compensate the royal treasury with plunder.

The talent was a common element in the two-part book of Kings, set about 970–586 B.C. In II Kings 5:5, Naaman, an army captain under the Syrian king, heeded the words of his wife's Hebrew maid and went to the prophet Elisha in Israel to be healed of leprosy. In payment, he carried with him 6,000 gold pieces, ten silver talents, and ten suits of clothing. Most impressive in the account was Elisha's refusal to take money for a miracle wrought by God.

In the book of Exodus, the epic narrative that comprises the second part of the Hebrew pentateuch, the adornment of the tabernacle required a precise list of bowls, candlesticks, and lamps. In Exodus 25:39, Moses followed godly injunctions to mold the holy articles from a talent of pure gold. Chapters 27 and 38 repeated the list by explaining how Bezaleel obeyed each element of God's instructions.

The gospel of Matthew created indelible stories of piety and human worth through mention of the talent. Drawn from a work by Mark around A.D. 80, the text appears to be the Aramaic writings of a publican — a tax accountant or customs agent. At the beginning of the wonder-working section, Jesus used the talent and the *denarius* as relative monetary values in the parable of the unmerciful servant, the teaching text on forgiveness read in Christian churches on the 31st Sunday after Pentecost. After a lord forgives a servant the loan of a talent, worth about $1,000, the servant turns on an underling in Matthew 18: 28–30 and demands a *denarius*, worth about 20 cents. For his wickedness, the lord jails the evil servant until he can produce the talent he owed.

Matthew's most memorable story of talents appears in chapter 25, in which Jesus expresses the importance of using gifts from God. Jesus structures the story around three gifts of five, two, and one talent from a man to the three servants he trusted to guard his property. The first two invest and double their money. The third, fearful of the lord's judgment, buries his talent. On the man's return, he lauds the faithfulness of the first two and condemns the third to penury and perpetual darkness.

The talent retained its importance to military history during the rise of republican Rome. Tributary states funneled huge quantities of precious metals weighed in talents, which an expanded market in slaves converted into coins. The boost to the Roman treasury was considerable:

country	*dates*	*amount in talents*
Carthage	264–241, 218–201 B.C.	14,000
Greece, Macedon	201–167 B.C.	15,000
Sidon	189–177 B.C.	15,000
Spain	206–196 B.C.	3,300

In addition to these terms of surrender, which added 47,300 talents to the treasury over a span of 68 years, nations also gave up their gold and silver mines to the state.

When Rome menaced Palestine, one of the most stirring of Jewish victories occurred at Jerusalem under Judas Maccabaeus, a legendary leader who warred against the Seleucid king Antiochus IV Epiphanes until 160 B.C. The Jews hung on to their religion and liberty until 63 B.C., when Pompey the Great conquered the city and annexed it to the Roman Empire. Part of the penalties paid by the losers was a fine of 10,000 talents. Another 6,000 talents bought a realm for Tigranes, whom Pompey set up as king of Armenia.

Pompey was so awed by the holy aura of the temple at Jerusalem that he viewed it like a tourist and left untouched its sacred treasury. When Crassus, a Roman notorious for greed, marched on Judea, he lacked his predecessor's sensibilities. According to *The History of the Jews* (A.D. 94), by the Romanized Hebrew historian Flavius Josephus:

> [Crassus] carried off the money that was in the temple, which Pompey had left, being two thousand talents, and disposed to spoil it of all the gold belonging to it, which was eight thousand talents. He also took a beam, which was made of solid beaten gold [Josephus 1960, p. 294].

As a sop to halt the looting of temple ornaments, the priest Eleazar, guardian of sacred treasure, had presented the beam, which was concealed in a wood sheathe. The ploy failed. Crassus broke his word and stripped the temple of the rest of its gold.

The Jews, ruled by a series of procurators or client kings appointed by Rome's emperor, chafed under hard-handed tyranny and taxation. During a revolt in A.D. 67, Gessius Florus, the Gentile governor under Nero, removed 17 talents from the temple as a means of satisfying the emperor's demands for cash. Young hotheads mimicked the sticky-fingered ruler by brandishing alms baskets at peasants in the street and begging donations for Florus. The governor dispatched legionaries into the moiling crowd, but failed to locate the culprits. In retaliation, Florus had others seized and crucified. As the Jewish War began, the death toll rose into the thousands of devout Jews willing to die for the sanctity of their sacred temple.

***See also* bible currency; shekel; trade and barter.**

SOURCES: Abbott, Walter M., et al. *The Bible Reader*. New York: Bruce Publishing Co., 1969. • Alexander, David, and Pat Alexander, eds. *Eerdmans' Handbook to the World's Religions*. Grand Rapids, Mich.: William B. Eerdmans Publishing Co., 1982. • Anderson, Bernhard W. *Understanding the Old Testament*. Englewood Cliffs, N.J.: Prentice-Hall, Inc., 1966. • Davies, Glyn. *A History of Money from Ancient Times to the Present Day*. Cardiff: University of Wales Press, 1994. • Einzig, Paul. *Primitive Money*. Oxford: Pergamon Press, 1966. • *Encyclopedia of the Ancient Greek World*. New York: Facts on File, Inc., 1995. • Herodotus. *The Histories*. London: Penguin Books, 1954. • Jeffrey, David Lyle, gen. ed. *A Dictionary of Biblical Tradition in English Literature*. Grand Rapids, Mich.: William B. Eerdmans Publishing Co., 1992. • Josephus. *Complete Works*. Grand Rapids, Mich.: Kregel Publications, 1960. • Kee, Howard Clark, Franklin W. Young, and Karlfried Froehlich. *Understanding the New Testament*. Englewood Cliffs, N.J.: Prentice-Hall, 1965. • Lockyer, Herbert. *All the Women of the Bible*. Grand Rapids, Mich.: Zondervan Publishing, 1988. • Maxey, Al. "The Lord's Supper: A Historical Overview." http://www.zianet.com/maxey/Supper5.htm. • May, Herbert G., and Bruce M. Metzger, eds. *The Oxford Annotated Bible*. New York: Oxford University Press, 1962. • Meshorer, Ya'akov. *Coins of the Ancient World*. Jerusalem: Jerusalem Publishing House, 1974. • Reinfeld, Fred. *Treasury of the World's Coins*. New York: Sterling Publishing, 1953. • Severy, Merle, ed. *Greece & Rome*. Washington, D.C.: National Geographic Society, 1977. • Snodgrass, Mary Ellen. *Encyclopedia of World Scripture*. Jefferson, N.C.: McFarland, 2001.

tally

Recognized into prehistory, a tally was a wood dowel, stick, or rod the length of a human hand and scored or notched with a V to record the amount of a debt or repayment in transactions between parties. The material itself was the source of the term "tally": it comes from the Latin *talea* meaning "wood slip." When the tally was split lengthwise, debtor and creditor could maintain a sure record of charges and installment payments. By matching up the two sides, both parties could guarantee an official, tamper-proof tally. When third parties accepted them, tallies advanced to a form of token money.

In Anglo-Saxon time, the shire reeve, later called the "sheriff," received a tally stick as a receipt for sums turned over to tellers at the exchequer's upper room. The notches hacked into the wood recorded the amount. The teller filled out a bill of receipt and dropped it through a pipe to the ground floor, where the tally-cutter struck a wood tally with the details on two of its faces. The junior deputy chamberlain split the stick end to end with a mallet or cleaver while the senior officer steadied it. The senior read aloud the data to the junior as a means of cross-checking for accuracy.

For England's treasury, the record of units sold was kept by a tallier, an Anglo-Norman term that evolved into "teller." The exchequer also issued tally sticks as receipts of taxes and loans. As described by Richard FitzNigel (also Son of Nigel or Fitzneale) in *Dialogus de Scaccario* (*The Course of the Exchequer*) (1179), a treatise on biennial treasury sessions, the original sticks were lengths of hazel around 9 inches long. Symbolically, each stroke stood for a monetary amount:

notch	*amount*
hole punched in the stick	half-penny
straight cut	1 penny
a narrow groove	1 shilling
a groove the width of a grain of barley	£1
a V the width of the tip of the little finger	£20
a curve the width of a thumb	£100
an indentation as wide as the palm	£1,000

This primitive, but effective system was an essential when one or both parties was illiterate. The creditor maintained the larger half with handle unsplit; the debtor kept the sliced half of the handle or shaft, called the "foil." If one person suspected conniving, he could demand a match-up of the two halves of the tally. The wood-notching system was still in use by Charles II in 1665, when small change was scarce. Ironically, in 1834, the burning of antique tally sticks caused a serious fire in Westminster Palace.

In China, a similar tally piece functioned as money from 1735 to 1936. The vertical slat was carved from bamboo with a string of Chinese letters and a hole at one end to accommodate a lanyard for easy portability. Worth from ⅕ to ⅒ of a penny, it served shoppers and merchants as a form of small change.

***See also* Exchequer.**

SOURCES: Allen, Larry. *Encyclopedia of Money.* New York: Checkmark Books, 2001. • Angell, Norman. *The Story of Money.* Garden City, N.Y.: Garden City Publishing, 1929. • Davies, Glyn. *A History of Money from Ancient Times to the Present Day.* Cardiff: University of Wales Press, 1994. • "Medieval Sourcebook: The Dialogue concerning the Exchequer." http://www. medievalhistory.net/excheq1.htm. • Opitz, Charles J. *Odd and Curious Money.* Ocala, Fla.: First Impressions, 1986. • *Probert Encyclopedia.* http://www.probertencyclopaedia.com/money.htm. • Sinclair, David. *The Pound.* London: Century Books, 2000. • *66 Centuries of Measurement.* Dayton, Ohio: Sheffield Measurement Division, 1984. • Snodgrass, Mary Ellen. *Encyclopedia of Kitchen History.* London: Fitzroy-Dearborn, 2002.

Tanner, Johann Sigismund

An engraver and coin maker under George II and George III of England, Johann (or John) Sigismund Tanner set the tone of coin art for the era. Trained at carving gunlocks and snuffboxes in his youth in Saxe-Gotha, he emigrated from Germany to England in 1728 and worked at the Tower Mint in London. Under the direction of mintmaster Richard Arundell, his contributions to coins covered dies for gold pieces in 1739, for coppers in 1740, and for silver coins after 1743. Some of his work emulated that of Thomas Simon, pattern maker for Oliver Cromwell.

In collaboration with engraver John Coker, Tanner made a crown coin and medals of George II and his family. The crown summarized in the word "Lima" the victory of Admiral George Anson and the crew of the *Centurion* near the Philippines. He captured Captain Jerónimo de Montero and the *Nuestra Señora de Covadonga*, a treasure ship departing from Lima, Peru, in June 1743, and returned to England with 1.25 million pounds of Spanish silver, the largest trove seized by any naval commander.

In addition, Tanner completed Milton's monument medal and the Copley medal for the Royal Society, a classical scenario featuring Pallas Athena holding a wreath and protecting a nature symbol. Biographers have logged few details of Tanner's career. He signed his work with his last name or with only the initial. He remained at work until his death in 1775. His name appears to survive in the use of "tanner" as slang for the sixpence.

***See also* treasure ships.**

SOURCES: "Admiral Anson." *Biographies*, http://blupete.com/Hist/BiosNS/1700-63/Anson.htm. • Davies, Glyn. *A History of Money from Ancient Times to the Present Day*. Cardiff: University of Wales Press, 1994. • Kemp, Peter, ed. *The Oxford Companion to Ships and the Sea*. Oxford: Oxford University Press, 1988. • "Landscape Issues." *New Arcadian Journal*, 1993. • Stephen, Sir Leslie, and Sir Sidney Lee, eds. *Dictionary of National Biography*. London: Oxford University Press, 1922.

thaler

The dollar originated from the German *thaler*, a popular silver coin influenced by the Spanish *de a ocho reales* (pieces of eight). After two centuries of minting, some 800 million of the coins had circulated, making the *thaler* the most minted silver piece in numismatic history. Early in the 16th century, Frederick III the Wise obtained cheap silver ore for minting from a major silver discovery three years earlier by Stephen, Count of Schlick, in Joachimsthal, Bohemia. In the first year of operation, the mine's rich veins produced ore, which Archduke Sigismund the Rich of Tyrol spread across western Europe. At peak production, the strike yielded 3 million ounces annually.

German coinsmiths turned the native silver into specie called *Joachimsthalers*, or *thalers* for short, the name that is the basis for the many modern currencies called "dollars." They struck the first 250,000 with the likeness of the area's patron St. Joachim, father of the Virgin Mary. The coin featured a cross and heraldic escutcheon, source of the Brazilian *cruzeiro* and the Portuguese *escudo*. By 1545, more than five million *thalers* had gone into circulation; by 1600, there were 7 million more for a total of 12 million Austrian dollar coins.

The ubiquitous term *thaler* was spelled a variety of ways in different countries:

thaler currency	*language*
daalder, rijksdaalder	Dutch
dala	Hawaiian
dalar	Norwegian
daler	Danish, Swedish
dollar	English
jefimok	Russian
jocandale	French
rigsdaler	Danish
tala	Samoan
talar	Polish
talari	Ethiopian
taler	German
tallero	Italian
tolar	Slovenia

Throughout the 1500s, German-speaking nations issued some 1,500 varieties of the coin. By the 20th century, the total number of varieties stood at 10,000. So many *thalers* entered the world coin market that the term became a synonym for currency.

Designers of *thalers* presented a variety of images of life in north central Europe. Many of these balanced, appealing coins captured the architecture and portrait artistry of the German Renaissance. A Saxon version, the silver *klappmutzentaler* (literally "folding hat dollar") was commissioned in 1519 by Frederick III the Wise, who struck dignified coins with the aid of die-masters Hans Kraft and Hans Krug at the Nürnberg mint.

In 1547, the German city of Luneburg struck a grand *thaler* picturing a somber man in the moon, an emblem drawn from the city's name, which derives from the Latin *luna* ("moon"). Picturing August, Christian, and Johann Georg of the Albertine line under their father, Christian I, one *thaler* presented the trio on the front and the royal shield on the reverse inside the inscription "*Frat. et. Duces. Saxon*" ("Brothers and Saxon Leaders"). The theme of military might influenced the engraving of other coins, notably that of Johann Wilhelm, Duke of Saxony, posed in armor in 1569.

A more complex symbolism explains the *wespentaler* ("wasp *thaler*"), also called the *mueckentaler* ("gnat *thaler*"). Minted in 1599 by Duke Heinrich Julius of Brunswick, founder of the monetary reserve system, it portrayed an eagle soaring above a lion beset by ten wasps, symbols of ten clans that rebelled and of the imperial eagle that protected the duke during the revolt. The duke also issued the *wahrheitstaler* ("truth *thaler*"), a coin minted in 1597 featuring the image of the allegorical figures of Truth overwhelming Untruth. The vast ores dug from his Harz Mountain mines enabled him to strike large *thalers*, which earned the name *Loesers* for their legend, "*Genannt Braunschweigische Julius Loeser*" ("Named the Redeemable of Julius of Brunswick").

Other interesting folk names attached to *thalers*. In 1510, the *rubentaler* ("turnip *taler*"), pictured a turnip on the crest of an archbishop. After 1616, the *thaler* of Duke Christian of Brunswick, Bishop of Halberstadt, carried the legend "*Gottes Freundt, der Pfaffen Feindt*" ("God's friend, the priests' enemy"). For this sentiment and because the mint struck the coins with silver plate from Paderborn Cathedral, the *thalers* were called *Gottesfreundtalers* ("God's friend *thaler*"). A parallel coin, the *pfarrenfeindtaler* ("priests' enemy *thaler*"), made sly reference to a feud between the Bishop of Münster and Rudolf Augustus. The Purim *thaler*, produced at Erfurt in 1631, displayed a complex obverse in Hebrew honoring the celebration of Queen Esther's triumph over anti-semitism. On the back, a lengthy statement in Latin commemorated Gustavus Adolphus's victory at Breitenfeld. Under Elector John George II of Saxony after 1656, the *beichttaler* ("confession *thaler*") earned it nickname for the amount given to church confessors by repentant sinners. Less decorous was the oversized *thaler* of Leopold the Hogmouth of Austria, a finely incised piece produced after 1658 on a roller press.

The *thaler* served the British, French, German, Italian, and Portuguese territories of Africa. After the onset of the Thirty Year's War in 1618, the coin lost its value as currency, but retained importance as an egregious show piece, displaying such as the portrait of General Eusebius Wallenstein, the crest of Rudolph II of Tyrol, hand-painted religious scenes, and images of Martin Luther, his wife Catharine von Bora, and Belgian religious reformer John Hus. Soldiers carried St. George *thalers* like St. Christopher medals and rabbits' feet as good luck pieces strong enough to deflect bullets.

In 1662, Christian Ludwig, Duke of Brunswick-Luneburg, issued a pictorial *thaler* featuring a horse bearing a crowned monogram on its flank and receiving a laurel wreath from the hand of God overhead. As though elevated from the common realm, the horse rose above a scene of ordinary life picturing miners digging silver ore for minting. Framing the scenario was an incised raised edge. Less uplifting was the ⅔ *thaler* issued by Elector Ernst August of Hanover in 1693. It received snickers from Germans who thought the portrait figure looked like it had a nosebleed, for which they dubbed it the *basenblutengulden* ("nosebleed guilder").

Eighteenth-century *thalers* perpetuated the use of coinage for self-aggrandizement and for celebrating the Protestant Reformation. Constantine Brancoveanu, founder of Transylvania's Horezu Monastery, displayed himself in striking pose with cockaded hat and national uniform on a showpiece minted in 1713 and backed with a crown and massive blazon featuring the Christian cross. The nationalism depicted by the coin was damning evidence at his trial in Istanbul on charges of treason, for which he and his heirs were decapitated. By 1750, Frederick the Great had reestablished the dignity of Prussian coinage with emphasis on the *thaler* and *pfennig* with himself pictured in glory on the gold ten-*thaler* piece. The *thaler* dominated Prussia's economy until the rise of Wilhelm I, who restructured finance in 1871 with the *mark* as its basis.

A late version, the Austrian *Maria-There-*

sien-Taler ("Maria Theresa *thaler*"), minted at Günzburg in 1773 and again at her death in 1780 by her adoring husband, Holy Roman Emperor Francis I, survived as a colonial currency until 1854. It featured a shield superimposed on a two-headed eagle and topped with a crown. A grand Prussian design, it honored a strong female ruler who was also the daughter and mother of emperors. The rimless coin proved so popular that it circulated in the Middle East and North Africa from Algeria to the Tuareg Oasis and the Sultanate of Bonou in Nigeria, always bearing the death date of 1780.

When Napoleon closed the Günzburg mint in 1805, the Vienna mint took up the task of striking Maria Theresa *thalers* and retained the old mint mark. The sentimental value of the coins prompted traveler C. F. Rey, author of *In the Country of the Blue Nile* (1927), to remark that the "Maria Theresa *Thaler* is more a commodity of facile use than a medium of exchange" (Einzig, 1966, p. 113). Subsequent reports from R. C. Cheeseman, author of *Lake Tana and the Blue Nile* (1936), noted that remote villagers preferred edible rock salt to *thalers*, which they couldn't eat.

An unusual thaler, the *schlafrockthaler* ("nightshirt *thaler*"), was the humorous name for the convention *thaler* of 1816 in ridicule of the blousy dress uniform of Frederick Augustus I of Saxony. Another, the *angsttaler* ("taler of fear") originated under Grand Duke Friedrich Franz II of Mecklenburg-Schwerin in 1845. Because he chose to omit the initials V. G. G., standing for "*Von Gottes Gnaden*" ("At God's Mercy"), and struck only a few coins, citizens interpreted his decision as terror of revolt. In 1829, coin sculptor Karl Voigt, mintmaster at Munich, featured the history of King Louis I of Bavaria in *thalers*. Scenes of his rise to power and landmarks and buildings he raised congratulated him for his patronage of the arts and for turning Munich into a world-class city.

The approach of World War II resulted in alterations to coinage and the spelling of specie names. In 1937, the year before Hitler overran Austria, the British Royal Mint manufactured the Maria Theresa *thaler* for trade in North and East Africa. In 1936, Mussolini challenged the Ethiopian *talari* with an Italian version, the *tallero*, minted at Rome. Picturing the Emperor Haile Selassie I, modernizer of Ethiopia, the paper *thalers* accorded dignity to a national hero who introduced his nation to the League of Nations and United Nations and established Addis Ababa as the center of the Organization of African Unity. Among his innovations were a strong police force, schools and public health care for all, and an end to feudal taxation. The Ethiopian *thaler* remained legal tender until 1948.

See also **dollar; Frederick the Great; *gulden; klippe; mark;* pfennig; pieces of eight; Rix dollars; siege money.**

SOURCES: Allen, Larry. *Encyclopedia of Money*. New York: Checkmark Books, 2001. • "The Artistry of African Currency." http://www.nmafa.si.edu/exhibits/site/manillas.htm. • Cribb, Joe. *Money*. Toronto: Stoddart, 1990. • "Curious Names." http://www.moneymuseum.ch/standard_english/raeume/geld–lieben/ueberlieferung/sprachliches/ • Davies, Glyn. *A History of Money from Ancient Times to the Present Day*. Cardiff: University of Wales Press, 1994. • Einzig, Paul. *Primitive Money*. Oxford: Pergamon Press, 1966. • Kiernan, Philip. "Alfred Petrie Leaves His Coins to the National Currency Collection." *Canadian Numismatic Association Journal*, October 2001, 389–395. • Lewis, Brenda Ralph. *Coins & Currency*. New York: Random House, 1993. • Reinfeld, Fred. *Treasury of the World's Coins*. New York: Sterling Publishing, 1953. • Weatherford, Jack. *The History of Money: From Sandstone to Cyberspace*. Pittsburgh, Pa.: Three Rivers Press, 1998.

Throckmorton, Peter

Author and historian Peter Throckmorton was a founder of marine archeology and discoverer of the two oldest sunken ships ever excavated, dating to 2500 B.C. and 1300 B.C. Born on July 30, 1928, in boyhood, he loved sea lore and combed the Maine shores for shipwrecks. He prepared for his unusual career as research associate at the University of Pennsylvania Museum at the University of Hawaii, University of the Americas in Mexico City, and the Institute of Ethnology at the University of Paris. In addition to theory, he mastered carpentry, sailing, and six foreign languages — French, German, Greek, Italian, Spanish, and Turkish — and picked up a working knowledge of Japanese and Tahitian.

Throckmorton's early interest in salvage furthered his work as a tanker engineer and deep-sea fishing boat manager in Honolulu. He moved closer to his childhood love of shipwrecks with a salvage business in the Hawaiian Islands. As a teacher at the University of Chicago, Villa Giulia Museum, and the Hellenic Institute of Nautical Archaeology, he educated students in ship history and launched marine projects and produced television documentaries on the science of undersea salvage.

In 1958, Turkish diver Kemal Aras informed Throckmorton of the discovery of an eastern trading vessel from 1200 B.C. in the "Ship Trap," a naval graveyard off the west coast of the Bodrum peninsula at Yassiada, Turkey. A team began the world's first undersea archeological excavation in 1960 and completed the first seabed study directed by a diving archeologist. Downed after striking a submerged pinnacle in the reign of Emperor Heraclius during a siege on Constantinople, the trader bore 1,000 wine amphorae, the stock of owner and merchant Giorgios Presbyteros Naukleros, as well as scarabs from Syria.

With advice from the University of Pennsylvania, Throckmorton initiated the first application of land-based archeological method to sea-floor artifacts. He, fellow salvor George Bass, and museum curator Oguz Alpozen established a base of operations aboard the *Lutfi Gelil* and set to work recovering relics. Among the rocks on the sandy bottom was a load of tin and copper. Because these elements were the makings of bronze weapons, Throckmorton and team mused on the possibility that the trader may have been supplying Greeks or Trojans fighting at Troy in the war that supplied Homer with the plot of the *Iliad* (ca. 850 B.C.).

In addition to recovering pottery, pine planking, iron spikes, a grill and firebox, and roof tiles, the team hammmered away a lump of concrescence eight inches thick to reveal the gold and copper coins that substantiated the date of the wreckage. The Cypriot copper consisted of 34 flat, four-handled ingots, forerunners of modern currency shaped like tanned ox hides, the type of barter media that prefigured money. Specialists surmised that the ox hide ingots represented the worth of a cow or an ox. The salvors placed their finds in the Bodrum Museum of Underwater Archaeology, a dilapidated castle transformed by Throckmorton and Bass into a modern public facility.

One of the high points of Throckmorton's career was his management of the National Maritime Historical Society. He expounded on his discoveries in numerous published works, including *The Lost Ships* (1964), *Surveying in Archaeology Underwater* (1969), *Shipwrecks and Archaeology: The Unharvested Sea* (1970), *Diving for Treasure* (1977), *The Sea Remembers: Shipwrecks and Archaeology from Homer's Greece to the Rediscovery of the Titanic* (1987), and articles for *Archaeology, Argosy, Atlantic Monthly, Expedition, Greek Heritage, Journal of Nautical Archaeology*, and *National Geographic*. After establishing the foundations of undersea excavation, Throckmorton added to the world's knowledge of ancient ship-building, navigational methods, commerce, and trade routes. In the 1970s, he searched for ancient ships off the Falkland Islands near Cape Horn, the dreaded graveyard of ships rounding the Americas in the centuries preceding the building of the Panama Canal. He died in Newcastle, Maine, on June 5, 1990.

***See also* George F. Bass; underwater archeology.**

SOURCES: Bass, George F., ed. *Ships and Shipwrecks of the Americas: A History Based on Underwater Archaeology*. London: Thames and Hudson, 1996. • *Contemporary Authors Online*. Farmington Hills, Mich.: Gale Group, 2000. • Fowler, Glenn. "Peter Throckmorton, Archeologist of Ancient Shipwrecks, Dies at 61." *New York Times*, June 11, 1990. • Norton, Trevor. *Stars Beneath the Sea*. London: Random House, 1999. • Sullivan, Mark, "Sunken Vessel near Turkey Believed to Date to 1,500 B.C." *New York Times*, October 30, 1982. • Throckmorton, Peter. "Oldest Known Shipwreck Yields Bronze Age Cargo." *National Geographic*, May 1962, pp. 696–711.

tokens

Tokens resemble coins, but serve as substitutes for legal tender, as with gambling tokens from Monaco after 1860, mining company tokens produced in Greenland after 1910, German *Rechenpfennige* (reckoning counters), and the wood chips used as gambling markers in Puerto Rico. The use of tokens as propaganda or tools of public relations dates to the disk-shaped *tesserae* ("tickets") of the Romans. They served as admission tokens for athletic contests and circuses and bore the number of the tier and seat in a theater or amphitheater. One class, the copper and brass *spintria* (literally, "male prostitute"), exhibited titillating designs of sexual organs and coital positions and appear to have allowed the bearer entrance to the *lupinaria* (bordello). According to Suetonius's *De Vita Caesarum* (ca. A.D. 110), the nickname "spintria" was also the nickname of the dissolute emperor Vitellius, who was murdered in A.D. 69. Roman politicians currying favor distributed to the lowest class traditional *congiarium* ("gifts") consisting of coins, bronze *tesserae frumentariae* ("food tokens"), or *tesserae nummariae* ("coin tokens"), which they threw to mobs and crowds following a procession on public streets. The tokens often commemorated a crowning, military victory, or imperial birthday.

From the first century B.C., Celtic monetary systems relied on tokens, stamped metal disks made of *potin,* an alloy of copper, lead, zinc, and tin. These vouchers or scrip were tangible representations of abstract credit that suited the transactions of individuals with employers, companies, and traders. The amount indicated or stamped on the surface equaled the face value or exchange rate for legal tender.

Under Henry VIII, the need for tokens for small market transactions derived from a lack of small change. At meat stalls, the price of a pound of beef was a half-penny, mutton was three farthings, and veal the most complicated at ⅝ of a penny. The only way for butchers to make change was with tokens. Swiss tourist Thomas Platter, author of *Journal of a Younger Brother: The Life of Thomas Platter as a Medical Student in Montpellier at the Close of the Sixteenth Century* (1599), found the system still in use in 1599, when London tradesmen were issuing pieces valued down to 1⁄12 of a penny. Grocer Edward Bryan at Gargrave, Yorkshire, commissioned his own penny portion in 1671, as did officials of the city of Bath. Under James I, the number of English tokens rose as some 3,000 merchants ordered their own small change.

The system of circulating metallic token moneys intensified during the rise of banking in the early 1700s. In the village of Bilston, England, issuance of copper and iron token coins allowed a closed system of flow through the Midlands and North Wales. In 1787, the Anglesey Copper company of Wales ordered a Druid penny made from ore from the local Parys mine. The token penny, featuring the cowled head of a druid enwreathed in branches, was good only for purchases at company offices and shops. The Parys Mines Company copied the idea in 1791 with a Druid penny of its own. Other towns emulated the system by purchasing planchets, choosing die designs, and producing such pieces as the Lady Godiva coin stamped at Coventry.

In 1796, Philip Parry Price Myddelton, an English developer of land in Kentucky, had Conrad Küchler design dies for the Myddelton token. Struck in silver at the Boulton & Watt steam-operated system in Birmingham, England, the token advertised employment possibilities to hundreds of farm workers seeking opportunity in America. Myddelton failed to carry through on the promise of his tokens after he was jailed at Newgate Prison for treason because of the pro–American bias of the motif. However, the crown was so intrigued at the quality of private minting that, in 1797, its minting agents contracted with Matthew Boulton to turn 50 tons of copper into pence and twopence coins.

In June 1797, the Bank of England produced silver tokens from confiscated Spanish and Spanish-American dollars that the mint counterstamped. The stop-gap measure failed as the price of silver rose, forcing a recall after three months. In 1799, the measure once more became feasible after England captured two Spanish treasure ships laden with New World specie and forced down the price of silver. In 1802, as the price continued to tumble, private entrepreneurs began emulating the bank by manufacturing their own dollars. The rise of silver prices in 1804 ended the flood of tokens.

A second rise in copper and silver token stamping in 1811 forced the English government to acknowledge its loss of authority as producer of legal tender. One piece, the Merthyr silver piece, carried the names of Leeds, London, Swansea, and York along with the disclaimer, "To Facilitate Trade Change Being Scarce" (Davies 1994, p. 296). The Bank of England's loss of control provoked dishonest manufacturers to circulate counterfeit coins. For forging sheaf tokens and three-shilling pieces resembling the issue of the Bank of England, farmer William Booth went to the gallows in 1812. A stiffer law prohibiting tokens passed in 1817, yet the government extended token rights, such as those of the Poor Law unions. When coinage finally met demand in 1821, makeshift change was no longer needed.

English tokens influenced mercantile and industrial concerns in Australia, Canada, and New Zealand to issue tokens, including an 1874 Thames Goldfields token featuring the mining office and derrick and the 1881 penny portrait disk of a Maori warrior from New Zealand. The in-house porcelain *salung* issued by the casinos of Thailand in 1850 remained in circulation late in the century. Observed at Zimmé between Siam and Burma by British imperial publicist Holt S. Hallett, author of *A Thousand Miles on an Elephant in the Shan States* (1890), octagonal gaming counters served as informal small change late in the 19th century. Marked with Chinese lettering, the pieces were worth from two to four *annas*.

The value of the unofficial tokens depended on the solvency of the Chinese gaming house owners who monopolized trade. When one owner lost his hold on business, he hired a crier to walk the streets, beating a gong and calling in token money for exchange. The grace period extended over three days, after which the tokens were worthless. The Far Eastern token remained in circulation until replaced by coppers from Bangkok.

One Canadian token producer, entrepreneur William Cowan, wholesaler in liquors and tobacco and builder of the Victoria Hotel in Revelstoke, British Columbia, issued a brass disk marked with his name and city on the front and "Good for One 15¢ Drink" on the reverse. The trade piece served salesmen passing through on the Canadian Pacific Railway after 1885 and was redeemable at the Central Hotel and Cowan's hotel. Around 1903, Alexander C. Cummins, merchant and owner of a general store in Ferguson, B.C., commissioned a similar brass token stamped with his name and town on the front and "Good for 12½¢ in Trade" on the back.

In the United States, hoarding produced a coin shortage during the depression of 1837–1838. To supply change, individuals and companies issued copper pennies, which citizens dubbed "Hard Times" tokens during the two-year period of high unemployment. Some bore political slogans, advertisements, and merchants' names. During the Civil War, 50 million private-issue pennies came into use in over 8,000 designs in 22 states. Arising from the need for small change to facilitate commerce, the Civil War token helped to bridge a gap in legal tender.

Struck at the same thickness and diameter as a U.S. penny, the pieces featured an array of legends, designs, and images. They matched a motif and date on the front with advertisements, for example:

- E. Townley Hives & Bees, Mount Auburn, Cincinnati
- If you get sick use Dr. Bennett's Medicine
- M. L. Marshall, Oswego, New York, Toys, fancy goods, fishing tackle, and rare coin
- H. B. Xelar Wine & Beer Saloon
- Brighton House, Lew. Boman
- Benjamin & Herrick Fruit Dealers, Albany, New York.

- C. Runyon Groceries, Market Street, Springfield, Ohio
- Straight's Elephantine Shoe Store, Broadway, Albany, New York
- John Grether, importer of china & queensware, Columbus, Ohio
- The Federal Union, It must and shall be preserved.

One unusual token was a metal dish bearing a postage stamp. In April 1864, Congress prohibitied further issue of pennies, tokens, or other monetary substitutions. In June 1964, a law halted all private coinage.

During World War I, tokens solved the problem of locating suitable material for coinage. While German manufacturers were melting down bronze coins to make military equipment, the treasury tried issuing *Notmünzen* ("emergency coins") in aluminum, iron, and zinc, as well as tokens. At the height of the shortage of money, the government printed *Notgelden* ("emergency money"), which survived a brief circulation until hard currency returned to use. A familiar token in France, Italy, Israel, Poland, and Hungary from the 20th century, the *gettone* or *jeton* substitutes for coins in accessing a pay telephone. In the 1970s, Italian merchants were so short on small coins that they used *gettones* or hard candies for making change.

See also **Matthew Boulton; Celtic money; colonial coins; Confederate money; elephant token; English money; food stamps; Muhammad ibn Tughluq; penny; Peter I;**

Tokens such as this 1971 advertisement piece for Top of the Mart in New Orleans commemorate local history.

The reverse of the New Orleans token reflects local pride in Mississippi history with a picture of the Delta Queen, a tourist sternwheeler in the tradition of nineteenth-century river transportation.

The Hawaiian Chamber of Commerce issued this 1975 Kona dollar token as an advertisement encouraging tourism.

The reverse of the Kona dollar summarizes Hawaii's natural attractions—mountains, palm trees, and miles of sandy beaches.

postage currency; Roman coins — Monarchy and republic; tally.

SOURCES: Cribb, Joe. *Money*. Toronto: Stoddart, 1990. • Cribb, Joe, Barrie Cook, and Ian Carradice. *The Coin Atlas*. London: Little, Brown and Co., 1999. • Davies, Glyn. *A History of Money from Ancient Times to the Present Day*. Cardiff: University of Wales Press, 1994. • Einzig, Paul. *Primitive Money*. Oxford: Pergamon Press, 1966. • *Encyclopedia of the Roman Empire*. New York: Facts on File, Inc., 1994. • Green, Ronald. "A. C. Cummins of Ferguson, B.C." *Canadian Numismatic Association Journal*, October 2001, 386–388. • Green, Ronald. "W. Cowan, Revelstoke, B.C." *Canadian Numismatic Association Journal*, November 2001, 428–431. • Grierson, Philip. *Numismatics*. London: Oxford University Press, 1975. • Jacobs, Wayne L. "Canada's First Coinage." *Canadian Numismatic Association Journal*, July/August 1995. • Jacobs, Wayne L. "The Mystery of the Disappearing P.E.I. 'Dumps.'" *Canadian Numismatic Association Journal*, November 2001, 433–438. • Lewis, Brenda Ralph. *Coins & Currency*. New York: Random House, 1993. • Powell, John. "The Birmingham Coiners, 1770–1816." *History Today*, July 1993, pp. 49–55. • Reed, Mort. *Cowles Complete Encyclopedia of U.S. Coins*. New York: Cowles Book Company, 1969. • Reinfeld, Fred. *Treasury of the World's Coins*. New York: Sterling Publishing, 1953. • Shanks, Hershel. "Solomon's Blessings." *Biblical Archaeology Review*, September/October 2001, pp. 46–47.

tooth money

The assessment of the worth of objects from nature has boosted such objects as stones, hides, elephant tusks, and the teeth of dogs, whales, and boars to the equivalent of legal tender. Ivory, a valuable commodity for its scarcity and low gloss, served some Africans as money, particularly in Uganda and Gabon. In his book *Journal of the Discovery of the Source of the Nile* (1863), explorer John Hanning Speke, gold medalist of the French Geographical Society and discoverer of Lake Victoria in 1858, witnessed ivory exchanged like coins. Explorer of the Congo and Uganda and author of *In Darkest Africa* (1890) Henry M. Stanley himself offered ivory as money.

Unlike rare ivory tusks, the teeth of other animals are more common in monetary history. In Alaska and British Columbia, Pacific Coast tribes relied on bear teeth for currency; the Bannock and Shoshone of the northern plains used elk tooth currency for adorning future brides. Solomon Islanders combined large numbers of porpoise, dog, or flying fox teeth and strings of shells in negotiations for the purchase of a wife. Because each porpoise produced up to 150 teeth, to halt inflation, taboos limited the slaughter of the porpoise to ritual ceremonies only on set days. Equivalents in other commodities offered alternatives to teeth. For one wife or a slave boy, a buyer on San Christobal might pay 100 dogs' teeth, 1,000 sticks of tobacco, 5,000 porpoise teeth, or 10,000 coconuts. A parallel system on the Admiralty Islands in 1900 set bride price at 100 strings of dogs' teeth or 3,000 shell strings. By 1929, the value of a dog's tooth equated with 10 taro roots or coconuts or 40 betel nuts.

In New Guinea, big purchases required the expenditure of boar tusks or many dog canines. In the New Hebrides, boars with their tusks intact served as livestock money and symbols of wealth and power. The removal of upper canines ended wear from grinding and produced tusks in overlapping circles beyond 360 degrees. These rounds earned up to thirty pounds each in the years preceding World War II. Another method of payment was a string of bat teeth, used for the purchase of nets and spears. The Yap of Micronesia maintained five styles of payment — in *ray* or round limestone money pierced at center, *reng* or turmeric compressed into a ball, *yar* or shell money, *mbul* or betel nut sheaths, and *gaw*, necklaces strung with scrimshaw carved onto shells and whale teeth.

On Fiji, islanders valued *tambua* (or *tabua)*, sperm whale teeth used as currency and presented polished teeth in payment of a bride price or for the purchase of a canoe. As ambassadorial gifts to chiefs at meetings and discussions of war and peace, the teeth served as symbols of dignity and sincerity. As guest gifts to respected visitors or an introduction of business meetings, funerals, or marital arrangements, the teeth broke the ice between parties. Recipients judged the gifts in terms of size and luster. The teeth were so sacred and so integral a part of island wealth that laws forbade their export.

As described in Glyn Davies's *A History of Money from Ancient Times to the Present Day* (1994), Fijians tossed the contents of a chest of gold coins like frisbees or tiddly winks. Devalued because they had no established prestige, the captured loot lacked the allure of polished whale teeth, a sacred item that Captain James Cook's seagoing contemporaries observed dyed red and strung on a necklace. In the *Journals of Captain James Cook on His Voyages of Discovery* (1774), Cook reported that natives of Fiji and Tonga valued *tambua* for religious and ritual purposes. The derivation of "taboo" relates to *tambua* and its relation to proper or ethical behavior. In 1874, a Fijian official requested that the British bureaucracy pay him in tooth money. During a royal visit of Queen Elizabeth II in 1982, greeters presented her with a whale tooth.

See also **shell money.**

SOURCES: Allen, Larry. *Encyclopedia of Money.* New York: Checkmark Books, 2001. • Clain-Stefanelli, Elvira, and Vladimir Clain-Stefanelli. *The Beauty and Lore of Coins, Currency, and Medals.* Croton-on-Hudson, N.Y.: Riverwood Publishers, 1974. • Davies, Glyn. *A History of Money from Ancient Times to the Present Day.* Cardiff: University of Wales Press, 1994. • Einzig, Paul. *Primitive Money.* Oxford: Pergamon Press, 1966. • Opitz, Charles J. *Odd and Curious Money.* Ocala, Fla.: First Impressions, 1986. • Weatherford, Jack. *The History of Money: From Sandstone to Cyberspace.* Pittsburgh, Pa.: Three Rivers Press, 1998.

touch coins

The touch coin, an element of faith healing, replaced the laying on of hands in a medieval English ceremony involving the king's power to cure scrofula, a tubercular condition of the glands causing lumps to arise on throat and neck and to suppurate and burst. The cure for the disease, called the "King's Evil," resulted from contact with a monarch's hand, the recitation of biblical passages by the royal chaplain, and receipt of intercessory prayer and an amulet coin.

Initiated in England by the saintly Edward the Confessor, the laying on of hands was a simple blessing, a parallel to acts of the biblical suffering servant and the ministrations of Christ. Under Henry II in the 12th century, the English version of the ceremony involved the certification of illness by parish clergy and church wardens. Sufferers carrying their signed permissions letters approached the chair where the king sat among courtiers. After the reading of Mark 16, the account of Christ's resurrection, the chief surgeon escorted each subject forward for the king to stroke along face and neck. For each patient, the attendants repeated the last half of verse 18, "They shall lay hands on the sick, and they shall recover." The Clerk of the Closet presented the ritual gold coin on a white silk ribbon for the king to drape around the patient's throat as the chaplain read verse 9, which mentions Christ's casting out of demons. After prayers, the lord chamberlain held a ewer of water for the king to rinse his hands.

Attractive touch coins survive from centuries of the laying on of hands and distribution of talisman coins or the sketching of a cross with a coin over the body of the sick to confer healing. Late in the 1300s, Richard II issued a half-groat touch piece featuring a cross with equal arms extending to the rim. A century later, English jurist Sir John Fortescue spoke of the healing touch and amulet coins in *De Laudibus Legum Angliae* (*On Praise of English Law*) (ca. 1475):

> And sithen the Kinges of England ben enoynted in theyre hands, and by vertue and meane thereof God commonlie healeth sickness, by putting to and touching the maladie, by the nontinge hands; and also gould and silver handled by them; and so offered on Good Friday have ben the meane and cause of great cures [Hastings 1951, VII, p. 737].

He added that the success of these sessions of faith healing raised a demand for healing coins, but noted that the accession of a queen would halt the practice, because women could not be anointed with holy oil.

By 1549, the *Book of Common Prayer* contained the liturgy of healing, which incorporated the Lord's Prayer. The Tudors continued the healing touch, which remained one on one and personal into the reign of Henry VII, who performed hands-on healing to a reading of the ceremony in Latin. He ended each personal ministration with a gift of a small gold coin in token of the alms once bestowed by Edward I.

Henry had the touch coins struck especially for the relief of sickness. The coin, called an "angel," was pierced and threaded on a lanyard for hanging about the seeker's neck. To the superstitious, the power to heal was a public proof of the divine right of kings, a concept that the royal line carried God's blessing. The ceremonies usually took place in London during the cool seasons of Easter, Whitsuntide, and Michaelmas, but additional rituals could be scheduled at Bath, Chester, Langley, Newmarket, Oxford, and Salisbury.

Henry VIII's gift of seven shillings and sixpence appears in *Breviarie of Health* (1547), compiled by the royal physician Andrew Boorde. Henry's daughter, Queen Elizabeth I, gloried in the ritual as a method of securing the love and thanks of her subjects. William Tooker's *Charisma* (1597) declared that she healed thousands of sick subjects by touching. Historians differ over her agreement or refusal to make the sign of the cross over the sick. A surgeon, William Clowes, author of *Treastise for the Artificial Cure of the Malady Called in Latin Struma* (1602), corroborated cures claimed by Elizabeth's staff.

Elizabeth's successor, James I, the former James VI of Scotland, disdained the notion of a healing touch. Nonetheless, an eyewitness, Thomas Fuller, was present in childhood when King James alleviated the sick at Salisbury Cathedral with the touch of his hand. James reinstated the ceremony in 1605, when his minter produced the first angel coins of his reign, lucky amulets known as touch coins or touchpieces.

The playwright William Shakespeare acknowledge the resumption of the kingly act, which is the subject of a speech by Malcolm, son of the murdered King Duncan in Act IV, Scene iii, ll. 140–159 of *Macbeth* (ca. 1603–1606). Malcolm explains to Macduff, a rebel against Macbeth, the nature and purpose of the healing touch:

> A most miraculous work in this good king,
> Which often, since my here-remain in England,
> I have seen him do. How he solicits heaven,
> Himself best knows; but strangely-visited people,
> All swol'n and ulcerous, pitiful to the eye,
> The mere despair of surgery, he cures,
> Hanging a golden stamp about their necks,
> Put on with holy prayers; and 'tis spoken,
> To the succeeding royalty he leaves
> The healing benediction [Shakespeare 1964, p. 59].

The speech concludes with other virtues of the king, including the gift of prophecy, blessings, and grace.

Charles I issued a proclamation inviting his ailing subjects to a private audience for the touch ceremony. Because the treasury could ill afford gold, the king substituted silver touchpieces. Most powerful were the portrait crown pieces of Charles I, who conferred healing for paralysis and rheumatism as well as scrofula. Superstitious sufferers collected coins at church entrances and hammered them into silver rings to ease infirmity.

After the 11-year Commonwealth, Charles's son and successor, Charles II, brought the touch ceremony to its height. As summarized in Thomas Babington Macaulay's *History of England from the Accession of James I* (1848), the king conducted the healing ceremony at the banquet hall of Whitehall, where he touched over time a total of 92,107 patients, beginning with only 2,983 in 1669. Sir John Evelyn notes in his *Diary* (1706) that, on March 28, 1684, so great a mob arose seeking admission tickets to the ritual that they trampled underfoot six or seven of the smallest and weakest.

James II, who came to the throne in 1685, restored the original holy office and the sign of the cross for use in public and private healing audiences. In addition to publishing the ceremony in 1686, he struck an elegant, spiritual touchpiece depicting the archangel Michael slaying a dragon with a pike topped with a cross. The designer ringed the scene with the pious phrase "*Soli Deo Gloria*" ("To God Alone Be the Glory"). James conferred healing on throngs of people, as noted in the journal of Bishop Cartwright on August 27, 1687, when the king began welcoming the sick at 9:00 A.M. and saw 350 patients. For those who could not afford to travel to the laying on of hands ritual, guilds and individual donors defrayed the cost. James's modified ceremony was printed in Hamon L'Estrange's *Alliance of Divine Offices Exhibiting all the Liturgies of the Church of England since the Reformation* (1699).

Britain's issuance of touch coins to the sick faltered under the skeptic William III, who failed to heal with his touch. The special mintage continued into the time of Queen Anne, England's last Stuart monarch and the last to claim divine right of rule. She touched 200 victims for disease. The last suppliant was Dr. Samuel Johnson as a toddler in 1712. The coin she applied carried the likeness of England's patron St. George slaying the dragon with a ship on reverse. The inscription read "*Anna D. G. M. Br. F. et H. Reg.*" ("Anne, by the Grace of God, Queen of Great Britain, France, and Ireland"). The first Hanoverian, King George I, a cold and distant German ruler, brought ignominy on himself from Jacobites for abolishing the practice of touching the sick.

Copies of touchpieces were part of the ritual of Stuart pretenders. In 1745, Prince Charles Edward ministered to an ailing child at Holyrood Palace in Edinburgh. Additional touch coins were issued under the orders of James III and Henry IX, Cardinal Duke of York, the last legitimate heir of James II. The ceremony also flourished in Holland, Hungary, Scandinavia, and Spain.

In France, the healing touch first emerged during the reign of Anne of Clovis in A.D. 481 Philip I, the Capetian monarch who came to power in 1059, was the first king to touch the sick. He applied the phrase, "*Le roi te touche, Dieu te guérit*" ("The king touches thee, God heals thee"). He lost his healing power because of immorality. Under St. Louis IX, the touch returned after the king made a pilgrimage to Corbeny to the shrine of St. Marcoul, who was Abbot of Nanteuil until A.D. 552. At throngs of the sick in a church, cloisters, or park, he continued the ritual faith healing and distributed through the grand almoner a coin to each.

Endowed with the hands-on power against St. Marcoul's Evil, the French name for scrofula, later kings — Charles VII, Louis XI, Charles VIII, Francis I — continued to make the pilgrimage to assure their healing power. After the crowning of Henri IV at Chartres in 1594, the king ministered to 1,500 sufferers, among whom the royal physician Laurentius identified over 750 cures. At the hospital of Saint-Marcoul, as pictured in Peter Lowe's *Discourse of the Whole Art of Chyrurgie* (1612), Henry received the sick on his knees and made a sign of the cross on the sufferer's forehead. The king altered the formulaic phrase to "*Le roi te touche, Dieu te guerisse*" ("The king touches thee, may God heal thee") (Brewer).

Later French monarchs had mixed feelings about faith healing. Louis XIV treated 2,600 after his crowning and, on Easter 1686, around 1,600 patients, to whom he intoned a tender, comforting phrase. He presented French seekers 15 *sous* in coin and twice that amount to foreigners. His successor, Louis XV, shortened the distance of the annual pilgrimage to Corbeny by transferring St. Marcoul's relics to the Abbey of Saint-Remi, where the king touched over 2,000. Louis XVIII declined to confer healing, but, after 1824, Charles X restored the ceremony.

***See also* Edward the Confessor.**

SOURCES: "Brewer Dictionary of Phrase and Fable." http://www.bibliomania.com. • Cavendish, Richard, ed. *Man, Myth & Magic*. New York: Marshall Cavendish, 1970. • Clain-Stefanelli, Elvira, and Vladimir Clain-Stefanelli. *The Beauty and Lore of Coins, Currency, and Medals*. Croton-on-Hudson, N.Y.: Riverwood Publishers, 1974. • *Encyclopedia of World Biography*. Detroit: Gale Group, 1998. • Farmer, David Hugh. *The Oxford Dictionary of Saints*. Oxford: Oxford University Press, 1992. • Freeman, Anthony. *The Moneyer and the Mint in the Reign of Edward the Confessor*. Oxford: B. A. R. British Series 145, 1985. • Hastings, James, ed. *Encyclopedia of Religion and Ethics*. New York:

Charles Scribner's Sons, 1951. • "The Life of King Edward the Confessor." http://www.lib.cam.ac.uk/cgi-bin/Ee.3.59/bytext. • Magnusson, Magnus. *Cambridge Biographical Dictionary*. Cambridge: University of Cambridge, 1990. • *New Catholic Encyclopedia*. San Francisco: Catholic University of America, 1967. • Parker, Michael St. John. *Britain's Kings and Queens*. Andover, Hants: Pitkin, 1994. • Pollak, Henry. *Coinage & Conflict*. Clifton, N.J.: Coin & Currency Institute, 2001. • Shakespeare, William. *Macbeth Complete Study Edition*. Lincoln, Neb.: Cliffs Notes, 1964. • Snodgrass, Mary Ellen. *Who's Who in the Middle Ages*. Jefferson, N.C.: McFarland, 2001.

touchstone

In the Middle Ages, merchants, moneylenders, and government agents in the field tested the purity and fineness of metal coins by submitting them to the touchstone test. Most common were touch pieces of opaque brown, red, or yellow quartz or jasper or a lump of fine-grained schist called Lydian stone or basanite, a striated crystallize rock easily split into layers. The subject drew the coin over the stone surface and studied the trace of metal in the streak removed by friction. The coloration proved the purity of a metal or alloy. To determine variance, the tester used proven metals assembled for the purpose of comparison. Unlike assaying, which determined purity by weight and chemical makeup, the touchstone test was a suitable alternative for on-the-spot questions about the authenticity of coinage, particularly international moneys.

The final word on value in England was the Worshipful Company of Goldsmiths, a guild organized in 1281 under Edward I. As arbiters of minting, they maintained test pieces for silver and gold called "touch needles," which offered colors for comparison with suspect metals. Combined with the trial by the pyx, the analysis of metal established the monetary standards of the realm, which officials applied most meticulously at the Royal Mint in London. In the 20th century, except in the Near East and India, the touchstone test gave place to ocular and x-ray spectrometry, the nitric acid test, and microchemical analysis.

See also **hallmark; Sir Isaac Newton; trial of the pyx.**

SOURCES: Allen, Larry. *Encyclopedia of Money*. New York: Checkmark Books, 2001. • Davies, Glyn. *A History of Money from Ancient Times to the Present Day*. Cardiff: University of Wales Press, 1994. • Grierson, Philip. *Numismatics*. London: Oxford University Press, 1975. • Sinclair, David. *The Pound*. London: Century Books, 2000. • Weatherford, Jack. *The History of Money: From Sandstone to Cyberspace*. Pittsburgh, Pa.: Three Rivers Press, 1998.

trade and barter

The need for an exchange medium began around 9000 B.C., when traders used uncoined precious metal as well as grain, hides, mahogany and sandalwood, jade, ivory, feathers, eggs, sugar, beads, canoes, quartz, salt, nails, axes, even rats, body paint, and slave women as a means of paying for goods and services. Among the Lapps of northern Norway, the standard trade was either furs or reindeer. For native Americans, wampum belts or strings and weapons were the common exchange on a par with sugar money and leaf tobacco in Barbados, Jamaica, and the Leeward Islands. In Oceania until the 1940s, Palau islanders carved *toluk* dish money from turtle shells and polished them with sand and sandstone. The saucers were gender specific and used only for women's purchases. Sumba islanders of Indonesia wove copper wire into chains with thick blunted ends. Owners pledged the chains at the signing of a contract or the negotiation of a bride price. For storing value, the Anakalang, Lamboya, and Lauli of Sumba wear brass or bronze *mamuli*, earrings shaped like female genitalia. Families accept the ornaments as betrothal gifts along with livestock, weapons, and gold.

The creation of an abstract unit of account in a standard measure simplified exchange and made payment easier and less often a cause for quarrels. Trade in identifiable units simplified deferred payment and the storage and securing of money upon its receipt as well as subsequent taxation and duties, which were also figured in monetary amounts.

The trade of commodities in money units impacted language as well as the economy. From the Roman *pecus* ("cow"), counted by the head, came the general term *pecunia* ("money"), the generic Latin term for all currency.

Standardized metrology replaced guessing with the exact proportions or weight of a single unit. It was the Sumerians, Babylonians, Egyptians, and Harappans of the Indus Valley who standardized weights and measures as a means of quantifying expenditures and receipts. As a marketing aid, around 5000 B.C., Egyptian inventors crafted a rudimentary balance beam or equal-arm balance with which to weigh the copper rings they used as coins. A primitive hand-held, dual-pan scale, it applied the physics of equal weight suspended from a central post on two trays dangling from cords on which they weighed ring money. In 3500 B.C., Egyptian traders systematized weights and measures for dry and liquid purchases:

Egyptian Term	*Current Equivalent*
hekat	5.2 quarts
khar (one sack)	20 hekats or 103.4 quarts
deben	3.2 ounces

In Thebes around 1650 B.C., Ahmes (or Ahmose), scribe of Amenemhet III, wrote out a summary of Egyptian weights and measures recording storage and sale of beer and bread.

To measure units of compensation, the dual-pan scale, named in the *Arthashastra* and the *Vajanaseyi Samhita*, became the standard for market transactions among the Harappans, residents of the Indus Valley from 2900 to 2600 B.C. Marketers assembled polished cube weights ranging from one, two, five, ten, and 20 to 100 or more units. Mesopotamians further simplified monetary exchange by inviting a writing system for keeping accounts. The Egyptians, Greeks, Babylonians, and Hebrews established the cubit, the distance from the elbow to the tip of the extended middle finger, as the first stage in metrology. According to a limestone stele of King Ur-Nammu, the Sumerians created a scale of linear measure:

Sumerian Term	*Current Equivalent*
cubit	19.5 inches
digit	0.6 inches or 1/30 of a cubit
reed	6 cubits
pole	12 cubits

Around 2400 B.C., tradesmen formalized a weighing system that prefaced the quantification of ore, nuggets, grains, or other mediums of exchange:

Babylonian Term	*Current Equivalent*
gerah	½ gram
bekah	10 gerahs
shekel	2 bekahs
mina	50 shekels
talent	60 minas

Through adaptations in the Egyptian and Babylonian system came the measurements invented by Hittites, Assyrians, and Phoenicians.

The Hebrews of the Old Testament had their own problems with weights and measures, as described about 750 B.C. during the reign of King Uzziah of Judah in the book of Isaiah. The Jews used the following methods of measuring dry and liquid ingredients:

Unit	*Metric Equivalent*
(liquid measure)	
log	0.3 liters
kab	1.2 liters
hin	3.66 liters
bath	22 liters
homer	10 baths
(dry measure)	
log	0.3 liters
kab	1.2 liters
omer	2.2 liters
seah	7.3 liters
ephah	22 liters

The New Testament standard included these:

Unit	*Metric Equivalent*
(liquid measure)	
xestes	0.3 liters
batos or metretes	39.5 liters

Unit	*Metric Equivalent*
(dry measure)	
choinixl	2 liters
modios	8.7 liters
saton	13 liters

When trades could not be arranged in kind, item for item, service for service, or item for service, people resorted to valuable objects, such as gardening or hand tools, weapons, shells, nails, or ingots of precious metals, the forerunners of money.

Greek merchants carried on trade in cattle and oxen, as did other Indo-Europeans. The word for "cow" evolved in many places into a synonym for money:

language	*word for cow*	*word for money*
Anglo-Saxon	*vieh/feoh*	fee
German	*skatts*	*Schatz* [value]
Gothic	*faihu*	*faihu* [money]
Icelandic	*kugildi*	*kugildi* [monetary unit]
Latin	*pecus*	*pecunia* [money]
Sanskrit	*rupa*	*rupee* [monetary unit]

In the mid-ninth century B.C., the epicist Homer recorded the value of the gold shield of Pallas Athena by describing it as decked with one hundred tassels, each valued at one hundred oxen. In the *Iliad*, Trojans valued slave women at 20 oxen, but ransomed a royal prince for 15 times that amount.

South of Athens, the disbursal of bribes to customs officials at Piraeus harbor was a major source of city revenue. To avoid the heavy-handed customs agent at the *emporion* (commercial port), ship captains often saw the wisdom of avoiding the stone quay and colonnade, the area's business center dealing in oil, wine, ceramics, preserved fish, timber, and pitch. Instead, they sought a nearby landing, an unregulated cove more to the tastes of swindlers, pirates, and smugglers.

By the sixth century B.C., city builders saw the advantage of using coin, which allowed them more latitude in choosing the style and timing of their trade. Rapidly, minting spread from Athens and Corinth west to Sicily. For Greek marketers, *metronomoi* (weight measurers), a group of authorities appointed to standardize transactions, verified weights and measures in public use to assure integrity. They marked a unit of weight with a turtle, dolphin, or other natural emblems, which found their way onto coins.

In his *Histories* (ca. 450 B.C.), Herodotus observed the level of cooperation involved in North African trade. He learned from the Carthaginians that they dealt indirectly with Libyans living beyond the Pillars of Hercules:

> On reaching this country, they unload their goods, arrange them tidily along the beach, and then, returning to their boats, raise a smoke. Seeing the smoke, the natives come down to the beach, place on the ground a certain quantity of gold in exchange for the goods, and go off again to a distance. The Carthaginians then come ashore and take a look at the gold; and if they think it represents a fair price for their wares, they collect it and go away [Herodotus 1954, p. 307].

This honor system had a built-in fail-safe. If the Libyans offered too little gold, the Carthaginians waited at their boats until the Libyans came back to shore with more gold. Herodotus marveled at the honesty of both parties: "The Carthaginians never touch the gold until it equals in value what they have offered for sale, and the natives never touch the goods until the gold has been taken away" (*ibid.*).

In the third century B.C., mathematician and engineer Archimedes simplified volume purchasing with the liquid displacement method. For measuring odd-shaped commodities such as a fish, fruit or vegetables, he set the goods in a container, filled it to the top with a liquid, and decanted the liquid to calculate how much of the total was water. A century later, Hebrew hermits in the Qumran desert used a stone measuring cup, twine, plates and bowls, and woven baskets as means of policing the sale of dry and liquid goods.

As explained in Adolphe Duhart-Fauvet's *The Pantropheon: History of Food in All Ages* (1853), Roman metrology set up a mediation system. Like children playing a finger game, both parties in a transaction held out closed fists, then thrust them open to reveal fingers. If they showed the same number, the seller named the price. When the number differed, the buyer's price ruled. The mediation method survived until A.D. 360, when standardized weights replaced the hand battle.

It was the Roman refinement of the balance beam scale in the first century A.D. that produced English words applying to weignts. The scale itself was the *libra*, forerunner of a sign of the zodiac and the English abbreviation lb. for pound. By setting the *bilanx* (dual pans) on a pin at the top of the central post, consumers initiated the word "balance." They countered the weight of the object in question with a series of heavy stones — the *pondus* and *unica*, roots of the English "pound" and "ounce." The Roman system of weights and measures illustrates the use of these two counterweights in determining price or weighing out precious metals in payment:

Roman unit	*Modern equivalent*
(dry weight)	
libra, a Roman pound or 12 ounces	¾ pound
semilibra or ½ Roman pound	6 ounces
unica, a Roman ounce	0.96 ounce
(liquid measure)	
scripulum or scruple, ¹⁄₂₄ ounce	a dash or ⅙ teaspoon
coclearum, a spoonful	1 teaspoon or 6 scruples or ¼ ounce
coclearum dimidium, half a spoonful	½ teaspoon or 3 scruples or ⅛ ounce
sextarius, a Roman pint	14.75 fluid ounces or 24 tablespoons
hemina or ½ pint	7.4 fluid ounces or 12 tablespoons
quartarius or ¼ pint	3.7 fluid ounces or 6 tablespoons
acetabulum or ⅛ pint	3 tablespoons
cyathus or ¹⁄₁₂ pint	1.5 tablespoons
modius	104.4 quarts

For linear measure, Roman metrology reverted to the anatomical unit as a means of measure:

Roman unit	*Modern equivalent*
pes (foot)	11.5 inches
passus (pace)	5 pedes (feet)
mile passuum (mile)	1000 passus or 0.95 miles

Roman money supplanted the Celtic coinage of Gallia and Britannia. However, at the fall of the Roman Empire, Britons faced a moneyless economy that dominated trade for two centuries. They resorted to barter until the invading Anglo-Saxons set up a minting and currency system.

From the Middle Ages, trading in Indonesia involved exchange of human heads. Described in a tale collected by Buzurg ibn Shahriyar, a tenth-century Persian sea captain and author of *Kitab 'Aja'ib al-Hind* (*Book of the Marvels of India*), Sumatran trade in skulls treated the heads as currency. Five centuries later, merchant traveler Niccolo di Conti of Venice, who spent a year in Sumatra in 1421, discovered the island monetary medium still circulating and valued like money. Borneo's headhunters apparently used heads in similar fashion to trade for merchandise; likewise, among the Jivaro (or Jibaro) of Peru and Ecuador's jungles, a shrunken human skull was worth the price of two rifles.

During the European colonization of Africa and the Americas, guns became a standard trade item. Valued at a fixed rate in ammunition, brass wire, iron hoops, cloth and blankets, salt, powder, rum, and ivory, rifles maintained their value in pre-industrial societies, in particular, among native American tribes of the American West and on the rubber plantations of Brazil. In the Congo, where display of rifles established prestige, natives priced merchandise with their equivalent in guns.

In the 18th century, barter remained the standard of trade in far-flung communities, particularly those of Australia, British Honduras, and New Zealand. In the 1700s, Scots carried pocketfuls of nails to spend on food items and ale. In British Honduras, mahogany logs served as legal currency after 1765, when citizens paid legal fines and settled debts in unmarred lengths of wood. A century later,

Hawaiians were still computing value in terms of sandalwood. In lieu of coins, citizens of Sydney Cove, New South Wales, used rum delivered by the American vessel *Hope* in 1792. By 1813, Australians followed the example of North American colonists by legitimizing Latin American *pesos*.

In Oceania, traders from the American South presented *lempeng*, compact leaves or sticks of tobacco as currency. The most common form was Lord Beaconsfield Native Twist Tobacco, manufactured after 1818 by Maclin-Zimmer-McGill Tobacco Company of Petersburg, Virginia. With only one or two twists, outsiders could hire a guide to paddle a canoe or fell trees for firewood.

A more unusual exchange medium greeted American journalist George Wilkins Kendall, author of *Narrative of the Texan Santa Fé Expedition* (1844), on his arrival in Mexico in 1841. Shoppers made change with bars of soap, each stamped with the name of the town that issued it. In an ungoverned economy, the soap moneys of different municipalities bore no relation to each other in size and worth. Kendall added that the bars were worn from use in wash tubs, but remained legal tender so long as the stamp was decipherable.

In 1976, Pennsylvania-born cultural anthropologist Annette Barbara Weiner described a late 20th-century gender-specific currency in *Women of Value, Men of Renown: New Perspectives in Trobriand Exchange* (1976) and *Inalienable Possessions: The Paradox of Keeping-While-Giving* (1992). On fellowship from Bryn Mawr, she studied primitive currency in Papua New Guinea as an element of female tribal membership. She characterized the use of grass skirts and bundles of banana leaves decorated with cut-outs as women's money. The bundles, consisting of ten leaves each, served as ritual gifts at funerals as well as for daily purchases.

***See also* banking; drum money; feather money; fishhook money; tooth money.**

SOURCES: Alexander, David, and Pat Alexander, eds. *Eerdmans' Handbook to the World's Religions*. Grand Rapids, Mich.: William B. Eerdmans Publishing Co., 1982. • Allen, Larry. *Encyclopedia of Money*. New York: Checkmark Books, 2001. • Angell, Norman. *The Story of Money*. Garden City, N.Y.: Garden City Publishing, 1929. • Casson, Lionel. *The Ancient Mariners*. Princeton, N.J.: Princeton University Press, 1991. • Clain-Stefanelli, Elvira, and Vladimir Clain-Stefanelli. *The Beauty and Lore of Coins, Currency, and Medals*. Croton-on-Hudson, N.Y.: Riverwood Publishers, 1974. • Clark, Jeffrey. " Review: Inalienable Possessions: The Paradox of Keeping-While-Giving." *Oceania*, September 1993, pp. 91–93. • Cribb, Joe. *Money*. Toronto: Stoddart, 1990. • Davies, Glyn. *A History of Money from Ancient Times to the Present Day*. Cardiff: University of Wales Press, 1994. • Edwards, Mike. "Indus Civilization." *National Geographic*, June 2000, 108–131. • Einzig, Paul. *Primitive Money*. Oxford: Pergamon Press, 1966. • Gabriel, Judith. "Among the Norse Tribes." *Aramco World*, November-December 1999, 36–42. • Grimbley, Shona, ed. *Encyclopedia of the Ancient World*. London: Fitzroy Dearborn, 2000. • Head, Barclay V. *A Guide to the Principal Coins of the Greeks*. London: British Museum, 1959. • Head, Barclay V. *Historia Numorum*. Chicago: Argonaut, 1911. • Herodotus. *The Histories*. London: Penguin Books, 1954. • Insoll, Timothy A. "The Road to Timbuktu: Trade & Empire." *Archaeology*, November/December 2000, 48–52. • Lewis, Brenda Ralph. *Coins & Currency*. New York: Random House, 1993. • Moore, Anderley, proj. ed. *Smithsonian Visual Timeline of Inventions*. New York: Dorling Kindersley, 1994. Reinfeld, Fred. *Treasury of the World's Coins*. New York: Sterling Publishing, 1953. • Snodgrass, Mary Ellen. *Encyclopedia of Kitchen History*. London: Fitzroy-Dearborn, 2002. • Thomas, Edward. *Numismata Orientalia*. London: Trübner & Co., 1874. • Weiner, Annette B. *Women of Value, Men of Renown: New Perspectives in Trobriand Exchange*. Austin: University of Texas Press, 1976.

treasure ships

The transporter of 17th- and 18th-century Spanish coins minted in the New World was the fabled treasure ship, the faithful galleon that plied the waves between Central and South American minting operations and ports of call in Cuba and Spain. Annually from 1530 to 1735, two *flota* ("fleets") of as few as 30 or as many as 90 ships moved between Seville and the New World colonies over an expanse of water that the English called the Spanish Main. Each fleet consisted of designated components:

ship	*purpose*
capitana (flagship)	front ship to lead the vanguard and carry the captain-general
gobiernador (armed ship)	cannon-decked warship to transport marines to defend the fleet
urca (storeship)	flat-bottomed cargo vessels to ferry general cargo
armadas	guardian ships that escorted the fleet on the outward journey from Spain to the Canary Islands
almiranta (vice-flagship)	lookout vessel to protect the rear of the fleet and carry the admiral, the military leader of the fleet

Underwriting the massive expense of convoys was the crown *avería* (tax) levied on goods, which grew from 2 percent in the 1500s to 12 percent by the 1600s.

The largest transatlantic transport preceding World War II, these treasure fleets delivered Spanish goods to the Western colonies in the "American Mediterranean," an early name for the Caribbean Sea. On the return trip east, they bore local produce, passengers, and a treasure in coin sufficient to alter Europe's economy. On the way from the mother country, the fleets followed the clockwise patterns of wind and current, a navigational aid discovered by Christopher Columbus and other explorers of the New World. The convoys moved down the African coast to the Canaries, where they took on provisions before crossing to the Western Hemisphere. The trade winds blew the fleet to Trinidad or the Windward Islands and into the Caribbean Basin. Additional shipping to the west took Spanish galleons from Acapulco around South America to Manila. Traders bore their silver from there to Pacific coast cities from Siberia south to Siam.

In the Caribbean Sea, the treasure fleets, controlled by the Casa de Contratación (House of Trade), divided into three convoys and their escort of guardian warships. The *flota* of New Spain picked up spices, silks, and porcelain from China at Vera Cruz, loaded Mexican gold and silver, and sailed northeast to Havana by way of western Florida. In fall, the *Tierra Firme* fleet of galleons loaded Mesoamerican goods at Cartagena, Colombia, and continued to Porto Bello, Panama, to pick up pearls from Margarita Island, Peruvian silver coins, Ecuadorian gold, Guatemalan bullion, and Colombian emeralds, a king's ransom that one Dominican priest saw heaped in the market square like stones. The remainder of the ships, the Honduran Fleet, docked at Trujillo to load indigo. After harboring in the Western Hemisphere during winter, the three components rendezvoused with warships at Havana harbor, the clearinghouse of Spanish vessels, and plotted their course via westerly trade winds across the Atlantic to Spain.

Security was tight. Guarding the treasures in port was Havana's Castillo de los Tres Reyes del Morro, a fort with walls ten feet thick. The convoy proceeded east to Havana and through the Florida straits up the Gulf Stream to Bermuda and back to Spain. Because they were heavily laden and without adequate military protection, the treasure ships offered enemy nations a ready source of cash. In 1628, Admiral Piet Heyn (or Hein), director of the Dutch West India Company, seized an entire Spanish fleet on the return voyage from Cuba and confiscated four million *ducats* of gold and twelve million silver florins. The plunder bankrolled the Dutch Republican army and navy against Spain during a heated competition for the Spanish Netherlands, the part of southern Holland that preceded the independent nations of Belgium and Luxembourg.

The English were also eager to waylay and loot Spanish treasure fleets, whose coins proved valuable to the national treasure for counterstamping as English currency. With the aid of Captain Richard Stayner, Robert Blake, the commander of the navy of Oliver Cromwell's Commonwealth, captured another convoy in 1656 off Cadiz. Blake's apprehension of an additional fleet in the bay of Santa Cruz de Tenerife in the Canary Islands boosted him to England's most renowned seaman of the age. In another half century, Spain worked out the logistics of moving coins from colonial mints to Europe by patrolling sea lanes and varying the standard routing of flotillas.

Despite good intentions, Spain still lost ships because it failed to correct top-heavy and unmanageable design, to recruit top pilots and seamen, or to control naval maintenance, shipworm damage, and routes. English Admiral George Anson, captain of the *Centurion* during a four-year circumnavigation of the globe, seized 1,313,843 pieces of eight, gold bars, and silver ingots worth £500,000 from the *Nuestra Señora de Covadonga* in June 1743 near the Philippines. The theft of the massive trove ended a four-year circumnavigation of the globe. In 1744, he transported the coins safely to England and carted them in 32 wagons to the Tower Mint for use in coining crowns stamped with the portrait of George II, incised by German engraver Johann Sigismund Tanner. Anson's treasure, the largest ever captured by a naval commander, is the subject of his journal, *A Voyage Round the World,* illustrated by Lieutenant Piercy Brett and published in 1748 by Anson's chaplain, Richard Walter. In 1956, novelist Patrick O'Brian fictionalized the event in *The Golden Ocean.* The blow to Spanish commerce in the Pacific was mortal as England gained supremacy over Pacific routes. By 1778, Spain ceased to launch its world-famous *flota.*

Havana, the great nexus of the transatlantic gold route, acquired hundreds of offshore wrecks scuttled by reefs, inept pilots, pirates, war, and hurricanes. Late in the 1990s, as the economy of Cuba worsened to the point of national despair, Communist dictator Fidel Castro sponsored a joint effort to recover ships from the Caribbean graveyard as a means of enriching the island treasury. Offering to share the take, Cuban officials partnered with salvors knowledgeable in the location and looting of sunken treasure fleets.

***See also Admiral Gardner; Atocha;* Samuel Bellamy; counterstamp; Mel Fisher; Piet Heyn; *Palemón;* piracy; shipwrecks; Johann Sigismund Tanner; tokens; underwater archeology.**

SOURCES: "Admiral Anson." *Biographies,* http://blupete.com/Hist/BiosNS/1700-63/Anson.htm. • Allen, Thomas B. "Cuba's Golden Past." *National Geographic,* July 2001, 74–91. • "Atocha Dive Expeditions." *Skin Diver,* December 1999, 96. • Bass, George F., ed. *Ships and Shipwrecks of the Americas: A History Based on Underwater Archaeology.* London: Thames and Hudson, 1996. • Bowden, Tracy. "Gleaning Treasure from the Silver Bank." *National Geographic,* July 1996, 90–105. • Bowers, Q. David. *Adventures with Rare Coins.* Los Angeles: Bowers & Ruddy Galleries, Inc., 1979. • Cockburn, Alexander. "Beat the Devil: Imperial Addictions." *Nation,* August 3, 1985, 70–71. • *Contemporary Newsmakers 1985.* Detroit: Gale Research, 1986. • Cribb, Joe. *Money.* Toronto: Stoddart, 1990. • Kemp, Peter, ed. *The Oxford Companion to Ships and the Sea.* Oxford: Oxford University Press, 1988. • Marx, Robert F., "Discovery of the Admiral's Flagship," *Sea Frontiers,* March-April 1982, 80–86. • Peterson, Mendel. "Graveyard of the Quicksilver Galleons." *National Geographic,* December 1979, 850–876. • Pickford, Nigel. *The Atlas of Ship Wrecks & Treasure.* New York: Dorling Kindersley, 1994. • "Treasure Hunter Who Went for the Gold." *U.S. News & World Report,* August 5, 1985, 13. • Weatherford, Jack. *The History of Money: From Sandstone to Cyberspace.* Pittsburgh, Pa.: Three Rivers Press, 1998.

Tregwynt hoard

On September 17, 1996, Roy Lewis announced discovery of the massive Tregwynt hoard at Tregwynt Mansion at Granston, Pembrokeshire, Wales, the finest ever recovered. In the ruined wall of an outbuilding and its environs, where Anne and Michael Sayer were building a tennis court, Lewis located a gold ring inscribed "Rather death [than] falce of fayth" ("Tregwynt Hoard"). Under the cover of a lead sheet, he located 467 silver pieces and 33 gold coins minted primarily at London's Tower Mint from the 1500s and 1600s. Lewis received the full value of the trove and placed the coins at the National Museums & Galleries of Wales in Cardiff.

Rich in examples commissioned by Edward VI, Philip and Mary, Elizabeth I, James I, Charles I, and the Puritans of the Commonwealth, the coins represented some of the most stirring eras of England's past. Historians deduced that the hoard was buried around 1647 during the English Civil War. Included in it was siege coinage hastily struck at a temporary mint at Shrewsbury, the work of master coiner Thomas Bushell and his staff from the branch mint at Aberystwyth Castle; the pieces were made from Cardiganshire silver. Other coins bore Bushell's markings from operations at Bristol and Oxford.

Six of the rarest coins may have been part of military pay for an infantryman on October 21, 1642, two days before the battle of Edgehill. Royalist pieces professed the Latin motto of the doomed Charles I: "*Religio Protestantium Leges Angliae Libertas Parliamenti*" ("The Protestant Faith, Laws of England and Freedom of Parliament"). They appealed to the citizen to "*Exurgat Deus et Dissipenhr Inimici Eius*" ("Let God Arise and Let His Enemies Be Scattered"), a reference to the divine right of kings.

Additional royalist pieces include coins struck by Sir Thomas Cary in 1644 in the Welsh Marches and a rare half-crown, the work of Sir Richard Vyvyan, a loyal Cornishman from Trelowarren, at the Exeter mint in 1646. Also produced during the fray were Irish half-crowns that may have been commissioned by the rebel Catholic Confederacy in 1642 and a siege crown struck at Dublin the following year. Analysts of the trove surmised that the west Midlands coins may have followed royalist commander Charles Gerard west after 1644. The arrival of Oliver Cromwell at the siege of Pembroke Castle in 1648 may have caused the trove's owner — perhaps farmer Llewellin Harrie (or Harries) — to stash a redware pot of coins before they were seized for use against the crown.

SOURCES: Grierson, Philip. *Numismatics*. London: Oxford University Press, 1975. • "The Tregwynt Hoard." http://www.aocc.ac.uk/archaeology/tre_int.html. • "Tregwynt Mansion." http://www.europetraditions.com/england/int/322.html.

trial by the pyx

The arbitrary selection of English coins from the Royal Mint for public sampling of metal content began during the reign of Edward I in 1282. Called the trial by the pyx, the ritual test, conducted by twelve discreet and law-abiding Londoners of the Star Chamber council and twelve guildsmen of the Worshipful Company of Goldsmiths, demonstrated the necessity of proving that a run of coins was truly worth the stated value. The test mediated two vested interests — the Crown, which wanted coins to offer an honest weight, quality design, and fineness for the sake of citizens and international trade; and the mintmaster, who kept the overage of coins that were lighter than the prescribed weight.

Over the centuries, the trial by the pyx enhanced the quality control of England's money. In 1799, 100 gold guineas pulled at random from a year's minting went into the pyx, a ceremonial case or money box from the Latin *pyxis* or "chest." The guildsmen stored the box in the Pyx Chamber at Westminster Abbey, where they conducted the procedure. The keys of the master coiner, comptroller, and mint warden opened the box.

Before the assembly, the trio of key-holders began the process of weighing samples from each month's work. The total weight had to fall within a set margin of variance, called the "remedy." Failure to satisfy standards resulted in a fine levied against the master coiner. In that year, the tolerance was 1/400 or 32 grains of a total 12,800 grains. In 1878, guildsmen moved the trial to Goldsmiths' Hall, where the Queen's Remembrancer, a justice of the high court, conducted the test.

Under the Coinage Act of 1971, English treasury authorities continued the trial of the pyx in the late 20th century. To mark seven centuries of assurance to the public of quality coinage, in 1982, Queen Elizabeth II attended the annual sampling. In 1993, random selection of ten pence pieces at the rate of one from every 20,000 minted that year resulted in 60,000 set aside for weighing. At the ritual, overseers deemed the new coins within limits of composition, diameter, and weight and issued their verdict in May to the mintmaster, who is the Chancellor of the Exchequer. A change in the order of the trial of the pyx occurred in February 1998 at court at Buckingham Palace to cover the testing of cupronickel, nickel brass, and gold-plated silver coin to assure standard composition of bimetallic coins.

See also **hallmark; Sir Isaac Newton; touchstone.**

SOURCES: Allen, Larry. *Encyclopedia of Money*. New York: Checkmark Books, 2001. • "Eight Centuries of Sampling Inspection: The Trial of the Pyx." *Journal of the American Statistical Association*, September 1977, 493–500. • Sinclair, David. *The Pound*. London: Century Books, 2000. • Stigler, Stephen. "Stephen Stigler's New Book Challenges Researchers to Show Him the Numbers." *University of Chicago Magazine*, December 1999. • "The Trial by Pyx Order 1998." http://www.hmso. gov. uk/si/si1998/ 19980264.htm.

Triana, Roderigo de

The cheating of Roderigo de Triana constitutes the first of a pattern of theft and deception in the history of the American frontier. Upon Christopher Columbus's departure for India with the *Pinta, Niña*, and *Santa Maria*, Spain's King Ferdinand and Queen Isabella pledged an annuity of 10,000 *maravedís* to the sailor in the fleet who first spotted land. Columbus promised a silk jacket as an additional prize. According to his extended journal entry for Tuesday, October 11, 1492, after sunset, the fleet steered west toward what the captain assumed was China. At 2:00 A.M., the *Pinta*, which led the fleet because of its speed, signaled that land was ahead.

The text credits navigator Rodrigo de Triana of Lepe, Spain, as the first to spy the island of San Salvador, but Columbus added that he spotted light at ten o'clock the previous evening from the quarter-deck and had his sighting confirmed by his groom, Pero Gutierrez. Rodrigo de Triana was the true winner of the prize, but Columbus demanded the reward for himself. The trickery earned Columbus a life annuity that the crown underwrote with a tax on Seville's butchers. According to Bartolomé de las Casas (or Casaus), the Dominican missionary who wrote *Historia de las Indias* (*History of the Indies*), first printed in 1875 by the Royal Academy of Madrid, Triana was so enraged that he converted to Islam. In 1999, in honor of the man whom Columbus cheated, the National Aeronautical and Space Administration (NASA) named a climate-sensing space satellite the *Triana*.

SOURCES: Cordingly, David. *Under the Black Flag*. San Diego, Calif.: Harvest Books, 1995. • de las Casas, Bartolomé. *History of the Indies*. New York: Harper & Row, 1971. • Dunn, Oliver, and James Kelley, eds. *The Diario of Christopher Columbus' First Voyage, 1492–1493*. Norman: University of Oklahoma Press, 1989. • Jordan, Louis. "The Coins of Colonial and Early America." http://www.coins.nd.edu/ColCoin/ColCoinContents/Introduction.html. • Pickford, Nigel. *The Atlas of Ship Wrecks & Treasure*. New York: Dorling Kindersley, 1994.

tughra

In the 1200s, the Ottoman Turks devised a unique symbol called the *tughra* (also *toughra* or *tugra)* an elaborate knotted monogram evolved from the ruler's secret signature. It stated the sultan's name, patronymic, and titles and a tribute to Allah, the Islamic god. The *tughra*, also called *damga*, or imprint, carried authority as well as dynastic significance. Dating to animal signs of the Oghuz Turks in Central Asia and similar to a crest, coat of arms, or signet stamp, these symbols possess beauty and flow from the Arabic tradition of artistic calligraphy.

The systematizing of Arabic cursive writing dates to A.D. 908 and the *khatt al-mansub* ("proportioned script") devised by Ibn Muqlah. Heightened to a religious art by calligrapher and writing teacher Ibn al-Bawwab, who hand-lettered 64 copies of the Koran around A.D. 1000 with artistic *nakshi* writing. After 1370, Tamur (or Tamberlane) united Iran and replaced Mongolian coin script with the cursive flow and complex interwoven strikes that stressed grandeur and unity. Drawing on the work of court artists and illuminators, mintmasters incised these imperial ciphers on pictureless coins according to an Islamic custom discouraging portraits.

The glamor and stateliness of the *tughra*'s epigraphy appears on the silver pieces and coppers minted after 1695 by Mustafa II of Turkey, who commissioned *tughra* designs on his gold *ashrafi altin*. The complex knot motif suited Suleiman I the Magnificent, Mustafa III, and Abdul Aziz, the Ottoman sultan at Constantinople in 1864, but it was Ahmed III who legitimized the design as a state symbol in 1703. In 1891, Afghan king Abdur Rahman imported a coining machine to Kabul that refined images on copper, silver, and gold specie. For his majestic coins, he presented the shrine of the 'Ali Mosque at Mazar-i-Sharif and backed the coin with the king's personal *tughra*.

The *tughra* influenced the numismatic iconography of the phoenix, Prussian eagle, Russian double eagle, and British royal crown. Circulated from Hungary south to Algeria and east to Iraq and Yemen, Islamic *tughra* coins incorporated with their royal insignia a spiraled edging, as found on the silver *kurus* minted in 1769 at Istanbul and in the ornate arabesques on the *ghirsh* struck in 1929 by the Saudi king, Sa'ud ibn 'Abd al-'Azia.

SOURCES: Baker, Phil. "Ottoman Art." *New Statesman*, July 26, 1996. • Cribb, Joe. *Money*. Toronto: Stoddart, 1990. • Cribb, Joe, Barrie Cook, and Ian Carradice. *The Coin Atlas*. London: Little, Brown and Co., 1999. • Grierson, Philip. *Numismatics*. London: Oxford University Press, 1975. • "The Nature of Islamic Ornament: Calligraphy." http://www.metmuseum.org/toah/hd/cali/hod_38.149.1.htm. • Pastan, E. C. "The Formation of Islamic Art." http://www.cc.emory.edu/HART/HART345S98/ Section3.html, 1988. • Sellin, Eric, and Hedi Abdel-Jaouad. "The Art and Design of Arabic Calligraphy." *Ethnic News Watch*, January 31, 1997.

tympf

The *tympf*, created in the mid–17th century, was an unprecedented blend of majestic, Renaissance-style pose and cheap metal. The issue of coiner Andreas Tympf, the ⅓ *gulden-tympf* silver coin entered circulation in Poland and Russia, and it was issued from the treasury of Prussia's Jan II Kazimierz (also John II Casimir), famed fighter of Cossacks, from 1652 to his abdication in 1667. The Prussian version, a portrait coin, pictured the king's laureate bust and the joint arms of Poland and Lithuania along with the date of their union. The *tympf* (or *chekh)* struck by Peter I of Russia paired his likeness with the double-headed eagle on back.

Because the *tympf* continued to be struck in billon during the baroque era and sank in worth from 30 to 18 *groschen* or *groszy*, the name of the coin earned ridicule and contempt. In 1749, a reissue of *tympfs* from Prussia's mints until the Seven Years' War reprised the same slide in value. After citizens stopped accepting them, minting halted in 1765.

SOURCES: Cribb, Joe. *Money*. Toronto: Stoddart, 1990. • Cribb, Joe, Barrie Cook, and Ian Carradice. *The Coin Atlas*. London: Little, Brown and Co., 1999. • "Curious Names," http://www.money museum.ch/standard_english/raeume/geld–lieben/ueberlieferung/sprachliches/

underwater archeology

An innovation enhanced by the oceanography that the U.S. Navy conducted during World War II, underwater archaeology carries reconnaissance and excavation under fresh or salt water by the same methods of observation, discovery, and recording that govern land-based searches. Much of the work begins in libraries, which often house eyewitness accounts of shipwrecks, passengers lists, cargo manifests, maps, and carpenters' schematic drawings and building plans of ships. To the detriment of historical inquiry, many caches of information have been lost to fire, theft, floods, earthquakes, and humidity:

date	*source*	*cause of loss*
1551	House of Trade, Seville, Spain	fire
1670	archives in Panama City, Panama	burned by pirates
1755	Casa de India Depository of Historical	earthquake

date	*source*	*cause of loss*
	Documents, Lisbon, Portugal	
1810	archives in Bogotá and Cartagena, Colombia	destroyed in war
1821	archives in Mexico City and Veracruz, Mexico	destroyed in war
1940s	archives in Amsterdam, London, Paris, Rotterdam	bombing
1962	Archives of the Indies, Seville, Spain	flood

Some divers carry on underwater exploration without special tools. In 1968, Bermudan diver Harry Cox located riches from a Portuguese treasure ship of the late 1500s by fanning away sand to disclose a gold bracelet and gold coins, bars, and chains worth $200,000. More strenuous excavation of a site often begins with aerial survey by small plane, helicopter, or helium balloon attached to a boat, which can spot anchors, piles of ballast stones, and cannon outlined in dark sand or by coral colonies in shallows. To work under oceans or large lakes and rivers, skilled divers emulate the techniques evolved by French scientist Captain Jacques-Yves Cousteau, inventor of the scuba or aqualung. Beginning his career at Le Grand Congloué outside Marseilles, France, he pioneered sea-floor observation of cultural resources, a new science furthered off the shores of southern Turkey by American marine archeologist George F. Bass and historian, amateur archeologist, and photo-journalist Dr. Peter Throckmorton.

In the early 1900s, attitudes toward salvage and get-rich-quick treasure hunting forced lawmakers to establish protective measures on behalf of archeological resources. The first legislation, the Antiquities Act of 1906, guarded national monuments and created a permit system to regulate excavations and punish despoilers of artifacts from nonrenewable sites. After discovery of a late Bronze Age eastern Roman ship in Yassiada, Turkey, in 1958, a team led by Dr. Peter Throckmorton began the world's first undersea archeological excavation in 1960 and completed the first seabed work directed by a diving archaeologist and the first project governed by the standards of terrestrial excavation. Aiding divers in the swift current off Cape Gelidonya was the two-man "Asherah," the first submarine crafted for archaeological investigation and launched in 1964. Increasingly stringent laws proposed by the Society for American Archeology resulted in the Archeological Resource Protection Act of 1979, which governed land use and conservation to preserve historic resources.

Among the divers who followed Mel Fisher's example was Teddy Tucker. In 1961, he explored the remains of the *Eagle*, an English Merchantman that wrecked off Bermuda on January 12, 1659. Using an airlift, he disclosed stores of trade goods, including a wood chest containing thousands of clay pipes. An undersea tremor prompted Tucker to grab Bob Canton, his brother-in-law and fellow diver, and flee before a massive coral boulder fell on them.

After the salvage boom in Florida in the 1960s, regulation was necessary to halt the despoliation of such shallow wrecks as the three treasure ships run aground off Padre Island, Texas, in 1554 and the coin-rich fleet of 11 galleons sunk in 1715 off Vero Beach, Florida. One of the ships of the lost fleet, the flat-bottomed *urca* (storeship) of Miguel de Lima, became Florida's first underwater archeological preserve in 1987. Anchored at Fort Pierce, it provides amateur divers and photographers a view of a real underwater relic.

Undersea exploration, which was once the province of Admiralty law, passed to the U.S. Abandoned Shipwreck Act of 1987, the beginning of historic conservation of sea-floor relics. Federal statutes accorded states the title to historic wreckage older than 50 years and the right to regulate salvage, diving, recreation, tourism, photography, and amateur exploration in regard to the wreck sites. These laws halted the looting of old wrecks for the purpose of selling for huge profits antiquities, precious metals, and rare or historic coins.

Among the important techniques of professional marine archeologists are radiocarbon and potassium-argon dating, thermoluminescence study, paleobotanic surveys of mud from food containers and amphoras to determine what substances they once held, preservation of fragile wood and natural fibers in polyethylene glycol to prevent shrinkage and warpage, and neutron activated studies of clayware to determine their sources. Adding to the efficiency of undersea archeology are a number of study methods and physical tools:

- metal probe, a graduated iron rod that an excavator forces into sediment to determine the depth of solid objects, such as the tool used by Norman Scott to study buildings and streets of Port Royal, Jamaica, a pirate city destroyed by earthquake on July 7, 1692
- photographic mosaic, an underwater mapping strategy introduced in 1873 by French diver Louis Bouton off the coast of France
- closed-circuit television cameras and bright lights mounted on sea sleds to illuminate objects on the ocean bottom
- hand-held sonar units, which chart solid objects in water where silt obscures visibility and which set up a pattern of beeps and a graph to alert divers
- sub-bottom sonar profiler, which locates non-ferrous relics concealed by sediment, a method that enabled underwater archeologists to map the entire sunken city of Port Royal, Jamaica, which yielded two historic silver coin hoards
- cofferdams, walls of sandbags or stones surrounding an area under exploration to retain items *in situ*
- core samples of mud and silt, which can unearth bone fragments, ceramic bits, flint, glass, gold dust and flakes, iron nails, rock, tacks, and wood
- magnetometers for locating large deposits of metal concealed by coral or sediment in shallow water
- underwater metal detectors, which locate ferrous and non-ferrous metals like gold and silver by generating a sub-bottom profile
- radiography, an x-ray of coral-encrusted conglomerates to disclose ship fittings, coins, religious medals, buttons, buckles, and jewelry
- archeomagnetic dating of clay vessels, such as olive jars, pipes, and storage containers
- air jet or water jet, a pipe used as a probe to direct compressed air or water toward sedimentary sand and mud obscuring objects
- lift bag, a retrieval pouch that carries objects to the surface for identification
- airlifts of compressed air in water deeper than 15 feet to force silt upward
- hydrolift, a dredge with screen basket that collects gold from crevices in river bottoms
- prop wash, also called a blaster or mail box, a metal elbow that covers a ship's propellor to direct its wake to the sea floor to dislodge sediment. A smaller version, the thruster, attaches to a submersible vehicle.
- towvane, a diving chamber that searches down to 600 feet
- photogrammetric mapping with stereophotographs and aluminum grids to maintain the integrity of historic items *in situ*
- remote operated vehicle (ROV), an unmanned observation vehicle like the Jason Jr. or J.J., a vessel designed by Woods Hole Oceanographic Institute. Explorer Dr. Robert Ballard of the Woods Hole Oceanographic Institution used an ROV to make 60,000 photographs of the *Titanic* over a 12-day period in 1986. Another ROV, the Merlin, assisted in the retrieval of pearls and other artifacts from the *Atocha*, a Spanish galleon that sank off Florida in 1622.
- midget submarines, manned craft such as the Alvin used by the U.S. Navy after 1964 and the Johnson Sea-Link I & II, which explored the *Monitor*, a Civil War relic. These submersibles extend the time that divers can examine relics on the sea floor, especially in environments of severe cold such as that surrounding the *Titanic*.

These methods disclose precious fragments of the past that Dr. Throckmorton called "the raw material of history" (Throckmorton 1962, p. 698).

Reclamation of coins and bullion, navigation tools, and filigreed jewelry is a tedious business begun by lifting amorphous lumps by hand and by air-filled balloons to add buoyancy. Experts transform concretions of salt and calcium carbonate with water jets; with electrolysis, they remove corrosive chlorides. The process concludes with the boiling of base metal in microcrystalline wax to seal surfaces against further deterioration. Museums clean and restore coins and bullion for sale to acquire the funds to build models, create educational exhibits on maritime history, and preserve ancient wood beams, galley housings, and other endangered structures that decay rapidly on return to the air from the deep.

See also Admiral Gardner;* assay marks; George Bass; Blackbeard; *La Capitana;* Mel Fisher; Captain William Kidd; *Palemón;* shipwrecks; Peter Throckmorton; treasure ships; *Whydah.

SOURCES: Allen, Thomas B. "Cuba's Golden Past." *National Geographic*, July 2001, 74–91. • "Atocha Dive Expeditions." *Skin Diver*, December 1999, 96. • Babits, Lawrence E., and Hans Van Tilburg, eds. *Maritime Archaeology: A Reader of Substantive and Theoretical Contributions*. London: Plenum, 1998. • Bass, George F., ed. *Ships and Shipwrecks of the Americas: A History Based on Underwater Archaeology*. London: Thames and Hudson, 1996. • Bowden, Tracy. "Gleaning Treasure from the Silver Bank." *National Geographic*, July 1996, 90–105. • Bowers, Q. David. *Adventures with Rare Coins*. Los Angeles: Bowers & Ruddy Galleries, Inc., 1979. • Cockburn, Alexander. "Beat the Devil: Imperial Addictions." *Nation*, August 3, 1985, 70–71. • *Contemporary Newsmakers 1985*. Detroit: Gale Research, 1986. • Cribb, Joe. *Money*. Toronto: Stoddart, 1990. • Crittenden, Jules. "Treasure Island: Explorers May Have Located Sunken Pirate Ships." *Boston Herald*, January 19, 2001. • Defoe, Daniel. *Robinson Crusoe*. New York: Airmont Books, 1963. • Jones, Bart. "Modern Day Pirates?" *Hannibal Post-Courier*, June 27, 1998. • Laing, Lloyd R. *Coins and Archaeology*. New York: Schocken Books, 1969. • Lewis, Brenda Ralph. *Coins & Currency*. New York: Random House, 1993. • Norton, Trevor. *Stars Beneath the Sea*. London: Random House, 1999. • Peterson, Mendel. "Graveyard of the Quicksilver Galleons." *National Geographic*, December 1979, 850–876. • Pickford, Nigel. *The Atlas of Ship Wrecks & Treasure*. New York: Dorling Kindersley, 1994. • Randall, Lorelei. "Our Marine Heritage." *Nordic Underwater Archaeology*, May 1999. • Reinfeld, Fred. *Treasury of the World's Coins*. New York: Sterling Publishing, 1953. • Ritchie, David. *Shipwrecks: An Encyclopedia of the World's Worst Disasters at Sea*. New York: Checkmark Books, 1996. • Sandz, Victoria. *Encyclopedia of Western Atlantic Shipwrecks and Sunken Treasure*. Jefferson, N.C.: McFarland, 2001. • Schemo, Diana Jean. "Recovery of Spanish Galleon off Ecuador's Coast Raises Controversy and Romance." *New York Times*, April 14, 1997. • Stemm, Greg. "Thirty-First Annual Law of the Sea Institute." *Odyssey News*, March 30, 1998. • Throckmorton, Peter. "Oldest Known Shipwreck Yields Bronze Age Cargo." *National Geographic*, May 1962, pp. 696–711. • "Treasure Hunter Who Went for the Gold." *U.S. News & World Report*, August 5, 1985, 13. • Velazquez, José. "Salvagers Recover Thousands of Coins from Galleon Sunk off Ecuador." *News Times*, April 4, 1997. • Wilson, Scott. "Castro Forms a New Alliance — With Treasure Hunters." *Washington Post*, December 27, 2000, p. A16.

U.S. Bureau of Engraving and Printing

Printed money was already in circulation before the U.S. government set up its own money press, forerunner of the U.S. Bureau of Engraving and Printing (BEP). In 1837, a bank in Ypsilanti, Michigan, produced a three-dollar banknote featuring ornate lettering, portraits of George Washington and Benjamin Franklin, romantic pictures of a woman churning and a man gathering corn, and a seated pose of Lady Liberty facing the American eagle. On August 29, 1862, in the basement and attic of the U.S. Treasury Building on Pennsylvania Avenue, the government began separating and packaging one- and two-dollar bills that they contracted to private printshops. For the duration of the Civil War, to prevent hoarding, the department replaced coins with paper bills worth three, five, ten, 25, and 50 cents.

The BEP contributed to American numismatics over the next century. In 1865, ten-year-old Emma S. Brown became the youngest person employed by the operation when her congressman learned that her family was poor and that her brother had been killed at

Petersburg fighting on the Union side. She remained an employee until 1924 as a trimmer of paper bills. After the Civil War, Congress began looking for a site for a free-standing print operation.

The BEP operation grew in 1876 with the printing of revenue stamps. On October 1, 1877, six members of the staff at offices in the basement of the Department of the Treasury began working with graver, burnisher, and hand-held magnifying glass and produced currency and postage stamps on Milligan steam-powered plate-printing presses, a four-plate machine installed in 1878. To protect the bills from fire, the agency hired its own in-house fire brigade, which was less harried in 1888 when the agency dispensed with gas lights and installed electricity. By 1894, the BEP was also turning out postage stamps as well as special currency for Hawaii and foreign currencies for Cuba, Korea, the Philippines, and Siam.

In 1928, the BEP selected the basic face and back designs for all denominations, which, by law, may not feature living subjects. The designs for paper money include the following:

denomination	*face*	*back*
$1	George Washington first U.S. president	Great Seal of the United States
$2	Thomas Jefferson third U.S. president	Signing of the Declaration of Independence
$5	Abraham Lincoln 16th U.S. president	Lincoln Memorial, circa 1922
$10	Alexander Hamilton first secretary of the treasury	U.S. Treasury Building
$20	Andrew Jackson 7th U.S. president	White House
$50	Ulysses S. Grant 18th U.S. president	U.S. Capitol
$100	Benjamin Franklin U.S. statesman	Independence Hall
$500	William McKinley 25th U.S. president	500/"Five Hundred Dollars"
$1000	Grover Cleveland 22rd & 24th U.S. president	1000/"One Thousand Dollars"
$5000	James Madison 4th U.S. president	5000/"Five Thousand Dollars"
$10,000	Salmon P. Chase U.S. Treasury secretary	10,000/"Ten Thousand Dollars"
$100,000	Woodrow Wilson 28th U.S. president	100,000/"One Hundred Thousand Dollars"

In 1929, the BEP saved on expenses and foiled counterfeiters by reducing paper money size by ⅓. Added responsibility fell to the bureau in 1939, when it began printing food stamps. In 1935, the BEP began imprinting paper money with the Great Seal of the United States, which originated in 1782 and first appeared on the one-dollar Silver Certificate, which became the world's most widely recognized and used currency. In 1957, the agency added the phrase "In God We Trust."

The operation grew to a 25-acre printworks comprised of 23 high-speed rotary presses that manufacture round the clock. Daily, in 65 steps, the staff turns out 37 million notes worth $696 million. Workers begin with a soft steel master die hand-engraved with a portrait, vignette, ornamentation, and lettering. By a process of siderography, the printer transfers multiple images of the die to a plate, then stores the die for later use. A copy of the image requires heat and great downward force to make an impression. The printer then makes an alto, a raised image of the die, in plastic. After dipping the plastic altos into an electrolytic tank, the printer shapes plates, which must be individually cleaned, polished, and approved by an engraver, who inspects them microscopically.

The printer uses the likeness to craft a chromium coated basso plate. Its recessed images are used for intaglio printing with green ink on high-speed, sheet-fed rotary presses, which turn out more than 8,000 sheets an hour under 20 tons of pressure. After up to 48 hours of drying, the sheets return to an examiner before being numbered and processed in an overprinter, a letterpress that applies the U.S. Treasury seal and serial numbers. The paper consists of 75 percent cotton and the rest linen, which replaced the silk fibers used before World War I.

Paper notes emerge at a weight per bill of .032 troy ounces and a physical size of 2.61 by 6.14 inches and .0043 inches thick. Guillotine cutters slice the sheets of 32 notes each into individual bills for banding and packaging in bricks of 4,000 bills to a stack and distribution to Federal Reserve banks. Any bills that contain errors or imperfections are replaced by a "star note," a duplicate bearing an independent series of serial numbers.

In 1991, the BEP installed a web press, which sped the process and reduced costs by imprinting both sides of a note in one operation. The new press delivered 10,000 sheets every 35 minutes. However, the fragility of the press ended its use in 1996. A web-press bill called a "web bill" bore no plate location or check number on the face. The press imprinted a plate number on the reverse.

An auxiliary printworks, the Western Currency Facility at Fort Worth, Texas, opened in 1991 and employs 600 workers to operate 12 additional high-speed presses. By 1997, 9.6 billion notes entered the Federal Reserve System to support growth and replace outdated bills. The breakdown of the system's productivity reflects the economy:

proportion of bills	*denomination*
26%	$1
1%	$2
9%	$5
11%	$10
19%	$20
5%	$50
7%	$100

Of the $539,890,223,079 in paper money circulating globally, $364,724,397,100 was in the highest denomination as of July 31, 2000. The presses also turn out federal certificates, commissions, invitations, naturalization documents, and visas.

United States paper currency has featured the signatures of five African Americans — Blanche K. Bruce, Judson W. Lyons, Azie Taylor Morton, James C. Napier, and William T. Vernon, all of whom served as registers of the Treasury. Morton, the 36th U.S. Treasurer, served from September 12, 1977, to January 20, 1981. In addition to these representations of nonwhite citizens, two 50-cent pieces have commemorated agronomist George Washington Carver and educator Booker T. Washington. In 2001, a third black American, baseball player Jackie Robinson, the first black athlete to play for the major leagues, was featured on a U.S. coin.

Paper money has a predictable lifespan figured at 22 months for the one-dollar bill, two years for the five-dollar bill, three years for the ten-dollar bill, four years for the 20-dollar bill, and nine years each for 50- and 100-dollar bills. As a service to citizens, the BEP, currently located next to the Holocaust Museum and across from the Potomac River Tidal Basin, redeems partially destroyed or badly damaged bills if the owner can produce more than half of the original. The annual turnover in ruined paper money involves redemption of 30,000 claims valued at more than $30 million. To determine authenticity, experts at the Office of Currency Standards examine mangled paper money and issue checks for the value of each claim. Additional services involve tours of the site in English, Chinese, French, German, Hebrew, Japanese and Spanish and online forums on such topics as the history of the treasury seal and the return of gold notes. A bureau store sells historic portraits, currency portfolios, shredded money, souvenirs, videos, and collector's items.

See also **continental currency; paper money; Anthony C. Paquet; pieces of eight.**

SOURCES: "The Bureau of Engraving and Printing." http://www.bep.treas.gov/. • Davies, Glyn. *A History of Money from Ancient Times to the Present Day*. Cardiff: University of Wales Press, 1994. • Griffin, Gary. "The Bureau's Flat-Plate Press." *Stamp Collector*, December 18, 2000. • Taxay, Don. *The U.S. Mint and Coinage*. New York: Arco Publishing, 1966. • "The U.S. Mint." http://www.usmint.gov. • Van Ryzin, Robert R. *Twisted Tails: Sifted Fact, Fantasy and Fiction from U.S. Coin History*. Iola, Wisc.: Krause Publications, 1995.

U.S. coins

In the beginning, settlements in the New World were extensions of the newcomers' origin, whether England, France, Portugal, Scotland, or Spain. After gaining independence from England, the colonies of New England set up a new and independent federal government. However, because they lacked the facilities to mint their own money, they had no choice but to rely on English tokens and on Spanish pieces of eight until silver for small change became available. In 1776, Mexican coiners produced North America's first silver dollar picturing Charles III of Spain. Surviving coins from this issue often bear the chop marks of Chinese merchants who tested them to determine if they were solid silver or clad coins with brass or copper inner layers.

After the Articles of Confederation authorized states to coin money in 1781, the Connecticut, Massachusetts, and New Jersey mints went into operation. In 1785, Vermont added to New World moneys by issuing copper pennies. Robert Morris, financier of the American Revolution and delegate to the Continental Congress, became Superintendent of Finance in the Continental Congress in 1781. After a four-year study, he submitted too confusing and impractical a plan to suit the nation's needs.

Thomas Jefferson's criteria for the best coinage required that it be convenient size, easily changed into arithmetic multiples and parts, and similar to moneys used in the colonies. On his advice, in 1784, the government chose a decimal basis rather than the eight-base standard of the Spanish *real*. With the passage of a national constitution, government planners lodged all power of coinage with Congress. When authorities discussed placing George Washington's portrait on new coinage, he refused the honor because he believed that the choice compromised democratic principles. As a result, Congress never authorized the portrait of a living person to appear on a coin for general circulation.

On July 6, 1785, the United States replaced colonial and state coinage with an official monetary system based on the dollar. The national mint produced the Franklin penny from 300 tons of "fugio" coppers, struck at New Haven, Connecticut. It had a simple design featuring a sundial and the inscription "*Fugio*" ("I fly") with a circle of 13 links for the original colonies on the front, and "We are one" and 1787 on the back. Generated during English industrialist Matthew Boulton's experimentation with minting by steam engine rather than by screw press, the first penny was the issue of James Jarvis, a private contractor. Production began in April 1787 from dies incised by Abel Buell (or Buel). The failure of the project resulted in a conviction of Buell for forgery and bribery charges against Jarvis. That same year, New York goldsmith Ephraim Brasher produced the nation's first gold coin with the Latin legend "*Nova Eboraca*" ("New York").

In 1789, Alexander Hamilton, Secretary of the Treasury, established a bimetallic standard based on gold and silver. Congress set up an official trimetallic national coin system on April 2, 1792, with ten denominations:

coin	*worth*
copper half-cent	$.005
copper cent	$.01
silver half-*disme* [dime]	$.05
silver *disme*	$.10
silver quarter	$.25

coin	*worth*
silver half-dollar	$.50
silver dollar	$1.00
gold quarter-eagle	$2.50
gold half-eagle	$5.00
gold eagle	$10.00

Legislators mandated that mintmasters stamp coins with an allegorical symbol of Liberty, the word "Liberty," the year, and "United States of America" on the back. Still following the original orders, the current mechanized minting process turns out over 50 million coins per day at the Philadelphia and Denver mints.

The Treasury opened its first mint in Philadelphia in 1792 and added others as demand increased:

mint	*mintmark*	*years of service*
Philadelphia	P	1792 to present
New Orleans	O	1830–1861, 1879–1909
Charlotte, N.C.	C	1838–1861
Dahlonega, Georgia	D	1838–1861
San Francisco	S	1854–1955, 1965
Carson City, Nevada	CC	1870–1893
Washington, D.C. (headquarters)		1873
Denver	D	1906 to present

For convenience of trade, the national mint supplied the populace with copper pennies and half pennies, two- and three-cent pieces, and other coins ranging upward to a $20 gold piece, such as that struck from gold nuggets and dust after the strike at Sutter's Mill, California, in 1848.

Coins came into and out of popularity for temporal reasons:

- In 1795, U.S. Mint director Henry William DeSaussure hired portrait artist Gilbert Stuart to replace flowing hair designs on coins. The sculptor of the original Lady Liberty on the penny, half-dollar, and silver dollar, Robert Scot created in art the nation's democratic ideal. In 1795, he produced the draped bust for a silver dollar, designed on portrait artist Gilbert Stuart's pose of socialite Anne Willing "Nancy" Bingham, granddaughter of Edward Shippen, mayor of Philadelphia. Assistant engraver John Eckstein adapted the drawings for a draped bust. The figure remained in use until 1807, when John Reich's Liberty replaced it.
- The chubby Miss Liberty on engraver John Reich's 1807 capped bust brought charges that he posed his overweight mistress for the image. The coin design resurfaced periodically on dimes and quarters.
- The 1844 Seated Liberty dime found an unusual place in jewelry history during the Mexican War, which began in April 1846. Soldiers hoping to capture the hearts of Hispanic women amassed the shiny new dimes from small change and pierced them to attach to bracelets.
- The issuance of a splendid ten-dollar gold eagle in 1795 resulted in a popular coin. Because of hoarding, the coin's scarcity forced citizens to rely on the Spanish silver dollar, which circulated in quantity.
- Most popular was the Indian head penny, issued in 1859 in a copper-nickel alloy and in bronze in 1864.

From widespread hoarding of silver specie during the Civil War, mine owner Joseph Wharton pressed the U.S. Mint to add nickel ores to copper for a cupro-nickel penny. Nickel was a good choice for adding strength to specie. Called "Kupfer-Nickel" (or "Devil's copper"), it had possibilities for saving on recoining and, at the same time, enriched Wharton, who held a monopoly on ores from the Western Hemisphere. Because of demand for the nickel coin, under mint director James Pollock, the U.S. government quickly exhausted Wharton's ore sources along with ores from Canadian deposits. Because of his bias against the metal's dull gloss, he pressed Congress to abolish the use of nickel and to replace it with French bronze. In April 1864, he succeeded in squelching nickel. He also proposed a three-cent coin to replace the obnoxious small change notes, a suggestion that Congress took in March 1865. By the end of the year, the mint shipped 11 million of the coins.

In 1864, the inscription "In God We Trust" was added to most denominations. The availability of cash and cash services per citizen increased rapidly:

year	*population*	*banks*	*banknotes*	*specie*	*total per capita*
1830	12,866,000	330	$61,000,000	$33,000,000	$9
1840	17,069,000	901	$107,000,000	$83,000,000	$15
1850	23,192,000	824	$131,000,000	$154,000,000	$13
1860	31,443,000	1562	$207,000,000	$253,000,000	$23

At war's end, issuance of the Shield nickel, struck in 1867, presented a noble laurel-draped image on the front with the number five on the reverse encircled with stars separated by rays of glory. Strong anti–Confederates complained that the coin looked too much like a rebel battle flag.

In 1879, John A. Kasson, U.S. ambassador to Austria and former chair of the Committee of Coinage, Weights and Measures, urged the U.S. Mint to strike a four-dollar gold piece. He based his proposal on a study of world currency. Such a coin, he surmised would be beneficial in a global market controlled by the Spanish *peseta*, Dutch and Austrian *florins*, and French *franc*. Coin designer Charles Edward Barber incised dies for a Miss Liberty coin featuring long tresses. George T. Morgan complied with a Miss Liberty Stella coin with prim braids, produced until 1880.

Early in the 20th century, Americans discovered the convenience of the nickel and the coin-operated machine. Caille Brothers Company of Detroit, Michigan, manufactured numerous gaudy slot machines, which salesmen guaranteed would boost the sale of liquor, food, cigars, and games of billiards. The company gave its machines colorful names — Ben Hur, Big Star Six, Black Cat, Bull Frog, Check Boy, Detroit, Eclipse, Liberty Bell, Lone Star, Owl, Puck, Silver Cup, Special Tiger, and Yankee. Other machines turning out amusement for five cents included ornate carillons and calliopes, the latter a kind of hurdy-gurdy music-maker found in the home of circus promoter P. T. Barnum and the Vanderbilt railroad barons of New York. In 1898, Roth & Engelhardt marketed a player piano that cranked out tunes for a nickel. The Mills Novelty Company of Chicago, founded in 1890, turned slot machines into a line of arcade goods — strength testers, horoscope machines, fortune tellers, and girlie peep shows.

In a long series of productions, notable 20th-century sculptors contributed to the dignity and esthetics of American coinage:

- In 1906, the U.S. Congress commissioned the original Lincoln penny, which Lithuanian-American medalist and sculptor Victor D. Brenner designed. The coin achieved two firsts — it was the first to feature a president and the first to display the motto "In God We Trust," which was first authorized during Lincoln's presidency. When the coin came up for redesign after a half century of use, in 1959, Frank Gasparro, chief engraver of the U.S. Mint, proposed the Lincoln Memorial for the reverse to mark Lincoln's 150th birthday. The design was unique in that it was the first time a U.S. coin honored the same figure on both sides.
- In 1913, James Earle Fraser of Winona, Minnesota, a student of Augustus Saint-Gaudens, designed the buffalo nickel, a uniquely American coin that popularized Fraser's art. For the Indian profile on the reverse, he made a composite sketch from the sittings of movie star Chief John Big Tree of the Onondaga, Cheyenne tribesman Two Moons, and Iron Tail, a Sioux. For the buffalo, he studied Black Diamond, an

American bison housed at the Bronx Park Zoo.

- The Mercury dime of classical sculptor Adolph Alexander Weinman, another protégé of Saint-Gaudens, came into circulation in 1916 and remained a standard for three decades. The placement of the Roman fasces, a bundle of sticks bound around an ax blade as a symbol of unity, brought laughs for the nicknames "battle-ax dime" and the "golf bag coin," for the emblem's resemblance to a set of clubs. More frivolous conjecture linked Weinman's W-over-A emblem with "Woodrow Wilson" and "watchful waiting" as the U.S. tried to remain out of World War I. In the late 1930s, the fasces launched a new wave of suspicions during the rise of fascism in Italy under Mussolini.
- That same year, Hermon Atkins MacNeil incised the standing Liberty quarter, a popular coin until 1930. The original, which featured a standing Liberty displaying one bare breast, caused outrage among the prudish. The U.S. Mint ceased coining the piece until staff could incise chain mail to clothe the figure's upper body.
- John Flanagan commemorated the father of the country with a quarter, issued in 1932, the bicentenary of the birth of George Washington, who had appeared on a portrait dollar in 1899 along with the Marquis de Lafayette and on a copper-nickel clad quarter with an eagle on the reverse.

The string of American numismatic beauties established a national coinage that was both artistic and reflective of deeply ingrained values and pride.

Nostalgia and respect for the American presidency sparked demand for portrait coinage. In 1938, the U.S. Mint began circulating a copper-nickel Jefferson nickel, a design by Felix Schlag that replaced the buffalo nickel with the president's portrait and his home, Monticello, on the reverse. A critic at the *Chicago Daily News* complained that the severe lines of Jefferson's mansion resembled advertisements on beer tokens. The mint honored Franklin D. Roosevelt, the nation's only four-term president, by featuring his likeness on a copper-nickel clad dime in 1946, the year after his sudden death in Warm Springs, Georgia, near the end of World War II. Coiners backed Dr. Selma H. Burke's famous presidential portrait with a torch, olive frond, and oak branch.

During the McCarthy era of red-baiting, the initials "JS" on the Roosevelt dime spread a rumor that they stood for Joseph Stalin. Embroiderers of the folk tale added that President Franklin D. Roosevelt had agreed to the mintage in February 1945 as a political concession at the Yalta Conference. The mounting furor caused Mint director Nellie Taylor Ross to acknowledge engraver John R. Sinnock as the source of the initials. In 1949, Sinnock's half-dollar featuring inventor and statesman Benjamin Franklin honored the Liberty Bell on the reverse. The initials "JRS" revived the post–World War II fabrication about a deal between Roosevelt and Stalin and added a new kink, a claim that the U.S. Mint harbored a Communist mole.

A similar furor arose over the Kennedy half-dollar. In 1964, a nation still mourning the assassination of President John Fitzgerald Kennedy welcomed a portrait half-dollar in copper and nickel designed by Gilroy Roberts with Frank Gasparro's U.S. presidential coat of arms on the reverse. The rumor that the initials "GR" identified a lurking Communist was short-lived. Seven years later, Gasparro's Eisenhower dollar coin, created in 1971, lost public support because of its inconvenience and weight.

Another failure, the 1979 Susan B. Anthony dollar, the first likeness of a woman on a U.S. coin, was also the work of Frank Gasparro, who worked from several portraits of the famed suffragist orator. He pictured the eagle of the Apollo 11 moon landing on the reverse. The disk, called a sandwich coin, was a tri-level stack of copper-nickel at top and bottom with pure copper at center. Because the coin was nearly the same size and weight as a quarter, it received public rejection. The most vocal complainers referred to the coin as the "agony dollar."

More popular were bicentennial quarters, half-dollars, and dollars issued in 1976 picturing the colonial drummer and Washington's portrait. Connecting the scene with the colonies was a circlet of thirteen stars centered with the torch of liberty. The Dollar Coin Act of 1997 replaced the Susan B. Anthony dollar coin with a new manganese brass clad dollar honoring Sacagawea, the Shoshone translator and guide of the Lewis and Clark expedition, issued in 2000. Her likeness commemorated the explorers' use of peace medals as tokens of good will.

See also **American eagle; Joseph A. Bailly; Charles Edward Barber; Ephraim Brasher; Victor D. Brenner; Abel Buell; Dr. Selma Burke; Confederate money; 50 state quarters; Fort Knox; James Earle Fraser; Frank Gasparro; Thomas Jefferson; James Barton Longacre; Hermon Atkins MacNeil; Mercury dime; George T. Morgan; Anthony C. Paquet; Robert Maskell Patterson; Peace dollar; Bela Lyon Pratt; Sacagawea coin; Augustus Saint-Gaudens; tokens; U.S. Bureau of Engraving and Printing; U.S. coins; U.S. Mint; Adolph Alexander Weinman; Joseph Wright.**

SOURCES: Bowers, Q. David. *Adventures with Rare Coins*. Los Angeles: Bowers & Ruddy Galleries, Inc., 1979. • Bowers, Q. David. "American Gold." *American Heritage*, December 1984, 43–49. • "The Bureau of Engraving and Printing." http://www.bep.treas.gov/. • Davies, Glyn. *A History of Money from Ancient Times to the Present Day*. Cardiff: University of Wales Press, 1994. • Kageleiry, Jamie. "The Other Side of the Coin." *Yankee*, September 1993, p. 58. • Lewis, Brenda Ralph. *Coins & Currency*. New York: Random House, 1993. • Lewis, Michael J. "Of Kitsch and Coins." *Commentary*, October 1999. • Reed, Mort. *Cowles Complete Encyclopedia of U.S. Coins*. New York: Cowles Book Company, 1969. • Reiter, Ed. "Circulated Coins." *New York Times*, November 4, 1984. • Reiter, Ed. "New Coin May Place Washington on Horseback." *New York Times*, February 21, 1982. • Rochette, Ed. "Meeting the Man with the Five-cent Profile." *Hobbies*, January 1984, p. 82. • Stephen, Sir Leslie, and Sir Sidney Lee, eds. *Dictionary of National Biography*. London: Oxford University Press, 1922. • Taxay, Don. *The U.S. Mint and Coinage*. New York: Arco Publishing, 1966. • "The U.S. Mint." http://www.usmint.gov. • Van Ryzin, Robert R. *Twisted Tails: Sifted Fact, Fantasy and Fiction from U.S. Coin History*. Iola, Wisc.: Krause Publications, 1995. • Wu, Corinna. "The Buck Starts Here." *Science News*, April 1, 2000. • Zielinski, Graeme. "Frank Gasparro Dies." *Washington Post*, October 4, 2001.

U.S. Mint

As the American colonies were transforming themselves into a nation, commerce depended on a motley array of moneys — English shillings, English and French guineas and crowns, Dutch johannes and half-johannes, Spanish and French *pistoles* and doubloons, and Spanish milled dollars. On May 11, 1775, the second day of the Second Continental Congress, May 11, 1775, John Hancock, the Massachusetts delegate, proposed using Spanish milled silver dollars or pieces of eight to back federal notes in lieu of an official U.S. currency. Thereafter, the need for national coinage spurred an interest in creating a minting operation, even if it had to be stocked with colonial plate for bullion. On December 24, 1776, the *London Chronicle* noted that members of the U.S. Congress "have established a Mint at Philadelphia, where they coin copper and silver pieces about the size of half a crown: In silver for twelve shillings, in copper for fourteen pence" (Taxay 1966, p. 8).

The shift from contract coinage to a federal operation was slow and fraught with disagreements. Congress, on the advice of Alexander Hamilton, Secretary of the Treasury, enacted the Coinage Act of 1792. The legislation established the official U.S. Mint and spelled out the appointment of officers, their salaries and duties, and use of facilities for free stamping of gold and silver belonging to U.S. citizens. The mother mint, which opened in Philadelphia on April 2, 1792, in the basement of a sawmaker named Harper, became the nation's first government building. The mint later housed one of the nation's oldest law enforcement agencies, the United States Mint Police.

President George Washington appointed as director scientist and mathematician David Rittenhouse of Paper Mill Run, Pennsylvania, with Henry Voigt serving as coinsmith and John Birch as designer. A precision maker of clocks, compasses, levels, thermometers, barometers, and surveying instruments, Rittenhouse also set up the nation's first telescope and supervised the surveys of state boundaries and the Mason-Dixon Line, which separates Philadelphia and Maryland. Using horse-powered machines, he supervised the hand-striking of commemorative half-dimes. Rittenhouse remained on the job until 1795. The current mint honors his expertise with a coin collection displayed in the David Rittenhouse Room.

According to first U.S. Mint officer Adam Eckfeldt, the president and his wife, who lived down the street from the mint, supplied $100 in family silver in October 1792. The figure of Liberty allegedly pictured first lady Martha Washington, although there is no proof of this bit of coin lore. A letter reputedly written by U.S. Mint technician Jonas R. McClintock in 1844 remarked on the active role that the Washingtons played in the coinage of the first half-*dismes*. The letter comments that the coins "were struck at the request of Gen. Washington to the extent of one hundred dollars which sum he deposited in bullion or specie" (Van Ryzin, 1995, p. 96). The text adds that the president sent some of the new coins to Europe and others to friends in Virginia. McClintock makes clear that "they were never designed as currency — the mint was not at the time fully ready for going into operation" (*ibid.*).

The first official coins were 11,178 copper cents, completed in March 1793. Because acquisition of copper bullion was irregular, the mintmaster solicited scrap copper and worn-out household plate. For the next two years, the reserves mounted with silver *écus* from the Bank of Maryland and gold from a Boston citizen. With metals on hand, the mint could then issue gold and silver five-, ten-, and 25-dollar pieces and small change in five-, ten-, 25-, and 50-cent denominations.

Cognizant of the egotism of European monarchs pictured on *ducats, sovereigns,* and *florins*, U.S. officials chose from the outset to avoid portrait coinage based on the likeness of the first president. Artistic in style and imitative of allegorical European coins, the 1794 silver dollar featured Liberty, a long-haired female profile within a circle of stars and the date. The silhouette emulated the bust on the Libertas Americana medal, the work of French medalist Augustin Dupré. With the success of the first coinage, the treasury chose to hire its first professional engraver, Robert Scot.

The next year, the first gold eagle featured a bird with outspread wings. Its beak held a laurel wreath and its talons an olive branch. By 1805, the mint had produced 1,439,517 silver dollars. The striking required the heating of ore in a furnace and flattening it into sheet metal by passing between rollers. After workers punched out coin planchets or disks, they hand-stamped them with dies and incised reeded edging.

The mint's mechanical success paralleled a rise in the value of precious metals. Because coins were worth more as raw metal than their face value, citizens began hoarding them and speculating on trades with worn Spanish coins from the West Indies. To return coinage to function in the U.S. economy, Secretary of State James Madison reduced the amount of silver in coins in 1806 and ended the production of gold eagles while increasing the circulation of paper bills backed by the silver specie on hand.

In 1836, installation of heavy steam-powered coining machines at the Philadelphia mint sped the coining operation while elevating quality and uniformity. In a fierce din, operators fed metal strips into the machines that cut planchets for stamping. Metal left over from cutting went back into melt-down, like dough after the cutting of cookies and biscuits. Workers returned strips into cast ingots and rolled strips for the next trip through the planchet cutter.

At the striking machine, the operator pressed down on each coin with dies. An ejection mechanism tossed the finished shape into a wooden hopper. In the adjusting room, women seated at balance-beam scales weighed each coin to determine proper value. Because coiners could remove, but couldn't add metal, they stamped planchets slightly heavier than necessary. Technicians finding excess weight used files to adjust the weight. Their vertical operation against the rims left parallel striations from the friction of metal against metal.

In 1837, President Andrew Jackson expanded the mint system with three branches, which struck gold and silver in New Orleans and gold alone in Charlotte, North Carolina, and Dahlonega, Georgia. These auxiliary mints, under the mint marks O, C, and D, allowed prospectors to coin their ore close to home without risking a long overland transfer to Philadelphia. When Confederate forces seized the three branches, President Jefferson Davis minted a half-million dollars in gold and silver ore into coins and applied the machinery to the manufacture of cannon. In Charlotte, the Confederate War Department transformed the mint into army headquarters and a hospital. After the war, the mint flourished from new demands for coins and established assay offices in Boise, Carson City, Deadwood, Helena, New York, Salt Lake City, Seattle, and St. Louis.

Additional changes marked mint operation in the last portion of the nineteenth century and into the 20th century. By 1873, the mint became a department of the U.S. Treasury. After the Spanish-American War in 1898, the U.S. Mint also produced military decorations — Bronze Star, Congressional Medal of Honor, Navy Cross, Purple Heart, Silver Star — and the coins of Mexico, Panama, Peru, and the Philippines. In 1932, the mint chose to honor George Washington, whom designers had passed over during his lifetime to avoid the mistakes made by European coiners in lauding egotistical monarchs. For the portrait on the quarter, the mint chose the work of John Flanagan. Six years later, a nickel pictured third U.S. president Thomas Jefferson and his beloved Virginia estate, Monticello.

Because of bullion shortages during the Great Depression, in 1933, the United States began printing silver certificates, which were redeemable at the U.S. Treasury on demand in standard silver dollars. The next year, Congress revoked the gold standard and reclaimed all of the nation's monetary gold, including bullion and coins held by Federal Reserve banks. The treasury began storing its gold bullion and historic documents at the U.S. Gold Bullion Depository at Fort Knox, Kentucky, in 1938 in a precaution against seizure if World War II involved the nation.

Additional portrait art celebrated American patriarchs, including John R. Sinnock's image of Franklin D. Roosevelt, the only four-term president, in 1946; the Franklin half-dollar two years later; the Frank Gasparro and Gilroy Robert design of the popular Kennedy half-dollar in 1964; and Gasparro's Eisenhower dollar in 1971. Another major shift in coin art occurred in 1961, when the mint first struck silver coins with multiple designs. In 1965, a silver crisis forced Congress to pass the Coinage Act authorizing the mintmaster to replace silver with base metal in dimes and quarters and to reduce it in half-dollars. In 1970, President Richard M. Nixon amended the Coinage Act of 1965 by removing silver from the dollar coin and replacing it with a cupronickel clad coin bearing a portrait of Dwight D. Eisenhower and the Apollo 11 landing on the moon.

Heightened security by the U.S. Mint Police has proved its worth. The Denver mint sustained a robbery attempt in 1864 when an employee hid $80,000 in gold in a secret compartment in his wooden leg. A foiled robbery in 1922 involved a bold daylight holdup of a Federal Reserve Bank truck parked at the receiving entrance to transport $200,000 in five-dollar bills to a branch bank. Two men in a black Buick brandished sawed-off shotguns and targeted mint guards, killing one. A third gang member stole the money. Secret Service agents discovered $80,000 of the original heist in 1923 in St. Paul, Minnesota. Although the robbery took place outside the mint, it is still called the Great Mint Robbery. Bullet holes in the marble walls of the building's foyer serve as reminders of the robbery.

In 1998, the U.S. Mint began considering new alloys, in particular, Nordic gold, a blend of aluminum, copper, tin, and zinc, the choice of the European Monetary Union for some of its ten-, 20-, and 50-cent euro coins replacing the Swedish *kroner*. Other possibilities for new American coins included the low-nickel alloy used in a gold-toned British pound coin, copper-based alloys, and an aluminum bronze alloy in the new U.S. dollar coin. Sources outside the mint surmised that the federal government planned to remove dollar bills from circulation and replace them with some nine billion coins. To determine the best metal, the mint subjected alloyed disks to chemical and electrical tests replicating exposure to sweat and normal handling.

For a design, the mint featured Sacagawea, Shoshone guide for the 1804–1806 westward expedition of George Rogers Clark and Meriwether Lewis, the second female likeness on a U.S. coin. The coin was a wise investment. For an initial outlay of 12 cents per coin, consumers gained a currency item which could last three decades, as compared to the dollar bill, which costs 3.5 cents to manufacture, but lasts only 18 months. Another plus for coins is that they enable clerks to make change quicker and avoid errors in reading a printed denomination. Contributing to the reception of the Sacagawea coin was the fact that it emulated the size and feel of the Susan B. Anthony dollar so vendors would not have to retool machines. Because Congress had dawdled for fifteen years on the issue of taking dollar notes out of circulation, the mint proposed a dual circulation. Their suggestion required only five months of discussion.

***See also* American eagle; Joseph Alexis Bailly; Charles Edward Barber; bas-relief; Matthew Boulton; Dr. Selma Burke; commemorative issue; 50 state quarters; Thomas Jefferson; James Barton Longacre; Robert Morris; pantograph; Robert Maskell Patterson; Sacagawea coin; U.S. coins; Wells Fargo; Charles Cushing Wright; Joseph Wright.**

SOURCES: Bowers, Q. David. *Adventures with Rare Coins*. Los Angeles: Bowers & Ruddy Galleries, Inc., 1979. • "The Bureau of Engraving and Printing." http://www.bep.treas.gov/. • Clain-Stefanelli, Elvira, and Vladimir Clain-Stefanelli. *The Beauty and Lore of Coins, Currency, and Medals*. Croton-on-Hudson, N.Y.: Riverwood Publishers, 1974. • Davies, Glyn. *A History of Money from Ancient Times to the Present Day*. Cardiff: University of Wales Press, 1994. • Kertes, Noella. "Mint Mulls Metals for Dollar Coin." *American Metal Market*, March 3, 1998. • Lewis, Michael J. "Of Kitsch and Coins." *Commentary*, October 1999. • McAdams, Robert. "David Rittenhouse." *Smithsonian*, December 1986, p. 10. • Taxay, Don. *The U.S. Mint and Coinage*. New York: Arco Publishing, 1966. • "The U.S. Mint." http://www.usmint.gov. • Van Ryzin, Robert R. *Twisted Tails: Sifted Fact, Fantasy and Fiction from U.S. Coin History*. Iola, Wisc.: Krause Publications, 1995. • Wu, Corinna. "The Buck Starts Here." *Science News*, April 1, 2000.

U.S. Secret Service

On July 5, 1865, the U.S. government established the Secret Service Division, a law-enforcement agency that suppressed "koniackers," a slang name for counterfeiters of coins, currency or stamps, securities of the United States, checks, and government bonds. Secretary of the Treasury Hugh McCulloch selected as chief Colonel William P. Wood, a veteran of the Mexican War. The choice was inspired. As a eulogist for the Washington *Evening Star* declared in Wood's obituary on March 21, 1903, he was a valuable agent to President Abraham Lincoln and Secretary of War Edwin M. Stanton. More than a dozen attempts were made on Wood's life, with one stalker crossing an ocean to dispatch him. The eulogist added, "The Confederates were determined to capture and hang him, and dozens of times he escaped from apparently inextricable dangers by his extraordinary nerve, adroitness, and audacity, coupled with prodigious physical strength and activity" (Davis 1988, p. 111).

The son of an immigrant coin engraver and die-maker, Wood was born on March 11, 1824, in Alexandria, Virginia, and grew up in Washington, D.C. He learned mechanics and model making in boyhood and, at age 23, joined the infantry during the Mexican War. After accepting a peace-time job as a die sinker, he returned to service raising troops to raid Harpers Ferry in 1859. After a solid war record during the Civil War, he accepted a summons from William Pitt Fessenden, Secretary of the Treasury, to take a security post in Washington.

In summer 1865, Wood assembled private detectives experienced at collaring counterfeiters along with potential security officers he had encountered during the Civil War. At their swearing-in, the new operatives and assistant operatives promised to work 24 hours a day, take any assignment in any locale, waste no government funds in travel and subsistence, remain fit and honest, and request pay on a daily basis of five dollars plus three dollars for meals and lodging. Each agent who captured a suspect earned a $25 bonus. Within a year, the new Secret Service arrested over 200 counterfeiters. Within three years, Wood added to the requirements vows of circumspection and sobriety, lawful conduct in making arrests, thrift, confidentiality, and abstention from graft or bribes. Men reported all official activities weekly to the department by mail rather than telegraph. Of particular interest to Wood was a rule requiring that agents guard confiscated specie and counterfeit materials.

Supervised by the Solicitor of the Treasury, the agency headquartered in New York City from 1870 to 1874, then moved to Washington in 1875. Eight years later, it became an official part of the Treasury Department. Agency duties increased to halting fraud against the government by mail robbers, phony land agents, smugglers, and distillers of illegal whiskey. In addition to protecting money, the agency investigated counterfeit U.S. currency passed in foreign countries, money laundering, racketeering, and unauthorized use of credit cards, telecommunication devices and computers, food stamps, and identification documents.

One of the oustanding forgers in the agency's history, Connecticut-born plate printer William E. "Long Bill" Brockway, whom the media dubbed the "king of counterfeiters," passed $1,000 bonds that fooled even Chief Wood. In 1850, Brockway launched a career that lasted four decades and defrauded the U.S. Treasury Department of $75,000. One of the victims, the Wall Street investment firm of Jay Cooke and Company, advertised a reward of $20,000 to stop the Brockway gang from passing bogus government bonds.

Secretary of the Treasury Hugh McCulloch offered Wood a $15,000 bonus if he left his official duties and personally arrested Brockway. Wood trailed his man, made a deal with Brockway's crony, Charles Adams, to halt Brockway in the act of passing $80,000 in federal bonds. Wood arrested the mastermind in Philadelphia, retrieved the plates from Long Island, and, by July 1868, obtained Brockway's confessions. Although Wood lived up to his part of the bargain, both the Treasury Department and Jay Cooke and Company refused to reward him. Brockway's assertion that Wood arrested him illegally cost Wood his job.

One of the chief counterfeiters of the late 19th century, Baldwin S. Brendell (or Bredell) passed 97 high quality $100 silver certificates from 1897 to 1899. In partnership with Arthur Taylor, he ran a cigar shop as a cover for the engraving of counterfeiting plates. The skillful notes circulated for over four months before the U.S. Treasury Department discovered that the official seal had lost its original color. The staff searched for the technician who had produced a low-grade seal and discovered that the certificates were phony. Before the forgers could order more paper and reach their goal of ten million dollars in fake certificates, Secret Service agents apprehended them.

While in prison, Brendell, who shared a cell with Taylor, continued his trade by duplicating 20-dollar bills by candlelight using makeshift materials. Brendell printed them on an iron that he tricked his father into sending to the prison cell and slipped the forged paper money to Arthur Taylor's brother Harry. The Secret Service halted the operation and gained a confession from the confederates, who drew seven-year sentences.

In 1894, agents began guarding the president, Grover Cleveland, and became full-time guards after the assassination of President William McKinley in 1901. The first officer killed in service was Joseph A. Walker, murdered on November 3, 1907, while investigating western land fraud. Agents added counter-espionage to their responsibilities in 1915 at the order of President Woodrow Wilson. Additional duties required the protection of the vice president, president-elect, former presidents, presidential nominees, diplomatic missions, visiting heads of state, and members of the immediate families of presidents and former presidents. The agency also investigated espionage and threats against the president. In 1922, during the presidency of Warren G. Harding, the White House obtained its own police force.

See also **Hugh McCulloch; Emanuel Ninger; U.S. Treasury.**

SOURCES: Davis, Curtis Carroll. "The Craftiest of Men: William P. Wood and the Establishment of the United States Secret Service." *Maryland Historical Magazine*, Summer 1988, pp. 111–126. • Hulse, Carl. "Forgotten Sleuth Is Honored at Last." *New York Times*, May 29, 2001, p. A12. • McLaughlin, Abraham. "20 Ways to Foil Forgers." *Christian Science Monitor*, September 24, 1998. • Nash, Jay Robert. *Encyclopedia of World Crime*. 6 vols. Wilmette, Ill.: CrimeBooks Inc., 1990. • "United States Secret Service." http://www.treas.gov/usss.

U.S. Treasury

Regulation of money, customs, and taxes occupied the founders of the United States from its colonial beginnings. In 1700, one colonial customs agent was killed while pursuing a pirate ship. By 1775, the Continental Congress issued its first currency, but the development of the U.S. Treasury did not begin until a year later with the appointment of a five-member Board of Treasury, also called the Treasury Office of Accounts. Within five years, the board gave place to a Superintendent of Finance.

The evolution of an official treasury seal parallels the design of the Great Seal of the United States and the selection of the dollar as a national monetary unit. In 1778, when the colonies received their first federal budget, auditor, comptroller, and chambers of accounts, Virginia planter Richard Henry Lee, New York Governor Robert Morris, and John Witherspoon, a Scottish Presbyterian minister, formed a committee of the Continental Congress to design seals for the treasury and navy. They completed the navy seal by 1780 and, with the aid of former Treasurer of Loans Francis Hopkinson, a New Jersey judge, composer, and poet, worked out a design for the treasury seal.

The finished icon pictured a large shield topped with a bow and surrounded by garlands. On the shield, a chevron separated a balance-beam scale and key. The Latin legend read "*Thesaur Amer Septent Sigil*" ("Seal of the North American Treasury"). It was first used in 1782. In 1968, the seal underwent redesign that removed the figured background, the bow, and garlands and replaced the old legend with "The Department of the Treasury" and "1789."

The workings of the treasury department grew complex and far-reaching, beginning in 1782, when the Superintendent of Finance began naming army inspectors to report fraud and cut waste. In 1784, the Continental Congress named three members of the Board of Treasury; the following year, on the advice of Thomas Jefferson, it adopted decimal coinage and the dollar as the national monetary unit. In 1789, the Treasury Department became the nation's second oldest governing department after the executive branch and began supervising the postmaster general and postal department.

A year after the drafting of the Constitution, President George Washington instructed Congress and Alexander Hamilton, Secretary of the Treasury, to systematize a uniform currency. The Treasury opened the first Bank of the United States and began collecting excise taxes in 1791 and, in 1792, opened the Philadelphia mint and named a Commissioner of Revenue. Until the Treasury could supply a national specie, Congress authorized foreign currency as legal tender. One of the first new additions to small change was a half-dime, issued in 1795, and the first U.S. dime, struck in 1796. The following year, the treasury held a first meeting of the Assay Commission.

Security was important from the beginning. In 1793, the Treasury staff installed Nero, the dog of the yard, to join the night watchman in patrolling the property. Nero came under the care of Henry Voigt, first superintendent and chief coiner. A mock Treasury seal pictured a wreathed circle centered with a grim-visaged dog with paw atop the key to the vault. When the Treasury caught fire in 1801, President John Adams joined a bucket brigade that saved the structure. It did succumb to fire in 1814, when British arsonists sat across the street at Rhodes Tavern to watch the blaze.

The construction of a custom house in New York City on Wall Street in 1834 eased some of the congestion of Treasury offices. A custom house in Galveston, Texas, which opened in 1858, checked shipments of goods over the Rio Grande. In 1855, the U.S. Mint opened a department of medals and, in five years, began sale of commemorative medals to the public. In 1862, the Congress placed within the Treasury a Bureau of Internal Revenue to codify tax laws and collect taxes on citizen earnings; two years later, the National Bank Act initiated a system of bank charters.

In the last weeks of the Civil War, one of the last acts performed by President Abraham Lincoln was the formation of the U.S. Secret Service. When actor John Wilkes Booth shot Lincoln during a performance of *Our American Cousin* at Ford Theater, the killer tangled his spur in the Treasury Guard flag decorating the presidential box, fell to the stage, and broke an ankle. Newly sworn-in President Andrew Johnson lodged in the Treasury building for two months while the Lincoln family, still occupying the White House, mourned their husband and father.

In 1872, customs collectors began protecting sailors in port and, two years later, added enforcement of copyright to their duties. The Bureau of Printing and Engraving took shape in 1877. In 1910, Congress authorized Postal Savings Depositories. The Internal Revenue Service added to its responsibilities in 1913, when a uniform income tax was passed, and seven years later, when it began superintending prohibition, which had become law on October 28, 1919, when the U.S. Congress passed the National Prohibition Act or Volstead Act. Treasury agents seized illicit alcohol, distilling equipment, and the cash that changed hands between rum runners and their customers. Under the presidency of Franklin Delano Roosevelt, prohibition ended on December 5, 1933.

In 1873, U.S. Treasury officials took charge of the Bureau of the Mint, which included branch mints in Charlotte, North Carolina; New Orleans, Louisiana; and Dahlonega, Georga, all created in 1835. To ease problems of assaying precious metals from mining operations in the western states, the Treasury opened a series of branch assay offices:

year	*place*
1853	New York City
1863	Carson City, Nevada
1869	Boise, Idaho
1877	Helena, Montana
1881	St. Louis, Missouri
1895	Denver, Colorado
1897	Deadwood, South Dakota
1909	Salt Lake City, Utah

A string of changes in the U.S. government added to the responsibilities of the U.S. Treasury:

date	*alteration*
1908	formation of the National Monetary Commission preceded establishment of the Federal Reserve System
1921	the Bureau of the Budget was established
1927	Treasury operation of the Bureau of Customs, which first monitored airports the previous year
1930	supervision of narcotics investigation through the Bureau of Narcotics
1933	founding of the Home Owners' Loan Corporation and the Federal Deposit Insurance Corporation
1934	addition of the Office of the General Counsel to offer legal advice to the Secretary of the Treasury. Also, the National Gun Law placed firearm regulation under Treasury supervision

date	alteration
1940	establishment of the Bureau of Public Debt
1941	supervision of the security of U.S. documents.

In the first month of World War II, President Franklin D. Roosevelt set a worthy example in buying the first Series E Savings Bond marketed to the public. Others supported the war effort by following his lead. Irving Berlin advertised the importance of bonds with an original song, "Any Bonds Today" (1941); 556 daily newspapers promoted defense savings stamps. In 1946, the Treasury added a U.S. Savings Bond Division as a means of financing war and defense. In 1949, the Treasury began enforcing the Export Control Act. The reduction of bills to only those worth $100 or less in 1969 removed largely uncirculating $500 and $1000 notes, which checks and credit cards made obsolete.

By 1955, the U.S. Treasury was computerized to simplify the collection and storage of data. In the '50s and the next decades, Treasury duties and the number of internal bureaucracies grew:

year	bureau
1951	Office of Price Stabilization
1951	United States Customs Service enforced Fur Products Labeling
1952	United States Customs Service enforcement of the Immigration and Nationality Act
1960	regulation of mergers and consolidations under the Bank Merger Act
1962	Tariff Commission began outlining a U.S. Tariff Schedule
1963	Cuban Assets Control Regulation
1967	observance of the U.S. government's foreign loans
1970	Federal Law Enforcement Training Center in Glynco, Georgia
1970	Executive Protective Service
1970	United States Customs Service enforced Currency and Foreign Transactions Reporting
1970	United States Customs Service Detector Dog Training Center
1970	United States Customs Service Sector Communications Unit
1971	Overseas Private Investment Corporation (OPIC)
1974	The Bureau of Government Financial Operations
1974	Congressional Budget and Impoundment Control
1983	African Development Bank
1987	Government Securities Act
1988	Multilateral Investment Guarantee Agency

In 1974, the Treasury moved the U.S. Customs Service to the World Trade Center in New York City.

See also **Fort Knox; greenbacks; Alexander Hamilton; In God We Trust; Robert Morris.**

SOURCES: Allen, Larry. *Encyclopedia of Money.* New York: Checkmark Books, 2001. • Brookhiser, Richard. "A Founding Father's Return to Grace." *U.S. News & World Report,* November 10, 1997, pp. 71–72. • *Encyclopedia of World Biography.* Detroit: Gale Group, 1998. • Lind, Michael. "Hamilton's Legacy." *Wilson Quarterly,* Summer 1994, 40–52. • Reed, Mort. *Cowles Complete Encyclopedia of U.S. Coins.* New York: Cowles Book Company, 1969.

Varin, Jean

Engraver and medalist Jean Varin (or Warin) served European royalty as coin artist and portraitist. Born in Liège in 1607, he followed a family tradition in sculpture and bas-relief. At age 22, he found employment on the staff at the Paris Mint. Within seven years, he obtained control of most royal coinage and bronze commemorative medals produced by the mints of Louis XIII le Juste, who refashioned the nation's minting system in 1640, and Louis XIV, a great manipulator of coin art as a propaganda tool over his extraordinary 73-year reign.

Among Varin's portraits are likenesses of Anne of Austria, Armand Cardinal Richelieu, and Louis XIII and Louis XIV in a variety of views — full-length, bust, and facial profiles at different ages. The scenarios of Varin's pieces include historic events from the rule of the Sun King, who was Varin's friend and fellow coin collector, as pictured in a painting. Two of Varin's contributions to the king's reign were the *Louis d'Or* ("gold Louis"), an impressive portrait coin struck near the end of l'Ancien Régime, and the *écu* or *denier d'or*, a gold or silver coin named for the French for "shield." The valuable coins figured in the treasure trove of a pirate's chest in Chapter IV of Robert Louis Stevenson's *Treasure Island* (1883).

In 1670, the Paris mint struck Varin's designs on silver 1⁄12 *écu* pieces for use as small change in France's American colonies. Featuring Louis XIV with loose hair and a brief garland, the coins stressed authority and grandeur in his profile, the crest with royal *fleurs-de-lis*, and the encircling legend, "Gloriam Regni Tui Dicent" ("They Will Speak the Glory of Your Reign"). In 1672, the year of Varin's death, he further glorified his king with a grand statue of Louis in Roman emperor's dress and pose, displayed in an alcove of the Venus Drawing Room at Versailles.

***See also* coinage; *écu*.**

SOURCES: Babbitt, John S., "Coins and Currency on U.S. Stamps," *Stamps*, January 21, 1995. • Clain-Stefanelli, Elvira, and Vladimir Clain-Stefanelli. *The Beauty and Lore of Coins, Currency, and Medals*. Croton-on-Hudson, N.Y.: Riverwood Publishers, 1974. • "Dossiers," http://www.artcult.com/hrb12. html. • Reinfeld, Fred. *Treasury of the World's Coins*. New York: Sterling Publishing, 1953.

wampum

Like beaded shell money of Africa and Oceania, the Algonquian and Iroquoian wampum or *wampumpeag* ("white beads") was a tubular form of cash that could be polished and strung on thongs for convenience or woven into unique artistic forms, a specialty of the Narragansett. Called *sewan* or *seawant* from the Algonquian *siwan* for "unstrung bead," the individual circlet, varying from 1⁄8 to 1⁄4 inch, required tedious sawing of whirls from the inner shell of the whelk (*Buccinum undatum*), quahog clam (*Venus mercenaria*), or other bivalve and concluded with coring each cylinder with a flint point. Thus, the smallest beads displayed more intricate craft and acquired more worth. Another measure of value was the clam's shading, from a common white to a rare deep purple, which produced the most valuable beads.

The work of producing wampum may date to 2500 B.C. In Long Island Sound, the summer work of gathering shells and the winter chore of sawing, grinding, piercing with a stone drill, and polishing beads involved men and women of the Montauk, Narragansett, and Quinnepiac. For stringing, they chose hemp or animal tendon and tied the finished lengths into edgings on moccasins and capes, aprons, necklaces, earrings, and headpieces. A single belt four inches wide, such as that worn by Massasoit on his visit to Plymouth for William Bradford's wedding in July 1623, could require 10,000 beads. By 1400, the concept of wampum as money had traveled inland to the Iroquois League. From there, traders carried the strings to the Dakotas and the Great Lakes tribes of Canada.

Pre-Columbian Indians from New Brunswick south to the Caribbean valued wampum for important rituals:

- to pledge to a treaty or territorial agreement
- to pay tribute or ransom moneys
- to display wealth and position
- as prizes and trophies for sports and games
- to invite guests or announce and honor the death of a chief
- as fines and compensation for crime
- to acknowledge selection of a tribal official
- as a badge or burial token
- to pay bribes or bride prices
- as gifts exchanged between friends
- as payments to priests, shamans, or entertainers at feasts.

On June 24, 1610, a wampum belt commemorated the baptism of the Memberteau and 100 other Micmac by Jessé Fléché, a French missionary at Port Royal on the Annapolis River. For the Pequot of Connecticut and Rhode Island, wampum facilitated long-distance trade in clayware, wood bowls and utensils, and rush baskets and strengthened their position during the Pequot War of 1636–1637. The Abenaki of northern New England and Quebec beaded wampum as a record of council decisions; the Mohawk recorded tribal history or natural events in symbolic beadwork.

After contact with whites, the Oneida of the Great Lakes region, the Passamoquoddy of Maine, and the Mahican of the northern Hudson River used shell beads as currency. In 1627, wampum entered the New England economy through native trade of Dutch merchant Isaac de Razier with the Manhata, who used beads valued at 50 English pounds for buying corn in Plymouth, Massachusetts. By 1637, wampum was colonial legal tender. Peter Stuyvesant, director of New Netherland, raised the value of wampum to around 6,000 *guilders* in 1644 to reimburse workers erecting a fort in New York. In general, colonists, who lacked their own coinage until the establishment of a mint at Boston in 1652, accepted the portable currency substitute, giving rise to the slang term "to shell out."

In 1644, Dutch missionary Johannes Megapolensis, author of "A Short Account of the Mohawk Indians," remarked on the Mohawk style of manufacturing wampum:

> Their money consists of certain little bones, made of shells or cockles, which are found on the sea-beach; a hole is drilled through the middle of the little bones, and these they string upon thread, or they make of them belts as broad as a hand, or broader, and hang them on their necks, or around their bodies. They have also several holes in their ears, and there they likewise hang some. They value these little bones as highly as many Christians do gold, silver and pearls [Megapolensis 1909].

After Megapolensis presented a Rix dollar to a chief, he laughed at Christians, whom he considered foolish for valuing little pieces of iron. The chief sneered that he would throw such coins in the river.

As wampum took on the significance of coins, the colonial authorities accepted beaded strips for government fines and fees and evaluated each string at ⅙ pence for use in purchasing goods costing no more than twelve pence. In Connecticut, each bead was equal to ¼ pence and suitable for the payment of taxes. The colonial court later differentiated between white and blue beads, with blue worth ½ pence, twice the value of white. Most valuable were the rare blue-black beads, which brought more than blue beads.

Throughout New England, New York, New Jersey, Pennsylvania, and Virginia, wampum came in its own denominations. The most common was the single strand or *peag*. Merchants had to examine each string in strong light to determine if the beads were consistent in color and quality and bore no cracks or splits. General circulation of metal coins gradually phased out shell money. By 1661, wampum was voted too cumbrous for payment of debts. Nonetheless, in 1682, William Penn's receipt of wampum belts confirmed the Treaty of Shackamaxon and the agreement was embodied in beaded pictographs. Into the 1690s, ferrymen carrying cargo and passengers from Brooklyn to Connecticut accepted as fare either ninepence or eight strings of wampum.

The Dutch of Long Island in New Amsterdam streamlined native bead making by turning clam shells on a lathe, thereby robbing natives of their monopoly on wampum beads. In 1746, John W. Campbell founded a family business at his beadworks in Pascack, New Jersey. Machine manufacture, which cranked out 20 feet per day, quickly deflated wampum on the Atlantic seaboard. In the interior of the Western Hemisphere into the lower Ohio Valley, far from white settlements, natives still accepted strings and strips as currency and traded them with fur trappers in the employ of John Jacob Astor. At century's end, paper money and coins supplanted wampum entirely as colonial specie. Nevertheless, Campbell's bead works remained in business into the mid–1800s, when Henry Wadsworth Longfellow romanticized wampum in his American epic *The Song of Hiawatha* (1855).

In the 18th and 19th centuries, wampum continued to intersect with historic occasions. In April 1710, when the Iroquois League sent four Mohawk dignitaries to visit Queen Anne in London, court artist Johannes Verelst painted the noblest, Tee Yee Neen Ho Ga Row (also Tiyanoga or Hendrick), holding a wampum sash in his right hand. In 1761, Guyasuta, a Seneca spokesman, carried a red wampum belt from the Onondaga Council to Fort Detroit as a declaration of war. By the early 1800s, phony porcelain beads circulated by fur traders devalued wampum.

In the mid–1800s, a wampum bag and crown established the importance of Paiute spokeswoman Sarah Winnemucca, who journeyed to Eastern seats of power to plead for the welfare and sovereignty of her people. Cherokee wampum makers depicted a tribal council meeting held at Tahlequah, Oklahoma, in 1843, to end an era of war with the Iroquois. In the late 20th century, Leon Shenandoah, speaker for the Onondaga, worked for three decades toward the return of 74 wampum belts displayed in museums. A fellow tribesman, Jake Thomas, interpreted the symbols on the belts as a respected part of native record-keeping.

Around the Great Lakes, a similar economy derived from the carving of copper into tubes, beads, and axes. On the Pacific coast, far from the quahog and whelk grounds of New England, according to ethnologer Alfred L. Kroeber's *Handbook of the Indians of California* (1925), Indians made similar shell money out of *dentalia*, *haliotis*, and *olivella*. The use of *dentalium* shell money extended north to Queen Charlotte and Vancouver islands in British Columbia, where value was determined by quantity rather than quality of beads.

An unusual reference to a "band of guineas" parallels the Algonquian wampum in Robert Louis Stevenson's adventure novel *Kidnapped* (1886). He depicted the belt on Highlander Alan Stewart as a symbol of a passé monetary economy no longer in use by lowlanders. Both valuable and decorative as a folk touch, the belt confers a majesty and statesmanship on the fictional Stewart, who later bargains with the guineas as though they were ordinary coins.

Native Americans are not the only people who have relied on bead money. In the Palau Island group southwest of Saipan, native currency consisted of varied styles of beads:

type	*source*
adelobok	green or white glass polished into 20 unusual shapes as small change
brak	rare yellow stone of unknown origin
kaldoir	beads of commoners
kalebukub	agate cylinders in 25 varieties
kaymon a kvae	green or white glass polished into unusual shapes as small change
kluk	polished enamel spheres in 26 varieties for major expenditure
mungugau	red jasper stone that confers prestige to royal females at state occasions

In addition, island currency also extends to exchange of betel nuts and leaves, shells, tortoise shell, tobacco, and mats, the inter-island currency throughout Oceania. The islanders appear to have derived their style of coinage from trade with the Yap, makers of huge stone wheels.

Europeans discovered the bead specie on contact with Pacific nations. The Pelew were trading in bead currency in 1783, when British army Captain Henry Wilson, author of *An Account of the Pelew Islands,* observed local commerce in glass beads and baked earthenware beads worn by royalty. After islanders of Mologojok looted the wrecked ship of Captain David Dean O'Keefe, in 1882, the British admiralty dispatched two battleships to seek damages. Islanders offered bead money to satisfy a fine of $4,600. In 1954, a British film, *His Majesty O'Keefe*, starring Burt Lancaster, fictionalized the historic event.

***See also* colonial coins; fur money; Rix dollars; St. Patrick coppers.**

SOURCES: Cantor, George. *North American Indian Landmarks*. Detroit: Gale Research, 1993. • Champagne, Duane, ed. *Chronology of Native North American History*. Detroit: Gale Research, 1994. • Clain-Stefanelli, Elvira, and Vladimir

Clain-Stefanelli. *The Beauty and Lore of Coins, Currency, and Medals*. Croton-on-Hudson, N.Y.: Riverwood Publishers, 1974. • Cribb, Joe. *Money*. Toronto: Stoddart, 1990. • Davies, Glyn. *A History of Money from Ancient Times to the Present Day*. Cardiff: University of Wales Press, 1994. • Einzig, Paul. *Primitive Money*. Oxford: Pergamon Press, 1966. • Gustafson, Eleanor H. "Swarthy Monarchs." *Antiques*, September 2000. • Johansen, Bruce E., and Donald A. Grinde. *The Encyclopedia of Native American Biography*. New York: Da Capo Press, 1998. • Jordan, Louis. "The Coins of Colonial and Early America." http://www.coins.nd.edu/ColCoin/ColCoinContents/Introduction.html. • McClure, Andres S. "Sarah Winnemuccca: Post Indian Princess and Voice of the Paiutes." *Melus*, Summer 1999. • Megapolensis, Johannes. "A Short Account of the Mohawk Indians." In J. Franklin Jameson's *Narratives of New Netherland, 1609–1664*. New York: Charles Scribner's Sons, 1909. • Opitz, Charles J. *Odd and Curious Money*. Ocala, Fla.: First Impressions, 1986. • Patterson, Lotsee, and Mary Ellen Snodgrass. *Indian Terms of the Americas*. Englewood, Colo.: Libraries Unlimited, 1994. • Pritzker, Barry M. *A Native American Encyclopedia: History, Culture, and Peoples*. Oxford: Oxford University Press, 2000. • Sorenson, Janet. "'Belts of Gold' and 'Twenty-Pounders': Robert Louis Stevenson's Textualized Economies." *Criticism*, Summer, 2000. • Weatherford, Jack. *The History of Money: From Sandstone to Cyberspace*. Pittsburgh, Pa.: Three Rivers Press, 1998.

Weinman, Adolph A.

One of America's most prominent practitioners of neo-classical representative symbolism, Adolph Alexander Weinman left his mark on notable buildings and coins. Born on December 11, 1870, in Karlsruhe, Germany, he immigrated to the United States at age ten and learned ivory and wood carving from a master carver while studying at night at the Cooper Union and the Art Students League. A student of human form from weekly sessions sketching skeletons and cadavers, he trained with Philip Martiny before assisting in the studios of Daniel Chester French, Olin Warner, and Augustus Saint-Gaudens. Later, Weinman and Malvina Hoffman, sculptor for Chicago's Field Museum, founded anatomy classes for artists at Columbia University's College of Physicians and Surgeons.

Weinman first gained fame for completion of the Roosevelt Inaugural Medal, a noble, but warmly human profile. In 1904, Weinman branched out as a freelance sculptor and medalist and was elected two years later to the National Academy. Through his association with Saint-Gaudens, he received Theodore Roosevelt's commission to design a classical Liberty coin featuring Greek and Roman draping. The result of his sketch was the Mercury dime, which carried the initials AW. To represent unfettered thought, he placed the winged Phrygian cap of Mercury, messenger of the gods, on Liberty's head. The reverse side featured a fasces, the Roman symbol of unity and strength comprised of a bundle of rods holding an axhead.

In 1915, Weinman designed the Walking Liberty half-dollar, a romanticized figure that quickly won the applause of citizens. The emblematic pose featured a young, assertive female form striding confidently into the dawn with her hand stretched forth in a gesture of generosity. Her other arm clutched laurel and oak leaves, symbols of achievement and victory. Sculptor John Mercanti supplied the noble eagle for the reverse side. The popular Walking Liberty coin, bearing the whimsically overlaid monogram of AAW, stayed in production for 31 years.

Weinman's artistry graced the 1919 World's Fair as well as streets of many cities — the Lincoln Memorial in Madison, Wisconsin; the statue of General Macomb on Michigan Avenue in Detroit, *Night* and *Day* for New York City's Pennsylvania Station and bas-reliefs and medallions for the city's Municipal Building; and a bas-relief for the Jefferson Memorial and Statue on the Potomac Tidal Basin, *The Arts of War* and *The Arts of Peace* for the National Archives Building, and the facade for the Post Office Department building in Washington, D.C. For New York City's Municipal Building, he created the gold-surfaced *Civic Fame*, Manhattan's largest statue. In 1929, a film, *The Medal Maker*, featured Weinman's coin artistry along with that of James Earle Fraser and Harmon MacNeil. After Weinman died on August 8, 1952, in Port Chester, New York, his papers, correspondence, photos, negatives, clippings, and sketchbook passed to the Smithsonian Institution.

Early in the 21st century, Weinman's name resurfaced during a controversy over his frieze of 18 great lawgivers of history for the Supreme Court Building in Washington, D.C. Completed in 1935, the tribute to justice on the four walls of the South Courtroom placed in chronological order Menes, Hammurabi, Moses, Solomon, Lycurgus, Solon, Draco, Confucius, Augustus, Justinian, Mohammed, Charlemagne, King John, St. Louis, Hugo Grotius, William Blackstone, John Marshall, and Napoleon. Because likenesses of deities or religious figures conflict with Islamic law, protesters demanded the removal of Mohammed from the group. Government officials replied that Weinman merely honored Islam's great prophet and lawgiver and in no way intended the figure to be a portrait.

***See also* Mercury dime; Peace dollar; Augustus Saint-Gaudens; U.S. coins.**

SOURCES: Bowers, Q. David. *Adventures with Rare Coins*. Los Angeles: Bowers & Ruddy Galleries, Inc., 1979. • Clain-Stefanelli, Elvira, and Vladimir Clain-Stefanelli. *The Beauty and Lore of Coins, Currency, and Medals*. Croton-on-Hudson, N.Y.: Riverwood Publishers, 1974. • Gohmann, Stephan F. "The End of Liberty." *The Freeman*, November 1999. • "Looking at Art: Arts Community Reflects on Significant 20th Century Artists." *Baton Rouge Advocate*, January 9, 2000. • Marotta, Michael E. "The Mercury Dime." *The Shinplaster*, March 1994. • Olert, Chris. "Buried Treasure Faceless Statue Gets a Name and a Rich History." *Fort Worth Star-Telegram*, April 5, 1998. • Reed, Mort. *Cowles Complete Encyclopedia of U.S. Coins*. New York: Cowles Book Company, 1969. • Reiter, Ed. "The Silver Bullion." *New York Times*, December 14, 1986, p. H43. • Silver, Constance S., et al. "U.S. Custom House, New York City: Overview of Analyses and Interpretation of Altered Architectural Finishes." *Journal of the American Institute of Conservation*, Vol. 32, No. 2, 141–152. • Soderberg, Susan C. "Maryland's Civil War Monuments." *The Historian*, Spring 1996. • Starita, Angela. "On the Map: From the Ruins, a Granite Couple Will Stand Over Newark." *New York Times*, December 24, 2000. • "Visual Thinking: Sketchbooks from the Archives of American Art." http://artarchives.si.edu/exhibits/sketchbk/weinman.htm. • Vitello, Barbara. "Undiscovered Gems: The Epitome of Modernism." *Daily Herald*, April 23, 1999.

Wells Fargo

A source of cash for highwaymen of dime novels and Western movies, Wells Fargo & Company prospered from its inception as a freighting and banking firm. Established in March 1852 in New York City, it was the concept of expressmen William G. Fargo and Henry Wells, founder of Western Express. By the first summer, Wells Fargo successfully linked its Montgomery Street office in San Francisco with the Atlantic seaboard as a means of posting news, letters, packages, and crates to and from the East. By buying up smaller, less profitable stage lines, including Adams and Company of California, within three years, Wells Fargo dominated delivery service with 55 offices in mining districts. The company soon grew to 147 outlets. Wells Fargo transported cash and gold dust, which pony express riders ferried to the line for transportation to the U.S. Mint. To survive the completion of the transcontinental railroad in 1869, the company reorganized and liquidated stage vehicles.

Guarding the green strongboxes were private police and detectives who halted stagecoach robberies by capturing 240 road agents, notably, the infamous Black Bart, the nickname of Charles E. Bolton (also Boles or Bole), who is credited with engineering 28 Wells Fargo Stage heists. He began his career in thievery near Fort Ross in 1877, when he seized $300 in cash. Dressed in flour-sack head covering and duster and armed with a shotgun, he plagued California coach drivers and escaped on foot with his loot in a suitcase. He eluded pursuers until his 28th robbery. After a passenger shot at him, he left behind a handkerchief with a laundry mark. For multiple hits on Wells Fargo, he served over four years in prison, then vanished from history, most likely in his hometown, New York City.

Still a source of cash and goods, Wells Fargo remained a likely target of criminals into the 20th century. On September 12, 1983, Argentinian Jorge Masetti, a former Cuban intelligence officer, claimed that the Cuban government masterminded the robbery of a Wells

Fargo armored truck in Hartford, Connecticut, netting $7.2 million. Executed by Juan Segarra Palmer and 11 other Puerto Rican members of the Armed Forces of National Liberation, the robbery was one of the largest in the United States. The perpetrators stashed the money in compartments of a getaway car, drove it to Mexico City, and dispatched four million dollars in cash to Havana through the Cuban embassy. Palmer received a 55-year prison sentence.

SOURCES: "Cuba Financed 1983 Wells Fargo Robbery, Former Cuban Agent Says," *Puerto Rico Herald,* January 4, 2000. • Lamar, Howard R., ed. *The Reader's Encyclopedia of the American West.* New York: Harper & Row, 1977. • "Wells Fargo," http://www.wellsfargo.com.

Whydah

In February 1717, English pirate Samuel Bellamy, formerly of the British Royal Navy, captured the 110-foot ship *Whydah*, which surrendered after a three-day chase from the Windward passage separating Cuba and Puerto Rico northeast to the Bahamian harbor of Long Island. Called "Black Sam" for his shoulder-length hair and long beard, Bellamy was known for bold ventures, including grand theft and piracy on the high seas, which he carried out with the help of American Paul Williams, Louis Lebous, and Benjamin Hornigold. A sea-going brigand during the height of Caribbean-based robberies on the high seas, Bellamy had emigrated to the New World to make his name and fortune. In 1715, he found a silent partner and sailed with his own ship and crew to Florida to search for sunken Spanish treasure ships. To Maria Hallet, a Massachusetts beauty, he promised to distinguish himself by sailing home to New England in the most impressive ship of the era.

When honorable career building failed, Bellamy turned to piracy, a short step down in the days of rampant privateering. His crew looted some 50 vessels. He commandeered the 300-ton, three-masted slaver *Whydah*, launched in 1715, on its way from Cuba and Hispaniola in part of the triangular trade that took slave ships from England to the Bight of Benin on Africa's west coast, west to Jamaica, and home to England. Without loss of life, he sent his crew aboard to capture sugar, quinine, indigo, gold Akan beads made by the lost wax method in Africa, and ivory as well as tons of gold and silver. Sharing the bulk of the Spanish *escudos* and silver *reales* were Bellamy, his carpenter, and the ship's doctor. Ordinary sailors earned shares worth $75 each.

At the end of Bellamy's plundering the *Whydah*, he transformed the ship from slaver to pirate vessel. Because his own vessel needed repair, he abandoned it and continued on his way home aboard the *Whydah*. Adding to the heist was the accumulated loot of some 50 other seizures in the year since Bellamy had turned from legitimate sailor to sea parasite. At the head of the fleet, the ship bore him back to New England in April 1717.

The *Whydah* set sail for Block Island off Rhode Island for a rendezvous with Paul Williams, who had gone ahead. When Bellamy's Indian pilot, John Julian, encountered harsh winds off Sluttsbush, Massachusetts, on April 26, 1717, he lost control of the *Whydah*, which foundered in a gale off the sandbars of Wellfleet, Cape Cod. Huge waves splintered the mainmast and rocked the cannons free, sending them plunging belowdecks. Bellamy and most of his 144 men, including any African captives from the *Whydah* who chose to turn pirate, were too drunk on Madeira wine captured from the stock of the three-masted English vessel *Mary Anne* to save themselves or their cargo.

Historical details of the *Whydah* were sketchy. Only Julian and the ship's carpenter, Thomas Davis, saved themselves by swimming to shore and avoided arrest by claiming that they were pressed into service against their will. A week later when the colonial governor dispatched Captain Cyprian Southack, an artist and cartographer, to salvage goods from the *Whydah*, the ship, which had turned upside down only 1,200 feet off Cape Cod's Marconi Beach, was already picked clean by local islanders. Southhack, who submitted a map of the shipwreck's location, snorted in his journal, "Pepol very Stife and will not [surrender] one thing of what they Gott on the Rack" (Pickford 1994, p. 69). Adding to his foul mood were suspicions that Thomas Davis and Samuel Harding managed to retrieve most of the treasure. In October, authorities hanged six of the pirates at Charlestown Ferry, Boston; the court exonerated Davis and Thomas South, a sailor aboard the *Mary Anne*.

Coins washed up on shore from time to time, piquing interest in the famed treasure ship that broke apart in the gale. In 1982, Cape Cod high school teacher Barry Clifford, who had heard of the treasure ship from his uncle's yarns, determined to locate the *Whydah*. He hired a crew of divers and incorporated his operation the following year as Maritime Explorations. Licensed to comb some two square miles of sea, he examined the area eroded in subsequent years by storms and savage currents. He was to receive one quarter of any marketable salvage, with the remainder going to the state. To facilitate the work, he refurbished the *Vast Explorer II*, a 60-foot Navy research vessel, and equipped it with magnetometer metal detectors and Loran charting equipment to comb the ocean floor in extremely low visibility.

On July 20, 1984, Clifford located the wreck off South Wellfleet, Massachusetts. The state board of underwater archaeological resources authenticated the find by examining the ship's 18-in. bronze bell bearing the legend "The Whydah Gally 1716" and valued artifacts at five million dollars. The only sunken pirate ship ever found, the *Whydah* restored historical data to a subject that had long been romanticized and denigrated by swashbuckling fiction. Among the items retrieved from ten feet of shifting sand on the ocean floor were cannonballs, cannon, musket balls, and a silver Peruvian coin dated 1684. To protect his find, Clifford immediately employed a security specialist and full-time watch to guard against dishonest divers as well as modern pirates and potential hijackers of daily transports of material dispatched from the site to the Maritime Explorations' laboratory in Chatham for processing and preservation.

In subsequent dives, Clifford, his son Brandon, and the other divers located brass dividers, navigational rulers, leadsman's rope and weights, a ring dial for determining latitudes, 4,000 silver pieces of eight, and gold ingots, as well as pirate garb, a pair of pistols tied to a silk sash, shoes, buttons, and plates. Some of the half-million coins found in the wreckage bore mint marks from England, France, the Netherlands, Scotland, and Spain dating from 1638 to 1715, two years before the *Whydah* sank. One coin from 1653 was valued at $40,000. The worth of Bellamy's cargo of 180 bags of treasure was estimated at $400 million.

Much of the haul resides in a museum, the Expedition Whydah Sea Lab and Learning Center, established in Provincetown, Massachusetts. A second historical museum, the three-story, 70 million-dollar Whydah Pirate Complex in Tampa, Florida, opened in 1995 during the annual Gasparilla festival, which celebrates the legendary pirate José "Gasparilla" Gaspar, a quasi-historical figure. The museum features a replica of the *Whydah*, a shipwreck simulation, trial of the surviving pirates, and historical re-creation of the ship's sinking. The Chamber of Commerce predicted that the Florida exhibition would draw 1.5 million tourists per year.

SOURCES: Burgan, Michael, "Lost and Found Treasure," *National Geographic World*, April 2000, 19. • "Cape Cod's Bounty," *Time*, November 11, 1985, p. 37. • Clifford, Barry. *Expedition Whydah*. New York: Cliff Street Books, 1999. • Clifford, Barry. *The Pirate Prince*. New York: Simon & Schuster, 1993. • Cordingly, David. *Under the Black Flag*. San Diego, Calif.: Harvest Books, 1995. • Mitchell, Mary A., "Tampa Lands New Pirate Attraction," *Travel Weekly*, November 23, 1992, 28. • Murphy, Jamie, "Down into the Deep," *Time*, August 11, 1986, 48–54. • Nash, Jay Robert. *Encyclopedia of World Crime*. 6 vols. Wilmette, Ill.: CrimeBooks Inc., 1990. • *Outlaws, Mobsters & Crooks: From the Old West to the Internet*. Farmington Hills, Mich.: U*X*L, 1998. • Pickford, Nigel. *The Atlas of Ship Wrecks & Treasure*. New York: Dorling Kindersley, 1994. • Rediker, Marcus. *Between the Devil and the Deep Blue Sea*. Cambridge: Cambridge University Press, 1987. • Sandz, Victoria. *Encyclopedia of Western Atlantic Shipwrecks and Sunken Treasure*. Jefferson, N.C.: McFarland, 2001. • Skerry, Brian, "Pirates of the *Whydah*," *National Geographic*, May 1999, 64. • Wheeler, Richard. *In Pirate Waters*. New York: Thomas Y. Crowell, 1969.

William the Conqueror

The first of England's Norman dynasty, William I the Conqueror halted multiple claimants to the English throne and established a solid dynasty and royal treasury. Born in 1028 to Herleva and Robert II, Duke of Normandy, he came of age in difficult times for royal children. At age 21, he and Henri I of France settled a French rebellion that netted William Alençon and Domfront. After stating his claim on England, he fought his way to full kingship of that country, a shift of power that introduced to the Anglo-Saxon language the other two elements — French and Latin — that produced Middle English.

After seizing English rule from Harold at Hastings on October 14, 1066, and receiving a crown from Aldred on Christmas Day at Westminster, William held Saxon residents in tight rein. By superintending an efficient system of tax collection, he avoided debasing currency. Following his example, subsequent English kings ended inflation by maintaining the value of money in circulation. By the time he called for the compilation of the *Domesday Book* (1086), England's fiscal health was stable.

William also maintained the customary Peter's pence, called "the Lord's penny," a tax in support of the Roman pope. William declared that any freeholder owning 30 pence or more should pay the annual stipend as a tithe. Lords paid the tax for their serfs. Burgesses and freemen owning one-half *mark* in property also paid the tax. All who cheated the tax collector suffered a fine of 30 pence to a church court or 40 shillings to a royal court plus thirty pence to the bishop.

***See also* English money.**

SOURCES: Baugh, Albert C. *A History of the English Language*. New York: Appleton-Century-Crofts, 1957. • Cantor, Norman F., ed. *The Civilization of the Middle Ages*. New York: HarperPerennial, 1993. • Davies, Glyn. *A History of Money from Ancient Times to the Present Day*. Cardiff: University of Wales Press, 1994. • Hollister, C. Warren. *Medieval Europe: A Short History*. New York: McGraw-Hill, 1994. • "Medieval Sourcebook: William the Conqueror: Provision for Peter's Pence." http://www. fordham.edu/halsall/source/1087william1-peterspence. html. • Montague-Smith, Patrick W. *The Royal Line of Succession: The British Monarchy from Cerdic to Queen Elizabeth II*. Andover, England: Pitkin, 1986. • Parker, Michael St. John. *Britain's Kings and Queens*. Andover, Hants: Pitkin, 1994. • Snodgrass, Mary Ellen. *Who's Who in the Middle Ages*. Jefferson, N.C.: McFarland, 2001. • Tyerman, Christopher. *Who's Who in Early Medieval England*. London: Shepheard-Walwyn Publishers, 1996.

Wizard of Oz

According to high school teacher Henry M. Littlefield, in 1900, fantasy writer L. Frank Baum, a supporter of bimetallism, allegorized in *The Wonderful Wizard of Oz* the furor over the gold standard that waged from 1880 to the end of the century, when James Fisk and Jay Gould nearly cornered the gold market. A children's adventure classic, the story was also a populist parable depicting courageous, optimistic heroine Dorothy against a forbidding Kansas landscape stirred up by a cyclone, the symbol of the "free and unlimited coinage of silver" mania (Parker 1994, p. 49). The Wicked Witch of the East dies after the whirling storm plunks a house on her. Dorothy, wearing the witch's magic silver shoes, treks through the land of Oz, which Baum named for the O–Z marking on the spine of a reference book, mocking at the same time the abbreviation for ounce.

Guiding Dorothy's way is the yellow brick road that leads to the Emerald City, emblems of the gold standard trail leading to Washington, D.C. Her companions link to principal figures in the gold standard controversy — a groaning, compassionless tin woodman (factory labor), a brainless scarecrow (farmers), and a cowardly lion, a caricature of pompous orator William Jennings Bryan, populist spokesman for free silver. The lion ennobles himself largely by his roar, a cover for fright. He confides to Dorothy, "I'm such a coward; but just as soon as they hear me roar they all try to get away from me, and of course I let them go" (Baum 1956, p. 54). The remark illuminates the number of times that Bryan ran unsuccessfully for public office.

Like a knight errant of the Gilded Age,

Dorothy bears the standard of Midwesterners. In one insightful conversation, she challenges the scarecrow, who can't understand why she wants to leave Oz to return to "the dry, gray place you call Kansas" (*ibid.*, p. 33). She replies that he hasn't enough brains to realize that "No matter how dreary and gray our homes are, we people of flesh and blood would rather live there than in any other country, be it ever so beautiful. There is no place like home" (*ibid.*).

The plot thickens with satiric digs at imperialism, materialism, and monomania, represented by the green-lensed glasses that fasten with two gold bands locked with a key, a jab at the illusion of permanence that Washington money produces. Through a green tinge, visitors to the dazzling Emerald City gaze at the terrain. At the throne room in the rear of the Palace of Oz (representing the White House or the white city at Chicago's 1893 Columbian Exposition), Dorothy meets the wizard (President William McKinley's campaign manager Marcus Alonzo Hanna). A symbol of public trickery, the wizard fools his adoring fans by speaking through the painted lips of a *papier-mâché* mask that he suspended from the ceiling on a wire. He explains to Dorothy, "I am a ventriloquist ... and I can throw the sound of my voice wherever I wish; so that you thought it was coming out of the Head" (Baum 1983, p. 265). When he wearies of manipulating his voice, he travels by hot-air balloon far from his native Omaha.

The wizard, who chooses to send a minion to do battle with rebellious Westerners, assigns Dorothy a quest to overthrow the Wicked Witch of the West. Along the way, Dorothy loses one of her slippers to the witch, a compromise of magic that parallels Republican attempts to weaken the outcry for free silver. Kept waiting on return to the wizard, the narrator comments with overt irritation at Washington's high-handedness: "The waiting was tiresome and wearing, and at last they grew vexed that Oz should treat them in so poor a fashion, after sending them to undergo hardships and slavery" (*ibid.*, p. 153).

On discovering that the wizard is a humbug, Dorothy locates Glinda, the Good Witch of the South, a tie to Southern sympathies toward the crusade for free silver coinage. Glinda assures Dorothy of the powers of the silver shoes, which "can carry you to any place in the world in three steps" (*ibid.*, p. 216). Once more in possession of both magic silver slippers, Dorothy clicks her heels and returns to Kansas, an agrarian ideal far from the materialistic, money-driven urban centers of the East. The whole Littlefieldian theory intrigued some, but others pointed to gaps in his understanding of a complex political scenario.

SOURCES: Allen, Larry. *Encyclopedia of Money.* New York: Checkmark Books, 2001. • Baum, L. Frank. *The Annotated Wizard of Oz.* New York: Schocken Books, 1983. • Baum, L. Frank. *The Wizard of Oz.* New York: Ballantine Books, 1956. • "The Bureau of Engraving and Printing." http://www.bep.treas.gov/. • Davies, Glyn. *A History of Money from Ancient Times to the Present Day.* Cardiff: University of Wales Press, 1994. • Littlefield, Henry M. "The Wizard of Oz: Parable on Populism." *American Quarterly*, 16, Spring, 47–58. • Mannix, Daniel P. "The Father of the Wizard of Oz." *American Heritage*, December 1964, 36. • Parker, David B. "The Rise and Fall of The Wonderful Wizard of Oz as a 'Parable on Populism.'" *Journal of the Georgia Association of Historians*, 1994, pp. 49–63. • Snodgrass, Mary Ellen. *Late Achievers.* Englewood, Colo.: Libraries Unlimited, 1992. • Snow, Jack. *Who's Who in Oz.* Chicago: Reilly & Lee, 1954. • Weatherford, Jack. *The History of Money: From Sandstone to Cyberspace.* Pittsburgh, Pa.: Three Rivers Press, 1998. • "The Wonderful Wizard of Oz." http://www.people.cornell.edu/pages/dbj5/oz.html.

world currency

World currency carries hints of colonialism in the names of currencies and monetary symbols. Many link former possessions and territories with their mother countries. For example, some African, Caribbean, and Pacific nations still label their currencies as franc/Fr. Currencies of the Western Hemisphere divested themselves of European nomenclature and instead honored expeditioners:

- the *bolivar* of Venezuela and *boliviano* of Bolivia, commemorating freedom fighter Simón Bolívar, Venezuela's native son

- the Panamanian *balboa,* named for Spanish explorer Vasco Nuñez de Balboa, the first European to cross the Isthmus of Panama and to glimpse the Pacific Ocean
- the Nicaraguan *cordoba*, the surname of Governor Fernández de Córdoba
- the *colón* of Costa Rica and El Salvador, which preserves the ingenuity of Spain's New World discoverer Christopher Columbus.

The spread of monetary units into newly settled regions required an expedient financial system, for example, the cupro-nickel *franc* issued from Brussels in 1922 for use in the Belgian Congo, afterward the independent nation of Zaire and now called the Democratic Republic of the Congo. The influence of the United States and the United Kingdom is particularly apparent in the large number of currencies based on the dollar ($) and the pound (£). Also suggesting U.S. and U.K. influence in traditional world currencies is the number of nations breaking their basic currency into one hundredths, as shown in the following table:

nation	*basic currency*	*symbol*
Afghanistan	100 puls=afghani	Afg
Albania	100 qindarka=lek	Lk
Algeria	100 centimes= Algerian dinar	Da
American Samoa	100 cents=dollar	$
Andorra	100 centimes=franc 100 céntimos=peseta	Fr
Angola	100 lwei=kwanza	Kzrl
Anguilla	100 cents=East Caribbean dollar	EC$
Antigua	100 cents=East Caribbean dollar	EC$
Argentina	10,000 australes= peso	
Armenia	100 louma=dram	
Aruba	florin	
Ascension Island	100 pence=St. Helena pound	£
Australia	100 cents= Australian dollar	$A
Austria	100 groschen= Schilling	
Azerbaijan	100 gopik=manat	
Bahamas	100 cents= Bahamian dollar	B$
Bahrain	1,000 fils=Bahraini dinar	BD
Bangladesh	100 poisha=taka	Tk
Barbados	100 cents=Barbados dollar	BD$

The reverse of this Barbadian 25-cent coin features the Morgan Lewis sugar mill, honoring the technology that brought wealth to the island.

***Left:* This seven-sided dollar coin from Barbados honors a national dish, flying fish, which islanders grill at breakfast with a dressing of salt and lime juice. *Right:* The reverse of this seven-sided dollar coin from Barbados features the island's national emblem and motto, "Pride and Industry."**

This 100-dollar bill of Barbados pictures the stone architecture of Bridgetown, the capital city.

nation	*basic currency*	*symbol*
Barbuda	100 cents=East Caribbean dollar	EC$
Belarus	100 kopeks=rouble	
Belgium	100 centimes=Belgian franc	
Belize	100 cents=Belize dollar	BZ$
Benin	franc	CFA
Bermuda	100 cents=Bermuda dollar	

Left: A five-cent piece struck in Bermuda in 1981 pictures a youthful bust of Queen Elizabeth II of England. **Right:** The reverse of the Bermuda five-cent piece pictures the graceful Bermuda angelfish, a favorite with snorkelers and scuba divers.

Bhutan	100 chetrum=ngultrum	
	100 paisa=Indian rupee	Rs
Bolivia	100 centavos=boliviano	$b
Bosnia-Hercegovina	marka	
	Deutschemark	DM
Botswana	100 thebe=pula	P
Brazil	100 centavos=real	
British Virgin Islands	100 cents=U.S. dollar	US$
	100 pence=pound sterling	£
	100 cents=East Caribbean dollar	EC$
Brunei	100 sen=Brunei dollar	B$
	100 cents=Singapore dollar	S$
Bulgaria	100 stotinki=lev	
Burkina Faso	franc	CFA
Burundi	100 centimes=Burundi franc	
Caicos Islands	100 cents=dollar	$
Cambodia	100 sen=riel	
Cameroon	franc	CFA
Canada	100 cents=Canadian dollar	C$
Cape Verde	100 centavos=escudo caboverdiano	
Cayman Islands	100 cents=Cayman Islands dollar	CI$

nation	*basic currency*	*symbol*
Central African Republic	franc	CFA
Chad	franc	CFA
Chile	100 centavos=Chilean peso	
China	100 fen=10 jiao=renminbi yuan	
Colombia	100 centavos=Colombian peso	
Comoros	100 centimes=Comorian franc	KMF
Congo, Dem. Rep. of	Congolese franc	
Congo, Rep. of	franc	CFA
Cook Islands	100 cents=dollar	
Costa Rica	100 céntimos=Costa Rican colón	#
Côte d'Ivoire	franc	CFA
Croatia	100 lipas=kuna	
Cuba	100 centavos=Cuban peso	
Cyprus	100 cents=Cyprus pound	C£
Czech Republic	100 haléru=koruna	Kcs
Denmark	100 øre=Danish krone	
Djibouti	100 centimes=Djibouti franc	
Dominica	100 cents=East Caribbean dollar	EC$
Dominican Republic	100 centavos=Dominican Republic peso	RD$
Ecuador	100 centavos=sucre	
Egypt	1,000 millièmes=100 piastres=Egyptian pound	£E
El Salvador	100 centavos=El Salvador colón	#
Equatorial Guinea	franc	CFA
Eritrea	nakfa	
Estonia	100 sents=kroon	
Ethiopia	100 cents=Ethiopian birr	EB
Falkland Islands	100 pence=Falkland pound	
Faroe Islands	100 øre=Danish krone	
Fiji	100 cents=Fiji dollar	F$
Finland	100 pennia=markka	Mk
France	100 centimes=franc	Fr
French Guiana	100 centimes=franc	Fr
French Polynesia	franc	CFP
Futuna Islands	franc	CFP
Gabon	franc	CFA
Gambia	100 butat=dalasi	D

In the 20th century, French Polynesia chose as coin art native blossoms and fruits from island flora.

In the 20th century, French Polynesia chose as coin art an island scene depicting palm-edged shores, a mountain peak, and a sailing vessel.

Tahitian money reflects the European influence in Polynesia by displaying Marianne, the female emblem of France who is the equivalent of Britannia in Great Britain, Hibernia in Ireland, and Lady Liberty and Uncle Sam in the United States.

nation	*basic currency*	*symbol*
Georgia	100 tetri=lari	
Germany	100 pfennig=Deutschemark	DM
Ghana	100 pesewas=cedi	
Gibraltar	100 pence=Gibraltar pound	

After 1948, West Germany's coins bore the inscription "Bundesrepublik Deutschland."

nation	*basic currency*	*symbol*
Greece	100 leptae=drachma	
Greenland	100 øre=Danish krone	
Grenada	100 cents=East Caribbean dollar	EC$
The Grenadines	100 cents=East Caribbean dollar	EC$
Guadeloupe	100 centimes=franc	Fr
Guam	100 cents=dollar	$
Guatemala	100 centavos=quetzal	Q
Guernsey	100 pence=pound sterling	£
Guinea	100 centimes=Guinea franc	
Guinea-Bissau	franc	CFA
Guyana	100 cents=Guyana dollar	G$
Haiti	100 centimes=gourde	
Honduras	100 centavos=lempira	
Hong Kong	100 cents=Hong Kong dollar	HK$
Hungary	100 fillér=forint	
Iceland	100 aurar=Icelandic króna	Kr
India	100 paisa=Indian rupee	Rs
Indonesia	100 sen=rupiah	Rp
Iran	rial	
Iraq	1,000 fils=Iraqi dinar	ID
Ireland, Rep. of	100 pence=punt	IR£
Israel	100 agorot=shekel (sheqalim)	
Italy	100 centesimi=lira	
Jamaica	100 cents=Jamaican dollar	J$
Japan	100 sen=yen	
Jersey	100 pence=pound	£
Jordan	1,000 fils=Jordanian dinar	JD
Kazakhstan	tenge	

Twentieth-century Italian coinage revived the grace of the classic image of the Greek goddess Athena and the laurel tree.

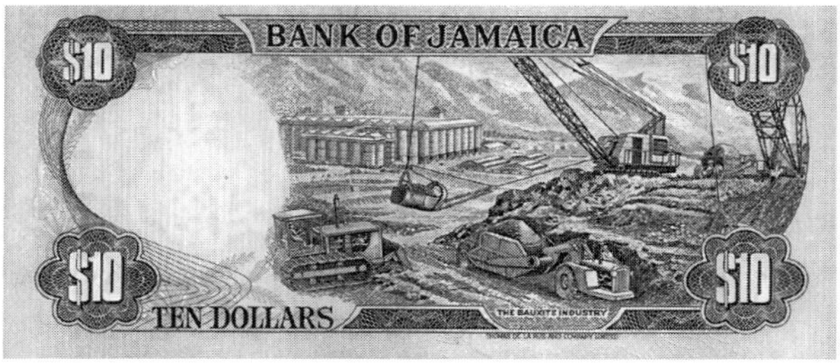

The reverse of this ten-dollar Jamaican note presents a scene of hard labor in the island bauxite industry.

The reverse of the Jamaican one-dollar note stresses the flora of the island and its placid waters.

nation	*basic currency*	*symbol*
Kenya	100 cents=Kenya shilling	Ksh
Kiribati	100 cents=Australian dollar	$A
Kuwait	1,000 fils=Kuwaiti dinar	KD
Kyrgyzstan	som	
Laos	100 santimes=kip	K
Latvia	100 santimes=lat	
Lebanon	100 piastres=Lebanese pound	L£
Lesotho	100 lisente=loti	M
Liberia	100 cents=Liberian dollar	L$

nation	*basic currency*	*symbol*
Libya	1,000 dirhams=Libyan dinar	LD
Liechtenstein	100 rappen=Swiss franc	
	100 centimes=Swiss franc	
Lithuania	litas	
Luxembourg	100 centimes= Luxembourg franc	LF
	100 centimes=Belgian franc	
Macao	100 avos=pataca	
Macedonia	100 paras=dinar	
Madagascar	100 centimes=franc malgache	FMG
Malawi	100 tambala=kwacha	K
Malaysia	100 sen=Malaysian dollar	M$
	100 sen=ringgit	

This 50-*sen* Malaysian coin is a modern design with the 18-story tower of Parliament House near Lake Gardens in Kuala Lampur alongside a crescent moon and star, a pair of Islamic symbols.

nation	*basic currency*	*symbol*
Maldives	100 laaris=rufiyaa	
Mali	franc	CFA
Malta	1,000 mils=100 cents= Maltese lira	LM
Marshall Islands	100 cents=dollar	$
Martinique	100 centimes=franc	Fr
Mauritania	5 khoums=ouguiya	UM
Mauritius	100 cents=Mauritius rupee	
Mayotte	100 centimes=franc	Fr
Mexico	100 centavos=peso	
Micronesia	100 cents=dollar	$
Miquelon	100 centimes=franc	Fr
Moldova	leu	
Monaco	100 centimes=French franc	Fr
Mongolia	100 möngö=tugrik	

The reverse of the 50-*centavo* coin of Mexico pictures a native profile in Incan headdress.

nation	*basic currency*	*symbol*
Montenegro	New dinar	
Montserrat	100 cents=East Caribbean dollar	EC$
Morocco	100 centimes=dirham	DH
Mozambique	100 centavos= metical	MT
Myanmar	100 pyas=kyat	K
Namibia	100 cents=Namibian dollar	
Nauru	100 cents=Australian dollar	$A
Nepal	100 paisa=Nepalese rupee	
Netherlands	100 cents=*gulden* (guilder)	
	100 cents=florin	
Netherlands Antilles	100 cents=Netherlands Antilles guilder	
Nevis	100 cents=East Caribbean dollar	EC$
New Caledonia	franc	CFP
New Zealand	100 cents=New Zealand dollar	NZ$

Below, left: **The Dutch ten-cent piece, called a *dubbeltje*, is the world's tiniest coin. *Right:* The Dutch 25-cent piece pictures Juliana, Queen of the Netherlands from 1948 to 1980.**

nation	*basic currency*	*symbol*
Nicaragua	100 centavos=córdoba	C$
Niger	franc	CFA
Nigeria	100 kobo=naira	N
Niue of the Cook Islands	tokelau	
Norfolk Island	100 cents=Australian dollar	$A
Northern Mariana Islands	100 cents=dollar	$
North Korea	100 chon=won	
Norway	100 øre=krone	
Oman	1,000 baiza=rial Omani	OR
Pakistan	100 paisa=Pakistan rupee	
Palau	100 cents=dollar	$
Panama	100 centésimos= balboa	
	100 cents=dollar	$
Papua–New Guinea	100 toea=kina	K
Paraguay	100 céntimos=guarani	Gs
Peru	100 cénts=new sol	
Philippines	100 centavos= Philippine peso	P
Pitcairn Islands	100 cents=New Zealand dollar	NZ$
Poland	100 groszy=zloty	
Portugal	100 centavos=escudo	Esc
Principe	100 centavos=dobra	

The reverse of the 100-*escudo* note from Portugal depicts Rossio Square, which was Lisbon's fashionable center of town in the nineteenth century.

Puerto Rico	100 cents=dollar	$
Qatar	1000 dirhams=Qatar riyal	
Réunion	100 centimes=franc	Fr
Romania	100 bani=leu (lei)	
Russia	100 kopeks=new rouble	
Rwanda	100 centimes=Rwanda franc	
St. Christopher (St. Kitts)	100 cents=East Caribbean dollar	EC$

nation	*basic currency*	*symbol*
St. Helena	100 pence= St. Helena pound	£
St. Lucia	100 cents=East Caribbean dollar	EC$
St. Pierre	100 centimes=franc	Fr
St. Vincent	100 cents=East Caribbean dollar	EC$
Samoa	100 sene=tala	S$
San Marino	100 centesimi=lira	
São Tomé	100 centavos=dobra	
Saudi Arabia	10 qursh= Saudi riyal 100 halala=Saudi riyal	SR
Scotland	100 pence=pound	£
Senegal	franc	CFA
Seychelles	100 cents=Seychelles rupee	
Sierra Leone	100 cents=leone	Le
Singapore	100 cents=Singapore dollar	S$
Slovakia	100 haliers=koruna	Sk
Slovenia	100 stotin=tolar	SIT
Solomon Islands	100 cents=Solomon Islands dollar	SI$
Somalia	100 cents=Somali shilling	
South Africa	100 cents=rand	R
South Korea	100 jeon=won	
Spain	100 céntimos=peseta	
Sri Lanka	100 cents=Sri Lanka rupee	
Sudan	10 pounds=Sudanese dinar	SD
Suriname	100 cents=Suriname guilder	
Swaziland	100 cents=lilangeni 100 cents=rand	E R
Sweden	100 öre=Swedish krona	
Switzerland	100 rappen=Swiss franc 100 centimes=Swiss franc	

Left: **This one-dollar coin from Singapore, struck in 1937 and adorned with a periwinkle blossom, exhibits the influence of Chinese geomancy or feng shui in the *pak kwa* or *pa kua* shape, a symbolic octagon that combats negative energy. *Right:* The reverse of the one-dollar coin from Singapore depicts lions holding the city shield.**

This two-franc coin from Switzerland retains the beaded circle around a classic garland.

Left: **This modern ten-cent piece from Singapore bears the old city name "Singapura," which means "lion city." *Right:* The reverse of this ten-cent piece from Singapore pictures native blossoms.**

This twentieth-century Swiss five-franc piece echoes the even-armed cross found on the Swiss flag and on the emblem of the International Red Cross, a relief agency that Swiss humanitarian Henri Dunant founded at the battle of Solferino in June 1859.

nation	basic currency	symbol
Syria	100 piastres=Syrian pound	S$
Taiwan	100 cents=new Taiwan dollar	NT$
Tajikistan	100 tanga=Tajik rouble	TJR
Tanzania	100 cents=Tanzanian shilingi	
Thailand	100 satang=baht	
Tobago	100 cents=Trinidad and Tobago dollar	TT$
Togo	franc	CFA
Tokelau	100 cents=dollar	
Tonga	100 seniti=pa'anga	T$
Transdniestra	New Ruble	
Trinidad	100 cents=Trinidad and Tobago dollar	TT$
Tristan da Cunha	100 pence=pound sterling	£
Tunisia	1,000 millimes=Tunisian dinar	
Turkey	100 kurus=Turkish lira	TL
Turkmenistan	100 tenesi=manat	
Turks	100 cents=dollar	$
Tuvalu	100 cents=Australian dollar	$A
Uganda	100 cents=Uganda shilling	
Ukraine	100 kopiykas=hryvna	
United Arab Emirates	100 fils=UAE dirham	
United Kingdom	100 pence=pound sterling	£
United States of America	100 cents=U.S. dollar	US$
Uruguay	100 centésimos= Uruguayan peso	
U.S. Virgin Islands	100 cents=U.S. dollar	US$
Uzbekistan	sum	
Vanuatu	100 centimes=vatu	
Vatican City State	100 centesimi=lira	
Venezuela	100 céntimos=bolivar	Bs
Vietnam	10 hào=dông 100 xu=dông	
Wallis	franc	CFP
Yemen	100 fils=riyal	
Yugoslavia	100 paras=new dinar	
Zambia	100 ngwee=kwacha	K
Zimbabwe	100 cents=Zimbabwe dollar	Z$

The names of world monetary denominations came from interesting and varied sources:

coin	source and/or meaning	nations (or other geographical entities)
afghani	Pashto, native people	Afghanistan
agorot	Hebrew, small coin	Israel
aurar	Latin, gold	Iceland
australes	Latin, southern	Argentina
avo	Latin, bird	Macao
baht	Thai, coin	Thailand
baiza		Oman
balboa	Spanish, name of Vasco Nuñez de Balboa, discoverer of the Pacific Ocean	Panama
bani	Romanian, coin	Romania
birr	Amharic, coin	Ethiopia
bolivar	Spanish, name of Símon Bolívar, freedom fighter	Venezuela
boliviano	Spanish, name of Símon Bolívar, freedom fighter and father of the Bolivian state	Bolivia
butat		Gambia
cedi	Ghanaian, shilling	Ghana
cent	Latin, one-hundredth	American Samoa, Anguilla, Antigua, Australia, Bahamas, Barbados, Barbuda, Belize,

coin	*source and/or meaning*	*nations (or other geographical entities)*
		Bermuda, British Virgin Islands, Brunei, Caicos Islands, Canada, Cayman Islands, Cook Islands, Cyprus, Dominica, Ethiopia, Fiji, Grenada, Grenadines, Guam, Guyana, Hong Kong, Jamaica, Kenya, Kiribati, Liberia, Malta, Marshall Islands, Mauritius, Micronesia, Montserrat, Namibia, Nauru, Netherlands, Netherlands Antilles, Nevis, New Zealand, Norfolk Island, Northern Mariana Islands, Palau, Pitcairn Island, Puerto Rico, St. Christopher, St. Lucia, St. Vincent, Seychelles, Sierra Leone, Singapore, Solomon Islands, Somalia, South Africa, Sri Lanka, Suriname, Swaziland, Taiwan, Tanzania, Tobago, Tokelau, Trinidad, Turks, Tuvalu, Uganda, United States of America, U.S. Virgin Islands, Zimbabwe
cént	Latin, one-hundredth	Peru
centavo	Latin, one-hundredth	Bolivia, Brazil, Cape Verde, Chile, Colombia, Cuba, Dominican Republic, Ecuador, El Salvador, Guatemala, Honduras, Mexico, Mozambique, Nicaragua, Philippines, Portugal, Principe, São Tomé
centesimi	Latin, one-hundredth	Italy, San Marino, Vatican City State
centésimo	Latin, one-hundredth	Panama, Paraguay, Uruguay
centime	Latin, one-hundredth	Algeria, Andorra, Belgium, Burundi, Comoros, Djibouti, France, French Guiana, Guadeloupe, Guinea, Haiti, Liechtenstein, Luxembourg, Madagascar, Martinique, Mayotte, Miquelon, Monaco, Morocco, Réunion, Rwanda, St. Pierre, Switzerland, Vanuatu
céntimo	Latin, one-hundredth	Andorra, Costa Rica, Spain, Venezuela
chetrum		Bhutan
chon	Korean, money	North Korea
colón	Spanish, name of Christopher Columbus, Spanish discoverer of the New World	Costa Rica, El Salvador
córdoba	Spanish, name of Governor Fernández de Córdoba	Nicaragua
dalasi	Gambian, coin	Gambia
Deutsche	German, of Germany	Bosnia-Hercegovina, Germany
mark	Italian, score	
dinar	Latin, coin	Algeria, Bahrain, Iraq, Jordan, Kuwait, Libya, Macedonia, Montenegro, Sudan, Tunisia, Yugoslavia
dirham	Greek, weight or coin	Libya, Morocco, Qatar, United Arab Emirates
dobra	Latin, double	Principe, São Tomé
dollar	German, valley	American Samoa, Anguilla, Antigua, Australia, Barbuda, Bahamas, Barbados, Belize, Bermuda, British Virgin Islands, Brunei, Caicos Islands, Canada, Cayman Islands, Cook Islands, Dominica, Fiji, Grenada, Grenadines, Guam, Guyana, Hong Kong, Jamaica, Kiribati, Liberia, Malaysia, Marshall Islands, Micronesia,

coin	*source and/or meaning*	*nations (or other geographical entities)*
		Montserrat, Namibia, Naura, Nevis, New Zealand, Norfolk Island, Northern Mariana Islands, Palau, Panama, Pitcairn Island, Puerto Rico, St. Christopher, St. Lucia, St. Vincent, Singapore, Solomon Islands, Taiwan, Tobago, Tokelau, Trinidad, Turks, Tuvalu, United States of America, U.S. Virgin Islands, Zimbabwe
dông	Vietnamese, money	Vietnam
drachma	Greek, handful	Greece
dram	Greek, handful	Armenia
escudo	Latin, shield	Cape Verde, Portugal
fen	Chinese, one hundredth	China
fillér	Hungarian, money	Hungary
fils	Arabian, copper coin	Bahrain, Iraq, Jordan, Kuwait, United Arab Emirates, Yemen
florin	Latin, flower	Aruba, Netherlands
forint	Latin, flower	Hungary
franc	French, Frankish	Andorra, Belgium, Benin, Burkina Faso, Burundi, Cameroon, Central African Republic, Chad, Comoros, Congo, Côte d'Ivoire, Djibouti, Equatorial Guinea, France, French Guiana, French Polynesia, Futuna Islands, Gabon, Guadeloupe, Guinea, Guinea-Bissau, Liechtenstein, Luxembourg, Mali, Martinique, Mayotte, Miquelon, Monaco, New Caledonia, Niger, Réunion, Rwanda, St. Pierre, Senegal, Switzerland, Togo, Wallis
gopik		Azerbaijan
gourde	Latin, a cucurbit	Haiti
groschen	Latin, thick	Austria
groszy	Latin, thick	Poland
guarani	Spanish, a people	Paraguay
guilder	Dutch, gold	Netherlands Antilles, Suriname
gulden	Dutch, gold	Netherlands
halala	Arabic, money	Saudi Arabia
haléru	German, a town	Czech Republic
halier	German, a town	Slovakia
hào		Vietnam
hryvna		Ukraine
jeon	Korean, money	South Korea
jiao	Chinese, a coin	China
khoum	Arabic, one-fifth	Mauritania
kina	Tok, money	Papua New Guinea
kip	Thai, money	Laos
kobo	Nigerian, copper	Nigeria
kopek	Russian, lance	Belarus, Russia
kopiyka	Russian, lance	Ukraine
koruna	Czech, crown	Czech Republic, Slovakia
króna	Swedish, crown	Iceland
krone	German, crown	Denmark, Faroe Islands, Greenland, Norway, Sweden
kroon	Estonian, crown	Estonia
kuna		Croatia
kuru	Turkish, thick	Turkey
kwacha	Bantu, dawn	Malawi, Zambia

coin	*source and/or meaning*	*nations (or other geographical entities)*
kwanza	Swahili, first	Angola
kyat	Burmese, money	Myanmar
laari	Persian, a town	Maldives
lari	Persian, a town	Georgia
lat	Latvian, of Latvia	Latvia
lek	Albanian, money	Albania
lempira	Indian, name of a chief who opposed Spanish invaders	Honduras
leone	Latin, lion	Sierra Leone
lepta	Greek, small	Greece
leu	Latin, lion	Moldova, Romania
lev	Latin, lion	Bulgaria
lilangeni	Bantu, family	Swaziland
lipa		Croatia
lira	Latin, pound	Italy, Malta, San Marino, Turkey, Vatican City State
lisente	Sesotho, money	Lesotho
lita		Lithuania
loti	Sesotho, money	Lesotho
louma		Armenia
lwei	Angolan, a name	Angola
malgache		Madagascar
manat		Azerbaijan, Turkmenistan
marka	Italian, score	Bosnia-Hercegovina
markka	Finnish, money	Finland
metical	Arabic, weigh	Mozambique
mil	Latin, thousand	Malta
millième	Latin, thousand	Egypt
millime	Latin, thousand	Tunisia
möngö	Mongolian, silver	Mongolia
naira	Nigerian, money	Nigeria
nakfa		Eritrea
ngultrum		Bhutan
ngwee	Bantu, money	Zambia
øre	Germanic, metal	Denmark, Faroe Islands, Greenland, Norway, Sweden
ouguiya	Latin, ounce	Mauritania
pa'anga	Tongan, money	Tonga
paisa	Hindi, money	Bhutan, India, Nepal, Pakistan
para	Persian, piece	Macedonia, Yugoslavia
pataca	Portuguese, dollar	Macao
pence	Middle English, coins	Ascension Island, British Virgin Islands, Falkland Islands, Gibraltar, Ireland, St. Helena, Tristan da Cunhan, United Kingdom
pennia	Finnish, coins	Finland
peseta	Latin, weigh	Andorra, Spain
pesewa	Fante/Twi, penny	Ghana
peso	Latin, weigh	Argentina, Chile, Colombia, Cuba, Dominican Republic, Mexico, Philippines, Uruguay
pfennig	Middle English, coin	Germany
piastre	Latin, plaster	Egypt, Lebanon, Syria
poisha	Bengali, money	Bangladash
pound	Latin, weight	Ascension Island, British Virgin Islands, Cyprus, Egypt, Falkland Islands, Gibraltar, Guernsey, Jersey, Lebanon, St. Helena, Scotland, Sudan, Syria, Tristan da Cunha, United Kingdom

coin	*source and/or meaning*	*nations (or other geographical entities)*
pul	Pashto, copper	Afghanistan
pula	Setswana, rain	Botswana
punt	Irish, pound	Ireland
pya	Burmese, money	Myanmar
qindarka	Albanian, one-hundredth	Albania
quetzal	Aztec, tail feather	Guatemala
qursh	Slavic, thick	Saudi Arabia
rand	Dutch, edge	South Africa, Swaziland
rappen	German, raven's head	Liechtenstein, Switzerland
real	Spanish, royal	Brazil
rial	Arabic, royal	Iran, Oman
riel	Khmer, money	Cambodia
ringgit	Malaysian, money	Malaysia
riyal	Arabic, royal	Qatar, Saudi Arabia, Yemen
rouble	Russian, money	Belarus, Russia, Tajikistan
ruble	Russian, money	Transdniestra
rufiyaa	Sanskrit, wrought silver	Maldives
rupee	Sanskrit, wrought silver	Bhutan, India, Mauritius, Nepal, Pakistan, Seychelles, Sri Lanka
rupiah	Sanskrit, wrought silver	Indonesia
santime		Laos, Latvia
satang	Pali, hundred	Thailand
schilling	Dutch, silver coin	Austria
sen	Japanese, money	Brunei, Cambodia, Indonesia, Japan, Malaysia
sene	Samoan, cent	Samoa
seniti	Tongan, cent	Tonga
sent		Estonia
shekel (sheqalim)	Hebrew, weight	Israel
shilingi	Germanic, silver coin	Tanzania
shilling	Germanic, silver coin	Kenya, Somalia, Uganda
sol	Spanish, sun	Peru
som		Kyrgyzstan
stotin	Bulgarian, one-hundredth	Slovenia
stotinki	Bulgarian, one-hundredth	Bulgaria
sucre	Spanish, José de Sucre	Ecuador
sum		Uzbekistan
taka	Sanskrit, weight	Bangladash
tala	Samoan, money	Samoa
tambala	Nyanja, cockerel	Malawi
tanga	Sanskrit, weight	Tajikistan
tenesi		Turkmenistan
tenge		Kazakhstan
tetri		Georgia
thebe	Setswana, shield	Botswana
toea	Motu, shell armlet	Papua New Guinea
tokelau		Niue
tolar		Slovenia
tugrik	Mongolian, money	Mongolia
vatu		Vanuatu
won	Korean, money	North Korea, South Korea
xu	Vietnamese, coin (*sou*)	Vietnam
yen	Japanese, round coins	Japan
yuan	Chinese, round coins	China
zloty	Polish, gold	Poland

For convenience in expressing monetary amounts, most nations have developed their own symbols or abbreviations:

symbol/currency	*nation (or other geographical entity)*
Afg/afghani	Afghanistan
Bd/Bahraini dollar	Bahrain
B$/Brunei dollar	Brunei
Bs/bolivar	Venezuela
C$/Canadian dollar	Canada
C$/córdoba	Nicaragua
CFA/franc	Benin, Burkina Faso, Cameroon, Central African Republic, Chad, Congo, Côte d'Ivoire, Equatorial Guinea, Gabon, Guinea-Bissau, Mali, Niger, Senegal, Togo
CFP/pound	French Polynesia, Futuna Islands, New Caledonia, Wallis
CI$/Cayman Islands dollar	Cayman Islands
C£/Cyprus pound	Cyprus
Da/dinar	Algeria
D/dalasi	Gambia
DH/dirham	Morocco
DM/Deutschemark	Bosnia-Hercegovina, Germany
$/dollar	American Samoa, Anguilla, Antigua, Australia, Bahamas, Barbados, Barbuda, Belize, Bermuda, British Virgin Islands, Brunei, Caicos Islands, Canada, Cayman Islands, Cook Islands, Dominica, Fiji, Grenada, Grenadines, Guam, Guyana, Hong Kong, Jamaica, Kiribati, Liberia, Malaysia, Marshall Islands, Micronesia, Montserrat, Namibia, Nauru, Nevis, New Zealand, Norfolk Island, Northern Mariana Islands, Palau, Panama, Pitcairn Island, Puerto Rico, St. Christopher, St. Lucia, St. Vincent, Singapore, Solomon Islands, Taiwan, Tobago, Tokelau, Trinidad, Turks, Tuvalu, United States of America, U.S. Virgin Islands, Zimbabwe
$A/Australian dollar	Kiribati, Nauru, Norfolk Island, Tuvalu
$B/dollar boliviano	Bolivia
E/lilangeni	Swaziland
EB/Ethiopian birr	Ethiopia
EC$/East Caribbean dollar	British Virgin Islands, Dominica, Grenada, Grenadines, Montserrat, Nevis, St. Christopher, St. Lucia, St. Vincent
Esc/escudo	Portugal
F$/Fiji dollar	Fiji
FMG/Franc malgache	Madagascar
Fr/franc	Andorra, Belgium, Benin, Burkina Faso, Burundi, Cameroon, Central African Republic, Chad, Comoros, Congo, Côte d'Ivoire, Djibouti, Equatorial Guinea, France, French Guiana, French Polynesia, Futuna Islands, Gabon, Guadeloupe, Guinea, Guinea-Bissau, Liechtenstein, Luxembourg, Mali, Martinique, Mayotte, Miquelon, Monaco, New Caledonia, Niger, Réunion, Rwanda, St. Pierre, Senegal, Switzerland, Togo, Wallis
Gs/guarani	Paraguay
HK$/Hong Kong dollar	Hong Kong
ID/Iraqi dinar	Iraq
IR£/punt	Ireland
JD/Jordanian dinar	Jordan
J$/Jamaican dollar	Jamaica
K/kip	Laos

symbol/currency	*nation (or other geographical entity)*
K/kina	Papua New Guinea
K/kwacha	Malawi, Zambia
K/kyat	Myanmar
Kcs/Koruna	Czech Republic
KD/Kuwaiti dollar	Kuwait
KMF/Comorian franc	Comoros
Kr/króna	Iceland
Ksh/Kenya shilling	Kenya
Kzrl/kwanzas	Angola
LD/Libyan dinar	Libya
L$/Liberian dollar	Liberia
Le/Leone	Sierra Leone
LF/Luxembourg franc	Luxembourg
Lk/lek	Albania
LM/Maltese lira	Malta
L£/Lebanese pound	Lebanon
M/loti	Lesotho
M$/Malaysian dollar	Malaysia
Mk/markka	Finland
MT/metical	Mozambique
N/naira	Nigeria
NT$/New Taiwan dollar	Taiwan
NZ$/New Zealand dollar	New Zealand, Pitcairn Islands
OR/rial omani	Oman
P/Philippine peso	Philippines
£/pound	Ascension Island, British Virgin Islands, Cyprus, Egypt, Falkland Islands, Gibraltar, Guernsey, Jersey, Lebanon, St. Helena, Scotland, Sudan, Syria, Tristan da Cunha, United Kingdom
£E/Egyptian pound	Egypt
P/pula	Botswana
Q/quetzal	Guatemala
R/rand	South Africa, Swaziland
RD$/Dominican Republic dollar	Dominican Republic
Rp/rupiah	Indonesia
Rs/rupee	Bhutan, India
SD/Sudanese dinar	Sudan
S$/Singapore dollar	Brunei
S$/Syrian pound	Syria
S$/tala	Samoa
SI$/Solomon Islands dollar	Solomon Islands
SIT/tolar	Slovenia
Sk/koruna	Slovakia
SR/Saudi riyal	Saudi Arabia
T$/pa'anga	Tonga
TJR/Tajik rouble	Tajikistan
Tk/taka	Bangladesh
TL/Turkish lira	Turkey
TT$/Tobago dollar	Tobago
TT$/Trinidad dollar	Trinidad
UM/ouguiya	Mauritania
Z$/Zimbabwe dollar	Zimbabwe
#/colón	Costa Rica, El Salvador

To accommodate strands of national heritage within a nation, some nations mint bilingual coins, for example, parallel sets of Flemish and French coins and coins stamped in two languages to serve the bilingual nation of Belgium. The loss of the national currencies of twelve countries — Austria, Belgium, Finland, France, Germany, Greece, Ireland, Italy, Luxembourg, the Netherlands, Portugal, and Spain plus Monaco, San Marino, and the Vatican — on January 1, 2002, stemmed from the European Union's choice of the euro as a shared currency. As a result, the Austrian schilling and *groschen*, Belgian and French and Luxemburger *franc* and *centime*, Dutch *gulden* and *florin*, Finnish *markka*, German *Deutschemark*, Greek *drachma* and *lepta*, Italian *lira*, Portuguese *escudo* and *centavo*, and Spanish *peseta* and *centimo* became obsolete.

See also **counterfeiting; dollar; euro; *franc;* krugerrand; *lira; mark; markka;* paper money, *peso;* penny; shilling.**

SOURCES: "The British Royal Mint." http://www.royalmint.com. • Cribb, Joe. *Money*. Toronto: Stoddart, 1990. • Cribb, Joe, Barrie Cook, and Ian Carradice. *The Coin Atlas*. London: Little, Brown and Co., 1999. • Krause, Chester L., and Clifford Mishler. *2002 Standard Catalog of World Coins*. Iola, Wisc.: Krause Publications, 2001. • Lewis, Brenda Ralph. *Coins & Currency*. New York: Random House, 1993. • Reinfeld, Fred. *Treasury of the World's Coins*. New York: Sterling Publishing, 1953.

Wright, Charles Cushing

The sculptor of presidents, medalist and engraver Charles Cushing Wright is best known for his likenesses of George Washington and Zachary Taylor. Wright was born in Damariscotta, Maine, on May 1, 1796. At age 21, he worked at silversmithing in Utica, New York, and migrated south in his mid–20s to Savannah, Georgia, and Charleston, South Carolina.

After teaming with James Bale at the New York City engraving firm of Wright and Bale in 1823, Wright first earned attention for his 1824 medal of George Washington and the Marquis de Lafayette. Wright based his profile of Washington on portrait busts by Pierre Simon Benjamin Du Vivier and Jean Antoine Houdon. The Washington-Lafayette medal produced valuable dies used on five coins — a cent, dime, half-dollar, one *real* and two *reales*— and for a reprised Washington-Lafayette pairing on medals in 1829 and 1833. After forming a partnership with Asher Brown Durand, Wright completed the 1826 Erie Canal medal, a classic design featuring Pan and Poseidon beneath the legend "Union of the Erie with the Atlantic." Wright also won acclaim for his medals featuring Colonel William S. Bliss and, in 1848, a bas-relief of Zachary Taylor, based on an oil painting by Salathiel Ellis.

Wright's rise to greatness in coinage coincided with in-house politics at the U.S. Mint in Philadelphia, where James Barton Longacre had been chief engraver since 1844. After the California Gold Rush of 1849, demand for gold coins during the development of the American West caused N.C. Representative James Iver McKay of the House Ways and Means Committee to begin proceedings authorizing a small gold dollar. Historic need to mint new shipments of gold into a larger coin required an amendment to his bill calling for a 20-dollar gold piece called the double eagle.

When the legislation passed on March 3, 1849, Robert Maskell Patterson, mint director, plotted to replace Longacre with Wright. Because Longacre hung onto his post, Wright returned to his job as underling and, in a prolific period preceding his death on June 7, 1854, produced some of the finest dies of the period. He also earned an exhibition at the American Art-Union.

SOURCES: *Biography Resource Center*. Farmington Hills, Mich.: Gale Group. 2001. • Taxay, Don. *The U.S. Mint and Coinage*. New York: Arco Publishing, 1966. • *Who Was Who in America*. Chicago: Marquis Who's Who, Inc., 1968.

Wright, Joseph

Famed English die-sinker and portraitist Joseph Wright, first engraver at the U.S. Mint in Philadelphia, set the standard for the first U.S. coinage. Born to wax modeler Patience Lovell and Joseph Wright, in Bordentown, New Jersey, on July 16, 1756, Wright lived in London with his mother and two sisters in 1772. After his father's death, his mother, who spied for the colonial patriots, supported the family by opening an art gallery featuring the busts of famous people. Well educated and encouraged to learn clay and wax modeling, Wright studied under John Trumbull and Benjamin West. At age 24, he exhibited original works at the Royal Academy. In 1782, he produced a portrait of George IV and, supported by Benjamin Franklin, resettled in Paris to do similar work for fashionable women.

Shipwrecked on his way from Nantes to Massachusetts, Wright limped into Spain and then made his way to Boston, a trip requiring ten weeks. Introductions from Franklin earned Wright a position at Princeton, New Jersey, as portraitist for both George and Martha Washington. Wright made a second oil painting of Washington in military dress and a casual crayon drawing that Wright developed into a popular etching. After subsequent plaster casts of Washington's face crumbled, the president refused to sit through another plastering.

While living in New York, Wright married a Miss Vandervoort in 1787, whom he depicted in a family setting with their three children in 1790. Issuance of Wright's Washington portrait as a medal in 1790 preceded the artist's appointment in 1792 as the first draftsman and engraver at the U.S. Mint, for which he designed a penny as well as other coins and medals, including a likeness of Henry "Lighthorse Harry" Lee, father of Robert E. Lee, and portraits of John Jay and James Madison and his family.

SOURCES: *Columbia Encyclopedia*, Edition 6. Farmington, Mich.: Gale Group, 2000. • Johnson, Allen, ed. *Dictionary of American Biography*. New York: Charles Scribner's Sons, 1928. • *Merriam-Webster's Biographical Dictionary*. Springfield, Mass.: Merriam-Webster, 1995. • Taxay, Don. *The U.S. Mint and Coinage*. New York: Arco Publishing, 1966. • "The U.S. Mint." http://www.usmint.gov.

Wu-Ti

The enlightened fifth emperor of Han Dynasty, Wu-Ti (also Han Wudi or Han Liu Ch'e) introduced state coinage to China. Born Liu Che in Chang'an, Shaanxi province, in 156 B.C., Wu-Ti came to power at age 15 and remained on the throne for 54 years. Educated and advised for six years by his grandmother Dou, the Empress Dowager, he quickly displayed the genius and drive of a facile ruler. The nation flourished under his innovations, particularly the elevation of Confucianism to the state cult in 136 B.C. and the selection of Confucius's *Analects* (ca. 438 B.C.) as the state-adopted curriculum for educating young men at the first state university.

An able autocrat, Wu-Ti took charge of an unwieldy bureaucracy and, by giving civil service exams, selected aides to control operations at the inner court. He mandated the division of property among the heirs of nobles, an act that vitiated large fiefdoms. Under his military guidance, China extended to northern Korea and to central, southern, and southwestern Asia into Afghanistan and onto the steppes as far as Mongolia. His ambassadors brought him news of Parthia and Rome's eastern empire, where he traded silk for alfalfa and wine.

To upgrade his nation, Wu-Ti established an income tax, initiated flood control, and built the Shanglin hunting park. His poets, musicians, and chroniclers kept detailed records of his achievements in engineering and the arts. In addition to stabilizing prices and monopolizing traffic in iron, liquor, and salt, he seized control of private coinage and established a state mint. His command of commerce enriched his people, but he burdened them with personal greed for horses, ivory, and precious jewels.

Late in his life, Wu-Ti retreated from view and sought eternal life through alchemy derived from Taoist sorcery. Following decades of palace intrigue over the selection of a successor, he died on March 29, 87 (or 86) B.C.

***See also* Chinese money.**

SOURCES: Angell, Norman. *The Story of Money*. Garden City, N.Y.: Garden City Publishing, 1929. • Hastings, James, ed. *Encyclopedia of Religion and Ethics*. New York: Charles Scribner's Sons, 1951. • *Historic World Leaders*. Detroit: Gale Research, 1994.

Wyon family

The Wyons, a dynasty of talented coin and seal engravers, served British royalty throughout the 19th century. The founder of the line, Thomas Wyon I (also Thomas Wyon Senior or Thomas Wyon the elder) was born in 1767 and sired Thomas Wyon II and Benjamin Wyon. The elder Thomas Wyon partnered with his brother, Peter Wyon, in sculpting coins and tokens. After the death of chief engraver of royal seals Nathaniel Marchant in 1816, Thomas Wyon I held the title until 1830.

- Thomas Wyon II (also Thomas Wyon the Younger), a native of Birmingham, apprenticed under his father at age 14 and, in 1806, studied with Marchant, who revived classical and contemporary engraving in England. The young Thomas created an unprecedented reputation at the Royal Academy's school of sculpture by winning two silver prizes. By age 16, he was engraving dies and won two gold medals from the Royal Society of Arts and a probationary position on the London Tower Mint staff by age 18. His early works included dies for tokens commissioned by the banks of England and Ireland. He served as chief mint engraver from 1815 to 1817, when he died at Hastings of consumption.

  Young Thomas Wyon is best known for incising a royal portrait die for the half crown of George III from an original carved by Benedetto Pistrucci. Wyon designed the Waterloo medal, gold *pistoles* and *gulden*, and silver and copper coins. He also made stamps for the coinage of the British colonies, Ceylon, Ireland, Jersey, and France. The 20-*franc* gold piece he cut in 1815 displayed the likeness of Louis XVIII and the French crest. Of the 871,581 pieces minted, many went into the payroll of regiments commanded by the Duke of Wellington.
- Benjamin Wyon assumed his father's post as chief engraver of seals in 1831 and designed medals and a seal for William IV. Benjamin held the position until his death in 1858.
- Benjamin Wyon's son, Joseph Shepherd Wyon, was the next chief engraver of seals, a title he held from 1858 to 1873. His output included medals, the Great Seal of Queen Victoria, and the official seal of Canada.
- Joseph's brother, Alfred Benjamin Wyon, next inherited the title of chief engraver of seals, which he held from 1873 to 1884.
- The position passed to Alfred's brother, Allan Wyon, who was chief engraver from 1884 to 1901, the last year of Queen Victoria's reign. Allan incised a gold presentation coin for the Institution of Mining and Metallurgy and completed and published his brother Alfred's book, *The Great Seals of England* (1887).

Another member of the Wyon dynasty, William Wyon, a nephew of Thomas the elder, was born in Birmingham in 1795. William was so skilled at neoclassic bas-relief that he earned membership in the Royal Academy. Early in his career, he struck an original likeness of Queen Adelaide on the coronation medal and followed with the image of Maria II of Portugal. In 1817, he produced the incorrupt crown coin, signed with his name and inscribed "*Incorrupta Fides Veritasque*" ("Unsullied Faith and Truth.") He served George IV and Victoria as chief engraver of the mint from 1828 to 1851 and produced coins for Britain and the colonies.

William Wyon is best known for his images of the young Queen Victoria, who first sat for him at age 13. He replicated her youth and vigor for the "young head" shieldback sovereign in 1838, the year after her accession to the throne and the year of her coronation. In 1839, he added to his achievements a view of the queen as the allegorical Una of Edmund Spenser's *The Faerie Queene* (1590) extending her scepter and leading a lion, a regal pose carved on a five-pound coin. In 1847, he sculpted a head-and-shoulders pose of Victoria with Gothic crown and furled braid that the mint applied to *florins* two years later. Critics sneered at the pun on the queen's crown on a crown coin. In 1851, Wyon incised paired portraits of the queen and Prince Albert, who modelled for the nation and empire a contented marriage and profitable partnership. Pleased with his representations, Victoria remarked that Wyon always depicted her favorably.

- William Wyon's eldest son, Leonard Charles Wyon, was born at one of the mint cottages in 1826 and studied at Merchant Taylors School. After apprenticing with his father in die making, from age 16, Leonard designed coins of the Victorian era as well as the Albert medal and commemoratives for India and South Africa. In his late teens, he was named deputy engraver at the London Mint and succeeded his father in 1851 as modeller and engraver.

Productive at his trade until his death in 1891, Leonard Charles Wyon produced the bronze "bun" penny, named for Queen Victoria's primly knotted hair. The styling retained the image of Britannia, symbol of the nation's command of the seas. After Victoria posed for Wyon, a mail carrier unintentionally destroyed the pattern die. The sculptor began again and created the originals of the bronze penny.

Leonard Charles Wyon also produced an unpopular "Jubilee Head" coin in 1887 for the queen's half-century anniversary. She posed for him in widow's veil and a tiny crown that understated her accomplishments as Britain's regent since 1837. Wyon thrived at his job, turning out portrait coins, numerous medals, and pieces for Africa, Australia, Canada, Ceylon, Cyprus, Guiana, Honduras, Hong Kong, India, Jamaica, Jersey, Malta, Mauritius, New Brunswick, Newfoundland, Nova Scotia, Prince Edward Island, and the West Indies.

***See also* Benedetto Pistrucci; Rix dollars.**

SOURCES: Clain-Stefanelli, Elvira, and Vladimir Clain-Stefanelli. *The Beauty and Lore of Coins, Currency, and Medals*. Croton-on-Hudson, N.Y.: Riverwood Publishers, 1974. • Davies, Glyn. *A History of Money from Ancient Times to the Present Day*. Cardiff: University of Wales Press, 1994. • "Getting in Touch." *Evening Mail*, August 13, 2001. • "Late Victorian Coinage." *Studium Magazine*, November 23, 2001. • Magnusson, Magnus. *Cambridge Biographical Dictionary*. Cambridge: University of Cambridge, 1990. • Reinfeld, Fred. *Treasury of the World's Coins*. New York: Sterling Publishing, 1953. • Stephen, Sir Leslie, and Sir Sidney Lee, eds. *Dictionary of National Biography*. London: Oxford University Press, 1922.

Time Line of Coins and Currency in History

3500 B.C	Sumerians coin shell money.
3100 B.C	Banking begins in Uruk, Mesopotamia.
1950 B.C	Abraham purchases a burial plot for Sarah at Hebron.
1800 B.C	Joseph's brothers sell him to Ishmaelite traders.
	Chinese consumers use cowries for money.
1750 B.C	The Code of Hammurabi sets Babylonian banking procedures.
1300 B.C	Egyptian financiers determine standard weight of metals.
1000 B.C	Chinese consumers use leather money.
950 B.C	The Queen of Sheba presents 120 gold talents to Solomon.
760 B.C	Chinese coinsmiths create bronze knife money.
687 B.C	Lydians turn precious metals into bean-shaped coins.
650 B.C	Athenians mint the gold *drachma*.
	Pheidon of Argos issues the first hammered disk coins.
598 B.C	Yacob Egibi founds modern moneylending.
578 B.C	Servius Tullius makes Rome's first proto-coins.
570 B.C	Croesus reforms Lydian money.
550 B.C	Darius standardizes the *daric*.
500 B.C	The first genuine coins struck in Africa appear in Libya.
413 B.C	Syracusans design the most artful Greek coins.
394 B.C	Pasion of Acharnae sets up a bank at Athens.
332 B.C	Alexander III the Great circulates Greek coins as soldiers' pay.
325 B.C	Celtic moneys imitate Greek designs of Philip II of Macedon.
323 B.C	Alexander III the Great pays a mustering-out bonus in talents.
	Egyptians develop private banking firms.
304 B.C	Ptolemy I Soter of Egypt creates the first portrait coin.
100 B.C	Roman *equites* operate banks.
67 B.C	Tribune Aulus Gabinius enacts laws controlling banking.
50 B.C	Roman troops introduce gold *solidi* in Britain.
44 B.C	Julius Caesar becomes the first living Roman pictured on a coin.
A.D. 14	Tiberius orders a coin that Jesus's disciples spend for food.

A.D. 26	Pontius Pilate commissions the *lepton*, the widow's mite.
30	Jesus uses Tiberius's coin to answer a trick question.
100	Ts'ai Lun turns mulberry bark into paper money.
100	The Maya and Aztec use cocoa beans for currency.
200	Aksum introduces the first indigenous African coinage.
290	Carausius attempts to legitimize his empire with portrait coins.
314	The first Christian cross marks Roman coins.
320	Ezana replaces pagan symbols on Aksumite coins with crosses.
398	John Chrystostom denounces Greek amulet coins.
450	Marcian reforms coinage during Byzantium's Golden Age.
560	Bishop Liudard revives coinage in Britain.
	Ethelbert refines a system of blood money.
630	Saxons stimulate commerce with gold coins.
632	Pada makes the first penny for King Penda of Kent.
600s (late)	Saxons create the silver *sceat*.
696	Abd al-Malik plans a true Arabic coinage.
711	Moors issue Islamic coins in Spain.
726	Leo III removes holy images during an era of iconoclasm.
752	Pepin III issues the first *denier*.
765	Heaberth of Kent issues the first English *denier*.
800	Charlemagne becomes the first original medieval European coiner.
ca. 800	Muhammad Ibn Musa Al-Khwarizmi creates modern number theory.
811	The Byzantine *nomisma* replaces the Roman *solidus*.
871	Alfred the Great increases coinages to pay mercenaries.

880s	Scandinavians copy the pennies of Alfred the Great.
900s	The Chinese make amulet coins from holy scrap metal.
	Japanese shoppers use packets of gold dust for money.
928	Athelstan standardizes England's money.
978	Ethelred the Unready supports 75 royal mints to pay the *danegeld*.
988	Christianity and Byzantine coins reach Kiev.
	Russian mints issue the area's first indigenous coins.
	Mahmud of Ghazna brings Islamic coinage to central India.
1000s	Arab merchants introduce Islamic coins in Kenya.
1016	Canute I inherits the *heregeld*.
1065	Edward the Confessor initiates hands-on healing of scrofula.
1096	Alexius I Comnenus debases coins to support the First Crusade.
	Crusaders initiate the wearing of St. George coins.
	The First Crusade stimulates European banking.
1154	Henry II of England fights coin clipping with the short-cross penny.
1156	Genoese bankers sign the first country-to-country coinless deal.
1173	Jewish diemasters coin bracteates for King Mieszko III of Cracow.
1179	The Third Lateran Council forbids usury.
1187	Richard the Lion-Hearted redeems sacred relics with *bezants*.
1200s	Ramkamhaeng of Siam invents bullet money.
ca. 1202	Leonardo Fibonacci democratizes math.
1210	King John Lackland distributes the first maundy money.

1231	Frederick II commissions the *augustalis.*
1247	Henry III fights coin clipping with the long-cross penny.
ca. 1250	Florence initiates the *florin.*
1252	Venetians stamp the first *florin.*
1279	William de Turnmire strikes the first sterling groat.
1280	Doge Giovanni Dandalo introduces the *grosso matapan* in Venice.
1282	English authorities institute the trial by the pyx to test coins.
1284	Doge Giovanni Dandolo issues the first *ducat.*
1298	The Genoan Casa di San Giorgio devises promissory notes.
1324	Mansa Musa of Mali displays his wealth at Mecca.
1325	Bohemia and Hungary adopt a money system union.
1327	The Goldsmiths' Company is chartered.
1346	Edward III commissions the first gold noble.
1352	Ibn Battuta observes wealth from the gold mines at Mali.
1360	John the Good is depicted on the first *franc.*
1380	Dmitri Ivanovich Donskoi launches minting in Moscow.
1400	The Iroquois League adopts the concept of wampum as money.
1450	Matteo de Pasti pioneers the medal of Christ.
1453	Constantine XI Palaeologus melts sacred vessels for soldier pay.
1457	Coins of Matthias I of Hungary protect children from cramp.
1489	Henry VIII issues the first pound coin, the rose noble.
1491	Lorenzo the Magnificent ruins the de' Medici banking cartel.
1492	Lodisio d'Oria and Jacobo di Negro bankroll Columbus's voyage.
1494	Fra Luca Pacioli creates double-entry bookkeeping.
1498	Henry VII introduces the shilling.
1500s	French-Canadian *coureurs de bois* trade in fur money.
1500s (early)	Julius II commissions Donato Bramante to erect a new papal mint.
1504	The Anjou kings of Naples produce bimetallic coins.
1508	Donato Bramante designs a screw press for coinage.
1530	The Knights Hospitallers begin minting coins on Malta.
	Spain begins its annual convoy of treasure ships.
1534	Sweden's King Gustav I creates the first silver *daler.*
1538	Benvenuto Cellini coins money with a screw press.
1541	Duarte Lopez explains elephant hair money from the Congo.
1550	Marx Schwab of Augsburg makes a heavy-duty screw press.
1565	Native slaves operate the silver mints in Lima, Peru.
1567	Scots popularize the English word "dollar."
1571	Elizabeth I presides over the opening of the Royal Exchange.
1574	William of Orange issues paper siege money at Leiden.
1579	The Royal Exchange opens in London.
1585	The Bank of Amsterdam establishes money-marketing.
ca. 1596	William Shakespeare's Shylock maligns Jewish moneylenders.
1600	Tokugawa Ieyasu sets up Tokyo's Kinza and Ginza mints.
1604	James I orders the "unite" sovereign.
1616	Nicholas Briot tests one-stroke coining.
1622	Spanish cobs go down with the *Atocha* and *Santa Margarita.*

1625	Nicholas Briot introduces the screw press at the London mint.
1627	Wampum enters the New England economy.
1628	Dutch privateer Piet Heyn captures a Spanish silver fleet.
1633	English bankers found premodern services.
1650	Rama restores money that Gopanna skimmed in Hyderabad.
1652	John Hull produces New England's first indigenous coins.
1654	The treasure ship *La Capitana* sinks off Ecuador.
1661	Kangxi orders a series of healing coins in China.
1662	Charles II installs coining mills that stamp edges.
1663	The gold guinea is England's first fully mechanized coinage.
1670	The Hudson Bay Company issues tokens in Canada.
1673	Quebec settlers legitimize moose- and bearskin money.
1675	Mexico becomes the first New World producer of gold *escudos*.
1685	Jacques de Meulles issues playing card money in Canada.
1688	Lloyd's of London is established.
	Scottish financier William Paterson saves England from debt.
1690	American colonists issue their first paper money.
1700	Peter I ends Russia's dependence on commodities currency.
1701	Blackbeard begins his career in piracy.
1707	Sir Isaac Newton supervises the recoinage of old Scottish money.
1712	The royal touch ritual ends with Anne, the last Stuart monarch.
1717	The *Whydah* sinks off Wellfleet, Cape Cod.
1718	John Law influences the founding of the first French bank.
1763	Chief Pontiac produces bark token notes.
1766	Catherine II of Russia initiates new coinage.
1767	Matthew Boulton and James Watt make coins by steam engine.
1772	The Ayr Bank of Scotland founders.
1775	American colonial authorities back the continental note.
1776	Adam Smith writes on political economy in *Wealth of Nations*.
1780	Robert Morris takes control of colonial finance.
1782	Charles Thomson selects "*E Pluribus Unum*" as the U.S. motto.
1785	Abel Buell invents a coining machine.
1787	Abel Buell strikes the postcolonial Fugio cent, the first U.S. coin.
	Ephraim Brasher makes coppers for New York.
	The U.S. Constitution ends printing of state and colonial moneys.
1790	The French print paper *assignats* to fund an interim government.
1791	Alexander Hamilton superintends the first U.S. national bank.
1792	The U.S. Mint opens in Philadelphia.
	The U.S. Mint Police are established.
	The New York Stock Exchange is formalized.
1797	Napoleon restores French metal coinage.
1798	Joseph Hilarius Eckhel systematizes numismatics.
1800	Napoleon creates the Bank of France.
1803	The Bank of France monopolizes printed banknotes.
1804	Matthew Boulton overstrikes Spanish dollars.
1809	The *Admiral Gardner* sinks in the English Channel with coppers.

1831	Christoph Bechtler begins assaying and minting gold coins.
1832	Welsh socialist Robert Owen proposes a moneyless world.
1836	Christian Gobrecht creates the Seated Liberty dollar.
1840	Workers discover the Cuerdale hoard of Anglo-Saxon coins.
1840s	Peter the mint bird nests at the U.S. Mint.
1843	Charles Dickens creates the miser Scrooge in *A Christmas Carol.*
1848	Gold is discovered at Sutter's Mill, California.
1852	Wells Fargo & Company begins delivering money and freight.
1857	Mongkut orders the first modern Thai coin, the *bannakarn.*
	The steamer *Central America* sinks off North Carolina.
1858	Canada adopts the U.S. decimal-based system of coinage.
1859	The Indian head penny becomes the most popular U.S. coin.
	Washington P. Brink founds Brinks, Incorporated, in Chicago.
1860	Victor Emmanuel II makes the *lira* Italy's national currency.
1861	B. F. Taylor becomes chief coiner of Confederate specie.
1862	The U.S. Treasury accepts postage stamp notes in lieu of coins.
	The U.S. Treasury issues the first greenbacks.
1863	Congress establishes a Nevada mint to coin silver.
1864	Maximilian creates Mexico's decimal currency based on the *peso.*
	The motto "In God We Trust" appears on a two-cent piece.
1865	With Jefferson Davis's departure from Richmond, Confederate gold disappears.
1865	The U.S. Secret Service is formed.

1868	The Currency Act makes the dollar Canada's monetary unit.
1870s	Charles George Gordon introduces British coins in Sudan.
1871	A Reef Islander uses feather money to compensate for murder.
1873	A U.S. coinage act establishes the gold standard.
	Joseph Bailly creates Miss Liberty for the trade dollar.
1886	Congress proposes a coin honoring Abraham Lincoln.
1891	Western Electric hires Brinks, Incorporated, to transport its payroll.
1896	William Jennings Bryan delivers the "Cross of Gold" speech.
	A gold rush begins in the Klondike.
1908	The Canadian Royal Mint opens in Ottawa.
1909	Victor Brenner completes the Lincoln penny.
1914	Interpol is founded.
1917	Russian Communists use coins to spread Marxist propaganda.
	Brinks, Incorporated, begins designing its own vehicles.
1933	Chiang Kai-shek modernizes Chinese specie.
1934	Eddie Cantor names the March of Dimes.
1935	Martha Washington is the only U.S. female pictured on a note.
1936	The International Numismatic Commission is established.
1937	U.S. gold is deposited at Fort Knox.
1938	Lord William Malcolm Hailey trains Africans in the use of coins.
1939	The Sutton Hoo hoard preserves coins of Raedwald of East Anglia.
	The U.S. Department of Agriculture creates food stamps.

1944	Dr. Selma Burke sculpts an image for the Roosevelt dime.
	Nazis counterfeit British money via Operation Bernhard.
1945	The *Deutschemark* replaces the Nazi *Reichsmark.*
1946	Hungarian financiers create the *forint.*
	John R. Sinnock claims credit for the Roosevelt dime image.
1948	Eliezer Kaplan proclaims the *lira* Israel's national currency.
1950	A Brinks robbery nets $2,775,395.
1958	Dr. Peter Throckmorton founds underwater archeology.
1970	South Africa introduces the *Krugerrand.*
1973	England passes the Protection of Wrecks Act of 1973.
	George Bass founds the Institute of Nautical Archaeology.
1976	Robbers in Montreal steal $2.8 million from a Brink's truck.
1980	The *shekel* becomes Israel's national currency.
1980s	Angolans trade in beer money.
1985	Mel Fisher begins recovery of cobs from the *Atocha.*
	Salvors recover coppers from the *Admiral Gardner.*
1986	Thomas G. Thompson locates the *Central America.*
1993	A cyclone destroys rare Santa Cruz feather money.
1995	Dr. Selma Burke begins designing a coin featuring Rosa Parks.
1996	England passes the Treasure Act that protects troves of historic value from salvors.
	Mike Daniel finds wreckage that may be Blackbeard's ship.
1997	Bill Clinton begins the issuance of 50 U.S. state quarters.
	Bob McClung locates the Spanish treasure ship *La Capitana.*
	Phil Collins and Bert Douch discover the Appledore hoard.
2000	Fidel Castro supports the Visa Gold Explorations coin salvage operations.
	Glenda Goodacre designs the Sacagawea coin.
2001	Adolf Burger helps locate Bank of England cash counterfeited by Nazis during World War II.
	Bill Clinton initiates plans for a Lincoln bicentennial penny.
2002	Greece replaces the *drachma* with the euro.
	The *euro* goes into circulation on January 1.

Glossary

alto a raised image of a die

Arabic numerals a system introduced by Leonardo Fibonacci that simplified accounting with a place-value decimal system. It rid bookkeeping of cumbrous Roman numerals and the need to use an abacus in business dealings.

archeomagnetic dating a chemical means of dating artifacts by comparing their magnetic data with known changes in the earth's magnetic field

assay to determine the weight, fineness, and purity of precious metals

basso plate a print plate with recessed images used in intaglio printing

bezant a saucer-shaped Byzantine coin

billon silver blended with equal or more parts of copper or other base metal for the manufacture of small change

bimetallism a monetary system based on silver and gold coins

bracteate a European coin hammered out of a thin silver sheet and pressed on one side with a single die, which produces an imprint on the front and its reverse on the opposite side

bullion precious metal in pure form

casting forming coins in molds by pouring molten metal into depressions

clipping profiteering on coinage by shaving or trimming metal from edges

cob a crude coin struck from an irregular blank, producing jagged edges

cofferdam an underwater wall that retains coins and other artifacts lodged in silt during archeological exploration

coinsmithy a workshop producing coins

commemorative a coin struck to honor an individual, phenomenon, or event

commodity money goods and produce such as leaf tobacco and lump sugar that is used like a medium of exchange; also "country pay"

counterstamp a distinctive punch mark or stamp that alters a coin from its original intent to a new coinage

country pay ***see*** **commodity money**

currency any form of money circulating as legal tender during a period of time

debasement lowering the worth of coins by reducing the amount of precious metal in the content while retaining the face value

decimalization introduction a monetary system based on an anchor unit that divides evenly by tens or hundreds

denomination the name of a coin that reflects its value

die hardened metal implements incised with designs for stamping into metal

electrum white gold; a mix of gold and silver occurring in nature; also, a manufactured alloy reflecting the makeup of natural electrum

fiat or fiduciary money money lacking intrinsic worth and backed by the issuer's promise of redemption

flan a blank metal disk that is used in the stamping of coins

gold standard a monetary system based on the accumulation of gold in a national treasury

guillotine cutter a weighted drop blade that slices sheets of printed notes into individual bills

hammered coin specie made one at a time by placing a die or punch over a flan and striking with a maul to imprint a surface with a design or legend

incuse a coin design that sinks into a plane rather than rises above it. *See also* intaglio.

ingot a bar or lump of precious metal bearing a stamp authenticating weight and fineness

intaglio die a stamp with a flat surface bearing a design carved into the plane. *See also* incuse.

legend an inscription or motto encircling or arching over the design on a coin

letter press a printing system that transfers an image from an inked raised surface onto paper bills

milled edge outer edge of a coin with a grained, incised, milled, or stamped design

Milligan press a four-stage printing machine that passes plates through inking, wiping, polishing, and impression on paper bills and postage stamps

milling the mechanical production of coins

mint mark a symbol or letter indicating the origin of a coin

moneyer the person manufacturing coins; also coiner or coinsmith

money laundering the passing of illicit funds through legitimate businesses and banks enabling criminals to turn cash into investments, lines of credit, and foreign bank deposits

mute coin a coin featuring no motto or legend

obverse the front of a two-sided coin

overprinter a letterpress that applies the U.S. Treasury seal and serial numbers

phantom medium a monetary unit or standard that does not exist in the form of coins or paper money

photogrammetric mapping the use of stereophotographs and aluminum grids in underwater archeology to maintain the integrity of historic items *in situ*

photographic mosaic an underwater mapping strategy during excavation of wreckage

planchet a blank metal disc that is stamped into a coin

plate money coinage achieved by stamping rectangular copper plates rather than round disks

punch a tool containing a bas-relief coin design and used to create a die

reeding a coin edging that replaces a smooth edge with parallel vertical grooves intended to halt counterfeiting and coin shaving

reverse the back of a two-sided coin

rocker press a coin press that applies curved dies that rock back and forth to engrave an image. Aligned with the obverse die is a parallel die to strike the reverse side of each coin.

roller press a coin press that turns out specie from metal strips. Hand-cranked by a single operator, the press positions a pair of dies to strike opposite sides of the metal. A planchet-cutter separates each coin from the strip.

sceat (also ***sceatta***) a small, lightweight hammered coin of low quality silver, few inscriptions, and little artistic appeal

screw press a vise invented by Donato Bramante in 1514 to apply pressure on a coin blank simultaneously from upper and lower dies.

scrip a short-term currency printed on a scrap of paper, playing card, wood, silk, buckskin, leather, aluminum foil, or other flimsy material as a substitute for legal tender; a form of token

scyphate a dish-shaped coin

siderography engraving on steel plates

siege money coins or paper money of limited value created during wartime to pay the cost of warfare and defense

sonar profiler a device that emits sound waves to locate non-ferrous relics concealed in underwater sediment

specie a general term for coins

speculum an alloy of bronze and tin used in the first English coins

star note a duplicate bearing an independent series of serial numbers to replace an imperfect or erroneous paper note

sweating shaking coins in a leather bag to generate gold dust

token a coin of limited worth valued only by the guarantee of the company or institution issuing it. *See also* scrip.

tughra an ornate symbol consisting of a signature written with artful calligraphy to create a single glyph

tympf a mid–17th century coin displaying a majestic pose on low-quality metal

underwater archeology reconnaissance and excavation under fresh or salt water by the same methods of observation, discovery, and recording that govern land-based searches

underwater metal detector an electronic device that locates ferrous and non-ferrous metals like gold and silver by generating a sub-bottom profile

uniface coinage stamped on one side only. *See also* incuse, intaglio.

web press a printing system that feeds a continuous roll of paper in the style of a newspaper press. The system speeds the process and reduces costs by imprinting both sides of a note in one operation.

Bibliography

Aaron, Robert. "'Invisible' 25-cent Coins Are Celebrations of Millennium." *Toronto Star*, July 1, 2000.

_____. "Let a Canadian Redesign Our Penny." *Toronto Star,* September 26, 2000.

_____. "Coins." *Toronto Star*, October 30, 2000.

Abbott, Walter M., et al. *The Bible Reader*. New York: Bruce Publishing Co., 1969.

Abrahams, Israel. *Jewish Life in the Middle Ages*. Philadelphia: The Jewish Publication Society of America, 1896.

Acar, Ozgen. "Mammoth Ottoman Hoard." *Archaeology*, January/February 2002, p. 8.

Achaya, K. T. *Indian Food: A Historical Companion*. Delhi: Oxford University Press, 1998.

"ACLU Asks Federal Court to Dismiss 'In God We Trust' Lawsuit Filed Against Kansas County." *Business Wire*, October 3, 2000.

Adams, Henry. *The Education of Henry Adams*. Boston: Houghton-Mifflin, 1961.

"Admiral Anson." *Biographies*, http://blupete.com/Hist/BiosNS/1700-63/Anson.htm.

"*Admiral Gardner*." http://www.ships.clara.net/lost/lost_a/admgard/index.htm.

"Adolph Weinman." http://www.kargesfineart.com/links2/Adolph-Weinman.htm.

"Advanced Encryption Technology." *Business Wire*, September 28, 1998.

"Aethelred II the Unready: The Laws of London 978." http://www.britannia.com/history/docs/unready.html.

Ahwash, Kamal M. *Encyclopedia of United States Liberty Seated Dimes 1837–1891*. Wallingford, Pa.: Kamal Press, 1974.

Akers, David W. *United States Gold Coins*. Englewood, Ohio: Paramount Publications, 1975.

Akimichi, Tomoya. "Okinawa and the Sea Roads of East Asia." *Japan Echo*, August 2000.

Alexander, David, and Pat Alexander, eds. *Eerdmans' Handbook to the World's Religions*. Grand Rapids, Mich.: William B. Eerdmans Publishing Co., 1982.

Alexander, David T., Thomas K. DeLorey, and P. Bradley Reed. *Coin World Comprehensive Catalog & Encyclopedia of United States Coins*. New York: World Almanac-Pharos Books, 1990.

Allen, Larry. *Encyclopedia of Money*. New York: Checkmark Books, 2001.

Allen, Robert. *William Jennings Bryan*. Milford, Mich.: Mott Media, 1992.

Allen, Thomas B. "Cuba's Golden Past." *National Geographic*, July 2001, 74–91.

Almanac of Famous People. 6th ed. Farmington Hills, Mich.: Gale Group, 1998.

"Americans for Common Cents." http://www.pennies.org/.

"America's Lost Treasure: The S.S. *Central America*." http://www.sscentralamerica.com/.

"Among Our Key People." *The Key Reporter*, Winter 2002, 8–9.

Amt, Emilie. *Women's Lives in Medieval Europe*. London: Routledge, 1993.

"Anchors Aweigh for Rhode Island's New Quarter — Last of the Original 13 Colonies." *PR Newswire,* May 21, 2001.

"Ancient History Sourcebook: A Collection of Contracts from Mesopotamia, c. 2300–428 BCE." http://www.fordham.edu/HALSALL/ANCIENT/mesopotamia-contracts.html.

Anderson, Bernhard W. *Understanding the Old Testament*. Englewood Cliffs, N.J.: Prentice-Hall, Inc., 1966.

Andrews, Tamra. *Nectar and Ambrosia: An Encyclopedia of Food in World Mythology*. Santa Barbara, Calif.: ABC-Clio, 2000.

Angell, Norman. *The Story of Money*. Garden City, N.Y.: Garden City Publishing, 1929.

"The Anglo-Saxon Chronicle." http://sunsite.berkeley.edu/OMACL/Anglo/.

Anthony, Susan B. "Women's Right to Vote." *The American Reader*. New York: HarperCollins, 1990.

"Anthony C. Paquet." http://www.uspatterns.com/uspatterns/anthonycpaquet.html.

The Apocrypha of the Old Testament. New York: American Bible Society, n.d.

Arberry, Arthur J., trans. *The Koran Interpreted*. New York: Macmillan, 1970.

"Archaeological Resource Guide for Europe." http://odur.let.rug.nl/arge/General/oldlinks.html.

Aristophanes. *Frogs in Classics in Translation*, ed. Paul MacKendrick and Herbert M. Howe, Vol. I. Madison: University of Wisconsin Press, 1952.

Armstrong, Karen. *A History of God*. New York: Alfred A. Knopf, 1994.

"The Artistry of African Currency." http://www.nmafa.si.edu/exhibits/site/manillas.htm.

Ashby, Thomas A. *The Valley Campaigns*. New York: Neale Publishing Co., 1914.

"Atocha Dive Expeditions." *Skin Diver*, December 1999, 96.

"ATS Money Systems." http://www.atsmoney.com/index.asp.

"Augustus Saint-Gaudens," http://www.sgnhs.org/Augustus.html.

Ausubel, Nathan. *The Book of Jewish Knowledge*. New York: Crown, 1964.

Avary, Myrta Lockett. *A Virginia Girl in the Civil War*. New York: D. Appleton & Co., 1903.

Aven, Paula. "Mint Guards Gold Bullion Worth Billions." *Denver Business Journal*, February 9, 1996, 16A.

Avirett, James Battle. *The Old Plantation: How We Lived in Great House and Cabin Before the War*. New York: F. Tennyson Neely Co., 1901.

Ayton, Andrew. *Knights and Warhorses: Military Service and the English Aristocracy Under Edward III*. Woodbridge, Suffolk: Boydell Press, 1994.

Babbitt, John S. "Coins and Currency on U.S. Stamps." *Stamps*, January 21, 1995.

Babits, Lawrence E., and Hans Van Tilburg, eds. *Maritime Archaeology: A Reader of Substantive and Theoretical Contributions*. London: Plenum, 1998.

Bacon, Francis. "Of Usury." http://www.orst.edu/instruct/phl302/texts/bacon/bacon_essays.html#OF USURY.

Baer, Yitzhak. *A History of the Jews in Christian Spain*. Philadelphia: The Jewish Publication Society of America, 1961.

Baker, Bernard. "Confederate Gold." *Danville Register & Bee*, June 29, 1996.

Baker, Phil. "Ottoman Art." *New Statesman*, July 26, 1996.

Balch, T. B. *My Manse, During the War*. Baltimore: Sherwood & Co., 1866.

Balzaretti, Ross. "Charlemagne in Italy." *History Today*, February 1996, 28–35.

Bancroft, Hubert Howe. *The Book of the Fair*. Chicago: The Bancroft Company, 1893.

_____. *The Works of Hubert Howe Bancroft*. San Francisco: The History Company, 1887.

"Banking on Children." *Chicago Sun-Times*, April 7, 2000.

"Banknotes and Banking." http://www.bankofengland.co.uk/banknotes/printworks.htm.

"The Bank of England." http://www.bankofengland.co.uk/history.htm.

Banks, Suzy. "George F. Bass." *Texas Monthly*, September 2000, p. 171.

Banks, William C. "The Curious Deals Behind the Key West Treasure." *Money*, September 1985, 46–50.

Baring-Gould, William S., intro. and notes. *The Annotated Mother Goose*. New York: Clarkson N. Potter, 1962.

Baronowski, Donald Walter. "Review: From Rome to Byzantium: The Fifth Century A.D." *Canadian Journal of History*, August 1999, 265.

Bartlett, John. *Familiar Quotations*. Boston: Little, Brown & Co., 1992.

Bartlett, Sarah, et al. "Money Laundering: Who's Involved, How It Works, and Where It's Spreading." *Business Week*, March 18, 1985, 74–80.

Barton, George Aaron. *Assyrian and Babylonian Literature*. New York: D. Appleton & Company, 1904.

Basbanes, Nicholas A. "Talk about Books 'Ship of Gold' Is Tale of History." *Patriot Ledger*, July 25, 1998.

Bascom, Willard. *Deep Water, Ancient Ships: The Treasure Vault of the Mediterranean*. Garden City, N.Y.: Doubleday and Co., 1976.

Baskins, Kevin. "It's a Krugerrand Christmas in Mason City, Too." *North Iowa Globe-Gazette*, January 23, 2001.

Bass, George F. "Cape Gelidonya: A Bronze Age Shipwreck." *Transactions of the American Philosophical Society* 57, Part 8, Philadelphia, 1967

_____. "25 Year History of INA Research." http://ina.tamu.edu/25yearhis1.htm.

_____. ed. *Ships and Shipwrecks of the Americas: A History Based on Underwater Archaeology*. London: Thames and Hudson, 1996.

Baugh, Albert C. *A History of the English Language*. New York: Appleton-Century-Crofts, 1957.

_____. *A Literary History of England*. New York: Appleton-Century-Crofts, 1948.

Baum, L. Frank. *The Annotated Wizard of Oz*. New York: Schocken Books, 1983.

_____. *The Wizard of Oz*. New York: Ballantine Books, 1956.

Bauman, Richard. "The Lady and the Peace Prize." *Modern Maturity*, January 1984, p. 89.

Beavis, Bill, and Richard G. McCloskey. *Salty Dog Talk: The Nautical Origins of Everyday Expressions*. Dobbs Ferry, N.Y.: Sheridan House, 1995.

Becatoros, Elena. "Greece Bids Farewell to Link with Ancient Past." *Bergen County Record*, December 31, 2000.

"The Bechtler Private Mint." http://www.raregold.com/r-bech.htm.

Becker, Martin B. *Medieval Italy: Constraints and Creativity*. Bloomington: Indiana University Press, 1981.

"Bédoyère, Guy de la. "Carausius, Rebel Emperor of Roman Britain." *The Numismatic Chronicle*, 1998, 79–88.

"Beginnings of the Bhikkuni Sasanaya." *London Times*, October 2, 2001.

"Belgian Graphic Designer Creates Euro Coins." *Newsbytes*, January 17, 1999.

Bell, Robert E. *Women of Classical Mythology: A Biographical Dictionary*. Santa Barbara, Calif.: ABC-Clio, 1991.

Bentley, James. *A Calendar of Saints*. London: Little, Brown & Co., 1993.

Berger, Stefan. "Historians and Nation-building in Germany after Reunification." *Past & Present*, August 1995.

Bernier, Olivier. *The World in 1800*. New York: John Wiley & Sons, 2001.

Betts, A. D. *Experience of a Confederate Chaplain, 1861–1864*. Greenville, S. C.: n.p., 190?.

Bevan, Wilson Lloyd. "Sir William Petty: A Study in English Economic Literature" (monograph). Publications of the American Economic Association, 1894.

Biedermann, Hans. *Dictionary of Symbolism*. New York: Facts on File, 1992.

Biography.Com, http://search.biography.com.

Biography Resource Center. Farmington Hills, Mich.: Gale Group, 2001.

Bloch, David. "Salt and the Evolution of Money." *Journal of Salt History*, Vol. 7, 1999.

Blythe, Al. *The Complete Guide to Liberty Seated Half Dimes*. Virginia Beach, Va.: DLRC Press, 1992.

Boggs, William Robertson. *Military Reminiscences of Gen. Wm. R. Boggs, C. S. A.* Durham, N.C.: Seeman Printery, 1913.

Bond, Constance. "A Fury from Hell or Was He?" *Smithsonian*, February 2000, p. 62.

_____. "Islamic Metalwork at Freer Gallery." *Smithsonian*, October 1985, p. 225.

Boorstin, Daniel J. *The Creators: A History of Heroes of the Imagination*. New York: Vintage Books, 1992.

_____. *The Discoverers: A History of Man's Search to Know His World and Himself*. New York: Vintage Books, 1983.

Bordsen, John. "Prowling with Pirates." *Charlotte Observer*, August 12, 2001, 1G, 8G.

Bowden, Tracy. "Gleaning Treasure from the Silver Bank." *National Geographic*, July 1996, 90–105.

Bowder, Diana, ed. *Who's Who in the Greek World*. New York: Washington Square Press, 1982.

_____. *Who's Who in the Roman World*. New York: Washington Square Press, 1980.

Bowers, Q. David. *Adventures with Rare Coins*. Los Angeles: Bowers & Ruddy Galleries, Inc., 1979.

_____. "American Gold." *American Heritage*, December 1984, 43–49.

_____. "Christian Gobrecht: American Coin Die Engraver Extraordinaire." *Rare Coin Review*, November/December 1998.

_____. *The History of United States Coinage as Illustrated by the Garrett Collection*. Wolfeboro, N. H.: Bowers & Merena Galleries, 1979.

_____. "Jacob Perkins, Early Die Cutter." *Hobbies*, July 1981, pp. 123–124.

Boyce, Charles. *Shakespeare A to Z*. New York: Facts on File, 1990.

Brand, Paul. "Jews and the Law in England, 1275–1290." *English Historical Review*, November 2000.

_____. *The Making of the Common Law*. Rio Grande, Ohio: Hambledon Press, 1992.

Braudel, Fernand. *The Wheels of Commerce*. New York: Harper and Row, 1982.

Breen, Walter. *Walter Breen's Complete Encyclopedia of U.S. and Colonial Coins*. New York: F. C. I. Press/Doubleday, 1988.

"Brewer Dictionary of Phrase and Fable." http://www.bibliomania.com.

Briggs, Larry. *The Comprehensive Encyclopedia of United States Liberty Seated Quarters*. Lima, Ohio: Larry Briggs Rare Coins, 1991.

"The Brinks Robbery." http://www.fbi.gov/fbinbrief/historic/famcases/brinks/brinks.htm.

Bristow, Sallie. "Penny That Ended Up Jewelry." *Hobbies*, July 1981, p. 124.

"The British Royal Mint." http://www.royalmint.com.

Broad, William. "Archaeologists Revise Portrait of Buccaneers as Monsters." *New York Times*, March 11, 1997, C1, 9.

Brookhiser, Richard. "A Founding Father's Return to Grace." *U.S. News & World Report*, November 10, 1997, 71–72.

Brothwell, Don and Patricia. *Food in Antiquity: A Survey of the Diet of Early Peoples*. New York: Frederick A. Praeger, 1969.

Brown, R. Allen. *The Origins of Modern Europe: The Medieval Heritage of Western Civilization*. New York: Barnes & Noble, 1972.

Brusher, Joseph. *Popes Through the Ages*. Denver, Colo.: New Advent, 1996.

Bryant, Arthur. *The Medieval Foundation of England*. Garden City, N.Y.: Doubleday & Co., 1967.

Bullis, Douglas. "The Longest Hajj: The Journeys of Ibn Battuta." *Aramco World*, July/August 2000, 2–39.

Bunson, Matthew. *A Dictionary of the Roman Empire*. New York: Oxford University Press, 1991.

_____. *Encyclopedia of the Middle Ages*. New York: Facts on File, 1995.

"The Bureau of Engraving and Printing." http://www.bep.treas.gov/.

Burgan, Michael. "Lost and Found Treasure." *National Geographic World*, April 2000, p. 19.

Burge, Dolly Sumner. *A Woman's Wartime Journal: An Account of the Passage Over a Georgia Plantation of Sherman's Army on the March to the Sea*. New York: The Century Co., 1918.

Burke, Daniel. "Questions behind Locked Doors." *Maclean's*, February 11, 1985, p. 12.

Burke, James. "On Track." *Scientific American*, November 23, 2001.

Burns, Thomas. *A History of the Ostrogoths*. Indianapolis: Indiana University Press, 1984.

Butler, Alban. *Lives of the Saints*. New York: Barnes & Noble, 1997.

Butler, Lindley S. "Blackbeard's Revenge." *American History*, August 2000, p. 18.

Byrom, Thomas. *The Dhammapada: The Sayings of the Buddha*. New York: Alfred A. Knopf, 1976.

Cabet, Étienne. *Voyage en Icarie*. New York: Kelley, 1973.

Cahill, Thomas, intro. *The Gospel According to Luke*. New York: Grove Press, 1999.

Calder, William M. "Is the Mask a Hoax." *Archaeology*, July/August 1999.

Campbell, Oscar James, ed. *The Reader's Encyclopedia of Shakespeare*. New York: MJF Books, 1966.

"The Canadian Coin Reference Site." http://www.canadiancoin.com/.

Cannon, John, and Ralph Griffiths. *Oxford Illustrated History of the British Monarchy*. Oxford: Oxford University Press, 1988.

Cantor, George. *North American Indian Landmarks*. Detroit: Gale Research, 1993.

Cantor, Norman F., ed. *The Civilization of the Middle Ages*. New York: HarperPerennial, 1993.

_____. *The Jewish Experience*. New York: HarperCollins, 1996.

_____. *The Medieval Reader*. New York: HarperCollins, 1994.

"Cape Cod's Bounty." *Time*, November 11, 1985, 37.

Carey, Joseph. "New Insight into Genes: Now the Payoff." *U.S. News & World Report*, August 6, 1984, 57.

Casson, Lionel. *The Ancient Mariners*. Princeton, N.J.: Princeton University Press, 1991.

Castle, Stephen. "Last Rites of the French Franc Marked by Confident Display of Gallic Indifference." *London Independent*, February 18, 2002.

Cavendish, Richard. "Founding of the Darien Colony." *History Today*, November 1998.

_____. ed. *Man, Myth & Magic*. New York: Marshall Cavendish, 1970.

Cawthorne, Andrew. "Cuban Sea Treasures Surface." *Toronto Star*, November 30, 2000.

"Cecilia Wertheimer, Curator of the Bureau of Engraving and Printing." *Montgomery Coin Club Bulletin*, October 1997.

"Celebrating the American Medal." *American Numismatic Society Newsletter*, Fall 1997.

"Celtic Gold 'Ring Money' Sells for (Pounds) 2,800." *Irish Times*, February 28, 1998.

"CGB.Fr Numismatiques." http://www.ordonnances.org/regnes/louis13/1622_1632.html.

Champagne, Duane, ed. *Chronology of Native North American History*. Detroit: Gale Research, 1994.

"Change Is Exciting." *Kipling's Personal Finance Magazine*, October 1, 2000.

Chappell, Kevin. "Sculptor Who Created Roosevelt's Imprint on the Dime Tells Kids How Love of Art Has Shaped Her Life." Knight-Ridder/Tribune News Service, December 7, 1994.

"Characteristics of Food Stamp Households." http://www.fns.usda.gov/OANE/MENU/Published/FSP/FILES/Participation/2000Characteristics.htm.

Chaucer, Geoffrey. *The Canterbury Tales*. London: Cresset Press, 1992.

_____. *Chaucer's Canterbury Tales: The Prologue*. Cliffs Notes: Lincoln, Neb.: 1966.

_____. *Chaucer's Canterbury Tales: The Wife of Bath*. Cliffs Notes: Lincoln, Neb.: 1966.

_____. *Selected Canterbury Tales*. New York: Holt, Rinehart and Winston, 1969.

_____. *The Works of Geoffrey Chaucer*. Boston: Houghton Mifflin, 1961.

Chesnut, Mary Boykin. *A Diary from Dixie*. New York: D. Appleton and C., 1905.

Cheyney, Edward P. *The Dawn of a New Era: 1250–1453*. New York: Harper & Brothers, 1936.

Chilvers, Ian. *The Concise Oxford Dictionary of Art and Artists*. Oxford: Oxford University Press, 1996.

"The Chinese Connection." *Banker*, October 1994, pp. 14–15.

Chute, Marchette. *Geoffrey Chaucer of England*. New York: E. P. Dutton, 1946.

Cirlot, J. E. *A Dictionary of Symbols*. New York: Dorset Press, 1971.

Clain-Stefanelli, Elvira. "Donors and Donations: The Smithsonian's National Numismatic Collection," *Perspectives in Numismatics*, 1986.

_____, and Vladimir Clain-Stefanelli. *The Beauty and Lore of Coins, Currency, and Medals*. Croton-on-Hudson, N.Y.: Riverwood Publishers, 1974.

Clark, Jeffrey. "Review: Inalienable Possessions:

The Paradox of Keeping-While- Giving." *Oceania*, September 1993, pp. 91–93.
Clark, John. *A History of Epic Poetry*. New York: Haskell House, 1973.
Clarke, Howard B., Máire ní Mhaonaigh, and Raghnall O'Floinn, eds. *Ireland and Scandinavia in the Early Viking Age*. Dublin: Four Courts Press, 1998.
Clarke, Mary Stetson, comp. *Women's Rights in the United States* (poster packet). Amawalk, N.Y.: Jackdaw, 1974.
Clifford, Barry. *Expedition Whydah*. New York: Cliff Street Books, 1999.
_____. *The Pirate Prince*. New York: Simon & Schuster, 1993.
Clifton, Chas S. *Encyclopedia of Heresies and Heretics*. Santa Barbara, Calif.: ABC-Clio, 1992.
"Clues Pointing Toward Ship As Blackbeard's Researchers '95 Percent Certain.'" *Washington Daily News*, October 30, 1997.
Cockburn, Alexander. "Beat the Devil: Imperial Addictions." *Nation*, August 3, 1985, 70–71.
Codrington, H. W. *Ceylon Coins and Currency*. Colombo, 1924.
Coe, Sophie D., and Michael D. Coe. *The True History of Chocolate*. London: Thames & Hudson Ltd., 1996.
Cohen, Roger S., Jr. *American Half Cents, the "Little Half Sisters."* Arlington, Va.: Wigglesworth & Ghatt, 1982.
Cohn-Sherbok, Lavinia. *Who's Who in Christianity*. London: Routledge, 1998.
"Coins of the Louis Kings." http://www.cgb.fr/monnaies/articles/monnaiesfrance/roislouisgb.html.
Cole, Michael. "Cellini's Blood." *Art Bulletin*, June 1999, pp. 215–216.
Collins, Miki. "Fierce and Beautiful World — Life on an Alaskan Trapline." *Pacific News Service*, April 22, 1997.
Columbia Encyclopedia, Edition 6. Farmington, Mich.: Gale Group, 2000.
Comay, Joan, and Lavinia Cohn-Sherbok. *Who's Who in Jewish History*. London: Routledge, 1995.
The Complete Marquis Who's Who. New Providence, N.J.: Marquis Who's Who, 2001.
Connors, Martin, and Jim Craddock, eds. *Video Hound's Golden Movie Retriever*. Detroit: Visible Ink, 1999.
Conrad, Joseph. *Lord Jim*. London: Penguin, 1989.
Considine, Bob. *The Men Who Robbed Brinks*. New York: Random House, 1961.
Contemporary Authors Online. Farmington Hills, Mich.: Gale Group, 2000.
Contemporary Black Biography. Detroit: Gale Research, 1997.
Contemporary Newsmakers 1985. Detroit: Gale Research, 1986.
Cooper, J. C., ed. *Dictionary of Christianity*. Chicago: Fitzroy Dearborn, 1996.
Cordingly, David. *Under the Black Flag*. San Diego, Calif.: Harvest Books, 1995.
Cordone, Bonnie J. "In Memoriam: Mel Fisher 1922–1998." *Skin Diver*, March 1999, 42–44.
Coulton, G. G. *Medieval Panorama*. New York: Meridian Books, 1955.
Crain, Stephen A. "Half Dimes Inspection of the First Coins of the United States Mint." *John Reich Journal*, January 1907.
Cribb, Joe. *Money*. Toronto: Stoddart, 1990.
_____, Barrie Cook, and Ian Carradice. *The Coin Atlas*. London: Little, Brown and Co., 1999.
Crichton, Michael. *The Great Train Robbery*. New York: Ballantine Books, 1995.
Cristal, Ronald J. *Siamese Coins from Funan to the Fifth Reign*. Bangkok: National Museum, 1996.
Crittenden, Jules. "Treasure Island: Explorers May Have Located Sunken Pirate Ships." *Boston Herald*, January 19, 2001.
Crombie, A. C. *Medieval and Early Modern Science*. Cambridge, Mass.: Harvard University Press, 1967.
Cross, F. L., and E. A. Livingston. *Dictionary of the Christian Church*. Oxford: Oxford University Press, 1997.
Crossen, Cynthia. "Progenitor of the Paper Millionaires; John Law's Currency System Devastated Royal France, Transformed World Trade." *Wall Street Journal*, July 19, 2000, B1.
Crow, John A. *Spain: The Root and the Flower*. Berkeley: University of California Press, 1985.
Crozier, Ronald. "A History of the Chloride Leach Process." *Bulletin of the Canadian Institute of Mining and Metallurgy*, July 1993.
Crystal, David, ed. *The Cambridge Biographical Dictionary*. Cambridge: University of Cambridge, 1996.
_____. *The Cambridge Encyclopedia of the English Language*. Cambridge: University of Cambridge, 1995.
"Cuba Financed 1983 Wells Fargo Robbery, Former Cuban Agent Says." *Puerto Rico Herald*, January 4, 2000.
"The Cuerdale Hoard." http://www.treasure-hunting.co.uk.
Cummins, John. "'That Golden Knight' Drake and His Reputation." *History Today*, January 1996, 14–22.
"Curious Names." http://www.moneymuseum.ch/standard_english/raeume/geld–lieben/ueberlieferung/sprachliches/.
Curry, J. L. M. *The South in the Olden Time*. Harrisburg, Pa.: Harrisburg Publishing Co., 1901.
Dahmas, Joseph. *Dictionary of Medieval Civilization*. New York: Macmillan, 1984.
Daly, John. "Solving Old Mysteries." *Maclean's*, March 20, 1989, 45.

Davenport, William. "Red-Feather Money." *Scientific American*, March 1962, 94–104.
Davidson, Alan. *The Oxford Companion to Food.* Oxford: Oxford University Press, 1999.
Davidson, Basil. *African Kingdoms.* New York: Time, Inc., 1966.
Davidson, Cathy N., and Linda Wagner-Martin, eds. in chief. *The Oxford Companion to Women's Writing in the United States.* New York: Oxford University Press, 1995.
Davies, Glyn. *A History of Money from Ancient Times to the Present Day.* Cardiff: University of Wales Press, 1994.
Davies, Norman. *God's Playground: A History of Poland.* New York: Columbia University Press, 1982.
da Vinci, Leonardo. *The Codex Leicester, Notebook of a Genius.* Sydney, Aust.: Powerhouse Publishing, 2000.
Davis, Andrew McFarland. *Colonial Currency Reprints, 1682–1751.* Boston: The Prince Society, 1911.
Davis, Curtis Carroll. "The Craftiest of Men: William P. Wood and the Establishment of the United States Secret Service." *Maryland Historical Magazine*, Summer 1988, pp. 111–126.
Davis, Mark. "Selma Burke, the 'Grande Dame' of African American Artists, Is Honored." Knight-Ridder/Tribune News Service, December 8, 1993.
Deaux, George. *The Black Death 1347.* New York: Weybright & Talley, 1969.
Defoe, Daniel. *Robinson Crusoe.* New York: Airmont Books, 1963.
de Jersey, Philip. *Coinage in Iron Age Armorica.* Oxford: Oxford University Press, 1994.
de las Casas, Bartolomé. *History of the Indies.* New York: Harper & Row, 1971.
Delehaye, Hippolyte. *The Legends of the Saints.* Dublin: Four Courts Press, 1955.
De Lorey, Thomas. "George T. Morgan Remembered." *COINage*, September, 1996.
_____. "Longacre, Unsung Engraver of the U.S. Mint." *The Numismatist*, October 1985.
"Les Dernières Volontés de Sir Thomas Gresham." http://u2.u-strasbg.fr/lexis/a992000/frame_txt_fichiers/F3_fichiers/gresham/lwill_ward_ok.html.
"The Deserter." *Freemasons Monthly Magazine*, 1842.
Dewaraja, Lorna S. "Rhys Davids: His contribution to Pali and Buddhist Studies." (Sri Lanka) *Daily News*, July 15, 1998.
Diamant, Lincoln. *Yankee Doodle Days.* Fleischmanns, N.Y.: Purple Mountain Press, 1996.
Dickens, Charles. *A Christmas Carol.* New York: Airmont, 1963.
Dictionary of Roman Religion. New York: Facts on File, Inc., 1996.
Dictionary of the Middle Ages. New York: Scribner's, 1989.
"Directory of Royal Genealogical Data." http://www.dcs.hull.ac.uk/cgi- bin/gedidex.
Doren, Eugene T. "Vegetable Ivory and Other Palm Nuts." *Principes*, Vol. 41, No. 4, 1997.
"Dossiers." http://www.artcult.com/hrb12.html.
Douglas, George William. *The American Book of Days.* New York: H. W. Wilson Co., 1948.
Drabble, Margaret, ed. *The Oxford Companion to English Literature.* Oxford: Oxford University Press, 1985.
Draper, John William. *History of the Conflict Between Religion and Science.* New York: D. Appleton, 1897.
Du Bois, Cora. *The People of Alor.* Cambridge, Mass.: Harvard University Press, 1960.
Duisenberg, Willem F. "European Central Bank." *Journal of the European Communities*, August 31, 2001.
Dunn, Oliver, and James Kelley, eds. *The Diario of Christopher Columbus' First Voyage, 1492–1493.* Norman: University of Oklahoma Press, 1989.
Dupree, Nancy Hatch. "Museum Under Siege." *Archaeology,* April 20, 1998.
Durant, Will. *The Life of Greece.* New York: Simon and Schuster, 1939.
_____. *Our Oriental Heritage.* New York: Simon and Schuster, 1942.
"Early Monetary Systems of Lanka." http://lakdiva.com/coins/lanka_monetary.html.
East, W. G. *An Historical Geography of Europe.* London: Methuen & Co., 1966.
Eastman, Lloyd. *Gods, Ghosts and Ancestors: The Popular Religion.* New York: Oxford, 1988.
Edwards, Mike. "Indus Civilization." *National Geographic*, June 2000, 108–131.
"Eight Centuries of Sampling Inspection: The Trial of the Pyx." *Journal of the American Statistical Association*, September 1977, 493–500.
Einzig, Paul. *Primitive Money.* Oxford: Pergamon Press, 1966.
Ekstrom, Reynolds R. *Concise Catholic Dictionary.* Dublin: Columba Press, 1995.
Elgood, Cyril. *The Medical History of Persia and the Eastern Caliphate.* London: Cambridge University Press, 1952.
Eliot, George. *Silas Marner.* New York: Signet, 1981.
Encyclopedia Americana (CD-ROM). Danbury, Conn.: Grolier Inc., 1999.
Encyclopedia Britannica (on-line). Britannica Corporation, 1999.
Encyclopedia of African History and Culture. New York: Facts on File, Inc., 2001.
Encyclopedia of Art. New York: McGraw-Hill Book Co., 1968.
Encyclopedia of Occultism and Parapsychology, 5th ed. Farmington Hills, Mich.: Gale Group, 2001.
Encyclopedia of the Ancient Greek World. New York: Facts on File, Inc., 1995.

Encyclopedia of the Roman Empire. New York: Facts on File, Inc., 1994.
Encyclopedia of World Art. New York: McGraw-Hill, 1967.
Encyclopedia of World Biography. Detroit: Gale Group, 1998.
Englebert, Omer. *The Lives of the Saints*. New York: Barnes & Noble, 1994.
Erkelenz, Michael. "The Genre and Politics of Shelley's 'Swellfoot the Tyrant.'" *Review of English Studies*, November 1996.
"The Euro." http://www.euro.ecb.int.
"Euro: Printing of 13 Billion Euro Banknotes Gets Under Way." *Europe Information Service*, July 17, 1999.
Evans, James Allan. "View from a Turkish Monastery: An Overview of the Byzantine World." *Athena Review*, Vol. 3, 2001, 16–25.
Evans, Joan. *Life in Medieval France*. Leicester, Eng.: Phaidon Press, 1957.
Explorers and Discoverers of the World. Detroit: Gale Research, 1993.
"Exploring Ethnomathematics in the Maldives." http://www.mcst.gov.mv/sitefiles/science-tech/research/counting.htm.
Faderman, Lillian. *To Believe in Women: What Lesbians Have Done for America*. Boston: Houghton Mifflin, 1999.
"Family Archives from Neo-Babylonian and Early Achaemenid Babylon." *Centre for the Study of Ancient Documents Newsletter*, June 3, 1998.
Fanthorpe, Lionel, and Patricia Fanthorpe. *The Oak Island Mystery: The Secret of the World's Greatest Treasure*. Toronto: Hounslow Press, 1995.
Farmer, David Hugh. *The Oxford Dictionary of Saints*. Oxford: Oxford University Press, 1992.
Fearn, Frances. *Diary of a Refugee*. New York: Moffatt, Yard & Co., 1910.
Ffoulkes, Charles. *The Armourer and His Craft*. New York: Dover Books, 1988.
Fielding, Andrew. "History from the Sea." *New Scientist*, January 14, 1988.
"50 State Quarters." http://catalog.usmint.gov/.
"Finally — A New Design for Quarters." *America's Community Banker*, February 1, 1999.
"Finally, the Payoff." *Life*, September 1985, 47.
Fine, John V. A., Jr. *The Late Medieval Balkans*. Ann Arbor: University of Michigan, 1994.
"The First Printed Currency." http://www.coins.nd.edu/ColCurrency/CurrencyIntros/IntroEarliest.html.
Fleming, Arline A., "Ann Franklin (1696–1763), 'The Widow Franklin,' Printer to R. I." *Journal-Bulletin*, May 7, 2002.
"Florida County Rejects 'In God We Trust' Posters." *Church & State*, October 1, 2001.
Foege, Alec. "Sunken Dream: Barry Clifford Has Found Captain Kidd's Long-Lost Pirate Ship — Maybe." *People Weekly*, May 22, 2000, 169.
"Forensic Laboratory." *Royal Canadian Mounted Police*, http://www.rcmp-grc.gc.ca/html/labs.htm.
"Forget the Titanic: Everyone Really Wants a Piece of the Hunley." *Wall Street Journal*, March 23, 2001.
"Fort Knox." http://library.louisville.edu/ekstrom/govpubs/states/kentucky/ftknox.html.
Foss, Michael. *People of the First Crusade*. New York: Arcade Publishing, 1997.
Fourier, Charles. *Selections from the Works of Fourier*. New York: Gordon Press, 1972.
Fowler, Glenn. "Peter Throckmorton, Archeologist of Ancient Shipwrecks, Dies at 61." *New York Times*, June 11, 1990.
"France, 1793." http://www.napoleonicmedals.org/coins/fran93-2.htm.
Franck, Irene M., and David M. Brownstone. *Women's World: A Timeline of Women in History*. New York: HarperPerennial, 1995.
Frankel, Bruce, and Tim Roche. "Good As Gold?" *People Weekly*, June 15, 1998, p. 89.
Franklin, Benjamin. "A Modest Enquiry into the Nature and Necessity of a Paper Currency." http://www.people.virginia.edu/~rwm3n/webdoc6.html.
_____. "The Writings of Benjamin Franklin." http://www.historycarper.com/resources/twobf2/paper1.htm.
Frawley-Holler, Janis. "The Coconut Palm." *Islands*, November 2000, 28.
Freeman, Anthony. *The Moneyer and the Mint in the Reign of Edward the Confessor*. Oxford: B. A. R. British Series 145, 1985.
Fremantle, Anne. *The Age of Faith*. New York: Time Incorporated, 1965.
Friedenberg, Daniel M. "Early Jewish History in Italy." *Judaism: A Quarterly Journal of Jewish Life and Thought*, Winter 2000.
Fritz, David. "Who's the Real Father of Economics?" *Across the Board*, January 1988, 62–63.
Fry, Maxwell J. "Choosing a Money for Europe." *Journal of Common Market Studies*, September 1991, 481–527.
Gabriel, Judith. "Among the Norse Tribes." *Aramco World*, November-December 1999, 36–42.
Galbraith, John Kenneth. *Money: Whence It Came, Where It Went*. Boston: Houghton Mifflin, 1975.
Gale Encyclopedia of U.S. Economic History. Farmington Hills, Mich.: Gale Group, 1999.
Gardner, Bill. "Futile Hunt for Film Loot Turns Fatal." *Charlotte Observer*, December 9, 2001, 18A.
Gardner, John. *The Life and Times of Chaucer*. New York: Alfred A. Knopf, 1977.
Garraty, John. *The Columbia History of the World*. New York: Harper & Row, 1972.
Gay & Lesbian Biography. Detroit: St. James Press, 1997.
Geiger, Rusty. "Elephant Tokens One Legacy of

N.C. Colony." *Coin World*, February 25, 1987, p. 38.
George, Leonard. *The Encyclopedia of Heresies and Heretics*. London: Robson Books, 1995.
"George Hill." http://www.amnumsoc.org/inc/hill bio.html.
"Germany Reviews Design of Its Euro Coins," *Europe Information Service*, October 7, 1998.
"Getting In Touch." *Evening Mail*, August 13, 2001.
Gifford, John A. "Ships and Shipwrecks of the Americas." *American Antiquity*, April 1998, pp. 361–362.
"The Gift of History." http://www.scripophily.net/mohvalban.html./
Gilbert, Martin. *Atlas of the Holocaust*. New York: William Morrow and Co., 1993.
Gillispie, Charles Couleston, ed. *Dictionary of Scientific Biography*. New York: Charles Scribner's Sons, 1981.
"Giovanni Villani: Florentine Chronicle." http://www.fordham.edu/halsall/source/villani.html.
Given-Wilson, Chris, and Francois Beriac. "Edward III's Prisoners of War: The Battle of Poitiers and Its Context." *English Historical Review*, September 1, 2001.
Glasgow, Eric. "The Gold of Troy Emerges from the Cold War." *Contemporary Review*, June 1996, pp. 312–314.
Glueck, Grace. "The Nature of Islamic Ornament, Part 1: Calligraphy." *New York Times*, April 24, 1998, p. B32.
Goethe. *Faust*. http://www.levity.com/alchemy/faust idx.html.
Gohmann, Stephan F. "The End of Liberty." *The Freeman*, November 1999.
"Gold Coin Hoard Unveiled." *BBC News*, January 10, 2001.
Goldstein, Steve. "Early Casualty of War on Terrorism Is Easy Sharing of Information." Knight-Ridder/Tribune News Service, November 4, 2001 p. 453.
"Goodbye Faraday, Hello Elgar." *London Daily Mail*, February 24, 2001.
Gowing, Lawrence, ed. *A Biographical Dictionary of Artists*. New York: Facts on File, 1995.
Graham-Campbell, James, ed. *Cultural Atlas of the Viking World*. Abingdon, Oxfordshire: Andromeda Oxford Limited, 1994.
Graves, Robert. *The Greek Myths*. London: Penguin Books, 1955.
"The Great Seal of the United States." http://greatseal.com/.
"The Great Seal of the United States." Washington, D.C.: U.S. Department of State Dispatch, 1996.
Green, Ronald. "A. C. Cummins of Ferguson, B.C." *Canadian Numismatic Association Journal*, October 2001, 386–388.
_____. "W. Cowan, Revelstoke, B.C." *Canadian Numismatic Association Journal*, November 2001, 428–431.
Greene, Bob. "Heads You Lose, Tails You Lose." *Esquire*, April 1981.
Greenspan, Karen. *The Timetables of Women's History*. New York: Touchstone, 1994.
"Gresham College." http://www.gresham.ac.uk/special/history.html.
Grierson, Philip. *Numismatics*. London: Oxford University Press, 1975.
Griffin, Gary. "The Bureau's Flat-Plate Press." *Stamp Collector*, December 18, 2000.
Grimbley, Shona, ed. *Encyclopedia of the Ancient World*. London: Fitzroy Dearborn, 2000.
Grosvenor, Melville Bell, ed. in chief. *Everyday Life in Bible Times*. Washington, D.C.: National Geographic Society, 1967.
Grotz, Alfred Fisk. "Notes on the Coins of the Grand Masters of the Knights of Malta." http://users.bigpond.net.au/jagatt/notes_on_the_coins_of_the_grand_.htm.
Grumbacher, Armin. "The Early Years of a German Institution: The Kreditanstalt fur Wiederaufbau in the 1950s." *Business History*, October 1, 2001.
Grun, Bernard. *The Timetables of History*. 3rd edition. New York: Touchstone, 1991.
"Guatemalan Government Honors Renowned UT Austin Scholar for Her Work in Deciphering Hieroglyphics." *University of Texas at Austin News*, March 18, 1998.
Gunderson, Craig, and Victor Oliveira. "The Food Stamp Program and Food Insufficiency." *American Journal of Agricultural Economics*, November 1, 2001.
Gustafson, Eleanor H. "Swarthy Monarchs." *Antiques*, September 2000.
Gustaitis, Joseph. "The Lady of the Tower." *American History*, June 1999, 44– 60.
Hadas, Moses. *Ancilla to Classical Reading*. New York: Columbia University Press, 1954.
_____. *A History of Latin Literature*. New York: Columbia University Press, 1952.
Hale, Ellen. "Europeans Make Change to Euro." *USA Today*, December 26, 2001, 3B.
_____. "Europe Makes Switch to Euro." *USA Today*, December 31, 2001, 1A.
Hallam, Elizabeth, ed. *Chronicles of the Crusades*. Wayne, N.J.: CLB, 1997.
_____. gen. ed. *Saints: Who They Are and How They Help You*. New York: Simon & Schuster, 1994.
Hallwood, Paul, Ronald MacDonald, and Ian W. Marsh. "An Assessment of the Causes of the Abandonment of the Gold Standard by the U.S. in 1933." *Southern Economic Journal*, October 2000, p. 448.
Hamilton, Franklin. *The Crusades*. New York: Dial Press, 1965.

Hammett, A. B. J. *The History of Gold*. Kerriville, Tex.: Braswell Printing, Co., 1966.
Hammond, N. G. L., and H. H. Scullard, eds. *The Oxford Classical Dictionary*. Oxford: Clarendon Press, 1992.
Handbook to Life in Ancient Egypt. New York: Facts on File, Inc., 1998.
Handbook to Life in Ancient Greece. New York: Facts on File, Inc., 1997.
Handbook to Life in Ancient Rome. New York: Facts on File, Inc., 1994.
Hardy, Thomas. *The Thomas Hardy Omnibus*. New York: St. Martin's Press, 1979.
Harnik, Eva. "The Land of Eternal Spring." *World & I*, August 1, 2001.
The Harper Encyclopedia of Military Biography. New York: HarperCollins, 1992.
Harpine, William D. "Bryan's "Cross of Gold": The Rhetoric and Polarization at the 1896 Democratic Convention." *Quarterly Journal of Speech*, August 1, 2001, 291–304.
Harpur, James. *Revelations: The Medieval World*. New York: Henry Holt & Co., 1995.
Harrington, Karl Pomeroy, ed. *Mediaeval Latin*. Boston: Allyn & Bacon, 1925.
Harris, Graham, et al. *Oak Island and Its Lost Treasure*. Victoria, B.C.: Formac, 2000.
Harris, Maurice H. *History of the Mediaeval Jews*. New York: Bloch Publishing Co., 1924.
Harrison, Paul. "Rational Equity Valuation at the Time of the South Sea Bubble." *History of Political Economy*, July 1, 2001, 269–281.
Hartley, Dorothy. *Food in England*. Boston: Little, Brown & Co., 1999
_____. *The Land of England*. London: Macdonald & Janes' Publishers Ltd., 1979.
Hastings, James, ed. *Encyclopedia of Religion and Ethics*. New York: Charles Scribner's Sons, 1951.
Hay, Denys. *The Medieval Centuries*. New York: Harper Torchbooks, 1964.
Head, Barclay V. *A Guide to the Principal Coins of the Greeks*. London: British Museum, 1959.
_____. *Historia Numorum*. Chicago: Argonaut, 1911.
Heilbroner, Robert L. *Behind the Veil of Economics: Essays in the World Philosophy*. New York: W. W. Norton & Co., 1989.
Henneberger, Melinda. "Reluctance in Greece to Let Go of the Coin of History." *New York Times*, December 31, 2001, p. A4.
Herbert, Jimmy, and Bertel Tingström. *The Plate Money Treasure of Nicobar*. Stockholm: Royal Coin Cabinet, 1999.
Heer, Friedrich. *The Medieval World*. New York: Mentor Books, 1961.
Henderson, Ernest F. *Select Historical Documents of the Middle Ages*. London: George Bell and Sons, 1896.
Hermann, Captain I. *Memoirs of a Veteran*. Atlanta, Ga.: Byrd Printing Company, 1911.
Herodotus. *The Histories*. London: Penguin Books, 1954.
"Hey Wiseguy — A Head Puzzler." *Peoria Journal Star*, December 4, 2000.
Hezel, Francis X. "A Yankee Trader in Yap: Crayton Philo Holcomb." *Journal of Pacific History*, 1975, 3–19.
Hibbert, Christopher. *The English: A Social HIstory, 1066–1945*. New York: W. W. Norton & Co., 1987.
Hicks, Brian. "Hunley Team Hoping to Find Fabled Coin." (Charleston, S.C.) *Post and Courier*, May 24, 2001.
_____. "Union Private's Tale Adds to Hunley Lore." (Charleston, S.C.) *Post and Courier*, May 1, 2001.
Hicks, Michael. *Who's Who in Late Medieval England*. London: Shepheard-Walwyn, 1991.
Highfill, John W., and Walter H. Breen. *The Comprehensive U.S. Silver Dollar Encyclopedia*. Broken Arrow, Okla.: Highfill Press, Inc., 1992.
Hill, G. F. *The Ancient Coinage of Southern Arabia*. Chicago: Ares Publishers, 1969.
_____. *Historical Greek Coins*. Chicago: Argonaut, Inc., 1966.
_____. *Historical Roman Coins*. Chicago: Argonaut, Inc., 1966.
Hine, Darlene Clark, et al., eds. *Black Women in America*. Bloomington: Indiana University Press, 1993.
Hipkiss, Edwin J. "A Florentine Coin of the Sixteenth Century." *Bulletin of the Museum of Fine Arts*, February 1937.
Historic World Leaders. Detroit: Gale Research, 1994.
"History of the Motto 'In God We Trust.'" http://www.ustreas.gov/opc/opc0011.html.
Ho, Erling. "The Things Kidds Do." *Geographical*, February 2001, 61.
"Hoard Returned." *Archaeology*, May/June 1999.
"Hoards of Coins." *Coins and Currency Weekly*, December 6, 1998.
"Hog Money Discovery at Castle Island." http://www.insiders.com/bermuda/sb-history.htm.
Hollister, C. Warren. *Medieval Europe: A Short History*. New York: McGraw-Hill, 1994.
Holmes, George, ed. *The Oxford Illustrated History of Medieval Europe*. Oxford: Oxford University Press, 1988.
Hopper, R. J. *The Early Greeks*. New York: Harper & Row, 1976.
Howarth, William. "The Work of Augustus Saint-Gaudens." *Smithsonian*, June 1983, 124–125.
Howatson, M. C., ed. *The Oxford Companion to Classical Literature*. Oxford: Oxford University Press, 1991.
Howe, Marvine. "Teresa Da Francisci, Miss Liberty

Model for Coin, Dies at 92." *New York Times*, October 21, 1990, 38.
"How Popular Will Sacagawea Be?" *USA Today Magazine*, November 2000.
Hughes, Merritt Y., ed. *John Milton: Complete Poems and Major Prose*. New York: Odyssey Press, 1957
Huizinga, J. *The Waning of the Middle Ages*. Garden City, N.Y.: Doubleday Anchor, 1956.
Hulse, Carl. "Forgotten Sleuth Is Honored at Last." *New York Times*, May 29, 2001, A12.
"Hungary: Government Grants 55 Billion Forints for Projects Boosting Economy." *BBC Monitoring European Economic*, October 25, 2001.
"The Hunley.com," http://www.thehunley.com/coinfound.htm.
Ibn Battuta. *The Travels of Ibn Battuta*. Cambridge: Cambridge University Press, 1971.
"I Had a Little Nut Tree." http://www.zelo.com/family/nursery/nuttree.asp.
"Infant Well Being." *Soap & Cosmetics*, November 2001, 9–10.
"'In God We Trust' Motto for Mississippi Schools." *New York Times*, March 25, 2001.
"In God We Trust on U.S. Coinage." http://www.coinlibrary.com/info/ingodwetrust.html.
Insoll, Timothy A. "The Road to Timbuktu: Trade & Empire." *Archaeology*, November/December 2000, 48–52.
"Instructions to Robert Evans." http://www.xmission.com/~drudy/mtman/html/fthall/instruct.html.
International Dictionary of Art and Artists. Detroit: St. James Press, 1990.
"Islamic Coins." http://www.islamiccoinsgroup.50g.com/jims.htm.
"Islamization of Central Asia." http://baskurt.homestead.com/Islamization.html.
Jack, R. Ian. *Medieval Wales*. Ithaca, N.Y.: Cornell University Press, 1972.
Jackson, Gerard. "Net Stocks and the South Sea Bubble." *New Australian*, February 21–27, 1999.
Jacobs, Wayne L. "Canada's First Coinage." *Canadian Numismatic Association Journal*, July/August 1995.
_____. "The Mystery of the Disappearing P. E. I. 'Dumps.'" *Canadian Numismatic Association Journal*, November 2001, 433–438.
James, Michael. "Counterfeiters Using Desktop Printers to Churn Out a Cascade of High-Quality Bogus Cash." *Buffalo News*, July 12, 1998.
James, Peter, and Nick Thorpe. *Ancient Inventions*. New York: Ballantine, 1994.
Jansen, H. W., and Anthony F. Janson. *History of Art*. New York: Harry N. Abrams, Incorporated, 1997.
Jeffrey, David Lyle, gen. ed. *A Dictionary of Biblical Tradition in English Literature*. Grand Rapids, Mich.: William B. Eerdmans Publishing Co., 1992.
"Jem Sultan Collection Donated to ANS." *American Numismatic Society Newsletter*, Winter 1997.
Jenner, Michael. *Journeys into Medieval England*. London: Michael Joseph, 1991.
Johansen, Bruce E., and Donald A. Grinde. *The Encyclopedia of Native American Biography*. New York: Da Capo Press, 1998.
Johnson, Allen, ed. *Dictionary of American Biography*. New York: Charles Scribner's Sons, 1928.
Johnston, Megan. "Death of the Drachma." *Money*, March 1, 2001, 28.
Jones, Bart. "Modern Day Pirates?" *Hannibal Post-Courier*, June 27, 1998.
Jones, Peter M. "Fighting World Crime." *Scholastic Update*, December 4, 1987, 22–23.
Jordan, Louis. "The Coins of Colonial and Early America." http://www.coins.nd.edu/ColCoin/ColCoinContents/Introduction.html.
"Joseph Alexis Bailly." *Philadelphia Public Art*, http://www.philart.net/cgi-bin/control.cgi.
Josephus. *Complete Works*. Grand Rapids, Mich.: Kregel Publications, 1960.
Jurdjevig, Mark. "Civic Humanism and the Rise of the Medici." *Renaissance Quarterly*, Winter 1999.
Kageleiry, Jamie. "The Other Side of the Coin." *Yankee*, September 1993, p. 58.
Kagin, Donald H. *Private Gold Coins and Patterns of the United States*. New York: Arco Publishing, 1981.
Kaiser, Thomas E. "Money, Despotism, and Public Opinion." *Journal of Modern History*, March 1991, pp. 1–28.
Kamen, Henry. *The Spanish Inquisition*. London: Weidenfeld & Nicolson, 1997.
Kaufman, R. "The Sea Remembers." *Library Journal*, January 1988, 85.
Kee, Howard Clark, Franklin W. Young, and Karlfried Froehlich. *Understanding the New Testament*. Englewood Cliffs, N.J.: Prentice-Hall, 1965.
Kelleher, Terry. "Pirate Tales." *People Weekly*, August 25, 1997, 18.
Kemp, Peter, ed. *The Oxford Companion to Ships and the Sea*. Oxford: Oxford University Press, 1988.
Kertes, Noella. "Mint Mulls Metals for Dollar Coin." *American Metal Market*, March 3, 1998.
Keys, David. "Buried 1,800 Years Ago, 43 Coins Offer Clues to High-Society Roman London." *Independent*, January 10, 2001.
Kibler, William W., and Grover A. Zinn, eds. *Medieval France: An Encyclopedia*. New York: Garland, 1995.
Kieckhefer, Richard. *Magic in the Middle Ages*. Cambridge: Cambridge University Press, 1989.
Kiernan, Philip. "Alfred Petrie Leaves His Coins to the National Currency Collection." *Canadian Numismatic Association Journal*, October 2001, 389–395.

Kinder, Gary. *Ship of Gold in the Deep Blue Sea.* New York: Atlantic Monthly Press, 1998.

Klare, Normand E. *The Final Voyage of the "Central America," 1857.* Spokane, Wash.: Arthur H. Clark Company, 1992.

Kleeberg, John, ed. *The Money of Pre-Federal America.* New York: American Numismatic Society, 1992.

Kline, Morris. *Mathematical Thought from Ancient to Modern Times.* New York: Oxford University Press, 1972.

Klingman, Lawrence, and Gerald Green. *His Majesty O'Keefe.* New York: Charles Scribner's Sons, 1950.

Klinkenborg, Verlyn. "The West Indies as Freshly Seen in the 16th Century." *Smithsonian,* January 1988, 89–98.

Komroff, Manuel, ed. *The Apocrypha or Non-Canonical Books of the Bible.* New York: Tudor Publishing Co., 1937.

Krasner-Khait, Barbara. "The South Sea Bubble." *History,* March 2002, 47–51.

Krause, Chester L., and Clifford Mishler. *2002 Standard Catalog of World Coins.* Iola, Wisc.: Krause Publications, 2001.

Kropf, Schuyler, and Brian Hicks. "Dixon's Coin Found." (Charleston, S.C.) *Post and Courier,* May 25, 2001.

"Krugerrands." http://www.krugerrand.org/.

Kumar, Bachchan. "Dongson Culture of Vietnam." http://www.ignca.nic.in/nl_00404.htm.

Kummer, Corby. "The Pull of Puglia." *Atlantic Monthly,* April 1994, 54–58.

Kumpikevicius, Gordon. "The Art of the Coin Forger." *Canadian Coin News,* May 27, 2000.

Kunzig, Robert. "Euroland or Bust." *Discover,* October 1998.

Labbé, Dominic. "The Hudson Bay Company Tokens." *Tasmanian Numismatist,* July 1999.

Lacroix, Paul. *Science and Literature in the Middle Ages.* New York: Frederick Ungar, 1964.

Laing, Lloyd R. *Coins and Archaeology.* New York: Schocken Books, 1969.

"Lake Search Yields Counterfeit Bills, but No Nazi Gold." (Bergen, N.J.) *Record,* November 23, 2000.

Lamar, Howard R., ed. *The Reader's Encyclopedia of the American West.* New York: Harper & Row, 1977.

"Landscape Issues." *New Arcadian Journal,* 1993.

Langly, Mike. "Sir Stanley's Famous Fivers." *Johannesburg Mail and Guardian,* March 3, 2000.

"Late Victorian Coinage." *Studium Magazine,* November 23, 2001.

"LaVere Redfield and His Dollars." http://coin-shop.com/gold26.htm.

Law, Steven. "Sculptors of Cape Ann." *American Art Review,* October 1997.

"The Law of the Twelve Tables." http://members.aol.com/pilgrimjon/private/LEX/12tables.html.

"The Law of Treasure Trove in England and Wales," http://www.amnumsoc.org/inc/treasur2.htm.

Lea, Henry Charles. *History of the Inquisition of the Middle Ages.* New York: Harbor Press, 1955.

Lee, J. Edward, and Ron Chepesiuk. *South Carolina in the Civil War.* Jefferson, N.C.: McFarland, 2000.

Lee, Robert E. *Blackbeard the Pirate.* Winston-Salem, N.C.: John F. Blair, 1974.

"Leeds Junior Chamber." http://www.cjirish.demon.co.uk/cityofleeds.htm.

"Legacy of Gold." *Charlotte Observer,* March 15, 1999.

Lemonick, Michael D. "Troy's Lost Treasure." *Time,* April 22, 1996, 78–80.

"Leo Africanus: Description of Timbuktu." *The Description of Africa,* http://www.wsu.edu:8080/~wldciv/world_civ_reader/world_civ_reader_2/leo_africanus.html.

"Lesher Dollars in Demand." *Victor Daily Record,* November 14, 1900.

Levy, Alan. "Adolf Burger: The Forger as a Work of Art." *Prague Post,* November 1, 2000.

Lewis, Brenda Ralph. *Coins & Currency.* New York: Random House, 1993.

Lewis, Michael J. "Of Kitsch and Coins." *Commentary,* October 1999.

"The Life of King Edward the Confessor." http://www.lib.cam.ac.uk/cgi-bin/Ee.3.59/bytext.

"Lincoln Bicentennial Commission Asked To Consider Minting New Penny." *PR Newswire,* April 7, 2000.

Lind, Michael. "Hamilton's Legacy." *Wilson Quarterly,* Summer 1994, 40–52.

Link, Marion Clayton. "Exploring the Drowned City of Port Royal." *National Geographic,* February 1960, 151, 158–182.

Littlefield, Henry M. "The Wizard of Oz: Parable on Populism." *American Quarterly,* 16, Spring, 47–58.

Llewellin, Philip, and Ann Saunders. *Book of British Towns.* London: Drive Publications, Ltd., 1979.

Lockyer, Herbert. *All the Women of the Bible.* Grand Rapids, Mich.: Zondervan Publishing, 1988.

Loesch, Robert K. "Seven Nobel Women." *Christian Century,* November 17, 1982, pp. 1158–1159.

"Looking at Art: Arts Community Reflects on Significant 20th Century Artists." *Baton Rouge Advocate,* January 9, 2000.

Lopez, Robert S. *The Birth of Europe.* New York: M. Evans & Co., 1967.

Lothar, Corinna. "Sun Shines brightly on Liguria La Superba." *Washington Times,* April 21, 2001.

Loud, G. A. "Coinage, Wealth and Plunder in the Age of Robert Guiscard." *English Historical Review,* September 1999.

"Louis XIII Le Juste." http://www.cgb.fr/monnaies/vso/v12/fr/monnaies8287.html.

Lowsley, Colonel B. "Coins of Lanka." *Numismatic Chronicle Series*, 1895, 211–223.

Lyttelton, Margaret, and Werner Forman. *The Romans: Their Gods and Their Beliefs*. London: Orbis Publishing, 1984.

MacDonnell, Joseph F. *The Jesuit Family Album*. Fairfield, Conn.: The Clavius Mathematics Group, 1997.

Mackay, Angus, and David Ditchburn, eds. *Atlas of Medieval Europe*. London: Routledge, 1997.

Madariaga, Isabel de. "Catherine the Great: A Personal View." *History Today*, November 1, 2001.

Maggio, Rosalie. *The New Beacon Book of Quotations by Women*. Boston: Beacon Press, 1996.

Magic and Medicine of Plants. Pleasantville, N.Y.: Reader's Digest, 1986.

Magill, Frank N., ed. *Dictionary of World Biography*. Chicago: Fitzroy Dearborn, 1998.

"Magna Carta." http://www.fh-augsburg.de/~harsch/Chronologia/Lspost13/MagnaCarta/mag_cart.html.

Magnusson, Magnus. *Cambridge Biographical Dictionary*. Cambridge: University of Cambridge, 1990.

_____. *Larousse Biographical Dictionary*. New York: Larousse, 1994.

Mannix, Daniel P. "The Father of the Wizard of Oz." *American Heritage*, December 1964, 36.

Mantello, F. A. C., and A. G. Rigg, eds. *Medieval Latin: An Introduction and Bibliographical Guide*. Washington, D.C.: Catholic University Press of America, 1996.

Mantinband, James H. *Dictionary of Latin Literature*. New York: Philosophical Library, 1956.

"The Man with the Midas Touch." (London) *Times*, March 14, 1998, 16.

"March of Dimes." http://www.modimes.org/.

"March of Dimes Holds WalkAmerica 30th Anniversary Continuing the Fight to Save Babies' Lives." *Fund Raising Management*, June 2000, 30.

Marks, Claude. *Pilgrims, Heretics, and Lovers: A Medieval Journey*. New York: Macmillan, 1975.

Marks, Geoffrey, and William K. Beatty. *Epidemics*. New York: Charles Scribner's Sons, 1976.

Marotta, Michael E. "Coin Gallery Online." http://www.coin-gallery.com/cgmarotta.htm.

_____. "The Mercury Dime." *The Shinplaster*, March 1994.

Marr, John. "The Death of Themistocles." *Greece & Rome*, October 1995.

Martin, Douglas. "Frank Gasparro, 92, of Mint." *New York Times*, October 3, 2001.

Martindale, Nancy E. "The Cash Notes of 'The Oldest Colony.'" *Canadian Numismatic Association Journal*, November 2001, 424–427.

_____. "War of 1812 Spurred the Need for Army Bills." *Canadian Numismatic Association Journal*, October 2001, 73–377.

Martinez, Alejandro J. "U.K.'s Mint Molds New Image for Sovereign Coins." *Wall Street Journal*, January 14, 2002, p. C11.

"Mathematics in Medieval Europe." http://www.csusm.edu/public/DJBarskyWebs/330CollageOct08.html.

Mathisen, Ralph W. "De Imperitoribus Romanis." http://www.salve.edu/~dimaiom/galla.html.

Marx, Robert F. "Discovery of the Admiral's Flagship." *Sea Frontiers*, March-April 1982, 80–86.

"Matthew Boulton and the Development of Modern Coinage." http://www.geocities.com/mboulton1797/.

"Maundy Money." *The Royal Report*, May 2000.

"Maundy Money for Pensioners." *Coventry Evening Telegraph*, April 13, 2001.

"The Maundy Tradition." http://www.royalinsight.gov.uk/200004/focus/index.html.

"Mausaeus Carausius." http://www.roman-empire.net/decline/carausius-index.html.

Maxey, Al. "The Lord's Supper: A Historical Overview." http://www.zianet.com/maxey/Supper5.htm.

May, Herbert G., and Bruce M. Metzger, eds. *The Oxford Annotated Bible*. New York: Oxford University Press, 1962.

McAdams, Robert, "David Rittenhouse," *Smithsonian*, December 1986, p. 10.

McCabe, Joseph, "Religious Controversy," http://freethought.org/library/historical/joseph_mccabe/religious_controversy/chapter_30.html, 1999.

McCall, Andrew. *The Medieval Underworld*. New York: Dorset Press, 1979.

McCarthy, Carlton. *Detailed Minutiae of Soldier Life*. New York: Time-Life Books, 1982.

McClanathan, Richard. *The Pageant of Medieval Art and Life*. Philadelphia: Westminster Press, 1966.

McClure, Andres S. "Sarah Winnemuccca: Post Indian Princess and Voice of the Paiutes." *Melus*, Summer 1999.

McCrum, Robert, William Cran, and Robert Mac Neil. *The Story of English*. New York: Viking, 1986.

McCusker, John J. *How Much Is That in Real Money?* Worcester, Mass.: American Antiquarian Society, 2001.

McGuire, Bill, "The Man Who Chained the Hudson," *Townline*, Fall 2000.

McKinnon, E. Edwards. "The Sambas Hoard: Bronze Drums, and Gold Ornaments Found in Kalimantan in 1991." *Journal of the Malaysian Branch of the Royal Asiatic Society*, 1994, 9–28.

McKisack, May. *The Fourteenth Century, 1307–1399*. New York: Oxford University Press, 1991.

McLeod, Marcia. "Crime Watch." *Computer Weekly*, February 27, 1997, 48.
McMurtry, Jo. *Understanding Shakespeare's England*. Hamden, Conn.: Archon Books, 1989.
Meale, Carol M., ed. *Women and Literature in Britain, 1150–1500*. Cambridge: Cambridge University Press, 1993.
"Medical History Time Line." http://tqd.advanced.org/2961/timeline.html.
"Medieval Latin." http://patriot.net/~lillard/cp/cred.html.
"The Medieval Period." http://wwwkc.nhmccd.edu/employee/jsamuels/medievel_period.htm.
"Medieval Philosophy: The Scholastic Period." http://radicalacademy.com/adiphilscholastic.htm.
"Medieval Sourcebook: Anna Comnena: The Alexiad." http://www.fordham.edu/HALSALL/basis/annacomnena-alexiad00.html.
"Medieval Sourcebook: Barcelona Jewish Court Documents: A Daughter's Inheritance, 1293." http://www.fordham.edu/halsall/source/1293belladona.html, 1998.
"Medieval Sourcebook: Barcelona Jewish Court Documents: A Jewish Widow and Her Daughter, 1261–1262." http://www.fordham.edu/halsall/source/1262cruxia.html.
"Medieval Sourcebook: Christopher Columbus: Extracts from Journal." http://www.fordham.edu/halsall/source/columbus1.html.
"Medieval Sourcebook: Corpus Iuris Civilis, 6th Century." http://www.fordham.edu/halsall/source/corpus1.html.
"Medieval Sourcebook: Henry II of England: Concerning Loans from the Jews." http://www.fordham.edu/halsall/source/hen2-jewsloans.html.
"Medieval Sourcebook: James I of Aragon: Grant of Trade Privileges to Barcelona, 1232." http://www.fordham.edu/halsall/source/1232barcelona3.html.
"Medieval Sourcebook: James I of Aragon: Improvement of Harbor Facilities in Barcelona, 1243." http://www.fordham.edu/halsall/source/1243barcelona1.html.
"Medieval Sourcebook: James I of Aragon: The Barcelona Navigation Act of 1227." http://www.fordham.edu/halsall/source/1227barcelona2.htm.
"Medieval Sourcebook: John of Monte Corvino: Report from China." http://www.fordham.edu/halsall/source/corvino1.html.
"Medieval Sourcebook: Jocelin de Brakelond: Concerning Loans to the Abbey of Bury St. Edmunds, 1173." http://www.fordham.edu/halsall/source/1173badloans.html.
"Medieval Sourcebook: List of Tolls Exacted at Billingsgate, c. 978–1016." http://www.fordham.edu/halsall/source/billingsgate-tolls.html.
"Medieval Sourcebook: Marsiglio of Padua." http://www.fordham.edu/halsall/source/marsiglio1.htm.
"Medieval Sourcebook: Martin Luther (1483–1546): The Jews and Their Lies, excerpts (1543)." http://www.fordham.edu/halsall/source/luther-jews.html.
"Medieval Sourcebook: Matthew of Paris: The Usury of the Cahorsins, 1235." http://www.fordham.edu/halsall/source/1235cahorsins.html.
"Medieval Sourcebook: Nennius: The History of the Britons." http://www.fordham.edu/halsall/source/nennius.html,
"Medieval Sourcebook: Tales of Relics." http://www.forham.edu/halsall/source/tales-relics.html, 1997.
"Medieval Source Book: The Anglo-Saxon Dooms, 560–975." http://www.fordham.edu/halsall/source/560-975dooms.html.
"Medieval Sourcebook: The Dialogue Concerning the Exchequer." http://www. medievalhistory.net/excheq1.htm.
"Medieval Sourcebook: William the Conqueror: Provision for Peter's Pence." http://www.fordham.edu/halsall/source/1087william1-peterspence.html.
Medovoy, George. "Merchant Runs Holocaust Museum with Price Tags." *Jewish Bulletin of Northern California*, October 27, 1995.
Meek, C. E., and M. K. Simms, eds. *The Fragility of Her Sex?: Medieval Irish Women in Their European Context*. Dublin: Four Courts Press, 1996.
Megapolensis, Johannes. "A Short Account of the Mohawk Indians." In J. Franklin Jameson's *Narratives of New Netherland, 1609–1664*. New York: Charles Scribner's Sons, 1909.
Mehl, B. Max. "The Petition Crown of Thomas Simon." *The Star Rare Coin Encyclopedia and Premium Catalog: An Elaborate Encyclopedia of the Coins of the World*. Fort Worth: The Numismatic Company of Texas, 1923.
"Mel Fisher's Payoff: Sinkin' Treasure." *Money*, November 1986, 15.
Melville, Herman. *Moby Dick*. New York: New American Library, 1961.
The Memorial Book for the Jewish Community of Yurburg, Lithuania. Tel Aviv, Israel: Organization of Former Residents of Yurburg, 1991.
Merriam-Webster's Biographical Dictionary. Springfield, Mass.: Merriam-Webster, 1995.
Mervin, Sabrina, and Carol Prunhuber. *Women Around the World and Through the Ages*. Wilmington, Del.: Atomium Books, 1990.
Meshorer, Ya'akov. *Ancient Jewish Coinage*. New York: Amphora Books, 1982.
______. *Coins of the Ancient World*. Jerusalem: Jerusalem Publishing House, 1974.
"Metallic Analysis of the 1730–1754 Polushka." *Journal of the Russian Numismatic Society*, Winter 1991-1992, 45.
Metzger, Bruce M. *The Apocrypha of the Old Testament*. New York: Oxford University Press, 1965.
"Mexican Cocoa Bean Money." *Money Talks*, 1972.

Michener, James. *Centennial.* New York: Random House, 1974.

Miksic, John N. "Evolving Archaeological Perspectives on Southeast Asia, 1970–95." *Journal of Southeast Asian Studies*, March 1995, 46–62.

"Milestones." *Time*, October 15, 2001.

Milton, Joyce, et al. *The Cross and the Crescent.* Boston: Boston Publishing Co., 1987.

Mitchell, Mary A. "Tampa Lands New Pirate Attraction." *Travel Weekly*, November 23, 1992, 28.

Mitchiner, Michael. *Oriental Coins.* London: Hawkins, 1978.

"Modern History Sourcebook: Oswald Spengler: The Decline of the West, 1922." http://www.fordham.edu/halsall/mod/spengler-decline.html.

Molnar, Michael R. *The Star of Bethlehem: The Legacy of the Magi.* New Brunswick, N.J.: Rutgers University Press, 1999.

"Monnaies Royales Françaises." http://www.epromat.com/poindessault/ve26/p2605.htm.

Monroe, Sylvester. "The Trouble with Treasure." *Time*, May 11, 1998, 30.

Montague-Smith, Patrick W. *The Royal Line of Succession: The British Monarchy from Cerdic to Queen Elizabeth II.* Andover, England: Pitkin, 1986.

Moore, Anderley, proj. ed. *Smithsonian Visual Timeline of Inventions.* New York: Dorling Kindersley, 1994.

Moorehead, Caroline. *Lost and Found: The 9,000 Treasures of Troy.* London: Penguin Books, 1994.

Morris, Richard B. *Encyclopedia of American History.* New York: Harper & Row, 1976.

Mossman, Philip L. "The Circulation of Irish Coinage in Pre-Federal America." *The Colonial Newsletter*, April 1999, 1899–1917.

_____. *Money of the American Colonies and Confederation.* New York: American Numismatic Society, 1993.

"Mrs. A. B. Marshall." http://www.canalmuseum.org.uk/marshall.htm.

Mumford, Lewis. *The Story of Utopias.* Gloucester, Mass.: Peter Smith, 1959.

Murphy, Antoin E. "The Evolution of John Law's Theories and Policies, 1707–1715." *European Economic Review*, July 1991, 1109–1126.

Murphy, Jamie. "Down into the Deep." *Time*, August 11, 1986, 48–54.

Murray, Peter, and Linda Murray. *A Dictionary of Art and Artists.* New York: Penguin Books, 1976.

"Muslim Scientists, Mathematicians, and Astronomers." http://salam.muslimsonline.com/~azahoor/.

"Muslim Spain." http://www.DocuWeb.ca/SiSpain/english/history/muslim.html.

Myers, John. "Priest Cracks Carol's Secret Code." Evening Standard, December 23, 2000.

Napier, H. Albert, et al. *Creating a Winning E-Business.* Detroit: Thomson Learning, 2001.

Nash, Jay Robert. *Encyclopedia of World Crime.* 6 vols. Wilmette, Ill.: CrimeBooks Inc., 1990.

Nashabe, Hisham, ed. *Studia Palaestina.* Beirut: Institute for Palestine Studies, Beirut, 1988.

National Women's Hall of Fame, http://www.greatwomen.org.

"The Nature of Islamic Ornament: Calligraphy." http://www.metmuseum.org/toah/hd/cali/hod_38.149.1.htm.

Newark, Tim. *Warlords, Ancient, Celtic, Medieval.* London: Brockhampton Press, 1996.

New Catholic Encyclopedia. San Francisco: Catholic University of America, 1967.

"New Krugerrand 2000 Coin Issued in South Africa." *African Mining Monitor,* October 25, 1999.

Newman, Eric. "Coinage for Colonial Virginia." *Numismatic Notes and Monographs*, No. 135, 1956.

_____. "The Earliest Money Using the Dollar as a Unit of Value." *Perspectives in Numismatics*, 1996.

_____. *The Early Paper Money of America.* Iola, Wisc: Krause, 1997.

Newman, Ewell L. "Abel Buell: Errant Genius." *Imprint*, February 1976, 7–8.

Newman, Louis I., and Samuel Spitz, eds. *The Talmudic Anthology.* West Orange, N.J.: Behrman House, 1945.

"Newsmakers." *Life,* January 1986, 26.

Newsom, John. "Legendary Treasure Beckons." *Greensboro News & Record*, August 12, 1996.

"New Yorkers Uncover Major Variety of Buffalo Nickel." *Coin World*, March 16, 1962, 1, 2.

Nicholas, John. "Gold Coin Appears in Salvation Army Kettle." *South Bend Tribune,* December 13, 1998.

Nicholls, C. S., ed. *Encyclopedia of Biography.* Oxford, Eng.: Helicon Publishing Ltd., 1996.

Nickell, Joe. "The Secrets of Oak Island." *Skeptical Inquirer*, March 2000, 14.

Nickerson, Colin. "Canadian Divers Agree to Share Their Undersea Finds with Cuba." *Boston Globe*, March 9, 2001.

"Nigeria: The Free Giant." *Time Europe*, October 10, 1960.

Noot, Arthur E. "Carausius Carved an Empire from Within an Empire." *The Celator*, February 1996.

"The North Carolina Collection's Currency Holdings," *North Carolina Collection Gallery,* http://www.lib.unc.edu/ncc/gallery/currency.html.

Norton, Trevor. *Stars Beneath the Sea.* London: Random House, 1999.

Norwich, John Julius. *A History of Venice.* New York: Alfred A. Knopf, 1982.

_____. *A Short History of Byzantium.* New York: Alfred A. Knopf, 1997.

Nostradamus. "Centurie VII." http://was.kewlhair.com/nostra/cent7.html.

Notable Mathematicians. Detroit: Gale Research, 1998.
"Numismatics." http://www.hermitage.museum.ru/en/numizmat/en_grosso_col.htm.
"Numismatics in the Age of Grolier." http://www.grolierclub.org/ExNumismatics.htm.
Nuthall, Keith. "Interpol Most-Wanted Goes Online." *Computer Weekly*, November 23, 2000, 20.
"Obituary." *Jet*, September 18, 1995, 58.
O'Ceirin, Kit, and Cyril O'Ceirin. *Women of Ireland: A Biographical Dictionary*. Galway: Tir Eolas, 1996.
O'Croinin, Daibhi. *Early Medieval Ireland, 400–1200*. London: Longman, 1995.
"An Official Report on Swedish and Norwegian Immigration, 1870." *Norwegian-American Studies*, Vol. 13, 1943.
Olcott, William. "The Roots of Fund Raising." *Fund Raising Management*, April 1989, 25–30.
"Old Fritz Returns to Prussia." *Economist*, July 27, 1991, 44.
Olert, Chris. "Buried Treasure Faceless Statue Gets a Name and a Rich History." *Fort Worth Star-Telegram*, April 5, 1998.
Opitz, Charles J. *Odd and Curious Money*. Ocala, Fla.: First Impressions, 1986.
"The Order of St. John of Jerusalem, Knights Hospitaller." http://www2.prestel.co.uk/church/oosj/history.htm.
O'Reilly, Jane. "From Davy Jones, a Tax Shelter." *Time*, April 11, 1983, 77.
Orr, Francine, and Tim Engle. "Yap Facts: A Primer of Yapese Culture." *Kansas City Star*, 1998.
Outlaws, Mobsters & Crooks: From the Old West to the Internet. Farmington Hills, Mich.: U*X*L, 1998.
"Over 10,000 Han Dynasty Coins Found in Central China." *Xinhua News Agency*, August 23, 2001.
The Oxford Companion to Art. Oxford: Clarendon Press, 1970.
"Paladins and Princes." http://www.legends.dm.net/paladins/roland.html, 1998.
Paris, Sheldon. "Sir Henry Morgan: Pirate or Patriot?" *Stamps*, June 17, 1995, 3.
Parker, David B. "The Rise and Fall of the Wonderful Wizard of Oz as a 'Parable on Populism.'" *Journal of the Georgia Association of Historians*, 1994, 49–63.
Parker, John. "Happy E-Day, Europe." *Traffic World*, September 10, 2001.
Parker, Michael St. John. *Britain's Kings and Queens*. Andover, Hants: Pitkin, 1994.
Parry, Melanie, ed. *Larousse Dictionary of Women*. New York: Larousse Kingfisher Chambers, 1994.
Parsons, John Carmi, ed. *Medieval Queenship*. New York: St. Martin's Press, 1998.
"The Parthenon Sculptures." *The British Museum*, http://www.thebritishmuseum.ac.uk/parthenon/7.html.
Pastan, E. C. "The Formation of Islamic Art." http://www.cc.emory.edu/HART/HART345S98/Section3.html, 1988.
"The Patching Hoard." http://www-wrds.uwyo.edu/coinnet/hoards/Britain/Patching/release.html.
Patterson, Lotsee, and Mary Ellen Snodgrass. *Indian Terms of the Americas*. Englewood, Colo.: Libraries Unlimited, 1994.
Paul, Ron. "Greenspan Go Home." *Liberty*, March 2000.
Paunov, Evgeni I. "Ancient Treasures from Thracian Tombs." *Athena Review*, 1998, 76–82.
Pavlenko, Nikolai. "A Woman of Substance." *Russian Life*, November 1996.
Pearl, Daniel. "Amid Global Turmoil, Wild Times in Trading Afghanis." *Wall Street Journal*, November 14, 2001, C1, C13.
Penguin Dictionary of Decorative Art. New York: Viking Penguin, 1989.
Pepys, Samuel. *The Diary of Samuel Pepys*. New York: Harper Torchbooks, 1960.
Peterson, Mendel. "Graveyard of the Quicksilver Galleons." *National Geographic*, December 1979, 850–876.
Petterwood, Graeme. "The Shamrock and the Harp." *Tasmanian Numismatist*, July 1999.
Pickford, Nigel. *The Atlas of Ship Wrecks & Treasure*. New York: Dorling Kindersley, 1994.
Plagens, Peter. "The Golden Hoard." *Newsweek*, April 8, 1996, 72–73.
"Plate Money from the *Nicobar*." http://www.tranquebar.dk/nicobar.htm#.
Platt, Colin. *The Abbeys and Priories of Medieval England*. New York: Barnes & Noble, 1996.
Platt, Gordon. "Europe/Africa: Hungary Widens Band for Forint." *Global Finance*, June 1, 2001.
Pliny. *The Natural History*. New York: McGraw-Hill, 1962.
Poe, Edgar Allan. *Selected Stories and Poems*. New York: Airmont, 1962.
Pollak, Henry. *Coinage & Conflict*. Clifton, N.J.: Coin & Currency Institute, 2001.
Pomerleau, Charlie. "Tall Tales of Buried Treasures Run Deep." *Bangor Daily News*, August 27, 1998.
Potok, Chaim. *Wanderings: Chaim Potok's History of the Jews*. New York: Alfred A. Knopf, 1978.
Powell, John. "The Birmingham Coiners, 1770–1816." *History Today*, July 1993, 49–55.
Power, Eileen. *Medieval Women*. Cambridge: Cambridge University Press, 1995.
"Powered Coining Press." *Inquiry Attic*, February 2000.
"The Power of Gold: The History of an Obsession." *Traders*, December 1, 2001.
Prebble, John. *The Lion in the North*. New York: Coward, McCann & Geoghegan, Inc., 1971.

"Pressing — Full Steam Ahead." *Franklin Institute*, http://fi.edu/qa00/attic2/index.html.

Preston, Douglas. "Death Trap Defies Treasure Seekers." *Smithsonian*, June 1988, 52–61.

_____. "Is Oak Island Ready to Yield Its Treasure?" *Reader's Digest* (Canadian), October 1988, 58–62.

Pringle, Heather. "The Cradle of Cash." *Discover*, October 1998.

Pritzker, Barry M. *A Native American Encyclopedia: History, Culture, and Peoples*. Oxford: Oxford University Press, 2000.

Probert Encyclopedia, http://www.probertencyclopaedia.com/money.htm.

Proctor, Steve. "Island of Controversy." *Maclean's*, August 21, 1995, p. 54.

Pruzan, Todd. "The Almighty Euro." *Print*, March-April 1999, pp. 138–143.

Quigley, Christine. *The Corpse: A History*. Jefferson, N.C.: McFarland, 1996.

Raby, F. J. E., ed. *A History of Christian-Latin Poetry*. Oxford: Clarendon Press, 1953.

_____. *The Oxford Book of Medieval Latin Verse*. Oxford: Clarendon Press, 1959.

Radice, Betty, ed. *Who's Who in the Ancient World*. New York: Penguin Books, 1973.

Randall, Lorelei. "Our Marine Heritage." *Nordic Underwater Archaeology*, May 1999.

Ranft, Patricia. *Women and the Religious Life in Premodern Europe*. New York: St. Martin's Press, 1996.

Rawlinson, George. *History of Phoenicia*. London: Longmans, Green, and Company, 1889.

Reden, Sita von. "The Piraeus — A World Apart." *Greece & Rome*, April 1995, 24–39.

Rediker, Marcus. *Between the Devil and the Deep Blue Sea*. Cambridge: Cambridge University Press, 1987.

_____. "When Women Pirates Sailed the Seas," *Wilson Quarterly*, Autumn 1993, 102–111.

Reed, Mort. *Cowles Complete Encyclopedia of U.S. Coins*. New York: Cowles Book Company, 1969.

Reid, Ronald F. *Three Centuries of American Rhetorical Discourse*. Prospect Heights, Ill.: Waveland Press, 1988.

Reid, T. R. "The New Europe." *National Geographic*, January 2002, 32–47.

Reif, Rita. "Islamic Calligraphy Makes a Statement." *New York Times*, December 16, 1990, H48.

Reinfeld, Fred. *Treasury of the World's Coins*. New York: Sterling Publishing, 1953.

Reiter, Ed. "Circulated Coins." *New York Times*, November 4, 1984.

_____. "Grading Service under Fire." *New York Times*, June 17, 1984, H35.

_____. "Historic Lesher House Recalls a Bygone Era." *New York Times*, June 16, 1985, H35.

_____. "New Coin May Place Washington on Horseback." *New York Times*, February 21, 1982.

_____. "Numismatics: The Roman Touch." *New York Times*, January 16, 1983.

_____. "A Quick Sale for Yale's Brasher Doubloon." *New York Times*, January 18, 1981, D32.

_____. "The Silver Bullion." *New York Times*, December 14, 1986, H43.

Reno, Frank D. *The Historic King Arthur*. Jefferson, N.C.: McFarland, 1996.

"Renowned Artist Glenna Goodacre Creates Sculpture for New Gold-Colored Dollar Coin for Year 2000." *People Weekly*, June 14, 1999.

Rice, David Talbot, ed. *The Dawn of European Civilization: The Dark Ages*. New York: McGraw-Hill, 1965.

Richter, Michael. *Ireland and Her Neighbours in the Seventh Century*. Bodmin, Cornwall: MPG Books, 1999.

Ritchie, David. *Shipwrecks: An Encyclopedia of the World's Worst Disasters at Sea*. New York: Checkmark Books, 1996.

Ritchie-Calder, Lord. "The Lunar Society of Birmingham." *Scientific American*, June 1982, 136–145.

Roberts, Nancy. *Blackbeard and Other Pirates of the Atlantic Coast*. New York: John F. Blair, Publisher, 1993.

Robinson, F. N., ed. *The Works of Geoffrey Chaucer*. Boston: Houghton Mifflin, 1957.

Rocco, Fiammetta. "Keeping the Flame." *Institutional Investor*, December 1988, 31–32.

Rochette, Ed. "Four Hundred Cents to the Stella Dollar!" *Antiques & Collecting Hobbies*, December 1986, 72.

_____. "Meeting the Man with the Five-cent Profile." *Hobbies*, January 1984, 82–83.

Römer, Joachim, and Michael Ditter, chief eds. *Culinaria: European Specialties*. Cologne, Ger.: Könemann, 1995.

Romey, Kristin M. "Canned Remains." *Archaeology*, May/June 2001, 25.

"Ronald Noble Picked to Head Interpol; First American to Hold Post." *Jet*, July 26, 1999, 4.

Rowley, Trevor. *The High Middle Ages, 1200–1550*. London: Routledge & Kegan Paul, 1986.

_____. *The Norman Heritage, 1066–1200*. London: Routledge & Kegan Paul, 1983.

"The Royal Exchange." *Scottish Country Life*, July 1917.

"The Royal Feast." http://www.acronet.net/~robokopp/english/godsavet.htm.

"Royal Mint Unveils Results of First Ever Public Consultation on New Coin Design." *PR Newswire*, October 24, 2000.

Royce, Sarah. *A Frontier lady: Recollections of the Gold Rush and Early California*. Lincoln: University of Nebraska Press, 1977.

Russell, Osborne. *Journal of a Trapper*. Lincoln: University of Nebraska Press, 1965.

Rust, William, and Amy Cushing. "Buried Cities of Khotan." *Athena Review*, Vol. 3, 2001, 78–88.

"Saint-Gaudens National Historic Site." http://www.nps.gov/saga/.

Sandz, Victoria. *Encyclopedia of Western Atlantic Shipwrecks and Sunken Treasure*. Jefferson, N.C.: McFarland, 2001.

Sardin, Frédérique. "Les légendes en creux fautées sur les tranches des monnaies françaises en or et en argent du XIXe siècle," http://www.amisdufranc.org/articles/varietes/tranches_fautees.html.

Sargent, Thomas J., and Francois R. Velde. *The Evolution of Small Change*. Chicago: Federal Reserve Bank, 1997.

Sarianidi, Viktor Ivanovich. "The Golden Hoard of Bactria." *National Geographic*, March 1990, 50–75.

Savaiko, Bernard C. "The International Glitter in the World of Gold Coins." *Barron's*, December 15, 1986, 36.

Sawyer, Peter, ed. *The Oxford Illustrated History of the Vikings*. Oxford: Oxford University Press, 1997.

Sawyer, P. H. *The Age of Vikings*. New York: St. Martin's Press, 1962.

"Saxon Coins Could Be Worth £750,000." *Weekly Telegraph*, August 20, 1997.

Scarr, Deryck, ed. *More Pacific Island Portraits*. Canberra: ANU Press, 1979.

Schaff, Philip. *History of the Christian Church*. New York: Scribner's, 1888.

Schapiro, Meyer. *Romanesque Art*. London: Thames & Hudson, 1993.

Schärer, Martin, and Alexander Fenton, eds. *Food and Material Culture*. East Lothian, Scotland: Tuckwell Press, 1998.

Scheibla, Shirley Hobbs. "Where Hot Money Hides." *Barron's*, July 11, 1983, 16–18.

Schemo, Diana Jean. "Recovery of Spanish Galleon off Ecuador's Coast Raises Controversy and Romance." *New York Times*, April 14, 1997.

Schena, Eric R. "The Influence of Islamic Coins on the Russian Monetary System." *Journal of the Islamic Coins Group*, Winter 1999/2000.

Schiff, Bennett. "From the Midlands, a Unique Master of Light and Color." *Smithsonian*, September 1990, 50–60.

Schofield, Robert E. *The Lunar Society of Birmingham: A Social History of Provincial Science and Industry in Eighteenth-Century England*. Oxford: Clarendon Press, 1963.

Schuiling, M., and H. C. Harries., "The Coconut Palm in East Africa." *Principes*, Vol. 38, No. 1, 1994.

Schwarz, Frederic D. "Drake Sees the Pacific." *American Heritage*, February-March 1998, 94–95.

Schwarz, Ted. *Coins as Living History*. New York: Arco Publishing, 1976.

Scott, A. F. *Who's Who in Chaucer*. New York: Hawthorn Books, 1974.

Scott, Franklin D. *Sweden: The Nation's History*. Minneapolis: University of Minnesota, 1977.

"The Search for Answers." *CBS News*, November 21, 2001.

Sears, Stuart D. "An Introduction to Early Muslim Drahms." *As-Sikka*, Winter 2000.

Sellin, Eric, and Hedi Abdel-Jaouad. "The Art and Design of Arabic Calligraphy." *Ethnic News Watch*, January 31, 1997.

Setton, Kenneth M., ed. *The Middle Ages*. Washington, D.C.: National Geographic, 1977.

Severy, Merle, ed. *Greece & Rome*. Washington, D.C.: National Geographic Society, 1977.

_____. ed. *The Middle Ages*. Washington, D.C.: National Geographic Society, 1977.

_____. ed. *The Renaissance*. Washington, D.C.: National Geographic Society, 1977.

"Shah Tahmasb." http://isfahan.anglia.ac.uk/oldsite/glossary/tahmasb.html.

Shakespeare, William. *Macbeth Complete Study Edition*. Lincoln, Neb.: Cliffs Notes, 1964.

_____. *The Riverside Shakespeare*. Boston: Houghton-Mifflin, 1974.

Shanks, Hershel. "Solomon's Blessings." *Biblical Archaeology Review*, September/October 2001, 46–47.

Shappell, Chris. "Y Notes and Y News." *American Numismatic Association Newsletter*, November 14, 2001.

"Shapur II." http://bcd.britannica.com/bcom/eb/.../0,5716,68882,00.html.

Shaw, Christine. "Counsel and Consent in Fifteenth-Century Genoa." *English Historical Review*, September 1, 2001.

"Sheffield Assay Office — A History." http://www.assayo‡ce.co.uk/history.htm.

Sheehan, John. "The Viking-Age Gold and Silver of Scotland: A.D. 850–1100." *Antiquity*, December 1995.

Sheets, Tara E., ed. *Encyclopedia of Associations*. Farmington Hills, Mich.: Gale Group, 1999.

"Shell and Feather Money of the Solomons." http://www.melanesianhandcraft.com/The_Shell_Money.htm.

Sherr, Lynn, and Jurate Kazickas. *Susan B. Anthony Slept Here: A Guide to American Women's Landmarks*. New York: Times Books, 1976.

Sherrill, Sarah B. "North Carolina Gold Coins." *Antiques*, October 1980, 638–639.

"Ship of Gold." http://www.shipofgoldinfo.com/.

"The Significance of Celtic Coinage." http://www.ex.ac.uk/~RDavies/arian/celtic.html.

Silver, Constance S., et al. "U.S. Custom House, New York City: Overview of Analyses and Interpretation of Altered Architectural Finishes." *Journal of the American Institute of Conservation*, Vol. 32, No. 2, 141–152.

Simmons, Donald C. *Confederate Settlements in British Honduras*. Jefferson, N.C.: McFarland, 2001.

Simms, Jeptha R. *History of Schoharie County, and Border Wars of New York*. Albany, N.Y.: Munsell & Tanner, Printers, 1845.

Simon, James. *The World of the Celts*. London: Thomas & Hudson, 1993.

Simpson, John. "Arresting a Diplomat." *History Today*, January 1985, 32–37.

Sims, G. Thomas, and David Woodruff. "Distribution of Euros to Start Tomorrow." *Wall Street Journal*, December 13, 2001, A10.

Sinclair, David. *The Pound*. London: Century Books, 2000.

"Sir Francis Drake's Secret Voyage to the North Coast of America, A.D. 1579." *Mercator's World*, September 2001, 17.

"1694 Elephant Token." http://www.lib.unc.edu/ncc/gallery/elephant.html.

66 Centuries of Measurement. Dayton, Ohio: Sheffield Measurement Division, 1984.

Skerry, Brian. "Pirates of the *Whydah*." *National Geographic*, May 1999, 64–77.

Smith, Aquila. "On the Ormonde Money." *Journal of the Kilkenny and Southeast of Ireland Archaeological Society*, 1854.

Smith, Jane S., and Paul Wagner. *A Paralyzing Fear: The Triumph over Polio in America*. New York: TV Books Inc., 1998.

Smith, Margaret Supplee, and Emily Herring Wilson. *North Carolina Women: Making History*. Chapel Hill: University of North Carolina Press, 1999.

Snodgrass, Mary Ellen. *Encyclopedia of Fable*. Santa Barbara, Calif.: ABC-Clio, 1998.

_____. *Encyclopedia of Frontier Literature*. Santa Barbara, Calif.: ABC-Clio, 1997.

_____. *Encyclopedia of Kitchen History*. London: Fitzroy-Dearborn, 2003.

_____. *Encyclopedia of World Scripture*. Jefferson, N.C.: McFarland, 2001.

_____. "Grace O'Malley: Pirate Extraordinaire." *Islands*, July/August 1986, 18–21.

_____. *Late Achievers*. Englewood, Colo.: Libraries Unlimited, 1992.

_____. *Religious Sites in America*. Santa Barbara, Calif.: ABC-Clio, 2000.

_____. *Signs of the Zodiac*. Westport, Conn.: Greenwood, 1997.

_____. *Voyages in Classical Mythology*. Santa Barbara, Calif.: ABC-Clio, 1994.

_____. *Who's Who in the Middle Ages*. Jefferson, N.C.: McFarland, 2001.

Snow, Jack. *Who's Who in Oz*. Chicago: Reilly & Lee, 1954.

Snyder, Christopher. "The Age of Arthur: Some Historical and Archaeological Background." *Heroic Age*, Spring/Summer 1999.

Soderberg, Susan C. "Maryland's Civil War Monuments." *The Historian*, Spring 1996.

"So Long to the Lira." *BBC News*, October 31, 2001.

"Sommer Islands 'Hogge Money' the First Coinage in the English-Speaking New World." *Money Talks*, American Numismatic Association, December 1996.

Sophocles. *Antigone*. New York: Longman, 1962.

Sorenson, Janet. "'Belts of Gold' and 'Twenty-Pounders': Robert Louis Stevenson's Textualized Economies." *Criticism*, Summer, 2000.

Southern, R. W. *The Middle Ages*. London: Penguin, 1970.

Spadone, Frank G. *Major Variety and Oddity Guide of United States Coins*. Wisconsin: Krause Publications, 1967.

Stall, Sam. "Treasures of the 'Atocha.'" *Saturday Evening Post*, November 1986, 50–56.

Standish, David. *The Art of Money*. San Francisco: Chronicle Books, 2000.

Stanton, Lucia C. "Realms of a Coin." *Monticello Newsletter*, Summer 1994.

Stapleton, Cy. "Small Talk." *Southern Graphics*, January 2001.

Starita, Angela. "On the Map: From the Ruins, a Granite Couple Will Stand Over Newark." *New York Times*, December 24, 2000.

Starr, Chester G. *A History of the Ancient World*. New York: Oxford University Press, 1991.

"State Quarters." http://www.statequarters.com.

"States Must Standardize Food Stamp Systems." *Government Computer News*, April 2000, 16.

Steelman, Ben. "Author Strikes 'Gold' with New Book." Wilmington, N.C., *Star-News*, August 8, 1999.

Steinmetz, Greg. "The Euro Designer's Art Is Sure to Have Wide Currency." *Wall Street Journal*, July 7, 1998, B1.

Stelten, Leo F. *Dictionary of Ecclesiastical Latin*. Peabody, Mass.: Hendrickson Publications, 1995.

Stemm, Greg. "Thirty-First Annual Law of the Sea Institute." *Odyssey News*, March 30, 1998.

Stephen, Sir Leslie, and Sir Sidney Lee, eds. *Dictionary of National Biography*. London: Oxford University Press, 1922.

Stevenson, Jed. "A Bite of Gold." *New York Times*, September 1, 1991, 57.

Stevenson, Robert Louis. *Treasure Island*. New York: Airmont, 1962.

Stewart, Gail B. *Life During the Spanish Inquisition*. San Diego, Calif.: Lucent Books, 1998.

Stigler, Stephen. "Stephen Stigler's New Book

Challenges Researchers to Show Him the Numbers." *University of Chicago Magazine*, December 1999.
St. James Guide to Crime & Mystery Writers, 4th ed. Detroit: St. James Press, 1996.
Stone, Alexander. "Illegal Tender." *Harvard International Review*, Summer 2001, 7.
Storey, Sallie L. "Understanding the Market for Gold Bullion Coins." *Barron's*, January 26, 1987, 56.
"The Story of the Sixpence." http://www.24carat.co.uk/sixpencesstory.html.
Stow, Kenneth R. *Alienated Minority: The Jews of Medieval Latin Europe*. Cambridge, Mass.: Harvard University Press, 1992.
"The Strange Tale of the Iowa Soldiers Who Guarded Confederate Gold." http://www.iowa-counties.com/civilwar/gold.htm.
Strayer, Joseph R., ed. *Dictionary of the Middle Ages*. New York: Charles Scribner's Sons, 1983.
Sturluson, Snorri. "Heimskringla or the Chronicle of the Kings of Norway Saga of Olaf Kyrre." http://sunsite.berkeley.edu/OMACL/Heimskringla/kyrre.html.
"A Submarine Sinks Myths About the Confederacy." *Christian Science Monitor*, July 25, 2001.
"Subsea Recovery." http://www.subsearecovery.com/ssr.html.
Sullivan, Mark. "Sunken Vessel Near Turkey Believed to Date to 1,500 B.C." *New York Times*, October 30, 1982.
"The Sutro Tunnel Company." http://www.library.unr.edu/specoll/mss/NC7.html.
Sutter, John August. *The Diary of Johann August Sutter*. San Francisco: Grabhorn Press, 1932.
Swift, Jonathan. *Gulliver's Travels and Other Writings*. New York: Modern Library, 1958.
"Tales from the Crypt." *Time*, April 18, 1994, 67.
Tan, Amy. *The Kitchen God's Wife*. New York: Ivy Books, 1991.
Tarpley, Cassie. "A Golden Touch." *Shelby* [Illinois] *Star*, December 10, 2001.
Tatum, W. Jeffrey. "The Lex Papiria de Dedicationibus: A Clarification." *Ancient History Bulletin*, 1997.
Taxay, Don. *An Illustrated History of U.S. Commemorative Coinage*. New York: Arco Publishing, 1967.
_____. *The U.S. Mint and Coinage*. New York: Arco Publishing, 1966.
Taylor, Michael. "Yep, They're Still Digging." *Forbes*, September 25, 1995, 138–142.
Taylor, Paul. "Wholesale Corruption." *Washington Post*, September 28, 1993, A29.
Taylor, Richard. *Destruction and Reconstruction: Personal Experiences of the Late War*. New York: D. Appleton & Co., 1879.
Tebben, Gerald. "On My Way to California." *Coin World*, July 19, 1999, 74–76.
"Terrorism Added to Interpol Agenda." *Washington Post*, September 23, 2001, 36.
"There's a New Flip Side to Quarters." *Omaha World Herald*, February 1, 1999.
Thomas, Edward. *Numismata Orientalia*. London: Trübner & Co., 1874.
Thorncroft, Tony. "The Great Charms of Old Money." *Financial Times*, January 20, 2001.
Throckmorton, Peter. "Oldest Known Shipwreck Yields Bronze Age Cargo." *National Geographic*, May 1962, 696–711.
Tibbles, Anthony. "Transatlantic Slavery." *Antiques*, June 1999.
Tingley, J. V. "Salt and Silver." *Nevada Geology*, Summer 1990.
Tompsett, Brian. "Directory of Royal Genealogical Data." http://www.dcs.hull.ac.uk/public/genealogy/royal/#Italy, 1999.
"Tradesmen's Tokens." http://www.ee.surrey.ac.uk/Contrib/manx/manxsoc/msvol17/ch05.htm.
"Trading with Europeans." http://educate.si.edu/resources/lessons/siyc/currency/essay5.html.
Trager, James. *The People's Chronology*. New York: Henry Holt, 1992.
_____. *The Women's Chronology*. New York: Henry Holt, 1995.
Traill, David A., and Paul C. Appleton. "Letters from Troy." *Archaeology*, January/February 2002, 54.
"Treasure Found in Southern Kyrgyzstan." *BBC Monitoring Service*, June 1, 2001.
"Treasure Hunter Who Went for the Gold." *U.S. News & World Report*, August 5, 1985, 13.
"Treasure News." http://www.treasurelore.com/florida/treasure_news.htm.
"Treasure of Rio Formoso." http://www.heraldstar.u-net.com/botija.htm.
"The Tregwynt Hoard." http://www.aocc.ac.uk/archaeology/tre_int.html.
"Tregwynt Mansion." http://www.europetraditions.com/england/int/322.html.
"The Trial by Pyx Order 1998." http://www.hmso.gov.uk/si/si1998/ 19980264.htm.
"Tribute to Leonard Matters Miscellaneous." *The Hindu*, November 2, 1951.
Trupp, Philip. "Ancient Shipwrecks Yield Both Prizes and Bitter Conflict." *Smithsonian*, October 1983, 79–89.
Tuchman, Barbara W. *A Distant Mirror: The Calamitous 14th Century*. New York: Alfred A. Knopf, 1978.
Turner, Jane Shoaf. *Grove Dictionary of Art*. New York: St. Martin's Press, 2000.
Twain, Mark. *A Connecticut Yankee in King Arthur's Court*. New York: Signet, 1963.
Tyerman, Christopher. *Who's Who in Early Medieval England*. London: Shepheard-Walwyn Publishers, 1996.

Tyler, Elizabeth. "Treasures and Convention in Old English Verse." *Notes and Queries*, March 1996.

"United States Pattern Coins: The Bass Collection." http://www.harrybassfoundation.org/basscatalogs/BASSSALE1/b1-2-a.htm.

"United States Secret Service." http://www.treas.gov/usss.

"Unlocking the Secrets of the Kinor and the bar Kochba Coins." http://www.harpofdavid.com/barkochba.htm.

"The U.S. Mint." http://www.usmint.gov.

Van Ryzin, Robert R. *Twisted Tails: Sifted Fact, Fantasy and Fiction from U.S. Coin History*. Iola, Wisc.: Krause Publications, 1995.

Varchaver, Nicholas. "Hiding Dirty Money." *Fortune*, March 4, 2002, 44.

Vaughan, Rice. *A Discourse of Coin and Coinage*. London: Th. Dawks, 1675.

Velasco, Andres. "Dollar Diplomacy." *Time*, February 8, 1999.

Velazquez, José. "Salvagers Recover Thousands of Coins from Galleon Sunk off Ecuador." *News Times*, April 4, 1997.

Vermeule, Cornelius. *Numismatic Art in America*. Cambridge, Mass.: Harvard University Press, 1971.

"Victor Man Starts a Mint." *American Numismatic Association Newsletter*, September 1998.

Vigdor, Irving. "The Euro, a New Profit Engine." *Bobbin Group*, September 1999.

Virgil. *The Aeneid*. New York: Mentor Classic, 1961.

"Virginia City in Ruins." *Territorial Enterprise*, October 27, 1875.

"Visa Gold Announces Patrimony Evaluations of 'Palemon Artifacts' to Be Completed by August 8th 2001." *Business Wire*, July 24, 2001.

"Visual Thinking: Sketchbooks from the Archives of American Art." http://artarchives.si.edu/exhibits/sketchbk/weinman.htm.

Vitello, Barbara. "Undiscovered Gems: The Epitome of Modernism." *Daily Herald*, April 23, 1999.

Vitullo-Martin, Julia. "Monkey Business: What Really Happened in Tennessee." *Commonweal*, October 8, 1999.

Volo, Dorothy Denneen, and James M. Volo. "Daily Life in Civil War America." *Daily Life Through History* (database), http://greenwood.scbbs.com:8080.

von Nothaus, Bernard. "Pre-Constitutional Concept of Money." *Norfed Report*, August 2000.

Waldman, Carl. *Who Was Who in Native American History*. New York: Facts on File, 1990.

Walker, John, ed. *Halliwell's Film & Video Guide*. New York: HarperPerennial, 1999.

Warmington, E. H. *Remains of Old Latin: Volume IV, Archaic Inscriptions*. Cambridge, Mass.: Harvard University Press, 1967.

Wasilewska, Ewa. "On the Money." *The World & I*, November 1, 1998, 222.

"Waterfront Used at Synod of Chelsea." *British Archaeology*, September 1997.

Weatherford, Jack. *The History of Money: From Sandstone to Cyberspace*. Pittsburgh, Pa.: Three Rivers Press, 1998.

Webster, Hutton. *Early European History*. New York: D. C. Heath, 1924.

Webster's Dictionary of American Women. New York: Merriam-Webster Incorporated, 1996.

Weida, Lorraine. "The Bankers Magazine Bankers Hall of Fame." *Bankers Magazine*, September-October 1982, 58–67.

Weiner, Annette B. *Women of Value, Men of Renown: New Perspectives in Trobriand Exchange*. Austin: University of Texas Press, 1976.

Weller, Anthony. "Bond at 40." *Forbes*, November 22, 1993, 133–143.

"Wells Fargo." http://www.wellsfargo.com.

Wenick, Robert. "When the Bubble Burst." *Smithsonian*, December 1989, 155–165.

Weston, John. "Sir Henry Morgan." http://www.data-wales.co.uk/morgan.htm.

Wheal, Elizabeth-Anne, Stephen Pope, and James Taylor. *Encyclopedia of the Second World War*. New York: Castle Books, 1989.

Wheeler, Richard. *In Pirate Waters*. New York: Thomas Y. Crowell, 1969.

White, Weimar W. *The Liberty Seated Dollar 1840–1873*. New York: Sanford J. Durst, 1985.

"Who Can Get Food Stamps." http://www.ssa.gov/pubs/10100.html.

Who Was Who in America. Chicago: Marquis Who's Who, Inc., 1968.

Wickramasinhe, Rajah M. "Minted Legacy." *Sunday Observer*, June 10, 2001.

Wigoder, Geoffrey. *The Encyclopedia of Judaism*. New York: Macmillan, 1989.

Wilde, Adna G. "Lesher Referendum Medals." *The Numismatist*, November 1978.

Wilentz, Amy. "We Found It! We Found It!" *Time*, August 5, 1985, 21–22.

Wilfong, Tara N. "Coining a New Era." *Arts and Antiques*, September 1999.

"William Paterson." *Significant Scots*. http://www.electricscotland.com/history/other/paterson.htm.

Williams, George L. *Papal Genealogy: The Families and Descendants of the Popes*. Jefferson, N.C.: McFarland, 1998.

Williams, Marty Newman, and Anne Echols. *Between Pit and Pedestal: Women in the Middle Ages*. Princeton, N.J.: Markus Wiener Publishers, 1994.

Williams, Trevor. *The History of Invention*. New York: Facts on File, 1987.

Willoughby, Jack. "What Your Country Can Do for You." *Forbes*, October 23, 1989, 104–106.

Wilson, James Grant, and John Fiske, eds. *Appleton's Cyclopedia of American Biography.* Detroit: Gale Research, Detroit, 1968.

Wilson, Scott. "Castro Forms a New Alliance — With Treasure Hunters." *Washington Post,* December 27, 2000, A16.

Winchester, Simon. "Sir Francis Drake Is Still Capable of Kicking Up a Fuss." *Smithsonian,* January 1997, 82–91.

Winters, Douglas, and Lawrence Cutler. *Gold Coins of the Old West: The Carson City Mint 1870–1893.* Wolfeboro, N. H.: Bowers & Merena Galleries, 1994.

_____. *New Orleans Mint Gold Coins 1839–1909.* Wolfeboro, N. H.: Bowers & Merena Galleries, 1992.

Wolff, Philippe. *The Awakening of Europe.* New York: Penguin Books, 1968.

"Woman's Suffrage: Women's History Month." *Voter,* March 2001.

Women and Social Movements in the United States, 1830–1930, http://womhist.binghamton.edu/index.html.

"Women's History." *The History Net,* http://womenshistory.about.com/mbody.htm.

"The Wonderful Wizard of Oz." http://www.people.cornell.edu/pages/dbj5/oz.html.

World of Invention, 2nd ed. Farmington Hills, Mich.: Gale Group, 1999.

Wu, Corinna. "The Buck Starts Here." *Science News,* April 1, 2000.

Wyman, J. N. *Journey to the Koyukuk.* Missoula, Mont.: Pictorial Histories Publishing, 1988.

Xu, Jay. "The Enigmatic Art of Sanxingdui." *Natural History,* November 1, 2001, 72–79.

"Yale Sells Storied Coin." *American Libraries,* February 1981, 65.

"Year 2000 25-cent Coins Unveiled by RCM." *Canadian Coin News,* January 25–February 7, 2000.

Yeoman, R. S. *A Guide Book of United States Coins.* Racine, Wisc.: Western Publishing, 1993.

Yoffee, Norman. "Sippar-Amnanum: The Ur-Utu Archive." *Journal of the American Oriental Society,* October 12, 1997.

Young, Douglas. "Local Coin Collector Builds $1 Billion Firm." *Los Angeles Business Journal,* August 21, 1995, 45–46.

"Yvette Gastauer-Claire." *British Art Medal Society,* http://www.bams.org.uk/artists/gast_claire.htm.

Yzábal, María Dolores, and Shelton Wiseman. *The Mexican Gourmet.* McMahons Point, Australia: Thunder Bay, 1995.

Zielinski, Graeme. "Frank Gasparro Dies." *Washington Post,* October 4, 2001.

Index

Main entries are in **boldface**; illustrations are bracketed.